ADOLESCENCE

ADOLESCENCE

Fourteenth Edition

JOHN W. SANTROCK

University of Texas at Dallas

The McGraw-Hill Companies

Published by McGraw-Hill, an imprint of The McGraw-Hill Companies, Inc., 1221 Avenue of the Americas, New York, NY 10020.

This book is printed on acid-free paper.

2 3 4 5 6 7 8 9 0 DOW/DOW 1 0 9 8 7 6 5 4 3 2

ISBN: 978-0-07-811716-9
MHID: 0-07-811716-X

Sponsoring Editor: *Allison McNamara*
Marketing Manager: *Julia Larkin*
Development Editors: *Cara Labell and Elisa Adams*
Editorial Coordinator: *Sarah Kiefer*
Production Editor: *Brett Coker*
Production Service: *Aaron Downey, Matrix Productions, Inc.*
Manuscript Editor: *Kate Petrella*
Cover Designer: *Preston Thomas*
Interior Designers: *Pam Verros and Preston Thomas*
Photo Researcher: *Janet Robbins*
Buyer: *Carol Bielski*
Composition: *9.5/12 Meridien Roman by Aptara®, Inc.*
Printing: *45# New Era Thin Plus by R.R. Donnelley*

Vice President Editorial: *Michael Ryan*
Publisher: *Michael J. Sugarman*
Director of Development: *Dawn Groundwater*

Credits: The credits section for this book begins on page C-1 and is considered an extension of the copyright page.

Library of Congress Cataloging-in-Publication Data

Santrock, John W.
Adolescence / John W. Santrock. — 14th ed.
p. cm.
Includes bibliographical references and index.
ISBN 978-0-07-811716-9 (pbk. : acid-free paper)
1. Adolescence. 2. Adolescent psychology. I. Title.
HQ796.S26 2012
305.235—dc23

2011037874

Printed in the USA

www.mhhe.com

To Tracy and Jennifer, who, as they matured, helped me appreciate the marvels of adolescent development.

about the **author**

John W. Santrock

John Santrock received his Ph.D. from the University of Minnesota in 1973. He taught at the University of Charleston and the University of Georgia before joining the program in Psychology and Human Development at the University of Texas at Dallas, where he currently teaches a number of undergraduate courses.

John has been a member of the editorial boards of Child Development and Developmental Psychology. His research on father custody is widely cited and used in expert witness testimony to promote flexibility and alternative considerations in custody disputes. John also has authored these exceptional McGraw-Hill texts: *Psychology* (seventh edition), *Children* (eleventh edition), *Life-Span Development* (thirteenth edition), and *Educational Psychology* (fifth edition).

John Santrock, teaching an undergraduate class.

For many years John was involved in tennis as player, a teaching professional, and a coach of professional tennis players. At the University of Miami (Florida), the tennis team on which he played still holds the NCAA Division I record for most consecutive wins (137) in any sport. His wife, Mary Jo, has a Master's degree in special education and has worked as a teacher and a Realtor. He has two daughters—Tracy, who also is a Realtor, and Jennifer, who is a medical sales specialist. He has one granddaughter, Jordan, age 20, currently an undergraduate student at Southern Methodist University, and two grandsons, Alex, age 7, and Luke, age 5. In the last decade, John also has spent time painting expressionist art.

brief contents

contents

CHAPTER 1 INTRODUCTION 1

CHAPTER 2 PUBERTY, HEALTH, AND BIOLOGICAL FOUNDATIONS 49

CHAPTER 6 SEXUALITY 186

CHAPTER 7 MORAL DEVELOPMENT, VALUES, AND RELIGION 223

CHAPTER 8 FAMILIES 252

CHAPTER 9 PEERS, ROMANTIC RELATIONSHIPS, AND LIFESTYLES 294

CHAPTER 10 SCHOOLS 330

CHAPTER 11 ACHIEVEMENT, WORK, AND CAREERS 361

CHAPTER 12 CULTURE 391

CHAPTER 13 PROBLEMS IN ADOLESCENCE AND EMERGING ADULTHOOD 422

Making Connections . . . From My Classroom to *Adolescence* to You

Having taught an undergraduate class on adolescent development every year for three decades, I'm always looking for ways to improve my course and texts. Just as McGraw-Hill looks to those who teach the adolescence course for input, each year I ask the 50 to 75 students in my adolescent development course to tell me what they like about the course and the text, and what they think could be improved. What have my students told me lately about my course, this text, and themselves?

One word highlights what students have been talking about in the last several years when I ask them about their lives and observe them more than in earlier decades: **Connecting.** Connecting and communicating have always been important themes of adolescents' lives, but the more I've talked with students recently, the more the word *connecting* comes up in conversations with them. How this connecting is done is changing dramatically. As part of a new discussion of the current generation of adolescents and emerging adults, the Millennials, in the text, I describe the results of a recent Pew Research Center survey on the digitally mediated world of adolescents (Lenhart & others, 2010a,b). The poll revealed that the main way adolescents now connect with their friends is through text messaging, surpassing face-to-face contact (Lenhart & others, 2010b)! In this survey, 81 percent of 18- to 24-year-olds have created a profile on a social networking site, such as Facebook.

With these new changes in adolescents' and emerging adults' lives in mind, I explored with students how they thought I could improve the course and the text by using *connecting* as a theme. Following is an outgrowth of those conversations focused on a *connections* theme and how I have incorporated it into the main goals of this text in this new, fourteenth edition:

1. **Connecting topical processes in development** to guide students in making *topical connections* across different aspects of adolescent development.
2. **Connecting research to what we know about development** to provide students with the best and most recent *theory and research* in the world today about adolescence and emerging adulthood.
3. **Connecting development to the real world** to help students understand ways to *apply* content about adolescence and emerging adulthood to the real world and improve the lives of youth; and to motivate them to think deeply about *their own personal journeys of youth* and better understand who they were, are, and will be.

MAKING

Connections

Connections play a key role in student learning and are a driving force behind *Adolescence*.

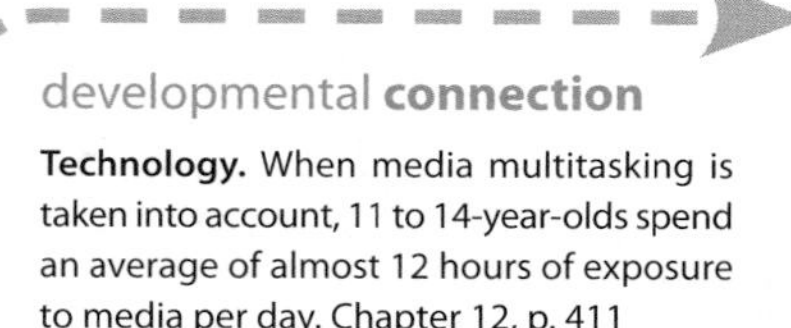
developmental **connection**

Technology. When media multitasking is taken into account, 11 to 14-year-olds spend an average of almost 12 hours of exposure to media per day. Chapter 12, p. 411

Connecting Topical Processes in Adolescent Development

✷ ***Developmental Connections*** highlight links across topics of adolescent development *and* connections between biological, cognitive, and socioemotional processes.

✷ ***Connect*** questions within chapters and in the chapter Review, Connect, and Reflect sections allow students to practice making connections among development topics.

Connecting Research to What We Know about Adolescent Development

✷ ***Connections with Research*** describes a study or program to illustrate how research in adolescent development is conducted and how it influences our understanding of the discipline.

✷ ***Leading experts*** in the field provided detailed input on the content and provided key insights on new research and findings in their fields of study. (See pp. xvii–xx for their bios and photos.)

✷ ***The most current coverage of research***—with over 1,000 citations from 2009, 2010, 2011, and 2012.

The text presents very concise and current overviews of key issues and very current research concerning important themes of adolescence and emerging adulthood. The book gives the student an excellent, well-written introduction to a number of topics that can be linked through guiding questions to the students' own experiences.

Jane Kroger
University of Western Washington and the University of Tromsø, Norway

Connecting Adolescent Development to the Real World

✳ ***Connecting with Health and Well-Being*** describes the influence of development in a real world context on topics that include increasing adolescents' self-esteem (Chapter 4), effective sex education (Chapter 6), parenting moral children and adolescents (Chapter 7), strategies for emerging adults and their parents (Chapter 8), effective and ineffective strategies for making friends (Chapter 9), and coping strategies in adolescence and emerging adulthood (Chapter 13).

✳ ***Connecting with Careers*** **and the** ***Careers in Adolescent Development*** appendix profile careers that require education and training in various areas of human development to show students where knowledge of human development could lead them.

✳ ***Connecting with Adolescents*** **and** ***Connecting with Emerging Adults*** share personal experiences from real adolescents and emerging adults.

✳ ***Reflect: Your Own Personal Journey of Life*** in the end-of-section reviews in each chapter asks students to reflect on some aspect of the discussion in the section they have just read and connect it to their own life.

✳ ***Connecting with Resources for Improving the Lives of Adolescents*** at the end of each chapter describes numerous resources such as books, websites, and organizations that provide valuable information for improving the lives of adolescents in many different areas.

✳ ***Self-Assessments*** on the Online Learning Center (www.mhhe.com/santrocka14e) allow students to explore their own experiences. For example, for Chapter 4, the self-assessment exercises include Exploring My Identity; for Chapter 8, How Much Did My Parents Monitor My Behavior During Adolescence?; and for Chapter 11, Evaluating My Career Interests.

expert consultants

Adolescent development has become an enormous, complex field, and no single author, or even several authors, can possibly keep up with all of the rapidly changing content in the many different areas of adolescent development. To solve this problem, author John Santrock sought the input of leading experts about content in a number of areas of adolescent development. The experts provided detailed evaluations and recommendations in their area(s) of expertise.

The following individuals were among those who served as expert consultants for one or more of the previous six editions of this text: Susan Harter, Charles Irwin, Elizabeth Susman, James Marcia, Nancy Guerra, Gerald Patterson, Catherine Cooper, Reed Larson, Daniel Keating, Ruth Chao, Luc Goosens, Shirley Feldman, Kathryn Wentzel, Joseph Allen, Nancy Galambos, L. Monique Ward, Lisa Crockett, John Schulenberg, Wyndol Furman, Mitchell Prinstein, Bonnie Leadbetter, James Rest, Lisa Diamond, Diane Halpern, Jennifer Connolly, Allan Wigfield, Lorah Dorn, Allison Ryan, Lawrence Walker, John Gibbs, and Bonnie Barber.

Following are the biographies and photographs of the expert consultants for the fourteenth edition of this text, who, like the expert consultants for the previous six editions, literally represent a who's who in the field of adolescent development:

Peter Benson

Peter Benson is one of the world's leading experts on social policy, community initiatives, and positive aspects of adolescent development. Dr. Benson is president and CEO of Minneapolis-based Search Institute, one of the world's leading research centers on positive human development. He joined the staff of Search Institute after several years in academia and became the Institute's president in1985. He holds doctorate and master's degrees in social psychology from the University of Denver as well as a master's degree from Yale University in the psychology of religion. In 1990, he premiered the research-based framework of Developmental Assets, which now is the most widely recognized approach to positive youth development in the United States and around the world. This framework is now utilized by 600 community initiatives and more than 10,000 schools, agencies, and programs in 60 nations. Most recently, he has focused on conceptualizing a new understanding of "thriving." His work on this topic was first published in 2008 by Jossey-Bass as *Sparks: How Parents Can Help Ignite the Hidden Strengths of Teenagers*. Dr. Benson is the author or editor of fifteen books on child and adolescent development, including, most recently, *All Kids Are Our Kids: What Communities Must Do to Raise Caring and Responsible Children and Adolescents; The Handbook of Spiritual Development in Childhood and Adolescence*; and *Parent, Teacher, Mentor, Friend: How Every Adult Can Change Kids' Lives*. Among his many honors, Dr. Benson was the first visiting scholar at the William T. Grant Foundation and also has received the William James Award for Career Contributions to the Psychology of Religion from the American Psychological Association.

"John Santrock's Adolescence *has been, for many years, at the top of the class. Not resting on its laurels, this new 14th edition includes many important changes. On the one hand, it updates every chapter with the latest research. On the other, it creatively and powerfully adds substantial material that connects theory and research to the real world experiences of students. Students are sure to find this new edition both intellectually engaging and personally rewarding.* Adolescence, *in its new incarnation, has jumped ahead of its competitors."* **—Dr. Peter Benson,** *The Search Institute*

Nina Mounts

Nina Mounts is a leading expert on family and peer relations in adolescence. Dr. Mounts obtained her Ph.D. in child and family studies from the University of Wisconsin–Madison. She currently is a professor in the Department of Psychology at Northern Illinois University, where she also is director of the Northern Illinois University Collaborative on Early Adolescence. Her research focuses on links between parent and peer contexts during adolescence. Dr. Mounts research has been funded by the National Institutes of Health and the National Science Foundation. Her publications have appeared in numerous child and adolescent development journals, and she also serves on several journal editorial boards.

". . . The narrative provides some of the latest information in the field. . . . John Santrock has worked hard to make the text relevant to today's undergraduate. The 'Through the Eyes . . .' sections seem like a good way to make the information more clear and relevant. I also like the 'Developmental Connections' idea that should help students understand how concepts talked about early in the course are linked to concepts later in the course." **—Dr. Nina Mounts,** *Northern Illinois University*

Deborah Capaldi

Deborah Capaldi is one of the world's leading experts on the development of adolescent problems. Originally from England, she obtained her Ph.D. from the University of Oregon and is currently a Senior Scientist at the Oregon Social Learning Center. Her main research interests focus on factors involved in the developmental trajectories of antisocial and co-occurring behaviors such as sexual risk taking and substance use. A further emphasis is understanding the formation and stability/instability of romantic relationships and explaining the development of aggression in such relationships. Dr. Capaldi has served on the editorial board of a number of journals, including *Child Development* and *Journal of Family Psychology*, as well as on a number of NIH and CDC review committees.

"This is an excellent chapter [Chapter 8, "Families"] *with a number of strengths—it presents a balanced picture overall, and it has a good treatment of cultural issues. The section on parenting in differing family types, such as stepfather families, is well presented. . . . This is a very comprehensive chapter* [13, "Problems in Adolescence and Emerging Adulthood"]. *The problems presented are well chosen, including important issues such as nutrition and obesity. The section on substance use in particular provides succinct important information on the range of substances used by adolescents and emerging adults. It is a strong feature that the chapter addresses successful interventions."* **—Dr. Deborah Capaldi,** *University of Oregon*

Bonnie Halpern-Felsher

Bonnie Halpern-Felsher is one of the world's leading experts on adolescent health and sexuality. Dr. Halpern obtained her Ph.D. in developmental psychology from the University of California, San Francisco, where she also completed a postdoctoral degree in health. She currently is a professor in the Division of Adolescent Medicine, Department of Pediatrics, University of California, San Francisco. Dr. Halpern-Felsher also is a faculty member at UCSF's Psychology and Medicine Postdoctoral Program, Center for Health and Community, and Center for Tobacco Control Research and Education. Her research focuses on cognitive and psychosocial factors involved in health-related decision making, perceptions of risk and vulnerability, health communication, and risk behavior. Dr. Halpern-Felsher has been the Principal Investigator or Co-Principal Investigator on several grants concerning adolescent risk behavior. She also has served as a consultant to a number of community-based adolescent health promotion programs and on national committees for reducing underage drinking, underage tobacco use, and teen motor crashes. She is currently a member of the editorial board of the *Journal of Adolescent Health.*

"The revised Preface and Chapters 2 ["Puberty, Health, and Biological Foundations"] *and* 6 ["Sexuality"] *were well-updated and well-written."* **—Dr. Bonnie Halpern-Felsher,** *University of California, San Francisco*

Daniel Lapsley

Daniel Lapsley is a leading expert on adolescent cognitive and moral development. He obtained his Ph.D. at the University of Wisconsin and currently is the ACE Collegiate Professor and Chair of the Department of Psychology at the University of Notre Dame. He also is the Coordinator of Academic Programs for Notre Dame's Alliance for Catholic Education. Dr. Lapsley is the editor or author of seven books, and numerous articles and chapters on various topics in child and adolescent development, especially in the areas of adolescent personality, individuation, risk behavior and decision making. He also studies the moral dimensions of personality and other topics in moral psychology, and has written extensively on moral and character education. Dr. Lapsley currently serves on the editorial boards of *Developmental Psychology, Journal of Educational Psychology,* and the *Journal of Early Adolescence*.

"I read the chapter [Chapter 3, "The Brain and Cognitive Development"] *with anticipation and found it to be a very good read indeed. . . . It was well-written and accessible—an historical trademark of John Santrock—as well as pleasingly substantive. It is a nice balance between topics that seem obligatory (such as Piaget's formal operations) and those that are more exciting and cutting edge. The chapter seems very much upgraded with new themes, citations, and articles."* **—Dr. Daniel Lapsley** *University of Notre Dame*

Jane Kroger

Jane Kroger is one of the world's leading experts on identity development in adolescence and adulthood. She received her Ph.D. from Florida State University and is currently research associate at Western Washington University and professor emeritus from University of Tromsø, Norway. Dr. Kroger has been a visiting fellow at the Erik H. and Joan M. Erikson Center, Harvard University; the Henry A. Murray Center, Radcliffe College; and research affiliate at the Norwegian Institute of Public Health. She is former president of the Society for Research on Identity Formation, and has published numerous articles, book chapters, monographs, and books in the areas of adolescent and adult identity development. Her most recent book is *Identity Development: Adolescence through Adulthood* (2nd Ed.) and she has served on the editorial boards of journals in the field of adolescent development and identity formation. Dr. Kroger's current work focuses on meta-analyses of adolescent and young adult identity statuses as well as the process of identity development among unaccompanied minor refugees moving to Norway from countries experiencing war and conflict.

"The book gives the student an excellent, well-written introduction to a number of topics that can be linked through guiding questions to the student's own experiences. . . . Chapter 4 ["The Self, Identity, Emotions, and Personality"] *is very well-written and presents material on key issues in very interesting ways. References are very current and study aids seem well presented and thought-provoking for students."* **—Dr. Jane Kroger** *Western Washington University and the University of Tromsø, Norway*

Moin Syed

Moin Syed is a leading expert on the development of the self and identity development in adolescence and emerging adulthood. He obtained his Ph.D. from the University of California, Santa Cruz, and currently is a professor in the Department of Psychology at the University of Minnesota. His research focuses on identity development among ethnically and culturally diverse adolescents and emerging adults, with a special emphasis on the development of multiple personal and social identities (ethnicity, socioeconomic status, and gender, for example) and the implications of identity development for educational experiences and career orientation. He has served as editor or co-editor of special issues of *New Directions for Child and Adolescent Development* on interdisciplinary conceptions of identity development, an issue of *Journal of Social Issues* focused on the under-representation of ethnic minority students in science and engineering fields, and an issue of *Identity* highlighting recent advances in Erik Erikson's theory of identity development.

"Overall, I think the chapter [Chapter 4, "The Self, Identity, Emotions, and Personality"] *is great. My comments are meant to improve upon an already fine work. It is easy to read, covers a lot of territory, and is very current. . . . The chapter reads very 'fresh' and current. This is particularly the case for the section on identity, where John Santrock does a nice job of discussing some of the current issues and debates in the field."* **—Dr. Moin Syed,** *University of Minnesota*

Pamela King

Pamela King is one of the world's leading experts on religious and spiritual development in adolescence and emerging adulthood. Dr. King obtained her undergraduate degree in psychology from Stanford University and a Master's of Divinity and Ph.D. in family studies from Fuller Theological Seminary. She also completed postdoctoral work at the Center on Adolescence at Stanford University. Dr. King currently is a professor in the area of family studies in the Center for Research and Child and Adolescent Development in the School of Psychology at Fuller Theological Seminary and ordained in the Presbyterian Church (USA). She also has been a visiting scholar at Cambridge University. Dr. King's main research areas are positive youth development, spiritual and moral development, and theological perspectives of development. She is a co-author of *The Reciprocating Self* and co-editor of the *Handbook of Spiritual Development in Childhood and Adolescence*. Her research has been published in a number of leading journals.

". . . Great work on the text. I am thrilled to see that John Santrock is expanding the text in the area of religion and spirituality. I believe this edition of the text will mark the most thorough and advanced coverage of this burgeoning topic and will further distinguish this text from other developmental texts." **—Dr. Pamela King,** *Fuller Theological Seminary*

Robert Laird

Robert Laird is a leading expert on family processes, peer relations, and the development of adolescent problems. He obtained his Ph.D. in human development and family studies from Auburn University and currently is a professor in the Department of Psychology at the University of New Orleans. Dr. Laird previously held faculty positions at Louisiana State University and the University of Rhode Island. His research interests focus on the contexts in which children and adolescents develop social and behavioral competencies with an emphasis on parent-child and peer relationships. Recently, Dr. Laird's research program has focused on young adolescents' decisions to keep parents informed versus restrict parents' access to information.

"This text is very comprehensive and attempts to incorporate as many recent publications as possible. It is clear from the preface and citations that there was an extensive effort to update the sources used in the text." **—Dr. Robert Laird,** *University of New Orleans*

Valerie Reyna

Valerie Reyna is one of the world's leading experts on cognitive processes in adolescent development. Dr. Reyna obtained her Ph.D. in experimental psychology from Rockefeller University and currently is co-director of the Center for Behavioral Economics and Decision Research and professor of human development, psychology, cognitive science and neuroscience at Cornell University. She publishes regularly in a wide range of journals, including *Psychological Science* and *Medical Decision Making*. Her research focuses on a number of aspects of memory, human judgment, and decision making. Dr. Reyna developed fuzzy-trace theory, a model of the relation between mental representations and decision making that has been widely applied in law, medicine, and public health. She is past president of the Society for Judgment and Decision Making, and also is a Fellow of the Division of Experimental Psychology, the Division of Developmental Psychology, the Division of Educational Psychology, and the Division of Health Psychology of the American Psychological Association. Dr. Reyna is a permanent member of the study sections of the National Institutes of Health and also has been a member of advisory panels for the National Science Foundation and the National Academy of Sciences.

"John Santrock has done a remarkable job of maintaining the currency of this book, updating the narrative and references, reflecting cutting-edge issues in the field. . . . I read the cognitive development chapter carefully, certain that I could add some 2010 or 2011 references, but most were already there, and well-integrated into the text. The emphasis on the latest research and the up-to-the-minute currency make this book head and shoulders above most undergraduate textbooks in the area. . . . The author's number one aim is to provide students with the most current theory and research about adolescence and emerging adulthood, and he succeeds admirably. . . . John Santrock has a keen appreciation for the topics that interest students, such as choosing a career or finding a purpose in life." **—Dr. Valerie Reyna,** *Cornell University*

content **revisions**

Numerous content changes were made in each of the 13 chapters in *Adolescence,* fourteenth edition. Here are some of the main ones.

Chapter 1: Introduction

- Extensive updating of research citations
- Much expanded coverage of cohort effects (Schaie, 2011a,b)
- New material on Millennials and how they are experiencing adolescence and emerging adulthood differently than did their counterparts in prior eras
- Inclusion of recent research and commentary on Millennials based on a recent national survey by the Pew Research Center (Lenhart & others, 2010a,b)
- Expanded discussion of poverty and adolescent development, including updated statistics on the percentage of U.S. children and adolescents under 18 years of age living in poverty (Childstats.gov, 2010)
- New Connecting with Adolescents feature: Doly Akter, Improving the Lives of Adolescent Girls in the Slums of Bangladesh
- Coverage of a recent national study on adolescent striving that focused on sparks, relational support for those sparks, and empowerment (Scales, Benson, & Roehlkepartain, 2011)
- Expanded and updated coverage of the importance of having meaningful relationships with adults beyond parents or guardians, such as coaches, neighbors, teachers, and so on (Benson, 2010)
- Description of a recent survey that found only 20 percent of U.S. 15-year-olds reported that they have had meaningful relationships outside their family that have helped them succeed in life (Search Institute, 2010)
- Added information about family obligation possibly helping immigrant adolescents to develop a positive pattern of adaptation (van Geel & Vedder, 2010)
- New material on the high percentage of deaths of the world's adolescents occurring in just two regions: sub-Saharan Africa and southeast Asia (Fatusi & Hindin, 2010)
- Discussion of a recent cross-cultural study of adolescents in 12 countries around the world focused on the importance of parental support (McNeely & Barber, 2010)
- Coverage of a recent Belgian study indicating that continued co-residence with parents during emerging adulthood slows down the process of becoming a self-sufficient and independent adult (Kins & Beyers, 2010)
- Expanded discussion of emerging adulthood, including material on whether it is likely to be universal or not, and its occurrence in European countries and Australia, as well as the United States (Kins & Beyers, 2010; Sirsch & others, 2009)
- Inclusion of recent research indicating that the majority of 18- to 26-year-olds in India felt that they had achieved adulthood (Seiter & Nelson, 2011)
- New coverage of Joseph and Claudia Allen's (2009) ideas about whether the road to adult maturity is being harmed by adolescence taking too long; includes their recommendations on how to provide adolescents with experiences that will help them mature more effectively
- New commentary about how extensively research on adolescent and emerging adulthood expanded in the first decade of the twenty-first century (Russell, Card, & Susman, 2011)
- New Figure 1.14 showing neuroimages of the brains of two adolescents (one a non-drinker, the other a heavy drinker) while they are engaging in a memory task
- New entries in the section on Connecting with Resources for Improving the Lives of Adolescents: (1) Brown, B. B., & M. Prinstein (Ed.). (2011). *Encyclopedia of Adolescence* (Vols. 1, 2, 3). New York: Elsevier. (2) Allen, J., & Allen, C. W. (2009). *Escaping the endless adolescence.* New York: Ballantine.

Chapter 2: Puberty, Health, and Biological Foundations

- Expanded commentary about puberty being a process, not a specific event, as well as the complexity of neuroendocrine changes being involved in pubertal change (Dorn & Biro, 2011)
- New conclusion based on a recent research review that the onset of menarche has not fallen as much as the onset of puberty (Dorn & Biro, 2011)
- Inclusion of recent information on a longitudinal study of the sequence of pubertal events in boys and girls (Susman & others, 2010)
- Updated commentary on the recent interest in molecular genetic studies that seek to identify genes that are linked to the onset of puberty (Elks & Ong, 2011; Paris & others, 2010)
- Description of a recent study of the role of weight in girls' pubertal development (Christensen & others, 2010)
- Inclusion of information from a recent research review on the role of early growth acceleration and its predictions of very early pubertal onset in girls and overweight

and obesity later in childhood and adolescence (Papadimitriou & others, 2010)

- Coverage of a recent research review indicating puberty does seem to be occurring earlier for overweight girls but that obesity delays pubertal onset in boys; earlier puberty in girls appears to be due to the increase in overweight and obesity (Walvoord, 2010)
- New paragraph on an individual ultimate height usually being at about the midpoint between the biological mother's and the biological father's heights, including a commentary about when the growth spurt typically ends
- Discussion of a recent study of gender differences in the aesthetic aspects of adolescents' body image (Abbott & Barber, 2010)
- Inclusion of information about a recent study of adolescents with the most positive body images, which was linked to their health-enhancing behavior, especially regular exercise (Frisen & Holmqvist, 2010)
- Description of a recent study of the links between body image and psychological well-being in non-Latino White, Latino, African American, and Asian American adolescents (Yuan, 2010)
- Coverage of a recent longitudinal study of early- and late-maturing girls from adolescence through emerging adulthood (Copeland & others, 2010)
- Discussion of a recent study on early maturing girls' higher level of depression and its link to a heightened sensitivity to interpersonal stress (Natsuaki & others, 2010)
- Coverage of recent research on the developmental pathway of early pubertal timing, early sexual activity, and delinquency in girls (Negriff, Susman, & Trickett, 2011)
- Discussion of recent research that found a higher level of internalizing problems in early maturing non-Latino White girls but not in early maturing African American girls (DeRose & others, 2011)
- Description of recent research linking maternal harshness in early childhood with early maturation and sexual risk taking in adolescence (Belsky & others, 2010)
- Coverage of a recent study that found a link between early maturation and substance abuse as well as early sexual intercourse (Gaudineau & others, 2010)
- Inclusion of information about recent research that concluded having a motor vehicle crash in adolescence was linked to a general tendency to take risks (Dunlop & Romer, 2010)
- Description of a recent study of different types of sensation-seeking young adolescents and links to whether they engaged in problem behaviors (Lynne-Landsman & others, 2010)
- Updated and expanded information about the increase in health problems in emerging adulthood compared to adolescence (Fatusi & Hindin, 2010; Irwin, 2010)
- New material on the role of schools in promoting adolescents' eating patterns, including a recent intervention study that increased vegetable consumption (Wang & others, 2010)
- Coverage of a recent study linking a low level of exercise to cardiovascular disease risk (Lobelo & others, 2010)
- Description of recent research linking a higher level of exercise in adolescence with a lower level of alcohol, cigarette, and marijuana use (Terry-McElrath, O'Malley, & Johnston, 2011)
- Discussion of a recent study linking low levels of exercise to depressive symptoms in young adolescents (Sund, Larsson, & Wichstrom, 2011)
- Description of recent research showing links between aerobic exercise and a number of children's and adolescents' cognitive skills (Best, 2011)
- Inclusion of information from a recent study indicating that high exercise levels in adolescence were related better sleep patterns, less tiredness, and improved concentration (Brand & others, 2010)
- Description of a recent study that found vigorous physical activity was related to lower drug use in adolescents (Delisle & others, 2010)
- New discussion of links between screen-based activity and physical exercise in adolescents, including recent research indicating that adolescents who combine low physical activity and high screen-based activity are nearly twice as likely to be overweight (Sisson & others, 2010)
- Description of four recent studies that found adolescent sleep was related to negative developmental outcomes (Beebe, Rose, & Amin, 2010; Clinkinbeard & others, 2011; Dregan & Armstrong, 2010; McHale & others, 2010)
- Coverage of a recent research review comparing adolescent bedtimes, total sleep, and daytime sleepiness on school days in North American, European, and Asian adolescents (Gradisar, Gardner, & Dohnt, 2011)
- Description of a recent study on delaying school start time for ninth- to twelfth-grade students and their improved sleep, alertness, mood, and health (Owens, Belon, & Moss, 2010)
- Discussion of a recent study of emerging adults' sleep patterns and indications that first-year college students have bedtimes and rise times that are later than those of seniors in high school but that bedtimes and rise times become earlier by the third and fourth year of college (Lund & others, 2010)
- Expanded discussion of criticisms of evolutionary psychology to include it being on a time scale that does not allow its empirical study
- New introductory material connecting the discussion of evolution and genetics
- New discussion of the concept of gene-gene interaction (Bapat & others, 2010)
- Updated coverage of the concept of $G \times E$, which involves the interaction of a specific measured variation in the DNA sequence and a specific measured aspect of the environment (Caspi & others, 2011; Rutter & Dodge, 2011)

- Inclusion of information about a G $\times$ E study linking an interaction between a genetic plasticity index based on five genes and supportive parenting with adolescent self-regulation (Belsky & Beaver, 2011)
- Inclusion of a new resource—The National Adolescent Health Information Center—in the section on Connecting with Resources for Improving the Lives of Adolescents

Chapter 3: The Brain and Cognitive Development

- Updated coverage of the development of the brain in adolescence (Casey, Jones, & Somerville, 2011)
- New entrees added to Connecting to Resources for Improving the Lives of Adolescents, including the December 2010 isssue of *Brain and Cognition* that presents a very up-to-date portrait of what is currently known about adolescent brain development.
- New material on the distinction between white matter and gray matter, including an explanation of their developmental changes in adolescence and a new Figure 3.3 (Gogtay & Thompson, 2010; Paus, 2010)
- Expanded discussion of the role that an increase in dopamine production in adolescence plays in reward seeking (Doremus-Fitzwater, Valrinskaya, & Spear, 2010)
- Inclusion of Laurence Steinberg and his colleagues' (Albert & Steinberg, 2011a,b; Cauffman & others, 2010; Steinberg & others, 2008, 2009) recent research and theorizing on changes during adolescence in preference for immediate rewards, benefits versus costs of engaging in risk taking, and impulse control
- New discussion of the potential positive outcomes of some aspects of risk taking in adolescence (Allen & Allen, 2009)
- New section, "Cognition and Emotion," in the discussion of cognitive changes in emerging and early adulthood
- New discussion of Labouvie-Vief and her colleagues' (Labouvie-Vief, 2006; Labouvie-Vief, Gruhn, & Studer, 2010) view of developmental changes in the integration and complexity of cognition and emotion, as well as increasing internal reflection and less context-dependent thinking in those who are middle-aged than in young adults
- Revision of the definition of postformal thought to include Labouvie-Vief and her colleagues' (2010) view on the role of emotion in cognitive changes
- Inclusion of recent information about the assessment of postformal thinking, including new Figure 3.5, that gives students an opportunity to evaluate their postformal thinking (Cartwright & others, 2009)
- Discussion of a recent study indicating that college students with a higher number of cross-category friends have a higher level of postformal thinking than do their counterparts with fewer cross-category friends (Galupo, Cartwright, & Savage, 2010)
- Coverage of a recent study that compared the wisdom of college students and older adults on three dimensions: cognitive, reflective, and affective (Ardelt, 2010)
- Added examples of different aspects of wisdom to provide students an indication of the types of items that are assessed in studies of wisdom (Ardelt, 2010)
- New discussion of a recent study linking working memory competence in elementary school with foreign language achievement in early adolescence (Andersson, 2010)
- New research on the prefrontal cortex's increasing role in working memory during late adolescence (Finn & others, 2010)
- Extensively updated and expanded coverage of cognitive control, including new sections on the roles of controlling attention, inhibiting distracting thoughts, and being cognitively flexible (Diamond, Casey, & Munakata, 2011; Galinsky, 2010)
- New Figure 3.11, which lets students evaluate how good they are at cognitive flexibility (Galinsky, 2010)
- Expanded discussion of creative thinking, including recent research indicating a decline in creative thinking by U.S. children and adolescents, and increased interest in teaching creative thinking in Chinese schools (Kim, 2010; Plucker, 2010)
- Description of a recent study with college students indicating that metacognition is a key factor in the ability to engage effectively in critical thinking (Magno, 2010)
- Description of a recent study of predicting academic performance with measures of general mental abilities and emotional intelligence (Song & others, 2010)
- Description of a recent research study indicating that adolescents envision that they are vulnerable to experiencing a premature death (de Bruin, Parker, & Fischhoff, 2007; Fischhoff & others, 2010)
- Expanded and updated coverage of the importance of perspective taking and ego development in explaining the imaginary audience and personal fable (Lapsley & Hill, 2010)
- Inclusion of recent research on the importance of distinguishing between two types of invulnerability (danger and psychological), which have different outcomes (Lapsley & Hill, 2010)
- New coverage of the view of Daniel Lapsley and his colleagues (Hill, Duggan, & Lapsley, 2011; Lapsley & Stey, 2012) that adolescents' personal fables are the result of the individuation-separation process and are not due to cognitive developmental changes

Chapter 4: The Self, Identity, Emotion, and Personality

- Added definitions of the self, identity, and personality
- Updated material on adolescents' social comparison, including comments about the looking glass self (Sebastian, Burnett, & Blakemore, 2010)

- Coverage of a recent longitudinal study linking childhood traits with narcissism in adolescence and emerging adulthood, as well as description of developmental changes in narcissism from14 to 23 years of age (Carlson & Gjerde, 2010)
- Updated material on the controversy over whether today's youth are more narcissistic than were their counterparts in the past (Arnett, 2010; Donnellan & Trzesniewski, 2010; Twenge & Campbell, 2010)
- Inclusion of recent research indicating that age differences are stronger than generational differences in narcissism (Roberts, Edmonds, & Grijaiva, 2010)
- New Figure 4.5, which gives students the opportunity to explore their identity status on a number of identity dimensions.
- Coverage of a recent study indicating that as individuals age from 12 to 20 years they increasingly engage in in-depth exploration of their identity (Klimstra & others, 2010)
- Description of a recent study on the consistency of identity over the course of adolescence and the percentage of adolescents who have identity conflicts throughout adolescence (Meeus & others, 2010)
- Coverage of a recent meta-analysis of 124 studies focused on developmental changes in Marcia's identity statuses (Kroger, Martinussen, & Marcia, 2010)
- Description of a recent study on an increase in engaging in thinking about meaning in life related to one's identity, especially meaning related to the self as changing (McLean, Breen, & Fournier, 2010)
- Discussion of a recent large-scale study of emerging adults that linked identity statuses to various measures of psychological well-being and health (Schwartz & others, 2011)
- Description of a recent meta-analysis that found links between secure attachment and identity achievement (Arseth & others, 2009)
- Coverage of a recent study of 14- to 21-year-olds' responses to the label "White" (Marks, Patton, & Garcia Coll, 2011)
- Inclusion of information from a recent study linking cultural socialization to higher self-esteem through a pathway of ethnic centrality (Rivas-Drake, 2011)
- Description of a recent research review that concluded a mature identity in adolescence is linked to high levels of adjustment and positive personality traits (Meeus, 2011)
- Coverage of a recent research review indicating that identity is more stable in adults than adolescents (Meeus, 2011)
- Discussion of a recent study indicating that ethnic identity in adolescents was linked to adjustment primarily through its role in fostering a positive sense of meaning (Kiang & Fuligni, 2010)
- Description of recent research confirming Erikson's theory that identity development in adolescence is a precursor of intimacy in romantic relationships in emerging adulthood (Beyers & Seiffge-Krenke, 2011)
- Inclusion of material on links between the Big Five factors of personality and identity development in college students
- Discussion of recent research on developmental changes in the Big Five factors in adolescence indicating negative trends for early adolescence and positive trends for late adolescence and the beginning of emerging adulthood (Soto & others, 2011)
- Updated material on possible alternatives to the Big Five factors of personality, including a sixth factor (honesty-humility) (Lee & Ashton, 2008) and three of the Big Five as possibly the best conceptualization across most cultures (De Raad & others 2010)
- New section, "Optimism," to reflect the increased interest that an optimistic thinking style can have in improving adolescent adjustment and development (Duke & others, 2011; Hirsch & others, 2009; Patton & others, 2011)

Chapter 5: Gender

- Discussion of a recent study of gender differences in college students' near and distant future selves in terms of family (economic provider, caregiver) and career (Brown & Diekman, 2010)
- New material on gender segregation in adolescence involving "hanging out" (Mehta & Strough, 2010)
- New commentary about friendships mainly being same-sex in adolescence through late adulthood (Mehta & Strough, 2009, 2010)
- Coverage of a recent study of how gender is displayed in MTV music videos (Wallis, 2011)
- Inclusion of information about a recent meta-analysis that revealed no gender differences in math for adolescents (Lindberg & others, 2010)
- Description of a recent study regarding cognitive gender differences and the extent to which adults stereotype these differences (Halpern, Straight, & Stephenson, 2011)
- Updated material on gender differences in high school dropout rates (National Center for Education Statistics, 2011)
- Update on the increasing gender difference in college enrollment, with more women than men going to college after high school (Women in Academia, 2011)
- Coverage of a recent large-scale study linking girls' positive attitudes about school to their higher grades and boys' negative attitudes toward school to their lower grades (Orr, 2011)
- Description of a recent research review focused on girls' negative attitudes about math and the negative expectations that parents and teachers have for girls' math competence (Gunderson, 2011)

- Discussion of a recent study indicating that relational aggression increases in middle and late childhood (Dishion & Piehler, 2009)
- Inclusion of information from a recent research review that girls engage in more relational aggression than do boys in adolescence but not in childhood (Smith, Rose, & Schwartz-Mette, 2010)
- Description of a recent study linking parents' psychological control to a higher incidence of relational aggression in their children (Kuppens & others, 2009)
- Updated and expanded discussion of gender differences in emotion (Hertenstein & Keltner, 2011)
- Revised and updated discussion of gender differences in relationships, including information from recent research reviews (Galambos & others, 2009; Perry & Pauletti, 2011)
- Coverage of a recent research review indicating that gender differences in adolescence are small (Perry & Pauletti, 2011)
- Inclusion of information about a recent study that indicated hyper-gender behavior in boys and girls was linked to a lower level of school engagement and school attachment (Ueno & McWilliams, 2010)
- Coverage of a recent study that found no intensification of masculinity or femininity in early adolescence (Priess, Lindberg, & Hyde, 2009)

Chapter 6: Sexuality

- New material on adolescents' use of Internet resources for information about sexuality, including description of a recent study of the quality and degree of accuracy of 177 sexual health websites (Buhi & others, 2010)
- Coverage of the American Academy of Pediatrics' (2010) recent policy statement regarding sexuality, contraception, and the media
- Revised and updated data (Figure 6.1) on the percentage of adolescents who reported that they have had sexual intercourse, including a recent gender reversal for twelfth-graders, with a higher percentage of twelfth-grade girls reporting that they have had sex than do twelfth-grade boys (Eaton & others, 2010)
- Updated data on the percentage of U.S. adolescents who report that they are currently sexually active (Eaton & others, 2010)
- Revised and updated data on the percentage of non-Latino White, African American, and Latino adolescents who report that they have had sexual intercourse (Eaton & others, 2010)
- New information about the pluses and minuses of oral versus vaginal sex based on a recent editorial by Bonnie Halpern-Felsher (2008) in the *Journal of Adolescent Health*
- Description of a recent study identifying the temporal order between oral and vaginal sex in adolescence (Song & Halpern-Felsher, 2010)
- Coverage of a study of adolescents' more positive outcomes when they have only oral sex versus vaginal sex (Brady & Halpern-Felsher, 2007)
- Discussion of a recent study that linked alcohol use, early menarche, and poor parent-child communication to early sexually intimate behavior in girls (Hipwell & others, 2011)
- Coverage of a recent study of early initiation of sexual intercourse in five countries (Madkour & others, 2010)
- Reorganized, updated, and expanded material on risk factors in adolescent sexuality
- Discussion of a recent study that revealed a link between neighborhood poverty concentration and 15- to 17-year-old boys' and girls' sexual initiation (Cubbin & others, 2010)
- Description of the results from a recent research review of a number of aspects of connectedness, such as family connectedness and parent-adolescent communication about sexuality, and links to adolescent sexuality outcomes (Markham & others, 2010)
- Coverage of a recent study linking family strengths in childhood with delayed initiation of sexual activity and less likelihood of adolescent pregnancy (Hillis & others, 2010)
- Description of recent research linking deviant peer relations in early adolescence with an increase in multiple sexual partners at age 16 (Lansford & others, 2010)
- New information from a recent research review on the role of prosocial norms and spirituality as protective factors in reducing negative sexual outcomes in youth (House & others, 2010)
- Description of a recent study linking parents' religiosity to a lower level of adolescents' risky sexual behavior (Landor & others, 2010)
- New discussion of recent interest in positive youth development programs in reducing negative sexual outcomes (Catalano, Gavin, & Markham, 2010; Gavin & others, 2010)
- Inclusion of information from a recent study of the sexual double standard at the societal, school, and friendship level for adolescent girls (Lyons & others, 2010)
- Inclusion of information about a recent national survey indicating that sexual minority youth engage in a higher number of health-risk behaviors than do their heterosexual counterparts (Kann & others, 2011)
- Expanded coverage of causes of homosexual behavior, including a recent large-scale study in Sweden (King, 2011; Langstrom & others, 2010)
- Description of a recent study that examined the percentage of adolescents who reported that they had masturbated at some point (Fortenberry & others, 2010)
- Updated information about the percentage of sexually active adolescents at different grade levels who used a condom the last time they had sexual intercourse (Eaton & others, 2010)

- Updated data on adolescent pregnancy trends indicating that in 2009 the U.S. adolescent pregnancy rate reached its lowest level since data have been recorded; includes update of Figure 6.5 (National Center for Health Statistics, 2011)
- Updated Figure 6.6 with recent data comparing birth rates of 15- to 19-year-old girls from different ethnic groups in the United States (National Center for Health Statistics, 2011)
- New coverage of information comparing ethnic groups on the likelihood of having a second child in adolescence (Rosengard, 2009)
- Updated Figure 6.7 with recent data on the continuing decline in the percentage of 15- to 19-year-old girls in the United States who give birth but are unmarried (Hamilton, Martin, & Ventura, 2010)
- Updated data on the percentage of U.S. adolescent girls' pregnancies that end in an abortion (Alan Guttmacher Institute, 2010)
- Description of a recent study that found abortion did not lead to mental health problems in adolescent girls (Warren & others, 2010)
- Inclusion of a recent meta-analysis of studies on gender differences in sexuality (Petersen & Hyde, 2010)
- Inclusion of a recent estimate that while 15- to 24-year-olds represent only 25 percent of the sexually experienced population in the United States, they acquire almost 50 percent of all new STIs (Centers for Disease Control and Prevention, 2009a)
- Updated description of HIV and AIDS in the United States (National Center for Health Statistics, 2010)
- Inclusion of information from an extensive research review indicating the effectiveness of behavioral interventions in reducing HIV in U.S. adolescents (Johnson & others, 2011)
- Updated data on the percentage of ninth- to twelfth-grade U.S. students who have been physically forced to have sex (Eaton & others, 2010)
- Coverage of a recent study that indicated sexual assault was more likely to occur if the offender was using substances, regardless of whether or not the victim was (Brecklin & Ullman, 2010)
- New description of the red zone on college and university campuses and the time in their college years when women are most likely to have unwanted sexual experiences (Kimble & others, 2008)
- New data on the percentage of U.S. adolescents who have been taught in school about AIDS or HIV (Eaton & others, 2010)
- Inclusion of information about some sex education programs that are abstinence-plus sexuality, in which programs promote abstinence, as well as contraceptive use (Realini & others, 2010)

Chapter 7: Moral Development, Values, and Religion

- Description of a recent study of children's unwillingness to donate any money after watching a UNICEF film on children suffering from poverty until an adult gently probed their intentions, which supports the situational nature of moral behavior (van IJzendoorn & others, 2010)
- Discussion of recent research by Gustavo Carlo and his colleagues (2010) that illustrated the importance of considering the multidimensional aspects of prosocial behavior
- Coverage of a recent study that revealed links between a higher level of multicultural experience and a lower level of closed mindedness, a growth mindset, and higher moral judgment (Narváez & Hill, 2010)
- Expanded discussion of moral identity with an emphasis on Darcia Narváez' (2010a) recent view that moral metacognition, especially through self-monitoring and self-reflection, is linked to moral maturity
- Description of a recent study that found adolescents' moral motivation was related to the quality of their relationship with their parents (Malti & Buchmann, 2010)
- Coverage of a recent study that linked authoritative parenting to an increase in adolescents' moral identity (Hardy & others, 2010)
- Much expanded, revised, and updated material on the domain theory of moral development and social conventional reasoning (Helwig & Turiel, 2011; Nucci & Gingo, 2011; Smetana, 2011)
- Discussion of two recent studies that revealed an important role of early secure attachment in children's and adolescents' future outcomes (Kochanska & others, 2010a,b)
- Description of a recent study linking college students' personality traits and engagement in academic cheating (Williams, Nathanson, & Paulhus, 2010)
- New introduction discussion of the history and current efforts of the U.S. government to engage students in service to the community and nation
- Updated coverage of the percentage of college freshmen who view being well-off financially versus pursuing a meaningful philosophy of life a very important or essential goal (Pryor & others, 2010)
- Updated material on the percentage of college freshmen who estimate that there is a very good chance they will participate in volunteer or community work (Pryor & others, 2010)
- New coverage of distinctions between religion, religiousness, and spirituality based on a recent analysis by Pamela King and her colleagues (2011)
- Update of college freshmen's religious activities and preference (Pryor & others, 2010)

- Description of a recent study of religious activity across the first three semesters of college (Stoppa & Lefkowitz, 2010)
- Coverage of a recent study linking religious attendance and a lower level of substance abuse in adolescents (Good & Willoughby, 2010)
- Discussion of recent research on church engagement and a lower level of depression in adolescents (Kang & Romo, 2011)
- Description of recent research linking parents' religiosity with adolescents' lower level of risky sexual behavior (Landor & others, 2011)
- Inclusion of recent research that found spirituality was related to a number of positive adolescent sexual outcomes (House & others, 2010)

Chapter 8: Families

- New coverage of a recent study of young adolescents who spent a lot of time unsupervised that revealed parental solicitation at age 11 predicted a lower level of antisocial behavior at age 12 (Laird, Marrero, & Sentse, 2010)
- Description of a recent cross-cultural study of adolescent self-disclosure to parents and adolescents' social competence (Hunter & others, 2011)
- Expanded and updated discussion of adolescents' management of their parents' access to information; includes recent research (Laird & Marrero, 2010; Smetana, 2011a,b)
- New description of a recent study of problematic neighborhoods and mothers' knowledge of their adolescents' whereabouts (Byrnes & others, 2011)
- Coverage of a recent study that found delinquency was lowest in families with at least one authoritative parent and highest in families with two neglectful parents (Hoeve & others, 2011)
- Discussion of recent research focused on parent-adolescent relationships of Asian American parents and their adolescents (Russell, Crockett, & Chao, 2010)
- New section, "Parenting Styles in Emerging Adulthood," including discussion of a recent study of mothers' and fathers' parenting styles and their links to emerging adult outcomes (Nelson & others, 2011)
- New information about the estimated number of youth who run away from home in the United States each year (Walsh & Donaldson, 2010)
- Description of a recent study of homeless youth and deterioration of their resilience associated with how long they did not have stable housing (Cleverley & Kidd, 2011)
- Coverage of a recent longitudinal study of factors that predict whether adolescents will run away from home, and outcomes for runaways at age 21 (Tucker & others, 2011)
- New discussion of National Safe Place, a partnership of youth-serving agencies, businesses, and community organizations, which provides immediate safety and access to service providers (Walsh & Donaldson, 2010)
- Description of a recent analysis that concluded the most consistent outcomes of secure attachment in adolescence involve positive peer relations and the development of emotion regulation capacities (Allen & Miga, 2010)
- Revised and updated discussion of adult attachment styles, including an opportunity for students to evaluate their own attachment style
- Updated and expanded material on the stability of adult attachment styles
- Inclusion of recent research on emerging adults' attachment security and the quality of their romantic relationships (Holland & Roisman, 2010)
- Discussion of recent research on links between anxious and avoidant attachment styles and various health problems (McWilliams & Bailey, 2010)
- Coverage of a recent study that revealed the importance of parents acting as "scaffolding" and "safety nets" to support their children's successful transition through emerging adulthood (Swartz & others, 2011)
- New information about a recent study of mothers' and fathers' parenting styles and their links to emerging adult outcomes (Nelson & others, 2011)
- Description of a recent study of developmental changes in adolescents and emerging adults' attachments to important people in their lives and links to behavioral problems (Rosenthal & Kobak, 2010)
- Coverage of a recent analysis that revealed a link between insecure attachment in adults and depression (Bakersmans-Kranenburg & van IJzendoorn, 2009)
- Discussion of a recent study that revealed attachment-anxious individuals show strong ambivalence toward a romantic partner (Mikulincer & others, 2010)
- Description of a recent study linking recent secure attachment to parents with ease in forming friendships in college (Parade, Leerkes, & Blankson, 2010)
- Coverage of a newly developed concept, *troubled ruminations about parents,* and its link to a number of negative outcomes for emerging adults (Schwartz & Finley, 2010)
- Inclusion of recent research on adolescents' perception of their parents' promotion of more psychological autonomy and less psychological control, and links to adolescent adjustment (Sher-Censor, Parke, & Coltrane, 2011)
- Description of a recent study of emerging and young adults with and without children and how frequently they see their parents (Bucx, Raaijmakers, & Van Wel, 2010)
- New discussion of immigrant adolescents as cultural brokers for their parents (Villanueva & Buriel, 2010)

- Expanded and updated coverage of the relationship between divorced parents and its link to visitations by the noncustodial parent (Fabricus & others, 2010)
- New discussion of E. Mark Cummings and his colleagues' (Cummings & Davies, 2010; Cummings, El-Sheikh, & Kouros, 2009) emotional security theory and its focus on the type of marital conflict that is negative for children's and adolescents' development
- Description of recent research revealing that an intervention in divorced families that focused on improving the mother-child relationship was linked to increases in children's and adolescents' short-term (6 months) and long-term (6 years) coping skills (Velez & others, 2011)
- Added comment about father involvement dropping off more than mother involvement following a divorce, especially for fathers of girls
- Inclusion of information about joint custody working best for children when the divorced parents can get along with each other (Parke & Clarke-Stewart, 2011)
- Added commentary about parental work's effect on adolescents not being only a maternal employment issue, but often involving the father as well (Parke & Clarke-Stewart, 2011)
- Description of a recent national survey indicating that 15.1 million children and adolescents in the United States are alone and unsupervised after school (Afterschool Alliance, 2009)
- Coverage of a recent within-family design of families with a biological child and an adopted child indicating only a slight trend in more internalized and externalized problems for adopted children (Glover & others, 2010)
- Discussion of a recent study of improved cognitive development in children who were adopted after they had lived in foster homes and institutions (van den Dries & others, 2010)
- Coverage of recent information about child and adolescent outcomes conceived by new reproductive technologies, which are increasingly used by gay and lesbian adults (Golombok, 2011a,b; Golombok & Tasker, 2010)
- New coverage of the concept of the middle generation more often functioning as a "pivot" generation than a "sandwich" generation (Fingerman & Birditt, 2011)
- Discussion of recent research linking the transmission of divorce across generations, although this transmission has decreased in recent years (Wolfinger, 2011)
- Description of a recent study of how often middle-aged parents provide support to their children who are 18 years and older (Fingerman & others, 2011)
- Expanded and updated coverage of social policy recommendations for adolescents and families with a focus on four of the best organizations in this regard: The Annie E. Casey Foundation, First Focus, the Institute for Youth, Education, and Families at the National League of Cities, and the National Collaboration for Youth
- Three new entries in Connecting with Resources for Improving the Lives of Adolescents: (1) Sheryl Feinstein's (2010) *101 Insights and Strategies for Parenting Teenagers*, (2) Laurence Steinberg's (2011) *You and Your Adolescent*, and (3) *Building a Brighter Future* (National Collaboration for Youth, 2011)

Chapter 9: Peers, Romantic Relationships, and Lifestyles

- Discussion of a recent short-term longitudinal study of links between parental management of adolescents' peer relations, precursors of parental management dimensions, and adolescents' social skills (Mounts, 2011)
- Coverage of recent analysis indicating that one of the most consistent outcomes of attachment research in adolescence is that secure attachment to parents is linked to positive peer relations (Allen & Miga, 2010)
- Description of a recent study linking adolescents' social intelligence with their peer popularity (Meijs & others, 2010)
- Inclusion of a recent study that focused on adolescents' grade point averages and links to having in-school and out-of-school friends (Witkow & Fuligni, 2010)
- Discussion of a recent study of young adolescents' friendships and depression (Brendgen & others, 2010)
- Description of recent research indicating benefits of mixed-age friendships for some young adolescents who don't have friends in their grade (Bowker & Spencer, 2010)
- Coverage of recent research on the characteristics of effective youth programs (Larson & Angus, 2011)
- Description of a recent study of loneliness in Latino high school students and its link to academic difficulties, as well as the buffering influence of friends (Benner, 2011)
- Description of recent research on the negative outcomes of adolescent girls having an older romantic partner (Haydon & Halpern, 2010)
- Discussion of a recent study of adolescent romantic partners and delinquency outcomes (Lonardo & others, 2009)
- Inclusion of recent research indicating the importance of physical appearance in romantic relationships (Furman & Winkles, 2010)
- Description of a recent study of 18- to 20-year-olds that found an increase in heavy drinking, marijuana use, and cigarette smoking following the dissolution of a romantic relationship (Fleming & others, 2010)
- Description of recent research linking the mother's marital satisfaction with the adolescent's romantic competence (Shulman, Davila, & Shachar-Shapira, 2011)
- New coverage of sociologist Andrew Cherlin's (2009) recent analysis of how Americans move in and out of relationship lifestyles more than is the case in other countries

- Updated data on single adults in the United States—for the first time, in 2009 the number of U.S. single adults from 25 to 34 years of age surpassed the number of married adults (U.S. Census Bureau, 2010)
- New coverage of Bella DePaulo's (2007, 2011) conclusion that there is widespread bias against unmarried adults
- Discussion of a recent large-scale study of U.S. singles that found women are not more likely than men to want their independence in relationships (Match.com, 2011)
- Coverage of a recent study of cohabiting couples that found men were more concerned about their loss of freedom while women were more concerned with delays in marriage (Huang & others, 2011)
- Description of a recent meta-analysis of links between cohabitation and marital quality/stability (Jose, O'Leary, & Moyer, 2010)
- Discussion of recent research that found a link between cohabitation prior to becoming engaged and negative marital outcomes for first marriages but not second marriages (Stanley & others, 2010)
- Further clarification of factors involved in whether cohabiting has negative marital outcomes with no negative effects if there were no previous live-in lovers and no children (Cherlin, 2009)
- Updated coverage of the continuing decline in the rate of marriage in the United States from 2007 to 2009 (National Vital Statistical Reports, 2010)
- Revised and updated analysis of marriage trends, including recent research on the percentage of U.S. adults under 30 who think marriage is headed for extinction and the percentage of those young adults who still plan to get married (Pew Research Center, 2010)
- New section on the benefits of a good marriage, including a recent study on a lower proportion of time spent in marriage being linked to a likelihood of earlier death (Henretta, 2010)
- Updated coverage on the resumption of a decline in the rate of divorce in the United States from 2007 to 2009 following an increase from 2005 to 2007 (National Vital Statistical Reports, 2010)
- Inclusion of two new resource recommendations: (1) Andrew Cherlin's recent book on trends in cohabitation, marriage, and divorce and (2) John Gottman and Nan Silver's excellent book on what makes marriages work

Chapter 10: Schools

- Updated coverage of school dropout rates, including new Figure 10.1, which show dropout rates by gender and ethnicity, as well the significant decrease of Latino dropouts in the first decade of the twenty-first century (National Center for Education Statistics, 2010)
- Expanded discussion of schools in low-income areas, including several characteristics of teachers in these areas that can reduce the quality of education experience (Eccles & Roeser, 2011)
- Description of a recent study linking behavioral control and caring with positive student outcomes, such as engagement in learning, which reflects Baumrind's concept of authoritative teaching (Nie & Lau, 2009)
- Description of three recent suicides in middle and late childhood and early adolescence that likely were influenced by bullying (Meyers, 2010)
- New emphasis on the importance of contexts in the study of bullying (Salmivalli, Peets, & Hodges, 2011; Schwartz & others, 2010)
- Coverage of two recent studies of bullies' popularity in the peer group (Veenstra & others, 2010; Witvliet & others, 2010)
- Description of a recent study of peer victimization and the extent of its link to lower academic achievement (Nakamoto & Schwartz, 2010)
- Discussion of a recent study of negative outcomes for bullies, victims, and bully-victims (Fitzpatrick, Dulin, & Piko, 2010)
- New information about the current trend in multicultural education not to focus exclusively on ethnicity but rather cover a diversity of differences, including religion, sexual orientation, disability, and others (Howe, 2010)
- New coverage of the view that too often individuals think that multicultural education is reserved only for students of color; rather, all students, including non-Latino White students, can benefit from multicultural education (Howe, 2010)
- Updated data on the percentage of college students who feel overwhelmed with what they have to do (Pryor & others, 2010)
- Updated statistics on the percentage of students with various disabilities who receive special education services in U.S. schools (National Center for Education Statistics, 2010)
- Expanded coverage of learning disabilities, including new information about dysgraphia and dyscalculia
- Coverage of a recent study indicating delayed development in the frontal lobes of children with ADHD, likely due to delayed or decreased myelination (Nagel & others, 2011)
- Description of a recent study that linked cigarette smoking during pregnancy to ADHD in children (Sciberras, Ukoumunne, & Efron, 2011)
- Updated discussion of the role of neurotransmitters in ADHD to include dopamine (Beaulieu & Gainetdinov, 2011; Mahmoudi-Gharaei & others, 2011)
- New coverage of executive functioning deficits in children and adolescents with ADHD (Jacobson & others, 2011; Rinsky & Hinshaw, 2011)
- Considerable expansion and updating of the discussion of adolescents who are gifted

- New coverage of the roles of nature and nurture in giftedness
- New information about the domain-specific aspects of giftedness (Horowitz, 2009; Winner, 2009)
- New discussion of the importance of identifying individuals who are gifted prior to adolescence (Keating, 2009)
- Expanded material on the education of adolescents who are gifted (Ambrose, Sternberg, & Sriraman, 2012; Sternberg, Grigorenko, & Jarvin, 2011)
- Two new entries in Connecting with Resources for Improving the Lives of Adolescents: (1) *Handbook of Learning and Instruction*, edited by Patricia Alexander and Richard Mayer (2011); (2) *Confronting Dogmatism in Gifted Education*, edited by Don Ambrose, Robert Sternberg, & Bharath Sriraman (2012)

Chapter 11: Achievement, Work, and Careers

- New commentary about Ryan and Deci's (2009) description of teachers who create circumstances for students to engage in self-determination as autonomy-supportive teachers
- New discussion of a recent study of parental intrinsic/extrinsic motivational practices and their link to children's and adolescents' motivation (Gottfried & others, 2009)
- Coverage of a longitudinal study linking children's intrinsic motivation in math and science from 9 to 17 years of age to their parents' motivational practices (Gottfried & others, 2009)
- New coverage of Carol Dweck's recent research and ideas about improving students' growth mindset by teaching them about the brain's plasticity and the brain changes that occur when one puts considerable effort into learning (Blackwell & others, 2007; Dweck & Master, 2009)
- New material about Carol Dweck's recent development of computer modules, called "Brainology," that explain how the brain works and how, through work and effort, students can make their brain work better (Blackwell & Dweck, 2008; Dweck & Master, 2009)
- New discussion of personal goals and their importance in students' motivation (Ford & Smith, 2007; Wigfield & Cambria, 2010)
- Description of a recent study of the importance of intentional self-regulation and extracurricular activities in positive developmental outcomes for young adolescents from low-income backgrounds (Urban, Lewin-Bizan, & Lerner, 2010)
- Discussion of a recent study of positive developmental outcomes for adolescents with high self-efficacy parents (Steca & others, 2011)
- Expanded material on expectations, including information about the roles of values in in adolescents' expectations (Wigfield & Cambria, 2010)
- Coverage of a recent large-scale longitudinal study focused on the importance of academic resources at home, especially in African American or low-SES students' achievement (Xia, 2010)
- Inclusion of recent international comparisons of 15-year-olds' reading, math, and science achievement in 65 countries, including new Figure 11.3 (OECD, 2010)
- Updated statistics on the percentage of college students who work while going to college (National Center for Education Statistics, 2010)
- Description of a recent study of 18- to 20-year-old urban Latinos and their school/work transitions (Sanchez & others, 2011)
- Discussion of recent research involving a re-analysis of data from an earlier study using more stringent matching of groups that revealed working part-time more than 20 hours a week in high school is linked with a decrease in school engagement and an increase in problems (Monahan, Lee, & Steinberg, 2011)
- New entry in Connecting with Resources for Improving the Lives of Adolescents: *Handbook of Self-Regulation of Learning and Performance*, edited by Barry Zimmerman and Dale Schunk (2011)

Chapter 12: Culture

- Updated coverage of poverty statistics for female-headed households and for ethnic groups (Federal Interagency Forum on Child and Family Statistics, 2010)
- Expanded discussion of poverty interventions, including recent research on outcomes of 9- to 19-year-old African American boys after experiencing the New Hope anti-poverty program (McLoyd & others, 2011)
- Expanded coverage of negative outcomes of poverty for adolescents, including links to other chapters where these links are described
- Expanded and updated material on immigrant families and their bicultural orientation including recent research by Ross Parke and his colleagues (2011)
- New discussion of immigrant adolescents as cultural brokers for their parents (Villanueva & Buriel, 2010)
- Discussion of a recent study of the outcomes of discrimination in Latino and Asian American adolescents (Huynh & Fuligni, 2010)
- Coverage of a recent longitudinal study of the educational and occupational aspirations of ethnic groups from 14 to 26 years of age that illustrated the importance of teasing apart SES and ethnicity (Mello, 2009)
- Description of a recent study indicating that adolescents' perceived racial discrimination was linked to the broader

society's negative views of African Americans (Seaton, Yip, & Sellers, 2009)

- Discussion of a recent study that found African American adolescents' perceived racial discrimination was linked to their higher level of delinquency (Martin & others, 2011)
- Substantial updating of media use based on the 2009 national survey of more than 2,000 U.S. adolescents, including comparisons with earlier national surveys to show trends in media use by adolescents (Rideout, Foehr, & Roberts, 2010)
- New information about a recent study of heavy media multitaskers and their problem with interference from irrelevant stimuli (Ophir, Nass, & Wagner, 2009)
- Inclusion of information about adolescents' use of music media and perceptions of their physical attractiveness and self-worth (Kistler & others, 2010)
- Coverage of a recent study of college students' Internet use that found outcomes for college students depended on what they used the Internet for (Padilla-Walker & others, 2010)
- Discussion of recent research that illustrated a link between playing prosocial video games and an increase in prosocial behavior (Gentile & others, 2009)
- Inclusion of information from recent research on video game use and outcomes for college men and women (Padilla-Walker & others, 2010)
- Description of a recent study that found a relation between media violence exposure and an increase in relational aggression in children (Gentile, Mathieson, & Crick, 2010)
- Coverage of recent national surveys of trends in adolescents' use of social media, including dramatic increases in social networking and text messaging, and declines in tweeting and blogging (Lenhart & others, 2010a,b)
- New commentary about text messaging now being the main way that adolescents prefer to connect with their friends (Lenhart & others, 2010b)
- Description of a recent study of the significant threats adolescents encounter both through offline and online bullying (Palfrey & others, 2009)
- Discussion of recent research on the negative outcomes of both online and school victimization (Fredstrom, Adams, & Gilman, 2011)
- Inclusion of information about a recent study of adolescents' involvement in Internet aggression (Werner, Bumpus, & Rock, 2010)
- Inclusion of information that Facebook replaced Google as the most frequently visited Internet site in 2010
- Discussion of recent research linking friendship and behavioral adjustment in early adolescence to emerging adults' communication on social networking sites (Mikami & others, 2010)
- Coverage of a recent study of the low level of parental monitoring of adolescents' online behavior and identification of the parenting style most likely to be linked to adolescents' risky online behavior (Rosen, Cheever, & Carrier, 2008)
- Description of a recent study of parenting predictors of adolescent media use (Padilla-Walker & Coyne, 2011)
- Inclusion of recent research linking problematic mother–early adolescent relationships with negative peer relations on the Internet in emerging adulthood (Szwedo, Mikami, & Allen, 2011)
- New entry in Connecting with Resources for Improving the Lives of Adolescents: *Generation M^2: Media in the Lives of 8- to 18-Year-Olds* (Rideout, Foehr, & Roberts, 2010)

Chapter 13: Problems in Adolescence and Emerging Adulthood

- Important new discussion of the developmental cascade approach in the study of developmental psychopathology (Masten & Cicchetti, 2010)
- New material on the developmental cascade approach of Gerald Patterson and his colleagues (2010) that links inept parenting to the development of antisocial behavior in children, which in turn connects children and adolescents to negative experiences in peer and school contexts.
- Expanded and updated coverage relationship stress and coping in adolescence, including gender differences (Seiffge-Krenke, 2011)
- New description of a prospective study of young adolescents that found links between an optimistic thinking style and subsequent lower levels of depressive symptoms and higher levels of substance abuse and antisocial behavior (Patton & others, 2011a)
- New content on coping with severe stressors, such as the sudden death of a friend or classmate in adolescence (Seiffge-Krenke, 2011)
- New discussion of avoidant coping and a recent study that found avoidant coping and emotion-focused coping were linked with an increased likelihood of depression and engaging in suicide ideation (Horwitz, Hill, & King, 2011)
- Updated coverage of recent trends in use of any illicit drug by adolescents in 2010 (Johnston & others, 2011)
- Updated coverage of drug trends by college students, including gender differences (Johnston & others, 2010)
- Description of recent research indicating that early smoking was predicted by peer and sibling smoking rather than parental smoking (Kelly & others, 2011)
- New data indicating an increase in marijuana use by U.S. adolescents from 2008 through 2010, and a decline

in perceived danger of using marijuana, including new information in Figure 13.5 on adolescents' perceived risk of using marijuana at three grade levels (Johnston & others, 2011)

- New information about the increase in Ecstasy use by U.S. adolescents in 2010 (Johnston & others, 2011)
- New data on the significant drop in Vicodin use by U.S. twelfth-graders in 2010 (Johnston & others, 2011)
- Discussion of a longitudinal study that revealed onset of alcohol use prior to 11 years of age was related to adult alcohol dependence (Guttmannova & others, 2011)
- Coverage of recent research that found parental monitoring was linked to lower substance abuse in adolescence (Tobler & Komro, 2010)
- Description of a recent research review that indicated adolescents who more frequently ate dinner with their family were less likely to have substance abuse problems (Sen, 2010)
- Discussion of recent research on positive and negative aspects of adolescents' interaction and relationships with parents and adolescent drinking and smoking (Guttmannova & others, 2011)
- New coverage of pregaming and gaming as becoming increasingly common rituals on college campuses, including recent research (DeJong, DeRicco, & Schneider, 2010; Read, Merrill, & Bytschkow, 2010)
- Discussion of recent research on the role of parental monitoring and support during adolescence in reducing criminal behavior in emerging adulthood (Johnson & others, 2011)
- Inclusion of recent research on the role of engaged parenting and mothers' social network support in reducing delinquency in low-income families (Ghazarian & Roche, 2010)
- Description of a recent study that found repeated poverty was a high risk factor for delinquency (Najman & others, 2010)
- Discussion of recent research on school connectedness serving as a protective factor in the development of conduct problems in young adolescents (Loukas, Roalson, & Herrera, 2010)
- Updated coverage of outcomes for the Fast Track delinquency intervention study through age 19 that found the program was successful in reducing juvenile arrest rates (Conduct Problems Prevention Research Group, 2010a)
- Coverage of a recent study that revealed male Chinese adolescents and emerging adults experience more depression than do their female counterparts (Sun & others, 2010)
- New material on the developmental cascade approach of Deborah Capaldi and her colleagues, which connects multiple relationships and contexts at different points in development to predict whether adolescents will develop depressive symptoms
- Description of recent research indicating a protective effect of friendship in adolescence by not increasing depressive symptoms in children who avoided peers or were excluded from them (Bukowski, Laursen, & Hoza, 2010)
- Inclusion of recent research indicating that mother-daughter co-rumination was linked to increased anxiety and depression in adolescent daughters (Waller & Rose, 2010)
- Discussion of a recent study linking co-rumination to various aspects of depression two years later in adolescent girls (Stone & others, 2011)
- Coverage of research indicating that exposure to maternal depression prior to age 12 predicted risk processes during development (difficulties in family relationships, for example), which set the course for the development of the adolescent's depression (Garber & Cole, 2010)
- Discussion of recent research indicating that four types of bullying were all linked to adolescents' depression (Wang, Nansel, & Iannotti, 2011)
- Updated national data on the percentage of adolescents who seriously think about committing suicide (Eaton & others, 2010)
- Coverage of a recent study that found increased family support, peer support, and community connectedness was linked to a lower risk of suicidal tendencies (Matlin, Molock, & Tebes, 2011)
- Description of recent research from the National Longitudinal Study of Adolescent Health indicating that parental loss predicted an increase in suicide attempts one year later but not seven years later (Thompson & Light, 2011)
- Inclusion of recent research on suicide attempts by young Latinas (Zayas & others, 2010)
- Discussion of a recent study linking sexual victimization to suicide attempts in adolescence (Plener, Singer, & Goldbeck, 2011)
- New coverage of the leveling off in being overweight in adolescence in the last half of the first decade of the twenty-first century, not just in the United States but in other countries as well (Rokholm, Baker, & Sorensen, 2010)
- Inclusion of recent research linking obesity in adolescence with the development of severe obesity in emerging adulthood (The & others, 2010)
- Discussion of a recent longitudinal study of overweight and obesity over 10 years from 14 years of age to 24 years of age (Patton & others, 2011b)
- Description of a recent study indicating that the main reason adolescents who were overweight were depressed was because of their body dissatisfaction (Mond & others, 2011)
- New material involving a research study of gender differences in being teased for being overweight (Taylor, 2011)

- New coverage of the roles that being overweight and the stress of weight-related concerns play in explaining the increase in depression in adolescent girls, including recent research (Vaughan & Halpern, 2010)
- New description of a recent research review that indicated targeting family lifestyle changes was the most effective strategy for helping children and adolescents lose weight (Oude Luttikhuis & others, 2009)
- Discussion of recent research on the role of attachment insecurity, body dissatisfaction, and need for approval in anorexia nervosa and bulimia nervosa (Abbate-Daga & others, 2010)
- New chapter-ending commentary about the importance of adolescence and emerging adulthood in understanding the student's life
- New section on binge eating disorder (BED), including recent research that indicates characteristics and factors that differentiate BED from other eating disorders (White & Grilo, 2011; Zeeck & others, 2011)
- New recommended resource for improving the lives of adolescents: *Development and Psychopathology*, 2010, Volume 22, Issues 3 and 4, which provides an up-to-date account of theory and research on developmental cascades

acknowledgments

I very much appreciate the support and guidance provided to me by many people at McGraw-Hill. Mike Sugarman, Publisher, has brought a wealth of publishing knowledge and vision to bear on improving my texts. Allison McNamara, Senior Editor, deserves special mention for the superb work she has done as the new editor for this book. The Senior Development Editor, Cara Labell, and Development Editor, Elisa Adams, have done an excellent job of editing the manuscript and handling the page-by-page changes to this new edition. Sarah Kiefer, Editorial Coordinator, has done a very competent job of obtaining reviewers and handling many editorial chores. Julia Flohr, Marketing Manager, has contributed in numerous positive ways to this book. I so much appreciate the direction and guidance provided by Terry Schiesl, Vice-President of Electronic Data Processing, in producing this text. Kate Petrella did a superb job as the book's copy editor. Brett Coker and Aaron Downey did a terrific job in coordinating the book's production.

I also want to thank my wife, Mary Jo, our children, Tracy and Jennifer, and our grandchildren, Jordan, Alex, and Luke, for their wonderful contributions to my life and for helping me to better understand the marvels and mysteries of life-span development.

REVIEWERS

I owe a special gratitude to the reviewers who provided detailed feedback on *Adolescence*.

Expert Consultants

Adolescent development has become an enormous, complex field, and no single author can possibly be an expert in all areas of the field. To solve this problem, I have sought the input of leading experts in many different areas of adolescent development. The experts have provided me with detailed recommendations of new research to include. The panel of experts is literally a who's who in the field of adolescent development. The experts' photographs and biographies appear on pp. xvii–xx.

General Text Reviewers

I also owe a great deal of thanks to the instructors teaching the adolescence course who have provided feedback about the book. Many of the changes in *Adolescence*, fourteenth edition, are based on their input. For their suggestions, I thank these individuals:

Reviewers for the Fourteenth Edition

Janine Buckner, *Seton Hall University;* **Laura Crosetti,** *Monroe Community College;* **Mark Durm,** *Athens State University;* **Celina Echols,** *Southern Louisiana University;* **Lisa Farkas,** *Rowan University;* **Sam Hardy,** *Brigham Young University;* **Andrew Peiser,** *Mercy College;* **Melinda Russell-Stamp,** *Weber State University;* **Patti Tolar,** *University of Houston;* **Traci Sachteleben,** *Southwestern Illinois College;* **Paul Schwartz,** *Mt. St. Mary College;* **Andrea Wesley,** *University of Southern Mississippi.*

Reviewers for Previous Editions

Alice Alexander, *Old Dominion University;* **Sandy Arntz,** *Northern Illinois University;* **Frank Ascione,** *Utah State University;* **Carole Beale,** *University of Massachusetts;* **Luciane A. Berg,** *Southern Utah University;* **David K. Bernhardt,** *Carleton University;* **Fredda Blanchard-Fields,** *Louisiana State University;* **Kristi Blankenship,** *University of Tennessee;* **Belinda Blevins-Knabe,** *University of Arkansas;* **Robert Bornstein,**

Miami University; **Ioakim Boutakidis,** *Fullerton State University;* **Geraldine Brookins,** *University of Minnesota;* **Jane Brower,** *University of Tennessee at Chattanooga;* **Deborah Brown,** *Friends University;* **Nancy Busch-Rossnagel,** *Fordham University;* **James I. Byrd,** *University of Wisconsin at Stout;* **Cheryl A. Camenzuli,** *Hofstra University;* **Elaine Cassel,** *Marymount University;* **Mark Chapell,** *Rowan University;* **Stephanie M. Clancy,** *Southern Illinois University at Carbondale;* **Ronald K. Craig,** *Cincinnati State College;* **Gary Creasey,** *Illinois State University;* **Rita Curl,** *Minot State University;* **Peggy A. DeCooke,** *Northern Illinois University;* **Nancy Defates-Densch,** *Northern Illinois University;* **Gypsy Denzine,** *Northern Arizona University;* **Imma Destefanis,** *Boston College;* **R. Daniel DiSalvi,** *Kean College;* **James A. Doyle,** *Roane State Community College;* **Mark W. Durm,** *Athens State University;* **Laura Duvall,** *Heartland Community College;* **Kimberly DuVall-Early,** *James Madison University;* **Celina Echols,** *Southern Louisiana State University;* **Richard M. Ehlenz,** *Lakewood Community College;* **Gene Elliot,** *Glassboro State University;* **Steve Ellyson,** *Youngstown State University;* **Robert Enright,** *University of Wisconsin at Madison;* **Jennifer Fager,** *Western Michigan University;* **Douglas Fife,** *Plymouth State College;* **Urminda Firlan,** *Michigan State University;* **Leslie Fisher,** *Cleveland State University;* **Martin E. Ford,** *Stanford University;* **Gregory T. Fouts,** *University of Calgary;* **Mary Fraser,** *San Jose State University;* **Rick Froman,** *John Brown University;* **Charles Fry,** *University of Virginia;* **Anne R. Gayles-Felton,** *Florida A&M University;* **Margaret J. Gill,** *Kutztown University;* **Sam Givham,** *Mississippi State University;* **Page Goodwin,** *Western Illinois University;* **William Gnagey,** *Illinois State University;* **Nicole Graves,** *South Dakota State University;* **B. Jo Hailey,** *University of Southern Mississippi;* **Dick E. Hammond,** *Southwest Texas State University;* **Frances Harnick,** *University of New Mexico, Indian Children's Program, and Lovelace-Bataan Pediatric Clinic;* **Dan Houlihan,** *Minnesota State University;* **Kim Hyatt,** *Weber State University;* **June V. Irving,** *Ball State University;* **Beverly Jennings,** *University of Colorado at Denver;* **Joline Jones,** *Worcester State College;* **Linda Juang,** *San Francisco State University;* **Alfred L. Karlson,** *University of Massachusetts at Amherst;* **Lynn F. Katz,** *University of Pittsburgh;* **Carolyn Kaufman,** *Columbus State Community College;* **Michelle Kelley,** *Old Dominion University;* **Marguerite D. Kermis,** *Canisius College;* **Roger Kobak,** *University of Delaware;* **Tara Kuther,** *Western Connecticut State University;* **Emmett C. Lampkin,** *Scott Community College;* **Royal Louis Lange,** *Ellsworth Community Center;* **Philip Langer,** *University of Colorado;* **Heidi Legg-Burross,** *University of Arizona;* **Tanya Letourneau,** *Delaware County College;* **Neal E. Lipsitz,** *Boston College;* **Nancy Lobb,** *Alvin Community College;* **Daniel Lynch,** *University of Wisconsin at Oshkosh;* **Joseph G. Marrone,** *Siena College;* **Ann McCabe,** *University of Windsor;* **Susan McCammon,** *East Carolina University;* **Sherri McCarthy-Tucker,** *Northern Arizona University;* **E. L. McGarry,** *California State University at Fullerton;* **D. Rush McQueen,** *Auburn University;* **Sean Meegan,** *Western Illinois University;* **Jessica Miller,** *Mesa State College;* **John J. Mirich,** *Metropolitan State College;* **John J. Mitchell,** *University of Alberta;* **Suzanne F. Morrow,** *Old Dominion University;* **Lloyd D. Noppe,** *University of Wisconsin at Green Bay;* **Delores Vantrice Oates,** *Texas Southern University;* **Daniel Offer,** *University of Michigan;* **Shana Pack,** *Western Kentucky University;* **Michelle Paludi,** *Michelle Paludi & Associates;* **Joycelyn G. Parish,** *Kansas State University;* **Ian Payton,** *Bethune-Cookman College;* **Peggy G. Perkins,** *University of Nevada;* **Richard Pisacreta,** *Ferris State University;* **Gayle Reed,** *University of Wisconsin at Madison;* **James D. Reid,** *Washington University;* **Vicki Ritts,** *St. Louis Community College;* **Anne Robertson,** *University of Wisconsin at Milwaukee;* **Tonie E. Santmire,** *University of Nebraska;* **Douglas Sawin,** *University of Texas;* **Mary Schumann,** *George Mason University;* **Jane Sheldon,** *University of Michigan at Dearborn;* **Kim Shifren,** *Towson University;* **Susan Shonk,** *State University of New York;* **Ken Springer,** *Southern Methodist University;* **Ruby Takanishi,** *Foundation for Child Development;* **Vern Tyler,** *Western Washington University;* **Rhoda Unger,** *Montclair State College;* **Angela Vaughn,** *Wesley College;* **Elizabeth Vozzola,** *Saint Joseph's College;* **Barry Wagner,** *Catholic University of America;* **Rob Weisskrich,** *California State University at Fullerton;* **Deborah Welsh,** *University of Tennessee;* **Wanda Willard,** *State University of New York at Oswego;* **Carolyn L. Williams,** *University of Minnesota;* **Shelli Wynants,** *California State University.*

instructor and **student resources**

The resources listed here may accompany *Adolescence*, fourteenth edition. Please contact your McGraw-Hill representative for details concerning policies, prices, and availability.

For the Instructor

The Online Learning Center The instructor side of the Online Learning Center at http://www.mhhe.com/santrocka14e contains the Instructor's Manual, Test Bank files, PowerPoint slides, Image Gallery, and other valuable material to help you design and enhance your course. Ask your local McGraw-Hill representative for your password.

Instructor's Manual revised by Patti Tolar at the University of Houston, is a flexible planner with an introduction to the chapter, outline, suggested lecture topics, classroom discussion and activities, critical thinking exercises, research articles, essay questions, and video and film recommendations.

Create Craft your teaching resources to match the way you teach! With McGraw-Hill Create, www.mcgrawhillcreate.com, you can easily rearrange chapters, combine material from other content sources, and quickly upload content you have written, like your course syllabus or teaching notes. Find the content you need in Create by searching through thousands of leading McGraw-Hill textbooks. Arrange your book to fit your teaching style. Create even allows you to personalize your book's appearance by selecting the cover and adding your name, school, and course information. Order a Create book and you'll receive a complimentary print review copy in 3–5 business days or a complimentary electronic review copy (eComp) via email in about one hour. Go to www.mcgrawhillcreate.com today and register. Experience how McGraw-Hill Create empowers you to teach your students your way.

Blackboard McGraw-Hill Higher Education and Blackboard have teamed up. What does this mean for you?

1. **Your life, simplified.** Now you can access McGraw-Hill's Create™ right from within your Blackboard course—all with one single sign-on. Say goodbye to the days of logging in to multiple applications.
2. **Deep integration of content and tools.** Not only do you get single sign-on with Create™, you also get deep integration of McGraw-Hill content and content engines right in Blackboard.
3. **A solution for everyone.** Whether your institution is already using Blackboard or you just want to try Blackboard on your own, we have a solution for you. McGraw-Hill and Blackboard can now offer you easy access to industry-leading technology and content, whether your campus hosts it, or we do. Be sure to ask your local McGraw-Hill representative for details.

Tegrity Tegrity Campus is a service that makes class time available all the time by automatically capturing every lecture in a searchable format for students to review when they study and complete assignments. With a simple one-click start and stop process, you capture all computer screens and corresponding audio. Students replay any part of any class with easy-to-use browser-based viewing on a PC or Mac.

Educators know that the more students can see, hear, and experience class resources, the better they learn. With Tegrity Campus, students quickly recall key moments by using Tegrity Campus' unique search feature. This search helps students efficiently find what they need, when they need it across an entire semester of class recordings. Help turn all your students' study time into learning moments immediately supported by your lecture.

Test Bank and Computerized Test Bank revised by Paul Schwartz at Mt. St. Mary College, has questions specifically related to the main text, including multiple-choice, short-answer, and essay questions, many of which are applied assessment.

PowerPoint Slides revised by Traci Sachteleben at Southwestern Illinois College, cover every chapter and concept presented in the text.

McGraw-Hill's Visual Asset Database for Development ("VAD") McGraw-Hill's Visual Assets Database for Development (VAD 2.0) (www.mhhe.com/vad) is an online database of videos for use in the developmental psychology classroom, created specifically for instructors. You can customize classroom presentations by downloading the videos to your computer and showing the videos on their own or insert them into your course cartridge or PowerPoint presentations. All of the videos are available with or without captions. Ask your McGraw-Hill representative for access information.

Student Resources

Online Learning Center The Online Learning Center, at http://www.mhhe.com/santrocka14e offers a wide variety of student resources. Multiple-Choice and Matching Tests for each chapter reinforce key principles, terms, and ideas, and cover all the major concepts discussed throughout the text. Entirely different from the test items in the Test Bank, the questions have been written to quiz students but also to help them learn. Key terms from the text are reproduced in a Glossary of Key Terms where they can be accessed in alphabetical order for easy reference and review. Decision-Making Scenarios present students with the opportunity to apply the information in the chapter to realistic situations, and see what effects their decisions will have. Streamable online Videos reinforce chapter content.

McGraw-Hill Contemporary Learning Series *Annual Editions: Human Development.* This reader is a collection of articles on topics related to the latest research and thinking in human development. Annual Editions are updated regularly and include useful features such as a topic guide, an annotated table of contents, unit overviews, and a topical index.

Taking Sides: Clashing Views on Controversial Issues in Adolescent Development Current controversial issues are presented in a debate-style format designed to stimulate student interest and develop critical-thinking skills. Each issue is thoughtfully framed with an issue summary, an issue introduction, and a postscript.

CourseSmart **CourseSmart** is a new way to find and buy eTextbooks. At CourseSmart you can save up to 50% off the cost of a print textbook, reduce your impact on the environment, and gain access to powerful web tools for learning. CourseSmart has the largest selection of eTextbooks available anywhere, offering thousands of the most commonly adopted textbooks from a wide variety of higher education publishers. CourseSmart eTextbooks are available in one standard online reader with full text search, notes and highlighting, and e-mail tools for sharing notes between classmates. For further details contact your sales representative or go to www.coursesmart.com.

ADOLESCENCE

chapter 1 INTRODUCTION

chapter **outline**

The Historical Perspective

Learning Goal 1 Describe the historical perspective of adolescence.

Early History
The Twentieth and Twenty-First Centuries
Stereotyping of Adolescents
A Positive View of Adolescence

Today's Adolescents in the United States and Around the World

Learning Goal 2 Discuss today's U.S. adolescents and adolescents around the world.

Adolescents in the United States
The Global Perspective

The Nature of Development

Learning Goal 3 Summarize the developmental processes, periods, transitions, and issues related to adolescence.

Processes and Periods
Developmental Transitions
Developmental Issues

The Science of Adolescent Development

Learning Goal 4 Characterize the science of adolescent development.

Science and the Scientific Method
Theories of Adolescent Development
Research in Adolescent Development

Jeffrey Dahmer's senior portrait in high school.

Jeffrey Dahmer had a troubled childhood and adolescence. His parents constantly bickered before they divorced. His mother had emotional problems and doted on his younger brother. He felt that his father neglected him, and he had been sexually abused by another boy when he was 8 years old. But the vast majority of people who suffered through a painful childhood and adolescence do not become serial killers as Dahmer did. Dahmer murdered his first victim in 1978 with a barbell and went on to kill 16 other individuals before being caught and sentenced to 15 life terms in prison.

A decade before Dahmer's first murder, Alice Walker, who would later win a Pulitzer Prize for her book *The Color Purple,* spent her days battling racism in Mississippi. Born the eighth child of Georgia sharecroppers, Walker knew the brutal effects of poverty. Despite the counts against her, she went on to become an award-winning novelist. Walker writes about people who, as she puts it, "make it, who come out of nothing. People who triumph."

Alice Walker.

Consider also the changing life of Michael Maddaus (Broderick, 2003; Masten, Obradovic, & Burt, 2006). During his childhood and adolescence in Minneapolis, his mother drank heavily and his stepfather abused him. He coped by spending increasing time on the streets, being arrested more than 20 times for his delinquency, frequently being placed in detention centers, and rarely going to school. At 17, he joined the Navy and the experience helped him to gain self-discipline and hope. After his brief stint in the Navy, he completed a GED and began taking community college classes. However, he continued to have some setbacks with drugs and alcohol. A defining moment as an emerging adult came when he delivered furniture to a surgeon's home. The surgeon became interested in helping Michael and his mentorship led to Michael volunteering at a rehabilitation center, then to a job with a neurosurgeon. Eventually, he obtained his undergraduate degree, went to medical school, got married, and started a family. Today, Michael Maddaus is a successful surgeon. One of his most gratifying volunteer activities is telling his story to troubled youth.

What leads one adolescent like Jeffrey Dahmer, so full of promise, to commit brutal acts of violence and another, like Alice Walker, to turn poverty and trauma into a rich literary harvest? How can we attempt to explain how one individual like Michael Maddaus can turn a childhood and adolescence shattered by abuse and delinquency into becoming a successful surgeon, whereas another one seems to come unhinged by life's minor hassles? Why is it that some adolescents are whirlwinds—successful in school, involved in a network of friends, and full of energy—whereas others hang out on the sidelines, mere spectators of life? If you have ever wondered what makes adolescents tick, you have asked yourself the central question we explore in this book.

Dr. Michael Maddaus, counseling a troubled youth.

preview

Adolescence, 14th edition, is a window into the nature of adolescent development—your own and that of every other adolescent. In this first chapter, you will read about the history of the field, the characteristics of today's adolescents, both in the United States and the rest of the world, and the way in which adolescents develop.

1 The Historical Perspective

LG1 Describe the historical perspective of adolescence.

- Early History
- The Twentieth and Twenty-First Centuries
- Stereotyping of Adolescents
- A Positive View of Adolescence

What have the portraits of adolescence been like at different points in history? When did the scientific study of adolescence begin?

In no order of things is adolescence the simple time of life.

—Jean Erskine Stewart, *American Writer, 20th Century*

EARLY HISTORY

In early Greece, the philosophers Plato and Aristotle both commented about the nature of youth. According to Plato (fourth century B.C.), reasoning doesn't belong to childhood but rather first appears in adolescence. Plato thought that children should spend their time in sports and music, whereas adolescents should study science and mathematics.

Aristotle (fourth century B.C.) argued that the most important aspect of adolescence is the ability to choose, and that self-determination is a hallmark of maturity. Aristotle's emphasis on the development of self-determination is not unlike some contemporary views that see independence, identity, and career choice as the key themes of adolescence. Aristotle also recognized adolescents' egocentrism, commenting once that adolescents think they know everything and are quite sure about it.

In the Middle Ages, children and adolescents were viewed as miniature adults and were subjected to harsh discipline. In the eighteenth century, French philosopher Jean-Jacques Rousseau offered a more enlightened view of adolescence, restoring the belief that being a child or an adolescent is not the same as being an adult. Like Plato, Rousseau thought that reasoning develops in adolescence. He said that curiosity should especially be encouraged in the education of 12- to 15-year-olds. Rousseau argued that, from 15 to 20 years of age, individuals mature emotionally, and their selfishness is replaced by an interest in others. Thus, Rousseau concluded that development has distinct phases. But his ideas were speculative; not until the beginning of the twentieth century did the scientific exploration of adolescence begin.

THE TWENTIETH AND TWENTY-FIRST CENTURIES

The end of the nineteenth century and the early part of the twentieth century saw the invention of the concept we now call adolescence. Between 1890 and 1920, a number of psychologists, urban reformers, educators, youth workers, and counselors began to develop the concept. At this time, young people, especially boys, were increasingly seen as being passive and vulnerable—qualities previously associated only with the adolescent female. When G. Stanley Hall's book on adolescence was published in 1904 (see the next section), it played a major role in restructuring thinking about adolescence.

G. Stanley Hall, father of the scientific study of adolescence.

G. Stanley Hall's Storm-and-Stress View G. Stanley Hall (1844–1924) pioneered the scientific study of adolescence. In 1904, Hall published his ideas in a two-volume set: *Adolescence*. Hall was strongly influenced by Charles Darwin, the famous evolutionary theorist. Applying Darwin's view to the study of adolescent development, Hall proposed that development is controlled primarily by biological factors.

The **storm-and-stress view** is Hall's concept that adolescence is a turbulent time charged with conflict and mood swings. In his view, adolescents' thoughts, feelings, and actions oscillate between conceit and humility, good intentions and temptation, happiness and sadness. An adolescent might be nasty to a peer one

storm-and-stress view G. Stanley Hall's concept that adolescence is a turbulent time charged with conflict and mood swings.

Anthropologist Margaret Mead (*left*) with a Samoan adolescent girl. Mead found that adolescence in Samoa was relatively stress-free, although recently her findings have been criticized. *How does Mead's view of adolescence contrast with Hall's view?*

moment and kind the next moment; in need of privacy one moment but seconds later want companionship.

Hall was a giant in the field of adolescence. He began the theorizing, systematizing, and questioning that went beyond mere speculation and philosophizing. Indeed, we owe the beginnings of the scientific study of adolescence to Hall.

Margaret Mead's Sociocultural View of Adolescence Anthropologist Margaret Mead (1928) studied adolescents on the South Sea island of Samoa. She concluded that the basic nature of adolescence is not biological, as Hall envisioned, but rather sociocultural. In cultures that provide a smooth, gradual transition from childhood to adulthood, which is the way adolescence is handled in Samoa, she found little storm and stress associated with the period. Mead's observations of Samoan adolescents revealed instead that their lives were relatively free of turmoil. Mead concluded that cultures that allow adolescents to observe sexual relations, see babies born, regard death as natural, do important work, engage in sex play, and know clearly what their adult roles will be tend to promote a relatively stress-free adolescence. However, in cultures like the United States, in which children are considered very different from adults, and adolescence is not characterized by the same experiences, the period is more likely to be stressful.

More than half a century after Mead's Samoan findings, her work was criticized as biased and error-prone (Freeman, 1983). Current criticism states that Samoan adolescence is more stressful than Mead suggested and that delinquency appears among Samoan adolescents just as it does among Western adolescents. Despite the controversy over Mead's findings, some researchers have defended Mead's work (Holmes,1987).

The Inventionist View Although adolescence has a biological base, as G. Stanley Hall argued, it also has a sociocultural base, as Margaret Mead maintained. Indeed, sociohistorical conditions contributed to the emergence of the concept of adolescence. According to the **inventionist view,** adolescence is a sociohistorical creation. Especially important in this view of adolescence are the sociohistorical circumstances at the beginning of the twentieth century, a time when legislation was enacted that ensured the dependency of youth and made their move into the economic sphere more manageable. These sociohistorical circumstances included a decline in apprenticeship; increased mechanization during the Industrial Revolution, which raised the level of skill required of laborers and necessitated a specialized division of labor; the separation of work and home; age-graded schools; urbanization; the appearance of youth groups such as the YMCA and the Boy Scouts; and the writings of G. Stanley Hall.

Schools, work, and economics are important dimensions of the inventionist view of adolescence. Some scholars argue that the concept of adolescence was invented mainly as a by-product of the movement to create a system of compulsory public education. In this view, the function of secondary schools is to transmit intellectual skills to youth. However, other scholars argue that the primary purpose of secondary schools is to deploy youth within the economic sphere. In this view, American society conferred the status of adolescence on youth through child-saving legislation (Lapsley, Enright, & Serlin, 1985). By developing special laws for youth, adults restricted their options, encouraged their dependency, and made their move into the world of work more manageable.

Historians now call the period between 1890 and 1920 the "age of adolescence." In this period, lawmakers enacted a great deal of compulsory legislation aimed at youth. In virtually every state, they passed laws that excluded youth from most employment and required them to attend secondary school. Much of this legislation included extensive enforcement provisions. Two clear changes resulted from this legislation: decreased employment and increased school attendance among youth. From 1910 to 1930, the number of 10- to 15-year-olds who were gainfully employed dropped about 75 percent. In addition, between 1900 and 1930 the number of high school graduates increased substantially. Approximately 600 percent more individuals graduated from high school in 1930 than in 1900. Let's take a closer look at

inventionist view The view that adolescence is a sociohistorical creation. Especially important in this view are the sociohistorical circumstances at the beginning of the twentieth century, a time when legislation was enacted that ensured the dependency of youth and made their move into the economic sphere more manageable.

how conceptions of adolescence and experiences of adolescents changed with the changing times of the twentieth century.

Further Changes in the Twentieth Century and the Twenty-First Century

Discussing historical changes in the way individuals have experienced adolescence involves focusing on changes in generations. A *cohort* is a group of people who are born at a similar point in history and share similar experiences as a result. For example, individuals who experienced the Great Depression as teenagers are likely to differ from their counterparts who were teenagers during the optimistic aftermath of World War II in the 1950s. In discussing and conducting research on such historical variations, the term **cohort effects** is used, which refers to effects due to a person's time of birth, era, or generation, but not to actual chronological age (Schaie, 2011; Schaie & Willis, 2012). Let's now explore potential cohort effects on the development of adolescents and emerging adults in the last half of the twentieth century and the early part of the twenty-first century.

1950s to 1970s By 1950, the developmental period referred to as adolescence had come of age. It had not only physical and social identities but a legal identity as well, for every state had developed special laws for youth between the ages of 16 and 18 to 20. Getting a college degree—the key to a good job—was on the minds of many adolescents during the 1950s, as was getting married, having a family, and settling down to the life of luxury displayed in television commercials.

Although adolescents' pursuit of higher education continued into the 1960s, many African American adolescents not only were denied a college education but received an inferior secondary education as well. Ethnic conflicts in the form of riots and sit-ins became pervasive, and college-age adolescents were among the most vocal participants.

Political protests reached a peak in the late 1960s and early 1970s, when millions of adolescents reacted violently to what they saw as the United States' immoral participation in the Vietnam War. By the mid-1970s, the radical protests of adolescents began to abate along with U.S. involvement in Vietnam. They were replaced by increased concern for upward mobility through achievement in high school, college, or vocational training. Material interests began to dominate adolescents' motives again, while ideological challenges to social institutions began to recede.

In the 1970s, the women's movement changed both the description and the study of adolescence. In earlier years, descriptions of adolescence had pertained more to males than to females. The dual family and career objectives that female adolescents have today were largely unknown to female adolescents of the 1890s and early 1900s.

Millennials In recent years, generations have been given labels by the popular culture. The most recent label is **Millennials,** the generation born after 1980, the first to come of age and enter emerging adulthood in the new millennium. Two characteristics of Millennials stand out: (1) their ethnic diversity, and (2) their connection to technology. A recent analysis also described Millennials as "confident, self-expressive, liberal, upbeat, and open to change" (Pew Research Center, 2010, p. 1).

Because their ethnic diversity has increased over prior generations, many Millennial adolescents and emerging adults are more tolerant and open-minded than their counterparts in previous generations. One survey indicated that 60 percent of today's adolescents say their friends include someone from diverse ethnic groups (Teenage Research Unlimited, 2004). Another survey found that 60 percent of U.S. 18- to 29-year-olds had dated someone from a different ethnic group (Jones, 2005).

Another major change that characterizes Millennials is the dramatic increase in their use of media and technology (Brown & Bobkowski, 2011). According to one analysis,

> They are history's first "always connected" generation. Steeped in digital technology and social media, they treat their multi-tasking hand-held gadgets almost like a body part—for better or worse. More than 8-in-10 say they sleep with a cell phone glowing

cohort effects Refers to effects due to a person's date of birth, era, or generation, but not to actual chronological age.

Millennials The generation born after 1980, the first to come of age and enter emerging adulthood in the new millennium. Two characteristics of Millennials stand out: (1) their ethnic diversity, and (2) their connection to technology.

by the bed, poised to disgorge texts, phone calls, e-mails, songs, news, videos, games, and wake-up jingles. But sometimes convenience yields to temptation. Nearly two-thirds admit to texting while driving (Pew Research Center, 2010, p. 1).

As just indicated, there likely are both positive and negative aspects to how the technology revolution is affecting youth. Technology can provide an expansive, rich set of knowledge that, if used in a constructive way, can improve adolescents' education (Smaldino, Lowther, & Russell, 2012; Taylor & Fratto, 2012). However, the possible downside of technology was captured in a recent book, *The Dumbest Generation: How the Digital Age Stupefies Young Americans and Jeopardizes Our Future (Or, Don't Trust Anyone Under 30)*, written by Emory University English professor Mark Bauerlein (2008). Among the book's themes are that many of today's youth are more interested in information retrieval than information formation, don't read books and aren't motivated to read them, can't spell without spellcheck, and have become encapsulated in a world of iPhones, text messaging, Facebook, YouTube, MySpace, *Grand Theft Auto* (the video's introduction in 2008 had first-week sales of $500 million, dwarfing other movie and video sales), and other technology contexts. In terms of retaining general information and historical facts, Bauerlein may be correct. And, in terms of some skills, such as adolescents' reading and writing, there is considerable concern—as evidenced by U.S. employers spending $1.3 billion a year to teach writing skills to employees (Begley & Interlandi, 2008). However, in terms of cognitive skills such as thinking and reasoning, he likely is wrong, given that IQ scores have been rising significantly since the 1930s (Flynn, 2007). Further, there is no research evidence that being immersed in a technological world of iPhones, Facebook, and YouTube impairs thinking skills (Begley & Interlandi, 2008). We will have much more to discuss about intelligence in Chapter 3 and about technology in Chapter 12.

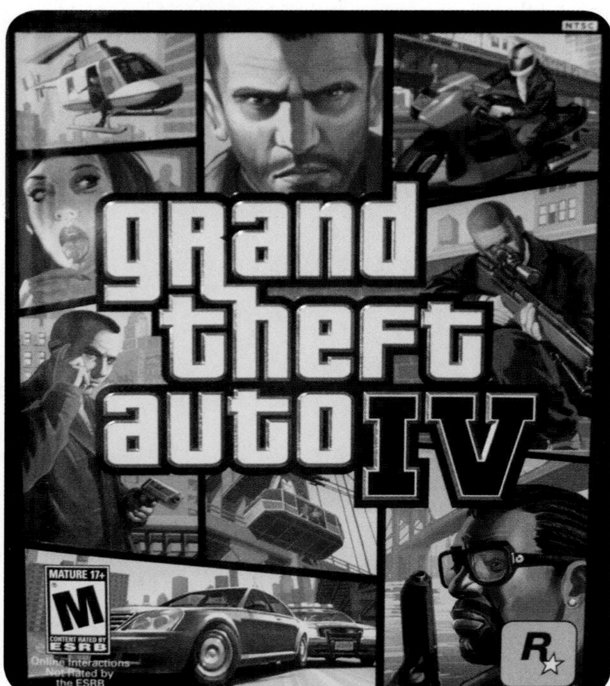

Another concern about the current generation of adolescents was recently voiced in *The Path to Purpose* by leading expert on adolescence William Damon (2008). Damon argues that many American adults have become effective at finding short-term solutions to various tasks and problems to get through their lives, and they are instilling the same desire for immediate gratification and shortsighted thinking in their children and adolescents. In Damon's view, although these short-term solutions (such as getting homework done, getting a good grade on a test tomorrow, and making a team) are often necessary adaptations to a situation, they can distract adolescents from thinking about their life purpose, such as "What kind of person do I want to be?" "What do I want to do with my life?" "Why should I try to be successful?" Damon further emphasizes that parents can help to remedy this problem by giving them options and guiding them through choices, as well as talking with them about paths, themes, and issues in their own lives that they find meaningful and communicating how they have coped with setbacks and dilemmas. We will expand on Damon's concept of the path to purpose later in the text in our discussion of identity exploration (Chapter 4), moral development, values, and religion (Chapter 7), and achievement and careers (Chapter 11).

We have considered the important sociohistorical circumstances surrounding the development of the concept of adolescence, evaluated how society has viewed adolescents at different points in history, and examined several main changes that characterize the current generation of adolescents. Next we explore why we need to exercise caution in generalizing about the adolescents of any era. As you read about the stereotyping of adolescents, think about how the book we just described—*The Dumbest Generation* (Bauerlein, 2008)—might reflect this stereotyping.

developmental **connection**

Technology. When media multitasking is taken into account, 11 to 14-year-olds spend an average of almost 12 hours of exposure to media per day. Chapter 12, p. 411

developmental **connection**

Identity. Damon argues that too many youths today are indecisive and aren't adequately moving toward identity resolution. Chapter 4, p. 142

STEREOTYPING OF ADOLESCENTS

A **stereotype** is a generalization that reflects our impressions and beliefs about a broad category of people. All stereotypes carry an image of what the typical member of a specific group is like. Once we assign a stereotype, it is difficult to abandon it, even in the face of contradictory evidence.

Stereotypes of adolescents are plentiful: "They say they want a job, but when they get one, they don't want to work." "They are all lazy." "All they think about is sex." "They are all into drugs, every last one of them." "Kids today don't have the moral fiber of my generation." "The problem with adolescents today is that they all have it too easy." "They are so self-centered." Indeed, during most of the twentieth century and the beginning of the twenty-first century, adolescents have been portrayed as abnormal and deviant rather than normal and nondeviant. Consider Hall's image of storm and stress. Consider, too, media portrayals of adolescents as rebellious, conflicted, faddish, delinquent, and self-centered. Especially distressing is that, when given evidence of youths' positive accomplishments—that a majority of adolescents participate in community service, for example—many adults either deny the facts or say that they must be exceptions (Youniss & Ruth, 2002).

Stereotyping of adolescents is so widespread that adolescence researcher Joseph Adelson (1979) coined the term **adolescent generalization gap,** which refers to generalizations that are based on information about a limited, often highly visible group of adolescents. Some adolescents develop confidence in their abilities despite negative stereotypes about them. And some individuals (like Alice Walker and Michael Maddaus, discussed in the opening of this chapter), triumph over poverty, abuse, and other adversities.

A POSITIVE VIEW OF ADOLESCENCE

The negative stereotyping of adolescents is overdrawn (Lerner & others, 2011; Lewin-Bizan, Bowers, & Lerner, 2011; O'Connor & others, 2010). In a cross-cultural study, Daniel Offer and his colleagues (1988) found no support for such a negative view. The researchers assessed the self-images of adolescents around the world—in the United States, Australia, Bangladesh, Hungary, Israel, Italy, Japan, Taiwan, Turkey, and West Germany—and discovered that at least 73 percent of the adolescents had a positive self-image. The adolescents were self-confident and optimistic about their future. Although there were some exceptions, as a group the adolescents were happy most of the time, enjoyed life, perceived themselves as capable of exercising

Have adolescents been stereotyped too negatively? Explain.

stereotype A generalization that reflects our impressions and beliefs about a broad group of people. All stereotypes refer to an image of what the typical member of a specific group is like.

adolescent generalization gap Adelson's concept of generalizations about adolescents based on information regarding a limited, often highly visible group of adolescents.

self-control, valued work and school, expressed confidence in their sexuality, showed positive feelings toward their families, and felt they had the capacity to cope with life's stresses—not exactly a storm-and-stress portrayal of adolescence.

> In case you're worried about what's going to become of the younger generation, it's going to grow up and start worrying about the younger generation.
>
> —ROGER ALLEN
> *Contemporary American Writer*

Old Centuries and New Centuries For much of the last century in the United States and other Western cultures, adolescence was perceived as a problematic period of the human life span in line with G. Stanley Hall's (1904) storm-and-stress portrayal. But as the research study just described indicates, a large majority of adolescents are not nearly as disturbed and troubled as the popular stereotype suggests.

The end of an old century and the beginning of the next has a way of stimulating reflection on what was, as well as visions of what could and should be. In the field of psychology in general, as in its subfield of adolescent development, psychologists have looked back at a century in which the discipline became too negative (Seligman & Csikszentmihalyi, 2000). Psychology had become an overly grim science in which people were too often characterized as being passive victims. Psychologists are now calling for a focus on the positive side of human experience and greater emphasis on hope, optimism, positive individual traits, creativity, and positive group and civic values, such as responsibility, nurturance, civility, and tolerance (King, 2011).

Generational Perceptions and Misperceptions Adults' perceptions of adolescents emerge from a combination of personal experience and media portrayals, neither of which produces an objective picture of how typical adolescents develop (Feldman & Elliott, 1990). Some of the readiness to assume the worst about adolescents likely involves the short memories of adults. Adults often portray today's adolescents as more troubled, less respectful, more self-centered, more assertive, and more adventurous than they were.

However, in matters of taste and manners, the youth of every generation have seemed radical, unnerving, and different from adults—different in how they look, how they behave, the music they enjoy, their hairstyles, and the clothing they choose. It is an enormous error to confuse adolescents' enthusiasm for trying on new identities and indulging in occasional episodes of outrageous behavior with hostility toward parental and societal standards. Acting out and boundary testing are time-honored ways in which adolescents move toward accepting, rather than rejecting, parental values.

Positive Youth Development What has been called *positive youth development* (PYD) in adolescence reflects the positive psychology approach. Positive youth development emphasizes the strengths of youth and the positive qualities and developmental trajectories that are desired for youth (Benson & Scales, 2009, 2011; Larson, 2011; Larson & Angus, 2011; Sullivan & Larson, 2010). Positive youth development has especially been promoted by Jacqueline Lerner and her colleagues (2009), who recently described the "Five Cs" of PYD:

- *Competence,* which involves having a positive perception of one's actions in domain-specific areas—social, academic, physical, career, and so on.
- *Confidence,* which consists of having an overall positive sense of self-worth and self-efficacy (a sense that one can master a situation and produce positive outcomes)
- *Connection,* which is characterized by having positive relationships with others, including family, peers, teachers, and individuals in the community
- *Character,* which is comprised of having respect for societal rules, an understanding of right and wrong, and integrity
- *Caring/compassion,* which encompasses showing emotional concern for others, especially those in distress

connecting with adolescents

Wanting to Be Treated as an Asset

Many times teenagers are thought of as a problem that no one really wants to deal with. People are sometimes intimidated and become hostile when teenagers are willing to challenge their authority. It is looked at as being disrespectful. Teenagers are, many times, not treated like an asset and as innovative thinkers who will be the leaders of tomorrow. Adults have the power to teach the younger generation about the world and allow them to feel they have a voice in it.

—Zula, age 16
Brooklyn, New York

Which perspective on adolescent development does this comment appear to take?

Lerner and her colleagues (2009) conclude that to develop these five positive characteristics, youth need access to positive social contexts—such as youth development programs and organized youth activities—and competent people—such as caring teachers, community leaders, and mentors. We will further explore youth development programs in Chapter 9, and in Chapter 13 we will examine Peter Benson's emphasis on the importance of developmental assets in improving youth development, which reflects the positive youth development approach.

A recent emphasis in the movement to increasingly study positive youth development rather than only the risks and challenges adolescents face is that of *thriving* (Benson & Scales, 2009, 2011; Lerner & others, 2011). A national study of more than 1,800 15-year-olds that focused on adolescent thriving examined the importance of identifying and supporting adolescents' *sparks*, defined as their deep passions or interests (Scales, Benson, & Roehlkepartain, 2011). In this study, the 15-year-olds who had accumulated a stronger level of sparks, opportunities in relationships to nurture those sparks (such as experiencing supportive relationships with adults), and empowerment (assessed by asking adolescents to name the things they wanted the next U.S. president to deal with) were more likely to be characterized by positive individual outcomes (such as grade point average and leadership) and interest in making prosocial contributions (such as volunteering and ethnic respect).

developmental **connection**

Youth Development. Many youth activities and organizations provide adolescents opportunities to develop positive qualities. Chapter 9, p. 309

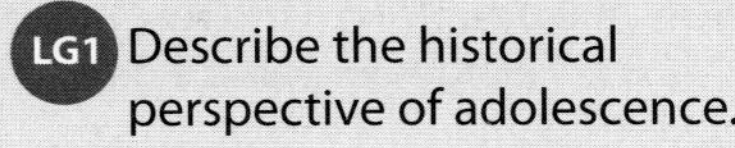

LG1 Describe the historical perspective of adolescence.

Review

- What was the early history of interest in adolescence?
- What characterized adolescence in the twentieth century, and how are adolescents changing in the twenty-first century?
- How extensively are adolescents stereotyped?
- Why is a more positive view of adolescence needed?

Connect

- How have the social changes of the twentieth century, as described in this section, changed society's views of adolescence?

Reflect *Your Own Personal Journey of Life*

- You likely experienced some instances of stereotyping as an adolescent. What are some examples of circumstances in which you think you were stereotyped as an adolescent?

2 Today's Adolescents in the United States and Around the World

Discuss today's U.S. adolescents and adolescents around the world.

Adolescents in the United States

The Global Perspective

You should now have a good sense of the historical aspects of adolescence, the stereotyping of adolescents, and the importance of considering the positive aspects of many adolescents' development. Now let's further explore the current status of adolescents.

ADOLESCENTS IN THE UNITED STATES

Growing up has never been easy. In many ways, the developmental tasks today's adolescents face are no different from those of adolescents 50 years ago. For a large majority of youth, adolescence is not a time of rebellion, crisis, pathology, and deviance. Rather it is a time of evaluation, decision making, commitment, and finding a place in the world.

However, adolescents are not a homogeneous group. Most adolescents successfully negotiate the lengthy path to adult maturity, but a large minority do not (McLoyd & others, 2009). Socioeconomic, ethnic, cultural, gender, age, and lifestyle differences influence the developmental trajectory of every adolescent.

Social Contexts Of special interest to researchers is how social contexts influence adolescent development (Chen & others, 2011; Parke & Clarke-Stewart, 2011). **Contexts** are the settings in which development occurs; they are influenced by historical, economic, social, and cultural factors. To understand how important contexts are in adolescent development, consider the task of a researcher who wants to discover whether today's adolescents are more racially tolerant than those of a decade or two ago. Without reference to the historical, economic, social, and cultural aspects of race relations, adolescents' racial tolerance cannot be fully evaluated. Each adolescent's development occurs against a cultural backdrop of contexts that includes family, peers, school, religion, neighborhood, community, region, and nation, each with its cultural legacies (Fung, 2011; Schlegel & Hewlett, 2011).

The cultural context for U.S. adolescents is changing with the dramatic increase in the number of adolescents immigrating from Latino and Asian countries (Cheah & Yeung, 2011; G. N. Hall, 2010). Figure 1.1 shows the projected percentage increase for non-Latino White, Latino, African American, and Asian American adolescents through 2100. Notice that Asian Americans are expected to be the fastest-growing ethnic group of adolescents, with a growth rate of more than 500 percent by 2100. Latino adolescents are projected to increase almost 400 percent by 2100. Figure 1.2 shows the actual numbers of adolescents in different ethnic groups in the year 2000, as well as the projected numbers projected through 2100. Notice that by 2100 Latino adolescents are expected to outnumber non-Latino White adolescents. Recent research indicates that a strong sense of family obligations may help immigrants achieve a positive pattern of adaptation (van Geel & Vedder, 2010).

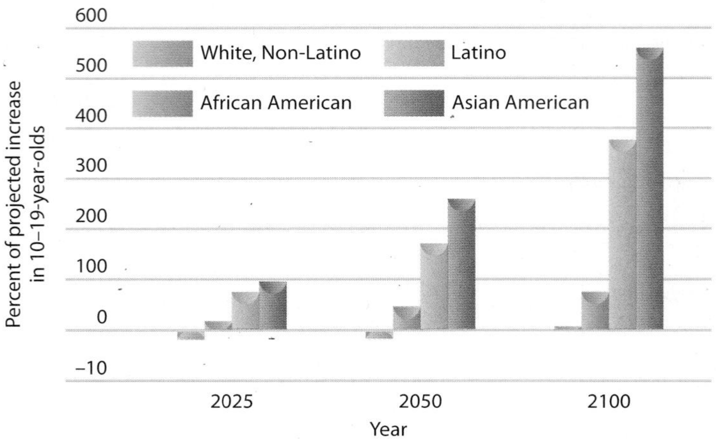

FIGURE **1.1**

PROJECTED PERCENTAGE INCREASE IN ADOLESCENTS AGED 10–19, 2025–2100. An actual decrease in the percentage of non-Latino White adolescents 10 to 19 years of age is projected through 2050. By contrast, dramatic percentage increases are projected for Asian American (233% in 2050 and 530% in 2100) and Latino (175% in 2050 and 371% in 2100) adolescents.

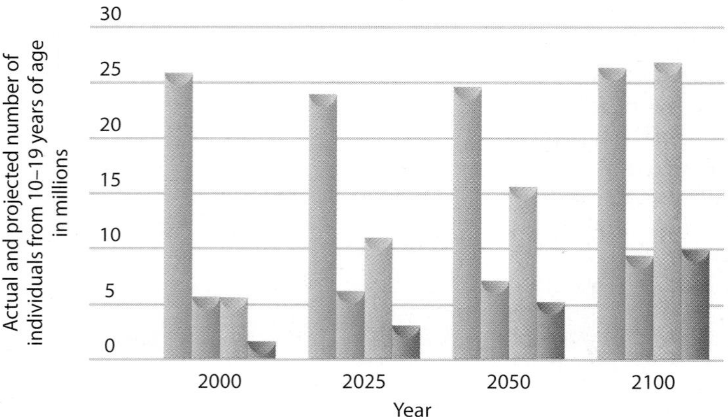

FIGURE **1.2**

ACTUAL AND PROJECTED NUMBER OF U.S. ADOLESCENTS AGED 10–19, 2000–2100. In 2000, there were more than 25 million White, non-Latino adolescents 10–19 years of age in the United States, while the numbers for ethnic minority groups were substantially lower. However, projections for 2025 through 2100 reveal dramatic increases in the number of Latino and Asian American adolescents to the point at which in 2100 it is projected that there will be more Latino than White non-Latino adolescents in the United States and more Asian American than African American adolescents.

contexts The settings in which development occurs. These settings are influenced by historical, economic, social, and cultural factors.

These changing social contexts receive special attention in this book. Chapters 8 to 12 are devoted to contexts, with separate emphasis on families, peers, schools, work, and culture. As we see next, some experts argue that the social policy of the United States should place stronger emphasis on improving the contexts in which adolescents live.

Social Policy and Adolescents' Development **Social policy** is the course of action designed by the national government to influence the welfare of its citizens. Currently, many researchers in adolescent development are attempting to design studies whose results will lead to wise and effective social policy decision making (Larson & Angus, 2011).

Peter Benson and his colleagues (Benson, 2010; Benson & Scales, 2009, 2011; Benson & others, 2006; Scales, Benson, & Roehlkepartain, 2011) argue that the United States has a fragmented social policy for youth that too often has focused only on the negative developmental deficits of adolescents, especially health-compromising behaviors such as drug use and delinquency, and not enough on positive strength-based approaches. According to Benson and his colleagues (2004, p. 783), a strength-based approach to social policy for youth

> adopts more of a wellness perspective, places particular emphasis on the existence of healthy conditions, and expands the concept of health to include the skills and competencies needed to succeed in employment, education, and life. It moves beyond the eradication of risk and deliberately argues for the promotion of well-being.

In their view, what the United States needs is a *developmentally attentive* youth policy, which would emphasize "the family, neighborhood, school, youth organization, places of work, and congregations as policy intervention points. Transforming schools into more developmentally rich settings, building linkages across multiple socializing institutions, launching community-wide initiatives organized around a shared vision of strength building, and expanding funding for quality out-of-school programs" would reflect this policy (Benson & others, 2004, p. 798). In a recent survey, only 20 percent of U.S. 15-year-olds reported that they have had meaningful relationships outside of their family that help them to succeed in life (Search Institute, 2010).

Research indicates that youth benefit enormously when they have caring adults in their lives in addition to parents or guardians. Caring adults—such as coaches, neighbors, teachers, mentors, and after-school leaders—can serve as role models, confidantes, advocates, and resources. Caring-adult relationships are powerful when youth know they are respected, that they matter to the adult, and that the adult wants to be a resource in their lives. Too often, though, adolescents report that they have no significant and lasting relationships outside their family (Benson, 2010).

To read about Peter Benson's career and work, see the *Connecting with Careers* profile.

Children and adolescents who grow up in poverty represent a special concern (Huston & Bentley, 2010). In 2008, 19 percent of U.S. children were living in families below the poverty line (Childstats.gov, 2010). This is an increase from 2001 (16.2 percent) but down from a peak of 22.7 percent in 1993. One study revealed that the more years 7- to 13-year-olds spent living in poverty, the more their physiological indices of stress were elevated (Evans & Kim, 2007).

The U.S. figure of 19 percent of children and adolescents living in poverty is much higher than figures from other industrialized nations. For example, Canada has a child poverty rate of 9 percent and Sweden has a rate of 2 percent.

The well-being of adolescents should be one of America's foremost concerns (Benson & Scales, 2011). The future of our youth is the future of our society. Adolescents who do not reach their full potential, who make fewer contributions to society than it needs, and who do not take their place in society as productive adults diminish our society's future.

developmental **connection**

Socioeconomic Status. Adolescents growing up in poverty experience widespread environmental inequities. Chapter 12, p. 401

social policy A national government's course of action designed to influence the welfare of its citizens.

connecting with careers

Peter Benson, President, Search Institute

Peter Benson has been the president of the Search Institute in Minneapolis since 1985. The Search Institute is an independent, non-profit organization whose mission is to advance the well-being of children and adolescents. The Institute conducts applied scientific research, provides information about many aspects of improving adolescents' lives, gives support to communities, and trains people to work with youth.

Peter obtained his undergraduate degree in psychology from Augustana College, master's degree in the psychology of religion from Yale University, and Ph.D. in social psychology from the University of Denver. Peter directs a staff of 80 individuals at the Search Institute, lectures widely about youth, and consults with a number of communities and organizations on adolescent issues.

Peter Benson talking with adolescents.

Under Peter's direction, the Search Institute has determined through research that a number of assets (such as family support and good schools) serve as a buffer to prevent adolescents from developing problems and increase the likelihood that adolescents will competently make the transition from adolescence to adulthood. We further discuss these assets in Chapter 13.

THE GLOBAL PERSPECTIVE

The way adolescence is presented in this text is based largely on the writing and research of scholars in the Western world, especially Europe and North America. In fact, some experts argue that adolescence is typically thought of in a "Eurocentric" way (Nsamenang, 2002). Others note that advances in transportation and telecommunication are spawning a global youth culture in which adolescents everywhere wear the same type of clothing and have similar hairstyles, listen to the same music, and use similar slang expressions (Larson, Wilson, & Rickman, 2009). But cultural differences among adolescents have by no means disappeared (Chen & others, 2011; Fung, 2011; Schlegel & Hewlett, 2011). Consider some of the following variations of adolescence around the world (Brown & Larson, 2002):

- Two-thirds of Asian Indian adolescents accept their parents' choice of a marital partner for them.
- In the Philippines, many female adolescents sacrifice their own futures by migrating to the city to earn money that they can send home to their families.
- Street youth in Kenya and other parts of the world learn to survive under highly stressful circumstances. In some cases abandoned by their parents, they may engage in delinquency or prostitution to provide for their economic needs.
- In the Middle East, many adolescents are not allowed to interact with the other sex, even in school.
- Youth in Russia are marrying earlier to legitimize sexual activity.

developmental **connection**

Culture. Cross-cultural studies compare a culture with one or more other cultures. Chapter 12, p. 393

Thus, depending on the culture being observed, adolescence may involve many different experiences (Cheah & Yeung, 2011; Patton & others, 2010).

Rapid global change is altering the experience of adolescence, presenting new opportunities and challenges to young people's health and well-being. Around the

connecting with adolescents

Doly Akter, Improving the Lives of Adolescent Girls in the Slums of Bangladesh

Doly Akter, age 17, lives in a slum in Dhaka, Bangladesh, where sewers overflow, garbage rots in the streets, and children are undernourished. Nearly two-thirds of young women in Bangladesh get married before they are 18. Doly recently organized a club supported by UNICEF in which girls go door-to-door to monitor the hygiene habits of households in their neighborhoods. The monitoring has led to improved hygiene and health in the families. Doly's group has also managed to stop several child marriages by meeting with parents and convincing them that the marriages are not in their daughters' best interests. When talking with parents in their neighborhoods, the girls in the club emphasize how important it is for their daughters to stay in school and how doing so will improve their future. Doly says the girls in her UNICEF group are far more aware of their rights than their mothers ever were (UNICEF, 2007).

What insights might U.S. adolescents draw from Doly's very different experience of growing up?

Doly Akter, a 17-year-old from Bangladesh, who is highly motivated to improve the lives of youth in her country.

world, adolescents' experiences may differ depending on their gender, families, schools, peers, and religion. However, some adolescent traditions remain the same in various cultures. Brad Brown and Reed Larson (2002) summarized some of these changes and traditions in the world's youth:

- *Health and well-being.* Adolescent health and well-being have improved in some areas but not in others. Overall, fewer adolescents around the world die from infectious diseases and malnutrition now than in the past (UNICEF, 2011). However, a number of adolescent health-compromising behaviors (especially illicit drug use and unprotected sex) continue to be at levels that place adolescents at risk for serious developmental problems (Hyde & DeLamater, 2011). Extensive increases in the rates of HIV in adolescents have occurred in many sub-Saharan countries (UNICEF, 2011). Almost two-thirds of the adolescent deaths in the world occur in just two regions, sub-Saharan Africa and southeast Asia, yet only 42 percent of the world's adolescents live in those regions (Fatusi & Hindin, 2010).
- *Gender.* Around the world, the experiences of male and female adolescents continue to be quite different (Eagly & Wood, 2011; UNICEF, 2011). Except in a few areas, such as Japan and Western countries, males have far greater access to educational opportunities than females do. In many countries, adolescent females have less freedom to pursue a variety of careers and engage in various leisure acts than males do. Gender differences in sexual expression are widespread, especially in India, Southeast Asia, Latin America, and Arab countries, where there are far more restrictions on the sexual activity of adolescent females than that of males. These gender differences do appear to be narrowing over time. In some countries, educational and career opportunities for women are expanding, and in some parts of the world control over adolescent girls' romantic and sexual relationships is decreasing.

Boys-only Muslim school in Middle East.

Asian Indian adolescents in a marriage ceremony.

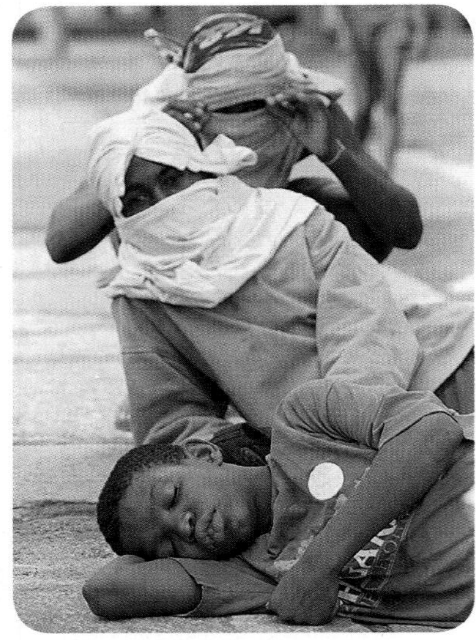
Street youth in Rio de Janeiro.

- *Family*. A recent study revealed that in 12 countries around the world (located in Africa, Asia, Australia, Europe, the Middle East, and the Americas), adolescents validated the importance of parental support in their lives (McNeely & Barber, 2010). However, variations in families across countries also characterize adolescent development. In some countries, adolescents grow up in closely knit families with extensive extended kin networks that provide a web of connections and reflect a traditional way of life. For example, in Arab countries, "adolescents are taught strict codes of conduct and loyalty" (Brown & Larson, 2002, p. 6). However, in Western countries such as the United States, many adolescents grow up in divorced families and stepfamilies. Parenting in many families in Western countries is less authoritarian than in the past. Other trends that are occurring in many countries around the world "include greater family mobility, migration to urban areas, family members working in distant cities or countries, smaller families, fewer extended-family households, and increases in mothers' employment" (Brown & Larson, 2002, p. 7). Unfortunately, many of these changes may reduce the ability of families to provide time and resources for adolescents.
- *School*. In general, the number of adolescents in school in developing countries is increasing. However, schools in many parts of the world—especially Africa, South Asia, and Latin America—still do not provide education to all adolescents (UNICEF, 2011). Indeed, there has been a decline in recent years in the percentage of Latin American adolescents who have access to secondary and higher education (Welti, 2002). Further, many schools do not provide students with the skills they need to be successful in adult work.
- *Peers*. Some cultures give peers a stronger role in adolescence than other cultures (Bagwell & Schmidt, 2011; B. B. Brown & Larson, 2009). In most Western nations, peers figure prominently in adolescents' lives, in some cases taking on responsibilities that are otherwise assumed by parents. Among street youth in South America, the peer network serves as a surrogate family that supports survival in dangerous and stressful settings. In other regions of the world, such as in Arab countries, peers have a very restrictive role, especially for girls.

In sum, adolescents' lives are characterized by a combination of change and tradition. Researchers have found both similarities and differences in the experiences of adolescents in different countries (Fatusi & Hindin, 2010; Larson, Wilson, & Rickman, 2009). In Chapter 12, we discuss these cross-cultural comparisons further.

Review *Connect* Reflect

LG2 Discuss today's U.S. adolescents and adolescents around the world.

Review

- What is the current status of today's adolescents? What is social policy? What are some important social policy issues concerning today's adolescents?
- How is adolescence changing for youth around the globe?

Connect

- Do you think adolescents in other countries experience stereotyping, as described earlier in the chapter? If so, why or how?

Reflect *Your Own Personal Journey of Life*

- How was your adolescence likely similar to, or different from, the adolescence of your parents and grandparents?

3 The Nature of Development

LG3 Summarize the developmental processes, periods, transitions, and issues related to adolescence.

Processes and Periods | Developmental Transitions | Developmental Issues

In certain ways, each of us develops like all other individuals; in other ways, each of us is unique. Most of the time, our attention focuses on our individual uniqueness, but researchers who study development are drawn to our shared as well as our unique characteristics. As humans, we travel some common paths. Each of us—Leonardo da Vinci, Joan of Arc, George Washington, Martin Luther King, Jr., you, and I—walked at about the age of 1, talked at about the age of 2, engaged in fantasy play as a young child, and became more independent as a youth.

What do we mean when we speak of an individual's development? **Development** is the pattern of change that begins at conception and continues through the life span. Most development involves growth, although it also includes decay (as in death and dying). The pattern is complex because it is the product of several processes.

PROCESSES AND PERIODS

Human development is determined by biological, cognitive, and socioemotional processes. It is often described in terms of periods.

Biological, Cognitive, and Socioemotional Processes **Biological processes** involve physical changes in an individual's body. Genes inherited from parents, the development of the brain, height and weight gains, advances in motor skills, and the hormonal changes of puberty all reflect biological processes. We discuss these biological processes extensively in Chapter 2.

Cognitive processes involve changes in an individual's thinking and intelligence. Memorizing a poem, solving a math problem, and imagining what being a movie star would be like all reflect cognitive processes. Chapter 3 discusses cognitive processes in detail.

Socioemotional processes involve changes in an individual's emotions, personality, relationships with others, and social contexts. Talking back to parents, aggression toward peers, assertiveness, enjoyment of social events such as an adolescent's senior prom, and gender-role orientation all reflect the role of socioemotional processes. Chapters 4 through 12 focus on socioemotional processes in adolescent development.

Biological, cognitive, and socioemotional processes are intricately interwoven. Socioemotional processes shape cognitive processes; cognitive processes advance or restrict socioemotional processes; and biological processes influence cognitive processes. Although you read about these processes in separate chapters of the book, keep in mind that you are studying about the development of an integrated human being who has only one interdependent mind and body (see Figure 1.3).

Nowhere is the connection across biological, cognitive, and socioemotional processes more obvious than in two rapidly emerging fields:

- *Developmental cognitive neuroscience,* which explores links between development, cognitive processes, and the brain (Diamond, Casey, & Munakata, 2011)
- *Developmental social neuroscience,* which examines connections between socioemotional processes, development, and the brain (Bell, Greene, & Wolfe, 2010)

Periods of Development Human development is commonly described in terms of periods. We consider developmental periods that occur in childhood, adolescence, and adulthood. Approximate age ranges are given for the periods to provide a general idea of when they begin and end.

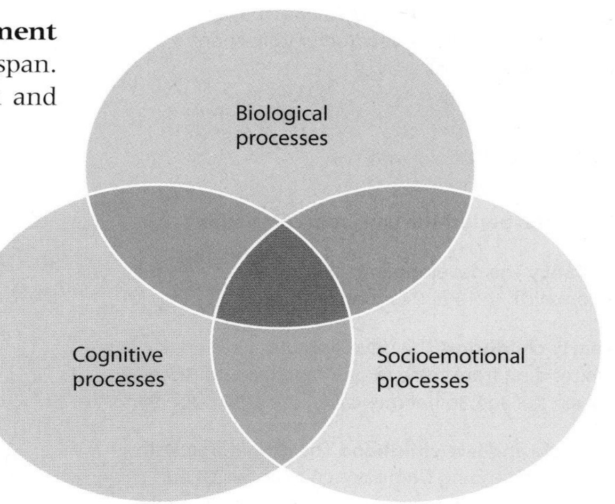

FIGURE **1.3**
DEVELOPMENTAL CHANGES ARE THE RESULT OF BIOLOGICAL, COGNITIVE, AND SOCIOEMOTIONAL PROCESSES. These processes interact as individuals develop.

developmental **connection**

Brain Development. Is there a link between changes in the adolescent's brain and mood swings and sensation seeking? Chapter 2, p. 65

development The pattern of change that begins at conception and continues through the life span. Most development involves growth, although it also includes decay (as in death and dying).

biological processes Physical changes in an individual's body.

cognitive processes Changes in an individual's thinking and intelligence.

socioemotional processes Changes in an individual's personality, emotions, relationships with other people, and social contexts.

"This is the path to adulthood. You're here."

Childhood Childhood includes the prenatal period, infancy, early childhood, and middle and late childhood.

The **prenatal period** is the time from conception to birth—approximately 9 months. It is a time of tremendous growth—from a single cell to an organism complete with a brain and behavioral capabilities.

Infancy is the developmental period that extends from birth to 18 or 24 months of age. Infancy is a time of extreme dependency on adults. Many psychological activities—for example, language, symbolic thought, sensorimotor coordination, social learning, and parent-child relationships—begin in this period.

Early childhood is the developmental period that extends from the end of infancy to about 5 or 6 years of age, sometimes called the preschool years. During this time, young children learn to become more self-sufficient and to care for themselves. They develop school readiness (following instructions, identifying letters) and spend many hours in play and with peers. First grade typically marks the end of early childhood.

Middle and late childhood is the developmental period that extends from the age of about 6 to 10 or 11 years of age. In this period, sometimes called the elementary school years, children master the fundamental skills of reading, writing, and arithmetic, and they are formally exposed to the larger world and its culture. Achievement becomes a central theme of the child's development, and self-control increases.

Adolescence As our developmental timetable suggests, considerable development and experience have occurred before an individual reaches adolescence. No girl or boy enters adolescence as a blank slate, with only a genetic code to determine thoughts, feelings, and behaviors. Rather, the combination of heredity, childhood experiences, and adolescent experiences determines the course of adolescent development. As you read through this book, keep in mind this continuity of development between childhood and adolescence.

A definition of adolescence requires a consideration not only of age but also of sociohistorical influences: recall our discussion of the inventionist view of adolescence. With the sociohistorical context in mind, we define **adolescence** as the period of transition between childhood and adulthood that involves biological, cognitive, and socioemotional changes. A key task of adolescence is preparation for adulthood. Indeed, the future of any culture hinges on how effective this preparation is.

Although the age range of adolescence can vary with cultural and historical circumstances, in the United States and most other cultures today adolescence begins at approximately 10 to 13 years of age and ends in the late teens. The biological, cognitive, and socioemotional changes of adolescence range from the development of sexual functions to abstract thinking processes to independence.

Increasingly, developmentalists describe adolescence in terms of early and late periods. **Early adolescence** corresponds roughly to the middle school or junior high school years and includes most pubertal change. **Late adolescence** refers

prenatal period The time from conception to birth.

infancy The developmental period that extends from birth to 18 or 24 months of age.

early childhood The developmental period extending from the end of infancy to about 5 or 6 years of age; sometimes called the preschool years.

middle and late childhood The developmental period extending from about 6 to about 10 or 11 years of age; sometimes called the elementary school years.

adolescence The developmental period of transition from childhood to adulthood; it involves biological, cognitive, and socioemotional changes. Adolescence begins at approximately 10 to 13 years of age and ends in the late teens.

early adolescence The developmental period that corresponds roughly to the middle school or junior high school years and includes most pubertal change.

late adolescence The developmental period that corresponds approximately to the latter half of the second decade of life. Career interests, dating, and identity exploration are often more pronounced in late adolescence than in early adolescence.

Bloom County used with the permission of Berkeley Breathed, the Washington Post Writers Group, and the Cartoonist Group.

approximately to the latter half of the second decade of life. Career interests, dating, and identity exploration are often more pronounced in late adolescence than in early adolescence. Researchers often specify whether their results generalize to all of adolescence or are specific to early or late adolescence.

The old view of adolescence was that it is a singular, uniform period of transition resulting in entry to the adult world. Current approaches emphasize a variety of transitions and events that define the period, as well as their timing and sequence. For instance, puberty and school events are key transitions that signal entry into adolescence; completing school and taking one's first full-time job are key transitional events that signal an exit from adolescence and entry into adulthood.

Today, developmentalists do not believe that change ends with adolescence (Park, 2011; Schaie, 2011; Schaie & Willis, 2012). Remember that development is defined as a lifelong process. Adolescence is part of the life course and as such is not an isolated period of development. Though it has some unique characteristics, what takes place during adolescence is connected with development and experiences in both childhood and adulthood (Collins, Welsh, & Furman, 2009).

Adulthood Like childhood and adolescence, adulthood is not a homogeneous period of development. Developmentalists often describe three periods of adult development: early adulthood, middle adulthood, and late adulthood.

Early adulthood usually begins in the late teens or early twenties and lasts through the thirties. It is a time of establishing personal and economic independence, and career development intensifies.

Middle adulthood begins at approximately 35 to 45 years of age and ends at some point between approximately 55 and 65 years of age. This period is especially important in the lives of adolescents whose parents are either in, or about to enter, this adult period. Middle adulthood is a time of increasing interest in transmitting values to the next generation, increased reflection about the meaning of life, and enhanced concern about one's body. In Chapter 8, "Families," we see how the maturation of both adolescents and parents contributes to the parent-adolescent relationship.

Eventually, the rhythm and meaning of the human life span wend their way to **late adulthood,** the developmental period that lasts from approximately 60 or 70 years of age until death. This is a time of adjustment to decreasing strength and health and to retirement and reduced income. Reviewing one's life and adapting to changing social roles also characterize late adulthood, as do lessened responsibility and increased freedom. Figure 1.4 summarizes the developmental periods in the human life span and their approximate age ranges.

> One's children's children's children. Look back to us as we look to you; we are related by our imaginations. If we are able to touch, it is because we have imagined each other's existence, our dreams running back and forth along a cable from age to age.
>
> —Roger Rosenblatt
> *Contemporary American Writer*

DEVELOPMENTAL TRANSITIONS

Developmental transitions are often important junctures in people's lives. Such transitions include moving from the prenatal period to birth and infancy, from infancy to early childhood, and from early childhood to middle and late childhood. For our purposes, two important transitions are from childhood to adolescence and from adolescence to adulthood. Let's explore these transitions.

Childhood to Adolescence The transition from childhood to adolescence involves a number of biological, cognitive, and socioemotional changes. Among the biological changes are the growth spurt, hormonal changes, and sexual maturation that come with puberty. In early adolescence, changes take place in the brain that allow for more advanced thinking. Also at this time, adolescents begin to stay up later and sleep later in the morning.

Among the cognitive changes that occur during the transition from childhood to adolescence are increases in abstract, idealistic, and logical thinking. As they make this transition, adolescents begin to think in more egocentric ways, often sensing that they are onstage, unique, and invulnerable. In response to these

early adulthood The developmental period beginning in the late teens or early twenties and lasting through the thirties.

middle adulthood The developmental period that is entered at about 35 to 45 years of age and exited at about 55 to 65 years of age.

late adulthood The developmental period that lasts from about 60 to 70 years of age until death.

Periods of Development

Prenatal period (conception to birth)	Infancy (birth to 18–24 months)	Early childhood (2–5 years)	Middle and late childhood (6–11 years)	Adolescence (10–13 to late teens)	Early adulthood (20s to 30s)	Middle adulthood (35–45 to 55–65)	Late adulthood (60s–70s to death)
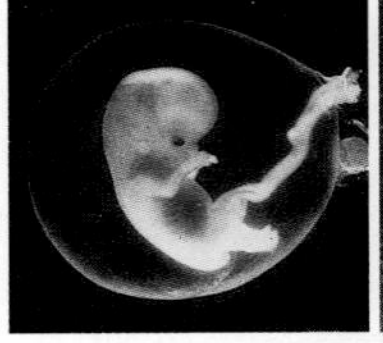							

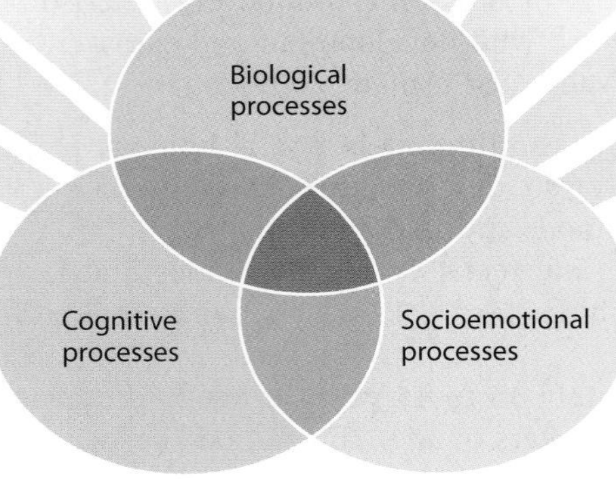

Processes of Development

FIGURE **1.4**

PROCESSES AND PERIODS OF DEVELOPMENT. The unfolding of life's periods of development is influenced by the interaction of biological, cognitive, and socioemotional processes.

changes, parents place more responsibility for decision making on the young adolescents' shoulders.

Among the socioemotional changes adolescents undergo are a quest for independence, conflict with parents, and a desire to spend more time with peers. Conversations with friends become more intimate and include more self-disclosure. As children enter adolescence, they attend schools that are larger and more impersonal than their neighborhood grade schools. Achievement becomes more serious business,

Development transitions from childhood to adolescence involve biological, cognitive, and socioemotional changes. *What are some of these changes?*

connecting with emerging adults

Chris Barnard

Emerging adult Chris Barnard is a single 24-year-old. Two years ago he moved back in with his parents, worked as a temp, and thought about his next step in life. One of the temp jobs became permanent. Chris now works with a trade association in Washington, D.C. With the exception of technology, he says that his life is similar to what his parents' lives must have been like as they made the transition to adulthood. Chris' living arrangements reflect the "instability" characteristic of emerging adulthood. While in college, he changed dorms each year; then as a senior he moved to an off-campus apartment. Following college, Chris moved back home, then moved to another apartment, and now is in yet another apartment. In Chris' words, "This is going to be the longest stay I've had since I went to college. . . . I've sort of settled in" (Jayson, 2006, p. 2D).

Chris Barnard, 24-year-old emerging adult, in the apartment he shares with two roommates.

Would you characterize Chris' life experiences since college as continuous or discontinuous?

and academic challenges increase. Also at this time, increased sexual maturation produces a much greater interest in romantic relationships. Young adolescents also experience greater mood swings than they did when they were children.

In sum, the transition from childhood to adolescence is complex and multidimensional, involving change in many different aspects of an individual's life. Negotiating this transition successfully requires considerable adaptation and thoughtful, sensitive support from caring adults.

developmental **connection**

Schools. The transition to middle or junior high school can be difficult and stressful for many students. Chapter 10, p. 334

Adolescence to Adulthood Another important transition occurs from adolescence to adulthood (Hamilton & Hamilton, 2009). It has been said that adolescence begins in biology and ends in culture. That is, the transition from childhood to adolescence begins with the onset of pubertal maturation, whereas the transition from adolescence to adulthood is determined by cultural standards and experiences.

Emerging Adulthood Recently, the transition from adolescence to adulthood has been referred to as **emerging adulthood,** approximately 18 to 25 years of age. Experimentation and exploration characterize the emerging adult. At this point in their development, many individuals are still exploring which career path they want to follow, what they want their identity to be, and which lifestyle they want to adopt (for example, single, cohabiting, or married).

Jeffrey Arnett (2006) recently concluded that five key features characterize emerging adulthood:

- *Identity exploration,* especially in love and work. Emerging adulthood is the time during which key changes in identity take place for many individuals (Kroger, Martinussen, & Marcia, 2010).
- *Instability.* Residential changes peak during emerging adulthood, a time during which there also is often instability in love, work, and education.

emerging adulthood The developmental period occurring from approximately 18 to 25 years of age; this transitional period between adolescence and adulthood is characterized by experimentation and exploration.

Rhymes with Orange used with the permission of Hilary Price, King Features Syndicate, and the Cartoonist Group.

- *Self-focused.* According to Arnett (2006, p. 10), emerging adults "are self-focused in the sense that they have little in the way of social obligations, little in the way of duties and commitments to others, which leaves them with a great deal of autonomy in running their own lives."
- *Feeling in-between.* Many emerging adults don't consider themselves adolescents or full-fledged adults.
- *The age of possibilities, a time when individuals have an opportunity to transform their lives.* Arnett (2006) describes two ways in which emerging adulthood is the age of possibilities: (1) many emerging adults are optimistic about their future; and (2) for emerging adults who have experienced difficult times while growing up, emerging adulthood presents an opportunity to direct their lives in a more positive direction (Masten & Wright, 2009).

Recent research indicates that these five aspects characterize not only individuals in the United States as they make the transition from adolescence to early adulthood, but also their counterparts in European countries and Australia (Buhl & Lanz, 2007; Sirsch & others, 2009). Although emerging adulthood does not characterize development in all cultures, it does appear to occur in those in which assuming adult roles and responsibilities is postponed (Kins & Beyers, 2010).

Does life get better for individuals when they become emerging adults? To read about this question, see the *Connecting with Health and Well-Being* interlude.

Becoming an Adult Determining just when an individual becomes an adult is difficult. In the United States, the most widely recognized marker of entry into adulthood is holding a more or less permanent, full-time job, which usually happens when an individual finishes school—high school for some, college for others, graduate or professional school for still others. However, other criteria are far from clear. Economic independence is one marker of adult status but achieving it is often a long process. College graduates are increasingly returning to live with their parents as they attempt to establish themselves economically. A longitudinal study found that at age 25 only slightly more than half of the participants were fully financially independent of their family of origin (Cohen & others, 2003). The most dramatic findings in this study, though, involved the extensive variability in the individual trajectories of adult roles across ten years from 17 to 27 years of age; many of the participants moved back and forth between increasing and decreasing economic dependency. A recent study revealed that continued co-residence with parents during emerging adulthood slowed down the process of becoming a self-sufficient and independent adult (Kins & Beyers, 2010).

Other studies show us that taking responsibility for oneself is likely an important marker of adult status for many individuals. In one study, more than 70 percent of college students said that being an adult means accepting responsibility for the consequences of one's actions, deciding on one's own beliefs and values, and establishing a relationship with parents as an equal adult (Arnett, 1995). And, in a recent study, both parents and college students agreed that taking responsibility for one's actions and developing emotional control are important aspects of becoming an adult

connecting with health and well-being

Do Health and Well-Being Change in Emerging Adulthood?

What are the health and well-being of individuals in emerging adulthood like, compared to adolescence? John Schulenberg and his colleagues (Johnston, O'Malley, & Bachman, 2004; Schulenberg & Zarrett, 2006) have examined this question. For the most part, life does get better for most emerging adults. For example, Figure 1.5 shows a steady increase in self-reported well-being from 18 years of age through 26 years of age. Figure 1.6 indicates that risk taking decreases during the same time frame.

Why does the health and well-being of emerging adults improve over their adolescent levels? One possible answer is the increasing choices individuals have in their daily living and life decisions during emerging adulthood. This increase can lead to more opportunities for individuals to exercise self-control in their lives. Also, as we discussed earlier, emerging adulthood provides an opportunity for individuals who engaged in problem behavior during adolescence to get their lives together. However, the lack of structure and support that often characterizes emerging adulthood can produce a downturn in health and well-being for some individuals (Schulenberg & Zarrett, 2006).

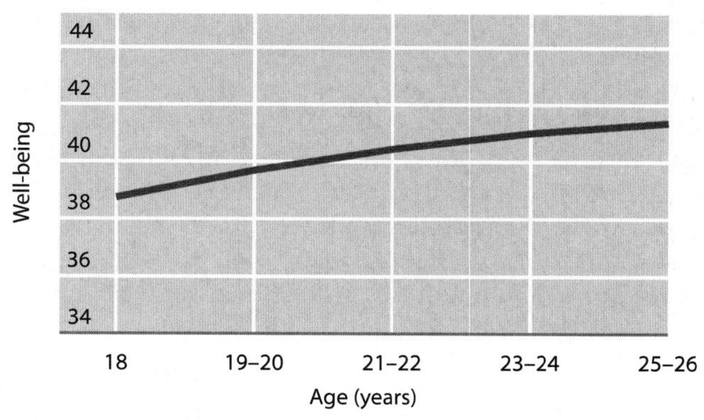

FIGURE **1.5**

WELL-BEING THROUGH EMERGING ADULTHOOD.
Note: Scores based on a combination of self-esteem (8 items), self-efficacy (5 items), and social support (6 items); possible responses ranged from disagree (1) to agree (5).

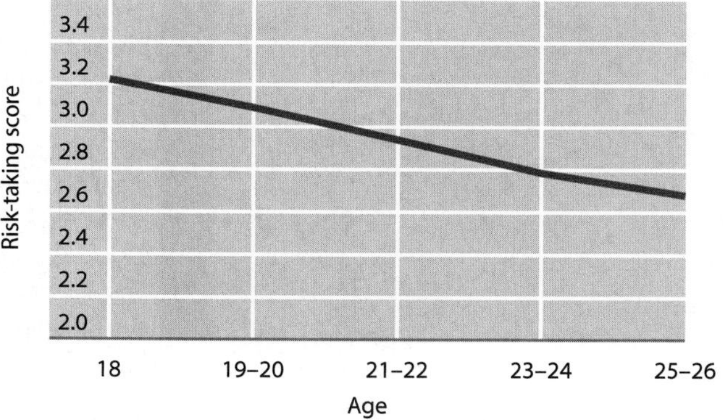

FIGURE **1.6**

RISK TAKING THROUGH EMERGING ADULTHOOD. *Note:* The two Risk-Taking Scale items ranged from 1 (disagree) to 5 (agree). The risk-taking score was the average of the two items that assessed whether the emerging adult got a kick out of doing things that are a little dangerous and enjoyed doing something a little risky.

What factors can emerging adults control that might influence whether their health and well-being improve over their adolescent levels?

(Nelson & others, 2007). However, parents and college students didn't always agree on other aspects of what it takes to become an adult. For example, parents were more likely than college students to emphasize that driving safely and not getting drunk are important aspects of becoming an adult.

At some point in the late teens through the early twenties, then, individuals reach adulthood. In becoming an adult, they accept responsibility for themselves, become capable of making independent decisions, and gain financial independence from their parents (Arnett, 2006). The new freedoms and responsibilities of emerging adulthood represent major changes in individuals' lives. Keep in mind, though, that considerable continuity still glues adolescence and adulthood together. For example, a longitudinal study found that religious views and behaviors of emerging adults were especially stable and that their attitudes toward drugs were stable to a lesser degree (Bachman & others, 2002).

What characterizes emerging adulthood? Even when emerging adults have experienced a troubled childhood and adolescence, what are some factors that can help them become competent?

What we have said so far about the determinants of adult status mainly addresses individuals in industrialized societies, especially the United States. In developing countries, marriage is often a more significant marker for entry into adulthood than in the United States, and it usually occurs much earlier than in the United States (Arnett, 2007; Eccles, Brown, & Templeton, 2008). Thus, some developmentalists argue that the term "emerging adulthood" applies more to Western countries, such as the United States and European countries, and some Asian countries, such as Japan, but less to developing countries (Arnett, 2007). In a recent study, the majority of 18- to 26-year-olds in India felt that they had achieved adulthood (Seiter & Nelson, 2011).

Contextual variations in emerging adulthood also may occur in cultures within a country (Arnett & Brody, 2008). For example, in the United States, "Mormons marry early and begin having children . . . so they have a briefer period of emerging adulthood before taking on adult roles" (Arnett, 2004, p. 22). Further, in some countries, such as China and India, emerging adulthood is more likely to occur in urban areas but less so in rural areas because young people in the urban areas of these countries "marry later, have children later, obtain more education, and have a greater range of occupational and recreational opportunities" (Arnett, 2004, p. 23).

What determines an individual's well-being in the transition to adulthood? In the view of Jacquelynne Eccles and her colleagues (Eccles, Brown, & Templeton, 2008; Eccles & Gootman, 2002), three types of assets are especially important in making a competent transition through adolescence and emerging adulthood: intellectual, psychological/emotional, and social. Figure 1.7 describes examples of these three types of assets.

Resilience At the beginning of the chapter, you read about the captivating story of Michael Maddaus, who got his life together as an emerging adult following a troubled childhood and adolescence. Michael Maddaus was resilient. What do we mean by the term *resilience?* **Resilience** refers to adapting positively and achieving successful outcomes in the face of significant risks and adverse circumstances. In Project Competence, Ann Masten and her colleagues (Masten, 2009; Masten, Obradovic, & Burt, 2006; McCormick, Kuo, & Masten, 2011) examined the resilience of individuals from childhood through adulthood. They found that adults who experienced considerable adversity while growing up—but became competent young adults—were characterized by certain individual and contextual factors. Competence was assessed in such areas as achievement, conduct, and social relationships. In emerging adulthood (assessed at 17 to 23 years of age), individuals who became competent after experiencing difficulties while growing up were more intelligent, experienced higher parenting quality, and were less likely to have grown up in poverty or low-income circumstances than their counterparts who did not become competent as emerging adults.

A further analysis focused on individuals who were still showing maladaptive patterns in emerging adulthood but had gotten their lives together by the time they were in the late twenties and early thirties. The three characteristics shared by these "late-bloomers" were support by adults, being planful, and showing positive aspects of autonomy. In other longitudinal research, "military service, marriage and romantic relationships, higher education, religion affiliations, and work opportunities may provide turning-point opportunities for changing the life course during emerging adulthood" (Masten, Obradovic, & Burt, 2006, p. 179).

Is Adolescence Taking Too Long? Joseph and Claudia Allen (2009) titled their recent book *Escaping the Endless Adolescence: How We Can Help Our Teenagers Grow Up Before They Grow Old*, and opened the book with a chapter titled, "Is twenty-five the

resilience Adapting positively and achieving successful outcomes in the face of significant risks and adverse circumstances.

nature-nurture issue Issue involving the debate about whether development is primarily influenced by an organism's biological inheritance (nature) or by its environmental experiences (nurture).

new fifteen?" They argue that in recent decades adolescents have experienced a world that places more challenges on maturing into a competent adult. In their words (p. 17)

> Generations ago, fourteen-year-olds used to drive, seventeen-year-olds led armies, and even average teens contributed labor and income that helped keep their families afloat. While facing other problems, those teens displayed adultlike maturity far more quickly than today's, who are remarkably well kept, but cut off from most of the responsibility, challenge, and growth-producing feedback of the adult world. Parents of twenty-somethings used to lament, "They grow up so fast." But that seems to be replaced with, "Well, . . . Mary's living at home a bit while she sorts things out."

The Allens conclude that what is happening to the current generation of adolescents is that after adolescence, they are experiencing "more adolescence," instead of adequately being launched into the adult years. Even many adolescents who have gotten good grades and then as emerging adults continued to achieve academic success in college later find themselves in their mid-twenties not having a clue about how to find a meaningful job, manage their finances, or live independently.

The Allens recommend the following to help adolescents become more mature on their way to adulthood:

- *Provide them with opportunities to be contributors.* Help them move away from being consumers by creating more effective work experiences (quality work apprenticeships, for example), or service learning opportunities, that allow adolescents to make meaningful contributions.
- *Give candid, quality feedback to adolescents.* Don't just shower praise and material things on them, but let them see how the real world works. Don't protect them from criticism, constructive or negative. Protecting them in this way only leaves them ill-equipped to deal with the ups and downs of the real world of adulthood.
- *Create positive adult connections with adolescents.* Many adolescents deny that they need parental support or attachment to parents, but to help them develop maturity on the way to adulthood, they do. Exploring a wider social world than in childhood, adolescents need to be connected to parents and other adults in positive ways to be able to handle autonomy in a mature way.
- *Challenge adolescents to become more competent.* Adults need to do fewer things for adolescents that they can accomplish for themselves. Providing adolescents with opportunities to engage in tasks that lie just beyond their current level stretches their minds and helps to move them farther along the road to maturity.

Intellectual development

Knowledge of essential life and vocational skills
Rational habits of mind—critical thinking and reasoning skills
Good decision-making skills
In-depth knowledge of more than one culture
Knowledge of skills necessary to navigate through multiple cultures
School success

Psychological and emotional development

Good mental health including positive self-regard
Good emotional self-regulation and coping skills
Good conflict resolution skills
Mastery motivation and positive achievement motivation
Confidence in one's personal efficacy
Planfulness
Sense of personal autonomy/responsibility for self
Optimism coupled with realism
Coherent and positive personal and social identity
Prosocial and culturally sensitive values
Spirituality and/or a sense of purpose in life
Strong moral character

Social development

Connectedness—perceived good relationships and trust with parents, peers, and some other adults
Sense of social place/integration—being connected and valued by larger social networks
Attachment to prosocial/conventional institutions such as school, church, out-of-school youth development centers
Ability to navigate in multiple cultural contexts
Commitment to civic engagement

FIGURE **1.7**
PERSONAL ASSETS THAT FACILITATE POSITIVE YOUTH DEVELOPMENT

DEVELOPMENTAL ISSUES

Is development due more to nature (heredity) or to nurture (environment)? Is it more continuous and smooth or discontinuous and stage-like? Is it due more to early experience or to later experience? These are three important issues raised in the study of adolescent development.

Nature and Nurture The **nature-nurture issue** involves the debate about whether development is primarily influenced by nature or nurture. Nature refers to an organism's biological inheritance, nurture to its environmental experiences. "Nature" proponents claim that the most important influence on development is biological inheritance. "Nurture" proponents claim that environmental experiences are the most important influence.

According to the nature advocates, just as a sunflower grows in an orderly way—unless flattened by an unfriendly environment—so does the human grow in

developmental **connection**

Community. Service learning is linked to many positive outcomes for adolescents. Chapter 7, p. 241

developmental **connection**

Families. Secure attachment to parents increases the likelihood that adolescents will be socially competent. Chapter 8, p. 267

an orderly way. The range of environments can be vast, but the nature approach argues that the genetic blueprint produces commonalities in growth and development (Mader, 2011). We walk before we talk, speak one word before two words, grow rapidly in infancy and less so in early childhood, experience a rush of sexual hormones in puberty, reach the peak of our physical strength in late adolescence and early adulthood, and then physically decline. The nature proponents acknowledge that extreme environments—those that are psychologically barren or hostile—can depress development. However, they believe that basic growth tendencies are genetically wired into humans.

By contrast, other psychologists emphasize the importance of nurture, or environmental experiences, in development (Grusec, 2011; Phillips & Lowenstein, 2011). Experiences run the gamut from the individual's biological environment—nutrition, medical care, drugs, and physical accidents—to the social environment—family, peers, schools, community, media, and culture.

Some adolescent development researchers maintain that, historically, too much emphasis has been placed on the biological changes of puberty as determinants of adolescent psychological development. They recognize that biological change is an important dimension of the transition from childhood to adolescence, one that is found in all primate species and in all cultures throughout the world. However, they argue that social contexts (nurture) play important roles in adolescent psychological development as well, roles that until recently have not been given adequate attention (Reich & Vandell, 2011; Russell, 2011).

FIGURE **1.8**
CONTINUITY AND DISCONTINUITY IN DEVELOPMENT. *Is human development like a seedling gradually growing into a giant oak? Or is it more like a caterpillar suddenly becoming a butterfly?*

Continuity and Discontinuity Think for a moment about your development. Was your growth into the person you are today gradual, like the slow, cumulative growth of a seedling into a giant oak? Or did you experience sudden, distinct changes in your growth, like the remarkable change from a caterpillar into a butterfly (see Figure 1.8)? The **continuity-discontinuity issue** focuses on the extent to which development involves gradual, cumulative change (continuity) or distinct stages (discontinuity). For the most part, developmentalists who emphasize experience have described development as a gradual, continuous process; those who emphasize nature have described development as a series of distinct stages.

In terms of continuity, a child's first word, while seemingly an abrupt, discontinuous event, is actually the result of weeks and months of growth and practice. Similarly, puberty, while also seeming to be abrupt and discontinuous, is actually a gradual process that occurs over several years.

In terms of discontinuity, each person is described as passing through a sequence of stages in which change is qualitatively, rather than quantitatively, different. As the oak moves from seedling to giant tree, it becomes more oak—its development is continuous. As a caterpillar changes into a butterfly, it does not become more caterpillar; it becomes a different kind of organism—its development is discontinuous. For example, at some point a child moves from not being able to think abstractly about the world to being able to. This is a qualitative, discontinuous change in development, not a quantitative, continuous change.

Early and Later Experience Another important debate is the **early-later experience issue,** which focuses on the degree to which early experiences (especially early in childhood) or later experiences are the key determinants of development (Schaie, 2011; Smith & Hart, 2011). That is, if infants or young children experience negative, stressful circumstances in their lives, can those experiences be overcome by later, more positive experiences in adolescence? Or are the early experiences so critical, possibly because they are the infant's first, prototypical experiences, that they cannot be overridden by a later, more enriched environment in childhood or adolescence?

continuity-discontinuity issue Issue regarding whether development involves gradual, cumulative change (continuity) or distinct stages (discontinuity).

early-later experience issue Issue focusing on the degree to which early experiences (especially early in childhood) or later experiences are the key determinants of development.

The early-later experience issue has a long history, and developmentalists continue to debate it (Schaie, 2011; Thompson, 2012). Some emphasize that unless infants experience warm, nurturant caregiving in the first year or so of life, their

To what extent is an adolescent's development due to earlier or later experiences?

development will never be optimal (Cassidy & others, 2011). Plato was sure that infants who were rocked frequently became better athletes. Nineteenth-century New England ministers told parents in Sunday sermons that the way they handled their infants would determine their children's future character. The emphasis on the importance of early experience rests on the belief that each life is an unbroken trail on which a psychological quality can be traced back to its origin.

The early-experience doctrine contrasts with the later-experience view that, rather than achieving statuelike permanence after change in infancy, our development continues to be like the ebb and flow of a river. The later-experience advocates argue that children and adolescents are malleable throughout development and that later sensitive caregiving is just as important as earlier sensitive caregiving (Antonucci, Birditt, & Ajrouch, 2011). A number of life-span developmentalists, who focus on the entire life span rather than only on child development, stress that too little attention has been given to later experiences in development (Almeida, 2011; Staudinger & Gluck, 2011). They accept that early experiences are important contributors to development, but no more important than later experiences. Jerome Kagan (1992, 2000, 2010) points out that even children who show the qualities of an inhibited temperament, which is linked to heredity, have the capacity to change their behavior.

Evaluating the Developmental Issues As we consider further these three salient developmental issues—nature and nurture, continuity and discontinuity, and early and later experience—it is important to realize that most developmentalists consider it unwise to take an extreme position on these issues. Development is not all nature or all nurture, not all continuity or discontinuity, and not all early experience or all later experience. Nature and nurture, continuity and discontinuity, and early and later experience all affect our development throughout the human life span. For example, in considering the nature-nurture issue, the key to development is the interaction of nature and nurture rather than either factor alone (Gottlieb, 2007; Mandelman & Grigorenko, 2011). An individual's cognitive development, for instance, is the result of heredity-environment interaction, not heredity or environment alone. Much more about the role of heredity-environment interaction appears in Chapter 2.

developmental **connection**

Nature and Nurture. The epigenetic view emphasizes the ongoing, bidirectional interchange between heredity and environment. Chapter 2, p. 81

Although most developmentalists do not take extreme positions on the developmental issues we have discussed, this consensus has not meant the absence of spirited debate about how strongly development is determined by these factors (Kagan, 2010; Schaie & Willis, 2012). Consider adolescents who, as children, experienced poverty, parental neglect, and poor schooling. Could enriched experiences in adolescence overcome the "deficits" they encountered earlier in development? The answers developmentalists give to such questions reflect their stance on the issues of nature and nurture, continuity and discontinuity, and early and later experiences. The answers also influence public policy about adolescents and how each of us lives throughout the human life span.

Review *Connect* Reflect

 Summarize the developmental processes, periods, transitions, and issues related to adolescence.

Review

- What are the key processes involved in adolescent development? What are the main childhood, adolescent, and adult periods of development?
- What is the transition from childhood to adolescence like? What is the transition from adolescence to adulthood like?
- What are three important developmental issues?

Connect

- Describe how nature and nurture might each contribute to an individual's degree of resilience.

Reflect *Your Own Personal Journey of Life*

- As you go through this course, ask yourself questions about how you experienced various aspects of adolescence. Be curious. Ask your friends and classmates about their experiences in adolescence and compare them with yours. For example, ask them how they experienced the transition from childhood to adolescence. Also ask them how they experienced, or are experiencing, the transition from adolescence to adulthood.

4 The Science of Adolescent Development

 Characterize the science of adolescent development.

- Science and the Scientific Method
- Theories of Adolescent Development
- Research in Adolescent Development

How can we answer questions about the roles of nature and nurture, stability and change, and continuity and discontinuity in development? How can we determine, for example, whether an adolescent's achievement in school changes or stays the same from childhood through adolescence, or how can we find out whether positive experiences in adolescence can repair the harm done by neglectful or abusive parenting in childhood? To effectively answer such questions, we need to turn to science (Jackson, 2011; Stangor, 2011).

SCIENCE AND THE SCIENTIFIC METHOD

Some individuals have difficulty thinking of adolescent development as being a science in the same way that physics, chemistry, and biology are sciences. Can a discipline that studies pubertal change, parent-adolescent relationships, or adolescent thinking be equated with disciplines that investigate how gravity works and the molecular structure of compounds? The answer is yes, because science is not defined by what it investigates but by how it investigates. Whether you are studying photosynthesis, Saturn's moons, or adolescent development, it is the way you study the subject that matters.

> There is nothing quite so practical as a good theory.
>
> —Kurt Lewin
>
> *American Social Psychologist, 20th Century*

Oral stage	Anal stage	Phallic stage	Latency stage	Genital stage
Infant's pleasure centers on the mouth.	Child's pleasure focuses on the anus.	Child's pleasure focuses on the genitals.	Child represses sexual interest and develops social and intellectual skills.	A time of sexual reawakening; source of sexual pleasure becomes someone outside the family.
Birth to 1 1/2 Years	1 1/2 to 3 Years	3 to 6 Years	6 Years to Puberty	Puberty Onward

FIGURE **1.9**
FREUDIAN STAGES

In taking a scientific path to study adolescent development, it is important to follow the *scientific method*, which is essentially a four-step process: (1) conceptualize a process or problem to be studied, (2) collect research information (data), (3) analyze data, and (4) draw conclusions.

In step 1, when researchers are formulating a problem to study, they often draw on theories and develop hypotheses. A **theory** is an interrelated, coherent set of ideas that helps to explain phenomena and make predictions. It may suggest **hypotheses,** which are specific assertions and predictions that can be tested. For example, a theory on mentoring might state that sustained support and guidance from an adult make a difference in the lives of children from impoverished backgrounds because the mentor gives the children opportunities to observe and imitate the behavior and strategies of the mentor.

THEORIES OF ADOLESCENT DEVELOPMENT

This section discusses key aspects of four theoretical orientations to development: psychoanalytic, cognitive, behavioral and social cognitive, and ecological. Each contributes an important piece to the adolescent development puzzle. Although the theories disagree about certain aspects of development, many of their ideas are complementary rather than contradictory. Together they let us see the total landscape of adolescent development in all its richness.

Psychoanalytic Theories

Psychoanalytic theories describe development as primarily unconscious (beyond awareness) and heavily colored by emotion. Psychoanalytic theorists emphasize that behavior is merely a surface characteristic and that a true understanding of development requires analyzing the symbolic meanings of behavior and the deep inner workings of the mind. Psychoanalytic theorists also stress that early experiences with parents extensively shape development. These characteristics are highlighted in the main psychoanalytic theory, that of Sigmund Freud (1856–1939).

Sigmund Freud, the pioneering architect of psychoanalytic theory. *What are some characteristics of Freud's theory?*

Freud's Theory As Freud listened to, probed, and analyzed his patients, he became convinced that their problems were the result of experiences early in life. He thought that as children grow up, their focus of pleasure and sexual impulses shifts from the mouth to the anus and eventually to the genitals. As a result, according to Freud's theory, we go through five stages of psychosexual development: oral, anal, phallic, latency, and genital (see Figure 1.9). Our adult personality, Freud (1917) claimed, is determined by the way we resolve conflicts between sources of pleasure at each stage and the demands of reality.

Freud stressed that adolescents' lives are filled with tension and conflict. To reduce the tension, he thought adolescents bury their conflicts in their unconscious mind. Freud said that even trivial behaviors can become significant when the unconscious forces behind them are revealed. A twitch, a doodle, a joke, a smile—each might betray unconscious conflict. For example, 17-year-old Barbara, while kissing and hugging Tom, exclaims, "Oh, *Jeff*, I love you so much." Repelled, Tom explodes: "Why did you call me Jeff? I thought you didn't think about him anymore. We

theory An interrelated, coherent set of ideas that helps explain phenomena and make predictions.

hypotheses Specific assertions and predictions that can be tested.

psychoanalytic theories Theories that describe development as primarily unconscious and heavily colored by emotion. Behavior is merely a surface characteristic, and the symbolic workings of the mind have to be analyzed to understand behavior. Early experiences with parents are emphasized.

need to have a talk!" You probably can remember times when such a "Freudian slip" revealed your own unconscious motives.

Freud (1917) divided personality into three structures: the id, the ego, and the superego. The *id* consists of instincts, which are an individual's reservoir of psychic energy. In Freud's view, the id is totally unconscious; it has no contact with reality. As children experience the demands and constraints of reality, a new structure of personality emerges—the *ego,* which deals with the demands of reality. The ego is called the "executive branch" of personality because it makes rational decisions.

The id and the ego have no morality—they do not take into account whether something is right or wrong. The *superego* is the moral branch of personality. The superego takes into account whether something is right or wrong. Think of the superego as what we often refer to as our "conscience." You probably are beginning to sense that both the id and the superego make life rough for the ego. Your ego might say, "I will have sex only occasionally and be sure to take the proper precautions because I don't want a child to interfere with the development of my career." However, your id is saying, "I want to be satisfied; sex is pleasurable." Your superego is at work, too: "I feel guilty about having sex."

Freud considered personality to be like an iceberg. Most of personality exists below our level of awareness, just as the massive part of an iceberg is beneath the water's surface. The ego resolves conflict between its reality demands, the id's wishes, and the superego's constraints through *defense mechanisms.* These are unconscious methods of distorting reality that the ego uses to protect itself from the anxiety produced by the conflicting demands of the three personality structures. When the ego senses that the id's demands may cause harm, anxiety develops, alerting the ego to resolve the conflict by means of defense mechanisms.

According to Freud, *repression* is the most powerful and pervasive defense mechanism. It pushes unacceptable id impulses out of awareness and back into the unconscious mind. Repression is the foundation on which all other defense mechanisms rest, since the goal of every defense mechanism is to repress, or push, threatening impulses out of awareness. Freud thought that early childhood experiences, many of which he believed are sexually laden, are too threatening and stressful for people to deal with consciously, so they repress them.

However, Peter Blos (1989), a British psychoanalyst, and Anna Freud (1966), Sigmund Freud's daughter, argued that defense mechanisms provide considerable insight into adolescent development. Blos stated that regression during adolescence is actually not defensive at all, but rather an integral, normal, inevitable, and universal aspect of puberty. The nature of regression may vary from one adolescent to the next. It may involve compliance, and cleanliness, or it may involve a sudden return to the passiveness that characterized the adolescent's behavior during childhood.

Anna Freud, Sigmund Freud's daughter. *How did her view differ from her father's?*

Anna Freud (1966) developed the idea that defense mechanisms are the key to understanding adolescent adjustment. She maintained that the problems of adolescence are not rooted in the id, or instinctual forces, but in the "love objects" in the adolescent's past. Attachment to these love objects, usually parents, is carried forward from the infant years and merely toned down or inhibited during the childhood years, she argued. During adolescence, these urges might be reawakened, or, worse, newly acquired urges might combine with them.

Bear in mind that defense mechanisms are unconscious; adolescents are not aware they are using them to protect their egos and reduce anxiety. When used temporarily and in moderation, defense mechanisms are not necessarily unhealthy. However, defense mechanisms should not be allowed to dominate an individual's behavior and prevent a person from facing reality. Sigmund Freud's theory has been significantly revised by a number of other psychoanalytic theorists as well. Many contemporary psychoanalytic theorists stress that he overemphasized sexual instincts; they place more emphasis on cultural experiences as determinants of an individual's development. Unconscious thought remains a central theme, but most contemporary psychoanalysts argue that conscious thought plays a greater role than Freud envisioned. Next, we outline the ideas of an important revisionist of Freud's ideas—Erik Erikson.

Erikson's Psychosocial Theory Erik Erikson recognized Freud's contributions but argued that Freud misjudged some important dimensions of human development. For one thing, Erikson (1950, 1968) said we develop in *psychosocial* stages, rather than in *psychosexual* stages, as Freud maintained. According to Freud, the primary motivation for human behavior is sexual in nature; according to Erikson, it is social and reflects a desire to affiliate with other people. According to Freud, our basic personality is shaped in the first five years of life; according to Erikson, developmental change occurs throughout the life span. Thus, in terms of the early- versus later-experience issue we discussed earlier in the chapter, Freud argued that early experience is far more important than later experiences, whereas Erikson emphasized the importance of both early and later experiences.

In **Erikson's theory,** eight stages of development unfold as we go through life (see Figure 1.10). At each stage, a unique developmental task confronts individuals with a crisis that must be resolved. According to Erikson, this crisis is not a catastrophe but a turning point marked by both increased vulnerability and enhanced potential. The more successfully an individual resolves the crises, the healthier development will be.

Trust versus mistrust is Erikson's first psychosocial stage, which is experienced in the first year of life. Trust in infancy sets the stage for a lifelong expectation that the world will be a good and pleasant place to live.

Autonomy versus shame and doubt is Erikson's second stage, occurring in late infancy and toddlerhood. After gaining trust, infants begin to discover that their behavior is their own, and they start to assert their independence.

Initiative versus guilt, Erikson's third stage of development, occurs during the preschool years. As preschool children encounter a widening social world, they face new challenges that require active, purposeful, responsible behavior. Feelings of guilt may arise, though, if the child is irresponsible and is made to feel too anxious.

Industry versus inferiority is Erikson's fourth developmental stage, occurring approximately in the elementary school years. Children now need to direct their energy toward mastering knowledge and intellectual skills. The negative outcome is that the child can develop a sense of inferiority—feeling incompetent and unproductive.

During the adolescent years, individuals face finding out who they are, what they are all about, and where they are going in life. This is Erikson's fifth developmental stage, *identity versus identity confusion.* If adolescents explore roles in a healthy manner and arrive at a positive path to follow in life, they achieve a positive identity; if not, identity confusion reigns.

Intimacy versus isolation is Erikson's sixth developmental stage, which individuals experience during the early adulthood years. At this time, individuals face the developmental task of forming intimate relationships. If young adults form healthy friendships and an intimate relationship with another individual, intimacy will be achieved; if not, isolation will result.

Generativity versus stagnation, Erikson's seventh developmental stage, occurs during middle adulthood. By generativity Erikson means primarily a concern for helping the younger generation to develop and lead useful lives. The feeling of having done nothing to help the next generation is stagnation.

Integrity versus despair is Erikson's eighth and final stage of development,

Erik Erikson with his wife, Joan, an artist. Erikson generated one of the most important developmental theories of the twentieth century. *Which stage of Erikson's theory are you in? Does Erikson's description of this stage characterize you?*

Erikson's Stages	Developmental Period
Integrity versus despair	Late adulthood (60s onward)
Generativity versus stagnation	Middle adulthood (40s, 50s)
Intimacy versus isolation	Early adulthood (20s, 30s)
Identity versus identity confusion	Adolescence (10 to 20 years)
Industry versus inferiority	Middle and late childhood (elementary school years, 6 years to puberty)
Initiative versus guilt	Early childhood (preschool years, 3 to 5 years)
Autonomy versus shame and doubt	Infancy (1 to 3 years)
Trust versus mistrust	Infancy (first year)

FIGURE **1.10**
ERIKSON'S EIGHT LIFE-SPAN STAGES

developmental **connection**

Identity. Adolescents and emerging adults can be classified as having one of four identity statuses: diffusion, foreclosure, moratorium, or achievement. Chapter 4, p. 143

Erikson's theory Theory that includes eight stages of human development. Each stage consists of a unique developmental task that confronts individuals with a crisis that must be faced.

Sensorimotor stage	Preoperational stage	Concrete operational stage	Formal operational stage
The infant constructs an understanding of the world by coordinating sensory experiences with physical actions. An infant progresses from reflexive, instinctual action at birth to the beginning of symbolic thought toward the end of the stage.	The child begins to represent the world with words and images. These words and images reflect increased symbolic thinking and go beyond the connection of sensory information and physical action.	The child can now reason logically about concrete events and classify objects into different sets.	The adolescent reasons in more abstract, idealistic, and logical ways.
Birth to 2 Years of Age	**2 to 7 Years of Age**	**7 to 11 Years of Age**	**11 Years of Age Through Adulthood**

FIGURE **1.11**

PIAGET'S FOUR STAGES OF COGNITIVE DEVELOPMENT

which individuals experience in late adulthood. During this stage, a person reflects on the past. If the person's life review reveals a life well spent, integrity will be achieved; if not, the retrospective glances likely will yield doubt or gloom—the despair Erikson described.

Jean Piaget, the famous Swiss developmental psychologist, changed the way we think about the development of children's minds. *What are some key ideas in Piaget's theory?*

Piaget's theory A theory stating that children actively construct their understanding of the world and go through four stages of cognitive development.

Evaluating Psychoanalytic Theories Contributions of psychoanalytic theories include an emphasis on a developmental framework, family relationships, and unconscious aspects of the mind. Criticisms include a lack of scientific support, too much emphasis on sexual underpinnings, and an image of people that is too negative.

Cognitive Theories Whereas psychoanalytic theories stress the importance of the unconscious, cognitive theories emphasize conscious thoughts. Three important cognitive theories are Piaget's cognitive developmental theory, Vygotsky's sociocultural cognitive theory, and information-processing theory.

Piaget's Cognitive Developmental Theory **Piaget's theory** states that individuals actively construct their understanding of the world and go through four stages of cognitive development. Two processes underlie this cognitive construction of the world: organization and adaptation. To make sense of our world, adolescents organize their experiences. For example, they separate important ideas from less important ideas, and connect one idea to another. In addition to organizing their observations and experiences, they *adapt,* adjusting to new environmental demands (Miller, 2011).

Piaget (1954) also maintained that people go through four stages in understanding the world (see Figure 1.11). Each stage is age-related and consists of a distinct way of thinking, a *different* way of understanding the world. Thus, according to Piaget, cognition is *qualitatively* different in one stage compared with another. What are Piaget's four stages of cognitive development like?

The *sensorimotor stage,* which lasts from birth to about 2 years of age, is the first Piagetian stage. In this stage, infants construct an understanding of the world by coordinating sensory experiences (such as seeing and hearing) with physical, motoric actions—hence the term *sensorimotor.*

The *preoperational stage,* which lasts from approximately 2 to 7 years of age, is Piaget's second stage. In this stage, children begin to go beyond simply connecting sensory information with physical action and represent the world with words, images, and drawings. However, according to Piaget, preschool children still lack the ability to perform what he calls *operations,* which are internalized mental actions that allow children to do mentally what they previously could only do physically. For example, if you imagine putting two sticks together to see whether they would be as long as another stick without actually moving the sticks, you are performing a concrete operation.

The *concrete operational stage,* which lasts from approximately 7 to 11 years of age, is the third Piagetian stage. In this stage, children can perform operations that involve objects, and they can reason logically as long as they can apply reasoning to specific or concrete examples. For instance, concrete operational thinkers cannot imagine the steps necessary to complete an algebraic equation, which is too abstract for thinking at this stage of development.

The *formal operational stage,* which appears between the ages of 11 and 15 and continues through adulthood, is Piaget's fourth and final stage. In this stage, individuals move beyond concrete experiences and think in abstract and more logical terms. As part of thinking more abstractly, adolescents develop images of ideal circumstances. They might think about what an ideal parent is like and compare their parents to this ideal standard. They begin to entertain possibilities for the future and are fascinated with what they can be. In solving problems, they become more systematic, developing hypotheses about why something is happening the way it is and then testing these hypotheses. We examine Piaget's cognitive developmental theory further in Chapter 3.

There is considerable interest today in Lev Vygotsky's sociocultural cognitive theory of child development. *What were Vygotsky's basic claims about children's development?*

Vygotsky's Sociocultural Cognitive Theory Like Piaget, the Russian developmentalist Lev Vygotsky (1896–1934) emphasized that individuals actively construct their knowledge. However, Vygotsky (1962) gave social interaction and culture far more important roles in cognitive development than Piaget did. **Vygotsky's theory** is a sociocultural cognitive theory that emphasizes how culture and social interaction guide cognitive development.

Vygotsky portrayed development as inseparable from social and cultural activities (Daniels, 2011). He stressed that cognitive development involves learning to use the inventions of society, such as language, mathematical systems, and memory strategies. Thus, in one culture, individuals might learn to count with the help of a computer; in another, they might learn by using beads. According to Vygotsky, children's and adolescents' social interaction with more-skilled adults and peers is indispensable to their cognitive development (Gauvain, 2011). Through this interaction, they learn to use the tools that will help them adapt and be successful in their culture. In Chapter 3, we examine ideas about learning and teaching that are based on Vygotsky's theory.

Information-Processing Theory **Information-processing theory** emphasizes that individuals manipulate information, monitor it, and strategize about it. Unlike Piaget's theory, but like Vygotsky's theory, information-processing theory does not describe development as stage-like. Instead, according to this theory, individuals develop a gradually increasing capacity for processing information, which allows them to acquire increasingly complex knowledge and skills (Halford & Andrews, 2011; Sternberg, 2012).

Robert Siegler (2006), a leading expert on children's information processing, states that thinking is information processing. In other words, when adolescents perceive, encode, represent, store, and retrieve information, they are thinking. Siegler emphasizes that an important aspect of development is learning good strategies for processing information. For example, becoming a better reader might involve learning to monitor the key themes of the material being read.

Evaluating Cognitive Theories Contributions of cognitive theories include a positive view of development and an emphasis on the active construction of understanding. Criticisms include skepticism about the pureness of Piaget's stages and too little attention to individual variations.

Vygotsky's theory A sociocultural cognitive theory that emphasizes how culture and social interaction guide cognitive development.

information-processing theory A theory emphasizing that individuals manipulate information, monitor it, and strategize about it. Central to this approach are the processes of memory and thinking.

Behavioral and Social Cognitive Theories *Behaviorism* essentially holds that we can study scientifically only what we can directly observe and measure. Out of

developmental **connection**

Social Cognitive Theory. Bandura emphasizes that self-efficacy is a key person/cognitive factor in adolescents' achievement. Chapter 11, p. 368

the behavioral tradition grew the belief that development is observable behavior that can be learned through experience with the environment (Spiegler & Guevremont, 2010). In terms of the continuity-discontinuity issue we discussed earlier in this chapter, the behavioral and social cognitive theories emphasize continuity in development and argue that development does not occur in stage-like fashion. Let's explore two versions of behaviorism: Skinner's operant conditioning and Bandura's social cognitive theory.

Albert Bandura, developed social cognitive theory.

Skinner's Operant Conditioning According to B. F. Skinner (1904–1990), through *operant conditioning* the consequences of a behavior produce changes in the probability of the behavior's occurrence. A behavior followed by a rewarding stimulus is more likely to recur, whereas a behavior followed by a punishing stimulus is less likely to recur. For example, when an adult smiles at an adolescent after the adolescent has done something, the adolescent is more likely to engage in the activity again than if the adult gives the adolescent a nasty look.

In Skinner's (1938) view, such rewards and punishments shape development. For example, Skinner's approach argues that shy people learn to be shy as a result of experiences they have while growing up. It follows that modifications in an environment can help a shy adolescent become more socially oriented. Also, for Skinner the key aspect of development is behavior, not thoughts and feelings. He emphasized that development consists of the pattern of behavioral changes that are brought about by rewards and punishments.

Bandura's Social Cognitive Theory Some psychologists agree with the behaviorists' notion that development is learned and is influenced strongly by environmental interactions. However, unlike Skinner, they argue that cognition is also important in understanding development. **Social cognitive theory** holds that behavior, environment, and cognition are the key factors in development.

American psychologist Albert Bandura (1925–) is the leading architect of social cognitive theory. Bandura (1986, 2001, 2004, 2009, 2010a,b) emphasizes that cognitive processes have important links with the environment and behavior. His early research program focused heavily on *observational learning* (also called *imitation*, or *modeling*), which is learning that occurs through observing what others do. For example, a young boy might observe his father yelling in anger and treating other people with hostility; with his peers, the young boy later acts very aggressively, showing the same characteristics as his father's behavior. Social cognitive theorists stress that people acquire a wide range of behaviors, thoughts, and feelings through observing others' behavior and that these observations form an important part of adolescent development.

What is *cognitive* about observational learning in Bandura's view? He proposes that people cognitively represent the behavior of others and then sometimes adopt this behavior themselves.

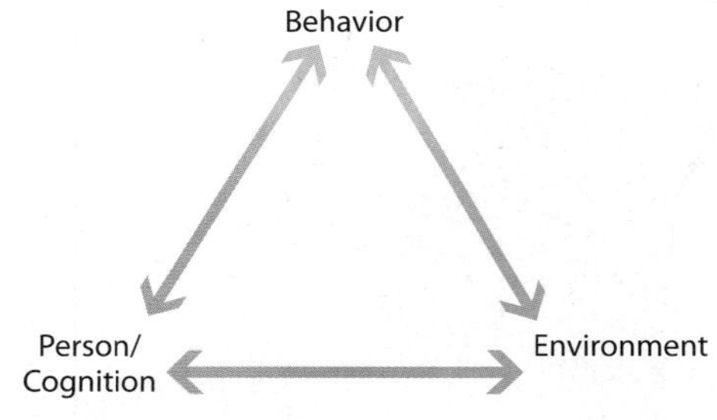

FIGURE **1.12**

BANDURA'S SOCIAL COGNITIVE THEORY. Bandura's social cognitive theory emphasizes reciprocal influences of behavior, environment, and person/cognitive factors.

Bandura's (2009, 2010a,b) most recent model of learning and development includes three elements: behavior, the person/cognition, and the environment. An individual's confidence that he or she can control his or her success is an example of a person factor; strategies are an example of a cognitive factor. As shown in Figure 1.12, behavior, person/cognitive, and environmental factors operate interactively.

Evaluating Behavioral and Social Cognitive Theories Contributions of the behavioral and social cognitive theories include an emphasis on scientific research and environmental determinants of behavior. Criticisms include too little emphasis on cognition in Skinner's views and giving inadequate attention to developmental changes.

social cognitive theory The view that behavior, environment, and cognition are the key factors in development.

Bronfenbrenner's ecological theory A theory focusing on the influence of five environmental systems: microsystem, mesosystem, exosystem, macrosystem, and chronosystem.

Ecological Theory One ecological theory that has important implications for understanding adolescent development was created by Urie Bronfenbrenner (1917–2005). **Bronfenbrenner's ecological theory** (1986, 2004; Bronfenbrenner

& Morris, 1998, 2006) holds that development reflects the influence of five environmental systems: microsystem, mesosystem, exosystem, macrosystem, and chronosystem (see Figure 1.13).

The *microsystem* is the setting in which the adolescent lives. These contexts include the adolescent's family, peers, school, and neighborhood. It is in the microsystem that the most direct interactions with social agents take place—with parents, peers, and teachers, for example. The adolescent is not a passive recipient of experiences in these settings but someone who helps to construct the settings.

The *mesosystem* involves relations between microsystems or connections between contexts. Examples are the relation of family experiences to school experiences, school experiences to religious experiences, and family experiences to peer experiences. For example, adolescents whose parents have rejected them may have difficulty developing positive relations with teachers.

The *exosystem* consists of links between a social setting in which the adolescent does not have an active role and the individual's immediate context. For example, a husband's or an adolescent's experience at home may be influenced by a mother's experiences at work. The mother might receive a promotion that requires more travel, which might increase conflict with the husband and change patterns of interaction with the adolescent.

The *macrosystem* involves the culture in which adolescents live. *Culture* refers to the behavior patterns, beliefs, and all other products of a group of people that are passed on from generation to generation.

The *chronosystem* consists of the patterning of environmental events and transitions over the life course, as well as sociohistorical circumstances. For example, divorce is one transition. Researchers have found that the negative effects of divorce on children often peak in the first year after the divorce (Hetherington, 2006). By two years after the divorce, family interaction is less chaotic and more stable. As an example of sociohistorical circumstances, consider how the opportunities for adolescent girls to pursue a career have increased during the last fifty years.

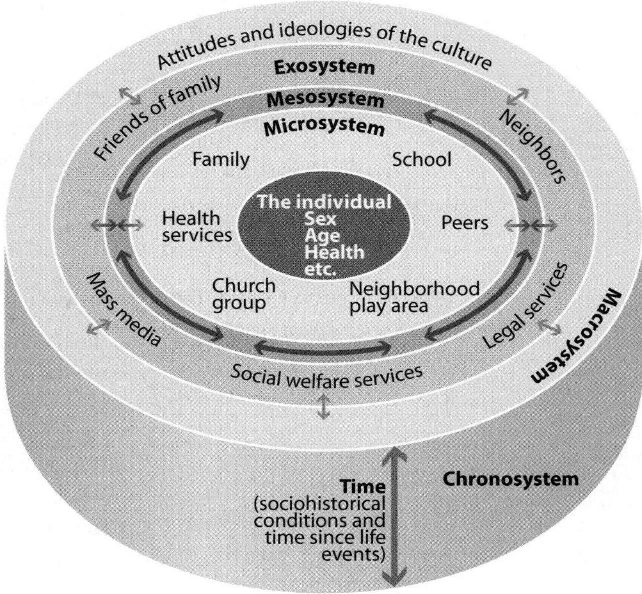

FIGURE **1.13**

BRONFENBRENNER'S ECOLOGICAL THEORY OF DEVELOPMENT. Bronfenbrenner's ecological theory consists of five environmental systems: microsystem, mesosystem, exosystem, macrosystem, and chronosystem. Kopp, *Child Development Social Context,* 1st Ed. © 1982. Electronically reproduced by permission of Pearson Education, Inc., Upper Saddle River, New Jersey.

Bronfenbrenner (2004; Bronfenbrenner & Morris, 2006) has added biological influences to his theory and describes the newer version as a bioecological theory. Nonetheless, ecological, environmental contexts still predominate in Bronfenbrenner's theory.

Contributions of the theory include a systematic examination of macro and micro dimensions of environmental systems, and attention to connections between environmental systems. Criticisms include giving inadequate attention to biological factors, as well as too little emphasis on cognitive factors.

Urie Bronfenbrenner developed ecological theory, a perspective that is receiving increased attention. *What is the nature of ecological theory?*

An Eclectic Theoretical Orientation No single theory described in this chapter can explain entirely the rich complexity of adolescent development, but each has contributed to our understanding of development. Psychoanalytic theory best explains the unconscious mind. Erikson's theory best describes the changes that occur in adult development. Piaget's, Vygotsky's, and the information-processing views provide the most complete description of cognitive development. The behavioral and social cognitive and ecological theories have been the most adept at examining the environmental determinants of development.

In short, although theories are helpful guides, relying on a single theory to explain adolescent development is probably a mistake. This book instead takes an **eclectic theoretical orientation,** which does not follow any one theoretical approach but rather selects from each theory whatever is considered its best features. In this way, you can view the study of adolescent development as it actually exists—with different theorists making different assumptions, stressing different empirical problems, and using different strategies to discover information.

eclectic theoretical orientation An orientation that does not follow any one theoretical approach but rather selects from each theory whatever is considered the best in it.

RESEARCH IN ADOLESCENT DEVELOPMENT

If scholars and researchers follow an eclectic orientation, how do they determine that one feature of a theory is somehow better than another? The scientific method discussed earlier provides the guide. Through scientific research, the features of theories can be tested and refined.

> Truth is arrived at by the painstaking process of eliminating the untrue.
>
> —Sir Arthur Conan Doyle
>
> *British Physician and Detective-Story Writer, 20th Century*

Generally, research in adolescent development is designed to test hypotheses, which in some cases are derived from the theories just described. Through research, theories are modified to reflect new data and occasionally new theories arise.

In the twenty-first century, research on adolescent and emerging adult development has expanded a great deal (Russell, Card, & Susman, 2011). Also, research on adolescent development has increasingly examined applications to the real worlds of adolescents (Brown, 2012; R. M. Lerner & Steinberg, 2009). This research trend involves a search for ways to improve the health and well-being of adolescents. The increased application emphasis in research on adolescent development is described in all of the chapters in this text. Let's now turn our attention to how data on adolescent development are collected and to research designs that are used to study adolescent development.

Methods for Collecting Data Whether we are interested in studying pubertal change, cognitive skills, or parent-adolescent conflict, we can choose from several ways of collecting data. Here we consider the measures most often used, beginning with observation.

Observation Scientific observation requires an important set of skills. For observations to be effective, they have to be systematic (Stangor, 2011). We have to have some idea of what we are looking for. We have to know whom we are observing, when and where we will observe, how we will make the observations, and how we will record them.

Where should we make our observations? We have two choices: the laboratory and the everyday world.

When we observe scientifically, we often need to control certain factors that determine behavior but are not the focus of our inquiry (Gravetter & Forzano, 2012; Langston, 2011). For this reason, some adolescent development research is conducted in a **laboratory,** a controlled setting with many of the complex factors of the "real world" removed. Laboratory research does have some drawbacks, however. First, it is almost impossible to conduct research without the participants' knowing they are being studied. Second, the laboratory setting is unnatural and therefore can cause the participants to behave unnaturally. Third, people who are willing to come to a university laboratory may not fairly represent groups from diverse cultural backgrounds. In addition, people who are unfamiliar with university settings, and with the idea of "helping science," may be intimidated by the laboratory setting.

Naturalistic observation provides insights that we sometimes cannot achieve in the laboratory (Jackson, 2011). **Naturalistic observation** means observing behavior in real-world settings, making no effort to manipulate or control the situation. Life-span researchers conduct naturalistic observations in neighborhoods, at schools, sporting events, work settings, and malls, and in other places adolescents frequent.

Survey and Interview Sometimes the best and quickest way to get information about adolescents is to ask them for it. One technique is to *interview* them directly. A related method is the *survey* (sometimes referred to as a questionnaire), which is especially useful when information from many people is needed (Babbie, 2011). A standard set of questions is used to obtain people's self-reported attitudes or beliefs about a specific topic. In a good survey, the questions are clear and unbiased, allowing respondents to answer unambiguously.

Surveys and interviews can be used to study a wide range of topics from religious beliefs to sexual habits to attitudes about gun control to beliefs about how to

laboratory A controlled setting in which many of the complex factors of the "real world" are removed.

naturalistic observation Observation of behavior in real-world settings.

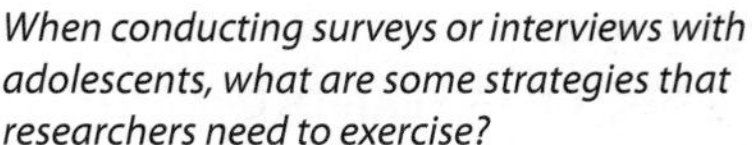

When conducting surveys or interviews with adolescents, what are some strategies that researchers need to exercise?

improve schools. Surveys and interviews today are conducted in person, over the telephone, and over the Internet.

One problem with surveys and interviews is the tendency of participants to answer questions in a way that they think is socially acceptable or desirable rather than telling what they truly think or feel (Leedy & Ormrod, 2010). For example, on a survey or in an interview, some adolescents might say that they do not take drugs even though they do.

Standardized Test A **standardized test** has uniform procedures for administration and scoring. Many standardized tests allow a person's performance to be compared with the performance of other individuals; thus they provide information about individual differences among people (Drummond & Jones, 2010). One example is the Stanford-Binet intelligence test, which we discuss in Chapter 3. Your score on the Stanford-Binet test tells you how your performance compares with that of thousands of other people who have taken the test.

One criticism of standardized tests is that they assume a person's behavior is consistent and stable, yet personality and intelligence—two primary targets of standardized testing—can vary with the situation. For example, adolescents may perform poorly on a standardized intelligence test in an office setting but score much higher at home, where they are less anxious.

Physiological Measures Researchers are increasingly using physiological measures when they study adolescent development. One type of physiological measure involves an assessment of the hormones in an adolescent's bloodstream. As puberty unfolds, glandular secretions in the blood increase, raising the blood levels of hormone samples. To determine the nature of these hormonal changes, researchers take blood samples from willing adolescents (Dorn & Biro, 2011). The body composition of adolescents also is a focus of physiological assessment. There is a special interest in the increase in fat content in the body during pubertal development. Until recently, little research had focused on the brain activity of adolescents. However, the development of neuroimaging techniques has led to a flurry of research studies. One technique that is being used in a number of them is *magnetic resonance imaging (MRI)*, in which radio waves are used to construct images of a person's brain tissue and biochemical activity (Nelson, 2011). Figure 1.14 compares the brain images of two adolescents—one a non-drinker, the other a heavy drinker—while engaged in a memory task.

Experience Sampling In the **experience sampling method (ESM),** participants in a study are given electronic pagers. Then, researchers "beep" them at random times. When they are beeped, the participants report on various aspects of their immediate situation, including where they are, what they are doing, whom they are with, and how they are feeling.

standardized test A test with uniform procedures for administration and scoring. Many standardized tests allow a person's performance to be compared with the performance of other individuals.

experience sampling method (ESM) Research method that involves providing participants with electronic pagers and then beeping them at random times, at which point they are asked to report on various aspects of their lives.

FIGURE **1.14**

BRAIN IMAGING OF 15-YEAR-OLD ADOLESCENTS. The two brain images indicate how alcohol can influence the functioning of an adolescent's brain. Notice the pink and red coloring (which indicates effective brain functioning involving memory) in the brain of the 15-year-old non-drinker while engaging in a memory task, and the lack of those colors in the brain of the 15-year-old under the influence of alcohol.

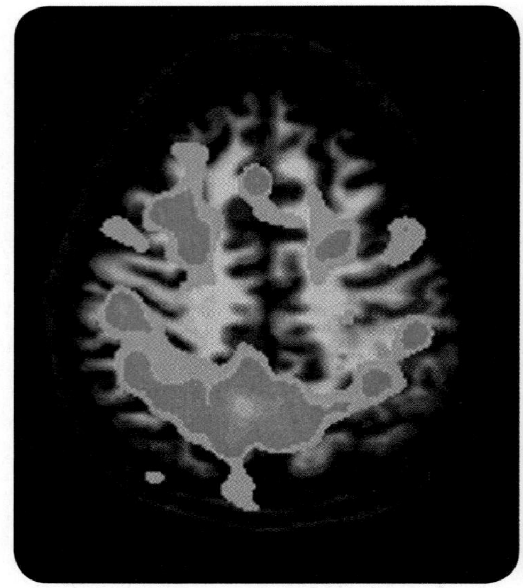

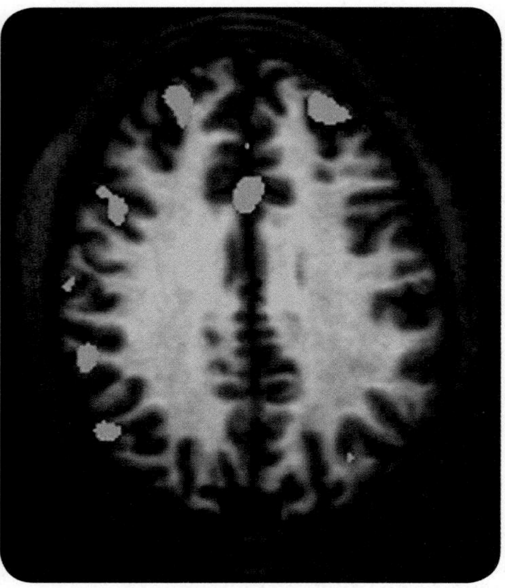

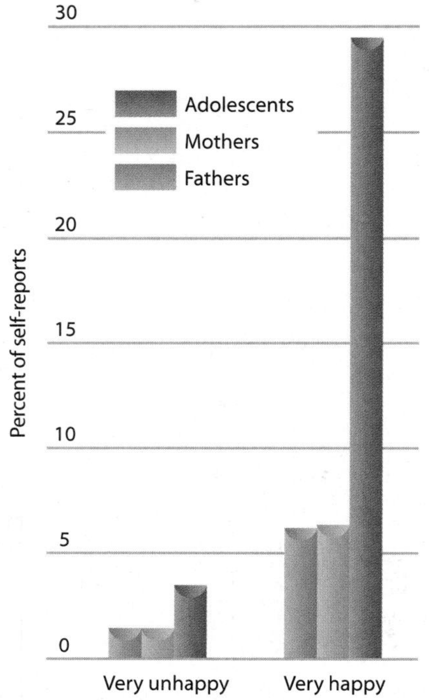

FIGURE **1.15**

SELF-REPORTED EXTREMES OF EMOTION BY ADOLESCENTS, MOTHERS, AND FATHERS USING THE EXPERIENCE SAMPLING METHOD. In the study by Reed Larson and Maryse Richards (1994), adolescents and their mothers and fathers were beeped at random times by researchers using the experience sampling method. The researchers found that adolescents were more likely to report more emotional extremes than their parents.

The ESM has been used in a number of studies to determine the settings in which adolescents are most likely to spend their time, the extent to which they spend time with parents and peers, and the nature of their emotions. Using this method, Reed Larson and Maryse Richards (1994) found that across the thousands of times they reported their feelings, adolescents experienced emotions that were more extreme and more fleeting than those of their parents. For example, adolescents were five times more likely than their parents to report being "very happy" when they were beeped, and three times more likely to feel "very unhappy" (see Figure 1.15).

Case Study A **case study** is an in-depth look at a single individual. Case studies are performed mainly by mental health professionals, when for practical or ethical reasons the unique aspects of an individual's life cannot be duplicated and tested in other individuals. A case study provides information about one person's fears, hopes, fantasies, traumatic experiences, upbringing, family relationships, health, or anything else that helps the psychologist to understand the person's mind and behavior (Babbie, 2011).

Consider the case study of Michael Rehbein, which illustrates the flexibility and resilience of the developing brain. At age 7, Michael began to experience uncontrollable seizures—as many as 400 a day. Doctors said that the only solution was to remove the left hemisphere of his brain where the seizures were occurring. Though Michael's recovery was slow, eventually his right hemisphere began to reorganize and take over functions that normally reside in the brain's left hemisphere, such as speech. The neuroimage in Figure 1.16 shows this reorganization of Michael's brain vividly. Although case histories provide dramatic, in-depth portrayals of people's lives, we must be cautious in generalizing from them. The subject of a case study is unique, with a genetic makeup and personal history that no one else shares. In addition, case studies involve judgments of unknown reliability. Psychologists who conduct case studies rarely check to see whether other psychologists agree with their observations.

case study An in-depth look at a single individual.

descriptive research Research that aims to observe and record behavior.

correlational research Research whose goal is to describe the strength of the relationship between two or more events or characteristics.

correlation coefficient A number based on a statistical analysis that is used to describe the degree of association between two variables.

Research Designs

In conducting research on adolescent development, in addition to a method for collecting data you also need a research design. There are three main types of research design: descriptive, correlational, and experimental.

Descriptive Research All of the data-collection methods that we have discussed can be used in **descriptive research,** which aims to observe and record behavior. For example, a researcher might observe the extent to which adolescents are altruistic or aggressive toward each other. By itself, descriptive research cannot prove what causes some phenomena, but it can reveal important information about people's behavior (Babbie, 2011).

Correlational Research In contrast to descriptive research, correlational research goes beyond describing phenomena to provide information that will help us to predict how people will behave (Heiman, 2012). In **correlational research,** the goal is to describe the strength of the relationship between two or more events or characteristics. The more strongly the two events are correlated (or related or associated), the more effectively we can predict one event from the other.

For example, to study whether adolescents of permissive parents have less self-control than other adolescents, you would need to carefully record observations of parents' permissiveness and their children's self-control. You could then analyze the data statistically to yield a numerical measure, called a **correlation coefficient,** a number based on a statistical analysis that is used to describe the degree of association between two variables. The correlation coefficient ranges from −1.00 to +1.00. A negative number means an inverse relation. For example, researchers often find a negative correlation between permissive parenting and adolescents' self-control. By contrast, they often find a positive correlation between parental monitoring of children and adolescents' self-control.

The higher the correlation coefficient (whether positive or negative), the stronger the association between the two variables. A correlation of 0 means that there is no association between the variables. A correlation of −.40 is stronger than a correlation of +.20 because we disregard whether the correlation is positive or negative in determining the strength of the correlation.

A caution is in order, however (Spatz, 2012). Correlation does not equal causation. The correlational finding just mentioned does not mean that permissive parenting necessarily causes low self-control in adolescents. It could mean that, but it also could mean that an adolescent's lack of self-control caused the parents to simply throw up their arms in despair and give up trying to control the adolescent. It also could mean that other factors, such as heredity or poverty, caused the correlation between permissive parenting and low self-control in adolescents. Figure 1.17 illustrates these possible interpretations of correlational data.

(a)

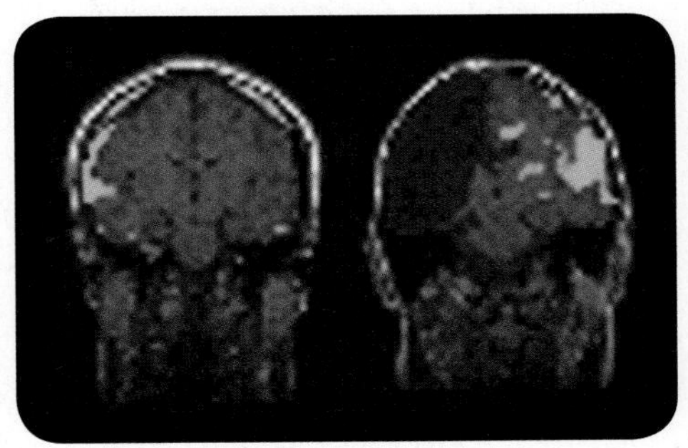
(b)

FIGURE **1.16**

PLASTICITY IN THE BRAIN'S HEMISPHERES. (a) Michael Rehbein at 14 years of age. (b) Michael's right hemisphere (*left*) has reorganized to take over the language functions normally carried out by corresponding areas in the left hemisphere of an intact brain (*right*). However, the right hemisphere is not as efficient in processing speech as the left, and more areas of the brain are recruited to process speech.

Experimental Research To study causality, researchers turn to **experimental research.** An experiment is a carefully regulated procedure in which one or more factors believed to influence the behavior being studied are manipulated, while all other factors are held constant (Gravetter & Forzano, 2012). If the behavior under study changes when a factor is manipulated, researchers say that the manipulated factor has caused the behavior to change. In other words, the experiment has demonstrated cause and effect. The cause is the factor that was manipulated. The effect is the behavior that changed because of the manipulation. Nonexperimental research methods (descriptive and correlational research) cannot establish cause and effect because they do not involve manipulating factors in a controlled way (Stangor, 2011).

All experiments involve at least one independent variable and one dependent variable. The **independent variable** is the factor that is manipulated. The term *independent* indicates that this variable can be manipulated independently of all other factors. For example, suppose we want to design an experiment to establish the effects of peer tutoring on adolescents' achievement. In this example, the amount and type of peer tutoring could be the independent variable.

The **dependent variable** is the factor that is measured; it can change as the independent variable is manipulated. The term *dependent* indicates that this variable depends on what happens as the independent variable is manipulated. In the peer tutoring study, adolescents' achievement would be the dependent variable. It might be assessed in a number of ways, perhaps by scores on a nationally standardized achievement test.

In an experiment, researchers manipulate the independent variable by giving different experiences to one or more experimental groups and one or more control

experimental research Research that involves an experiment, a carefully regulated procedure in which one or more of the factors believed to influence the behavior being studied are manipulated while all other factors are held constant.

independent variable The factor that is manipulated in experimental research.

dependent variable The factor that is measured in experimental research.

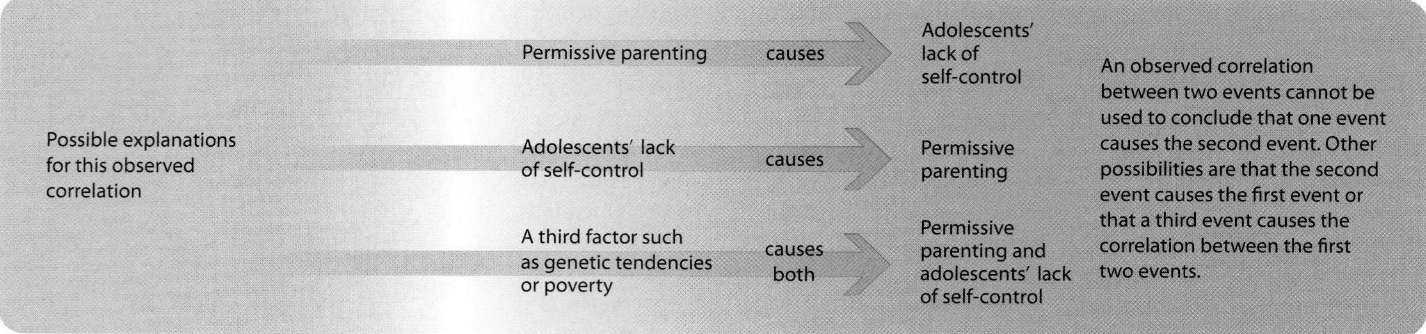

FIGURE **1.17**
POSSIBLE EXPLANATIONS OF CORRELATIONAL DATA

groups. An *experimental group* is a group whose experience is manipulated. A *control group* is a group that is treated like the experimental group in every other way except for the manipulated factor. The control group serves as a baseline against which the effects on the manipulated group can be compared. In the peer tutoring study, we would need to have one group of adolescents that got peer tutoring (experimental group) and one that didn't (control group).

An important principle of experimental research is *random assignment*—assigning participants to experimental and control groups by chance (Gravetter & Forzano, 2012). This practice reduces the likelihood that the results of the experiment will be affected by preexisting differences between the groups. In our study of peer tutoring, random assignment would greatly reduce the probability that the two groups differed in age, family background, initial achievement, intelligence, personality, or health.

To summarize, in our study of peer tutoring and adolescent achievement, we would assign participants randomly to two groups. One (the experimental group) would be given peer tutoring and the other (the control group) would not. The different experiences that the experimental and control groups receive would be the independent variable. After the peer tutoring had been completed, the adolescents would be given a nationally standardized achievement test (the dependent variable). Figure 1.18 applies the experimental research method to a different problem: whether a time management program can improve adolescents' grades.

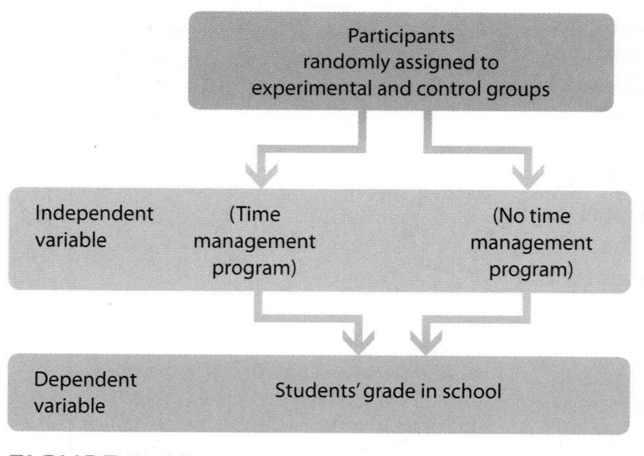

FIGURE **1.18**
RANDOM ASSIGNMENT AND EXPERIMENTAL DESIGN

Time Span of Research

A special concern of developmentalists is the time span of a research investigation (Schaie, 2011; Schaie & Willis, 2012). Studies that focus on the relation of age to some other variable are common. Researchers have two options: They can study different individuals of different ages and compare them, or they can study the same individuals as they age over time.

Cross-Sectional Research

Cross-sectional research involves studying people all at one time. For example, a researcher might study the self-esteem of 10-, 15-, and 20-year-olds. In a cross-sectional study, all participants' self-esteem would be assessed at one time.

The main advantage of a cross-sectional study is that researchers do not have to wait for the individuals to grow older. Despite its time efficiency, however, the cross-sectional approach has its drawbacks. It gives no information about how individuals change or about the stability of their characteristics. The increases and decreases of development—the hills and valleys of growth and development—can become obscured in the cross-sectional approach. For example, in a cross-sectional study of self-esteem, average increases and

cross-sectional research A research strategy that involves studying people all at one time.

decreases might be revealed. But the study would not show how the life satisfaction of individual children waxed and waned over the years. It also would not tell us whether younger children who had high or low self-esteem as young adults continued to have high or low self-esteem, respectively, when they became older.

Longitudinal Research **Longitudinal research** involves studying the same individuals over a period of time, usually several years or more. In a longitudinal study of self-esteem, the researcher might examine the self-esteem of a group of 10-year-olds, then assess their self-esteem again when they are 15, and then again when they are 20.

Longitudinal studies provide a wealth of information about such important issues as stability and change in development and the importance of early experience for later development (Little & others, 2009). However, they are not without their problems (Gibbons, Hedeker, & DuToit, 2010). They are expensive and time consuming. The longer the study lasts, the more participants drop out—they move, get sick, lose interest, and so forth. Participants can bias the outcome of a study, because those who remain may be dissimilar to those who drop out. Those individuals who remain in a longitudinal study over a number of years may be more compulsive and conformity-oriented, for example, or they might have more stable lives.

Conducting Ethical Research Ethics in research may affect you personally if you ever serve as a participant in a study. In that event, you need to know your rights as a participant and the responsibilities of researchers to assure that these rights are safeguarded.

If you ever become a researcher in life-span development yourself, you will need an even deeper understanding of ethics. Even if you carry out experimental projects only in psychology courses, you must consider the rights of the participants in those projects. A student might think, "I volunteer in a home for the mentally retarded several hours per week. I can use the residents of the home in my study to see if a specific treatment helps improve their memory for everyday tasks." But, without proper permissions, the most well-meaning, kind, and considerate studies still violate the rights of the participants.

Today, proposed research at colleges and universities must pass the scrutiny of a research ethics committee before the research can be initiated. In addition, the American Psychological Association (APA) has developed ethics guidelines for its members. The code of ethics instructs psychologists to protect their participants from mental and physical harm. The participants' best interests need to be kept foremost in the researcher's mind (Jackson, 2011). APA's guidelines address four important issues. First, *informed consent*—all participants must know what their research participation will involve and what risks might develop. Even after informed consent is given, participants must retain the right to withdraw from the study at any time and for any reason. Second, *confidentiality*—researchers are responsible for keeping all of the data they gather on individuals completely confidential and, when possible, completely anonymous. Third, *debriefing*—after the study has been completed, participants should be informed of its purpose and the methods that were used. In most cases, the experimenter also can inform participants in a general manner beforehand about the purpose of the research without leading participants to behave in a way they think that the experimenter is expecting. Fourth, *deception*—in some circumstances, telling the participants beforehand what the research study is about substantially alters the participants' behavior and invalidates the researcher's data. In all cases of deception, however, the psychologist must ensure that the deception will not harm the participants and that the participants will be told the complete nature of the study (will be debriefed) as soon as possible after the study is completed.

Minimizing Bias Studies of adolescent development are most useful when they are conducted without bias or prejudice toward any particular group of people. Of special concern is bias based on gender and bias based on culture or ethnicity.

longitudinal research A research strategy in which the same individuals are studied over a period of time, usually several years or more.

Gender Bias Society continues to have a **gender bias,** a preconceived notion about the abilities of females and males that prevents individuals from pursuing their own interests and achieving their potential. But gender bias also has had a less obvious effect within the field of adolescent development. For example, too often researchers have drawn conclusions about females' attitudes and behaviors from research conducted with males as the only participants.

When gender differences are found, they sometimes are unduly magnified (Matlin, 2012). For example, a researcher might report in a study that 74 percent of the boys had high achievement expectations versus only 67 percent of the girls and go on to talk about the differences in some detail. In reality, this might be a rather small difference. It also might disappear if the study were repeated, or the study might have methodological problems that don't allow such strong interpretations.

developmental **connection**

Gender. Research continues to find that gender stereotyping is pervasive. Chapter 5, p. 170

Cultural and Ethnic Bias At the same time as researchers have been struggling with gender bias, the realization that research needs to include more people from diverse ethnic groups has also been building (Cheah & Yeung, 2011). Historically, members of ethnic minority groups (African American, Latino, Asian American, and Native American) have been discounted from most research in the United States and simply thought of as variations from the norm or average. Because their scores don't always fit neatly into measures of central tendency (such as a mean score to reflect the average performance of a group of participants), minority individuals have been viewed as confounds or "noise" in data. Consequently, researchers have deliberately excluded them from the samples they have selected. Given the fact that individuals from diverse ethnic groups were excluded from research on adolescent development for so long, we might reasonably conclude that adolescents' real lives are perhaps more varied than research data have indicated in the past.

Researchers also have tended to overgeneralize about ethnic groups (Cheah & Yeung, 2011). **Ethnic gloss** is using an ethnic label such as African American or Latino in a superficial way that portrays an ethnic group as being more homogeneous than it really is. For example, a researcher might describe a research sample like this: "The participants were 20 Latinos and 20 Anglo-Americans." A more complete description of the Latino group might be something like this: "The 20 Latino participants were Mexican Americans from low-income neighborhoods in the southwestern area of Los Angeles. Twelve were from homes in which Spanish is the dominant language spoken, 8 from homes in which English is the main language

gender bias A preconceived notion about the abilities of females and males that prevents individuals from pursuing their own interests and achieving their potential.

ethnic gloss Use of an ethnic label such as African American or Latino in a superficial way that portrays an ethnic group as being more homogeneous than it really is.

Look at the two photographs, one of all non-Latino White males (*left*) and one of a diverse group of females and males from different ethnic groups, including some non-Latino White individuals (*right*). Consider a topic in adolescent development, such as parenting, identity, or cultural values. *If you were conducting research on this topic, might the results be different depending on whether the participants in your study were the individuals in the left photograph or the individuals in the right photograph?*

connecting with careers

Pam Reid, Educational and Developmental Psychologist

When she was a child, Pam Reid liked to play with chemistry sets. Reid majored in chemistry during college and wanted to become a doctor. However, when some of her friends signed up for a psychology class as an elective, she also decided to take the course. She was intrigued by learning about how people think, behave, and develop—so much so that she changed her major to psychology. Reid went on to obtain her Ph.D. in psychology (American Psychological Association, 2003, p. 16).

For a number of years, Reid, was a professor of education and psychology at the University of Michigan, where she also was a research scientist at the Institute for Research on Women and Gender. Her main focus has been on how children and adolescents develop social skills with a special interest in the development of African American girls (Reid & Zalk, 2001). In 2004, Reid became provost and executive vice-president at Roosevelt University in Chicago, and in 2007 she became president of Saint Joseph College in Hartford, Connecticut.

Pam Reid (center, back row) with some of the graduate students she mentored at the University of Michigan.

For more information about the work that educational psychologists do, see page 47 in the "Careers in Adolescent Development" appendix.

spoken. Ten were born in the United States, 10 in Mexico. Ten described themselves as Mexican American, 4 as Mexican, 3 as American, 2 as Chicano, and 1 as Latino." Ethnic gloss can cause researchers to obtain samples of ethnic groups that are not representative of the group's diversity, which can lead to overgeneralization and stereotyping.

Pam Reid is a leading researcher who studies gender and ethnic bias in development. To read about her interests, see the *Connecting with Careers* profile.

developmental **connection**

Diversity. Too often differences between ethnic minority groups and the non-Latino White majority group have been characterized as deficits on the part of ethnic minority groups. Chapter 12, p. 408

Review *Connect* Reflect

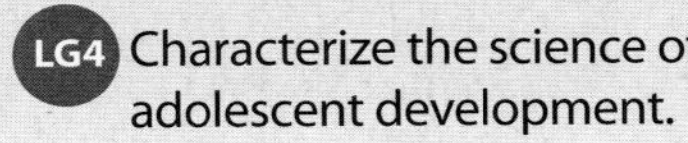

LG4 Characterize the science of adolescent development.

Review

- What is the nature of the scientific study of adolescent development? What is meant by the concept of theory?
- What are four main theories of adolescent development?
- What are the main methods used to collect data on adolescent development? What are the main research designs? What are some concerns about potential bias in research on adolescents?

Connect

- Which research method do you think would best address the question of whether adolescents around the world experience stereotyping?

Reflect *Your Own Personal Journey of Life*

- Which of the theories of adolescent development do you think best explains your own adolescent development?

reach your **learning goals**

1 The Historical Perspective

LG1 Describe the historical perspective of adolescence.

Early History

- Plato said that reasoning first develops in adolescence, and Aristotle argued that self-determination is the hallmark of maturity. In the Middle Ages, knowledge about adolescence moved a step backward: children were viewed as miniature adults. Rousseau provided a more enlightened view of adolescence, including an emphasis on different phases of development.

The Twentieth and Twenty-First Centuries

- Between 1890 and 1920, a cadre of psychologists, urban reformers, and others began to mold the concept of adolescence. G. Stanley Hall is the father of the scientific study of adolescence. In 1904, he proposed the storm-and-stress view of adolescence, which has strong biological foundations. In contrast to Hall's biological view, Margaret Mead argued for a sociocultural interpretation of adolescence. In the inventionist view, adolescence is a sociohistorical invention. Legislation was enacted early in the twentieth century that ensured the dependency of adolescents and delayed their entry into the workforce. From 1900 to 1930, there was a 600 percent increase in the number of high school graduates in the United States. Adolescents gained a more prominent place in society from 1920 to 1950. By 1950, every state had developed special laws for adolescents. Barriers prevented many ethnic minority individuals and females from entering the field of studying adolescent development in the early and middle part of the twentieth century. Leta Hollingworth was a pioneering female in studying adolescents. Two changes in the current generation of adolescents and emerging adults—called Millennials—involve their increasing ethnic diversity and their connection to technology. Cohort effects refer to effects due to a person's time of birth, era, or generation, but not to actual chronological age.

Stereotyping of Adolescents

- Negative stereotyping of adolescents in any historical era has been common. Joseph Adelson described the concept of the "adolescent generalization gap," which states that generalizations are often based on a limited set of highly visible adolescents.

A Positive View of Adolescence

- For too long, adolescents have been viewed in negative ways. Research shows that a considerable majority of adolescents around the world have positive self-esteem. The majority of adolescents are not highly conflicted but rather are searching for an identity.

2 Today's Adolescents in the United States and Around the World

LG2 Discuss today's U.S. Adolescents and adolescents around the world.

Adolescents in the United States

- Adolescents are heterogeneous. Although a majority of adolescents successfully make the transition from childhood to adulthood, too large a percentage do not and are not provided with adequate opportunities and support. Different portraits of adolescents emerge depending on the particular set of adolescents being described. Contexts, the settings in which development occurs, play important roles in adolescent development. These contexts include families, peers, schools, and culture. Social policy is a national government's course of action designed to influence the welfare of its citizens. The U.S. social policy on adolescents needs revision to provide more services for youth. Benson and his colleagues argue that U.S. youth social policy has focused too much on developmental deficits and not enough on strengths.

The Global Perspective

- There are both similarities and differences in adolescents across different countries. Much of what has been written and researched about adolescence comes from

American and European scholars. With technological advances, a youth culture with similar characteristics may be emerging. However, there still are many variations in adolescents across cultures. In some countries, traditions are being continued in the socialization of adolescence, whereas in others, substantial changes in the experiences of adolescents are taking place. These traditions and changes involve health and well-being, gender, families, schools, and peers.

3 The Nature of Development

LG3 Summarize the developmental processes, periods, transitions, and issues related to adolescence.

Processes and Periods

- Development is the pattern of movement or change that occurs throughout the life span. Biological processes involve physical changes in the individual's body. Cognitive processes consist of changes in thinking and intelligence. Socioemotional processes focus on changes in relationships with people, in emotion, in personality, and in social contexts. Development is commonly divided into these periods: prenatal, infancy, early childhood, middle and late childhood, adolescence, early adulthood, middle adulthood, and late adulthood. Adolescence is the developmental period of transition between childhood and adulthood that involves biological, cognitive, and socioemotional changes. In most cultures, adolescence begins at approximately 10 to 13 years of age and ends at about 18 to 22 years of age. Developmentalists increasingly distinguish between early adolescence and late adolescence.

Developmental Transitions

- Two important transitions in development are from childhood to adolescence and from adolescence to adulthood. In the transition from childhood to adolescence, pubertal change is prominent, although cognitive and socioemotional changes occur as well. It sometimes has been said that adolescence begins in biology and ends in culture. The concept of emerging adulthood has been proposed to describe the transition from adolescence to adulthood. Five key characteristics of emerging adulthood are identity exploration (especially in love and work), instability, being self-focused, feeling in-between, and experiencing possibilities to transform one's life. Competent individuals in emerging adulthood who experienced difficulties while growing up are often characterized by having supportive adults, intelligence, and planfulness. Among the criteria for determining adulthood are self-responsibility, independent decision making, and economic independence. A recent proposal argues that adolescence is taking too long and that adolescents aren't being provided with adequate opportunities to mature.

Developmental Issues

- Three important issues in development are (1) the nature-nurture issue (is development mainly due to heredity [nature] or environment [nurture]?), (2) the continuity-discontinuity issue (is development more gradual and cumulative [continuity] or more abrupt and sequential [discontinuity]?), and (3) the early-later experience issue (is development due more to early experiences, especially in infancy and early childhood, or to later experiences?). Most developmentalists do not take extreme positions on these issues, although they are extensively debated.

4 The Science of Adolescent Development

Characterize the science of adolescent development.

Science and the Scientific Method

- To answer questions about adolescent development, researchers often turn to science. They usually follow the scientific method, which involves four main steps: (1) conceptualize a problem, (2) collect data, (3) analyze data, and (4) draw conclusions. Theory is often involved in conceptualizing a problem. A theory is an interrelated, coherent set of ideas that helps to explain phenomena and to make predictions. Hypotheses are specific assertions and predictions, often derived from theory, that can be tested.

Theories of Adolescent Development

- According to psychoanalytic theories, development primarily depends on the unconscious mind and is heavily couched in emotion. Two main psychoanalytic theories were proposed by Freud and Erikson. Freud theorized that individuals go through five psychosexual stages. Erikson's theory emphasizes eight psychosocial stages of development. Cognitive theories emphasize thinking, reasoning, language, and other cognitive processes. Three main cognitive theories are Piaget's, Vygotsky's, and information processing. Piaget's cognitive developmental theory proposes four stages of cognitive development with the formal operational stage being entered from 11 to 15 years of age. Vygotsky's sociocultural cognitive theory emphasizes how culture and social interaction guide human development. The information-processing approach stresses that individuals manipulate information, monitor it, and strategize about it. Two main behavioral and social cognitive theories are Skinner's operant conditioning, and social cognitive theory. In Skinner's operant conditioning, the consequences of a behavior produce changes in the probability of the behavior's occurrence. In social cognitive theory, observational learning is a key aspect of life-span development. Bandura emphasizes reciprocal interactions among person/cognition, behavior, and environment. Ecological theory is Bronfenbrenner's environmental systems view of development. It proposes five environmental systems. An eclectic orientation does not follow any one theoretical approach but rather selects from each theory whatever is considered the best in it.

Research in Adolescent Development

- The main methods for collecting data about life-span development are observation (in a laboratory or a naturalistic setting), survey (questionnaire) or interview, standardized test, physiological measures, experience sampling method, and case study. Three main research designs are descriptive, correlational, and experimental. Descriptive research aims to observe and record behavior. In correlational research, the goal is to describe the strength of the relationship between two or more events or characteristics. Experimental research involves conducting an experiment, which can determine cause and effect. To examine the effects of time and age, researchers can conduct cross-sectional or longitudinal studies. Researchers' ethical responsibilities include seeking participants' informed consent, ensuring confidentiality, debriefing them about the purpose and potential personal consequences of participating, and avoiding unnecessary deception of participants. Researchers need to guard against gender, cultural, and ethnic bias in research.

key terms

storm-and-stress view 3
inventionist view 4
cohort effects 5
Millennials 5
stereotype 7
adolescent generalization gap 7
contexts 10
social policy 11
development 15
biological processes 15
cognitive processes 15
socioemotional processes 15
prenatal period 16
infancy 16
early childhood 16
middle and late childhood 16
adolescence 16
early adolescence 16
late adolescence 16
early adulthood 17
middle adulthood 17
late adulthood 17
emerging adulthood 19
resilience 22
nature-nurture issue 22
continuity-discontinuity issue 24
early-later experience issue 24
theory 27
hypotheses 27
psychoanalytic theories 27
Erikson's theory 29
Piaget's theory 30
Vygotsky's theory 31
information-processing theory 31
social cognitive theory 32
Bronfenbrenner's ecological theory 32
eclectic theoretical orientation 33
laboratory 34
naturalistic observation 34
standardized test 35
experience sampling method (ESM) 35
case study 36
descriptive research 36
correlational research 36
correlation coefficient 36
experimental research 37
independent variable 37
dependent variable 37
cross-sectional research 38
longitudinal research 39
gender bias 40
ethnic gloss 40

key people

G. Stanley Hall 3
Margaret Mead 4
Mark Bauerlein 6
William Damon 6
Joseph Adelson 7
Daniel Offer 7
Jacqueline Lerner 9
Peter Benson 11
Brad Brown and Reed Larson 13
Jeffrey Arnett 19
Jacquelynne Eccles 22
Ann Masten 22
Joseph and Claudia Allen 22
Sigmund Freud 27
Peter Blos 28
Anna Freud 28
Erik Erikson 29
Jean Piaget 30
Lev Vygotsky 31
Robert Siegler 31
B. F. Skinner 32
Albert Bandura 32
Urie Bronfenbrenner 32
Reed Larson and Maryse Richards 36

resources for improving the lives of adolescents

Encyclopedia of Adolescence
B. Bradford Brown and Mitch Prinstein (Eds.) (2011)
New York: Elsevier

A three-volume set with more than 140 articles written by leading experts in the field of adolescent development. Providing a very contemporary overview, topics include various biological, cognitive, and socioemotional processes.

Escaping the Endless Adolescence
by Joe Allen and Claudia Allen (2009)
New York: Ballantine

A superb, well-written book on the lives of emerging adults, including extensive recommendations for parents on how to effectively guide their children through the transition from adolescence to adulthood.

Adolescence: Growing Up in America
by Joy Dryfoos and Carol Barkin (2006)
New York: Oxford University Press

A follow-up to Dryfoos' (1990) earlier landmark book on adolescent problems, in *Adolescence: Growing Up in America*, the authors examine the problems adolescents are having today and the prevention and intervention strategies that work.

Children's Defense Fund ***www.childrensdefense.org***

The Children's Defense Fund, headed by Marian Wright Edelman, exists to provide a strong and effective voice for children and adolescents who cannot vote, lobby, or speak for themselves.

The Search Institute ***www.search-institute.org***

The Search Institute conducts large, comprehensive research projects to help define the pathways to healthy development for 12- to 25-year-olds. The Institute develops practical resources based on this research to foster reform, parent education, effective after-school programs, and community mobilization. Many resources are available for downloading on the Institute's website.

Handbook of Adolescent Psychology
edited by Richard Lerner and Laurence Steinberg (2009, 3rd ed.)
New York: John Wiley

An outstanding collection of articles by leading researchers in the field of adolescent development. Includes chapters on social policy, health, parent-adolescent relationships, peers, delinquency, sex, puberty, and many other topics.

self-assessment

The student Online Learning Center includes the following self-assessments for further exploration:

- *Do I Have the Characteristics of an Emerging Adult?*
- *Models and Mentors in My Life*
- *Evaluating My Interest in a Career in Adolescent Development*

appendix

Careers in Adolescent Development

Some of you may be quite sure about what you plan to make your life's work. Others may not have decided on a major yet and are uncertain about which career path you want to follow. Each of us wants to find a rewarding career and enjoy the work we do. The field of adolescent development offers an amazing breadth of career options that can provide extremely satisfying work.

If you decide to pursue a career in adolescent development, what career options are available to you? There are many. College and university professors teach courses in adolescent development, education, family development, and medicine. Middle school and high school teachers impart knowledge, understanding, and skills to adolescents. Counselors, clinical psychologists, and physicians help adolescents to cope more effectively with the unique challenges of adolescence. And various professionals work with families of adolescents to improve the adolescent's development.

By choosing one of these career options, you can guide youth in improving their lives, help others to understand them better, or even advance the state of knowledge in the field. You can have an enjoyable time while you are doing these things. Although an advanced degree is not absolutely necessary in some areas of adolescent development, you usually can expand your opportunities (and income) considerably by obtaining a graduate degree. Many careers in adolescent development pay reasonably well. For example, psychologists earn well above the median salary in the United States.

If you are considering a career in adolescent development, as you go through this term, try to spend some time with adolescents of different ages. Observe their behavior; talk with them about their lives. Think about whether you would like to work with youth in your life's work.

Another worthwhile activity is to talk with people who work with adolescents. For example, if you have some interest in becoming a school counselor, call a school, ask to speak with a counselor, and set up an appointment to discuss the counselor's career path and work. Be prepared with a list of questions to ask, and take notes if you wish.

Working in one or more jobs related to your career interests while you are in college can also benefit you. Many colleges and universities offer internships or work experiences for students who major in fields such as development. In some instances, these opportunities are for course credit or pay; in others, they are strictly on a volunteer basis. Take advantage of these opportunities. They can provide you with valuable experiences to help you decide if this is the right career area for you, and they can help you get into graduate school, if you decide you want to go.

In the following sections, we profile careers in three areas: education/research; clinical/counseling/medical; and families/relationships. These are not the only career options in the field of adolescent development, but they should provide you with an idea of the range of opportunities available and information about some of the main career avenues you might pursue. In profiling these careers, we address the amount of education required, the nature of the training, and a description of the work.

Education/Research

Education and research offer a wide range of career opportunities to work with adolescents. These range from being a college professor to secondary school teacher to school psychologist.

College/University Professor

Courses in adolescent development are taught in different programs and schools in college and universities, including psychology, education, child and family studies, social work, and medicine. They are taught at research universities that offer one or more master's or Ph.D. programs in development; at four-year colleges with no graduate programs; or at community colleges. The work college professors do includes teaching courses either at the undergraduate or graduate level (or both); conducting research in a specific area; advising students and/or directing their research; and serving on college or university committees. Some college instructors do not conduct research but instead focus mainly on teaching. Research is most likely to be part of the job description at universities with master's and Ph.D. programs.

A Ph.D. or master's degree almost always is required to teach in some area of adolescent development in a college or university. Obtaining a doctoral degree usually takes four to six years of graduate work. A master's degree requires approximately two years of graduate work. The training involves taking graduate courses, learning to conduct research, and attending and presenting papers at professional meetings. Many graduate students work as teaching or research assistants to professors, an apprenticeship relationship that helps them to develop their teaching and research skills.

If you are interested in becoming a college or university professor, you might want to make an appointment with your instructor to learn more about the profession and what his or her career/work is like. You can also read a profile of a counseling psychologist and university professor on page 178 (Chapter 5).

Researcher

In most instances, individuals who work in research positions will have either a master's degree or Ph.D. in some area of adolescent development. They might work at a university, perhaps in a research program; in government at agencies such as the National Institute of Mental Health; or in private industry. Those who have full-time research positions generate innovative research ideas, plan studies, and carry out research by collecting data, analyzing the data, and then interpreting it. Some spend much of their time in a laboratory; others work outside the lab in schools, hospitals, and other settings. Researchers usually attempt to publish their research in a scientific journal. They often work in collaboration with other researchers and may present their work at scientific meetings, where they learn about other research.

Secondary School Teacher

Secondary school teachers teach one or more subjects, prepare the curriculum, give tests, assign grades, monitor students' progress, conduct parent-teacher conferences, and attend in-service workshops. At minimum, becoming a secondary school teacher requires an undergraduate degree. The training involves taking a wide range of courses, with a major or concentration in education, as well as completion of a supervised practice-teaching internship. Read profiles of secondary school teachers on pages 110 and 369 (Chapters 3 and 11).

Exceptional Children (Special Education) Teacher

Teachers of exceptional children concentrate their efforts on individual children who either have a disability or are gifted. Among the children they might work with are children with learning disabilities, ADHD (attention deficit hyperactivity disorder), mental retardation, or a physical disability such as cerebral palsy. Some of their work is done outside of the regular classroom, some of it in the regular classroom. The exceptional children teacher works closely with both the regular classroom teacher and parents to create the best educational program for each student. Becoming a teacher of exceptional children requires a minimum of an undergraduate degree. The training consists of taking a wide range of courses in education with a concentration of courses in educating children with disabilities or children who are gifted. Teachers of exceptional children often continue their education after obtaining their undergraduate degree, and many attain a master's degree in special education.

Family and Consumer Science Educator

Family and consumer science educators may specialize in early childhood education or instruct middle and high school students about matters such as nutrition, interpersonal relationships, human sexuality, parenting, and human development. Hundreds of colleges and universities throughout the United States offer two- and four-year degree programs in family and consumer science. These programs usually include an internship requirement. Additional education courses may be needed to obtain a teaching certificate. Some family and consumer science educators go on to graduate school for further training, which provides preparation for jobs in college teaching or research. Read a profile of a family and consumer science educator on page 207 (Chapter 6).

Educational Psychologist

Most educational psychologists teach in a college or university setting and conduct research on learning, motivation, classroom management, or assessment. These professors help to train students to enter the fields of educational psychology, school psychology, and teaching. Many educational psychologists have a doctorate in education, which requires four to six years of graduate work. Read a profile of an educational psychologist on page 41 (Chapter 1).

School Psychologist

School psychologists focus on improving the psychological and intellectual well-being of elementary and secondary school students. They may work in a school district's centralized office or in one or more schools where they give psychological tests, interview students and their parents, consult with teachers, and provide counseling to students and their families. School psychologists usually have a master's or doctoral degree in school psychology. In graduate school, they take courses in counseling, assessment, learning, and other areas of education and psychology.

Clinical/Counseling/Medical

A wide variety of clinical, counseling, and medical professionals work with adolescents, from clinical psychologists to adolescent drug counselors and adolescent medicine specialists.

Clinical Psychologist

Clinical psychologists seek to help people with their psychological problems. They work in a variety of settings, including colleges and universities, clinics, medical schools, and private practice. Most clinical psychologists conduct psychotherapy; some perform psychological assessment as well; and some do research.

Clinical psychologists must obtain either a Ph.D. that involves clinical and research training or a Psy.D. degree, which involves only clinical training. This graduate training, which usually takes five to seven years, includes courses in clinical psychology and a one-year supervised internship in an accredited setting. In most cases, candidates for these degrees must pass a test to become licensed to practice and to call themselves clinical psychologists. Read a profile of a clinical psychologist on page 433 (Chapter 13).

Psychiatrist

Like clinical psychologists, psychiatrists might specialize in working with adolescents. They might work in medical schools, both as teachers and researchers, in medical clinics, and in private practice. Unlike psychologists, however, psychiatrists can administer psychiatric drugs to clients. Psychiatrists must first obtain a medical degree and then do a residency in psychiatry. Medical school takes approximately four years to complete and the psychiatric residency another three to four years.

Psychiatric Nurse

Psychiatric nurses work closely with psychiatrists to improve adolescents' mental health. This career path requires two to five years of education in a certified nursing program. Psychiatric nursing students take courses in the biological sciences, nursing care, and psychology and receive supervised clinical training in a psychiatric setting. Designation as a clinical specialist in adolescent nursing requires a master's degree or higher in nursing.

Counseling Psychologist

Counseling psychologists go through much the same training as clinical psychologists and work in the same settings. They may do psychotherapy, teach, or conduct research, but they normally do not treat individuals with severe mental disorders, such as schizophrenia. Counseling psychologists must have either a master's degree or a doctoral degree, as well as a license to practice their profession. One type of master's degree in counseling leads to the designation of licensed professional counselor. Read a profile of a counseling psychologist on page 178 (Chapter 5).

School Counselor

School counselors help students to identify their abilities and interests, and then guide them in developing academic plans and exploring career options. High school counselors advise students on choosing a major, meeting the admissions requirements for college, taking entrance exams, applying for financial aid, and obtaining vocational and technical training. School counselors may also help students to cope with adjustment problems, working with them individually, in small groups, or even in the classroom. They often consult with parents, teachers, and school administrators when trying to help students with their problems. School counselors usually have a master's degree in counseling. Read a profile of a high school counselor on page 386 (Chapter 11).

Career Counselor

Career counselors help individuals to identify their career options and guide them in applying for jobs. They may work in private industry or at a college or university, where they usually interview individuals to identify careers that fit their interests and abilities. Sometimes career counselors help individuals to create professional résumés, or they conduct mock interviews to help them prepare for a job interview. They may also create and promote job fairs or other recruiting events to help individuals obtain jobs. Read a profile of a career counselor on page 384 (Chapter 11).

Social Worker

Social workers are often involved in helping people with their social or economic problems. They may investigate, evaluate, and attempt to rectify reported cases of abuse, neglect, endangerment, or domestic disputes. They can intervene in families if necessary and provide counseling and referral services to individuals and families. They often work for publicly funded agencies at the city, state, or national level, although increasingly they work in the private sector in areas such as drug rehabilitation and family counseling. In some cases, social workers specialize in certain types of work. For example, family-care social workers often work with families in which a child, adolescent, or older adult needs support services. Social workers must have at least an undergraduate degree from a school of social work, including course work in various areas of sociology and psychology. Some social workers also have a master's or doctoral degree.

Drug Counselor

Drug counselors provide counseling to individuals with drug-abuse problems, either on an individual basis or in group therapy sessions. They may work in private practice, with a state or federal agency, for a company, or in a hospital setting. Some specialize in working with adolescents. At a minimum, drug counselors must have an associate degree or certificate. Many have an undergraduate degree in substance-abuse counseling, and some have master's and doctoral degrees. In most states, drug counselors must fulfill a certification procedure to obtain a license to practice.

Health Psychologist

Health psychologists work with many different health-care professionals, including physicians, nurses, clinical psychologists, psychiatrists, and social workers, in an effort to improve the health of adolescents. They may conduct research, perform clinical assessments, or give treatment. Many health psychologists focus on prevention through research and clinical interventions designed to foster health and reduce the risk of disease. More than half of all health psychologists provide clinical services. Among the settings in which health psychologists work are primary care programs, inpatient medical units, and specialized care programs in areas such as women's health, drug treatment, and smoking cessation.

Health psychologists typically have a doctoral degree (Ph.D. or Psy.D.) in psychology. Some receive training in clinical psychology as part of their graduate work. Others have obtained their doctoral degree in some area other than health psychology and then pursue a postdoctoral degree in health psychology. A postdoctoral degree usually takes about two additional years of graduate study. Many doctoral programs in clinical, counseling, social, and experimental psychology have specialized tracks in health psychology.

Adolescent Medicine Specialist

Adolescent medicine specialists evaluate the medical and behavioral problems that are common among adolescents, including growth disorders (such as delayed puberty), acne, eating disorders, substance abuse, depression, anxiety, sexually transmitted infections, contraception and pregnancy, and sexual identity concerns. They may work in private practice, in a medical clinic, in a hospital, or in a medical school. As a medical doctor, they can administer drugs and may counsel parents and adolescents on ways to improve the adolescent's health. Many adolescent medicine specialists on the faculty of medical schools also teach and conduct research on adolescents' health and diseases.

Adolescent medicine specialists must complete medical school and then obtain further training in their specialty, which usually involves at least three more years of schooling. They must become board certified in either pediatrics or internal medicine.

Families/Relationships

Adolescents sometimes benefit from help that is provided to the entire family. One career that involves working with adolescents and their families is marriage and family therapy.

Marriage and Family Therapist

Many individuals who have psychological problems benefit when psychotherapy is provided within the context of a marital or family relationship. Marriage and family therapists may provide marital therapy, couple therapy to those individuals who are not married, and family therapy to two or more members of a family.

Marriage and family therapists must have a master's or doctoral degree. Their training is similar to that of a clinical psychologist but with a focus on marital and family relationships. In most states, professionals must go through a licensing procedure to practice marital and family therapy. Read a profile of a marriage and family therapist on page 264 (Chapter 8).

chapter 2 PUBERTY, HEALTH, AND BIOLOGICAL FOUNDATIONS

chapter **outline**

Puberty

Learning Goal 1 Discuss the determinants, characteristics, and psychological dimensions of puberty.

Determinants of Puberty
Growth Spurt
Sexual Maturation
Secular Trends in Puberty
Psychological Dimensions of Puberty
Are Puberty's Effect's Exaggerated?

Health

Learning Goal 2 Summarize the nature of adolescents' and emerging adults' health.

Adolescence: A Critical Juncture in Health
Emerging Adults' Health
Nutrition
Exercise and Sports
Sleep

Evolution, Heredity, and Environment

Learning Goal 3 Explain the contributions of evolution, heredity, and environment to adolescent development.

The Evolutionary Perspective
The Genetic Process
Heredity-Environment Interaction

I am pretty confused. I wonder whether I am weird or normal. My body is starting to change, but I sure don't look like a lot of my friends. I still look like a kid for the most part. My best friend is only 13, but he looks like he is 16 or 17. I get nervous in the locker room during PE class because when I go to take a shower, I'm afraid somebody is going to make fun of me since I'm not as physically developed as some of the others.

—ROBERT, AGE 12

I don't like my breasts. They are too small, and they look funny. I'm afraid guys won't like me if they don't get bigger.

—ANGIE, AGE 13

I can't stand the way I look. I have zits all over my face. My hair is dull and stringy. It never stays in place. My nose is too big. My lips are too small. My legs are too short. I have four warts on my left hand, and people get grossed out by them. So do I. My body is a disaster!

—ANN, AGE 14

I'm short and I can't stand it. My father is six feet tall, and here I am only five foot four. I'm 14 already. I look like a kid, and I get teased a lot, especially by other guys. I'm always the last one picked for sides in basketball because I'm so short. Girls don't seem to be interested in me either because most of them are taller than I am.

—JIM, AGE 14

The comments of these four adolescents in the midst of pubertal change underscore the dramatic upheaval in their bodies following the calm, consistent growth of middle and late childhood. Young adolescents develop an acute concern about their bodies.

preview

Puberty's changes are perplexing to adolescents. Although these changes bring forth doubts, fears, and anxieties, most adolescents eventually overcome them. We will explore many aspects of pubertal change in this chapter from growth spurts and sexual maturation to the psychological aspects of puberty. We will also examine other topics related to adolescent physical development, including health and the roles of evolution, heredity, and environment in adolescent development.

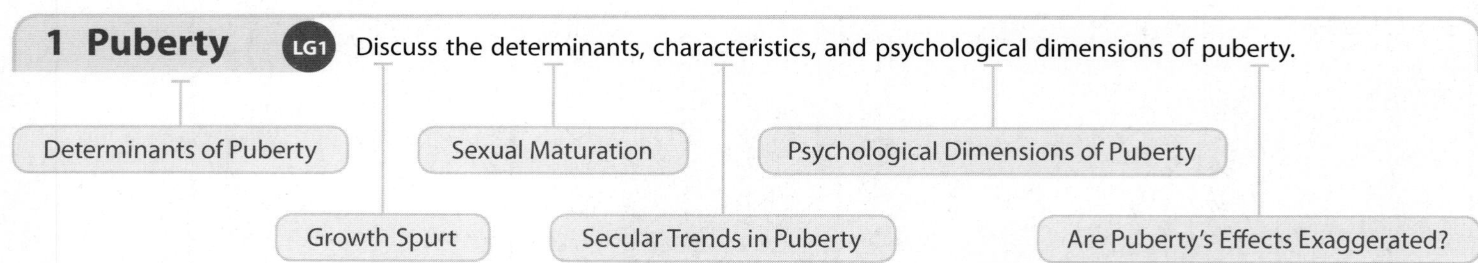

puberty A period of rapid physical maturation involving hormonal and bodily changes that take place primarily in early adolescence.

Puberty can be distinguished from adolescence. For virtually everyone, puberty ends long before adolescence is exited. Puberty is often thought of as the most important marker for the beginning of adolescence. **Puberty** is a period of rapid physical maturation involving hormonal and bodily changes that take place primarily in early adolescence.

In youth, we clothe ourselves with rainbows and go brave as the zodiac.

—Ralph Waldo Emerson
American Poet and Essayist, 19th Century

DETERMINANTS OF PUBERTY

Although we do not know precisely what initiates puberty, a number of complex factors are involved. Puberty is accompanied by changes in the endocrine system, weight, body fat, and leptin, but we don't know if these are a cause or a consequence of puberty (Dorn & Biro, 2011; Marceau & others, 2011). Also, there is increased interest in the role that birth weight, rapid weight gain in infancy, obesity, and sociocultural factors might play in pubertal onset and characteristics. As discussed next, heredity is an important factor in puberty.

Heredity Puberty is not an environmental accident. Programmed into the genes of every human being is the timing for the emergence of puberty (Mueller & others, 2010). Puberty does not take place at 2 or 3 years of age and it does not occur in the twenties. Recently, scientists have begun to conduct molecular genetic studies in an attempt to identify specific genes that are linked to the onset and progression of puberty (Elks & Ong, 2011; Elks & others, 2010; Paris & others, 2010). Nonetheless, as we see later, puberty takes place between about 9 and 16 years of age for most individuals. Environmental factors can also influence its onset and duration (Belsky & others, 2011).

Hormones Behind the first whisker in boys and the widening of hips in girls is a flood of **hormones,** powerful chemical substances secreted by the endocrine glands and carried throughout the body by the bloodstream (Pfaffle & Klammt, 2011). Two classes of hormones have significantly different concentrations in males and females: **androgens,** the main class of male sex hormones, and **estrogens,** the main class of female hormones. Note that although these hormones function more strongly in one sex or the other, they are produced by both males and females.

Testosterone is an androgen that plays an important role in male pubertal development. Throughout puberty, rising testosterone levels are associated with a number of physical changes in boys, including the development of external genitals, an increase in height, and voice changes (Goji & others, 2009). Testosterone level in adolescent boys is also linked to sexual desire and activity (Cameron, 2004). *Estradiol* is an estrogen that plays an important role in female pubertal development. As estradiol levels rise, breast development, uterine development, and skeletal changes occur. The identity of hormones that contribute to sexual desire and activity in adolescents is less clear for girls than it is for boys (Cameron, 2004). Boys and girls experience an increase in both testosterone and estradiol during puberty. However,

hormones Powerful chemicals secreted by the endocrine glands and carried through the body by the bloodstream.

androgens The main class of male sex hormones.

estrogens The main class of female sex hormones.

From *Penguin Dreams and Stranger Things* by Berkeley Breathed. Copyright © 1985 by The Washington Post Company. By permission of Little, Brown and Co. Copyright © 1985 by Berkeley Breathed. Reprinted by permission of International Creative Management, Inc.

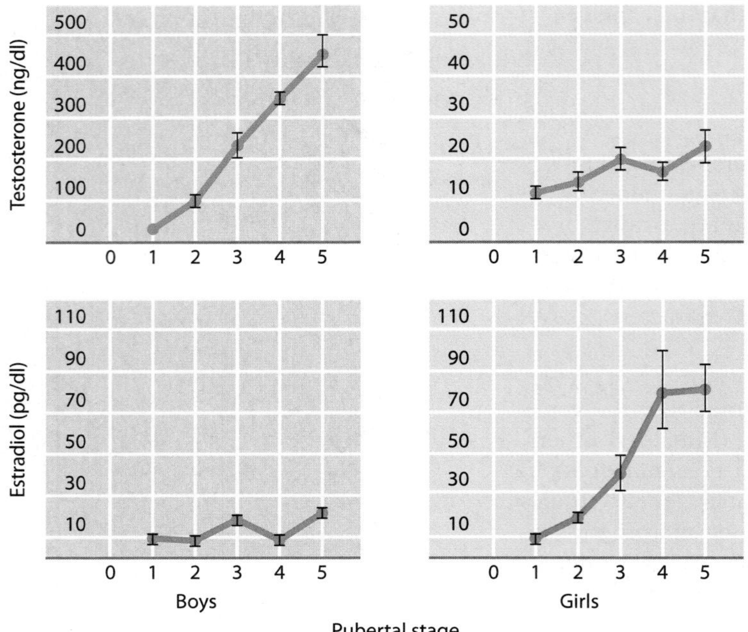

FIGURE **2.1**

HORMONE LEVELS BY SEX AND PUBERTAL STAGE FOR TESTOSTERONE AND ESTRADIOL. The five stages range from the early beginning of puberty (stage 1) to the most advanced stage of puberty (stage 5). Notice the significant increase in testosterone in boys and the significant increase in estradiol in girls.

in one study, testosterone levels increased 18-fold in boys but only 2-fold in girls during puberty; estradiol levels increased 8-fold in girls but only 2-fold in boys during puberty (Nottelmann & others, 1987) (see Figure 2.1).

The Endocrine System Puberty is not a specific event but rather a process that unfolds through a series of coordinated neuroendocrine changes (Dorn & Biro, 2011). Puberty onset involves the activation of the hypothalamic-pituitary-gonadal (HPG) axis (see Figure 2.2). The *hypothalamus* is a structure in the higher portion of the brain that monitors eating, drinking, and sex. The *pituitary gland* is the endocrine gland that controls growth and regulates other glands. The *gonads* are the sex glands—the testes in males, the ovaries in females. How does the endocrine system work? The pituitary gland sends a signal via gonadotropins (hormones that stimulate sex glands) to the testes or ovaries to manufacture the hormone. Then, through interaction with the hypothalamus, the pituitary gland detects when the optimal level of hormones has been reached and maintains it with additional gonadotropin secretions (Pfaffle & Klammt, 2011; Wanakowska & Polkowska, 2010).

Levels of sex hormones are regulated by two hormones secreted by the pituitary gland: *FSH* (*follicle-stimulating hormone*) and *LH* (*luteinizing hormone*). FSH stimulates follicle development in females and sperm production in males. LH regulates estrogen secretion and ovum development in females

Hypothalamus: A structure in the brain that interacts with the pituitary gland to monitor the bodily regulation of hormones.

Pituitary: This master gland produces hormones that stimulate other glands. It also influences growth by producing growth hormones; it sends gonadotropins to the testes and ovaries and a thyroid-stimulating hormone to the thyroid gland. It sends a hormone to the adrenal gland as well.

Thyroid gland: It interacts with the pituitary gland to influence growth.

Adrenal gland: It interacts with the pituitary gland and likely plays a role in pubertal development, but less is known about its function than about sex glands. Recent research, however, suggests it may be involved in adolescent behavior, particularly for boys.

The gonads, or sex glands: These consist of the testes in males and the ovaries in females. The sex glands are strongly involved in the appearance of secondary sex characteristics, such as facial hair in males and breast development in females. The general class of hormones called estrogens is dominant in females, while androgens are dominant in males. More specifically, testosterone in males and estradiol in females are key hormones in pubertal development.

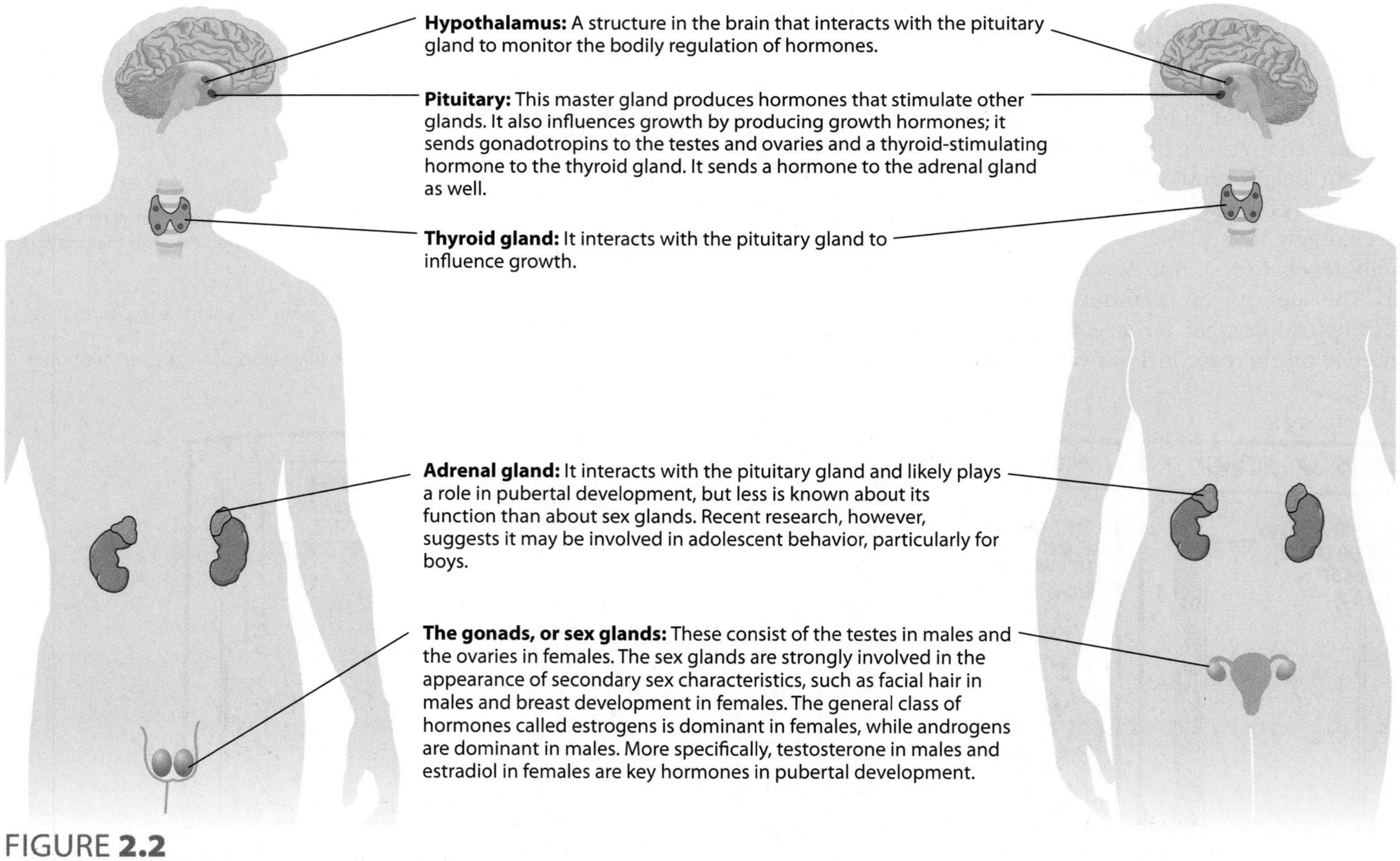

FIGURE **2.2**

THE MAJOR ENDOCRINE GLANDS INVOLVED IN PUBERTAL CHANGE

and testosterone production in males (Kuhn & others, 2010). In addition, the hypothalamus secretes a substance called *GnRH* (*gonadotropin-releasing hormone*), which is linked to pubertal timing.

These hormones are regulated by a *negative feedback system.* If the level of sex hormones rises too high, the hypothalamus and pituitary gland reduce their stimulation of the gonads, decreasing the production of sex hormones. If the level of sex hormones falls too low, the hypothalamus and pituitary gland increase their production of the sex hormones.

Figure 2.3 shows how the feedback system works. In males, the pituitary gland's production of LH stimulates the testes to produce testosterone. When testosterone levels rise too high, the hypothalamus decreases its production of GnRH, and this decrease reduces the pituitary's production of LH. When the level of testosterone falls as a result, the hypothalamus produces more GnRH and the cycle starts again. The negative feedback system operates in a similar way in females, except that LH and GnRH regulate the ovaries and the production of estrogen.

This negative feedback system in the endocrine system can be compared to a thermostat and furnace. If a room becomes cold, the thermostat signals the furnace to turn on. The action of the furnace warms the air in the room, which eventually triggers the thermostat to turn off the furnace. The room temperature gradually begins to fall again until the thermostat once again signals the furnace to turn on, and the cycle is repeated. This type of system is called a *negative* feedback loop because a *rise* in temperature turns *off* the furnace, while a *decrease* in temperature turns *on* the furnace.

The level of sex hormones is low in childhood but increases in puberty (Dorn & Biro, 2011). It is as if the thermostat is set at 50°F in childhood and now becomes set at 80°F in puberty. At the higher setting, the gonads have to produce more sex hormones, and they do so during puberty.

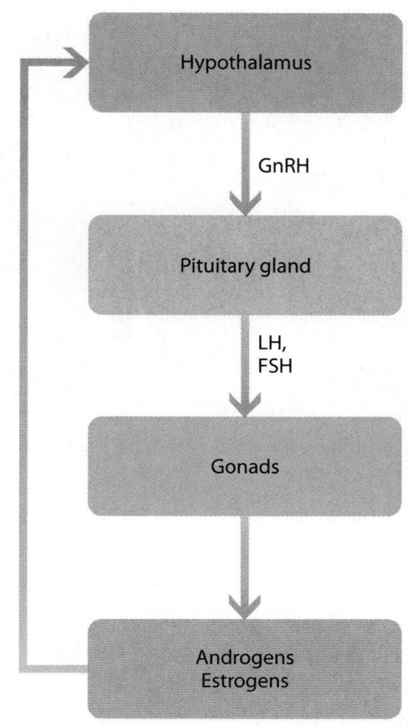

FIGURE **2.3**
THE FEEDBACK SYSTEM OF SEX HORMONES

Growth Hormones We know that the pituitary gland releases gonadotropins that stimulate the testes and ovaries (Enea & others, 2011; Stukenborg, Colon, & Soder, 2010). In addition, through interaction with the hypothalamus, the pituitary gland also secretes hormones that lead to growth and skeletal maturation either directly or through interaction with the *thyroid gland,* located in the neck region (see Figure 2.2).

At the beginning of puberty, growth hormone is secreted at night. Later in puberty, it also is secreted during the day, although daytime levels are usually very low (Susman, Dorn, & Schiefelbein, 2003). Cortisol, a hormone that is secreted by the adrenal cortex, also influences growth, as do testosterone and estrogen (Stroud & others, 2011).

Adrenarche and Gonadarche Two phases of puberty are linked with hormonal changes: adrenarche and gonadarche (Dorn & Biro, 2011; Idkowiak & others, 2011). **Adrenarche** involves hormonal changes in the adrenal glands, located just above the kidneys. These changes occur surprisingly early, from about 6 to 9 years of age in girls and about one year later in boys, before what is generally considered the beginning of puberty (Dorn & others, 2006). During adrenarche and continuing through puberty, the adrenal glands secrete adrenal androgens, such as dehydroepiandrosterone (DHEA) (Miller, 2008). Adrenarche is still not well understood (Dorn & Biro, 2011).

Gonadarche, which follows adrenarche by about two years, is the period most people think of as puberty. Gonadarche involves the maturation of primary sexual characteristics (ovaries in females, testes in males) and secondary sexual characteristics (pubic hair, breast, and genital development) (Dorn & others, 2006). "The hallmark of gonadarche is reactivation of the hypothalamic-pituitary-gonadal axis (HPG). . . . The initial activation of the HPG axis was during the fetal and neonatal period" (Dorn & others, 2006, p. 35).

In the United States, the gonadarche period begins at approximately 9 to 10 years of age in non-Latino White girls, and 8 to 9 years in African American girls (Herman-Giddens, Kaplowitz, & Wasserman, 2004). In boys, gonadarche begins at about 10 to

adrenarche Puberty phase involving hormonal changes in the adrenal glands, which are located just above the kidneys. These changes occur from about 6 to 9 years of age in girls and about one year later in boys, before what is generally considered the beginning of puberty.

gonadarche Puberty phase involving the maturation of primary sexual characteristics (ovaries in females, testes in males) and secondary sexual characteristics (pubic hair, breast, and genital development). This period follows adrenarche by about two years and is what most people think of as puberty.

What are some of the differences in the ways girls and boys experience pubertal growth?

11 years of age. **Menarche,** the first menstrual period, occurs in mid- to late gonadarche in girls. In boys, **spermarche,** a boy's first ejaculation of semen, occurs in early to mid-gonadarche. Robert, Angie, Ann, and Jim, the adolescents we described at the beginning of this chapter, are each in various phases of adrenarche and gonadarche.

Weight, Body Fat, and Leptin Some researchers argue that a child must reach a critical body mass before puberty, especially menarche, emerges (Ackerman & others, 2006). A number of studies have found that higher weight, especially obesity, is linked to earlier pubertal development (Kaplowitz, 2009). For example, a recent study revealed that being overweight or obese was linked with more advanced breast development and pubic hair growth in 8- to 14-year-olds (Christensen & others, 2010). Some have even proposed that a body weight of 106 +/− 3 pounds triggers menarche and the end of the pubertal growth spurt (Friesch, 1984). However, this specific weight target is not well documented (Susman, 2001).

Other scientists have hypothesized that the onset of menarche is influenced by the percentage of body fat in relation to total body weight. They say that for menarche to occur, a minimum of 17 percent of a girl's body weight must be comprised of body fat. As with the weight target, this percentage has not been consistently verified. However, both anorexic adolescents whose weight drops dramatically and females who participate in certain sports (such as gymnastics and swimming) may not menstruate. In boys, undernutrition may delay puberty (Susman, Dorn, & Schiefelbein, 2003).

The hormone *leptin* may signal the beginning and progression of puberty. Leptin concentrations, which are higher in girls than in boys, are related to the amounts of fat in girls and androgen in boys (Lecke, Morshc, & Spritzer, 2011; Xi & others, 2011). Thus, a rise in leptin may indicate adequate fat stores for reproduction and the maintenance of pregnancy (Hillman & Biro, 2010). Some researchers conclude that leptin by itself may be a necessary but not sufficient cause for puberty (Kaplowitz, 2009).

Weight at Birth and in Infancy Might puberty's onset and characteristics be influenced by birth weight and weight gain during infancy? There is increasing research evidence for this link (Ibanez & others, 2011; Ong, 2010). Low birth weight girls experience menarche approximately 5 to 10 months earlier than normal birth weight girls, and low birth weight boys are at risk for small testicular volume during adolescence (Ibanez & de Zegher, 2006). A recent research review concluded that early growth acceleration soon after birth that reaches a peak in the first 2 to 4 years of life predicts very early pubertal onset for girls (Papadimitriou & others, 2010). This review also concluded that this early growth acceleration is present in children who become overweight and obese later in childhood and adolescence.

How might birth weight and weight gain in infancy be linked to pubertal onset?

Sociocultural and Environmental Factors Might sociocultural and environmental factors be linked to pubertal timing? Recent research indicates that cultural variations and early experiences may be related to earlier pubertal onset. Adolescents in developed countries and large urban areas reach puberty earlier than their counterparts in less developed countries and rural areas (Graham, 2005). Children who have been adopted from developing countries to developed countries often enter puberty earlier than their counterparts who continue to live in developing countries (Teilmann & others, 2002). African American females enter puberty earlier than Latina and non-Latino females, and African American males enter puberty earlier than non-Latino males (Biro & others, 2006; Talpade, 2008).

Early experiences that are linked to earlier pubertal onset include adoption, father absence, low socioeconomic status, family conflict, maternal harshness, child maltreatment, and early substance use (Arim & others, 2011; Deardorff & others, 2011; Ellis & others, 2011). In many cases, puberty comes months earlier in these

menarche A girl's first menstrual period.

spermarche A boy's first ejaculation of semen.

situations, and this earlier onset of puberty is likely explained by high rates of conflict and stress in these social contexts. A recent study revealed that maternal harshness in early childhood was linked to early maturation as well as sexual risk taking in adolescence (Belsky & others, 2010). Another recent study found that girls who used alcohol before puberty were more likely to experience delayed puberty (Peck & others, 2011).

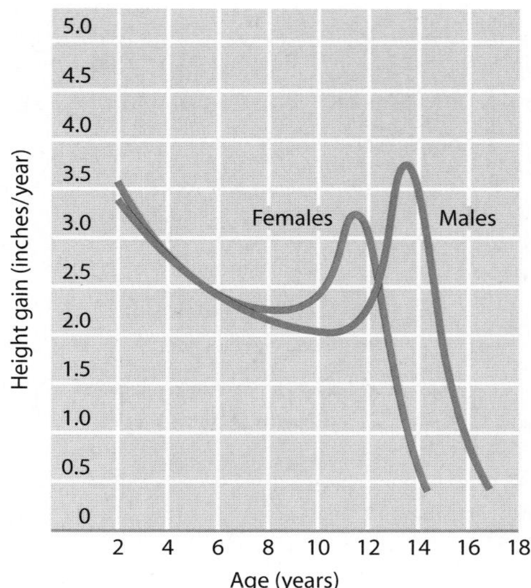

FIGURE **2.4**

PUBERTAL GROWTH SPURT. On the average, the peak of the growth spurt that characterizes pubertal changes occurs two years earlier for girls (11½) than for boys (13½).

GROWTH SPURT

Growth slows throughout childhood, then puberty brings forth the most rapid increases in growth since infancy. Figure 2.4 shows that the growth spurt associated with puberty occurs approximately two years earlier for girls than for boys. For girls, the mean beginning of the growth spurt is 9 years of age; for boys, it is 11 years of age. The peak of pubertal change occurs at 11½ years for girls and 13½ years for boys. During their growth spurt, girls increase in height about 3½ inches per year; boys, about 4 inches.

An individual's ultimate height is often a midpoint between the biological mother's and the biological father's height, adjusted a few inches down for a female and a few inches up for a male. The growth spurt typically ends around menarche for girls, later for boys.

Boys and girls who are shorter or taller than their peers before adolescence are likely to remain so during adolescence. At the beginning of adolescence, girls tend to be as tall as or taller than boys of their age, but by the end of the middle school years most boys have caught up with them, or in many cases even surpassed them in height. Though height in elementary school is a good predictor of height later in adolescence, as much as 30 percent of an individual's height in late adolescence is unexplained by the child's height in elementary school.

The rate at which adolescents gain weight follows approximately the same developmental timetable as the rate at which they gain height. Marked weight gains coincide with the onset of puberty (Dorn & Biro, 2011; Marceau & others, 2011). Fifty percent of adult body weight is gained during adolescence (Rogol, Roemmich, & Clark, 1998). At the peak of this weight gain, girls gain an average of 18 pounds in one year at roughly 12 years of age (approximately six months after their peak height increase). Boys' peak weight gain per year (20 pounds) occurs about the same time as their peak increase in height, about 13 to 14 years of age. During early adolescence, girls tend to outweigh boys, but—just as with height—by about 14 years of age, boys begin to surpass girls in weight.

In addition to increases in height and weight, puberty brings changes in hip and shoulder width. Girls experience a spurt in hip width, whereas boys undergo an

ZITS By Jerry Scott and Jim Borgman

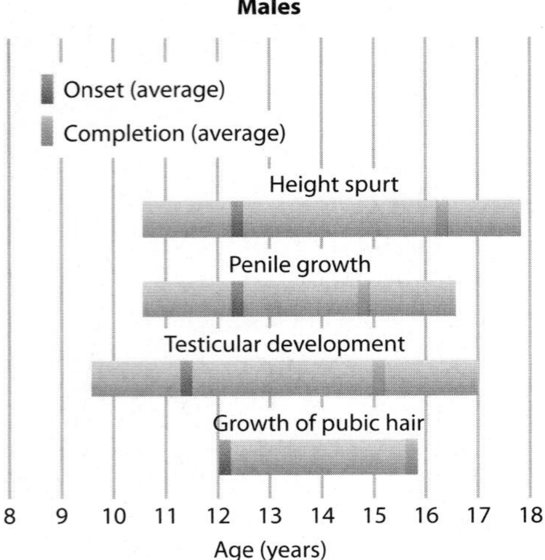

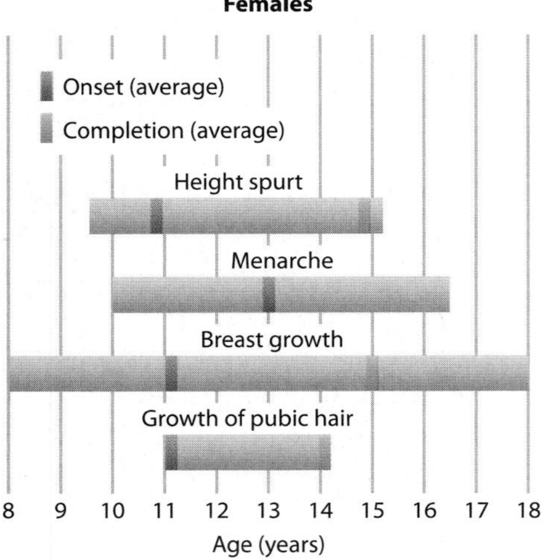

FIGURE **2.5**
NORMAL RANGE AND AVERAGE DEVELOPMENT OF SEXUAL CHARACTERISTICS IN MALES AND FEMALES

increase in shoulder width. In girls, increased hip width is linked with an increase in estrogen. In boys, increased shoulder width is associated with an increase in testosterone (Susman & Dorn, 2009).

Finally, the later growth spurt of boys produces a greater leg length in boys than in girls. In many cases, boys' facial structure becomes more angular during puberty, whereas girls' facial structure becomes rounder and softer.

SEXUAL MATURATION

Think back to the onset of your puberty. Of the striking changes that were taking place in your body, what was the first that occurred? Researchers have found that male pubertal characteristics develop in this order: increased penis and testicle size; appearance of straight pubic hair; minor voice change; first ejaculation (spermarche—this usually occurs through masturbation or a wet dream); appearance of kinky pubic hair; onset of maximum growth; growth of hair in armpits; more detectable voice changes; and growth of facial hair. Three of the most noticeable signs of sexual maturation in boys are penis elongation, testes development, and growth of facial hair. The normal range and average age of development for these sexual characteristics, along with height spurt, are shown in Figure 2.5.

Figure 2.6 illustrates the typical course of male sexual development during puberty. The five numbers in Figure 2.6 reflect the five stages of secondary sexual characteristics known as the Tanner stages (Tanner, 1962). A recent longitudinal study revealed that on average, boys' genital development preceded their pubic development by about 4 months (Susman & others, 2010). In this study, African American boys and girls began puberty almost one year earlier than non-Latino White boys and girls.

What is the order of appearance of physical changes in females? On average, breast development occurs first, followed by the appearance of pubic hair. Later, hair appears in the armpits. As these changes occur, the female grows in height, and her hips become wider than her shoulders. Her first menstruation (menarche) occurs rather late in the pubertal cycle. Initially, her menstrual cycles may be highly irregular, and for the first several years she might not ovulate every cycle. In some instances, a female does not become fertile until two years after her period begins. No voice changes occur that are comparable to those in pubertal males. By the end of puberty, the female's breasts have become more fully rounded. Two of the most noticeable aspects of female pubertal change are pubic hair and breast development. Figure 2.5 shows the normal range and average development for two of these female sexual characteristics and provides information about menarche and height spurt. Figure 2.6 illustrates the typical course of female sexual development during puberty. A longitudinal study revealed that on average, girls' breast development preceded their pubic hair development by about two months (Susman & others, 2010).

Note that there may be wide individual variations in the onset and progression of puberty. For boys, the pubertal sequence may begin as early as 10 years of age or as late as 13½. It may end as early as 13 years or as late as 17. The normal range is wide enough that given two boys of the same chronological age, one might complete the pubertal sequence before the other one has begun it. For girls, the normal age range for menarche is even wider, between 9 and 15 years of age.

Precocious puberty is the term used to describe the very early onset and rapid progression of puberty. Judith Blakemore and her colleagues (2009, p. 58) recently described the following characteristics of precocious puberty. Precocious puberty is usually diagnosed when pubertal onset occurs before 8 years of age in girls and before 9 years of age in boys. Precocious puberty occurs approximately 10 times more often in girls than in boys. When precocious puberty occurs, it usually is treated by medically suppressing gonadotropic secretions, which temporarily stops pubertal change (Kaplowitz, 2009). The reasons for this treatment is that children who experience precocious puberty are ultimately likely to have short stature, early

precocious puberty The very early onset and rapid progression of puberty.

MALE SEXUAL DEVELOPMENT

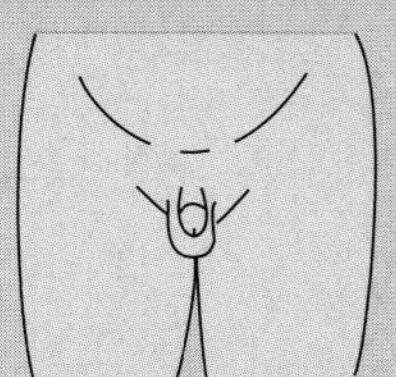

1.
No pubic hair. The testes, scrotum, and penis are about the same size and shape as those of a child.

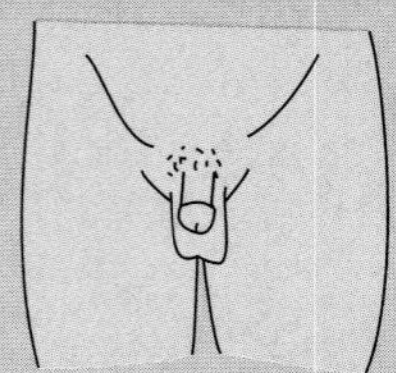

2.
A little soft, long, lightly colored hair, mostly at the base of the penis. This hair may be straight or a little curly. The testes and scrotum have enlarged, and the skin of the scrotum has changed. The scrotum, the sack holding the testes, has lowered a bit. The penis has grown only a little.

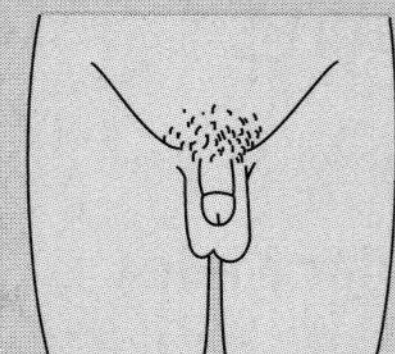

3.
The hair is darker, coarser, and more curled. It has spread to thinly cover a somewhat larger area. The penis has grown mainly in length. The testes and scrotum have grown and dropped lower than in stage 2.

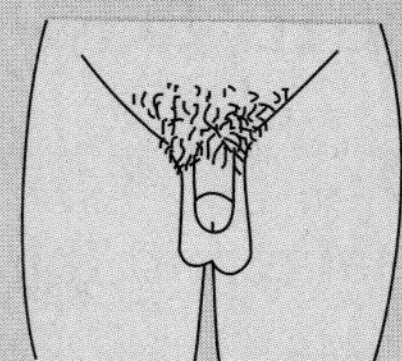

4.
The hair is now as dark, curly, and coarse as that of an adult male. However, the area that the hair covers is not as large as that of an adult male; it has not spread to the thighs. The penis has grown even larger and wider. The glans (the head of the penis) is bigger. The scrotum is darker and bigger because the testes have gotten bigger.

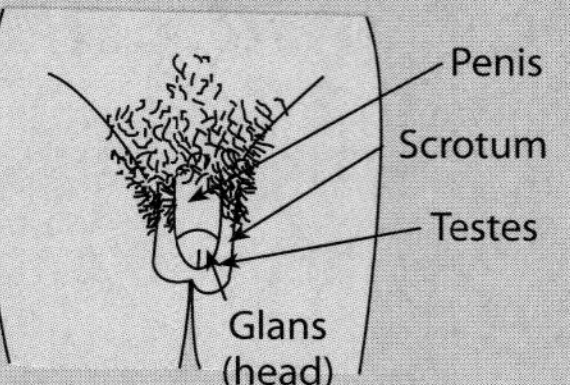

5.
The hair has spread to the thighs and is now like that of an adult male. The penis, scrotum, and testes are the size and shape of those of an adult male.

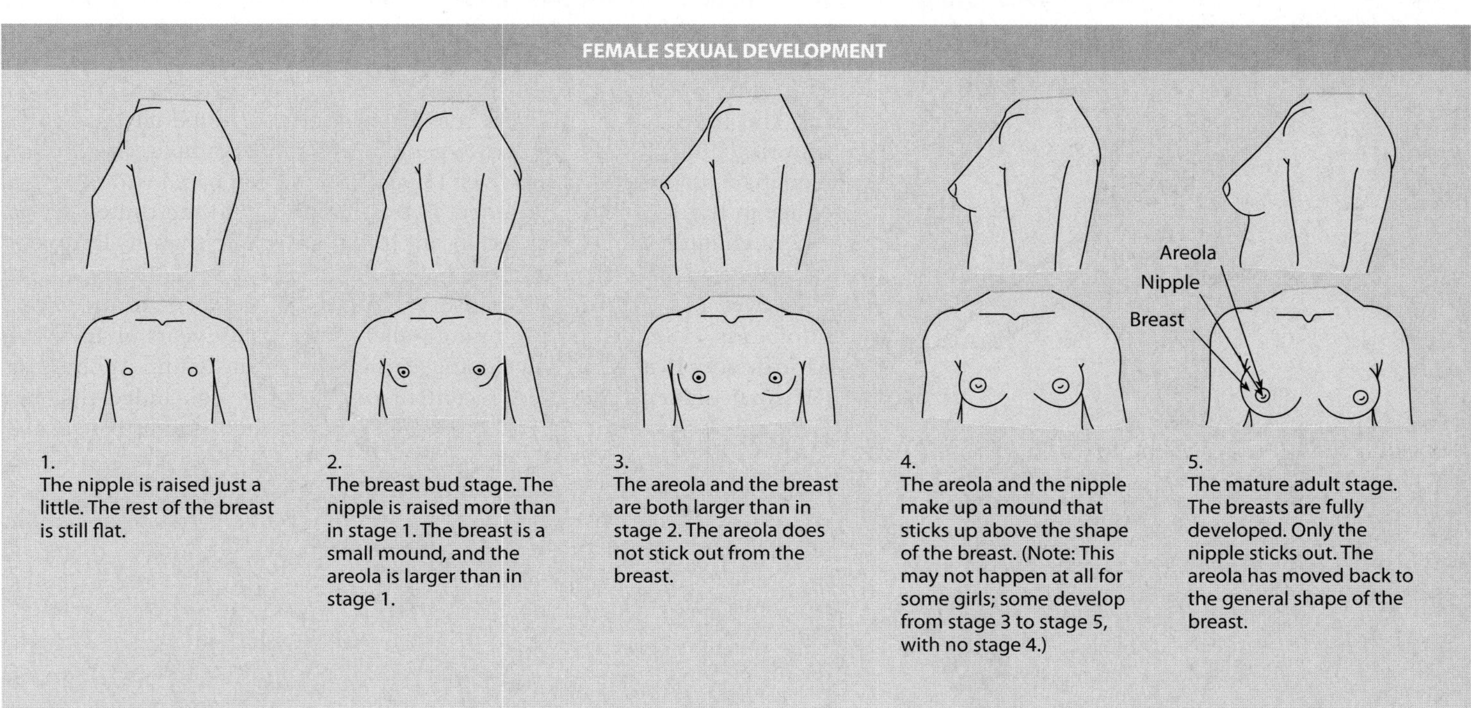

FIGURE **2.6**
THE FIVE PUBERTAL STAGES OF MALE AND FEMALE SEXUAL DEVELOPMENT

sexual capability, and the potential for engaging in age-inappropriate behavior (Blakemore, Berenbaum, & Liben, 2009).

SECULAR TRENDS IN PUBERTY

Imagine a toddler displaying all the features of puberty—a 3-year-old girl with fully developed breasts, or a boy just slightly older, with a deep male voice. One proposal

connecting with adolescents

Attractive Blond Females and Tall Muscular Males

When columnist Bob Greene (1988) called Connections in Chicago, a chatline for teenagers, to find out what young adolescents were saying to each other, the first things the boys and girls asked—after first names—were physical descriptions. The idealism of the callers was apparent. Most of the girls described themselves as having long blond hair, being 5 feet 5 inches tall, and weighing 110 pounds. Most of the boys said that they had brown hair, lifted weights, were 6 feet tall, and weighed 170 pounds.

Would current research on gender differences predict these responses? Why or why not?

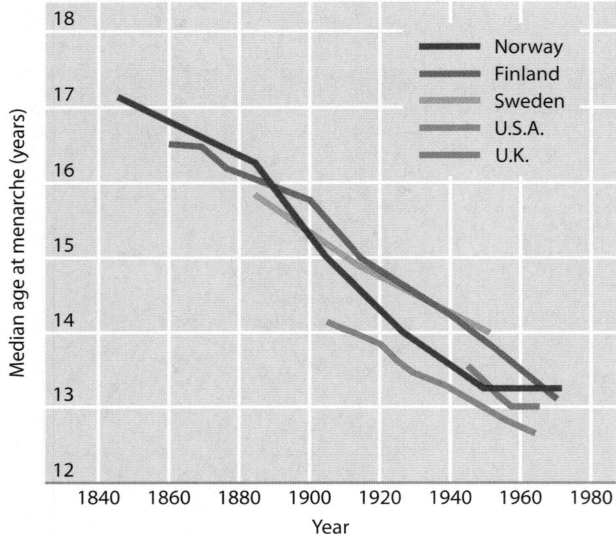

FIGURE **2.7**

MEDIAN AGES AT MENARCHE IN SELECTED NORTHERN EUROPEAN COUNTRIES AND THE UNITED STATES FROM 1845 TO 1969. Notice the steep decline in the age at which girls experienced menarche in five different countries. Recently the age at which girls experience menarche has been leveling off.

was that this is what we would likely see by the year 2250 if the age at which puberty arrives continued to drop at the rate at which it occurred for much of the twentieth century (Petersen, 1987). However, we are unlikely to ever see pubescent toddlers because of genetic limits on how early puberty can occur (Elks & Ong, 2011).

The term **secular trends** refers to patterns of pubertal onset over historical time, especially across generations. For example, in Norway, menarche now occurs at just over 13 years of age, compared with 17 years of age in the 1840s (Ong, Ahmed, & Dunger, 2006). In the United States, where children mature physically up to a year earlier than in European countries, menarche now occurs at about 12½ years of age compared with over 14 years of age a century ago (see Figure 2.7). An increasing number of U.S. girls are beginning puberty at 8 and 9 years of age, with African American girls developing earlier than non-Latino White girls (Herman-Giddens, 2007). A recent research review concluded that age at menarche has not fallen as much as the onset of puberty (Dorn & Biro, 2011). The earlier arrival of pubertal onset historically is believed to be due to improved health and nutrition.

However, recent analyses call into question blanket statements that puberty has continued to rise in recent years. For example, a panel of experts recently examined pubertal timing data and agreed that breast development onset and menarche occurred earlier in girls from 1940 to 1994 but that current data are insufficient to conclude that earlier pubertal development took place for boys across this time frame (Euling & others, 2008). Further, a recent research review concluded that early puberty does seem to be occurring only in overweight girls but that obesity delays pubertal onset in boys (Walvoord, 2010). In this review, it was concluded that earlier puberty in girls is directly linked to the increase in overweight and obesity.

So far, we have been concerned mainly with the physical dimensions of puberty. As we see next, the psychological dimensions of puberty are also important.

secular trends Patterns of the onset of puberty over historical time, especially across generations.

PSYCHOLOGICAL DIMENSIONS OF PUBERTY

A host of psychological changes accompanies an adolescent's pubertal development. Try to remember when you were entering puberty. Not only did you think of yourself differently, but your parents and peers also began treating you differently. Maybe you were proud of your changing body, even though it perplexed you. Perhaps your

Adolescents show a strong preoccupation with their changing bodies and develop images of what their bodies are like. *Why might adolescent males have more positive body images than adolescent females?*

parents felt they could no longer sit in bed and watch television with you or even kiss you good night.

Far less research has been conducted on the psychosocial aspects of male pubertal transitions than on female pubertal transitions, possibly because of the difficulty in detecting when the male transitions occur. Wet dreams are one marker, yet there has been little research on the topic. Not only are the effects of puberty easier to study in girls, they also are more likely to have a strong effect on girls because they are more obvious than the pubertal changes in boys. For girls—having your breasts enlarge is very detectable.

Body Image One psychological aspect of puberty is certain for both boys and girls: Adolescents are preoccupied with their bodies (Lawler & Nixon, 2010; Markey, 2010; Murray, Byrne, & Rieger, 2011). Perhaps you looked in the mirror on a daily, and sometimes even hourly, basis to see if you could detect anything different about your changing body. Preoccupation with one's body image is strong throughout adolescence, but it is especially acute during puberty, a time when adolescents are more dissatisfied with their bodies than in late adolescence.

Gender Differences Gender differences characterize adolescents' perceptions of their bodies (Murray, Byrne, & Rieger, 2010; Natsuaki & others, 2010). In general, throughout puberty girls are less happy with their bodies and have more negative body images than do boys (Crespo & others, 2010). As pubertal change proceeds, girls often become more dissatisfied with their bodies, probably because their body fat increases (Markey, 2010; Yuan, 2010). In contrast, boys become more satisfied as they move through puberty, probably because their muscle mass increases. The following recent studies shed further light on gender differences in body image during adolescence:

- Adolescent girls placed a higher aesthetic value on body image but had a lower aesthetic satisfaction with their bodies than did adolescent boys (Abbott & Barber, 2010).

- The profile of adolescents with the most positive body images was characterized by health-enhancing behaviors, especially regular exercise (Frisen & Holmqvist, 2010).
- Among non-Latino White, Latino, African American, and Asian American adolescents, the psychological well-being (self-esteem and depression, for example) of non-Latino White girls was the most influenced and that of non-Latino White boys the least influenced by body perceptions (Yuan, 2010).
- The negative aspects of puberty for girls appeared in a study that explored 400 middle school boys' and girls' perceptions of the best and worst aspects of being a boy or a girl (Zittleman, 2006). In the views of the middle school girls, at the top of the list of the worst things about being a girl was the biology of being female, which included such matters as childbirth, PMS, periods, and breast cancer. The middle school boys said certain aspects of discipline—getting into trouble, being disciplined, and being blamed more than girls even when they were not at fault—were the worst things about being a boy. However, another aspect of physical development was at the top of the girls' list of the best things about being a girl—appearance (which included choosing clothes, hairstyles, and beauty treatments). Boys said the best thing about being a boy was playing sports.

Use of body art, such as tattoos and body piercing, is increasing in adolescence and emerging adulthood. *Why do youth engage in such body modification?*

Body Art An increasing number of adolescents and college students are obtaining tattoos and getting parts of their body pierced (Beznos & Coates, 2007; Mayers & Chiffriller, 2008). Many of these youth engage in such body modification to be different, to stamp their identity as unique. In one study of adolescents, 60 percent of the students with tattoos had academic grades of A's and B's (Armstrong, 1995). In this study, the average age at which the adolescents got their first tattoo was 14 years of age. Some studies indicate that tattoos and body piercings are markers for risk taking in adolescence (Deschesnes, Fines, & Demers, 2006). A recent study revealed that having multiple body piercings is especially a marker for risk-taking behavior (Suris & others, 2007). However, other researchers argue that body art is increasingly used to express individuality and self-expression rather than rebellion (Armstrong & others, 2004).

Hormones and Behavior Are concentrations of hormones linked to adolescent behavior? Hormonal factors are thought to account for at least part of the increase in negative and variable emotions that characterize adolescents (Vermeersch & others, 2008). In boys higher levels of androgens are associated with violence and acting-out problems (Van Goozen & others, 1998). There is also some indication that increased estrogen levels are linked to depression in adolescent girls (Blakemore, Berenbaum, & Liben, 2009). Further, high levels of adrenal androgens are associated with negative affect in girls (Susman & Dorn, 2009). One recent study found that early-maturing girls with high levels of adrenal androgens had higher emotional arousal and depressive affect than did other girls (Graber, Brooks-Gunn, & Warren, 2006).

However, hormonal factors alone are not responsible for adolescent behavior (DeRose & Brooks-Gunn, 2008). For example, one study found that social factors accounted for two to four times as much variance as hormonal factors in young adolescent girls' depression and anger (Brooks-Gunn & Warren, 1989). Another study found little direct connection between adolescent males' and females' testosterone levels and risk behavior or depression (Booth & others, 2003). In contrast, a link with risk behavior depended on the quality of parent-adolescent relations. When relationship quality decreased, testosterone-linked risk-taking behavior and symptoms of depression increased. And, in a recent study, negative life events mediate links between hormones (estradiol and an adrenal hormone) and aggression in 10- to 14-year-old girls (Graber, Brooks-Gunn, & Warren, 2006). Thus, hormones do not function independently; hormonal activity is influenced by many environmental factors, including parent-adolescent relationships. Stress, eating patterns, sexual activity, and depression can also activate or suppress various aspects of the hormone system (DeRose & Brooks-Gunn, 2008).

developmental **connection**

Nature of Development. Biological, cognitive, and socioemotional processes interact in development. Chapter 1, p. 15

Early and Late Maturation Did you enter puberty early, late, or on time? When adolescents mature earlier or later than their peers, they often perceive themselves differently (de Rose & others, 2011; Graber, Nichols, & Brooks-Gunn, 2010; Negriff, Susman, & Trickett, 2011). In the Berkeley Longitudinal Study conducted many years ago, early-maturing boys perceived themselves more positively and had more successful peer relations than did late-maturing boys (Jones, 1965). The findings for early-maturing girls were similar but not as strong as for boys. When the late-maturing boys were in their thirties, however, they had developed a more positive identity than the early-maturing boys had (Peskin, 1967). Perhaps the late-maturing boys had had more time to explore life's options, or perhaps the early-maturing boys continued to focus on their physical status instead of paying attention to career development and achievement.

An increasing number of researchers have found that early maturation increases girls' vulnerability to a number of problems (Blumenthal & others, 2011; de Rose & others, 2011; Graber, Nichols, & Brooks-Gunn, 2010; Negriff, Susman, & Trickett, 2011). Early-maturing girls are more likely to smoke, drink, be depressed, have an eating disorder, engage in delinquency, struggle for earlier independence from their parents, and have older friends; and their bodies are likely to elicit responses from males that lead to earlier dating and earlier sexual experiences (Copeland & others, 2010; de Rose & others, 2011; Negriff, Susman, & Trickett, 2011). And early-maturing girls are less likely to graduate from high school and more likely to cohabit and marry earlier (Cavanagh, 2009). Apparently the combination of their social and cognitive immaturity and early physical development result in early-maturing girls being more easily lured into problem behaviors, not recognizing the possible long-term effects of these on their development. The following recent studies document the negative outcomes of early pubertal timing in girls:

- Early-maturing girls were more likely to engage in substance abuse and early sexual intercourse (Gaudineau & others, 2010).
- A study of 9- to 13-year-old girls found that early pubertal timing was linked to a higher level of sexual activity and delinquency later in adolescence (Negriff, Susman, & Trickett, 2011).
- Early-maturing girls' higher level of internalizing problems (depression, for example) was linked to their heightened sensitivity to interpersonal stress (Natsuaki & others, 2010).
- A longitudinal study revealed that in adolescence early-maturing girls were more likely than on-time or late-maturing girls to engage in a number of problems—self-reported criminality, substance use, and early sexual behavior (Copeland & others, 2010). In emerging adulthood (assessed when they were 19 and 21 years of age), functioning of the early-maturing girls improved in some areas; however, early-maturing girls who exhibited conduct disorder in adolescence were more likely to be depressed in emerging adulthood, and early-maturing girls were more likely to have had many sexual partners.
- Although early-maturing non-Latino White girls showed more internalizing of problems (depression, for example), early-maturing African American girls did not have a higher level of internalizing problems (de Rose & others, 2011).

What are some risk factors associated with early maturation in girls?

connecting with health and well-being

How Can Early and Late Maturers at Risk for Health Problems Be Identified?

Adolescents whose development is extremely early or late are likely to come to the attention of a physician. Children who experience precocious puberty, which we discussed earlier in this chapter, and a boy who has not had a growth spurt by age 16 or a girl who has not menstruated by age 15, are likely to come to the attention of a physician. Girls and boys who are early or late maturers, but are still well within the normal range, are less likely to be seen by a physician. Nonetheless, these boys and girls may have doubts and fears about being normal that they will not raise unless a physician, counselor, or other health-care provider does. A brief discussion of the usual sequence and timing of events, and the large individual variations in them, may be all that is required to reassure many adolescents who are maturing very early or late.

Health-care providers may want to discuss an adolescent's early or late development with parents as well. Information about peer pressures can be helpful, especially the peer pressures on early-maturing girls to date and to engage in adult-like behavior. For girls and boys who are in the midst of puberty, the transition to middle school, junior high school, or high school may be more stressful (Wigfield & others, 2006).

If pubertal development is extremely late, a physician may recommend hormonal treatment. This approach may or may not be helpful (Richmond & Rogol, 2007). In one study of extended pubertal delay in boys, hormonal treatment helped to increase height, dating interest, and peer relations in several boys but brought little or no improvement in other boys (Lewis, Money, & Bobrow, 1977).

In sum, most early- and late-maturing individuals manage to weather puberty's challenges and stresses. For those who do not, discussions with sensitive and knowledgeable health-care providers and parents can improve the adolescent's coping abilities.

How might a sensitive health-care provider connect with the concerns of an adolescent boy or girl regarding early or late pubertal development?

When does early or late maturation become a health issue? To read further about early and late maturation, see the *Connecting with Health and Well-Being* interlude.

ARE PUBERTY'S EFFECTS EXAGGERATED?

Some researchers question whether puberty's effects are as strong as was once believed. Have the effects of puberty been exaggerated? Puberty affects some adolescents more strongly than others, and some behaviors more strongly than others. Body image, interest in dating, and sexual behavior are quite clearly affected by pubertal change. In one study, early-maturing boys and girls reported more sexual activity and delinquency than late maturers (Flannery, Rowe, & Gulley, 1993). Yet, if we look at overall development and adjustment over the human life span, puberty and its variations have less dramatic effects than is commonly thought for most individuals. For some young adolescents, the path through puberty is stormy, but for most it is not. Each period of the human life span has its stresses and puberty is no different. Although puberty poses new challenges, the vast majority of adolescents weather the stresses effectively. Besides the biological influences on adolescent development, cognitive and social or environmental influences also shape who we become (DeRose & Brooks-Gunn, 2008; Sontag & others, 2008). Singling out biological changes as the dominant influence during adolescence may not be wise.

Although extremely early and late maturation may be risk factors in development, we have seen that the overall effects of early or late maturation often are not great. Not all early maturers will date, smoke, and drink, and not all late maturers will have difficulty with peer relations. In some instances, the effects of an adolescent's grade level in school are stronger than maturational timing (Petersen & Crockett, 1985). Because the adolescent's social world is organized by grade level rather than physical development, this finding is not surprising.

connecting with careers

Anne Petersen, Researcher and Administrator

Anne Petersen has had a distinguished career as a researcher and administrator with a main focus on adolescent development. Petersen obtained three degrees (B.A., M.A., and Ph.D.) from the University of Chicago in math and statistics. Her first job after she obtained her Ph.D. was as a research associate/professor involving statistical consultation, and it was on this job that she was introduced to the field of adolescent development, which became the focus of her subsequent work.

Petersen moved from the University of Chicago to Pennsylvania State University, where she became a leading researcher in adolescent development. Her research included a focus on puberty and gender. Petersen also has held numerous administrative positions. In the mid-1990s, Petersen became deputy director of the National Science Foundation and from 1996 to 2005 was senior vice-president for programs at the W.K. Kellogg Foundation. In 2006, Anne Petersen became the deputy director of the Center for Advanced Study in the Behavioral Sciences at Stanford University and also assumed the position of professor of psychology at Stanford.

Anne Petersen, interacting with adolescents.

Petersen says that what inspired her to enter the field of adolescent development and take her current position at the Kellogg Foundation was her desire to make a difference for people, especially youth. In her position at Kellogg, Petersen is responsible for all programming and services provided by the foundation for adolescents. Her goal is to make a difference for youth in this country and around the world. She believes that too often adolescents have been neglected.

However, it does not mean that age of maturation has no influence on development. Rather, we need to evaluate puberty's effects within the larger framework of interacting biological, cognitive, and socioemotional contexts (Graber, Nichols, & Brooks-Gunn, 2010).

Anne Petersen has made numerous contributions to our understanding of puberty and adolescent development. To read about her work and career, see the *Connecting with Careers* profile.

Review *Connect* Reflect

LG1 Discuss the determinants, characteristics, and psychological dimensions of puberty.

Review

- What are puberty's main determinants?
- What characterizes the growth spurt in puberty?
- How does sexual maturation develop in puberty?
- What are some secular trends in puberty?
- What are some important psychological dimensions of puberty?
- Are puberty's effects exaggerated?

Connect

- How do nature and nurture (described in Chapter 1) affect pubertal timing?

Reflect *Your Own Personal Journey of Life*

- Think back to when you entered puberty. How strong was your curiosity about the pubertal changes that were taking place? What misconceptions did you have about those changes?

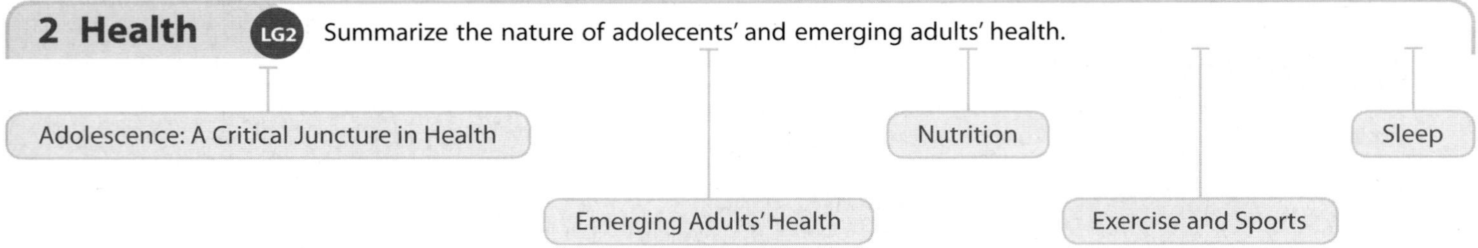

Why might adolescence be a critical juncture in health? What characterizes emerging adults' health? What are some concerns about adolescents' eating habits? How much do adolescents exercise, and what role do sports play in their lives? Do adolescents get enough sleep? These are among the questions we explore in this section.

ADOLESCENCE: A CRITICAL JUNCTURE IN HEALTH

Adolescence is a critical juncture in the adoption of behaviors that are relevant to health (Fatusi & Hindin, 2010; Yancey & others, 2011). Many of the behaviors that are linked to poor health habits and early death in adults begin during adolescence. Conversely, the early formation of healthy behavior patterns, such as regular exercise and a preference for foods low in fat and cholesterol, not only has immediate health benefits but helps in adulthood to delay or prevent disability and mortality from heart disease, stroke, diabetes, and cancer (Hahn, Payne, & Lucas, 2011).

Unfortunately, even though the United States has become a health-conscious nation, many adolescents (and adults) still smoke, have poor nutritional habits, and spend too much of their lives as "couch potatoes" (Sparling & Redican, 2011). Why might many adolescents develop poor health habits? In adolescence, many individuals reach a level of health, strength, and energy that they will never match during the remainder of their lives. Given this high level of physical strength, good health, and high energy, it is not surprising that many adolescents develop poor health habits.

Many health experts conclude that improving adolescents' health involves far more than taking them to the doctor's office when they are sick (Boyce & others, 2008). Increasingly, experts recognize that whether or not adolescents develop health problems depends primarily on their behavior (Turbin & others, 2006). These experts' goals are (1) to reduce adolescents' *health-compromising behaviors*, such as drug abuse, violence, unprotected sexual intercourse, and dangerous driving; and (2) to increase adolescents' *health-enhancing behaviors*, such as exercising, eating nutritiously, wearing seat belts, and getting adequate sleep.

One study found these activities, resources, and relationships to promote adolescents' health-enhancing behaviors (Youngblade & others, 2006): (1) participation in school-related organized activities, such as sports; (2) availability of positive community resources, such as Boys & Girls Clubs, and volunteering; and (3) secure attachment to parents. In this study, health-enhancing behavior was assessed by asking adolescents the extent to which they engaged in such behaviors as wearing a seat belt and engaging in physical activities in and out of school.

Risk-Taking Behavior One type of health-compromising behavior that increases in adolescence is risk taking (Rao & others, 2011). A recent study revealed that sensation seeking increased from 10 to 15 years of age and then declined or remained stable through the remainder of adolescence and into early adulthood (Steinberg & others, 2008). However, even 18-year-olds are "more impulsive, less future-oriented, and more susceptible to peer influence" than adults in their mid- to late twenties (Steinberg, 2009).

A recent study of adolescents concluded that increased risk of having a motor vehicle crash was due to a general tendency to take risks (Dunlop & Romer, 2010). Of course, not all adolescents are high risk takers and sensation seekers. A recent study classified young adolescents as stable high, moderately increasing, and stable low sensation seekers (Lynn-Landsman & others, 2010). In this study, the stable low sensation-seeking young adolescents engaged in low levels of substance use, delinquency, and aggression.

What are some characteristics of adolescents' risk-taking behavior?

> Beginning in early adolescence, many individuals seek experiences that create high intensity feelings. . . . Adolescents like intensity, excitement, and arousal. They are drawn to music videos that shock and bombard the senses. Teenagers flock to horror and slasher movies. They dominate queues waiting to ride the high-adrenaline rides at amusement parks. Adolescence is a time when sex, drugs, very loud music, and other high-stimulation experiences take on great appeal. It is a developmental period when an appetite for adventure, a predilection for risks, and a desire for novelty and thrills seem to reach naturally high levels. While these patterns of emotional changes are evident to some degree in most adolescents, it is important to acknowledge the wide range of individual differences during this period of development. (Dahl, 2004, p. 6)

Researchers also have found that the more resources there are in the community, such as youth activities and adults as role models, the less likely adolescents are to engage in risky behavior (Jessor, 1998; Yancey & others, 2011). One study found that a higher level of what was labeled *social capital* (in this study, number of schools, number of churches/temples/synagogues, and number of high school diplomas) was linked with lower levels of adolescent risky behavior (in this study, gunshot wounds, pregnancy, alcohol and drug treatment, and sexually transmitted infections) (Youngblade & Curry, 2006). Another recent study revealed that "hanging out" with peers in unstructured contexts was linked with an increase in adolescents' risk-taking behavior (Youngblade & Curry, 2006). Also in this study, risk taking by siblings was related to the likelihood that an adolescent would engage in risk taking. Further, adolescents who had better grades were less likely to engage in risk taking than their counterparts with lower grades. And parental monitoring and communication skills are linked to a lower level of adolescent risk taking (Chen & others, 2008).

Recently, neurobiological explanations of adolescent risk taking have been proposed (Steinberg, 2009). The *prefrontal cortex*, the brain's highest level that is involved in reasoning, decision making, and self-control, matures much later (continuing to develop in late adolescence and emerging adulthood) than the *amygdala*, which is the main structure involved in emotion in the brain. The later development of the prefrontal cortex combined with the earlier maturity of the amygdala may explain the difficulty younger adolescents have in putting the brakes on their risk-taking adventures. These developmental changes in the brain provide one explanation of why risk taking declines as adolescents get older (Steinberg, 2008). We will consider much more about these developmental changes in the adolescent brain in Chapter 3.

What can be done to help adolescents satisfy their motivation for risk taking without compromising their health? One strategy is to increase the social capital of a community, as was recommended in the study previously described (Youngblade & others, 2006). As Laurence Steinberg (2004, p. 58) argues, another strategy is to limit

> opportunities for immature judgment to have harmful consequences. . . . Thus, strategies such as raising the price of cigarettes, more vigilantly enforcing laws governing the sale of alcohol, expanding access to mental health and contraceptive services, and raising the driving age would likely be more effective in limiting adolescent smoking, substance abuse, suicide, pregnancy, and automobile fatalities than strategies aimed at making adolescents wiser, less impulsive, and less short-sighted.

It also is important for parents, teachers, mentors, and other responsible adults to effectively monitor adolescents' behavior (Fang, Schinke, & Cole, 2010). In many cases, adults decrease their monitoring of adolescents too early, leaving them to cope with tempting situations alone or with friends and peers

developmental **connection**

Brain Development. Although the prefrontal cortex shows considerable development in childhood, it is still not fully mature in adolescence. Chapter 3, p. 89

developmental **connection**

Social Cognition. The social context plays an important role in adolescent decision making. Chapter 3, p. 108

(Masten, 2004). When adolescents are in tempting and dangerous situations with minimal adult supervision, their inclination to engage in risk-taking behavior combined with their lack of self-regulatory skills can make them vulnerable to a host of negative outcomes (Johnson & others, 2010).

Health Services Adolescents underutilize health-care systems (Hoover & others, 2010). Health services are especially unlikely to meet the needs of younger adolescents, ethnic minority adolescents, and adolescents living in poverty. However, not all of the blame should be placed on health-care providers. Many adolescents don't believe that health-care providers can help them. And some health-care providers may want to provide better health care for adolescents but lack adequate training and/or time during their visit.

Professional guidelines for adolescents recommend annual preventive visits with screening and guidance for health-related behaviors. However, a recent large-scale survey revealed that only 38 percent of adolescents had a preventive visit in the previous 12 months, and among those adolescents few were given guidance for health-related behaviors (Irwin & others, 2009). Of special concern is the low use of health services by older adolescent males (Hoover & others, 2010). A U.S. study found that 16- to 20-year-old males have significantly less contact with health-care services than 11- to 15-year-old males (Marcell & others, 2002). In contrast, 16- to 20-year-old females have more contact with health-care services than do younger females. And one study found that adolescents were much more likely to seek health care for problems related to disease than problems related to mental health, tobacco use, or sexual behavior (Marcell & Halpern-Felsher, 2011).

What is the pattern of adolescent's use of health services?

Among the chief barriers to better health care for adolescents are cost, poor organization and availability of health services, lack of confidentiality, and reluctance on the part of health-care providers to communicate with adolescents about sensitive health issues (Hoover & others, 2010). Few health-care providers receive any special training in working with adolescents. Many say they feel unprepared to provide services such as contraceptive counseling or to evaluate what constitutes abnormal behavior in adolescents. Health-care providers may transmit to their patients their discomfort in discussing topics such as sexuality and drugs, causing adolescents to avoid discussing sensitive issues with them (Marcell & Millstein, 2001).

Leading Causes of Death Medical improvements have increased the life expectancy of today's adolescents and emerging adults compared with their counterparts in the early twentieth century. Still, life-threatening factors do exist in adolescents' and emerging adults' lives (Irwin, 2010; Park & others, 2008).

Students comfort each other in Canisteo, New York, at a memorial on the bridge where four adolescents from Jasper, New York, were killed in a car crash in 2007.

The three leading causes of death in adolescence and emerging adults are accidents, homicide, and suicide (National Center for Health Statistics, 2010). Almost half of all deaths from 15 to 24 years of age are due to unintentional injuries, approximately three-fourths of them involving motor vehicle accidents. Risky driving habits, such as speeding, tailgating, and driving under the influence of alcohol or other drugs, may be more important contributors to these accidents than lack of driving experience. In about 50 percent of motor vehicle fatalities involving adolescents, the driver has a blood alcohol level of 0.10 percent—twice the level needed to be designated as "under the influence" in some states. A high rate of intoxication is also found in adolescents who die as pedestrians, or while using recreational vehicles.

The Society for Adolescent Health and Medicine recently published a position paper on adolescents and driving (D'Angelo, Halpern-Felsher, & Anisha, 2010). The Society recommends a three-stage process to begin after the sixteenth birthday with each stage requiring a minimum of 6 months to finish. One recommended course for this three-stage approach is learner's permit, restricted provisional license, and full license. Also recommended is an increase in the number of hours the adolescent is observed driving before moving to the next stage. Further information about graduated driver licensing (GDL) programs for adolescents appears in Chapter 3 in the context of adolescent decision making (Keating & Halpern-Felsher, 2008).

Homicide also is another leading cause of death in adolescence and emerging adults, especially among African American males, who are three times more likely to be killed by guns than by natural causes. Suicide is the third leading cause of death in adolescence and emerging adulthood. Since the 1950s, the adolescent and emerging adult suicide rate has tripled, although it has declined in recent years. We further discuss suicide in adolescence and emerging adulthood in Chapter 13.

developmental **connection**

Problems and Disorders. Both early and later experiences may be involved in suicide attempts. Chapter 13, p. 451

EMERGING ADULTS' HEALTH

Emerging adults have more than twice the mortality rate of adolescents (Park & others, 2008). As indicated in Figure 2.8, males are mainly responsible for the higher mortality rate of emerging adults.

Also, compared to adolescents, emerging adults engage in more health-compromising behaviors, have more chronic health problems, are more likely to be obese, and are more likely to have a mental health disorder (Irwin, 2010). Although emerging adults may know what it takes to be healthy, they often don't apply this information to their own behavior (Furstenberg, 2006). In many cases, emerging adults are not as healthy as they seem (Fatusi & Hindin, 2010).

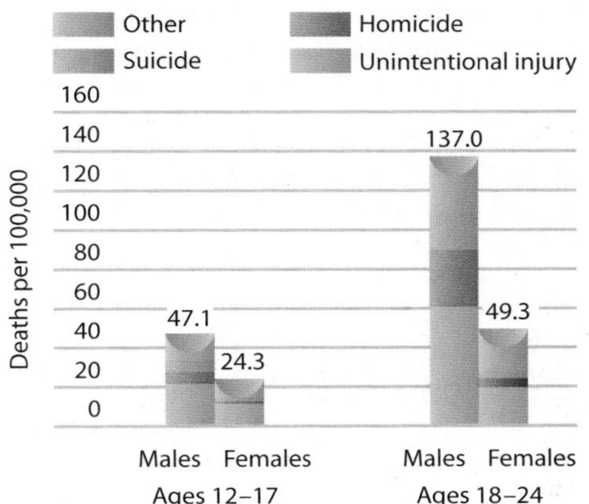

FIGURE **2.8**

MORTALITY RATES OF U.S. ADOLESCENTS AND EMERGING ADULTS

Few emerging adults stop to think about how their personal lifestyles will affect their health later in their adult lives (Sakamaki & others, 2005). As emerging adults, many of us develop a pattern of not eating breakfast, not eating regular meals, and relying on snacks as our main food source during the day; eating excessively to the point where we exceed the normal weight for our age; smoking moderately or excessively; drinking moderately or excessively; failing to exercise; and getting by with only a few hours of sleep at night (American College Health Association, 2008). These lifestyles are associated with poor health (Rimsza & Moses, 2005). In the Berkeley Longitudinal Study—in which individuals were evaluated over a period of 40 years—physical health at age 30 predicted life satisfaction at age 70, more so for men than for women (Mussen, Honzik, & Eichorn, 1982).

There are some hidden dangers in the peaks of performance and health in early adulthood. Young adults can draw on physical resources for a great deal of pleasure, often bouncing back easily from physical stress and abuse. However, this behavior can lead them to push their bodies too far. The negative effects of abusing one's body might not show up in emerging adulthood, but they probably will surface later in early adulthood or in middle adulthood (Rathunde & Csikszentmihalyi, 2006).

NUTRITION

Nutrition is an important aspect of health-compromising and health-enhancing behaviors (Seo & Sa, 2010; Schiff, 2011; Spruijt-Metz, 2011). The eating habits of many adolescents are health-compromising, and an increasing number of adolescents have an eating disorder (Haley, Hedberg, & Leman, 2010; Thompson, Manore, & Vaughn, 2011). A comparison of adolescents in 28 countries found that U.S. and British adolescents were more likely to eat fried food and less likely to eat fruits and vegetables than adolescents in most other countries that were studied (World Health Organization, 2000).

Concern is often expressed over adolescents' tendency to eat between meals. However, their choice of foods is much more important than the time or place of eating. Fresh vegetables and fruits as well as whole-grain products are needed to complement the foods adolescents commonly

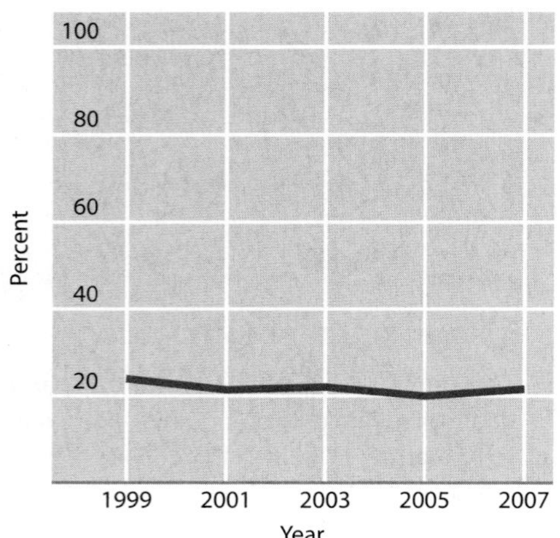

FIGURE **2.9**

PERCENTAGE OF U.S. HIGH SCHOOL STUDENTS WHO ATE FRUITS AND VEGETABLES FIVE OR MORE TIMES A DAY, 1999 TO 2007. *Note:* The graph shows the percentage of high school students over time who had eaten fruits and vegetables (100% fruit juice, fruit, green salad, potatoes–excluding french fries, fried potatoes, or potato chips–carrots, or other vegetables) five or more times per day during the preceding seven days (Eaton & others, 2008).

choose, which tend to be high in protein and energy value. U.S. adolescents are decreasing their intake of fruits and vegetables. The National Youth Risk Survey found that U.S. high school students decreased their intake of fruits and vegetables from 1999 through 2007 (Eaton & others, 2008) (see Figure 2.9). A recent research review found that these two family factors were linked to increased fruit and vegetable consumption by adolescents: availability of fruits and vegetables in the home and consumption of fruits and vegetables by parents (Pearson, Biddle, & Gorely, 2009). And a recent study revealed that eating regular family meals during early adolescence was linked to healthy eating habits five years later (Burgess-Champoux & others, 2009). Thus, parents play an important role in adolescents' nutrition through the food choices they make available to adolescents, serving as models for healthy or unhealthy nutrition, and including adolescents in regular family meals.

Schools also can play an important role in adolescents' eating patterns. A recent study revealed that a comprehensive school intervention in the fourth and fifth grades resulted in increased vegetable consumption two years later (Wang & others, 2010).

A special concern in American culture is the amount of fat in our diet. Many of today's adolescents virtually live on fast-food meals, which contribute to the high fat levels in their diet (Blake, 2011). A longitudinal study revealed that frequent intake of fast food (three or more times a week) was reported by 24 percent of males and 21 percent of 15-year-old females (Larson & others, 2008). At 20 years of age, the percent increased to 33 percent for males but remained at 21 percent for the females.

We have much more to discuss about nutrition in Chapter 13. There we also examine three eating disorders: obesity, anorexia nervosa, and bulimia nervosa.

EXERCISE AND SPORTS

Do American adolescents get enough exercise? How extensive is the role of sports in adolescent development? The answers to these questions influence adolescents' health and well-being.

Exercise In the fourth century B.C., Aristotle commented that the quality of life is determined by its activities. Today, we know that exercise is one of the principal activities that improves the quality of life, both in adolescence and adulthood (Cleland & Venn, 2010; Powers, Dodd, & Jackson, 2011).

Developmental Changes Researchers have found that individuals become less active as they reach and progress through adolescence (Pate & others, 2009). A recent national study of U.S. 9- to 15-year-olds revealed that almost all 9- and 11-year-olds met the federal government's moderate to vigorous exercise recommendations per day (a minimum of 60 minutes a day), but only 31 percent of 15-year-olds met the recommendations on weekdays and only 17 percent met the recommendations on weekends (Nader & others, 2008). The recent national study also found that adolescent boys were more likely to engage in moderate to vigorous exercise than were girls. Another recent national study of U.S. adolescents revealed that physical activity increased until 13 years of age in boys and girls but then declined through 18 years of age (Kahn & others, 2008). In this study, adolescents were more likely to engage in regular exercise when they perceived it was important to present a positive body image to their friends and when exercise was important to their parents. Yet another recent study documented that physical activity declined from 12 to 17 years age in U.S. adolescents (Duncan & others, 2007). In this study, having physically active friends was linked to higher physical activity levels for adolescents.

developmental **connection**

Problems and Disorders. The percentage of overweight and obese adolescents has increased dramatically in recent years. Chapter 13, p. 453

Ethnic differences in exercise participation rates of U.S. adolescents also occur and these rates vary by gender. As indicated in Figure 2.10, in the National Youth Risk Survey, non-Latino White boys exercised the most, African American girls the least (Eaton & others, 2008). Do U.S. adolescents exercise less than their counterparts in other countries? A comparison of adolescents in 28 countries found that U.S. adolescents exercised less and ate more junk food than did adolescents in most of the other countries (World Health Organization, 2000). Just two-thirds of U.S. adolescents exercised at least twice a week compared with 80 percent or more of adolescents in Ireland, Austria, Germany, and the Slovak Republic. U.S. adolescents were more likely to eat fried food and less likely to eat fruits and vegetables than were adolescents in most other countries studied. U.S. adolescents' eating choices were similar to those of adolescents in England.

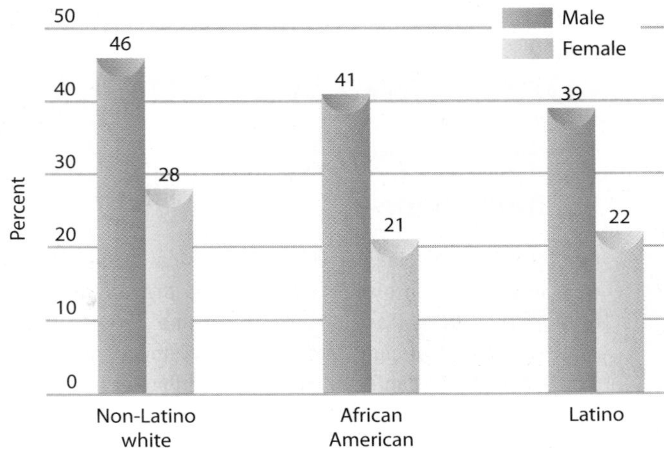

FIGURE **2.10**

EXERCISE RATES OF U.S. HIGH SCHOOL STUDENTS: GENDER AND ETHNICITY. *Note:* Data are for high school students who were physically active doing any kind of physical activity that increased their heart rate and made them breathe hard some of the time for a total of at least 60 minutes per day on five or more of the seven days preceding the survey.

Positive Benefits of Exercise in Adolescence Exercise is linked to a number of positive outcomes in adolescence (Sund, Larsson, & Wichstrom, 2011). Regular exercise has a positive effect on adolescents' weight status. A recent study revealed that regular exercise from 9 to 16 years of age especially was associated with normal weight in girls (McMurray & others, 2008). Other positive outcomes of exercise in adolescence are reduced triglyceride levels, lower blood pressure, and a lower incidence of type 2 diabetes (Butcher & others, 2008; Lobelo & others, 2010). A recent study found that adolescents in the lowest 20 percent of cardiorespiratory fitness were at risk for cardiovascular disease (Lobelo & others, 2010). Other recently reported research indicated that eighth-, tenth-, and twelfth-grade students who engaged in higher levels of exercise had lower levels of alcohol, cigarette, and marijuana use (Teery-McElrath, O'Malley, & Johnston, 2011).

Research studies also underscore other positive benefits of exercise for adolescents. One study revealed that physical fitness in adolescence was linked to physical fitness in adulthood (Mikkelsson & others, 2006). Another study revealed that adolescents who were more physically fit had electrophysiological brain profiles indicative

In 2007, Texas became the first state to test students' physical fitness. The student shown here is performing the trunk lift. Other assessments include aerobic exercise, muscle strength, and body fat. Assessments will be done annually.

connecting with adolescents

In Pitiful Shape

A lot of kids in my class are in pitiful physical shape. They never exercise, except in gym class, and even then they hardly break a sweat. During lunch hour, I see some of the same loafers hanging out and smoking a bunch of cigarettes. Don't they know what they are doing to their bodies? All I can say is that I'm glad I'm not like them. I'm on the basketball team, and during the season, the coach runs us until we are exhausted. In the summer, I still play basketball and swim often. I don't know what I would do without exercise. I couldn't stand to be out of shape.

—Brian, age 14

What are some of the lifelong benefits of the positive health habits cited in this passage?

of a higher level of task preparation and response inhibition (which benefit learning and academic achievement) than their less physically fit counterparts (Stroth & others, 2009). And a recent study found that vigorous physical exercise was linked to lower drug use in adolescence (Delisle & others, 2010). Yet another recent study revealed that high exercise levels in adolescence are related to positive sleep patterns (higher sleep quality, shorter time to sleep onset after going to bed, fewer awakenings after sleep onset) and being less tired and having better concentration during the day (Brand & others, 2010).

An exciting possibility is that physical exercise might act as a buffer against the stress adolescents experience and improve their mental health and life satisfaction (Butcher & others, 2008). Consider these studies, which support this possibility:

- A nine-month physical activity intervention with sedentary adolescent girls improved their self-image (Schneider, Dunton, & Cooper, 2008).
- Higher physical activity at 9 and 11 years of age predicted higher self-esteem at 11 and 13 years of age (Schmalz & others, 2007).
- High school seniors who exercised frequently had higher grade-point averages, used drugs less frequently, were less depressed, and got along better with their parents than those who rarely exercised (Field, Diego, & Sanders, 2001).
- Low levels of exercise were related to depressive symptoms in young adolescents (Sund, Larsson, & Wichstrom, 2010).

A recent research review concluded that aerobic exercise also increasingly is linked to children's and adolescents' cognitive skills (Best, 2011). Researchers have found that aerobic exercise has benefits for children's and adolescents' attention, memory, effortful and goal-directed thinking and behavior, and creativity (Best, 2011; Budde & others, 2008; Davis & others, 2007, 2011; Hillman & others, 2009; Hinkle, Tuckman, & Sampson, 1993; Pesce & others, 2009).

Roles of Families, Schools, and TV/Computers in Adolescent Exercise What contextual factors influence whether adolescents engage in regular exercise? Three factors are the influences of families, of schools, and of TV/computers.

Families Parents play an important role in influencing adolescents' exercise patterns (Dugan, 2008). Children and adolescents benefit when parents engage in regular exercise and are physically fit. Children whose parents got them involved in regular exercise and sports during the elementary school years are likely to continue engaging in exercise on a regular basis as adolescents. A recent study revealed that 9- to 13-year-olds were more likely to engage in physical activity during their free time when the children felt safe, had a number of places to be active, and had parents who participated in physical activities with them (Heitzler & others, 2006).

Schools Some of the blame for the poor physical condition of U.S. children and adolescents falls on U.S. schools, many of which fail to provide physical education class on a daily basis (Schmottiach & McManama, 2010). A recent national survey revealed that only 30 percent of U.S. ninth- through twelfth-graders participated in physical education classes five days in an average school week (Eaton & others, 2008). Males (33 percent) were more likely to participate at this level than females (27 percent). Tenth-graders were most likely to regularly take a PE class (47 percent); eleventh-graders (30 percent) and twelfth-graders (31 percent), the least likely.

Does pushing children and adolescents to exercise more vigorously in school make a difference? In one study, sedentary adolescent females were assigned to one of two groups: (1) a special physical education class that met five times a week with about 40 minutes of activity daily (aerobic dance, basketball, swimming, or Tae Bo) for four of the five days and a lecture/discussion on the importance of physical activity and ways to become more physically active on the fifth day; or (2) a control group that did not take a physical education class (Jamner & others, 2004). After four months, the participants in the physical education class had improved their cardiovascular fitness and lifestyle activity (such as walking instead of driving short distances). Other research studies have found positive benefits for programs designed to improve the physical fitness of students (Timperio, Salmon, & Ball, 2004; Veugelers & Fitzgerald, 2005).

What roles might schools play in improving the exercise habits of adolescents?

Screen-Based Activity Screen-based activity (watching television, using computers, talking on the phone, texting, and instant messaging for long hours) may be involved in lower levels of physical fitness in adolescence (Leatherdale, 2010; Rey-Lopez & others, 2008; Sisson & others, 2010). A recent study revealed that children and adolescents who engaged in the highest amount of daily screen-based activity (TV/video/video game in this study) were less likely to exercise daily (Sisson & others, 2010). In this study, children and adolescents who engaged in low physical activity and high screen-based activity were almost twice as likely to be overweight as their more active, less sedentary counterparts (Sisson & others, 2010).

developmental **connection**

Technology. When media multitasking is taken into account, U.S. 11- to 14-year olds use media an average of nearly 12 hours a day. Chapter 12, p. 411

Sports Sports play an important role in the lives of many adolescents. A recent national study revealed that 56 percent of ninth- through twelfth-grade U.S. students played on at least one sports team at school or in the community (Eaton & others, 2008). Boys (62 percent) were more likely to play on a sports team than girls (50 percent).

Sports can have both positive and negative influences on adolescent development (Adie, Duda, & Ntoumanis, 2010; Busseri & others, 2011). Many sports activities can improve adolescents' physical health and well-being, self-confidence, motivation to excel, and ability to work with others (Gaudreau & others, 2009). Adolescents who spend considerable time in sports are less likely than others to engage in risk-taking behaviors, such as taking drugs. The following recent studies confirmed the positive benefits of organized sports for adolescents:

- Adolescents who participated in sports were less likely to engage in such risk-taking activities as truancy, cigarette smoking, sexual intercourse, and delinquency than nonsports participants (Nelson & Gordon-Larsen, 2006).
- Adolescents who participated in sports plus other activities had more positive outcomes (competence, self-concept, and connectedness, for example) than adolescents who participated in sports alone, school groups alone, or religious groups alone, or who engaged in no group activities (Linver, Roth,

developmental **connection**

Schools. Adolescents who participate in extracurricular activities have higher grades, are more engaged in school, and are less likely to drop out of school. Chapter 10, p. 344

developmental connection

Achievement. Carol Dweck argues that a mastery orientation (focusing on the task and process of learning) produces more positive achievement outcomes than a performance orientation in which the outcome—winning—is the most important aspect of achieving. Chapter 11, p. 366

& Brooks-Gunn, 2009). However, participating in sports had more positive outcomes than no involvement in activities.

- Young adolescents who participated both in sports programs and youth development programs were characterized by positive development (academic competence, confidence, character, caring, and social connection, for example) (Zarrett & others, 2009).

Sports also can have negative outcomes for children: the pressure to achieve and win, physical injuries, a distraction from academic work, and unrealistic expectations for success as an athlete. One downside of the extensive participation in sports by American adolescents includes pressure by parents and coaches to win at all costs. Researchers have found that adolescents' participation in competitive sports is linked with competition anxiety and self-centeredness (Smith & Smoll, 1997). Furthermore, some adolescents spend so much time in sports that their academic skills suffer.

Injuries are common when adolescents play sports (Stein & Micheli, 2010). A recent national study of ninth- through twelfth-graders revealed that of the 80 percent of adolescents who exercised or played sports during the 30 previous days, 22 percent had seen a doctor or nurse for an exercise- or sports-related injury (Eaton & others, 2008). Ninth-graders were most likely to incur exercise- or sports-related injuries; twelfth-graders, the least likely.

What are some positive and negative aspects of sports participation in adolescence?

Increasingly, adolescents are pushing their bodies beyond their capabilities, stretching the duration, intensity, and frequency of their training to the point that they cause overuse injuries (Patel & Baker, 2006). Another problem that has surfaced is the use of performance-enhancing drugs, such as steroids, by adolescent athletes (Elliot & others, 2007).

Some of the problems adolescents experience in sports involve their coaches (Coatsworth & Conway, 2009). Many youth coaches create a performance-oriented motivational climate that is focused on winning, public recognition, and performance relative to other participants. But other coaches place more emphasis on mastery motivation that focuses adolescents' attention on the development of their skills and self-determined standards of success. Researchers have found that athletes who have a mastery focus are more likely than others to see the benefits of practice, to persist in the face of difficulty, and to show significant skill development over the course of a season (Roberts, Treasure, & Kavussanu, 1997).

A final topic involving sports that needs to be examined is the **female athlete triad,** which involves a combination of disordered eating (weight loss), amenorrhea (absent or irregular menstrual periods), and osteoporosis (thinning and weakening of bones) (Misra, 2008). Once menstrual periods have become somewhat regular in adolescent girls, not having a menstrual period for more than three or four months can reduce bone strength. Fatigue and stress fractures may develop. The female athlete triad often goes unnoticed (Bonci & others, 2008; Joy, 2009). Recent research studies suggest that the incidence of the female athlete triad is low, but that a significant number of female adolescents and college students have one of the characteristics of the disorder, such as disordered eating or osteoporosis (Nichols & others, 2006).

female athlete triad A combination of disordered eating, amenorrhea, and osteoporosis that may develop in female adolescents and college students.

SLEEP

Might changing sleep patterns in adolescence contribute to adolescents' health-compromising behaviors? There has been a surge of interest in adolescent sleep patterns (Beebe, 2011; Carskadon, 2011; Fakier & Wild, 2011; Hart, Cairns, & Jelalian, 2011; McHale & others, 2010).

In a recent national survey of youth, only 31 percent of U.S. adolescents got eight or more hours of sleep on an average school night (Eaton & others, 2008). In this study, the percentage of adolescents getting this much sleep on an average school night decreased as they got older (see Figure 2.11).

Another recent study also found that adolescents are not getting adequate sleep. The National Sleep Foundation (2006) conducted a U.S. survey of 1,602 caregivers and their 11- to 17-year-olds. Forty-five percent of the adolescents got inadequate sleep on school nights (less than 8 hours). Older adolescents (ninth- to twelfth-graders) got markedly less sleep on school nights than younger adolescents (sixth- to eighth-graders)—62 percent of the older adolescents got inadequate sleep compared to 21 percent of the younger adolescents. Adolescents who got inadequate sleep (8 hours or less) on school nights were more likely to feel more tired or sleepy, more cranky and irritable, fall asleep in school, be in a depressed mood, and drink caffeinated beverages than their counterparts who got optimal sleep (9 or more hours).

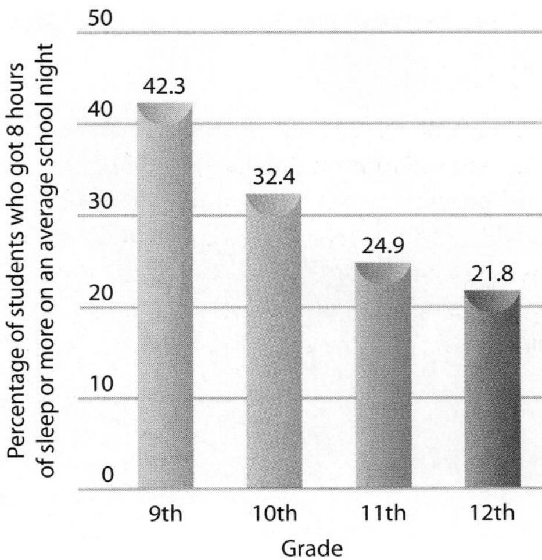

FIGURE **2.11**

DEVELOPMENTAL CHANGES IN U.S. ADOLESCENTS' SLEEP PATTERNS ON AN AVERAGE SCHOOL NIGHT

The following recent studies document the negative link between getting too little sleep during adolescence and adolescent problems:

- Adolescents who slept 7 hours or less per night engaged in more delinquent acts than their counterparts who slept 8 to 10 hours per night (Clinkinbeard & others, 2011).
- Night-to-night variability in sleep and napping were related to depressive symptoms and risk-taking behavior in Mexican American adolescents (McHale & others, 2010).
- Sleep disturbances (insomnia, for example) at 16 years of age predicted sleep disturbances at 23, 33, and 42 years of age (Dregan & Armstrong, 2010).
- In a recent experimental study, 16 adolescents underwent a sleep manipulation that included five consecutive nights of sleep deprivation (6½ hours in bed) and five nights of healthy sleep duration (10 hours in bed) (Beebe, Rose, & Amin, 2010). The two types of sleep were counterbalanced by administering them in varied sequences. At the end of each session, the participants watched educational films and took related quizzes in a simulated classroom. The adolescents who had experienced the unhealthy sleep condition had lower quiz scores and were less attentive to the films.
- A recent research review found that Asian adolescents' bedtimes were even later than those of their peers in North America and Europe, which results in less total sleep and more daytime sleepiness on school nights for the Asian adolescents (Gradisar, Gardner, & Dohnt, 2011).

Many adolescents, especially older adolescents, stay up later at night and sleep longer in the morning than they did when they were children. These findings have implications for the hours during which adolescents learn most effectively in school (Colrain & Baker, 2011).

Mary Carskadon and her colleagues (Carskadon 2002, 2004, 2006, 2011; Crowley & Carskadon, 2010; Jenni & Carskadon, 2007; Kurth & others, 2010; Tarokh & Carskadon, 2008, 2010; Tarokh, Carskadon, & Achermann, 2011) have conducted a number of research studies on adolescent sleep patterns. They found that when given the opportunity adolescents will sleep an average of 9 hours and 25 minutes a night. Most get considerably less than 9 hours of sleep, especially during the week. This shortfall creates a sleep deficit, which adolescents often attempt to make up on the weekend. The researchers also found that older adolescents tend to be sleepier during the day than younger adolescents. They theorized that this sleepiness was not due to academic work or social pressures. Rather, their research suggests that adolescents' biological clocks undergo a shift as they get older, delaying their period of wakefulness by about one hour. A delay in the nightly release of the sleep-inducing hormone melatonin, which is produced in the brain's pineal gland, seems

In Mary Carskadon's sleep laboratory at Brown University, an adolescent girl's brain activity is being monitored. Carskadon (2005) says that in the morning, sleep-deprived adolescents' "brains are telling them it's night time . . . and the rest of the world is saying it's time to go to school" (p. 19).

to underlie this shift. Melatonin is secreted at about 9:30 p.m. in younger adolescents and approximately an hour later in older adolescents.

Carskadon has suggested that early school starting times may cause grogginess, inattention in class, and poor performance on tests. Based on her research, school officials in Edina, Minnesota, decided to start classes at 8:30 a.m. rather than the usual 7:25 a.m. Since then there have been fewer referrals for discipline problems, and the number of students who report being ill or depressed has decreased. The school system reports that test scores have improved for high school students but not for middle school students. This finding supports Carskadon's suspicion that early start times are likely to be more stressful for older than for younger adolescents. Also, a recent study found that just a 30-minute delay in school start time was linked to improvements in adolescents' sleep, alertness, mood, and health (Owens, Belon, & Moss, 2010).

Do sleep patterns change in emerging adulthood? Research indicates that they do (Kloss & others, 2011; Wolfson, 2010; Galambos, Howard, & Maggs, 2011). In a recent study, which revealed that more than 60 percent of college students were categorized as poor quality sleepers, it appears that the weekday bedtimes and rise times of first-year college students are approximately 1 hour and 15 minutes later than those of seniors in high school (Lund & others, 2010). However, the first-year college students had later bedtimes and rise times than third- and fourth-year college students, indicating that at about 20 to 22 years of age, a reverse in the timing of bedtimes and rise times occurs. In this study, poor quality sleep was linked to worse physical and mental health, and the students reported that emotional and academic stress negatively impacted their sleep.

Review *Connect* Reflect

LG2 Summarize the nature of adolescents' and emerging adults' health.

Review

- Why is adolescence a critical juncture in health? How extensive is risk taking in adolescence? How good are adolescents at using health services? What are the leading causes of death in adolescence?
- What characterizes emerging adults' health?
- What are some concerns about adolescents' eating habits?
- What roles do exercise and sports play in adolescents' lives?
- What are some concerns about adolescent sleep patterns?

Connect

- Compare adolescents' health issues with those of emerging adults.

Reflect *Your Own Personal Journey of Life*

- What were your health habits like from the time you entered puberty to the time you completed high school? Describe your health-compromising and health-enhancing behaviors during this time. Since high school, have you reduced your health-compromising behaviors? Explain.

3 Evolution, Heredity, and Environment

LG3 Explain the contributions of evolution, heredity, and environment to adolescent development.

The Evolutionary Perspective — The Genetic Process — Heredity-Environment Interaction

The size and complexity of the adolescent's brain emerged over the long course of evolution. Let's explore the evolutionary perspective on adolescent development and then examine how heredity and environment interact to influence adolescent development.

THE EVOLUTIONARY PERSPECTIVE

In terms of evolutionary time, humans are relative newcomers to the Earth. If we think of the broad expanse of time as a calendar year, then humans arrived on Earth in the last moments of December (Sagan, 1977). As our earliest ancestors left the forest to feed on the savannahs, and finally to form hunting societies on the open plains, their minds and behaviors changed. How did this evolution come about?

> There are one hundred and ninety-three living species of monkeys and apes. One hundred and ninety-two of them are covered with hair. The exception is the naked ape, self-named Homo sapiens.
>
> —DESMOND MORRIS
> *British Zoologist, 20th Century*

Natural Selection and Adaptive Behavior *Natural selection* is the evolutionary process that favors those individuals of a species who are best adapted to survive and reproduce. To understand natural selection, let's return to the middle of the nineteenth century, when the British naturalist Charles Darwin (1809–1882) was traveling the world, observing many different species of animals in their natural habitats. In his groundbreaking book, *On the Origin of Species* (1859), Darwin noted that most species reproduce at rates that would cause enormous increases in their population and yet populations remained nearly constant. He reasoned that an intense struggle for food, water, and resources must occur among the many young born in each generation, because many of them do not survive. Darwin believed that those who do survive to reproduce and pass on their genes to the next generation are probably superior to others in a number of ways. In other words, the survivors are better adapted to their world than the nonsurvivors (Raven, 2011; Starr, 2011). Over the course of many generations, Darwin reasoned, organisms with the characteristics needed for survival would compose a larger and larger percentage of the population, producing a gradual modification of the species. If environmental conditions changed, however, other characteristics might be favored by natural selection, moving the evolutionary process in a different direction.

To understand the role of evolution in behavior, we need to understand the concept of adaptive behavior (Brooker, 2011; Mader, 2011). In evolutionary conceptions of psychology, **adaptive behavior** is a modification of behavior that promotes an organism's survival in the natural habitat. All organisms must adapt to specific places, climates, food sources, and ways of life in order to survive. In humans, attachment ensures an infant's closeness to the caregiver for feeding and protection from danger. This behavioral characteristic promotes survival just as an eagle's claw, which facilitates predation, ensures the eagle's survival.

Evolutionary Psychology Although Darwin introduced the theory of evolution by natural selection in 1859, his ideas only recently have been used to explain behavior. The field of **evolutionary psychology** emphasizes the importance of adaptation, reproduction, and "survival of the fittest" in explaining behavior. Because evolution favors organisms that are best adapted to survive and reproduce in a specific environment, evolutionary psychology focuses on the conditions that allow individuals to survive or perish. In this view, the process of natural selection favors those behaviors that increase organisms' reproductive success and their ability to pass their genes on to the next generation (Cosmides, 2011).

David Buss' (2000, 2008, 2012) ideas on evolutionary psychology have produced a wave of interest in how evolution can explain human behavior. Buss argues that just as evolution shapes our physical features, such as our body shape and height, it also influences our decision making, our aggressive behavior, our fears, and our mating patterns.

Evolutionary Developmental Psychology There is growing interest in using the concepts of evolutionary psychology to understand human development (Bjorklund, 2012; Buss, 2012; Hawley, 2011). Following are some ideas proposed by evolutionary developmental psychologists (Bjorklund & Pellegrini, 2002).

One important concept is that an extended childhood period evolved because humans require time to develop a large brain and learn the complexity of human societies. Humans take longer to become reproductively mature than any other

adaptive behavior A modification of behavior that promotes an organism's survival in the natural habitat.

evolutionary psychology An approach that emphasizes the importance of adaptation, reproduction, and "survival of the fittest" in explaining behavior.

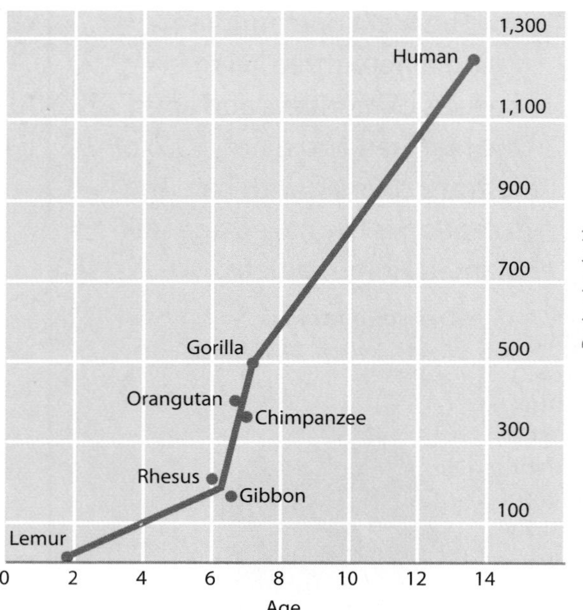

FIGURE **2.12**

THE BRAIN SIZES OF VARIOUS PRIMATES AND HUMANS IN RELATION TO THE LENGTH OF THE JUVENILE PERIOD

developmental **connection**

Social Cognitive Theory. Bandura's social cognitive theory emphasizes reciprocal connections between behavior, environment, and person (cognitive) factors. Chapter 1, p. 32

mammal (see Figure 2.12). During this extended childhood period, they develop a large brain and the experiences needed to become competent adults in a complex society.

Another key idea is that many evolved psychological mechanisms are *domain-specific*. That is, the mechanisms apply only to a specific aspect of a person's makeup. According to evolutionary psychology, information processing is one example. In this view, the mind is not a general-purpose device that can be applied equally to a vast array of problems. Instead, as our ancestors dealt with certain recurring problems such as hunting and finding shelter, specialized modules evolved that process information related to those problems: for example, a module for physical knowledge for tracking animals, a module for mathematical knowledge for trading, and a module for language.

Evolved mechanisms are not always adaptive in contemporary society (Hawley, 2011). Some behaviors that were adaptive for our prehistoric ancestors may not serve us well today. For example, the food-scarce environment of our ancestors likely led to humans' propensity to gorge when food is available and to crave high-caloric foods, a trait that that might lead to an epidemic of obesity when food is plentiful (Hawley, 2011).

Evaluating Evolutionary Psychology Albert Bandura (1998), whose social cognitive theory was described in Chapter 1, has criticized the "biologizing" of psychology. Bandura acknowledges the influence of evolution on human adaptation and change. However, he rejects what he calls "one-sided evolutionism," in which social behavior is seen as the product of evolved biology. Bandura stresses that evolutionary pressures favored biological adaptations that encouraged the use of tools, allowing humans to manipulate, alter, and construct new environmental conditions. In time, humans' increasingly complex environmental innovations produced new pressures that favored the evolution of specialized brain systems to support consciousness, thought, and language.

In other words, evolution gave humans body structures and biological potentialities, not behavioral dictates. Having evolved our advanced biological capacities, we can use them to produce diverse cultures—aggressive or pacific, egalitarian, or autocratic. As American scientist Stephen Jay Gould (1981) concluded, in most domains, human biology allows a broad range of cultural possibilities. The sheer pace of social change, Bandura (1998) notes, underscores the range of possibilities biology permits.

The "big picture" idea of natural selection leading to the development of human traits and behaviors is difficult to refute or test because it is on a time scale that does not lend itself to empirical study. Thus, studying specific genes in humans and other species—and their links to traits and behaviors—may be the best approach for testing ideas coming out of the evolutionary psychology perspective.

THE GENETIC PROCESS

Genetic influences on behavior evolved over time and across many species. The many traits and characteristics that are genetically influenced have a long evolutionary history that is retained in our DNA. In other words, our DNA is not just inherited from our parents; it's also what we've inherited as a species from the species that came before us. Let's take a closer look at DNA and its role in human development.

How are characteristics that suit a species for survival transmitted from one generation to the next? Darwin did not know because genes and the principles of genetics had not yet been discovered. Each of us carries a "genetic code" that we inherited from our parents. Because a fertilized egg carries this human code, a fertilized human egg cannot grow into an egret, eagle, or elephant.

DNA and the Collaborative Gene Each of us began life as a single cell weighing about one twenty-millionth of an ounce! This tiny piece of matter housed our entire

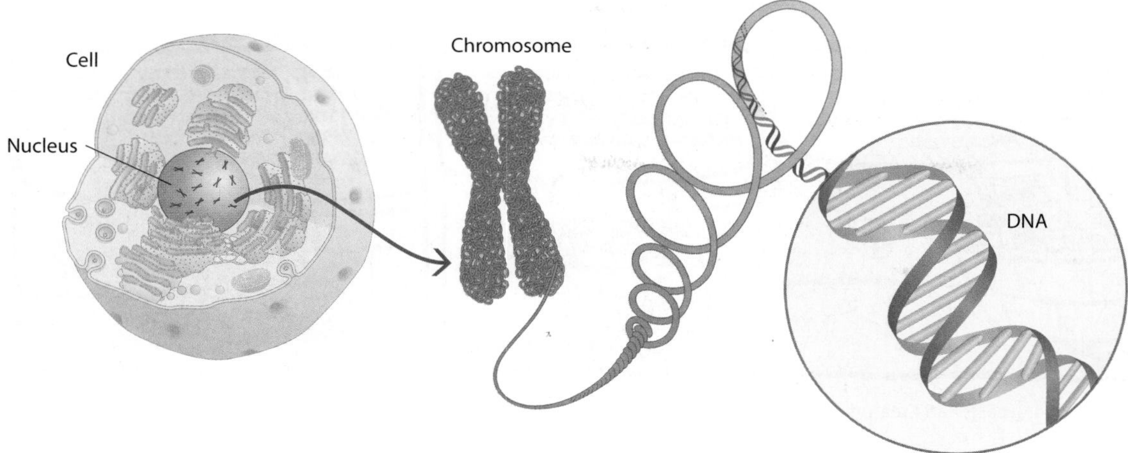

FIGURE **2.13**

CELLS, CHROMOSOMES, GENES, AND DNA. (*Left*) The body contains trillions of cells, which are the basic structural units of life. Each cell contains a central structure, the nucleus. (*Middle*) Chromosomes and genes are located in the nucleus of the cell. Chromosomes are made up of threadlike structures composed of DNA molecules. (*Right*) A gene, a segment of DNA that contains the hereditary code. The structure of DNA is a spiraled double chain.

genetic code—instructions that orchestrated growth from that single cell to a person made of trillions of cells, each containing a perfect replica of the original genetic code. That code is carried by our genes. What are they and what do they do?

The nucleus of each human cell contains **chromosomes,** which are threadlike structures that contain the remarkable substance deoxyribonucleic acid, or DNA. **DNA** is a complex molecule that contains genetic information. It has a double helix shape, like a spiral staircase. **Genes,** the units of hereditary information, are short segments composed of DNA, as you can see in Figure 2.13. They direct cells to reproduce themselves and to assemble proteins. Proteins, in turn, serve as the building blocks of cells, as well as the regulators that direct the body's processes (Starr, 2011).

Each gene has its own function, and each gene has its own location, its own designated place on a specific chromosome. Today, there is a great deal of enthusiasm about efforts to discover the specific locations of genes that are linked to certain functions (Goodenough & McGuire, 2012; Plomin & Davis, 2009). An important step in this direction was accomplished when the Human Genome Project and the Celera Corporation completed a preliminary map of the human *genome*—the complete set of instructions for making a human organism (U.S. Department of Energy, 2001).

One of the big surprises of the Human Genome Project was a report indicating that humans have only about 30,000 genes (U.S. Department of Energy, 2001). More recently, the number of human genes has been revised further downward to approximately 21,500 (Ensembl Human, 2008). Scientists had thought that humans had as many as 100,000 or more genes. They had also believed that each gene programmed just one protein. In fact, humans appear to have far more proteins than they have genes, so there cannot be a one-to-one correspondence between them (Commoner, 2002; Moore, 2001). Each segment of DNA is not translated, in automation-like fashion, into one and only one protein. It does not act independently, as developmental psychologist David Moore (2001) emphasized by titling his book *The Dependent Gene*.

Rather than being an independent source of developmental information, DNA collaborates with other sources of information to specify our characteristics (Diamond, 2009; Diamond, Casey, & Munakata, 2011). The collaboration operates at many points. Small pieces of DNA are mixed, matched, and linked by the cellular machinery. That machinery is sensitive to its context—that is, it is influenced by what is going on around it. Whether a gene is turned "on," working to assemble proteins, is also a matter of collaboration. The activity of genes (genetic *expression*) is affected by their

chromosomes Threadlike structures that contain deoxyribonucleic acid, or DNA.

DNA A complex molecule that contains genetic information.

genes The units of hereditary information, which are short segments composed of DNA.

THE WIZARD OF ID

By permission of John L. Hart FLP, and Creators Syndicate, Inc.

environment (Gottlieb, 2007; Kahn & Fraga, 2009). For example, hormones that circulate in the blood make their way into the cell, where they can turn genes "on" and "off." And the flow of hormones can be affected by environmental conditions, such as light, day length, nutrition, and behavior. Numerous studies have shown that external events outside the cell and the person, and internal events inside the cell, can excite or inhibit gene expression (Gottlieb, Wahlsten, & Lickliter, 2006). For example, one recent study revealed that an increase in the concentration of stress hormones such as cortisol produced a 5-fold increase in DNA damage (Flint & others, 2007).

In short, a single gene is rarely the source of a protein's genetic information, much less of an inherited trait (Gottlieb, 2007). Rather than being a group of independent genes, the human genome consists of many collaborative genes.

The term *gene-gene interaction* is increasingly used to describe studies that focus on the interdependence of two or more genes in influencing characteristics, behavior, diseases, and development (Li & others, 2008). For example, recent studies have documented gene-gene interaction in cancer (Bapat & others, 2010) and cardiovascular disease (Jylhava & others, 2009).

Genotype and Phenotype No one possesses all the characteristics that his or her genetic structure makes possible. A person's genetic heritage—the actual genetic material—is called a **genotype.** Not all of this genetic material is apparent in our observed and measurable characteristics. The way an individual's genotype is expressed in observed and measurable characteristics is called a **phenotype.** Phenotypes include physical traits, such as height, weight, eye color, and skin pigmentation, as well as psychological characteristics, such as intelligence, creativity, personality, and social tendencies.

For each genotype, a range of phenotypes can be expressed (Brooker, 2011; Hartwell, 2011; Johnson, 2012). Imagine that we could identify all the genes that would make an adolescent introverted or extraverted. Could we predict measured introversion or extraversion in a specific person from our knowledge of those genes? The answer is no, because even if our genetic model was adequate, introversion and extraversion are characteristics that are shaped by experience throughout life. For example, a parent might push an introverted child into social situations, encouraging the child to become more gregarious. Or the parent might support the child's preference for solitary play.

HEREDITY-ENVIRONMENT INTERACTION

So far, we have discussed genes and how they work, and one theme is apparent: Heredity and environment interact to produce development. Whether we are studying how genes produce proteins or what their influence is on how tall a person is, we end up discussing heredity-environment interactions. Is it possible, though, to untangle the influence of heredity from that of environment and discover the role

genotype A person's genetic heritage; the actual genetic material.

phenotype The way an individual's genotype is expressed in observed and measurable characteristics.

of each in producing individual differences in development? When heredity and environment interact, how does heredity influence the environment, and vice versa?

Twin studies compare identical twins with fraternal twins. Identical twins develop from a single fertilized egg that splits into two genetically identical organisms. Fraternal twins develop from separate eggs, making them genetically no more similar than nontwin siblings. *What is the nature of the twin study method?*

Behavior Genetics **Behavior genetics** is the field that seeks to discover the influence of heredity and environment on individual differences in human traits and development (Gregory, Ball, & Button, 2011; Koskinen & others, 2011). If you think about all of the people you know, you have probably realized that people differ in terms of their level of introversion/extraversion. What behavior geneticists try to do is to figure out what is responsible for those differences—that is, to what extent do people differ because of differences in genes, environment, or a combination of these?

To study the influence of heredity on behavior, behavior geneticists often use either twins or adoption situations. In the most common **twin study,** the behavioral similarity of identical twins is compared with the behavioral similarity of fraternal twins. *Identical twins* (called monozygotic twins) develop from a single fertilized egg that splits into two genetically identical replicas, each of which becomes a person. *Fraternal twins* (called dizygotic twins) develop from separate eggs and separate sperm. Although fraternal twins share the same womb, they are no more alike genetically than are nontwin brothers and sisters, and they may be of different sexes.

By comparing groups of identical and fraternal twins, behavior geneticists capitalize on the basic knowledge that identical twins are more similar genetically than are fraternal twins (Silberg & others, 2010; van Soelen & others, 2011). For example, one study found that conduct problems were more prevalent in identical twins than fraternal twins; the researchers concluded that the study demonstrated an important role for heredity in conduct problems (Scourfield & others, 2004).

However, several issues complicate interpretation of twin studies (Mandelman & Grigorenko, 2011). For example, perhaps the environments of identical twins are more similar than the environments of fraternal twins. Adults might stress the similarities of identical twins more than those of fraternal twins, and identical twins might perceive themselves as a "set" and play together more than fraternal twins do. If so, observed similarities in identical twins could be more strongly influenced by the environment than the results suggested.

In an **adoption study,** investigators seek to discover whether the behavior and psychological characteristics of adopted children are more like those of their adoptive parents, who have provided a home environment, or more like those of their biological parents, who have contributed their heredity (Loehlin, Horn, & Ernst, 2007). Another form of the adoption study involves comparing adopted and biological siblings.

Heredity-Environment Correlations The difficulties that researchers encounter when they interpret the results of twin studies and adoption studies reflect the complexities of heredity-environment interaction. Some of these interactions are heredity-environment correlations—that is, individuals' genes influence the types of environments to which they are exposed. In a sense, individuals "inherit" environments that are related or linked to genetic propensities (Plomin & others, 2009). Behavior geneticist Sandra Scarr (1993) described three ways that heredity and environment are correlated (see Figure 2.14):

- **Passive genotype-environment correlations** occur because biological parents, who are genetically related to the child, provide a rearing environment for the child. For example, the parents might have a genetic predisposition to be intelligent and read skillfully. Because they read well and enjoy reading, they provide their children with books to read. The likely outcome is that their children, given their own inherited predispositions from their parents, will become skilled readers.

behavior genetics The field that seeks to discover the influence of heredity and environment on individual differences in human traits and development.

twin study A study in which the behavioral similarity of identical twins is compared with the behavioral similarity of fraternal twins.

adoption study A study in which investigators seek to discover whether the behavior and psychological characteristics of adopted children are more like their adoptive parents, who have provided a home environment, or more like those of their biological parents, who have contributed their heredity. Another form of adoption study involves comparing adopted and biological siblings.

passive genotype-environment correlations Correlations that occur because biological parents, who are genetically related to the child, provide a rearing environment for the child.

Heredity-Environment Correlation	Description	Examples

developmental **connection**

Nature and Nurture. The nature and nurture debate is one of the main issues in the study of adolescent development. Chapter 1, p. 22

intelligent girl is elected president of her senior class in high school, is her success due to heredity or to environment? Of course, the answer is both.

The relative contributions of heredity and environment are not additive. That is, we can't say that such-and-such a percentage of nature and such-and-such a percentage of experience make us who we are. Nor is it accurate to say that full genetic expression happens once, around conception or birth, after which we carry our genetic legacy into the world to see how far it takes us. Genes produce proteins throughout the life span, in many different environments. Or they don't produce these proteins, depending in part on how harsh or nourishing those environments are.

The emerging view is that many complex behaviors likely have some genetic loading that gives people a propensity for a specific developmental trajectory (Plomin & others, 2009). However, the actual development requires more: an environment. And that environment is complex, just like the mixture of genes we inherit (Grusec, 2011). Environmental influences range from the things we lump together under "nurture" (such as parenting, family dynamics, schooling, and neighborhood quality) to biological encounters (such as viruses, birth complications, and even biological events in cells).

Imagine for a moment that a cluster of genes is somehow associated with youth violence (this example is hypothetical because we don't know of any such combination). The adolescent who carries this genetic mixture might experience a world of loving parents, regular nutritious meals, lots of books, and a series of masterful teachers. Or the adolescent's world might include parental neglect, a neighborhood in which gunshots and crime are everyday occurrences, and inadequate schooling. In which of these environments are the adolescent's genes likely to manufacture the biological underpinnings of criminality?

If heredity and environment interact to determine the course of development, is that all there is to answering the question of what causes development? Are adolescents completely at the mercy of their genes and environment as they develop? Genetic heritage and environmental experiences are pervasive influences on adolescents' development. But in thinking about what causes development, adolescents not only are the outcomes of their heredity and the environment they experience, but they also can author a unique developmental path by changing the environment. As one psychologist recently concluded:

> In reality, we are both the creatures and creators of our worlds. We are . . . the products of our genes and environments. Nevertheless, . . . the stream of causation that shapes the future runs through our present choices . . . Mind matters. . . . Our hopes, goals, and expectations influence our future. (Myers, 2010, p. 168)

Review *Connect* Reflect

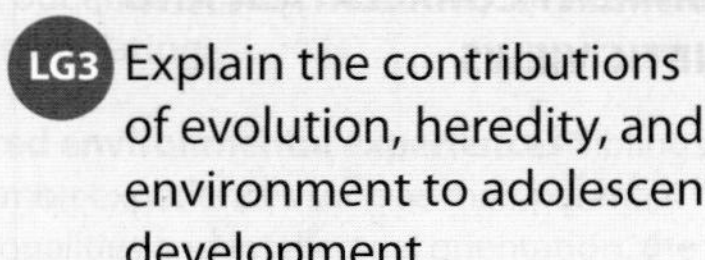

LG3 Explain the contributions of evolution, heredity, and environment to adolescent development.

Review

- What role has evolution played in adolescent development? How do the fields of evolutionary psychology and evolutionary developmental psychology describe evolution's contribution to understanding adolescence?
- What is the genetic process?
- What is the nature of heredity-environment interaction?

Connect

- Which side of the nature and nurture issue does evolutionary developmental psychology take? Explain.

Reflect *Your Own Personal Journey of Life*

- Someone tells you that she has analyzed your genetic background and environmental experiences and reached the conclusion that the environment definitely has had little influence on your intelligence. What would you say to this person about her ability to make this diagnosis?

reach your **learning goals**

1 Puberty

LG1 Discuss the determinants, characteristics, and psychological dimensions of puberty.

Determinants of Puberty

- Puberty is a period of rapid physical maturation involving hormonal and bodily changes that take place primarily in early adolescence. Puberty's determinants include heredity, hormones, and possibly weight, percentage of body fat, and leptin. Two classes of hormones that are involved in pubertal change and have significantly different concentrations in males and females are androgens and estrogens. The endocrine system's role in puberty involves the interaction of the hypothalamus, pituitary gland, and gonads. FSH and LH, which are secreted by the pituitary gland, are important aspects of this system. So is GnRH, which is produced by the hypothalamus. The sex hormone system is a negative feedback system. Growth hormone also contributes to pubertal change. Low birth weight and rapid weight gain in infancy are linked to earlier pubertal onset. Puberty has two phases: adrenarche and gonadarche. The culmination of gonadarche in boys is spermarche; in girls, it is menarche.

Growth Spurt

- The onset of pubertal growth occurs on the average at 9 years of age for girls and 11 years for boys. The peak of pubertal change for girls is 11½ years; for boys it is 13½ years. Girls grow an average of 3½ inches per year during puberty; boys grow an average of 4 inches.

Sexual Maturation

- Sexual maturation is a key feature of pubertal change. Individual variation in puberty is extensive and is considered to be normal within a wide age range.

Secular Trends in Puberty

- Secular trends in puberty took place in the twentieth century with puberty coming earlier. Recently, there are indications that earlier puberty is occurring only for overweight girls.

Psychological Dimensions of Puberty

- Adolescents show heightened interest in their bodies and body images. Younger adolescents are more preoccupied with these images than are older adolescents. Adolescent girls often have a more negative body image than adolescent boys do. Adolescents and college students increasingly have tattoos and body piercings (body art). Some scholars conclude that body art is a sign of rebellion and is linked to risk taking, whereas others argue that increasingly body art is used to express uniqueness and self-expression rather than rebellion. Researchers have found connections between hormonal change during puberty and behavior, but environmental influences need to be taken into account. Early maturation often favors boys, at least during early adolescence, but as adults late-maturing boys have a more positive identity than early-maturing boys. Early-maturing girls are at risk for a number of developmental problems. Some scholars doubt that puberty's effects on development are as strong as once envisioned. Most early- and late-maturing adolescents weather the challenges of puberty successfully. For those who do not adapt well to pubertal changes, discussions with knowledgeable health-care providers and parents can improve the coping abilities of off-time adolescents.

Are Puberty's Effects Exaggerated?

- Puberty has important influences on development, but the significance of these influences needs to be considered in terms of the entire life span. Some scholars argue that too much emphasis has been given to the biological changes of puberty.

2 Health

LG2 Summarize the nature of adolescents' and emerging adults' health.

Adolescence: A Critical Juncture in Health

- Many of the behaviors that are linked to poor health habits and early death in adults begin during adolescence. Engaging in healthy behavior patterns in adolescence, such as regular exercise, helps to delay disease in adulthood. Important goals are to reduce adolescents' health-compromising behaviors and to increase their health-enhancing behaviors. Risk-taking behavior increases during adolescence and combined with a delay in developing self-regulation makes adolescents vulnerable to a number of problems. Developmental changes in the brain have recently been proposed to help explain adolescent risk-taking behavior. Among the strategies for keeping increased motivation for risk taking from compromising adolescents' health are to limit their opportunities for harm and monitor their behavior. Adolescents underutilize health services. The three leading causes of death in adolescence are (1) accidents, (2) homicide, and (3) suicide. Although emerging adults have a higher death rate than adolescents, emerging adults have few chronic health problems. However, many emerging adults don't stop to think about how their personal lifestyles will affect their health later in their lives.

Nutrition

- Special nutrition concerns in adolescence are eating between meals, the amount of fat in adolescents' diets, and increased reliance on fast-food meals.

Exercise and Sports

- A majority of adolescents are not getting adequate exercise. At approximately 13 years of age, their regular exercise often begins to decline. American girls especially have a low rate of exercise. Regular exercise has many positive outcomes for adolescents, including a lower risk of being overweight and higher self-esteem. Family, school, and TV/computer contexts influence adolescents' exercise patterns. Sports play an important role in the lives of many adolescents. Sports can have positive (improved physical health and well-being, confidence, ability to work with others) or negative (intense pressure by parents and coaches to win at all costs, injuries) outcomes. Recently, the female athlete triad has become a concern.

Sleep

- Adolescents like to go to bed later and get up later than children do. This pattern may be linked to developmental changes in the brain. A special concern is the extent to which these changes in sleep patterns in adolescents affect academic behavior and achievement. Developmental changes in sleep continue to occur in emerging adulthood.

3 Evolution, Heredity, and Environment

Explain the contributions of evolution, heredity, and environment to adolescent development.

The Evolutionary Perspective

- Natural selection—the process that favors the individuals of a species that are best adapted to survive and reproduce—is a key aspect of the evolutionary perspective. Evolutionary psychology is the view that adaptation, reproduction, and "survival of the fittest" are important in explaining behavior. Evolutionary developmental psychology has promoted a number of ideas, including the view that an extended "juvenile" period is needed to develop a large brain and learn the complexity of human social communities. Critics argue that the evolutionary perspective does not give adequate attention to experience and humans as a culture-making species.

The Genetic Process

- The nucleus of each human cell contains chromosomes, which contain DNA. Genes are short segments of DNA that direct cells to reproduce and manufacture proteins that maintain life. DNA does not act independently to produce a trait or behavior. Rather, it acts collaboratively. Genotype refers to the unique configuration of genes, whereas phenotype involves observed and measurable characteristics.

Heredity-Environment Interaction

- Behavior genetics is the field concerned with the degree and nature of behavior's hereditary basis. Methods used by behavior geneticists include twin studies and adoption studies. In Scarr's heredity-environment correlations view, heredity directs the types of environments that children experience. She describes three genotype-environment correlations: passive, evocative, and active (niche-picking). Scarr argues that the relative importance of these three genotype-environment correlations changes as children develop. Shared environmental experiences refer to siblings' common experiences, such as their parents' personalities and intellectual orientation, the family's socioeconomic status, and the neighborhood in which they live. Nonshared environmental experiences involve the adolescent's unique experiences, both within a family and outside a family, that are not shared with a sibling. Many behavior geneticists argue that differences in the development of siblings are due to nonshared environmental experiences (and heredity) rather than to shared environmental experiences. The epigenetic view emphasizes that development is the result of an ongoing, bidirectional interchange between heredity and environment. Many complex behaviors have some genetic loading that gives people a propensity for a specific developmental trajectory. However, actual development also requires an environment, and that environment is complex. The interaction of heredity and environment is extensive. Much remains to be discovered about the specific ways that heredity and environment interact to influence development.

key terms

puberty 50
hormones 51
androgens 51
estrogens 51
adrenarche 53
gonadarche 53
menarche 54
spermarche 54
precocious puberty 56
secular trends 58
female athlete triad 72
adaptive behavior 75
evolutionary psychology 75
chromosomes 77
DNA 77
genes 77
genotype 78
phenotype 78
behavior genetics 79
twin study 79
adoption study 79
passive genotype-environment correlations 79
evocative genotype-environment correlations 80
active (niche-picking) genotype-environment correlations 80
shared environmental experiences 80
nonshared environmental experiences 80
epigenetic view 81
gene × environment (G × E) interaction 81

key people

Mary Carskadon 73
David Buss 75
Albert Bandura 76
David Moore 77
Sandra Scarr 79
Robert Plomin 81

resources for improving the lives of adolescents

The Society for Adolescent Health and Medicine ***www.adolescenthealth.com***

This organization is a valuable source of information about competent physicians who specialize in treating adolescents. It maintains a list of recommended adolescent specialists across the United States. The society also publishes the *Journal of Adolescent Health,* which contains articles on a wide range of health-related and medical issues involving adolescents.

National Adolescent Health Information Center (NAHIC) ***http://nahic.ucsf.edu/***

This organization, associated with the University of California–San Francisco, has an excellent website that includes adolescent health data; recommendations for research, policy, and programs; health-care services resources; and information about a national initiative to improve adolescent health.

Journal of School Health ***www.blackwellpublishing.com***

This journal publishes articles that pertain to the school-related aspects of children's and adolescents' health, including a number of health education programs.

self-assessment

The Student Online Learning Center includes the following self-assessments for further exploration:

- *Is My Lifestyle Good for My Health?*
- *My Health Habits*
- *Do I Get Enough Sleep?*

chapter 3 THE BRAIN AND COGNITIVE DEVELOPMENT

chapter outline

The Brain

Learning Goal 1 Describe the developmental changes in the brain during adolescence.

Neurons
Brain Structure, Cognition, and Emotion
Experience and Plasticity

The Cognitive Developmental View

Learning Goal 2 Discuss the cognitive developmental view of adolescence.

Piaget's Theory
Vygotsky's Theory

The Information-Processing View

Learning Goal 3 Characterize the information-processing view of adolescence.

Cognitive Resources
Attention and Memory
Executive Functioning

The Psychometric/Intelligence View

Learning Goal 4 Summarize the psychometric/intelligence view of adolescence.

Intelligence Tests
Multiple Intelligences
Heredity and Environment

Social Cognition

Learning Goal 5 Explain how social cognition is involved in adolescent development.

Adolescent Egocentrism
Social Cognition in the Rest of the Text

One of my most vivid memories of my oldest daughter, Tracy, is from when she was 12 years of age. I had accompanied her and her younger sister, Jennifer (10 at the time), to a tennis tournament. As we walked into a restaurant to have lunch, Tracy bolted for the restroom. Jennifer and I looked at each other, wondering what was wrong. Five minutes later Tracy emerged, looking calmer. I asked what had happened. Her response: "This one hair was out of place and every person in here was looking at me!"

Consider another adolescent—Margaret. During a conversation with her girlfriend, 16-year-old Margaret says, "Did you hear about Catherine? She's pregnant. Do you think I would ever let that happen to me? Never."

Also think about 13-year-old Adam as he describes himself: "No one understands me, especially my parents. They have no idea of what I am feeling. They have never experienced the pain I'm going through."

Comments like Tracy's, Margaret's, and Adam's reflect the emergence of egocentric thought during adolescence. When we think about thinking, we usually consider it in terms of school subjects like math and English, or of solutions to intellectual problems. But people's thoughts about social circumstances also are important. Later in the chapter we will further explore adolescents' social thoughts.

preview

When we think about adolescence, we often focus on the biological changes of puberty or socioemotional changes, such as the motivation for independence, relations with parents and peers, and problems such as drug abuse and delinquency. Further, when developmentalists have studied cognitive processes, their main focus has been on infants and young children, not on adolescents. We will see in this chapter, however, that adolescents also display some impressive cognitive changes and that increasingly researchers are finding that these changes are linked to the development of the brain. Indeed, to begin this chapter, we will explore the explosion of interest in the changing adolescent brain and then study three different views of cognitive development: cognitive developmental, information processing, and psychometric. At the chapter's close we will examine social cognition, including the emergence of adolescent egocentrism.

1 The Brain

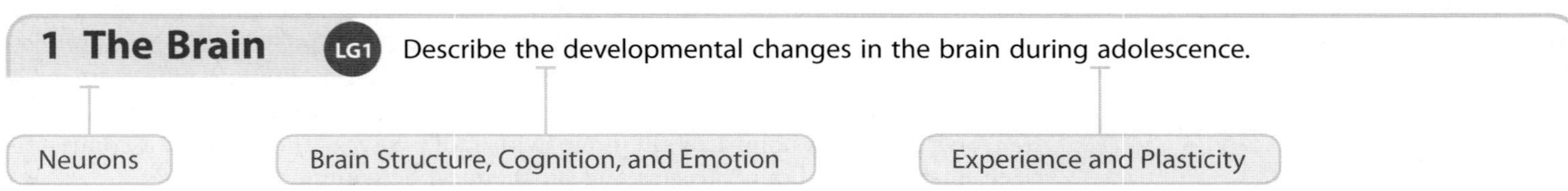

Until recently, little research had been conducted on developmental changes in the brain during adolescence. Although research in this area is still in its infancy, an increasing number of studies are under way (Burnett & others, 2011; Forbes & Dahl, 2010). Scientists now note that the adolescent's brain is different from the child's brain, and that in adolescence the brain is still developing (Casey, Jones, & Somerville, 2011; Luciana, 2010; Nelson, 2011).

> The thoughts of youth are long, long thoughts.
>
> —Henry Wadsworth Longfellow, *American Poet, 19th Century*

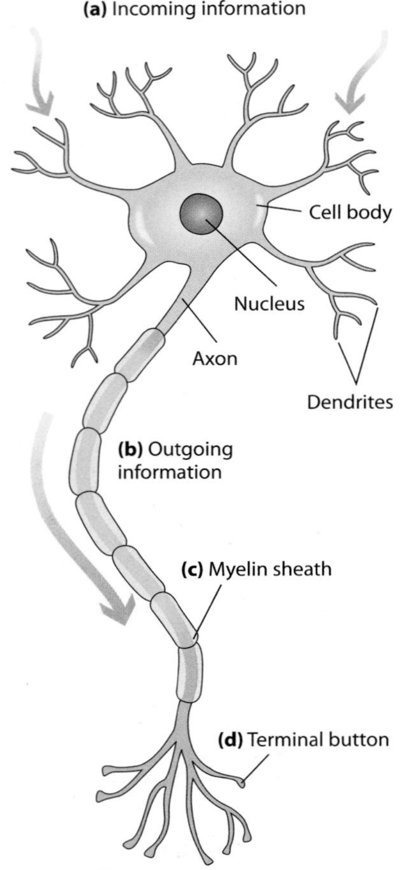

FIGURE **3.1**

THE NEURON. (a) The dendrites of the cell body receive information from other neurons, muscles, or glands. (b) An axon transmits information away from the cell body. (c) A myelin sheath covers most axons and speeds information transmission. (d) As the axon ends, it branches out into terminal buttons.

NEURONS

Neurons, or nerve cells, are the nervous system's basic units. A neuron has three basic parts: the cell body, dendrites, and axon (see Figure 3.1). The *dendrite* is the receiving part of the neuron, and the *axon* carries information away from the cell body to other cells. Through a process called **myelination,** the axon portion of a neuron becomes covered and insulated with a layer of fat cells (called the myelin sheath), increasing the speed and efficiency of information processing in the nervous system. Myelination continues to increase through adolescence and emerging adulthood (Casey, Jones, & Somerville, 2011).

In the language of neuroscience, the term *white matter* is used to describe the whitish color of myelinated axons, and the term *gray matter* refers primarily to dendrites and the cell body of the neuron (see Figure 3.2). A significant developmental change in adolescence is the increase in white matter and the decrease in gray matter in the prefrontal cortex (Gogtay & Thompson, 2010). Most accounts emphasize that the increase in white matter across adolescence is due to increased myelination, although a recent analysis proposed that the white matter increase also might be due to an increase in the diameter of axons (Paus, 2010).

In addition to the encasement of axons through myelination, another important aspect of the brain's development is the dramatic increase in connections between neurons, a process that is called *synaptogenesis* (Gogtay & Thompson, 2010). **Synapses** are gaps between neurons, where connections between the axon and dendrites take place. Synaptogenesis begins in infancy and continues through adolescence.

Researchers have discovered that nearly twice as many synaptic connections are made than will ever be used (Huttenlocher & Dabholkar, 1997). The connections that are used are strengthened and survive, while the unused ones are replaced by other pathways or disappear. That is, in the language of neuroscience, these connections will be "pruned." What results from this pruning is that by the end of adolescence individuals have "fewer, more selective, more effective neuronal connections than they did as children" (Kuhn, 2009, p. 153). And this pruning indicates that the activities adolescents choose to engage in and not to engage in influence which neural connections will be strengthened and which will disappear.

With the onset of puberty, the levels of *neurotransmitters*—chemicals that carry information across the synaptic gap between one neuron and the next—change. For example, an increase in the neurotransmitter dopamine occurs in both the prefrontal cortex and the limbic system during adolescence (Ernst & Spear, 2009). Increases in dopamine have been linked to increased risk taking and the use of addictive drugs (Stansfield & Kirstein, 2006; Wahlstrom & others, 2010). Researchers have found that dopamine plays an important role in reward seeking (Doremus-Fitzwater, Varlinskaya, & Spear, 2010; Ernst & Spear, 2009).

BRAIN STRUCTURE, COGNITION, AND EMOTION

Neurons do not simply float in the brain. Connected in precise ways, they form the various structures in the brain. Using functional magnetic resonance imaging (fMRI) to scan the brain, scientists have recently discovered that adolescents' brains undergo significant structural changes (Blakemore & others, 2011; Luna, Padmanabhan, & O'Hearn, 2010; Smith & others, 2011). An fMRI creates a magnetic field around a person's body and bombards the brain with radio waves. The result is a computerized image of the brain's tissues and biochemical activities.

Among the most important structural changes in the brain during adolescence are those involving the corpus callosum, the prefrontal cortex, and the amygdala. The **corpus callosum,** a large bundle of axon fibers that connects the brain's left and right hemispheres, thickens in adolescence, and this thickening improves adolescents' ability to process information (Giedd, 2008). Advances in the development of the **prefrontal cortex**—the highest level of the frontal lobes that is involved in reasoning, decision making, and self-control—continue through the emerging adult years,

neurons Nerve cells, which are the nervous system's basic units.

myelination The process by which the axon portion of the neuron becomes covered and insulated with a layer of fat cells, which increases the speed and efficiency of information processing in the nervous system.

synapses Gaps between neurons, where connections between the axon and dendrites occur.

corpus callosum A large bundle of axon fibers that connect the brain's left and right hemispheres.

prefrontal cortex The highest level of the brain's frontal lobes that is involved in reasoning, decision making, and self-control.

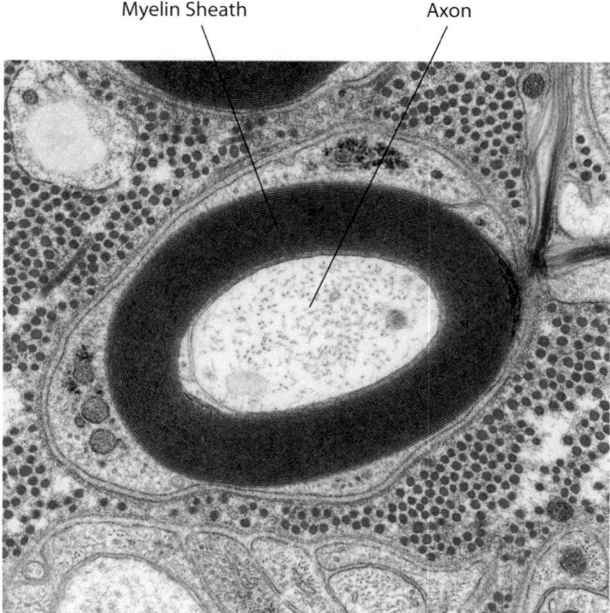

FIGURE **3.2**

A MYELINATED NERVE FIBER. The myelin sheath, shown in brown, encases the axon (white). This image was produced by an electron microscope that magnified the nerve fiber 12,000 times. *What role does myelination play in the brain's development?*

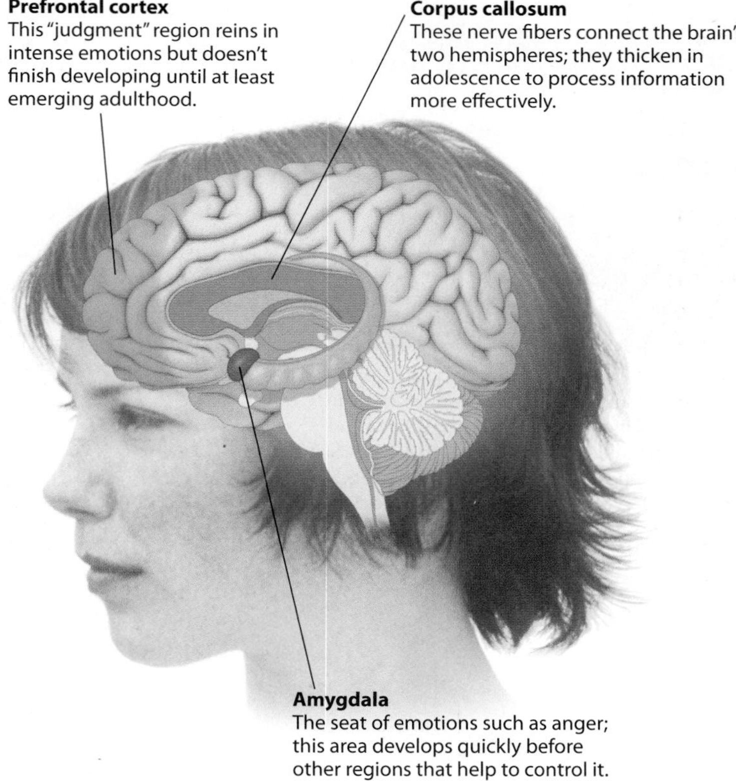

FIGURE **3.3**

THE PREFRONTAL CORTEX, AMYGDALA, AND CORPUS CALLOSUM

approximately 18 to 25 years of age, or later (Gogtay & Thompson, 2010; Luciana, 2010). However, the **amygdala**—a part of the brain's limbic system that is the seat of emotions such as anger—matures much earlier than the prefrontal cortex (Casey, Duhoux, & Malter Cohen, 2010; Casey, Jones, & Somerville, 2011). Figure 3.3 shows the locations of the corpus callosum, prefrontal cortex, and amygdala.

Leading researcher Charles Nelson (2003) points out that although adolescents are capable of very strong emotions, their prefrontal cortex hasn't adequately developed to the point at which they can control these passions. It is as if the prefrontal cortex doesn't yet have the brakes to slow down the amygdala's emotional intensity. Or consider this interpretation of the development of emotion and cognition in adolescents: "early activation of strong 'turbo-charged' feelings with a relatively unskilled set of 'driving skills' or cognitive abilities to modulate strong emotions and motivations" (Dahl, 2004, p. 18).

developmental **connection**

Brain Development. Developmental social neuroscience is a recently developed field that focuses on connections between development, socioemotional factors, and neuroscience. Chapter 1, p. 15

Recall from the earlier discussion of neurotransmitters, that dopamine production increases in early adolescence, which produces increased reward seeking and risk taking. In recent research conducted by Laurence Steinberg and his colleagues (Albert & Steinberg, 2011a,b; Cauffman & others, 2010; O'Brien & others, 2010; Steinberg, 2010, 2011; Steinberg & others, 2008, 2009), preference for immediate rewards (assessed in such contexts as a gambling task and a video driving game) increased from 14 to 16 years of age and then declined. Also, in Steinberg's (2010, 2011) research, adolescents' belief that the benefits of risk taking override its potential negative outcomes peaks at about 14 to 16 years of age. By contrast, in research conducted by Steinberg and his colleagues (2008, 2009), impulse control increased in a linear fashion from preadolescence to emerging adulthood.

The increase in risk taking in adolescence is usually thought to result in negative outcomes. However, there are some aspects of risk taking that benefit

amygdala A portion of the brain's limbic system that is the seat of emotions such as anger.

Lee Malvo was 17 years old when he and John Muhammad, an adult, went on a sniper spree in 2002, terrorizing the Washington, D.C., area and killing 10 people. A 2005 U.S. Supreme Court ruling stated that individuals who are 18 years of age and under, like Malvo, cannot be given the death penalty. *Are there implications regarding what scientists are learning about the adolescent's brain for legal decisions, such as the death penalty?*

adolescents. Being open to new experiences and challenges, even risky ones, can help adolescents to stretch themselves to learn about aspects of the world they would not have encountered if they had shied away from such exploration (Allen & Allen, 2009). Later in the chapter, we will revisit the issue of risk taking in the context of adolescents' sense of invulnerability and recent research that distinguishes between different types of vulnerability (Lapsley & Hill, 2010; Lapsley & Stey, 2012).

Of course, a major issue is which comes first—biological changes in the brain or experiences that stimulate these changes (Lerner, Boyd, & Du, 2008). Consider a study in which the prefrontal cortex thickened and more brain connections formed when adolescents resisted peer pressure (Paus & others, 2007). Scientists have yet to determine whether the brain changes come first or whether the brain changes are the result of experiences with peers, parents, and others. Once again, we encounter the nature-nurture issue that is so prominent in examining development through the life span.

According to leading expert Jay Giedd (2007, pp. 1–2D), "Biology doesn't make teens rebellious or have purple hair or take drugs. It does not mean you are going to do drugs, but it gives you more of a chance to do that."

Are there implications of what we now know about changes in the adolescent's brain for the legal system? For example, can the recent brain research we have just discussed be used to argue that because the adolescent's brain, especially the higher-level prefrontal cortex, is still developing, adolescents are less mature than adults and therefore should not be given a death penalty? Leading expert Elizabeth Sowell (2004) says that scientists can't just do brain scans on adolescents and decide if they should be tried as adults. In 2005, the death penalty for adolescents (under the age of 18) was prohibited by the U.S. Supreme Court, but it still continues to be debated (Ash, 2006).

EXPERIENCE AND PLASTICITY

Scientists are especially interested in the extent to which environmental experiences influence the brain's development. They also want to know how much plasticity the brain retains as individuals progress through their childhood, adolescent, and adult years (Diamond, Casey, & Munakata, 2011). A recent analysis indicated that early adolescence is a time of considerable plasticity in the brain (Gogtay & Thompson, 2010). Let's examine three questions involving the roles of experience and plasticity in the development of the brain in adolescence:

- *Can new brain cells be generated in adolescence?* Until close to the end of the twentieth century, scientists argued that the brain generated no new cells (neurons) after the early childhood years. However, researchers have recently discovered that people can generate new brain cells throughout their lives (Marlatt, Lucassen & van Pragg, 2010). Currently, researchers have documented neurogenesis in only two brain regions, the hippocampus, which is involved in memory, and the olfactory bulb, which functions in smell (Arenkiel, 2011; Glasper, Schoenfeld, & Gould, 2011). It also is not known what functions these new brain cells perform, and at this point researchers have documented that they last for only several weeks. Researchers currently are studying factors that might inhibit and promote neurogenesis, including various drugs, stress, exercise, and cognitive fitness (Dranovsky & Leonardo, 2011; Shors & others, 2011; Wolf, Melnik, & Kempermann, 2011). And they are exploring how the grafting of neural stem cells to various regions of the brain, such as the hippocampus, might increase neurogenesis (Szulwach & others, 2010).
- *Can the adolescent's brain recover from injury?* In childhood and adolescence, the brain has a remarkable ability to repair itself (Nelson, 2011). In Chapter 1, you read about Michael Rehbein, whose left hemisphere was removed

because of brain seizures. The plasticity of the human brain was apparent as his right hemisphere reorganized itself to take over functions, such as speech, that normally take place in the left hemisphere. Although the brain retains considerable plasticity in adolescence, the earlier a brain injury occurs, the higher the likelihood of a successful recovery (Yen & Wong, 2007). *What do we know about applying information about brain development to adolescents' education?* Unfortunately, too often statements about the implications of brain science for secondary education are speculative and far removed from what neuroscientists know about the brain (Blakemore, 2010; Fischer & Immordino-Yang, 2008). We don't have to look any further than the hype about "left-brained" individuals being more logical and "right-brained" individuals being more creative to see that links between neuroscience and brain education are incorrectly made (Sousa, 1995).

Another commonly promoted link between neuroscience and brain education is that most of the key changes in the brain occur prior to adolescence (Fischer & Immordino-Yang, 2008). However, the recent research on the plasticity of the adolescent's brain and the continuing development of the prefrontal cortex through adolescence support the view that education can considerably benefit adolescents (Blakemore, 2010; Casey, Jones, & Somerville, 2011).

Review *Connect* Reflect

Describe the developmental changes in the brain during adolescence.

Review

- What are neurons? How do the brain's neurons change in adolescence?
- What changes involving brain structure, cognition, and emotion occur in adolescence?
- How much plasticity does the brain have in adolescence?

Connect

- Relate the structural changes in the brain that occur during adolescence to the psychological dimensions of puberty discussed in Chapter 2.

Reflect *Your Own Personal Journey of Life*

- Evaluate your lifestyle in terms of such factors as your exercise, eating habits, whether you get adequate sleep, and how much you challenge yourself to learn and achieve. Considering what you have learned about the brain's plasticity, what implications are there for your lifestyle's influence on the development of your brain in adolescence and emerging adulthood?

2 The Cognitive Developmental View

Discuss the cognitive developmental view of adolescence.

Piaget's Theory

Vygotsky's Theory

The development of the brain that we have just discussed provides a biological foundation for the cognitive changes that characterize adolescence. Reflect for a moment about your thinking skills as a young adolescent. Were your thinking skills as good as they are now? Could you solve difficult abstract problems and reason logically about complex topics? Or did those skills improve in your high school years? Can you describe any ways in which your thinking skills are better now than they were in high school?

Jean Piaget, the main architect of the field of cognitive development, at age 27.

In Chapter 1, we briefly examined Jean Piaget's theory of cognitive development. Piaget was intrigued by the changes in thinking that take place through childhood and adolescence. In this section, we further explore his ideas about adolescent cognition, as well as the increasingly popular sociocultural cognitive theory of Lev Vygotsky.

PIAGET'S THEORY

We begin our coverage of Piaget's theory by describing the main processes he stressed as responsible for cognitive changes in development. Then we turn to his cognitive stages, giving special attention to concrete operational and formal operational thought.

Cognitive Processes Piaget's theory is the best-known, most widely discussed theory of adolescent cognitive development. According to his theory, adolescents are motivated to understand their world because doing so is biologically adaptive. Adolescents actively construct their own cognitive worlds; information doesn't just pour into their minds from the environment. To make sense of the world, adolescents organize their experiences, separating important ideas from less important ones and connecting one idea to another. They also adapt their thinking to include new ideas because the additional information furthers their understanding.

In actively constructing their world, adolescents use schemas. A **schema** is a mental concept or framework that is useful in organizing and interpreting information. Piaget was especially interested in how children and adolescents use schemas to organize and make sense out of their current experiences.

Piaget (1952) found that children and adolescents use and adapt their schemas through two processes: assimilation and accommodation. **Assimilation** is the incorporation of new information into existing knowledge. In assimilation, the schema does not change. **Accommodation** is the adjustment of a schema to new information. In accommodation, the schema changes.

Suppose, for example, that a 13-year-old girl wants to learn how to use a new smartphone her parents have given her for her birthday. Although she has never had the opportunity to use one, from her experience and observation she realizes that she needs to press a button to turn on the phone. This behavior fit into an existing conceptual framework (assimilation). Once the phone is activated, she presses an icon on the screen but it doesn't get her to the screen she wants. She also wants to add an application but can't figure out how to do that. Soon she realizes that she needs help in learning how to use the smartphone—either by studying the instructions further or getting help from a friend who has experience using this type of phone. This adjustment in her approach shows her awareness of the need to alter her conceptual framework (accommodation).

Equilibration, another process Piaget identified, is a shift in thought from one state to another. At times adolescents experience cognitive conflict or a sense of disequilibrium in their attempt to understand the world. Eventually they resolve the conflict and reach a balance, or equilibrium, of thought. Piaget maintained that individuals move back and forth between states of cognitive equilibrium and disequilibrium. Consider Margaret's comment at the beginning of the chapter that she will never get pregnant. Eventually, Margaret will resolve these conflicts as her thought becomes more advanced. In the everyday world, adolescents constantly face such cognitive inconsistencies.

schema A mental concept or framework that is useful in organizing and interpreting information.

assimilation The incorporation of new information into existing knowledge.

accommodation An adjustment of a schema to new information.

equilibration A mechanism in Piaget's theory that explains how individuals shift from one state of thought to the next. The shift occurs as individuals experience cognitive conflict or a disequilibrium in trying to understand the world. Eventually, the individual resolves the conflict and reaches a balance, or equilibrium, of thought.

Stages of Cognitive Development Piaget theorized that individuals develop through four cognitive stages: sensorimotor, preoperational, concrete operational, and formal operational (see Figure 3.4). Each of these age-related stages consists of distinct ways of thinking. This *different* way of understanding the world is what makes one stage more advanced than another; simply knowing more information does not make an adolescent's thinking more advanced. Thus, in Piaget's theory, a person's cognition is *qualitatively* different in one stage compared with another.

Sensorimotor Stage

Infants gain knowledge of the world from the physical actions they perform on it. Infants coordinate sensory experiences with these physical actions. An infant progresses from reflexive, instinctual action at birth to the beginning of symbolic thought toward the end of the stage.

Preoperational Stage

The child begins to use mental representations to understand the world. Symbolic thinking, reflected in the use of words and images, is used in this mental representation, which goes beyond the connection of sensory information with physical action. However, there are some constraints on the child's thinking at this stage, such as egocentrism and centration.

2 to 7 Years of Age

Concrete Operational Stage

The child can now reason logically about concrete events, understands the concept of conservation, organizes objects into hierarchical classes (classification), and places objects in ordered series (seriation).

7 to 11 Years of Age

Formal Operational Stage

The adolescent reasons in more abstract, idealistic, and logical (hypothetical-deductive) ways.

11 Years of Age Through Adulthood

FIGURE **3.4**
PIAGET'S FOUR STAGES OF COGNITIVE DEVELOPMENT

Sensorimotor and Preoperational Thought The **sensorimotor stage,** which lasts from birth to about 2 years of age, is the first Piagetian stage. In this stage, infants construct an understanding of the world by coordinating sensory experiences (such as seeing and hearing) with physical, motoric actions—hence the term sensorimotor.

The **preoperational stage,** which lasts approximately from 2 to 7 years of age, is the second Piagetian stage. In this stage, children begin to represent the world with words, images, and drawings. Symbolic thought goes beyond simple connections of information and action.

We are born capable of learning.

—Jean-Jacques Rousseau
Swiss-Born French Philosopher, 18th Century

Concrete Operational Thought The **concrete operational stage,** which lasts approximately from 7 to 11 years of age, is the third Piagetian stage. Logical reasoning replaces intuitive thought as long as the reasoning can be applied to specific or concrete examples. According to Piaget, concrete operational thought involves *operations*—mental actions that allow individuals to do mentally what earlier they did physically.

Piaget used the term *conservation* to refer to an individual's ability to recognize that the length, number, mass, quantity, area, weight, and volume of objects and substances does not change through transformations that alter their appearance. Concrete operational thinkers have conservation skills; preoperational thinkers don't.

Another characteristic of concrete operational thought is *classification,* or class inclusion reasoning. Children who engage in classification can systematically organize objects into hierarchies of classes and subclasses.

Although concrete operational thought is more advanced than preoperational thought, it has its limitations. Logical reasoning replaces intuitive thought as long as the principles can be applied to specific, *concrete* examples. For example, the concrete operational child cannot imagine the steps necessary to complete an algebraic equation, an abstract statement with no connection to the concrete world.

sensorimotor stage Piaget's first stage of development, lasting from birth to about 2 years of age. In this stage, infants construct an understanding of the world by coordinating sensory experiences with physical, motoric actions.

preoperational stage Piaget's second stage, which lasts approximately from 2 to 7 years of age. In this stage, children begin to represent their world with words, images, and drawings.

concrete operational stage Piaget's third stage, which lasts approximately from 7 to 11 years of age. In this stage, children can perform operations. Logical reasoning replaces intuitive thought as long as the reasoning can be applied to specific or concrete examples.

"Ben is in his first year of high school, and he's questioning all the right things." © Edward Koren/The New Yorker Collection/ www.cartoonbank.com.

Formal Operational Thought The **formal operational stage** is Piaget's fourth and final stage of cognitive development. Piaget argued that this stage emerges at 11 to 15 years of age. Adolescents' developing power of thought opens up new cognitive and social horizons. What are the characteristics of formal operational thought? Most significantly, formal operational thought is more abstract than concrete operational thought. Adolescents are no longer limited to actual, concrete experiences as anchors for thought. They can conjure up make-believe situations—events that are purely hypothetical possibilities or strictly abstract propositions—and try to reason logically about them.

The abstract quality of the adolescent's thought at the formal operational level is evident in the adolescent's verbal problem-solving ability. Whereas the concrete operational thinker would need to see the concrete elements A, B, and C to be able to make the logical inference that if A = B and B = C, then A = C, the formal operational thinker can solve this problem merely through verbal representation.

Another indication of the abstract quality of adolescents' thought is their increased tendency to think about thought itself. As one adolescent commented, "I began thinking about why I was thinking what I was. Then I began thinking about why I was thinking about why I was thinking about what I was." If this statement sounds abstract, it is, and it characterizes the adolescent's enhanced focus on thought and its abstract qualities. Later in this chapter, we return to the topic of thinking about thinking, which is called *metacognition*.

Might adolescents' ability to reason hypothetically and to evaluate what is ideal versus what is real lead them to engage in demonstrations, such as this protest related to better ethnic relations? What other causes might be attractive to adolescents' new found cognitive abilities of hypothetical-deductive reasoning and idealistic thinking?

Besides being abstract, formal operational thought is full of idealism and possibilities. Whereas children frequently think in concrete ways about what is real and limited, adolescents begin to engage in extended speculation about ideal characteristics—qualities they desire in themselves and others. Such thoughts often lead adolescents to compare themselves and others in regard to such ideal standards. And, during adolescence, the thoughts of individuals are often fantasy flights into future possibilities. It is not unusual for the adolescent to become impatient with these newfound ideal standards and perplexed over which of many ideals to adopt. At the same time that adolescents think more abstractly and idealistically, they also think more logically. Adolescents begin to reason more as a scientist does, devising ways to solve problems and test solutions systematically. Piaget gave this type of problem solving an imposing name, **hypothetical-deductive reasoning**—that is, the ability to develop hypotheses, or best guesses, about how to solve problems, such as algebraic equations. Having developed a hypothesis, the formal operational thinker then systematically deduces, or concludes, the best path to follow in solving the problem. In contrast, children are more likely to solve problems by trial and error.

Piaget maintained that formal operational thought is the best description of how adolescents think. Formal operational thought is not a homogeneous stage of development, however. Not all adolescents are full-fledged formal operational thinkers. Instead, some developmentalists argue that formal operational thought consists of two subperiods (Broughton, 1983):

- *Early formal operational thought.* Adolescents' newfound ability to think in hypothetical ways produces unconstrained thoughts with unlimited possibilities. In this early period, flights of fantasy may submerge reality and the world is perceived too subjectively and idealistically. Assimilation is the dominant process in this subperiod.
- *Late formal operational thought.* As adolescents test their reasoning against experience, intellectual balance is restored. Through accommodation, adolescents begin to adjust to the upheaval they have experienced. Late formal thought may appear in the middle adolescent years.

In this two-subperiod view, assimilation characterizes early formal operational thought; accommodation characterizes late formal operational thought (Lapsley, 1990).

formal operational stage Piaget's fourth and final stage of cognitive development, which he argued emerges at 11 to 15 year of age. It is characterized by abstract, idealistic, and logical thought.

hypothetical-deductive reasoning Piaget's term for adolescents' ability, in the formal operational stage, to develop hypotheses, or best guesses, about ways to solve problems; they then systematically deduce, or conclude, the best path to follow in solving the problem.

In his early writings, Piaget (1952) indicated that both the onset and consolidation of formal operational thought are completed during early adolescence, from about 11 to 15 years of age. Later, Piaget (1972) revised his view and concluded that formal operational thought is not completely achieved until later in adolescence, between approximately 15 and 20 years of age.

Still, his theory does not adequately account for the individual differences that characterize the cognitive development of adolescents, which have been documented in a number of investigations (Kuhn, 2009). Some young adolescents are formal operational thinkers; others are not. For instance, a review of investigations about formal operational thought revealed that only about one of every three eighth-grade students is a formal operational thinker (Strahan, 1983). Some investigators have found that formal operational thought increased with age in adolescence; others have not found this result. In fact, many college students and adults do not think in formal operational ways, either. Investigators have revealed that from 17 to 67 percent of college students think on the formal operational level (Elkind, 1961; Tomlinson-Keasey, 1972).

At the same time that many young adolescents are just beginning to think in a formal operational manner, others are at the point of consolidating their concrete operational thought, using it more consistently than they did in childhood. By late adolescence, many youth are beginning to consolidate their formal operational thought, using it more consistently. And there often is variation across the content areas of formal operational thought, just as there is in concrete operational thought in childhood. A 14-year-old adolescent might reason at the formal operational level when analyzing algebraic equations but not when solving verbal problems or when reasoning about interpersonal relations.

Evaluating Piaget's Theory What were Piaget's main contributions? Has his theory withstood the test of time? In this section, we examine both Piaget's contributions and the criticisms of his work.

Contributions Piaget has been a giant in the field of developmental psychology. We owe to him the present field of cognitive development as well as a long list of masterful concepts of enduring power and fascination: assimilation, accommodation, conservation, and hypothetical-deductive reasoning, among others. We also owe to Piaget the current vision of children as active, constructive thinkers (Miller, 2011).

Piaget was a genius when it came to observing children. His careful observations documented inventive new ways to discover how children act on and adapt to their world. Piaget showed us some important things to look for in cognitive development, such as the shift from preoperational to concrete operational thinking. He also pointed out that children need to make their experiences fit their schemas, or cognitive frameworks, yet they can simultaneously adapt their schemas to experience. He also revealed that cognitive change is likely to occur if the context is structured to allow gradual movement to the next higher level. We owe to Piaget the current belief that a concept does not emerge all of a sudden, full blown, but develops instead through a series of partial accomplishments that lead to an increasingly comprehensive understanding.

Criticisms Piaget's theory has not gone unchallenged (Miller, 2011). Questions are raised about the timing and nature of his stage view of cognitive development, whether he failed to adequately study in detail key cognitive processes, and the effects of culture on cognitive development. Let's consider each of these criticisms in turn.

In terms of timing and stages, some cognitive abilities have been found to emerge earlier than Piaget had thought (Miller, 2011). For example, conservation of number (which Piaget said emerged at approximately 7 years of age in the concrete operational stage) has been demonstrated as early as age 3 (which instead is early in his preoperational stage). Other cognitive abilities often emerge later than

An outstanding teacher and education in the logic of science and mathematics are important cultural experiences that promote the development of operational thought. *Might Piaget have underestimated the roles of culture and schooling in children's cognitive development?*

Piaget indicated. Many adolescents still think in concrete operational ways or are just beginning to master formal operations. Even as adults, many individuals are not formal operational thinkers. The evidence does not support Piaget's view that prior to age 11 children don't engage in abstract thinking and that from 11 years on they do (Kuhn, 2009). Thus, adolescents' cognitive development is not as stage-like as Piaget thought.

One group of cognitive developmentalists, the **neo-Piagetians,** conclude that Piaget's theory does not adequately focus on attention, memory, and cognitive strategies that adolescents use to process information, and that Piaget's explanations of cognitive changes are too general. They especially maintain that a more accurate vision of children's and adolescents' thinking requires more knowledge of the strategies they use, how fast and automatically they process information, the particular cognitive tasks involved in processing information, and the division of cognitive problems into smaller, more precise steps.

The leading proponent of the neo-Piagetian view has been Canadian developmental psychologist Robbie Case (1992, 2000). Case accepts Piaget's four stages of cognitive development but emphasizes that a more precise description of changes within each stage is needed. He notes that children's and adolescents' growing ability to process information efficiently is linked to their brain growth and memory development. In particular, Case cites the increasing ability to hold information in working memory (a workbench for memory similar to short-term memory) and to manipulate it more effectively as critical to understanding cognitive development.

Finally, culture exerts stronger influence on development than Piaget envisioned. For example, the age at which individuals acquire conservation skills is associated to some extent with the degree to which their culture provides relevant educational practice (Cole, 2006). In many developing countries, educational opportunities are limited and formal operational thought is rare. You will read shortly about Lev Vygotsky's theory of cognitive development, in which culture is given a more prominent role than in Piaget's theory.

Cognitive Changes in Adulthood As we discussed earlier, according to Piaget adults and adolescents use the same type of reasoning. Adolescents and adults think in *qualitatively* the same way. Piaget did acknowledge that adults can be *quantitatively* more advanced in their knowledge. What are some ways that adults might be more advanced in their thinking than adolescents?

Realistic and Pragmatic Thinking Some developmentalists have proposed that as young adults move into the world of work, their way of thinking does change. One idea is that as they face the constraints of reality, which work promotes, their idealism decreases (Labouvie-Vief, 1986).

Reflective and Relativistic Thinking William Perry (1970, 1999) also described changes in cognition that take place in early adulthood. He said that adolescents often view the world in terms of polarities—right/wrong, we/they, or good/bad. As youth age into adulthood, they gradually move away from this type of absolutist thinking as they become aware of the diverse opinions and multiple perspectives of others. Thus, in Perry's view, the absolutist, dualistic thinking of adolescence gives way to the reflective, relativistic thinking of adulthood.

Expanding on Perry's view, Gisela Labouvie-Vief (2006) recently proposed that the increasing complexity of cultures in the past century has generated a greater need for more reflective, complex thinking that takes into account the changing nature of

neo-Piagetians Theorists who argue that Piaget got some things right but that his theory needs considerable revision. In their revision, they give more emphasis to information processing that involves attention, memory, and strategies; they also seek to provide more precise explanations of cognitive changes.

knowledge and challenges. She also emphasizes that the key aspects of cognitive development in emerging adulthood include deciding on a specific worldview, recognizing that the worldview is subjective, and understanding that diverse worldviews should be acknowledged. In her perspective, considerable individual variation characterizes the thinking of emerging adults with the highest level of thinking attained by only some. She argues that the level of education emerging adults achieve especially influences how likely they will maximize their cognitive potential.

Cognition and Emotion Labouvie-Vief and her colleagues (Labouvie-Vief, 2009; Labouvie-Vief, Gruhn, & Studer, 2010) also argue that to understand cognitive changes in adulthood it is necessary to consider how emotional maturity might affect cognitive development. They conclude that although emerging and young adults become more aware that emotions influence their thinking, at this point thinking is often swayed too strongly by negative emotions that can produce distorted and self-serving thinking. In this research, a subset of emerging adults who are high in empathy, flexibility, and autonomy are more likely to engage in complex, integrated cognitive-emotional thinking. Labouvie-Vief and her colleagues have found that the ability to think in this cognitively and emotionally balanced, advanced manner increases in middle adulthood. Further, they emphasize that in middle age, individuals become more inwardly reflective and less context-dependent in their thinking than they were as young adults. In the work of Labouvie-Vief and her colleagues, we see the effort to discover connections between cognitive and socioemotional development, which was described as an increasing trend in the field of life-span development in Chapter 1.

developmental **connection**

Health. Emotional fluctuations in early adolescence may be linked to hormone levels. As adolescents move into adulthood, their emotions become less extreme. Chapter 2, p. 60, Chapter 4, p. 151

Is There a Fifth, Postformal Stage? Some theorists have pieced together these descriptions of adult thinking and have proposed that young adults move into a new qualitative stage of cognitive development, postformal thought (Sinnott, 2003). **Postformal thought** is:

- *Reflective, relativistic, and contextual.* As young adults engage in solving problems, they might think deeply about many aspects of work, politics, relationships, and other areas of life (Labouvie-Vief, 1986). They find that what might be the best solution to a problem at work (with a boss or co-worker) might not be the best solution at home (with a romantic partner). Thus, postformal thought holds that the correct answer to a problem requires reflective thinking and may vary from one situation to another. Some psychologists argue that reflective thinking continues to increase and becomes more internal and less contextual in middle age (Labouvie-Vief, Gruhn, & Studer, 2010; Mascalo & Fischer, 2010).
- *Provisional.* Many young adults also become more skeptical about the truth and seem unwilling to accept an answer as final. Thus, they come to see the search for truth as an ongoing and perhaps never-ending process.
- *Realistic.* Young adults understand that thinking can't always be abstract. In many instances, it must be realistic and pragmatic.
- *Recognized as being influenced by emotion.* Emerging and young adults are more likely than adolescents to understand that their thinking is influenced by emotions. However, too often negative emotions produce thinking that is distorted and self-serving at this point in development.

What are some characteristics that have been proposed for a fifth stage of cognitive development called postformal thought?

One effort to assess postformal thinking is the 10-item Complex Postformal Thought Questionnaire (Sinnott & Johnson, 1997). Figure 3.5 presents the questionnaire and gives you an opportunity to evaluate your thinking at the postformal level. A recent study found that the questionnaire items reflect three main categories of postformal thinking: (1) Taking into account multiple aspects of a problem or situation,

postformal thought Thought that is reflective, relativistic, and contextual; provisional; realistic; and open to emotions and subjective.

Respond to each of the items below in terms of how well they characterize your thinking from 1 = Not True (of Self) to 7 = Very True (of Self).	Not True 1	2	3	4	5	6	Very True 7
1. I see the paradoxes in life.							
2. I see more than one method that can be used to reach a goal.							
3. I am aware that I can decide which reality to experience at a particular time; but I know that reality is really multi-level and more complicated.							
4. There are many "right" ways to define any life experience; I must make a final decision on how I define the problems of life.							
5. I am aware that sometimes "succeeding" in the everyday world means finding a concrete answer to one of life's problems; but sometimes it means finding a correct path that would carry me through any problems of this type.							
6. Almost all problems can be solved by logic, but this may require different types of "logics."							
7. I tend to see several causes connected with any event.							
8. I see that a given dilemma always has several good solutions.							
9. I realize that I often have several goals in mind, or that life seems to have several goals in mind for me. So I go toward more than one in following my path in life.							
10. I can see the hidden logic in others' solutions to the problem of life, even if I don't agree with their solutions and follow my own path.							

FIGURE **3.5**

COMPLEX POSTFORMAL THOUGHT QUESTIONNAIRE. After you have responded to the items, total your score, which can range from 10 to 70. The higher your score, the more likely you are to engage in postformal thinking.

(2) Making a subjective choice in a particular problem situation , and (3) Perceiving underlying complexities in a situation (Cartwright & others, 2009).

One study using the Complex Postformal Thought Questionnaire revealed that college students who had more cross-category friends (based on categories of gender, age, ethnicity, socioeconomic status, and sexual orientation) scored higher on the postformal thought measure than did their counterparts who had fewer cross-category friends (Galupo, Cartwright, & Savage, 2010).

Cross-category friendships likely stimulate individuals to move beyond either/or thinking, critically evaluate stereotypical thinking, and consider alternative explanations.

How strong is the evidence for a fifth, postformal stage of cognitive development? Researchers have found that young adults are more likely to engage in postformal thinking than adolescents are (Commons & Richards, 2003). But critics argue that research has yet to document that postformal thought is a qualitatively more advanced stage than formal operational thought.

Wisdom Paul Baltes and his colleagues (2006) define **wisdom** as expert knowledge about the practical aspects of life that permits excellent judgment about important matters. This practical knowledge involves exceptional insight about human development and life matters, good judgment, and an understanding of how to cope with difficult life problems. Thus, wisdom, more than standard conceptions of intelligence, focuses on life's pragmatic concerns and human conditions (Sternberg, in press).

In regard to wisdom, research by Baltes and his colleagues (Baltes & Kunzmann, 2007; Baltes, Lindenberger, & Staudinger, 2006; Baltes & Smith, 2008) has found that:

wisdom Expert knowledge about the practical aspects of life that permits excellent judgment about important matters.

- *High levels of wisdom are rare.* Few people, including older adults, attain a high level of wisdom. That only a small percentage of adults show wisdom supports the contention that it requires experience, practice, or complex skills.

- *The time frame of late adolescence and early adulthood is the main age window for wisdom to emerge.* No further advances in wisdom have been found for middle-aged and older adults beyond the level they attained as young adults, but this may have been because the problems studied were not sufficiently relevant to older adults' lives.
- *Factors other than age are critical for wisdom to develop to a high level.* For example, certain life experiences, such as being trained and working in a field concerned with difficult life problems and having wisdom-enhancing mentors, contribute to higher levels of wisdom. Also, people higher in wisdom have values that are more likely to consider the welfare of others rather than their own happiness.
- *Personality-related factors, such as openness to experience and creativity, are better predictors of wisdom than cognitive factors such as intelligence.*

A recent study compared college students and older adults on a wisdom scale, which consisted of three dimensions: cognitive, reflective, and affective (Ardelt, 2010, p. 199):

- *Cognitive* scale items measured the absence of cognitive wisdom and included items about not having the ability or being unwilling to understand something thoroughly ("ignorance is bliss," for example), and tending to perceive the world as either/or instead of more complex ("People are either good or bad," for example), and being unaware of ambiguity and uncertainty in life ("There is only one right way to do anything," for example).
- *Reflective* scale items evaluated having the ability and being willing to examine circumstances and issues from different perspectives ("I always try to look at all sides of a problem," for example) and the lack of self-examination and self-insight ("Things often go wrong for me through no fault of my own," for example).
- *Affective* scale items assessed positive and caring emotions ("Sometimes I feel a real compassion for everyone," for example) and the lack of those characteristics ("It's not really my problem if others are in trouble and need help," for example).

On the overall wisdom scale, which included an assessment of all three dimensions combined, no differences were found between the two age groups. However, older adults who were college educated scored higher on the reflective and affective, but not the cognitive, dimensions of wisdom than did the college students.

Robert J. Sternberg (1998, 2011a), whose theory of intelligence we will consider later in the chapter, argues that wisdom is linked to both practical and academic intelligence. In his view, academic intelligence is a necessary but in many cases insufficient requirement for wisdom. Practical knowledge about the realities of life also is needed for wisdom. For Sternberg, balance between self-interest, the interests of others, and contexts produces a common good. Thus, wise individuals don't just look out for themselves—they also need to consider others' needs and perspectives, as well as the specific context involved. Sternberg assesses wisdom by presenting problems to individuals that require solutions highlighting various intrapersonal, interpersonal, and contextual interests. He also emphasizes that such aspects of wisdom should be taught in schools (Sternberg, 2011a; Sternberg, Jarvin, & Reznitskaya, 2011). It is Sternberg's emphasis on using knowledge for the common good in a manner that addresses competing interests that mainly differentiates it from Baltes and his colleagues' view of wisdom.

VYGOTSKY'S THEORY

Lev Vygotsky's (1962) theory was introduced in Chapter 1, and it has stimulated considerable interest in the view that knowledge is *situated* and *collaborative* (Daniels, 2011). That is, knowledge is distributed among people and their environments, which include objects, artifacts, tools, books, and the communities in which people live. This distribution suggests that knowing can best be advanced through interaction with others in cooperative activities.

One of Vygotsky's most important concepts is the **zone of proximal development (ZPD),** which refers to the range of tasks that are too difficult for an individual to master alone, but that can be mastered with the guidance and assistance of adults or more-skilled peers. Thus, the lower level of the ZPD is the level of problem solving reached by an adolescent working independently. The upper limit is the level of thinking the adolescent can accept with the assistance of an able instructor (see Figure 3.6). Vygotsky's emphasis on the ZPD underscored his belief in the importance of social influences on cognitive development (Levykh, 2008).

Upper limit

Level of additional responsibility child can accept with assistance of an able instructor

Zone of proximal development (ZPD)

Lower limit

Level of problem solving reached on these tasks by child working alone

FIGURE **3.6**

VYGOTSKY'S ZONE OF PROXIMAL DEVELOPMENT (ZPD). Vygotsky's zone of proximal development has a lower limit and an upper limit. Tasks in the ZPD are too difficult for the child or adolescent to perform alone. They require assistance from an adult or a more-skilled youth. As children and adolescents experience the verbal instruction or demonstration, they organize the information in their existing mental structures so they can eventually perform the skill or task alone.

In Vygotsky's approach, formal schooling is but one of the cultural agents that determine an adolescent's growth (Daniels, 2011). Parents, peers, the community, and the culture's technological orientation also influence adolescents' thinking (Rogoff & others, 2011). For example, parents' and peers' attitudes toward intellectual competence affect adolescents' motivation to acquire knowledge. So do the attitudes of teachers and other adults in the community.

Even though their theories were proposed about the same time, most of the world learned about Vygotsky's theory later than they learned about Piaget's theory, so Vygotsky's theory has not yet been evaluated as thoroughly. Vygotsky's view of the importance of sociocultural influences on children's development fits with the current belief that it is important to evaluate the contextual factors in learning.

Although both theories are constructivist, Vygotsky's is a **social constructivist approach,** which emphasizes the social contexts of learning and the construction of knowledge through social interaction. In moving from Piaget to Vygotsky, the conceptual shift is from the individual to collaboration, social interaction, and sociocultural activity (Gauvain, 2011). The end point of cognitive development for Piaget is formal operational thought. For Vygotsky, the end point can differ, depending on which skills are considered to be the most important in a particular culture. For Piaget, children construct knowledge by transforming, organizing, and reorganizing previous knowledge. For Vygotsky, children and adolescents construct knowledge through social interaction (Holzman, 2009). The implication of Piaget's theory for teaching is that children need support to explore their world and discover knowledge. The main implication of Vygotsky's theory for teaching is that students need many opportunities to learn with the teacher and more-skilled peers (Daniels, 2011). In both Piaget's and Vygotsky's theories, teachers serve as facilitators and guides, rather than as directors and molders of learning. Figure 3.7 compares Vygotsky's and Piaget's theories.

Criticisms of Vygotsky's theory also have surfaced (Karpov, 2006). Some critics point out that Vygotsky was not specific enough about age-related changes (Gauvain & Parke, 2010). Another criticism focuses on Vygotsky not adequately describing how changes in socioemotional capabilities contribute to cognitive development (Gauvain, 2008). Yet another criticism is that he overemphasized the role of language in thinking. Also, his emphasis on collaboration and guidance has potential pitfalls. Might facilitators be too helpful in some cases, as when a parent becomes too overbearing and controlling? Further, some adolescents might become lazy and expect help when they might have done something on their own.

zone of proximal development (ZPD) Vygotsky's concept that refers to the range of tasks that are too difficult for an individual to master alone, but that can be mastered with the guidance or assistance of adults or more-skilled peers.

social constructivist approach Approach that emphasizes the social contexts of learning and the construction of knowledge through social interaction.

	Vygotsky	Piaget
Sociocultural Context	Strong emphasis	Little emphasis
Constructivism	Social constructivist	Cognitive constructivist
Stages	No general stages of development proposed	Strong emphasis on stages (sensorimotor, preoperational, concrete operational, and formal operational)
Key Processes	Zone of proximal development, language, dialogue, tools of the culture	Schema, assimilation, accommodation, operations, conservation, classification
Role of Language	A major role; language plays a powerful role in shaping thought	Language has a minimal role; cognition primarily directs language
View on Education	Education plays a central role, helping children learn the tools of the culture	Education merely refines the child's cognitive skills that have already emerged
Teaching Implications	Teacher is a facilitator and guide, not a director; establish many opportunities for children to learn with the teacher and more-skilled peers	Also views teacher as a facilitator and guide, not a director; provide support for children to explore their world and discover knowledge

FIGURE **3.7**
COMPARISON OF VYGOTSKY'S AND PIAGET'S THEORIES

Review *Connect* Reflect

LG2 Discuss the cognitive developmental view of adolescence.

Review

- What is Piaget's view of adolescence? What are some contributions and criticisms of Piaget's theory? What are some possible cognitive changes in adulthood?
- What is Vygotsky's view of adolescence?

Connect

- Compare the concepts of postformal thought and wisdom.

Reflect *Your Own Personal Journey of Life*

- Think back to when you were 8 years old and 16 years old. Imagine that you are watching a political convention on television at these two different ages. In terms of Piaget's stages of cognitive development, how would your perceptions of the proceedings likely have differed when you were at these two different ages? What would you have "seen" and comprehended as an 8-year-old? What would you have "seen" and comprehended as a 16-year-old? What Piagetian concepts would these differences in your cognition reflect?

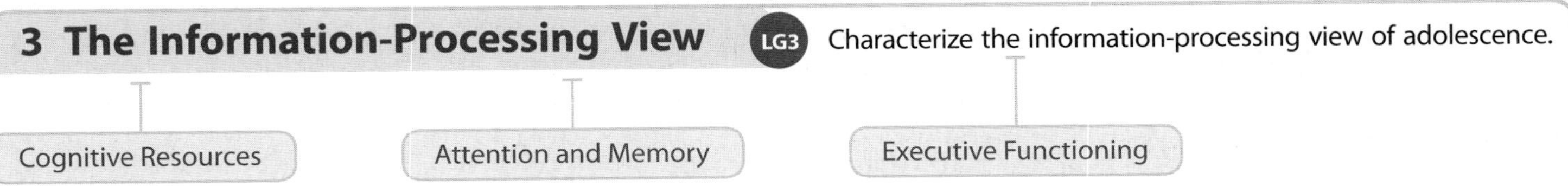

In Chapter 1, we briefly discussed the information-processing view. We saw that information processing includes how information gets into adolescents' minds, how it is stored, and how adolescents retrieve information to think about and solve problems.

Information processing is both a framework for thinking about adolescent development and a facet of that development. As a framework, the information-processing view includes certain ideas about how adolescents' minds work and how best to study those workings (Kuhn, 2009). As a facet of development, information processing changes as children make the transition from adolescence to adulthood. Changes in attention and memory, for example, are essentially changes in the way individuals process information (Mayer, 2008).

Deanna Kuhn (2009) recently discussed some important characteristics of adolescent's information processing and thinking. In her view, in the later years of childhood, and continuing in adolescence, individuals approach cognitive levels that may or may not be achieved, in contrast to the largely universal cognitive levels that young children attain. By adolescence, considerable variation in cognitive functioning is present across individuals. This variability supports the argument that adolescents are producers of their own development to a greater extent than are children.

In our exploration of information processing, we discuss developmental changes in attention, memory, and a number of higher-order cognitive processes involved in executive functioning. But first let's examine the importance of cognitive resources in processing information.

COGNITIVE RESOURCES

Information processing is influenced by both the capacity and the speed of processing (Frye, 2004). These two characteristics are often referred to as *cognitive resources,* and adolescents are better than children at managing and deploying these resources in controlled and purposeful ways (Kuhn & Franklin, 2006).

Most information-processing psychologists argue that an increase in capacity improves processing of information (Halford & Andrews, 2011). For example, as adolescents' information-processing capacity increases, they likely can hold in mind several dimensions of a topic or problem simultaneously, whereas younger children are more prone to focus on only one dimension.

What is the role of processing speed? Generally, fast processing is linked with good performance on cognitive tasks. However, some compensation for slower processing speed can be achieved through effective strategies.

There is abundant evidence that the speed with which such tasks are completed improves dramatically across the childhood and adolescent years (Hommel, Li, & Li, 2004; Kail, 2007; Kuhn, 2009). In one study, 10-year-olds were approximately 1.8 times slower at processing information than young adults on such tasks as

connecting with adolescents

We Think More Than Adults Think We Do

I don't think adults understand how much kids think today. We just don't take something at face value. We want to understand why things are the way they are and the reasons behind things. We want it to be a better world and we are thinking all of the time how to make it that way. When we get be adults, we will make the world better.

—Jason, age 15
Dallas, Texas

How does this comment reflect the argument that adolescents can hold several dimensions of a topic or problem in mind simultaneously?

reaction time and abstract matching (Hale, 1990). Twelve-year-olds were approximately 1.5 times slower than young adults, but 15-year-olds processed information on the tasks as fast as the young adults. Also, a recent study of 8- to 13-year-old children revealed that processing speed increased with age, and further that the developmental change in processing speed preceded an increase in working memory capacity (Kail, 2007).

ATTENTION AND MEMORY

When adolescents process information quickly, they have to focus their attention on the information. And, if they need to use the information later, they will have to remember it. Attention and memory are key aspects of adolescents' information processing.

Attention

Attention is the concentration and focusing of mental effort. Individuals can allocate their attention in different ways. Psychologists have labeled these types of allocation as selective attention, divided attention, sustained attention, and executive attention.

- **Selective attention** is focusing on a specific aspect of experience that is relevant while ignoring others that are irrelevant. Focusing on one voice among many in a crowded room is an example of selective attention.
- **Divided attention** involves concentrating on more than one activity at the same time. An example of divided attention is text messaging while listening to an instructor's lecture.
- **Sustained attention** is the ability to maintain attention to a selected stimulus for a prolonged period of time. Staying focused on reading this chapter from start to finish without interruption is an example of sustained attention.
- **Executive attention** involves action planning, allocating attention to goals, error detection and compensation, monitoring progress on tasks, and dealing with novel or difficult circumstances. An example of executive attention is effectively deploying attention to effectively engage in the aforementioned cognitive tasks while writing a 10-page paper for a history course.

Let's further explore divided, sustained, and executive attention. In one investigation, 12-year-olds were markedly better than 8-year-olds, and slightly worse than

What are some changes in attention during childhood and adolescence?

attention Concentration and focusing of mental resources.

selective attention Focusing on a specific aspect of experience that is relevant while ignoring others that are irrelevant.

divided attention Concentration on more than one activity at the same time.

sustained attention The ability to maintain attention to a selected stimulus for a prolonged period of time.

executive attention Type of attention that involves action planning, allocating attention to goals, error detection and compensation, monitoring progress on tasks, and dealing with novel or difficult circumstances.

developmental **connection**

Media. A recent study revealed that when media multitasking is taken into account, 11- to 14-year-olds use media nearly 12 hours a day (Rideout, Foehr, & Roberts, 2010). Chapter 12, p. 411

Is multitasking beneficial or distracting for adolescents?

20-year-olds, at dividing their attention between two tasks (Manis, Keating, & Morrison, 1980). Adolescents may have more resources available to them than children (through increased processing speed, capacity, and automaticity), or they may be more skilled at directing the resources.

As we described in Chapter 1, one trend involving divided attention is adolescents' multitasking, which in some cases involves dividing attention not just between two activities, but between even three or more (Bauerlein, 2008). A major influence on the increase in multitasking is the availability of multiple electronic media. If a key task is at all complex and challenging, such as trying to figure out how to solve a homework problem, multitasking considerably reduces attention to the key task (Myers, 2008).

Sustained and executive attention also are very important aspects of adolescent cognitive development. As adolescents are required to engage in larger, increasingly complex tasks that require longer time frames to complete, their ability to sustain attention is critical for succeeding on the tasks. An increase in executive attention supports the rapid increase in effortful control required to effectively engage in these complex academic tasks (Rothbart, 2011).

developmental **connection**

Brain Development. One study revealed that peak thickness of the cerebral cortex occurs 3 years later (10.5 years) in children with ADHD (Shaw & others, 2007). Chapter 10, p. 353

As with any cognitive process, there are wide individual differences in how effectively adolescents use these different types of attention in their everyday lives. For example, in Chapter 10, we will discuss *attention deficit hyperactivity disorder (ADHD)*, a disability in which adolescents have severe problems in effectively allocating attention.

Memory There are few moments when adolescents' lives are not steeped in memory. Memory is at work with each step adolescents take, each thought they think, and each word they utter. *Memory* is the retention of information over time. It is central to mental life and to information processing. To successfully learn and reason, adolescents need to hold on to information and retrieve it when necessary. Three important memory systems—short-term memory, working memory, and long-term memory—are involved in adolescents' learning.

Short-Term Memory *Short-term memory* is a limited-capacity memory system in which information is retained for as long as 30 seconds, unless the information is rehearsed, in which case it can be retained longer. A common way to assess short-term memory is to present a list of items to remember, which is often referred to as a memory span task. If you have taken an IQ test, you probably were asked to remember a string of numbers or words. You simply hear a short list of stimuli—usually digits—presented at a rapid pace (one per second, for example). Then you are asked to repeat the digits back. Using the memory span task, researchers have found that short-term memory increases extensively in early childhood and continues to increase in older children and adolescents, but at a slower pace. For example, in one investigation, memory span increased by 1½ digits between the ages of 7 and 12 (Dempster, 1981) (see Figure 3.8). Keep in mind, though, memory span's individual differences, which explain the use of IQ and various aptitude tests.

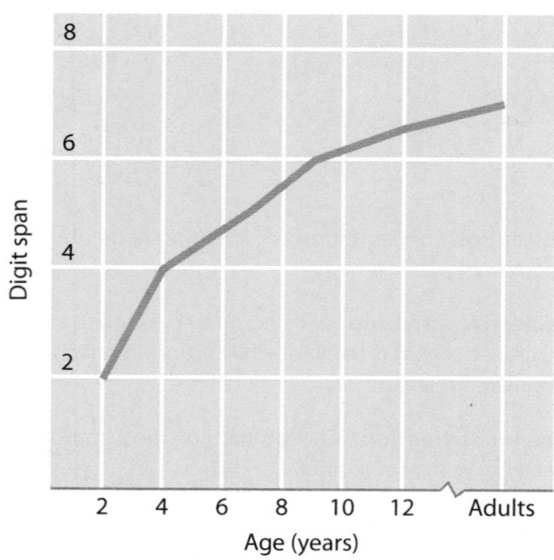

FIGURE **3.8**
DEVELOPMENTAL CHANGES IN MEMORY SPAN. In one study, memory span increased about 3 digits from 2 years of age to 5 digits at 7 years of age (Dempster, 1981). By 12 years of age, memory span had increased on average another 1½ digits.

Working Memory Short-term memory is like a passive storehouse with shelves to store information until it is moved to long-term memory. *Working memory* is a kind of mental "workbench" where individuals manipulate and assemble information when they make decisions, solve problems, and comprehend written and spoken language (Baddeley, 2008, 2010a,b, 2012) (see Figure 3.9). Many psychologists prefer the term *working memory* over *short-term memory* to describe how memory works. Working memory is described as more active and powerful in modifying information than is short-term memory. A recent study revealed that working memory capacity at 9 to 10 years of age predicted foreign language comprehension two years later, at 11 to 12 years of age (Andersson, 2010). Another recent study found that the prefrontal cortex plays a more important role in working memory in late adolescence than early adolescence (Finn & others, 2010).

In one study, the performances of individuals from 6 to 57 years of age were examined on both verbal and visuospatial working memory tasks (Swanson, 1999). As shown in Figure 3.10, working memory increased substantially from 8 through 24 years of age no matter what the task. Thus, the adolescent years are likely to be an important developmental period for improvement in working memory. Note that working memory continues to improve through the transition to adulthood and beyond.

Long-Term Memory *Long-term memory* is a relatively permanent memory system that holds huge amounts of information for a long period of time. Long-term memory increases substantially in the middle and late childhood years and improvement likely continues during adolescence, although this has not been well documented by researchers. If anything at all is known about long-term memory, it is that it depends on the learning activities engaged in when an individual is learning and remembering information (Pressley & Hilden, 2006). Most learning activities fit under the category of *strategies*, activities under the learner's conscious control. There are many such activities, but one of the most important is organization, the tendency to group or arrange items into categories. We have more to discuss about strategies shortly.

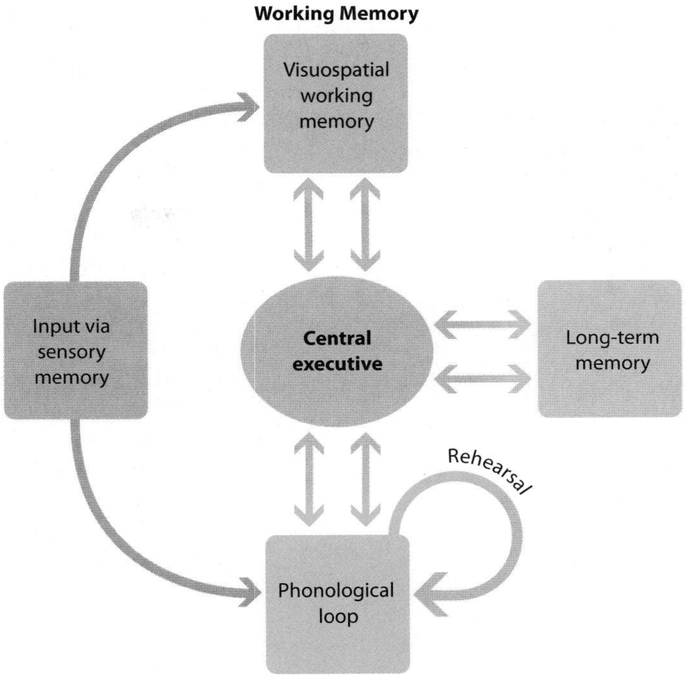

Working Memory
Visuospatial working memory
Input via sensory memory
Central executive
Long-term memory
Rehearsal
Phonological loop

FIGURE **3.9**

WORKING MEMORY. In Baddeley's working memory model, working memory is like a mental workbench where a great deal of information processing is carried out. Working memory consists of three main components: the phonological loop and visuospatial working memory serve as assistants, helping the central executive do its work. Input from sensory memory goes to the phonological loop, where information about speech is stored and rehearsal takes place, and to visuospatial working memory, where visual and spatial information, including imagery, is stored. Working memory is a limited-capacity system, and information is stored there for only a brief time. Working memory interacts with long-term memory, using information from long-term memory in its work and transmitting information to long-term memory for longer storage.

EXECUTIVE FUNCTIONING

Attention and memory are important dimensions of information processing, but other dimensions also are important. These other dimensions involve engaging in a number of higher-order cognitive activities, such as exercising cognitive control, making decisions, thinking critically, thinking creatively, and engaging in metacognition. These types of higher-order, complex cognitive processes involve an umbrella-like concept called **executive functioning.** In his model of cognitive functioning

executive functioning An umbrella-like concept that involves higher-order, complex cognitive processes that include exercising cognitive control, making decisions, reasoning, thinking critically, thinking creatively, and metacognition.

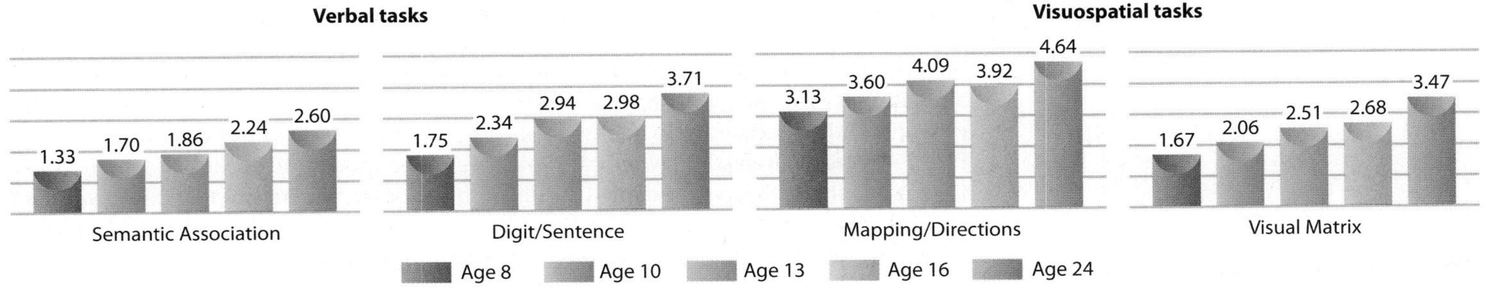

FIGURE **3.10**

DEVELOPMENTAL CHANGES IN WORKING MEMORY. *Note:* The scores shown here are the means for each age group and the age also represents a mean age. Higher scores reflect superior working memory performance.

described earlier in the chapter, Alan Baddeley (2008, 2010a,b, 2012) recognized the importance of these higher-order cognitive processes and actually called this aspect of his model the *central executive*.

Executive functioning becomes increasingly strong during adolescence (Kuhn, 2009; Kuhn & Franklin, 2006). This executive functioning

> assumes a role of monitoring and managing the deployment of cognitive resources as a function of task demands. As a result, cognitive development and learning itself become more effective. . . . Emergence and strengthening of this executive (functioning) is arguably the single most important and consequential intellectual development to occur in the second decade of life. (Kuhn & Franklin, 2006, p. 987)

Cognitive Control **Cognitive control** involves effective control and flexible thinking in a number of areas, including controlling attention, reducing interfering thoughts, and being cognitively flexible (Diamond, Casey, & Munakata, 2011). Cognitive control also has been referred to as *inhibitory control* or *effortful control* to emphasize the ability to resist a strong inclination to do one thing but instead to do what is most effective (Diamond, 2010; Rothbart, 2011).

Across childhood and adolescence, cognitive control increases with age (Casey, Jones, & Somerville, 2011; Luna, Padmanabhan, & O'Hearn, 2010). The increase in cognitive control is thought to be due to the maturation of brain pathways and circuitry we considered earlier in the chapter. For example, one study found less diffusion and more focal activation in the prefrontal cortex from 7 to 30 years of age (Durston & others, 2006). The activation change was accompanied by increased efficiency in cognitive performance, especially in *cognitive control*.

Think about all the times adolescents and emerging adults need to engage in cognitive control, such as (Galinsky, 2010):

- making a real effort to stick with a task, avoiding interfering thoughts or environmental events, and instead doing what is most effective.
- stopping and thinking before acting to avoid blurting out something a minute or two later they wished they hadn't said.
- continuing to work on something that is important but boring when there is something a lot more fun to do, but inhibiting their behavior and doing the boring but important task, saying to themselves, "I have to show the self-discipline to finish this."

Control Attention and Reduce Interfering Thoughts Controlling attention is a key aspect of learning and thinking in adolescence and emerging adulthood (Bjorklund, 2012). Distractions that can interfere with attention in adolescence and emerging adulthood come from the external environment (other students talking while the student is trying to listen to a lecture, or the student switching on a laptop during a lecture and looking at a new friend request on Facebook, for example) or intrusive distractions from competing thoughts in the individual's mind. Self-oriented thoughts, such as worrying, self-doubt, and intense emotionally laden thoughts may especially interfere with focusing attention on thinking tasks (Gillig & Sanders, 2011; Walsh, 2011).

Be Cognitively Flexible *Cognitive flexibility* involves being aware that options and alternatives are available and adapting to the situation. Before adolescents and emerging adults adapt their behavior in a situation, they need to become aware that they need to change their way of thinking and be motivated to do so. Having confidence in their ability to adapt their thinking to a particular situation, an aspect of *self-efficacy,* also is important in being cognitively flexible (Bandura, 2010a). To evaluate how cognitively flexible you are, see Figure 3.11 (Galinsky, 2010).

Decision Making Adolescence is a time of increased decision making—which friends to choose; which person to date; whether to have sex, buy a car, go to college; and so on (Albert & Steinberg, 2011a,b; Kuhn, 2009; Reyna & others, 2011). How

cognitive control Involves effective control and flexible thinking in a number of areas, including controlling attention, reducing interfering thoughts, and being cognitively flexible.

Circle the number that best reflects how you think for each of the four items:

	Exactly Like You	Very Much Like You	Somewhat Like You	Not Too Much Like You	Not At All Like You
1. When I try something that doesn't work, it's hard for me to give it up and try another solution.	1	2	3	4	5
2. I adapt to change pretty easily.	5	4	3	4	5
3. When I can't convince someone of my point of view, I can usually understand why not.	5	4	3	4	5
4. I am not very quick to take on new ideas.	1	2	3	4	5

Add your numbers for each of the four items: Total Score: ______
If your overall score is between 20 and 15, then you rate high on cognitive flexibility. If you scored between 9 and 14, you are in the middle category, and if you scored 8 or below, you likely could improve.

FIGURE **3.11**
HOW COGNITIVELY FLEXIBLE ARE YOU?

competent are adolescents at making decisions? In some reviews, older adolescents are described as more competent than younger adolescents, who in turn are more competent than children (Keating, 1990). Compared with children, young adolescents are more likely to generate different options, examine a situation from a variety of perspectives, anticipate the consequences of decisions, and consider the credibility of sources.

What are some of the decisions adolescents have to make? What characterizes their decision making?

One study documents that older adolescents are better at decision making than younger adolescents are (Lewis, 1981). Eighth-, tenth-, and twelfth-grade students were presented with dilemmas involving the choice of a medical procedure. The oldest students were most likely to spontaneously mention a variety of risks, to recommend consultation with an outside specialist, and to anticipate future consequences. For example, when asked a question about whether to have cosmetic surgery, a twelfth-grader said that different aspects of the situation need to be examined along with its effects on the individual's future, especially relationships with other people. In contrast, an eighth-grader presented a more limited view, commenting on the surgery's effects on getting turned down for a date, the money involved, and being teased by peers.

In sum, older adolescents often make better decisions than do younger adolescents, who in turn, make better decisions than do children. The ability to regulate one's emotions during decision making, to remember prior decisions and their consequences, and to adapt subsequent decision making on the basis of those consequences appears to improve with age at least through the early adulthood years (Klaczynski, Byrnes, & Jacobs, 2001).

However, older adolescents' decision-making skills are far from perfect, but of course, we also are not perfect decision makers as adults (Kuhn, 2009). Adolescents and adults who are impulsive and seek sensation are often not very effective decision makers, for example (Galvan & others, 2007).

Being able to make competent decisions does not guarantee that individuals will make them in everyday life, where breadth of experience often comes into play. As an example, driver-training courses improve adolescents' cognitive and motor skills to levels equal to, or sometimes superior to, those of adults. However, driver training has not been effective in reducing adolescents' high rate of traffic accidents, although recently researchers have found that implementing a graduated driver licensing (GDL) program can reduce crash and fatality rates for adolescent drivers (Keating, 2007). GDL components include a learner's holding period, practice-driving certification, night-driving restriction, and passenger restriction. In addition to GDL, parental monitoring and expectations can reduce adolescents' driving accidents (Keating & Halpern-Felsher, 2008). For example, parents can restrict and monitor the presence of adolescents' peers in the vehicle.

Most people make better decisions when they are calm rather than emotionally aroused, which may especially be true for adolescents (Rivers, Reyna, & Mills, 2008; Steinberg & others, 2009). Recall from our discussion of brain development earlier in the chapter that adolescents have a tendency to be emotionally intense. Thus, the same adolescent who makes a wise decision when calm may make an unwise decision when emotionally aroused (Casey, Getz, & Galvan, 2008; Giedd, 2008). In the heat of the moment, then, adolescents' emotions may especially overwhelm their decision-making ability.

The social context plays a key role in adolescent decision making (Albert & Steinberg, 2011a,b). For example, adolescents' willingness to make risky decisions is more likely to occur in contexts where substances and other temptations are readily available (Gerrard & others, 2008; Reyna & Rivers, 2008). Recent research reveals that the presence of peers in risk-taking situations increases the likelihood that adolescents will make risky decisions (Albert & Steinberg, 2011a,b). In one study of risk taking involving a simulated driving task, the presence of peers increased an adolescent's decision to engage in risky driving by 50 percent but had no effect on adults (Gardner & Steinberg, 2005). One view is that the presence of peers activates the brain's reward system, especially dopamine pathways (Albert & Steinberg, 2011a,b; Steinberg, 2010).

Adolescents need more opportunities to practice and discuss realistic decision making. Many real-world decisions on matters such as sex, drugs, and daredevil driving occur in an atmosphere of stress that includes time constraints and emotional involvement. One strategy for improving adolescent decision making in such circumstances is to provide more opportunities for them to engage in role-playing and group problem solving. Another strategy is that parents involve adolescents in appropriate decision-making activities.

One proposal to explain adolescent decision making is the **dual-process model,** which states that decision making is influenced by two cognitive systems—one analytical and one experiential, which compete with each other (Klacyznski, 2001; Reyna & Farley, 2006; Reyna & others, 2011). The dual-process model emphasizes that it is the experiential system—monitoring and managing actual experiences—that benefits adolescents' decision making, not the analytical system. In this view, adolescents don't benefit from engaging in reflective, detailed, higher-level cognitive analysis about a decision, especially in high-risk, real-world

How do emotions and social contexts influence adolescents' decision making?

dual-process model States that decision making is influenced by two systems—one analytical and one experiential, which compete with each other; in this model, it is the experiential system—monitoring and managing actual experiences—that benefits adolescent decision making.

contexts. In such contexts, adolescents just need to know that there are some circumstances that are so dangerous that they need to be avoided at all costs (Mills, Reyna, & Estrada, 2008). However, some experts on adolescent cognition argue that in many cases adolescents benefit from both analytical and experiential systems (Kuhn, 2009).

Critical Thinking **Critical thinking** is thinking reflectively and productively and evaluating evidence (Bonney & Sternberg, 2011; Galinsky, 2010). In one study of fifth-, eighth-, and eleventh-graders, critical thinking increased with age but still occurred only in 43 percent of eleventh-graders (Klaczynski & Narasimham, 1998). Many adolescents showed self-serving biases in their thinking.

Adolescence is an important transitional period in the development of critical thinking (Keating, 1990). Among the cognitive changes that allow improved critical thinking during this period are the following:

- Increased speed, automaticity, and capacity of information processing, which free cognitive resources for other purposes
- Greater breadth of content knowledge in a variety of domains
- Increased ability to construct new combinations of knowledge
- A greater range and more spontaneous use of strategies and procedures for obtaining and applying knowledge, such as planning, considering the alternatives, and cognitive monitoring

"For God's sake, think! Why is he being so nice to you?"

Although adolescence is an important period in the development of critical-thinking skills, if a solid basis of fundamental skills (such as literacy and math skills) was not developed during childhood, critical-thinking skills are unlikely to adequately develop in adolescence.

Considerable interest has developed in teaching critical thinking in schools (Fairweather & Cramond, 2011). Cognitive psychologist Robert J. Sternberg (1985) concludes that most school programs that teach critical thinking are flawed. He thinks that schools focus too much on formal reasoning tasks and not enough on the critical-thinking skills needed in everyday life. Among the critical-thinking skills that Sternberg notes adolescents need in everyday life are these: recognizing that problems exist, defining problems more clearly, handling problems with no single right answer or any clear criteria for the point at which the problem is solved (such as selecting a rewarding career), making decisions on issues of personal relevance (such as deciding to have a risky operation), obtaining information, thinking in groups, and developing long-term approaches to long-term problems.

One way to encourage students to think critically is to present them with controversial topics or articles that present both sides of an issue to discuss (Kuhn & Franklin, 2006). Some teachers shy away from having students engage in these types of critical-thinking debates or discussions because it is not "polite" or "nice" (Winn, 2004). However, critical thinking is promoted when students encounter conflicting accounts of arguments and debates, which can motivate them to delve more deeply into a topic and attempt to resolve an issue (Kuhn, 2009; Kuhn & Franklin, 2006).

Getting students to think critically is not always an easy task. Many students come into a class with a history of passive learning, having been encouraged to recite the correct answer to a question, rather than put forth the intellectual effort to think in more complex ways. By using more assignments that require students to focus on an issue, a question, or a problem, rather than just reciting facts, teachers stimulate students' ability to think critically.

To read about the work of one secondary school teacher who encourages students to think critically, see the *Connecting with Careers* profile.

critical thinking Thinking reflectively and productively and evaluating the evidence.

Creative Thinking **Creativity** is the ability to think in novel ways and discover unique solutions to problems. Thus, intelligence, which we discuss shortly, and

creativity The ability to think in novel and unusual ways and discover unique solutions to problems.

connecting with careers

Laura Bickford, Secondary School Teacher

Laura Bickford, working with students writing papers.

Laura Bickford teaches English and journalism in grades 9 to 12, and she is chair of the English Department at Nordhoff High School in Ojai, California.

Bickford especially believes it is important to encourage students to think. Indeed, she says that "the call to teach is the call to teach students how to think." She believes that teachers need to show students the value in asking their own questions, in having discussions, and in engaging in stimulating intellectual conversations. Bickford says that she also encourages students to engage in metacognitive strategies (knowing about knowing). For example, she asks students to comment on their learning after particular pieces of projects have been completed. She requires students to keep reading logs so they can observe their own thinking as it happens.

For more information about the work that secondary school teachers do, see page 46 in the Careers in Adolescent Development appendix.

"What do you mean 'What is it?' It's the spontaneous, unfettered expression of a young mind not yet bound by the restraints of narrative or pictorial representation."
Sidney Harris. ScienceCartoonsPlus.com. Used with permission.

convergent thinking A pattern of thinking in which individuals produce one correct answer; characteristic of the items on conventional intelligence tests; coined by Guilford.

divergent thinking A pattern of thinking in which individuals produce many answers to the same question; more characteristic of creativity than convergent thinking; coined by Guilford.

creativity are not the same thing. J. P. Guilford (1967) first made this distinction by contrasting **convergent thinking,** which produces one correct answer and is characteristic of the kind of thinking required on a conventional intelligence test, and **divergent thinking,** which produces many answers to the same question and is more characteristic of creativity. For example, a typical item on a conventional intelligence test is "How many quarters will you get in return for 60 dimes?" This question has only one correct answer. In contrast, the following questions have many possible answers: "What image comes to mind when you hear the phrase *sitting alone in a dark room?*" or "Can you think of some unique uses for a paper clip?"

Are intelligence and creativity related? Although most creative adolescents are quite intelligent, the reverse is not necessarily true (Lubart, 2003). Many highly intelligent adolescents are not very creative.

A special concern is that adolescents' creative thinking appears to be declining. A study of approximately 300,000 U.S. children, adolescents, and adults found that creativity scores rose until 1990, but since then have been steadily declining (Kim, 2010). Among the likely causes of the creativity decline are the number of hours U.S. children and adolescents watch TV, play video games, connect on Facebook, and text message instead of engaging in creative activities, as well as the lack of emphasis on creative-thinking skills in schools (Beghetto & Kaufman, 2011; Runco & Spritzker, 2011; Sternberg, 2011b,c) Some countries, though, are placing increasing emphasis on creative thinking in schools. For example, historically, creative thinking has typically been discouraged in Chinese schools. However, Chinese educators are now encouraging teachers to spend more classroom time on creative activities (Plucker, 2010).

An important teaching goal is to help students become more creative (Fairweather & Cramond, 2011; Hennesey, 2011; Sternberg, 2011b,c). Teachers need to recognize that students will show more creativity in some domains than in others (Runco &

Spritzker, 2011). A student who shows creative-thinking skills in mathematics may not exhibit these skills in art, for example.

School environments that encourage independent work, are stimulating but not distracting, and make resources readily available are likely to encourage students' creativity. There is mounting concern that the U.S. government's No Child Left Behind legislation has harmed the development of students' creative thinking by focusing attention on memorization of materials to do well on standardized tests (Kaufman & Sternberg, 2007).

Here are some good strategies for increasing adolescents' creative-thinking skills:

- *Have adolescents engage in brainstorming and come up with as many ideas as possible.* Brainstorming is a technique in which individuals are encouraged to come up with creative ideas in a group, play off each other's ideas, and say practically whatever comes to mind. However, recognize that some adolescents are more creative when they work alone. Indeed, one review of research on brainstorming concluded that for many individuals, working alone can generate more ideas and better ideas than working in groups (Rickards & deCock, 2003). One reason for this is that in groups, some individuals contribute only a few ideas, whereas others do most of the creative thinking. Nonetheless, there may be benefits to brainstorming, such as team building, that support its use.
- *Introduce adolescents to environments that stimulate creativity.* Some settings nourish creativity; others depress it (Csikszentmihalyi & Nakamura 2006; Sternberg, 2012; Strati, Shernoff, & Kackar, 2011). People who encourage creativity often rely on adolescents' natural curiosity. They provide exercises and activities that stimulate adolescents to find insightful solutions to problems, rather than asking a lot of questions that require rote answers. Adults also encourage creativity by taking adolescents to locations where creativity is valued.
- *Don't overcontrol.* Teresa Amabile (1993) says that telling individuals exactly how to do things leaves them feeling that any originality is a mistake and any exploration is a waste of time. Letting adolescents select their interests and supporting their inclinations are less likely to destroy their natural curiosity than dictating which activities they should engage in.
- *Encourage internal motivation.* The excessive use of prizes such as gold stars or money can stifle creativity by undermining the intrinsic pleasure adolescents derive from creative activities. Creative adolescents' motivation is the satisfaction generated by the work itself. Competition for prizes and formal evaluations often undermine intrinsic motivation and creativity (Amabile & Hennesey, 1992; Hennesey, 2011).
- *Build adolescents' confidence.* To expand adolescents' creativity, encourage them to believe in their own ability to create something innovative and worthwhile. Building adolescents' confidence in their creative skills aligns with Bandura's (2010a) concept of self-efficacy, the belief that one can master a situation and produce positive outcomes.
- *Guide adolescents to be persistent and delay gratification.* Most highly successful creative products take years to develop. Most creative individuals work on ideas and projects for months and years without being rewarded for their efforts (Sternberg & Williams, 1996). Adolescents don't become experts at sports, music, or art overnight. It usually takes many years working at something to become an expert at it; so it is with being a creative thinker who produces a unique, worthwhile product.

developmental **connection**

Schools. A number of criticisms of the government's No Child Left Behind legislation have been made. Chapter 10, p. 333

developmental **connection**

Work. Intrinsic motivation comes from such processes as self-determination and personal choice, optimal experiences, interest, and cognitive engagement. Chapter 11, p. 364

An adolescent boy painting in the streets of the African nation of Zanzibar. *If you were going to work with adolescents to encourage their creativity, what strategies would you adopt?*

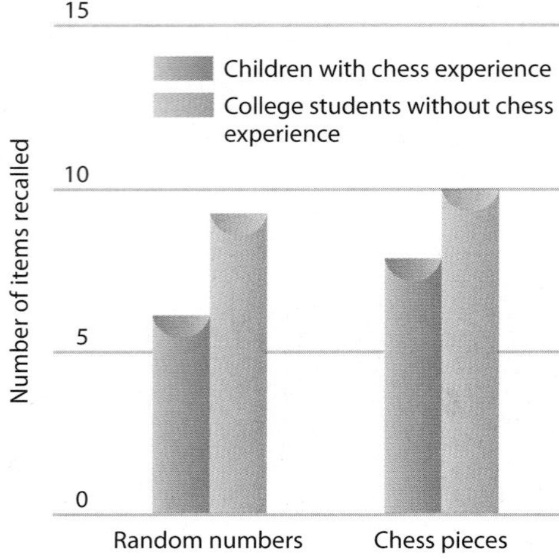

FIGURE **3.12**
MEMORY FOR NUMBERS AND CHESS PIECES

- *Encourage adolescents to take intellectual risks.* Creative individuals take intellectual risks and seek to discover or invent something never before discovered or invented (Sternberg & Williams, 1996). They risk spending extensive time on an idea or project that may not work. Adolescents' creativity benefits when they are not afraid of failing or getting something wrong (Sternberg, 2011b,c).
- *Introduce adolescents to creative people.* Think about the identity of the most creative people in your community. Teachers can invite these people to their classrooms and ask them to describe what helps them become creative or to demonstrate their creative skills. A writer, poet, musician, scientist, and many others can bring their props and productions to the class, turning it into a theater for stimulating students' creativity.

Expertise Recently, psychologists have shown an increased interest in experts and novices in a specific knowledge domain (Ackerman, 2011; Sternberg, 2012). An expert is the opposite of a novice (someone who is just beginning to learn a content area). What is it, exactly, that experts do so well? They are better than novices at (National Research Council, 1999):

- Detecting features and meaningful patterns of information
- Accumulating more content knowledge and organizing it in a manner that shows an understanding of the topic
- Retrieving important aspects of knowledge with little effort

In areas where children and adolescents are experts, their memory is often extremely good. In fact, it often exceeds that of adults who are novices in that content area. This superiority was documented in a study of 10-year-old chess experts (Chi, 1978). These children were excellent chess players, but not especially brilliant in other ways. As with most 10-year-olds, their memory spans for digits were shorter than an adult's. However, when they were presented chessboards, they remembered the configurations far better than did the adults who were novices at chess (see Figure 3.12).

Experts' knowledge is organized around important ideas or concepts more than novices' knowledge is (National Research Council, 1999). This ability provides experts with a much deeper understanding of knowledge than novices. Experts in a specific area usually have far more elaborate networks of information about that area than novices do. The information they represent in memory has more nodes, more interconnections, and better hierarchical organization.

What determines whether or not someone becomes an expert? Can motivation and practice get someone to expert status? Or does expertise also require a great deal of talent?

One perspective is that a specific kind of practice—*deliberate practice*—is required to become an expert. Deliberate practice involves practice that is at an appropriate level of difficulty for the individual, provides corrective feedback, and allows opportunities for repetition (Ericsson & others, 2006). In one study of violinists at a music academy, the extent to which children engaged in deliberate practice distinguished novices and experts (Ericsson, Krampe, & Tesch-Römer, 1993). The top violinists averaged 7,500 hours of deliberate practice by age 18, the good violinists only 5,300 hours. Many individuals give up on becoming an expert because they won't put forth the effort it takes to engage in extensive deliberate practice over a number of years.

Such extensive practice requires considerable motivation. Students who are not motivated to practice long hours are unlikely to become experts in a specific area. Thus, a student who complains about all of the work, doesn't persevere, and doesn't extensively practice solving math problems over a number of years is not going to become an expert in math. However, talent is also usually required to become an expert (Ruthsatz & others, 2008; Sternberg, 2012). Many individuals have attempted to become great musicians and athletes but have given up trying after only mediocre performances. Nonetheless, musicians such as Beethoven and athletes such as Tiger Woods would not have developed expertise in their fields without being highly motivated and engaging in extensive deliberate practice. Talent alone does not make an expert.

How are talent and deliberate practice involved in expertise?

Metacognition We have discussed some important ways in which adolescents process information. In this section, we explore how they monitor their information processing and think about thinking.

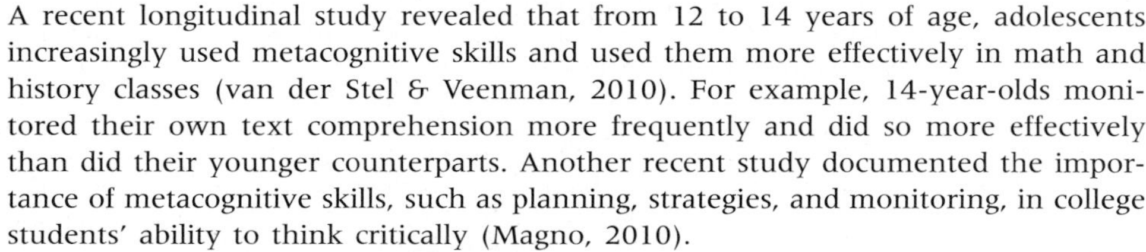

What Is Metacognition? Earlier in this chapter, in discussing Piaget's theory, we learned that adolescents increase their thinking about thinking. Cognitive psychologists call this kind of thought **metacognition**—that is, cognition about cognition, or "knowing about knowing" (Flavell, 2004).

Metacognition is increasingly recognized as a very important cognitive skill not only in adolescence but also in emerging adulthood. Compared to children, adolescents have an increased capacity to monitor and manage cognitive resources to effectively meet the demands of a learning task (Kuhn, 2009). This increased metacognitive ability results in improved cognitive functioning and learning. A recent longitudinal study revealed that from 12 to 14 years of age, adolescents increasingly used metacognitive skills and used them more effectively in math and history classes (van der Stel & Veenman, 2010). For example, 14-year-olds monitored their own text comprehension more frequently and did so more effectively than did their younger counterparts. Another recent study documented the importance of metacognitive skills, such as planning, strategies, and monitoring, in college students' ability to think critically (Magno, 2010).

Metacognitive skills have been taught to students to help them solve problems. In one study, for each of 30 daily lessons involving verbal math problems, a teacher guided low-achieving students in learning to recognize when they did not know the meaning of a word, did not have all the necessary information to solve a problem, did not know how to subdivide a problem into specific steps, or did not know how to carry out a computation (Cardelle-Elawar, 1992). After completing these lessons, the students who had received the metacognitive training had better math achievement and better attitudes toward math.

Strategies In addition to metamemory, metacognition includes knowledge about strategies. In the view of Michael Pressley (2003), the key to education is helping students learn a rich repertoire of strategies that result in solutions to problems. Good thinkers routinely use strategies and effective planning to solve problems. Good thinkers also know when and where to use strategies. Understanding when and where to use strategies often results from monitoring the learning situation.

Pressley and his colleagues (Pressley & others, 2001, 2003, 2004, 2007) spent considerable time in recent years observing strategy instruction by teachers and strategy use by students in elementary and secondary school classrooms. They conclude that strategy instruction is far less complete and intense than what students need in order to learn how to use strategies effectively. They argue that education needs to be restructured so that students are provided with more opportunities to become competent strategic learners.

As an example of how important strategies are for adolescents, a recent meta-analysis (use of statistical techniques to combine the results of studies) revealed that the most successful intervention in improving fourth- through twelfth-grade students' writing quality was strategy instruction (Graham & Perin, 2007).

Domain-Specific Thinking Skills Our coverage of metacognition mainly emphasized the importance of some general cognitive skills, such as strategies and self-regulation, in becoming a better thinker. Indeed, researchers have found that

metacognition Cognition about cognition, or "knowing about knowing."

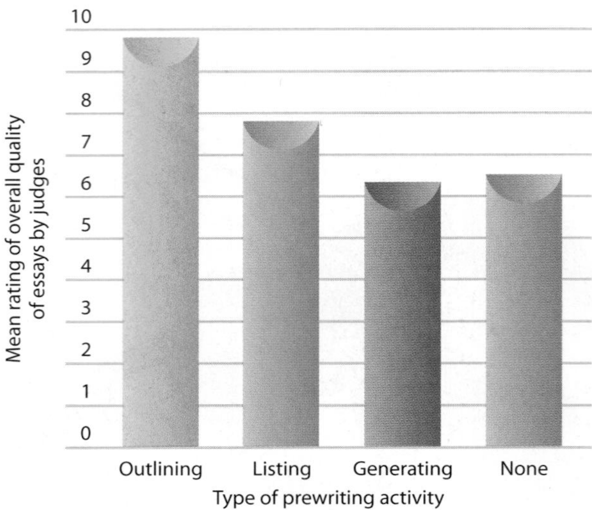

FIGURE 3.13

THE RELATION OF PREWRITING ACTIVITIES TO ESSAY QUALITY. The most effective prewriting activity for college students was outlining, which involved creating an outline with relevant ideas under multilevel headings. Judges rated the quality of each essay from 1 (lowest) to 10 (highest).

metacognitive skills can be taught. For example, adolescents have been effectively taught to become aware of their thinking processes and engage in self-regulation of their learning (Schunk, 2011; Veenman, 2011).

However, it also is very important to teach domain-specific thinking skills to adolescents (De La Paz & McCutchen, 2011; Duschl & Hamilton, 2011). In this regard, a review concluded that one of educational psychology's greatest accomplishments is the teaching of domain-specific thinking skills (Mayer & Wittrock, 2006). Thus, a rich tradition in quality education programs has been the teaching of thinking skills within specific subjects, such as writing, mathematics, science, and history (Alexander & Mayer, 2011; Edwards, Esmonde, & Wagner, 2011; Levstik, 2011). Researchers have found that "it is possible to analyze and teach the underlying cognitive processes required in tasks such as comprehending a passage, writing an essay, solving an arithmetic word problem, answering a scientific question, or explaining an historical event . . ." (Mayer & Wittrock, 2006).

Planning is an important general cognitive skill for adolescents and emerging adults to use, but they also benefit when they apply this and other cognitive skills to specific subjects (Halonen & Santrock, 2012; Mayer, 2008, 2012). For example, one study examined how prewriting activities can affect the quality of college students' writing (Kellogg, 1994). As indicated in Figure 3.13, the planning activity of outlining was the prewriting activity that helped writers the most.

Review *Connect* Reflect

 Characterize the information-processing view of adolescence.

Review

- What characterizes the development of cognitive resources?
- What developmental changes characterize attention and memory in adolescence?
- What is executive functioning? How can adolescent decision making be described? What characterizes critical thinking in adolescence? What distinguishes experts from novices and how do individuals become experts? What is metacognition and how does it change developmentally? What is self-regulatory learning? How important is domain-specific thinking?

Connect

- How does research on cognitive control shed light on adolescents' risk-taking behavior, described in Chapter 2?

Reflect *Your Own Personal Journey of Life*

- What were your study skills like during adolescence? How have your study skills changed since adolescence? Has metacognition played a role in improving your study skills?

4 The Psychometric/Intelligence View

 Summarize the psychometric/intelligence view of adolescence.

Intelligence Tests | Multiple Intelligences | Heredity and Environment

psychometric/intelligence view A view that emphasizes the importance of individual differences in intelligence; many advocates of this view also argue that intelligence should be assessed with intelligence tests.

The two views of adolescent cognition that we have discussed so far—cognitive developmental and information processing—do not emphasize individual variations in intelligence. The **psychometric/intelligence view** does emphasize the importance of individual differences in intelligence; many advocates of this view favor the use of intelligence tests. An increasing issue in the field of intelligence involves pinning down what the components of intelligence really are.

How can intelligence be defined? **Intelligence** is the ability to solve problems and to adapt and learn from everyday experiences. But even this broad definition doesn't satisfy everyone. As you will see shortly, Robert Sternberg (2011b,c; 2012) proposes that practical know-how should be considered part of intelligence. In his view, intelligence involves weighing options carefully and acting judiciously, as well as developing strategies to improve shortcomings. Also, a definition of intelligence based on a theory such as Lev Vygotsky's, which we discussed earlier in the chapter, would have to include the ability to use the tools of the culture with help from more-skilled individuals. Because intelligence is such an abstract, broad concept, it is not surprising that there are so many different ways to define it.

Interest in intelligence has often focused on individual differences and assessment. *Individual differences* are the stable, consistent ways in which people are different from each other. We can talk about individual differences in personality or any other domain, but it is in the domain of intelligence that the most attention has been directed at individual differences. For example, an intelligence test purports to inform us about whether an adolescent can reason better than others who have taken the test (Lohman & Lakin, 2011; Stanovich, West, & Toplak, 2011).

INTELLIGENCE TESTS

Robert Sternberg recalls being terrified of taking IQ tests as a child. He literally froze, he says, when the time came to take such tests. Even as an adult, Sternberg is stung by humiliation when he recalls in the sixth grade being asked to take an IQ test with fifth-graders. Sternberg eventually overcame his anxieties about IQ tests. Not only did he begin to perform better on them, but at age 13 he devised his own IQ test and began using it to assess his classmates—that is, until the chief school-system psychologist found out and scolded him. Sternberg became so fascinated by intelligence that he made its study one of his lifelong pursuits. Later in this chapter, we discuss his theory of intelligence. To begin, though, let's step back in time to examine the first valid intelligence test.

Alfred Binet constructed the first intelligence test after being asked to create a measure to determine which children would benefit from instruction in France's schools.

The Binet Tests In 1904, the French Ministry of Education asked psychologist Alfred Binet to devise a method of identifying children who were unable to learn in school. School officials wanted to reduce crowding by placing students who did not benefit from regular classroom teaching in special schools. Binet and his student Theophile Simon developed an intelligence test to meet this request. The test is called the 1905 Scale. It consisted of 30 questions on topics ranging from the ability to touch one's ear to the ability to draw designs from memory and define abstract concepts.

Binet developed the concept of **mental age (MA),** an individual's level of mental development relative to others. Not much later, in 1912, William Stern created the concept of **intelligence quotient (IQ),** a person's mental age divided by chronological age (CA), multiplied by 100. That is: $IQ = MA/CA \times 100$. If mental age is the same as chronological age, then the person's IQ is 100. If mental age is above chronological age, then IQ is more than 100. If mental age is below chronological age, then IQ is less than 100.

The Binet test has been revised many times to incorporate advances in the understanding of intelligence and intelligence tests. These revisions are called the *Stanford-Binet tests* (Stanford University is where the revisions have been done). By administering the test to large numbers of people of different ages from different backgrounds, researchers have found that scores on the Stanford-Binet approximate a normal distribution (see Figure 3.14). A **normal distribution** is symmetrical, with a majority of the scores falling in the middle of the possible range of scores, and few scores appearing toward the extremes of the range.

intelligence The ability to solve problems and to adapt to and learn from everyday experiences; not everyone agrees on what constitutes intelligence.

mental age (MA) An individual's level of mental development relative to others; a concept developed by Binet.

intelligent quotient (IQ) A person's tested mental age divided by chronological age, multiplied by 100.

normal distribution A symmetrical distribution of values or scores, with a majority of scores falling in the middle of the possible range of scores and few scores appearing toward the extremes of the range.

FIGURE **3.14**

THE NORMAL CURVE AND STANFORD-BINET IQ SCORES. The distribution of IQ scores approximates a normal curve. Most of the population falls in the middle range of scores, between 84 and 116. Notice that extremely high and extremely low scores are rare. Only about 1 in 50 individuals has an IQ of more than 132 or less than 68.

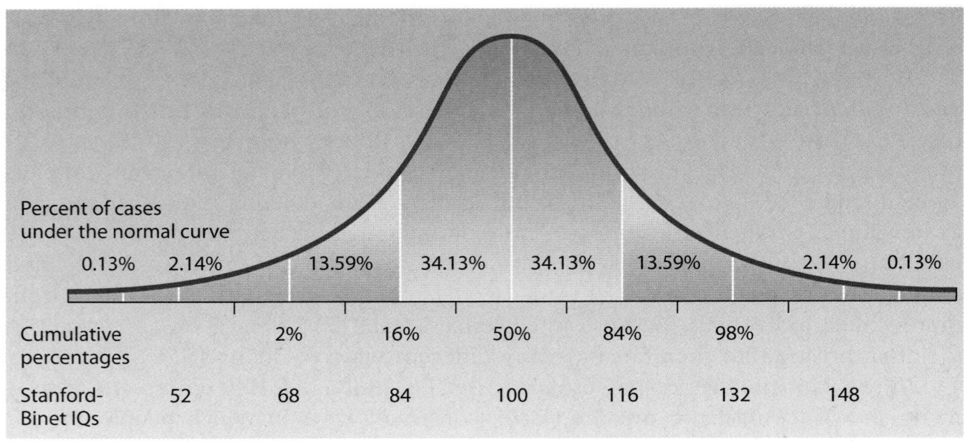

Verbal Subscales

Similarities

An individual must think logically and abstractly to answer a number of questions about how things might be similar.

Example: "In what way are a lion and a tiger alike?"

Comprehension

This subscale is designed to measure an individual's judgment and common sense.

Example: "What is the advantage of keeping money in a bank?"

Nonverbal Subscales

Block Design

An individual must assemble a set of multicolored blocks to match designs that the examiner shows.
Visual-motor coordination, perceptual organization, and the ability to visualize spatially are assessed.

Example: "Use the four blocks on the left to make the pattern on the right."

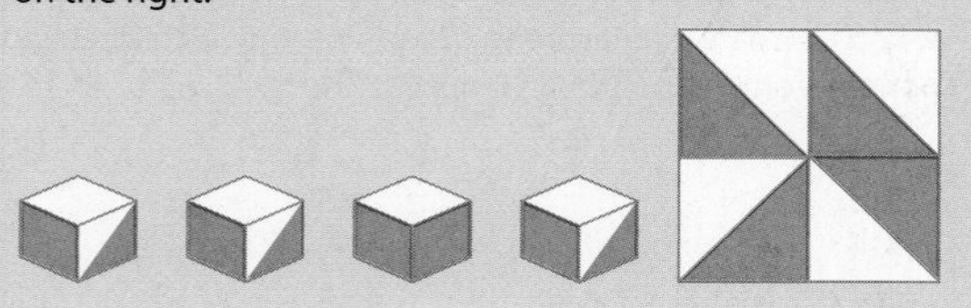

FIGURE **3.15**

SAMPLE SUBSCALES OF THE WECHSLER ADULT INTELLIGENCE SCALE—THIRD EDITION (WAIS-III). The Wechsler includes 11 subscales, 6 verbal and 5 nonverbal. Three of the subscales are shown here. Simulated items similar to those found in the *Wechsler Adult Intelligence Scale—Third Edition (WAIS-III). Copyright © 1997 NCS Pearson, Inc. Reproduced with permission. All rights reserved. "Wechsler Adult Intelligence Scale" and "WAIS" are trademarks, in the USA and/or other countries, of Pearson Education, Inc. or its affiliates(s).*

In 2004, the test—now called the Stanford-Binet 5—was revised to analyze an individual's response in five content areas: fluid reasoning, knowledge, quantitative reasoning, visual-spatial reasoning, and working memory. A general composite score also is still obtained.

The Wechsler Scales Another set of widely used tests is called the *Wechsler scales*, developed by David Wechsler. They include the Wechsler Preschool and Primary Scale of Intelligence—Third Edition (WPPSI-III) to test children 2 years 6 months to 7 years 3 months of age; the Wechsler Intelligence Scale for Children—Fourth Edition (WISC-IV) for children and adolescents 6 to 16 years of age; and the Wechsler Adult Intelligence Scale—Third Edition (WAIS-III) for adolescents and adults 16 to 89 years of age.

Not only do the Wechsler scales provide an overall IQ, but they also yield a number of additional composite scores (for example, the Verbal Comprehension Index, the Working Memory Index, and the Processing Speed Index), allowing the examiner to quickly see patterns of strengths and weaknesses in different areas of the student's intelligence. Three of the Wechsler subscales are shown in Figure 3.15.

Using Intelligence Tests Psychological tests are tools. Like all tools, their effectiveness depends on the knowledge, skill, and integrity of the user. A hammer can be used to build a beautiful kitchen cabinet, or it can be used as a weapon of assault. Like a hammer, psychological tests can be used for positive purposes, or they can be badly abused. Here are some cautions about IQ that can help you avoid the pitfalls of using information about an adolescent's intelligence in negative ways:

- *Avoid stereotyping and expectations.* A special concern is that the scores on an IQ test easily can lead to stereotypes and expectations about adolescents. Sweeping generalizations are too often made on the basis of an IQ score. An IQ test should always be considered a measure of current performance. It is not a measure of fixed potential. Maturational changes and enriched environmental experiences can advance an adolescent's intelligence.
- *Know that IQ is not a sole indicator of competence.* Another concern about IQ tests occurs when they are used as the main or sole assessment of competence. A high IQ is not the ultimate human value. It is important to

triarchic theory of intelligence Sternberg's view that intelligence comes in three main forms: analytical, creative, and practical.

consider not only students' competence in such areas as verbal skills but also their practical skills, their relationship skills, and their moral values (Mayer & others, 2011).

MULTIPLE INTELLIGENCES

Is it more appropriate to think of an adolescent's intelligence as a general ability or as a number of specific abilities? Robert Sternberg and Howard Gardner have proposed influential theories that describe specific types of intelligence. The concept of emotional intelligence also has been proposed as a different type of intelligence than that measured by traditional intelligence tests.

Robert J. Sternberg, who developed the triarchic theory of intelligence.

Sternberg's Triarchic Theory Robert J. Sternberg (1986, 2004, 2009, 2010, 2011a,b,c, 2012) developed the **triarchic theory of intelligence,** which states that intelligence comes in three forms: (1) *analytical intelligence,* which refers to the ability to analyze, judge, evaluate, compare, and contrast; (2) *creative intelligence,* which consists of the ability to create, design, invent, originate, and imagine; and (3) *practical intelligence,* which involves the ability to use, apply, implement, and put ideas into practice.

Sternberg (2010, 2012) says that students with different triarchic patterns perform differently in school. Students with high analytic ability tend to be favored in conventional schools. They often do well in classes in which the teacher lectures and gives objective tests. They often are considered smart students, typically get good grades, do well on traditional IQ tests and the SAT, and later gain admission to competitive colleges.

Students who are high in creative intelligence often are not in the top rung of their class. Creatively intelligent students might not conform to the expectations that teachers have about how assignments should be done. They give unique answers, for which they might get reprimanded or marked down.

Like students high in creative intelligence, students who are practically intelligent often do not relate well to the demands of school. However, these students frequently do well outside the classroom's walls. Their social skills and common sense may allow them to become successful managers, entrepreneurs, or politicians, despite undistinguished school records.

Sternberg (2010, 2012) argues that it is important for classroom instruction to give students opportunities to learn through all three types of intelligence.

"You're wise, but you lack tree smarts."

Gardner's Eight Frames of Mind Howard Gardner (1983, 1993, 2002) suggests there are eight types of intelligence, or "frames of mind." These are described here, with examples of the types of vocations in which they are reflected as strengths (Campbell, Campbell, & Dickinson, 2004):

- *Verbal.* The ability to think in words and use language to express meaning (occupations: authors, journalists, speakers)
- *Mathematical.* The ability to carry out mathematical operations (occupations: scientists, engineers, accountants)
- *Spatial.* The ability to think three-dimensionally (occupations: architects, artists, sailors)
- *Bodily-kinesthetic.* The ability to manipulate objects and be physically adept (occupations: surgeons, craftspeople, dancers, athletes)
- *Musical.* A sensitivity to pitch, melody, rhythm, and tone (occupations: composers, musicians, and sensitive listeners)
- *Interpersonal.* The ability to understand and effectively interact with others (occupations: successful teachers, mental health professionals)
- *Intrapersonal.* The ability to understand oneself (occupations: theologians, psychologists)

Which of Gardner's eight intelligences are adolescent girls using in this situation?

- *Naturalist*: The ability to observe patterns in nature and understand natural and human-made systems (occupations: farmers, botanists, ecologists, landscapers)

According to Gardner, everyone has all of these intelligences but to varying degrees. As a result, we prefer to learn and process information in different ways. People learn best when they can apply their strong intelligences to the task.

Both Gardner's and Sternberg's theories include one or more categories related to social intelligence. In Gardner's theory, the categories are interpersonal intelligence and intrapersonal intelligence; in Sternberg's theory, practical intelligence. Another theory that emphasizes interpersonal, intrapersonal, and practical aspects of intelligence is called **emotional intelligence,** which has been popularized by Daniel Goleman (1995) in his book *Emotional Intelligence*. The concept of emotional intelligence was initially developed by Peter Salovey and John Mayer (1990), who define it as the ability to perceive and express emotion accurately and adaptively (such as taking the perspective of others), to understand emotion and emotional knowledge (such as understanding the roles that emotions play in friendship and marriage), to use feelings to facilitate thought (such as being in a positive mood, which is linked to creative thinking), and to manage emotions in oneself and others (such as being able to control one's anger). In one study, assessment of emotional intelligence predicted high school students' final grades in their courses (Gil-Olarte Marquez, Palomera Martin, & Brackett, 2006).

There continues to be considerable interest in the concept of emotional intelligence (Lomas & others, 2011; Mayer & others, 2011; Parker, Keefer, & Wood, 2011; Takeuchi & others, 2011). A recent study of college students revealed that both a general mental abilities test and an emotional intelligence assessment were linked to academic performance, although the general mental abilities test was a better predictor (Song & others, 2010). In this study, emotional intelligence was related to the quality of peer relations. Critics argue that too often emotional intelligence broadens the concept of intelligence too far and has not been adequately assessed and researched (Matthews, Zeidner, & Roberts, 2006, 2011).

Do People Have One or Many Intelligences? Figure 3.16 provides a comparison of Sternberg's, Gardner's, and Mayer/Salovey/Goleman's views. Notice that Sternberg's view is unique in emphasizing creative intelligence and that Gardner's includes a number of types of intelligence that are not addressed by the other views. These theories of multiple intelligence have much to offer. They have stimulated us to think more broadly about what makes up people's intelligence and competence (Sternberg, 2011b,c, 2012). And they have motivated educators to develop programs that instruct students in different domains (Campbell, 2008).

Sternberg	Gardner	Mayer/ Salovey/Goleman
Analytical	Verbal Mathematical	
Creative	Spatial Movement Musical	
Practical	Interpersonal Intrapersonal	Emotional
	Naturalistic	

FIGURE **3.16**
COMPARISON OF STERNBERG'S, GARDNER'S, AND MAYER/SALOVEY/GOLEMAN'S VIEWS

Theories of multiple intelligences have their critics (Jensen, 2008). Some critics argue that the research base to support these theories has not yet developed. In particular, some critics say that Gardner's classification seems arbitrary. For example, if musical skills represent a type of intelligence, why don't we also refer to chess intelligence, prize-fighter intelligence, and so on?

A number of psychologists still support the concept of *g* (general intelligence) (Davis, Arden, & Plomin, 2008; Jensen, 2008). For example, one expert on intelligence, Nathan Brody (2007) argues that people who excel at one type of intellectual task are likely to excel in other intellectual tasks. Thus, individuals who do well at memorizing lists of digits are also likely to be good at solving verbal problems and spatial layout problems. This general intelligence includes abstract reasoning or thinking, the capacity to acquire knowledge, and problem-solving ability (Brody, 2007; Carroll, 1993).

emotional intelligence The ability to perceive and express emotion accurately and adaptively, to understand emotion and emotional knowledge, to use feelings to facilitate thought, and to manage emotions in oneself and others.

Some experts who argue for the existence of general intelligence conclude that individuals also have specific intellectual abilities (Brody, 2007; Chiappe &

MacDonald, 2005; Hunt, 2011). In one study, John Carroll (1993) conducted an extensive examination of intellectual abilities and concluded that all intellectual abilities are related to each other, a view that supports the concept of general intelligence, but adds that there are many specialized abilities as well. Some of these specialized abilities, such as spatial abilities and mechanical abilities, are not adequately reflected in the curriculum of most schools. In sum, controversy still characterizes whether it is more accurate to conceptualize intelligence as a general ability, as specific abilities, or as both (Davis & others, 2011; Sternberg, 2011b,c, 2012). Sternberg (2011a,b, 2012) actually accepts that there is a *g* in the kinds of analytical tasks that traditional IQ tests assess but thinks that the range of intellectual tasks those tests measure is too narrow.

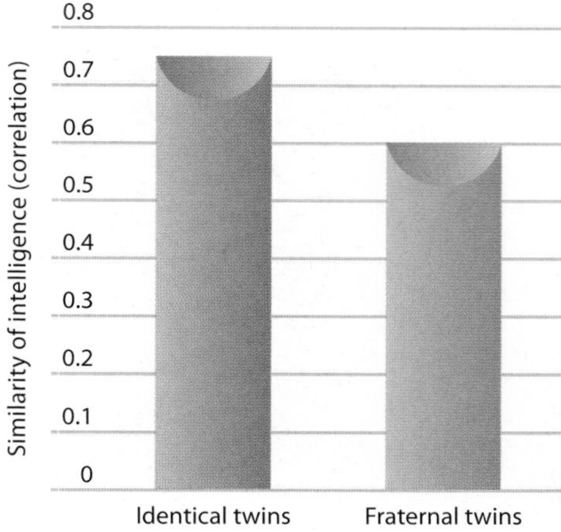

FIGURE **3.17**

CORRELATION BETWEEN INTELLIGENCE TEST SCORES AND TWIN STATUS. The graph represents a summary of research findings that have compared the intelligence test scores of identical and fraternal twins. An approximate 0.15 difference has been found with a higher correlation for identical twins (0.75) and a lower correlation for fraternal twins (0.60).

HEREDITY AND ENVIRONMENT

An ongoing issue involving intelligence is the extent to which it is due to heredity or to environment. In Chapter 2, we indicated how difficult it is to tease apart these influences, but that has not kept psychologists from trying to untangle them.

Heredity How strong is the effect of heredity on intelligence? A committee of respected researchers convened by the American Psychological Association concluded that by late adolescence, research studies reveal a strong influence of heredity on intelligence (Neisser & others, 1996). However, most research on heredity and environment does not include environments that differ radically. Thus, it is not surprising that many studies of heredity, environment, and intelligence show environment to be a fairly weak influence on intelligence (Fraser, 1995).

One strategy for examining the role of heredity in intelligence is to compare the IQs of identical and fraternal twins. Recall from Chapter 2 that identical twins have exactly the same genetic makeup, but fraternal twins do not. If intelligence is genetically determined, say some investigators, identical twins' IQs should be more similar than the intelligence of fraternal twins. Researchers have found that the IQs of identical twins are more similar than those of fraternal twins, but in some studies the difference is not very large (Grigorenko, 2000) (see Figure 3.17).

Environment One way to study the environment's influence on intelligence is to compare adolescents who have experienced different amounts of schooling. Schooling does influence intelligence, with the largest effects occurring when adolescents have had no formal education for an extended period, which is linked to lower intelligence (Ceci & Gilstrap, 2000).

Another possible effect of education can be seen in rapidly increasing IQ test scores around the world (Flynn, 1999, 2007, 2011). IQ scores have been increasing so fast that a high percentage of people regarded as having average intelligence at the turn of the century would be considered below average in intelligence today (see Figure 3.18). If a representative sample of people today took the Stanford-Binet test used in 1932, about one-fourth would be defined as having very superior intelligence, a label usually accorded to fewer than 3 percent of the population. Because the increase has taken place in a relatively short time, it can't be due to heredity, but rather may be due to increasing levels of education attained by a much greater percentage of the world's population or to other environmental factors such as the explosion of information to which people are exposed (Rönnlund & Nilsson, 2008). The worldwide increase in intelligence test scores that has occurred over a short time frame has been called the *Flynn effect,* after the researcher who discovered it—James Flynn (1999, 2007, 2011).

developmental **connection**

Nature and Nurture. The epigenetic view emphasizes that development is an ongoing, bidirectional interchange between heredity and environment. Chapter 2, p. 81

Heredity and Environment Interaction Today, most researchers agree that genetics and environment interact to influence intelligence (Mandelman & Grigorenko, 2011). For many adolescents, this means that positive modifications in environment

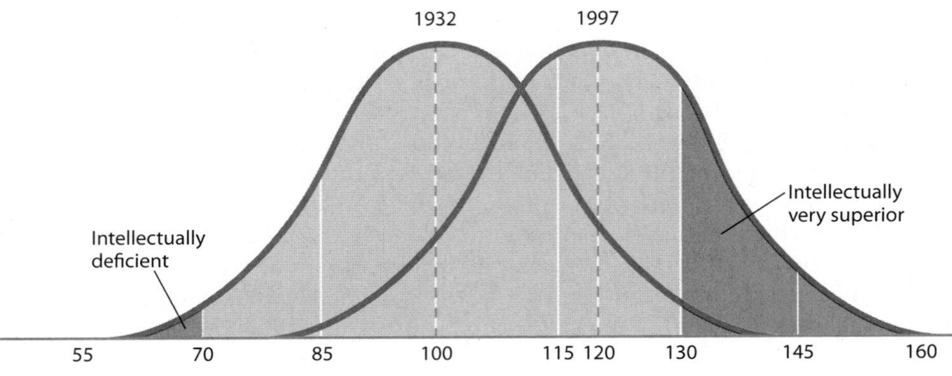

FIGURE **3.18**

THE INCREASE IN IQ SCORES FROM 1932 TO 1997. As measured by the Stanford-Binet intelligence test, American children seem to be getting smarter. Scores of a group tested in 1932 fell along a bell-shaped curve with half below 100 and half above. Studies show that if children took that same test today, half would score above 120 on the 1932 scale. Very few of them would score in the "intellectually deficient" end, on the left side, and about one-fourth would rank in the "very superior" range.

can change their IQ scores considerably. Although genetic endowment may always influence adolescents' intellectual ability, the environmental influences and opportunities provided to adolescents do make a difference.

Review *Connect* Reflect

LG4 Summarize the psychometric/intelligence view of adolescence.

Review

- What is intelligence? What are the main individual tests of intelligence? What are some strategies in interpreting intelligence test scores?
- What theories of multiple intelligences have been developed? Do people have one intelligence or many intelligences?
- What roles do heredity and environment play in intelligence?

Connect

- Compare creative and critical thinking.

Reflect *Your Own Personal Journey of Life*

- Apply Gardner's, Sternberg's, and Salovey, Mayer, and Goleman's categories of intelligence to yourself as an adolescent and emerging adult. Write a description of yourself based on each of these views.

5 Social Cognition

 Explain how social cognition is involved in adolescent development.

Adolescent Egocentrism | Social Cognition in the Remainder of the Text

social cognition The way individuals conceptualize and reason about their social worlds—the people they watch and interact with, their relationships with those people, the groups they participate in, and the way they reason about themselves and others.

adolescent egocentrism The heightened self-consciousness of adolescents, which is reflected in their belief that others are as interested in them as they themselves are, and in their sense of personal uniqueness and invulnerability.

Social cognition refers to the way individuals conceptualize and reason about their social worlds—the people they watch and interact with, their relationships with those people, the groups they participate in, and the way they reason about themselves and others. Our discussion will focus on adolescent egocentrism and our coverage of social cognition in the remainder of the text.

ADOLESCENT EGOCENTRISM

Adolescent egocentrism is the heightened self-consciousness of adolescents, which is reflected in their belief that others are as interested in them as they are in themselves, and in their sense of personal uniqueness and invulnerability. David Elkind (1976) argues that adolescent egocentrism can be dissected into two types of social thinking—imaginary audience and personal fable.

The *imaginary audience* refers to the aspect of adolescent egocentrism that involves attention-getting behavior—the attempt to be noticed, visible, and "onstage." An adolescent boy might think that others are as aware of a few hairs that are out of place as he is. An adolescent girl walks into her classroom and thinks that all eyes are riveted on her complexion. Adolescents especially sense that they are onstage in early adolescence, believing they are the main actors and all others are the audience. You may recall the story of my daughter, Tracy, from the beginning of the chapter. Tracy was exhibiting adolescent egocentrism when she perceived that every person in the restaurant was looking at her single out-of-place hair.

What characterizes adolescent egocentrism?

According to Elkind, the *personal fable* is the part of adolescent egocentrism that involves an adolescent's sense of personal uniqueness and invulnerability. Adolescents' sense of personal uniqueness makes them feel that no one can understand how they really feel. For example, an adolescent girl thinks that her mother cannot possibly sense the hurt she feels because her boyfriend has broken up with her. As part of their effort to retain a sense of personal uniqueness, adolescents might craft stories about themselves that are filled with fantasy, immersing themselves in a world that is far removed from reality. Personal fables frequently show up in adolescent diaries.

Elkind (1985) argued that the imaginary audience and personal fable are due to the cognitive egocentrism involved in the transition to formal operational thought. However, Daniel Lapsley and his colleagues (Hill, Duggan, & Lapsley, 2011; Hill & Lapsley, 2010; Lapsley & Hill, 2010; Lapsley & Stey, 2012) conclude that the distortions in the imaginary audience and personal fable involve the adolescent's ego. As they increasingly develop their own self and identity apart from their parents, their personal fable ideation likely reflects an adaptive narcissism that supports their ego. What role, then, does the personal fable play in adolescent adjustment? See the *Connecting with Health and Well-Being* interlude.

In early research, Elkind found that adolescent egocentrism did peak in early adolescence and then declined (Elkind & Bowen, 1979). However, a recent study of more than 2,300 adolescents and emerging adults from 11 to 21 years of age revealed that adolescent egocentrism was still prominent in the 18- to 21-year-olds (emerging adults) and the results varied by gender (Schwartz, Maynard, & Uzelac, 2008). For example, emerging adult males scored higher on the imaginary audience scale than did late adolescence males (15- to 18-year-olds), but no age differences on this scale occurred for females.

SOCIAL COGNITION IN THE REMAINDER OF THE TEXT

Interest in social cognition has blossomed, and the approach has infiltrated many aspects of the study of adolescent development. In the overview of the self and identity in Chapter 4, social cognition's role in understanding the self and identity is explored. In the evaluation of moral development in Chapter 7, considerable time is devoted to discussing Kohlberg's theory, which is a prominent aspect of the study of social cognition in adolescence. Further, in the discussion of families in Chapter 8, the emerging cognitive abilities of the adolescent are evaluated in concert with parent-adolescent conflict and parenting strategies. Also, in the description of peer relations in Chapter 9, the importance of social knowledge and social information processing in peer relations is highlighted.

developmental **connection**

Identity. Major changes in self-understanding take place in the adolescent years. Chapter 4, p. 130

connecting with health and well-being

What Role Does the Personal Fable Play in Adolescent Adjustment?

Some developmentalists conclude that the sense of uniqueness and invincibility that egocentrism generates is responsible for some of the seemingly reckless behavior of adolescents, including drag racing, drug use, failure to use contraceptives during intercourse, and suicide (Dolcini & others, 1989). For example, one study found that eleventh- and twelfth-grade females who were high in adolescent egocentrism were more likely to say they would not get pregnant from engaging in sex without contraception than were their counterparts who were low in adolescent egocentrism (Arnett, 1990).

A study of sixth- through twelfth-graders examined whether aspects of the personal fable were linked to various aspects of adolescent adjustment (Aalsma, Lapsley, & Flannery, 2006). A sense of invulnerability was linked to engaging in risky behaviors, such as smoking cigarettes, drinking alcohol, and delinquency, whereas a sense of personal uniqueness was related to depression and suicidal thoughts. A subsequent study confirmed the findings of the first with regard to the correlation between personal uniqueness, depression, and suicidal thoughts. (Goossens & others, 2002).

How are personal uniqueness and invulnerability linked to adolescent adjustment and problems?

These findings indicate that personal uniqueness fables should be treated as a risk factor for psychological problems, especially depression and suicidal tendencies in girls (Aalsma, Lapsley, & Flannery, 2006). Treating invulnerability as a risk factor for adjustment problems is less certain because in the earlier study just described (Aalsma, Lapsley, & Flannery, 2006), a sense of invulnerability was associated not only with risky behavior but also with some positive aspects of adjustment, such as coping and self-worth.

Further reason to question the accuracy of the invulnerability aspect of the personal fable is provided by other research that reveals many adolescents don't consider themselves invulnerable (de Bruin, Parker, & Fischhoff, 2007). Indeed, an increasing number of research studies suggest that, rather than perceiving themselves to be invulnerable, adolescents tend to portray themselves as vulnerable to experiencing a premature death (Jamieson & Romer, 2008; Reyna & Rivers, 2008). For example, in a recent study, 12- to 18-year-olds were asked about their chance of dying in the next year and prior to age 20 (Fischhoff & others, 2010). The adolescents greatly overestimated their chance of dying.

Some researchers have questioned the view that invulnerability is a unitary concept and argued rather that it consists of two dimensions (Duggan & others, 2000; Lapsley & Hill, 2010):

- *Danger invulnerability,* which describes adolescents' sense of indestructibility and tendency to take on physical risks (driving recklessly at high speeds, for example).
- *Psychological invulnerability,* which captures an adolescent's felt invulnerability related to personal or psychological distress (getting one's feelings hurt, for example).

A recent study revealed that adolescents who scored high on a danger invulnerability scale were more likely to engage in juvenile delinquency and/or substance abuse, or to be depressed (Lapsley & Hill, 2010). In this study, adolescents who scored high on psychological invulnerability were less likely to be depressed, had higher self-esteem, and engaged in better interpersonal relationships. In terms of psychological invulnerability, adolescents often benefit from the normal developmental challenges of exploring identity options, making new friends, asking someone to go out on a date, and learning a new skill. All of these important adolescent tasks include risk and failure as an option, but if successful result in enhanced self-image.

In the view of Daniel Lapsley and his colleagues (Hill, Duggan, & Lapsley, 2011; Lapsley & Stey, 2012), the separation-individuation process—which involves adolescents separating from their parents and developing independence and identity—is responsible for the findings just discussed rather than cognitive developmental changes. With respect to personal fables, they argue that invulnerability and personal uniqueness are forms of adolescent narcissism.

Do these findings about the two dimensions of perceived invulnerability have practical applications? For instance, could they help identify adolescents at risk for engaging in self-destructive behavior such as delinquency and substance abuse?

Review *Connect* Reflect

LG5 Explain how social cognition is involved in adolescent development.

Review

- What characterizes adolescent egocentrism?
- How is social cognition related to other topics discussed in this text?

Connect

- Compare and contrast the concepts of the imaginary audience and the personal fable.

Reflect *Your Own Personal Journey of Life*

- Think about your friends in early adolescence, late adolescence, and emerging adulthood. Did adolescent egocentrism decline for all of them as they moved through late adolescence and emerging adulthood? Explain how it might especially be maladaptive if the characteristics of adolescent egocentrism still strongly characterize individuals in the emerging adult years.

reach your **learning goals**

1 The Brain

LG1 Describe the developmental changes in the brain during adolescence.

Neurons

- Neurons, the basic units of the nervous system, are made up of a cell body, dendrites, and an axon. Myelination is the process by which the axon portion of the neuron becomes covered and insulated with a layer of fat cells, which increases the speed and efficiency of information processing in the nervous system. Myelination continues to increase during adolescence. Synaptogenesis in the prefrontal cortex, where reasoning and self-regulation occur, also continues through adolescence.

Brain Structure, Cognition, and Emotion

- The corpus callosum, a large bundle of axon fibers that connects the brain's left and right hemispheres, thickens in adolescence, and this thickening improves the adolescent's ability to process information. The prefrontal cortex, the highest level of the frontal lobes that is involved in reasoning, decision making, and self-control, matures much later (continuing to develop in emerging adulthood) than the amygdala, the part of the limbic system that is the seat of emotions such as anger. The later development of the prefrontal cortex combined with the earlier maturity of the amygdala may explain the difficulty adolescents have in putting the brakes on their emotional intensity.

Experience and Plasticity

- Experience plays an important role in development of the brain in childhood and adolescence. Although early experiences are very important in the development of the brain, the brain retains considerable plasticity in adolescence. New brain cells may be generated during adolescence. The earlier brain injury occurs, the more successful recovery is likely to be.

2 The Cognitive Developmental View

Discuss the cognitive developmental view of adolescence.

Piaget's Theory

- Piaget's widely acclaimed theory stresses the concepts of adaptation, schemas, assimilation, accommodation, and equilibration. Piaget said that individuals develop through four cognitive stages: sensorimotor, preoperational, concrete operational, and formal operational. Formal operational thought, which Piaget emphasized appears from 11 to 15 years of age, is characterized by abstract, idealistic, and hypothetical-deductive thinking. Some experts argue that formal operational thought has two phases: early and late. Individual variation in adolescent cognition is extensive. Many young adolescents are still consolidating their concrete operational thought or are early formal operational thinkers rather than full-fledged ones. Piaget's ideas have been applied to education. In terms of Piaget's contributions, we owe to him the entire field of cognitive development and a masterful list of concepts. He also was a genius at observing children. Criticisms of Piaget's theory focus on estimates of competence, stages, training to reason at higher stages, and the role of culture and education. Neo-Piagetians have proposed some substantial changes in Piaget's theory. Some experts argue that the idealism of Piaget's formal operational stage declines in young adults, being replaced by more realistic, pragmatic thinking. Perry said that adolescents often engage in dualistic, absolutist thinking, whereas young adults are more likely to think reflectively and relativistically. Postformal thought is reflective, relativistic, and contextual; provisional; realistic; and open to emotions and subjective.

Wisdom is expert knowledge about the practical aspects of life that permits excellent judgment about important matters. Baltes and his colleagues have found that high levels of wisdom are rare, the time frame of late adolescence and early adulthood is the main age window for wisdom to emerge, factors other than age are critical for a high level of wisdom to develop, and personality-related factors are better predictors of wisdom than cognitive factors such as intelligence. Sternberg argues that wisdom involves both academic and practical aspects of intelligence. His balance theory emphasizes making competent decisions that take into account self-interest, the interests of others, and contexts to produce a common good. Sternberg argues that wisdom should be taught in schools.

Vygotsky's Theory

- Vygotsky's view stimulated considerable interest in the idea that knowledge is situated and collaborative. One of his important concepts is the zone of proximal development, which involves guidance by more skilled peers and adults. Vygotsky argued that learning the skills of the culture is a key aspect of development. Piaget's and Vygotsky's views are both constructivist, although Vygotsky's view is a stronger social constructivist view than Piaget's. In both views, teachers should be facilitators, not directors, of learning. Criticisms of Vygotsky's view focus on facilitators possibly being too helpful and adolescents expecting others to do things for them.

3 The Information-Processing View

LG3 Characterize the information-processing view of adolescence.

Cognitive Resources

- Capacity and speed of processing, often referred to as cognitive resources, increase across childhood and adolescence. Changes in the brain serve as biological foundations for developmental changes in cognitive resources. In terms of capacity, the increase is reflected in older children and adolescents being able to hold in mind simultaneously several dimensions of a topic. A reaction-time task has often been used to assess speed of processing. Processing speed continues to improve in adolescence.

Attention and Memory

- Attention is the focusing of mental resources. Adolescents typically have better attentional skills than children do, although there are wide individual differences in how effectively adolescents deploy their attention. Four ways that adolescents can allocate their attention are selective attention, divided attention, sustained attention, and executive attention. Multitasking is an example of divided attention and it can harm adolescents' attention when they are engaging in a challenging task. Adolescents have better short-term memory, working memory, and long-term memory than children do.

Executive Functioning

- Higher-order cognitive processes such as exercising cognitive control, making decisions, reasoning, thinking critically, thinking creatively, and metacognition are often called executive functioning. Adolescence is characterized by a number of advances in executive functioning. Cognitive control involves effective control and flexible thinking in a number of areas, including controlling attention, reducing interfering thoughts, and being cognitively flexible. Across childhood and adolescence, cognitive control (inhibition) increases with age and this increase is likely due to the maturation of the prefrontal cortex. Older adolescents make better decisions than younger adolescents, who in turn are better at this than children are. Being able to make competent decisions, however, does not mean they actually will be made in everyday life, where breadth of experience comes into play. Adolescents often make better decisions when they are calm than when emotionally aroused. Social contexts, especially the presence of peers, influence adolescent decision making. Critical thinking involves thinking reflectively and productively and evaluating the evidence. Adolescence is an important transitional period in critical thinking because of such cognitive changes as increased speed, automaticity, and capacity of information processing; more breadth of content knowledge; increased ability to construct new combinations of knowledge; and a greater range and spontaneous use of strategies. Thinking creatively is the ability to think in novel and unusual ways and discover unique solutions to problems. Guilford distinguished between convergent and divergent thinking. A number of strategies, including brainstorming, not overcontrolling, encouraging internal control, and introducing adolescents to creative people, can be used to stimulate creative thinking. An expert is the opposite of a novice (someone who is just beginning to learn a content area). Experts are better than novices at detecting features and meaningful patterns of information, accumulating more content knowledge and organizing it effectively, and retrieving important aspects of knowledge with little effort. Becoming an expert usually involves talent and deliberate practice and motivation. Metacognition is cognition about cognition, or knowing about knowing. In Pressley's view, the key to education is helping students learn a rich repertoire of strategies that results in solutions to problems. Adolescents' thinking skills benefit when they are taught general metacognitive skills and domain-specific thinking skills.

4 The Psychometric/Intelligence View

Summarize the psychometric/intelligence view of adolescence.

Intelligence Tests

- Intelligence is the ability to solve problems and to adapt and learn from everyday experiences. A key aspect of intelligence focuses on its individual variations. Traditionally, intelligence has been measured by tests designed to compare people's performance on cognitive tasks. Alfred Binet developed the first intelligence test and created the concept of mental age. William Stern developed the concept of IQ for use with the Binet test. Revisions of the Binet test are called the Stanford-Binet. The test scores on the Stanford-Binet approximate a normal distribution. The Wechsler scales, created by David Wechsler, are the other main intelligence assessment tool. These tests provide an overall IQ and other composite scores, including the Working Memory Index and the Information Processing Speed Index. The single number provided by many IQ tests can lead to false expectations, and IQ test scores should be only one type of information used to evaluate an adolescent.

Multiple Intelligences

- Sternberg's triarchic theory states that there are three main types of intelligence: analytical, creative, and practical. Gardner has proposed that there are eight types of intelligence: verbal, mathematical, spatial, bodily-kinesthetic, musical, interpersonal, intrapersonal, and naturalist. Emotional intelligence is the ability to perceive and express emotion accurately and adaptively, to understand emotion and emotional knowledge, to use feelings to facilitate thought, and to manage emotions in oneself and others. The multiple intelligences approaches have broadened the definition of intelligence and motivated educators to develop programs that instruct students in different domains. Critics maintain that the multiple intelligence theories have classifications that seem arbitrary and factors that really aren't part of intelligence, such as musical skills and creativity.

Heredity and Environment

- Many studies show that by late adolescence intelligence is strongly influenced by heredity, but many of these studies do not reflect environments that are radically different. A well-documented environmental influence on intelligence is schooling.

Also, probably because of increased education, intelligence test scores have risen considerably around the world in recent decades—an increase called the Flynn effect—and this supports the role of environment in intelligence. In sum, intelligence is influenced by heredity and environment.

5 Social Cognition

Explain how social cognition is involved in adolescent development.

Adolescent Egocentrism

- Social cognition refers to how people conceptualize and reason about their social world, including the relation of the self to others. Adolescent egocentrism is adolescents' heightened self-consciousness, mirrored in their belief that others are as interested in them as they are. According to Elkind, adolescent egocentrism consists of an imaginary audience and a personal fable. Researchers have recently found that adolescents actually overestimate their chance of experiencing a premature death, indicating that they perceive themselves to be less invulnerable than Elkind's personal fable indicates. An alternative to Elkind's cognitive egocentrism view is the view that the imaginary audience and personal fable are mainly the result of changes in perspective taking and the adolescent's ego. Also, recently invulnerability has been described as having two dimensions—danger invulnerability and psychological invulnerability—which have different outcomes for adolescence.

Social Cognition in the Remainder of the Text

- We study social cognition throughout this text, especially in chapters on the self and identity, moral development, peers, and families.

key terms

neurons 88
myelination 88
synapses 88
corpus callosum 88
prefrontal cortex 88
amygdala 89
schema 92
assimilation 92
accommodation 92
equilibration 92
sensorimotor stage 93
preoperational stage 93
concrete operational stage 93
formal operational stage 94
hypothetical-deductive reasoning 94
neo-Piagetians 96
postformal thought 97
wisdom 98
zone of proximal development (ZPD) 100
social constructivist approach 100
attention 103
selective attention 103
divided attention 103
sustained attention 103
executive attention 103
executive functioning 105
cognitive control 106
dual-process model 108
critical thinking 109
creativity 109
convergent thinking 110
divergent thinking 110
metacognition 113
psychometric/intelligence view 114
intelligence 115
mental age (MA) 115
intelligence quotient (IQ) 115
normal distribution 115
triarchic theory of intelligence 116
emotional intelligence 118
social cognition 120
adolescent egocentrism 120

key people

Laurence Steinberg 89
Charles Nelson 89
Jay Giedd 90
Elizabeth Sowell 90
Jean Piaget 92
Robbie Case 96
William Perry 96
Gisela Labouvie-Vief 96
Paul Baltes 98
Robert Sternberg 99
Lev Vygotsky 100
Deanna Kuhn 102
Alan Baddeley 106
J. P. Guilford 110
Michael Pressley 113
Alfred Binet 115
William Stern 115
David Wechsler 116
Howard Gardner 117
Peter Salovey and John Mayer 118
Daniel Goleman 118
Nathan Brody 118
David Elkind 121
Daniel Lapsley 121

resources for **improving the lives of adolescents**

Brain and Cognition
(2010, December, Vol. 72, 1-164)

This journal issue brought together leading experts in the field of brain development in adolescence to write about the current state of knowledge and research in this area.

Adolescent Thinking
Deanna Kuhn
in R. M. Lerner & L. Steinberg (Eds.)
Handbook of Adolescent Psychology (2009, 3rd ed.)
New York: Wiley

An up-to-date, in-depth examination of the important changes in executive functioning and other cognitive changes in adolescence.

Adolescent Thinking
Developmental Review
(2008, Vol. 28, 1–152)

A number of leading experts examine the nature of risk and rational decision making during adolescence.

self-**assessment**

The Student Online Learning Center includes the following self-assessments for further exploration:

- *Exploring Changes in My Thinking from Adolescence to Adulthood*
- *My Study Skills*
- *Examining My Creative Thinking*
- *Evaluating Myself on Gardner's Eight Types of Intelligence*
- *How Emotionally Intelligent Am I?*

understanding of different personality characteristics (Thompson & Goodman, 2011; Thompson, Winer, & Goodvin, 2011). Several aspects of the self have been studied more than others. These include self-understanding, self-esteem, and self-concept.

More so than as children, adolescents carry with them a sense of who they are and what makes them different from everyone else. Consider one adolescent boy's self-description: "I am male, bright, an athlete, a political liberal, an extravert, and a compassionate individual." He takes comfort in his uniqueness: "No one else is quite like me. I am 5 feet 11 inches tall and weigh 160 pounds. I live in a suburb and plan to attend the state university. I want to be a sports journalist. I am an expert at building canoes. When I am not going to school and studying, I write short stories about sports figures, which I hope to publish someday." Real or imagined, an adolescent's developing sense of self and uniqueness is a motivating force in life. Our exploration of the self begins with information about adolescents' self-understanding and then turns to their self-esteem and self-concept.

SELF-UNDERSTANDING

Know thyself, for once we know ourselves, we may learn how to care for ourselves, but otherwise we never shall.

—Socrates

Greek Philosopher, 5th Century B.C.

Though individuals become more introspective in adolescence and even more so in emerging adulthood, this self-understanding is not completely internal; rather, self-understanding is a social cognitive construction (Harter, 2006). That is, adolescents' and emerging adults' developing cognitive capacities interact with their sociocultural experiences to influence their self-understanding. These are among the questions we examine in this section: What is self-understanding? What are some important dimensions of adolescents' and emerging adults' self-understanding?

What Is Self-Understanding? **Self-understanding** is the individual's cognitive representation of the self, the substance and content of self-conceptions. For example, a 12-year-old boy understands that he is a student, a football player, a family member, and a video game lover. A 14-year-old girl understands that she is a soccer player, a student council member, a movie fan, and a rock music fan. An adolescent's self-understanding is based, in part, on the various roles and membership categories that define who adolescents are (Harter, 2006). Though self-understanding provides the rational underpinnings, it is not the whole of personal identity.

What Are Some Important Dimensions of Adolescents' and Emerging Adults' Self-Understanding? The development of self-understanding in adolescence is complex and involves a number of aspects of the self (Harter, 2006). Let's examine how the adolescent's self-understanding differs from the child's, then describe some changes in self-understanding during emerging adulthood.

developmental **connection**

Cognitive Theory. In Piaget's fourth stage of cognitive development, thought becomes more abstract, idealistic, and logical. Chapter 3, p. 94

Abstraction and Idealism Remember from our discussion of Piaget's theory of cognitive development in Chapter 1 and Chapter 3 that many adolescents begin to think in more abstract and *idealistic* ways. When asked to describe themselves, adolescents are more likely than children to use abstract and idealistic terms. Consider 14-year-old Laurie's abstract description of herself: "I am a human being. I am indecisive. I don't know who I am." Also consider her idealistic description of herself: "I am a naturally sensitive person who really cares about people's feelings. I think I'm pretty good-looking." Not all adolescents describe themselves in idealistic ways, but most adolescents distinguish between the real self and the ideal self.

Differentiation Over time, an adolescent's self-understanding becomes increasingly *differentiated* (Harter, 2006). Adolescents are more likely than children to note contextual or situational variations in describing themselves (Harter, Waters, & Whitesell, 1996). For example, a 15-year-old girl might describe herself by

self-understanding The individual's cognitive representation of the self; the substance and content of self-conceptions.

using one set of characteristics in connection with her family and another set of characteristics in connection with her peers and friends. Yet another set of characteristics might appear in her self-description of her romantic relationship. In sum, adolescents are more likely than children to understand that they possess several different selves, each one varying to some degree according to a specific role or context.

What are some characteristics of self-understanding in adolescence?

The Fluctuating Self Given the contradictory nature of the self in adolescence, it is not surprising that the self fluctuates across situations and across time (Harter, 1990a). The 15-year-old girl who was quoted at the beginning of this chapter remarked that she could not understand how she could switch from being cheerful one moment, to being anxious the next, and then sarcastic a short time later. One researcher has referred to the fluctuating adolescent's self as "the barometric self" (Rosenberg, 1979). In most cases, the self continues to be characterized by instability until late adolescence or even early adulthood, when a more unified theory of self is constructed. We have more to consider about fluctuations in adolescents' emotions later in the chapter.

Contradictions Within the Self As adolescents begin to differentiate their concept of the self into multiple roles in different relationship contexts, they sense potential contradictions between their differentiated selves. In one study, Susan Harter (1986) asked seventh-, ninth-, and eleventh-graders to describe themselves. She found that the number of contradictory self-descriptions they mentioned (moody *and* understanding, ugly *and* attractive, bored *and* inquisitive, caring *and* uncaring, introverted *and* fun-loving) increased dramatically between the seventh and ninth grades. Though the number of contradictory self-descriptions students mentioned declined in the eleventh grade, they still outnumbered those noted in the seventh grade. Adolescents develop the cognitive ability to detect these inconsistencies as they strive to construct a general theory of the self (Harter & Monsour, 1992).

Real Versus Ideal, True Versus False Selves Adolescents' emerging ability to construct ideal selves can be perplexing to them. Although the capacity to recognize a discrepancy between the *real* and *ideal* selves represents a cognitive advance, the humanistic theorist Carl Rogers (1950) argued that a strong discrepancy between the real and ideal selves is a sign of maladjustment. Too great a discrepancy between one's actual self and one's ideal self—the person one wants to be—can produce a sense of failure and self-criticism and can even trigger depression.

Although some theorists consider a strong discrepancy between the ideal and real selves maladaptive, others argue that it need not always be, especially in adolescence. In one view, an important aspect of the ideal or imagined self is the **possible self:** what individuals might become, what they would like to become, and what they are afraid of becoming (Markus & Nurius, 1986). Thus, adolescents' possible selves include both what they hope to be as well as what they dread they could become (Quinlan, Jaccard, & Blanton, 2006). In this view, the presence of both hoped-for and dreaded ideal selves is psychologically healthy, lending balance to an adolescent's perspective and motivation. That is, the attributes of the future positive self—getting into a good college, being admired, having a successful career—can direct an adolescent's positive actions, whereas the attributes of the future negative self—being unemployed, being lonely, not getting into a good college—can identify behaviors to be avoided.

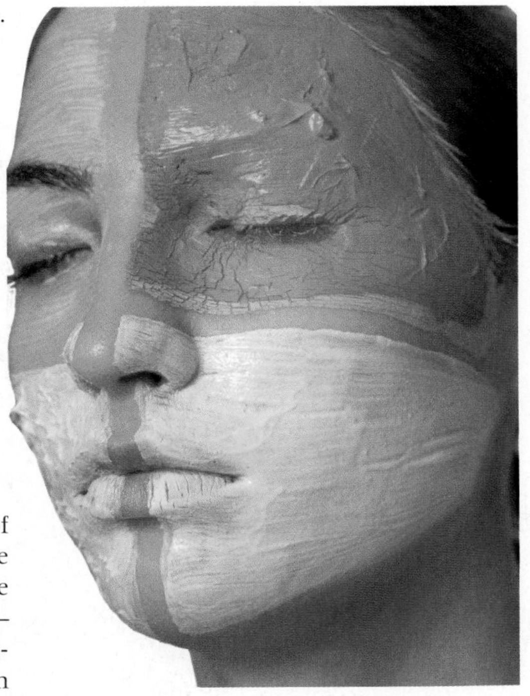

What characterizes adolescents' possible selves?

Can adolescents distinguish between their *true* and *false* selves? In one research study, they could (Harter & Lee, 1989). Adolescents are most likely to show their false selves with classmates and in romantic or dating situations; they are least likely to show their false selves with close friends. Adolescents may display a false self to impress others or to try out new behaviors or roles. They may feel that others do not understand their true selves or that others force them to behave in false ways. Some adolescents report that they do not like their false-self behavior, but others

possible self What individuals might become, what they would like to become, and what they are afraid of becoming.

say that it does not bother them. One study found that experienced authenticity of the self is highest among adolescents who say they receive support from their parents (Harter, Stocker, & Robinson, 1996).

Social Comparison Young adolescents are more likely than children to compare themselves with others and to understand that others are making comparisons about them (Ruble & others, 1980; Sebastian, Burnett, & Blakemore, 2010). An individual's beliefs about how he or she is viewed by others is referred to as the *looking glass* self. However, most adolescents are unwilling to *admit* that they engage in social comparison because they view social comparison as socially undesirable. That is, they think that acknowledging their social comparison motives will endanger their popularity. Relying on social comparison information can be confusing to adolescents because of the large number of reference groups available to them. Should adolescents compare themselves to classmates in general? To friends of their own gender? To popular adolescents, good-looking adolescents, athletic adolescents? Considering all of these social comparison groups simultaneously can be perplexing for adolescents.

Self-Consciousness Adolescents are more likely than children to be *self-conscious* about, and preoccupied with, their self-understanding (Harter, 2006). Although adolescents become more introspective, they do not always develop their self-understanding in social isolation. Adolescents turn to their friends for support and self-clarification, including their friends' opinions in their emerging self-definitions. As one researcher on self-development commented, adolescents' friends are often the main source of reflected self-appraisals, the social mirror into which adolescents anxiously stare (Rosenberg, 1979).

Self-Protection In adolescence, the sense of confusion and conflict that is stimulated by the efforts to understand oneself is accompanied by a need to *protect the self*. In an attempt to protect the self, adolescents are prone to deny their negative characteristics. For example, in Harter's investigation of self-understanding, adolescents were more likely than not to see positive self-descriptions such as *attractive, fun-loving, sensitive, affectionate,* and *inquisitive* as central, important aspects of the

How does self-consciousness change as individuals go through adolescence?

self, and to see negative self-descriptions such as *ugly, mediocre, depressed, selfish,* and *nervous* as peripheral, less important aspects of the self (Harter, 1986). This tendency is consistent with adolescents' tendency to describe the self in idealistic ways.

How does self-understanding change in emerging adulthood?

The Unconscious Self In adolescence, self-understanding involves greater recognition that the self includes unconscious as well as conscious components. This recognition is not likely to occur until late adolescence, however. That is, older adolescents are more likely than younger adolescents to believe that certain aspects of their mental experience are beyond their awareness or control.

Not Quite Yet a Coherent, Integrated Self Because of the proliferation of selves and unrealistic self-portraits during adolescence, the task of integrating these varying self-conceptions becomes problematic (Harter, 2006). Only later, usually in emerging adulthood, do individuals successfully integrate the many aspects of the self (Luyckx & others, 2010).

Emerging Adulthood and Adulthood In emerging adulthood, self-understanding becomes more integrative, with the disparate parts of the self pieced together more systematically. Emerging adults may detect inconsistencies in their earlier self-descriptions as they attempt to construct a general theory of self, an integrated sense of identity.

As we saw in Chapter 3, Gisela Labouvie-Vief (2006) concludes that considerable restructuring of the self can take place in emerging adulthood. She emphasizes that key aspects of self-development in emerging adulthood involve an increase in self-reflection and a decision about a specific worldview.

However, Labouvie-Vief (2006) argues that although emerging adults engage in more complex and critical thinking than when they were adolescents, many still have difficulty integrating their complex view of the world. She says this difficulty results because emerging adults are still easily influenced by their emotions, which can distort their thinking and cause them to be too self-serving and self-protective. In her research, it is not until 30 to 39 years of age that adults effectively develop a coherent, integrated worldview.

developmental **connection**

Cognitive Theory. Understanding cognitive changes in emerging adulthood and early adulthood requires consideration of how emotional maturity might affect cognitive development. Chapter 3, p. 97

Self-Understanding and Social Contexts We have seen that the adolescent's self-understanding can vary across relationships and social roles. Researchers have found that adolescents' portraits of themselves can differ depending on whether they describe themselves when they are with their mother, father, close friend, romantic partner, or peer. They also can differ depending on whether they describe themselves in the role of student, athlete, or employee. Similarly, adolescents might create different selves depending on their ethnic and cultural background and experiences (Lalonde & Chandler, 2004).

The multiple selves of ethnically diverse youth reflect their experiences in navigating their multiple worlds of family, peers, school, and community (Cooper & others, 2002; Rossiter, 2008). As U.S. youth from different ethnic backgrounds move from one culture to another, they can encounter barriers related to language, racism, gender, immigration, and poverty. In each of their different worlds, however, they also can find resources—in institutions, in other people, and in themselves. Youth who have difficulty moving between worlds can experience alienation from their school, family, or peers. This in turn can lead to other problems. However, youth who can navigate effectively between different worlds can develop bicultural or multicultural selves and become "culture brokers" for others.

The contemporary perspective on the self emphasizes the construction of multiple self-representations across different relational contexts.

—Susan Harter

Contemporary Psychologist, University of Denver

Hazel Markus and her colleagues (Markus & Kitayama, 2010; Markus, Mullally, & Kitayama, 1999) stress that understanding how multiple selves emerge through

This lack of awareness contributes to their adjustment problems (Hill & Lapsley, 2011; Lapsley & Stey, 2012). Narcissists are excessively self-centered and self-congratulatory, viewing their own needs and desires as paramount. As a result, narcissists rarely show any empathy toward others. In fact, narcissists often devalue people around them to protect their own precarious self-esteem, yet they often respond with rage and shame when others do not admire them and treat them in accordance with their grandiose fantasies about themselves. Narcissists are at their most grandiose when their self-esteem is threatened. Narcissists may fly into a frenzy if they have given an unsatisfactory performance.

What characterizes narcissistic individuals?

One study revealed that narcissistic adolescents were more aggressive than other adolescents but only when they were shamed (Thomaes & others, 2008). Low self-esteem was not linked to aggression, but narcissism combined with high self-esteem was related to exceptionally high aggression. And a recent longitudinal study found that narcissistic adolescents and emerging adults were more impulsive, histrionic (acting, being affected), active, and self-focused as young children than were others (Carlson & Gjerde, 2010). In this study, narcissism increased from 14 to 18 years of age, then slightly declined from 18 to 23.

So far, narcissism has been portrayed as a negative aspect of adolescent and emerging adult development. However, Daniel Lapsley and Matthew Aalsma (2006) found that college students' adjustment varied according to the type of narcissism. In their research, moderate narcissists showed healthy adjustment, whereas covert and overt narcissists were characterized by poor adjustment. Covert narcissists were described as reflecting "narcissistic grandiosity and entitlement lurking behind a façade of personal inadequacy, inferiority, and vulnerability" (p. 68). Overt narcissists openly displayed their grandiosity and exploitativeness at a high level.

developmental **connection**

Social Cognition. Adolescent egocentrism increases in early adolescence. Chapter 3, p. 121

Are today's adolescents and emerging adults more self-centered and narcissistic than their counterparts in earlier generations? Research by Jean Twenge and her colleagues (2008a,b) indicated that compared with baby boomers who were surveyed in 1975, twelfth-graders surveyed in 2006 were more self-satisfied overall and far more confident they would be very good employees, mates, and parents. They call today's adolescents *generation me.* However, other recent large-scale analyses have revealed no increase in high school and college students' narcissism from the 1976 through 2006 (Trzesniewski & Donnellan, 2010; Trzesniewski, Donnellan, & Robins, 2008a,b). In sum, the extent to which recent generations of adolescents have higher self-esteem and are more narcissistic than earlier generations is controversial (Arnett, 2010; Donnellan & Trzesniewski, 2010; Eckersley, 2010; Roberts, Edmonds, & Grijaiva, 2010; Twenge & Campbell, 2010).

In one recent analysis, age changes in narcissism were much stronger than generational changes (Roberts, Edmonds, & Grijaiva, 2010). In this study, across three generations, college students were the most narcissistic, followed by their parents, and then students' grandparents were the least narcissistic. These researchers say that it is more accurate to label today's adolescents and emerging adults *developmental me* rather than *generational me*.

Does Self-Esteem Change During Adolescence and Emerging Adulthood?

Researchers have found that self-esteem often decreases when children make the transition from elementary school to middle or junior high school (Twenge & Campbell, 2001). Indeed, during and just after many life transitions, individuals' self-esteem often decreases. This decrease in self-esteem may occur during the transition from middle or junior high school to high school, and from high school to college.

Self-esteem fluctuates across the life span. One cross-sectional study assessed the self-esteem of a very large, diverse sample of 326,641 individuals from 9 to 90 years of age (Robins & others, 2002). About two-thirds of the participants were from the United States. The individuals were asked to respond to the item, "I have

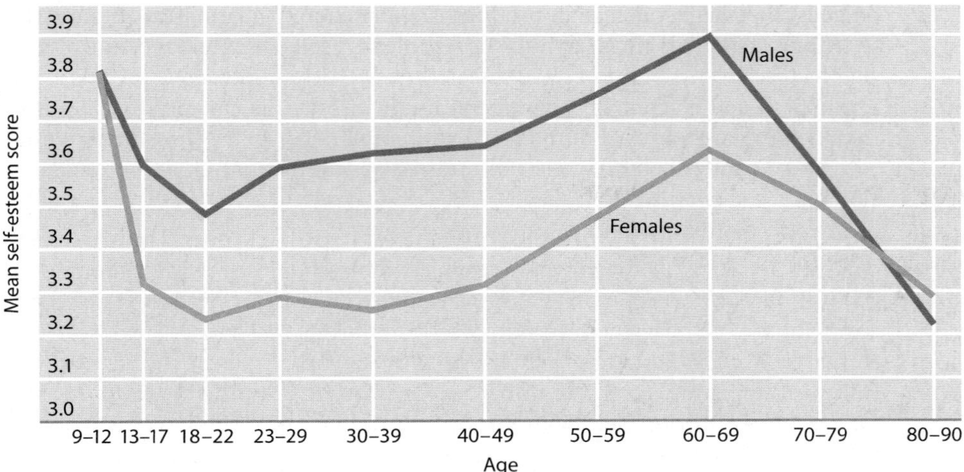

FIGURE **4.2**

SELF-ESTEEM ACROSS THE LIFE SPAN. One large-scale study asked more than 300,000 individuals to rate the extent to which they have high self-esteem on a 5-point scale, 5 being "strongly agree" and 1 being "strongly disagree." Self-esteem dropped in adolescence and late adulthood. Self-esteem of females was lower than self-esteem of males through most of the life span.

high self-esteem" on a 5-point scale in which 5 stood for "strongly agree" and 1 stood for "strongly disagree." Self-esteem decreased in adolescence, increased in the twenties, leveled off in the thirties, rose in the forties through the mid-sixties, and then dropped in the seventies and eighties (see Figure 4.2). At most ages, males reported higher self-esteem than females did.

Another study also found that the gender gap (lower for females) in self-esteem decreased as individuals went through emerging adulthood from 18 to 25 years of age (Galambos, Barker, & Krahn, 2006). In this study, social support and marriage were linked with an increase in self-esteem, whereas unemployment was related to a decrease in self-esteem.

Some researchers argue that although there may be a decrease in self-esteem during adolescence, the drop is actually very slight and not nearly as pronounced as presented in the media (Hyde, 2005, 2011; Kling & others, 1999). Also note in Figure 4.2 that, despite the drop in self-esteem among adolescent girls, their average score (3.3) was still slightly higher than the neutral point on the scale (3.0).

One explanation for the decline in the self-esteem among females during early adolescence focuses on girls' more negative body images during pubertal change compared with boys (Harter, 2006). Another explanation involves the greater interest young adolescent girls take in social relationships and society's failure to reward that interest.

A current concern is that too many of today's college students grew up receiving empty praise and as a consequence have inflated self-esteem (Graham, 2005; Stipek, 2005). Too often they were given praise for performance that was mediocre or even poor. Now in college, they may have difficulty handling competition and criticism. The title of a book, *Dumbing Down Our Kids: Why American Children Feel Good About Themselves But Can't Read, Write, or Add* (Sykes, 1995), vividly captured the theme that many U.S. students' academic problems may stem at least in part from unmerited praise as part of an effort to prop up their self-esteem. Despite these concerns, as indicated earlier, whether recent generations of adolescents and emerging adults are more narcissistic than earlier generations remains controversial (Trzesniewski & Donnellan, 2010; Twenge & Campbell, 2010).

Is Self-Esteem Linked to Success in School and Initiative? School performance and self-esteem are only moderately correlated, and these correlations do not

Domain	Harter's U.S. samples	Other countries
Physical Appearance	.65	.62
Scholastic Competence	.48	.41
Social Acceptance	.46	.40
Behavioral Conduct	.45	.45
Athletic Competence	.33	.30

FIGURE **4.3**

CORRELATIONS BETWEEN GLOBAL SELF-ESTEEM AND DOMAINS OF COMPETENCE. *Note:* The correlations shown are the average correlations computed across a number of studies. The other countries in this evaluation were England, Ireland, Australia, Canada, Germany, Italy, Greece, the Netherlands, and Japan. Recall from Chapter 1 that correlation coefficients can range from −1.00 to +1.00. The correlations between physical appearance and global self-esteem (.65 and .62) are moderately high.

suggest that high self-esteem produces better school performance (Baumeister & others, 2003). Efforts to increase students' self-esteem have not always led to improved school performance (Davies & Brember, 1999). Adolescents with high self-esteem have greater initiative, but this can produce positive or negative outcomes (Baumeister & others, 2003). High-self-esteem adolescents are prone to both prosocial and antisocial actions.

Are Some Domains More Closely Linked to Self-Esteem Than Others? In Chapter 2, we saw how preoccupied many adolescents are about their body image (Markey, 2010). Physical appearance is an especially powerful contributor to self-esteem in adolescence (Harter, 2006). In Harter's (1999) research, for example, global self-esteem was correlated most strongly with physical appearance, a link that has been found in both the United States and other countries (see Figure 4.3). In another study, adolescents' concept of their physical attractiveness was the strongest predictor of their overall self-esteem (Lord & Eccles, 1994). This strong association between perceived appearance and general self-worth is not confined to adolescence but holds across most of the life span, from early childhood through middle age (Harter, 1999).

developmental **connection**

Gender. Gender differences characterize adolescents' body images. Chapter 2, p. 59

Social Contexts and Self-Esteem Social contexts such as the family, peers, and schools contribute to the development of an adolescent's self-esteem (Roustit & others, 2010). One study found that as family cohesiveness increased, adolescents' self-esteem increased over time (Baldwin & Hoffman, 2002). In this study, family cohesion was based on the amount of time the family spent together, the quality of their communication, and the extent to which the adolescent was involved in family decision making. In another investigation, the following parenting attributes were associated with boys' high self-esteem: expression of affection; concern about the boys' problems; harmony in the home; participation in joint family activities; availability to give competent, organized help when the boys needed it; setting clear and fair rules; abiding by the rules; and allowing the boys freedom within well-prescribed limits (Coopersmith, 1967).

Peer judgments gain increasing importance in adolescence (Prinstein & Dodge, 2010; Villanti, Boulay, & Juon, 2011). The link between peer approval and self-worth increases during adolescence (Harter, 1990a). The transition from elementary school to middle or junior high school is associated with lowered self-esteem (Harter, 2006). Self-esteem is higher in the last year of elementary school than in middle or junior high school, especially in the first year after the transition (Simmons & Blyth, 1987). We have much more to say about the transition from elementary to middle or junior high school in Chapter 10.

developmental **connection**

School. The transition to middle or junior high school is stressful for many individuals because it coincides with a number of physical, cognitive, and socioemotional changes. Chapter 10, p. 334

Consequences of Low Self-Esteem For most adolescents and emerging adults, the emotional discomfort of low self-esteem is only temporary, but for some, low self-esteem can develop into other problems. Low self-esteem has been implicated in depression, anorexia nervosa, delinquency, and other adjustment problems, and even suicide (Kuhlberg, Pena, & Zayas, 2010).

An important point needs to be made about much of the research on self-esteem: It is correlational rather than experimental. Remember from Chapter 1, that correlation does not equal causation. Thus, if a correlational study finds an association between self-esteem and depression, it could be equally likely that depression causes low self-esteem or low self-esteem causes depression.

Also keep in mind that the seriousness of the problem depends not only on the nature of the adolescent's and emerging adult's low self-esteem, but on other conditions as well. When low self-esteem is compounded by difficult school transitions, a troubled family life, or other stressful events, an individual's problems can intensify.

connecting with health and well-being

How Can Adolescents' Self-Esteem Be Increased?

Four ways to improve adolescents' and emerging adults' self-esteem are to (1) identify the causes of low self-esteem and the domains of competence important to the self, (2) provide emotional support and social approval, (3) foster achievement, and (4) help adolescents to cope.

Identifying an adolescent's and emerging adult's sources of self-esteem—that is, the domains that are important to the self—is critical to improving self-esteem. Self-esteem theorist and researcher Susan Harter (1990a) points out that the self-esteem enhancement programs of the 1960s, in which self-esteem itself was the target and individuals were encouraged to simply feel good about themselves, were ineffective. Rather, Harter (1998) concludes that intervention must occur at the level of the *causes* of self-esteem if self-esteem is to improve significantly. Adolescents and emerging adults have the highest self-esteem when they perform competently in domains important to the self. Therefore, adolescents and emerging adults should be encouraged to identify and value their domains of competence. For example, some adolescents and emerging adults might have artistic strengths, others academic strengths, and yet others might excel in sports.

What are some strategies for increasing self-esteem?

Emotional support and social approval in the form of confirmation from others can also powerfully influence self-esteem (Harter, 1990a,b). Some youth with low self-esteem come from conflicted families or conditions in which they experienced abuse or neglect—situations in which support is unavailable. In some cases, alternative sources of support can be implemented, either informally through the encouragement of a teacher, a coach, or another significant adult, or more formally, through programs such as Big Brothers and Big Sisters. While peer approval becomes increasingly important during adolescence, both adult and peer support are important influences on the adolescent's self-esteem. In one study, both parental and peer support were related to the adolescent's general self-worth (Robinson, 1995).

Achievement can also improve adolescents' and emerging adults' self-esteem (Bednar, Wells, & Peterson, 1995). For example, the straightforward teaching of real skills to adolescents and emerging adults often results in increased achievement and, thus, in enhanced self-esteem. Adolescents and emerging adults develop higher self-esteem because they know what tasks are important for achieving goals, and they have experienced performing them or similar behaviors. The emphasis on the importance of achievement in improving self-esteem has much in common with Albert Bandura's (2010a) social cognitive concept of *self-efficacy,* which refers to individuals' beliefs that they can master a situation and produce positive outcomes.

Self-esteem often increases when adolescents face a problem and try to cope with it rather than avoid it (Dyson & Renk, 2006). Facing problems realistically, honestly, and nondefensively produces favorable self-evaluative thoughts, which lead to the self-generated approval that raises self-esteem.

Can individuals have too much self-esteem? How can research address this question?

Does self-esteem in adolescence foreshadow adjustment and competence in adulthood? A New Zealand longitudinal study assessed self-esteem at 11, 13, and 15 years of age and adjustment and competence of the same individuals when they were 26 years old (Trzesniewski & others, 2006). The results revealed that adults characterized by poorer mental and physical health, worse economic prospects, and higher levels of criminal behavior were more likely to have low self-esteem in adolescence than their better adjusted, more competent adult counterparts.

Given the potential consequences of low self-esteem, how can the low self-esteem of adolescents and emerging adults be increased? To explore this question, see the *Connecting with Health and Well-Being* interlude.

developmental **connection**

Achievement. High self-efficacy adolescents show advances in a number of aspects of achievement. Chapter 11, p. 368

Review *Connect* Reflect

LG1 Describe the development of the self in adolescence.

Review

- What is self-understanding? What are the key dimensions of self-understanding in adolescence?
- What are self-esteem and self-concept? How can they be measured? Are some domains more salient than others to adolescents' self-esteem? How are social contexts linked with adolescents' self-esteem? What are the consequences of low self-esteem? How can adolescents' self-esteem be increased?

Connect

- Contrast self-esteem, self-concept, and narcissism.

Reflect *Your Own Personal Journey of Life*

- Think about what your future selves might be. What do you envision will make you the happiest about the future selves you aspire to become? What prospective selves hold negative possibilities?

2 Identity

LG2 Explain the many facets of identity development.

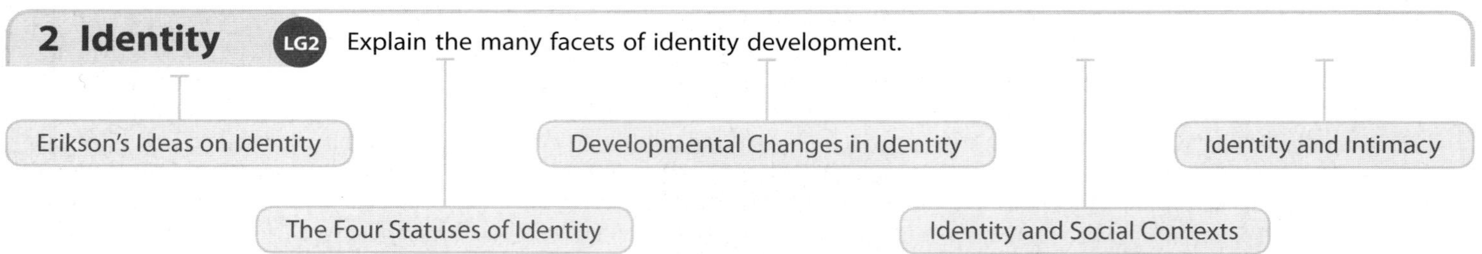

Identity is who a person is, representing a synthesis and integration of self-understanding. By far the most comprehensive and provocative theory of identity development is that of Erik Erikson. In fact, some experts on adolescence consider Erikson's ideas to be the single most influential theory of adolescent development. Erikson's theory was introduced in Chapter 1; here we expand on that introduction, beginning with an analysis of his ideas on identity.

> "Who are you?" said the Caterpillar. Alice replied, rather shyly, "I—I hardly know, Sir, just at present—at least I know who I was when I got up this morning, but I must have changed several times since then."
>
> —Lewis Carroll
> *English Writer, 19th Century*

ERIKSON'S IDEAS ON IDENTITY

Who am I? What am I all about? What am I going to do with my life? What is different about me? How can I make it on my own? These questions, not usually considered in childhood, surface as a common, virtually universal concern during adolescence. Adolescents clamor for solutions to questions of identity. Erik Erikson (1950, 1968) was the first to realize how central such questions are to understanding adolescent development. That today identity is believed to be a key concept in adolescent development results directly from Erikson's masterful thinking and analysis.

identity Who a person is, representing a synthesis and integration of self-understanding.

identity versus identity confusion Erikson's fifth developmental stage, which occurs during adolescence. At this time, individuals are faced with deciding who they are, what they are all about, and where they are going in life.

psychosocial moratorium Erikson's term for the gap between childhood security and adult autonomy that adolescents experience as part of their identity exploration.

Revisiting Erikson's Views on Identity

Identity versus identity confusion, Erikson's fifth developmental stage, occurs during the adolescent years. At this time, adolescents are faced with deciding who they are, what they are all about, and where they are going in life. They confront many new roles, from vocational to romantic. As part of their identity exploration, adolescents experience a **psychosocial moratorium,** Erikson's term for the gap between childhood security and adult autonomy. In the course of exploring and searching their culture's identity files, they often experiment with different roles. Youth who successfully cope with these conflicting roles and identities emerge with a new sense of self that is both refreshing and acceptable. But adolescents who do not successfully resolve the identity crisis suffer what Erikson calls *identity confusion*. Either they withdraw, isolating themselves from peers and family, or they immerse themselves in the world of peers and lose their identity in the crowd.

Personality and Role Experimentation Two core ingredients in Erikson's theory of identity development are personality and role experimentation. As we have seen, Erikson stressed that adolescents face an overwhelming number of choices, and at some point during their youth enter a period of psychological moratorium. During this moratorium and before they reach a stable sense of self, they try out different roles and personalities. They might be argumentative one moment, cooperative the next. They might dress neatly one day and sloppily the next day. One week they might like a particular friend, the next week they might despise the friend. This personality experimentation is a deliberate effort on the part of adolescents to find their place in the world.

As adolescents gradually come to realize that they will soon be responsible for themselves and their lives, they search for what those lives are going to be. Many parents and other adults, accustomed to having children go along with what they say, may be bewildered or incensed by the wisecracks, rebelliousness, and rapid mood changes that accompany adolescence. But it is important for these adults to give adolescents the time and opportunity to explore different roles and personalities. In turn, most adolescents eventually discard undesirable roles.

Erik Erikson.

There are literally hundreds of roles for adolescents to try out and probably just as many ways to pursue each role. Erikson argued that by late adolescence, vocational roles become central to identity development, especially in a highly technological society like that of the United States. Youth who have been well trained to enter a workforce that offers the potential of reasonably high self-esteem will experience the least stress during this phase of identity development. Some youth may reject jobs offering good pay and traditionally high social status, choosing instead work that allows them to be more genuinely helpful to others, perhaps in the Peace Corps, a mental health clinic, or a school for children in a low-income neighborhood. Some youth may prefer unemployment to the prospect of work they feel they could not perform well or would make them feel useless. To Erikson, such choices reflect the desire to achieve a meaningful identity by being true to oneself, rather than by burying one's identity in the larger society.

developmental **connection**

Theories. Erikson proposed that individuals go through eight stages in the course of human development. Chapter 1, p. 29

Identity is a self-portrait that is composed of many pieces:

- The career and work path a person wants to follow (vocational/career identity)
- Whether a person is politically conservative, liberal, or middle of the road (political identity)
- A person's spiritual beliefs (religious identity)
- Whether a person is single, married, divorced, or cohabiting (relationship identity)
- The extent to which a person is motivated to achieve and is intellectual (achievement, intellectual identity)
- Whether a person is heterosexual, homosexual, or bisexual (sexual identity)
- Which part of the world or country a person is from and how intensely the person identifies with his or her cultural heritage (cultural/ethnic identity)
- The things a person likes to do, including sports, music, and hobbies (interests)
- An individual's personality characteristics (introverted or extraverted, anxious or calm, friendly or hostile, and so on) (personality)
- A person's body image (physical identity)

One of Erik Erikson's strategies for explaining the nature of identity development was to analyze the lives of famous individuals. One such individual was Mahatma Gandhi (*center*), the spiritual leader of India in the mid-twentieth century, about whom Erikson (1969) wrote in *Gandhi's Truth*.

Some Contemporary Thoughts on Identity Contemporary views of identity development suggest that it is a lengthy process, in many instances more gradual and less cataclysmic than Erikson's term *crisis* implies (Phinney, 2008). Today's

As long as one keeps searching, the answers come.

—JOAN BAEZ
American Folk Singer, 20th Century

theorists note that this extraordinarily complex process neither begins nor ends with adolescence (Coté, 2009; Kroger, 2007; McAdams, 2011). It begins in infancy with the appearance of attachment, the development of a sense of self, and the emergence of independence. It ends with a life review and integration in old age. What is important about identity development in adolescence and emerging adulthood is that for the first time, physical, cognitive, and socioemotional development advance to the point at which the individual can sort through and synthesize childhood identities and identifications to construct a viable path toward adult maturity (Marcia & Carpendale, 2004). Resolution of the identity issue during adolescence and emerging adulthood does not mean that identity will be stable through the remainder of one's life. An individual who develops a healthy identity is flexible and adaptive, open to changes in society, in relationships, and in careers. This openness assures numerous reorganizations of identity throughout the individual's life.

What are some contemporary thoughts about identity formation and development?

Just as researchers increasingly describe adolescents' and emerging adults' self-understanding in terms of multiple selves, there also is a trend in characterizing adolescents' and emerging adults' identity in terms of multiple identities (Phinney, 2008). Although adolescent and emerging adult identities are preceded by childhood identities, central questions such as "Who am I?" come up more frequently in the adolescent and emerging adult years. During adolescence and emerging adulthood, identities are characterized more strongly by the search for balance between the needs for autonomy and for connectedness.

Identity formation neither happens neatly nor is it usually cataclysmic. At the bare minimum, it involves commitment to a vocational direction, an ideological stance, and a sexual orientation. Synthesizing the components of identity can be a long, drawn-out process, with many negations and affirmations of various roles. Identity development gets done in bits and pieces. Decisions are not made once and for all but must be made again and again. Although the decisions might seem trivial at the time—whom to date, whether or not to have intercourse, whether to break up; whether to take drugs; to go to college or get a job, to study or play; to be politically active or not—over the years, they begin to form the core of what an individual is all about.

A current concern about the development of identity in adolescence and emerging adulthood was voiced in William Damon's (2008) book, *The Path to Purpose*, which we discussed in Chapter 1. Damon acknowledges that successful identity development is a long-term process of extended exploration and reflection, and in some instances it can involve postponing decisions for a number of years. However, what concerns Damon is that too many of today's youth aren't moving toward any identity resolution. In Damon's (2008, pp. 5, 7) words,

> Their delay is characterized more by indecision than by motivated reflection, more by confusion than by pursuit of clear goals, more by ambivalence than by determination. Directionless shift is not a constructive moratorium in either a developmental or a societal sense. Without a sense of direction, opportunities are lost, and doubt and self-absorption can set in. Maladaptive habits are established and adaptive ones not built. . . . What is too often missing is . . . the kind of wholehearted dedication to an activity or interest that stems from serious purpose, a purpose that can give meaning and direction to life.

developmental **connection**

Achievement. In interviews with 12- to 22-year-olds, Damon found that only about 20 percent had a clear vision of where they wanted to go in life, what they wanted to achieve, and why. Chapter 11, p. 370

In Damon's (2008, p. 47) view, too many youth are left to their own devices in dealing with some of life's biggest questions: "What is my calling? What do I have to contribute to the world? What am I here for?" Damon acknowledges that adults can't make youths' decisions for them, but he emphasizes that it is very important for parents, teachers, mentors, and other adults to provide guidance, feedback, and contexts that will improve the likelihood youth will develop a positive identity.

Youth need a cultural climate that inspires rather than demoralizes them and supports their chances of reaching their aspirations.

THE FOUR STATUSES OF IDENTITY

James Marcia (1980, 1994, 2002) stresses that Erikson's theory of identity development implies four identity statuses, or ways of resolving the identity crisis: identity diffusion, identity foreclosure, identity moratorium, and identity achievement. That is, Marcia uses the extent of an adolescent's crisis and commitment to classify individuals according to these four identity statuses. He defines the term **crisis** as a period of identity development during which the adolescent is choosing among meaningful alternatives. (Most researchers use the term *exploration*.) By **commitment,** he means a personal investment in what an individual is going to do.

Let's examine each of Marcia's four identity statuses:

- **Identity diffusion** is Marcia's term for the state adolescents are in when they have not yet experienced an identity crisis (that is, have not yet explored meaningful alternatives) and have not made any commitments. Not only are adolescents in this status undecided about occupational and ideological choices, they usually show little interest in such matters.
- **Identity foreclosure** is Marcia's term for the state adolescents are in when they have made a commitment but have not experienced an identity crisis. This status occurs most often when parents hand down commitments to their adolescents, usually in an authoritarian way. Thus, adolescents with this status have not had adequate opportunities to explore different approaches, ideologies, and vocations on their own.
- **Identity moratorium** is Marcia's term for the state of adolescents who are in the midst of an identity crisis, but who have not made a clear commitment to an identity.
- **Identity achievement** is Marcia's term for the status of adolescents who have undergone an identity crisis and made a commitment. Figure 4.4 summarizes Marcia's four statuses of identity development.

Let's explore some specific examples of Marcia's identity statuses. A 13-year-old adolescent has neither begun to explore her identity in a meaningful way nor made an identity commitment; she is *identity diffused*. An 18-year-old boy's parents want him to be a doctor, so he is planning on majoring in premedicine in college and has not adequately explored any other options; he is *identity foreclosed*. Nineteen-year-old Sasha is not quite sure what life path she wants to follow, but she recently went to the counseling center at her college to find out about different careers; she is in an *identity moratorium*. Twenty-one-year-old Marcelo extensively explored a number of different career options in college; eventually got his degree in science education and is looking forward to his first year of teaching high school; he is *identity achieved*. Although these examples of identity statuses focus on careers, remember that the whole of identity has multiple dimensions.

	Identity Status			
Position on Occupation and Ideology	**Identity Diffusion**	**Identity Foreclosure**	**Identity Moratorium**	**Identity Achievement**
Crisis	Absent	Absent	Present	Present
Commitment	Absent	Present	Absent	Present

FIGURE **4.4**
MARCIA'S FOUR STATUSES OF IDENTITY

crisis A period of identity development during which the adolescent is choosing among meaningful alternatives.

commitment The part of identity development in which adolescents show a personal investment in what they are going to do.

identity diffusion Marcia's term for the state adolescents are in when they have not yet experienced an identity crisis or made any commitments.

identity foreclosure Marcia's term for the state adolescents are in when they have made a commitment but have not experienced an identity crisis.

identity moratorium Marcia's term for the state of adolescents who are in the midst of an identity crisis but who have not made a clear commitment to an identity.

identity achievement Marcia's term for an adolescent who has undergone an identity crisis and made a commitment.

FIGURE **4.5**

EXPLORING YOUR IDENTITY. If you checked diffused or foreclosed for any areas, take some time to think about what you need to do to move into a moratorium identity status in those areas.

Think deeply about your exploration and commitment in the areas listed here. For each area, check whether your identity status is diffused, foreclosed, moratorium, or achieved.

Identity Component	Identity Status			
	Diffused	Foreclosed	Moratorium	Achieved
Vocational (career)				
Political				
Religious				
Relationships				
Achievement				
Sexual				
Gender				
Ethnic/Cultural				
Interests				
Personality				
Physical				

Earlier in this chapter we described a number of dimensions of identity. To explore your your identity status on a number of identity's dimensions, see Figure 4.5.

Marcia's approach has been sharply criticized by some researchers who conclude that it distorts and overly simplifies Erikson's concepts of crisis and commitment (Coté, 2009; Luyckx, Schwartz, Goossens, & others, 2008). Erikson emphasized that youth question the perceptions and expectations of their culture and the development of an autonomous position with regard to one's society. In Marcia's approach, these complex questions are reduced to whether a youth has thought about certain issues and considered the alternatives. Similarly, in Marcia's approach, Erikson's idea of commitment loses its meaning of investing oneself in certain lifelong projects and is interpreted simply as having made a firm decision. Other researchers still maintain that Marcia's approach is a valuable contribution to understanding identity (Berzonsky & Adams, 1999).

Recently, Luc Goossens, Koen Luyckx, and their colleagues (Goossens & Luyckx, 2007; Luyckx, Schwartz, Berzonsky, & others, 2008; Luyckx & others, 2010) have proposed an extension of Marcia's concepts of exploration and commitment. The revisionist theorizing stresses that effective identity development involves evaluating identity commitments on a continuing basis. Two that have been devised to capture this ongoing identity examination are (1) *exploration in depth,* which involves "gathering information and talking to others about current commitments"; and (2) *identification with commitment,* which consists of "the degree of security and certainty one experiences with regard to current commitments" (Luyckx, 2006, p. i).

For example, consider a first-year college student who makes a commitment to become a lawyer. Exploring this commitment in depth might include finding out as much as possible about what is involved in being a lawyer, such as educational requirements, the work conducted by lawyers in different areas, what types of college classes might be beneficial for this career, and so on. It might also include talking with several lawyers about their profession. As a result of this in-depth exploration, the college student may become more confident that being a lawyer is the career that best suits her, which reflects identification with commitment (Goossens, 2006). As she goes through the remainder of her college years, she will continue to evaluate the commitment she has made to becoming a lawyer and may change her commitment as she continues to gather new information and reflect on the life path she wants to take.

More recently, a third dimension—*ruminative* (or *excessive*) *exploration*—indicates how identity exploration can sometimes become too distressful and possibly produce depression (Luyckx, Schwartz, Berzonsky, & others, 2008).

One way that researchers are examining identity changes in depth is to use a *narrative approach*. This involves asking individuals to tell their life stories and evaluate the extent to which their stories are meaningful and integrated (McAdams, 2011; McLean, Breen, & Fournier, 2010; McLean & Pasupathi, 2010; Syed, 2010, 2011). The term *narrative identity* "refers to the stories people construct and tell about themselves to define who they are for themselves and others. Beginning in adolescence and young adulthood, our narrative identities are the stories we live by" (McAdams, Josselson, & Lieblich, 2006, p. 4). A recent study using the narrative identity approach revealed that from age 11 to 18, boys increasingly engaged in thinking about the meaningfulness of their lives, especially meaning related to the self as changing (McLean, Breen, & Fournier, 2010). In other research, relationship, autonomy, and mortality events were important contributors to searching for a meaningful identity in late adolescence and emerging adulthood (McLean & Pratt, 2006; McLean & Thorne, 2006). There also is increasing evidence that the effective management of difficult life events and circumstances contributes to the development of a meaningful identity in emerging adulthood (Pals, 2006).

DEVELOPMENTAL CHANGES IN IDENTITY

During early adolescence, most youth are primarily in the identity statuses of *diffusion, foreclosure,* or *moratorium*. According to Marcia (1987, 1996), at least three aspects of the young adolescent's development are important to identity formation. Young adolescents must be confident that they have parental support, must have an established sense of industry, and must be able to take a self-reflective stance toward the future.

A recent study found that as individuals aged from early adolescence to emerging adulthood, they increasingly engaged in in-depth exploration of their identity (Klimstra & others, 2010). And a recent study of 1,200 Dutch 12- to 20-year-olds revealed that the majority did not often experience identity conflicts and that their identity development proceeded more smoothly than is commonly thought (Meeus & others, 2010). In this study, though, approximately one in eight adolescents struggled with identity conflicts throughout adolescence.

Researchers have developed a consensus that many of the key changes in identity are most likely to take place in emerging adulthood, the period from about 18 to 25 years of age, not in adolescence (Juang & Syed, 2010; Moshman, 2011; Swanson, 2010; Syed, 2010, 2011). For example, Alan Waterman (1985, 1992) has found that from the years preceding high school through the last few years of college, the number of individuals who are identity achieved increases, whereas the number of individuals who are identity diffused decreases. Many young adolescents are identity diffused. College upperclassmen are more likely than high school students or college freshmen to be identity achieved.

How does identity change in emerging adulthood?

Why might college produce some key changes in identity? Increased complexity in the reasoning skills of college students combined with a wide range of new experiences that highlight contrasts between home and college and between themselves and others stimulates them to reach a higher level of integrating various dimensions of their identity (Phinney, 2008). Recall

developmental **connection**

Emerging Adulthood. Emerging adults have few social obligations, which allows them considerable autonomy in running their lives (Arnett, 2006). Chapter 1, p. 20

from Chapter 1, that one of emerging adulthood's themes is not having many social commitments, which gives individuals considerable independence in developing a life path (Arnett, 2006, 2010). James Coté (2006, 2009) argues that, because of this freedom, developing a positive identity in emerging adulthood requires considerable self-discipline and planning. Without this self-discipline and planning, emerging adults are likely to drift and not follow any particular direction. Coté also stresses that emerging adults who obtain a higher education are more likely to be on a positive identity path. Those who don't obtain a higher education, he says, tend to experience frequent job changes, not because they are searching for an identity but rather because they are just trying to eke out a living in a society that rewards higher education.

A recent meta-analysis of 124 studies by Jane Kroger and her colleagues (2010) revealed that during adolescence and emerging adulthood, identity moratorium status rose steadily to age 19 and then declined; identity achievement rose across late adolescence and emerging adulthood; and foreclosure and diffusion statuses declined across the high school years but fluctuated in the late teens and emerging adulthood. The studies also found that a large portion of individuals were not identity achieved by the time they reached their twenties. This important finding—that so few older adolescents and emerging adults had reached an identity achieved status—suggests that mastering identity development by the end of adolescence is more elusive for most individuals than Erikson (1968) envisioned.

A recent study of more than 9,000 emerging adult students at 30 U.S. universities examined various identity statuses and their links to psychological adjustment (Schwartz & others, 2011). The clusters of identity status that emerged included all four of Marcia's identity statuses (diffusion, foreclosure, moratorium, and achievement), although in some cases variations appeared that provided more specific dimensions. For example, two types of diffusion appeared: diffused diffusion (low commitment but high ruminative exploration and exploration in depth) and carefree diffusion (low commitment, low exploration, low synthesis, and high confusion). The diffused-status emerging adults had the lowest self-esteem, internal control, and psychological well-being. The carefree diffused cluster had the highest level of externalizing problems (antisocial, alienated) and health-compromising behaviors (dangerous drug use, for example) of all identity clusters. More males than females were categorized as carefree diffused. The achievement cluster was high on exploration and commitment, and the identity-achieved emerging adults had the highest scores on all of the positive aspects of psychological functioning (self-esteem, internal locus of control, psychological well-being, satisfaction with life, and happiness that results from life pursuits, for example). A recent research review also concluded that adolescents who have a mature identity show high levels of adjustment and a positive personality profile (Meeus, 2011). For example, adolescents who are highly committed in their identity development are characterized by higher levels of conscientiousness and emotional stability (Meeus, 2011).

A recent research review concluded that identity is more stable in adulthood than in adolescence (Meeus, 2011), but resolution of the identity issue during adolescence and emerging adulthood does not mean that identity will be stable through the remainder of life (McAdams & Cox, 2010). Many individuals who develop positive identities follow what are called "MAMA" cycles; that is, their identity status changes from *m*oratorium to *a*chievement to *m*oratorium to *a*chievement (Marcia, 1994). These cycles may be repeated throughout life (Francis, Fraser, & Marcia, 1989). Marcia (2002) points out that the first identity is just that—it is not, and should not be expected to be, the final product.

Researchers have shown that identity consolidation—the process of refining and enhancing the identity choices that are made in emerging adulthood—continues well into early adulthood and possibly the early part of middle adulthood (Kroger, 2007). One research study found that women and men continued to show identity development from 27 through 36 years of age with the main changes in the direction of greater commitment (Pulkkinen & Kokko, 2000). In this study, adults more often moved into achieved and foreclosed identities than into moratorium or diffused identities. Further, as individuals move from early to middle adulthood, they become more certain about their identity. For example, a longitudinal study of Smith College women found that identity certainty increased from the thirties through the fifties (Stewart, Ostrove, & Helson, 2001).

IDENTITY AND SOCIAL CONTEXTS

Social contexts influence an adolescent's identity development (Nishina & others, 2010). Questions we will explore in this regard are: Do family relationships influence identity development? How are culture and ethnicity linked to identity development? Is the identity development of females and males different?

developmental **connection**

Attachment. Even while adolescents seek autonomy, attachment to parents is important; secure attachment in adolescence is linked to a number of positive outcomes. Chapter 8, p. 268

Family Influences on Identity Parents are important figures in the adolescent's development of identity (Cooper, 2011). For example, one study found that poor communication between mothers and adolescents, as well as persistent conflicts with friends, was linked to less positive identity development (Reis & Youniss, 2004). Catherine Cooper and her colleagues (Cooper, 2011; Cooper, Behrens, & Trinh, 2009; Cooper & Grotevant, 1989) have found that a family atmosphere that promotes *both* individuality and connectedness is important in the adolescent's identity development:

- **Individuality** consists of two dimensions: self-assertion, which is the ability to have and communicate a point of view; and separateness, which is the use of communication patterns to express how one is different from others.
- **Connectedness** also consists of two dimensions: mutuality, which involves sensitivity to and respect for others' views; and permeability, which involves openness to others' views.

How might parents influence the adolescent's identity development?

Research interest also has increased in the role that attachment to parents might play in identity development. A meta-analysis found weak to moderate correlations between attachment to parents in adolescence and identity development (Arseth & others, 2009). In this study, though, securely attached adolescents were far more likely to be identity achieved than their counterparts who were identity diffused or identity foreclosed.

developmental **connection**

Culture and Ethnicity. Historical, economic, and social experiences produce differences between various ethnic groups and the majority non-Latino White group in the United States. Chapter 12, p. 408

Ethnic Identity Throughout the world, ethnic minority groups have struggled to maintain their ethnic identities while blending in with the dominant culture (Erikson, 1968). **Ethnic identity** is an enduring aspect of the self that includes a sense of membership in an ethnic group, along with the attitudes and feelings related to that membership (Phinney, 2006). Thus, for adolescents from ethnic minority groups, the process of identity formation has an added dimension: the choice between two or more sources of identification—their own ethnic group and the mainstream, or dominant, culture (Seaton, 2010). Many adolescents resolve this choice by developing a **bicultural identity.** That is, they identify in some ways with their ethnic group and in other ways with the majority culture (Cooper, 2011; Marks, Patton, & Garcia Coll, 2011; Phinney & Baldelomar, 2011). A study of Mexican American and Asian American college students found that they identified both with the American mainstream culture and with their culture of origin (Devos, 2006).

A recent study explored bicultural identity in 14- to 21-year-olds (Marks, Patton, & Garcia Coll, 2011). Younger bicultural adolescents primarily responded to the label "White" with an inhibited response, suggesting hesitation in determining whether the label was "like me" or "not like me."

Time is another aspect of the context that influences ethnic identity. The indicators of identity often differ for each succeeding generation of immigrants (Phinney, 2006; Phinney & Baldelomar, 2011). First-generation immigrants are likely to be

individuality An important element in adolescent identity development. It consists of two dimensions: self-assertion, the ability to have and communicate a point of view; and separateness, the use of communication patterns to express how one is different from others.

connectedness An important element in adolescent identity development. It consists of two dimensions: mutuality, sensitivity to and respect for others' views; and permeability, openness to others' views.

ethnic identity An enduring, basic aspect of the self that includes a sense of membership in an ethnic group and the attitudes and feelings related to that membership.

bicultural identity Identity formation that occurs when adolescents identify in some ways with their ethnic group and in other ways with the majority culture.

secure in their identities and unlikely to change much; they may or may not develop a new identity. The degree to which they begin to feel "American" appears to be related to whether or not they learn English, develop social networks beyond their ethnic group, and become culturally competent in their new country. Second-generation immigrants are more likely to think of themselves as "American"—possibly because citizenship is granted at birth. For second-generation immigrants, ethnic identity is likely to be linked to retention of their ethnic language and social networks. In the third and later generations, the issues become more complex. Broad social factors may affect the extent to which members of this generation retain their ethnic identities. For example, media images may either discourage or encourage members of an ethnic group from identifying with their group or retaining parts of its culture. Discrimination may force people to see themselves as cut off from the majority group and encourage them to seek the support of their own ethnic culture.

Michelle Chin, age 16: "Parents do not understand that teenagers need to find out who they are, which means a lot of experimenting, a lot of mood swings, a lot of emotions and awkwardness. Like any teenager, I am facing an identity crisis. I am still trying to figure out whether I am a Chinese American or an American with Asian eyes."

The immediate contexts in which ethnic minority youth live also influence their identity development (Cooper, 2011; Markstrom, 2011; Umana-Taylor & Guimond, 2010). In the United States, many ethnic minority youth live in pockets of poverty, are exposed to drugs, gangs, and crime, and interact with youth and adults who have dropped out of school or are unemployed. Support for developing a positive identity is scarce. In such settings, programs for youth can make an important contribution to identity development.

As indicated in the following studies, researchers are also increasingly finding that a positive ethnic identity is related to positive outcomes for ethnic minority adolescents (Umana-Taylor, Updegraff, & Gonzales-Bracken, 2011):

- Navajo adolescents' positive ethnic heritage was linked to higher self-esteem, school connectedness, and social functioning (Jones & Galliher, 2007).
- Exploration was an important aspect of establishing a secure sense of one's ethnic identity, which in turn was linked to a positive attitude toward one's own group and other groups (Whitehead & others, 2009).
- Cultural socialization (measured by items such as, "How often have your parents said it was important to follow the traditions of your racial or ethnic group?") was linked to higher self-esteem through a pathway of ethnic centrality (assessed by items such as the importance of ethnicity in "how I see myself") in Latino college students (Rivas-Drake, 2011).
- Ethnic identity was linked to adjustment in adolescents primarily by fostering a positive sense of meaning (Kiang & Fuligni, 2010). In this study, Asian American adolescents reported engaging in a search for meaning in life more than did non-Latino White and Latino adolescents.

> Many ethnic minority youth must bridge "multiple worlds" in constructing their identities.
>
> —Catherine Cooper
> *Contemporary Developmental Psychologist, University of California–Santa Cruz*

The Contexts of Ethnic Identity Development The contexts in which ethnic minority youth live influence their identity development (Chao & Otsuki-Clutter, 2011; Cooper, 2011; Markstrom, 2011; Moshman, 2011; Syed & Azmitia, 2010; Updegraff & others, 2010). In the United States, many ethnic minority youth live in low-SES urban settings where support for developing a positive identity is lacking. Many of these youth live in pockets of poverty; are exposed to drugs, gangs, and criminal activities; and interact with youth and adults who have dropped out of school or are unemployed. In such settings, support organizations and programs for youth can make an important contribution to their identity development.

developmental **connection**

Poverty. Living in poverty involves a number of environmental inequities for adolescents. Chapter 12, p. 401

intimacy versus isolation Erikson's sixth developmental stage, which individuals experience during the early adulthood years. At this time, individuals face the developmental task of forming intimate relationships with others.

Might there be aspects of the social contexts in which adolescents live that increase the likelihood they will develop a positive ethnic identity? One study analyzed 60 youth organizations that involved 24,000 adolescents over a period of five years and found that these organizations were especially good at building a sense of ethnic pride in inner-city youth (Heath & McLaughlin, 1993). Many inner-city youth have too much time on their hands, too little to do, and too few places to go. Organizations that nurture youth and respond positively to their needs and interests can enhance their identity development. And organizations that perceive youth as capable, worthy, and eager to have a healthy and productive life contribute in positive ways to the identity development of ethnic minority youth.

How do social contexts influence adolescents' ethnic identity?

Ethnic Identity in Emerging Adulthood Jean Phinney (2006) described how ethnic identity may change in emerging adulthood, especially highlighting how certain experiences of ethnic minority individuals may shorten or lengthen emerging adulthood. For ethnic minority individuals who have to take on family responsibilities and do not go to college, identity formation may occur earlier. By contrast, especially for ethnic minority individuals who go to college, identity formation may take longer because of the complexity of exploring and understanding a bicultural identity. The cognitive challenges of higher education likely stimulate ethnic minority individuals to reflect on their identity and examine changes in the way they want to identify themselves. This increased reflection may focus on integrating parts of one's ethnic minority culture and the mainstream non-Latino White culture. For example, some emerging adults have to come to grips with resolving a conflict between family loyalty and interdependence emphasized in one's ethnic minority culture and the values of independence and self-assertion emphasized by the mainstream non-Latino White culture (Arnett, 2006).

Moin Syed and Margarita Azmitia (Syed, 2010, 2011; Syed & Azmitia, 2008, 2009) have recently examined ethnic identity in emerging adulthood. In one study, they found that ethnic identity exploration and commitment increased from the beginning to the end of college (Syed & Azmitia, 2009). Exploration especially began to increase in the second year of college and continued to increase into the senior year. In another study, Syed and Azmitia (2008) found that the narrative stories told by identity moratorium and achieved-status emerging adults involved more personally meaningful experiences that linked to their sense of identity and self-integration. Identity-achieved emerging adults told about more experiences involving prejudice and cultural connections than did their counterparts in an unexamined identity status.

What characterizes ethnic identity development in emerging adulthood?

Gender and Identity Erikson's (1968) classic presentation of identity development reflected the traditional division of labor between the sexes that was common at the time. Erikson wrote that males were mainly oriented toward career and ideological commitments, whereas females were mainly oriented toward marriage and childbearing. In the 1960s and 1970s, researchers found support for this assertion of gender differences in identity. For example, they found that vocational concerns were more central to male identity, whereas affiliative concerns were more central to female identity (LaVoie, 1976). In the last several decades, however, as females have developed stronger vocational interests, these gender differences have begun to disappear (Hyde, 2005; Sharp & others, 2007).

IDENTITY AND INTIMACY

Erikson (1968) argued that intimacy should develop after individuals are well on their way to establishing a stable and successful identity. **Intimacy versus isolation** is Erikson's sixth developmental stage, which individuals experience during early adulthood. At this time, individuals face the task of forming intimate relationships with others. Erikson describes intimacy as finding oneself, yet losing oneself in another. If young adults form healthy friendships and an intimate relationship with another individual, intimacy will be achieved; if not, isolation will result.

In one study of unmarried college students 18 to 23 years of age, a strong sense of self, expressed through identity achievement and an instrumental orientation, was an important factor in forming intimate connections, for both males and females (Madison & Foster-Clark, 1996). However, insecurity and a defensive posture in

developmental **connection**

Gender. Debate continues about gender similarities and differences in adolescents and their causes. Chapter 5, p. 170

relationships were expressed differently in males' and females' relationships, with males displaying greater superficiality and females more dependency. Another study also found that a higher level of intimacy was linked to a stronger identity for both male and female college students, although the intimacy scores of the college females were higher than for the males (Montgomery, 2005). A recent study confirmed Erikson's theory that identity development in adolescence is a precursor to intimacy in romantic relationships during emerging adulthood (Beyers & Seiffge-Krenke, 2011). And a meta-analysis revealed a positive link between identity development and intimacy with the connection being stronger for men than for women (Arseth & others, 2009).

Review *Connect* Reflect

LG2 Explain the many facets of identity development.

Review

- What is Erikson's view of identity development?
- What are the four statuses of identity development?
- What developmental changes characterize identity?
- How do social contexts influence identity development?
- What is Erikson's view on identity and intimacy?

Connect

- Compare the influence of family and of ethnicity/culture on identity development.

Reflect *Your Own Personal Journey of Life*

- How would you describe your identity in adolescence? How has your identity changed since adolescence?

3 Emotional Development

LG3 Discuss the emotional development of adolescents.

The Emotions of Adolescence | Hormones, Experience, and Emotions | Emotional Competence

Defining emotion is difficult because it is not easy to tell when an adolescent is in an emotional state. For our purposes, we will define **emotion** as feeling, or affect, that occurs when a person is in a state or an interaction that is important to the individual, especially to his or her well-being. Emotion is characterized by behavior that reflects (expresses) the pleasantness or unpleasantness of the state the individual is in, or the transactions he or she is experiencing.

How are emotions linked to the two main concepts we have discussed so far in this chapter—the self and identity? Emotion is closely connected to self-esteem. Negative emotions, such as sadness, are associated with low self-esteem, whereas positive emotions, such as joy, are linked to high self-esteem. The emotional experiences involved in events such as emerging sexual experiences, dating and romantic encounters, and driving a car contribute to the adolescent's developing identity (Rosenblum & Lewis, 2003).

THE EMOTIONS OF ADOLESCENCE

Adolescence has long been described as a time of emotional turmoil (Hall, 1904). In its extreme form, this view is too stereotypical because adolescents are not constantly in a state of "storm and stress." Nonetheless, early adolescence is a time when emotional highs and lows occur more frequently (Rosenblum & Lewis, 2003). Young adolescents can be on top of the world one moment and down in the dumps the next. In many instances, the intensity of their emotions seems out of proportion to the events that elicit them (Steinberg, 2011). Young adolescents may sulk a lot,

emotion Feeling, or affect, that occurs when a person is in a state or an interaction that is important to the individual, especially to his or her well-being.

not knowing how to express their feelings adequately. With little or no provocation, they may blow up at their parents or siblings, projecting their unpleasant feelings onto another person.

As we saw in Chapter 1, adolescents reported more extreme emotions and more fleeting emotions than did their parents (Larson & Richards, 1994). For example, adolescents were five times more likely than their parents to report being "very happy" and three times more likely to report being "very sad." These findings lend support to the perception that adolescents are moody and changeable (Rosenblum & Lewis, 2003). Researchers have also found that from the fifth through the ninth grades, both boys and girls experience a 50 percent decrease in the state of being "very happy" (Larson & Lampman-Petraitis, 1989). In this study, adolescents were more likely than preadolescents to report mildly negative mood states.

It is important for adults to recognize that moodiness is a *normal* aspect of early adolescence, and that most adolescents eventually emerge from these moody times and become competent adults. Nonetheless, for some adolescents, intensely negative emotions can reflect serious problems. For example, rates of depressed moods become more frequent in girls during adolescence (Nolen-Hoeksema, 2011). We have much more to say about depression in adolescence in Chapter 13.

What characterizes adolescents' emotions?

HORMONES, EXPERIENCE, AND EMOTIONS

As we saw in Chapter 2, significant hormonal changes occur during puberty. The emotional fluctuations of early adolescence may be related to variability in hormone levels during this period. As adolescents move into adulthood, their moods become less extreme, perhaps because of their adaptation to hormone levels over time or to maturation of the prefrontal cortex (Rosenblum & Lewis, 2003; Somerville, Jones, & Casey, 2010).

Researchers have discovered that pubertal change is associated with an increase in negative emotions (Dorn & others, 2006). However, most researchers conclude that such hormonal influences are small and are usually associated with other factors, such as stress, eating patterns, sexual activity, and social relationships (Susman & Dorn, 2009). Indeed, environmental experiences may contribute more to the emotions of adolescence than do hormonal changes. Recall from Chapter 2, that in one study, social factors accounted for two to four times as much variance as hormonal factors in young adolescent girls' depression and anger (Brooks-Gunn & Warren, 1989).

Among the stressful experiences that might contribute to changes in emotion during adolescence are the transition to middle or junior high school and the onset of sexual experiences and romantic relationships. In one study, real and fantasized sexual/romantic relationships were responsible for more than one-third of ninth- to twelfth-graders' strong emotions (Wilson-Shockley, 1995).

In sum, both hormonal changes and environmental experiences are involved in the changing emotions of adolescence. So is the young person's ability to manage emotions (Casey, Duhoux, & Malter Cohen, 2010). In Chapter 3, we studied the concept of emotional intelligence. Now let's examine a closely related concept, emotional competence.

developmental **connection**

Intelligence. Emotional intelligence includes managing one's emotions effectively. Chapter 3, p. 118

EMOTIONAL COMPETENCE

In adolescence, individuals are more likely to become aware of their emotional cycles, such as feeling guilty about being angry. This new awareness may improve their ability to cope with their emotions. Adolescents also become more skillful at presenting their emotions to others. For example, they become aware of the importance of covering up their anger in social relationships. And they are more likely to understand the importance of being able to communicate their emotions constructively to improve the quality of a relationship (Saarni & others, 2006).

What are some characteristics of emotional competence in adolescence and emerging adulthood?

Although the increased cognitive abilities and awareness of adolescents prepare them to cope more effectively with stress and emotional fluctuations, many adolescents do not effectively manage their emotions (Somerville, Jones, & Casey, 2010). As a result, they may become prone to depression, anger, and poor emotional regulation, which in turn can trigger problems such as academic difficulties, drug abuse, juvenile delinquency, or eating disorders. For example, one study illustrated the importance of emotion regulation and mood in academic success (Gumora & Arsenio, 2002). Even when their level of cognitive ability was controlled for, young adolescents who said they experienced more negative emotion regarding academic routines had lower grade-point averages.

The emotional competencies that are important for adolescents to develop include the following (Saarni, 1999):

Emotional Competence	Example
• Being aware that the expression of emotions plays a major role in relationships.	Knowing that expressing anger toward a friend on a regular basis can harm the friendship.
• Adaptively coping with negative emotions by using self-regulatory strategies that reduce intensity and duration of such emotional states.	Reducing anger by walking away from a negative situation and enagaging in an activity that takes one's mind off it.
• Understanding that inner emotional states do not have to correspond to outer expressions. (As adolescents become more mature, they begin to understand how their emotionally expressive behavior may impact others, and to take that understanding into account in the way they present themselves.)	Recognizing that one can feel anger yet manage one's emotional expression so that it appears neutral.
• Being aware of one's emotional states without becoming overwhelmed by them.	Differentiating between sadness and anxiousness, and focusing on coping rather than being overwhelmed by these feelings.
• Being able to discern others' emotions.	Perceiving that another person is sad rather than afraid.

Review *Connect* Reflect

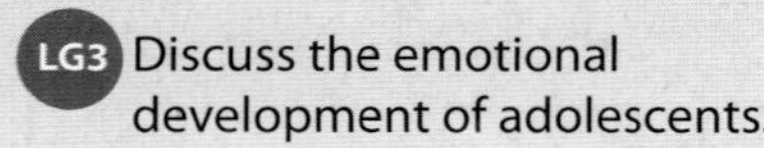

LG3 Discuss the emotional development of adolescents.

Review

- How would you characterize adolescents' emotions?
- How extensively are adolescents' emotions linked to their hormones and experiences?
- What does it take to be emotionally competent in adolescence?

Connect

- Connect the development of emotional competence to the development of self-esteem, as described in the preceding section of this chapter.

Reflect *Your Own Personal Journey of Life*

- How would you describe your emotions in early adolescence? Did you experience more extremes of emotion when you were in middle or junior high school than you do today? Have you learned how to control your emotions better now than you did in early adolescence? Explain.

4 Personality Development

Characterize the personality development of adolescents.

Personality | Temperament

So far in this chapter, we have discussed the development of the self, identity, and emotion in adolescence and emerging adulthood. In this section, we explore the nature of personality and temperament in adolescence and emerging adulthood.

PERSONALITY

How can personality be defined? **Personality** refers to the enduring personal characteristics of individuals. How is personality linked to the self, identity, and emotion? Personality is usually viewed as encompassing the self and identity. The description of an individual's personality traits sometimes involves emotions. For example, an adolescent may be described in terms of emotional stability/instability and positive/negative affectivity. How are such traits manifested in adolescence? Which traits are most important?

Big Five Factors of Personality The search for the core personality traits that characterize people has a long history (Olson & Hergenhahn, 2011). In recent years, researchers have focused on the **Big Five factors of personality:** openness to experience, conscientiousness, extraversion, agreeableness, and neuroticism (emotional stability) (see Figure 4.6). If you create an acronym from these trait names, you get the word OCEAN.

Much of the research on the Big Five factors has used adults as the participants in studies (Church, 2010; Lucas & Donnellan, 2009; Smits & others, 2011; McCrae & Costa, 2006). However, an increasing number of studies involving the Big Five factors focus on adolescents (Caprara & others, 2011; Hendriks & others, 2008; Ortet & others, 2011; Selfhout & others, 2010).

The major finding in the study of the Big Five factors in adolescence is the emergence of conscientiousness as a key predictor of adjustment and competence (Roberts & others, 2009). Following is a sampling of recent research documenting this link:

- Of the Big Five factors, conscientiousness was the best predictor of both high school and college grade-point average (Noftle & Robins, 2007).
- Conscientiousness was linked to better interpersonal relationships: higher-quality friendships, better acceptance by peers, and less victimization by peers in fifth- to eighth-graders (Jenson-Campbell & Malcolm, 2007).
- A longitudinal study of more than 1,200 individuals across seven decades revealed that conscientious individuals lived longer from childhood through late adulthood (Martin, Friedman, & Schwartz, 2007).

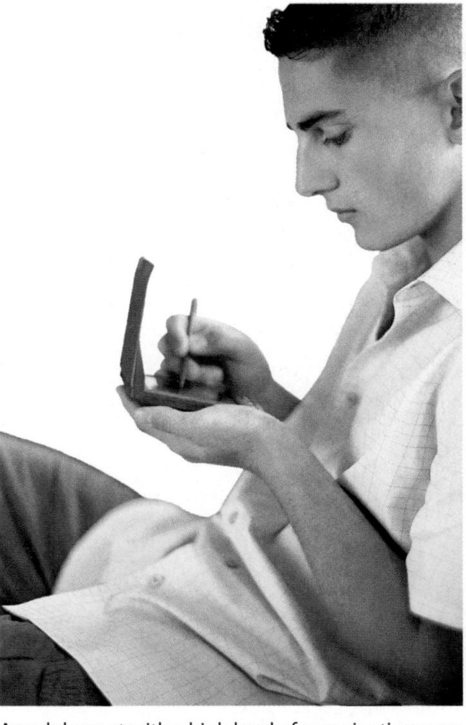

An adolescent with a high level of conscientiousness organizes his daily schedule and plans how to use his time effectively. *What are some characteristics of conscientiousness? How is it linked to adolescents' competence?*

personality The enduring personal characteristics of individuals.

Big Five factors of personality Five core traits of personality: openness to experience, conscientiousness, extraversion, agreeableness, and neuroticism (emotional stability).

Openness
- Imaginative or practical
- Interested in variety or routine
- Independent or conforming

Conscientiousness
- Organized or disorganized
- Careful or careless
- Disciplined or impulsive

Extraversion
- Sociable or retiring
- Fun-loving or somber
- Affectionate or reserved

Agreeableness
- Softhearted or ruthless
- Trusting or suspicious
- Helpful or uncooperative

Neuroticism (emotional stability)
- Calm or anxious
- Secure or insecure
- Self-satisfied or self-pitying

FIGURE **4.6**

THE BIG FIVE FACTORS OF PERSONALITY. Each of the broad supertraits encompasses more narrow traits and characteristics. Use the acronym OCEAN to remember the Big Five personality factors (openness, conscientiousness, and so on).

How do the Big Five factors change during adolescence? A recent large-scale cross-sectional study found that several of the Big Five factors show negative trends in early adolescence (Soto & others, 2011). In this study, young adolescents showed a decrease in conscientiousness, extraversion, and agreeableness. However, conscientiousness and agreeableness increased in late adolescence and beginning of emerging adulthood.

Are the Big Five factors linked to identity development? One study of more than 2,000 college students found that being emotionally stable and extraverted were related to identity achievement (Lounsbury & others, 2007).

Debate continues about whether the Big Five is the best way to conceptualize the personality traits of people (Veselka, Schermer, & Vernon, 2011). One analysis proposed a model of six traits—the Big Five plus an honesty-humility dimension (Lee & Ashton, 2008). And some cross-cultural researchers conclude that only three (extraversion, agreeableness, and conscientiousness) of the Big Five factors consistently portray people's personality traits in different cultures (De Raad & others, 2010).

Optimism Researchers increasingly are finding that optimism is an important personality trait in the development of adolescents and emerging adults (Duke & others, 2011; Oberle, Schonert-Reichl, & Zumbo, 2011). **Optimism** involves having a positive outlook on the future and minimizing problems. In the study of more than 2,000 college students discussed earlier, the personality trait of optimism was more strongly linked to identity achievement than were any of the Big Five factors (Lounsbury & others, 2007). A recent study revealed that having an optimistic style of thinking was related to reduced suicide ideation in adolescents who experienced negative and potentially traumatic life events (Hirsch & others, 2009). And adolescents who have an optimistic thinking style are at reduced risk for developing depressive symptoms (Patton & others, 2011; Sawyer, Pfeiffer, & Spense, 2009).

Traits and Situations Many psychologists argue that it is better to view personality not only in terms of traits but also in terms of contexts and situations (Friedman & Schustack, 2011). They conclude that the trait approach ignores environmental factors and places too much emphasis on stability and lack of change. This criticism was first leveled by social cognitive theorist Walter Mischel (1968), who argued that personality varies according to the situation. Thus, adolescents might behave quite differently when they are in a library than when they are at a party.

Today, most psychologists are interactionists, arguing that both traits and situations need to be taken into account in understanding personality (Berecz, 2009). Let's again consider the situations of being in a library or at a party and consider the preferences of two adolescents: Jane, who is an introvert, and Sandra, who is an extravert. Jane, the introvert, is more likely to enjoy being in the library, whereas Sandra, the extravert, is more likely to enjoy herself at the party.

TEMPERAMENT

Although the study of personality has focused mainly on adults, the study of temperament has been primarily confined to infants and children (Rothbart, 2011; Sanson & others, 2011). However, both personality and temperament are important in understanding adolescent development. **Temperament** can be defined as an individual's behavioral style and characteristic way of responding. Many psychologists emphasize that temperament forms the foundation of personality. Through increasing capacities and interactions with the environment, temperament evolves or becomes elaborated across childhood and adolescence into a set of personality traits (Caspi & Shiner, 2006).

The close link between temperament and personality is supported by research that connects some of the Big Five personality factors to temperament categories (Caspi & Shiner, 2006). For example, the temperament category of positive emotionality is related to the personality trait of extraversion, negative emotionality

optimism Involves having a positive outlook on the future and minimizing problems.

temperament An individual's behavioral style and characteristic way of responding.

maps onto neuroticism (emotional instability), and effortful control is linked to conscientiousness (Putnam, Sanson, & Rothbart, 2002).

Temperament Categories Just as with personality, researchers are interested in discovering what the key dimensions of temperament are (Rothbart, 2011; Sanson & others, 2011). Psychiatrists Alexander Chess and Stella Thomas (Chess & Thomas, 1977; Thomas & Chess, 1991) followed a group of infants into adulthood and concluded that there are three basic types, or clusters, of temperament:

- An **easy child** is generally in a positive mood, quickly establishes regular routines, and adapts easily to new experiences.
- A **difficult child** reacts negatively to many situations and is slow to accept new experiences.
- A **slow-to-warm-up child** has a low activity level, is somewhat negative, and displays a low intensity of mood.

New classifications of temperament continue to be forged (Rothbart, 2011). In a review of temperament research, Mary Rothbart and John Bates (1998) concluded that the best framework for classifying temperament involves a revision of Chess and Thomas' categories of easy, difficult, and slow to warm up. The general classification of temperament now focuses more on the following:

- *Positive affect and approach.* This category is much like the personality trait of extraversion/introversion.
- *Negative affectivity*. This involves being easily distressed. Children with a temperament that involves negative affectivity may fret and cry often. Negative affectivity is closely related to the personality traits of introversion and neuroticism (emotional instability).
- *Effortful control (self-regulation)*. This involves the ability to control one's emotions. Thus, adolescents who are high on effortful control show an ability to keep their arousal from getting too high and have strategies for soothing themselves. By contrast, adolescents who are low on effortful control often show an inability to control their arousal, and they become easily agitated and intensely emotional (Eisenberg & others, 2002).

What temperament categories have been used to describe adolescents?

easy child A child who generally is in a positive mood, quickly establishes regular routines, and adapts easily to new experiences.

difficult child A child who reacts negatively to many situations and is slow to accept new experiences.

slow-to-warm-up child A child who has a low activity level, is somewhat negative, and displays a low intensity of mood.

A recent study revealed that adolescents characterized by high positive affectivity, low negative affectivity, and high effortful control had lower levels of depressive symptoms (Verstraeten & others, 2009).

Developmental Connections and Contexts How stable is temperament from childhood to adulthood? Do young adults show the same behavioral style and characteristic emotional responses that they did when they were infants or young children? For instance, activity level is an important dimension of temperament. Are children's activity levels linked to their personality in emerging and early adulthood? In one longitudinal study, children who were highly active at age 4 were likely to be very outgoing at age 23, a finding that reflects continuity (Franz, 1996, p. 337). Yet, in other ways, temperament may change. From adolescence into early adulthood, most individuals show fewer emotional mood swings, become more responsible, and engage in less risk-taking behavior, characteristics reflecting discontinuity of temperament (Caspi, 1998).

Is temperament in childhood linked to adjustment in adolescence and adulthood? Here is what is known based on the few longitudinal studies that have been conducted on this topic (Caspi, 1998). A longitudinal study using Chess and Thomas' categories found a link between temperament assessed at 1 year of age and adjustment at 17 years of age (Guerin & others, 2003). Those with easier temperaments as infants showed more optimal development across behavioral and intellectual domains in late adolescence. The individuals with easier temperaments experienced a family environment that was more stimulating and cohesive and had more positive relationships with their parents during adolescence than did their counterparts with more difficult temperaments. When the participants were characterized by a difficult temperament in combination with a family environment that was high in conflict, an increase in externalizing behavior problems (conduct problems, delinquency) occurred.

With regard to a link between temperament in childhood and adjustment in adulthood, in one longitudinal study children who had an easy temperament at 3 to 5 years of age were likely to be well adjusted as young adults (Chess & Thomas, 1977). In contrast, many children who had a difficult temperament at 3 to 5 years of age were not well adjusted as young adults. Other researchers have found that boys who have a difficult temperament in childhood are less likely than others to continue their formal education as adults; girls with a difficult temperament in childhood are more likely to experience marital conflict as adults (Wachs, 2000).

In sum, across a number of longitudinal studies, an easy temperament in childhood is linked with more optimal development and adjustment in adolescence and adulthood. When the contexts in which individuals live are problematic, such as living in a family environment high in conflict, the long-term outcomes of having a difficult temperament are exacerbated.

Inhibition is another temperament characteristic that has been studied extensively (Kagan, 2010). Researchers have found that individuals with an inhibited temperament in childhood are less likely to be assertive or experience social support as adolescents and emerging adults, and more likely to delay entering a stable job track (Wachs, 2000).

Yet another aspect of temperament is emotionality and the ability to control one's emotions (Rothbart, 2011). In one longitudinal study, individuals who as 3-year-old children showed good control of their emotions and were resilient in the face of stress were likely to continue to handle their emotions effectively as adults (Block, 1993). In contrast, individuals who as 3-year-olds had low emotional control and were not very resilient were likely to show those same problems as young adults.

In sum, these studies reveal some continuity between certain aspects of temperament in childhood and adjustment in early adulthood. Keep in mind, however, that these connections between childhood temperament and adult adjustment are based on only a small number of studies; more research is needed to verify the links.

	Initial Temperament Trait: Inhibition	
	Child A	**Child B**
	Intervening Context	
Caregivers	Caregivers (parents) who are sensitive and accepting, and let child set his or her own pace.	Caregivers who use inappropriate "low-level control" and attempt to force the child into new situations.
Physical Environment	Presence of "stimulus shelters" or "defensible spaces" that the children can retreat to when there is too much stimulation.	Child continually encounters noisy, chaotic environments that allow no escape from stimulation.
Peers	Peer groups with other inhibited children with common interests, so the child feels accepted.	Peer groups consist of athletic extroverts, so the child feels rejected.
Schools	School is "undermanned," so inhibited children are more likely to be tolerated and feel they can make a contribution.	School is "overmanned," so inhibited children are less likely to be tolerated and more likely to feel undervalued.
	Personality Outcomes	
	As an adult, individual is closer to extraversion (outgoing, sociable) and is emotionally stable.	As an adult, individual is closer to introversion and has more emotional problems.

FIGURE **4.7**

TEMPERAMENT IN CHILDHOOD, PERSONALITY IN ADULTHOOD, AND INTERVENING CONTEXTS. Varying experiences with caregivers, the physical environment, peers, and schools may modify links between temperament in childhood and personality in adulthood. The example given here is for inhibition.

Indeed, Theodore Wachs (1994, 2000) has proposed ways that the links between childhood temperament and adult personality might vary, depending on the intervening contexts an individual experiences (see Figure 4.7).

The match between an individual's temperament and the environmental demands the individual must cope with, called **goodness of fit,** can be important to an adolescent's adjustment (Rothbart, 2011; Sanson & others, 2011). In general, the temperament characteristics of effortful control, manageability, and agreeableness reduce the effects of adverse environments, whereas negative emotionality increases their effects (Rothbart, 2011).

In this chapter, we examined many aspects of the self, identity, emotions, and personality. In our discussion of identity and emotion, we evaluated the role of gender. Chapter 5 is devoted exclusively to the topic of gender.

goodness of fit The match between an individual's temperament style and the environmental demands the individual must cope with.

Review *Connect* Reflect

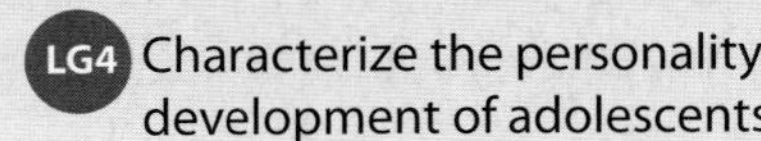

LG4 Characterize the personality development of adolescents.

Review

- What are some key personality traits in adolescence? Is personality influenced by situations?
- What is temperament, and how is it linked to personality? What are some key temperament categories? What developmental connections and contexts characterize temperament?

Connect

- How might the Big Five factors of personality be linked to the concept of risk taking that was discussed in Chapter 3?

Reflect *Your Own Personal Journey of Life*

- Consider your own temperament. We described a number of different temperament categories. Which one best describes your temperament? Has your temperament changed as you have grown older, or is it about the same as when you were a child or an adolescent? If your temperament has changed, what factors contributed to the changes?

reach your learning goals

1 The Self

LG1 Describe the development of the self in adolescence.

Self-Understanding

- Self-understanding is the adolescent's cognitive representation of the self, the substance and content of the adolescent's self-conceptions. Dimensions of the adolescent's self-understanding include abstract and idealistic; differentiated; contradictions within the self; real and ideal, true and false selves; social comparison; self-conscious; unconscious; and not yet being self-integrative. The increasing number of selves in adolescence can vary across relationships with people, social roles, and sociocultural contexts. In emerging adulthood, self-understanding becomes more integrative, reflective, and more complex, and is characterized by decisions about a worldview. However, it is not until the thirties that a coherent and integrative worldview develops for many individuals.

Self-Esteem and Self-Concept

- Self-esteem is the global, evaluative dimension of the self, and also is referred to as self-worth, or self-image. Self-concept involves domain-specific self-evaluations. For too long, little attention was given to developing measures of self-esteem and self-concept specifically tailored to adolescents. Harter's Self-Perception Profile is one adolescent measure. Self-esteem reflects perceptions that do not always match reality. Thus, high self-esteem may be justified or it might reflect an arrogant, grandiose view of one's self that is not warranted. An increasing number of studies document the problems of adolescents who are narcissistic. Controversy characterizes the extent to which self-esteem changes during adolescence and whether there are gender differences in self-esteem. Researchers have found that self-esteem often drops during and just after developmental transitions, such as going from elementary school to middle or junior high school. Some researchers have found that the self-esteem of girls declines in adolescence, especially during early adolescence, although other researchers argue that this decline has been exaggerated and actually is only modest in nature. Self-esteem is only moderately linked to school success. Adolescents with high self-esteem have greater initiative, but this can produce positive or negative outcomes. Perceived physical appearance is an especially strong contributor to global self-esteem. Peer acceptance also is linked to global self-esteem in adolescence. In Coopersmith's study, children's self-esteem was associated with such parenting practices as affection and allowing children freedom within well-prescribed limits. Peer and friendship relations also are linked with self-esteem. Self-esteem is higher in elementary school than in middle or junior high school. For most adolescents, low self-esteem results in only temporary emotional discomfort. However, for others, especially when low self-esteem persists, it is linked with depression, anorexia nervosa, delinquency, and even suicide. Four ways to increase adolescents' self-esteem are to (1) identify the causes of low self-esteem and which domains of competence are important to the adolescent, (2) provide emotional support and social approval, (3) help the adolescent to achieve, and (4) improve the adolescent's coping skills.

2 Identity

LG2 Explain the many facets of identity development.

Erikson's Ideas on Identity

- Identity versus identity confusion is Erikson's fifth developmental stage, which individuals experience during adolescence. As adolescents are confronted with new roles, they enter a psychosocial moratorium. Personality and role experimentation are two key ingredients of Erikson's view. In technological societies like that of the United States, the vocational role is especially important. Identity development is extraordinarily complex and is done in bits and pieces. A current concern voiced by William Damon is the difficulty too many youth today have in developing a purposeful identity.

The Four Statuses of Identity

- Marcia proposed four identity statuses: diffused, foreclosed, moratorium, and achieved. A combination of crisis (exploration) and commitment yields one of the statuses. Some critics argue that Marcia's four identity statuses oversimplify identity development. Recently, emphasis has been given to expanding Marcia's concepts of exploration and commitment to focus more on in-depth exploration and ongoing evaluation of one's commitment.

Developmental Changes in Identity

- Some experts argue that the main identity changes take place in late adolescence or youth, rather than in early adolescence. College upperclassmen are more likely to be identity achieved than are freshmen or high school students, although many college students are still wrestling with ideological commitments. Individuals often follow MAMA ("*m*oratorium–*a*chievement–*m*oratorium–*a*chievement") cycles.

Identity and Social Contexts

- Parents are important figures in adolescents' identity development. Researchers have found that democratic parenting, individuality, connectedness, and enabling behaviors are linked with positive aspects of identity. Erikson was especially sensitive to the role of culture in identity development, underscoring the fact that throughout the world ethnic minority groups have struggled to maintain their cultural identities while blending into majority culture. Adolescence is often a special juncture in the identity development of ethnic minority individuals because for the first time they consciously confront their ethnic identity. Many ethnic minority adolescents have a bicultural identity. Ethnic identity increases with age during adolescence and emerging adulthood, and higher levels of ethnic identity are linked to more positive attitudes. The contexts in which ethnic minority youth live influence their identity development. The cognitive challenges of higher education likely stimulate ethnic minority individuals to reflect on their identity. Erikson noted that adolescent males have a stronger vocational identity, female adolescents a stronger social identity. However, researchers are finding that these gender differences are disappearing.

Identity and Intimacy

- Intimacy versus isolation is Erikson's sixth stage of human development, which individuals experience during early adulthood. Erikson argued that an optimal sequence is to develop a positive identity before negotiating the intimacy versus isolation stage.

3 Emotional Development

LG3 Discuss the emotional development of adolescents.

The Emotions of Adolescence

- Emotion is feeling, or affect, that occurs when a person is in a state or an interaction that is important to the individual, especially to his or her well-being. Adolescents report more extreme and fleeting emotions than those of their parents, and as individuals go through early adolescence they are less likely to report being very happy. However, it is important to view moodiness as a normal aspect of early adolescence.

Hormones, Experience, and Emotions

- Although pubertal change is associated with an increase in negative emotions, hormonal influences are often small, and environmental experiences may contribute more to the emotions of adolescence than do hormonal changes.

Emotional Competence

- Adolescents' increased cognitive abilities and awareness provide them with the opportunity to cope more effectively with stress and emotional fluctuations. However, the emotional burdens of adolescence can be overwhelming for some adolescents. Among the emotional competencies that are important for adolescents to develop are being aware that the expression of emotions plays a major role in relationships, adaptively coping with negative emotions by using self-regulatory strategies, understanding how emotionally expressive behavior influences others, being aware of one's emotional states without being overwhelmed by them, and being able to discern others' emotions.

4 Personality Development

LG4 Characterize the personality development of adolescents.

Personality

- There has been a long history of interest in discovering the core traits of personality, and recently that search has focused on the Big Five factors of personality: openness to experience, conscientiousness, extraversion, agreeableness, and neuroticism (emotional instability). Much of the research on the Big Five factors has focused on adults, but an increasing number of these studies focus on adolescents. Having an optimistic thinking style is linked to positive adjustment in adolescents. Researchers continue to debate what the core characteristics of personality are. Critics of the trait approach argue that it places too much emphasis on stability and not enough on change and situational influences. Today, many psychologists stress that personality is best described in terms of both traits and situational influences.

Temperament

- Many psychologists emphasize that temperament forms the foundation for personality. Chess and Thomas described three basic types of temperament: easy child, difficult child, and slow-to-warm-up child. New classifications of temperament include positive affect and approach, negative affectivity, and effortful control (self-regulation). Connections between the temperament of individuals from childhood to adulthood have been found, although these links may vary according to the contexts of people's lives. Goodness of fit refers to the match between an individual's temperament and the environmental demands of individuals.

key terms

self 129
self-understanding 130
possible self 131
self-esteem 134
self-concept 135
narcissism 135
identity 140
identity versus identity confusion 140
psychosocial moratorium 140
crisis 143
commitment 143
identity diffusion 143
identity foreclosure 143
identity moratorium 143
identity achievement 143
individuality 147
connectedness 147
ethnic identity 147
bicultural identity 147
intimacy versus isolation 148
emotion 150
personality 153
Big Five factors of personality 153
optimism 154
temperament 154
easy child 155
difficult child 155
slow-to-warm-up child 155
goodness of fit 157

key people

Susan Harter 131
Gisela Labouvie-Vief 133
Daniel Lapsley and Matthew Aalsma 136
Erik Erikson 140
William Damon 142
James Marcia 143
Luc Goossens and Koen Luyckx 144
Alan Waterman 145
James Coté 146
Jane Kroger 146
Catherine Cooper 147
Jean Phinney 149
Moin Syed and Margarita Azmitia 149
Walter Mischel 154
Alexander Chess and Stella Thomas 155

resources for improving the lives of adolescents

The Development of Self-Representations in Childhood and Adolescence
by Susan Harter
in W. Damon and R. Lerner (Eds.)
Handbook of Child Psychology (2006, 6th ed.)
New York: Wiley

Leading self theorist and researcher Susan Harter provides an in-depth analysis of how the self develops in childhood and adolescence.

Emotional Development
by Carolyn Saarni, Joseph Campos, Linda Camras, and David Witherspoon
in W. Damon and R. Lerner (Eds.)
Handbook of Child Psychology (2006, 6th ed.)
New York: Wiley

Read about up-to-date research and views on how emotions develop in children and adolescents.

Gandhi's Truth
by Erik Erikson (1969)
New York: W. W. Norton

This Pulitzer Prize–winning book by Erik Erikson, who developed the concept of identity as a central aspect of adolescent development, analyzes the life of Mahatma Gandhi, the spiritual leader of India in the middle of the twentieth century.

Identity Development: Adolescence Through Adulthood
by Jane Kroger (2007, 2nd ed.)
Thousand Oaks, CA: Sage

Leading expert Jane Kroger provides a contemporary analysis of identity development research.

Bridging Multiple Worlds
by Catherine Cooper (2011)
New York: Oxford University Press

This excellent book by a leading expert explores the development of cultural identities and ways to improve the educational opportunities of immigrant, minority, and low-income youth as they develop through adolescence and emerging adulthood.

Intersections of Personal and Social Identities
by Margarita Azmitia, Moin Syed, and Kimberley Radmacher (Eds.) (2008)
New Directions for Child and Adolescent Development, 120, 1–16

A number of leading experts discuss research and theory on numerous aspects of identity, including the roles of the media, gender, and ethnicity.

Personality Development
by Avshalom Caspi and Rebecca Shiner
in W. Damon and R. Lerner (Eds.)
Handbook of Child Psychology (2006, 6th ed.)
New York: Wiley

Leading experts describe recent research on how personality develops.

self-assessment

The Online Learning Center includes the following self-assessments for further exploration:

- *My Self-Esteem*
- *Exploring My Identity*
- *Am I Extraverted or Introverted?*

chapter 5 GENDER

chapter **outline**

Biological, Social, and Cognitive Influences on Gender

Learning Goal 1 Describe the biological, social, and cognitive influences on gender.

Biological Influences on Gender
Social Influences on Gender
Cognitive Influences on Gender

Gender Stereotypes, Similarities, and Differences

Learning Goal 2 Discuss gender stereotypes, similarities, and differences.

Gender Stereotyping
Gender Similarities and Differences
Gender Controversy
Gender in Context

Gender-Role Classification

Learning Goal 3 Characterize the variations in gender-role classification.

Masculinity, Femininity, and Androgyny
Context, Culture, and Gender Roles
Androgyny and Education
Traditional Masculinity and Problem Behaviors in Adolescent Males
Gender-Role Transcendence

Developmental Changes and Junctures

Learning Goal 4 Summarize developmental changes in gender.

Early Adolescence and Gender Intensification
Is Early Adolescence a Critical Juncture for Females?

"You know it seems like girls are more emotionally sensitive than guys, especially teenage guys. We don't know all the reasons, but we have some ideas about why this might be true. Once a girl reaches 12 or so and begins to mature physically, it seems as though nature is preparing her to be sensitive to others the way a mother might be to her baby, to feel what others feel so she can provide love and support to her children. Our culture tells boys different things. They are expected to be 'tough' and not get carried away with their feelings . . . In spite of this, don't think that girls cannot be assertive and boys cannot be sensitive. In fact, boys do feel emotions but many of them simply don't know how to express their feelings or fear that they will be teased."

—Zoe, age 13 (Zager & Rubenstein, 2002, pp. 21–22)

"With all the feminist ideas in the country and the equality, I think guys sometimes get put on the spot. Guys might do something that I think or they think might not be wrong at all, but they still get shot down for it. If you're not nice to a girl, she thinks you don't care. But if you are nice, she thinks you are treating her too much like a lady. Girls don't understand guys, and guys don't understand girls very well."

—Toby, age 17 (Pollack, 1998, p. 164)

The comments of these two adolescents—one female, one male—reflect the confusion that many adolescents feel about how to act as a female or a male. Nowhere in adolescents' socioemotional development have more sweeping changes occurred in recent years than in the area of gender, and these changes have led to the confusion about gender behavior just described.

preview

What exactly is meant by gender? **Gender** refers to the characteristics of people as males and females. Few aspects of adolescents' lives are more central to their identity and to their social relationships than gender. One aspect of gender bears special mention: a **gender role** is a set of expectations that prescribes how females and males should think, act, and feel. For example, should males be more assertive than females, and should females be more sensitive than males to others' feelings? Though individuals become aware of gender early in childhood, a new dimension is added to gender with the onset of puberty and the sexual maturation it brings. This chapter begins with a discussion of the biological, as well as the social and cognitive influences on gender. We will distinguish gender stereotypes from actual differences between the sexes and examine the range of gender roles that adolescents can adopt. The chapter closes by exploring the developmental changes in gender that characterize adolescence.

1 Biological, Social, and Cognitive Influences on Gender

LG1 Describe the biological, social, and cognitive influences on gender.

Biological Influences on Gender | Social Influences on Gender | Cognitive Influences on Gender

Gender development is influenced by biological, social, and cognitive factors. Our discussion of these influences focuses on such questions as: How strong is biology's influence on gender? How extensively does experience shape children's and adolescents' gender development? To what extent do cognitive factors influence gender development?

gender The characteristics of people as males or females.

gender role A set of expectations that prescribes how females and males should think, act, and feel.

It is fatal to be man or woman pure and simple; one must be woman-manly or man-womanly.

—Virginia Woolf
English Novelist, 20th Century

BIOLOGICAL INFLUENCES ON GENDER

Pubertal change is a biological influence on gendered behavior in adolescence. Freud and Erikson also argued that the physical characteristics of males and females influence their behavior. And evolutionary psychologists emphasize the role of gender in the survival of the fittest.

Pubertal Change and Sexuality Puberty intensifies the sexual aspects of adolescents' gender attitudes and behavior (Galambos, Berenbaum, & McHale, 2009). As their bodies flood with hormones, young adolescent boys and girls incorporate sexuality into their gender attitudes and behaviors, especially when they interact with the other sex or with a same-sex individual to whom they are sexually attracted. Thus, adolescent girls might behave in a sensitive, charming, and soft-spoken manner with a boy they are sexually attracted to, whereas boys might behave in an assertive, cocky, and forceful way, perceiving that such behaviors enhance their sexuality.

developmental **connection**

Biological Processes. Hormones are powerful chemical substances secreted by the endocrine glands and carried through the body by the bloodstream. Chapter 2, p. 51

Few attempts have been made to relate puberty's sexual changes to gender behavior. Researchers have found, however, that sexual behavior is related to hormonal changes during puberty, at least for boys. For example, in one study, rising androgen levels were related to boys' increased sexual activity (Udry, 1990). For adolescent girls, androgen levels and sexual activity were associated, but girls' sexual activity was more strongly influenced by the type of friends they had than by their hormone levels. The same study also evaluated whether hormone increases in puberty were related to gender behaviors, such as being affectionate, charming, assertive, or cynical, but a significant link was not found.

In sum, pubertal changes may result in masculinity and femininity being renegotiated during adolescence, and much of the renegotiation likely involves sexuality. Toward the end of the chapter, we return to the role that puberty plays in gender attitudes and behavior.

Freud and Erikson—Anatomy Is Destiny Both Sigmund Freud and Erik Erikson argued that an individual's genitals influence his or her gender behavior and, therefore, that anatomy is destiny. One of Freud's basic assumptions was that human behavior is directly related to reproductive processes. From this assumption arose his belief that gender and sexual behavior are essentially unlearned and instinctual. Erikson (1968) extended Freud's argument, claiming that the psychological differences between males and females stem from their anatomical differences. Erikson argued that, because of genital structure, males are more intrusive and aggressive, females more inclusive and passive. Critics of the anatomy-is-destiny view stress that experience is not given enough credit. The critics say that females and males are more free to choose their gender roles than Freud and Erikson allow. In response to the critics, Erikson modified his view, saying that females in today's world are transcending their biological heritage and correcting society's overemphasis on male intrusiveness.

Evolutionary Psychology and Gender In Chapter 2, we discussed the approach of evolutionary psychology, which emphasizes that adaptation during the evolution of humans produced psychological differences between males and females (Buss, 2008, 2012). Evolutionary psychologists argue that primarily because of their differing roles in reproduction, males and females faced different pressures in primeval environments when the human species was evolving (Geary, 2010). In particular, because having multiple sexual liaisons improves the likelihood that males will pass on their genes, natural selection favored males who adopted short-term mating strategies. These males competed with other males to acquire more resources in order to access females. Therefore, say evolutionary psychologists, males evolved dispositions that favor violence, competition, and risk taking.

developmental **connection**

Theories. Evolutionary psychology emphasizes the importance of adaptation, reproduction, and "survival of the fittest" in shaping behavior. Chapter 2, p. 75

In contrast, according to evolutionary psychologists, females' contributions to the gene pool were improved by securing resources for their offspring, which was promoted by obtaining long-term mates who could support a family. As a consequence, natural selection favored females who devoted effort to parenting and chose mates who could provide their offspring with resources and protection (Bjorklund, 2006). Females developed preferences for successful, ambitious men who could provide these resources (Geary, 2010).

This evolutionary unfolding, according to some evolutionary psychologists, explains key gender differences in sexual attitudes and sexual behavior. For example, in one study, men said that ideally they would like to have more than 18 sexual partners in their lifetime, whereas women stated that ideally they would like to have only 4 or 5 (Buss & Schmitt, 1993). In another study, 75 percent of the men but none of the women approached by an attractive stranger of the opposite sex consented to a request for sex (Clark & Hatfield, 1989).

Such gender differences, says David Buss (2008, 2012), are exactly the type predicted by evolutionary psychology. Buss argues that men and women differ psychologically in those domains in which they have faced different adaptive problems during evolutionary history. In all other domains, predicts Buss, the sexes will be psychologically similar.

Critics of evolutionary psychology argue that its hypotheses are backed by speculations about prehistory, not evidence, and that in any event people are not locked into behavior that was adaptive in the evolutionary past. Critics also claim that the evolutionary view pays little attention to cultural and individual variations in gender differences (Brannon, 2012; Matlin, 2012).

"It's a guy thing."
© Donald Reilly/The New Yorker Collection/ www.cartoonbank.com

SOCIAL INFLUENCES ON GENDER

Many social scientists do not locate the cause of psychological gender differences in biological dispositions. Rather, they argue that these differences are due mainly to social experiences. Alice Eagly (2001, 2010) proposed **social role theory,** which states that gender differences mainly result from the contrasting roles of females and males. In most cultures around the world, females have less power and status than males have, and they control fewer resources (UNICEF, 2011). Compared with men, women perform more domestic work, spend fewer hours in paid employment, receive lower pay, and are more thinly represented in the highest levels of organizations. In Eagly's view, as women adapted to roles with less power and less status in society, they showed more cooperative, less dominant profiles than men. Thus, the social hierarchy and division of labor are important causes of gender differences in power, assertiveness, and nurture (Eagly, 2010).

As the man beholds
the woman,
As the woman sees
the man,
Curiously they note
each other,
As each other they only can.

—Bryan Procter
English Poet, 19th Century

Parental Influences Parents, by action and example, influence their children's and adolescents' gender development (Maccoby, 2007). During the transition from childhood to adolescence, parents allow boys more independence than they allow for girls, and concern about girls' sexual vulnerability may cause parents to monitor their behavior more closely and ensure that they are chaperoned. Families with young adolescent daughters indicate that they experience more intense conflict about sex, choice of friends, and curfews than do families with young adolescent sons (Papini & Sebby, 1988).

developmental **connection**

Achievement. Parents' and teachers' expectations are important influences on adolescents' achievement. Chapter 11, p. 368

Parents may also have different achievement expectations for their adolescent sons and daughters, especially in academic areas such as math and science (Leaper & Friedman, 2007). For example, many parents believe that math is more important to their sons' futures than to their daughters'. These beliefs influence the value that adolescents place on math achievement (Eccles, 1987). We consider more about gender and achievement later in this chapter.

Mothers and fathers often interact differently with their adolescents. Mothers are more involved with their children and adolescents than are fathers, although fathers increase the time they spend in parenting when they have sons and are less

social role theory Theory stating that gender differences mainly result from the contrasting roles of females and males, with females having less power and status and controlling fewer resources than males.

How do mothers and fathers interact differently with their daughters and sons?

likely to become divorced when they have sons (Diekman & Schmidheiny, 2004). Mothers' interactions with their adolescents often center on caregiving and teaching activities, whereas fathers' interactions often involve leisure activities (Galambos, Berenbaum, & McHale, 2009).

Mothers and fathers also often interact differently with their sons and daughters. In a research review, the following conclusions were reached (Bronstein, 2006):

- *Mothers' socialization strategies.* In many cultures, mothers socialize their daughters to be more obedient and responsible than their sons. They also place more restrictions on daughters' autonomy.
- *Fathers' socialization strategies.* Fathers show more attention to sons than daughters, engage in more activities with sons, and put forth more effort to promote sons' intellectual development.

Thus, despite an increase in more egalitarian gender roles in many aspects of society, many mothers and fathers showed marked differences in the way they interact with boys and girls, and these differences persist through adolescence (Bronstein, 2006; Galambos, Berenbaum, & McHale, 2009).

Recent research provided further support for the belief that some aspects of gender roles are still not egalitarian (E. R. Brown & Diekman, 2010). College students were interviewed about their future selves in the near future (1 year) and the distant future (10–15 years). Stronger gender patterns were found for distant than near selves. For distant selves, females were more likely to list "family" while men were more likely to list "career." In terms of "family" selves in the future, males were more likely to list "economic provider" while females were more likely to list "caregiver."

Social cognitive theory has been especially important in understanding social influences on gender (Bussey & Bandura, 1999). The **social cognitive theory of gender** emphasizes that children's and adolescents' gender development is influenced by their observation and imitation of others' gender behavior, as well as by the rewards and punishments they experience for gender-appropriate and gender-inappropriate behavior. By observing parents and other adults, as well as peers, at home, at school, in the neighborhood, and in the media, adolescents are exposed to a myriad of models that display masculine and feminine behavior. And parents often use rewards and punishments to teach their daughters to be feminine ("Karen, that dress you are wearing makes you look so beautiful.") and their sons to be masculine ("Bobby, you were so aggressive in that game. Way to go!").

developmental **connection**

Social Cognitive Theory. Social cognitive theory holds that behavior, environment, and person/cognitive factors are the key aspects of development. Chapter 1, p. 32

Siblings Siblings also play a role in gender socialization (Galambos, Berenbaum, & McHale, 2009). One study revealed that over a two-year time frame in early adolescence, younger siblings became more similar to their older siblings in terms of gender-role and leisure activity (McHale & others, 2001). For example, if a younger sibling had an older sibling who was masculine and engaged in masculine leisure activities, over the two years the younger sibling became more masculine

social cognitive theory of gender Theory emphasizing that children's and adolescents' gender development occurs through observation and imitation of gender behavior, and through rewards and punishments they experience for gender-appropriate and gender-inappropriate behavior.

and participated in more masculine leisure activities. In contrast, older siblings became less like their younger siblings over the two-year period.

What role does gender play in adolescent peer relations?

Peers Parents provide the first models of gender behavior, but before long peers also are responding to and modeling masculine and feminine behavior (Rubin & others, 2011). In middle and late childhood, children show a clear preference for being with and liking same-sex peers (Maccoby, 1998, 2002). After extensive observations of elementary school playgrounds, two researchers characterized the play settings as "gender school," pointing out that boys teach one another the required masculine behavior and reinforce it, and that girls also teach one another the required feminine behavior and reinforce it (Luria & Herzog, 1985).

Adolescents spend increasing amounts of time with peers (B. B. Brown & others, 2008). In adolescence, peer approval or disapproval is a powerful influence on gender attitudes and behavior (Prinstein & Dodge, 2010). Peer groups in adolescence are more likely to be a mix of boys and girls than they were in childhood. However, a recent study of 15- to 17-year-olds indicated that gender segregation characterizes some aspects of adolescents' social life (Mehta & Strough, 2010). In this study, 72 percent of peers said they were most likely to "hang out" with the same gender of adolescents as themselves.

Peers can socialize gender behavior partly by accepting or rejecting others on the basis of their gender-related attributes. Continuing in adolescence and the adulthood years through late adulthood, friendships also mainly consist of same-sex peers (Mehta & Strough, 2009, 2010). We will have much more to discuss about gender and peer relations in Chapter 9.

Schools and Teachers There are concerns that schools and teachers have biases against both boys and girls (Arms, Bickett, & Graf, 2008). What evidence exists that the classroom is biased against boys? Here are some factors to consider (DeZolt & Hull, 2001):

- Compliance, following rules, and being neat and orderly are valued and reinforced in many classrooms. These are behaviors that usually characterize girls more than boys.
- A large majority of teachers are females, especially in the elementary school. This trend may make it more difficult for boys than for girls to identify with their teachers and model their teachers' behavior.
- Boys are more likely than girls to have learning problems.
- Boys are more likely than girls to be criticized.
- School personnel tend to ignore that many boys are clearly having academic problems, especially in the language arts.
- School personnel tend to stereotype boys' behavior as problematic.

What evidence is there that the classroom is biased against girls? Consider the views of Myra and David Sadker (2005):

- In a typical classroom, girls are more compliant, boys more rambunctious. Boys demand more attention, girls are more likely to quietly wait their turn. Teachers are more likely to scold and reprimand boys, as well as send boys to school authorities for disciplinary action. Educators worry that girls' tendency to be compliant and quiet comes at a cost: diminished assertiveness.

How are gender and schools linked during adolescence?

- In many classrooms, teachers spend more time watching and interacting with boys, whereas girls work and play quietly on their own. Most teachers don't intentionally favor boys by spending more time with them, yet somehow the classroom frequently ends up with this type of gendered profile.
- Boys get more instruction than girls and more help when they have trouble with a question. Teachers often give boys more time to answer a question, more hints at the correct answer, and further tries if they give the wrong answer.
- Boys are more likely than girls to get lower grades and to be grade repeaters, yet girls are less likely to believe that they will be successful in college work.
- Girls and boys enter first grade with roughly equal levels of self-esteem. Yet by the middle school years, girls' self-esteem is lower than boys'.
- When elementary school children are asked to list what they want to do when they grow up, boys describe more career options than girls do.

Thus, there is evidence of gender bias against both males and females in schools. Many school personnel are not aware of their gender-biased attitudes. These attitudes are deeply entrenched in and supported by the general culture. Increasing awareness of gender bias in schools is clearly an important strategy in reducing such bias.

Might same-sex education be better for children than coed education? The research evidence related to this question is mixed (Blakemore, Berenbaum, & Liben, 2009). Some research indicates that same-sex education has positive outcomes for girls' achievement, whereas other research does not show any improvements in achievement for girls or boys in same-sex education (Feniger, 2011; Mael, 1998; Warrington & Younger, 2003). A recent study revealed that girls who took a physics class in a same-sex education school had a more positive physics-related self-concept than girls who took a physics class in a coed school (Kessels & Hannover, 2008).

Mass Media Influences As already described, adolescents encounter gender roles in their everyday interactions with parents, peers, and teachers. The messages about gender roles carried by the mass media also are important influences on adolescents' gender development (Straubhaar, LaRose, & Davenport, 2011). Television shows directed at adolescents are extremely stereotyped in their portrayal of the sexes, especially teenage girls (Comstock & Scharrer, 2006). One study found that teenage girls were portrayed as being concerned primarily with dating, shopping, and their appearance (Campbell, 1988). They rarely were shown as being interested in school or career plans. Attractive girls were often typed as "airheads" and intelligent girls as unattractive.

Another highly stereotyped form of programming that specifically targets teenage viewers is music videos (Roberts & Foehr, 2008). What adolescents see on MTV and some other TV shows is highly stereotyped and slanted toward a male audience. A recent study of MTV videos reinforced stereotypical notions of women as sexual objects and females as subordinate to males (Wallis, 2011). MTV has been described as a teenage boy's "dreamworld," filled with beautiful, aroused women who outnumber men, seek out and even assault them to have sex, and always mean yes, even when they say no (Jhally, 1990).

Females are often portrayed in sexually provocative ways on MTV and in rock videos.

Early adolescence may be a period of heightened sensitivity to television messages about gender roles. Increasingly, young adolescents view programs designed for adults that include messages about gender-appropriate behavior, especially in heterosexual relationships. Cognitively, adolescents engage in more idealistic thoughts than children do, and television certainly has its share of idealized characters with whom adolescents can identify and imitate—highly appealing models who are young, glamorous, and successful.

The world of television is highly gender-stereotyped and conveys clear messages about the relative power and importance of women and men (Calvert, 2008). Men are portrayed as more powerful than women on many TV shows. On music videos, male characters are portrayed more often than female characters as aggressive, dominant, competent, autonomous, and active, whereas female characters are more often portrayed as passive. In one study of prime-time commercials, women were underrepresented as primary characters except in commercials for health and beauty products (Ganahl, Prinsen, & Netzley, 2003).

The media influence adolescents' body images, and some studies reveal gender differences in this area (Grabe & Hyde, 2009). For example, one study of 10- to 17-year-olds found that girls more so than boys perceived that the media influence their body images (Polce-Lynch & others, 2001). Another study revealed that the more adolescent girls and boys watched entertainment television, the more negative their body images were (Anderson & others, 2001).

developmental **connection**

Identity. Girls have more negative body images than do boys during adolescence. Chapter 2, p. 59

COGNITIVE INFLUENCES ON GENDER

Observation, imitation, rewards and punishment—these are the mechanisms by which gender develops according to social cognitive theory. Interactions between the child/adolescent and the social environment are the main keys to gender development in this view. Some critics who adopt a cognitive approach argue that this explanation pays too little attention to the child's own mind and understanding, and portrays the child as passively acquiring gender roles (Martin, Ruble, & Szkrybalo, 2002).

One influential cognitive theory is **gender schema theory,** which states that gender-typing emerges as children and adolescents gradually develop gender schemas of what is gender-appropriate and gender-inappropriate in their culture (Martin & Ruble, 2010). A *schema* is a cognitive structure, a network of associations that guide an individual's perceptions. A gender schema organizes the world in terms of female and male. Children and adolescents are internally motivated to perceive the world and to act in accordance with their developing schemas. Bit by bit, children and adolescents pick up what is gender-appropriate and gender-inappropriate in their culture, and develop gender schemas that shape how they perceive the world and what they remember. Children and adolescents are motivated to act in ways that conform with these gender schemas.

In sum, cognitive factors contribute to the way adolescents think and act as males and females (Blakemore, Berenbaum, & Liben, 2009). Through biological, social, and cognitive processes, children develop their gender attitudes and behaviors (Galambos, Berenbaum, & McHale, 2009).

Regardless of the factors that influence gender behavior, the consequences of gender have become the subject of intense focus and research over the last several decades. Next, we explore the myths and realities of how females and males do or do not differ.

gender schema theory Theory stating that an individual's attention and behavior are guided by an internal motivation to conform to gender-based sociocultural standards and stereotypes. Females are often portrayed in sexually provocative ways on MTV and in rock videos.

Review *Connect* Reflect

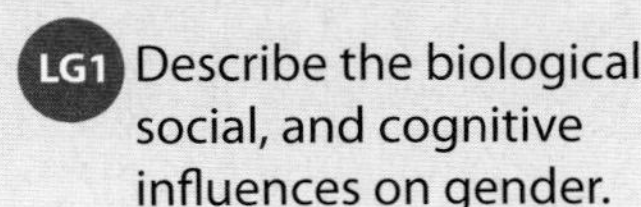

Describe the biological, social, and cognitive influences on gender.

Review

- How can gender and gender roles be defined? What are some important biological influences on gender?
- What are some important social influences on gender?
- What are some important cognitive influences on gender?

Connect

- How might the characteristics of Piaget's formal operational thought, discussed in Chapter 3, be linked to the way adolescents think about gender?

Reflect *Your Own Personal Journey of Life*

- Which theory do you think best explains your gender development through adolescence? What might an eclectic view of gender development be like? (You might want to review the discussion of an eclectic theoretical orientation in Chapter 1.)

2 Gender Stereotypes, Similarities, and Differences

LG2 Discuss gender stereotypes, similarities, and differences.

Gender Stereotyping | Gender Similarities and Differences | Gender Controversy | Gender in Context

How pervasive is gender stereotyping? What are the real differences between boys and girls, and why is this issue such a controversial one? In this section, our goal is not just to answer these questions but also to discuss controversy regarding gender and to place gender behavior in context.

GENDER STEREOTYPING

Gender stereotypes are general impressions and beliefs about females and males. For example, men are powerful; women are weak. Men make good mechanics; women make good nurses. Men are good with numbers; women are good with words. Women are emotional; men are not. All of these are stereotypes. They are generalizations about a group that reflect widely held beliefs. Recent research has found that gender stereotypes are, to a great extent, still present in today's world, in the lives of both children and adults (Best, 2010; Matlin, 2012; Wood, 2011). Researchers also have found that boys' gender stereotypes are more rigid than girls' (Blakemore, Berenbaum, & Liben, 2009).

A classic study in the early 1970s assessed which traits and behaviors college students believed were characteristic of females and which they believed were characteristic of males (Broverman & others, 1972). The traits associated with males were labeled *instrumental:* They included characteristics such as being independent, aggressive, and power-oriented. The traits associated with females were labeled *expressive:* They included characteristics such as being warm and sensitive.

Thus, the instrumental traits associated with males suited them for the traditional masculine role of going out into the world as the breadwinner. The expressive traits associated with females paralleled the traditional feminine role of being the sensitive, nurturing caregiver in the home. These roles and traits, however, are not just different; they also are unequal in terms of social status and power. The traditional feminine characteristics are childlike, suitable for someone who is dependent and subordinate to others. The traditional masculine characteristics suit one to deal competently with the wider world and to wield authority.

Researchers continue to find that gender stereotyping is pervasive (Blakemore, Berenbaum, & Liben, 2009; Leaper & Bigler, 2011; Matlin, 2012). For example, one study found extensive differences in the stereotyping of females' and males' emotions (Durik & others, 2006). Females were stereotyped as expressing more fear, guilt, love, sadness, shame, surprise, and sympathy than their male counterparts. Males were stereotyped as expressing more anger and pride than their female counterparts.

GENDER SIMILARITIES AND DIFFERENCES

What is the reality behind gender stereotypes? Let's now examine some of the differences between the sexes, keeping the following in mind:

- The differences are average and do not apply to all females or all males.
- Even when gender differences occur, there often is considerable overlap between males and females, especially in cognitive and socioemotional development.
- The differences may be due primarily to biological factors, to sociocultural factors, or to both.

First, we examine physical similarities and differences, and then we turn to cognitive and socioemotional similarities and differences.

gender stereotypes Broad categories that reflect our impressions and beliefs about females and males.

Physical Similarities and Differences We could devote numerous pages to describing physical differences between the average man and woman. For example, women have about twice the body fat of men, most concentrated around breasts and hips. In males, fat is more likely to go to the abdomen. On the average, males grow to be 10 percent taller than females. Males have greater physical strength than females.

Many physical differences between men and women are tied to health. From conception on, females have a longer life expectancy than do males, and females are less likely than males to develop physical or mental disorders. Females are more resistant to infection, and their blood vessels are more elastic than males'. Males have higher levels of stress hormones, which cause faster clotting and higher blood pressure. For example, a recent study of emerging adults found that the hypothalamic-pituitary-adrenal (HPA) axis responses in males were greater than in females following a psychological stress test (Uhart & others, 2006). This greater response of the HPA axis in males was reflected in elevated levels of such stress-related hormones as cortisol.

Much of the research on gender similarities and differences in the brain have been conducted with adults rather than children or adolescents (Lenroot & Giedd, 2010). Among the differences that have been discovered in studies with adults are the following:

- One part of the hypothalamus involved in sexual behavior tends to be larger in men than in women (Swaab & others, 2001).
- An area of the parietal lobe that functions in visuospatial skills tends to be larger in males than in females (Frederikse & others, 2000).
- Female brains are smaller than male brains but female brains have more folds; the larger folds (called *convolutions*) allow more surface brain tissue within the skulls of females than of males (Luders & others, 2004).

Although some gender differences in brain structure and function have been found, many of these differences are either small or research is inconsistent regarding the differences (Hyde, 2007). Also, when gender differences in the brain have been revealed, in many cases they have not been directly linked to psychological differences (Blakemore, Berenbaum, & Liben, 2009). Although research on gender differences in the brain is still in its infancy, it is likely that there are far more similarities than differences in the brains of females and males (Halpern, 2006; Hyde, 2007). Similarities and differences in the brains of males and females could be due to evolution and heredity, as well as social experiences.

Cognitive Similarities and Differences No gender differences occur in overall intellectual ability—but in some cognitive areas, gender differences do appear (Blakemore, Berenbaum, & Liben, 2009; Galambos, Berenbaum, & McHale, 2009). Many years ago, Eleanor Maccoby and Carol Jacklin (1974) concluded that males have better math and visuospatial skills (the kinds of skills an architect needs to design a building's angles and dimensions) than do females, whereas females have better verbal abilities than do males. Subsequently, Maccoby (1987) concluded that the verbal differences between females and males had virtually disappeared but that the math and visuospatial differences persisted.

In the National Assessment of Educational Progress in the United States, fourth- and eighth-grade males continued to slightly outperform females in math through 2007 (National Assessment of Educational Progress, 2005, 2007). However, not all recent studies have shown differences. A recent very large-scale study of more than 7 million U.S. students in grades 2 through 11 revealed no differences in math scores for boys and girls (Hyde & others, 2008). And a recent meta-analysis found no gender differences in math for adolescents (Lindberg & others, 2010).

One area of math that has been examined for possible gender differences is visuospatial skills, which include being able to rotate objects mentally and determine

"So according to the stereotype, you can put two and two together, but I can read the handwriting on the wall." © 1994 Joel Pett. Reprinted with permission.

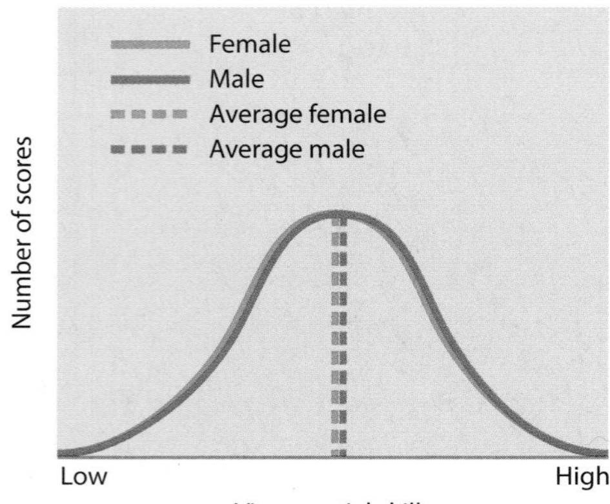

FIGURE **5.1**

VISUOSPATIAL SKILLS OF MALES AND FEMALES. Notice that, although an average male's visuospatial skills are higher than an average female's, scores for the two sexes almost entirely overlap. Not all males have better visuospatial skills than all females—the overlap indicates that, although the average male score is higher, many females outperform most males on such tasks.

what they would look like when rotated. These types of skills are important in courses such as plane and solid geometry and geography. A recent research review revealed that boys have better visuospatial skills than do girls (Halpern & others, 2007). For example, despite equal participation in the National Geography Bee, in most years all 10 finalists were boys (Liben, 1995).

However, some experts in gender, such as Janet Shibley Hyde (2005, 2007), conclude that the cognitive differences between females and males have been exaggerated. For example, Hyde points out that there is considerable overlap in the distributions of female and male scores on math and visuospatial tasks (see Figure 5.1).

Debate continues about how extensive cognitive gender differences are and the extent to which there are stereotypes about the differences (Else-Quest, Hyde, & Linn, 2010; Jussim & others, 2009). In a recent study, highly educated adults gave estimates of male and female success for 12 cognitive tasks (Halpern, Straight, & Stephenson, 2011). Their estimates were compared with published research on the tasks. The adults were generally accurate about the direction of the differences but underestimated the size of the differences.

Are there gender differences in reading and writing skills? There is strong evidence that females outperform males in reading and writing. In national studies, girls had higher reading achievement than did boys in grades 4, 8, and 12, with the gap widening as students progressed through school (Coley, 2001; National Assessment of Educational Progress, 2005). Girls also have consistently outperformed boys in writing skills in the National Assessment of Educational Progress in fourth-, eighth-, and twelfth-grade assessments. Figure 5.2 shows the gender gap in writing for U.S. eighth-grade students (National Asssessment of Educational Progress, 2007).

Keep in mind that measures of achievement in school or scores on standardized tests may reflect many factors besides cognitive ability. For example, performance in school may in part reflect attempts to conform to gender roles or differences in motivation, self-regulation, or other socioemotional characteristics (Watt, 2008; Watt & Eccles, 2008).

Let's further explore gender difference related to schooling and achievement. In 2009, males were more likely to drop out of school than were females (9 percent versus 7 percent) (National Center for Education Statistics, 2011). Boys predominate in the academic bottom half of high school classes. That is, although many boys perform at the average or advanced level, the bottom 50 percent academically is made up mainly of boys. Half a century ago, in 1961, less than 40 percent of women who graduated from high school went on to attend college. Beginning in 1996, women were more likely to enroll in college than were men. In 2009, almost 75 percent of women attended college after high school compared to 66 percent of men (Women in Academia, 2011).

Piecing together the information about school dropouts, the percentage of males in the bottom half of their high school classes, and the percentage of males in college classes, we can conclude that currently females show greater overall academic interest and achievement than do males in the United States. Females are more likely to be engaged with academic material, be attentive in class, put forth more academic effort, and participate more in class than boys are (DeZolt & Hull, 2001). A recent large-scale study revealed that girls had more positive attitudes about school than boys did (Orr, 2011). And, further, girls' positive attitudes about school were linked to their higher grades; boys' negative attitudes about school were related to their lower grades.

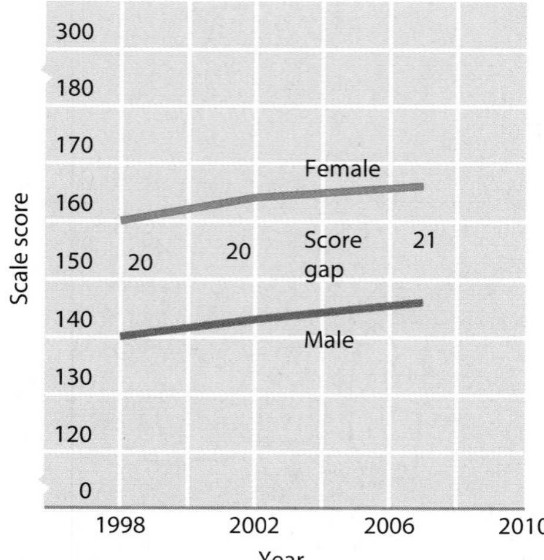

FIGURE **5.2**

GENDER DIFFERENCES IN U.S. EIGHTH-GRADE STUDENTS' WRITING SKILLS, 1998 TO 2007

Despite these positive characteristics of girls, the increasing evidence that there is similarity in the math and science skills of girls and boys, and the legislative efforts to attain gender equality in recent years, gender differences in science, technology, and math careers continue to favor males (Watt, 2008; Watt & Eccles, 2008). Toward the end of high school, girls are less likely to be taking high-level math courses and less likely to plan to enter the so-called "STEM" fields of science, technology, engineering, and math. A recent research review concluded that girls have more negative math attitudes and that parents' and teachers' expectancies for children's math competence are often gender-biased in favor of boys (Gunderson & others, 2011). We will have more to say about the topic of gender disparity in career development in Chapter 11.

What are little boys
made of?
Frogs and snails
and puppy dogs' tails.
What are little girls made of?
Sugar and spice
And all that's nice.

—J. O. HALLIWELL
English Author, 19th Century

Socioemotional Similarities and Differences Are "men from Mars" and "women from Venus"? This question was posed in the title of John Gray's (1992) highly popular book on gender differences in relationships. The answer to the question is no. Males and females are not so different that they should be thought of as being from different planets (Perry & Pauletti, 2011). For just about every imaginable socioemotional characteristic, researchers have examined whether there are differences between males and females. Here we examine four: aggression, communication in relationships, prosocial behavior (behavior that is intended to benefit other people), and self-regulation of emotion and behavior.

Aggression One of the most consistent gender differences is that boys are more physically aggressive than girls. The difference occurs in all cultures and appears very early in children's development (Kistner & others, 2010). The difference in physical aggression is especially pronounced when children are provoked. Although boys are consistently more physically aggressive than girls, might girls show as much or more verbal aggression, such as yelling, than boys? When verbal aggression is examined, gender differences typically either disappear or are sometimes even more pronounced in girls (Eagly & Steffen, 1986).

Recently, increased interest has been shown in *relational aggression,* which involves harming someone by manipulating a relationship (Hemphill & others, 2010; Werner & Hill, 2010). Relational aggression includes such behaviors as trying to make others dislike a certain individual by spreading malicious rumors about the person or ostracizing him or her (Underwood, 2011). Relational aggression increases in middle and late childhood (Dishion & Piehler, 2009). Mixed findings have characterized research on whether girls show more relational aggression than boys, but one consistency in findings is that relational aggression comprises a greater percentage of girls' overall aggression than is the case for boys (Putallaz & others, 2007). And a recent research review revealed that girls engage in more relational aggression than boys in adolescence but not in childhood (Smith, Rose, & Schwartz-Mette, 2010). A recent study also found links between parenting and children's relational aggression (Kuppens & others 2009). In this study, parents' psychological control was linked to a higher incidence of relational aggression in their children.

Are there gender differences in emotion? Girls are more likely to express their emotions openly and intensely than are boys, especially in displaying sadness and fear (Blakemore, Berenbaum, & Liben, 2009). Girls also are better at reading others' emotions and more likely to show empathy than are boys (Blakemore, Berenbaum, & Liben, 2009).

An important skill is to be able to regulate and control one's emotions and behavior (Eisenberg, Spinrad, & Eggum, 2010; Thompson & Goodman, 2011). Boys usually show less self-regulation than girls (Blakemore, Berenbaum, & Liben, 2009). This low self-control can translate into behavior problems

Communication in Relationships Sociolinguist Deborah Tannen (1990) distinguishes between rapport talk and report talk:

- **Rapport talk** is the language of conversation and a way of establishing connections and negotiating relationships. Females enjoy rapport talk and conversation that is relationship-oriented more than boys do.
- **Report talk** is talk that gives information. Public speaking is an example of report talk. Males hold center stage through report talk with such verbal performances as storytelling, joking, and lecturing with information.

rapport talk The language of conversation, establishing connections and negotiating relationships.

report talk Talk that gives information; public speaking is an example.

Tannen says that boys and girls grow up in different worlds of talk—parents, siblings, peers, teachers, and others talk differently to boys and girls. The play of

What have researchers found about gender similarities and differences in children's and adolescents' talkativeness, affiliative speech, and self-assertive speech?

boys and girls is also different. Boys tend to play in large groups that are hierarchically structured, and their groups usually have a leader who tells the others what to do and how to do it. Boys' games have winners and losers and often are the subject of arguments. And boys often boast of their skill and argue about who is best at what. In contrast, girls are more likely to play in small groups or pairs, and at the center of a girl's world is often a best friend. In girls' friendships and peer groups, intimacy is pervasive. Turn-taking is more characteristic of girls' games than of boys' games. And, much of the time, girls simply like to sit and talk with each other, concerned more about being liked by others than jockeying for status in some obvious way.

Researchers have found that girls are more "people oriented" and adolescent boys are more "things oriented" (Galambos, & others, 2009; Su, Rounds, & Armstrong, 2009). In a recent research review, this conclusion was supported by findings that girls spend more time in relationships, while boys spend more time alone, playing video games, and playing sports; that girls work at part-time jobs that are people-oriented such as waitressing and baby-sitting, while boys are more likely to take part-time jobs that involve manual labor and using tools; and that girls are interested in careers that are more people-oriented, such as teaching and social work, while boys are more likely to be interested in object-oriented careers, such as mechanics and engineering (Perry & Pauletti, 2011). Also, in support of Tannen's view, researchers have found that adolescent girls engage in more self-disclosure (communication of intimate details about themselves) in close relationships and are better at actively listening in a conversation than are boys (Leaper & Friedman, 2007).

However, Tannen's view has been criticized on the grounds that it is overly simplified and that communication between males and females is more complex than Tannen suggests (Edwards & Hamilton, 2004). Further, some researchers have found similarities in males' and females' relationship communication strategies. In one study, in their talk, men and women described and responded to relationship problems in ways that were more similar than different (MacGeorge, 2004).

developmental **connection**

Moral Development. Prosocial behavior is behavior intended to benefit other people. Chapter 7, p. 234

Prosocial Behavior Are there gender differences in prosocial behavior? Girls view themselves as more prosocial and empathic (Eisenberg & others, 2009). Across childhood and adolescence, girls engage in more prosocial behavior than do boys (Hastings, Utendale, & Sullivan, 2007). The biggest gender difference occurs for kind and considerate behavior, with a smaller difference for sharing.

Emotion and Its Regulation Gender differences occur in some aspects of emotion (Hertenstein & Keltner, 2011). Females express emotion more than do males, are better than males at decoding emotion, smile more, cry more, and are happier (Gross, Fredrickson, & Levenson, 1994; LaFrance, Hecht, & Paluck, 2003). Males report experiencing and expressing more anger than do females (Kring, 2000).

An important skill is to be able to regulate and control one's emotions and behavior (Thompson, Winer, & Goodvin, 2011). Boys usually show less self-regulation than girls (Eisenberg, Spinrad, & Eggum, 2010). This low self-control can translate into behavior problems. In one study, children's low self-regulation was linked with greater aggression, teasing of others, overreaction to frustration, low cooperation, and inability to delay gratification (Block & Block, 1980).

GENDER CONTROVERSY

Controversy continues about the extent of gender differences and what might cause them. As we saw earlier, evolutionary psychologists such as David Buss

(2012) argue that gender differences are extensive and caused by the adaptive problems they have faced across their evolutionary history. Alice Eagly (2010) also concludes that gender differences are substantial but reaches a very different conclusion about their cause. She emphasizes that gender differences are due to social conditions that have resulted in women having less power and controlling fewer resources than men.

By contrast, Janet Shibley Hyde (2005, 2007) concludes that gender differences have been greatly exaggerated, especially fueled by popular books such as John Gray's (1992) *Men Are from Mars, Women Are from Venus* and Deborah Tannen's (1990) *You Just Don't Understand*. She argues that the research shows that females and males are similar on most psychological factors. In a research review, Hyde (2005) summarized the results of 44 meta-analyses of gender differences and similarities. In most areas, gender differences either were nonexistent or small, including math ability and communication. The largest difference occurred on motor skills (favoring males), followed by sexuality (males masturbate more and are more likely to endorse sex in a casual, uncommitted relationship) and physical aggression (males are more physically aggressive than females). A recent research review also concluded that gender differences in adolescence are quite small (Perry & Pauletti, 2011).

There is more difference within the sexes than between them.

—IVY COMPTON-BURNETT
English Novelist, 20th Century

Hyde's summary of meta-analyses and the recent research review (Perry & Pauletti, 2011) is still not likely to quiet the controversy about gender differences and similarities, but further research should continue to provide a basis for more accurate judgments about this controversy.

GENDER IN CONTEXT

In thinking about gender, it is important to consider the context of behavior, as gender behavior often varies across contexts (Eagly, 2010; Perry & Pauletti, 2011). Consider helping behavior. Males are more likely to help in contexts in which a perceived danger is present and they feel competent to help (Eagly & Crowley, 1986). For example, males are more likely than females to help a person who is stranded by the roadside with a flat tire; automobile problems are an area about which many males feel competent. In contrast, when the context involves volunteering time to help a child with a personal problem, females are more likely to help than males are because there is little danger present and females feel more competent at nurturing. In many cultures, girls show more caregiving behavior than boys do. However, in the few cultures where they both care for younger siblings on a regular basis, girls and boys are similar in their tendencies to nurture (Whiting, 1989).

developmental **connection**

Theories. Bronfenbrenner's ecological theory emphasizes the importance of contexts; in his theory, the macrosystem includes cross-cultural comparisons. Chapter 1, p. 33

Adolescent girls in Iran. *How might gender-role socialization for girls in Iran compare with that in the United States?*

Context is also relevant to gender differences in the display of emotions. Consider anger. Males are more likely to show anger toward strangers, especially other males, when they think they have been challenged. Males also are more likely than females to turn their anger into aggressive action, especially when the culture endorses such action (Tavris & Wade, 1984).

We find contextual variations regarding gender in specific situations not only within a particular culture but also across cultures (Shiraev & Levy, 2010). Although in recent decades roles assumed by males and females in the United States have become increasingly similar, in many countries gender roles have remained more gender-specific (UNICEF, 2011). For example, in a number of Middle Eastern countries, the division of labor between males and females is dramatic: Males are socialized to work in the public sphere, females in the private world of home and child rearing; a man's duty is to provide for his family, the woman's to care for her family and household. Any deviations from this traditional gender-role orientation are severely disapproved of.

developmental **connection**

Culture and Ethnicity. East Asian children and adolescents consistently outperform their U.S. counterparts in math achievement. Chapter 11, p. 374

Review *Connect* Reflect

LG2 Discuss gender stereotypes, similarities, and differences.

Review

- How extensive is gender stereotyping?
- How similar or different are adolescent males and females in their physical, cognitive, and socioemotional development?
- What is the controversy about the cause of gender differences?
- How extensively is gender development influenced by contexts?

Connect

- How do socioemotional similarities and differences between girls and boys relate to the development of self-esteem, discussed in Chapter 4?

Reflect *Your Own Personal Journey of Life*

- Some decades ago, the word *dependency* was used to describe the relational orientation of femininity. Dependency took on a negative connotation for females—for instance, that females can't take care of themselves whereas males can. Today, the term *dependency* is being replaced by the term *relational abilities,* which has more positive connotations (Caplan & Caplan, 1999). Rather than being thought of as dependent, women are now more often described as skilled in forming and maintaining relationships. Make up a list of words that you associate with masculinity and femininity. Do these words have any negative connotations for males and females? For the words that do have negative connotations, are there words that could be used to replace them?

3 Gender-Role Classification

Characterize the variations in gender-role classification.

- Masculinity, Femininity, and Androgyny
- Context, Culture, and Gender Roles
- Androgyny and Education
- Traditional Masculinity and Problem Behaviors in Adolescent Males
- Gender-Role Transcendence

Not long ago, it was accepted that boys should grow up to be masculine and girls to be feminine, that boys are made of "frogs and snails" and girls are made of "sugar and spice and all that's nice." Let's further explore such gender classifications of boys and girls as "masculine" and "feminine."

MASCULINITY, FEMININITY, AND ANDROGYNY

In the past, a well-adjusted boy was supposed to be independent, aggressive, and powerful. A well-adjusted girl was supposed to be dependent, nurturant, and uninterested in power. The masculine characteristics were considered to be healthy and good by society; the feminine characteristics were considered undesirable.

In the 1970s, as both males and females became dissatisfied with the burdens imposed by their stereotyped roles, alternatives to "masculinity" and "femininity" were explored. Instead of thinking of masculinity and femininity as a continuum, with more of one meaning less of the other, it was proposed that individuals could show both expressive and instrumental traits. This thinking led to the development of the concept of **androgyny,** the presence of a high degree of masculine and feminine characteristics in the same individual (Bem, 1977; Spence & Helmreich, 1978). The androgynous individual might be a male who is both assertive (masculine) and sensitive to others' feelings (feminine), or a female who is both dominant (masculine) and caring (feminine).

androgyny The presence of a high degree of desirable feminine and masculine characteristics in the same individual.

Measures have been developed to assess androgyny. One of the most widely used gender measures, the *Bem Sex-Role Inventory*, was constructed by a leading early proponent of androgyny, Sandra Bem (1977). Figure 5.3 shows examples of masculine and feminine items on the Bem Sex-Role Inventory. Based on their responses to the items in this inventory, individuals are classified as having one of four gender-role orientations—masculine, feminine, androgynous, or undifferentiated (see Figure 5.4):

- The androgynous individual is simply a female or a male who has a high degree of both feminine and masculine traits. No new characteristics are used to describe the androgynous individual.
- A feminine individual is high on feminine traits and low on masculine traits.
- A masculine individual is high on instrumental traits and low on expressive traits.
- An undifferentiated person is low on both feminine and masculine traits.

Androgynous women and men, according to Bem, are more flexible and more mentally healthy than either masculine or feminine individuals; undifferentiated individuals are the least competent. One study found that androgyny was linked to well-being and lower levels of stress (Stake, 2000). Another study with emerging adults revealed that androgynous individuals reported better health practices (such as safety belt use, less smoking) than masculine, feminine, or undifferentiated individuals (Shifren, Furnham, & Bauserman, 2003).

Examples of masculine items

Defends open beliefs
Forceful
Willing to take risks
Dominant
Aggressive

Examples of feminine items

Does not use harsh language
Affectionate
Loves children
Understanding
Gentle

FIGURE **5.3**

THE BEM SEX-ROLE INVENTORY (BSRI). These items are from the Bem Sex-Role Inventory. When taking the BSRI, a person is asked to indicate on a 7-point scale how well each of the 60 characteristics describes herself or himself. The scale ranges from 1 (never or almost never true) to 7 (always or almost always true). The items are scored on independent dimensions of masculinity and femininity as well as androgyny and undifferentiated classifications. Reproduced by special permission of the Publisher, Mind Garden, Inc., www.mindgarden.com from the *Bem Sex Role Inventory* by Sandra Bem. Copyright 1978, 1981 by Consulting Psychologists Press, Inc. Further reproduction is prohibited without the Publisher's written consent.

CONTEXT, CULTURE, AND GENDER ROLES

The concept of gender-role classification involves a personality-trait-like categorization of a person. However, it is important to think of personality in terms of both traits and contexts rather than personality traits alone (Friedman & Schustack, 2011). In close relationships, a feminine or androgynous gender role may be more desirable because of the expressive nature of close relationships. However, a masculine or androgynous gender role may be more desirable in academic and work settings because of their demands for action and assertiveness. For example, one study found that masculine and androgynous individuals had higher expectations for being able to control the outcomes of their academic efforts than did feminine or undifferentiated individuals (Choi, 2004).

The importance of considering gender in context is nowhere more apparent than when examining what is culturally prescribed behavior for females and males in different countries around the world (Gibbons, 2000). Increasing numbers of children and adolescents in the United States and other modernized countries such as Sweden are being raised to behave in androgynous ways. In the last 30 to 40 years in the United States, a decline in the adoption of traditional gender roles has occurred. For example, in recent years U.S. female college students have shown a propensity for turning in their aprons for careers. In 1967, more than 40 percent of college females and more than 60 percent of college males agreed with the statement, "The activities of married women are best confined to home and family." In 2005, those percentages had dropped to 15 percent for college females and 26 percent for college males (Pryor & others, 2005). As shown in Figure 5.5, the greatest change in these attitudes occurred in the 1960s and early 1970s.

But traditional gender roles continue to dominate the cultures of many countries around the world today. In such cultures, the man's duty is to provide for his family; the woman's duty to care for her family and household. Any deviations from this traditional gender-role orientation are severely disapproved of. In the United States, the cultural backgrounds of adolescents influence how boys and girls will be socialized. In one study, Latino and Latina adolescents were socialized differently as they were growing

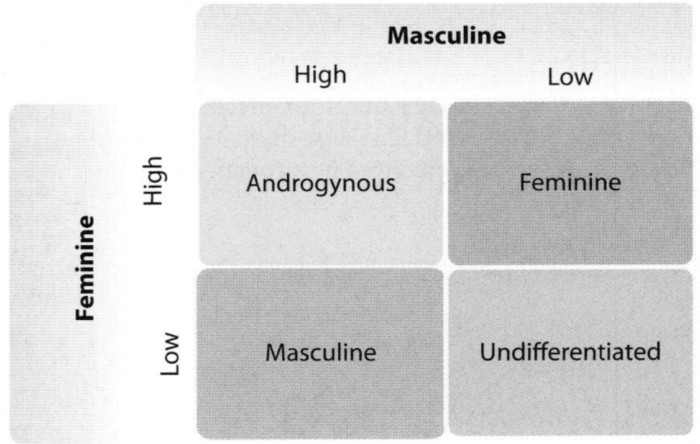

FIGURE **5.4**

GENDER-ROLE CLASSIFICATION

connecting with careers

Cynthia de las Fuentes, College Professor and Counseling Psychologist

Cynthia de las Fuentes is a professor at Our Lady of the Lake University in San Antonio. She obtained her undergraduate degree in psychology and her doctoral degree in counseling psychology at the University of Texas in Austin. Among the courses she teaches are the psychology of women, Latino psychology, and counseling theories.

Cynthia is president of the Division of the Psychology of Women in the American Psychological Association. "Many young women," she says, "take for granted that the women's movement has accomplished its goals—like equal pay for women, or reproductive rights—and don't realize that there is still work to be done." She is interested in "learning about people's intersecting identities, like female and Latina, and how the two work together." (Winerman, 2005, pp. 66–67).

Cynthia de las Fuentes.

For more information about the work that college professors and counseling psychologists do, see pages 46 and 47 in the Careers in Adolescent Development appendix.

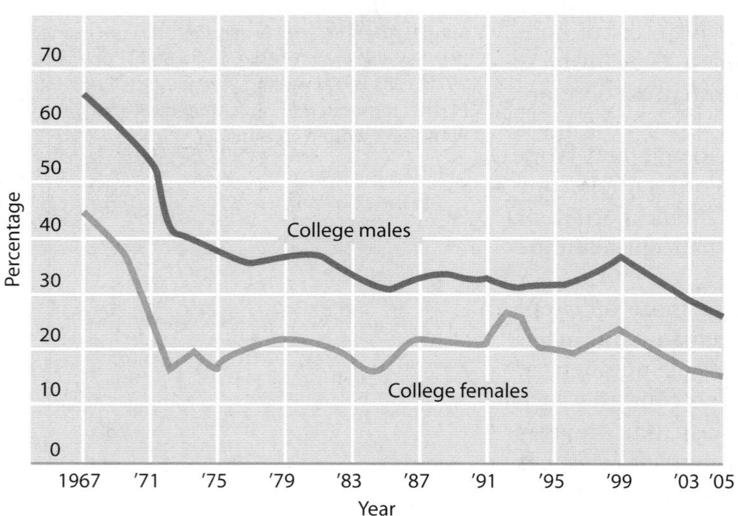

FIGURE **5.5**

CHANGING ATTITUDES ABOUT GENDER ROLES. *Note:* Data show the percentage of first-year U.S. college students agreeing with the statement, "The activities of married women are best confined to home and family" from 1967 through 2005.

up (Raffaelli & Ontai, 2004). Latinas experienced far greater restrictions than Latinos in curfews, interaction with members of the other sex, acquisition of a driver's license, job possibilities, and involvement in after-school activities. To read about the work of one individual who is interested in Latinas, see the *Connecting with Careers* profile.

Access to education for girls has improved somewhat around the world, but girls' education still lags behind boys' education. For example, according to a UNICEF (2003) analysis of education around the world, by age 18, girls have received, on average, 4.4 years less education than boys have. This lack of education reduces their chances of developing to their future potential. Exceptions to lower participation and completion rates in education for girls occur in Western nations, Japan, and the Philippines (Brown & Larson, 2002). Gaining advanced training or advanced degrees is higher in most countries for males (Fussell & Greene, 2002).

Despite these gender gaps, evidence of increasing gender equality is appearing. For example, "among upper income families in India and Japan, fathers are assuming more child-rearing responsibilities. Rates of employment and career opportunities for women are expanding in many parts of the globe. Control over adolescent girls' social relationships, especially romantic and sexual relationships, is easing in some nations" (Brown & Larson, 2002, p. 16).

ANDROGYNY AND EDUCATION

Can and should androgyny be taught to students? In general, it is easier to teach androgyny to girls than to boys and easier to teach it before the middle school grades. For example, in one study, a gender curriculum was put in place for one year in the kindergarten, fifth, and ninth grades (Guttentag & Bray, 1976). It involved books, discussion materials, and classroom exercises with an androgynous bent. The program was most successful with the fifth-graders, least successful with the ninth-graders. The ninth-graders, especially the boys, showed a boomerang effect, in which they had more traditional gender-role attitudes after the year of androgynous instruction than before it.

Despite such mixed findings, the advocates of androgyny programs argue that traditional sex-typing is harmful for all students and especially has prevented many girls from experiencing equal opportunity. The detractors respond that androgynous educational programs are too value-laden and ignore the diversity of gender roles in our society.

TRADITIONAL MASCULINITY AND PROBLEM BEHAVIORS IN ADOLESCENT MALES

In our discussion of masculinity so far, we have considered how the masculine role has been accorded a prominent status in the United States, as well as in most other cultures. However, might there be a negative side to traditional masculinity, especially in adolescence? An increasing number of gender theorists and researchers conclude that there is (Levant, 2001).

What are some concerns about boys who adopt a strong masculine role?

Concern about the ways boys have been brought up in traditional ways has been called a "national crisis of boyhood" by William Pollack (1999) in his book *Real Boys*. He says that, although there has been considerable talk about the "sensitive male," little has been done to change what he calls the "boy code."

Pollack argues that this code tells boys they should show little if any emotion as they are growing up. Too often boys are socialized to not show their feelings and to act tough, says Pollack. Boys learn the boy code in many different contexts—sandboxes, playgrounds, schoolrooms, camps, hangouts—and are taught the code by parents, peers, coaches, teachers, and other adults. Pollack, as well as many others, notes that boys would benefit from being socialized to express their anxieties and concerns rather than keep them bottled up, as well as to learn how to better regulate their aggression.

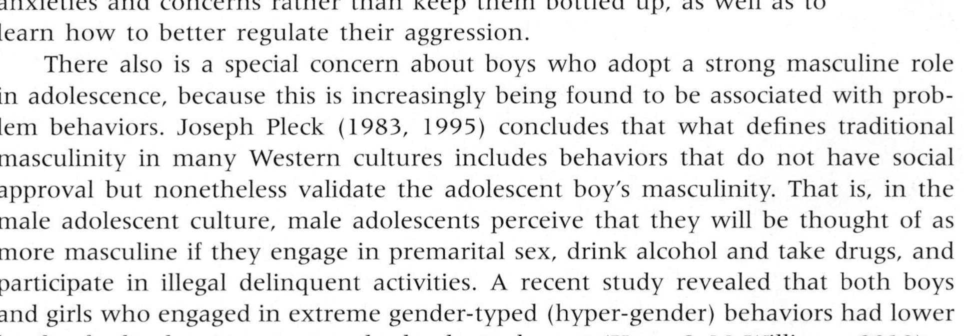

There also is a special concern about boys who adopt a strong masculine role in adolescence, because this is increasingly being found to be associated with problem behaviors. Joseph Pleck (1983, 1995) concludes that what defines traditional masculinity in many Western cultures includes behaviors that do not have social approval but nonetheless validate the adolescent boy's masculinity. That is, in the male adolescent culture, male adolescents perceive that they will be thought of as more masculine if they engage in premarital sex, drink alcohol and take drugs, and participate in illegal delinquent activities. A recent study revealed that both boys and girls who engaged in extreme gender-typed (hyper-gender) behaviors had lower levels of school engagement and school attachment (Ueno & McWilliams, 2010).

GENDER-ROLE TRANSCENDENCE

Some critics of androgyny say enough is enough and that there is too much talk about gender. They stress that androgyny is less of a panacea than originally envisioned (Paludi, 2002). An alternative is **gender-role transcendence,** the view that when an individual's competence is at issue, it should be conceptualized on a person basis rather than on the basis of masculinity, femininity, or androgyny (Pleck, 1983). That is, we should think about ourselves as people, not as masculine, feminine, or androgynous. Parents should rear their children to be competent boys and girls, not masculine, feminine, or androgynous, say the gender-role critics. They argue that such gender-role classification leads to too much stereotyping.

gender-role transcendence The belief that, when an individual's competence is at issue, it should be conceptualized not on the basis of masculinity, femininity, or androgyny but, rather, on a person basis.

Review *Connect* Reflect

LG3 Characterize the variations in gender-role classification.

Review

- How can traditional gender roles be described? What is androgyny? How is androgyny related to social competence?
- How do context and culture influence gender roles?
- How effectively can androgyny be taught in schools?
- How is traditional masculinity linked with the behavior of adolescent males?
- What is gender-role transcendence?

Connect

- Compare and contrast the concepts of androgyny and gender-role transcendence.

Reflect ***Your Own Personal Journey of Life***

- How would you describe your gender-role classification today? How satisfied are you with your gender-role classification? What factors contributed to your classification?

4 Developmental Changes and Junctures

LG4 Summarize development changes in gender.

Early Adolescence and Gender Intensification

Is Early Adolescence a Critical Juncture for Females?

What changes take place during early adolescence that might affect gender roles? Is early adolescence a critical juncture in girls' development?

EARLY ADOLESCENCE AND GENDER INTENSIFICATION

Toward the beginning of this chapter, we considered how pubertal changes might be linked to gendered behavior. Here we expand on the earlier discussion. During early adolescence, individuals develop the adult, physical aspects of their sex. Some theorists and researchers have proposed that, with the onset of puberty, girls and boys experience an intensification in gender-related expectations (Basow, 2006). The **gender intensification hypothesis** states that psychological and behavioral differences between boys and girls become greater during early adolescence because of increased socialization pressures to conform to traditional masculine and feminine gender roles (Hill & Lynch, 1983; Lynch, 1991). Puberty may signal to socializing others—parents, peers, and teachers—that an adolescent is approaching adulthood and should begin to act in stereotypical male or female ways. Some researchers have reported evidence of gender intensification in early adolescence (Hill & Lynch, 1983). However, a recent longitudinal study of individuals from 7 to 19 years of age revealed stable gender differences in activity interests but a decline in both male- and female-typed activity interests across the age range (McHale & others, 2009). And another recent study found no evidence for intensification in masculinity or femininity in young adolescents (Priess, Lindberg, & Hyde, 2009). The jury is still out on the validity of the gender-intensification hypothesis, but recent research has raised questions about its accuracy (Galambos, Berenbaum, & McHale, 2009).

What is the gender intensification hypothesis? How strong is the evidence for this hypothesis?

gender intensification hypothesis Hypothesis stating that psychological and behavioral differences between boys and girls become greater during early adolescence because of increased socialization pressure to conform to masculine and feminine gender roles.

As adolescent boys and girls grow older, they tend to show less stereotypic gender behavior. In one study of eighth- and eleventh-graders, the eleventh-graders were more similar to each other on both masculine and feminine traits than were the eighth-graders (Karniol & others, 1998). Irrespective of gender, the eleventh-graders showed less masculinity than the eighth-graders. The eleventh-grade girls were also lower on femininity than the eighth-grade girls, and the eleventh-grade boys higher on femininity than the eighth-grade boys. Indeed, no eighth-grade boys fell into the low-masculinity/high-femininity category.

IS EARLY ADOLESCENCE A CRITICAL JUNCTURE FOR FEMALES?

Carol Gilligan has conducted extensive interviews with girls from 6 to 18 years of age (Gilligan, 1982, 1996; Gilligan, Brown, & Rogers, 1990). She and her colleagues have reported that girls consistently reveal detailed knowledge of human relationships that is based on their experiences with others. According to Gilligan, girls are sensitive to different rhythms and emotions in relationships. Gilligan argues that girls experience life differently from boys; in her words, girls have a "different voice."

Gilligan also stresses that adolescence is a critical juncture in girls' development. In early adolescence (usually around 11 to 12 years of age), she says, girls become aware that the male-dominated culture does not value their intense interest in intimacy, even though society values women's caring and altruism. The dilemma, says Gilligan, is that girls are presented with a choice that makes them appear either selfish (if they become independent and self-sufficient) or selfless (if they remain responsive to others). As young adolescent girls struggle with this dilemma, Gilligan states, they begin to "silence" their "different voice," becoming less confident and more tentative in offering their opinions. This reticence often persists into adulthood. Some researchers note that the self-doubt and ambivalence girls experience in early adolescence translate into depression and eating disorders.

developmental **connection**

Moral Development. Gilligan argues that the care perspective, which emphasizes the importance of connectedness to others, is especially important in adolescent girls' moral development. Chapter 7, p. 231

Contextual variations influence the degree to which adolescent girls silence their "voice" (Ryan, 2003). In one study, Susan Harter and her colleagues (Harter, Waters, & Whitesell, 1996) found that feminine girls reported lower levels of voice in public contexts (at school with teachers and classmates) but not in more private interpersonal relationships (with close friends and parents). However, androgynous girls reported a strong voice in all contexts. Harter and her colleagues found that adolescent girls who buy into societal messages that females should be seen and not heard are at the greatest risk in their development. The greatest liabilities occurred for females who not only lacked a "voice" but who emphasized the importance of appearance. In focusing on their outer selves, these girls faced formidable challenges in meeting the punishing cultural standards of attractiveness.

Some critics argue that Gilligan and her colleagues overemphasize differences in gender (Dindia, 2006; Hyde, 2007). One of those critics is developmentalist Eleanor Maccoby, who says that Gilligan exaggerates the differences in intimacy and connectedness between males and females. Other critics fault Gilligan's research strategy, which rarely includes a comparison group of boys or statistical analysis. Instead, Gilligan conducts extensive interviews with girls and then provides excerpts from the girls' narratives to buttress her ideas. Other critics fear that Gilligan's findings reinforce stereotypes—females as nurturing and sacrificing, for example—that might undermine females' struggle for equality. These critics say that Gilligan's "different voice" perhaps should be called "the voice of the victim." What we should be stressing, say these critics, is more opportunities for females to reach higher levels of achievement and self-determination.

Carol Gilligan. *What is Gilligan's view of moral development?*

Whether you accept the connectionist arguments of Gilligan or the achievement/self-determination arguments of her critics, there is increasing evidence that adolescence is a critical juncture in the psychological development of females (Basow, 2006). In Chapter 4, we considered a large-scale national study that revealed a decrease in the self-esteem of boys and girls during adolescence, but a more substantial decrease for adolescent girls than boys (Robins & others, 2002). In another national survey that was conducted by the American Association of University Women (1992), girls revealed a significantly greater drop in self-esteem during adolescence than boys did. In yet another study, the self-esteem of girls declined during adolescence (Rosner & Rierdan, 1994). At ages 8 and 9, 60 percent of the girls were confident and assertive

connecting with health and well-being

How Can We Best Guide Adolescents' Gender Development?

Boys

- *Encourage boys to be more sensitive in relationships and to engage in more prosocial behavior.* An important socialization task is to help boys become more interested in having positive close relationships and become more caring. Fathers can play an especially important role for boys in this regard by being a model who is sensitive and caring.
- *Encourage boys to be less physically aggressive.* Too often, boys are encouraged to be tough, virile, and aggressive. A positive strategy is to encourage them to be self-assertive but not overly physically aggressive.
- *Encourage boys to handle their emotions more effectively.* This guideline involves not only helping boys to regulate their emotions, as in controlling their anger, but also helping them to learn to express their anxieties and concerns rather than to keep them bottled up.
- *Work with boys to improve their school performance.* Girls get better grades, put forth more academic effort, and are less likely than boys to be assigned to special/remedial classes. Parents and teachers can help boys by emphasizing the importance of school and expecting better academic effort from them.

Girls

- *Encourage girls to be proud of their relationship skills and caring.* The strong interest that girls show in relationships and caring should be rewarded by parents and teachers.
- *Encourage girls to develop their self-competencies.* While guiding girls to retain their relationship strengths, adults can help girls to develop their ambition and achievement.
- *Encourage girls to be more self-assertive.* Girls tend to be more passive than boys and can benefit from being encouraged to be more self-assertive.
- *Encourage girls' achievement.* This guideline can involve encouraging girls to have higher academic expectations and exposing them to a greater range of career options.

Boys and Girls

- *Help adolescents to reduce gender stereotyping and discrimination.* Don't engage in gender stereotyping and discrimination yourself—otherwise, you will be providing a model of gender stereotyping and discrimination for adolescents.

How can adopting one set of suggestions for girls and another for boys ensure that we do not "assign one set of values and behaviors to one sex and a different set to the other?"

developmental **connection**

Identity. Self-esteem, also referred to as self-worth or self-image, is the global evaluative dimension of the self. Chapter 4, p. 134

and felt positive about themselves, compared with 67 percent of the boys. However, over the next eight years, the girls' self-esteem fell 31 percentage points—only 29 percent of high school girls felt positive about themselves. Across the same age range, boys' self-esteem dropped 21 points—leaving 46 percent of the high school boys with high self-esteem, which makes for a gender gap of 17 percentage points. Another study found that the self-esteem of high school girls was lower than the self-esteem of elementary school girls and college women (Frost & McKelvie, 2004). Keep in mind, though, as we discussed in Chapter 4, that some psychologists conclude that gender differences in self-esteem during adolescence are quite small (Hyde, 2007).

We should also recognize that many experts emphasize the importance for adolescent girls and emerging adult women both to maintain their competency in relationships and to be self-motivated (Brabeck & Brabeck, 2006). In Phyllis Bronstein's (2006, p. 269) view, "It is beneficial neither to individuals nor to society as a whole to assign one set of values and behaviors to one sex and a different set to the other." How might we put this view into practice? The following *Connecting with Health and Well-Being* interlude provides some recommendations for improving the gendered lives of adolescents.

In this chapter, we have examined many aspects of gender. We saw that sexuality influences gender in adolescence more than in childhood. In Chapter 6, we explore adolescent sexuality more extensively.

Review *Connect* Reflect

LG4 Summarize developmental changes in gender.

Review

- How might early adolescence influence gender development?
- Is early adolescence a critical juncture for females?

Connect

- How might gender intensification be linked to media influences?

Reflect *Your Own Personal Journey of Life*

- Did your gender behavior change as you went through early adolescence? Explain.

reach your **learning goals**

1 Biological, Social, and Cognitive Influences on Gender

Describe the biological, social, and cognitive influences on gender.

Biological Influences on Gender

- Gender refers to the characteristics of people as females and males. A gender role is a set of expectations that prescribes how females and males should think, act, and feel. Because of pubertal change, sexuality plays a more important role in gender development for adolescents than for children. Freud's and Erikson's theories promote the idea that anatomy is destiny. Today's developmentalists are interactionists when biological and environmental influences on gender are at issue. In the evolutionary psychology view, evolutionary adaptations produced psychological sex differences, especially in the area of mate selection. However, criticisms of the evolutionary psychology view have been made, especially in terms of culture and gender. Gender differences have been found in the developmental trajectories of the brain in adolescence but overall there are more similarities than differences in the brains of males and females.

Social Influences on Gender

- In the social role view, women have less power and status than men do and control fewer resources. In this view, gender hierarchy and sexual division of labor are important causes of sex-differentiated behavior. The social cognitive theory of gender emphasizes that adolescents' gender development is influenced by their observation and imitation of others' gender behavior, as well as by rewards and punishments of gender-appropriate and gender-inappropriate behavior. Parents and siblings influence adolescents' gender roles. Mothers and fathers often interact with their adolescents differently and also interact differently with sons and daughters. Peers are especially adept at rewarding gender-appropriate behavior. There is still concern about gender inequity in education. Despite improvements, TV continues to portray males as more competent than females.

Cognitive Influences on Gender

- Gender schema theory states gender-typing emerges as individuals develop schemas for what is gender-appropriate and gender-inappropriate in their culture.

2 Gender Stereotypes, Similarities, and Differences

Discuss gender stereotypes, similarities, and differences.

Gender Stereotyping

- Gender stereotypes are general impressions and beliefs about males and females. Gender stereotypes are widespread.

Gender Similarities and Differences

- There are a number of physical differences in males and females. In the cognitive domain, gender differences in math are either small or nonexistent. However, girls significantly outperform boys in reading skills and writing skills, get better grades in school, and are less likely to drop out of school. Socioemotional differences include the following: males are more physically aggressive and active; females show a stronger interest in relationships, are better at self-regulation of behavior and emotion, and engage in more prosocial behavior.

Gender Controversy

- There continues to be controversy about the extent of gender differences and what causes them. Buss argues that gender differences are extensive and caused by an individual's evolutionary history. Eagly also concludes that gender differences are extensive but that they are caused by social conditions. Hyde states that gender differences have been exaggerated and that females and males are similar on most psychological factors.

Gender in Context

- Gender in context is an important concept. Gender roles can vary according to the culture in which adolescents develop and the immediate contexts in which they behave.

3 Gender-Role Classification

LG3 Characterize the variations in gender-role classification.

Masculinity, Femininity, and Androgyny

- In the past, the well-adjusted male was supposed to show instrumental traits, the well-adjusted female expressive traits. In the 1970s, alternatives to traditional gender roles were introduced. It was proposed that competent individuals could show both masculine and feminine traits. This thinking led to the development of the concept of androgyny, the presence of masculine and feminine traits in one individual. Gender-role measures often categorize individuals as masculine, feminine, androgynous, or undifferentiated. Most androgynous individuals are flexible and mentally healthy, although the specific context and the individual's culture also determine how adaptive a gender-role orientation is.

Context, Culture, and Gender Roles

- In thinking about gender, it is important to keep in mind the context in which gendered behavior is displayed. In many countries around the world, traditional gender roles are still dominant.

Androgyny and Education

- Androgyny education programs have been more successful with females than with males and more successful with children than with adolescents.

Traditional Masculinity and Problem Behaviors in Adolescent Males

- A special concern is that boys raised in a traditional manner are socialized to conceal their emotions. Researchers have found that problem behaviors often characterize highly masculine adolescents.

Gender-Role Transcendence

- One alternative to androgyny states that there has been too much emphasis on gender and that a better strategy is to think about competence in terms of people rather than gender.

4 Developmental Changes and Junctures

LG4 Summarize developmental changes in gender.

Early Adolescence and Gender Intensification

- The gender intensification hypothesis states that psychological and behavioral differences between boys and girls become greater during adolescence because of increased socialization pressures to conform to traditional gender roles. The jury is still out on the validity of the gender intensification hypothesis, although an increasing number of studies is not showing support for the hypothesis.

Is Early Adolescence a Critical Juncture for Females?

- Gilligan argues that girls come to a critical juncture in their development during early adolescence. Girls become aware that their intense interest in intimacy is not prized by the male-dominant society. Some critics say that Gilligan exaggerates gender differences in intimacy.

key terms

key people

resources for improving the lives of adolescents

Gender Development in Adolescence
by Nancy Galambos, Sheri Berenbaum, and Susan McHale
in R. Lerner and L. Steinberg (Eds.)
Handbook of Adolescence (2009, 3rd ed.)
New York: Wiley

A very up-to-date discussion of many different research areas of gender development in adolescence is provided.

Gender Development
by Judith Blakemore, Sheri Berenbaum, and Lynn Liben (2009)
New York: Psychology Press

Leading experts give a detailed, contemporary portrait of what is known about gender development.

The Inside Story on Teen Girls
by Karen Zager and Alice Rubenstein (2002)
Washington, DC: American Psychological Association

Provides insight into the lives of adolescent girls with many excellent recommendations about such topics as identity, puberty, sex, dating, school, peers, and relationships with parents.

Real Boys
by William Pollack (1999)
New York: Owl Books

Pollack examines the ways boys have been reared and concludes that there needs to be a major change in this rearing.

YMCA ***www.ymca.net***

The YMCA provides a number of programs for teenage boys. A number of personal health and sports programs are available. The website provides information about the YMCA closest to your location.

YWCA ***www.ywca.org***

The YWCA promotes health, sports participation, and fitness for women and girls. Its programs include instruction in health, teen pregnancy prevention, family life education, self-esteem enhancement, parenting, and nutrition. The website provides information about the YWCA closest to your location.

self-assessment

The Student Online Learning Center includes the following self-assessments for further exploration:

- *What Is My Gender-Role Orientation?*
- *My Attitudes Toward Women*

chapter 6 SEXUALITY

chapter outline

Exploring Adolescent Sexuality

Learning Goal 1 Discuss some basic ideas about the nature of adolescent sexuality.

A Normal Aspect of Adolescent Development
The Sexual Culture
Developing a Sexual Identity
Obtaining Research Information About Adolescent Sexuality

Sexual Attitudes and Behavior

Learning Goal 2 Summarize sexual attitudes and behavior in adolescence.

Heterosexual Attitudes and Behavior
Sexual Minority Attitudes and Behavior
Self-Stimulation
Contraceptive Use

Negative Sexual Outcomes in Adolescence

Learning Goal 3 Describe the main negative sexual outcomes that can emerge in adolescence.

Adolescent Pregnancy
Sexually Transmitted Infections
Forcible Sexual Behavior and Sexual Harassment

Sexual Literacy and Sex Education

Learning Goal 4 Characterize the sexual literacy of adolescents and sex education.

Sexual Literacy
Sources of Sex Information
Cognitive Factors
Sex Education in Schools

I guess when you give a girl a sexy kiss you're supposed to open your lips and put your tongue in her mouth. That doesn't seem very sexy to me. I can't imagine how a girl would like that. What if she has braces on her teeth and your tongue gets scratched? And how are you supposed to breathe? Sometimes I wish I had an older brother I could ask stuff like this.

—FRANK, AGE 12

I can't believe I'm so much in love! I just met him last week but I know this is the real thing. He is much more mature than the boys who have liked me before. He's a senior and has his own car. When he brought me home last night, we got so hot I thought we were going to have sex. I'm sure it will happen the next time we go out. It goes against everything I've been taught—but I can't see how it can be wrong when I'm so much in love and he makes me feel so fantastic!

—AMY, AGE 15

Ken and I went on a camping trip last weekend and now I'm sure that I'm gay. For a long time I've known I've been attracted to other guys, like in the locker room at school it would sometimes be embarrassing. Ken and I are great friends and lots of times we would mess around wrestling or whatever. I guessed that he felt the way I did. Now I know. Sooner or later, I'll have to come out, as they say, but I know that is going to cause a lot of tension with my parents and for me.

—TOM, AGE 15

I'm lucky because I have a good figure and I'm popular. I've had boyfriends since middle school and I know how to take care of myself. It's fun when you're out with a guy and you can be intimate. The only thing is, Dan and I had sex a few weeks ago and I'm wondering if I'm pregnant. He used a contraceptive, but maybe it didn't work. Or maybe I'm just late. Anyway, if I have a baby, I could deal with it. My aunt wasn't married when she got pregnant with my cousin, and it turned out okay.

—CLAIRE, AGE 16

About a month ago my mom's friend's daughter tested positive for HIV. Until then my mom and stepfather never talked about sex with me, but now they're taking turns lecturing me on the theme of "don't have sex until you're married." Give me a break! Nicole and I have been together for a year and a half. What do they think we do when we go out, just talk? Besides, my real father never remarried and has girlfriends all the time. All my life I've been seeing movies and TV shows where unmarried people sleep together and the worst that happens is maybe a broken heart. I don't know that woman's daughter, but she must have been mixed up with some pretty bad characters. Me, I always use a condom.

—SEAN, AGE 17

preview

During adolescence and emerging adulthood, the lives of adolescents are wrapped in sexuality. Adolescence and emerging adulthood are time frames when individuals engage in sexual exploration and incorporate sexuality into their identity. In Chapter 2, we studied the biological basis of sexual maturation, including the timing of these changes and the hormones that are involved. This chapter focuses on the sexual experiences, attitudes, and behaviors of adolescents and emerging adults. We begin with an overview of sexuality in adolescence and emerging adulthood and then examine some problems involving sexual activity, such as adolescent pregnancy, sexually transmitted infections, and forcible sex. Next, we explore the ways in which adolescents learn about sex.

1 Exploring Adolescent Sexuality

Discuss some basic ideas about the nature of adolescent sexuality.

A Normal Aspect of Adolescent Development | The Sexual Culture | Developing a Sexual Identity | Obtaining Research Information About Adolescent Sexuality

Sexual arousal emerges as new phenomenon in adolescence and it is important to view sexuality as a normal aspect of adolescent development.

—**Shirley Feldman**
Contemporary Psychologist, Stanford University

Adolescents have an almost insatiable curiosity about the mysteries of sex. They wonder whether they are sexually attractive, how to behave sexually, and what the future holds for their sexual lives. Most adolescents eventually manage to develop a mature sexual identity, even though, as adults can attest, there are always times of vulnerability and confusion along life's sexual journey.

A NORMAL ASPECT OF ADOLESCENT DEVELOPMENT

Much of what we hear about adolescent sexuality involves problems, such as adolescent pregnancy and sexually transmitted infections. Although these are significant concerns, it is important not to lose sight of the fact that sexuality is a normal part of adolescence (Tolman & McClelland, 2011).

An important theme of adolescence that is underscored in this book is that too often adolescents are negatively stereotyped (Lerner & others, 2011; Lewin-Bizan, Bowers, & Lerner, 2011). The themes of negative stereotyping and adolescent problems also apply to the topic of adolescent sexuality (Diamond & Savin-Williams, 2011). Although we will discuss a number of problems that can occur in the area of adolescent sexuality, it is important to keep in mind that the majority of adolescents have healthy sexual attitudes and engage in sexual behaviors that will not compromise their journey to adulthood.

Every society pays some attention to adolescent sexuality. In some societies, adults chaperone adolescent females to protect them from males; others promote very early marriage. Still other societies, such as the United States, allow some sexual experimentation, although there is a wide range of opinions about just how far this experimentation should be allowed to go.

developmental **connection**

Biological Processes. Early maturation in girls is linked with earlier sexual experiences. Chapter 2, p. 61

Chapters 2 through 5 introduced topics that are a backdrop for understanding sexual attitudes and behavior in adolescence. In Chapter 2, we saw that an important aspect of pubertal change involves sexual maturation and a dramatic increase in androgens in males and estrogens in females. And, we also discussed how puberty is coming earlier today than in previous generations, which can lead to early dating and early sexual activity.

In Chapter 3, we indicated that young adolescents tend to exhibit a form of egocentrism in which they perceive themselves as unique and invulnerable. This can lead them to take sexual risks. In emotional moments like those involved in sexual experimentation, adolescents' sexual urges can overwhelm their ability to make competent decisions.

In Chapter 4, we considered sexual identity as one of the dimensions of personal identity. Intimacy with another is an important aspect of the dyadic nature of adolescent sexuality.

In Chapter 5, we examined the physical and biological differences between females and males. We also saw that, according to the gender intensification hypothesis, pubertal changes can lead boys and girls to conform to traditional masculine and feminine behavior, respectively. Further, when college students are asked to rate the strength of their sex drive, men report higher levels of sexual desire than women. The adolescent developmental transition, then, may be seen as a bridge between the asexuality of childhood and the fully developed sexual identity of adulthood.

Chapters 8, 9, 10, and 12 also include discussions that are important for understanding adolescent sexuality. In Chapter 8, we learn that intense, prolonged conflict with parents is associated with adolescent sexual problems, as is a lack of parental monitoring. Better relationships with parents are correlated with the postponement of sexual intercourse, less frequent intercourse, and fewer partners in adolescence. Later in this chapter, we see that adolescents receive very little sex education from parents and that parents and adolescents rarely discuss sex.

In Chapter 9, we read about how same-sex siblings, peers, and friends often discuss sexuality. We also learn that early dating is associated with a number of adolescent problems and that romantic love is important (especially for girls) in adolescence.

In Chapter 10, we study how schools are playing an increasingly important role in adolescent sexuality. And, as we see later in this chapter, most parents now recognize that sex education in schools is an important aspect of education.

In Chapter 12, we describe the vast cultural variations in sexuality. In some cultures, sexuality is highly repressed; other cultures have far more liberal standards for sexuality.

As you can see, sexuality has ties to virtually all areas of adolescent development that we discuss in this book. Let's now explore the sexual culture American adolescents are exposed to.

developmental **connection**

Peers. Early dating and "going with" someone are linked with adolescent pregnancy. Chapter 9, p. 316

THE SEXUAL CULTURE

It is important to put adolescent sexuality into the broader context of sexuality in the American culture (King, 2012; Welch, 2011). Whereas 50 years ago sex was reserved for married couples, today adult sex is openly acknowledged among both married and single adults. Sex among unmarried teenagers is an extension of this general trend toward greater sexual permissiveness in the adult culture. In the U.S. culture, sex has mixed messages for youth—on the one hand, adolescents (especially girls) are told not to have sex—but on the other hand, they see sex portrayed in the media as positive (especially for boys). Thus, it is no wonder that adolescents find sexual development and choices so confusing. Consider the following recent portrayal of sex in the media:

> The messages conveyed about sexuality (in the media) are not always ideal . . . and they are often limited, unrealistic, and stereotypical. Dominating is a recreational orientation to sexuality in which courtship is treated as a competition, a battle of the sexes, characterized by dishonesty, game playing, and manipulation. . . . Also prominent are stereotypical sexual roles featuring women as sexual objects, whose value is based solely on their physical appearance, and men as sex-driven players looking to "score" at all costs. . . . (Ward, Day, & Epstein, 2006, p. 57)

Sex is explicitly portrayed in movies, TV shows, videos, lyrics of popular music, MTV, and Internet websites (Bersamin & others, 2010; Bleakley & others, 2011; Strasburger, 2010; Tolman & McClelland, 2011). A study of 1,762 12- to 17-year-olds found that those who watched more sexually explicit TV shows were more likely than their counterparts who watched these shows less to initiate sexual intercourse in the next 12 months (Collins & others, 2004). Adolescents in the highest 10 percent of viewing sexually explicit TV shows were twice as likely to engage in sexual intercourse as those in the lowest 10 percent. The results held regardless of whether the exposure to explicit sex involved sexual behavior or just talk about sex. In another study, U.S. high school students who frequently viewed talk shows and "sexy" prime-time programs were more likely to endorse sexual stereotypes than their counterparts who viewed these shows infrequently (Ward & Friedman, 2006). Also in this study, more frequent viewing and stronger identification with popular TV characters were linked with greater levels of sexual experience in adolescents. And, a recent research review concluded that

Adolescents are exposed to sex virtually everywhere in the American culture and sex is used to sell just about everything.

Adolescents are exposed to sex in many contexts, including TV and the Internet. *Is it surprising, then, that adolescents are so curious about sex and tempted to experiment with sex?*

adolescents who view more sexual content on TV are more likely to initiate sexual intercourse earlier than their peers who view less sexual content on TV (Brown & Strasburger, 2007). Further, a study of adolescents across a three-year period revealed a link between watching sex on TV and subsequent higher risk of pregnancy (Chandra & others, 2009).

Adolescents increasingly have had access to sexually explicit Web sites. A recent study revealed that adolescents who reported ever visiting a sexually explicit website were more sexually permissive and were more likely to have multiple lifetime sexual partners, more than one sexual partner in the last three months, used alcohol or other substances at their last sexual encounter, and engaged in anal sex more than their counterparts who reported that they never had visited a sexually explicit website (Braun-Courville & Rojas, 2009).

Adolescents and emerging adults also increasingly use the Internet as a resource for information about sexuality. A recent study of 177 sexual health website found that that inaccuracies were few but that the quality of the information (such as display of authorship and authors' credentials, clear sources, for example) was low (Buhi & others, 2010). The category with the lowest-rated quality was sexual assault.

The American Academy of Pediatrics (2010) recently issued a policy statement on sexuality, contraception, and the media. They pointed out that television, film, music, and the Internet are all becoming increasingly explicit, yet information about abstinence, sexual responsibility, and birth control rarely is included in these media outlets. We further explore media influences on adolescent sexuality in Chapter 12.

DEVELOPING A SEXUAL IDENTITY

Mastering emerging sexual feelings and forming a sense of sexual identity is multifaceted (Diamond & Savin-Williams, 2011; Savin-Williams, 2011; Tolman & McClelland, 2011). This lengthy process involves learning to manage sexual feelings, such as sexual arousal and attraction, developing new forms of intimacy, and learning the skills to regulate sexual behavior to avoid undesirable consequences. Developing a sexual identity also involves more than just sexual behavior. Sexual identities emerge in the context of physical factors, social factors, and cultural factors, with most societies placing constraints on the sexual behavior of adolescents. An adolescent's sexual identity is strongly influenced by *social norms* related to sex—the extent to which adolescents perceive that their peers are having sex, using protection, and so on. These social norms have important influences on adolescents' sexual behavior. For example, a recent study revealed that when adolescents perceived that their peers were sexually permissive, the adolescents had a higher rate of initiating sexual intercourse and engaging in risky sexual practices (Potard, Courtois, & Rusch, 2008).

> We are born twice over, the first time for existence, the second for life; Once as human beings and later as men and as women.
>
> —Jean-Jacques Rousseau
>
> *Swiss-Born French Philosopher, 18th Century*

An adolescent's sexual identity involves an indication of sexual orientation (whether an individual has same-sex or other-sex attractions), and it also involves activities, interests, and styles of behavior. A study of 470 tenth- to twelfth-grade Australian youth found considerable variation in their sexual attitudes and practices (Buzwell & Rosenthal, 1996). Some were virgins and sexually naive. Some had high anxiety about sex and perceived their bodies as underdeveloped and unappealing, whereas others had low anxiety about sex and an interest in exploring sexual options. Yet others felt sexually attractive, were sexually experienced, and had confidence in their ability to manage sexual situations.

OBTAINING RESEARCH INFORMATION ABOUT ADOLESCENT SEXUALITY

Assessing sexual attitudes and behavior is not always a straightforward matter (Saewyc, 2011). Consider how you would respond if someone asked you, "How often do you have intercourse?" or "How many different sexual partners have you had?" The individuals most likely to respond to sexual surveys are those with liberal sexual attitudes who engage in liberal sexual behaviors. Thus, research is limited by the reluctance of some individuals to answer candidly questions about extremely personal matters, and by researchers' inability to get any answer, candid or otherwise, from individuals who simply refuse to talk to strangers about sex. In addition, when asked about their sexual activity, individuals may respond truthfully or they may give socially desirable answers. For example, a ninth-grade boy might report that he has had sexual intercourse, even if he has not, because he is afraid someone will find out that he is sexually inexperienced. For example, one study of high school students revealed that 8 percent of the girls understated their sexual experience, while 14 percent of the boys overstated their sexual experience (Siegel, Aten, & Roghmann, 1998). Thus, boys tend to exaggerate their sexual experiences to increase perceptions of their sexual prowess, while girls tend to play down their sexual experience so they won't be perceived as irresponsible or promiscuous (Diamond & Savin-Williams, 2009).

developmental **connection**

Research Methods. One drawback of surveys and interviews is the tendency of some participants to answer questions in a socially desirable way. Chapter 1, p. 34

Review *Connect* Reflect

LG1 Discuss some basic ideas about the nature of adolescent sexuality.

Review

- How can sexuality be explained as a normal aspect of adolescent development?
- What kind of sexual culture are adolescents exposed to in the United States?
- What is involved in developing a sexual identity in adolescence?
- What are some difficulties in obtaining research information about adolescent sexuality?

Connect

- How does the sexual culture you learned about in this section contribute to gender stereotypes described in Chapter 5?

Reflect ***Your Own Personal Journey of Life***

- How would you describe your sexual identity as an adolescent and emerging adult? What contributed to this identity?

2 Sexual Attitudes and Behavior

LG2 Summarize sexual attitudes and behavior in adolescence.

- Heterosexual Attitudes and Behavior
- Sexual Minority Attitudes and Behavior
- Self-Stimulation
- Contraceptive Use

Let's now explore adolescents' sexual attitudes and behavior. First, we study heterosexual attitudes and behavior, and then sexual minority attitudes and behavior.

HETEROSEXUAL ATTITUDES AND BEHAVIOR

How early do adolescents engage in various sexual activities? What sexual scripts do adolescents follow? Are some adolescents more vulnerable than others to irresponsible sexual behavior? We examine each of these questions.

Development of Sexual Activities in Adolescents What is the current profile of sexual activity of adolescents? In a U.S. national survey conducted in 2009, 62 percent of twelfth-graders reported that they had experienced sexual intercourse compared with 32 percent of ninth-graders (Eaton & others, 2010). By

> How is it that, in the human body, reproduction is the only function to be performed by an organ of which an individual carries only one half so that he has to spend an enormous amount of time and energy to find another half?
>
> —François Jacob
>
> *French Biologist, 20th Century*

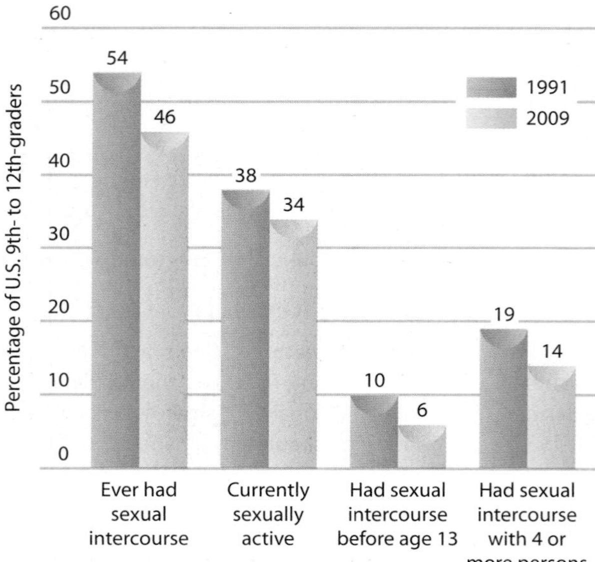

FIGURE **6.1**

SEXUAL ACTIVITY OF U.S. ADOLESCENTS FROM 1991 TO 2009. *Source:* After Eaton & others (2010). U.S. Government Data.

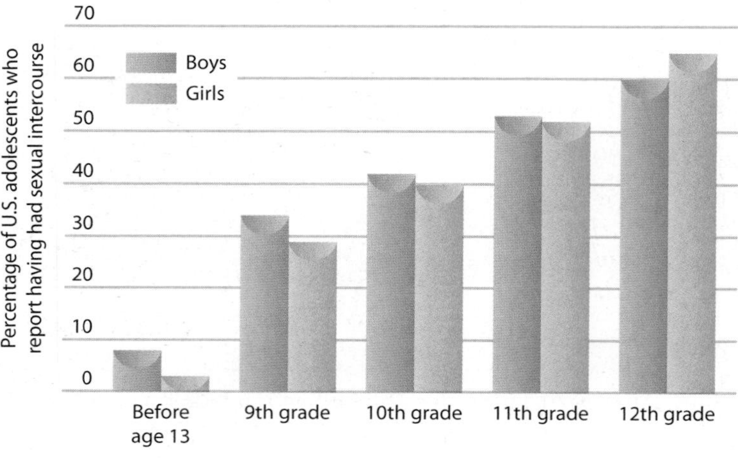

FIGURE **6.2**

TIMING OF SEXUAL INTERCOURSE IN U.S. ADOLESCENTS

Sexual timetable	Non-Latino White	African American	Latino	Asian American
Kiss	14.3	13.9	14.5	15.7
French kiss	15.0	14.0	15.3	16.2
Touch breast	15.6	14.5	15.5	16.9
Touch penis	16.1	15.0	16.2	17.8
Touch vagina	16.1	14.6	15.9	17.1
Sexual intercourse	16.9	15.5	16.5	18.0
Oral sex	17.1	16.9	17.1	18.3

FIGURE **6.3**

SEXUAL TIMETABLES OF NON-LATINO WHITE, AFRICAN AMERICAN, LATINO AND ASIAN AMERICAN ADOLESCENTS. *Note:* These data were reported in 1999. In the twenty-first century, adolescents are reporting that they engage in oral sex earlier in the sexual timetable. The numbers reflect the percentage of adolescents who reported engaging in the sexual activity.

age 20, 77 percent of U.S. youth have engaged in sexual intercourse (Dworkin & Santelli, 2007). Nationally, 49 percent of twelfth-graders, 40 percent of eleventh-graders, 29 percent of tenth-graders, and 21 percent of ninth-graders recently reported that they are currently sexually active (Eaton & others, 2010).

What trends in adolescent sexual activity have occurred in the last two decades? From 1991 to 2009, fewer adolescents reported any of the following: ever having had sexual intercourse, currently being sexually active, having had sexual intercourse before the age of 13, and having had sexual intercourse with four or more persons during their lifetime (Eaton & others, 2010) (see Figure 6.1).

Until very recently, at all grade levels, adolescent males reported that they are more likely than adolescent females to say that they have had sexual intercourse and are sexually active (MMWR, 2006a). However, in the 2009 national survey, a higher percentage of twelfth-grade females (65 percent) than twelfth-grade males (60 percent) reported that they had experienced sexual intercourse; a higher percentage of ninth-grade males (34 percent) than ninth-grade females (29 percent) reported that they had experienced sexual intercourse (Eaton & others, 2010) (see Figure 6.2). Adolescent males are more likely than their female counterparts to describe sexual intercourse as an enjoyable experience.

Sexual initiation varies by ethnic group in the United States (Santelli, Abraido-Lanza, & Melnikas, 2009). African Americans are more likely to engage in sexual behaviors earlier than other ethnic groups, whereas Asian Americans are more likely to engage in them later (Feldman, Turner, & Araujo, 1999) (see Figure 6.3). In a more recent national U.S. survey (2009) of ninth- to twelfth-graders, 67 percent of African Americans, 51 percent of Latinos, and 43 percent of non-Latino Whites said they had ever experienced sexual intercourse (Eaton & others, 2010). In this study, 15 percent of African Americans (compared with 7 percent of Latinos and 3 percent of non-Latino Whites) said they had their first sexual experience before 13 years of age.

Oral Sex Recent research indicates that oral sex is now a common occurrence for U.S. adolescents (Brewster & Harker Tillman, 2008; Salazar & others, 2011). In a national survey, 55 percent of U.S. 15- to 19-year-old boys and 54 percent of girls of the same age said they had engaged in oral sex (National Center for Health Statistics, 2002). Figure 6.4 shows the developmental trends in oral sex. Noteworthy is that in this survey, a slightly higher percentage of 15- to 19-year-olds (55 percent of boys, 54 percent of girls) said they had engaged in oral sex than had engaged in sexual intercourse (49 percent of girls, 53 percent of boys). Also in the survey, more than 20 percent of the adolescents who had not had sexual intercourse had engaged in oral sex.

In a recent editorial in the *Journal of Adolescent Health*, Bonnie Halpern-Felsher (2008) discussed the pluses and minuses of oral versus vaginal sex. Oral sex negates the risk of pregnancy and is linked to fewer negative outcomes than is vaginal sex. However, oral sex is not risk-free, being related to such negative health outcomes as sexually transmitted infections (herpes, chlamydia, and gonorrhea, for example). In recent research, Halpern-Felsher and her colleagues have examined the merits of engaging in oral versus vaginal sex (Brady & Halpern-Felsher, 2007; Song & Halpern-Felsher, 2010).

In one study, the temporal order between oral and vaginal sex in sexually active adolescents was examined (Song & Halpern-Felsher, 2010). In this study, most of the adolescents initiated vaginal sex after or within the same 6-month period of starting to have oral sex. Those who initiated oral sex at the end of the ninth grade had a 50 percent chance of having vaginal sex by the end of the eleventh grade, but those who delayed having oral sex until the end of the eleventh grade had less than a 20 percent chance of initiating vaginal sex by the end of the eleventh grade.

In another study, the consequences of having oral sex versus vaginal sex were explored (Brady & Halpern-Felsher, 2007). Compared to adolescents who engaged in oral sex and/or vaginal sex, adolescents who engaged only in oral sex were less likely to become pregnant or incur a sexually transmitted infection, feel guilty or used, have their relationship deteriorate, and get into trouble with their parents about sex. Adolescents who engaged only in oral sex also were more likely to report experiencing pleasure, feeling good about themselves, and having their relationship improve as a result of the sexual experience than did their counterparts who engaged only in vaginal sex or in both oral and vaginal sex.

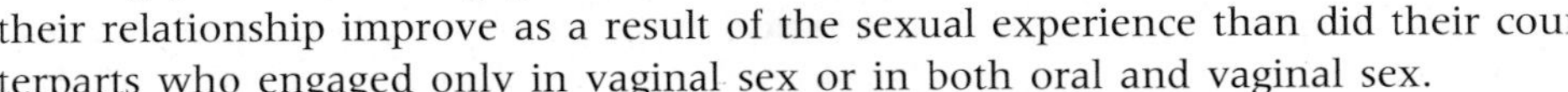

Age	Boys (%)	Girls (%)
15	35	26
16	42	42
17	58	56
18	65	70
19	74	74

FIGURE 6.4

PERCENTAGE OF U.S. 15- TO 19-YEAR-OLD BOYS AND GIRLS WHO REPORT ENGAGING IN ORAL SEX

Cross-Cultural Comparisons The timing of teenage sexual initiation varies widely by culture and gender, and in most instances is linked to the culture's values and customs (Carroll, 2010). In one study, among females, the proportion having first intercourse by age 17 ranged from 72 percent in Mali to 47 percent in the United States and 45 percent in Tanzania (Singh & others, 2000). The proportion of males who had their first intercourse by age 17 ranged from 76 percent in Jamaica to 64 percent in the United States and 63 percent in Brazil. Not all countries were represented in this study, and it is generally agreed that in some Asian countries, such as China and Japan, first intercourse occurs much later than in the United States.

What are some trends in the sexual behavior of adolescents?

Sexual activity patterns for 15- to 19-year-olds follow very different patterns for males and females in almost every geographic region of the world (Singh & others, 2000). In developing countries, the vast majority of sexually experienced males in this age group are unmarried, whereas two-thirds or more of the sexually experienced females at these ages are married. However, in the United States and in other developed nations such as the Netherlands, Sweden, and Australia, the overwhelming majority of 15- to 19-year-old females are unmarried.

Sexual Scripts As adolescents explore their sexual identities, they are guided by sexual scripts. A **sexual script** is a stereotyped pattern of role prescriptions for how individuals should behave sexually. By the time individuals reach adolescence, girls and boys have been socialized to follow different sexual scripts. Differences in female and male sexual scripting can cause problems and confusions for adolescents as they work out their sexual identities. Female adolescents learn to link sexual intercourse with love (Michael & others, 1994). They often rationalize their sexual behavior by telling themselves that they were swept away by the passion of the moment. A number of studies have found that adolescent girls are more likely than their male counterparts to report being in love as the main reason they are sexually active (Hyde & DeLamater, 2011). Other reasons that girls give for being sexually active include giving in to male pressure, gambling that sex is a way to get a boyfriend, curiosity, and sexual desire unrelated to loving and caring.

The majority of adolescent sexual experiences involve the males making sexual advances, and it is up to the female to set the limits on the male's sexual overtures.

sexual script A stereotyped pattern of role prescriptions for how individuals should sexually behave. Females and males have been socialized to follow different sexual scripts.

connecting with adolescents

Struggling with a Sexual Decision

Elizabeth is an adolescent girl who is reflecting on her struggle with whether to have sex with a guy she is in love with. She says it is not a question of whether she loves him or not. She does love him, but she still doesn't know if it is right or wrong to have sex with him. He wants her to have sex, but she knows her parents don't. Among her friends, some say yes, others say no. So Elizabeth is confused. After a few days of contemplation, in a moment of honesty, she admits that she is not his special love. This finally tilts the answer to not having sex with him. She realizes that if the relationship falls through, she will look back and regret it if she does have sex. In the end, Elizabeth decides not to have sex with him.

Elizabeth's reflections reveal her struggle to understand what is right and what is wrong, whether to have sex or not. In her circumstance, the fact that in a moment of honesty she admitted that she was not his special love made a big difference in her decision.

What sexual script probably lies behind Elizabeth's decision?

Adolescent boys experience considerable peer pressure to have sexual intercourse. As one adolescent remarked, "I feel a lot of pressure from my buddies to go for the score."

Deborah Tolman (2002) interviewed a number of girls about their sexuality and was struck by how extensively a double standard still restricts girls from experiencing and talking about sexuality but allows boys more free rein on their sexuality. In movies, magazines, and music, girls are often depicted as the object of someone else's desire but rarely as someone who has acceptable sexual feelings of their own. Tolman says that girls face a difficult challenge related to their sexual selves: to be the perfect sexual object, they are supposed to be sexy but control their desire. A recent study indicated that adolescent girls often recognized the existence of a sexual double standard on a societal or school level, but support or acceptance in their close friend network served as a buffer against the double standard (Lyons & others, 2010).

Risk Factors in Adolescent Sexuality Many adolescents are not emotionally prepared to handle sexual experiences, especially in early adolescence. Early sexual activity is linked with risky behaviors such as drug use, delinquency, and school-related problems (Jayakody & others, 2011; Yi & others, 2010). In a longitudinal study from 10 to 12 years of age to 25 years of age, early sexual intercourse and affiliation with deviant peers were linked to substance use disorders in emerging adulthood (Cornelius & others, 2007). A recent study of adolescents in five countries, including the United States, found that substance use was related to early sexual intercourse (Madkour & others, 2010). Another recent study revealed that alcohol use, early menarche, and poor parent-child communication were linked to early sexually intimate behavior in girls (Hipwell & others, 2010).

In addition to having sex in early adolescence, other risk factors for sexual problems in adolescence include contextual factors such as socioeconomic status (SES) and poverty, family/parenting and peer factors, and school-related influences (Van Ryzin & others, 2011). The percentage of sexually active young adolescents is higher in low-income areas of inner cities (Silver & Bauman, 2006). A recent study revealed that neighborhood poverty concentrations predicted 15- to 17-year-old girls' and boys' sexual initiation (Cubbin & others, 2010).

What are some risks for early initiation of sexual intercourse?

A number of family factors are linked to sexuality outcomes for adolescents. A recent research review indicated that the following aspects of connectedness predicted sexual and reproductive health outcomes for youth: family connectedness, parent-adolescent communication about sexuality, parental monitoring, and partner connectedness (Markham & others, 2010). A recent study found that family strengths (family closeness, support, and responsiveness to health needs, for example) in childhood were protective against early initiation of sexual activity and adolescent pregnancy (Hillis & others, 2010). Another recent study revealed that sexual risk-taking behavior was more likely to occur in girls living in single-parent homes (Hipwell & others, 2011). Also, having older sexually active siblings or pregnant/parenting teenage sisters places adolescent girls at risk for pregnancy (Miller, Benson, & Galbraith, 2001).

Peer and school contexts provide further information about sexual risk taking in adolescents (Young & Vazsonyi, 2011). A recent study found that adolescents who associated with more deviant peers in early adolescence were likely to have more sexual partners at age 16 (Lansford & others, 2010). And a recent research review found that school connectedness was linked to positive sexuality outcomes (Markham & others, 2010). Also, a study of middle school students revealed that better academic achievement was a protective factor in keeping boys and girls from engaging in early initiation of sexual intercourse (Laflin, Wang, & Barry, 2008).

Cognitive factors are increasingly implicated in sexual risk taking in adolescence (Fantasia, 2008). Two such factors are attention problems and self-regulation (the ability to control one's emotions and behavior). A longitudinal study revealed that attention problems and high rates of aggressive disruptive behavior at school entry increased the risk of multiple problem behaviors (school maladjustment, antisocial behavior, and substance use) in middle school, which in turn was linked to early initiation of sexual activity (Schofield & others, 2008). Another longitudinal study found that weak self-regulation at 8 to 9 years of age and risk proneness (tendency to seek sensation and make poor decisions) at 12 to 13 years of age set the stage for sexual risk taking at 16 to 17 years of age (Crockett, Raffaelli, & Shen, 2006).

developmental **connection**

Religious Development. Certain aspects of being religious are linked to lower sexual risk-taking. Chapter 7, p. 249

Might adolescents' character and spirituality protect them from negative sexual outcomes? A recent research review concluded that *prosocial norms* (providing youth with information about norms of risk behaviors; having youth make public commitments to behavior in a prosocial manner, such as avoiding risk behaviors; and having peers and older youth communicate positive aspects of prosocial behavior) and *spirituality* (being spiritual, religious, or believing in a higher power, for example) were linked to positive sexual outcomes for adolescents: less likely to intend to have sex, not likely to engage in early sex, having sex less frequently, and not becoming pregnant (House & others, 2010). A recent study also found that parents' religiosity was linked to a lower level of adolescents' risky sexual behavior, in part resulting from adolescents hanging out with less sexually permissive peers (Landor & others, 2010).

A recent effort to develop a strategy reducing negative outcomes for adolescent sexuality focuses on positive youth development (PYD), which we initially described in Chapter 1 (Lerner & others, 2010; Lewin-Bizan, Bowers, & Lerner, 2010). PYD programs seek to strengthen adolescents' relationships and skills and help them develop a more positive future outlook by enhancing academic, economic, and volunteer activities. An increasing number of efforts utilizing a PYD focus to improve sexual outcomes in adolescence are being implemented (Catalano, Gavin, & Markham, 2010; Gavin & others, 2010; House & others, 2010; Markham & others, 2010).

developmental **connection**

Positive Youth Development. The "Five Cs" of PYD are competence, confidence, connection, character, and caring/compassion. Chapter 1, p. 8

Further Exploration of Sexuality in Emerging Adults We already have covered some aspects of heterosexual attitudes and behavior in emerging adults. Here we consider further analysis and integration of information about patterns of heterosexual behavior in emerging adults.

Surveys indicate that at the beginning of emerging adulthood (age 18), just more than half of individuals have experienced sexual intercourse—but by the end of emerging adulthood (age 25), most individuals have had sexual intercourse (Lefkowitz & Gillen, 2006; Regenerus & Uecker, 2011). Also, the average age of marriage in the United States is currently 27 for males and 26 for females (Popenoe,

and verbal and physical harassment at school and in the community (Coker, Austin, & Schuster, 2010; Ryan & others, 2009; Saewyc, 2011). Between July and September, 2010, five sexual minority adolescents committed suicide, apparently the outcome of anti-gay bullying and abuse (Halpern, 2011).

In conclusion, many sexual minority adolescents experience discrimination and rejection in interactions with their families, peers, schools, and communities (Halpern, 2011). Sexual minority youths' exposure to stigma and discrimination is the main reason given as to why they are more likely to develop problems (Saewyc, 2011). For example, a recent study found that family rejection of coming out by sexual minority adolescents was linked to their higher rates of depression, substance use, and unprotected sex (Ryan & others, 2009). Despite these negative circumstances, many ethnic minority adolescents successfully cope with the challenges they face and develop levels of health and well-being that are similar to their heterosexual peers (Saewyc, 2011).

SELF-STIMULATION

Regardless of whether adolescents have a heterosexual or same-sex attraction, they must equally confront increasing feelings of sexual arousal. One way in which many youths who are not dating or who consciously choose not to engage in sexual intercourse or sexual explorations deal with these insistent feelings of sexual arousal is through self-stimulation, or masturbation.

As indicated earlier, a heterosexual continuum of kissing, petting, and intercourse or oral sex characterizes many adolescents' sexual experiences. Substantial numbers of adolescents, though, have sexual experience outside this heterosexual continuum through masturbation or same-sex behavior. Most boys have an ejaculation for the first time at about 12 to 13 years of age. Masturbation, genital contact with a same-sex or other-sex partner, or a wet dream during sleep are common circumstances for ejaculation.

Masturbation is the most frequent sexual outlet for many adolescents, especially male adolescents. A recent study of 14- to 17-year-olds revealed that 80 percent of the males and 48 percent of the females reported that they had masturbated at some point (Fortenberry & others, 2010). Adolescents today do not feel as guilty about masturbation as they once did, although they still may feel embarrassed or defensive about it. In past eras, masturbation was denounced as causing everything from warts to insanity. Today, as few as 15 percent of adolescents attach any stigma to masturbation (Hyde & DeLamater, 2011).

In one study, the masturbation practices of female and male college students were studied (Leitenberg, Detzer, & Srebnik, 1993). Almost twice as many males as females said they had masturbated (81 percent versus 45 percent), and the males who masturbated did so three times more frequently during early adolescence and early adulthood than did the females who masturbated during the same age periods. No association was found between the quality of sexual adjustment in adulthood and a history of engaging in masturbation during preadolescence and/or early adolescence.

Much of the existing data on masturbation are difficult to interpret because they are based on self-reports in which many adolescents may not be responding accurately. Most experts on adolescent sexuality likely would agree that boys masturbate more than girls—but masturbation is more stigmatized behavior for girls, so they may actually masturbate more than they indicate in self-reports (Diamond, 2004).

CONTRACEPTIVE USE

Sexual activity is a normal activity necessary for procreation, but if appropriate safeguards are not taken it brings the risk of unintended, unwanted pregnancy and sexually transmitted infections (Kelly, 2011; Welch, 2011). Both these risks can be reduced significantly by using certain forms of contraception and barriers (such as condoms) (Crooks & Baur, 2011).

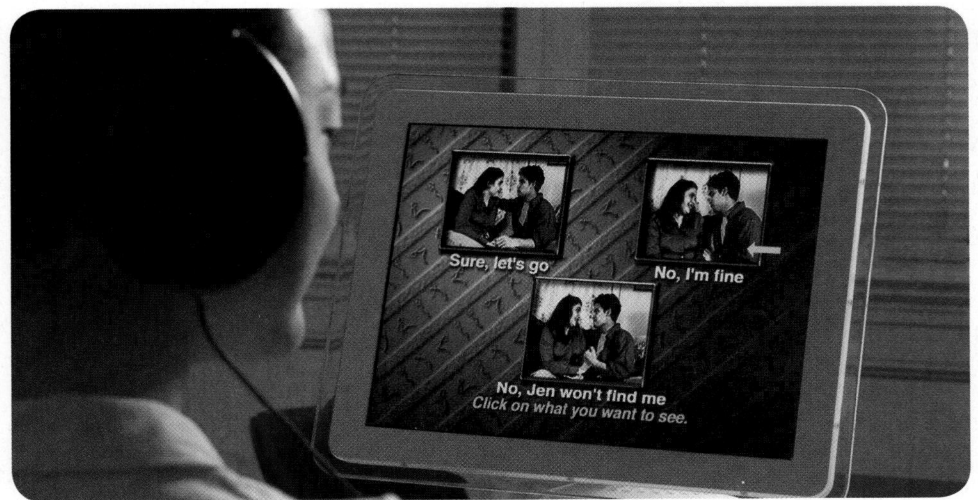

An adolescent participates in an interactive video session developed by Julie Downs and her colleagues at the Department of Social and Decision Sciences at Carnegie Mellon University. The videos help adolescents evaluate their responses and decisions in high-risk sexual contexts.

Are adolescents increasingly using condoms? A recent national study revealed a substantial increase in the use of a contraceptive (61 percent in 2009 compared with 46 percent in 1991) by U.S. high school students during the last time they had sexual intercourse (Eaton & others, 2010). However, in this study, condom use by U.S. adolescents did not significantly change from 2003 through 2009.

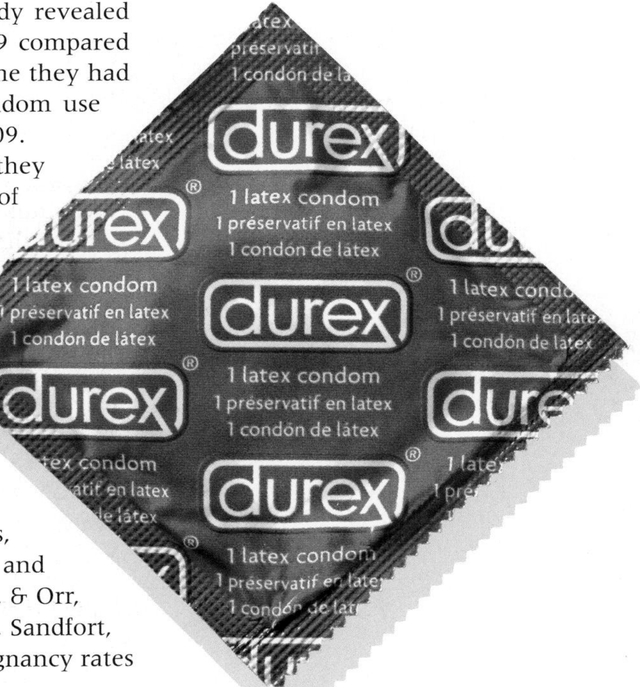

Many sexually active adolescents still do not use contraceptives, or they use them inconsistently (Tschann & others, 2010). In 2009, 34 percent of sexually active adolescents did not use a condom the last time they had sexual intercourse (Eaton & others, 2010). In the recent national U.S. survey (2009), among currently active adolescents, ninth-graders (64 percent) and tenth-graders (68 percent) reported that they had used a condom during their last sexual intercourse more than did eleventh-graders (61 percent) and twelfth-graders (55 percent) (Eaton & others, 2010).

Researchers also have found that U.S. adolescents use condoms less than their counterparts in Europe. Recent studies of 15-year-olds revealed that in Europe 72 percent of the girls and 81 percent of the boys used condoms at last intercourse (Currie & others, 2008); by comparison, in the United States, 62 percent of the girls and 75 percent of the boys used condoms at last intercourse (Santelli, Sandfort, & Orr, 2009). Pill use also continues to be higher in European countries (Santelli, Sandfort, & Orr, 2009). Such comparisons provide insight into why adolescent pregnancy rates are much higher in the United States than in European countries.

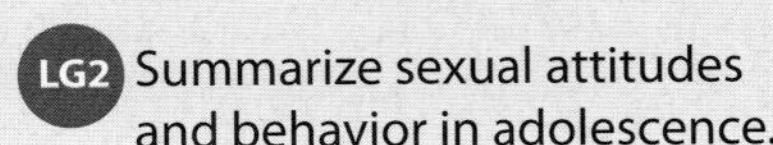

Review *Connect* Reflect

LG2 Summarize sexual attitudes and behavior in adolescence.

Review

- How would you describe adolescent heterosexual attitudes and behaviors?
- How would you characterize adolescent sexual minority behavior and attitudes?
- What is known about sexual self-stimulation in adolescence?
- How extensively do U.S. adolescents use contraceptives?

Connect

- Connect what you learned about identity in Chapter 4 with this section's discussion of gay or lesbian identity and disclosure.

Reflect *Your Own Personal Journey of Life*

- Think about your sexual experiences or lack of sexual experiences in adolescence. What would you change?

3 Negative Sexual Outcomes in Adolescence

LG3 Describe the main negative sexual outcomes that can emerge in adolescence.

Adolescent Pregnancy | Sexually Transmitted Infections | Forcible Sexual Behavior and Sexual Harassment

Negative sexual outcomes in adolescence include adolescent pregnancy, sexually transmitted infections, and forcible sexual behavior and sexual harassment. Let's begin by exploring adolescent pregnancy and its prevalence in the United States and around the world.

ADOLESCENT PREGNANCY

Angela is 15 years old. She reflects, "I'm three months pregnant. This could ruin my whole life. I've made all of these plans for the future, and now they are down the drain. I don't have anybody to talk with about my problem. I can't talk to my parents. There is no way they can understand." Pregnant adolescents were once virtually invisible and unmentionable, shuttled off to homes for unwed mothers where relinquishment of the baby for adoption was their only option, or subjected to unsafe and illegal abortions. But yesterday's secret has become today's dilemma. Our exploration of adolescent pregnancy focuses on its incidence and nature, its consequences, cognitive factors that may be involved, adolescents as parents, and ways in which adolescent pregnancy rates can be reduced.

Incidence of Adolescent Pregnancy Adolescent girls who become pregnant are from different ethnic groups and from different places, but their circumstances have the same stressfulness. To many adults, they represent a flaw in America's social fabric. Each year more than 200,000 females in the United States have a child before their eighteenth birthday. Like Angela, far too many become pregnant in their early or middle adolescent years. As one 17-year-old Los Angeles mother of a 1-year-old son said, "We are children having children."

In cross-cultural comparisons, the United States continues to have one of the highest adolescent pregnancy and childbearing rates in the industrialized world, despite a considerable decline in the 1990s (Cooksey, 2009). The U.S. adolescent pregnancy rate is eight times as high as in the Netherlands. This dramatic difference exists in spite of the fact that U.S. adolescents are no more sexually active than their counterparts in the Netherlands.

Why are U.S. adolescent pregnancy rates so high? Three reasons based on cross-cultural studies are as follows (Boonstra, 2002, pp. 9–10):

- *"Childbearing regarded as adult activity."* European countries, as well as Canada, give a strong consensus that childbearing belongs in adulthood "when young people have completed their education, have become employed and independent from their parents and are living in stable relationships. . . . In the United States, this attitude is much less strong and much more variable across groups and areas of the country."
- *"Clear messages about sexual behavior."* While adults in other countries strongly encourage teens to wait until they have established themselves before having children, they are generally more accepting than American adults of teens having sex. In France and Sweden, in particular, teen sexual expression is seen as normal and positive, but there is also widespread expectation that sexual intercourse will take place within committed relationships. (In fact, relationships among U.S. teens tend to be more sporadic and of shorter duration.) Equally strong is the expectation that young people who are having sex will take actions to protect themselves and their partners from pregnancy and sexually transmitted infections, an expectation that is much stronger in Europe than in the United States. "In keeping with this view, . . . schools in Great

Britain, France, Sweden, and most of Canada" have sex education programs that provide more comprehensive information about prevention than do U.S. schools. In addition, these countries use the media more often in "government-sponsored campaigns for promoting responsible sexual behavior."

- *"Access to family planning services.* In countries that are more accepting of teenage sexual relationships, teenagers also have easier access to reproductive health services. In Canada, France, Great Britain, and Sweden, contraceptive services are integrated into other types of primary health care and are available free or at low cost for all teenagers. Generally, teens (in these countries) know where to obtain information and services and receive confidential and nonjudgmental care. . . . In the United States, where attitudes about teenage sexual relationships are more conflicted, teens have a harder time obtaining contraceptive services. Many do not have health insurance or cannot get birth control as part of their basic health care."

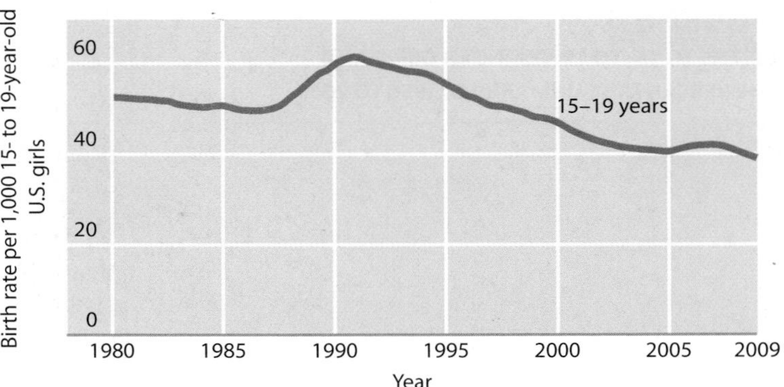

FIGURE **6.5**

BIRTH RATES FOR U.S. 15- TO 19-YEAR-OLD GIRLS FROM 1980 TO 2009. Centers for Disease Control and Prevention (2011). Vital signs: teen pregnancy—United States, 1981–2009. *MMWR, 60,* 414–420.

Trends in U.S. Adolescent Pregnancy Rates Despite the negative comparisons of the United States with many other developed countries, there have been some encouraging trends in U.S. adolescent pregnancy rates. In 2009, the U.S. birth rate for 15- to 19-year-olds was 39.1 births per 1,000 females, the lowest rate ever recorded, which represents a 37 percent decrease from 1991 (National Center for Health Statistics, 2011) (see Figure 6.5). Reasons for these declines include school/community health classes, increased contraceptive use, and fear of sexually transmitted infections such as AIDS (Joyner, 2009).

Ethnic variations characterize adolescent pregnancy (see Figure 6.6). Latina adolescents are more likely than African American and non-Latina White adolescents to become pregnant (Hamilton, Martin, & Ventura, 2010). For 15- to 19-year-old U.S. females in 2009, per 1,000 births, the birth rate for Latinas was 70.1, for African Americans 59.0, and for non-Latina Whites 25.6 (National Center for Health Statistics, 2011). Latina and African American adolescent girls who have a child are also more likely to have a second child than are non-Latina White adolescent girls (Rosengard, 2009). And daughters of teenage mothers are at risk for

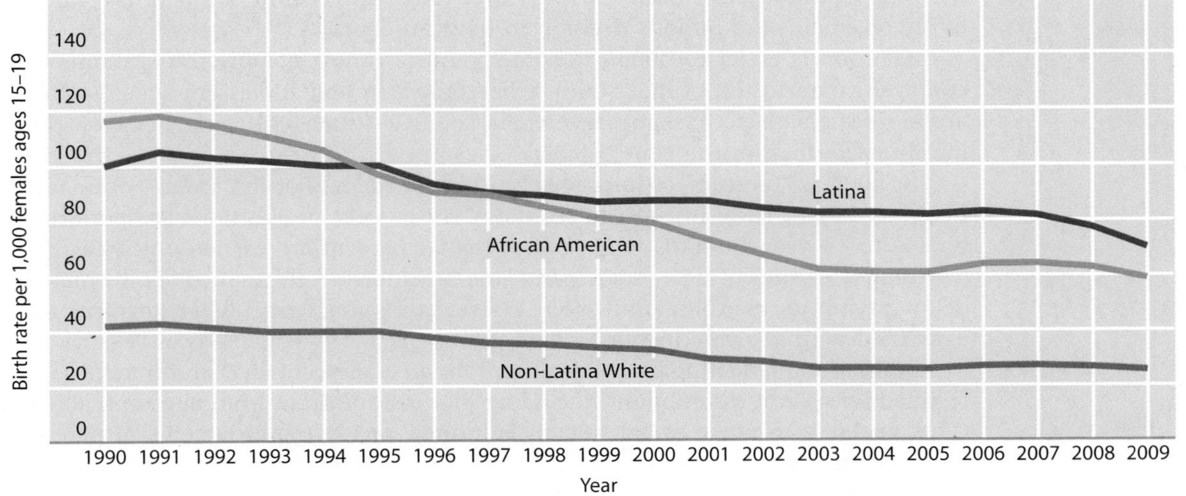

FIGURE **6.6**

ADOLESCENTS WHO GAVE BIRTH, 1990 TO 2009 BY ETHNICITY. National Center for Education Statistics (2011). Vital signs: teen pregnancy—United States, 1981–2009. *MMWR, 60,* 414–420.

FIGURE **6.7**

BIRTHS TO 15- TO 19-YEAR-OLD GIRLS AND THE PERCENTAGE UNMARRIED, 1950 TO 2008

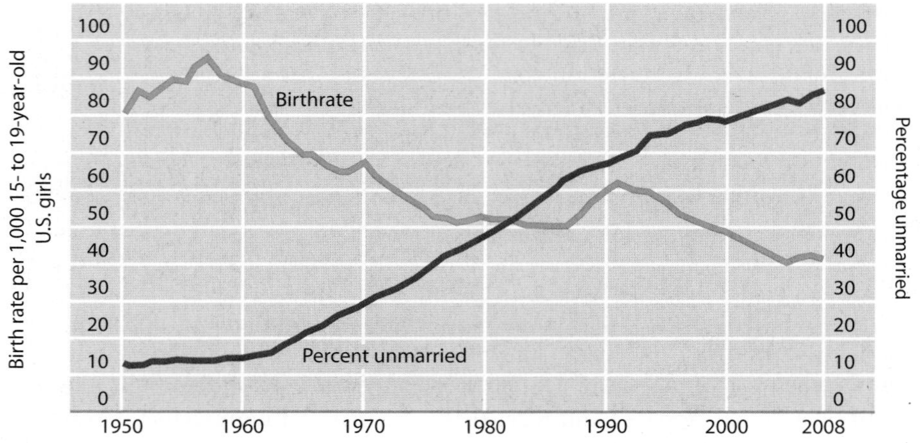

teenage childbearing, thus perpetuating an intergenerational cycle. A study using data from the National Longitudinal Survey of Youth revealed that daughters of teenage mothers were 66 percent more likely to become teenage mothers themselves (Meade, Kershaw, & Ickovics, 2008). In this study, risks that increased the likelihood that daughters of the teenage mothers would become pregnant included low parental monitoring and poverty.

Even though adolescent childbearing overall has declined steeply over the last half century, the proportion of adolescent births that are nonmarital has increased in equally dramatic fashion, from 13 percent in 1950 to 87 percent in 2008 (Hamilton, Martin, & Ventura, 2010 (see Figure 6.7). Two factors are responsible for this trend. First, marriage in adolescence has now become quite rare (the average age of first marriage in the United States is now 25 for women and 27 for men). Second, pregnancy is no longer seen as a reason for marriage. In contrast to the days of the "shotgun marriage" (when youth were forced to marry if a girl became pregnant), very few adolescents who become pregnant now marry before their baby is born.

Abortion Impassioned debate characterizes abortion in the United States today, and this debate is likely to continue in the foreseeable future. The experiences of U.S. adolescents who want to have an abortion vary by state and region. Thirty-eight states prohibit abortions after a specified point in pregnancy, most often fetal viability (Alan Guttmacher Institute, 2010). Thirty-four states require some form of parental involvement in a minor's decision to have an abortion.

Abortion is easier to obtain in some countries, most notably the Scandinavian countries, than in the United States, where abortion and adolescent sexual activity are more stigmatized. In many developing countries, such as Nigeria, abortion is far more unsafe than in the United States.

In 2006, 27 percent of teen pregnancies ended in abortion (Alan Guttmacher Institute, 2010). Also, in the United States, 19 percent of abortions are performed on 15- to 19-year-old girls, whereas less than 1 percent are carried out with those less than 15 years of age. Adolescent girls are more likely than older women to delay having an abortion until after 15 weeks of pregnancy, when medical risks associated with abortion increase significantly.

Legislation mandating parental consent for an adolescent girl's abortion has been justified by several assumptions, including high risk of harm from abortion, adolescents' inability to make an adequately informed decision, and benefits of parental involvement. Research related to each of these assumptions was the focus of a review (Adler, Ozer, & Tschann, 2003).

Legal abortion in the United States itself carries few medical risks if performed in the first trimester of pregnancy, especially compared with the risks of childbearing, for adolescent girls. And, in terms of psychological risks, a recent study revealed that abortion did not lead to mental health problems for adolescent girls (Warren & others, 2010). Other studies have found that adolescents are not psychologically harmed by their abortion experience (Pope, Adler, & Tschann, 2001; Quinton, Major, & Richards, 2001).

Regardless of research outcomes, pro-life and pro-choice advocates are convinced of the rightness of their positions (Hyde & DeLamater, 2011). Their conflict has a foundation in religious beliefs, political convictions, and morality. This conflict has no easy solutions.

What are some consequences of adolescent pregnancy?

Consequences of Adolescent Pregnancy The consequences of America's high adolescent pregnancy rate are cause for great concern (Welch, 2011). Adolescent pregnancy creates health risks for both the baby and the mother. Infants born to adolescent mothers are more likely to be born preterm and have low birth weights—a prominent factor in infant mortality—as well as neurological problems and childhood illness (Khashan, Baker, & Kenny, 2010). Adolescent mothers often drop out of school. Although many adolescent mothers resume their education later in life, they generally do not catch up economically with women who postpone childbearing until their twenties. A longitudinal study revealed that these characteristics of adolescent mothers were related to their likelihood of having problems as emerging adults: a history of school problems, delinquency, hard substance use, and mental health problems (Oxford & others, 2006).

Though the consequences of America's high adolescent pregnancy rate are cause for great concern, it often is not pregnancy alone that leads to negative consequences for an adolescent mother and her offspring. Adolescent mothers are more likely to come from low-SES backgrounds (Molina & others, 2010). Many adolescent mothers also were not good students before they became pregnant (Malamitsi-Puchner & Boutsikou, 2006). However, not every adolescent girl who bears a child lives a life of poverty and low achievement. Thus, although adolescent pregnancy is a high-risk circumstance, and adolescents who do not become pregnant generally fare better than those who do, some adolescent mothers do well in school and have positive outcomes (Ahn, 1994; Leadbeater & Way, 2000).

connecting with adolescents

Sixteen-Year-Old Alberto: Wanting a Different Kind of Life

Sixteen-year-old Alberto's maternal grandmother was a heroin addict who died of cancer at the age of 40. His father, who was only 17 when Alberto was born, had been in prison most of Alberto's life. His mother and stepfather are not married but have lived together for a dozen years and have four other children. Alberto's stepbrother dropped out of school when he was 17, fathered a child, and is now unemployed. But Alberto, who lives in the Bronx in New York City, has different plans for his own future. He wants to be a dentist, he said, "like the kind of woman who fixed his teeth at Bronx-Lebanon Hospital Center clinic when he was a child" (Bernstein, 2004, p. A22). And Alberto, along with his girlfriend, Jasmine, wants to remain a virgin until he is married.

What cultural influences, negative and positive, might be helping Alberto plan his future?

Alberto with his girlfriend.

These teenage mothers are involved in a program in Nebraska that is designed to help them care for their infants and keep them in school. *What are adolescents like as parents?*

Adolescents as Parents Children of adolescent parents face problems even before they are born (Chedraui, 2008). Only one of every five pregnant adolescent girls receives any prenatal care at all during the important first three months of pregnancy. Pregnant adolescents are more likely to have anemia and complications related to prematurity than are mothers aged 20 to 24. The problems of adolescent pregnancy double the normal risk of delivering a low birth weight baby (one that weighs under 5.5 pounds), a category that places that infant at risk for physical and mental deficits (Dryfoos & Barkin, 2006). In some cases, infant problems may be due to poverty rather than the mother's age.

Infants who escape the medical hazards of having an adolescent mother might not escape the psychological and social perils. Adolescent mothers are less competent at child rearing and have less realistic expectations for their infants' development than do older mothers (Osofsky, 1990). Children born to adolescent mothers do not perform as well on intelligence tests and have more behavioral problems than children born to mothers in their twenties (S. Silver, 1988). One longitudinal study found that the children of women who had their first birth during their teens had lower achievement test scores and more behavioral problems than did children whose mothers had their first birth as adults (Hofferth & Reid, 2002).

So far, we have talked exclusively about adolescent mothers. Although some adolescent fathers are involved with their children, the majority are not. In one study, only one-fourth of adolescent mothers with a 3-year-old child said the father had a close relationship with them (Leadbeater, Way, & Raden, 1994).

Adolescent fathers have lower incomes, less education, and more children than do men who delay having children until their twenties. One reason for these difficulties is that the adolescent father often compounds the problem of becoming a parent at a young age by dropping out of school (Resnick, Wattenberg, & Brewer, 1992).

Reducing Adolescent Pregnancy Serious, extensive efforts are needed to reduce adolescent pregnancy and to help pregnant adolescents and young mothers enhance their educational and occupational opportunities (Graves & others, 2011; Sieving & others, 2011; Tortolero & others, 2010). John Conger (1988) offered the following four recommendations for reducing the high rate of adolescent pregnancy: (1) sex education and family planning, (2) access to contraceptive methods, (3) the life options approach, and (4) broad community involvement and support. We consider each of these recommendations in turn.

Age-appropriate family-life education benefits adolescents (Fallon; 2011). One strategy that is used in some family-life education programs is the Baby Think It Over doll, a life-size computer-driven baby doll that engages in realistic responses and provides adolescents the opportunity to experience the responsibilities of being a parent. A recent study of primarily Latino ninth-grade students who took care of the Baby Think It Over doll found that the experience increased the age at which they said they wanted to have a child, produced a greater interest in career and educational planning, and raised their concerns about the possibility of how having a baby might interfere with those plans (de Ànda, 2006). To read about the work of one individual who incorporates the Baby Think It Over automated doll in her effort to educate adolescents about the reality of having a baby, see the *Connecting with Careers* profile.

In addition to age-appropriate family-life and sex education, sexually active adolescents need access to contraceptive methods (Crooks & Baur, 2011). These needs often can be handled through adolescent clinics that provide comprehensive, high-quality health services.

connecting with careers

Lynn Blankenship, Family and Consumer Science Educator

Lynn Blankenship is a family and consumer science educator. She has an undergraduate degree in this area from the University of Arizona. She has taught for more than 20 years, the last 14 at Tucson High Magnet School.

Blankenship was awarded the Tucson Federation of Teachers Educator of the Year Award for 1999–2000 and the Arizona Association of Family and Consumer Science Teacher of the Year in 1999.

Blankenship especially enjoys teaching life skills to adolescents. One of her favorite activities is having students care for an automated baby that imitates the needs of real babies. Blankenship says that this program has a profound impact on students because the baby must be cared for around the clock for the duration of the assignment. Blankenship also coordinates real-world work experiences and training for students in several child-care facilities in the Tucson area.

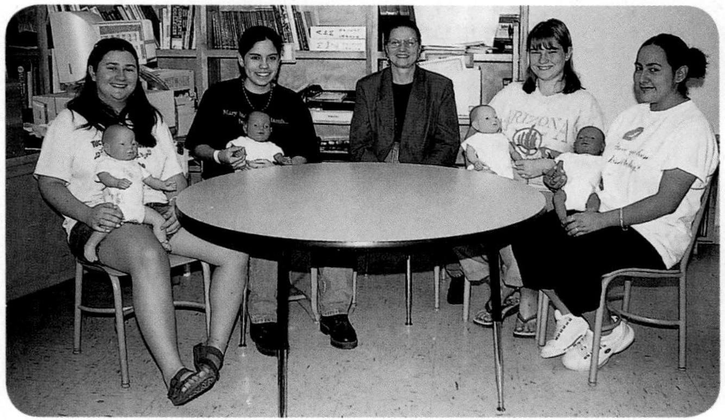

Lynn Blankenship, with students carrying their automated babies.

For more information about what a family and consumer science educator does, see page 47 in the Careers in Adolescent Development appendix.

Better sex education, family planning, and access to contraceptive methods alone will not remedy the adolescent pregnancy crisis, especially for high-risk adolescents. Adolescents have to become motivated to reduce their pregnancy risk. This motivation will come only when adolescents look to the future and see that they have an opportunity to become self-sufficient and successful. Adolescents need opportunities to improve their academic and career-related skills; job opportunities; life-planning consultation; and extensive mental health services.

Finally, for adolescent pregnancy prevention to ultimately succeed, we need broad community involvement and support. This support is a major reason for the success of pregnancy prevention efforts in other developed nations where rates of adolescent pregnancy, abortion, and childbearing are much lower than in America despite similar levels of sexual activity. In the Netherlands, as well as other European countries such as Sweden, sex does not carry the mystery and conflict it does in American society. The Netherlands does not have a mandated sex education program, but adolescents can obtain contraceptive counseling at government-sponsored clinics for a small fee. The Dutch media also have played an important role in educating the public about sex through frequent broadcasts focused on birth control, abortion, and related matters. Perhaps as a result, Dutch adolescents are unlikely to have sex without contraception.

Girls, Inc., has four programs that are intended to increase adolescent girls' motivation to avoid pregnancy until they are mature enough to make responsible decisions about motherhood (Roth & others, 1998). Growing Together, a series of five two-hour workshops for mothers and adolescents, and Will Power/Won't Power, a series of six two-hour sessions that focus on assertiveness training, are for 12- to 14-year-old girls. For older adolescent girls, Taking Care of Business provides nine sessions that emphasize career planning as well as information about sexuality, reproduction, and contraception. Health Bridge coordinates health and education

What are some strategies for reducing adolescent pregnancy?

These are not adolescent mothers, but rather adolescents who are participating in the Teen Outreach Program (TOP), which engages adolescents in volunteer community service. These adolescent girls are serving as volunteers in a child-care center for crack babies. Researchers have found that such volunteer experiences can reduce the rate of adolescent pregnancy.

services—girls can participate in this program as one of their club activities. Research on girls' participation in these programs revealed a significant drop in their likelihood of getting pregnant, compared with girls who did not participate (Girls, Inc., 1991).

So far, we have discussed four ways to reduce adolescent pregnancy: sex education and family planning, access to contraceptive methods, life options, and broad community involvement and support. A fifth consideration, which is especially important for young adolescents, is abstinence. Abstinence is increasingly being included as a theme in sex education classes, which we discuss later in this chapter; however, criticisms of abstinence-only sex education programs have recently been made (Constantine, 2008; Schalet, 2011).

SEXUALLY TRANSMITTED INFECTIONS

Tammy, age 15, has just finished listening to an expert lecture in her health class. We overhear her talking to one of her girlfriends as she walks down the school corridor: "That was a disgusting lecture. I can't believe all the infections you can get by having sex. I think she was probably trying to scare us. She spent a lot of time talking about AIDS, which I have heard that normal people do not get. Right? I've heard that only homosexuals and drug addicts get AIDS. And I've also heard that gonorrhea and most other sexual infections can be cured, so what is the big deal if you get something like that?" Tammy's view of sexually transmitted infections—that they always happen to someone else, that they can be easily cured without any harm done, that they are too disgusting for a nice young person to hear about, let alone get—is common among adolescents. Tammy's view is wrong. Adolescents who are having sex run the risk of getting sexually transmitted infections.

Sexually transmitted infections (STIs) are infections that are contracted primarily through sexual contact. This contact is not limited to vaginal intercourse but includes oral-genital and anal-genital contact as well. STIs are an increasing health problem. Recent estimates indicate that while 15- to 24-year-olds represent only 25 percent of the sexually experienced U.S. population, they acquire nearly 50 percent of all new STIs (Centers for Disease Control and Prevention, 2009a).

Among the main STIs adolescents can get are three STIs caused by viruses—acquired immune deficiency syndrome (AIDS), genital herpes, and genital warts—and three STIs caused by bacteria—gonorrhea, syphilis, and chlamydia.

HIV and AIDS

No single STI has caused more deaths, had a greater impact on sexual behavior, or created more public fear in recent decades, than HIV (Welch, 2011). We explore here its nature and incidence, how it is transmitted, and prevention.

AIDS stands for acquired immunodeficiency syndrome, a sexually transmitted infection that is caused by the human immunodeficiency virus (HIV), which destroys the body's immune system. Following exposure to HIV, an individual is vulnerable to germs that a normal immune system could destroy.

Through December 2005, there were 41,149 cumulative cases of AIDS in 13- to 24-year-olds in the United States (Centers for Disease Control and Prevention, 2009b). Worldwide, the greatest concern about AIDS is in sub-Saharan Africa, where it has reached epidemic proportions (Burnett & others, 2011; Renju & others, 2011; Sommer, 2011; UNICEF, 2011). Adolescent girls in many African countries are especially vulnerable to infection with the HIV virus by adult men (Cherutich & others, 2008). Approximately six times as many adolescent girls as boys have AIDS in these countries. In Kenya, 25 percent of 15- to 19-year-old girls are HIV-positive, compared with only 4 percent of this age group of boys. In Botswana, more than 30 percent of the adolescent girls who are pregnant are infected with HIV. In some sub-Saharan countries, less than 20 percent of women and 40 percent of 15- to 19-year-olds reported that they used a condom the last time they had sexual intercourse (Bankole & others, 2004).

sexually transmitted infections (STIs) Infections that are contracted primarily through sexual contact. This contact is not limited to vaginal intercourse but includes oral-genital contact and anal-genital contact as well.

AIDS Stands for acquired immunodeficiency syndrome, a sexually transmitted infection caused by the human immunodeficiency virus (HIV), which destroys the body's immune system.

A youth group presents a play in the local market place in Morogoro, Tanzania. The play is designed to educate the community about HIV and AIDS.

A 13-year-old boy pushes his friends around in his barrow during his break from his work as a barrow boy in a community in sub-Saharan Africa. He became the breadwinner in the family because both of his parents died of AIDS.

AIDS also has resulted in a dramatic increase in the number of African children and adolescents who are orphaned and left to care for themselves because their parents acquired the disease. In 2006, 12 million children and adolescents had become orphans because of the deaths of their parents due to AIDS (UNICEF, 2006). This figure is expected to increase to 16 million in the second decade of the twenty-first century; thus, AIDS orphans then could make up as many as 15 to 20 percent of the population of some sub-Saharan countries. As a result of the dramatic increase in AIDS orphans, more of these children and adolescents are being cared for by their grandmothers or by no one, in which case all too often they turn to a lifestyle of crime or prostitution.

There continues to be great concern about AIDS in many parts of the world, not just sub-Saharan Africa (UNICEF, 2011). In the United States, prevention is especially targeted at groups that show the highest incidence of AIDS. These include drug users, individuals with other STIs, young gay males, individuals living in low-income circumstances, Latinos, and African Americans (Centers for Disease Control and Prevention, 2009b). Also, in recent years, there has been increased heterosexual transmission of HIV in the United States.

There are some differences in AIDS cases in U.S. adolescents, compared with AIDS cases in U.S. adults:

- A higher percentage of adolescent AIDS cases are acquired by heterosexual transmission.
- A higher percentage of adolescents are asymptomatic individuals (but will become symptomatic in adulthood—that is, they are HIV-positive, but do not yet have AIDS).
- A higher percentage of African American and Latino AIDS cases occur in adolescence.
- A special set of ethical and legal issues is involved in testing and informing partners and parents of adolescents.
- Adolescents have less access to contraceptives and are less likely to use them than are adults.

Experts say that HIV can be transmitted only by sexual contact, the sharing of needles, or blood transfusion (which in recent years has been tightly monitored)

The HIV virus is not transmitted like colds or the flu, but by an exchange of infected blood, semen, or vaginal fluids. This usually occurs during sexual intercourse, in sharing drug needles, or to babies infected before or during birth.

You won't get the HIV virus from:	Everyday contact with individuals around you in school or the workplace, at parties, child-care centers, or stores Swimming in a pool, even if someone in the pool has the AIDS virus A mosquito bite, or from bedbugs, lice, flies, or other insects Saliva, sweat, tears, urine, or feces A kiss Clothes, telephones, or toilet seats Using a glass or eating utensils that someone else has used Being on a bus, train, or crowded elevator with an individual who is infected with the virus or who has AIDS
Risky behavior:	Your chances of coming into contact with the virus increase if you: Have more than one sex partner Share drug needles and syringes Engage in anal, vaginal, or oral sex without a condom Perform vaginal or oral sex with someone who shoots drugs Engage in sex with someone you don't know well or with someone who has several sex partners Engage in unprotected sex (without a condom) with an infected individual
Blood donations and transfusions:	You will not come into contact with the HIV virus by donating blood at a blood bank. The risk of getting AIDS from a blood transfusion has been greatly reduced. Donors are screened for risk factors, and donated blood is tested for HIV antibodies.
Safe behavior:	Not having sex Having sex that does not involve fluid exchange (rubbing, holding, massage) Sex with one mutually faithful, uninfected partner Sex with proper protection Not shooting drugs Source: *America Responds to AIDS*. U.S. Government educational pamphlet, 1988.

FIGURE **6.8**
UNDERSTANDING AIDS: WHAT'S RISKY, WHAT'S NOT

(Kelly, 2011). Approximately 90 percent of AIDS cases in the United States continue to occur among men who have sex with other men and intravenous drug users. Penile-anal sex involves a higher risk of microscopic tearing and therefore blood-semen contact. A disproportionate increase among females who are heterosexual partners of bisexual males or of intravenous drug users has recently been noted (Centers for Disease Control and Prevention, 2009a). This increase suggests that the risk of AIDS may be increasing among heterosexual individuals who have multiple sex partners. Figure 6.8 describes what is risky and what is not, regarding AIDS and HIV.

Merely asking a date about his or her sexual behavior, of course, does not guarantee protection from HIV or other STIs. For example, in one investigation, 655 college students were asked to answer questions about lying and sexual behavior (Cochran & Mays, 1990). Of the 422 respondents who said they were sexually active, 34 percent of the men and 10 percent of the women said they had lied so their partner would have sex with them. Much higher percentages—47 percent of the men and 60 percent of the women—said they had been lied to by a potential sexual partner. When asked what aspects of their past they would be most likely to lie about, more than 40 percent of the men and women said they would understate the number of their sexual partners. Twenty percent of the men, but only 4 percent of the women, said they would lie about their results from an HIV blood test. A recent study revealed that 40 percent of sexually active adolescents who were HIV-positive had not disclosed their status to their partners (Michaud & others, 2009).

Because it is possible, and even probable, among high-risk groups to have more than one STI at a time, efforts to prevent one infection help reduce the prevalence of other infections. Efforts to prevent AIDS can also help prevent adolescent pregnancy and other sexually related problems. An extensive recent research review revealed that behavioral interventions can succeed in reducing HIV through such methods as increasing condom use, reducing or delaying penetrative sex, and increasing partner communication skills involving safe sex (Johnson & others, 2011).

Genital Herpes **Genital herpes** is a sexually transmitted infection caused by a large family of viruses with many different strains, some of which produce other, nonsexually transmitted diseases such as cold sores, chicken pox, and mononucleosis. Three to five days after contact, itching and tingling can occur, followed by an eruption of painful sores and blisters. The attacks can last up to three weeks and can recur as frequently as every few weeks or as infrequently as every few years. The virus can also pass through nonlatex condoms as well as contraceptive foams and creams. It is estimated that approximately 20 percent of adolescents have genital herpes (Centers for Disease Control and Prevention, 2009a). It also is estimated that more than 600,000 new genital herpes infections are appearing in the 15- to 24-year-old age group in the United States each year.

Although drugs such as acyclovir can alleviate symptoms, there is no known cure for herpes. Thus, individuals infected with herpes often experience severe emotional distress in addition to the considerable physical discomfort. They may feel conflicted or reluctant about sex, angry about the unpredictability of the infection, and fearful that they won't be able to cope with the pain of the next attack. For these reasons, many communities have established support groups for victims of herpes.

Genital Warts **Genital warts** are caused by the human papillomavirus (HPV), which is difficult to test for and does not always produce symptoms but is very contagious nonetheless. Genital warts usually appear as small, hard, painless bumps on the penis, in the vaginal area, or around the anus. More than 9 million individuals in the United States in the 15- to 24-year-old age group are estimated to have an HPV infection, making HPV the most commonly acquired STI in this age group. Treatment involves the use of a topical drug, freezing, or surgery. Unfortunately, genital warts may return despite treatment, and in some cases they are linked to cervical cancer and other genital cancers. Condoms afford some protection against HPV infection. In 2010, the Centers for Disease Control and Prevention recommended that all 11- and 12-year-old girls as well as females 13 to 26 years of age be given a three-dose HPV vaccine, which helps to fight off HPV and cervical cancer (Friedman & others, 2011). Females as young as 9 years of age can be given the HPV vaccine.

We now turn to three STIs—gonorrhea, syphilis, and chlamydia—caused by bacteria.

Gonorrhea **Gonorrhea** is an STI that is commonly called the "drip" or the "clap." It is caused by a bacterium called *Neisseria gonorrhoeae*, which thrives in the moist mucous membranes lining the mouth, throat, vagina, cervix, urethra, and anal tract. The bacterium is spread by contact between the infected moist membranes of one individual and the membranes of another. Although the incidence

genital herpes A sexually transmitted infection caused by a large family of viruses of different strains. These strains produce other, nonsexually transmitted diseases such as chicken pox and mononucleosis.

genital warts An STI caused by the human papillomavirus; genital warts are very contagious and are the most common acquired STI in the United States in the 15- to 24-year-old age group.

gonorrhea A sexually transmitted infection caused by the bacterium *Neisseria gonorrhoeae*, which thrives in the moist mucous membranes lining the mouth, throat, vagina, cervix, urethra, and anal tract. This STI is commonly called the "drip" or the "clap."

of gonorrhea has declined, it is estimated that more than 400,000 new cases appear each year in the 15- to 24-year-old age group (Weinstock, Berman, & Cates, 2004). A recent large-scale study revealed that adolescents who were most likely to screen positive for gonorrhea were female, African American, and 16 years or older (Han & others, 2011).

Early symptoms of gonorrhea are more likely to appear in males, who are likely to have a discharge from the penis and burning during urination. The early sign of gonorrhea in females, often undetectable, is a mild, sometimes irritating vaginal discharge. Complications of gonorrhea in males include prostate, bladder, and kidney problems, as well as sterility. In females, gonorrhea may lead to infertility due to the abdominal adhesions or pelvic inflammatory disease (PID) that it can cause (Crooks & Baur, 2011). Gonorrhea can be successfully treated in its early stages with penicillin or other antibiotics.

Syphilis **Syphilis** is an STI caused by the bacterium *Treponema pallidum,* a member of the spirochaeta family. The spirochete needs a warm, moist environment to survive, and it is transmitted by penile-vaginal, oral-genital, or anal contact. It can also be transmitted from a pregnant woman to her fetus after the fourth month of pregnancy; if she is treated before this time with penicillin, the syphilis will not be transmitted to the fetus. Syphilis rates have increased in U.S. 15- to 24-year-old males and females from 2004 to 2008 (Centers for Disease Control and Prevention, 2009a).

If untreated, syphilis may progress through four phases: primary (chancre sores appear), secondary (general skin rash occurs), latent (can last for several years in which no overt symptoms are present), and tertiary (cardiovascular disease, blindness, paralysis, skin ulcers, liver damage, mental problems, and even death may occur) (Crooks & Baur, 2011). In its early phases, syphilis can be effectively treated with penicillin.

Chlamydia **Chlamydia,** one of most common of all STIs, is named for *Chlamydia trachomatis,* an organism that spreads by sexual contact and infects the genital organs of both sexes. Although fewer individuals have heard of chlamydia than have heard of gonorrhea and syphilis, its incidence is much higher. In 2007, more than 2.8 million new cases of chlamydia were estimated to have occurred in the United States (Centers for Disease Control and Prevention, 2009a). More than 50 percent of the new cases of chlamydia reported in 2007 were in 15- to 25-year-old females. A recent large-scale survey found that adolescents who screened positive for chlamydia were more likely to be female, African American, and 16 years and older (Han & others, 2011). About 10 percent of all college students have chlamydia. This STI is highly infectious; women run a 70 percent risk of contracting it in a single sexual encounter with an infected partner. The male risk is estimated at between 25 and 50 percent. The estimated annual incidence of chlamydia in the 15- to 24-year-old age group is 1 million individuals (Weinstock, Berman, & Cates, 2004).

Many females with chlamydia have few or no symptoms (McClure & others, 2006). When symptoms do appear, they include disrupted menstrual periods, pelvic pain, elevated temperature, nausea, vomiting, and headache. Possible symptoms of chlamydia in males are a discharge from the penis and burning during urination.

Because many females with chlamydia are asymptomatic, the infection often goes untreated and the chlamydia spreads to the upper reproductive tract, where it can cause pelvic inflammatory disease (PID). The resultant scarring of tissue in the fallopian tubes can result in infertility or in ectopic pregnancies (tubal pregnancies)—that is, a pregnancy in which the fertilized egg is implanted outside the uterus. One-quarter of females who have PID become infertile; multiple cases of PID increase the rate of infertility to half. Some researchers suggest that chlamydia is the number one preventable cause of female infertility.

Although they can occur without sexual contact and are therefore not classified as STIs, urinary tract or bladder infections and vaginal yeast infections (also called *thrush*) are common in sexually active females, especially those who have an intense

syphilis A sexually transmitted infection caused by the bacterium *Treponema pallidum,* a spirochete.

chlamydia One of most common sexually transmitted infections, named for *Chlamydia trachomatis,* an organism that spreads by sexual contact and infects the genital organs of both sexes.

"honeymoon" lovemaking experience. Both of these infections clear up quickly with medication, but their symptoms (urinary urgency and burning in urinary tract infections; itching, irritation, and whitish vaginal discharge in yeast infections) may be frightening, especially to adolescents who may already have considerable anxiety about sex. We discuss them because one of the non-STIs may be what brings an adolescent girl to a doctor, nurse practitioner, or family-planning clinic, providing an opportunity for her to receive sex education and contraception.

So far we have discussed the problems of adolescent pregnancy and sexually transmitted infections. Next, we explore these sexuality problems: forcible sexual behavior and sexual harassment.

FORCIBLE SEXUAL BEHAVIOR AND SEXUAL HARASSMENT

Most people choose to engage in sexual intercourse or other sexual activities—but, unfortunately, some people force others to engage in sex. Too many adolescent girls and young women report that they believe they don't have adequate sexual rights (East & Adams, 2002). These include the right not to have sexual intercourse when they don't wish to, the right to tell a partner that he is being too rough, or the right to use any form of birth control during intercourse. One study found that almost 20 percent of 904 sexually active 14- to 26-year-old females believed that they never have the right to make decisions about contraception; to tell their partner that they don't want to have intercourse without birth control; that they want to make love differently, or that their partner is being too rough; or to stop foreplay at any time, including at the point of intercourse (Rickert, Sanghvi, & Wiemann, 2002). In this study, poor grades in school and sexual inexperience were linked to a lack of sexual assertiveness in females.

Forcible Sexual Behavior **Rape** is forcible sexual intercourse with a person who does not give consent. Legal definitions of rape vary from state to state. In some states, for example, the law allows husbands to force their wives to have sex. Because of the difficulties involved in reporting rape, the actual incidence is not easily determined (Wolitzky-Taylor & others, 2011). A recent national study found that 7.4 percent of U.S. ninth- to twelfth-grade students reported that they had been physically forced to have intercourse against their will (Eaton & others, 2010). In this study, 10.5 percent of the female students and 4.5 percent of the male students reported they had been forced to have sexual intercourse.

What are some characteristics of date or acquaintance rape?

Why is rape so pervasive in the American culture? Feminist writers assert that males are socialized to be sexually aggressive, to regard females as inferior beings, and to view their own pleasure as the most important objective. Researchers have found the following characteristics common among rapists: Aggression enhances their sense of power or masculinity; they are angry at females generally; and they want to hurt their victims. Research indicates that rape is more likely to occur when alcohol and marijuana are being used (Fair & Vanyur, 2011; Testa, Hoffman, & Livingston, 2010). A recent study revealed that regardless of whether or not the victim was using substances, sexual assault was more likely to occur when the offender was using substances (Brecklin & Ullman, 2010).

A form of rape that went unacknowledged until recent decades is **date,** or **acquaintance, rape,** which is coercive sexual activity directed at someone whom the perpetrator knows. Acquaintance rape is an increasing problem in high schools and on college campuses (Alleyne & others, 2011; Ball, Kerig, & Rosenbluth, 2009). A major study that focused on campus sexual assault involved a phone survey of 4,446 women attending two- or four-year colleges (Fisher, Cullen, & Turner, 2000). In this study, slightly less than 3 percent said that they had

rape Forcible sexual intercourse with a person who does not give consent.

date, or **acquaintance, rape** Coercive sexual activity directed at someone whom the perpetrator knows.

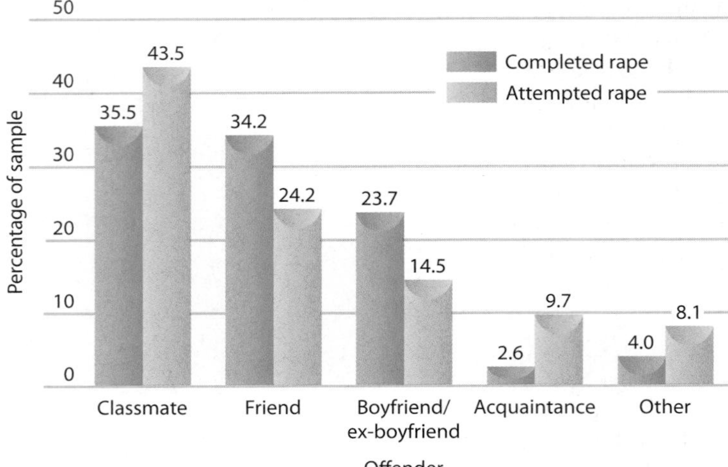

FIGURE **6.9**

COMPLETED RAPE AND ATTEMPTED RAPE OF COLLEGE WOMEN ACCORDING TO VICTIM-OFFENDER RELATIONSHIP

experienced either rape or an attempted rape during the academic year. About one of ten college women said that they had experienced rape in their lifetime. Unwanted or uninvited sexual contacts were widespread, with more than one-third of the college women reporting such incidents. As shown in Figure 6.9, in this study most women (about nine of ten) knew the person who sexually victimized them. Most of the women attempted to take protective actions against their assailants but were then reluctant to report the victimization to the police. Several factors were associated with sexual victimization: living on campus, being unmarried, getting drunk frequently, and having been sexually victimized on a prior occasion.

A number of colleges and universities describe the *red zone* as a period of time early in the first year of college when women are at especially high risk for unwanted sexual experiences. A recent study revealed that first-year women were more at risk for unwanted sexual experiences, especially early in the fall term, than were second-year women (Kimble & others, 2008).

developmental **connection**

Peers. Romantic relationships in adolescence often trigger positive and negative aspects of adjustment. Chapter 9, p. 315

In another study, about two-thirds of the sexual victimization incidents were perpetrated by a romantic acquaintance (Flanagan, 1996). In yet another study, approximately 2,000 ninth- through twelfth-grade girls were asked about the extent to which they had experienced physical and sexual violence (Silverman & others, 2001). About 20 percent of the girls said they had been physically or sexually abused by a dating partner. Further, the physical and sexual abuse was linked with substance use.

Rape is a traumatic experience for the victim and those close to her or him (Amstadter & others, 2011; Zinzow & others, 2011). The rape victim initially feels shock and numbness and often is acutely disorganized. Some women show their distress through words and tears; others show more internalized suffering. As victims strive to get their lives back to normal, they might experience depression, fear, and anxiety for months or years (Zinzow & others, 2010). Sexual dysfunctions, such as reduced sexual desire and the inability to reach orgasm, occur in 50 percent of rape victims. Many rape victims make lifestyle changes, moving to a new apartment or refusing to go out at night. About one-fifth of rape victims have made a suicide attempt—a rate eight times higher than that of women who have not been raped.

A girl's or woman's recovery depends on both her coping abilities and her psychological adjustment prior to the assault (Macy, Nurius, & Norris, 2006). Social support from parents, partner, and others close to her are also important factors in recovery, as is the availability of professional counseling, sometimes obtained through a rape crisis center. Many rape victims become empowered by reporting their rape to the police and assisting in the prosecution of the rapist if caught. However, women who take a legal approach are especially encouraged to use supportive counselors to aid them throughout the legal ordeal. Each female must be allowed to make her own, individual decision about whether to report the rape or not.

Although most victims of rape are girls and women, rape of boys and men does occur. Men in prisons are especially vulnerable to rape, usually by heterosexuals who are using homosexual rape to establish their domination and power within the prison.

Sexual Harassment Girls and women encounter sexual harassment in many different forms—ranging from sexist remarks and covert physical contact (patting, brushing against bodies) to blatant propositions and sexual assaults (Taylor, Stein, & Burden, 2010). Literally millions of girls and women experience such sexual harassment each year in educational and work settings. A recent study of adolescent girls indicated that most (90 percent) of the girls said they had experienced sexual harassment at least once (Leaper & Brown, 2008). In this study, 52 percent of the schools reported that they had experienced academic sexism (involving science, math, and computer technology) and 76 percent said that they had encountered athletic sexism.

A survey of 2,000 college women by the American Association of University Women (2006) revealed that 62 percent of them reported that they had experienced sexual harassment while attending college. Most of the college women said that the sexual harassment involved noncontact forms such as crude jokes, remarks, and gestures. However, almost one-third said that the sexual harassment was physical in nature. A recent study of almost 1,500 college women revealed that when they had been sexually harassed they reported an increase in psychological distress, greater physical illness, and an increase in disordered eating (Huerta & others, 2006).

The Office for Civil Rights in the U.S. Department of Education published a 40-page policy guide on sexual harassment. In this guide, a distinction is made between quid pro quo and hostile environment sexual harassment (Chmielewski, 1997):

- **Quid pro quo sexual harassment** occurs when a school employee threatens to base an educational decision (such as a grade) on a student's submission to unwelcome sexual conduct. For example, a teacher gives a student an A for allowing the teacher's sexual advances, or the teacher gives the student an F for resisting the teacher's approaches.
- **Hostile environment sexual harassment** occurs when students are subjected to unwelcome sexual conduct that is so severe, persistent, or pervasive that it limits the students' ability to benefit from their education. Such a hostile environment is usually created by a series of incidents, such as repeated sexual overtures.

Quid pro quo and hostile environment sexual harassment are illegal in the workplace as well as in educational settings, but potential victims are often not given access to a clear reporting and investigation mechanism where they can make a complaint.

Sexual harassment is a form of power and dominance of one person over another, which can result in harmful consequences for the victim. Sexual harassment can be especially damaging when the perpetrators are teachers, employers, and other adults who have considerable power and authority over students. As a society, we need to be less tolerant of sexual harassment (Das, 2009).

quid pro quo sexual harassment Sexual harassment in which a school employee threatens to base an educational decision (such as a grade) on a student's submission to unwelcome sexual conduct.

hostile environment sexual harassment Sexual harassment in which students are subjected to unwelcome sexual conduct that is so severe, persistent, or pervasive that it limits the students' ability to benefit from their education.

Review *Connect* Reflect

Describe the main negative sexual outcomes that can emerge in adolescence.

Review

- How would you characterize adolescent pregnancy?
- What are the main sexually transmitted infections in adolescence?
- What is the nature of forcible sexual behavior and sexual harassment in adolescence?

Connect

- Connect what you learned about sexually transmitted infections in this chapter to the discussion of adolescent health and well-being in Chapter 2.

Reflect *Your Own Personal Journey of Life*

- Have you experienced any of the negative sexual outcomes in adolescence and emerging adulthood that have just been described—adolescent pregnancy, sexually transmitted infections, forcible sexual behavior, or sexual harassment? If so, is there anything you could have done differently to avoid the negative outcome(s)? If you didn't experience these negative outcomes, what factors likely contributed to these outcomes?

4 Sexual Literacy and Sex Education

LG4 Characterize the sexual literacy of adolescents and sex education.

Sexual Literacy | Sources of Sex Information | Cognitive Factors | Sex Education in Schools

Given the high rate of STIs, a special concern is the knowledge that both adolescents and adults have about these infections and about other aspects of sexuality. How sexually literate are Americans? What are adolescents' sources of sex education? What cognitive factors might be involved in whether sex education is effective? What is the role of schools in sex education?

SEXUAL LITERACY

According to June Reinisch (1990), director of the Kinsey Institute for Sex, Gender, and Reproduction, U.S. citizens know more about how their automobiles function than about how their bodies function sexually. American adolescents and adults are not sheltered from sexual messages; indeed, Reinisch says, adolescents too often are inundated with sexual messages, but not sexual facts. Sexual information is abundant, but much of it is misinformation. In some cases, even sex education teachers display sexual ignorance. One high school sex education teacher referred to erogenous zones as "erroneous zones," causing students to wonder if their sexually sensitive zones were in error!

SOURCES OF SEX INFORMATION

Adolescents can get information about sex from many sources, including parents, siblings, other relatives, schools, peers, magazines, television, and the Internet. A special concern is the accuracy of sexual information adolescents have access to on the Internet. A recent study revealed that adolescents' most frequent sources of information about sexuality were friends, teachers, mothers, and the media (Bleakley & others, 2009). In this study, learning about sex from parents, grandparents, and religious leaders was linked with adolescent beliefs likely to delay having sexual intercourse, whereas learning about sex from friends, cousins, and the media was related to beliefs likely to increase the likelihood of having sexual intercourse earlier.

Many parents feel uncomfortable talking about sex with adolescents, and many adolescents feel uncomfortable about this as well (Guilamo-Ramos & others, 2008). One study revealed that 94 percent of fathers and 76 percent of mothers had never discussed sexual desire with their daughters (Feldman & Rosenthal, 1999).

Many adolescents say that they cannot talk freely with their parents about sexual matters, but those who can talk with their parents openly and freely about sex are less likely to be sexually active (Chia-Chen & Thompson, 2007). Contraceptive use by female adolescents also increases when adolescents report that they can communicate about sex with their parents (Fisher, 1987). Also, a recent study found that first semester college women who felt more comfortable talking openly about sex with their mothers were more likely to have positive beliefs about condoms and confidence in using them (Lefkowitz & Espinosa-Hernandez, 2006).

Adolescents are far more likely to have conversations about sex with their mothers than with their fathers (Kirkman, Rosenthal, & Feldman, 2002). This tendency is true of both female and male adolescents, although female adolescents report having more frequent conversations about sex with their mothers than their male counterparts do (Feldman & Rosenthal, 2002).

COGNITIVE FACTORS

Cognitive changes have intriguing implications for adolescents' sex education (Lipsitz, 1980). With their developing idealism and ability to think in more abstract and hypothetical ways, some young adolescents may become immersed in a mental world far removed from reality. They may see themselves as omnipotent and indestructible and believe that bad things cannot or will not happen to them, characteristics of adolescent egocentrism we discussed in Chapter 3. Consider the personal fable aspect of adolescent egocentrism reflected in this 14-year-old's words: "Hey, it won't happen to me." However, increasingly it is recognized that a majority of adolescents see themselves as more vulnerable than invulnerable (Fischhoff & others, 2010).

developmental **connection**

Social Cognition. The personal fable involves an adolescent's sense of personal uniqueness and invulnerability. Chapter 3, p. 121

Informing adolescents about contraceptives is not enough—what seems to predict whether or not they will use contraceptives is their acceptance of themselves and their sexuality. This acceptance requires not only emotional maturity but cognitive maturity.

Most discussions of adolescent pregnancy and its prevention assume that adolescents have the ability to anticipate consequences, to weigh the probable outcome of behavior, and to project into the future what will happen if they engage in certain acts, such as sexual intercourse. That is, prevention is based on the belief that adolescents have the cognitive ability to approach problem solving in a planned, organized, and analytical manner. However, although many adolescents 16 years of age and older have these capacities, it does not mean they use them, especially in emotionally charged situations, such as when they are sexually aroused or are being pressured by a partner.

Indeed, young adolescents (10 to 15 years of age) seem to experience sex in a depersonalized way that is filled with anxiety and denial. This depersonalized orientation toward sex is not likely to lead to preventive behavior. Middle adolescents (15 to 17 years of age) often romanticize sexuality. Late adolescents (18 to 19 years of age) are to some degree realistic and future-oriented about sexual experiences, just as they are about careers and marriage.

SEX EDUCATION IN SCHOOLS

A recent survey revealed that 89 percent of parents in Minnesota recommended teaching adolescents about both abstinence and comprehensive sex education that includes contraception information (Eisenberg & others, 2008). The parents said that most sex education topics should first be introduced in middle schools. Other surveys also indicate that a large percentage of U.S. parents want schools to provide adolescents with comprehensive sex education (Constantine, Jerman, & Juang, 2007; Ito & others, 2006). A recent study indicated that parents think adolescents too often get their information about sex from friends and the media (Lagus & others, 2011).

One survey found that 93 percent of Americans support the teaching of sex education in high schools, and 84 percent support its teaching in middle/junior high schools (SIECUS, 1999). The dramatic increase in HIV/AIDS and other STIs is the main reason that Americans have increasingly supported sex education in schools in recent years. This survey also found that more than eight of ten Americans think that adolescents should be given information to protect themselves from unwanted pregnancies and STIs, as well as about abstinence. In a recent national survey, 87 percent of ninth- to twelfth-grade students said that they had been taught in school about AIDS or HIV (Eaton & others, 2010).

The nature of sex education in schools is changing. U.S. schools today increasingly focus on abstinence and are less likely to present students with comprehensive teaching that includes information about birth control, abortion, and sexual orientation (Hampton, 2008). To read further about sex education in the United States and around the world, see the *Connecting with Health and Well-Being* interlude.

The AIDS epidemic has led to an increased awareness of the importance of sex education in adolescence.

In many countries, contraceptive knowledge is included in sex education. Here students in a sex education class in Beijing, China, learn about condoms.

connecting with health and well-being

What Is the Most Effective Sex Education?

Currently, a major controversy in sex education is whether schools should have an abstinence-only program or a program that emphasizes contraceptive knowledge. Two recent research reviews found that abstinence-only programs do not delay the initiation of sexual intercourse and do not reduce HIV risk behaviors (Kirby, Laris, & Rolleri, 2007; Underhill, Montgomery, & Operario, 2007). Further, a recent study revealed that adolescents who experienced comprehensive sex education were less likely to report adolescent pregnancies than those who were given abstinence-only sex education or no sex education (Kohler, Manhart, & Lafferty, 2008). Some sex education programs are starting to adopt an abstinence-plus sexuality approach that promotes abstinence as well as contraceptive use (Realini & others, 2010). A number of leading experts on adolescent sexuality now conclude that sex education programs that emphasize contraceptive knowledge do not increase the incidence of sexual intercourse and are more likely to reduce the risk of adolescent pregnancy and sexually transmitted infections than are abstinence-only programs (Constantine, 2008; Eisenberg & others, 2008; Hampton, 2008; Hyde & DeLamater, 2011).

U.S. sex education typically has focused on the hazards of sex and the need to protect adolescent females from male predators. The contrast between the United States and other Western nations is remarkable (Hampton, 2008). For example, the Swedish State Commission on Sex Education recommends that students gain knowledge to help them to experience sexual life as a source of happiness and fellowship with others. Swedish adolescents are sexually active at an earlier age than are American adolescents, and they are exposed to even more explicit sex on television. However, the Swedish National Board of Education has developed a curriculum to give every child, beginning at age 7, a thorough grounding in reproductive biology and, by the age of 10 or 12, information about various forms of contraception. Teachers handle the subject of sex whenever it becomes relevant, regardless of the subject they are teaching. The idea is to dedramatize and demystify sex so that familiarity will make students less vulnerable to unwanted pregnancy and STIs. Despite a relatively early onset of sexual activity, the adolescent pregnancy rate in Sweden is one of the lowest in the world.

Why do you suppose that, despite the evidence, sex education in U.S. schools today increasingly focuses on abstinence?

How is sex education in Sweden different from sex education in the United States?

Review *Connect* Reflect

 Characterize the sexual literacy of adolescents and sex education.

Review

- How sexually literate are U.S. adolescents?
- What are adolescents' sources of sexual information?
- What cognitive factors might be involved in the effectiveness of sex education?
- How would you describe sex education in schools?

Connect

- Recall what you learned in Chapter 3 about adolescent attention and memory. How does that information support this section's discussion of adolescents and sexual literacy?

Reflect *Your Own Personal Journey of Life*

- Think about how you learned the "facts of life." Did most of your information come from well-informed sources? Were you able to talk freely and openly with your parents about what to expect sexually? Did you acquire some false beliefs through trial-and-error efforts? As you grew older, did you discover that some of what you thought you knew about sex was inaccurate? Think also about the sex education you received in school. How adequate was it? What do you wish the schools you attended would have done differently in regard to sex education?

reach your **learning goals**

1 Exploring Adolescent Sexuality

LG1 Discuss some basic ideas about the nature of adolescent sexuality.

A Normal Aspect of Adolescent Development

- Too often the problems adolescents encounter with sexuality are emphasized rather than the fact that sexuality is a normal aspect of adolescent development. Adolescence is a bridge between the asexual child and the sexual adult. Adolescent sexuality is related to many other aspects of adolescent development, including physical development and puberty, cognitive development, the self and identity, gender, families, peers, schools, and culture.

The Sexual Culture

- Increased permissiveness in adolescent sexuality is linked to increased permissiveness in the larger culture. Adolescent initiation of sexual intercourse is related to exposure to explicit sex on TV.

Developing a Sexual Identity

- Developing a sexual identity is multifaceted. An adolescent's sexual identity involves an indication of sexual orientation, interests, and styles of behavior.

Obtaining Research Information About Adolescent Sexuality

- Obtaining valid information about adolescent sexuality is not easy. Much of the data are based on interviews and questionnaires, which can involve untruthful or socially desirable responses.

2 Sexual Attitudes and Behavior

 Summarize sexual attitudes and behavior in adolescence.

Heterosexual Attitudes and Behavior

- The progression of sexual behaviors is typically kissing, petting, sexual intercourse, and oral sex. The number of adolescents reporting having had sexual intercourse increased significantly in the twentieth century. The proportion of females engaging in intercourse increased more rapidly than for males. National data indicate that slightly more than half of all adolescents today have had sexual intercourse by age 17, although the percentage varies by sex, ethnicity, and context. Male, African American, and inner-city adolescents report the highest sexual activity. The percentage of 15- to 17-year-olds who have had sexual intercourse declined from 1991 to

2001. A common adolescent sexual script involves the male making sexual advances, and it is left up to the female to set limits on the male's sexual overtures. Adolescent females' sexual scripts link sex with love more than adolescent males' sexual scripts do. Risk factors for sexual problems include early sexual activity, having a number of sexual partners, not using contraception, engaging in other at-risk behaviors such as drinking and delinquency, living in a low-SES neighborhood, and ethnicity, as well as cognitive factors such as attentional problems and low self-regulation. Heterosexual behavior patterns change in emerging adulthood.

Sexual Minority Attitudes and Behavior

- An individual's sexual attraction—whether heterosexual or sexual minority—is likely caused by a mix of genetic, hormonal, cognitive, and environmental factors. Terms such as "sexual minority individuals" (who identify with being a gay, lesbian, or bisexual) and "same-sex attraction" are increasingly used, whereas the term "homosexual" is used less frequently. Developmental pathways for sexual minority youth are often diverse, may involve bisexual attractions, and do not always involve falling in love with a same-sex individual. Recent research has focused on adolescents' disclosure of same-sex attractions and the struggle they often go through in doing this. The peer relations of sexual minority youth differ from those of heterosexual youth. Sexual minority youth are more likely to engage in substance abuse, show sexual risk-taking behavior, and be the target of violence in a number of contexts. Discrimination and bias against same-sex attraction produce considerable stress for adolescents with a same-sex attraction. The stigma, discrimination, and rejection experienced by sexual minority youth are thought to explain why they may develop problems. Despite such negative experiences, many sexual minority youth successfully cope with the challenges they face and have health and well-being outcomes that are similar to their heterosexual counterparts.

Self-Stimulation

- Self-stimulation, or masturbation, is part of the sexual activity of virtually all adolescents and one of their most frequent sexual outlets.

Contraceptive Use

- Adolescents are increasing their use of contraceptives, but large numbers of sexually active adolescents still do not use them. Adolescents from low-SES backgrounds are less likely to use contraceptives than are their middle-SES counterparts.

3 Negative Sexual Outcomes in Adolescence

Describe the main negative sexual outcomes that can emerge in adolescence.

Adolescent Pregnancy

- The U.S. adolescent pregnancy rate is one of the highest in the Western world. Fortunately, the U.S. adolescent pregnancy rate has declined in the last two decades. A complex, impassioned issue involving an unintended pregnancy is the decision of whether to have an abortion. Adolescent pregnancy increases health risks for the mother and the offspring. Adolescent mothers are more likely to drop out of school and have lower-paying jobs than their adolescent counterparts who do not bear children. It is important to remember, though, that it often is not pregnancy alone that places adolescents at risk. Adolescent mothers frequently come from low-income families and were not doing well in school prior to their pregnancy. The infants of adolescent parents are at risk both medically and psychologically. Adolescent parents are less effective in rearing their children than older parents are. Many adolescent fathers do not have a close relationship with their baby and the adolescent mother. Recommendations for reducing adolescent pregnancy include sex education and family planning, access to contraception, life options, community involvement and support, and abstinence. In one study, volunteer community service was linked with a lower incidence of adolescent pregnancy.

Sexually Transmitted Infections

- Sexually transmitted infections (STIs) are contracted primarily through sexual contact with an infected partner. The contact is not limited to vaginal intercourse but includes oral-genital and anal-genital contact as well. AIDS stands for acquired immunodeficiency syndrome, a sexually transmitted infection that is caused by the human immunodeficiency virus (HIV), which destroys the body's immune system. Currently, the rate of AIDS in U.S. adolescents is relatively low, but it has reached epidemic proportions in sub-Saharan Africa, especially in adolescent girls. AIDS can be transmitted through sexual contact, sharing needles, and blood transfusions. A number of projects are focusing on AIDS prevention. Genital herpes is caused by a family of viruses with different strains. Genital warts, caused by a virus, is the most common STI in the 15- to 24-year-old age group. Commonly called the "drip" or "clap," gonorrhea is another common STI. Syphilis is caused by the bacterium *Treponema pallidum,* a spirochete. Chlamydia is one of the most common STIs.

Forcible Sexual Behavior and Sexual Harassment

- Some individuals force others to have sex with them. Rape is forcible sexual intercourse with a person who does not give consent. About 95 percent of rapes are committed by males. An increasing concern is date, or acquaintance, rape. Sexual harassment is a form of power of one person over another. Sexual harassment of adolescents is widespread. Two forms are quid pro quo and hostile environment sexual harassment.

4 Sexual Literacy and Sex Education

Characterize the sexual literacy of adolescents and sex education.

Sexual Literacy

- American adolescents and adults are not very knowledgeable about sex. Sex information is abundant, but too often it is misinformation.

Sources of Sex Information

- Adolescents can get their information about sex from many sources, including parents, siblings, schools, peers, magazines, TV, and the Internet.

Cognitive Factors

- Cognitive factors, such as idealism and the personal fable, can make it difficult for sex education to be effective, especially with young adolescents.

Sex Education in Schools

- A majority of Americans support teaching sex education in schools, and this support has increased in concert with increases in STIs, especially AIDS. Some experts believe that school-linked sex education that ties in with community health centers is a promising strategy.

key terms

sexual script 193
sexual minority 197
bisexual 197
homophobia 199
sexually transmitted infections (STIs) 208
AIDS 208
genital herpes 211
genital warts 211
gonorrhea 211
syphilis 212
chlamydia 212
rape 213
date, or acquaintance, rape 213
quid pro quo sexual harassment 215
hostile environment sexual harassment 215

key people

Bonnie Halpern-Felsher 192
Deborah Tolman 194
Ritch Savin-Williams 199
June Reinisch 216

resources for **improving the lives of adolescents**

AIDS Hotline
National AIDS Information Clearinghouse
800-342-AIDS
800-344-SIDA (Spanish)
800-AIDS-TTY (Deaf)

The people answering the hotline will respond to any questions children, youth, or adults have about HIV infection or AIDS. Pamphlets and other materials on AIDS are available.

Alan Guttmacher Institute ***www.guttmacher.org***
The Alan Guttmacher Institute is an especially good resource for information about adolescent sexuality. The Institute publishes a well-respected journal, *Perspectives on Sexual and Reproductive Health* (renamed in 2003, formerly *Family Planning Perspectives*), which includes articles on many dimensions of sexuality, such as adolescent pregnancy, statistics on sexual behavior and attitudes, and sexually transmitted infections.

Adolescent Sexuality
by Lisa Diamond and Ritch Savin-Williams (2009)
in R. M. Lerner & L. Steinberg (Eds.),
Handbook of Adolescent Psychology
New York: Wiley

Leading researchers on adolescent gay males and lesbians, Lisa Diamond and Ritch Savin-Williams examine many aspects of their development and relationships, as well as sexual behavior in heterosexual adolescents.

National Sexually Transmitted Diseases Hotline
800-227-8922

This hotline provides information about a wide variety of sexually transmitted infections.

Sex Information and Education Council of the United States (SIECUS) ***www.siecus.org***
This organization serves as an information clearinghouse about sex education. The group's objective is to promote the concept of human sexuality as an integration of physical, intellectual, emotional, and social dimensions.

self-**assessment**

The Student Online Learning Center includes the following self-assessments for further exploration:

- *My Knowledge of Sexual Myths and Realities*
- *How Much Do I Know About STIs?*

chapter 7 MORAL DEVELOPMENT, VALUES, AND RELIGION

chapter **outline**

Domains of Moral Development

Learning Goal 1 Discuss the domains of moral development.

Moral Thought
Moral Behavior
Moral Feeling
Moral Personality

Contexts of Moral Development

Learning Goal 2 Describe how the contexts of parenting and schools can influence moral development.

Parenting
Schools

Values, Religion, and Spirituality

Learning Goal 3 Explain the roles of values, religion, and spirituality in adolescents' and emerging adults' lives.

Values
Religion and Spirituality

Jewel Cash, seated next to her mother, participating in a crime-watch meeting at a community center. She is an exemplar of positive teenage community involvement.

The mayor of the city says that she is "everywhere." She recently persuaded the city's school committee to consider ending the practice of locking tardy students out of their classrooms. She also swayed a neighborhood group to support her proposal for a winter jobs program. According to one city councilman, "People are just impressed with the power of her arguments and the sophistication of the argument" (Silva, 2005, pp. B1, B4). She is Jewel E. Cash, and she is just 16 years old.

A junior at Boston Latin Academy, Jewel was raised in one of Boston's housing projects by her mother, a single parent. Today she is a member of the Boston Student Advisory Council, mentors children, volunteers at a woman's shelter, manages and dances in two troupes, and is a member of a neighborhood watch group—among other activities. Jewel told an interviewer from the *Boston Globe,* "I see a problem and I say, 'How can I make a difference?' . . . I can't take on the world, even though I can try. . . . I'm moving forward but I want to make sure I'm bringing people with me." (Silva, 2005, pp. B1, B4).

preview

Jewel Cash's caring for people in her community reflects the positive side of moral development, a major focus of this chapter. Moral development involves the distinction between what is right and wrong, what matters to people, and what people should do in their interactions with others. We begin by discussing the three main traditional domains of moral development—moral thoughts, behavior, and feeling—and the recent emphasis on moral personality. Next, we explore the contexts in which moral development takes place, focusing on families and schools. We conclude with an examination of adolescent values, religion, and spirituality.

1 Domains of Moral Development

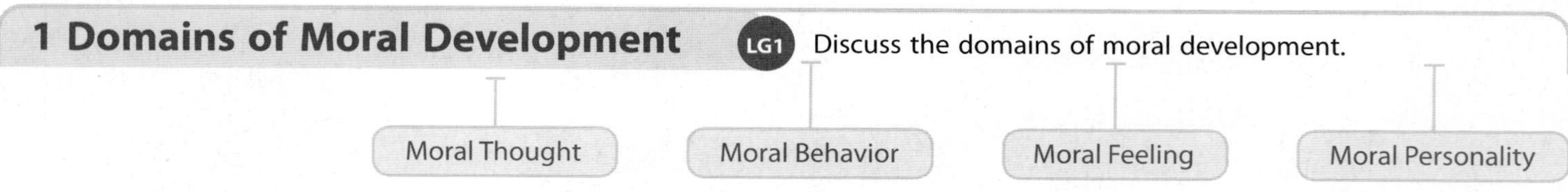

Moral development involves thoughts, behaviors, and feelings regarding standards of right and wrong. Moral development has an intrapersonal dimension (a person's basic values and sense of self) and an interpersonal dimension (a focus on what people should do in their interactions with other people). The intrapersonal dimension regulates a person's activities when she or he is not engaged in social interaction. The interpersonal dimension regulates people's social interactions and arbitrates conflict. Let's now further explore some basic ideas about moral thoughts, feelings, and behaviors.

moral development Thoughts, feelings, and behaviors regarding standards of right and wrong.

First, how do adolescents *reason*, or think, about rules for ethical conduct? For example, we might present an adolescent with a story in which someone has a conflict about whether or not to cheat in a specific situation, such as taking an exam in school. The adolescent is asked to decide what is appropriate for the character to do and why. The focus is placed on the reasoning adolescents use to justify their moral decisions.

Second, how do adolescents actually *behave* in moral circumstances? For example, with regard to cheating, we might observe adolescents' cheating and the environmental circumstances that produced and maintain the cheating. We could conduct our study through a one-way mirror as adolescents are taking an exam. We might note whether they take out "cheat" notes, look at another student's answers, and so on.

Third, how do adolescents *feel* about moral matters? In the example of cheating, do the adolescents feel enough guilt to resist temptation? If adolescents do cheat, do feelings of guilt after the transgression keep them from cheating the next time they face temptation?

The remainder of this discussion of moral development focuses on these three facets—thought, behavior, and feelings—and a new approach that emphasizes moral personality. Keep in mind that, although we have separated moral development into three components—thought, behavior, and feelings—the components often are interrelated. For example, if the focus is on the adolescent's behavior, it is still important to evaluate the adolescent's intentions (moral thought). Similarly, emotions accompany, and can distort, moral reasoning.

MORAL THOUGHT

How do adolescents think about standards of right and wrong? Piaget had some thoughts about this, but they applied to children's moral development. It was Lawrence Kohlberg (1958, 1976, 1986) who crafted a major theory of how adolescents think about right and wrong. He proposed that moral development is based primarily on moral reasoning and unfolds in a series of stages.

Kohlberg's Stages Central to Kohlberg's work on moral development were interviews with individuals of different ages. In the interviews, individuals were presented with a series of stories in which characters face moral dilemmas. The following is the most cited of the Kohlberg dilemmas:

> In Europe, a woman was near death from a special kind of cancer. There was one drug that the doctors thought might save her. It was a form of radium that a druggist in the same town had recently discovered. The drug was expensive to make, but the druggist was charging ten times what the drug cost him to make. He paid $200 for the radium and charged $2,000 for a small dose of the drug. The sick woman's husband, Heinz, went to everyone he knew to borrow the money, but he could only get together $1,000, which is half of what it cost. He told the druggist that his wife was dying and asked him to sell it cheaper or let him pay later. But the druggist said, "No, I discovered the drug, and I am going to make money from it." So Heinz got desperate and broke into the man's store to steal the drug for his wife. (Kohlberg, 1969, p. 379)

This story is one of eleven that Kohlberg devised to investigate the nature of moral thought. After reading the story, interviewees are asked a series of questions about the moral dilemma: Should Heinz have stolen the drug? Was stealing it right or wrong? Why? Is it a husband's duty to steal the drug for his wife if he can get it no other way? Would a good husband steal it? Did the druggist have the right to charge that much when there was no law setting a limit on the price? Why?

From the answers interviewees gave for this and other moral dilemmas, Kohlberg hypothesized three levels of moral development, each of which is characterized by two stages (see Figure 7.1). A key concept in understanding progression through the levels and stages is that their morality becomes more internal or mature. That is, their reasons for their moral decisions or values begin to go beyond the external or superficial reasons they gave when they were younger. Let's further examine Kohlberg's stages.

Lawrence Kohlberg.

LEVEL 1	LEVEL 2	LEVEL 3
Preconventional Level **No Internalization**	**Conventional Level** **Intermediate Internalization**	**Postconventional Level** **Full Internalization**
Stage 1 Heteronomous Morality *Individuals pursue their own interests but let others do the same. What is right involves equal exchange.*	**Stage 3** Mutual Interpersonal Expectations, Relationships, and Interpersonal Conformity *Individuals value trust, caring, and loyalty to others as a basis for moral judgments.*	**Stage 5** Social Contract or Utility and Individual Rights *Individuals reason that values, rights, and principles undergird or transcend the law.*
Stage 2 Individualism, Purpose, and Exchange *Children obey because adults tell them to obey. People base their moral decisions on fear of punishment.*	**Stage 4** Social System Morality *Moral judgments are based on understanding and the social order, law, justice, and duty.*	**Stage 6** Universal Ethical Principles *The person has developed moral judgments that are based on universal human rights. When faced with a dilemma between law and conscience, a personal, individualized conscience is followed.*

FIGURE **7.1**

KOHLBERG'S THREE LEVELS AND SIX STAGES OF MORAL DEVELOPMENT

Kohlberg's Level 1: Preconventional Reasoning **Preconventional reasoning** is the lowest level in Kohlberg's theory of moral development. Its two stages are punishment and obedience orientation; individualism, instrumental purpose, and exchange.

- Stage 1. *Punishment and obedience orientation* is the first Kohlberg stage of moral development. At this stage, moral thinking is often tied to punishment. For example, children and adolescents obey adults because adults tell them to obey.
- Stage 2. *Individualism, instrumental purpose, and exchange* is the second stage of Kohlberg's theory. At this stage, individuals pursue their own interests but also let others do the same. Thus, what is right involves an equal exchange. People are nice to others so that others will be nice to them in return. This stage has been described as reflecting an attitude of "What's in it for me?"

Kohlberg's Level 2: Conventional Reasoning **Conventional reasoning** is the second, or intermediate, level in Kohlberg's theory of moral development. Individuals abide by certain standards (internal), but they are the standards of others (external), such as parents or the laws of society. In conventional reasoning, individuals develop expectations about social roles. The conventional reasoning level consists of two stages: mutual interpersonal expectations, relationships, and interpersonal conformity; and social systems morality.

- Stage 3. *Mutual interpersonal expectations, relationships, and interpersonal conformity* is Kohlberg's third stage of moral development. At this stage, individuals value trust, caring, and loyalty to others as a basis of moral judgments. Children and adolescents often adopt their parents' moral standards at this stage, seeking to be thought of by their parents as a "good girl" or a "good boy."
- Stage 4. *Social systems morality* is the fourth stage in Kohlberg's theory of moral development. At this stage, moral judgments are based on understanding the social order, law, justice, and duty. For example, adolescents may say that, for a community to work effectively, it needs to be protected by laws that are adhered to by its members. Thus, in Stage 4 reasoning, individuals engage in social perspective taking that goes beyond intimate acquaintances to understanding the importance of being a good citizen.

Kohlberg's Level 3: Postconventional Reasoning **Postconventional reasoning** is the highest level in Kohlberg's theory of moral development. At this level, morality

preconventional reasoning The lowest level in Kohlberg's theory of moral development. At this level, morality is often focused on reward and punishment. The two stages in preconventional reasoning are punishment and obedience orientation (stage 1) and individualism, instrumental purpose, and exchange (stage 2).

conventional reasoning The second, or intermediate, level in Kohlberg's theory. Individuals abide by certain standards (internal), but they are the standards of others (external), such as parents or the laws of society. The conventional level consists of two stages: mutual interpersonal expectations, relationships, and interpersonal conformity (stage 3) and social systems morality (stage 4).

postconventional reasoning The third and highest level in Kohlberg's theory. At this level, morality is more internal. The postconventional level consists of two stages: social contract or utility and individual rights (stage 5) and universal ethical principles (stage 6).

Stage Description	Examples of Moral Reasoning that Support Heinz's Theft of the Drug	Examples of Moral Reasoning that Indicate that Heinz Should not Steal the Drug
	Preconventional Reasoning	
Stage 1: Punishment and obedience orientation	Heinz should not let his wife die; if he does, he will be in big trouble.	Heinz might get caught and sent to jail.
Stage 2: Individualism, instrumental purpose, and exchange	If Heinz gets caught, he could give the drug back and maybe they would not give him a long jail sentence.	The druggist is a businessman and needs to make money.
	Conventional Reasoning	
Stage 3: Mutual interpersonal expectations, relationships, and interpersonal conformity	Heinz was only doing something that a good husband would do; it shows how much he loves his wife.	If his wife dies, he can't be blamed for it; it is the druggist's fault. The druggist is the selfish one.
Stage 4: Social systems morality	It isn't morally wrong for Heinz to steal the drug in this case because the law is not designed to take into account every particular case or anticipate every circumstance.	Heinz should obey the law because laws serve to protect the productive and orderly functioning of society.
	Postconventional Reasoning	
Stage 5: Social contract or utility and individual rights	Heinz was justified in stealing the drug because a human life was at stake and that transcends any right the druggist had to the drug.	It is important to obey the law because laws represent a necessary structure of common agreement if individuals are to live together in society.
Stage 6: Universal ethical principles	Human life is sacred because of the universal principle of respect for the individual and it takes precedence over other values.	Heinz needs to decide whether or not to consider the other people who need the drug as badly as his wife does. He ought not to act based on his particular feelings for his wife, but consider the value of all the lives involved.

FIGURE **7.2**
MORAL REASONING AT KOHLBERG'S STAGES IN RESPONSE TO THE "HEINZ AND THE DRUGGIST" STORY

is more internal. The individual recognizes alternative moral courses, explores the options, and then decides on a moral code. In postconventional reasoning, individuals engage in deliberate checks on their reasoning to ensure it meets high ethical standards. The postconventional level of morality consists of two stages: social contract or utility and individual rights, and universal ethical principles.

- Stage 5. *Social contract or utility and individual rights* is the fifth Kohlberg stage. At this stage, individuals reason that values, rights, and principles undergird or transcend the law. A person evaluates the validity of actual laws and examines social systems in terms of the degree to which they preserve and protect fundamental human rights and values.
- Stage 6. *Universal ethical principles* is the sixth and highest stage in Kohlberg's theory of moral development. At this stage, the person has developed a moral standard based on universal human rights. When faced with a conflict between law and conscience, the person will follow conscience, even though the decision might involve personal risk.

How might individuals at each of the six Kohlberg stages respond to the "Heinz and the druggist" moral dilemma described earlier? Figure 7.2 provides some examples of these responses.

Kohlberg argued that these levels and stages occur in a sequence and are age-related: Before age 9, most children reason about moral dilemmas in a preconventional way; by early adolescence, they reason in more conventional ways. Most adolescents reason at stage 3, with some signs of stages 2 and 4. By early adulthood, a small number of individuals reason in postconventional ways. In a 20-year longitudinal investigation, the uses of stages 1 and 2 decreased (Colby & others, 1983)

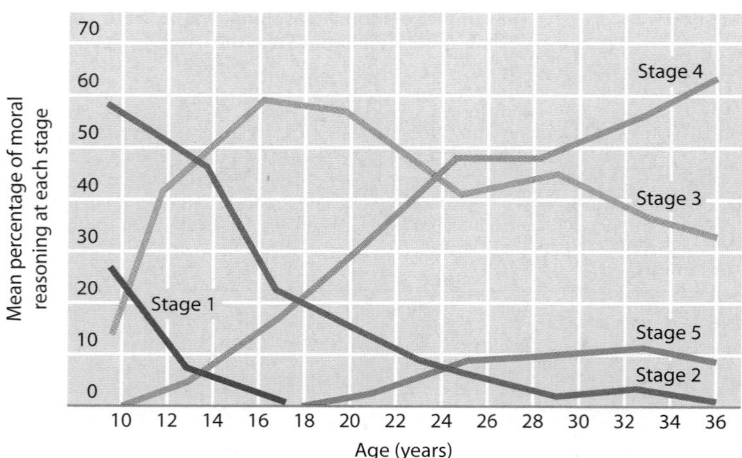

FIGURE **7.3**

AGE AND THE PERCENTAGE OF INDIVIDUALS AT EACH KOHLBERG STAGE. In one longitudinal study of males from 10 to 36 years of age, at age 10 most moral reasoning was at stage 2 (Colby & others, 1983). At 16 to 18 years of age, stage 3 became the most frequent type of moral reasoning and it was not until the mid-twenties that stage 4 became the most frequent. Stage 5 did not appear until 20 to 22 years of age and it never characterized more than 10 percent of the individuals. In this study, the moral stages appeared somewhat later than Kohlberg envisioned and stage 6 was absent.

(see Figure 7.3). Stage 4, which did not appear at all in the moral reasoning of 10-year-olds, was reflected in 62 percent of the moral thinking of 36-year-olds. Stage 5 did not appear until age 20 to 22 and never characterized more than 10 percent of the individuals. Thus, the moral stages appeared somewhat later than Kohlberg initially envisioned, and the higher stages, especially stage 6, were extremely elusive. Recently, stage 6 was removed from the Kohlberg moral judgment scoring manual, but it still is considered to be theoretically important in the Kohlberg scheme of moral development. A review of data from 45 studies in 27 diverse world cultures provided support for the universality of Kohlberg's first four stages but suggested that stages 5 and 6 tend to vary across cultures (Snarey, 1987).

Any change in moral reasoning between late adolescence and early adulthood appears to be relatively gradual (Eisenberg & others, 2009). One study found that when 16- to 19-year-olds and 18- to 25-year-olds were asked to reason about real-life moral dilemmas and coded using Kohlberg stages, there was no significant difference in their moral reasoning (Walker & others, 1995).

Influences on the Kohlberg Stages Kohlberg theorized that the individual's moral orientation unfolds as a consequence of cognitive development and exposure to appropriate social experiences. Children and adolescents construct their moral thoughts as they pass from one stage to the next, rather than passively accepting a cultural norm of morality. Investigators have sought to understand factors that influence movement through the moral stages, among them modeling, cognitive conflict, peer relations, and role-taking opportunities.

Several investigators have attempted to advance individuals' levels of moral development by having a model present arguments that reflect moral thinking one stage above the individuals' established levels. These studies are based on the cognitive developmental concepts of equilibrium and conflict (Walker & Taylor, 1991). By presenting moral information slightly beyond the individual's cognitive level, a disequilibrium is created that motivates a restructuring of moral thought. The resolution of the disequilibrium and conflict should be toward

Why did Kohlberg think peer relations are so important in moral development?

increased competence. In one study, participants did prefer stages higher than their own more than stages lower than their own (Walker, de Vries, & Bichard, 1984). In sum, moral thought can be moved to a higher level through exposure to models or discussion that is more advanced than the adolescent's level.

Like Piaget, Kohlberg emphasized that peer interaction is a critical part of the social stimulation that challenges individuals to change their moral orientation. Whereas adults characteristically impose rules and regulations on children, the mutual give-and-take in peer interaction provides the child with an opportunity to take the role of another person and to generate rules democratically (Rubin, Bukowski, & Parker, 2006). Kohlberg stressed that role-taking opportunities can, in principle, be engendered by any peer group encounter. Researchers have found that more advanced moral reasoning takes place when peers engage in challenging, even moderately conflicting, conversation (Berkowitz & Gibbs, 1983; Walker, Hennig, & Krettenauer, 2000).

Kohlberg did note that certain types of parent-child experiences can induce the child and adolescent to think at more advanced levels of moral reasoning. In particular, parents who allow or encourage conversation about value-laden issues promote more advanced moral thought in their children and adolescents. Unfortunately, many parents do not systematically provide their children and adolescents with such role-taking opportunities. Nonetheless, in one study, children's moral development was related to their parents' discussion style, which involved questioning and supportive interaction (Walker & Taylor, 1991). In recent years, there has been increasing emphasis on the role of parenting in moral development (Thompson & Newton, 2010).

Why Is Kohlberg's Theory Important for Understanding Moral Development in Adolescence? Kohlberg's theory is essentially a description of the progressive conceptions people use to understand social cooperation. In short, it tells the developmental story of people trying to understand things like society, rules and roles, and institutions and relationships. Such basic conceptions are fundamental to adolescents, for whom ideology becomes important in guiding their lives and making life decisions.

Kohlberg's Critics Kohlberg's theory provoked debate, research, and criticism (Gibbs, 2010; Helwig & Turiel, 2011; Narváez, 2010a,b; Walker & Frimer, 2011). The criticisms involve the link between moral thought and moral behavior, the quality of the research, inadequate consideration of culture's role in moral development, and underestimation of the care perspective.

Moral Thought and Moral Behavior Kohlberg's theory has been criticized for placing too much emphasis on moral thought and not enough emphasis on moral behavior. Moral reasons can always be a shelter for immoral behavior. Some bank embezzlers, presidents, and religious figures endorse the loftiest of moral virtues when commenting about moral dilemmas, but their own behavior may be immoral. No one wants a nation of cheaters and liars who can reason at the postconventional level. The cheaters and liars may know what is right and wrong yet still do what is wrong.

In evaluating the relation between moral thought and moral behavior, consider the corrupting power of rationalizations and other defenses that disengage us from self-blame; these include interpreting a situation in our favor and attributing blame to authorities, circumstances, or victims (Bandura, 1991). One area in which a link between moral judgment and behavior has been found involves antisocial behavior and delinquency. Researchers have found that less advanced moral reasoning in adolescence is related to antisocial behavior and delinquency (Gibbs, 2010; Taylor & Walker, 1997). One study also revealed that moral reasoning was related to self-reported altruism (Maclean, Walker, & Matsuba, 2004).

Given the terrorist attacks of September 11, 2001, and the continuing war on terrorism, it is intriguing to explore how heinous actions can be cloaked in a mantle

How does Bandura describe the way terrorists justify their actions?

of moral virtue and why that is especially dangerous. Social cognitive theorist Albert Bandura (1999, 2002) argues that people usually don't engage in harmful conduct until they have justified the morality of their actions to themselves. In this process of moral justification, immoral conduct is made personally and socially acceptable by portraying it as serving socially worthy or moral purposes. In many instances throughout history, perpetrators have twisted theology so that they see themselves as doing God's will. Bandura provides the example of Islamic extremists who mount their actions as self-defense against tyrannical, decadent people whom they see as seeking to enslave the Islamic world.

Assessment of Moral Reasoning Some developmentalists fault the quality of Kohlberg's research and stress that more attention should be paid to the way moral development is assessed. For example, James Rest (1986; Rest & others, 1999) argued that alternative methods should be used to collect information about moral thinking instead of relying on a single method that requires individuals to reason about hypothetical moral dilemmas. Rest also said that Kohlberg's stories are extremely difficult to score. To help remedy this problem, Rest developed his own measure of moral development, called the Defining Issues Test (DIT).

Unlike Kohlberg's procedure, the DIT attempts to determine which moral issues individuals feel are crucial in a given situation by presenting a series of dilemmas and a list of potential considerations in making a decision. In the dilemma of Heinz and the druggist, individuals are asked to rate such matters as whether a community's laws should be upheld or whether Heinz should be willing to risk being injured or caught as a burglar. They might also be asked to list the most important values that govern human interaction. They are given six stories and asked to rate the importance of each issue involved in deciding what ought to be done. Then they are asked to list what they believe are the four most important issues. Rest argued that this method provides a more valid and reliable way to assess moral thinking than does Kohlberg's method (Rest & others, 1999).

DIT researchers recently have described their theory as *neo-Kohlbergian*, reflecting a connection to Kohlberg's theory but an important shift away from his theory (Rest & others, 1999; Thoma, 2006). The departure from Kohlberg's theory includes replacement of his strong stage model with an emphasis on a gradual shift from lower-level to more complex moral thinking.

Researchers also have found that the hypothetical moral dilemmas posed in Kohlberg's stories do not match the moral dilemmas many children and adults face in their everyday lives (Walker, de Vries, & Trevethan, 1987; Yussen, 1977). Most of Kohlberg's stories focus on the family and authority. However, when one researcher invited adolescents to write stories about their own moral dilemmas, the adolescents generated dilemmas that were broader in scope, focusing on friends, acquaintances, and other issues, as well as family and authority (Yussen, 1977). The adolescents' moral dilemmas also were analyzed in terms of their content. As shown in Figure 7.4, the moral issue that concerned adolescents more than any other was interpersonal relationships.

	Grade		
Story subject	**7**	**9**	**12**
		Percentage	
Alcohol	2	0	5
Civil rights	0	6	7
Drugs	7	10	5
Interpersonal relations	38	24	35
Physical safety	22	8	3
Sexual relations	2	20	10
Smoking	7	2	0
Stealing	9	2	0
Working	2	2	15
Other	1	26	20

FIGURE **7.4**
ACTUAL MORAL DILEMMAS GENERATED BY ADOLESCENTS

Culture and Moral Development Kohlberg emphasized that his stages of moral reasoning are universal, but some critics claim his theory is culturally biased (Miller, 2007). Both Kohlberg and his critics may be partially correct. One review of forty-five studies in twenty-seven cultures around the world, mostly non-European, provided support for the universality of Kohlberg's first four stages (Snarey, 1987). Individuals in diverse cultures developed through these four stages in sequence as Kohlberg predicted. A more recent research review revealed support for the qualitative shift from stage 2 to stage 3 across cultures (Gibbs & others, 2007). Stages 5 and 6, however, have not been found in all cultures (Gibbs & others, 2007; Snarey, 1987). Furthermore, Kohlberg's scoring system does not recognize the higher-level moral reasoning of certain cultures and thus that moral reasoning is more culture-specific than Kohlberg envisioned (Snarey, 1987).

developmental **connection**

Research Methods. Cross-cultural studies provide information about the degree to which children's development is universal, or similar, across cultures or is culture-specific. Chapter 1, p. 12; Chapter 12, p. 393

In the view of John Gibbs (2010), most young adolescents around the world use the moral judgment of mutuality (stage 3) that makes intimate friendships possible. And by late adolescence, many individuals also are beginning to grasp the importance of agreed-upon standards and institutions for the common good (stage 4). A main exception, though, is the delayed moral judgment of adolescents who regularly engage in delinquency.

In sum, Kohlberg's approach captures much—but not all—of the moral reasoning voiced in various cultures around the world; as we have just seen, there are some important moral concepts in specific cultures that his approach misses or misconstrues (Miller, 2007).

A recent study explored links between culture, mindset, and moral judgment (Narváez & Hill, 2010). In this study, a higher level of multicultural experience was linked to closed mindedness (being cognitively inflexible), a growth mindset (perceiving that one's qualities can change and improve through effort), and higher moral judgment.

This 14-year-old boy in Nepal is thought to be the sixth holiest Buddhist in the world. In one study of 20 adolescent male Buddhist monks in Nepal, the issue of justice, a basic theme in Kohlberg's theory, was not a central focus in the monks' moral views (Huebner & Garrod, 1993). Also, the monks' concerns about prevention of suffering and the importance of compassion are not captured in Kohlberg's theory.

Gender and the Care Perspective The most publicized criticism of Kohlberg's theory has come from Carol Gilligan (1982, 1992, 1996), who argues that Kohlberg's theory reflects a gender bias. According to Gilligan, Kohlberg's theory is based on a male norm that puts abstract principles above relationships and concern for others and sees the individual as standing alone and independently making moral decisions. It puts justice at the heart of morality. In contrast to Kohlberg's **justice perspective,** Gilligan argues for a **care perspective,** which is a moral perspective that views people in terms of their connectedness with others and emphasizes interpersonal communication, relationships with others, and concern for others. According to Gilligan, Kohlberg greatly underplayed the care perspective, perhaps because he was a male, because most of his research was with males rather than females, and because he used male responses as a model for his theory.

In extensive interviews with girls from 6 to 18 years of age, Gilligan and her colleagues found that girls consistently interpret moral dilemmas in terms of human relationships and base these interpretations on listening and watching other people (Gilligan, 1992; Gilligan & others, 2003). However, a meta-analysis (a statistical analysis that combines the results of many different studies) casts doubt on Gilligan's claim of substantial gender differences in moral judgment (Jaffee & Hyde, 2000). And a recent analysis concluded that girls' moral orientations are "somewhat more likely to focus on care for others than on abstract principles of justice, but they can use both moral orientations when needed (as can boys . . .)" (Blakemore, Berenbaum, & Liben, 2009, p. 132).

developmental **connection**

Gender. Janet Shibley Hyde concluded that many views and studies of gender exaggerate differences. Chapter 5, p. 172

Domain Theory: Moral, Social Conventional, Personal Reasoning The **domain theory of moral development** states that there are different domains of social knowledge and reasoning, including moral, social conventional, and personal domains. In domain theory, children's and adolescents' moral, social conventional, and personal knowledge and reasoning emerge from their attempts to understand and deal with different forms of social experience (Helwig & Turiel, 2011; Nucci & Gingo, 2011; Smetana, 2011).

Some theorists and researchers argue that Kohlberg did not adequately distinguish between moral reasoning and social conventional reasoning (Helwig & Turiel, 2011; Nucci & Gingo, 2011; Smetana, 2011). **Social conventional reasoning** focuses on conventional rules that have been established by social consensus in order to control behavior and maintain the social system. The rules themselves are arbitrary, such as raising your hand in class before speaking, using one staircase at school to go up, the other to go down, not cutting in front of someone standing in line to buy movie tickets, and stopping at a stop sign when

justice perspective A moral perspective that focuses on the rights of the individual. Individuals independently make moral decisions.

care perspective The moral perspective of Carol Gilligan, which views people in terms of their connectedness with others and emphasizes interpersonal communication, relationships with others, and concern for others.

domain theory of moral development States that there are different domains of social knowledge and reasoning, including moral, social conventional, and personal domains. These domains arise from children's and adolescents' attempts to understand and deal with different forms of social experience.

social conventional reasoning Thoughts about social consensus and convention, as opposed to moral reasoning that stresses ethical issues.

driving. There are sanctions if we violate these conventions, although they can be changed by consensus.

In contrast, moral reasoning focuses on ethical issues and rules of morality. Unlike conventional rules, moral rules are not arbitrary. They are obligatory, widely accepted, and somewhat impersonal (Helwig & Turiel, 2011). Rules pertaining to lying, cheating, stealing, and physically harming another person are moral rules because violation of these rules affronts ethical standards that exist apart from social consensus and convention. Moral judgments involve concepts of justice, whereas social conventional judgments are concepts of social organization. Violating moral rules is usually more serious than violating conventional rules.

The social conventional approach is a serious challenge to Kohlberg's approach because Kohlberg argued that social conventions are a stop-over on the road to higher moral sophistication. For social conventional reasoning advocates, social conventional reasoning is not lower than postconventional reasoning but rather something that needs to be disentangled from the moral thread (Helwig & Turiel, 2011; Smetana, 2011).

Recently, a distinction also has been made between moral and conventional issues, which are viewed as legitimately subject to adult social regulation, and personal issues, which are more likely subject to the child's or adolescent's independent decision making and personal discretion (Helwig & Turiel, 2011; Nucci & Gingo, 2011; Smetana, 2011). Personal issues include control over one's body, privacy, and choice of friends and activities. Thus, some actions belong to a *personal* domain, not governed by moral strictures or social norms.

Moral, conventional, and personal domains of reasoning arise in families. Moral issues include such areas as lying to parents about engaging in a deviant behavior and stealing money from a sibling. Conventional issues involve such matters as curfews and who takes out the garbage. Personal issues involve such things as what music to like, styles of dress, what to put on the walls of one's bedroom, and which friends to choose.

In domain theory, boundaries are developed regarding adult authority, which can produce parent-adolescent conflict. Adolescents have a large personal domain and most parents can live with that; however, parents have a larger moral domain than adolescents think is reasonable (Smetana, 2011).

MORAL BEHAVIOR

We saw that one of the criticisms of Kohlberg's theory is that it does not give adequate attention to the link between moral thought and moral behavior. In our exploration of moral behavior, we focus on these questions: What are the basic processes that behaviorists argue are responsible for adolescents' moral behavior? How do social cognitive theorists view adolescents' moral development? What is the nature of prosocial behavior?

Basic Processes Behavioral views emphasize the moral behavior of adolescents. The familiar processes of reinforcement, punishment, and imitation have been invoked to explain how and why adolescents learn certain moral behaviors and why their behaviors differ from one another (Grusec, 2006). The general conclusions to be drawn are the same as those for other domains of social behavior. When adolescents are positively reinforced for behavior that is consistent with laws and social conventions, they are likely to repeat that behavior. When models who behave morally are provided, adolescents are likely to adopt their behavior. And, when adolescents are punished for immoral or unacceptable behavior, those behaviors can be eliminated, but at the expense of sanctioning punishment by its very use and of causing emotional side effects for the adolescent. For example, when adolescent drivers act responsibly and are praised by their parents for doing so, they are more likely to continue driving safely. If adolescents see their parents driving responsibly, they are more likely to follow the same patterns. If driving privileges are revoked from adolescents who do not drive responsibly, the behavior is eliminated, but the adolescent may feel humiliated by the punishment.

To these general conclusions, we can add several qualifiers. The effectiveness of reinforcement and punishment depends on how consistently they are administered and the schedule that is adopted. The effectiveness of modeling depends on the characteristics of the model (power, warmth, uniqueness, and so on) and the presence of cognitive processes, such as symbolic codes and imagery, to enhance retention of the modeled behavior.

What kind of adult moral models are adolescents being exposed to in American society? Do such models usually do what they say? Adolescents are especially alert to adult hypocrisy, and evidence indicates that they are right to believe that many adults display a double standard—their moral actions do not always correspond to their moral thoughts or pronouncements (Bandura, 1991).

In addition to emphasizing the role of environmental determinants and the gap between moral thought and moral action, behaviorists also emphasize that moral behavior is situationally dependent. That is, they say that adolescents are not likely to display consistent moral behavior in diverse social settings (Eisenberg & others, 2009). In a classic investigation of moral behavior—one of the most extensive ever conducted—Hugh Hartshorne and Mark May (1928–1930) observed the moral responses of 11,000 children and adolescents who were given the opportunity to lie, cheat, and steal in a variety of circumstances—at home, at school, at social events, and in athletics. A completely honest or a completely dishonest child or adolescent was difficult to find. Situation-specific moral behavior was the rule. Adolescents were more likely to cheat when their friends pressured them to do so and when the chance of being caught was slim. Other analyses suggest that some adolescents are more likely to lie, cheat, and steal than others, an indication of more consistency of moral behavior in some adolescents than in others (Burton, 1984).

In further support of the situational determinants of morality, a recent study found that very few 7-year-olds were willing to donate any money after watching a UNICEF film on children suffering from poverty (van IJzendoorn & others, 2010). However, after gentle probing by an adult, most children were willing to donate some of their money.

Social Cognitive Theory of Moral Development The **social cognitive theory of moral development** emphasizes a distinction between adolescents' moral competence—the ability to produce moral behaviors—and moral performance—the enactment of those behaviors in specific situations (Mischel & Mischel, 1975). Competence, or acquisition, is primarily the outgrowth of cognitive-sensory processes. Competencies include what adolescents are capable of doing, what they know, their skills, their awareness of moral rules and regulations, and their cognitive ability to construct behaviors. In contrast, adolescents' moral performance, or behavior, is determined by their motivation and the rewards and incentives to act in a specific moral way.

developmental **connection**

Social Cognitive Theory. What are the main themes of Bandura's social cognitive theory? Chapter 1, p. 32

Albert Bandura (1991, 2002) also concludes that moral development is best understood by considering a combination of social and cognitive factors, especially those involving self-control. He proposes that in developing a "moral self, individuals adopt standards of right and wrong that serve as guides and deterrents for conduct. In this self-regulatory process, people monitor their conduct and the conditions under which it occurs, judge it in relation to moral standards, and regulate their actions by the consequences they apply to themselves. They do things that provide them satisfaction and a sense of self-worth. They refrain from behaving in ways that violate their moral standards because such conduct will bring self-condemnation. Self-sanctions keep conduct in line with internal standards" (Bandura, 2002, p. 102). Thus, in Bandura's view, self-regulation rather than abstract reasoning is the key to positive moral development.

social cognitive theory of moral development The theory that distinguishes between moral competence (the ability to produce moral behaviors) and moral performance (enacting those behaviors in specific situations).

Overall, the findings are mixed with regard to the association of moral thought and behavior, although in one investigation with college students, individuals with both highly principled moral reasoning and high ego strength were less likely to cheat in a resistance-to-temptation situation than were their low-principled and low-ego-strength counterparts (Hess, Lonky, & Roodin, 1985).

Moral behavior includes both negative aspects of behavior—cheating, lying, and stealing, for example—and positive aspects of behavior—such as being considerate to others and giving to a worthy cause. Let's now explore the positive side of moral behavior—*prosocial behavior*.

Prosocial Behavior Many prosocial acts involve **altruism,** an unselfish interest in helping another person. Altruism is found throughout the human world and is a guiding principle in Christianity, Buddhism, Hinduism, Islam, and Judaism. Although adolescents have often been described as egocentric and selfish, adolescent acts of altruism are, nevertheless, plentiful (Grusec, Hastings, & Almas, 2011; Grusec & Sherman, 2011). We see examples daily in the hardworking adolescent who places a one-dollar bill in the church offering plate each week; the adolescent-sponsored car washes, bake sales, and concerts organized to make money to feed the hungry and help children with a disability; and the adolescent who takes in and cares for a wounded cat. How do psychologists account for such altruistic acts?

It is one of the beautiful compensations of this life that no one can sincerely try to help another without helping himself.

—Charles Dudley Warner
American Essayist, 19th Century

The circumstances most likely to involve altruism by adolescents are empathetic or sympathetic emotion for an individual in need or a close relationship between the benefactor and the recipient (Clark & others, 1987). Prosocial behavior occurs more often in adolescence than in childhood, although examples of caring for others and comforting someone in distress occur even during the preschool years (Eisenberg, Fabes, & Spinrad, 2006).

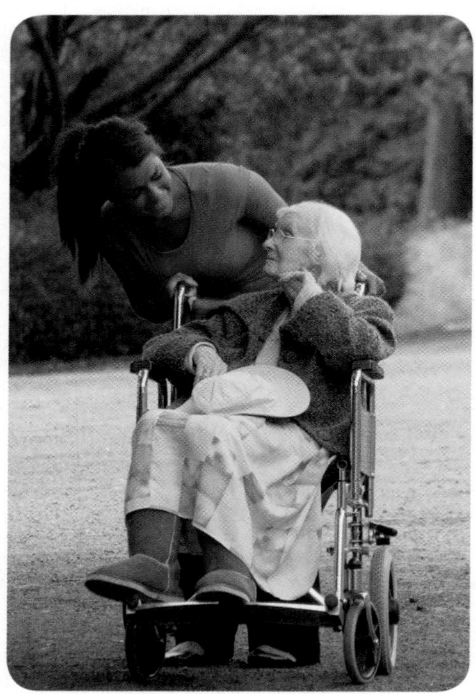

What are some characteristics of prosocial behavior in adolescence?

Are there gender differences in prosocial behavior during adolescence? Adolescent females view themselves as more prosocial and empathic, and also engage in more prosocial behavior than do males (Eisenberg & others, 2009). For example, a review of research found that across childhood and adolescence, females engaged in more prosocial behavior (Eisenberg & Fabes, 1998). The biggest gender difference occurred for kind and considerate behavior, with a smaller difference in sharing.

Are there different types of prosocial behavior? In a recent study, Gustavo Carlo and his colleagues (2010, pp. 340–341) investigated this question and confirmed the presence of these six types of prosocial behavior in young adolescents:

- altruism ("One of the best things about doing charity work is that it looks good.")
- public ("Helping others while I'm being watched is when I work best.")
- emotional ("I usually help others when they are very upset.")
- dire ("I tend to help people who are hurt badly.")
- anonymous ("I prefer to donate money without anyone knowing.")
- compliant ("I never wait to help others when they ask for it.")

In this study, adolescent girls reported more emotional, dire, compliant, and altruistic behavior than did boys, while boys engaged in more public prosocial behavior. Parental monitoring was positively related to emotional, dire, and compliant behavior but not to the other types of behavior. Compliant, anonymous, and altruistic prosocial behavior were positively related to religiosity.

Most research on prosocial behavior conceptualizes the concept in a global and unidimensional manner. The study by Carlo and colleagues (2010) illustrates the important point that in thinking about and studying prosocial behavior, it also is imporant to consider its dimensions.

Forgiveness is an aspect of prosocial behavior that occurs when the injured person releases the injurer from possible behavioral retaliation (Klatt & Enright, 2009). In one investigation, individuals from the fourth grade through college and adulthood were asked questions about forgiveness (Enright, Santos, & Al-Mabuk, 1989). The adolescents were especially swayed by peer pressure in their willingness to forgive others.

altruism Unselfish interest in helping another person.

forgiveness An aspect of prosocial behavior that occurs when an injured person releases the injurer from possible behavioral retaliation.

Gratitude is a feeling of thankfulness and appreciation, especially in response to someone doing something kind or helpful (Grant & Gino, 2010). A recent study of young adolescents revealed that gratitude was linked to a number of positive aspects of development, including satisfaction with one's family, optimism, and prosocial behavior (Froh, Yurkewicz, & Kashdan, 2009).

So far we have examined two of the three main domains of moral development: thought and behavior. Next, we explore the third main domain: moral feeling.

MORAL FEELING

Among the ideas formulated about the development of moral feelings are concepts central to psychoanalytic theory, the nature of empathy, and the role of emotions in moral development.

Psychoanalytic Theory As we discussed in Chapter 1, Sigmund Freud's psychoanalytic theory describes the superego as one of the three main structures of personality (the id and the ego being the other two). In Freud's classical psychoanalytic theory, an individual's *superego*—the moral branch of personality—develops in early childhood when the child resolves the Oedipus conflict and identifies with the same-sex parent. According to Freud, one reason why children resolve the Oedipus conflict is to alleviate the fear of losing their parents' love and of being punished for their unacceptable sexual wishes toward the opposite-sex parent. To reduce anxiety, avoid punishment, and maintain parental affection, children form a superego by identifying with the same-sex parent. In Freud's view, through this identification, children internalize the parents' standards of right and wrong that reflect societal prohibitions. At the same time, children turn inward the hostility that was previously aimed at the same-sex parent. This inwardly directed hostility is then experienced self-punitively (and unconsciously) as guilt. In the psychoanalytic account of moral development, self-punitiveness of guilt keeps children and, later on, adolescents from committing transgressions. That is, children and adolescents conform to societal standards to avoid guilt.

developmental **connection**

Psychoanalytic Theory. Freud theorized that individuals go through five main stages of psychosexual development. Chapter 1, p. 44

In Freud's view, the superego consists of two main components—the ego ideal and the conscience—which promote children's and adolescents' development of moral feelings. The **ego ideal** is the component of the superego that involves ideal standards approved by parents, whereas the **conscience** is the component of the superego that involves behaviors not approved of by parents. An individual's ego ideal rewards the individual by conveying a sense of pride and personal value when the individual acts according to moral standards. The conscience punishes the individual for acting immorally by making the individual feel guilty and worthless. In this way, self-control replaces parental control.

Erik Erikson (1970) outlined three stages of moral development: specific moral learning in childhood, ideological concerns in adolescence, and ethical consolidation in adulthood. According to Erikson, during adolescence individuals search for an identity. If adolescents become disillusioned with the moral and religious beliefs they acquired during childhood, they are likely to lose, at least temporarily, their sense of purpose and feel that their lives are empty. This loss may lead to adolescents' search for an ideology that will give some purpose to their lives. For the ideology to be acceptable, it must both fit the evidence and mesh with adolescents' logical reasoning abilities. If others share this ideology, a sense of community is felt. For Erikson, ideology surfaces as the guardian of identity during adolescence because it provides a sense of purpose, assists in tying the present to the future, and contributes meaning to the behavior (Hoffman, 1988).

Empathy Positive feelings, such as empathy, contribute to adolescents' moral development (Eisenberg & others, 2009; Malti & Latzko, 2010). Feeling **empathy** means reacting to another's feelings with an emotional response that is similar to that person's feelings. Although empathy is experienced as an emotional state, it

gratitude A feeling of thankfulness and appreciation, especially in response to someone doing something kind or helpful.

ego ideal The component of the superego that involves ideal standards approved by parents.

conscience The component of the superego that involves behaviors disapproved of by parents.

empathy Reaction to another's feelings with an emotional response that is similar to the other's feelings.

What characterizes empathy in adolescence?

often has a cognitive component—the ability to discern another's inner psychological states, or what we have previously called *perspective taking*.

At about 10 to 12 years of age, individuals develop an empathy for people who live in unfortunate circumstances (Damon, 1988). Children's concerns are no longer limited to the feelings of specific persons in situations they directly observe. Instead, 10- to 12-year-olds expand their concerns to the general problems of people in unfortunate circumstances—the poor, those with disabilities, the socially outcast, and so forth. This newfound sensitivity may lead older children to behave altruistically, and later may give a humanitarian flavor to adolescents' development of ideological and political views.

Although every adolescent may be capable of responding with empathy, not everyone does so. Adolescents' empathic behavior varies considerably. For example, in older children and adolescents, empathic dysfunctions can contribute to antisocial behavior. Some delinquents convicted of violent crimes show a lack of feeling for their victims' distress. A 13-year-old boy convicted of violently mugging a number of older adults, when asked about the pain he had caused one blind woman, said, "What do I care? I'm not her" (Damon, 1988).

The Contemporary Perspective We have seen that classical psychoanalytic theory emphasizes the power of unconscious guilt in moral development but that other theories, such as that of Damon, emphasize the role of empathy. Today, many developmentalists note that both positive feelings, such as empathy, sympathy, admiration, and self-esteem, and negative feelings, such as anger, outrage, shame, and guilt, contribute to adolescents' moral development (Damon, 1995; Eisenberg & others, 2009). When strongly experienced, these emotions influence adolescents to act in accord with standards of right and wrong. Such emotions as empathy, shame, guilt, and anxiety over other people's violations of standards are present early in development and undergo developmental change throughout childhood and adolescence.

These emotions provide a natural base for adolescents' acquisition of moral values, both orienting adolescents toward moral events and motivating them to pay close attention to such events (Thompson, 2009). However, moral emotions do not operate in a vacuum to build adolescents' moral awareness, and they are not sufficient in themselves to generate moral responsivity. They do not give the "substance" of moral regulation—the rules, values, and standards of behavior that adolescents need to understand and act on. Moral emotions are inextricably interwoven with the cognitive and social aspects of adolescents' development.

MORAL PERSONALITY

So far we have examined three key dimensions of moral development: thoughts, behavior, and feelings. Recently, there has been a surge of interest in a fourth dimension: personality (Frimer & others, 2011; Walker & Frimer, 2011). Thoughts, behavior, and feelings can all be involved in an individual's moral personality. For many years, skepticism characterized the likelihood that a set of moral characteristics or traits could be discovered that would constitute a core of moral personality. Much of this skepticism stemmed from the results of Hartshorne and May's (1928–1930) classic study, and Walter Mischel's (1968) social learning theory and research, which argued that situations trump traits when attempts are made to predict moral behavior. Mischel's (2004) subsequent research and theory and Bandura's (2010a,b) social cognitive theory have emphasized the importance of "person" factors while still recognizing situational variation. Until recently, though, there has been little interest in studying what might comprise a moral personality. Three aspects of moral personality that have recently been emphasized are (1) moral identity, (2) moral character, and (3) moral exemplars.

developmental **connection**

Personality. The contemporary view of personality emphasizes the interaction of traits and situations. Chapter 4, p. 154

moral identity An aspect of personality that is present when individuals have moral notions and commitments that are central to their lives.

Moral Identity A central aspect of the recent interest in the role of personality in moral development focuses on **moral identity.** Individuals have a moral identity when moral notions and commitments are central to their life. In this view, behaving in a manner that violates this moral commitment places the integrity of the self at risk (Aquino, McFarren, & Laven, 2011; Narváez & Lapsley, 2009; Walker & Frimer, 2011).

Recently, Darcia Narváez (2010a) concluded that a mature moral individual cares about morality and being a moral person. For these individuals, moral responsibility is central to their identity. Mature moral individuals engage in moral metacognition, including moral self-monitoring and moral self-reflection. Moral self-monitoring involves monitoring one's thoughts and actions related to moral situations, and engaging in self-control when it is needed. Moral self-reflection encompasses critical evaluations of one's self-judgments and efforts to minimize bias and self-deception.

developmental **connection**

Identity. According to James Marcia, what are the four statuses of identity development? Chapter 4, p. 143

Moral Character James Rest (1995) argued that moral character has not been adequately emphasized in moral development. In Rest's view, *moral character* involves having the strength of your convictions, persisting, and overcoming distractions and obstacles. If individuals don't have moral character, they may wilt under pressure or fatigue, fail to follow through, or become distracted and discouraged, and fail to behave morally. Moral character presupposes that the person has set moral goals and that achieving those goals involves the commitment to act in accord with those goals. Rest (1995) also concluded that motivation has not been adequately emphasized in moral development. In Rest's view, *moral motivation* involves prioritizing moral values over other personal values.

Lawrence Walker (2002) has studied moral character by examining people's conceptions of moral excellence. Among the moral virtues people emphasize are "honesty, truthfulness, and trustworthiness, as well as those of care, compassion, thoughtfulness, and considerateness. Other salient traits revolve around virtues of dependability, loyalty, and conscientiousness" (Walker, 2002, p. 74). In Walker's perspective, these aspects of moral character provide a foundation for positive social relationships and functioning.

developmental **connection**

Personality. Conscientiousness is linked to a number of positive outcomes in adolescence. Chapter 4, p. 153

Moral Exemplars **Moral exemplars** are people who have lived exemplary lives. Moral exemplars, such as Jewel Cash, who was portrayed at the beginning of the chapter, have a moral personality, identity, character, and set of virtues that reflect moral excellence and commitment (Frimer & others, 2011; Walker & Frimer, 2011).

In one study, three different exemplars of morality were examined—brave, caring, and just (Walker & Hennig, 2004). Different personality profiles emerged for the three exemplars. The brave exemplar was characterized by being dominant and extraverted, the caring exemplar by being nurturant and agreeable, and the just exemplar by being conscientious and open to experience. However, a number of traits characterized all three moral exemplars, considered by the researchers to reflect a possible core of moral functioning. This core included being honest and dependable.

moral exemplars People who have lived exemplary lives.

Rosa Parks (*left photo,* sitting in the front of a bus after the U.S. Supreme Court ruled that segregation was illegal on her city's bus system) and Andrei Sakharov (*right photo*) are moral exemplars. Parks (1913–2005), an African American seamstress in Montgomery, Alabama, became famous for her quiet, revolutionary act of not giving up her bus seat to a non-Latino White man in 1955. Her heroic act is cited by many historians as the beginning of the modern civil rights movement in the United States. Across the next four decades, Parks continued to work for progress in civil rights. Sakharov (1921–1989) was a Soviet physicist who spent several decades designing nuclear weapons for the Soviet Union and came to be known as the father of the Soviet hydrogen bomb. However, later in his life he became one of the Soviet Union's most outspoken critics and worked relentlessly to promote human rights and democracy.

Another study examined the personality of exemplary young adults to determine what characterized their moral excellence (Matsuba & Walker, 2004). Forty young adults were nominated by executive directors of a variety of social organizations (such as Big Brothers, AIDS Society, and Ronald McDonald House) as moral exemplars based on their extraordinary moral commitment to these social organizations. They were compared with 40 young adults matched in age, education, and other variables who were attending a university. The moral exemplars were more advanced in moral reasoning, further along in developing an identity, and more likely to be in close relationships.

Review *Connect* Reflect

LG1 Discuss the domains of moral development.

Review

- What is moral development? What are the main points of Kohlberg's theory of moral development? How has Kohlberg's theory been criticized?
- What are some basic processes in the behavioral view of moral development? What is the social cognitive view of moral development? What is the nature of prosocial behavior?
- What is the psychoanalytic view of moral development? What role does empathy play in moral development? What is the contemporary perspective on moral feeling?
- What is the moral personality approach to moral development?

Connect

- Considering what you learned about gender similarities and differences in Chapter 5, were you surprised by findings cited in this section about gender's role in moral development?

Reflect *Your Own Personal Journey of Life*

- Which of the four approaches we have discussed—cognitive, psychoanalytic, behavioral/social cognitive, and personality—do you think best describes the way you have developed morally? Explain.

2 Contexts of Moral Development

LG2 Describe how the contexts of parenting and schools can influence moral development.

Earlier in the chapter, we saw that both Piaget and Kohlberg maintained that peer relations are an important context for moral development. Adolescents' experiences in families and schools also are important contexts for moral development.

PARENTING

Both Piaget and Kohlberg held that parents do not provide any unique or essential inputs to children's moral development. They do believe that parents are responsible for providing general role-taking opportunities and cognitive conflict, but they reserve the primary role in moral development for peers. Researchers have revealed how both parents and peers contribute to the development of moral maturity (Day, 2010; Hastings, Utendale, & Sullivan, 2007). In general, higher-level moral reasoning in adolescence is linked with parenting that is supportive and encourages adolescents to question and expand on their moral reasoning (Eisenberg & others, 2009). Next, we focus on parental discipline and its role in moral development and then draw some conclusions about parenting and moral development.

In Freud's psychoanalytic theory, the aspects of child rearing that encourage moral development are practices that instill the fears of punishment and of losing parental love. Developmentalists who have studied child-rearing techniques and moral development have focused on parents' discipline techniques (Grusec, 2006). These include love withdrawal, power assertion, and induction (Hoffman, 1970):

- **Love withdrawal** comes closest to the psychoanalytic emphasis on fear of punishment and of losing parental love. It is a discipline technique in which a parent withholds attention or love from the adolescent, as when the parent refuses to talk to the adolescent or states a dislike for the adolescent.
- **Power assertion** is a discipline technique in which a parent attempts to gain control over the adolescent or the adolescent's resources. Examples include spanking, threatening, or removing privileges.
- **Induction** is the discipline technique in which a parent uses reason and explanation of the consequences for others of the adolescent's actions. Examples of induction include, "Don't hit him. He was only trying to help" and "Why are you yelling at her? She didn't mean to hurt your feelings."

Moral development theorist and researcher Martin Hoffman (1970) argues that any discipline produces arousal on the adolescent's part. Love withdrawal and power assertion are likely to evoke a very high level of arousal, with love withdrawal generating considerable anxiety and power assertion considerable hostility. Induction is more likely to produce a moderate level of arousal in adolescents, a level that permits them to attend to the cognitive rationales parents offer. When a parent uses power assertion or love withdrawal, the adolescent may be so aroused that, even if the parent gives accompanying explanations about the consequences for others of the adolescent's actions, the adolescent might not attend to them. Power assertion presents parents as weak models of self-control—as individuals who cannot control their feelings.

Accordingly, adolescents may imitate this model of poor self-control when they face stressful circumstances. The use of induction, however, focuses the adolescent's attention on the action's consequences for others, not on the adolescent's own shortcomings. For these reasons, Hoffman (1988) notes that parents should use induction to encourage adolescents' moral development. In research on parenting techniques, induction is more positively related to moral development than is love withdrawal or power assertion, although the findings vary according to developmental level and socioeconomic status. For example, induction works better with adolescents and older children than with preschool children (Brody & Schaffer, 1982) and better with middle-SES than with lower-SES children (Hoffman, 1970). Older children and adolescents are generally better able to understand the reasons given to them and better at perspective taking than younger children are. Some theorists believe the reason that internalization of society's moral standards is more likely among middle-SES than among lower-SES individuals is that internalization is more rewarding in the middle-SES culture (Kohn, 1977).

How can parents apply such findings to strategies for raising a moral child and adolescent? For some suggestions, see the *Connecting with Health and Well-Being* interlude.

SCHOOLS

Schools are an important context for moral development. Moral education is hotly debated in educational circles. We first study one of the earliest analyses of moral education and then turn to some contemporary views on moral education.

The Hidden Curriculum

More than 70 years ago, educator John Dewey (1933) recognized that even when schools do not have specific programs in moral education, they provide moral education through a "hidden curriculum." The **hidden curriculum** is conveyed by the moral atmosphere that is a part of every school.

The moral atmosphere is created by school and classroom rules, the moral orientation of teachers and school administrators, and text materials. Teachers serve as models of ethical or unethical behavior. Classroom rules and peer relations at school transmit attitudes about cheating, lying, stealing, and consideration for others. And,

love withdrawal A discipline technique in which a parent removes attention or love from the adolescent.

power assertion A discipline technique in which a parent attempts to gain control over the adolescent or the adolescent's resources.

induction A discipline technique in which a parent uses reason and explanation of the consequences for others of the adolescent's actions.

hidden curriculum The pervasive moral atmosphere that characterizes every school.

connecting with health and well-being

How Can We Raise Moral Children and Adolescents?

Parental discipline does contribute to children's moral development, but other aspects of parenting also play an important role, such as providing opportunities for perspective taking and modeling moral behavior and thinking. One research view concluded that, in general, moral children tend to have parents who do the following (Eisenberg & Valiente, 2002, p. 134):

- Are warm and supportive rather than punitive.
- Use inductive discipline.
- Provide opportunities for the children to learn about others' perspectives and feelings.
- Involve children in family decision making and in the process of thinking about moral decisions.
- Model moral behaviors and thinking themselves, and provide opportunities for their children to do so.
- Provide information about what behaviors are expected and why.
- Foster an internal rather than an external sense of morality.

What are some parenting characteristics and practices that are linked with children's and adolescents' moral development?

Parents who show this configuration of behaviors likely foster concern and caring about others in their children, and create a positive parent-child relationship. A recent study found that adolescents' moral motivation was positively linked to the quality of their relationship with their parents (Malti & Buchmann, 2010). Another recent study revealed that dimensions of authoritative parenting (such as a combination of responsiveness, autonomy-granting, and demandingness) predicted an increase in adolescents' moral identity (Hardy & others, 2010).

In terms of relationship quality, secure attachment may play an important role in children's and adolescents' moral development. A secure attachment can place children on a positive path for internalizing parents' socializing goals and family values. In a recent study, early secure attachment defused a maladaptive trajectory toward antisocial outcomes (Kochanska, & others, 2010a). In another recent study, securely attached children's willing, cooperative stance was linked to positive future socialization outcomes such as a lower incidence of externalizing problems (high level of aggression, for example) (Kochanska, 2010b).

Recently, an interest has developed in determining which parenting strategies work best when children and adolescents are confronted with situations in which they are exposed to values outside the home that conflict with parents' values (Grusec, 2006). Two strategies that parents often use in this regard are cocooning and pre-arming (Bugental & Goodnow, 2006). *Cocooning* occurs when parents protect children and adolescents from exposure to deviant behavior, and thus the temptation to engage in negative moral behavior. In adolescence, cocooning involves monitoring the contexts in which adolescents spend time and restricting their interaction with deviant peers. *Pre-arming* involves anticipating conflicting values and preparing adolescents to handle them in their lives outside their home. In using pre-arming, parents discuss strategies with adolescents to help them deal with harmful situations.

What type of studies do you think researchers might design to compare the relative effectiveness of cocooning and pre-arming?

through its rules and regulations, the school administration infuses the school with a value system.

character education A direct moral education approach that involves teaching students a basic moral literacy to prevent them from engaging in immoral behavior or doing harm to themselves or others.

Character Education Currently 40 of 50 states have mandates regarding **character education,** a direct education approach that involves teaching students a basic moral literacy to prevent them from engaging in immoral behavior and doing harm to themselves or others (Nucci & Narváez, 2008). The argument is that such behaviors as lying, stealing, and cheating are wrong, and students should be taught this throughout their education (Berkowitz, Battistich, & Bier, 2008; Davidson, Lickona, & Khmelkov, 2008).

Every school should have an explicit moral code that is clearly communicated to students. Any violations of the code should be met with sanctions. Instruction in specified moral concepts, such as cheating, can take the form of example and definition, class discussions and role playing, or rewarding students for proper behavior. More recently, an emphasis on the importance of encouraging students to develop a care perspective has been accepted as a relevant aspect of character education (Noddings, 2008). Rather than just instructing adolescents in refraining from engaging in morally deviant behavior, a care perspective advocates educating students in the importance of engaging in prosocial behaviors, such as considering others' feelings, being sensitive to others, and helping others (Roberts, 2010).

Lawrence Walker (2002) argues that it is important for character education to involve more than a listing of moral virtues on a classroom wall. Instead, he emphasizes that children and adolescents need to participate in critical discussions of values; they need to discuss and reflect on how to incorporate virtues into their daily lives. Walker also advocates exposing children to moral exemplars worthy of emulating and getting children to participate in community service. The character education approach reflects the moral personality domain of moral development we discussed earlier in the chapter (Walker, Frimer, & Dunlop, 2011).

Values Clarification A second approach to providing moral education is **values clarification,** which involves helping individuals to clarify what their lives are for and what is worth working for. Unlike character education, which tells students what their values should be, values clarification encourages students to define their own values and understand the values of others.

Advocates of values clarification say it is value-free. However, critics argue that its content offends community standards and that the values-clarification exercises fail to stress right behavior.

Cognitive Moral Education A third approach to moral education, **cognitive moral education,** is based on the belief that students should learn to value such things as democracy and justice as their moral reasoning develops. Kohlberg's theory has served as the foundation for a number of cognitive moral education programs (Snarey & Samuelson, 2008). In a typical program, high school students meet in a semester-long course to discuss a number of moral issues. The instructor acts as a facilitator rather than as a director of the class. The hope is that students will develop more advanced notions of such concepts as cooperation, trust, responsibility, and community (Power & Higgins-D'Alessandro, 2008).

Service Learning Over the last several decades, there has been a growing understanding that the quality of a society can be considerably enhanced when citizens become proactive in providing service to the community and the nation. The initial call to serve came in John F. Kennedy's inaugural address after he was sworn in as president on January 20, 1961. In his words, "Ask not what your country can do for you—ask what you can do for your country." This idea helped to increase the government's commitment to develop programs that emphasize service. Over time, this commitment has produced the Peace Corps, Americorps, Senior Corps, VISTA, and Learn and Serve America. This latter initiative provides grants to schools, universities, and communities to engage students in service to communities. Much of this effort is orchestrated through the Corporation for National and Community Service. For program descriptions and opportunities to volunteer, go to www.nationalservice.gov.

At the beginning of the chapter you read about 16-year-old Jewel Cash, who is strongly motivated to make a positive difference in the community. Jewel Cash has a sense of social responsibility that an increasing number of educational programs seek to promote in students through **service learning,** a form of education that promotes social responsibility and service to the community. In service learning, adolescents engage in activities such as tutoring, helping older adults, working in a

values clarification An educational approach that focuses on helping people clarify what is important to them, what is worth working for, and what purpose their lives are to serve. Students are encouraged to define their own values and understand others' values.

cognitive moral education An approach based on the belief that students should learn to value things like democracy and justice as their moral reasoning develops; Kohlberg's theory has been the basis for many of the cognitive moral education approaches.

service learning A form of education that promotes social responsibility and service to the community.

connecting with adolescents

Finding a Way to Get a Playground

Twelve-year-old Katie Bell more than just about anything else wanted a playground in her New Jersey town. She knew that other kids also wanted one too, so she put together a group that generated fund-raising ideas for the playground. They presented their ideas to the town council. Her group got more youth involved. They helped raise money by selling candy and sandwiches door-to-door. Katie says, "We learned to work as a community. This will be an important place for people to go and have picnics and make new friends." Katie's advice: "You won't get anywhere if you don't try."

What moral lessons from her family or school do you think Katie Bell had already learned when she undertook the playground project?

Katie Bell (*front*) and some of her volunteers.

What are some positive outcomes of service learning?

hospital, assisting at a child-care center, or cleaning up a vacant lot to make a play area. An important goal of service learning is that adolescents become less self-centered and more strongly motivated to help others (Davidson & others, 2010; Hart, Matsuba, & Atkins, 2008). Service learning is often more effective when two conditions are met (Nucci, 2006): (1) students are given some degree of choice in the service activities in which they participate, and (2) students are provided opportunities to reflect about their participation.

Service learning takes education out into the community (Zaff & others, 2010). Adolescent volunteers tend to be extraverted, committed to others, and have a high level of self-understanding (Eisenberg & Morris, 2004). Also, one study revealed that adolescent girls participated in service learning more than adolescent boys (Webster & Worrell, 2008).

Researchers have found that service learning benefits adolescents in a number of ways (Zaff & others, 2010). These improvements in adolescent development related to service learning include higher grades in school, increased goal setting, higher self-esteem, an improved sense of being able to make a difference for others, and an increased likelihood that they will serve as volunteers in the future. In one study, 74 percent of African American and 70 percent of Latino adolescents said that service-learning programs could have a "fairly or very big effect" on keeping students from dropping out of school (Bridgeland, Dilulio, & Wulsin, 2008).

An analysis revealed that 26 percent of U.S. public high schools require students to participate in service learning (Metz & Youniss, 2005). The benefits of service learning, both for the volunteer and the recipient, suggest that more adolescents should be required to participate in such programs (Enfield & Collins, 2008; Zaff & others, 2010).

Cheating A moral education concern is whether students cheat and how to handle the cheating if it is detected (Anderman & Anderman, 2010). Academic cheating can take many forms including plagiarism, using "cheat sheets" during an exam, copying from a neighbor during a test, purchasing papers, and falsifying lab results.

A 2006 survey revealed that 60 percent of secondary school students said they had cheated on a test in school during the past year, and one-third of the students reported that they had plagiarized information from the Internet in the past year (Josephson Institute of Ethics, 2006).

Why do students cheat? Among the reasons students give for cheating include the pressure for getting high grades, time pressures, poor teaching, and lack of interest (Stephens, 2008). In terms of poor teaching, "students are more likely to cheat when they perceive their teacher to be incompetent, unfair, and uncaring" (Stephens, 2008, p. 140).

A long history of research also implicates the power of the situation in determining whether students cheat or not (Hartshorne & May, 1928–1930; Vandehey, Diekhoff, & LaBeff, 2007). For example, students are more likely to cheat when they are not being closely monitored during a test; when they know their peers are cheating; when they know whether or not another student has been caught cheating; and when student scores are made public (Anderman & Murdock, 2007; Harmon, Lambrinos, & Kennedy, 2008). A recent study revealed that college students who engaged in academic cheating were characterized by the personality traits of low conscientiousness and low agreeableness (Williams, Nathanson, & Paulhus, 2010).

Among the strategies for decreasing academic cheating are preventive measures such as making sure students are aware of what constitutes cheating, making clear the consequences if they do cheat, closely monitoring students' behavior while they are taking tests, and emphasizing the importance of being a moral, responsible individual who engages in academic integrity. In promoting academic integrity, many colleges have instituted an honor code policy that emphasizes self-responsibility, fairness, trust, and scholarship. However, few secondary schools have developed honor code policies. The Center for Academic Integrity (www.academicintegrity.org) has extensive materials available to help schools develop academic integrity policies.

What are some factors that influence whether adolescents engage in cheating?

An Integrative Approach Darcia Narváez (2006, 2008, 2010a,b) emphasizes an *integrative approach* to moral education that encompasses both the reflective moral thinking and commitment to justice advocated in Kohlberg's approach, and the development of a particular moral character as advocated in the character education approach. She highlights the Child Development Project as an excellent example of an integrative moral education approach. In the Child Development Project, students are given multiple opportunities to discuss other students' experiences, which inspire empathy and perspective taking, and they participate in exercises that encourage them to reflect on their own behaviors in terms of such values as fairness and social responsibility (Battistich, 2008). Adults coach students in ethical decision making and guide them in becoming more caring individuals. Students experience a caring community, not only in the classroom, but also in after-school activities and through parental involvement in the program. Research evaluations of the Child Development Project indicate that it is related to an improved sense of community, an increase in prosocial behavior, better interpersonal understanding, and an increase in social problem solving (Battistich, 2008; Solomon & others, 1990).

Another integrative moral education program that is being implemented is called *integrative ethical education* (Narváez, 2006, 2008, 2010a,b; Narváez & others, 2004). This program builds on the concept of expertise with the goal of turning moral novices into moral experts by educating students about four ethical skills that moral experts possess: ethical sensitivity, ethical judgment, ethical focus, and ethical action (Narvaez, 2010a). Figure 7.5 further describes components of these four ethical skills.

Ethical Sensitivity	Understanding emotional expression Taking the perspective of others Connecting to others Responding to diversity Controlling social bias Interpreting situations Communicating effectively
Ethical Judgment	Understanding ethical problems Using codes and identifying judgment criteria Reasoning generally Reasoning ethically Understanding consequences Reflecting on the process and outcome Coping and being resilient
Ethical Focus	Respecting others Cultivating conscience Acting responsibly Helping others Finding meaning in life Valuing traditions and institutions Developing ethical identity and integrity
Ethical Action	Resolving conflicts and problems Asserting respectfully Taking initiative as a leader Implementing decisions Cultivating courage Persevering Working hard

FIGURE **7.5**
ETHICAL SKILLS IN INTEGRATIVE ETHICAL EDUCATION
Narvaez, D., *Handbook of Moral Development*. Copyright © 2006 by Taylor & Francis Group LLC-Books. Reproduced with permission of Taylor & Francis Group LLC Books in the format Books and Other book via Copyright Clearance Center.

Review *Connect* Reflect

LG2 Describe how the contexts of parenting and schools can influence moral development.

Review

- How does parental discipline affect moral development? What are some effective parenting strategies for advancing children's and adolescents' moral development?
- What is the hidden curriculum? What are some contemporary approaches to moral education used in schools? How does service learning affect adolescents?

Connect

- How might cultural and ethnic identity, which you studied in Chapter 4, influence parents' approaches to their children's moral development?

Reflect *Your Own Personal Journey of Life*

- What type of discipline did your parents use with you? What effect do you think this has had on your moral development?

3 Values, Religion, and Spirituality

LG3 Explain the roles of values, religion, and spirituality in adolescents' and emerging adults' lives.

Values | Religion and Spirituality

What are adolescents' and emerging adults' values like today? How powerful are religion and spirituality in adolescents' and emerging adults' lives?

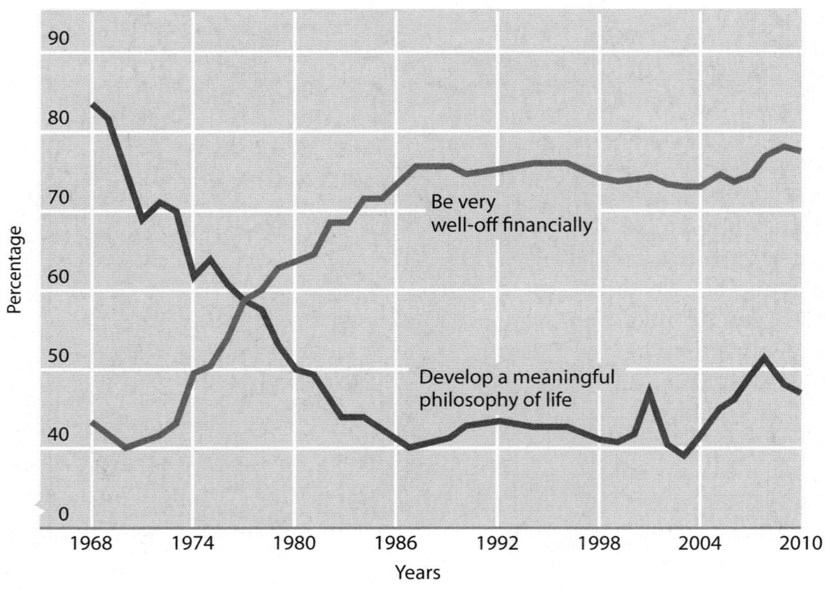

FIGURE **7.6**

CHANGING FRESHMEN LIFE GOALS, 1968 TO 2010. In the last three decades, a significant change has occurred in freshmen students' life goals. A far greater percentage of today's college freshmen state that an "essential" or "very important" life goal is to be well-off financially, and far fewer state that developing a meaningful philosophy of life is an "essential" or a "very important" life goal.

VALUES

Values are beliefs and attitudes about the way things should be. They involve what is important to us. We attach values to all sorts of things: politics, religion, money, sex, education, helping others, family, friends, career, cheating, self-respect, and so on. Values reflect the intrapersonal dimension of morality introduced at the beginning of the chapter.

One way of measuring what people value is to ask them what their goals are. Over the past three decades, traditional-aged college students have shown an increased concern for personal well-being and a decreased concern for the well-being of others, especially for the disadvantaged (Pryor & others, 2010). As shown in Figure 7.6, today's college freshmen are more strongly motivated to be well-off financially and less motivated to develop a meaningful philosophy of life than were their counterparts of 20 or even 10 years ago. In 2010, 77 percent of students viewed becoming well-off financially as an "essential" or a "very important" objective compared with only 42 percent in 1971.

There are, however, some signs that U.S. college students are shifting toward a stronger interest in the welfare of society. In the survey just described, interest in developing a meaningful philosophy of life increased from 39 percent to 47 percent of U.S. freshmen from 2001 through 2010 (Pryor & others, 2010) (see Figure 7.6). Also in this survey, the percentage of college freshmen who said the chances are very good that they will participate in volunteer or community service programs increased from 18 percent in 1990 to 32 percent in 2010 (Pryor & others, 2010).

values Beliefs and attitudes about the way things should be.

connecting with careers

Constance Flanagan, Professor of Youth Civic Development

Constance (Connie) Flanagan is a professor of youth civic development in the College of Agricultural Sciences at Pennsylvania State University. Her research focuses on youths' views about justice and the factors in families, schools, and communities that promote civic values, connections, and skills in youth (Flanagan, 2004).

Flanagan obtained her undergraduate degree in psychology from Duquesne University, her master's degree in education from the University of Iowa, and her Ph.D. from the University of Michigan. She has a special interest in improving the U.S. social policy for adolescents and serves as co-chair of the Committee on Child Development. In addition to teaching undergraduate and graduate classes, conducting research, and serving on various committees, Flanagan evaluates research for potential publication as a member of the editorial board of *Journal of Adolescent Research* and *Journal of Research on Adolescence*. She also presents her ideas and research at numerous national and international meetings.

Connie Flanagan with adolescents.

Other research on values has found that adolescents who are involved in groups that connect them to others in school, their communities, or faith-based institutions report higher levels of social trust, altruism, commitments to the common good of people, and endorsements of the rights of immigrants for full inclusion in society (Flanagan & Faison, 2001). In this research, adolescents who were uninvolved in such groups were more likely to endorse self-interest and materialistic values.

The research we have just discussed was conducted by Constance Flanagan and her colleagues. To read further about her work, see the *Connecting with Careers* profile.

Our discussion of values relates to the view William Damon (2008) proposed in *The Path to Purpose,* which we described in Chapter 1. Damon concluded that a major difficulty confronting today's youth is their lack of a clear sense of what they want to do with their lives—that too many youth are essentially "rudderless." Damon (2008, p. 8) found that only about 20 percent of 12- to 22-year-olds in the United States expressed "a clear vision of where they want to go, what they want to accomplish in life, and why." He argues that their goals and values too often focus on the short term, such as getting a good grade on a test this week and finding a date for a dance, rather than developing a plan for the future based on positive values. As we indicated in Chapter 1, the types of questions that adults can pose to youth to guide them in the direction of developing more purposeful values include *"What's most important in your life? Why do you care about those things? . . . What does it mean to be a good person?"* (Damon, 2008, p. 135).

developmental **connection**

Work and Achievement. Purpose is an important aspect of many aspects of adolescents' lives, including their identity, values, achievement, and careers. Chapter 1, p. 23; Chapter 11, p. 370

RELIGION AND SPIRITUALITY

In Damon's (2008) view, one long-standing source for discovering purpose in life is religion. Can religion and spirituality be distinguished? A recent analysis by Pamela King and her colleagues (2011) makes the following distinctions:

- **Religion** is an organized set of beliefs, practices, rituals, and symbols that increases an individual's connection to a sacred or transcendent other (God, higher power, or ultimate truth).
- **Religiousness** refers to the degree of affiliation with an organized religion, participation in its prescribed rituals and practices, connection with its beliefs, and involvement in a community of believers.

religion An organized set of beliefs, practices, rituals, and symbols that increases an individual's connection to a sacred or transcendent other (God, higher power, or higher truth).

religiousness The degree of affiliation with an organized religion, participation in prescribed rituals and practices, connection with its beliefs, and involvement in a community of believers.

connecting with adolescents

Nina Vasan, Superstar Volunteer and Fund-Raiser

Nina Vasan founded ACS Teens, a nationwide group of adolescent volunteers who support the efforts of the American Cancer Society (ACS). Nina's organization has raised hundreds of thousands of dollars for cancer research, helped change state tobacco laws, and conducted a number of cancer control programs. She created a national letter-writing campaign to obtain volunteers, established a website and set up an e-mail network, started a newsletter, and arranged monthly phone calls to communicate ideas and plan projects. In Nina's words,

> I realized that teenagers like myself could make a big difference in the fight against cancer. I knew that the best way to help was to start a teen organization. . . . To be a beneficial part of the human race, it is essential and fundamental to give back to the community and others. (Vasan, 2002, p. 1)

Nina Vasan's work on behalf of cancer involved pursuing a purpose. She says that the success of her work involving cancer far outweighs the many honors she has been awarded (Damon, 2008).

What values are likely to motivate Nina Vasan?

Nina Vasan.

Religion enlightens, terrifies, subdues; it gives faith, inflicts remorse, inspires resolutions, and inflames devotion.

—Henry Newman

English Churchman and Writer, 19th Century

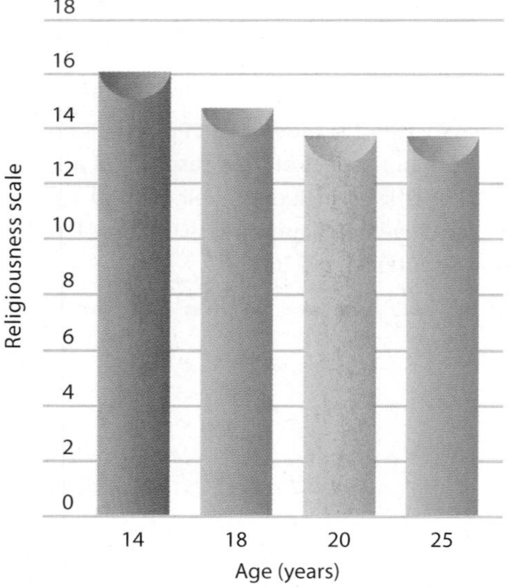

FIGURE **7.7**

DEVELOPMENTAL CHANGES IN RELIGIOUSNESS FROM 14 TO 25 YEARS OF AGE. *Note:* The religiousness scale ranged from 0 to 32 with higher scores indicating stronger religiousness.

- **Spirituality** involves experiencing something beyond oneself in a transcendent manner and living in a way that benefits others and society.

Religious issues are important to many adolescents and emerging adults (Day, 2010; King, Carr, & Boiter, 2011; Warren, Lerner, & Phelps, 2011). However, in the twenty-first century, a downtrend in religious interest among college students has occurred. In the national study of American freshmen described earlier in the chapter in our discussion of values, in 2010, 75 percent said they attended a religious service frequently or occasionally during the past year, down from a high of 85 percent in 1997 (Pryor & others, 2010). Further, in 2010, almost three times as many first-year students (23 percent) reported that they don't have a religious preference than did first-year students in 1978 (8 percent). A recent study found that across the first three semesters of college, students were less likely to attend religious services or engage in religious activities (Stoppa & Lefkowitz, 2010).

A recent developmental study revealed that religiousness declined from 14 to 20 years of age in the United States (Koenig, McGue, & Iacono, 2008) (see Figure 7.7). In this study, religiousness was assessed with items such as frequency of prayer, frequency of discussing religious teachings, frequency of deciding moral actions for religious reasons, and the overall importance of religion in everyday life. As indicated in Figure 7.7, more change in religiousness occurred from 14 to 18 years of age than from 20 to 24 years of age. Also, attending religious services was highest at 14 years of age, declining from 14 to 18 years of age and increasing at 20 years of age. More change occurred in attending religious services than in religiousness.

Analysis of the World Values Survey of 18- to 24-year-olds revealed that emerging adults in less-developed countries were more likely to be religious than their counterparts in more-developed countries (Lippman & Keith, 2006). For example, emerging adults' reports that religion is very important in their lives ranged from a low of 0 in Japan to 93 percent in Nigeria, and belief in God ranged from a low of 40 percent in Sweden to a high of 100 percent in Pakistan.

Researchers have found that adolescent girls are more religious than are adolescent boys (King & Roeser, 2009). One study of 13- to 17-year-olds revealed that girls are more likely to frequently attend religious services, perceive that religion shapes their daily lives, participate in religious youth groups, pray more alone, and feel closer to God (Smith & Denton, 2005).

Adolescents participating in a church youth group. *What are some positive aspects of religion in adolescents' lives?*

The Positive Role of Religion and Spirituality in Adolescents' and Emerging Adults' Lives Researchers have found that various aspects of religion are linked with positive outcomes for adolescents (Day, 2010; King & Roeser, 2009; Mellor & Freeborn, 2011). A recent study revealed that a higher level of church engagement (based on years of attendance, choice in attending, and participation in activities) was related to higher grades for male adolescents (Kang & Romo, 2011). Churchgoing may benefit students because religious communities encourage socially acceptable behavior, which includes doing well in school. Churchgoing also may benefit students because churches often offer positive role models for students.

Religion also plays a role in adolescents' health and whether they engage in problem behaviors (King & Roeser, 2009). In a national random sample of more than 2,000 11- to 18-year-olds, those who were higher in religiosity were less likely to smoke, drink alcohol, use marijuana, be truant from school, engage in delinquent activities, and be depressed than were their low-religiosity counterparts (Sinha, Cnaan, & Gelles, 2007). A recent study of ninth- to twelfth-graders revealed that more frequent religious attendance in one grade predicted lower levels of substance abuse in the next grade (Good & Willoughby, 2010).

Many religious adolescents also internalize their religion's message about caring and concern for people. For example, in one survey, religious youth were almost three times as likely to engage in community service as were nonreligious youth (Youniss, McLellan, & Yates, 1999).

How does religious thinking change in adolescence? How is religion linked to adolescents' health?

Developmental Changes Adolescence and emerging adulthood can be especially important junctures in religious development (Day, 2010; King & Roeser, 2009). Even if children have been indoctrinated into a religion by their parents, because of advances in their cognitive development adolescents and emerging adults may question what their own religious beliefs truly are.

Cognitive Changes Many of the cognitive changes thought to influence religious development involve Piaget's cognitive developmental theory, which we discussed in Chapter 3. More so than in childhood, adolescents think more abstractly, idealistically, and logically. The increase in abstract thinking lets adolescents consider various ideas about religious and spiritual concepts. For example, an adolescent might ask how a loving God can possibly exist given the extensive suffering of many people in the world (Good & Willoughby, 2008). Adolescents' increased idealistic thinking provides a foundation for thinking about whether religion provides the best route to a better, more ideal world than the present. And adolescents' increased logical reasoning gives them the ability to develop hypotheses and systematically sort through different answers to spiritual questions (Good & Willoughby, 2008).

spirituality Experiencing something beyond oneself in a transcendent manner and living in a way that benefits others and society.

Erikson's Theory During adolescence and emerging adulthood, especially emerging adulthood, identity development becomes a central focus (Erikson, 1968; Kroger, 2007). Adolescents and emerging adults want to know answers to questions like these: "Who am I?" "What am I all about as a person?" "What kind of life do I want to lead?" As part of their search for identity, adolescents and emerging adults begin to grapple in more sophisticated, logical ways with such questions as "Why am I on this planet?" "Is there really a God or higher spiritual being, or have I just been believing what my parents and the church imprinted in my mind?" "What really are my religious views?" One study found that college students' identity integration, defined as "the extent to which one's moral values have become integrated into identity," was related to intrinsic religious orientation, defined as "one's motivation for engaging in religious practice," and self-reported altruism (Maclean, Walker, & Matsuba, 2004, p. 429). In one analysis, it was proposed that the link between identity and spirituality in adolescence and emerging adulthood can serve as a gateway for developing a spiritual identity that "transcends, but not necessarily excludes, the assigned religious identity in childhood" (Templeton & Eccles, 2006, p. 261).

Religious Socialization and Parenting Religious institutions created by adults are designed to introduce certain beliefs to children and thereby ensure that they will carry on a religious tradition. Various societies utilize Sunday schools, parochial education, tribal transmission of religious traditions, and parental teaching of children at home to further this aim.

Many children and adolescents show an interest in religion, and many religious institutions created by adults (such as this Muslim school in Malaysia) are designed to introduce them to religious beliefs and ensure that they will carry on a religious tradition.

Does this religious socialization work? In many cases it does (Oser, Scarlett, & Bucher, 2006). In general, children and adolescents tend to adopt the religious teachings of their upbringing. If a religious change or reawakening occurs, it is most likely to take place during adolescence or emerging adulthood.

However, it is important to consider the quality of the parent-adolescent relationship and whether mothers or fathers are more influential (Granqvist & Dickie, 2006; King, Ramos, & Clardy, 2012; Ream & Savin-Williams, 2003). Adolescents who have a positive relationship with their parents or are securely attached to them are likely to adopt their parents' religious affiliation. But, when conflict or insecure attachment characterizes parent-adolescent relationships, adolescents may seek religious affiliation that is different from their parents' (Streib, 1999). A number of studies also have documented that mothers are more influential in their children's and adolescents' religious development than fathers are (King & Roeser, 2009). Mothers are likely more influential because they are more likely than fathers to go to church, lead family prayer, and converse with their children and youth about religion.

Religiousness and Sexuality in Adolescence and Emerging Adulthood One area of religion's influence on adolescent and emerging adult development involves sexual activity. Although variability and change in church teachings make it difficult to generalize about religious doctrines, most churches discourage premarital sex. Thus, the degree of adolescent and emerging adult participation in religious organizations may be more important than affiliation with a specific religion as a determinant of premarital sexual attitudes and behavior. Adolescents and emerging adults who frequently attend religious services are likely to hear messages about abstaining from sex. Involvement of adolescents and emerging adults in religious organizations also enhances the probability that they will become friends with adolescents who have restrictive attitudes toward premarital sex. A recent study revealed that adolescents with high religiosity were less likely to have had sexual intercourse (Gold & others, 2010).

As you read in Chapter 6, a recent study found that parents' religiosity was linked to a lower level of adolescents' risky sexual behavior, in part by adolescents hanging out with less sexually permissive peers (Landor & others, 2011). Also recall the discussion of a recent research review in Chapter 6, which concluded that *spirituality* was linked to these positive adolescent outcomes: less likely to intend to have sex, not engage in early sex, have sex less frequently, and not become pregnant (House & others, 2010).

developmental **connection**

Sexuality. An increasing number of positive youth development (PYD) programs include a focus on improving sexual outcomes in adolescence. Chapter 6, p. 195

Review *Connect* Reflect

LG3 Explain the roles of values, religion, and spirituality in adolescents' and emerging adults' lives.

Review

- What are values? What are some of today's college students' values, and how have they changed over the last three decades?
- How important are religion and spirituality in adolescents' and emerging adults' lives? What characterizes religious and spiritual development in adolescents and emerging adults?

Connect

- How might spirituality influence adolescents' identity development (Chapter 4)?

Reflect *Your Own Personal Journey of Life*

- What were your values, religious, and spiritual interests in middle school and high school? Have they changed since then? If so, how?

reach your **learning goals**

1 Domains of Moral Development

LG1 Discuss the domains of moral development.

Moral Thought

- Moral development involves thoughts, feelings, and behaviors regarding standards of right and wrong, and it consists of intrapersonal and interpersonal dimensions. Kohlberg developed a provocative theory of moral reasoning. He argued that moral development consists of three levels—preconventional, conventional, and postconventional—and six stages (two at each level). Increased internalization characterizes movement to levels two and three. Influences on the stages include modeling, cognitive conflict, peer relations, and role-taking opportunities. Kohlberg's critics say that he gave inadequate attention to moral behavior, did not adequately assess moral development, underestimated cultural influences, and underestimated the care perspective (Gilligan's theory). Research has found stronger links between gender-role classification and caring and prosocial behavior than between biological sex and caring and prosocial behavior. The domain theory of moral development states that there are different domains of social knowledge and reasoning, including moral, social conventional, and personal.

Moral Behavior

- Behaviorists argue that moral behavior is determined by the processes of reinforcement, punishment, and imitation. Situational variability in moral behavior is stressed by behaviorists. Hartshorne and May's classic study found considerable variation in moral behavior across situations. The social cognitive theory of moral development emphasizes a distinction between moral competence (the ability to produce moral behaviors) and moral performance (performing those behaviors in specific situations). Social cognitive theorists note that Kohlberg gave inadequate attention to moral behavior and situational variations. Prosocial behavior has especially been studied in the realm of altruism. Adolescents engage in more prosocial behavior than children do, and adolescent girls engage in prosocial behavior more than adolescent boys do. Forgiveness and gratitude are important aspects of prosocial behavior.

Moral Feeling

- In Freud's theory, the superego—the moral branch of personality—is one of personality's three main structures. Freud also argued that through identification children internalize a parent's standards of right and wrong. Children may conform to moral standards in order to avoid guilt, in the Freudian view. The two main components of the superego are the ego ideal and conscience. Feeling empathy means reacting to another's feelings with an emotional response that is similar to that person's feelings. Empathy involves perspective taking as a cognitive component. Empathy changes developmentally. The contemporary perspective on emotions and moral development is that both positive feelings (such as empathy) and negative feelings (such as guilt) contribute to adolescents' moral development. Emotions are interwoven with the cognitive and social dimensions of moral development.

Moral Personality

- Recently, there has been a surge of interest in studying moral personality. This interest has focused on moral identity, moral character, and moral exemplars. Blasi's view of moral identity emphasizes willpower (self-control), integrity, and moral desire. Moral character involves having the strength of your convictions, persisting, and overcoming distractions and obstacles. Moral character consists of having certain virtues, such as honesty, care, and conscientiousness. Moral exemplars are people who have lived exemplary lives.

2 Contexts of Moral Development

Describe how the contexts of parenting and schools can influence moral development.

Parenting

- Discipline can involve love withdrawal, power assertion, or induction. Induction has been the most effective technique, especially with middle-SES children. Children's moral development is advanced when parents are supportive, create opportunities for their children to learn about others' perspectives, include children in family decision making, model moral behavior and thinking, state the behaviors that are expected and why, and encourage an internal moral orientation.

Schools

- The hidden curriculum, initially described by Dewey, is the moral atmosphere of every school. Contemporary approaches to moral education include character education, values clarification, cognitive moral education, service learning, and integrative ethical education. Cheating is a moral education concern and can take many forms. Various aspects of the situation influence whether students will cheat or not.

3 Values, Religion, and Spirituality

Explain the roles of values, religion, and spirituality in adolescents' and emerging adults' lives.

Values

- Values are the beliefs and attitudes about the way things should be. Over the last two decades, adolescents have shown an increased concern for personal well-being and a decreased interest in the welfare of others. Recently, adolescents have shown an increased interest in community values and societal issues.

Religion and Spirituality

- Distinctions have been made between the concepts of religion, religiousness, and spirituality. Many children, adolescents, and emerging adults show an interest in religion, and religious institutions are designed to introduce them to religious beliefs. Adolescence and emerging adulthood may be special junctures in religious and spiritual development for many individuals. Various aspects of religion and spirituality are linked with positive outcomes in adolescent development. Cognitive changes—such as increases in abstract, idealistic, and logical thinking—influence adolescents' religious and spiritual development. Erikson's ideas on identity can be applied to understanding the increased interest in religion during adolescence and emerging adulthood. When adolescents have a positive relationship with parents and/or are securely attached to them, they often adopt their parents' religious beliefs. Links have been found between adolescent/emerging adult sexuality and religiousness.

key terms

moral development 224
preconventional reasoning 226
conventional reasoning 226
postconventional reasoning 226
justice perspective 231
care perspective 231
domain theory of moral development 231
social conventional reasoning 231
social cognitive theory of moral development 233
altruism 234
forgiveness 234
gratitude 235
ego ideal 235
conscience 235
empathy 235
moral identity 236
moral exemplars 237
love withdrawal 239
power assertion 239
induction 239
hidden curriculum 239
character education 240
values clarification 241
cognitive moral education 241
service learning 241
values 244
religion 245
religiousness 245
spirituality 247

key people

Lawrence Kohlberg 225
James Rest 230
John Gibbs 231
Carol Gilligan 231
Hugh Hartshorne and Mark May 233
Albert Bandura 233
Gustavo Carlo 234
Sigmund Freud 235
Erik Erikson 235
Walter Mischel 236
Lawrence Walker 237
Darcia Narváez 237
John Dewey 239
William Damon 245
Pamela King 245

resources for improving the lives of adolescents

Moral Development and Reality
by John C. Gibbs (2010, 2nd ed.)
Boston: Allyn & Bacon

Leading researcher and theorist John Gibbs provides an insightful, contemporary examination of many aspects of moral development, including treatment programs for antisocial youth.

Handbook of Moral and Character Education
edited by Larry Nucci and Darcia Narváez (2008)
New York: Routledge

A number of leading experts describe their views of many aspects of moral education.

Moral Cognitions and Prosocial Responding in Adolescence
by Nancy Eisenberg, Amanda Morris, Brenda McDaniel, and Tracy Spinrad in R. M. Lerner and L. Steinberg (Eds.)
Handbook of Adolescent Psychology (2009, 3rd ed.)
New York: Wiley

Leading experts provide an up-to-date look at theory and research on moral development in adolescence.

Spiritual Development
edited by Peter Benson, Eugene Roehlkepartain, and Kathryn Hong (2008)
Thousand Oaks, CA: Sage

Leading scholars describe a range of topics on spiritual development in youth.

self-assessment

The Student Online Learning Center includes the following self-assessment for further exploration:

- *My Spiritual Well-Being*

chapter 8 FAMILIES

chapter outline

Family Processes

Learning Goal 1 Discuss the nature of family processes in adolescence.

Reciprocal Socialization and the Family as a System
Maturation

Adolescents' and Emerging Adults' Relationships with Their Parents

Learning Goal 2 Describe adolescents' and emerging adults' relationships with their parents.

Parents as Managers
Parenting Styles
Coparenting
Parent-Adolescent Conflict
Autonomy and Attachment
Emerging Adults' Relationships with Their Parents
Intergenerational Relationships

Sibling Relationships

Learning Goal 3 Characterize sibling relationships in adolescence.

Sibling Roles
Birth Order

The Changing Family in a Changing Society

Learning Goal 4 Describe the changing family in a changing society.

Divorced Families
Stepfamilies
Working Parents
Adoption
Gay and Lesbian Parents
Culture and Ethnicity

Social Policy, Adolescents, and Families

Learning Goal 5 Explain what is needed for improved social policy involving adolescents and their families.

My mother and I depend on each other. However, if something separated us, I think I could still get along OK. I know that my mother continues to have an important influence on me. Sometimes she gets on my nerves, but I still basically like her, and respect her, a lot. We have our arguments, and I don't always get my way, but she is willing to listen to me.

—Amy, age 16

You go from a point at which your parents are responsible for you to a point at which you want a lot more independence. Finally, you are more independent, and you feel like you have to be more responsible for yourself; otherwise you are not going to do very well in this world. It's important for parents to still be there to support you, but at some point, you've got to look in the mirror and say, "I can do it myself."

—John, age 18

I don't get along very well with my parents. They try to dictate how I dress, who I date, how much I study, what I do on weekends, and how much time I spend talking on the phone. They are big intruders in my life. Why won't they let me make my own decisions? I'm mature enough to handle these things. When they jump down my throat at every little thing I do, it makes me mad and I say things to them I probably shouldn't. They just don't understand me very well.

—Ed, age 17

My father never seems to have any time to spend with me. He is gone a lot on business, and when he comes home, he is either too tired to do anything or plops down and watches TV and doesn't want to be bothered. He thinks I don't work hard enough and don't have values that were as solid as his generation. It is a very distant relationship. I actually spend more time talking to my mom than to him. I guess I should work a little harder in school than I do, but I still don't think he has the right to say such negative things to me. I like my mom a lot better because I think she is a much nicer person.

—Tom, age 14

We have our arguments and our differences, and there are moments when I get very angry with my parents, but most of the time they are like heated discussions. I have to say what I think because I don't think they are always right. Most of the time when there is an argument, we can discuss the problem and eventually find a course that we all can live with. Not every time, though, because there are some occasions when things just remain unresolved. Even when we have an unresolved conflict, I still would have to say that I get along pretty good with my parents.

—Ann, age 16

preview

Although parent-adolescent relationships can vary considerably, researchers are finding that for the most part, the relationships are both (1) very important aspects of development, and (2) more positive than once thought. This chapter examines families as a context for adolescent development. We begin by exploring family processes and then discuss parent-adolescent relationships, followed by relationships with siblings. Next, we consider the substantial changes of families in a changing society. The chapter concludes by focusing on social policy recommendations for the well-being of adolescents and their families.

1 Family Processes

Discuss the nature of family processes in adolescence.

Reciprocal Socialization and the Family as a System | Maturation

> It is not enough for parents to understand children. They must accord children the privilege of understanding them.
>
> —Milton Saperstein, *American Author, 20th Century*

Researchers are especially interested in the family processes that adolescents experience. We begin our exploration of family processes by examining how family members interact with one another.

RECIPROCAL SOCIALIZATION AND THE FAMILY AS A SYSTEM

For many years, socialization between parents and children/adolescents was considered to be a one-way process: Children and adolescents were seen as the products of their parents' socialization techniques. However, today parent-adolescent relationships are viewed as reciprocal (Gault-Sherman, 2011; Manongdo & Garcia, 2011; Parke & Clarke-Stewart, 2011). **Reciprocal socialization** is the process by which children and adolescents socialize parents, just as parents socialize them.

As a social system, the family can be thought of as a constellation of subsystems defined in terms of generation, gender, and role. Divisions of labor among family members define specific subunits, and attachments define others. Each family member is a participant in several subsystems—some dyadic (involving two people), some polyadic (involving more than two people). The father and the adolescent represent one dyadic subsystem, the mother and the father another; the mother-father-adolescent represent one polyadic subsystem, the mother and two siblings another. Thus, when the behavior of one family member changes, it can influence the behavior of other family members (Parke & Clarke-Stewart, 2011).

An organizational scheme that highlights the reciprocal influences of family members and family subsystems is illustrated in Figure 8.1 (Belsky, 1981). As the arrows in the figure show, marital relations, parenting, and adolescent behavior can have both direct and indirect effects on each other. An example of a direct effect is the influence of the parent's behavior on the adolescent. An example of an indirect effect is how the relationship between the spouses mediates the way a parent acts toward the adolescent. For example, marital conflict might reduce the efficiency of parenting, in which case marital conflict would have an indirect effect on the adolescent's behavior.

reciprocal socialization The process by which children and adolescents socialize parents, just as parents socialize them.

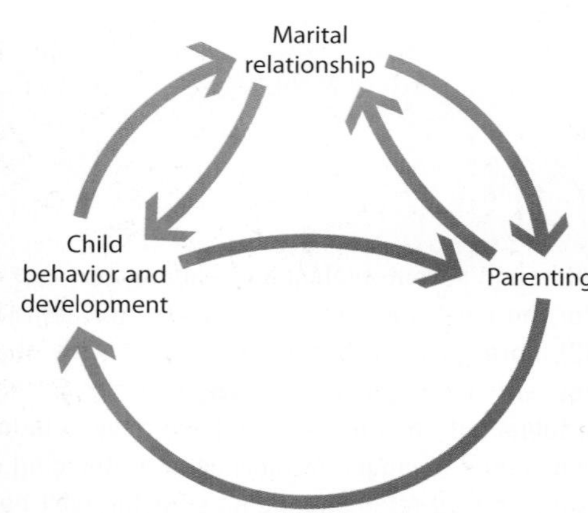

FIGURE **8.1**
INTERACTION BETWEEN ADOLESCENTS AND THEIR PARENTS: DIRECT AND INDIRECT EFFECTS

As researchers have broadened their focus in families beyond just studying the parent-adolescent relationship, an increasingly studied aspect of the family system involves the link between marital relationships and parenting (Carlson & others, 2011). The most consistent findings are that happily married parents are more sensitive, responsive, warm, and affectionate toward their children and adolescents (Fosco & Grych, 2010). Researchers have also found that marital satisfaction is often related to good parenting. The marital relationship is an important support for parenting (Cowan, Cowan, & Barry, 2011; Parent & others, 2011). When parents report more intimacy and better communication in their marriage, they are more affectionate to their children and adolescents (Grych, 2002). Thus, an important, if unintended, benefit of marriage enhancement programs is the improvement of parenting—and consequently healthier children and adolescents. Programs that focus on parenting skills might also benefit from including attention to the participants' marriages.

MATURATION

Nineteenth- and twentieth-century American author Mark Twain once remarked that when he was 14 his father was so ignorant he could hardly stand to have the man around him, but when Mark got to be 21, he was astonished at how much his father had learned in those seven years! Mark Twain's comments suggest that maturation is an important theme of parent-adolescent relationships. Adolescents change as they make the transition from childhood to adulthood, but their parents also change during their adult years.

Adolescent Changes Among the changes in the adolescent that can influence parent-adolescent relationships are puberty, expanded logical reasoning, increased idealistic thought, violated expectations, changes in schooling, peers, friendships, dating, and movement toward independence. Several investigations have shown that conflict between parents and adolescents, especially between mothers and sons, is the most stressful during the apex of pubertal growth (Steinberg, 1988). Also, early-maturing adolescents experience more conflict with their parents than do adolescents who mature late or on time (Collins & Steinberg, 2006).

In terms of cognitive changes, the adolescent can now reason in more logical ways with parents than in childhood. During childhood, parents may be able to get by with saying, "Okay. That is it. We do it my way or else," and the child conforms. But with increased cognitive skills adolescents no longer are likely to accept such a statement as a reason for conforming to parental dictates. Adolescents want to know, often in fine detail, why they are being disciplined. Even when parents give what seem to be logical reasons for discipline, adolescents' cognitive sophistication may call attention to deficiencies in the reasoning.

developmental **connection**

Cognitive Theory. In Piaget's formal operational stage, adolescents' thought becomes more abstract, idealistic, and logical. Chapter 3, p. 94

In addition, the adolescent's increasing idealistic thought comes into play in parent-adolescent relationships. Parents are now evaluated vis-à-vis what an ideal parent is. The very real interactions with parents, which inevitably involve some negative interchanges and flaws, are placed next to the adolescent's schema of an ideal parent. And, as part of their egocentrism, adolescents' concerns with how others view them are likely to produce overreactions to parents' comments. A mother may comment to her adolescent daughter that she needs a new blouse. The daughter might respond, "What's the matter? You don't think I have good taste? You think I look gross, don't you? Well, you are the one who is gross!" The same comment made to the daughter several years earlier in late childhood probably would have elicited a less intense response.

Another dimension of the adolescent's changing cognitive world related to parent-adolescent relations is the expectations parents and adolescents have for each other. Preadolescent children are often compliant and easy to manage. As they enter puberty, children begin to question or seek rationales for parental demands. Parents might perceive this behavior as resistant and oppositional because it departs from

To what extent is an adolescent's development likely to be influenced by early experiences with parents?

developmental **connection**

Peers. The transition to middle or junior high school can be stressful because it takes place when significant biological, cognitive, and socioemotional changes are occurring. Chapter 10, p. 334

the child's previously compliant behavior. Parents often respond to the lack of compliance with increased pressure for compliance. In this situation, expectations that were stabilized during a period of relatively slow developmental change are lagging behind the behavior of the adolescent in the period of rapid pubertal change.

What dimensions of the adolescent's socioemotional world contribute to parent-adolescent relationships? Adolescence brings with it new definitions of socially appropriate behavior. In our society, these definitions are associated with changes in schooling. As they make the transition to middle or junior high school, adolescents are required to function in a more anonymous, larger environment with multiple and varying teachers. More work is required, and students must show more initiative and responsibility to adapt successfully. Adolescents spend more time with peers than when they were children, and they develop more sophisticated friendships than in childhood. Adolescents also begin to push more strongly for independence. In sum, parents are called on to adapt to the changing world of the adolescent's schooling, peer relations, and push for autonomy.

Parental Changes Parental changes that contribute to parent-adolescent relationships involve marital satisfaction, economic burdens, career reevaluation and time perspective, and health and body concerns. For most parents, marital satisfaction increases after adolescents or emerging adults leave home (Fingerman, 2011). In addition, parents feel a greater economic burden when their children are in adolescence and emerging adulthood. During this time, parents may reevaluate their occupational achievement, deciding whether they have met their youthful aspirations of success. They may look to the future and think about how much time they have remaining to accomplish their life goals. Many adolescents, meanwhile, look to the future with unbound optimism, sensing that they have an unlimited amount of time to accomplish what they desire. Parents of adolescents may become preoccupied with concerns about their own health, body integrity, and sexual attractiveness (Almeida, 2011; Whitfield, 2011). Even when their body and sexual attractiveness are not deteriorating, many parents of adolescents perceive that they are. By contrast, many adolescents have reached or are beginning to reach the peak of their physical attractiveness, strength, and health. Although both adolescents and their parents show a heightened preoccupation with their bodies, adolescents' outcome probably is more positive.

What are some maturational changes in parents that might influence parent-adolescent relationships?

Multiple Developmental Trajectories The concept of **multiple developmental trajectories** refers to the fact that adults follow one trajectory and children and adolescents another one (Parke & Buriel, 2006; Parke & Clarke-Stewart, 2011). How adult and child/adolescent developmental trajectories mesh is important for understanding the timing of entry into various family tasks. Adult developmental trajectories include timing of entry into marriage, cohabitation, or parenthood; child developmental trajectories include timing of child care and entry into middle school. The timing of some family tasks and changes are planned, such as reentry into the workforce or delaying parenthood, whereas others are not, such as job loss or divorce (Parke & Buriel, 2006).

The changes in adolescents' parents we considered earlier are typical of development in middle adulthood (Fingerman & Birditt, 2011). Most adolescents' parents either are in middle adulthood or are rapidly approaching this period of life. However, in the last two decades, the timing of parenthood in the United States has undergone some dramatic shifts. Parenthood is taking place earlier for some, and later for others, than in previous decades. First, the number of adolescent pregnancies in the United States increased considerably in the 1970s and 1980s. Although the adolescent pregnancy rate has decreased since then, the U.S. adolescent pregnancy rate remains one of the highest in the developed world. Second, the number of women who postpone childbearing until their thirties and early forties simultaneously increased (Popenoe & Whitehead, 2008). We discussed adolescents as parents in Chapter 6. Here we focus on sociohistorical changes related to postponement of childbearing until the thirties or forties.

developmental **connection**

Sexuality. In ethnic comparisons in the United States, Latina adolescents have the highest adolescent pregnancy rate. Chapter 6, p. 203

There are many contrasts between becoming a parent in adolescence and becoming a parent 15 to 30 years later. Delayed childbearing allows for considerable progress in occupational and educational domains. For both males and females, education usually has been completed, and career development is well established.

The marital relationship varies with the timing of parenthood onset. In one investigation, couples who began childbearing in their early twenties were compared with those who began in their early thirties (Walter, 1986). The late-starting couples had more egalitarian relationships, with men more often participating in child care and household tasks.

Is parent-child interaction different for families in which parents delay having children until their thirties or forties? Investigators have found that older fathers are warmer, communicate better, encourage more achievement, place fewer demands on their children, are more lax in enforcing rules, and show less rejection with their children than younger fathers. However, older fathers also are less likely to engage in physical play or sports with their children (MacDonald, 1987). These findings suggest that sociohistorical changes are resulting in different developmental trajectories for many families, trajectories that involve changes in the way marital partners and parents and adolescents interact.

The generations of living things pass in a short time and like runners hand on the torch of life.

—Lucretius
Roman Poet, 1st Century B.C.

multiple developmental trajectories Concept that adults follow one trajectory and children and adolescents another one; how these trajectories mesh is important.

Review *Connect* Reflect

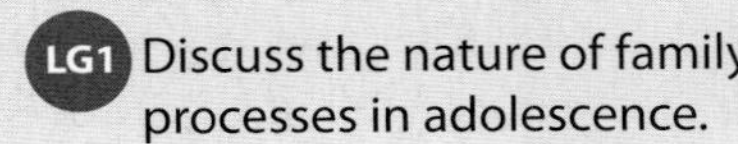

Discuss the nature of family processes in adolescence.

Review

- What is reciprocal socialization? How can the family be described as a system?
- What roles do maturation of the adolescent and maturation of parents play in understanding parent-adolescent relationships?

Connect

- What has the historical perspective on adolescence (Chapter 1) contributed to our view of the family as a system?

Reflect *Your Own Personal Journey of Life*

- Think about your family as a system as you developed through adolescence. How might your parents' marital relationship have influenced your development?

2 Adolescents' and Emerging Adults' Relationships with Their Parents

LG2 Describe adolescents' and emerging adults' relationships with their parents.

- Parents as Managers
- Parenting Styles
- Coparenting
- Parent-Adolescent Conflict
- Autonomy and Attachment
- Emerging Adults' Relationships with Their Parents
- Intergenerational Relationships

We have seen how the expectations of adolescents and their parents often seem violated as adolescents change dramatically during the course of puberty. Many parents see their child changing from a compliant being into someone who is noncompliant, oppositional, and resistant to parental standards. Parents often clamp down and put more pressure on the adolescent to conform to parental standards. Many parents often deal with the young adolescent as if they expect him or her to become a mature being within the next 10 to 15 minutes. But the transition from childhood to adulthood is a long journey with many hills and valleys. Adolescents are not going to conform to adult standards immediately. Parents who recognize that adolescents take a long time "to get it right" usually deal more competently and calmly with adolescent transgressions than do parents who demand immediate conformity to parental standards. Yet other parents, rather than placing heavy demands on their adolescents for compliance, do virtually the opposite, letting them do as they please in a very permissive manner.

Our discussion of parent-adolescent relationships will indicate that neither high-intensity demands for compliance nor an unwillingness to monitor and be involved in the adolescent's development is likely to be a wise parenting strategy. Further, we will explore another misperception that parents of adolescents sometimes entertain. Parents may perceive that virtually all conflict with their adolescent is bad. We will discover that a moderate degree of conflict with parents in adolescence is not only inevitable but may also serve a positive developmental function. We also will explore relationships between emerging adults and their parents, including examination of strategies that emerging adults and their parents can use to get along better. And, to conclude this section, we will discuss how adolescent development is influenced by intergenerational relationships.

connecting with adolescents

Needing Parents as Guides

Stacey Christensen, age 16: "I am lucky enough to have open communication with my parents. Whenever I am in need or just need to talk, my parents are there for me. My advice to parents is to let your teens grow at their own pace, be open with them so that you can be there for them. We need guidance; our parents need to help but not be too overwhelming.

Stacey Christensen.

PARENTS AS MANAGERS

Parents can play important roles as managers of adolescents' opportunities, as monitors of adolescents' social relationships, and as social initiators and arrangers (Brown & Bakken, 2011; Parke & Buriel, 2006; Parke & Clarke-Stewart, 2011). An important developmental task in adolescence is to develop the ability to make competent decisions in an increasingly independent manner. To help adolescents reach their full potential, parents can assume an important role as effective managers who find information, make contacts, help structure choices, and provide guidance (Gauvain & Perez, 2007). Parents who fulfill this important managerial role help adolescents to avoid pitfalls and to work their way through a myriad of choices and decisions they face (Mounts, 2007, 2011).

Parents can serve as regulators of opportunities for their adolescents' social contact with peers, friends, and adults. Mothers are more likely than fathers to have a managerial role in parenting. In adolescence, it could involve participating in a parent-teacher conference and subsequently managing the adolescent's homework activity.

Researchers have found that family-management practices are positively related to students' grades and self-responsibility, and negatively to school-related problems (Eccles, 2007). One of the most important family-management practices in this regard is maintaining a structured and organized family environment, such as establishing routines for homework, chores, bedtime, and so on. One study focused on African American families, examining links between mothers' reports of family-management practices, including routine, and adolescents' school-related behavior (Taylor & Lopez, 2005). Family routine (well managed and organized) was positively related to adolescents' school achievement, paying attention in class, and attendance, and negatively linked to their school-related problems.

A key aspect of the managerial role of parenting is effective monitoring, which is especially important as children move into the adolescent years (Laird, Marrero, & Sherwood, 2010; Smetana, 2010, 2011a,b). Monitoring includes supervising an adolescent's choice of social settings, activities, and friends. A research review of family functioning in African American students' academic achievement found that when African American parents monitored their son's academic achievement by ensuring that homework was completed, restricted time spent on nonproductive distractions (such as video games and TV), and participated in a consistent, positive dialogue with teachers and school officials, their son's academic achievement benefited (Mandara, 2006).

A recent study found that adolescent's perceptions of a higher level of parental solicitation (assessed by asking the adolescents how often in the last month their mother initiated a conversation about their free time) at age 11 predicted a lower level of antisocial behavior at age 12 among young adolescents reporting large amounts of unsupervised time (Laird, Marrero, & Sentse, 2010). Another recent study revealed that mothers who perceived that their neighborhood was problematic reported lower knowledge of their adolescents' whereabouts (Byrnes & others, 2011). In this study, knowledge of the adolescents' whereabouts was linked to adolescents' lower use of alcohol and a lower incidence of delinquency. As we will discuss in Chapter 13, a lack of adequate parental monitoring is the parental factor that is related to juvenile delinquency more than any other.

A current interest involving parental monitoring focuses on adolescents' management of their parents' access to information, especially disclosing or concealing strategies about their activities (Amsel & Smetana, 2011; Hamza & Willoughby, 2011; Laird & Marrero, 2011; Keijsers & Laird, 2010). Researchers have found that adolescents' disclosure to parents about their whereabouts, activities, and friends is linked to positive adolescent adjustment (Laird & Marrero, 2010; Smetana, 2011a,b). For example, a recent study revealed that adolescents in three countries—Costa Rica, Thailand, and South Africa—who engaged in a higher level of self-disclosure to parents were more competent (Hunter & others, 2011).

What characterizes adolescents' management of their parents' access to information?

Self-disclosure to parents varies according to the adolescent's developmental level and activities. One study found that, when concerned about parental disapproval, older adolescents fully disclosed less and lied somewhat more than younger adolescents (Smetana & others, 2009). Another study revealed that adolescents' reasons for not disclosing information to parents varied across activities (Smetana & others, 2007). Adolescents failed to disclose their engagement in risky activities, such as drinking alcohol or driving in a car with a teen driver, because they feared parental disapproval or punishment. By contrast, adolescents did not disclose many of their personal activities, such as privacy, personal preferences, how they spend their allowance, and what they talk about with friends on the phone, because they perceived these to be private matters.

A recent longitudinal study revealed that low levels of disclosure (telling all or telling if asked, for example) and high levels of concealment (keeping something secret or lying, for example) were related to increased antisocial and rule-breaking behavior one year later (Laird & Marrero, 2010). Also, disclosing strategies are connected to positive aspects of parent-adolescent relationships, such as trust, while concealing strategies are linked to negative aspects of parent-adolescent relationships, such as feeling controlled (Keijsers & Laird, 2010). Adolescents' willingness to disclose information to parents also is related to responsive parenting and a higher level of parental behavioral control, which are components of a positive parenting style, *authoritative parenting,* which we discuss in the next section.

PARENTING STYLES

Parents want their adolescents to grow into socially mature individuals, and they often feel a great deal of frustration in their role as parents. Psychologists have long searched for parenting ingredients that promote competent social development in adolescents (Garai, McKee, & Forehand, 2012; Parke & Clarke-Stewart, 2011; Phares & Rojas, 2012). For example, behaviorist John Watson (1930) urged parents not to be too affectionate with their children. Early research focused on a distinction between physical and psychological discipline, or between controlling and permissive parenting. More recently, there has been greater precision in unraveling the dimensions of competent parenting (Grusec, 2011).

Especially widespread is the view of Diana Baumrind (1971, 1991), who notes that parents should be neither punitive nor aloof from their adolescents, but rather should develop rules and be affectionate with them. She emphasizes four styles of parenting that are associated with different aspects of the adolescent's social behavior—authoritarian, authoritative, neglectful, and indulgent:

- **Authoritarian parenting** is a restrictive, punitive style in which the parent exhorts the adolescent to follow directions and to respect work and effort. The authoritarian parent places firm limits and controls on the adolescent and allows little verbal exchange. For example, an authoritarian parent might say, "You do it my way or else. There will be no discussion!" Authoritarian parenting is associated with adolescents' socially incompetent behavior. Adolescents of authoritarian parents often are anxious about social comparison, fail to initiate activity, and have poor communication skills.
- **Authoritative parenting** encourages adolescents to be independent but still places limits and controls on their actions. Extensive verbal give-and-take is allowed, and parents are warm and nurturant toward the adolescent. An authoritative father, for example, might put his arm around the adolescent in a comforting way and say, "You know you should not have done that. Let's talk about how you can handle the situation better next time." Authoritative parenting is associated with adolescents' socially competent behavior. The adolescents of authoritative parents are self-reliant and socially responsible.

authoritarian parenting A restrictive, punitive style in which the parent exhorts the adolescent to follow the parent's directions and to respect work and effort. Firm limits and controls are placed on the adolescent, and little verbal exchange is allowed. This style is associated with adolescents' socially incompetent behavior.

authoritative parenting A style encouraging adolescents to be independent but still placing limits and controls on their actions. Extensive verbal give-and-take is allowed, and parents are warm and nurturant toward the adolescent. This style is associated with adolescents' socially competent behavior.

CHEEVERWOOD by Michael Fry

- **Neglectful parenting** is a style in which the parent is very uninvolved in the adolescent's life. The neglectful parent cannot answer the question, "It is 10:00 p.m. Do you know where your adolescent is?" Neglectful parenting is associated with adolescents' socially incompetent behavior, especially a lack of self-control. Adolescents have a strong need for their parents to care about them; adolescents whose parents are neglectful develop the sense that other aspects of the parents' lives are more important than they are. Adolescents whose parents are neglectful are socially incompetent: they show poor self-control and do not handle independence well. Closely related to the concept of neglectful parenting is a lack of parental monitoring which, as we discussed earlier, is linked to a number of negative outcomes for adolescents.
- **Indulgent parenting** is a style in which parents are highly involved with their adolescents but place few demands or controls on them. Indulgent parents allow their adolescents to do what they want, and the result is that the adolescents never learn to control their own behavior and always expect to get their way. Some parents deliberately rear their adolescents in this way because they mistakenly believe that the combination of warm involvement with few restraints will produce a creative, confident adolescent. However, indulgent parenting is associated with adolescents' social incompetence, especially a lack of self-control.

	Accepting, responsive	Rejecting, unresponsive
Demanding, controlling	Authoritative	Authoritarian
Undemanding, uncontrolling	Indulgent	Neglectful

FIGURE **8.2**
FOURFOLD SCHEME OF PARENTING STYLES

In our discussion of parenting styles, we have talked about parents who vary along the dimensions of acceptance, responsiveness, demand, and control. As shown in Figure 8.2, the four parenting styles—authoritarian, authoritative, neglectful, and indulgent—can be described in terms of these dimensions (Maccoby & Martin, 1983).

In general, researchers have found authoritative parenting to be related to positive aspects of development (Milevsky, 2012; Steinberg & Silk, 2002). For example, a recent study revealed that delinquency was lowest in families with at least one authoritative parent and highest in families with two neglectful parents (Hoeve & others, 2011). Why is authoritative parenting likely to be the most effective style? These reasons have been given (Steinberg & Silk, 2002):

- Authoritative parents establish an appropriate balance between control and autonomy, giving adolescents opportunities to develop independence while providing the standards, limits, and guidance that children and adolescents need.
- Authoritative parents are more likely to engage adolescents in verbal give-and-take and allow adolescents to express their views. This type of family

neglectful parenting A style in which the parent is very uninvolved in the adolescent's life. It is associated with adolescents' social incompetence, especially a lack of self-control.

indulgent parenting A style in which parents are highly involved with their adolescents but place few demands or controls on them. This is associated with adolescents' social incompetence, especially a lack of self-control.

What parenting style do many Asian Americans practice?

discussion is likely to help adolescents to understand social relationships and the requirements for being a socially competent person.

- The warmth and parental involvement provided by authoritative parents make the adolescent more receptive to parental influence.

Parenting Styles and Ethnicity In general, African American, Latino, and Asian American parents use the authoritarian style more than do non-Latino White parents, who more often use an authoritative style (Fuligni, Hughes, & Way, 2009). Do the benefits of authoritative parenting transcend the boundaries of ethnicity, socioeconomic status, and household composition? Although some exceptions have been found, evidence linking authoritative parenting with competence on the part of the adolescent occurs in research across a wide range of ethnic groups, social strata, cultures, and family structures (Steinberg & Silk, 2002).

However, research with ethnic groups suggests that some aspects of the authoritarian style may be associated with positive child outcomes (Dixon, Graber, & Brooks-Gunn, 2008; Parke & Buriel, 2006). Elements of the authoritarian style may take on different meanings and have different effects, depending on the context.

Aspects of traditional Asian child-rearing practices are often continued by Asian American families. In some cases, these practices have been described as authoritarian. However, Ruth Chao (2001, 2005, 2007; Chao & Otsuki-Clutter, 2011) argues that the style of parenting used by many Asian American parents is best conceptualized as a type of training in which parents are concerned and involved in their children's lives rather than reflecting strict or authoritarian control. Thus, the parenting style Chao describes—training—is based on a type of parental control that is distinct from the more "domineering" control reflected in the authoritarian parenting style. The positive outcomes of the training parenting style in Asian American families occur in the high academic achievement of Asian American children (Stevenson & Zusho, 2002). In recent research on parenting adolescents, Chinese American parents endorsed parental control and the Confucian parental goals of perseverance, working hard in school, obedience, and being sensitive to parents' wishes (Chao & Otsuki-Clutter, 2011; Russell, Crockett, & Chao, 2010).

Latino child-rearing practices encourage the development of a self and identity that is embedded in the family and requires respect and obedience (Harwood & others, 2002). As in African American families, there is a high level of cross-generational and co-residence arrangements and assistance (Zinn & Wells, 2000).

Researchers have found that African American parents are more likely than non-Latino White parents to use physical punishment (Deater-Deckard & Dodge, 1997). However, the use of physical punishment is linked with more externalized child problems (such as acting out and high levels of aggression) in non-Latino White families but not in African American families. One explanation of this finding is the need for African American parents to enforce rules in the dangerous environments in which they are more likely to live (Harrison-Hale, McLoyd, & Smedley, 2004). In this context, requiring obedience to parental authority may be an adaptive strategy to keep children from engaging in antisocial behavior that can have serious consequences for the victim or the perpetrator.

Further Thoughts on Parenting Styles Several caveats about parenting styles are in order. First, the parenting styles do not capture the important themes of reciprocal socialization and synchrony (Parke & Clarke-Stewart, 2011). Keep in mind that adolescents socialize parents, just as parents socialize adolescents (Smetana, 2011a,b). Second, many parents use a combination of techniques rather than a single technique, although one technique may be dominant. Although consistent parenting is usually recommended, the wise parent may sense the importance of being more permissive in certain situations, more authoritarian in others, and yet more authoritative in others. Also, some critics argue that the concept of parenting style is too broad and that more research needs to be conducted to "unpack" parenting styles by studying various components that comprise the styles (Grusec, 2011). For example, is parental monitoring more important than warmth in predicting adolescent outcomes?

COPARENTING

The organizing theme of coparenting is that poor coordination, active undermining and disparagement of the other parent, lack of cooperation and warmth, and disconnection by one parenting partner—either alone or in combination with overinvolvement by the other—are conditions that place children and adolescents at developmental risk (Solmeyer & others, 2011). By contrast, parental solidarity, cooperation, and warmth show clear ties to children's and adolescents' prosocial behavior and competence in peer relations. When parents show cooperation, mutual respect, balanced communication, and attunement to each other's needs, these attributes help children and adolescents to develop positive attitudes toward both males and females (Tamis-LeMonda & Cabrera, 2002).

A longitudinal study examined the influence of coparenting conflict on parental negativity and adolescent maladjustment (Feinberg, Kan, & Hetherington, 2007). In this study, parents reported that child-rearing issues were a central aspect of coparenting conflict and that coparenting conflict was linked to parents' negativity and adolescent adjustment three years later.

PARENT-ADOLESCENT CONFLICT

A common belief is that a huge gulf separates parent and adolescents in the form of a so-called generation gap—that is, that during adolescence the values and attitudes of adolescents become increasingly distanced from those of their parents. For the most part, the generation gap is a stereotype. For example, most adolescents and their parents have similar beliefs about the value of hard work, achievement, and career aspirations (Gecas & Seff, 1990). They also often have similar religious and political beliefs. As you will see in our discussion of research on parent-adolescent conflict, a minority of adolescents (perhaps 20 to 25 percent) have a high degree of conflict with their parents, but for a substantial majority the conflict is moderate or low.

That said, the fact remains that early adolescence is a time when parent-adolescent conflict escalates beyond parent-child conflict (McKinney & Renk, 2011; Zeiders, Roosa, & Tein, 2011). This increase may be due to a number of factors already discussed involving the maturation of the adolescent and the maturation of parents: the biological changes of puberty; cognitive changes involving increased idealism and logical reasoning; social changes focused on independence and identity; violated expectations; and physical, cognitive, and social changes in parents associated with middle adulthood. A research review concluded that parent-adolescent conflict decreases from early adolescence through late adolescence (Laursen, Coy, & Collins, 1998).

Although conflict with parents does increase in early adolescence, it does not reach the tumultuous proportions envisioned by G. Stanley Hall at the beginning of the twentieth century (Laursen & Collins, 2009). Rather, much of the conflict involves the everyday events of family life, such as keeping a bedroom clean, dressing neatly, getting home by a certain time, not talking on the phone forever, and so on. The conflicts rarely involve major dilemmas like drugs and delinquency. In a study of middle-socioeconomic-status African American families, parent-adolescent conflict was common but low in intensity and focused on everyday living issues such as the adolescent's room, chores, choice of activities, and homework (Smetana & Gaines, 1999). Nearly all conflicts were resolved by adolescents' giving in to parents, but adolescent concession declined with age.

Conflict with parents increases in early adolescence. *What is the nature of this conflict in a majority of American families?*

connecting with careers

Martha Chan, Marriage and Family Therapist

Martha Chan is a marriage and family therapist who works for Adolescent Counseling Services in Palo Alto, California. She has been the program director of Adolescent Counseling Services for more than a decade.

Among her activities, Chan counsels parents and adolescents about family issues, conducts workshops for parents at middle schools, and writes a monthly column that addresses such topics as "I'm a single mom; How do I talk with my son about sex?" "My daughter wants to dye her hair purple." "My son is being bullied."

For more information about what a marriage and family therapist does, see page 48 in the Careers in Adolescent Development appendix.

In one study of conflict in a number of social relationships, adolescents reported having more disagreements with their mother than with anyone else—followed in order by friends, romantic partners, siblings, fathers, other adults, and peers (Laursen, 1995). In another study of 64 high school sophomores, interviews were conducted in their homes on three randomly selected evenings during a three-week period (Montemayor, 1982). The adolescents were asked to tell about the events of the previous day, including any conflicts they had with their parents. During a period of 192 days of tracking the 64 adolescents, an average of 68 arguments with parents was reported. This represents a rate of 0.35 argument with parents per day or about one argument every three days. The average length of the arguments was 11 minutes. Most conflicts were with mothers, and the majority were between mothers and daughters.

Still, a high degree of conflict characterizes some parent-adolescent relationships. It has been estimated that in about 20 to 25 percent of families, parents and adolescents engage in prolonged, intense, repeated, unhealthy conflict (Montemayor, 1982). Although this figure represents a minority of adolescents, it indicates that 4 to 5 million American families encounter serious, highly stressful parent-adolescent conflict. And this prolonged, intense conflict is associated with a number of adolescent problems—moving away from home, juvenile delinquency, school dropout rates, pregnancy and early marriage, membership in religious cults, and drug abuse (Brook & others, 1990). In a recent study of Latino families, higher levels of conflict with either the mother or the father were linked to higher levels of adolescent boys' and girls' internalizing (depression, for example) and externalizing (delinquency, for example) behaviors (Crean, 2008). In this study, emotional support of the adolescent from the other parent often served a protective function in reducing the likelihood that the adolescent will engage in problem behaviors. Also in this study, conflict with the mother was especially detrimental for Latina girls. To read about the career of one individual who counsels families with high parent-adolescent conflict, see the *Connecting with Careers* profile.

Although in some cases adolescent problems may be caused by intense, prolonged parent-adolescent conflict, in others the problems might have originated before the onset of adolescence (Darling, 2008). Simply because children are physically much smaller than parents, parents might be able to suppress oppositional behavior. But, by adolescence, increased size and strength—especially in boys—can result in an indifference to or confrontation with parental dictates. At the same time, some psychologists have argued that conflict is a normative part of adolescent development.

Cross-cultural studies reveal that parent-adolescent conflict is lower in some countries than in the United States. Two countries where parent-adolescent conflict is lower than in the United States are Japan and India (Larson, 1999; Rothbaum & others, 2000).

AUTONOMY AND ATTACHMENT

It has been said that there are only two lasting bequests that we can leave our children—one is roots, the other wings. These words reflect the importance of attachment and autonomy in the adolescent's successful adaptation to the world. Historically, developmentalists have shown far more interest in autonomy than in attachment during the adolescent period. Recently, however, interest has heightened in attachment's role in healthy adolescent and emerging adult development (Kerig, Swanson, & Ward, 2012). Adolescents and their parents live in a coordinated social world, one involving both autonomy and attachment. In keeping with the historical interest in these processes, we discuss autonomy first.

Autonomy The increased independence that typifies adolescence is interpreted as rebellion by some parents, but in many instances adolescents' push for autonomy has little to do with their feelings toward the parents. Psychologically healthy families adjust to adolescents' push for independence by treating the adolescents in more adult ways and including them more in family decision making. Psychologically unhealthy families often remain locked into power-oriented parental control, and parents move even more heavily toward an authoritarian posture in their relationships with their adolescents.

The adolescent's quest for autonomy and sense of responsibility creates puzzlement and conflict for many parents. Parents begin to see their teenagers slipping away from their grasp. As we have discussed, the urge is to take stronger control as the adolescent seeks autonomy and personal responsibility. Heated, emotional exchanges might ensue, with either side calling names, making threats, and doing whatever seems necessary to gain control. Parents can become frustrated because they expected their teenager to heed their advice, to want to spend time with the family, and to grow up to do what is right. To be sure, they anticipated that their teenager would have some difficulty adjusting to the changes adolescence brings, but few parents are able to imagine and predict the strength of adolescents' determination to spend time with their peers and to show that it is they, not the parents, who are responsible for their success or failure.

What are strategies that parents can use to guide adolescents in effectively handling their increased motivation for autonomy?

The Complexity of Adolescent Autonomy Defining adolescent autonomy is more complex and elusive than it might at first seem (McElhaney & others, 2009; Perez-Brena, Updegraff, & Umana-Taylor, 2011). The term *autonomy* generally connotes self-direction and independence. But what does it really mean? Is it an internal personality trait that consistently characterizes the adolescent's immunity from parental influence? Is it the ability to make responsible decisions for oneself? Does autonomy imply consistent behavior in all areas of adolescent life, including school, finances, dating, and peer relations? What are the relative contributions of peers and other adults to the development of an adolescent's autonomy?

One aspect of autonomy that is especially important is **emotional autonomy,** the capacity to relinquish childlike dependencies on parents. In developing emotional autonomy, adolescents increasingly de-idealize their parents, perceive them as people rather than simply as parenting figures, and become less dependent on them for immediate emotional support.

Gender and Culture Gender differences characterize autonomy granting in adolescence, with boys being given more independence than girls are. In one study, this

emotional autonomy The capacity to relinquish childlike dependence on parents.

was especially true in those U.S. families with a traditional gender-role orientation (Bumpus, Crouter, & McHale, 2001). Also, Latino families protect and monitor daughters more closely than sons than is the case in non-Latino White families (Allen & others, 2008).

Expectations about the appropriate timing of adolescent autonomy often vary across cultures, parents, and adolescents (Fuligni, Hughes, & Way, 2009; McElhaney & Allen, 2012). For example, expectations for early autonomy on the part of adolescents are more prevalent in non-Latino Whites, single parents, and adolescents themselves than they are in Asian Americans or Latinos, married parents, and parents themselves (Feldman & Rosenthal, 1999). In another study, young adolescents' perception that their parents promoted more psychological autonomy and less psychological control predicted fewer depressive symptoms two years later (Sher-Censor, Parke, & Coltrane, 2011).

In one study, adolescents in the United States sought autonomy from parents earlier than did adolescents in Japan (Rothbaum & others, 2000). Asian adolescents raised in the United States, however, usually do not seek autonomy as early as their Anglo-American peers (Greenberger & Chu, 1996). Also in the transition to adulthood, Japanese are less likely to live outside the home than are Americans (Hendry, 1999).

Developmental Transitions in Autonomy and Going Away to College Many emerging adults experience a transition in the development of autonomy when they leave home and go away to college (Kerig, Swanson, & Ward, 2012; Kloep & Hendry, 2010). The transition from high school to college involves increased autonomy for most individuals (Bucx & van Wel, 2008; Nelson & others, 2011). For some, homesickness sets in; for others, sampling the privileges of life without parents hovering around is marvelous. For the growing number of students whose families have been torn by separation and divorce, though, moving away can be especially painful. Adolescents in such families may find themselves in the roles of comforter, confidant, and even caretaker of their parents as well as their siblings. In the words of one college freshman, "I feel responsible for my parents. I guess I shouldn't, but I can't help it. It makes my separation from them, my desire to be free of others' problems, my motivation to pursue my own identity more difficult." For yet other students, the independence of being a college freshman is not always as stressful. According to 18-year-old Brian, "Becoming an adult is kind of hard. I'm having to learn to balance my own checkbook, make my own plane reservations, do my own laundry, and the hardest thing of all is waking up in the morning. I don't have my mother there banging on the door."

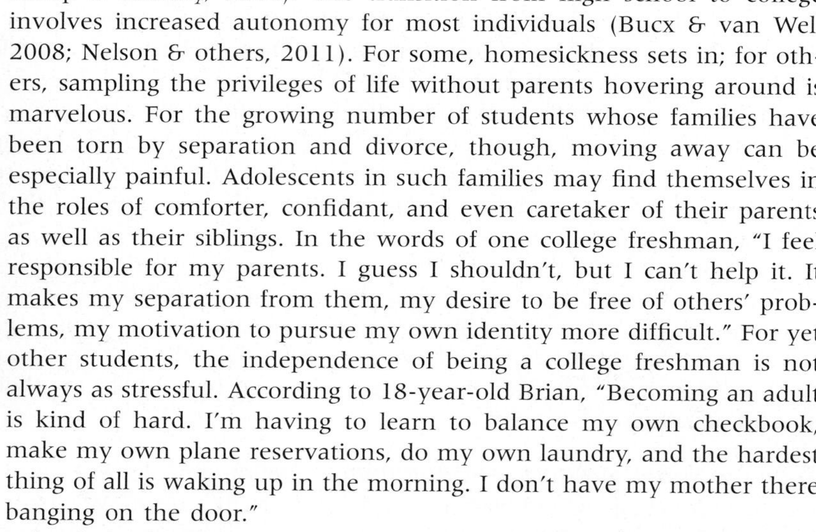

How do relationships with parents change when individuals go to college?

In one study, the psychological separation and adjustment of 130 college freshmen and 123 college upperclassmen were studied (Lapsley, Rice, & Shadid, 1989). As expected, freshmen showed more psychological dependency on their parents and poorer social and personal adjustment than did upperclassmen. Female students also showed more psychological dependency on their parents than male students did.

Adolescent Runaways An estimated 1.6 million youth run away from home each year in the United States (Walsh & Donaldson, 2010). Why do adolescents run away from their homes? Generally, runaways are desperately unhappy at home. The reasons many of them leave seem legitimate by almost anyone's standards. When they run away, they usually do not leave a clue as to their whereabouts—they just disappear.

Many runaways are from families in which a parent or another adult beats them or sexually exploits them (Chen & others, 2004). Their lives may be in danger daily. Their parents may be drug addicts or alcoholics. In some cases, the family may be so impoverished that the parents are unable to feed and clothe their teenagers adequately. The parents may be so overburdened by their own emotional and/or material inadequacies that they fail to give their adolescents the attention and understanding they need. So teenagers hit the streets in search of the emotional and material rewards they are not getting at home.

But runaways are not all from our society's lower-SES tier. Teenage lovers, confronted by parental hostility toward their relationship, might decide to elope and make it on their own. Or the middle-SES teenager might decide that he has seen enough of his hypocritical parents—people who try to make him live by an unrealistically high set of moral standards, while they live by a loose, false set of ideals. Another teen might live with parents who constantly bicker. Any of these adolescents might decide that they would be happier away from home.

This adolescent has run away from home. *What is it about family relationships that causes adolescents to run away from home? Are there ways society could better serve runaways?*

Running away often is a gradual process, as adolescents begin to spend less time at home and more time on the streets or with a peer group. The parents might be telling them that they really want to see them, to understand them; but runaways often feel that they are not understood at home and that the parents care much more about themselves. A recent study of homeless youth revealed that the longer they did not have stable housing, the more their resilience decreased and mental health deteriorated (Cleverley & Kidd, 2011).

A recent longitudinal study of more than 4,000 youth from grade 9 to age 21 found that running away from home was linked to lack of parental support, school disengagement, depressive symptoms, and substance use in grade 9 (Tucker & others, 2011). Also, runaways had higher drug dependence and depressive symptoms at age 21.

National Safe Place is a partnership of more than 360 youth serving agencies and more than 10,000 businesses and community organizations in the United States that provides immediate safety and access to runaways (Walsh & Donaldson, 2010). The Safe Place program educates youth about alternatives to running away and homelessness, and helps youth connect with service providers.

Conclusions In sum, the ability to attain autonomy and gain control over one's behavior in adolescence is acquired through appropriate adult reactions to the adolescent's desire for control. An individual at the onset of adolescence does not have the knowledge to make appropriate or mature decisions in all areas of life. As the adolescent pushes for autonomy, the wise adult relinquishes control in those areas in which the adolescent can make reasonable decisions and continues to guide the adolescent in areas where the adolescent's knowledge is more limited. Gradually, the adolescent acquires the ability to make mature decisions on his or her own (Harold, Colarossi, & Mercier, 2007). The discussion that follows reveals in greater detail how important it is to view the development of autonomy in relation to connectedness to parents.

Attachment and Connectedness Adolescents do not simply move away from parental influence into a decision-making world all on their own. As they become more autonomous, it is psychologically healthy for them to be attached to their parents.

Secure and Insecure Attachment Attachment theorists such as John Bowlby (1989) and Mary Ainsworth (1979) argue that secure attachment in infancy is central to the development of social competence. In **secure attachment,** infants use the caregiver, usually the mother, as a secure base from which to explore the environment. Secure attachment is theorized to be an important foundation for psychological development later in childhood, adolescence, and adulthood. In **insecure attachment,** infants either avoid the caregiver or show considerable resistance or ambivalence toward the caregiver. Insecure attachment is theorized to be related to difficulties in relationships and problems in later development (Sroufe, Coffino, & Carlson, 2010).

secure attachment Attachment pattern in which infants use their primary caregiver, usually the mother, as a secure base from which to explore the environment. Secure attachment is theorized to be an important foundation for psychological development later in childhood, adolescence, and adulthood.

insecure attachment Attachment pattern in which infants either avoid the caregiver or show considerable resistance or ambivalence toward the caregiver. This pattern is theorized to be related to difficulties in relationships and problems in later development.

Adolescence One of the most widely discussed aspects of socioemotional development in infancy is secure attachment to caregivers (Sroufe, Coffino, & Carlson,

2010). In the past decade, researchers have explored whether secure attachment also might be an important concept in adolescents' relationships with their parents (Laursen & Collins, 2009; Rosenthal & Kobak, 2010). For example, Joseph Allen and his colleagues (2009) found that adolescents who were securely attached at age 14 were more likely to report that they were in an exclusive relationship, comfortable with intimacy in relationships, and were achieving increasing financial independence at 21 years of age. A recent analysis concluded that the most consistent outcomes of secure attachment in adolescence involve positive peer relations and development of the adolescent's emotion regulation capacities (Allen & Miga, 2010).

Many studies that assess secure and insecure attachment in adolescence use the Adult Attachment Interview (AAI) (George, Main, & Kaplan, 1984). This measure examines an individual's memories of significant attachment relationships. Based on the responses to questions on the AAI, individuals are classified as secure-autonomous (which corresponds to secure attachment in infancy) or as being in one of three insecure categories:

- **Dismissing/avoidant attachment** is an insecure category in which individuals deemphasize the importance of attachment. This category is associated with consistent experiences of rejection of attachment needs by caregivers. One possible outcome of dismissing/avoidant attachment is that parents and adolescents mutually distance themselves from each other, a state that lessens parents' influence.
- **Preoccupied/ambivalent attachment** is an insecure category in which adolescents are hyperattuned to attachment experiences. This is thought to mainly occur because parents are inconsistently available to the adolescent. This state can result in a high degree of attachment-seeking behavior, mixed with angry feelings. Conflict between parents and adolescents in this type of attachment classification can be too high for healthy development.
- **Unresolved/disorganized attachment** is an insecure category in which the adolescent has an unusually high level of fear and might be disoriented. This can result from such traumatic experiences as a parent's death or abuse by parents.

A recent study using the Important People Interview (IPI) assessed attachments of high school students (14 to 18 years of age) and emerging adult college students (18 to 23 years of age) to the four most important people in their lives, followed by their four most important peers (Rosenthal & Kobak, 2010). After identifying the important people in their lives, the students rank-ordered the people in terms of these contexts: attachment bond (closeness, separation distress, and an emergency situation), support seeking (comfort or support in daily contexts), and affiliative (enjoyable social contact). College students placed romantic partners in higher positions and fathers in lower positions than did high school students. Friends' placements in higher positions and fathers' exclusion from the most important people list or as the fourth most important person were linked to increased behavior problems (internalizing, such as depression, for example, and externalizing, such as rule-breaking, for example).

Conclusions About Parent-Adolescent Conflict and Attachment in Adolescence In sum, the old model of parent-adolescent relationships suggested that, as adolescents mature, they detach themselves from parents and move into a world of autonomy apart from parents. The old model also suggested that parent-adolescent conflict is intense and stressful throughout adolescence. The new model emphasizes that parents serve as important attachment figures, resources, and support systems as adolescents explore a wider, more complex social world. The new model also emphasizes that, in the majority of families, parent-adolescent conflict is moderate rather than severe and that everyday negotiations and minor disputes are normal, serving the positive developmental function of promoting independence and identity (see Figure 8.3).

dismissing/avoidant attachment An insecure attachment category in which individuals deemphasize the importance of attachment. This category is associated with consistent experiences of rejection of attachment needs by caregivers.

preoccupied/ambivalent attachment An insecure attachment category in which adolescents are hyperattuned to attachment experiences. This is thought mainly to occur because parents are inconsistently available to the adolescents.

unresolved/disorganized attachment An insecure category in which the adolescent has an unusually high level of fear and is disoriented. This can result from such traumatic experiences as a parent's death or abuse by parents.

Old Model

Autonomy, detachment from parents; parent and peer worlds are isolated

Intense, stressful conflict throughout adolescence; parent-adolescent relationships are filled with storm and stress on virtually a daily basis

New Model

Attachment and autonomy; parents are important support systems and attachment figures; adolescent-parent and adolescent-peer worlds have some important connections

Moderate parent-adolescent conflict is common and can serve a positive developmental function; conflict greater in early adolescence

FIGURE **8.3**

OLD AND NEW MODELS OF PARENT-ADOLESCENT RELATIONSHIPS

Attachment in Emerging Adults Although relationships with romantic partners differ from those with parents, romantic partners fulfill some of the same needs for adults as parents do for their children (Shaver & Mikulincer, 2007, 2012). *Securely attached* infants are defined as those who use the caregiver as a secure base from which to explore the environment. Similarly, emerging and young adults may count on their romantic partners to be a secure base to which they can return and obtain comfort and security in stressful times.

Do adult attachment patterns with partners in emerging and early adulthood reflect childhood attachment patterns with parents? In a retrospective study, Cindy Hazan and Philip Shaver (1987) revealed that young adults who were securely attached in their romantic relationships were more likely to describe their early relationship with their parents as securely attached. In a longitudinal study, infants who were securely attached at 1 year of age were securely attached twenty years later in their adult romantic relationships (Steele & others, 1998). However, in another longitudinal study, links between early attachment styles and later attachment styles were lessened by stressful and disruptive experiences, such as the death of a parent or instability of caregiving (Lewis, Feiring, & Rosenthal, 2000).

Hazan and Shaver (1987, p. 515) measured attachment styles using the following brief assessment:

Read each paragraph and then place a check mark next to the description that best describes you:

____ **1.** I find it relatively easy to get close to others and I am comfortable depending on them and having them depend on me. I don't worry about being abandoned or about someone getting too close to me.

____ **2.** I am somewhat uncomfortable being close to others. I find it difficult to trust them completely and to allow myself to depend on them. I get nervous when anyone gets too close to me and it bothers me when someone tries to be more intimate with me than I feel comfortable with.

____ **3.** I find that others are reluctant to get as close as I would like. I often worry that my partner doesn't really love me or won't want to stay with me. I want to get very close to my partner, and this sometimes scares people away.

These items correspond to three attachment styles—secure attachment (option 1 above) and two insecure attachment styles (avoidant—option 2 above, and anxious—option 3 above):

- ***Secure attachment style.*** Securely attached adults have positive views of relationships, find it easy to get close to others, and are not overly concerned with or stressed out about their romantic relationships. These adults tend to enjoy sexuality in the context of a committed relationship and are less likely than others to have one-night stands.

- ***Avoidant attachment style.*** Avoidant individuals are hesitant about getting involved in romantic relationships and once in relationships tend to distance themselves from their partners.
- ***Anxious attachment style.*** These individuals demand closeness, are less trusting, and are more emotional, jealous, and possessive.

What are some key dimensions of attachment in emerging adulthood, and how are they related to relationship patterns and well-being?

The majority of adults (about 60 to 80 percent) describe themselves as securely attached, and not surprisingly adults prefer having a securely attached partner (Zeifman & Hazan, 2008).

Researchers are studying links between adults' current attachment styles and many aspects of their lives (Mikulincer & others, 2010). For example, securely attached adults are more satisfied with their close relationships than are insecurely attached adults, and the relationships of securely attached adults are more likely to be characterized by trust, commitment, and longevity (Feeney & Monin, 2008). A recent study of 18- to 25-year-olds revealed that attachment security predicted the perceived quality of romantic relationships (Holland & Roisman, 2010). Another recent study found that attachment-anxious individuals showed strong ambivalence toward a romantic partner (Mikulincer & others, 2010). Also, a study of 18- to 20-year-olds revealed that secure attachment to parents was linked to ease in forming friendships in college (Parade, Leerkes, & Blankson, 2010). A national survey indicated that insecure attachment in adults was associated with the development of disease and chronic illness, especially cardiovascular system problems such as high blood pressure, heart attack, and stroke (McWilliams & Bailey, 2010). And a research review of 10,000 adult attachment interviews found that attachment insecurity was related to depression (Bakersmans-Kranenburg & van IJzendoorn, 2009).

Recently, the label *troubled ruminations about parents* was proposed as an attachment-based concept that involves a negative attachment history, a sense of being rejected by parents, regrets about not having a better relationship with parents or not spending more time with them, and a general sense of dissatisfaction with parents (Schwartz & Finlay, 2010). In addition, a research study of more than 1,300 college students found that troubled ruminations about parents were linked to lower levels of self-esteem and life satisfaction as well as to psychological distress and problems in romantic relationships (Schwartz & Finlay, 2010).

developmental **connection**

Peers. Recent research revealed that co-rumination in adolescent girls' friendships predicted depressive symptoms. Chapter 13, p. 450

If you have an insecure attachment style, are you stuck with it and does it doom you to have problematic relationships? Attachment categories are somewhat stable in adulthood, but adults do have the capacity to change their attachment thinking and behavior. Although attachment insecurities are linked to relationship problems, attachment style makes only a moderate-size contribution to relationship functioning, and other factors contribute to relationship satisfaction and success (Ein-Dor & others, 2010; Shaver & Mikulincer, 2012).

EMERGING ADULTS' RELATIONSHIPS WITH THEIR PARENTS

For the most part, emerging adults' relationships with their parents improve when they leave home. They often grow closer psychologically to their parents and share more with them than they did before they left home (Arnett, 2007). However, challenges in the parent–emerging adult relationship involve the emerging adult's increasing autonomy by possessing adult status in many areas yet still depending on parents in some manner (Kerig, Swanson, & Ward, 2012). Many emerging adults can make their own decisions about where to live, whether to stay in college, which lifestyle to adopt, whether to get married, and so on. At the same time, parents often provide support for their emerging adult children, even after they leave home. This might be accomplished through loans and monetary gifts for education, purchase of a car, and financial contribution to living arrangements, as well as emotional support.

Doonesbury BY GARRY TRUDEAU

In successful emerging adulthood, individuals separate from their family of origin without cutting off ties completely or fleeing to some substitute emotional refuge. Complete cutoffs from parents rarely solve emotional problems. Emerging adulthood is a time for young people to sort out emotionally what they will take along from the family of origin, what they will leave behind, and what they will create.

The vast majority of studies of parenting styles have focused on outcomes for children and adolescents and have involved mothers rather than fathers. A recent study revealed parents act as "scaffolding" and "safety nets" to support their children's successful transition through emerging adulthood (Swartz & others, 2011). Another recent study examined mothers' and fathers' parenting styles with their emerging adult children (Nelson & others, 2011). An authoritative parenting style (defined in this study as high responsiveness, low control) by both mothers and fathers was linked with positive outcomes in emerging adulthood children (high self-worth and high social acceptance, and low depression, for example). The most negative outcomes for emerging adult children (low self-worth, high depression, and high anxiety, for example) were related to a controlling-indulgent style (low responsiveness, high control) on the part of both mothers and fathers. High control by parents may be especially detrimental with emerging adults who are moving toward more autonomy as they leave their parents' home. Negative outcomes for emerging adult children also resulted from an uninvolved parenting style (low responsiveness, low control) on the part of both mothers and fathers. The most positive outcomes for emerging adult children involved having fathers who parented with an authoritative style.

Many emerging adults no longer feel compelled to comply with parental expectations and wishes. They shift to learning to deal with their parents on an adult-to-adult basis, which requires a mutually respectful form of relating—in which, by the end of emerging adulthood, individuals can appreciate and accept their parents as they are.

In today's uncertain economic times, many emerging adults continue to live at home or return to live at home after several years of college or after graduating from college, or while saving money after taking a full-time job (Furman, 2005). Emerging and young adults also may move back in with their parents after an unsuccessful career or a divorce. And some individuals don't leave home at all until their middle to late twenties because they cannot financially support themselves. Numerous labels have been applied to emerging and young adults who return to their parents' homes to live, including "boomerang kids," and "B2B" (or Back-to-Bedroom) (Furman, 2005).

developmental **connection**

Environment. Residential changes peak during emerging adulthood, a time when there also is often instability in love, work, and education. Chapter 1, p. 19

As with most family living arrangements, there are both pluses and minuses when emerging adult children live at home or return to live at home. One of the most common complaints voiced by both emerging adults and their parents is a loss of privacy. Emerging adults complain that their parents restrict their independence, cramp their sex lives, reduce their music listening, and treat them as children rather than adults. Parents often complain that their quiet home has become noisy, that they stay up late worrying when their emerging adult children will come home,

connecting with health and well-being

Can Emerging Adults and Their Parents Coexist?

When emerging adults ask to return home to live, parents and their emerging adult children should agree on the conditions and expectations beforehand. For example, they might discuss and agree on whether the emerging adults will pay rent, wash their own clothes, cook their own meals, do any household chores, pay their phone bills, come and go as they please, be sexually active or drink alcohol at home, and so on. If these conditions aren't negotiated at the beginning, conflict often results because the expectations of parents and young adult children will likely be violated. Parents need to treat emerging adult children more like adults than children and let go of much of their parenting role. Parents should interact with emerging adult children not as if they are dependent children who need to be closely monitored and protected but rather as young adults who are capable of responsible, mature behavior. Emerging adults have the right to choose how much they sleep and eat, how they dress, who they choose as friends and lovers, what career they pursue, and how they spend their money. However, if the emerging adult children act in ways that interfere with their parents' lifestyles, parents need to say so. The discussion should focus not on emerging adults' choices but on how their activities are unacceptable while living together in the same home.

Some parents don't let go of their emerging adult children when they should. They engage in "permaparenting," which can impede not only their emerging adult children's movement toward independence and responsibility but also their own postparenting lives. "Helicopter parents" is another label used for parents who hover too closely in their effort to ensure that their children succeed in college and adult life (Paul, 2003). Although well intentioned, this intrusiveness by parents can slow the process by which their children become responsible adults.

What are some strategies that can benefit the relationship between emerging adults and their parents?

When they move back home, emerging adults need to think about how they will need to change their behavior to make the living arrangement work. Elina Furman (2005) provides some good recommendations in *Boomerang Nation: How to Survive Living with Your Parents . . . the Second Time Around.* She recommends that, when emerging adults move back home, they should expect to make adjustments. And, as recommended earlier, she urges emerging adults to sit down with their parents and negotiate the ground rules for living at home before they actually move back. Furman also recommends that emerging adults set a deadline for how long they will live at home and then stay focused on their goals (whether to save enough money to pay off their debts, save enough to start a business or buy their own home, finish graduate school, and so on). Too often emerging adults spend the money they save by moving home on such luxuries as spending binges, nights on the town, expensive clothes, and unnecessary travel, which only delay their ability to move out of their parents' home.

How do you think emerging adults' relationship with their parents differs if they do not have to live at home?

that meals are difficult to plan because of conflicting schedules, that their relationship as a married couple has been invaded, and that they have to shoulder too much responsibility for their emerging adult children. In sum, when emerging adults return home to live, a disequilibrium in family life is created, which requires considerable adaptation on the part of parents and their emerging adult children.

How can emerging adults and their parents get along better? See the *Connecting with Health and Well-Being* interlude for some ideas.

INTERGENERATIONAL RELATIONSHIPS

Connections between generations play important roles in development through the life span (Fingerman & Birditt, 2011; Shulman, Scharf, & Shachar-Shapira, 2012; Silverstein & Giarrusso, 2010). With each new generation, personality characteristics, attitudes, and values are replicated or changed. As older family members die, their biological, intellectual, emotional, and personal legacies are carried on in the next generation. Their children become the oldest generation and their grandchildren the second generation. A recent study revealed that emerging and young adults with children see their parents more frequently than do their counterparts who do not have children (Bucx, Raaijmakers, & Van Wel, 2010).

> In case you're worried about what's going to become of the younger generation, it's going to grow up and start worrying about the younger generation.
>
> —Roger Allen
> *American Writer, 20th Century*

Adults in midlife play important roles in the lives of the young and the old (Fingerman & Birditt, 2011; Martini & Bussèri, 2010). Middle-aged adults share their experience and transmit values to the younger generation. They may be launching adolescents into adulthood, adjusting to having grown children return home, or becoming grandparents. They also may be giving or receiving financial assistance, or caring for a widowed or sick parent.

Middle-aged adults have been described as the "sandwich," "squeezed," or "overload" generation because of the responsibilities they have for their adolescent and young adult children on the one hand and their aging parents on the other (Etaugh & Bridges, 2010; Pudrovska, 2009). However, an alternative view is that in the United States, a "sandwich" generation, in which the middle generation cares for both grown children and aging parents simultaneously, occurs less often than a "pivot" generation, in which the middle generation alternates attention between the demands of grown children and aging parents (Fingerman & Birditt, 2011).

Gender differences also characterize intergenerational relationships (Etaugh & Bridges, 2010). Females have an especially important role in connecting family relationships across generations. Females' relationships across generations are thought to be closer than other family bonds (Fingerman & Birditt, 2011; Merrill, 2009).

Culture and ethnicity also are important aspects of intergenerational relationships. For example, cultural brokering has increasingly occurred in the United States as children and adolescents serve as mediators (cultural and linguistic) for their immigrant parents (Villanueva & Buriel, 2010).

The following studies provide evidence of the importance of intergenerational relationships in the development of adolescents and emerging adults:

How do intergenerational relationships influence adolescents' development?

- In a longitudinal study, hostility and positive engagement by parents and adolescents during family interaction at age 14 were related to levels of hostility and positive engagement expressed by offspring and their spouses during marital interaction 17 years later (Whitton & others, 2008). A higher level of family-of-origin hostility during adolescence showed an especially strong link to a higher level of marital hostility and a lower level of positive engagement 17 years later.
- Supportive family environments and parenting in childhood (assessed when the children were 3 to 15 years of age) were linked with more positive relationships (in terms of contact, closeness, conflict, and reciprocal assistance) between the children and their middle-aged parents when the children were 26 years of age (Belsky & others, 2001).
- Adult children of divorce who were classified as securely attached were less likely to divorce in the early years of their marriage than were their insecurely attached counterparts (Crowell, Treboux, & Brockmeyer, 2009).
- Children of divorce were disproportionately likely to end their own marriage as compared to children from intact, never divorced families, although the

transmission of divorce across generations has declined in recent years (Wolfinger, 2011).

- Middle-aged parents are more likely to provide support to their grown children than to their parents (Fingerman & others, 2011).

So far in this chapter we have examined the nature of family processes, adolescent/emerging adult relationships with parents, and intergenerational relationships. In addition, there is another aspect to the family worlds of most adolescents and emerging adults—sibling relationships—which we discuss next.

Review *Connect* Reflect

LG2 Describe adolescents' and emerging adults' relationships with their parents.

Review

- How can parents be effective managers of adolescents?
- What are four important parenting styles, and how are they linked with adolescent development?
- How effective is coparenting?
- How can parent-adolescent conflict be accurately described?
- What roles do autonomy and attachment play in the development of adolescents and emerging adults?
- What are some issues involved in relationships between emerging adults and their parents?
- How do intergenerational relationships influence adolescent development?

Connect

- Connect the discussion of emotional development in Chapter 4 to this section's discussion of autonomy and attachment.

Reflect *Your Own Personal Journey of Life*

- What has characterized your own development of attachment and autonomy to this point in your life?

3 Sibling Relationships

 Characterize sibling relationships in adolescence.

Sibling Roles | Birth Order

What characterizes sibling roles? As we examine the roles siblings play in social development, you will discover that conflict is a common dimension of sibling relationships but that siblings also play many other roles in social development (McHale, Updegraff, & Whiteman, 2011; Whiteman, Jensen, & Bernard, 2012). And how influential is birth order in the adolescent's development?

SIBLING ROLES

Approximately 80 percent of American adolescents have one or more siblings—that is, sisters and brothers (Dunn, 2007). As anyone who has had a sibling knows, conflict is a common interaction style of siblings. However, conflict is only one of the many dimensions of sibling relations, (Conger & Kramer, 2010; Howe, Ross, & Recchia, 2011; Whiteman, McHale, & Soli, 2011). Adolescent sibling relations include helping, sharing, teaching, fighting, and playing—and adolescent siblings can act as emotional supports, rivals, and communication partners (East, 2009; Howe, Ross, & Recchia, 2011). One study found that adolescent siblings spent an average of 10 hours a week together, with an average of 12 percent of that time spent in constructive time (creative activities such as art, music, and hobbies; sports; religious activities; and games) and 25 percent in nonconstructive time (watching TV and hanging out) (Tucker, McHale, & Crouter, 2001). In Mexican American families, adolescent siblings spend even more time together—more than 17 hours a week (Updegraff & others, 2005). A recent review concluded that sibling relationships in adolescence are not as close, not as intense, and more egalitarian than in childhood (East, 2009).

About 80 percent of us have one or more siblings. *What are some characteristics of sibling relationships in adolescence?*

What do adolescent siblings talk about when they are together? One study revealed that siblings most often talked about extracurricular activities, media, and school (Tucker & Winzeler, 2007). Less than 10 percent of their time together, the focus of their discussion was friends, family, eating, and body image.

Judy Dunn (2007), a leading expert on sibling relationships, recently described three important characteristics of sibling relationships:

- *Emotional quality of the relationship.* Both intense positive and negative emotions are often expressed by siblings toward each other. Many children and adolescents have mixed feelings toward their siblings.
- *Familiarity and intimacy of the relationship.* Siblings typically know each other very well, and this intimacy suggests that they can either provide support or tease and undermine each other, depending on the situation.
- *Variation in sibling relationships.* Some siblings describe their relationships more positively than do others. Thus, there is considerable variation in sibling relationships. We've seen that many siblings have mixed feelings about each other, but some adolescents mainly describe their sibling in warm, affectionate ways, whereas others primarily talk about how irritating and mean a sibling is.

Do parents usually favor one sibling over others, and if so does it make a difference in an adolescent's development? One study of 384 adolescent sibling pairs revealed that 65 percent of their mothers and 70 percent of their fathers showed favoritism toward one sibling (Shebloski, Conger, & Widaman, 2005). When favoritism of one sibling occurred, it was linked to lower self-esteem and sadness in the less-favored sibling.

In some instances, siblings can be stronger socializing influences on the adolescent than parents or peers are (Dunn, 2007). Someone close in age to the adolescent—such as a sibling—might be able to understand the adolescent's problems and communicate more effectively than parents can. In dealing with peers, coping with difficult teachers, and discussing taboo subjects (such as sex), siblings can be more influential in socializing adolescents than parents are. In one study, both younger and older adolescent siblings viewed older siblings as sources of support for social and scholastic activities (Tucker, McHale, & Crouter, 2001).

High sibling conflict can be detrimental to adolescent development, especially when combined with ineffective parenting (East, 2009; Kramer, 2010; Milevsky, 2011). A longitudinal study revealed that a combination of ineffective parenting (poor problem-solving skills, weak supervision skills, parent-adolescent conflict) and sibling conflict (hitting, fighting, stealing, cheating) at 10 to 12 years of age was linked to antisocial behavior and poor peer relations from 12 to 16 years of age (Bank, Burraston, & Snyder, 2004). And another longitudinal study found that increased sibling conflict was linked to increased depression and that increased sibling intimacy was related to increased peer competence and, for girls, decreased depression (Kim & others, 2007).

As just indicated, negative aspects of sibling relationships, such as high conflict, are linked to negative outcomes for adolescents. The negative outcomes can develop not only through conflict but also through direct modeling of a sibling's behavior, as when a younger sibling has an older sibling who has poor study habits and engages in delinquent behavior. By contrast, close and supportive sibling relationships can buffer the negative effects of stressful circumstances in an adolescent's life (East, 2009).

What are sibling relationships like in emerging adulthood? Most siblings spend far less time with each other in emerging adulthood than they did in adolescence. Mixed feelings about siblings are still common in emerging adulthood. However, as siblings move out of their home and sibling contact becomes more optional, conflicted sibling relationships in adolescence often become less emotionally intense (Hetherington & Kelly, 2002).

BIRTH ORDER

Whether an adolescent has older or younger siblings has been linked to development of certain personality characteristics. For example, a recent review concluded that "firstborns are the most intelligent, achieving, and conscientious, while later-borns are the most rebellious, liberal, and agreeable" (Paulhus, 2008, p. 210). Compared with later-born children, firstborn children have also been described as more adult-oriented, helpful, conforming, and self-controlled. However, when such birth order differences are reported, they often are small.

Birth order also plays a role in siblings' relationships with each other (Vandell, Minnett, & Santrock, 1987). Older siblings invariably take on the dominant role in sibling interaction, and older siblings report feeling more resentful that parents give preferential treatment to younger siblings.

What are later-borns like? Characterizing later-borns is difficult because they can occupy so many different sibling positions. For example, a later-born might be the second-born male in a family of two siblings or a third-born female in a family of four siblings. In two-child families, the profile of the later-born child is related to the sex of his or her sibling. For example, a boy with an older sister is more likely to develop "feminine" interests than is a boy with an older brother. Overall, later-borns usually enjoy better relations with peers than firstborns. Last-borns, who are often described as the "baby" in the family even after they have outgrown infancy, run the risk of becoming overly dependent. Middle-borns tend to be more diplomatic, often performing the role of negotiator in times of dispute (Sutton-Smith, 1982).

The popular conception of the only child is that of a "spoiled brat" with such undesirable characteristics as dependency, lack of self-control, and self-centered behavior. But research presents a more positive portrayal of the only child, who often is achievement-oriented and displays a desirable personality, especially in comparison to later-borns and children from large families (Thomas, Coffman, & Kipp, 1993).

So far our consideration of birth-order effects suggests that birth order might be a strong predictor of adolescent behavior. However, family researchers have found that birth order has often been overemphasized. The critics argue that, when all of the factors that influence adolescent behavior are considered, birth order itself shows limited ability to predict adolescent behavior. Consider just sibling relationships alone. They vary not only in birth order, but also in number of siblings, age of siblings, age spacing of siblings, and sex of siblings. In one study, male sibling pairs had a less positive relationship (less caring, less intimate, and lower conflict resolution) than male/female or female/female sibling pairs (Cole & Kerns, 2001). Consider also the temperament of siblings. Researchers have found that siblings' temperamental traits (such as "easy" and "difficult"), as well as differential treatment of siblings by parents, influence how siblings get along (Brody, Stoneman, & Burke, 1987). Siblings with "easy" temperaments who are treated in relatively equal ways by parents tend to get along with each other the best, whereas siblings with "difficult" temperaments, or siblings whose parents gave one sibling preferential treatment, get along the worst.

The one-child family is becoming much more common in China because of the strong motivation to limit the population growth in the People's Republic of China. The effects of this policy have not been fully examined. *In general, what have researchers found the only child to be like?*

In addition to gender, temperament, and differential treatment of siblings by parents, think about some of the other important factors in adolescents' lives that influence their behavior beyond birth order. They include heredity, models of competency or incompetency that parents present to adolescents on a daily basis, peer influences, school influences, socioeconomic factors, sociohistorical factors, cultural variations, and so on. Although birth order itself may not be a good predictor of adolescent behavior, sibling relationships and interaction are important dimensions of family processes in adolescence (Dunn, 2005).

Review *Connect* Reflect

LG3 Characterize sibling relationships in adolescence.

Review

- What is the nature of sibling roles?
- How strongly is birth order linked to adolescent development?

Connect

- Contrast a family with siblings to a family with a single child in terms of the family-as-a-system perspective.

Reflect *Your Own Personal Journey of Life*

- If you grew up with one or more siblings, what was your relationship with your sibling(s) like? If you could have changed anything in your relationship with your sibling(s) in adolescence, what would that have been? If you are an only child, how do you think this sibling status influenced your development?

4 The Changing Family in a Changing Society

LG4 Describe the changing family in a changing society.

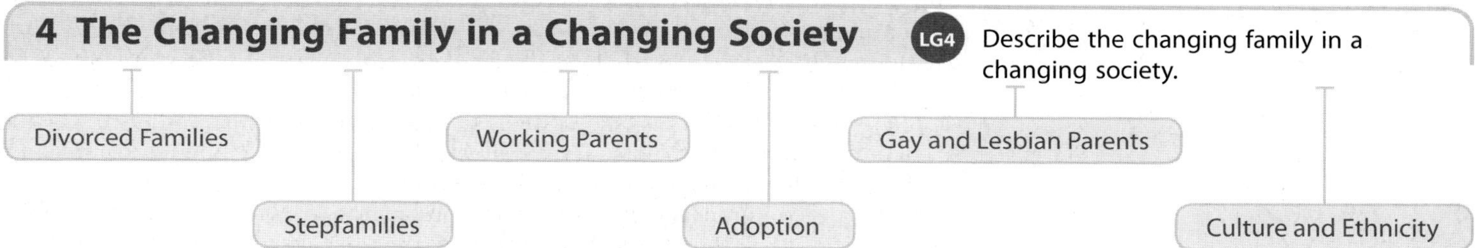

More U.S. adolescents are growing up in a wider variety of family structures than ever before in history. Many mothers spend the greater part of their day away from their children. More than one of every two mothers with a child under the age of 5, and more than two of every three with a child from 6 to 17 years of age, is in the labor force. The number of adolescents growing up in single-parent families is staggering. The United States has the highest percentage of single-parent families, compared with virtually all other countries (see Figure 8.4). And, by age 18, approximately one-fourth of all American children will have lived a portion of their lives in a stepfamily.

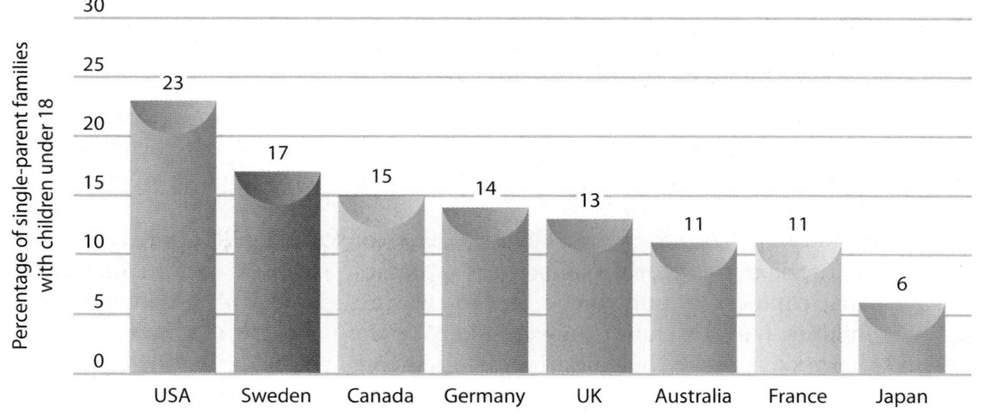

FIGURE **8.4**
SINGLE-PARENT FAMILIES IN DIFFERENT COUNTRIES

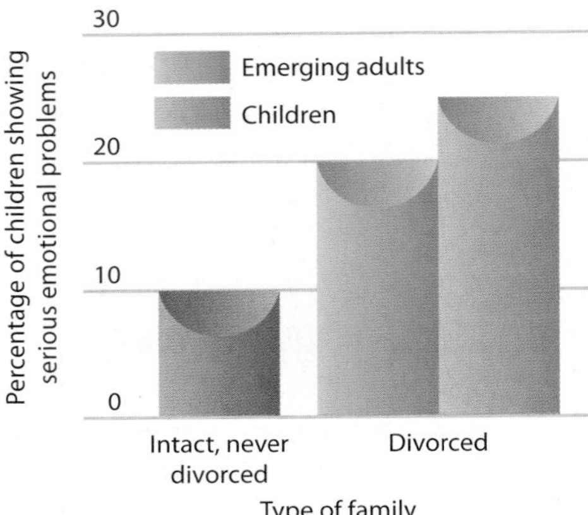

FIGURE **8.5**

EMOTIONAL PROBLEMS IN CHILDREN AND EMERGING ADULTS FROM DIVORCED FAMILIES. In Hetherington's longitudinal study, 25 percent of children from divorced families had emotional problems, but that figure decreased to 20 percent in emerging adulthood. Ten percent of children and emerging adults from nondivorced families had emotional problems.

DIVORCED FAMILIES

The U.S. divorce rate increased dramatically in the 1960s and 1970s but has declined since the 1980s (Amato & Dorius, 2010). Many other countries around the world have also experienced significant changes in their divorce rate. For example, Japan has experienced an increase in its divorce rate in the 1990s and the first decade of the twenty-first century. However, the divorce rate in the United States is still much higher than that in Japan and higher than that in most other countries as well. It is estimated that 40 percent of children born to married parents will experience their parents' divorce (Hetherington & Stanley-Hagan, 2002).

These are the questions that we now explore regarding the effects of divorce: Is the adjustment of adolescents and emerging adults better in intact, never-divorced families than in divorced families? Should parents stay together for the sake of their children and adolescents? How much do parenting skills matter in divorced families? What factors affect the adolescent's individual risk and vulnerability in a divorced family? What role does socioeconomic status play in the lives of adolescents in divorced families? (Hetherington, 2005, 2006; Hetherington and Kelly, 2002; Hetherington & Stanley-Hagan, 2002).

Adolescents' Adjustment in Divorced Families Most researchers agree that children, adolescents, and emerging adults from divorced families show poorer adjustment than their counterparts in nondivorced families (Hetherington, 2005, 2006; Lansford, 2009; Parke & Clarke-Stewart, 2011; Wallerstein, 2008) (see Figure 8.5). In the longitudinal study conducted by E. Mavis Hetherington and her colleagues (Hetherington, 2005, 2006; Hetherington, Cox, & Cox, 1982; Hetherington & Kelly, 2002), 25 percent of children from divorced families had emotional problems, but that figure decreased to 20 percent in emerging adulthood. In this study, 10 percent of children and emerging adults from nondivorced families had emotional problems.

In Hetherington's research, the 20 percent of emerging adults from divorced families who continued to have emotional problems were characterized by impulsive, irresponsible, antisocial behavior, or were depressed. Toward the end of emerging adulthood, this troubled group was having problems at work and difficulties in romantic relationships. The 10 percent of emerging adults from nondivorced families who had emotional problems mainly came from homes where family conflict was high and authoritative parenting was rare. As in childhood, emerging adults who had gone from a highly conflicted intact family to a more harmonious divorced family context with a caring, competent parent had fewer emotional problems. In another longitudinal study, parental divorce in childhood and adolescence was linked to poor relationships with fathers, unstable romantic or marital relationships, and low levels of education in adulthood (Amato, 2006).

> As marriage has become a more optional, less permanent institution in contemporary America, children and adolescents are encountering stresses and adaptive challenges associated with their parents' marital transitions.
>
> —E. Mavis Hetherington
>
> *Contemporary Psychologist, University of Virginia*

Those who have experienced multiple divorces are at greater risk. Adolescents and emerging adults in divorced families are more likely than adolescents from nondivorced families to have academic problems, to show externalized problems (such as acting out and delinquency) and internalized problems (such as anxiety and depression), to be less socially responsible, to have less competent intimate relationships, to drop out of school, to become sexually active at an earlier age, to take drugs, to associate with antisocial peers, and to have lower self-esteem (Conger & Chao, 1996; Hetherington, 2005, 2006; Hetherington & Kelly, 2002). A recent study revealed that adolescent girls with divorced parents were especially vulnerable to developing depressive symptoms (Oldehinkel & others, 2008).

Note that marital conflict may have negative consequences for children in the context of marriage or divorce (Cummings & Davies, 2010). A longitudinal study revealed that conflict in nondivorced families was associated with emotional problems in children (Amato, 2006). Indeed, many of the problems that children from divorced homes experience begin during the predivorce period, a time when parents are often in active conflict with each other. Thus, when children from divorced homes show problems, the problems may be due not only to the divorce, but to the marital conflict that led to it (Thompson, 2008).

E. Mark Cummings and his colleagues (Cummings & Davies, 2010; Cummings, El-Sheikh, & Kouros, 2009; Cummings & Kouros, 2008; Schermerhorn, Chow, & Cummings, 2010) have proposed *emotion security theory*, which has its roots in attachment theory and states that children appraise marital conflict in terms of their sense of security and safety in the family. They make a distinction between marital conflict that is negative for children (such as hostile emotional displays and destructive conflict tactics) and marital conflict that can be positive for children (such as marital disagreement that involves a calm discussion of each person's perspective and working together to reach a solution).

Despite the emotional problems that some adolescents and emerging adults from divorced families have, the weight of the research evidence underscores that most adolescents and emerging adults competently cope with their parents' divorce and that a majority of adolescents and emerging adults in divorced families do not have significant adjustment problems (Ahrons, 2007; Barber & Demo, 2006). For example, in one study of adults who were children when their parents divorced, approximately 80 percent concluded, 20 years after the divorce, that their parents' decision to divorce was a wise one (Ahrons, 2004).

What concerns are involved in whether parents should stay together for the sake of the children or become divorced?

Should Parents Stay Together for the Sake of the Children and Adolescents? Whether parents should stay in an unhappy or conflicted marriage for the sake of their children and adolescents is one of the most commonly asked questions about divorce (Hetherington, 2005, 2006). If the stresses and disruptions in family relationships associated with an unhappy, conflicted marriage that erode the well-being of the children and adolescents are reduced by the move to a divorced, single-parent family, divorce might be advantageous (Yu & others, 2010). However, if the diminished resources and increased risks associated with divorce also are accompanied by inept parenting and sustained or increased conflict, not only between the divorced couple but also between parents, children, and siblings, the best choice for the children would be for an unhappy marriage to be retained (Hetherington & Stanley-Hagan, 2002). These are "ifs," and it is difficult to determine how these will play out when parents either remain together in an acrimonious marriage or become divorced.

How Much Do Family Processes Matter in Divorced Families? In divorced families, family processes matter a great deal (Hetherington, 2006; Lansford, 2009; Parke & Clarke-Stewart, 2011; Sigal & others, 2011). When the divorced parents have a harmonious relationship and use authoritative parenting, the adjustment of adolescents is improved (Hetherington, 2006). When the divorced parents can agree on child-rearing strategies and can maintain a cordial relationship with each other, frequent visits by the noncustodial parent usually benefit the child (Fabricus & others, 2010).

However, two longitudinal studies revealed that conflict (especially when it is intense and prolonged) between divorced parents was linked to emotional problems, insecure social relationships, and antisocial behavior in adolescents (Hetherington, 2006). A secure attachment also matters. Researchers have shown that a disequilibrium, including diminished parenting skills, occurs in the year following the divorce, but that by two years after the divorce restabilization has occurred and parenting skills have improved (Hetherington, 1989). Father involvement with children drops off more than mother involvement, especially for fathers of girls. About one-fourth to one-third of adolescents in divorced families, compared with 10 percent in nondivorced families, become disengaged from their families, spending as little time as possible at home and in interaction with family members (Hetherington & Kelly,

connecting with emerging adults

College Students Reflect on Growing Up in a Divorced Family

College Student 1

"In my early adolescence, the lack of a consistent, everyday father figure in my life became a source of many problems. Because I felt deprived of a quality relationship with a man, I tried to satisfy this need by starting to date very young. I was desperate to please every boyfriend, and this often led to promiscuous behavior. I was anxious and seductive in my interactions with males. It seemed like no matter how hard I tried I could not make these relationships work. Just as with my dad—no matter how good I was, my father remained emotionally unavailable. I still feel a lot of anger that I did not deal with as a small child. As a young woman now, I am continuously struggling with these issues trying to get my life together.

College Student 2

"It has always been painful knowing that I have a father who is alive and perfectly capable of acting like a parent, but who does not care about me. As a child, I was often depressed and acted out. As I grew older I had very low self-esteem. In junior high school, although I was successful, I felt like I belonged to the 'loser crowd.' . . . After I graduated from high school, I decided I still needed to fill the emptiness in my life by finding out at least a little bit about my father. I was seventeen when I found his number and called to see if he would be willing to talk. After a long hesitation, he agreed. We met and spent the day together. He has called me regularly ever since. Today I am better able to understand what I was feeling all those years. Now I am able to say without guilt that the absence of my father caused me much pain. I no longer feel abandoned, but many of the scars still remain. I still haven't been able to bring myself to call him 'Dad.'

"There were two positive consequences of my parents' divorce for me: I discovered my own strength by living through this most difficult experience and surviving the loss of my father, and I developed this close bond with my mother from sharing the experience. She and I have become best friends.

"Fortunately I had my friends, my teachers, my grandparents, and my brother to help me through the whole crazy-making time after my parents' divorce. The most important people were my brother and a teacher I had in the sixth and seventh grades. My brother was important because he was the only constant in my life; we shared every experience. My teacher was important because she took an interest in me and showed compassion. My grandparents offered consistent support. They gave my mother money for rent and food and paid for private schools for my brother and me; they were like second parents to us."

(From Clarke-Stewart, A., & Brentano, C. (2006). *Divorce: Causes and Consequences*).

2002). This disengagement is higher for boys than for girls in divorced families. However, if there is a caring adult outside the home, such as a mentor, the disengagement can be a positive solution to a disrupted, conflicted family circumstance. Also, a recent study in divorced families revealed that an intervention focused on improving the mother-child relationship was linked to improvements in relationship quality that increased children's and adolescents' coping skills over the short term (6 months) and long term (6 years) (Velez & others, 2011).

What Factors Are Involved in the Adolescent's Individual Risk Vulnerability in a Divorced Family? Among the factors involved in individual risk vulnerability are the adolescent's adjustment prior to the divorce, personality and temperament, developmental status, gender, and custody. Children and adolescents whose parents later divorce show poorer adjustment before the breakup (Amato & Dorius, 2010).

Personality and temperament also play a role in adolescent adjustment in divorced families. Adolescents who are socially mature and responsible, who show few behavioral problems, and who have an easy temperament are better able to cope with their parents' divorce. Children and adolescents with a difficult temperament often have problems coping with their parents' divorce (Hetherington & Stanley-Hagan, 2002).

developmental **connection**

Personality. Easy, difficult, and slow to warm up represent one classification of temperament styles. Chapter 4, p. 155

Focusing on the developmental status of the child or adolescent involves taking into account the age of onset of the divorce and the time when the child's or adolescent's adjustment is assessed. In most studies, these factors are confounded with length of time since the divorce occurred. Some researchers have found that preschool children whose parents divorce are at greater risk for long-term problems than are older children (Zill, Morrison, & Coiro, 1993). The explanation for this focuses on their inability to realistically appraise the causes and consequences of divorce, their anxiety about the possibility of abandonment, their self-blame for the divorce, and their inability to use extrafamilial protective resources. However, problems in adjustment can emerge or increase during adolescence, even if the divorce occurred much earlier. As we discussed earlier, whether a divorce occurs earlier or later in children's or adolescents' development is linked to the type of problems the children and adolescents are likely to develop (Lansford & others, 2006).

In recent decades, an increasing number of children and adolescents have lived in father-custody and joint-custody families (Ziol-Guest, 2009). What is their adjustment like, compared with the adjustment of children and adolescents in mother-custody families? Although there have been few thorough studies of the topic, a review of studies concluded that children benefit from joint custody because it facilitates ongoing positive involvement with both parents (Bauserman, 2003). Joint custody works best for children when the parents can get along with each other (Parke & Clarke-Stewart, 2011).

Some studies have shown that boys adjust better in father-custody families and that girls adjust better in mother-custody families, but other studies have not shown these results. In one study, adolescents in father-custody families had higher rates of delinquency, believed to be due to less-competent monitoring by the fathers (Buchanan, Maccoby, & Dornsbusch, 1992).

Another factor involved in an adolescent's adjustment in a divorced family is relocation (Kelly & Lamb, 2003). One study found that when children and adolescents whose parents have divorced experience a move away of either of their parents, they show less effective adjustment (Braver, Ellman, & Fabricus, 2003).

What Role Does Socioeconomic Status Play in the Lives of Adolescents in Divorced Families? On average, custodial mothers' income decreases about 25 to 50 percent from their predivorce income, in comparison to a decrease of only 10 percent for custodial fathers (Emery, 1999). This income decrease for divorced mothers is typically accompanied by increased workloads, high rates of job instability, and residential moves to less desirable neighborhoods with inferior schools (Sayer, 2006).

STEPFAMILIES

Not only are parents divorcing more, they are also getting remarried more (Ganong, Coleman, & Jamison, 2011; Hetherington, 2006; Marsiglio & Hinojosa, 2010). It takes time for couples to marry, have children, get divorced, and then remarry. Consequently, there are far more elementary and secondary schoolchildren than infant or preschool children in stepfamilies.

The number of remarriages involving children has grown steadily in recent years. As a result of their parents' successive marital transitions, about half of all children whose parents divorce will have a stepfather within four years of parental separation. Furthermore, divorces occur at a 10 percent higher rate in remarriages than in first marriages (Cherlin & Furstenberg, 1994).

Types of Stepfamilies There are different types of stepfamilies. Some types are based on family structure, others on relationships. The stepfamily may have been preceded by a circumstance in which a spouse died. However, a large majority of stepfamilies are preceded by a divorce rather than a death.

Three common types of stepfamily structure are (1) stepfather, (2) stepmother, and (3) blended or complex. In stepfather families, the mother typically had custody of the children and became remarried, introducing a stepfather into her children's lives. In stepmother families, the father usually had custody and became remarried, introducing a stepmother into his children's lives. And, in a blended or complex stepfamily, both parents bring children from previous marriages to live in the newly formed stepfamily.

Adjustment As in divorced families, adolescents in stepfamilies have more adjustment problems than do their counterparts in nondivorced families (Hetherington, 2006; Hetherington & Kelly, 2002; Marsiglio & Hinojosa, 2010). The adjustment problems of adolescents in stepfamilies are much like those of adolescents in divorced families: academic problems, externalizing and internalizing problems, lower self-esteem, early sexual activity, delinquency, and so on (Hetherington, 2006). Adjustment for parents and children may take longer in stepfamilies (up to five years or more) than in divorced families, in which a restabilization is more likely to occur within two years (Anderson & others, 1999; Hetherington, 2006). One aspect of a stepfamily that makes adjustment difficult is **boundary ambiguity,** the uncertainty in stepfamilies about who is in or out of the family and who is performing or responsible for certain tasks in the family system.

Researchers have found that children's relationships with custodial parents (mother in stepfather families, father in stepmother families) are often better than with stepparents (Santrock, Sitterle, & Warshak, 1988). However, when adolescents have a positive relationship with their stepfather, it is related to fewer adolescent problems (Flouri, 2004). Also, adolescents in simple stepfamilies (stepfather, stepmother) often show better adjustment than their counterparts in complex (blended) families (Anderson & others, 1999; Hetherington, 2006).

How does living in a stepfamily influence a child's development?

There is an increase in adjustment problems of adolescents in newly remarried families (Hetherington, 2006; Hetherington & Clingempeel, 1992). In research conducted by James Bray and his colleagues (Bray, Berger, & Boethel, 1999; Bray & Kelly, 1998), the formation of a stepfamily often meant that adolescents had to move, and the move involved changing schools and friends. It took time for the stepparent to get to know the stepchildren. The new spouses had to learn how to cope with the challenges of their relationship and parenting together. In Bray's view, the formation of a stepfamily was like merging two cultures.

Bray and his colleagues also found that when the stepparent tried to discipline the stepchild, it often did not work well. Most experts recommend that in the early period of a stepfamily the biological parent should be the parent doing any disciplining of the child that is needed. The stepparent-stepchild relationship develops best when the stepparent spends time with the stepchild in activities that the child enjoys.

In Hetherington's (2006) most recent analysis, adolescents who had been in a simple stepfamily for a number of years were adjusting better than in the early years of the remarried family and were functioning well in comparison to adolescents in conflicted nondivorced families and adolescents in complex stepfamilies. More than 75 percent of the adolescents in long-established simple stepfamilies described their relationships with their stepparents as "close" or "very close." Hetherington (2006) concludes that in long-established simple stepfamilies adolescents seem eventually to benefit from the presence of a stepparent and the resources provided by the stepparent.

In terms of the age of the child, researchers have found that early adolescence is an especially difficult time for the formation of a stepfamily (Bray & Kelly, 1998; Hetherington & others, 1999). This may occur because the stepfamily circumstances exacerbate normal adolescent concerns about identity, sexuality, and autonomy.

boundary ambiguity The uncertainty in stepfamilies about who is in or out of the family and who is performing or responsible for certain tasks in the family system.

Now that we have considered the changing social worlds of adolescents when their parents divorce and remarry, we turn our attention to another aspect of the changing family worlds of adolescents—the situation when both parents work.

WORKING PARENTS

Interest in the effects of parental work on the development of children and adolescents has increased in recent years. Our examination of parental work focuses on the following issues: the role of working parents in adolescents' development and the adjustment of latchkey adolescents.

How might parents' work schedules and work stress issues influence adolescents' development?

Working Parents and Adolescent Adjustment More than one of every two U.S. mothers with a child under the age of 5 is in the labor force; more than two of every three with a child from 6 to 17 years of age is. Maternal employment is a part of modern life, but its effects are still debated.

Most of the research on parental work has focused on young children and on the mother's employment (Brooks-Gunn, Han, & Waldfogel, 2010). However, the effects of working parents involves the father as well when such matters as work schedules and work-family stress are considered (O'Brien & Moss, 2010; Parke & Clarke-Stewart, 2011).

Until recently, little attention has been given to the role of parents' work on adolescents (Crouter, 2006). Recent research indicates that what matters for adolescent development is the nature of parents' work rather than whether one parent works outside the home (Goodman & others, 2011; Han, 2009; Parke & Clarke-Stewart, 2011). Ann Crouter (2006) recently described how parents bring their experiences at work into their homes. She concluded that parents who have poor working conditions, such as long hours, overtime work, stressful work, and lack of autonomy at work, are likely to be more irritable at home and engage in less effective parenting than their counterparts who have better work conditions in their jobs. The negative work conditions of parents are linked to more behavior problems and lower grades in their adolescents. One study found that, when fathers worked more than 60 hours per week and perceived their work overload gave them too little time to do what they wanted, their relationship with their adolescents was more conflicted (Crouter & others, 2001). A consistent finding is the children (especially girls) of working mothers engage in less gender stereotyping and have more egalitarian views of gender (Goldberg & Lucas-Thompson, 2008).

Latchkey Adolescents Although the mother's working is not necessarily associated with negative outcomes for adolescents, a certain set of adolescents from working-mother families bears further scrutiny—those called *latchkey adolescents*. Latchkey adolescents typically do not see their parents from the time they leave for school in the morning until about 6:00 or 7:00 p.m. They are called "latchkey" children or adolescents because they carry a key to their home and let themselves into the home while their parents are still at work. Many latchkey adolescents are largely unsupervised for two to four hours a day during each school week, or for entire days, five days a week, during the summer months. A recent survey found that 15.1 million children and adolescents in the United States are alone and unsupervised after school (Afterschool Alliance, 2009).

In one study of 819 10- to 14-year-olds, out-of-home care, whether supervised or unsupervised, was linked to delinquency, drug and alcohol use, and school problems (Coley, Morris, & Hernandez, 2004). Some latchkey children may grow up too fast, hurried by the responsibilities placed on them. How do latchkey children handle the lack of limits and structure during the latchkey hours? Without limits and parental supervision, latchkey children find their way into trouble more easily, possibly stealing, vandalizing, or abusing a sibling. Joan Lipsitz (1983), in testifying before the Select Committee on Children, Youth, and Families, called the lack of adult supervision of children in the after-school hours a major problem. Lipsitz called it the "three-to-six o'clock problem" because it was during this time that the Center for Early Adolescence in North Carolina, when Lipsitz was director, experienced a peak of referrals for clinical help.

Although latchkey adolescents can be vulnerable to problems, keep in mind that the experiences of latchkey adolescents vary enormously, just as do the experiences of all adolescents with working mothers. Parents need to give special attention to the ways they can monitor their latchkey adolescents' lives effectively. Variations in latchkey experiences suggest that parental monitoring and authoritative parenting help the adolescent to cope more effectively with latchkey experiences, especially in resisting peer pressure (Galambos & Maggs, 1991; Steinberg, 1986). The degree to which latchkey adolescents are at developmental risk remains unsettled. A positive sign is that researchers are beginning to conduct more precise analyses of adolescents' latchkey experiences in an effort to determine which aspects of latchkey circumstances are the most detrimental and which aspects foster better adaptation. One study that focused on the after-school hours found that unsupervised peer contact, lack of neighborhood safety, and low monitoring were linked with externalizing problems (such as acting out and delinquency) in young adolescents (Pettit & others, 1999).

developmental **connection**

Schools. Adolescents who participate in high-quality extracurricular activities have positive developmental outcomes. Chapter 10, p. 345

ADOPTION

Another variation in the type of family in which children live involves adoption, the social and legal process by which a parent-child relationship is established between persons unrelated at birth. As we see next, an increase in diversity has characterized the adoption of children in the United States in recent years.

The Increased Diversity of Adopted Children and Adoptive Parents A number of changes have characterized adopted children and adoptive parents in the last three to four decades (Brodzinsky & Pinderhughes, 2002). In the first half of the twentieth century, most U.S. adopted children were healthy, non-Latino White infants who were adopted at birth or soon after; however, in recent decades as abortion became legal and contraception increased, fewer of these infants became available for adoption. Increasingly, U.S. couples have adopted a much wider diversity of children—from other countries, from other ethnic groups, children with physical and/or mental problems, and children who had been neglected or abused (Castle & others, 2010).

Changes also have characterized adoptive parents in the last three to four decades (Brodzinsky & Pinderhughes, 2002). In the first half of the twentieth century, most adoptive parents were from non-Latino White middle or upper socioeconomic status backgrounds who were married and did not have any type of disability. However, in recent decades, increased diversity has characterized adoptive parents. Many adoption agencies today have no income requirements for adoptive parents and now allow adults from a wide range of backgrounds to adopt children, including single adults, gay male and lesbian adults, and older adults.

What are some changes in adoption practice in recent decades in the United States?

Do these changes matter? They open opportunities for many adolescents and many couples, but possible effects of changes in the characteristics of parents on the outcomes for adolescents are still unknown. For example, in one study, adopted adolescents were more likely to have problems if the adoptive parents had low levels of education (Miller & others, 2000). In another study, international adoptees showed fewer behavior problems and were less likely to be using mental health services than were domestic adoptees (Juffer & van IJzendoorn, 2005). More research is needed before definitive conclusions can be reached about the changing demographic characteristics of adoption.

The changes in adoption practice over the last several decades make it difficult to generalize about the average adopted adolescent or average adoptive parent. As we see next, though, some researchers have provided useful comparisons between adopted adolescents and nonadopted adolescents and their families.

Developmental Outcomes for Adopted and Nonadopted Children How do adopted children and adolescents fare after they are adopted? Children and adolescents who are adopted very early in their lives are more likely to have positive outcomes than do their counterparts adopted later in life (Bernard & Dozier, 2008).

In general, adopted children and adolescents are more likely to experience psychological and school-related problems than are nonadopted children and adolescents (Bernard & Dozier, 2008). For example, a meta-analysis (a statistical procedure that combines the results of a number of studies) revealed that adoptees were far more likely to be using mental health services than were their nonadopted counterparts (Juffer & van IJzendoorn, 2005). Adopted children and adolescents also showed more behavior problems than did nonadoptees, but this difference was small. A recent large-scale study found that adopted children are more likely to have a learning disability than are nonadopted children (Altarac & Saroha, 2007).

Research that contrasts adopted and nonadopted adolescents has also found positive characteristics among the adopted adolescents. For example, in one study, although adopted adolescents were more likely than nonadopted adolescents to use illicit drugs and to engage in delinquent behavior, the adopted adolescents were also less likely to be withdrawn and more likely to engage in more prosocial behavior, such as being altruistic, caring, and supportive of others (Sharma, McGue, & Benson, 1996).

In short, the vast majority of adopted children and adolescents (including those adopted at older ages, transracially, and across national borders) adjust effectively, and their parents report considerable satisfaction with their decision to adopt (Brodzinsky & Pinderhughes, 2002; Castle & others, 2010). A research review of 88 studies also revealed no difference in the self-esteem of adopted and nonadopted children and adolescents, as well as no differences between transracial and same-race adoptees (Juffer & IJzendoorn, 2007).

Most studies of adopted and nonadopted children compare different families (adoptive and nonadoptive). A recent study used a different strategy: Studying families who had a biological child of their own and an adopted child (Glover & others, 2010). Findings similar to studies of between-family comparisons occurred with only a slight (but nonsignificant) trend for adopted children to show more internalized (depression, for example) and externalized (antisocial behavior, for example) problems.

In other comparisons, adopted children and adolescents fare much better than children and adolescents in long-term foster care or in an institutional environment (Bernard & Dozier, 2008). A recent study of infants in China revealed that their cognitive development improved by 2 to 6 months following their adoption from foster homes and institutions (van den Dries & others, 2010).

Parenting Adopted Adolescents Many of the keys to effectively parenting adopted adolescents are no different than those for effectively parenting biological adolescents: Be supportive and caring, be involved and monitor the adolescent's behavior and whereabouts, be a good communicator, and help the adolescent to learn to develop self-control. However, parents of adopted adolescents face some unique circumstances. These include recognizing the differences involved in adoptive family life, providing child rearing that supports open communication about these differences, showing respect for the birth family, and supporting the adolescent's search for self and identity (Wolfgram, 2008).

The emergence of more abstract and logical thinking in adolescence provides the foundation for adopted adolescents to reflect on their adoptive status in more complex ways. As pubertal change focuses adolescents' attention on their bodies, many adopted adolescents become preoccupied with the lack of physical resemblance between themselves and others in the family. The search for identity that characterizes adolescence may also give rise to extensive exploration of the fact that they are adopted and how this fits into their identity. Adoptive parents "need to be aware of these many complexities and provide teenagers with the support they need to cope with these adoption-related tasks" (Brodzinsky & Pinderhughes, 2002, p. 292).

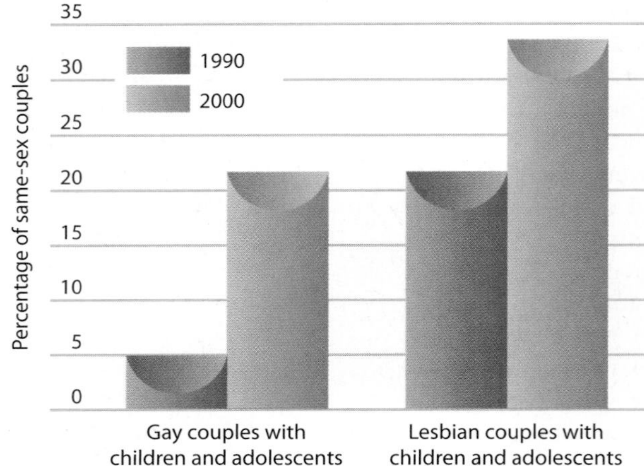

FIGURE **8.6**
PERCENTAGE OF GAY MALE AND LESBIAN COUPLES WITH CHILDREN AND ADOLESCENTS: 1990 AND 2000

GAY AND LESBIAN PARENTS

Another aspect of the changing family in a changing society focuses on adolescents raised by gay and lesbian parents (Patterson & Wainright, 2010). Increasingly, gay and lesbian couples are creating families that include children and adolescents (see Figure 8.6). There may be more than 1 million gay and lesbian parents in the United States today.

An important aspect of gay and lesbian families with adolescents is the sexual identity of parents at the time of a child's birth or adoption (Patterson, 2009). The largest group of adolescents with gay and lesbian parents are likely those who were born in the context of heterosexual relationships, with one or both parents only later identifying themselves as gay male or lesbian. Gay and lesbian parents may be single or they may have same-gender partners. In addition, gay and lesbians are increasingly choosing parenthood through donor insemination or adoption. Researchers have found that the children and adolescents created through new reproductive technologies—such as in vitro fertilization—are as well adjusted as their counterparts conceived by natural means (Golombok, 2011a,b; Golombok & Tasker, 2010). Custodial arrangements also may vary.

Another issue focuses on custody arrangements for adolescents. Many gays and lesbians have lost custody of their adolescents to heterosexual spouses following divorce. For this reason, many gay fathers and lesbian mothers are noncustodial parents.

Researchers have found few differences in children and adolescents growing up with gay fathers and lesbian mothers and in children and adolescents growing up with heterosexual parents (Patterson, 2009). For example, adolescents growing up in gay or lesbian families are just as popular with their peers, and there are no differences in the adjustment and mental health of adolescents living in these families when they are compared with adolescents in heterosexual families (Hyde & DeLamater, 2011). Also, the overwhelming majority of adolescents growing up in a gay or lesbian family have a heterosexual orientation (Golombok & Tasker, 2010).

CULTURE AND ETHNICITY

What are some variations in families across different cultures? How do families vary across different ethnic groups?

Cross-Cultural Comparisons Cultures vary on a number of issues involving families, such as what the father's role in the family should be, the extent to which support systems are available to families, and how children should be disciplined (Cheah & Yeung, 2011; Conger & others, 2012; Hewlett & Macfarlan, 2010). Although there are cross-cultural variations in parenting, in one study of parenting behavior in 186 cultures around the world, the most common pattern was a warm and controlling style, one that was neither permissive nor restrictive (Rohner & Rohner, 1981). The investigators commented that the majority of cultures have discovered, over many centuries, a "truth" that only recently emerged in the Western world—namely, that children's and adolescents' healthy social development is most effectively promoted by love and at least some moderate parental control.

Nonetheless, in some countries, authoritarian parenting continues to be widely practiced (Rothbaum & Trommsdorff, 2007). In the Arab world, families today are still very authoritarian and dominated by the father's rule (Booth, 2002). In Arab countries, adolescents are taught strict codes of conduct and family loyalty.

Cultural change is coming to many families around the world (Cheah & Yeung, 2011; Chen & others, 2011). There are trends toward greater family mobility, migration to urban areas, family members working in distant cities or countries, smaller families, fewer extended-family households, and increases in the mothers' employment (Brown & Larson, 2002). These trends can change the resources that are available to adolescents. For example, many families have fewer extended family members nearby, resulting in a decrease in support and guidance for adolescents. Also, smaller families may produce more openness and communication between parents and adolescents. We have much more to consider about culture and parenting in Chapter 12.

Ethnicity and Parenting Ethnic minority families differ from non-Latino White American families in their size, structure and composition, reliance on kinship networks, and level of income and education (Tamis-LeMonda & McFadden, 2010). Large and extended families are more common among ethnic minority groups than among non-Latino White Americans. For example, more than 30 percent of Latino families consist of five or more individuals. African American and Latino children interact more with grandparents, aunts, uncles, cousins, and more distant relatives than do non-Latino White American children (McAdoo, 2006).

Ethnic minority adolescents are more likely to come from low-income families than non-Latino White American adolescents are (Brandon, 2009). Single-parent families are more common among African Americans and Latinos than among non-Latino White Americans (Harris & Graham, 2007). In comparison with two-parent households, single-parent households often have more-limited resources of time, money, and energy. This shortage of resources can prompt parents to encourage autonomy among their adolescents prematurely. Ethnic minority parents, on average, are less well educated and engage in less joint decision making than non-Latino White American parents. Although impoverished families often raise competent youth, poor parents can have a diminished capacity for supportive and involved parenting (McLoyd & others, 2009).

Some aspects of home life can help to protect ethnic minority youth from social patterns of injustice. The community and family can filter out destructive racist messages, parents can provide alternate frames of reference than those presented by the majority, and parents can also provide competent role models and encouragement. And the extended-family system in many ethnic minority families provides an important buffer to stress (Gonzales & others, 2007).

A sense of family duty and obligation also varies across ethnic groups (Fuligni, Hughes, & Way, 2009; van Geel & Vedder, 2011). Asian American and Latino

The family reunion of the Limon family in Austin, Texas. Mexican American children often grow up in families with a network of relatives that runs into scores of individuals.

A 14-year-old adolescent, his 6-year-old sister, and their grandmother. The African American cultural tradition of an extended family household has helped many African American parents cope with adverse social conditions.

families place a greater emphasis on family duty and obligation than do non-Latino White families. In a study of 18- to 25-year-olds, Asian Americans said family interdependence was more important to them than did non-Latino Whites (Tseng, 2004). Researchers have found that Asian American and Latino adolescents believe that they should spend more time taking care of their siblings, helping around the house, assisting their parents at work, and being with their family than do adolescents with a European heritage (Fuligni, Tseng, & Lamb, 1999).

Of course, individual families vary, and how ethnic minority families deal with stress depends on many factors (Conger & others, 2012; Fuligni, Hughes, & Way, 2009; van Geel & Vedder, 2011). Whether the parents are native-born or immigrants, how long the family has been in this country, their socioeconomic status, and their specific national origin all make a difference (Hayashino & Chopra, 2009). The characteristics of the family's social context also influence its adaptation. What are the attitudes toward the family's ethnic group within its neighborhood or city? Can the family's children attend good schools? Are there community groups that welcome people from the family's ethnic group? Do members of the family's ethnic group form community groups of their own?

developmental **connection**

Culture and Ethnicity. Many families that have immigrated to the United States in recent decades, such as Mexican American and Asian American, come from collectivist cultures in which family obligation is strong. Chapter 12, p. 405

Review *Connect* Reflect

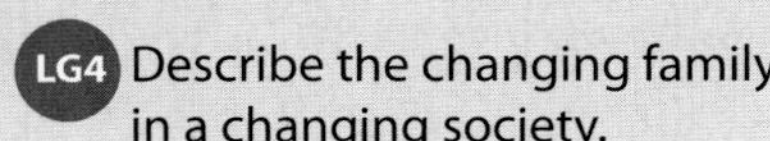

LG4 Describe the changing family in a changing society.

Review

- What are the effects of divorce on adolescents?
- How does growing up in a stepfamily influence adolescents' development?
- How do working parents influence adolescent development?
- How does being adopted affect adolescent development?
- What are the effects on adolescents of having gay or lesbian parents?
- What roles do culture and ethnicity play in families with adolescents?

Connect

- What did you learn about siblings earlier in this chapter that might inform your understanding of stepfamilies and the issues they face?

Reflect *Your Own Personal Journey of Life*

- You have studied many aspects of families and adolescents in this chapter. Imagine that you have decided to write a book describing life in your family when you were an adolescent. What would the title of the book be? What would be the main theme of the book?

5 Social Policy, Adolescents, and Families

LG5 Explain what is needed for improved social policy involving adolescents and their families.

We have seen in this chapter that parents play very important roles in adolescent development. Although adolescents are moving toward independence, they are still connected with their families, which are far more important to them than is commonly believed (McElhaney & others, 2009). We know that competent adolescent development is most likely to happen when adolescents have parents who do the following:

- Show them warmth and respect.
- Demonstrate sustained interest in their lives.

- Recognize and adapt to their changing cognitive and socioemotional development.
- Communicate expectations for high standards of conduct and achievement.
- Display authoritative, constructive ways of dealing with problems and conflict.

However, compared with families with young children, families with adolescents have been neglected in community programs and public policies. The Carnegie Council on Adolescent Development (1995) identified some key opportunities for improving social policy regarding families with adolescents. Even now, at the end of the first decade of the twenty-first century, the recommendations they made in 1995 still need to be followed:

Community programs such as this one in East Orange, New Jersey, can provide a monitored, structured context for adolescents to study in during the after-school hours. *In addition to improving after-school options for adolescents, what are some other ways that U.S. social policy could be improved to support families with adolescents?*

- School, cultural arts, religious and youth organizations, and health-care agencies should examine the extent to which they involve parents in activities with adolescents and should develop ways to engage parents and adolescents in activities they both enjoy.
- Professionals such as teachers, psychologists, nurses, physicians, youth specialists, and others who have contact with adolescents need not only to work with the individual adolescent but also to increase the time they spend interacting with the adolescent's family.
- Employers should extend to the parents of young adolescents the workplace policies now reserved only for the parents of young children. These policies include flexible work schedules, job sharing, telecommuting, and part-time work with benefits. This change in work/family policy would free parents to spend more time with their teenagers.
- Community institutions such as businesses, schools, and youth organizations should become more involved in providing after-school programs. After-school programs for elementary schoolchildren are increasing, but such programs for adolescents are rare. More high-quality, community-based programs for adolescents are needed in the after-school, weekend, and vacation time periods.

  Several national organizations develop and advocate supportive family policies at the federal, state, and local levels. Four of the best organizations in this regard are:

  —The Annie E. Casey Foundation (www.aecf.org)

  —First Focus, a Washington, D.C.-based policy center whose mission is to make children and families a major priority (www.firstfocus.net)

  —The Institute for Youth, Education, and Families at the National League of Cities (www.nlc.org)

  —The National Collaboration for Youth (www.collab4youth.org)

Review *Connect* Reflect

LG5 Explain what is needed for improved social policy involving adolescents and their families.

Review

- What is needed for improved social policy involving adolescents and their families?

Connect

- Do current social policies appear to view the family as a system?

Reflect *Your Own Personal Journey of Life*

- If you were a U.S. senator, what would you seek to do to improve social policy involving the families of adolescents? What would be your number one priority?

reach your **learning goals**

1 Family Processes

LG1 Discuss the nature of family processes in adolescence.

Reciprocal Socialization and the Family as a System

- The concept of reciprocal socialization is that adolescents socialize parents just as parents socialize adolescents. The family is a system of interacting individuals with different subsystems—some dyadic, some polyadic.

Maturation

- Relationships are influenced by the maturation of the adolescent and the maturation of parents. Adolescent changes include puberty, expanded logical reasoning, increased idealistic and egocentric thought, violated expectations, changes in schooling, peers, friendships, dating, and movement toward independence. Changes in parents might include marital satisfaction, economic burdens, career reevaluation, time perspective, and health/body concerns. Adults follow one developmental trajectory and children and adolescents another one. How these trajectories mesh is important for understanding timing of entry into various family tasks.

2 Adolescents' and Emerging Adults' Relationships with Their Parents

 Describe adolescents' and emerging adults' relationships with their parents.

Parents as Managers

- An increasing trend is to conceptualize parents as managers of adolescents' lives. This involves being a parent who finds information, makes contacts, helps structure choices, and provides guidance. Parents can serve as regulators of their adolescents' social contacts with peers, friends, and adults. A key aspect of the managerial role involves parental monitoring. A current interest focuses on adolescents' management of their parents' access to information.

Parenting Styles

- Authoritarian, authoritative, neglectful, and indulgent are four main parenting styles. Authoritative parenting, which encourages independence but places limits and controls, is associated with socially competent adolescent behavior more than the other styles. Some ethnic variations in parenting have been found, such as the positive relation between training by Asian American parents and the achievement of their adolescents. Recent research indicates that an authoritative parenting style also benefits emerging adults but a controlling-indulgent style is related to negative outcomes for emerging adults.

Coparenting

- Coparenting, father-mother cooperation, and mutual respect enhance the adolescent's development.

Parent-Adolescent Conflict

- Conflict with parents does increase in early adolescence, but such conflict is usually moderate and can serve a positive developmental function of increasing independence and identity exploration. The generation gap is exaggerated, although in as many as 20 percent of families parent-adolescent conflict is too high and is linked with adolescent problems.

Autonomy and Attachment

- Many parents have a difficult time handling the adolescent's push for autonomy. Autonomy is a complex concept with many referents. Developmental transitions in autonomy include the onset of early adolescence and the time when individuals leave home and go to college. A special concern about autonomy involves runaways. The wise parent relinquishes control in areas where the adolescent makes mature decisions and retains more control in areas where the adolescent makes immature decisions. Adolescents do not simply move away into a world isolated from parents. Attachment to parents in adolescence increases the probability that an adolescent will be socially competent and explore a widening social world in a healthy way. Increasingly, researchers classify attachment in adolescence into one secure category (secure-autonomous) and three insecure categories (dismissing/avoidant, preoccupied/ambivalent, and unresolved/disorganized). Increased interest in attachment during emerging adulthood is revealing that securely attached emerging adults have better social relationships than do insecurely attached emerging adults.

Emerging Adults' Relationships with Their Parents

- An increasing number of emerging adults are returning to live at home with their parents, often for economic reasons. Both emerging adults and their parents need to adapt when emerging adults return home to live.

Intergenerational Relationships

- Connections between parents play important roles in development through the life span. An increasing number of studies indicate that intergenerational relationships influence the development of adolescents. Marital interaction, a supportive family environment, divorce, and conduct disorder in the adolescent's family of origin are among the factors that are linked to later characteristics and relationships when the adolescent moves into the adulthood years.

3 Sibling Relationships

LG3 Characterize sibling relationships in adolescence.

Sibling Roles

- Sibling relationships often involve more conflict than do relationships with other individuals. However, adolescents also share many positive moments with siblings through emotional support and social communication.

Birth Order

- Birth order has been of special interest, and differences between firstborns and later-borns have been reported. The only child often is more socially competent than the stereotype "spoiled brat" suggests. An increasing number of family researchers believe that birth-order effects have been exaggerated and that other factors are more important in predicting the adolescent's behavior.

4 The Changing Family in a Changing Society

Describe the changing family in a changing society.

Divorced Families

- Adolescents in divorced families have more adjustment problems than their counterparts in nondivorced families, although the size of the effects is debated. Whether parents should stay together for the sake of the adolescent is difficult to determine, although conflict has a negative effect on the adolescent. Adolescents are better adjusted in divorced families when their parents have a harmonious relationship with each other and use authoritative parenting. Among other factors to be considered in adolescent adjustment are adjustment prior to the divorce, personality and temperament, and developmental status, gender, and custody. Income loss for divorced mothers is linked to a number of other stresses that can affect adolescent adjustment.

Stepfamilies

- An increasing number of adolescents are growing up in stepfamilies. Stepfamilies involve different types of structure (stepfather, stepmother, blended. Adolescents in stepfamilies have more adjustment problems than do children in nondivorced homes. Adjustment is especially difficult in the first several years of a stepfamily's existence and is difficult for young adolescents.

Working Parents

- It is the nature of parents' work, not whether one parent works outside the home or not, that is linked to adolescents' development. Latchkey experiences do not have a uniformly negative effect on adolescents. Parental monitoring and structured activities in the after-school hours benefit latchkey adolescents.

Adoption

- Although adopted adolescents have more problems than their nonadopted counterparts, the majority of adopted adolescents adapt effectively. When adoption occurs very early in development, the outcomes for the adolescent improve. Because of the dramatic changes that have occurred in adoption in recent decades, it is difficult to generalize about the average adopted adolescent or average adoptive family.

Gay and Lesbian Parents

- There is considerable diversity among lesbian mothers, gay fathers, and their adolescents. Researchers have found few differences in adolescents growing up in gay male or lesbian families and adolescents growing up in heterosexual families.

Culture and Ethnicity

- Authoritative parenting is the most common form of parenting around the world. Ethnic minority families differ from non-Latino White families in their size, structure, and composition, their reliance on kinship networks, and their levels of income and education.

5 Social Policy, Adolescents, and Families

Explain what is needed for improved social policy involving adolescents and their families.

- Families with adolescents have been neglected in social policy. A number of recommendations for improving social policy for families include the extent to which parents are involved in schools, youth organizations, and health-care agencies; the degree to which teachers and other professionals invite and encourage parents to be involved in schools and other settings that adolescents frequent; the extent to which policies are developed to allow employers to provide more flexible scheduling for parents; and the provision of greater funding by institutions such as businesses, schools, and youth organizations for high-quality programs for adolescents in after-school, weekend, and vacation time periods.

key terms

reciprocal socialization 254
multiple developmental trajectories 257
authoritarian parenting 260
authoritative parenting 260
neglectful parenting 261
indulgent parenting 261
emotional autonomy 265
secure attachment 267
insecure attachment 267
dismissing/avoidant attachment 268
preoccupied/ambivalent attachment 268
unresolved/disorganized attachment 268
boundary ambiguity 282

key people

Diana Baumrind 260
John Bowlby and Mary Ainsworth 267
Joseph Allen 268
Judy Dunn 275
E. Mavis Hetherington 278
E. Mark Cummings 279
Ann Crouter 283

resources for **improving the lives of adolescents**

101 Insights and Strategies for Parenting Teenagers
by Sheryl Feinstein (2010)
Monterey, CA: Healthy Learning

An excellent, easy-to-read book for parents that provides valuable strategies for guiding adolescents through the transition from childhood to emerging adulthood.

You and Your Adolescent
by Laurence Steinberg (2011)
New York: Simon and Schuster

Leading adolescence expert Laurence Steinberg provides a broad, developmental overview of adolescence, with good advice for parents along the way.

Building a Brighter Future
National Collaboration for Youth (2011)
Available at www.collab4youth.org

The National Collaboration for Youth is one of the most important national organizations in advocating positive social policy for youth and their families. In this up-to-date report, an essential agenda for America's youth is presented.

Big Brothers Big Sisters of America ***www.bbbsa.org***

Single mothers and single fathers who are having problems with a son or daughter might want to get a responsible adult to spend at least one afternoon every other week with the son or daughter.

Divorce Lessons: Real-Life Stories and What You Can Learn from Them
by Alison Clarke-Stewart and Cornelia Brentano (2006)
Charleston, SC: BookSurge

An outstanding book that gives special attention to emerging adults' experiences and development while growing up in divorced families.

National Stepfamily Resource Center ***www.stepfamilies.info***

This organization serves as a clearinghouse of information, resources, and support for stepfamilies.

self-**assessment**

The Student Online Learning Center includes the following self-assessment for further exploration:

- *How Much Did My Parents Monitor My Behavior During Adolescence?*

FIGURE **9.1**

GENERATION OF ALTERNATIVE SOLUTIONS AND ADAPTIVE PLANNING BY NEGATIVE- AND POSITIVE-PEER-STATUS BOYS. Notice that negative-peer-status boys were less likely to generate alternative solutions and plan ahead than were positive-peer-status counterparts.

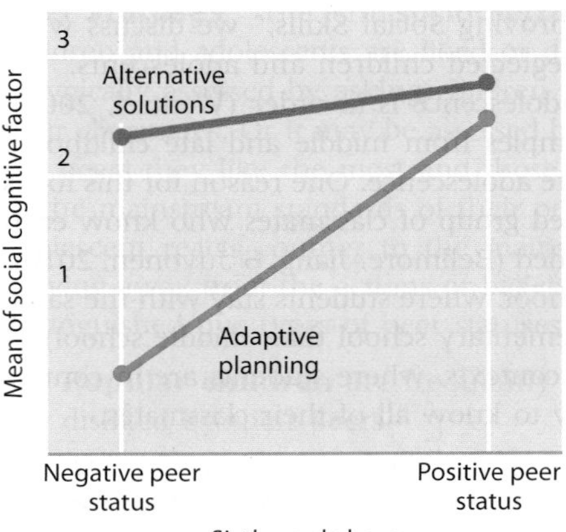

knocks a boy's soft drink out of his hand. The boy misinterprets the encounter as a hostile one, which leads him to retaliate aggressively against the peer. Through repeated encounters of this kind, peers come to perceive the boy as having a habit of acting inappropriately. Kenneth Dodge (1993) argues that adolescents go through five steps in processing information about their social world: decoding of social cues, interpretation, response search, selection of an optimal response, and enactment. Dodge has found that aggressive boys are more likely to perceive another child's actions as hostile when the peer's intention is ambiguous. And, when aggressive boys search for cues to determine a peer's intention, they respond more rapidly, less efficiently, and less reflectively than do nonaggressive children. These are among the social cognitive factors believed to be involved in adolescents' conflicts with one another.

Emotion Not only does cognition play an important role in peer relations, so does emotion (Bukowski, Buhrmester, & Underwood, 2011). For example, the ability to regulate emotion is linked to successful peer relations. Moody and emotionally negative individuals experience greater rejection by peers, whereas emotionally positive individuals are more popular (Saarni & others, 2006). Adolescents who have effective self-regulatory skills can modulate their emotional expressiveness in contexts that evoke intense emotions, as when a peer says something negative (Denham & others, 2011).

developmental **connection**

Personality. Emotional swings and intensity of emotion characterize adolescent development. Chapter 4, p. 150

One study focused on the emotional aspects of social information processing in aggressive boys (Orobio de Castro & others, 2005). Highly aggressive boys and a control group of less-aggressive boys listened to vignettes involving provocations involving peers. The highly aggressive boys expressed less guilt, attributed more hostile intent, and generated less adaptive emotion-regulation strategies than did the comparison group of boys.

Strategies for Improving Social Skills A number of strategies have been proposed for improving social skills that can lead to better peer relations (Ladd, Kochenderfer-Ladd, & Rydell, 2011). **Conglomerate strategies,** also referred to as coaching, involve the use of a combination of techniques, rather than a single approach, to improve adolescents' social skills. A conglomerate strategy might consist of demonstration or modeling of appropriate social skills, discussion, and reasoning about the social skills, as well as the use of reinforcement for their enactment in actual social situations.

In one study using a conglomerate strategy, middle school adolescents were instructed in ways to improve their self-control, stress management, and social problem solving (Weissberg & Caplan, 1989). For example, as problem situations arose, teachers modeled and students practiced six sequential steps:

conglomerate strategies The use of a combination of techniques, rather than a single approach, to improve adolescents' social skills; also called coaching.

1. Stop, calm down, and think before you act.
2. Go over the problem and state how you feel.

3. Set a positive goal.
4. Think of lots of solutions.
5. Plan ahead for the consequences.
6. Go ahead and try the best plan.

The adolescents who participated in the program improved their ability to devise cooperative solutions to problem situations, and their teachers reported that the students showed improved social relations in the classroom following the program.

More specifically, how can neglected children and adolescents be trained to interact more effectively with their peers? The goal of training programs with neglected children and adolescents is often to help them attract attention from their peers in positive ways and to hold their attention by asking questions, by listening in a warm and friendly way, and by saying things about themselves that relate to the peers' interests. They also are taught to enter groups more effectively. The goal of training programs with rejected children and adolescents is often to help them listen to peers and "hear what they say" instead of trying to dominate peer interactions. Rejected children and adolescents are trained to join peers without trying to change what is taking place in the peer group.

Despite the positive outcomes of some programs that attempt to improve the social skills of adolescents, researchers have often found it difficult to improve the social skills of adolescents who are actively disliked and rejected. Many of these adolescents are rejected because they are aggressive or impulsive and lack the self-control to keep these behaviors in check. Still, some intervention programs have been successful in reducing the aggressive and impulsive behaviors of these adolescents (Ladd, Kochenderfer-Ladd, & Rydell, 2011).

Social-skills training programs have generally been more successful with children 10 years of age or younger than with adolescents (Malik & Furman, 1993). Peer reputations become more fixed as cliques and peer groups become more significant in adolescence. Once an adolescent gains a negative reputation among peers as being "mean," "weird," or a "loner," the peer group's attitude is often slow to change, even after the adolescent's problem behavior has been corrected. Thus, researchers have found that skills interventions may need to be supplemented by efforts to change the minds of peers. One such intervention strategy involves cooperative group training (Slavin, 2012). In this approach, children or adolescents work toward a common goal that holds promise for changing reputations (Johnson & Johnson, 2009). Most cooperative group programs have been conducted in academic settings, but other contexts might be used. For example, participation in cooperative games and sports increases sharing and feelings of happiness. And some video games require cooperative efforts by the players.

FRIENDSHIP

Earlier we noted that peers are individuals who are about the same age or maturity level. **Friends** are a subset of peers who engage in mutual companionship, support, and intimacy. Thus, relationships with friends are much closer and more involved than are relationships with the peer group. Some adolescents have several close friends, others one, and yet others none.

A man's growth is seen in the successive choirs of his friends.

—Ralph Waldo Emerson
American Poet and Essayist, 19th Century

The Importance of Friendship The functions that adolescents' friendships serve can be categorized in six ways (Gottman & Parker, 1987) (see Figure 9.2):

1. *Companionship.* Friendship provides adolescents with a familiar partner, someone who is willing to spend time with them and join in collaborative activities.
2. *Stimulation.* Friendship provides adolescents with interesting information, excitement, and amusement.
3. *Physical support.* Friendship provides resources and assistance.

friends A subset of peers who engage in mutual companionship, support, and intimacy.

FIGURE **9.2**
THE FUNCTIONS OF FRIENDSHIP

4. *Ego support.* Friendship provides the expectation of support, encouragement, and feedback that helps adolescents to maintain an impression of themselves as competent, attractive, and worthwhile individuals.
5. *Social comparison.* Friendship provides information about where adolescents stand vis-á-vis others and whether adolescents are doing okay.
6. *Intimacy/affection.* Friendship provides adolescents with a warm, close, trusting relationship with another individual, a relationship that involves self-disclosure.

The importance of friendship was underscored in a two-year longitudinal study (Wentzel, Barry, & Caldwell, 2004). Sixth-grade students who did not have a friend engaged in less prosocial behavior (cooperation, sharing, helping others), had lower grades, and were more emotionally distressed (depression, low well-being) than did their counterparts who had one or more friends. Two years later, in the eighth grade, the students who did not have a friend in the sixth grade were still more emotionally distressed than their counterparts with one or more friends.

Friendship in Adolescence For most children, being popular with their peers is a strong motivator. The focus of their peer relations is on being liked by classmates and being included in games or lunchroom conversations. Beginning in early adolescence, however, teenagers typically prefer to have a smaller number of friendships that are more intense and intimate than those of young children.

Harry Stack Sullivan (1953) has been the most influential theorist in the study of adolescent friendships. Sullivan argued that friends are also important in shaping the development of children and adolescents. Everyone, said Sullivan, has basic social needs, such as the need for secure attachment, playful companionship, social acceptance, intimacy, and sexual relations. Whether or not these needs are fulfilled largely determines our emotional well-being. For example, if the need for playful companionship goes unmet, then we become bored and depressed; if the need for social acceptance is not met, we suffer a lowered sense of self-worth.

During adolescence, said Sullivan, friends become increasingly important in meeting social needs. In particular, Sullivan argued that the need for intimacy intensifies during early adolescence, motivating teenagers to seek out close friends. If adolescents fail to forge such close friendships, they experience loneliness and a reduced sense of self-worth.

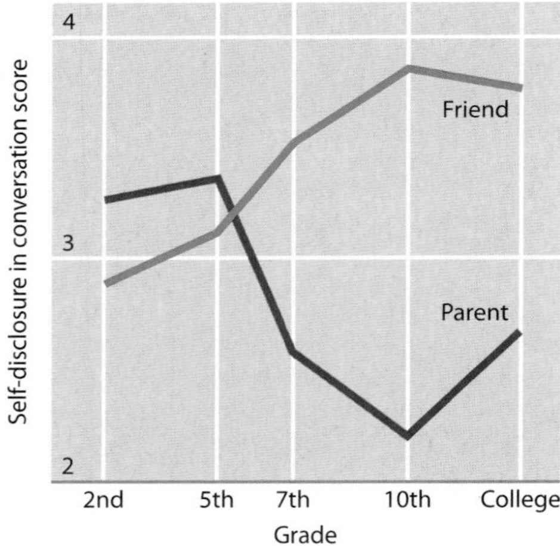

FIGURE **9.3**
DEVELOPMENTAL CHANGES IN SELF-DISCLOSING CONVERSATIONS. Self-disclosing conversations with friends increased dramatically in adolescence while declining in an equally dramatic fashion with parents. However, self-disclosing conversations with parents began to pick up somewhat during the college years. The measure of self-disclosure involved a 5-point rating scale completed by the children and youth, with a higher score representing greater self-disclosure. The data shown represent the means for each age group.

Many of Sullivan's ideas have withstood the test of time. For example, adolescents report disclosing intimate and personal information to their friends more often than do younger children (Buhrmester, 1998) (see Figure 9.3). Adolescents also say they depend more on friends than on parents to satisfy their needs for companionship, reassurance of worth, and intimacy.

Willard Hartup (1996), who has studied peer relations across four decades, concluded that children and adolescents use friends as cognitive and social resources on a regular basis. Hartup also commented that normative transitions, such as moving from elementary to middle school, are negotiated more competently by children who have friends than by those who don't.

Although having friends can be a developmental advantage, not all friendships are alike and the quality of friendship is also important to consider (Bukowski, Buhrmester, & Underwood, 2011). People differ in the company they keep—that is, who their friends are (Ali & Dwyer, 2011; Poulin & others, 2011). Developmental advantages occur when adolescents have friends who are socially skilled, supportive, and oriented toward academic achievement (Ryan, 2011). However, it is developmentally disadvantageous to have coercive, conflict-ridden, and poor-quality friendships (Salzinger & others, 2011).

Let's examine several studies that document how the characteristics of an adolescent's friends can influence whether the friends have a positive or negative influence on the adolescent. In one study, friends' grade-point average was a consistent predictor of positive school achievement and also was linked to less drug abuse and acting out (Cook, Deng, & Morgano, 2007). A recent study found that adolescents who had more in-school friends—compared to out-of-school friends—had higher grade point averages (Witkow & Fuligni, 2010).

Researchers have found that interacting with delinquent peers and friends greatly increases the risk of becoming delinquent (Salzinger & others, 2011). Further, not having a close relationship with a best friend, having less contact with friends, having friends who are depressed, and experiencing peer rejection all increase depressive tendencies in adolescents (Brendgen & others, 2010).

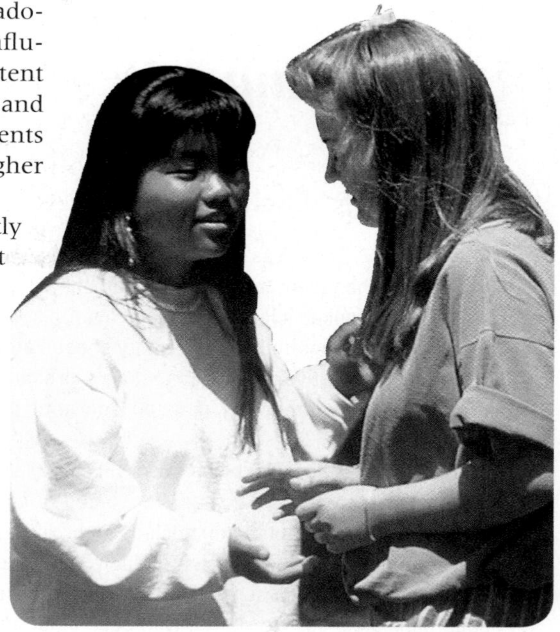

How do the characteristics of an adolescent's friends influence whether the friends have a positive or a negative influence on the adolescent?

Friendship in Emerging Adulthood Many aspects of friendship are the same in adolescence as in emerging adulthood. One difference between close relationships in adolescence and emerging adulthood was found in a longitudinal study (Collins & van Dulmen, 2006). Close relationships—between friends, family members, and romantic partners—were more integrated and similar than in adolescence. Also in this study, the number of friendships declined from the end of adolescence through emerging adulthood.

Another research study indicated that best friendships often decline in satisfaction and commitment in the first year of college (Oswald & Clark, 2003). In this study, maintaining communication with high school friends and keeping the same best friends across the transition to college lessened the decline.

Intimacy and Similarity Two important characteristics of friendship are intimacy and similarity.

Intimacy In the context of friendship, *intimacy* has been defined in different ways. For example, it has been defined broadly to include everything in a relationship that makes the relationship seem close or intense. In most research studies, though, **intimacy in friendship** is defined narrowly as self-disclosure, or sharing of private thoughts. Private or personal knowledge about a friend also has been used as an index of intimacy.

The most consistent finding in the last two decades of research on adolescent friendships is that intimacy is an important feature of friendship (Berndt & Perry, 1990). When young adolescents are asked what they want from a friend, or how they can tell if someone is their best friend, they frequently say that a best friend will share problems with them, understand them, and listen when they talk about their own thoughts or feelings. When young children talk about their friendships, comments about intimate self-disclosure or mutual understanding are rare. In one investigation, friendship intimacy was more prominent in 13- to 16-year-olds than in 10- to 13-year-olds (Buhrmester, 1990).

Similarity Another predominant characteristic of friendship is that, throughout the childhood and adolescent years, friends are generally similar—in terms of age, sex, ethnicity, and many other factors. Similarity is referred to as *homophily*, the tendency to associate with similar others (Brechwald & Prinstein, 2011). Friends often have similar attitudes toward school, similar educational aspirations, and closely aligned achievement orientations.

Mixed-Age Friendships Although most adolescents develop friendships with individuals who are close to their own age, some adolescents become best friends with younger or older individuals. Do older friends encourage adolescents to engage in delinquent behavior or early sexual behavior? Adolescents who interact with older youth do engage in these behaviors more frequently, but it is not known whether the older youth guide younger adolescents toward deviant behavior or whether the younger adolescents were already prone to deviant behavior before

intimacy in friendship In most research studies, this concept is defined narrowly as self-disclosure, or sharing of private thoughts.

connecting with adolescents

We Defined Each Other with Adjectives

"I was funky. Dana was sophisticated. Liz was crazy. We walked to school together, went for bike rides, cut school, got stoned, talked on the phone, smoked cigarettes, slept over, discussed boys and sex, went to church together, and got angry at each other. We defined each other with adjectives and each other's presence. As high school friends, we simultaneously resisted and anticipated adulthood and womanhood. . . ."

"What was possible when I was 15 and 16? We still had to tell our parents where we were going! We wanted to do excitedly forbidden activities like going out to dance clubs and drinking whiskey sours. Liz, Dana, and I wanted to do these forbidden things in order to feel: to have intense emotional and sensual experiences that removed us from the suburban sameness we shared with each other and everyone else we knew. We were tired of the repetitive experiences that our town, our siblings, our parents, and our school offered to us. . . ."

"The friendship between Dana, Liz, and myself was born out of another emotional need: the need for trust. The three of us had reached a point in our lives when we realized how unstable relationships can be, and we all craved safety and acceptance. Friendships all around us were often uncertain. We wanted and needed to be able to like and trust each other."

(*Source:* Garrod & others, 1992, pp. 199–200)

How do these excerpts demonstrate the roles of intimacy and similarity in friendship?

they developed the friendship with the older youth. A study also revealed that over time from the sixth through tenth grades girls were more likely to have older male friends, which places some girls on a developmental trajectory for engaging in problem behavior (Poulin & Pedersen, 2007). However, a recent study of young adolescents found that mixed-grade friends may protect same-grade friendless girls from feelings of loneliness and same-grade friendless and anxious-withdrawn boys from victimization (Bowker & Spencer, 2010).

Are there strategies that can help adolescents develop friendships? See the *Connecting with Health and Well-Being* interlude.

Loneliness can develop when individuals go through life transitions. *What are some strategies for reducing loneliness?*

LONELINESS

In some cases individuals who don't have friends are vulnerable to loneliness, and loneliness can set in when individuals leave a close relationship (Bowker, Rubin, & Coplan, 2012). Each of us has times in our lives when we feel lonely, but for some individuals loneliness is a chronic condition. More than just an unwelcome social situation, chronic loneliness is linked with impaired physical and mental health (Karnick, 2005). A recent study also found that increasing and chronic loneliness of Latino high school students was associated with academic difficulties (Benner, 2011). In this study, support from friends buffered the negative relation of loneliness to academic difficulties.

It is important to distinguish loneliness from the desire for solitude. Some individuals value solitary time. Loneliness is often interwoven with the passage through life transitions, such as a move to a different part of the country, a divorce, or the death of a close friend or family member. Another situation that often creates loneliness is the first year of college, especially if students leave the familiar world of their hometown and family to enter college. Freshmen rarely bring their popularity and social standing from high school into the college environment. There may be a dozen high school basketball stars, National Merit scholars, and former student council presidents in a single dormitory wing. Especially if students attend college away from home, they face the task of forming completely new social relationships.

connecting with health and well-being

What Are Effective and Ineffective Strategies for Making Friends?

Here are some strategies that adults can recommend to adolescents for making friends (Wentzel, 1997):

- *Initiate interaction.* Learn about a friend—ask for his or her name, age, favorite activities. Use these prosocial overtures: Introduce yourself, start a conversation, and invite him or her to do things.
- *Be nice.* Show kindness, be considerate, and compliment the other person.
- *Engage in prosocial behavior.* Be honest and trustworthy: Tell the truth, keep promises. Be generous, share, and be cooperative.
- *Show respect for yourself and others.* Have good manners, be polite and courteous, and listen to what others have to say. Have a positive attitude and personality.
- *Provide social support.* Show you care.

And here are some inappropriate strategies for making friends that adults can recommend that adolescents avoid using (Wentzel, 1997):

- *Be psychologically aggressive.* Show disrespect and have bad manners. Use others, be uncooperative, don't share, ignore others, gossip, and spread rumors.
- *Present yourself negatively.* Be self-centered, snobby, conceited, and jealous; show off; care only about yourself. Be mean, have a bad attitude, be angry, throw temper tantrums, and start trouble.
- *Behave antisocially.* Be physically aggressive, yell at others, pick on them, make fun of them, be dishonest, tell secrets, and break promises.

What are some effective and ineffective strategies for making friends?

Which of these positive strategies have been successful for you? Has someone befriended you using one of the recommended approaches?

In one study of more than 2,600 undergraduates, lonely individuals were less likely to actively cope with stress than were individuals who were able to make friends (Cacioppo & others, 2000). Also in this study, lonely college students had higher levels of stress-related hormones and poorer sleep patterns than did students who had positive relationships with others.

Review *Connect* Reflect

 LG1 Discuss the roles of peer relations, friendship, and loneliness in adolescent development.

Review

- What roles do peers play in adolescent development?
- How does friendship contribute to adolescent development?
- How would you distinguish between loneliness and the desire to be alone?

Connect

- Relate emotional competence, which was discussed in Chapter 4, to the topic of social cognition that was described in this section.

Reflect *Your Own Personal Journey of Life*

- How much time did you spend in adolescence with friends, and what activities did you engage in? What were your friends like? Were they similar to you or different? Has the nature of your friendships changed since adolescence? Explain.

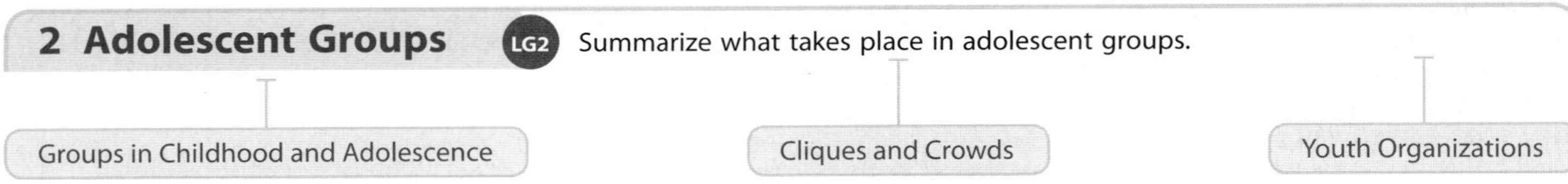

During your adolescent years, you probably were a member of both formal and informal groups. Examples of formal groups include the basketball team or drill team, the Girl Scouts or Boy Scouts, the student council, and so on. A more informal group could be a group of peers, such as a clique. Our study of adolescent groups focuses on differences between childhood groups and adolescent groups, cliques and crowds, and youth organizations.

GROUPS IN CHILDHOOD AND ADOLESCENCE

Childhood groups differ from adolescent groups in several important ways. The members of childhood groups often are friends or neighborhood acquaintances, and the groups usually are not as formalized as many adolescent groups. During the adolescent years, groups tend to include a broader array of members; in other words, adolescents other than friends or neighborhood acquaintances often are members of adolescent groups. Try to recall the student council, honor society, art club, football team, or another organized group at your junior high school. If you were a member of any of these organizations, you probably remember that they were made up of many individuals you had not met before and that they were a more heterogeneous group than were your childhood peer groups. Rules and regulations were probably well defined, and captains or leaders were formally elected or appointed in the adolescent groups.

A classic observational study by Dexter Dunphy (1963) indicates that opposite-sex participation in social groups increases during adolescence. In late childhood, boys and girls tend to form small, same-sex groups. As they move into the early adolescent years, the same-sex groups begin to interact with each other. Gradually, the leaders and high-status members form further groups based on mixed-sex relationships. Eventually, the newly created mixed-sex groups replace the same-sex groups. The mixed-sex groups interact with each other in large crowd activities, too—at dances and athletic events, for example. In late adolescence, the crowd begins to dissolve as couples develop more serious relationships and make long-range plans that may include engagement and marriage. A summary of Dunphy's ideas is presented in Figure 9.4.

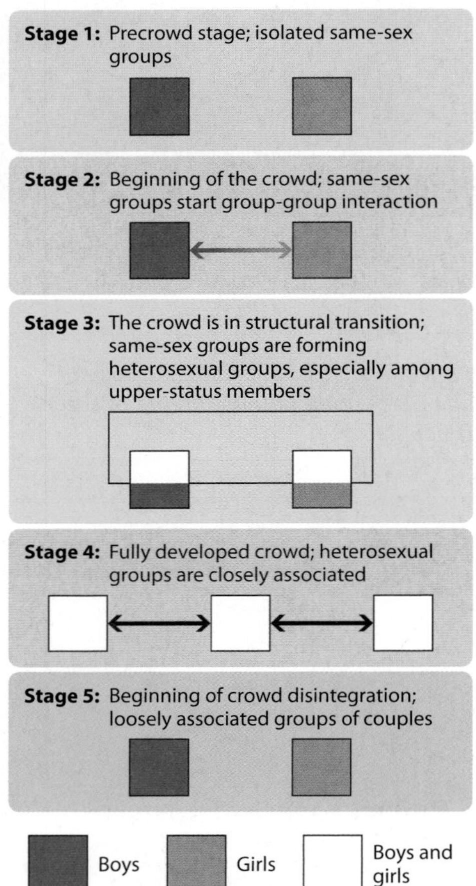

FIGURE **9.4**

DUNPHY'S PROGRESSION OF PEER GROUP RELATIONS IN ADOLESCENCE

CLIQUES AND CROWDS

In our discussion of Dunphy's work, the importance of heterosexual relationships in the evolution of adolescent crowds was noted. Let's now examine adolescent cliques and crowds in greater detail.

Cliques and crowds assume more important roles in the lives of adolescents than children (Brown, 2011; Daddis, 2010). **Cliques** are small groups that range from 2 to about 12 individuals and average about 5 to 6 individuals. The clique members are usually of the same sex and about the same age.

Cliques can form because adolescents engage in similar activities, such as being in a club or on a sports team (Brown, 2011; Brown & Dietz, 2009). Several adolescents may form a clique because they have spent time with each other and enjoy each other's company. Not necessarily friends, they often develop a friendship if they stay in the clique.

What do adolescents do in cliques? They share ideas and hang out together. Often they develop an in-group identity in which they believe that their clique is better than other cliques.

cliques Small groups that range from 2 to about 12 individuals and average about 5 to 6 individuals. Members are usually of the same sex and are similar in age; cliques can form because of similar interests, such as sports, and also can form purely from friendship.

Crowds are larger than cliques and less personal. Adolescents are usually members of a crowd based on reputation, and they may or may not spend much time together. Many crowds are defined by the activities adolescents engage in (such as "jocks," who are good at sports, or "druggies," who take drugs) (Brown, 2011; Brown & others, 2008). Reputation-based crowds often appear for the first time in early adolescence and usually become less prominent in late adolescence (Collins & Steinberg, 2006).

What characterizes adolescent cliques? How are they different from crowds?

In one study, crowd membership was associated with adolescent self-esteem (Brown & Lohr, 1987). The crowds included jocks (athletically oriented), populars (well-known students who led social activities), normals (middle-of-the-road students who made up the masses), druggies or toughs (known for illicit drug use or other delinquent activities), and nobodies (low in social skills or intellectual abilities). The self-esteem of the jocks and the populars was highest, whereas that of the nobodies was lowest. One group of adolescents not in a crowd had self-esteem equivalent to that of the jocks and the populars; this group was the independents, who indicated that crowd membership was not important to them. Keep in mind that these data are correlational; self-esteem could increase an adolescent's probability of becoming a crowd member, just as crowd membership could increase the adolescent's self-esteem.

YOUTH ORGANIZATIONS

Recall from Chapter 1 that the positive youth movement includes youth development programs and organized youth activities (Lerner & others, 2010). Youth organizations can have an important influence on the adolescent's development (Bathgate & Silva, 2010; Larson & Angus, 2011). Currently there are more than 400 national youth organizations in the United States. The organizations include career groups, such as Junior Achievement; groups aimed at building character, such as Girl Scouts and Boy Scouts; political groups, such as Young Republicans and Young Democrats; and ethnic groups, such as Indian Youth of America. They serve approximately 30 million young people each year. The largest youth organization is 4-H, with nearly 5 million participants. Among the smallest organizations are ASPIRA, a Latino youth organization that provides intensive educational enrichment programs for about 13,000 adolescents each year, and WAVE, a dropout-prevention program that serves about 8,000 adolescents each year.

developmental **connection**

Youth Development. The positive youth movement (PYD) emphasizes the strengths of youth and the positive developmental trajectories that are desired for youth. Chapter 1, p. 8

Adolescents who join such groups are more likely to participate in community activities in adulthood and have higher self-esteem, are better educated, and come from families with higher incomes than their counterparts who do not participate in youth groups (Erickson, 1982). Participation in youth groups can help adolescents practice the interpersonal and organizational skills that are important for success in adult roles.

The Search Institute (1995) conducted a study that sheds light on both the potential for and barriers to participation in youth programs. The study focused on Minneapolis, which faces many of the same challenges regarding youth as other major U.S. cities. After-school hours and summer vacations are important time slots during which adolescents could form positive relationships with adults and peers. Yet this study found that more than 50 percent of the youth said they don't participate in any type of after-school youth program in a typical week. More than 40 percent reported no participation in youth programs during the summer months.

These adolescents are participating in Boys & Girls Club activities. *What effects do youth organizations have on adolescents?*

About 350 youth programs were identified in Minneapolis, about one program for every 87 adolescents. However, about one-half of the youth and their parents agreed that there were not enough youth programs. Parents with the lowest incomes were the least satisfied with program availability. Some of the reasons given by middle school adolescents for not participating in youth programs were a lack of

crowds A larger group structure than cliques. Adolescents are usually members of a crowd based on reputation and may or may not spend much time together.

interest in available activities, a lack of transportation, and lack of awareness about what is available.

According to Reed Larson and his colleagues (Larson, 2000; Larson & Walker, 2010; Larson & others, 2011), structured voluntary youth activities are especially well suited for the development of initiative. One study of structured youth activities that led to increased initiative involved adolescents in low-income areas who began participating in art and drama groups, sports teams, Boys & Girls Clubs, YMCA gang intervention programs, and other community organizations (Heath, 1999; Heath & McLaughlin, 1993). When the adolescents first joined these organizations, they seemed bored. Within three to four weeks, though, they reported greater confidence in their ability to affect their world and adjusted their behavior in pursuit of a goal. In a recent study, how high school students come to see themselves as more responsible by participating in youth programs was examined (Wood, Larson, & Brown, 2009). The study revealed that participation in three of the programs increased the responsibility of half of the students in the programs. In these three programs, it was not the fun and games involved in the programs that increased the students' responsibility but rather showing persistence in completing demanding tasks.

In further research, successful youth programs had stable characteristics, such as positive relationships, trust, and commitment to youth (Larson & Angus, 2011). Successful programs also included learning experiences that were challenging, required reaching a demanding goal, and involved feedback to youth.

In sum, youth activities and organizations provide excellent developmental contexts in which to provide adolescents opportunities to develop many positive qualities (Flanagan, 2004). Participation in these contexts can help to increase achievement and decrease delinquency (Larson, 2000). For example, a study of vulnerable youth revealed that, when they participated in positive extracurricular activities in high school, they were more likely to subsequently enroll in college (Peck & others, 2008).

Review *Connect* Reflect

LG2 Summarize what takes place in adolescent groups.

Review

- How are childhood groups different from adolescent groups?
- What are cliques and crowds? What roles do they play in adolescent development?
- How can youth organizations be characterized?

Connect

- Contrast membership in a clique with the experience of loneliness discussed in the preceding section. What influence does each have on adolescent development?

Reflect *Your Own Personal Journey of Life*

- What would have been the ideal youth organization to support your needs when you were an adolescent?

3 Gender and Culture

LG3 Describe the roles of gender and culture in adolescent peer groups and friendships.

Gender | Socioeconomic Status and Ethnicity | Culture

The social worlds of adolescent peer groups and friendships are linked to gender and culture. In Chapter 5, we learned that during the elementary school years children spend a large majority of their free time with children of their own sex. Preadolescents spend an hour or less a week interacting with the other sex (Furman & Shaeffer, 2003). With puberty, though, more time is spent in mixed-sex peer groups, which was reflected in Dunphy's developmental view, which we just discussed (Buhrmester & Chong, 2009). And, by the twelfth grade, boys spend an average of five hours a week with the other sex, girls ten hours a week (Furman, 2002). Nonetheless, there are some significant differences between adolescent peer groups made up of males and those made up of females.

GENDER

There is increasing evidence that gender plays an important role in the peer group and friendships (Bukowski, Buhrmester, & Underwood, 2011; Coyne, Nelson, & Underwood, 2011; Rose & Smith, 2009). The evidence related to the peer group focuses on group size and interaction in same-sex groups (Maccoby, 2002):

- *Group size.* From about 5 years of age forward, boys are more likely than girls to associate in larger clusters. Boys are more likely to participate in organized games and sports than girls are.
- *Interaction in same-sex groups.* Boys are more often likely than girls to engage in competition, conflict, ego displays, and risk taking and to seek dominance. By contrast, girls are more likely to engage in "collaborative discourse," in which they talk and act in a more reciprocal manner.

developmental **connection**

Gender. Recent research indicates that relational aggression occurs more in girls than boys in adolescence, but not in childhood. Chapter 5, p. 173

Are the friendships of adolescent girls more intimate than the friendships of adolescent boys? Girls' friendships in adolescence are more likely to focus on intimacy; boys' friendships tend to emphasize power and excitement (Buhrmester & Chong, 2009). Boys may discourage one another from openly disclosing their problems because they perceive that self-disclosure is not masculine (Maccoby, 2002).

Recently, researchers have found that some aspects of girls' friendships may be linked to adolescent problems (Tompkins & others, 2011). For example, a study of third- through ninth-graders revealed that girls' co-rumination (as reflected in excessively discussing problems) predicted not only an increase in positive friendship quality but also an increase in further co-rumination as well as an increase in depressive and anxiety symptoms. One implication of the research is that some girls who are vulnerable to developing internalized problems may go undetected because they have supportive friendships.

What are some gender differences in peer relations and friendships in adolescence?

SOCIOECONOMIC STATUS AND ETHNICITY

In many schools, peer groups are strongly segregated according to socioeconomic status and ethnicity (Way & Silverman, 2012). In schools with large numbers of middle- and lower-SES students, middle-SES students often assume the leadership roles in formal organizations, such as student council, the honor society, fraternity-sorority groups, and so on. Athletic teams are one type of adolescent group in which African American adolescents and adolescents from low-income families have been able to gain parity or even surpass adolescents from middle- and upper-SES families in achieving status.

For many ethnic minority youth, especially immigrants, peers from their own ethnic group provide a crucial sense of brotherhood or sisterhood within the majority culture. Peer groups may form to oppose those of the majority peer groups and to provide adaptive supports that reduce feelings of isolation.

CULTURE

So far, we have considered adolescents' peer relations in regard to gender, socioeconomic status, and ethnicity. Are there also some foreign cultures in which the peer group plays a role different from that in the United States?

What are some cross-cultural variations in peer relations? How are American and Japanese adolescents socialized differently in regard to peer relations?

In some countries, adults restrict adolescents' access to peers. For example, in many areas of rural India and in Arab countries, opportunities for peer relations in adolescence are severely restricted, especially for girls (Brown & Larson, 2002). If girls attend school in these regions of the world, it is usually in sex-segregated schools. In these countries, interaction with the other sex or opportunities for romantic relationships are restricted if not totally prohibited (Booth, 2002).

In Chapter 8, we learned that Japanese adolescents seek autonomy from their parents later and have less conflict with them than American adolescents do. In a cross-cultural analysis, the peer group was more important to U.S. adolescents than to Japanese adolescents (Rothbaum & others, 2000). Japanese adolescents spend less time outside the home, have less recreational leisure time, and engage in fewer extracurricular activities with peers than U.S. adolescents do (White, 1993). Also, U.S. adolescents are more likely to put pressure on their peers to resist parental influence than Japanese adolescents are (Rothbaum & others, 2000).

A trend, though, is that in societies in which adolescents' access to peers has been restricted, adolescents are engaging in more peer interaction during school and in shared leisure activities, especially in middle-SES contexts (Brown & Larson, 2002). For example, in Southeast Asia and some Arab regions, adolescents are starting to rely more on peers for advice and share interests with them (Booth, 2002; Santa Maria, 2002).

In many countries and regions, though, peers play more prominent roles in adolescents' lives (Brown & Larson, 2002; Way & Silverman, 2012). For example, in sub-Saharan Africa, the peer group is a pervasive aspect of adolescents' lives (Nsamenang, 2002); similar results have been observed throughout Europe and North America (Arnett, 2002).

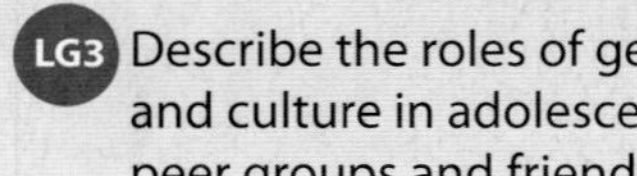

developmental **connection**

Culture. Cross-cultural variations not only characterize peer relationships but also parent-adolescent relationships. Chapter 1, p. 12; Chapter 12, p. 393

In some cultures, children are placed in peer groups for much greater lengths of time at an earlier age than they are in the United States. For example, in the Murian culture of eastern India, both male and female children live in a dormitory from the age of 6 until they get married (Barnouw, 1975). The dormitory is a religious haven where members are devoted to work and spiritual harmony. Children work for their parents, and the parents arrange the children's marriages. The children continue to live in the dormitory through adolescence, until they marry. In some cultural settings, peers even assume responsibilities usually assumed by parents. For example, street youth in South America rely on networks of peers to help them negotiate survival in urban environments (Welti, 2002).

Review *Connect* Reflect

LG3 Describe the roles of gender and culture in adolescent peer groups and friendships.

Review

- What role does gender play in adolescent peer groups and friendships?
- How are socioeconomic status and ethnicity linked to adolescent peer relations?
- How is culture involved in adolescent peer relations?

Connect

- Compare the influence of families, discussed in Chapter 8, to that of socioeconomic status in the development of adolescent peer relations.

Reflect *Your Own Personal Journey of Life*

- How did your peer relations and friendships during adolescence likely differ depending on whether you are a female or a male?

4 Dating and Romantic Relationships

LG4 Characterize adolescent dating and romantic relationships.

Functions of Dating

Types of Dating and Developmental Changes

Emotion, Adjustment, and Romantic Relationships

Romantic Love and Its Construction

Gender and Culture

Though many adolescent boys and girls have social interchanges through formal and informal peer groups, it is through dating that more serious contacts between the sexes occur (Shulman, Davila, & Shachar-Shapira, 2011). Let's explore the functions of dating.

FUNCTIONS OF DATING

Dating is a relatively recent phenomenon. It wasn't until the 1920s that dating as we know it became a reality, and even then, its primary role was to select and win a mate. Prior to this period, mate selection was the sole purpose of dating, and "dates" were carefully monitored by parents, who completely controlled the nature of any heterosexual companionship. Often, parents bargained with each other about the merits of their adolescents as potential marriage partners and even chose mates for their children. In recent times, of course, adolescents have gained much more control over the dating process and whom they go out with. Furthermore, dating has evolved into something far more than just courtship for marriage (Collins, Welsh, & Furman, 2009).

Dating today can serve at least eight functions (Paul & White, 1990):

1. Dating can be a form of recreation. Adolescents who date seem to have fun and see dating as a source of enjoyment and recreation.
2. Dating is a source of status and achievement. Part of the social comparison process in adolescence involves evaluating the status of the people one dates: Are they the best looking, the most popular, and so forth?
3. Dating is part of the socialization process in adolescence: It helps the adolescent to learn how to get along with others and assists in learning manners and sociable behavior.
4. Dating involves learning about intimacy and serves as an opportunity to establish a unique, meaningful relationship with a person of the opposite sex.
5. Dating can be a context for sexual experimentation and exploration.
6. Dating can provide companionship through interaction and shared activities in an opposite-sex relationship.
7. Dating experiences contribute to identity formation and development; dating helps adolescents to clarify their identity and to separate from their families of origin.
8. Dating can be a means of mate sorting and selection, thereby retaining its original courtship function.

In the first half of the twentieth century, dating served mainly as a courtship for marriage.

Today the functions of dating include courtship but also many others. *What are some of these other functions of dating?*

TYPES OF DATING AND DEVELOPMENTAL CHANGES

A number of dating variations and developmental changes characterize dating and romantic relationships. First, we examine heterosexual romantic relationships and then turn to romantic relationships in sexual minority youth (gay and lesbian adolescents).

Heterosexual Romantic Relationships Three stages characterize the development of romantic relationships in adolescence (Connolly & McIsaac, 2009):

1. *Entry into romantic attractions and affiliations at about 11 to 13 years of age.* This initial stage is triggered by puberty. From 11 to 13 years old, adolescents become intensely interested in romance, and it dominates many conversations with same-sex friends. Developing a crush on someone is common, and the crush often is shared with a same-sex friend. Young adolescents may or may not interact with the individual who is the object of their infatuation. When dating occurs, it usually occurs in a group setting.
2. *Exploring romantic relationships at approximately 14 to 16 years of age.* At this point in adolescence, casual dating and dating in groups—two types of romantic involvement—occur. *Casual dating* emerges between individuals who are mutually attracted. These dating experiences are often short-lived, last a few months at best, and usually endure for only a few weeks. *Dating in groups* is common and reflects embeddedness in the peer context. Friends often act as a third-party facilitator of a potential dating relationship by communicating their friend's romantic interest and confirming whether this attraction is reciprocated.
3. *Consolidating dyadic romantic bonds at about 17 to 19 years of age.* At the end of the high school years, more serious romantic relationships develop. This is characterized by strong emotional bonds more closely resembling those in adult romantic relationships. These bonds often are more stable and enduring than earlier bonds, typically lasting one year or more.

What are dating relationships like in adolescence?

Two variations on these stages in the development of romantic relationships in adolescence involve early and late bloomers (Connolly & McIsaac, 2009). *Early bloomers* include 15 to 20 percent of 11- to 13-year-olds who say that they currently are in a romantic relationship and 35 percent who indicate that they have had some prior experience in romantic relationships. *Late bloomers* comprise approximately 10 percent of 17- to 19-year-olds who say that they have had no experience with romantic relationships and another 15 percent who report that they have not engaged in any romantic relationships that lasted more than four months.

In one study, announcing that "I like someone" occurred by the sixth grade for about 40 percent of the individuals sampled (Buhrmester, 2001) (see Figure 9.5). However, it was not until the tenth grade that 50 percent of the adolescents had a sustained romantic relationship that lasted two months or longer. By their senior year, 25 percent still had not engaged in this type of sustained romantic relationship. In another study, a rather large portion of adolescents in a steady dating relationship said that their steady relationship had persisted 11 months or longer: 20 percent of adolescents 14 or younger, 35 percent of 15- to 16-year-olds, and almost 60 percent of 17- and 18-year-olds (Carver, Joyner, & Udry, 2003).

Adolescents often find comfort in numbers in their early exploration of romantic relationships (Connolly & McIsaac, 2009). They may begin hanging out together in heterosexual groups. Sometimes they just hang out at someone's house or get organized enough to ask an adult to drive them to a mall or a movie. A special concern in early dating and "going with" someone is the associated risk for adolescent pregnancy and problems at home and school.

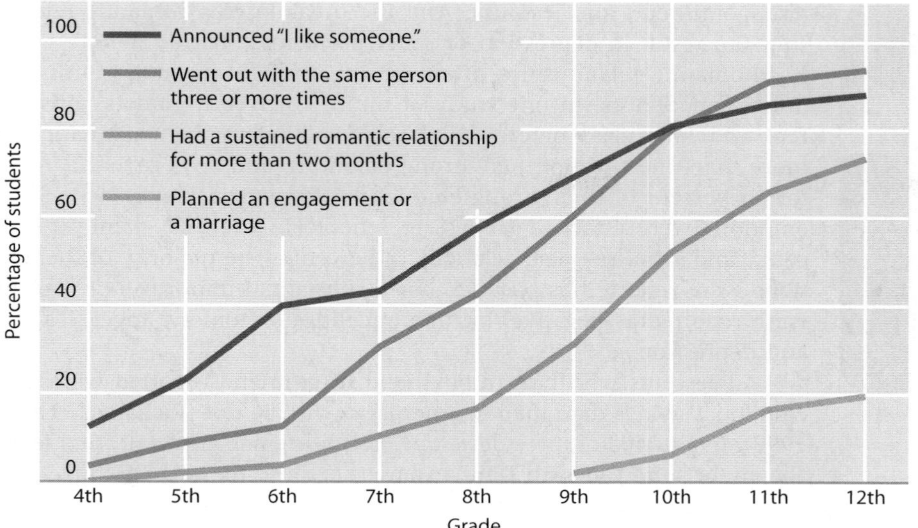

FIGURE **9.5**

AGE OF ONSET OF ROMANTIC ACTIVITY. In this study, announcing that "I like someone" occurred earliest, followed by going out with the same person three or more times, having a sustained romantic relationship for over two months, and finally planning an engagement or marriage (which characterized only a very small percentage of participants by the twelfth grade) (Buhrmester, 2001).

Romantic Relationships in Sexual Minority Youth Most research on romantic relationships in adolescence has focused on heterosexual relationships. Recently, researchers have begun to study romantic relationships in gay, lesbian, and bisexual youth (Diamond & Savin-Williams, 2009, 2011; Savin-Williams, 2011.

The average age of the initial same-sex activity for females ranges from 14 to 18 years of age and for males from 13 to 15 (Diamond & Savin-Williams, 2009, 2011). The most common initial same-sex partner is a close friend. More lesbian adolescents have sexual encounters with boys before same-sex activity, whereas gay adolescents show the opposite sequence (Savin-Williams, 2011).

Most sexual minority youth have same-sex sexual experience, but relatively few have same-sex romantic relationships because of limited opportunities and the social disapproval such relationships may generate from families or heterosexual peers (Diamond & Savin-Williams, 2009, 2011). The importance of romance to sexual minority youth was underscored in a study that found that they rated the breakup of a current romance as their second most stressful problem, second only to disclosure of their sexual orientation to their parents (D'Augelli, 1991). The romantic possibilities of sexual minority youth are complex (Diamond & Savin-Williams, 2009, 2011; Savin-Williams, 2011). To adequately address the relational interests of sexual minority youth, we can't generalize from heterosexual youth and simply switch the labels. Instead, we need to consider the full range of variation in sexual minority youths' sexual desires and romantic relationships for same- and other-sex partners.

What characterizes romantic relationships in sexual minority youth?

EMOTION, ADJUSTMENT, AND ROMANTIC RELATIONSHIPS

Romantic emotions can envelop adolescents' and emerging adults' lives (Crissey, 2009). In some cases, these emotions are positive, in others negative. A concern is that in some cases the negative emotions are so intense and prolonged they can lead to adjustment problems.

developmental **connection**

Sexuality. Sexual minority youth have diverse patterns of initial attraction. Chapter 6, p. 198

Emotions in Romantic Relationships A 14-year-old reports being in love and unable to think about anything else. A 15-year-old is distressed that "everyone else has a boyfriend but me." As we just saw, adolescents spend a lot of time thinking about romantic involvement. Some of this thought can involve positive emotions of compassion and joy, but it also can include negative emotions such as worry,

How is emotion involved in adolescent romantic relationships? How are romantic relationships linked to adolescent adjustment?

disappointment, and jealousy. And the breakup of a romantic relationship can result in depression or other problems (Sbarra, 2006).

Romantic relationships often are involved in an adolescent's emotional experiences. In one study of ninth- to twelfth-graders, girls gave real and fantasized heterosexual relationships as the explanation for more than one-third of their strong emotions, and boys gave this reason for 25 percent of their strong emotions (Wilson-Shockley, 1995). Strong emotions were attached far less to school (13 percent), family (9 percent), and same-sex peer relations (8 percent). The majority of the emotions were reported as positive, but a substantial minority (42 percent), were reported as negative, including feelings of anxiety, anger, jealousy, and depression.

Adolescents who have a boyfriend or girlfriend reported wider daily emotional swings than their counterparts who did not (Richards & Larson, 1990). In a period of three days, one eleventh-grade girl went from feeling "happy because I'm with Dan" to upset, because they had a "huge fight" and "he won't listen to me and keeps hanging up on me" to feeling "suicidal because of the fight" to feeling "happy because everything between me and Dan is fine."

Dating and Adjustment Researchers have linked dating and romantic relationships with various measures of how well adjusted adolescents are (Connolly & McIsaac, 2009; Furman & Collins, 2009; Vujeva & Furman, 2011). Consider the following studies:

- The more romantic experiences tenth graders had, the more they reported higher levels of social acceptance, friendship competence, and romantic competence; however, having more romantic experience also was linked to a higher level of substance use, delinquency, and sexual behavior (Furman, Low, & Ho, 2009).
- Adolescent girls' higher frequency of dating was linked to having depressive symptoms and emotionally unavailable parents (Steinberg & Davila, 2008).
- Adolescent girls who engaged in co-rumination (excessive discussion of problems with friends) were more likely to be involved in a romantic relationship, and together co-rumination and romantic involvement predicted an increase in depressive symptoms (Starr & Davila, 2009).
- Among adolescent girls, but not adolescent males, having an older romantic partner was linked to an increase in depressive symptoms, largely influenced by an increase in substance use (Haydon & Halpern, 2010).
- Adolescents with deviant romantic partners were more likely to engage in delinquency than were their counterparts with more prosocial partners, regardless of friends' or parents' behavior (Lonardo & others, 2009).

Dating and romantic relationships at an early age can be especially problematic (Connolly & McIsaac, 2009). Researchers have found that early dating and "going with" someone are linked with adolescent pregnancy and problems at home and school (Florsheim, Moore, & Edgington, 2003).

Dissolution of a Romantic Relationship When things don't go well in a romantic relationship, adolescents and emerging adults need to consider dissolving the relationship. In particular, falling out of love may be wise if you are obsessed with a person who repeatedly betrays your trust; if you are involved with someone who is draining you emotionally or financially; or if you are desperately in love with someone who does not return your feelings.

Being in love when love is not returned can lead to depression, obsessive thoughts, sexual dysfunction, inability to work effectively, difficulty in making new friends, and self-condemnation. Thinking clearly in such relationships is often difficult, because they are so often linked to arousing emotions.

Some individuals get taken advantage of in relationships. For example, without either person realizing it, a relationship can evolve in a way that creates dominant and submissive roles. Detecting this pattern is an important step toward learning either to reconstruct the relationship or to end it if the problems cannot be worked out.

Studies of romantic breakups have mainly focused on their negative aspects (Kato, 2005). For example, a recent study of 18- to 20-year-olds revealed that heavy drinking, marijuana use, and cigarette smoking increased following the dissolution of a romantic relationship (Fleming & others, 2010). Few studies, however, have examined the possibility that a romantic breakup might lead to positive changes (Sbarra & Ferrer, 2006). One study of college students assessed the personal growth that can follow the breakup of a romantic relationship (Tashiro & Frazier, 2003). The participants were 92 undergraduate students who had experienced a relationship breakup in the past nine months. They were asked to describe "what positive changes, if any, have happened as a result of your breakup that might serve to improve your future romantic relationships" (p. 118). Self-reported positive growth was common following the romantic breakups. The most commonly reported types of growth were feeling stronger emotionally and being more self-confident, being more independent, and developing new friendships. Women reported more positive growth than did men.

ROMANTIC LOVE AND ITS CONSTRUCTION

Romantic love, also called passionate love or eros, has strong sexual and infatuation components, and it often predominates in the early part of a love relationship. Romantic love characterizes most adolescent love, and romantic love is also extremely important among college students. In one investigation, unmarried college males and females were asked to identify their closest relationship (Berscheid, Snyder, & Omoto, 1989). More than half named a romantic partner, rather than a parent, sibling, or friend.

Another type of love is **affectionate love,** also called companionate love, which occurs when individuals desire to have another person near and have a deep, caring affection for that person. There is a strong belief that affectionate love is more characteristic of adult love than adolescent love and that the early stages of love have more romantic ingredients than the later stages (Berscheid, 2010).

developmental **connection**

Sexuality. Sexual interest plays an important role in adolescents' romantic relationships. Chapter 6, p. 192

Physical attractiveness and similarity are important aspects of romantic relationships. A recent study revealed that physically attractive adolescents were more satisfied with their romantic life (Furman & Winkles, 2010). In another study, girls and boys who were dating each other tended to be from the same ethnic group, come from similar socioeconomic backgrounds, and have similar academic success as measured by their grade point average (Furman & Simon, 2008). In another study, there were substantial pre-relationship similarities between adolescents and their future romantic partners on peer popularity, attractiveness, body appeal, and depressive symptoms (Simon, Aikins, & Prinstein, 2008). Also in this study, the influence of a dating partner on the adolescent was examined over time. Especially important was the positive influence of a high-functioning dating partner on a low-functioning dating partner as the relationship endured. For example, an adolescent who initially reported having a high level of depression but dated an adolescent who reported having a low level of depression indicated that she or he had a lower level of depression 11 months later.

> Love is a canvas furnished by nature and embroidered by imagination.
>
> —VOLTAIRE
> *French Philosopher, 18th Century*

To fully understand dating relationships in adolescence, we also need to know how experiences with family members and peers contribute to the way adolescents and emerging adults construct their dating relationships (Collins, Welsh, & Furman, 2009; Ivanova, Mills, & Veenstra, 2011; Nosko & others, 2011; Shulman, Davila, & Shachar-Shapira, 2011). Attachment history is linked to couple relationships in adolescence and emerging adulthood (Sroufe & others, 2005; Sroufe, Coffino, & Carlson, 2010). For example, infants who have an anxious attachment with their caregivers

romantic love Love that has strong sexual and infatuation components; also called passionate love or eros. It often predominates in the early part of a love relationship.

affectionate love Love occurring when an individual desires to have another person near and has a deep, caring affection for that person; also called companionate love.

developmental **connection**

Attachment. Researchers are discovering numerous links between attachment styles and romantic relationships in emerging adulthood. Chapter 8, p. 270

in infancy are less likely to develop positive romantic relationships in adolescence than are their securely attached counterparts. It might be that adolescents with a history of secure attachment are better able to control their emotions and more comfortable self-disclosing in romantic relationships. A recent study also found that a positive relationship with parents during adolescence was linked to better-quality romantic relationships in emerging adulthood (Madsen & Collins, 2011). Also in this study, better adolescent dating quality was related to a smoother romantic relationship process and less negative affect in emerging adult romantic relationships.

Wyndol Furman and Elizabeth Wehner (1998) discussed how specific insecure attachment styles might be related to adolescents' romantic relationships. Adolescents with a secure attachment to parents are likely to approach romantic relationships expecting closeness, warmth, and intimacy. Thus, they are likely to feel comfortable developing close, intimate romantic relationships. Adolescents with a dismissing/avoidant attachment to parents are likely to expect romantic partners to be unresponsive and unavailable. Thus, they might tend to behave in ways that distance themselves from romantic relationships. Adolescents with a preoccupied/ambivalent attachment to parents are likely to be disappointed and frustrated with intimacy and closeness in romantic relationships.

Adolescents' observations of their parents' marital relationship also contribute to their own construction of dating relationships. A recent study of 17-year-old Israeli girls and their mothers revealed that mothers who reported a higher level of marital satisfaction had daughters who were more romantically competent (based on multiple dimensions, such as maturity, coherence, and realistic perception of the romantic relationship) (Shulman, Davila, & Shachar-Shapira, 2011). Another study revealed that parents' marital conflict was linked to increased conflict in an emerging adult's romantic relationships (Cui, Fincham, & Pasley, 2008).

In a classic study, E. Mavis Hetherington (1972, 1977) found that divorce was associated with a stronger interest in boys on the part of adolescent daughters than was the death of a parent or living in an intact family. Further, the daughters of divorced parents had a more negative opinion of males than did the girls from other family structures. And girls from divorced and widowed families were more likely to marry images of their fathers than were girls from intact families. Hetherington stresses that females from intact families likely have had a greater opportunity to work through relationships with their fathers and therefore are more psychologically free to date and marry someone different from their fathers.

Recent research confirms that the divorce of parents influences adolescents' romantic relationships. For example, a recent study revealed that an adolescent's

How might experiences with family members influence the way adolescents construct the dating relationships?

first romantic relationship occurred earlier in divorced than never-divorced intact families but only when the divorce occurred in early adolescence (Ivanova, Mills, & Veenstra, 2011). One explanation for this timing of divorce impact is heightened sensitivity during transition periods, such as early adolescence.

Parents are also likely to be more involved or interested in their daughters' dating patterns and relationships than their sons'. For example, in one investigation, college females were much more likely than their male counterparts to say that their parents tried to influence whom they dated during adolescence (Knox & Wilson, 1981). They also indicated that it was not unusual for their parents to try to interfere with their dating choices and relationships.

Peer relations and friendships also provide the opportunity to learn modes of relating that are carried over into romantic relationships (Collins, Welsh, & Furman, 2009; Furman & Winkles, 2010). A longitudinal study revealed that friendship in middle childhood was linked with security in dating, as well as intimacy in dating, at age 16 (Collins, Hennighausen, & Sroufe, 1998; Collins & van Dulmen, 2006).

Research by Jennifer Connolly and her colleagues (Connolly, Furman, & Konarski, 2000; Connolly & Stevens, 1999; Connolly & others, 2004) documents the role of peers in the emergence of romantic involvement in adolescence. In one study, adolescents who were part of mixed-sex peer groups moved more readily into romantic relationships than their counterparts whose mixed-sex peer groups were more limited (Connolly, Furman, & Konarski, 2000). Another study also found that young adolescents increase their participation in mixed-gender peer groups (Connolly & others, 2004). This participation was "not explicitly focused on dating but rather brought boys and girls together in settings in which heterosocial interaction might occur but is not obligatory. . . . We speculate that mixed-gender groups are important because they are easily available to young adolescents who can take part at their own comfort level" (p. 201).

GENDER AND CULTURE

Dating and romantic relationships may vary according to gender and culture. Think back to your middle school/junior high and high school years and consider how gender likely influenced your romantic relationships.

Gender Do male and female adolescents bring different motivations to the dating experience? Candice Feiring (1996) found that they did. Fifteen-year-old girls were more likely to describe romance in terms of interpersonal qualities; boys described it in terms of physical attraction. For young adolescents, the affiliative qualities of companionship, intimacy, and support were frequently mentioned as positive dimensions of romantic relationships, but love and security were not. Also, the young adolescents described physical attraction more in terms of being cute, pretty, or handsome than in terms of sexuality (such as being a good kisser). Possibly, however, the failure to discuss sexual interests was due to the adolescents' discomfort in talking about such personal feelings with an unfamiliar adult.

What characterizes dating scripts in adolescence?

Dating scripts are the cognitive models that adolescents and adults use to guide and evaluate dating interactions. In one study, first dates were highly scripted along gender lines (Rose & Frieze, 1993). Males followed a proactive dating script, females a reactive one. The male's script involved initiating the date (asking for and planning it), controlling the public domain (driving and opening doors), and initiating sexual interaction (making physical contact, making out, and kissing). The female's script focused on the private domain (concern about appearance, enjoying the date), participating in the structure of the date provided by the male (being picked up, having doors opened), and responding to his sexual gestures. These gender differences give males more power in the initial stage of a relationship.

developmental **connection**

Gender. Gender differences have been found in sexual scripts. Chapter 6, p. 193

dating scripts The cognitive models that adolescents and adults use to guide and evaluate dating interactions.

Ethnicity and Culture The sociocultural context exerts a powerful influence on adolescent dating patterns and on mate selection. Values and religious beliefs of

connecting with careers

Susan Orenstein, Couples Counselor

Susan Orenstein provides counseling to emerging adults and young adults in Cary, North Carolina. She specializes in premarital and couple counseling to help couples increase their intimacy and mutual appreciation, and also works with couples to resolve long-standing conflicts, reduce destructive patterns of communication, and restore trust in the relationship. In addition to working privately with couples, she conducts workshops on relationships and gives numerous talks at colleges, businesses, and organizations.

Dr. Orenstein obtained an undergraduate degree in psychology from Brown University, a master's degree in counseling from Georgia Tech University, and a doctorate in counseling psychology from Temple University. Some couples therapists have advanced degrees in clinical psychology or marriage and family therapy rather than counseling, and some practice with a master's degree. After earning a master's or doctoral degree in an appropriate program, before practicing couples therapy, individuals are required to do an internship and pass a state licensing examination.

At most colleges, the counseling or health center has a counselor or therapist who works with couples to improve their relationship.

portion of adult life spent in marriage was linked to an increased likelihood of dying at an earlier age (Henretta, 2010). Further, an unhappy marriage can shorten a person's life by an average of four years (Gove, Style, & Hughes, 1990).

Premarital Education Premarital education occurs in a group and focuses on relationship advice. Might premarital education improve the quality of a marriage and possibly reduce the chances that the marriage will end in a divorce? Researchers have found that it can (Carroll & Doherty, 2003; Owen & others, 2011). For example, a recent survey of more than 3,000 adults revealed that premarital education was linked to a higher level of marital satisfaction and commitment to a spouse, a lower level of destructive marital conflict, and a 31 percent lower likelihood of divorce (Stanley & others, 2006). The premarital education programs in the study ranged from several hours to 20 hours with a median of 8 hours. It is recommended that premarital education begin approximately six months to a year before the wedding.

To improve their relationships, some couples seek counseling. To read about the work of couples counselor Susan Orenstein, see the *Connecting with Careers* profile.

DIVORCED ADULTS

Divorce has become an epidemic in the United States (Hoelter, 2009). However, the divorce rate declined in recent decades after peaking at 5.1 divorces per 1,000 people in 1981 and had declined by 2009 to 3.6 divorces per 1,000 people (National Center for Vital Statistics, 2010). Still, the United States has one of the highest divorce rates in the world.

Individuals in some groups have a higher incidence of divorce (Amato, 2010). Youthful marriage, low educational level, low income, not having a religious affiliation, having parents who are divorced, and having a baby before marriage are factors that are associated with increases in divorce (Hoelter, 2009). And these characteristics of one's partner increase the likelihood of divorce: alcoholism, psychological problems, domestic violence, infidelity, and inadequate division of household labor (Hoelter, 2009).

Earlier, we indicated that researchers have not been able to pin down a specific age that is the best time to marry so that the marriage is unlikely to end in a divorce. However, if a divorce is going to occur, it usually takes place early in a marriage; most occur in the fifth to tenth year of marriage (National Center for Health Statistics, 2000)

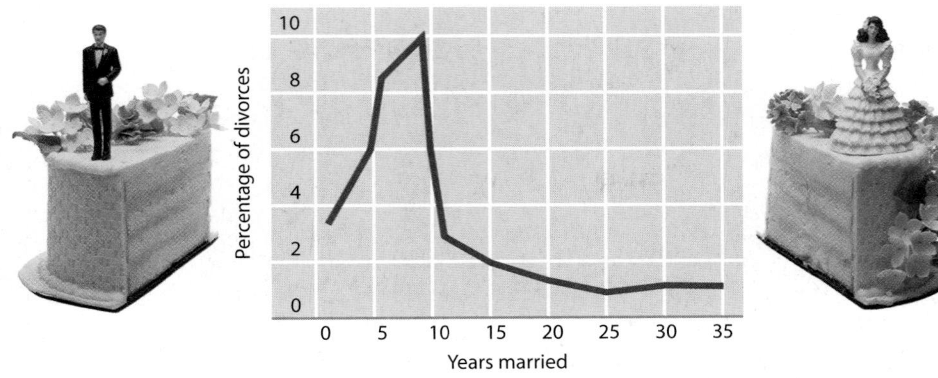

FIGURE **9.7**

THE DIVORCE RATE IN RELATION TO NUMBER OF YEARS MARRIED. Shown here is the percentage of divorces as a function of how long couples have been married. Notice that most divorces occur in the early years of marriage, peaking in the fifth to tenth years of marriage.

(see Figure 9.7). This timing may reflect an effort by partners in troubled marriages to stay in the marriage and try to work things out. If after several years these efforts don't improve the relationship, they may then seek a divorce.

Even those adults who initiated their divorce experience challenges after a marriage dissolves (Keyes, Hatzenbuehler, & Hasin, 2011; Lee & others, 2011). Both divorced women and divorced men complain of loneliness, diminished self-esteem, anxiety about the unknowns in their lives, and difficulty in forming satisfactory new intimate relationships.

Psychologically, one of the most common characteristics of divorced adults is difficulty in trusting someone else in a romantic relationship. Following a divorce, though, people's lives can take diverse turns (Tashiro, Frazier, & Berman, 2005). For example, in one research study, 20 percent of the divorced group "grew more competent, well-adjusted, and self-fulfilled" following their divorce (Hetherington & Kelly, 2002, p. 98). They were competent in multiple areas of life and showed a remarkable ability to bounce back from stressful circumstance and to create something meaningful out of problems.

GAY AND LESBIAN ADULTS

The legal and social context of marriage creates barriers to breaking up that do not usually exist for same-sex partners (Rostosky & others, 2010). But in other ways, researchers have found that gay and lesbian relationships are similar—in their satisfactions, loves, joys, and conflicts—to heterosexual relationships (Crooks & Baur, 2011). For example, like heterosexual couples, gay and lesbian couples need to find the balance of romantic love, affection, autonomy, and equality that is acceptable to both partners (Hope, 2009). An increasing number of gay and lesbian couples are creating families that include children.

Lesbian couples especially place a high priority on equality in their relationships (Fingerhut & Peplau, 2012). Indeed, some researchers have found that gay and lesbian couples are more flexible in their gender roles than heterosexual individuals are (Marecek, Finn, & Cardell, 1988). And a recent study of couples revealed that over the course of ten years of cohabitation, partners in gay male and lesbian relationships showed a higher average level of relationship quality than did heterosexual couples (Kurdek, 2008).

There are a number of misconceptions about gay and lesbian couples (Diamond, Fagundes, & Butterworth, 2010). Contrary to stereotypes, in only a small percentage of gay and lesbian couples is one partner masculine and the other feminine. Only a small segment of the gay population has a large number of sexual partners, and this is uncommon among lesbians. Furthermore, researchers have found that gay and lesbian couples prefer long-term, committed relationships (Fingerhut & Peplau, 2012). About half of committed gay couples do have an open relationship that allows the possibility of sex (but not affectionate love) outside of the relationship. Lesbian couples usually do not have this open relationship.

Review *Connect* Reflect

LG5 Explain the diversity of emerging adult lifestyles.

Review

- What characterizes single adults?
- What are the lives of cohabiting adults like?
- What are some key aspects of the lives of married adults?
- How does divorce affect adults?
- What characterizes the lifestyles of gay and lesbian adults?

Connect

- What are some similarities and differences between cohabitating relationships and marriages?

Reflect *Your Own Personal Journey of Life*

- Which type of lifestyle are you living today? What do you think are its advantages and disadvantages for you? If you could have a different lifestyle, which one would it be? Why?

reach your **learning goals**

1 Exploring Peer Relations and Friendship

Discuss the role of peer relations, friendship, and loneliness in adolescent development.

Peer Relations

- Peers are individuals who are about the same age or maturity level. Peers provide a means of social comparison and a source of information beyond the family. Contexts and individual difference factors influence peer relations. Good peer relations may be necessary for normal social development. The inability to "plug in" to a social network is associated with a number of problems. Peer relations can be negative or positive. Sullivan stressed that peer relations provide the context for learning the symmetrical reciprocity mode of relationships. Healthy family relations usually promote healthy peer relations. The pressure to conform to peers is strong during adolescence, especially around the eighth and ninth grades. Popular children are frequently nominated as a best friend and are rarely disliked by their peers. Average children receive an average number of both positive and negative nominations from their peers. Neglected children are infrequently nominated as a best friend but are not disliked by their peers. Rejected children are infrequently nominated as a best friend and are disliked by their peers. Controversial children are frequently nominated both as a best friend and as being disliked by peers. Social knowledge and social information-processing skills are associated with improved peer relations. Self-regulation of emotion is associated with positive peer relations. Conglomerate strategies, also referred to as coaching, involve the use of a combination of techniques, rather than a single strategy, to improve adolescents' social skills.

Friendship

- Friends are a subset of peers who engage in mutual companionship, support, and intimacy. The functions of friendship include companionship, stimulation, physical support, ego support, social comparison, and intimacy/affection. Sullivan argued that the psychological importance and intimacy of close friends increases dramatically in adolescence. Research supports this view. Children and adolescents who become close friends with older individuals engage in more deviant behaviors than do their counterparts with same-age friends. Early-maturing girls are more likely than late-maturing girls to have older friends, a characteristic that can contribute to problem behaviors. Some changes in friendship in emerging adulthood occur. Intimacy and similarity are two of the most important characteristics of friendships.

Loneliness

- Chronic loneliness is linked with impaired physical and mental health. Loneliness often emerges when people make life transitions, so it is not surprising that loneliness is common among college freshmen. Moderately or intensely lonely individuals never or rarely feel in tune with others and rarely or never find companionship when they want it, whereas other individuals may value solitary time.

2 Adolescent Groups

LG2 Summarize what takes place in adolescent groups.

Groups in Childhood and Adolescence

- Childhood groups are less formal, less heterogeneous, and less mixed-sex than adolescent groups. Dunphy's study found that adolescent group development proceeds through five stages.

Cliques and Crowds

- Cliques are small groups that range from two to about twelve individuals and average about five to six individuals. Clique members are similar in age, usually of the same sex, and often participate in similar activities, sharing ideas, hanging out, and developing an in-group identity. Crowds are a larger group structure than cliques and are less personal. Adolescents are members of crowds usually based on reputation and may or may not spend much time together. Many crowds are defined by adolescents' activities, such as jocks, druggies, populars, and independents.

Youth Organizations

- Youth organizations can have important influences on adolescent development. More than 400 national youth organizations currently exist in the United States. Boys & Girls Clubs are examples of youth organizations designed to increase membership in youth organizations in low-income neighborhoods. Participation in youth organizations may increase achievement and decrease delinquency. Youth activities and organizations also may provide opportunities for adolescents to develop initiative.

3 Gender and Culture

Describe the roles of gender and culture in adolescent peer groups and friendships.

Gender

- The social world of adolescent peer groups varies according to gender, socioeconomic status, ethnicity, and culture. In terms of gender, boys are more likely to associate in larger clusters and organized games than girls are. Boys also are more likely than girls to engage in competition, conflict, ego displays, and risk taking and to seek dominance. By contrast, girls are more likely to engage in collaborative discourse. Girls engage in more intimacy in their friendships than boys do.

Socioeconomic Status and Ethnicity

- In many cases, peer groups are segregated according to socioeconomic status. In some cases, ethnic minority adolescents in the United States rely on peers more than non-Latino White adolescents do.

Culture

- In some countries, such as rural India, Arab countries, and Japan, adults restrict access to the peer group. In North America and Europe, the peer group is a pervasive aspect of adolescents' lives.

4 Dating and Romantic Relationships

Characterize adolescent dating and romantic relationships.

Functions of Dating

- Dating can be a form of recreation, a source of social status and achievement, an aspect of socialization, a context for learning about intimacy and sexual experimentation, a source of companionship, and a means of mate sorting.

Types of Dating and Developmental Changes

- Three stages characterize the development of romantic relationships in adolescence: (1) entry into romantic attractions and affiliations at about 11 to 13 years of age, (2) exploring romantic relationships at approximately 14 to 16 years of age, and (3) consolidating dyadic romantic bonds at about 17 to 19 years of age. Younger adolescents often begin to hang out together in mixed-sex groups. A special concern is early dating, which is associated with a number of problems. In early adolescence, individuals spend more time thinking about the opposite sex than actually being with them, but this trend tends to reverse in the high school years. Most sexual minority youth have same-sex sexual experience, but relatively few have same-sex romantic relationships.

Emotion, Adjustment, and Romantic Relationships

- The emotions of romantic relationships can envelop adolescents' lives. Sometimes these emotions are positive, sometimes negative, and they can change very quickly. Adolescents who date have more problems, such as substance abuse, than those who do not date, but they also have more acceptance with peers.

Romantic Love and Its Construction

- Romantic love, also called passionate love, involves sexuality and infatuation more than affectionate love. Romantic love is especially prominent among adolescents and traditional-aged college students. Affectionate love is more common in middle and late adulthood, characterizing love that endures over time. The developmental construction view emphasizes how relationships with parents, siblings, and peers influence how adolescents construct their romantic relationships. Connolly's research revealed the importance of peers and friends in adolescent romantic relationships.

Gender and Culture

- Girls tend to view dating as an interpersonal experience; boys view dating more in terms of physical attraction. Culture can exert a powerful influence on dating. Many adolescents from immigrant families face conflicts with their parents about dating.

5 Emerging Adult Lifestyles

Explain the diversity of emerging adult lifestyles.

Single Adults

- Being single has become an increasingly prominent lifestyle. Myths and stereotypes about singles abound, ranging from "swinging single" to "desperately lonely, suicidal single." There are advantages and disadvantages to being single, autonomy being one of the advantages. Intimacy, loneliness, and finding a positive identity in a marriage-oriented society are concerns of single adults.

Cohabiting Adults

- Cohabitation is an increasing lifestyle for many adults. Cohabitation offers some advantages as well as problems. Cohabitation leads not to greater marital happiness but rather to no differences or differences suggesting that cohabitation is not good for a marriage.

Married Adults

- Even though adults are remaining single longer and the divorce rate is high, the majority of Americans still get married. The age at which individuals marry, expectations about what the marriage will be like, and the developmental course of marriage vary not only over time within a culture, but also across cultures. Premarital education is associated with positive relationship outcomes.

Divorced Adults

- The U.S. divorce rate increased dramatically in the twentieth century but began to decline in the 1980s. Divorce is complex and emotional. In the first year following divorce, a disequilibrium in the divorced adult's behavior occurs, but by several years after the divorce more stability has been achieved.

Gay and Lesbian Adults

- There are many misconceptions about gay and lesbian adults. One of the most striking findings about gay and lesbian couples is how similar they are to heterosexual couples.

key terms

peers 296
sociometric status 300
popular children 300
average children 300
neglected children 300
rejected children 300
controversial children 300
conglomerate strategies 302
friends 303
intimacy in friendship 305
cliques 308
crowds 309
romantic love 317
affectionate love 317
dating scripts 319
cohabitation 321

key people

Judith Smetana 298
Mitchell Prinstein 299
Kenneth Dodge 302
Harry Stack Sullivan 304
Willard Hartup 304
Dexter Dunphy 308
Reed Larson 310
Wyndol Furman 318
Elizabeth Wehner 318
Jennifer Connolly 319
Candice Feiring 319
Andrew Cherlin 321

resources for improving the lives of adolescents

Understanding Peer Influence in Children and Adolescents
edited by Mitchell Prinstein and Kenneth Dodge (2008)
New York: Guilford

Leading experts describe many facets of peer relations in adolescence, including current issues, peer influence processes, positive and negative aspects of peer relations, and bullying.

Adolescent Romantic Relationships
by W. Andrew Collins, Deborah Welsh, and Wyndol Furman (2009)
Annual Review of Psychology, Vol. 60
Palo Alto, CA: Annual Reviews

Experts provide an up-to-date overview of theory and research on the much-neglected topic of romantic relationships in adolescence.

Just Friends
by Lillian Rubin (1985)
New York: HarperCollins

Just Friends explores the nature of friendship and intimacy.

The Marriage-Go-Round
by Andrew Cherlin (2009)
New York: Random House

Leading sociologist Andrew Cherlin provides up-to-date information about trends in cohabitation, marriage, and divorce.

The Seven Principles for Making Marriages Work
by John Gottman and Nan Silver (1999)
New York: Crown

Leading relationship expert John Gottman provides valuable recommendations for what makes marriages work based on his extensive research.

self-assessment

The Online Learning Center includes the following self-assessment for further exploration:

- *The Characteristics I Desire in a Potential Mate*

chapter 10 SCHOOLS

chapter outline

Approaches to Educating Students

Learning Goal 1 Describe approaches to educating students.

Contemporary Approaches to Student Learning
Accountability

Transitions in Schooling

Learning Goal 2 Discuss transitions in schooling from early adolescence to emerging adulthood.

Transition to Middle or Junior High School
Improving Middle Schools
The American High School
High School Dropouts
Transition from High School to College
Transition from College to Work

The Social Contexts of Schools

Learning Goal 3 Explain how the social contexts of schools influence adolescent development.

Changing Social Developmental Contexts
Classroom Climate and Management
Person-Environment Fit
Teachers, Parents, Peers, and Extracurricular Activities
Culture

Adolescents Who Are Exceptional

Learning Goal 4 Characterize adolescents who are exceptional and their education.

Who Are Adolescents with Disabilities?
Learning Disabilities
Attention Deficit Hyperactivity Disorder
Educational Issues Involving Adolescents with Disabilities
Adolescents Who Are Gifted

To improve high school education in the United States, the National Research Council (2004) voiced a strong recommendation that teachers need to find ways to engage students' motivation for learning. Here are some strategies that several award-winning teachers use to get students engaged in learning:

Henry Brown teaches at-risk students real-world math skills to help them become more engaged in learning.

Pete Karpyk shrink-wrapped himself to demonstrate the effects of air pressure in his high school chemistry class.

- A former at-risk student himself, Henry Brown, a recent Florida Teacher of the Year, teaches math. Half of the students enter the high school where Brown teaches with math skills below the fifth-grade level. Brown engages them by teaching real-world math skills. In one project, he devised a dummy corporation and had students play different roles in it, learning important math skills as they worked and made decisions in the corporation (*USA Today,* 2001).
- Peter Karpyk, a West Virginia high school chemistry teacher, uses an extensive range of activities to bring science alive for students. He has students give chemistry demonstrations at elementary schools and has discovered that some students who don't do well on tests excel when they teach children. He also adapts his teaching based on feedback from former students and incorporates questions from their college chemistry tests as bonus questions on his high school tests to challenge and motivate them (Wong Briggs, 2005).
- Peggy Schweiger, a physics teacher in Texas, makes science interesting by giving students opportunities to explore everyday science problems. Among the projects she has students do are wiring a doll house and making replicas of boats for a regatta. One of her former students, Alison Arnett, 19, said:

  > She taught us how to think and learn, not to succeed in physics class. We were encouraged to stand on desks, tape things to the ceiling, and even drop an egg on her head to illustrate physics—anything to make us discover that we live with physics every day" (*USA Today,* 2001, p. 6).

- Carmella Williams Scott, a middle school teacher in Georgia, created Juvenile Video Court TV, a student-run judicial system, so that students could experience how such systems function. She especially targeted gang leaders for inclusion in the system because they ran the school. Scott likes to use meaningful questions to stimulate students' critical thinking. She believes that mutual respect is a key factor in her success as a teacher and the lack of discipline problems she has in her classes (Wong Briggs, 1999).

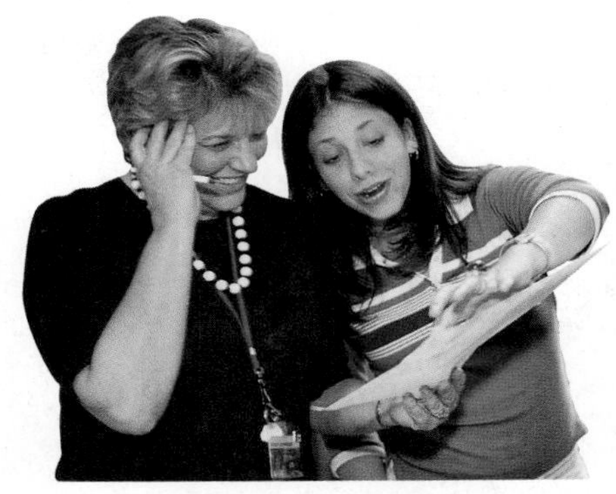

Peggy Schweiger with a student who is learning how to think and discover how physics works in people's everyday lives.

Carmella Williams Scott has been successful in creating a learning atmosphere that stimulates students' critical thinking.

preview

In youth, we learn. An important context for learning is school. Schools not only foster adolescents' academic learning, they also provide a social arena where peers, friends, and crowds can have a powerful influence on their development. Our exploration of schools in this chapter focuses on approaches to educating students, transitions in schooling, the social contexts of schools, and strategies for educating adolescents who are exceptional.

1 Approaches to Educating Students

LG1 Describe approaches to educating students.

Contemporary Approaches to Student Learning

Accountability

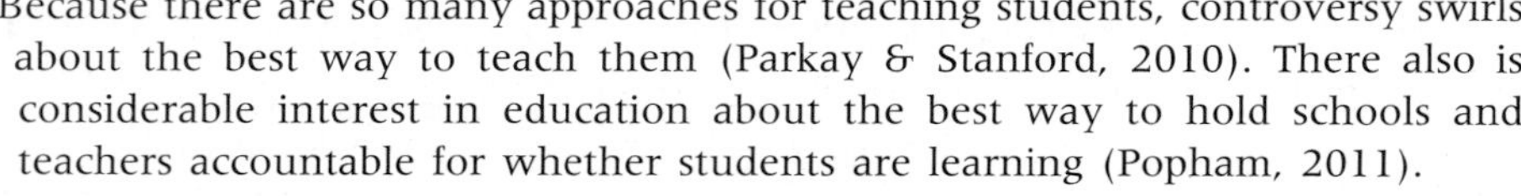

> The whole art of teaching is only the art of awakening the natural curiosity of young minds.
>
> —ANATOLE FRANCE
> *French Novelist, 20th Century*

Because there are so many approaches for teaching students, controversy swirls about the best way to teach them (Parkay & Stanford, 2010). There also is considerable interest in education about the best way to hold schools and teachers accountable for whether students are learning (Popham, 2011).

CONTEMPORARY APPROACHES TO STUDENT LEARNING

There are two main contemporary approaches to student learning: constructivist and direct instruction. We examine both approaches and then consider whether effective teachers use both approaches.

The **constructivist approach** is learner centered and it emphasizes the importance of individuals actively constructing their knowledge and understanding with guidance from the teacher. In the constructivist view, teachers should not attempt to simply pour information into students' minds. Rather, students should be encouraged to explore their world, discover knowledge, reflect, and think critically with careful monitoring and meaningful guidance from the teacher (Appleton, 2012; McCombs, 2010; Eby, Herrell, & Jordan, 2011). The constructivist belief is that for too long in American education students have been required to sit still, be passive learners, and rotely memorize irrelevant as well as relevant information.

Today, constructivism may include an emphasis on collaboration—students working with each other in their efforts to know and understand (Slavin, 2011). A teacher with a constructivist instructional philosophy would not have students memorize information rotely but would give them opportunities to meaningfully construct the knowledge and understand the material while guiding their learning (Appleton, 2012; Cruikshank, Jenkins, & Mectalf, 2012; Littleton, Scanlon, & Sharples, 2011).

> No one can be given an education. All you can give is the opportunity to learn.
>
> —CAROLYN WARNER
> *American Author, 20th Century*

By contrast, the **direct instruction approach** is structured and teacher centered. It is characterized by teacher direction and control, high teacher expectations for students' progress, maximum time spent by students on academic tasks, and efforts by the teacher to keep negative affect to a minimum. An important goal in the direct instruction approach is maximizing student learning time (Arends, 2012; Borich, 2011).

Advocates of the constructivist approach argue that the direct instruction approach turns students into passive learners and does not adequately challenge them to think in critical and creative ways (Abruscato & DeRosa, 2010). The direct instruction enthusiasts say that the constructivist approaches do not give enough attention to the content of a discipline, such as history or science. They also believe that the constructivist approaches are too relativistic and vague.

constructivist approach A learner-centered approach that emphasizes the adolescent's active, cognitive construction of knowledge and understanding with guidance from the teacher.

direct instruction approach A teacher-centered approach characterized by teacher direction and control, mastery of academic skills, high expectations for students, and maximum time spent on learning tasks.

Some experts in educational psychology believe that many effective teachers use both a constructivist *and* a direct instruction approach rather than either exclusively (Bransford & others, 2006). Further, some circumstances may call more for a constructivist approach, others for a direction instruction approach. For example, experts increasingly recommend an explicit, intellectually engaging direct instruction approach when teaching students with a reading or a writing disability (Berninger, 2006).

In the History Alive! program of the Teacher's Curriculum Institute, students work in cooperative groups of four to prepare one student to be the actor in a lively panel debate. *Is the History Alive! program more characteristic of a constructivist or direct instruction approach?*

ACCOUNTABILITY

Since the 1990s, the U.S. public as well as governments at every level have demanded increased accountability from schools. One result has been the spread of state-mandated tests to measure just what students had or had not learned (Popham, 2011). Many states identified objectives for students in their state and created tests to measure whether students were meeting those objectives. This approach became national policy in 2002 when the No Child Left Behind (NCLB) legislation was signed into law.

Advocates argue that statewide standardized testing will have a number of positive effects. These include improved student performance; more time teaching the subjects that are tested; high expectations for all students; identification of poorly performing schools, teachers, and administrators; and improved confidence in schools as test scores rise.

Critics argue that the NCLB legislation is doing more harm than good (Yell & Drasgow, 2009). One criticism stresses that using a single test as the sole indicator of students' progress and competence presents a very narrow view of students' skills (Lewis, 2007). This criticism is similar to the one leveled at IQ tests, which we described in Chapter 3. To assess student progress and achievement, many psychologists and educators emphasize that a number of measures should be used, including tests, quizzes, projects, portfolios, classroom observations, and so on. Also, the tests used as part of NCLB don't measure creativity, motivation, persistence, flexible thinking, and social skills (Stiggins, 2008). Critics point out that teachers end up spending far too much class time "teaching to the test" by drilling students and having them memorize isolated facts at the expense of teaching that focuses on thinking skills, which students need for success in life (Pressley, 2007). Also, some individuals are concerned that in the era of No Child Left Behind policy there is a neglect of students who are gifted in the effort to raise the achievement level of students who are not doing well (Clark, 2008).

developmental **connection**

Intelligence. The intelligence quotient (IQ) gives students a specific number to indicate their intelligence. Chapter 3, p. 115

Consider also the following: Each state is allowed to have different criteria for what constitutes passing or failing grades on tests designated for NCLB inclusion. An analysis of NCLB data indicated that almost every fourth-grade student in Mississippi knows how to read, but only half of Massachusetts' students do (Birman & others, 2007). Clearly, Mississippi's standards for passing the reading test are far below those of Massachusetts. In the recent analysis of state-by-state comparisons, many states have taken the safe route and kept the standard for passing low. Thus, while one of NCLB's goals was to raise standards for achievement in U.S. schools, apparently allowing states to set their own standards likely has lowered achievement standards.

What are some issues involved in the No Child Left Behind legislation?

Despite such criticisms, the U.S. Department of Education is committed to implementing No Child Left Behind, and schools are making accommodations to meet the requirement of this law. Indeed, most educators support the importance of high expectations and high standards of excellence for students and teachers. At issue, however, is whether the tests and procedures mandated by NCLB are the best ones for achieving these high standards (Darling-Hammond, 2011; Nitko & Brookhart, 2011).

Review *Connect* Reflect

Describe approaches to educating students.

Review

- What are the two main approaches to educating adolescents?
- What is involved in making schools more accountable?

Connect

- Relate the concept of multiple intelligences (Chapter 3) to this section's discussion of the constructivist and direct instruction approaches to student learning.

Reflect *Your Own Personal Journey of Life*

- When you were in secondary school, which approach did your teachers use more: direct instruction or constructivist? Which approach would you have liked your teachers to use more? Why?

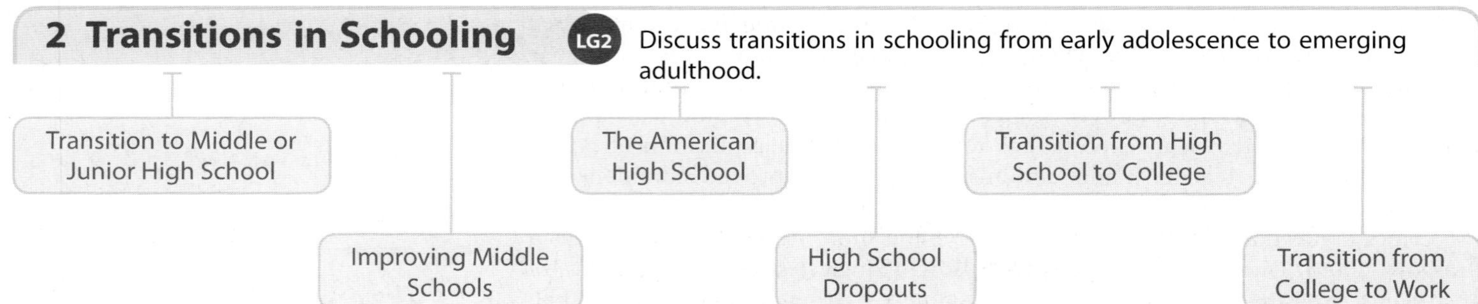

As children become adolescents, and as adolescents become adults, they experience transitions in schooling: from elementary school to middle school or junior high school, from school to work for noncollege youth, from high school to college, and from college to work.

TRANSITION TO MIDDLE OR JUNIOR HIGH SCHOOL

The transition to middle or junior high school can be difficult and stressful for many students (Anderman & Dawson, 2011; Eccles & Roeser, 2011; A. Howe & Richards, 2011). Why? The transition takes place at a time when many changes—in the individual, in the family, and in school—are occurring simultaneously. These changes include puberty and related concerns about body image; the emergence of at least some aspects of formal operational thought, including accompanying changes in social cognition; increased responsibility and decreased dependency on parents; change to a larger, more impersonal school structure; change from one teacher to many teachers and from a small, homogeneous set of peers to a larger, more heterogeneous set of peers; and an increased focus on achievement and performance and their assessment. Also, when students make the transition to middle or junior high school, they experience the **top-dog phenomenon,** moving from being the oldest, biggest, and most powerful students in the elementary school to being the youngest, smallest, and least powerful students in the middle or junior high school. Researchers have found that students' self-esteem is higher in the last year of elementary school and that they like school better than in the first year of middle or junior high school (Hawkins & Berndt, 1985; Hirsch & Rapkin, 1987). A recent study in North Carolina schools revealed that sixth-grade students attending middle schools were far more likely to be cited for discipline problems than were their counterparts

developmental **connection**

Cognitive Development. Formal operational thought is more abstract, idealistic, and logical than concrete operational thought. Chapter 3, p. 94

top-dog phenomenon The circumstance of moving from the top position (in elementary school, the oldest, biggest, and most powerful students) to the lowest position (in middle or junior high school, the youngest, smallest, and least powerful).

who were attending elementary schools (Cook & others, 2008). The transition to middle or junior high school is less stressful when students have positive relationships with friends and go through the transition in team-oriented schools in which 20 to 30 students take the same classes together (Hawkins & Berndt, 1985).

There can also be positive aspects to the transition to middle or junior high school (Bellmore, Villarreal, & Ho, 2011). Students are more likely to feel grown up, have more subjects from which to select, have more opportunities to spend time with peers and locate compatible friends, and enjoy increased independence from direct parental monitoring. They also may be more challenged intellectually by academic work.

The transition from elementary to middle or junior high school occurs at the same time as a number of other developmental changes. *What are some of these other developmental changes?*

IMPROVING MIDDLE SCHOOLS

In 1989 the Carnegie Council on Adolescent Development issued an extremely negative evaluation of U.S. middle schools. In the report—*Turning Points: Preparing American Youth for the Twenty-First Century*—the conclusion was reached that most young adolescents attend massive, impersonal schools; learn from seemingly irrelevant curricula; trust few adults in school; and lack access to health care and counseling. The Carnegie report recommended the following:

- Develop smaller "communities" or "houses" to lessen the impersonal nature of large middle schools.
- Lower student-to-counselor ratios from hundreds-to-1 to 10-to-1.
- Involve parents and community leaders in schools.
- Develop curricula that produce students who are literate, understand the sciences, and have a sense of health, ethics, and citizenship.
- Have teachers team-teach in more flexibly designed curriculum blocks that integrate several disciplines, instead of presenting students with disconnected, rigidly separated 50-minute segments.
- Boost students' health and fitness with more in-school programs and help students who need public health care to get it. (Carnegie Council on Adolescent Development, 1989.)

I touch the future. I teach.

—**Christa McAuliffe**
American Educator and Astronaut, 20th Century

Turning Points 2000 continued to endorse the recommendations set forth in *Turning Points 1989* (Jackson & Davis, 2000). One new recommendation in the 2000 report stated that it is important to teach a curriculum grounded in rigorous academic standards for what students should know. A second new recommendation was to engage in instruction to achieve higher standards and become lifelong learners. These new recommendations reflect the increasing emphasis on challenging students and having higher academic expectations for them.

THE AMERICAN HIGH SCHOOL

Many high school graduates not only are poorly prepared for college, they also are poorly prepared for the demands of the modern, high-performance workplace (Smith, 2009). In a review of hiring practices at major companies, it was concluded that many companies now have sets of basic skills they want their employees to have. These include the ability to read at relatively high levels, do at least elementary algebra, use personal computers for straightforward tasks such as word processing, solve semistructured problems in which hypotheses must be formed and tested, communicate effectively (orally and in writing), and work effectively in groups with persons of various backgrounds (Murnane & Levy, 1996).

The National Research Council (2004) made a number of recommendations for improving U.S. high schools. They especially emphasized the importance of finding ways to get students more engaged in learning. The council concluded that the best way to do so is to focus on the psychological factors involved in motivation. Increasing students' engagement in learning consists of promoting a sense of belonging "by personalizing instruction, showing an interest in students' lives, and creating a supportive, caring social environment" (National Research Council, 2004, p. 3). The council said that this description of engaging students applies to very few urban high schools, which too often are characterized by low expectations, alienation, and low achievement. You might recall from the chapter-opening vignette the four teachers who created exciting, real-world opportunities for students to increase their motivation to become more engaged in learning. We have much more to consider about strategies for improving adolescents' motivation in Chapter 11.

developmental **connection**

Achievement. Adolescence is a critical juncture in achievement that brings new social and academic pressures. Chapter 11, p. 363

HIGH SCHOOL DROPOUTS

Dropping out of high school has been viewed as a serious educational and societal problem for many decades. By leaving high school before graduating, adolescents approach adult life with educational deficiencies that severely curtail their economic and social well-being (White, 2010; Vaughn & others, 2011).

High School Dropout Rates In the last half of the twentieth century and the first several years of the twenty-first century, U.S. high school dropout rates declined (National Center for Education Statistics, 2010). In the 1940s, more than half of U.S. 16- to 24-year-olds had dropped out of school; by 2008, this figure had decreased to 8 percent. The dropout rates of Latino adolescents remains high, although it has been decreasing in the twenty-first century (from 28 percent in 2000 to 18 percent in 2008). The lowest dropout rate in 2008 occurred for Asian American adolescents (3.2 percent), followed by non-Latino White adolescents (6.2 percent), African American adolescents (10.4 percent), then Latino adolescents (18 percent). Native American adolescents also have a high dropout rate, although government statistics for this ethnic group have not been adequately assessed.

Gender differences characterize U.S. dropout rates, with males more likely to drop out than females (10.4 versus 7.9 percent) (data for 2008, National Center for Education Statistics, 2010). The gender gap in dropout rates is especially large for Latino adolescents (21.9 versus 15 percent). Figure 10.1 shows the dropout rates of 16- to 24-year-olds by ethnicity and gender in 2008.

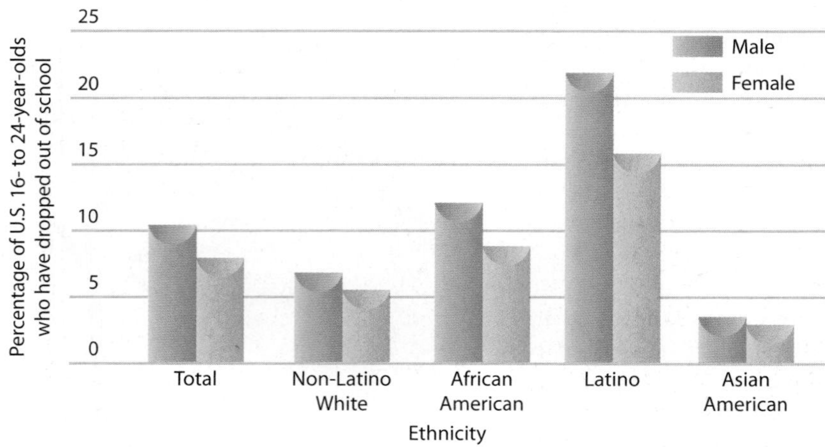

FIGURE **10.1**

SCHOOL DROPOUT RATES OF U.S. 16- TO 24-YEAR-OLDS BY GENDER AND ETHNICITY. National Center for Education Statistics (2010). *The condition education 2010.* Washington, D.C.: U.S. Department of Education.

The Causes of Dropping Out Students drop out of school for school-related, economic, family-related, peer-related, and personal reasons. School-related problems are consistently associated with dropping out of school (White, 2010). In one investigation, almost 50 percent of the dropouts cited school-related reasons for leaving school, such as not liking school, being suspended, or being expelled (Rumberger, 1995). Twenty percent of the dropouts (but 40 percent of the Latino students) cited economic reasons for dropping out. Many of these students quit school and go to work to help support their families. Students from low-income families are more likely to drop out than those from middle-income families. A recent study revealed that when children's parents were involved in their schools in middle and late childhood, and when parents and adolescents had good relationships in early adolescence, a positive trajectory toward academic success was the likely outcome (Englund,

Egeland, & Collins, 2008). By contrast, those who had poor relationships with their parents were more likely to drop out of high school despite doing well academically and behaviorally. Many school dropouts have friends who also are school dropouts. Approximately one-third of the girls who drop out of school do so for personal reasons, such as pregnancy or marriage.

Students in the technology training center at Wellpinit Elementary/High School, located on the Spokane Indian Reservation in Washington State. An important educational goal is to increase the high school graduation rate of Native American adolescents.

Reducing the Dropout Rate A review of school-based dropout programs found that the most effective programs provided early reading programs, tutoring, counseling, and mentoring (Lehr & others, 2003). They also emphasized the importance of creating caring environments and relationships and offered community-service opportunities.

Clearly, then, early detection of children's school-related difficulties, and getting children and youth engaged with school in positive ways, are important strategies for reducing the dropout rate. One successful dropout prevention program is Talent Search, which provides low-income high school students mentoring, academic tutoring, and training on test-taking and study skills, as well as career development coaching, financial aid application assistance for college, and visits to college campuses (Constantine & others, 2006). Talent Search students had high school completion rates that were 9 percent higher than a control group of students who were not in the Talent Search program.

Also, recently the Bill and Melinda Gates Foundation (2006, 2008) has funded efforts to reduce the dropout rate in schools where rates are high. One strategy that is being emphasized in the Gates' funding is keeping at-risk students with the same teachers through their high school years. The hope is that the teachers will get to know these students much better, their relationship with the students will improve, and they will be able to monitor and guide the students toward graduating from high school.

"I Have a Dream" (IHAD) is an innovative, comprehensive, long-term dropout prevention program administered by the National "I Have a Dream" Foundation in New York. Since the National IHAD Foundation was created in 1986, it has grown to over 180 projects in 64 cities and 27 states, Washington, D.C., and New Zealand serving more than 15,000 children ("I Have a Dream" Foundation, 2011). Local IHAD projects around the country "adopt" entire grades (usually the third or fourth) from public elementary schools, or corresponding age cohorts from public housing developments. These children—"Dreamers"—are then provided with a program of academic, social, cultural, and recreational activities throughout their elementary, middle school, and high school years. An important part of this program is that it is personal rather than institutional: IHAD sponsors and staff develop close long-term relationships with the children. When participants complete high school, IHAD provides the tuition assistance necessary for them to attend a state or local college or vocational school.

These adolescents participate in the "I Have a Dream" (IHAD) program, a comprehensive, long-term dropout prevention program that has been very successful. *What are some other strategies for reducing high school dropout rates?*

The IHAD program was created in 1981, when philanthropist Eugene Lang made an impromptu offer of college tuition to a class of graduating sixth-graders at P.S. 121 in East Harlem. Statistically, 75 percent of the students should have dropped out of school; instead, 90 percent graduated and 60 percent went on to college. Other evaluations of IHAD programs have found dramatic improvements in grades, test scores, and school attendance, as well as a reduction of behavioral problems of Dreamers. For example, in Portland, Oregon, twice as many Dreamers as control-group students had reached a math standard, and the Dreamers were less likely to be referred to the juvenile justice system (Davis, Hyatt, & Arrasmith, 1998). And in a recent analysis of the "I Have a Dream" program in Houston, 91 percent of the participants received passing grades in reading/English, 83 percent said they liked school, 98 percent said getting good grades is important to them, 100 percent said they plan to graduate from high school, and 94 percent reported they plan to go to college ("I Have a Dream" Foundation, 2008).

The transition from high school to college often involves positive as well as negative features. In college, students are likely to feel grown up, be able to spend more time with peers, have more opportunities to explore different lifestyles and values, and enjoy greater freedom from parental monitoring. However, college involves a larger, more impersonal school structure and an increased focus on achievement and its assessment. *What was your transition to college like?*

TRANSITION FROM HIGH SCHOOL TO COLLEGE

Just as the transition from elementary school to middle or junior high school involves change and possible stress, so does the transition from high school to college. In many ways, the two transitions involve parallel changes. Going from being a senior in high school to being a freshman in college replays the top-dog phenomenon of going from the oldest and most powerful group of students to the youngest and least powerful group of students. The transition from high school to college involves a move to a larger, more impersonal school structure, interaction with peers from more diverse geographical and sometimes more diverse ethnic backgrounds, and increased focus on achievement and performance, and their assessment.

However, as with the transition from elementary school to middle or junior high school, the transition from high school to college can have positive aspects. Students are more likely to feel grown up, have more subjects from which to select, have more time to spend with peers, have more opportunities to explore different lifestyles and values, enjoy greater independence from parental monitoring, and may be more challenged intellectually by academic work (Santrock & Halonen, 2009).

Today's college students experience more stress and are more depressed than in the past, according to a national study of more than 300,000 freshmen at more than 500 colleges and universities (Pryor & others, 2010). In 2010, 29 percent (up from 16 percent in 1985) said they frequently "felt overwhelmed with what I have to do." College females were more than twice as likely as their male counterparts (39 to 18 percent, respectively) to say that they felt overwhelmed with all they had to do. And college freshmen in 2010 indicated that they felt more depressed than their counterparts from the 1980s had indicated. The pressure to succeed in college, get a great job, and make lots of money were pervasive concerns of these students.

What makes college students happy? One study of 222 undergraduates compared the upper 10 percent of college students who were very happy with average and very unhappy college students (Diener & Seligman, 2002). The very happy college students were highly social, more extraverted, and had stronger romantic and social relationships than the less happy college students, who spent more time alone.

What characterizes the transition from college to work?

TRANSITION FROM COLLEGE TO WORK

Having a college degree is a strong asset. College graduates can enter careers that will earn them considerably more money in their lifetimes than those who do not go to college, and income differences between college graduates and high school graduates continue to grow (*Occupational Outlook Handbook, 2010–2011*). In the United States, individuals with a bachelor's degree make over $1,000 a month more on the average than those with only a high school degree. Over a lifetime, a college graduate will make approximately $600,000 more on average than a high school graduate will.

Nonetheless, in North American countries, the transition from college to work is often a difficult one. U.S. colleges train many students to develop general skills rather than vocationally specific skills, with the result that many college graduates are poorly prepared for specific jobs or occupations. After finishing college, many individuals have difficulty obtaining the type of job they desire, or any job. Bouncing from one job to another after college is also not unusual.

Accelerated technical and occupational change in the future may make it even more difficult for colleges to provide training that keeps up with a fluid and shifting job market. Thus, it is important for colleges and employers to become better connected with each other to provide improved training for changing job opportunities (Mortimer & Larson, 2002).

developmental **connection**

Work. A diversity of school and work patterns characterize emerging adults. Chapter 11, p. 381

Review *Connect* Reflect

LG2 Discuss transitions in schooling from early adolescence to emerging adulthood.

Review

- How can the transition to middle or junior high school be characterized?
- How can middle schools be improved?
- What is the American high school like? How can it be improved?
- What characterizes high school dropouts?
- How can the transition from high school to college be described?
- How can the transition from college to work be summarized?

Connect

- What impact might the concept of parents as "managers" (Chapter 8) have on reducing the high school dropout rate?

Reflect *Your Own Personal Journey of Life*

- What was your own middle or junior high school like? How did it measure up to the recommendations made by the Carnegie Council?

3 The Social Contexts of Schools

LG3 Explain how the social contexts of schools influence adolescent development.

- Changing Social Developmental Contexts
- Classroom Climate and Management
- Person-Environment Fit
- Teachers, Parents, Peers, and Extracurricular Activities
- Culture

Schools and classrooms vary along many dimensions, including size of school or class and school or class atmosphere. Adolescents' school life also involves thousands of hours of interactions with teachers. A special concern is parent involvement in the adolescent's schooling. Also, as we see next, the social context of schools changes with the developmental level of students.

CHANGING SOCIAL DEVELOPMENTAL CONTEXTS

The social context differs at the preschool, elementary, and secondary level. The preschool setting is a protected environment, whose boundary is the classroom. The classroom is still the major context for the elementary school child, although it is more likely to be experienced as a social unit than in the preschool. As children move into middle or junior high schools, the school environment increases in scope and complexity (Elmore, 2009). The social field is the school as a whole rather than the classroom. Adolescents socially interact with many different teachers and peers from a range of social and ethnic backgrounds. Students are often exposed to a greater mix of male and female teachers. And social behavior is heavily weighted toward peers, extracurricular activities, clubs, and the community. The student in secondary school is usually aware of the school as a social system and may be motivated to conform and adapt to the system or to challenge it (Minuchin & Shapiro, 1983).

CLASSROOM CLIMATE AND MANAGEMENT

It is important for classrooms to present a positive environment for learning (Charles, 2011; Jones, 2011). Two effective general strategies for creating positive classroom environments are using an authoritative strategy and effectively managing the group's activities.

The idea of an authoritative classroom management strategy is derived from Diana Baumrind's (1971) typology of parenting styles, which we discussed in Chapter 8. Like authoritative parents, authoritative teachers have students who tend to be self-reliant, delay gratification, get along well with their peers, and show high self-esteem. An **authoritative strategy of classroom management** encourages

authoritative strategy of classroom management A teaching strategy that encourages students to be independent thinkers and doers but still involves effective monitoring. Authoritative teachers engage students in considerable verbal give-and-take and show a caring attitude toward them. However, they still declare limits when necessary.

"How come when you say we have a problem, I'm always the one who has the problem?"
Phi Delta Kappan, Oct. 92. Used with permission.

students to be independent thinkers and doers but still involves effective monitoring. Authoritative teachers engage students in considerable verbal give-and-take and show a caring attitude toward them. However, they still declare limits when necessary. Teachers clarify rules and regulations, establishing these standards with input from students.

The authoritative strategy contrasts with two ineffective strategies: authoritarian and permissive. The **authoritarian strategy of classroom management** is restrictive and punitive. The focus is mainly on keeping order in the classroom rather than on instruction and learning. Authoritarian teachers place firm limits and controls on students and have little verbal exchange with them. Students in authoritarian classrooms tend to be passive learners, fail to initiate activities, express anxiety about social comparison, and have poor communication skills.

The **permissive strategy of classroom management** offers students considerable autonomy but provides them with little support for developing learning skills or managing their behavior. Not surprisingly, students in permissive classrooms tend to have inadequate academic skills and low self-control.

developmental **connection**

Diversity. Asian American parents recently have been characterized as training parents. Chapter 8, p. 262

Overall, an authoritative style benefits students more than do authoritarian or permissive styles. An authoritative style helps students become active, self-regulated learners. A recent study of ninth-grade English classrooms revealed that a combination of behavioral control and caring on the part of teachers was linked with positive student outcomes, such as students' engagement in learning, which is consistent with an authoritative style (Nie & Lau, 2009).

A well-managed classroom not only fosters meaningful learning but also helps prevent academic and emotional problems from developing. Well-managed classrooms keep students busy with active, appropriately challenging tasks. Well-managed classrooms have activities that encourage students to become absorbed and motivated and learn clear rules and regulations (Larrivee, 2009). In such classrooms, students are less likely to develop academic and emotional problems. By contrast, in poorly managed classrooms, students' academic and emotional problems are more likely to fester. The academically unmotivated student becomes even less motivated. The shy student becomes more reclusive. The bully becomes meaner.

What are some effective strategies teachers can use to manage the classroom? How is managing the classroom different in secondary school from managing it in elementary school?

Secondary school students' problems can be more long-standing and more deeply ingrained, and therefore more difficult to modify, than those of elementary school students (Weinstein, 2007). Also in secondary schools, discipline problems are frequently more severe, as the students are potentially more unruly and even dangerous. Because most secondary school students have more advanced reasoning skills than do elementary school students, they might demand more elaborate and logical explanations of rules and discipline. And in secondary schools, hallway socializing can carry into the classroom. Every hour there is another "settling down" process.

PERSON-ENVIRONMENT FIT

Some of the negative psychological changes associated with adolescent development might result from a mismatch between the needs of developing adolescents and the opportunities afforded them by the schools they attend (Anderman, 2011; Anderman & Dawson, 2011). Adolescent experts Jacquelynne Eccles, Allan Wigfield, and their colleagues (Eccles, 2004, 2007; Eccles & Roeser, 2009, 2011; Wigfield & others, 2006) have described ways in which developmentally appropriate school environments can be created that match up better with adolescents' needs. Their recommendations are based on a large-scale study of 1,500 young adolescents in middle-income communities in Michigan. These adolescents were studied as they made the change from the sixth grade in an elementary school to the seventh grade in a junior high school.

authoritarian strategy of classroom management A teaching strategy that is restrictive and punitive. The focus is mainly on keeping order in the classroom rather than on instruction and learning.

permissive strategy of classroom management A teaching strategy that offers students considerable autonomy but provides them with little support for developing learning skills or managing their behavior.

Eccles (2004, 2007) argues that a lack of fit between the middle school/junior high environment and the needs of young adolescents produces increasingly negative self-evaluations and attitudes toward school. Her research has revealed that teachers become more controlling just at the time when adolescents are seeking more autonomy, and the teacher-student relationship becomes more impersonal at a time when students are seeking more independence from their parents and need more support from other adults. At a time when adolescents are becoming more self-conscious, an increased emphasis on grades and other competitive comparisons only make things worse.

Although there is less research on the transition from middle school to high school, the existing research suggests that, like the transition from elementary to middle school, it can produce similar problems (Eccles & Roeser, 2009). High schools often are even larger and more bureaucratic than middle schools. In such schools, a sense of community usually is undermined, with little opportunity for students and teachers to get to know each other. As a consequence, distrust between students and teachers develops easily and there is little communication about students' goals and values. Such contexts can especially harm the motivation of students who are not doing well academically.

What lessons can be drawn from this discussion? Perhaps the single most important lesson is that middle school and junior high school students benefit when teachers think of ways to make their school settings more personal, less formal, and more intrinsically challenging.

TEACHERS, PARENTS, PEERS, AND EXTRACURRICULAR ACTIVITIES

Adolescents' development is influenced by teachers. In addition, two increasingly important issues are parent involvement in schooling and the roles that peers and extracurricular activities play in schooling and academic achievement.

Teachers Competent teachers of adolescents have a good understanding of their development and know how to create instructional materials that are appropriate for the developmental levels of the adolescents in their classroom (Wentzel, 2010).

Psychologists and educators have tried to compile a profile of a good teacher's personality traits, but the complexity of personality, education, learning, and individuals makes this a difficult task (Morrison, 2009). Nonetheless, some teacher traits—enthusiasm, ability to plan, poise, adaptability, warmth, flexibility, and awareness of individual differences—are associated with positive student outcomes more

connecting with adolescents

"You Are the Coolest"

I just want to thank you for all the extra time you took to help me. You didn't have to do that, but you did, and I want to thank you for it. Thanks also for being straight up with me and not beating around the bush, and for that you are the coolest. I'm sorry for the hard times I gave you. You take so much junk, but through all that you stay calm and you are a great teacher.

—Jessica, Seventh-Grade Student Macon, Georgia
Letter to Chuck Rawls, Her Teacher, at the End of the School Year

What classroom management strategy does teacher Chuck Rawls likely adopt?

than are other traits. And in one study, positive teacher expectations were linked with higher student achievement (Jussim & Eccles, 1993).

Parents and Schools Parents play important roles in the adolescent's success in schools. Among the ways that parents can positively contribute to adolescents' school success are through effective family management practices and involvement in adolescents' schooling.

developmental **connection**

Families. A key aspect of the management role of parenting is parental monitoring. Chapter 8, p. 259

Family Management Researchers have found that family management practices are positively related to grades and self-responsibility, and negatively to school-related problems (Taylor, 1996). Among the family management practices important in this regard is maintaining a structured and organized family environment, such as establishing routines for homework, chores, bedtime, and so on. Creating a family environment in which high expectations for achievement are present also is important (Jeynes, 2003).

As we saw in Chapter 8, one study focusing on African American families examined links between mothers' reports of family management practices, including routine and achievement expectations, and adolescents' school-related behavior (Taylor & Lopez, 2005). Family routine (well managed and organized) was positive related to adolescents' school achievement, paying attention in class, and attendance, and negatively linked to their school-related problems. Compared to mothers with low expectations for achievement, mothers with high expectations for achievement had adolescents who made higher grades and had better school attendance.

What are some important roles of parents in students' schooling?

Parental Involvement Even though parental involvement is minimal in elementary school, it is even less in secondary school (Casas, 2011). In one study, teachers listed parental involvement as the number one priority in improving education (Chira, 1993). In an analysis of 16,000 students, the students were more likely to get A's and less likely to repeat a grade or be expelled if both parents were highly involved in their schooling (National Center for Education Statistics, 1997).

Joyce Epstein (2001, 2005, 2007a,b, 2009) offers the following recommendations for increasing parental involvement in adolescents' schooling:

- *Families have a basic obligation to provide for the safety and health of their adolescents.* Many parents are not knowledgeable about the normal age-appropriate changes that characterize adolescents. School-family programs can help to educate parents about the normal course of adolescent development. Schools also can offer programs about health issues in adolescence, including sexually transmitted infections, depression, drugs, delinquency, and eating disorders. Schools also can help parents find safe places for their adolescents to spend time away from home. Schools are community buildings that could be used as program sites by youth organizations and social service agencies.
- *Schools have a basic obligation to communicate with families about school programs and the individual progress of their adolescents.* Teachers and parents rarely get to know each other in the secondary school years. Programs are needed to facilitate more direct and personalized parent-teacher communication. Parents also need to receive better information about how curricular choices can lead to eventual career choices. This goal is especially important with regard to girls and ethnic minority students enrolling in science and math courses.
- *Parents' involvement at school needs to be increased.* Parents and other family members may be able to assist teachers in the classroom in a variety of ways, such as tutoring, teaching special skills, and providing clerical or supervisory assistance. Such involvement is especially important in inner-city schools.

Peers We examined many aspects of adolescent peer relations in Chapter 9. Here we explore peer relations in school contexts.

Structure of Middle Schools Middle schools are structured in a way that encourages students to interact with larger numbers of peers on a daily basis (Wentzel, 2009; Wentzel & Watkins, 2011). The relative uncertainty and ambiguity of multiple classroom environments and more complex class schedules may result in middle school students turning to each other for information, social support, and strategies for coping.

Peer Statuses Peer statuses have been studied in relation to school success. Being popular or accepted by peers is usually associated with academic success, whereas being rejected by peers is related to more negative academic outcomes (Bellmore, Villarreal, & Ho, 2011; Wentzel, 2009).

developmental **connection**

Peers. Peer statuses include popular, rejected, neglected, controversial, and average children. Chapter 9, p. 300

Bullying Significant numbers of students are victimized by bullies (Espelage, Holt, & Poteat, 2010; Guerra, Williams, & Sadek, 2011; Salmivalli, Peets, & Hodges, 2011). In a national survey of more than 15,000 students in grades 6 through 10, nearly one of every three students said that they had experienced occasional or frequent involvement as a victim or perpetrator in bullying (Nansel & others, 2001). In this study, bullying was defined as verbal or physical behavior intended to disturb someone less powerful (see Figure 10.2). Boys are more likely to be bullies than are girls, but gender differences regarding victims of boys is less clear (Salmivalli & Peets, 2009).

Who is likely to be bullied? In the study just described, boys and younger middle school students were most likely to be affected (Nansel & others, 2001). Children who said they were bullied reported more loneliness and difficulty in making friends, while those who did the bullying were more likely to have low grades and to smoke and drink alcohol. Researchers have found that anxious, socially withdrawn, and aggressive children are often the victims of bullying (Hanish & Guerra, 2004). Anxious and socially withdrawn children may be victimized because they are nonthreatening and unlikely to retaliate if bullied, whereas aggressive children may be the targets of bullying because their behavior is irritating to bullies (Rubin & others, 2011).

Social contexts also influence bullying (Schwartz & others, 2010). Recent research indicates that 70 to 80 percent of victims and their bullies are in the same school classroom (Salmivalli & Peets, 2009). Classmates are often aware of bullying incidents and in many cases witness bullying. The larger social context of the peer group plays an important role in bullying (Salmivalli, Peets, & Hodges, 2011). In many cases, bullies torment victims to gain higher status in the peer group and bullies need others to witness their power displays. Many bullies are not rejected by the peer group (Peeters, Cillessen, & Scholte, 2010). In one study, bullies were only rejected by peers for whom they were a potential threat (Veenstra & others, 2010). In another study, bullies often affiliated with each other or in some cases maintained their position in the popular peer group (Witvliet & others, 2010).

What are the outcomes of bullying? One study indicated that bullies and their victims in adolescence were more likely to experience depression and engage in suicide ideation and attempt suicide than their counterparts who were not involved in bullying (Brunstein Klomek & others, 2007). A recent meta-analysis of 33 studies revealed a small but significant link between peer victimization and lower academic achievement (Nakamoto & Schwartz, 2010). Another study revealed that bullies, victims, or those who were both bullies and victims had more health problems (such as headaches, dizziness, sleep problems, and anxiety) than their counterparts who were not involved in bullying (Srabstein & others, 2006). And in a recent study, bullies, victims, and bully-victims reported higher levels of depressive symptoms than their nonbullied-nonvictimized counterparts (Fitzpatrick, Dulin, & Piko, 2010). Recently, bullying has been linked to these suicides: An 8-year-old jumped out of a two-story building in Houston; a 13-year-old girl hanged herself in Houston; and teenagers harassed a girl in Massachusetts so mercilessly that she killed herself (Meyers, 2010).

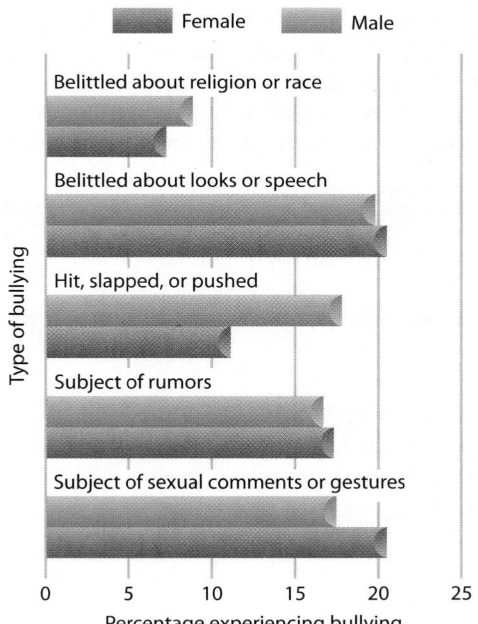

FIGURE **10.2**

BULLYING BEHAVIORS AMONG U.S. YOUTH. This graph shows the type of bullying most often experienced by U.S. youth. The percentages reflect the extent to which bullied students said that they had experienced a particular type of bullying. In terms of gender, note that when they were bullied, boys were more likely to be hit, slapped, or pushed than girls were.

connecting with health and well-being

Bullying Prevention/Intervention

Extensive interest is developing in preventing and treating bullying and victimization (Guerra & Williams, 2010; Salmivalli, Peets, & Hodges, 2011). A research review revealed mixed results for school-based intervention (Vreeman & Carroll, 2007). School-based interventions vary greatly, ranging from involving the whole school in an antibullying campaign to individualized social skills training. One of the most promising bullying intervention programs has been created by Dan Olweus. This program focuses on 6- to 15-year-olds with the goal of decreasing opportunities and rewards for bullying. School staff are instructed in ways to improve peer relations and make schools safer. When properly implemented, the program reduces bullying by 30 to 70 percent (Olweus, 2003).

To reduce bullying, schools can adopt these strategies (Cohn & Canter, 2003; Hyman & others, 2006; Limber, 2004):

- Get older peers to serve as monitors for bullying and intervene when they see it taking place.
- Develop school-wide rules and sanctions against bullying and post them throughout the school.
- Form friendship groups for adolescents who are regularly bullied by peers.
- Incorporate the message of the antibullying program into places of worship, schools, and other community activity areas where adolescents are involved.
- Encourage parents to reinforce their adolescent's positive behaviors and model appropriate interpersonal interactions.
- Identify bullies and victims early and use social skills training to improve their behavior.
- Encourage parents to contact the school's psychologist, counselor, or social worker and ask for help with their adolescent's bullying or victimization concerns.

What are some strategies to reduce bullying?

developmental **connection**

Technology. Recently there has been a substantial increase in youth harassment and cyberbullying on the Internet. Chapter 12, p. 414

A dramatic increase in *cyberbullying*—bullying on the Internet—has occurred recently (Fredstrom, Adams, & Gilman, 2011). We will explore the effects of cyberbullying on adolescents in Chapter 12. To read about a number of strategies for reducing bullying, see the *Connecting with Health and Well-Being* interlude.

Friendship Another aspect of peer relations that is linked with school success involves friendship (Wentzel & Watkins, 2011). Having friends, especially friends who are academically oriented and make good grades, is related to higher grades and test scores in adolescents (Ryan, 2011). One longitudinal study found that having at least one friend was related to academic success over a two-year period (Wentzel & Caldwell, 1997).

Extracurricular Activities Adolescents in U.S. schools usually have a wide array of extracurricular activities they can participate in beyond their academic courses. These adult-sanctioned activities typically occur in the after-school hours and can be sponsored by either the school or the community. They include such diverse activities as sports, honor societies, band, drama club, and various academic clubs (math and language, for example). Researchers have found that participation in extracurricular activities is linked to higher grades, school engagement, less likelihood of dropping out of school, improved probability of going to college, higher

How does participation in extracurricular activities influence development in adolescence and emerging adulthood?

self-esteem, and lower rates of depression, delinquency, and substance abuse (Eccles & Roeser, 2011; Kort-Butler & Hagewen, 2011). Adolescents benefit from a breadth of extracurricular activities more than they do when they focus on a single extracurricular activity (Morris & Kalil, 2006). Also, the more years adolescents spend in extracurricular activities, the stronger the link is with positive developmental outcomes (Fredricks & Eccles, 2006). For example, a longitudinal study revealed that youth who participated in organized school-sponsored activities (sports, cheerleading, music groups, plays, student government, honor societies, and service clubs, for example) and community-sponsored activities (religious activities, community youth groups, music/art/dance lessons, sports lessons, and community service, for example) for two years during adolescence had better educational and occupational outcomes in early adulthood than did those who participated for one year (Gardner, Roth, & Brooks-Gunn, 2008). In this study, more intensive participation was linked to more positive educational, occupational, and civic success in early adulthood.

Of course, the quality of the extracurricular activities matters (Blomfield & Barber, 2011; Mahoney & others, 2009). High-quality extracurricular activities that are likely to promote positive adolescent development include competent, supportive adult mentors, opportunities for increasing school connectedness, challenging and meaningful activities, and opportunities for improving skills (Fredricks & Eccles, 2006).

CULTURE

As we saw in Chapter 9, in some cultures—such as Arab countries and rural India—adults often restrict access to peers, especially for girls. The peer restriction includes the social setting of schools, where girls are educated separately from boys. Let's now explore these aspects of culture and schools: socioeconomic status, ethnicity, and cross-cultural comparisons.

Socioeconomic Status and Ethnicity Adolescents from low-income, ethnic minority backgrounds have more difficulties in school than do their middle-socioeconomic-status non-Latino White counterparts. Why? Critics argue that schools have not done a good job of educating low-income, ethnic minority adolescents and emerging adults to overcome the barriers to their achievement (Stulberg & Weinberg, 2011). Let's further explore the roles of socioeconomic status and ethnicity in schools.

The Education of Students from Low-Income Backgrounds Many adolescents in poverty face problems that present barriers to their learning (Eccles & Roeser, 2011; McLoyd & others, 2009, 2011). They might have parents who don't set high educational standards for them, who are incapable of reading to them, and who don't have enough money to pay for educational materials and experiences, such as books

developmental **connection**

Socioeconomic Status. Socioeconomic differences are a proxy for material, human, and social capital beyond the family. Chapter 12, p. 399

connecting with adolescents

Forensics Teacher Tommie Lindsey's Students

Tommie Lindsey teaches competitive forensics (public speaking and debate) at Logan High School in Union City, California. In U.S. schools, forensics classes are mainly offered in affluent areas, but most of Lindsey's students come from impoverished or at-risk backgrounds. His students have won many public speaking honors.

The following comments by his students reflect Lindsey's outstanding teaching skills:

> He's one of the few teachers I know who cares so much. . . . He spends hours and hours, evenings, and weekends, working with us.
>
> —Justin Hinojoza, 17

> I was going through a tough time. . . . Mr. Lindsey helped me out. I asked how I could pay him back and he said, "Just help someone the way I helped you."
>
> —Robert Hawkins, 21

> This amazing opportunity is here for us students and it wouldn't be if Mr. Lindsey didn't create it.
>
> —Michael Joshi, 17

As a ninth-grade student, Tommie Lindsey became a public speaker. He says that his English teacher doubted his ability, and he wanted to show her how good he could be at public speaking, preparing a speech that received a standing ovation. Lindsey remembers, "She was expecting me to fail, and I turned the tables on her. . . . And we do that with our forensic program. When we started a lot of people didn't believe our kids could do the things they do." For his outstanding teaching efforts, Tommie Lindsey was awarded a prestigious McArthur Fellowship in 2005.

Tommie Lindsey, working with his students on improving their public speaking and debate skills.

(*Source:* Seligson, 2005.)

and trips to zoos and museums. They might be malnourished and live in areas where crime and violence are a way of life.

Compared with schools in higher-income areas, schools in low-income areas are more likely to have more students with low achievement test scores, low graduation rates, and small percentages of students going to college; they are more likely to have young teachers with less experience, more noncredentialed or nonqualified teachers, and substitute teachers who regularly fill in to teach; they are more likely to encourage rote learning; and they don't provide adequate support for English language learners (Eccles & Roeser, 2011; Entwistle, Alexander, & Olson, 2010). Too few schools in low-income neighborhoods provide students with environments that are conducive to learning (Leventhal, Dupéré, & Brooks-Gunn, 2009). Many of the schools' buildings and classrooms are old and crumbling.

Living in economically disadvantaged families during adolescence may have more negative achievement outcomes than do corresponding circumstances in childhood (McLoyd & others, 2009, 2011). The possible timing difference in poverty effects might be due to the adolescents' greater awareness of barriers to their success and the difficulties they will encounter in becoming successful.

Some innovative programs indicate that improving certain characteristics of schools enhances the achievement of adolescents from economically disadvantaged backgrounds (McLoyd & others, 2011). For example, a study by the Center for Collaborative Education of a series of pilot schools in Boston revealed that the following changes were linked with higher levels of achievement in high school: smaller class sizes, longer classes, creating more advisory sessions, and allotting more time for teachers to explore teaching methods (Tung & Ouimette, 2007).

Ethnicity in Schools More than one-third of all African American and almost one-third of all Latino students attend schools in the 47 largest city school districts in the United States, compared with only 5 percent of all non-Latino White and 22 percent of all Asian American students. Many of these inner-city schools are still segregated, are grossly underfunded, and do not provide adequate opportunities for children to learn effectively. Thus, the effects of SES and the effects of ethnicity are often intertwined (Entwistle, Alexander, & Olson, 2010; Hill & Witherspoon, 2011).

In *The Shame of the Nation,* Jonathan Kozol (2005) described his visits to 60 U.S. schools in low-income areas of cities in 11 states. He saw many schools in which the minority population was 80 to 90 percent, concluding that school segregation is still present for many poor minority students. Kozol saw many of the inequities just summarized—poorly kept classrooms, hallways, and restrooms; inadequate textbooks and supplies; and lack of resources. He also saw teachers mainly instructing students to rotely memorize material, especially as preparation for mandated tests, rather than engage in higher-level thinking. Kozol also frequently observed teachers using threatening disciplinary tactics to control the classroom.

Even outside inner-city schools, school segregation remains a factor in U.S. education (Nieto & Bode, 2012). Almost one-third of all African American and Latino students attend schools in which 90 percent or more of the students are from minority groups (Banks, 2008).

The school experiences of students from different ethnic groups vary considerably (Banks, 2010; Nieto & Bode, 2012; Rowley, Kurtz-Costes, & Cooper, 2010). African American and Latino students are much less likely than non-Latino White or Asian American students to be enrolled in academic, college preparatory programs and are much more likely to be enrolled in remedial and special education programs. Asian American students are far more likely than other ethnic minority groups to take advanced math and science courses in high school. African American students are twice as likely as Latinos, Native Americans, or non-Latino Whites to be suspended from school.

Why is there a concern about the education of Latina adolescents?

Latina (the term used for Latino females) adolescents are a special concern (Ceballo, Huerta, & Ngo, 2010; Cooper, 2011). In one study, it was concluded that U.S. schools are doing an especially poor job of meeting the needs of America's fastest-growing minority population—Latinas (Ginorio & Huston, 2001). The study focuses on how Latinas' futures—or "possible selves"—are influenced by their families, culture, peers, teachers, and media. The report indicates that many high school counselors view success as "going away to college," yet some Latinas, because of family responsibilities, believe it is important to stay close to home. The high school graduation rate for Latinas lags behind that for girls of any other ethnic minority group, except Native Americans. Latinas also are less likely to take the SAT exam than are non-Latino White and other ethnic-group females. Thus, a better effort needs to be made at encouraging Latinas' academic success and involving their families more fully in the process of college preparation (Suarez-Orozco & Suarez-Orozco, 2010).

Following are some strategies for improving relationships among ethnically diverse students:

- *Turn the class into a jigsaw classroom.* When Elliot Aronson was a professor at the University of Texas at Austin, the school system contacted him for ideas on how to reduce the increasing racial tension in classrooms. Aronson (1986) developed the concept of the **jigsaw classroom,** in which students from different cultural backgrounds are placed in a cooperative group in which they have to construct different parts of a project to reach a common goal. Aronson used the term *jigsaw* because he saw the technique as much like a group of students cooperating to put different pieces together to complete a jigsaw puzzle. How might this work? Team sports, drama productions, and music performances are examples of contexts in which students cooperatively participate to reach a common goal.

jigsaw classroom A classroom strategy in which students from different cultural backgrounds are placed in a cooperative group in which, together, they have to construct different parts of a project to reach a common goal.

Cover of the spring 2007 issue of *Teaching Tolerance* magazine, which includes numerous resources for improving interethnic relationships.

- *Encourage students to have positive personal contact with diverse other students.* Contact alone does not do the job of improving relationships with diverse others. For example, busing ethnic minority students to predominantly non-Latino White schools, or vice versa, has not reduced prejudice or improved interethnic relations (Minuchin & Shapiro, 1983). What matters is what happens after children and adolescents get to school. Especially beneficial in improving interethnic relations is sharing one's worries, successes, failures, coping strategies, interests, and other personal information with people of other ethnicities. When such sharing takes place, people tend to look at others as individuals rather than as members of a homogeneous group.
- *Encourage students to engage in perspective taking.* Exercises and activities that help students see others' perspectives can improve interethnic relations. These help students "step into the shoes" of peers who are culturally different and feel what it is like to be treated in fair or unfair ways.
- *Help students think critically and be emotionally intelligent about cultural issues.* Students who learn to think critically and deeply about interethnic relations are likely to decrease their prejudice. Becoming more emotionally intelligent includes understanding the causes of one's feelings, managing anger, listening to what others are saying, and being motivated to share and cooperate.
- *Reduce bias.* Teachers can reduce bias by displaying images of children from diverse ethnic and cultural groups, selecting play materials and classroom activities that encourage cultural understanding, helping students resist stereotyping, and working with parents.

- *View the school and community as a team.* James Comer (2004, 2006, 2010) emphasizes that a community, team approach is the best way to educate children. Three important aspects of the Comer Project for Change are (1) a governance and management team that develops a comprehensive school plan, assessment strategy, and staff development plan; (2) a mental health or school support team; and (3) a parents' program. Comer holds that the entire school community should have a cooperative rather than an adversarial attitude. The Comer program is currently operating in more than 600 schools in 26 states. To read further about James Comer's work, see the *Connecting with Careers* profile.
- *Be a competent cultural mediator.* Teachers can play a powerful role as a cultural mediator by being sensitive to racist content in materials and classroom interactions, learning more about different ethnic groups, being sensitive to children's ethnic attitudes, viewing students of color positively, and thinking of positive ways to get parents of color more involved as partners with teachers in educating children (Kumar & Maehr, 2010).

Understanding the role of ethnicity in schooling also involves multicultural education. The hope is that multicultural education can contribute to making our nation more like what the late civil rights leader Martin Luther King, Jr., dreamed of: a nation where children and youth will be judged not by the color of their skin but by the quality of their character.

Multicultural education is education that values diversity and includes the perspectives of a variety of cultural groups. Its proponents believe that children and youth of color should be empowered and that multicultural education benefits all students (Banks, 2010; Grant & Sleeter, 2011). An important goal of multicultural education is equal educational opportunity for all students. This includes closing the gap in academic achievement between mainstream students and students from underrepresented groups (Florence, 2010).

multicultural education Education that values diversity and includes the perspectives of a variety of cultural groups.

Multicultural education grew out of the civil rights movement of the 1960s and the call for equality and social justice for women and people of color (Spring, 2010). As a field, multicultural education includes issues related to socioeconomic status, ethnicity, and gender. An increasing trend in multicultural education,

connecting with careers

James Comer, Child Psychiatrist

James Comer grew up in a low-income neighborhood in East Chicago, Indiana, and credits his parents with leaving no doubt about the importance of education. He obtained a B.A. degree from Indiana University. He went on to obtain a medical degree from Howard University College of Medicine, a Master of Public Health degree from the University of Michigan School of Public Health, and psychiatry training at the Yale University School of Medicine's Child Study Center. He currently is the Maurice Falk Professor of Child Psychiatry at the Yale University Child Study Center and an associate dean at the Yale University Medical School. During his years at Yale, Comer has concentrated his career on promoting a focus on child development as a way of improving schools. His efforts in support of healthy development of young people are known internationally.

Dr. Comer, perhaps, is best known for the founding of the School Development program in 1968, which promotes the collaboration of parents, educators, and community to improve social, emotional, and academic outcomes for children. His concept of teamwork is currently improving the educational environment in more than 600 schools throughout the United States.

James Comer (*left*) is shown with some of the inner-city African American children who attend a school that became a better learning environment because of Comer's intervention.

though, is not to make ethnicity a focal point but to also include socioeconomic status, gender, religion, disability, sexual orientation, and other forms of differences (Howe, 2010). Another important point about contemporary multicultural education is that many individuals think it is reserved for students of color. However, all students, including non-Latino White students, can benefit from multicultural education (Howe, 2010).

Cross-Cultural Comparisons Many countries recognize that quality, universal education of children and youth is critical for the success of any country. However, countries vary considerably in their ability to fulfill this mission (Feinstein & Peck, 2008).

Secondary Schools Secondary schools in different countries share a number of features but differ on others. Let's explore the similarities and differences in secondary schools in seven countries: Australia, Brazil, Germany, Japan, China, Russia, and the United States.

Most countries mandate that children begin school at 6 to 7 years of age and stay in school until they are 14 to 17 years of age. Brazil requires students to go to school only until they are 14 years old, whereas Russia mandates that students stay in school until they are 17. Germany, Japan, Australia, and the United States require school attendance until at least 15 to 16 years of age, with some states, such as California, recently raising the mandatory age to 18.

Most secondary schools around the world are divided into two or more levels, such as middle school (or junior high school) and high school. However, Germany's schools are divided according to three educational ability tracks: (1) the main school provides a basic level of education, (2) the middle school gives students a more

A young Bill Gates, founder of Microsoft and now one of the world's richest persons. Like many highly gifted students, Gates was not especially fond of school. He hacked a computer security system when he was 13, and as a high school student, he was allowed to take some college math classes. He dropped out of Harvard University and began developing a plan for what was to become Microsoft Corporation. *What are some ways that schools can enrich the education of such highly talented students as Gates to make it a more challenging, interesting, and meaningful experience?*

accomplished at the very latest by adolescence (Keating, 2009). During adolescence, individuals who are talented become less reliant on parental support and increasingly pursue their own interests.

Education of Children and Youth Who Are Gifted An increasing number of experts argue that in the United States the education of students who are gifted requires a significant overhaul (Ambrose, Sternberg, & Sriraman, 2012; Gardner, 2012; VanTassel-Baska, 2012). This concern is reflected in the titles of these books: *Genius Denied: How to Stop Wasting Our Brightest Young Minds* (Davidson & Davidson, 2004) and *A Nation Deceived: How Schools Hold Back America's Brightest Students* (Colangelo, Assouline, & Gross, 2004).

Underchallenged students who are gifted can become disruptive, skip classes, and lose interest in achieving. Sometimes they just disappear into the woodwork, becoming passive and apathetic toward school. It is extremely important for teachers to challenge children and youth who are gifted to reach high expectations (Ambrose, Sternberg, & Sriraman, 2012; Webb & others, 2007; Winner, 2006).

A number of experts argue that too often students who are gifted are socially isolated and underchallenged in the classroom (Ambrose, Sternberg, & Sriarman, 2012; Karnes & Stephens, 2008). It is not unusual for them to be ostracized and labeled "nerds" or "geeks." Ellen Winner (1996, 2006) concludes that a student who is truly gifted often is the only child in the room who does not have the opportunity to learn with students of like ability.

Many eminent adults report that school was a negative experience for them, that they were bored and sometimes knew more than their teachers (Bloom, 1985). Winner stresses that American education will benefit when standards are raised for all students. When some students are still underchallenged, she recommends that they be allowed to attend advanced classes in their domain of exceptional ability, such as allowing some especially precocious middle school students to take college classes in their area of expertise. For example, Bill Gates, founder of Microsoft, took college math classes and hacked a computer security system at 13; Yo-Yo Ma, a famous cellist, graduated from high school at 15 and attended Juilliard School of Music in New York City.

In this chapter, we have examined many aspects of schools for adolescents. An important aspect of the education of adolescents involves achievement. In Chapter 11, we examine the development of achievement in adolescents.

Review *Connect* Reflect

 Characterize adolescents who are exceptional and their education.

Review

- Who are adolescents with disabilities?
- How can learning disabilities be characterized?
- What is known about attention deficit hyperactivity disorder?
- What educational issues are involved in educating adolescents with disabilities?
- How can adolescents who are gifted be described?

Connect

- How does the concept of the family as a system (discussed in Chapter 8) support parents' efforts to seek the best for their children who are exceptional learners?

Reflect *Your Own Personal Journey of Life*

- Think back on your own schooling and how students with learning disabilities either were or were not diagnosed. Were you aware of such individuals in your classes? Were they helped by teachers and/or specialists? You might know one or more people with a learning disability. Interview them about their school experiences and what could have been done better to help them learn more effectively.

reach your **learning goals**

1 Approaches to Educating Students

Describe approaches to educating students.

Contemporary Approaches to Student Learning

- Two main contemporary approaches to student learning are constructivist and direct instruction. The constructivist approach is a learner-centered approach that emphasizes the adolescent's active, cognitive construction of knowledge and understanding. The direct instruction approach is a teacher-centered approach characterized by teacher direction and control, mastery of academic skills, high expectations for students, and maximum time spent on learning tasks. Many effective teachers use aspects of both approaches.

Accountability

- Accountability has become a major issue in U.S. education. Increased concern by the public and government in the United States has produced extensive state-mandated testing, which has both strengths and weaknesses, and is controversial. The most visible example of the increased state-mandated testing is the No Child Left Behind federal legislation.

2 Transitions in Schooling

Discuss transitions in schooling from early adolescence to emerging adulthood.

Transition to Middle or Junior High School

- The emergence of junior high schools in the 1920s and 1930s was justified on the basis of the developmental changes occurring in early adolescence and an effort to meet the needs of a growing student population. Middle schools have become more popular, and their appearance has coincided with earlier pubertal development. The transition to middle/junior high school is often stressful because it occurs at the same time as a number of physical, cognitive, and socioemotional changes. This transition involves going from the "top-dog" to the "bottom-dog" position.

Improving Middle Schools

- *Turning Points 1989* provided a very negative evaluation of U.S. middle school education. *Turning Points 2000* continued to express serious concerns about middle school education and added new emphases on teaching a curriculum grounded in rigorous academic standards and engaging in instruction that prepares all students to achieve higher standards.

The American High School

- An increasing number of educators believe that U.S. high schools need a new mission for the twenty-first century, one that involves more support for graduating with the knowledge and skills to succeed in college and a career, higher expectations for achievement, less time spent working in low-level service jobs, and better coordination of the K–12 curriculum. The National Research Council provided a number of recommendations for improving U.S. high school education that focus on engaging students to learn.

High School Dropouts

- Many school dropouts have educational deficiencies that limit their economic and social well-being for much of their adult lives. Progress has been made in lowering the dropout rate for African American youth, but the dropout rate for Native American and Latino youth remains very high. Dropping out of school is associated with demographic, family-related, peer-related, school-related, economic, and personal factors.

Transition from High School to College

- In many ways, the transition to college parallels the transition from elementary to middle/junior high school. Reduced interaction with parents is usually involved in this transition. A special problem today is the discontinuity between high schools and colleges.

Transition from College to Work

- Having a college degree is highly beneficial for increasing one's income. However, the transition from college to work is often a difficult one. One reason is that colleges train many students to develop general skills rather than job-specific skills.

3 The Social Contexts of Schools

Explain how the social contexts of schools influence adolescent development.

Changing Social Developmental Contexts

- The social context differs at the preschool, elementary school, and secondary school levels, increasing in complexity and scope for adolescents.

Classroom Climate and Management

- A positive classroom climate, which is promoted by an authoritative management strategy and effective management of group activities, improves student learning and achievement. An important teaching skill is managing the classroom to prevent problem behavior from developing and to maximize student learning. Some issues in classroom management in secondary schools are different from those in elementary schools.

Person-Environment Fit

- Person-environment fit involves the concept that some of the negative psychological changes associated with adolescent development might result from a mismatch between adolescents' developing needs and the lack of opportunities afforded by schools.

Teachers, Parents, Peers, and Extracurricular Activities

- Teacher characteristics involve many different dimensions, and compiling a profile of the competent teacher's characteristics has been difficult. Effective family management, especially routine and high achievement expectations, is positively linked to adolescents' success in school. Parent involvement usually decreases as the child moves into adolescence. Epstein argues that greater collaboration among schools, families, and communities is needed. The way middle schools are structured encourages students to interact with larger numbers of peers on a daily basis. A popular or accepted peer status is linked with academic success; a rejected status is related to less academic success. An increasing concern in schools is bullying. Victims of bullying can experience both short-term and long-term negative effects. Friendship is also related to school success. Participation in extracurricular activities is associated with positive academic and psychological outcomes.

Culture

- At home, in their neighborhoods, and at school, adolescents in poverty face problems that present barriers to effective learning. In comparison to schools in higher-SES neighborhoods, schools in low-SES neighborhoods have fewer resources, have less experienced teachers, and encourage rote learning more than thinking skills. The school experiences of students from different ethnic groups vary considerably. It is important for teachers to have positive expectations and challenge students of color to achieve. Strategies that teachers can use to improve relations among ethnically diverse students include turning the classroom into a "jigsaw," encouraging positive personal contact, stimulating perspective taking, viewing the school and community as a team, and being a competent cultural mediator. Multicultural education is education that values diversity and includes the perspectives of varying cultural groups. Schools vary across cultures. For example, U.S. schools have by far the strongest emphasis on athletics.

4 Adolescents Who Are Exceptional

Characterize adolescents who are exceptional and their education.

Who Are Adolescents with Disabilities?

- An estimated 14 percent of U.S. children and adolescents receive special education or related services. Slightly less than 45 percent of students with disabilities are classified as having a learning disability. In the federal government classification, this category includes attention deficit hyperactivity disorder, or ADHD.

Learning Disabilities

- Learning disabilities are characterized by difficulties in learning that involve understanding or using spoken or written language; the difficulty can appear in listening, thinking, reading, writing, and spelling. A learning disability also may involve difficulty in doing mathematics. To be classified as a learning disability, the learning problem is not primarily the result of visual, hearing, or motor disabilities; mental retardation; emotional disorders; or environmental, cultural, or economic disadvantage. Dyslexia is a category of learning disabilities that involves a severe impairment in the ability to read and spell. Dysgraphia and dyscalculia are two other categories of learning disabilities.

Attention Deficit Hyperactivity Disorder

- Attention deficit hyperactivity disorder (ADHD) involves problems in one or more of these areas: inattention, hyperactivity, and impulsivity. Most experts recommend a combination of interventions for ADHD—medical (stimulants such as Ritalin) and behavioral.

Educational Issues Involving Adolescents with Disabilities

- Public Law 94-142 requires that all students with disabilities be given a free, appropriate education. IDEA spells out broad mandates for services to all children and adolescents with disabilities. The concept of least restrictive environment (LRE) also has been set forth. Inclusion means educating students with disabilities in the regular classroom. Full inclusion has increasingly characterized U.S. schools, although some educators argue that this trend may not be best for some students with disabilities.

Adolescents Who Are Gifted

- Adolescents who are gifted have above-average intelligence (usually defined by an IQ of 130 or higher) and/or superior talent in some domain, such as art, music, or math. Characteristics of adolescents who are gifted include precocity, marching to their own drummer, a passion to master, and superior information-processing skills. Giftedness is likely a result of the interaction of heredity and environment, and for most individuals giftedness is domain-specific. Significant criticisms have been made of the way adolescents who are gifted have been educated in the U.S.

key terms

constructivist approach 332
direct instruction approach 332
top-dog phenomenon 334
authoritative strategy of classroom management 339
authoritarian strategy of classroom management 340
permissive strategy of classroom management 340
jigsaw classroom 347
multicultural education 348
learning disabilities 353
attention deficit hyperactivity disorder (ADHD) 353
Public Law 94-142 355
Individuals with Disabilities Education Act (IDEA) 355
least restrictive environment (LRE) 355
inclusion 355
adolescents who are gifted 355

key people

Jacquelynne Eccles and Allan Wigfield 340
Joyce Epstein 342
Jonathan Kozol 347
Elliot Aronson 347
James Comer 348
James Kauffman 354
Ellen Winner 355

resources for **improving the lives of adolescents**

Council for Exceptional Children (CEC) ***www.cec.sped.org***

The CEC maintains an information center on the education of children and adolescents who are exceptional and publishes materials on a wide variety of topics.

Encyclopedia of Educational Psychology
edited by Neal Salkind (2008, 2nd ed., Vols. 1 and 2)
Mahwah, NJ: Erlbaum

A number of leading experts provide in-depth coverage of many educational psychology topics, ranging from learning and cognition to the social and cultural aspects of schools.

Handbook of Learning and Instruction
Edited by Patricia Alexander and Richard Mayer (2011).
New York: Routledge

Leading experts in many areas of education discuss the latest research and applications in improving the education of children and adolescents.

National Dropout Prevention Center
www.dropoutprevention.org

The center operates as a clearinghouse for information about dropout prevention and at-risk youth and publishes the National Dropout Prevention Newsletter.

Turning Points 2000: Educating Adolescents in the 21st Century
by Anthony Jackson and Gayle Davis (2000)
New York: Teachers College Press

This follow-up to earlier *Turning Points* recommendations includes a number of strategies for meeting the educational needs of adolescents.

Confronting Dogmatism in Gifted Education
Edited by Don Ambrose, Robert Sternberg, and Bharath Sriraman (2012)
New York: Routledge

Leading experts discuss barriers that keep adolescents who are gifted from reaching their full potential.

self-**assessment**

The Online Learning Center includes the following self-assessment for further exploration:

- *The Best and Worst Characteristics of My Teachers*

chapter 11 ACHIEVEMENT, WORK, AND CAREERS

chapter **outline**

Achievement

Learning Goal 1 Discuss achievement in the lives of adolescents.

The Importance of Achievement in Adolescence
Achievement Processes
Social Relationships and Contexts
Some Motivational Obstacles to Achievement

Work

Learning Goal 2 Describe the role of work in adolescence and in college.

Work in Adolescence
Working During College
Work/Career-Based Learning
Work in Emerging Adulthood

Career Development

Learning Goal 3 Characterize career development in adolescence.

Developmental Changes
Cognitive Factors
Identity Development
Social Contexts

Kim-Chi Trinh was only 9 years old in Vietnam when her father used his savings to buy passage for her on a fishing boat. It was a costly and risky sacrifice for the family, who placed Kim-Chi on the small boat, among strangers, in the hope that she eventually would reach the United States, where she would get a good education and enjoy a better life.

Kim made it to the United States and coped with a succession of three foster families. When she graduated from high school in San Diego in 1988, she had a straight-A average and a number of college scholarship offers. When asked why she excels in school, Kim-Chi says that she has to do well because she owes it to her parents, who are still in Vietnam.

Kim-Chi is one of a wave of bright, highly motivated Asians who are immigrating to America. Asian Americans are the fastest-growing ethnic minority group in the United States—two out of five immigrants are now Asian. Although Asian Americans make up only 5 percent of the U.S. population, they constitute 17 percent of the undergraduates at Harvard, 18 percent at MIT, 27 percent at the University of California at Berkeley, and a staggering 35 percent at the University of California at Irvine.

Not all Asian American youth do this well, however. Poorly educated Vietnamese, Cambodian, and Hmong refugee youth are especially at risk for school-related problems. Many refugee children's histories are replete with losses and trauma. Thuy, a 12-year-old Vietnamese girl, has been in the United States for two years and resides with her father in a small apartment with a cousin's family of five in the inner city of a West Coast metropolitan area (Huang, 1989). While trying to escape from Saigon, "the family became separated, and the wife and two younger children remained in Vietnam. . . . Thuy's father has had an especially difficult time adjusting to the United States. He struggles with English classes and has been unable to maintain several jobs as a waiter" (Huang, 1989, p. 307). When Thuy received a letter from her mother saying that her 5-year-old brother had died, Thuy's schoolwork began to deteriorate, and she showed marked signs of depression—lack of energy, loss of appetite, withdrawal from peer relations, and a general feeling of hopelessness. At the insistence of the school, she and her father went to the child and adolescent unit of a community mental health center. It took the therapist a long time to establish credibility with Thuy and her father, but eventually they began to trust the therapist, who was a good listener and gave them competent advice about how to handle different experiences in the new country. The therapist also contacted Thuy's teacher, who said that Thuy had been involved in several interethnic skirmishes at school. With the assistance of the mental health clinic, the school initiated interethnic student panels to address cultural differences and discuss reasons for ethnic hostility. Thuy was selected to participate in these panels. Her father became involved in the community mutual assistance association, and Thuy's academic performance began to improve.

preview

This chapter focuses on achievement, work, and careers. As adolescence and emerging adulthood unfold, achievement takes a more central role in development, work becomes a major aspect of life, and careers play an increasing role. The chapter begins by examining why adolescence is a key period in achievement. Then, we turn to the development of adolescents and emerging adults. The chapter concludes with an evaluation of the major theories of career development and the contexts that influence adolescents' career choices.

Some developmentalists worry that the United States is rapidly becoming a nation of hurried, wired people who are raising their youth to become the same way—too uptight about success and failure, and far too preoccupied with how personal accomplishments compare with those of others. However, an increasing number of experts argue that achievement expectations for youth are low, that adolescents are not adequately challenged to achieve, and that too many adolescents aren't being given adequate support and guidance to reach their achievement aspirations.

Meredith MacGregor, here pictured as a senior at Fairview High School in Boulder, Colorado, is an aspiring scientist and was one of Colorado's top high school long-distance runners. She maintained a 4.0 grade point average, participated in a number of school organizations, and cofounded the AfriAid Club. She was named a USA Today High School Academic All-Star and was awarded the Intel Foundation Young Scientist Award (Wong Briggs, 2007). *What are some factors that were likely involved in Meredith's motivation to achieve?*

THE IMPORTANCE OF ACHIEVEMENT IN ADOLESCENCE

Adolescence is a critical juncture in achievement (Anderman, 2012; Eccles & Roeser, 2010, 2011). New social and academic pressures force adolescents toward different roles. These new roles often involve more responsibility. Achievement becomes a more serious business in adolescence, and adolescents begin to sense that the game of life is now being played for real. They even may begin to perceive current successes and failures as predictors of future outcomes in the adult world. And, as demands on adolescents intensify, different areas of their lives may come into conflict. Adolescents' social interests may cut into the time they need to pursue academic matters, or ambitions in one area may undermine the attainment of goals in another, as when academic achievement leads to social disapproval.

How effectively adolescents adapt to these new academic and social pressures is determined, in part, by psychological, motivational, and contextual factors (Anderman & Dawson, 2011; Wigfield, Klauda, & Cambria, 2011; Schunk, 2012; Zimmerman & Schunk, 2011). Indeed, adolescents' achievement is due to much more than their intellectual ability. Students who are not as bright as others may show an adaptive motivational pattern—being persistent at tasks and confident about their ability to solve problems, for example—and turn out to be high achievers. In contrast, some of the brightest students may have maladaptive achievement patterns—giving up easily and not having confidence in their academic skills, for example—and turn out to be low achievers.

ACHIEVEMENT PROCESSES

Achievement involves a number of motivational processes. We explore these processes next, beginning with the distinction between intrinsic and extrinsic motivation.

Life is a gift . . . Accept it.
Life is an adventure . . . Dare it.
Life is a mystery . . . Unfold it.
Life is a struggle . . . Face it.
Life is a puzzle . . . Solve it.
Life is an opportunity . . . Take it.
Life is a mission . . . Fulfill it.
Life is a goal . . . Achieve it.

—AUTHOR UNKNOWN

Intrinsic and Extrinsic Motivation **Intrinsic motivation** is based on internal factors such as self-determination, curiosity, challenge, and effort. **Extrinsic motivation** involves external incentives such as rewards and punishments. The humanistic and cognitive approaches stress the importance of intrinsic motivation in achievement. Some adolescents study hard because they are internally motivated to achieve high standards in their work (intrinsic motivation). Other adolescents study hard because they want to make good grades or avoid parental disapproval (extrinsic motivation).

Current evidence strongly favors establishing a classroom climate in which students are intrinsically motivated to learn (Weinstein, Deci, & Ryan, 2012). For example, a study of third- through eighth-grade students found that intrinsic motivation was positively linked with grades and standardized test scores, whereas extrinsic motivation was negatively related to achievement outcomes (Lepper, Corpus, & Iyengar, 2005). And a recent study of fifth- and sixth-grade students revealed that framing goals extrinsically was related to a lower level of independent motivation and lower persistence on achievement tasks (Vansteenkiste & others, 2008). Parental intrinsic/extrinsic motivational practices are also linked to children's motivation. In one study, children and adolescents had higher intrinsic motivation in math and science from 9 to 17 years of age when their parents engaged in task-intrinsic practices (encouraging children's pleasure and engagement in learning) than when their parents engaged in task-extrinsic practices (providing external rewards and consequences contingent on children's performance) (Gottfried & others, 2009).

Students are more motivated to learn when they are given choices, become absorbed in challenges that match their skills, and receive rewards that have informational value but are not used for control. Praise also can enhance students' intrinsic motivation. To understand the importance of these aspects of achievement in adolescent development, let's first explore these views of intrinsic motivation: (1) self-determination and personal choice, (2) optimal experiences and flow, and (3) cognitive engagement and self-responsibility. Then we offer some concluding thoughts about intrinsic and extrinsic motivation.

Self-Determination and Personal Choice One view of intrinsic motivation emphasizes that students want to believe that they are doing something because of their own will, not because of external success or rewards (Deci, Koestner, & Ryan, 2001; Mclellan & Remedios, 2011; Weinstein, Deci, & Ryan, 2012). Students' internal motivation and intrinsic interest in school tasks increase when they have opportunities to make choices and take responsibility for their learning (Stipek, 2002). In one study, students who were given some choice of activities and when to do them, and were encouraged to take personal responsibility for their behavior, had higher achievement gains and were more likely to graduate from high school than was a control group (deCharms, 1984). The architects of self-determination theory,

intrinsic motivation Internal motivational factors such as self-determination, curiosity, challenge, and effort.

extrinsic motivation External motivational factors such as rewards and punishments.

Richard Ryan and Edward Deci (2009), refer to teachers who create circumstances that allow students to engage in self-determination as *autonomy-supportive teachers*.

Optimal Experiences and Flow Mihaly Csikszentmihalyi (1990, 1993; Csikszentmihalyi & Csikszentmihalyi, 2006) has studied the optimal experiences of people for more than two decades. These optimal experiences occur when people report feelings of deep enjoyment and happiness. Csikszentmihalyi uses the term **flow** to describe optimal experiences in life. Flow occurs most often when people develop a sense of mastery and are absorbed in a state of concentration while they engage in an activity. He argues that flow occurs when individuals are engaged in challenges they find neither too difficult nor too easy.

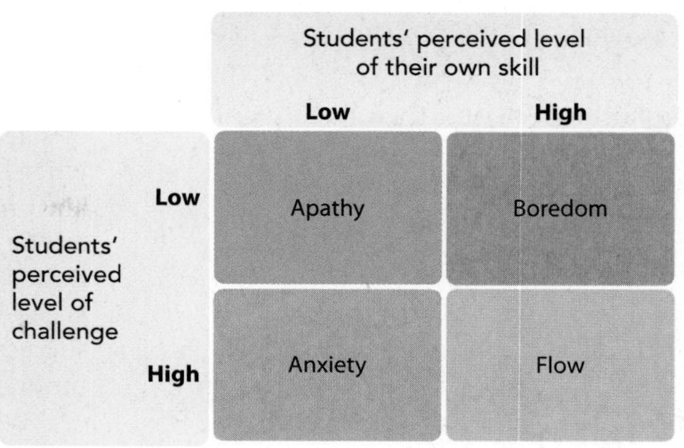

FIGURE **11.1**
OUTCOMES OF PERCEIVED LEVELS OF CHALLENGE AND SKILL

Perceived levels of challenge and skill can result in different outcomes (see Figure 11.1) (Brophy, 2004). Flow is most likely to occur in areas in which adolescents are challenged and perceive themselves as having a high degree of skill (Strati, Shernoff, & Kackar, 2012). When adolescents' skills are high, but the activity provides little challenge, the result is boredom. When both challenge and skill levels are low, apathy occurs. And when adolescents perceive themselves as not having adequate skills to master a challenging task they face, they experience anxiety. In a recent study, students were less engaged in classrooms than in other contexts (Shernoff, 2009). In this study, students were more engaged when they participated in contexts they found challenging, relevant, and enjoyable. After-school programs, especially those involving organized sports, academic enrichment, and arts enrichment activities, elicited the highest level of engagement in the after-school hours (Shernoff, 2009).

Cognitive Engagement and Self-Responsibility It is increasingly recognized that becoming cognitively engaged and developing self-responsibility are key aspects of achievement (Appleton, 2012). Phyllis Blumenfeld and her colleagues (Blumenfeld, Kempler, & Krajcik, 2006; Blumenfeld, Marx, & Harris, 2006) have proposed another variation on intrinsic motivation, which emphasizes the importance of creating learning environments that encourage students to become cognitively engaged and to take responsibility for their learning. The goal is to get students to become motivated to expend the effort to persist and master ideas rather than simply doing enough work to just get by and make passing grades. Especially important in encouraging students to become cognitively engaged and responsible for their learning is embedding subject matter content and skills learning within meaningful contexts, especially real-world situations that mesh with students' interests. Recall from the opening story in Chapter 10 how award-winning teachers created meaningful real-world experiences for students to engage their learning.

Some Final Thoughts About Intrinsic and Extrinsic Motivation An overwhelming conclusion is that it is important for parents and teachers to encourage students to become intrinsically motivated and to create learning environments that promote students' cognitive engagement and self-responsibility for learning (Blumenfeld, Marx, & Harris, 2006; Townsend, 2011). That said, the real world is not just one of intrinsic motivation, and too often intrinsic and extrinsic motivation have been pitted against each other as polar opposites. In many aspects of students' lives, both intrinsic and extrinsic motivation are at work (Anderman & Anderman, 2010; Cameron & Pierce, 2008; Schunk, 2012). Keep in mind, though, that many psychologists recommend that extrinsic motivation by itself is not a good strategy.

Our discussion of extrinsic and intrinsic motivation sets the stage for consideration of other cognitive processes involved in motivating students to learn. As we explore these additional cognitive processes, notice how intrinsic and extrinsic motivation continue to be important. The processes are: (1) attribution; (2) mastery motivation and mindset; (3) self-efficacy; (4) expectations; (5) goal setting, planning, and self-monitoring; and (6) purpose.

flow Csikszentmihalyi's concept of optimal life experiences, which he believes occur most often when people develop a sense of mastery and are absorbed in a state of concentration when they're engaged in an activity.

The student:

- Says "I can't"
- Doesn't pay attention to teacher's instructions
- Doesn't ask for help, even when it is needed
- Does nothing (for example, stares out the window)
- Guesses or answers randomly without really trying
- Doesn't show pride in successes
- Appears bored, uninterested
- Is unresponsive to teacher's exhortations to try
- Is easily discouraged
- Doesn't volunteer answers to teacher's questions
- Maneuvers to get out of or to avoid work (for example, has to go to the nurse's office)

FIGURE **11.2**
BEHAVIORS THAT SUGGEST HELPLESSNESS

Attribution **Attribution theory** states that individuals are motivated to discover the underlying causes of their own performance and behavior. Attributions are perceived causes of outcomes (Mclellan & Remedios, 2011). In a way, attribution theorists say, adolescents are like intuitive scientists, seeking to explain the cause behind what happens (Weiner, 2005). For example, a secondary school student asks, "Why am I not doing well in this class?" or "Did I get a good grade because I studied hard or the teacher made up an easy test, or both?" The search for a cause or explanation is often initiated when unexpected and important events end in failure, as when a good student gets a low grade. Some of the most frequently inferred causes of success and failure are ability, effort, task ease or difficulty, luck, mood, and help or hindrance from others.

What are the best strategies for teachers to use in helping students who attribute their poor performance to factors such as lack of ability, luck, and hindrance from others? Educational psychologists recommend getting adolescents to attribute their poor performance to internal factors such as a lack of effort rather than on external factors, such as bad luck, or blaming others, such as a teacher creating a test that was too difficult. They also emphasize getting adolescents to concentrate on the learning task at hand rather than worrying about failing; to retrace their steps to discover their mistake; and to analyze the problem to discover another approach.

Mastery Motivation and Mindset Becoming cognitively engaged and self-motivated to improve are reflected in adolescents with a mastery motivation. These adolescents also have a growth mindset and believe that they can produce positive outcomes if they put forth the effort.

Mastery Motivation Developmental psychologists Valanne Henderson and Carol Dweck (1990) have found that adolescents often show two distinct responses to difficult or challenging circumstances. Adolescents who display a **mastery orientation** are task-oriented; instead of focusing on their ability, they concentrate on learning strategies and the process of achievement rather than the outcome. Those with a **helpless orientation** seem trapped by the experience of difficulty, and they attribute their difficulty to lack of ability. They frequently say such things as "I'm not very good at this," even though they might earlier have demonstrated their ability through many successes. And, once they view their behavior as failure, they often feel anxious, and their performance worsens even further. Figure 11.2 describes some behaviors that might reflect helplessness (Stipek, 2002).

In contrast, mastery-oriented adolescents often instruct themselves to pay attention, to think carefully, and to remember strategies that have worked for them in previous situations. They frequently report feeling challenged and excited by difficult tasks, rather than being threatened by them (Anderman & Wolters, 2006; Dorn & others, 2011). One study revealed that seventh- to eleventh-grade students' mastery goals were linked to how much effort they put forth in mathematics (Chouinard, Karsenti, & Roy, 2007).

Another issue in motivation involves whether to adopt a mastery or a performance orientation. Adolescents with a **performance orientation** are focused on winning, rather than on achievement outcome, and believe that happiness results from winning. Does this mean that mastery-oriented adolescents do not like to win and that performance-oriented adolescents are not motivated to experience the self-efficacy that comes from being able to take credit for one's accomplishments? No. A matter of emphasis or degree is involved, though. For mastery-oriented individuals, winning isn't everything; for performance-oriented individuals, skill development and self-efficacy take a backseat to winning.

Recall from Chapter 10 that the No Child Left Behind Act (NCLB) emphasizes testing and accountability. Although NCLB may motivate some teachers and students to work harder, motivation experts worry that it encourages a performance rather than a mastery motivational orientation on the part of students (Meece, Anderman, & Anderman, 2006).

attribution theory The theory that in their effort to make sense of their own behavior or performance, individuals are motivated to discover its underlying causes.

mastery orientation An outlook in which individuals focus on the task rather than on their ability; they concentrate on learning strategies and the process of achievement instead of the outcome.

helpless orientation An outlook in which individuals seem trapped when experiencing difficulty and attribute their difficulty to a lack of ability. This orientation undermines performance.

performance orientation An outlook in which individuals are focused on winning rather than achievement outcome. For performance-oriented students, winning results in happiness.

A final point needs to be made about mastery and performance goals: They are not always mutually exclusive. Students can be both mastery- and performance-oriented, and researchers have found that mastery goals combined with performance goals often benefit students' success (Anderman & Anderman, 2010; Schunk, 2012).

Mindset Carol Dweck's (2006, 2007, 2012) most recent analysis of motivation for achievement stresses the importance of developing a **mindset,** which she defines as the cognitive view individuals develop for themselves. She concludes that individuals have one of two mindsets: (1) a *fixed mindset,* in which they believe that their qualities are carved in stone and cannot change; or (2) a *growth mindset,* in which they believe their qualities can change and improve through their effort. A fixed mindset is similar to a helpless orientation; a growth mindset is much like having mastery motivation.

In *Mindset,* Dweck (2006) argued that individuals' mindsets influence their outlook, whether optimistic or pessimistic; shape their goals and how hard they will strive to reach those goals; and affect many aspects of their lives, including achievement and success in school and sports. Dweck says that mindsets begin to be shaped when children and adolescents interact with parents, teachers, and coaches, who themselves have either a fixed mindset or a growth mindset.

Dweck and her colleagues (Blackwell & Dweck, 2008; Blackwell, Trzesniewski, & Dweck, 2007; Dweck, 2012; Dweck & Master, 2009) recently incorporated information about the brain's plasticity into their effort to improve students' motivation to achieve and succeed. In one study, they assigned two groups of students to eight sessions of either (1) study skills instruction or (2) study skills instruction plus information about the importance of developing a growth mindset (called *incremental theory* in the research) (Blackwell & others, 2007). One of the exercises in the growth mindset group was titled "You Can Grow Your Brain," which emphasized that the brain is like a muscle that can change and grow as it gets exercised and develops new connections. Students were informed that the more you challenge your brain to learn, the more your brain cells grow. Both groups had a pattern of declining math scores prior to the intervention. Following the intervention, the group who only received the study skills instruction continued to decline. The group who received the combination of study skills instruction plus the growth-mindset emphasis on how the brain develops when it is challenged reversed the downward trend and improved their math achievement.

In other work, Dweck has been creating a computer-based workshop, "Brainology," to teach students that their intelligence can change (Blackwell & Dweck, 2008). Students experience six modules about how the brain works and how the

developmental **connection**

Schools. A number of criticisms of No Child Left Behind have been made. Chapter 10, p. 333

Going into the virtual brain. A screen from Carol Dweck's "Brainology" program, which is designed to cultivate a growth mindset.

mindset The cognitive view, either fixed or growth, that individuals develop for themselves.

students can make their brain improve. After being tested in 20 New York City schools recently, students strongly endorsed the value of the computer-based brain modules. Said one student, "I will try harder because I know that the more you try the more your brain knows" (Dweck & Master, 2009, p. 137).

Self-Efficacy Like having a growth mindset, **self-efficacy,** the belief that one can master a situation and produce favorable outcomes, is an important cognitive view for adolescents to develop. Albert Bandura (1997, 2004, 2010a), whose social cognitive theory we discussed in Chapter 1, argues that self-efficacy is a critical factor in whether or not adolescents achieve. Self-efficacy has much in common with mastery motivation. Self-efficacy is the belief that "I can"; helplessness is the belief that "I cannot" (Stipek, 2002). Adolescents with high self-efficacy endorse such statements as "I know that I will be able to learn the material in this class" and "I expect to be able to do well at this activity."

developmental **connection**

Social Cognitive Theory. Social cognitive theory holds that behavior, environment, and person/cognitive factors are the key influences on development. Chapter 1, p. 32

Dale Schunk (2008, 2012) has applied the concept of self-efficacy to many aspects of students' achievement. In his view, self-efficacy influences a student's choice of activities. Students with low self-efficacy for learning might avoid many learning tasks, especially those that are challenging, whereas students with high self-efficacy eagerly approach these learning tasks. Students with high self-efficacy are more likely to persist with effort at a learning task than are students with low self-efficacy (Walsh, 2008). A recent study revealed that high-self-efficacy adolescents had higher academic aspirations, spent more time doing homework, and were more likely to associate learning activities with optimal experience than did their low self-efficacy counterparts (Bassi & others, 2007).

They can because they think they can.

—Virgil

Roman Poet, 1st Century B.C.

Expectations Expectations play important roles in adolescents' achievement. These expectations involve not only the expectations of adolescents themselves but also of the expectations of parents and teachers.

Adolescents How hard students will work can depend on how much they expect to accomplish. If they expect to succeed, they are more likely to work hard to reach a goal than if they expect to fail. Jacquelynne Eccles (1987, 1993) defined expectations for students' success as beliefs about how well they will do on upcoming tasks, either in the immediate or long-term future (Wigfield & others, 2006). Three aspects of ability beliefs, according to Eccles, are students' beliefs about how good they are at a particular activity, how good they are in comparison to other individuals, and how good they are in relation to their performance in other activities.

How hard students work also depends on the *value* they place on the goal (Wigfield & Cambria, 2010). Indeed, the combination of expectancy and value has been the focus of a number of efforts to better understand students' achievement motivation. In Jacquelynne Eccles' (1993, 2007) model, students' expectancies and values are assumed to directly influence their performance, persistence, and task choice.

A student and teacher at Langston Hughes Elementary School in Chicago, a school whose teachers have high expectations for students. *How do teachers' expectations influence students' achievement?*

Parents and Teachers A student's motivation is often influenced by the expectations that parents, teachers, and other adults have for the person's achievement. Children and adolescents benefit when both parents and teachers have high expectations for them and provide the necessary support for them to meet those expectations (Anderman & Anderman, 2010).

Researchers have found that parents' expectations are linked with children's and adolescents' academic achievement (Burchinal & others, 2002). One longitudinal study revealed that children whose mothers had higher academic expectations for them in the first grade were more likely to reach a higher level of educational attainment in emerging adulthood (age 23) than children whose mothers had lower expectations for them in the first grade (Englund, Luckner, & Whaley, 2003).

self-efficacy The belief that one can master a situation and produce positive outcomes.

Too often parents attempt to protect children's and adolescents' self-esteem by setting low standards (Graham, 2005; Stipek, 2005). In reality, it is more beneficial

connecting with careers

Jaime Escalante, Secondary School Math Teacher

Jaime Escalante in a classroom teaching math.

An immigrant from Bolivia, Jaime Escalante became a math teacher at Garfield High School in East Los Angeles in the 1970s. When he began teaching at Garfield, many of the students had little confidence in their math abilities, and most of the teachers had low expectations for the students' success. Escalante took it as a special challenge to improve the students' math skills and even get them to the point where they could perform well on the Educational Testing Service Advanced Placement (AP) calculus exam.

The first year was difficult. Escalante's calculus class began at 8 a.m. He told the students the doors would be open at 7 a.m. and that instruction would begin at 7:30 a.m. He also worked with them after school and on weekends. He put together lots of handouts, told the students to take extensive notes, and required them to keep a folder. He gave them a five-minute quiz each morning and a test every Friday. He started with fourteen students but within two weeks only half remained. Only five students lasted through the spring. One of the boys who quit said, "I don't want to come at seven o'clock. Why should I?"

Because of Escalante's persistent, challenging, and inspiring teaching, Garfield High—a school plagued by poor funding, violence, and inferior working conditions—became ranked seventh in the United States in calculus. Escalante's commitment and motivation were transferred to his students, many of whom no one believed in before Escalante came along. Escalante's contributions were portrayed in the film *Stand and Deliver.* Escalante, his students, and celebrity guests also introduce basic math concepts for sixth- to twelfth-grade students on the *Futures with Jaime Escalante* PBS series. Now retired from teaching, Escalante continues to work in a consulting role to help improve students' motivation to do well in math and improve their math skills. Escalante's story is testimony to how *one* teacher can make a major difference in students' motivation and achievement.

For more information about the work of secondary school teachers, see page 46 in the Careers in Adolescent Development appendix.

to set standards that challenge children and adolescents and to expect performance at the highest levels they are capable of achieving. Those who are not challenged may develop low standards for themselves, and the fragile self-confidence they develop from reaching these low expectations can be shattered the first time they encounter more challenging work and are held to higher standards.

Teachers' expectations also are important influences on children's achievement (Rubie-Davies, 2011). In an observational study of twelve classrooms, teachers with high expectations spent more time providing a framework for students' learning, asked higher-level questions, and were more effective in managing students' behavior than did teachers with average and low expectations (Rubie-Davies, 2007).

To read about the work of one individual who had high expectations for his students, see the *Connecting with Careers* profile.

Goal Setting, Planning, and Self-Monitoring Self-efficacy and achievement improve when individuals set goals that are specific, proximal, and challenging (Anderman & Anderman, 2010; Schunk, 2011). A nonspecific, fuzzy goal is "I want to be successful." A more concrete, specific goal is "I want to make the honor roll by the end of the semester."

Students can set both long-term (distal) and short-term (proximal) goals. It is okay for individuals to set some long-term goals, such as "I want to graduate from high school" or "I want to go to college," but they also need to create short-term goals, which are steps along the way. "Getting an A on the next math test" is an example of a short-term, proximal goal. So is "Doing all of my homework by 4 p.m. Sunday."

Another good strategy is to set challenging goals (Anderman & Anderman, 2010). A challenging goal is a commitment to self-improvement. Strong interest and involvement in activities are sparked by challenges. Goals that are easy to reach generate little interest or effort. However, goals should be optimally matched to the individual's skill level. If goals are unrealistically high, the result will be repeated failures that lower the individual's self-efficacy.

Yet another good strategy is to develop personal goals about desired and undesired future circumstances (Ford & Smith, 2007; Wigfield & Cambria, 2010). Personal goals can be a key aspect of an individual's motivation for coping and dealing with life's challenges and opportunities (Maehr & Zusho, 2009).

It is not enough just to set goals. In order to achieve, it also is important to plan how to reach those goals (Winne, 2011). Being a good planner means managing time effectively, setting priorities, and being organized.

Individuals should not only plan their next week's activities but also monitor how well they are sticking to their plan. Once engaged in a task, they need to monitor their progress, judge how well they are doing on the task, and evaluate the outcomes to regulate what they do in the future (Wigfield, Klauda, & Cambria, 2011). High-achieving youth are often self-regulatory learners (Schunk, 2011). For example, high-achieving youth monitor their learning and systematically evaluate their progress toward a goal more than low-achieving students do. Encouraging youth to monitor their learning conveys the message that they are responsible for their own behavior and that learning requires their active, dedicated participation.

An adolescent working with his daily planner. *How are goals, planning, and self-regulation involved in adolescent achievement?*

developmental **connection**

Identity. William Damon (2008) concludes that too many of today's youth aren't moving toward any identity resolution. Chapter 4, p. 142

One type of self-regulation is *intentional self-regulation*, which involves selecting goals or outcomes, optimizing the means to achieve desired outcomes, and compensating for setbacks along the path to goal achievement (Gestsdottir & others, 2009). A recent study found that intentional self-regulation was especially beneficial to young adolescents from low-income backgrounds (Urban, Lewin-Bizan, & Lerner, 2010). In this study, these high self-regulating adolescents were more likely to seek out extracurricular activities, which resulted in more positive developmental outcomes such as academic achievement. Selecting goals or outcomes was assessed by items such as, "When I decide upon a goal, I stick to it"; optimizing the means to achieve desired outcomes was assessed by items such as, "I think exactly about how I can best realize my plans"; and compensating for setbacks was assessed by items such as, "When things don't work the way they used to, I look for other ways to achieve them."

Purpose In earlier chapters, we considered the view of William Damon (2008) that he proposed in his book *The Path to Purpose.* For example, in Chapter 4 we discussed the importance of purpose in identity development, and in Chapter 7 we saw that purpose is a key aspect of values. Here we expand on Damon's view and explore how purpose is a missing ingredient in many adolescents' and emerging adults' achievement.

For Damon, *purpose* is an intention to accomplish something meaningful to one's self and to contribute something to the world beyond the self. Finding purpose involves answering such questions as "*Why* am I doing this? *Why* does it matter? *Why* is it important for me and the world beyond me? *Why* do I strive to accomplish this end?" (Damon, 2008, pp. 33–34).

In interviews with 12- to 22-year-olds, Damon found that only about 20 percent had a clear vision of where they want to go in life, what they want to achieve, and why. The largest percentage—about 60 percent—had engaged in some potentially purposeful activities, such as service learning or fruitful discussions with a career counselor, but they still did not have

William Damon. In Damon's view, purpose is a missing ingredient in many adolescents' and emerging adults' achievement. *What are some strategies adults can adopt to guide adolescents and emerging adults to incorporate purpose into their paths to achievement?*

a real commitment or any reasonable plans for reaching their goals. Slightly more than 20 percent expressed no aspirations and in some instances said they didn't see any reason to have aspirations.

Damon concludes that most teachers and parents communicate the importance of such goals as studying hard and getting good grades, but rarely discuss what the goals might lead to—the purpose for studying hard and getting good grades. Damon emphasizes that too often students focus only on short-term goals and don't explore the big, long-term picture of what they want to do with their life. These interview questions that Damon (2008, p. 135) has used in his research are good springboards for getting students to reflect on their purpose:

> What's most important to you in your life?
> Why do you care about those things?
> Do you have any long-term goals?
> Why are these goals important to you?
> What does it mean to have a good life?
> What does it mean to be a good person?
> If you were looking back on your life now, how would you like to be remembered?

connecting with emerging adults

Hari Prabhakar, Student on a Path to Purpose

Hari Prabhakar's ambition is to become an international health expert. Prabhakar graduated from Johns Hopkins University in 2006 with a double major in public health and writing. A top student (3.9 GPA), he took the initiative to pursue a number of activities outside the classroom in the health field. As he made the transition from high school to college, Hari created the Tribal India Health Foundation (www.tihf.org), which provides assistance in bringing low-cost health care to rural areas in India. Juggling his roles as a student and as the foundation's director, Prabhakar spent about 15 hours a week leading Tribal India Health throughout his four undergraduate years.

Prabhakar also applied for, and received, $16,500 in research fellowships from different Johns Hopkins programs to advance his knowledge of public health care. He sought the expertise of health specialists on the Hopkins faculty to expand his understanding of international health care. Prabhakar also worked an average of six hours each week conducting research on sickle-cell disease, which is prevalent among tribes in rural areas of India. He spent three months every summer during college in India working directly with the tribal people. In describing his work, Prabhakar said (Johns Hopkins University, 2006a):

> I have found it very challenging to coordinate the international operation. . . . It takes a lot of work, and there's not a lot of free time. But it's worth it when I visit our patients and see how they and the community are getting better.

As a reward for his undergraduate accomplishments, in 2007, Prabhakar received a Marshall scholarship to study in Great Britain. He completed two master's degrees at Oxford University's Health Services Research Unit and the London School of Hygiene and Tropical Medicine. Prabhakar seeks to combine clinical training with health systems management to improve the medical care of people in impoverished circumstances around the world. In 2010, Prabhakar began further education by entering Harvard Medical School.

Hari Prabhakar (*in rear*) at a screening camp in India that he created as part of his Tribal India Health Foundation.

(*Sources:* Johns Hopkins University, 2006a,b; Lunday, 2006; Marshall Scholarships, 2007; Prabhakar, 2007).

What kinds of goals did Prabhakar likely set for himself that strengthened his extraordinary sense of purpose?

SOCIAL RELATIONSHIPS AND CONTEXTS

What are some ways that peer relations can influence an adolescent's achievement?

Adolescents' relationships with parents, peers, teachers, and mentors are important aspects of their achievement. And socioeconomic status, ethnicity, and culture are social contexts that influence adolescents' achievement.

Parents Earlier we discovered that parents' expectations have an important influence on adolescents' achievement. A recent study revealed that adolescents with high self-efficacy parents reported more competence in learning activities, fewer problems, and more daily opportunities for optimal experiences (Steca & others, 2011). Here are some additional positive parenting practices that result in improved achievement in adolescents (Wigfield & others, 2006):

- Knowing enough about the adolescent to provide the right amount of challenge and the right amount of support
- Providing a positive emotional climate, which motivates adolescents to internalize their parents' values and goals
- Modeling motivated achievement behavior: working hard and persisting with effort at challenging tasks

Peers Peers can affect adolescents' achievement through social goals, social comparison, and peer status (Wentzel, 2009). In considering adolescents' achievement, it is important to consider not only academic goals but social goals as well. One study revealed that young adolescents motivated to engage in social dominance over their peers had a low achievement level (Kiefer & Ryan, 2008). Popularity goals were not linked to adolescents' achievement.

Adolescents often compare themselves with their peers on where they stand academically and socially. Adolescents are more likely than younger children to engage in social comparison, although adolescents are prone to deny that they ever compare themselves with others (Harter, 2006). For example, in social comparison, one adolescent might learn that another adolescent did not do well on a test in school and think, "I'm smarter than he is." Positive social comparisons usually result in higher self-esteem; negative comparisons in lower self-esteem. Adolescents are most likely to compare themselves with others who are most similar to them in age, ability, and interests.

Adolescents who are more accepted by their peers and who have good social skills often do better in school and have positive academic achievement motivation (Rubin, Bukowski, & Parker, 2006). In contrast, rejected adolescents, especially those who are highly aggressive, are at risk for a number of achievement problems, including getting low grades and dropping out of school (Dodge, Coie, & Lynam, 2006). A recent study revealed that having aggressive-disruptive friends in adolescence was linked to a lower likelihood of graduating from high school (Veronneau & others, 2008).

developmental **connection**

Peers. Adolescents with friends who are academically oriented have higher grades in school. Chapter 9, p. 305

Teachers Earlier we saw how important teachers' expectations for success are in adolescents' achievement. Here we further explore the key role that teachers play in adolescents' achievement. When researchers have observed classrooms, they have found that effective, engaging teachers provide support for them to make good progress, but they also encourage adolescents to become self-regulated achievers (Perry & Rahim, 2011). The encouragement takes place in a very positive environment, one in which adolescents are regularly being guided to become motivated to try hard and develop self-efficacy.

Nel Noddings (1992, 2001, 2006) stresses that students are most likely to develop into competent human beings when they feel cared for. This caring requires teachers to get to know students fairly well. She says that this is difficult in large schools with large numbers of adolescents in each class. She recommends that teachers remain with the same students for two to three years (voluntarily on the part of the teacher and the pupil) so that teachers would be better positioned to attend to the interests and capacities of each student. Recall from Chapter 10 that the same proposal is being examined in schools with high-risk adolescents, an effort that is being funded by the Bill and Melinda Gates Foundation (2008).

Mentors **Mentors** are usually older and more experienced individuals who are motivated to improve the competence and character of a younger person. Mentoring can involve demonstration, instruction, challenge, and encouragement over an extended period of time. As a positive mentoring experience proceeds, the mentor and the youth being mentored develop a bond of commitment, and the youth develops a sense of respect and identification with the mentor (Hamilton & Hamilton, 2006, 2009).

Mentoring may take place naturally or through a mentoring program (Hamilton & Hamilton, 2006). Natural mentoring doesn't involve any formal program but rather emerges out of an individual's existing relationships. Natural mentors might be family, friends, relatives, neighbors, coaches, extracurricular activity instructors, clergy, youth group leaders, bosses, or teachers. Mentoring programs, which are more formal arrangements than natural mentoring, involve matching an adult mentor with a young person. In many mentoring programs, a mentor assumes a quasi-parental role. A good mentor can help youth develop the sense of purpose William Damon (2008) describes as so critical for today's youth in their quest for achievement and success.

An effective mentoring program has been created at the St. Luke's Methodist Church in Dallas to address the special concern of a lack of ethnic minority role models for ethnic minority students. The program has signed up more than 200 men and 100 boys (ages 4 to 18). The mentoring program involves academic tutoring as well as trips to such activities as sporting and cultural events. The mentors also recently took the children and adolescents to the Johnson Space Center in Houston. Shown here is Dr. Leonard Berry, a mentor in the program, with Brandon Scarborough (age 13) in front, and his own son, Leonard (age 12). Brandon not only has benefited from Dr. Berry's mentoring but has become friends with his son.

Mentoring programs are increasingly being advocated as a strategy for improving the achievement of secondary school and college students who are at risk for failure (Herrera & others, 2011; Lindley, 2009; Rowley, 2009). One of the largest mentoring programs is Big Brothers Big Sisters (BBBS), which pairs caring, volunteer mentors with at-risk youth (Rhodes & DuBois, 2008). In a large-scale study of BBBS's recently developed school-based mentoring program, significant improvements occurred in the at-risk students' academic achievement, school conduct, attendance, and perceived academic self-efficacy (Herrera & others, 2007). Of course, some mentoring relationships are more effective than others, and the matching of an adolescent with a mentor requires careful selection and monitoring (Rhodes & Lowe, 2009).

College students can play important roles as mentors for at-risk children and adolescents. One study indicated that mentoring at-risk fourth-grade students improved their understanding of children and the value of mentoring and community work (Schmidt, Marks, & Derrico, 2004).

Sociocultural Contexts How extensively do ethnicity and socioeconomic status affect adolescents' achievement? How does culture influence adolescents' achievement?

Ethnicity and Socioeconomic Status The diversity that exists among ethnic minority adolescents is evident in their achievement (Cooper, 2011; Graham, 2011; Rowley, Kurtz-Costes, & Cooper, 2010). For example, many Asian American students have a strong academic achievement orientation, but some do not.

In addition to recognizing the diversity that exists within every cultural group in terms of adolescents' achievement, it also is important to distinguish between difference and deficiency. Too often the achievement of ethnic minority students—especially African American, Latino, and Native American students—has been interpreted as *deficits* by middle-socioeconomic-status non-Latino White standards, when they simply are *culturally different and distinct*.

At the same time, many investigations overlook the socioeconomic status (SES) of ethnic minority students (Graham & Taylor, 2001). Many studies have found that socioeconomic status predicts achievement better than does ethnicity. Regardless of their ethnic background, students from middle- and upper-income families fare better than their counterparts from low-income backgrounds in a host of achievement

developmental **connection**

Diversity. Ethnicity refers to characteristics rooted in cultural heritage, including nationality, race, religion, and language. Chapter 12, p. 404

mentors Individuals who are usually older and more experienced and are motivated to improve the competence and character of a younger person.

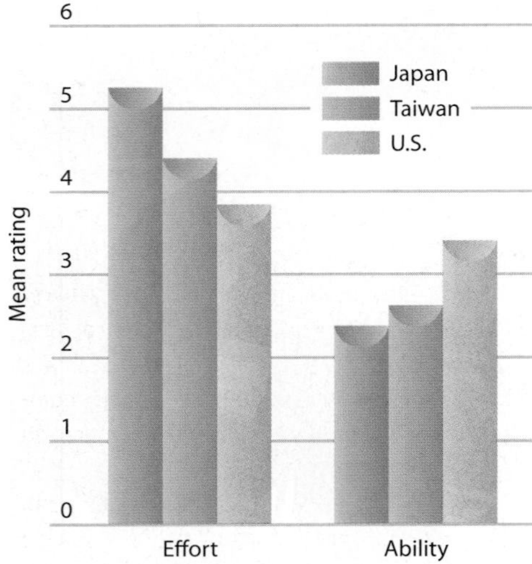

FIGURE **11.4**

MOTHERS' BELIEFS ABOUT THE FACTORS RESPONSIBLE FOR CHILDREN'S MATH ACHIEVEMENT IN THREE COUNTRIES. In one study, mothers in Japan and Taiwan were more likely to believe that their children's math achievement was due to effort rather than innate ability, whereas U.S. mothers were more likely to believe their children's math achievement was due to innate ability (Stevenson, Lee, & Stigler, 1986). If parents believe that their children's math achievement is due to innate ability and their children are not doing well in math, the implication is that they are less likely to think their children will benefit from putting forth more effort.

- Substituting a worthy but lower-priority activity. For example, you might clean your room instead of studying for a test.
- Believing that repeated minor delays won't hurt you.
- Dramatizing a commitment to a task rather than doing it. For example, you might take your books along for a weekend trip but never open them.
- Persevering on only part of the task. For example, you might write and rewrite the first paragraph of a paper but never get to the body of it.

Can you become better at reducing or eliminating procrastination? For some proven strategies, see the *Connecting with Health and Well-Being* interlude.

Anxiety **Anxiety** is a vague, highly unpleasant feeling of fear and apprehension. It is normal for students to be concerned or worried when they face school challenges, such as doing well on a test. Indeed, researchers have found that many successful students have moderate levels of anxiety (Bandura, 1997). However, some students have high levels of anxiety and worry constantly, characteristics that can significantly impair their ability to achieve (Parritz & Troy, 2011).

Some adolescents' high anxiety levels are the result of parents' unrealistic achievement expectations and pressure. For many individuals, anxiety increases across the school years as they "face more frequent evaluation, social comparison, and (for some) experiences of failure" (Eccles, Wigfield, & Schiefele, 1998, p. 1043). When schools create such circumstances, they likely increase students' anxiety.

A number of intervention programs have been created to reduce high anxiety levels (Miltenberger, 2012; Wigfield & Eccles, 1989). Some intervention programs emphasize relaxation techniques. These programs often are effective at reducing anxiety but do not always lead to improved achievement. Anxiety intervention programs linked to worrying emphasize modifying the negative, self-damaging thoughts of anxious students by getting them to engage in more positive, task-focused thoughts (Meichenbaum & Butler, 1980; Watson & Tharp, 2007). These programs have been more effective than the relaxation programs in improving students' achievement.

Protecting Self-Worth by Avoiding Failure Some individuals are so interested in protecting their self-worth and avoiding failure that they become distracted from pursuing goals and engage in ineffective strategies.

These strategies include the following (Covington, 2002; Covington & Teel, 1996):

- *Nonperformance.* The most obvious strategy for avoiding failure is not to try at all. In the classroom, nonperformance tactics include appearing eager to answer a teacher's question but hoping the teacher will call on another student, sliding down in the seat to avoid being seen by the teacher, and avoiding eye contact. These can seem like minor deceptions, but they might portend other, more chronic forms of noninvolvement such as excessive absences or dropping out.
- *Procrastination.* Individuals who postpone studying for a test until the last minute can blame failure on poor time management, thus deflecting attention away from the possibility that they are incompetent (Steel, 2007).
- *Setting unreachable goals.* By setting goals so high that success is virtually impossible, individuals can avoid the implication that they are incompetent, because virtually anyone would fail to reach this goal.

developmental **connection**

Self-Esteem. A number of strategies can be implemented to improve students' self-esteem, also referred to as self-worth or self-image. Chapter 4, p. 139

anxiety A vague, highly unpleasant feeling of fear and apprehension.

self-handicapping Use of failure avoidance strategies such as not trying in school or putting off studying until the last minute so that circumstances, rather than a lack of ability, will be seen as the cause of low-level performance.

Efforts to avoid failure often involve **self-handicapping** strategies (Urdan & Midgley, 2001). That is, some individuals deliberately handicap themselves by not making an effort, by putting off a project until the last minute, by fooling around the night before a test, and so on, so that if their subsequent performance is at a low level, these circumstances, rather than lack of ability, will be seen as the cause. Efforts to avoid failure often involve *self-handicapping strategies* (Leondari & Gonida, 2007). A recent study revealed that self-regulatory and in-depth learning strategies were negatively

connecting with health and well-being

Can You Tackle Procrastination?

Here are some good strategies for overcoming procrastination:

- *Acknowledge that procrastination is a problem.* Too often, procrastinators don't face up to their problem. When you admit that you are procrastinating, you can sometimes begin thinking about how to solve the problem.
- *Identify your values and goals.* Think about how procrastination can undermine your values and goals.
- *Work on your time management.* Make yearly (or term), monthly, weekly, and daily plans. Then monitor how you are using your time to find out ways to use it more wisely.
- *Divide the task into smaller parts.* Sometimes you might procrastinate because you view the task as so large and overwhelming that you will never be able to finish it. When this is the case, divide the task into smaller units and set subgoals for completing one unit at a time. This strategy can often make what seems to be a completely unmanageable task manageable.
- *Use behavioral strategies.* Identify the diversions that might be keeping you from focusing on the most important tasks and activities. Note when and where you engage in these diversions. Plan how to diminish and control their use. Another behavioral strategy is to make a contract with yourself or someone you see regularly related to your procrastination problem. And yet another behavioral strategy is to build in a reward for yourself, which gives you an incentive to complete all or part of the task. For example, if you complete all your math problems, treat yourself to a movie when you finish them.
- *Use cognitive strategies.* Watch for mental self-seductions that can lead to behavioral diversions, such as "I'll do it tomorrow," "What's the problem with watching an hour or so of TV now?" and "I can't do it." Dispute mental diversions (Watson & Tharp, 2007). For example, tell yourself, "I really don't have much time left and other things are sure to come up later," "If I get this done, I'll be able to better enjoy my time," or "Maybe if I just go ahead and get going on this, it won't be so bad."

Do you think these strategies are more effective in creating intrinsic or extrinsic motivation, or both? Which strategies are likely to be most effective in enabling you to overcome procrastination?

linked to students' use of self-handicapping and that surface-learning and test anxiety were positively linked to their use of self-handicapping (Thomas & Gadbois, 2007).

Here are some strategies to reduce preoccupation with protecting self-worth and avoiding failure (Covington, 2002):

- Set challenging but realistic goals.
- Strengthen the link between your effort and self-worth. Take pride in your effort and minimize social comparison.
- Have positive beliefs about your abilities.

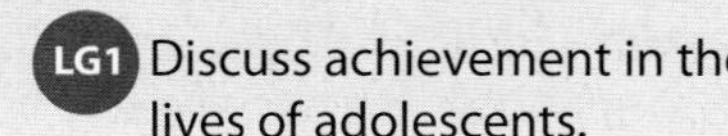

Review *Connect* Reflect

LG1 Discuss achievement in the lives of adolescents.

Review

- Why is achievement so important in adolescence?
- What are some important achievement motivation processes?
- What are some key social relationships and contexts that influence adolescents' achievement?
- What are some motivational obstacles to achievement and ways to deal with them?

Connect

- Which aspects of achievement might benefit young adolescents as they make the difficult transition through the first year of middle or junior high school (Chapter 10)?

Reflect *Your Own Personal Journey of Life*

- Would you consider yourself highly motivated to achieve? Or do you have trouble becoming motivated to achieve? Explain.

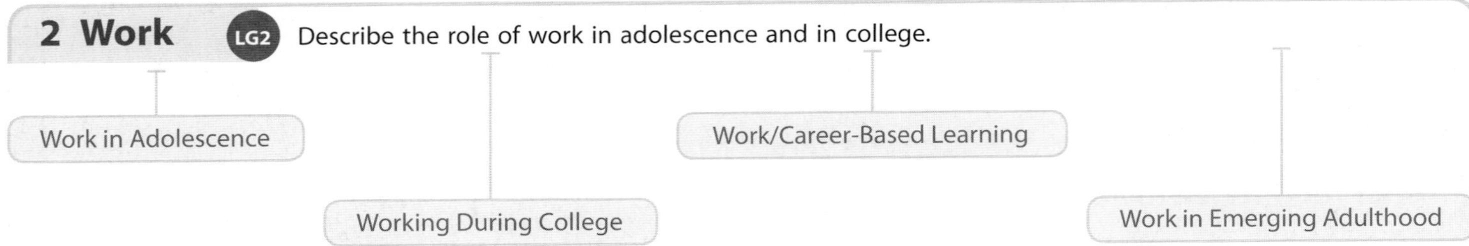

Achievement and motivation show up not only in school but also in work. One of the greatest changes in adolescents' lives in recent years has been the increased likelihood that they will work in some part-time capacity and still attend school on a regular basis. Our discussion of work focuses on various aspects of work during adolescence and college, work/career-based learning, and work in emerging adulthood.

WORK IN ADOLESCENCE

What is the sociohistorical context of work in adolescents' lives? What characterizes part-time work in adolescence? What are the work profiles of adolescents around the world?

Sociohistorical Context of Work During Adolescence Even though education keeps many of today's youth from holding full-time jobs, it has not prevented them from working part-time while going to school (Staff, Messersmith, & Schulenberg, 2009). In 1940, only 1 of 25 tenth-grade males attended school and simultaneously worked part-time. In the 1970s, the number had increased to 1 in 4. Today, it is estimated that 80 to 90 percent of adolescents are employed at some point during high school (Staff, Messersmith, & Schulenberg, 2009). As shown in Figure 11.5, as adolescents go from the eighth to the twelfth grade, their likelihood of working and the average number of hours they work during the school year increases (Staff, Messersmith, & Schulenberg, 2009). As shown in Figure 11.5, in the eighth and tenth grades, the majority of students don't work in paid employment during the school year, but in the twelfth grade only one-fourth don't engage in paid employment during the school year. Almost 10 percent of employed twelfth-graders work more than 30 hours each week during the school year.

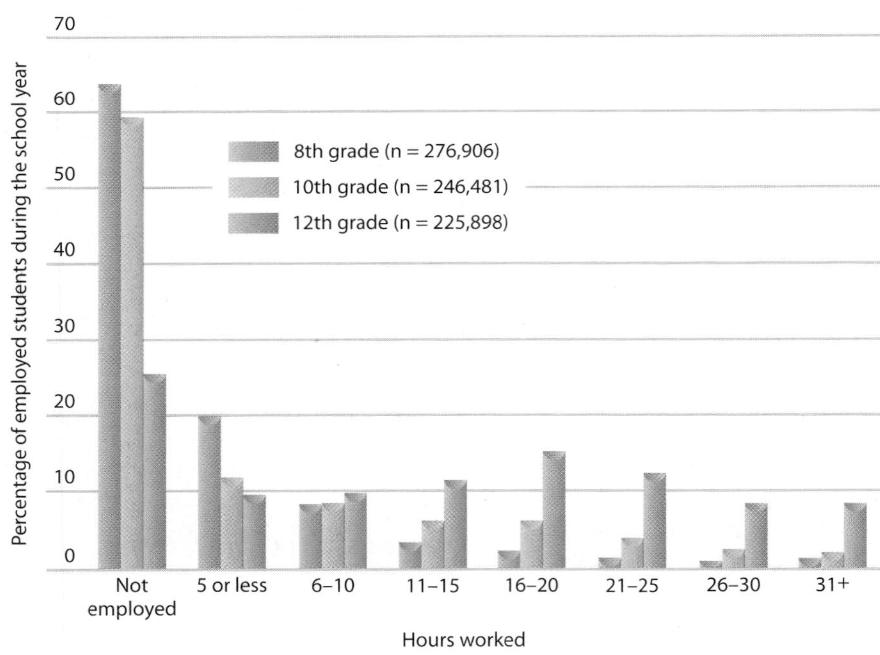

FIGURE **11.5**

ADOLESCENT EMPLOYMENT. Percentage of employed students and number of hours worked during the school year by eighth, tenth, and twelfth grade (combined data for 1991 to 2006 Monitoring the Future, Institute of Social Research, cohorts).

Part-Time Work in Adolescence What kinds of jobs are U.S. adolescents working at today? About 21 percent of U.S. twelfth-graders who work do so in restaurants, such as McDonald's and Burger King, waiting on customers and cleaning up (Staff, Messersmith, & Schulenberg, 2009). Other adolescents work in retail stores as cashiers or salespeople (23 percent), in offices as clerical assistants (7 percent), or as unskilled laborers (about 10 percent).

Overall, the weight of the evidence suggests that spending large amounts of time in paid labor has limited developmental benefits for youth, and for some it is associated with risky behavior and costs to physical health (Larson, Wilson, & Rickman, 2009). For example, one research study found that it was not just working that affected adolescents' grades—more important was how long they worked (Greenberger & Steinberg, 1986). Tenth-graders who worked more than 14 hours a week suffered a drop in grades. Eleventh-graders worked up to 20 hours a week before their grades dropped. When adolescents spend more than 20 hours per week working, there is little time to study for tests and to complete homework assignments. In addition, working adolescents felt less involved in school, were absent more, and said that they did not enjoy school as much as their non-working counterparts did. Adolescents who worked also spent less time with their families—but just as much time with their peers—as their nonworking counterparts. Adolescents who worked long hours also were more frequent users of alcohol and marijuana.

A recent re-analysis of the data in this study (Greenberger & Steinberg, 1986) included a better matched control group of students who did not work. Even with the more careful matching of groups, adolescents in the tenth and eleventh grades who worked more than 20 hours a week were less engaged in school and showed increases in substance abuse and delinquency (Monahan, Lee, & Steinberg, 2011). For adolescents who cut back their part-time work hours to 20 hours a week or less, negative outcomes disappeared.

Some youth, though, are engaged in challenging work activities, are provided constructive supervision by adults, and experience favorable work conditions (Staff, Messersmith, & Schulenberg, 2009). For example, work may benefit adolescents in low-income, urban contexts by providing them with economic benefits and adult monitoring. This may increase school engagement and decrease delinquency.

What are some advantages and disadvantages of part-time work during adolescence?

Work Profiles of Adolescents Around the World So far, our exploration of work during adolescence has primarily focused on U.S. adolescents. How does work in adolescence vary in different countries around the world?

In many developing countries, where it is common for adolescents not to attend school on a regular basis, boys often spend more time in income-generating labor than girls do, whereas girls spend more time in unpaid labor than boys (Larson & Verma, 1999; Larson, Wilson, & Rickman, 2009). Young adolescents work on average more than eight hours a day in many nonindustrial, unschooled populations. In the developed world, work averages less than one hour per day across childhood and adolescence except for U.S. adolescents. For example, U.S. adolescents are far more likely to participate in paid labor than European and East Asian adolescents. As we saw earlier, many U.S. high school students work 10 or even 20 hours or more per week. One study found that U.S. high school students spent an average of 50 minutes per day working at a job, whereas Northern European adolescents spent an average of only 15 minutes per day working at a job (Alsaker & Flammer, 1999). In this study, employment of adolescents was virtually nonexistent in France and Russia. In another study, 80 percent of Minneapolis eleventh-graders had part-time jobs compared with only 27 percent of Japanese eleventh-graders and 26 percent of Taiwanese eleventh-graders (Fuligni & Stevenson, 1995).

Overall, the weight of the evidence suggests that spending large amounts of time in paid labor has limited developmental benefits for youth, and for some it is associated with risk behavior and costs to physical health (Larson & Verma, 1999; Larson, Wilson, & Rickman, 2009). Some youth, though, are engaged in challenging work activities, are provided constructive supervision by adults, and experience favorable work conditions. However, in general, given the repetitive nature of most labor carried out by adolescents around the world, it is difficult to argue that working 15 to 25 hours per week in such labor provides developmental gains (Larson & Verma, 1999).

WORKING DURING COLLEGE

The percentage of full-time U.S. college students who were employed increased from 34 percent in 1970 to 47 percent in 2008 (down from a peak of 52 percent in 2000)

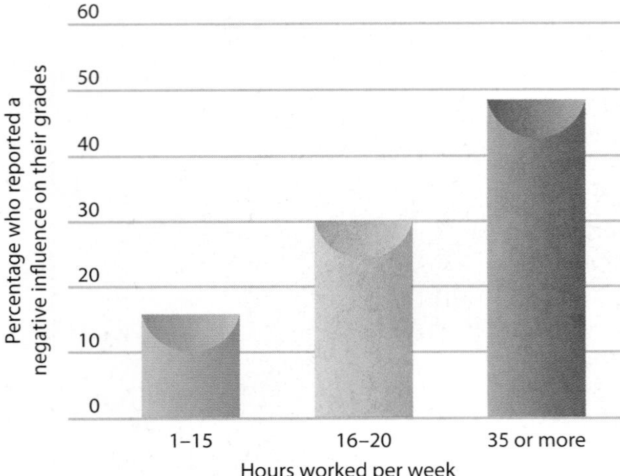

FIGURE **11.6**

THE RELATION OF HOURS WORKED PER WEEK IN COLLEGE TO GRADES. Among students working to pay for school expenses, 16 percent of those working 1 to 15 hours per week reported that working negatively influenced their grades (National Center for Education Statistics, 2002). Thirty percent of college students who worked 16 to 20 hours a week said the same, as did 48 percent who worked 35 hours or more per week.

(National Center for Education Statistics, 2010). In this recent survey, 81 percent of part-time U.S. college students were employed.

Working can pay or help offset some costs of schooling, but working can also restrict students' opportunities to learn and negatively influence grades. One national study found that as the number of hours worked per week increased for those who identified themselves primarily as students, their grades suffered and the number of classes, class choice, and library access became more limited (National Center for Education Statistics, 2002) (see Figure 11.6).

Other research has found that as the number of hours college students work increases the more likely they are to drop out of college (National Center for Education Statistics, 1998). Thus, college students need to carefully examine the number of hours they work and the extent the work is having a negative impact on their college success. Although borrowing to pay for education can leave students with considerable debt, working long hours reduces the amount of time students have for studying and can decrease the likelihood that these students will do well or even complete their college degree.

WORK/CAREER-BASED LEARNING

In our discussion of education in Chapter 10, we learned that a number of experts note that a better connection between school and work needs to be forged. One way to improve this connection is through work/career-based learning experiences—especially for those adolescents going directly from high school into the workforce.

High School Work/career-based learning increasingly has become part of the effort to help youth make the transition from school to employment. Each year, approximately 500,000 high school students participate in cooperative education or other arrangements where learning objectives are met through part-time employment in office occupations, retailing, and other vocational fields. Vocational classes also involve large numbers of adolescents in school-based enterprises, through which they build houses, run restaurants, repair cars, operate retail stores, staff child-care centers, and provide other services.

Some important changes have recently taken place in vocational education. Today's high school diploma provides access to fewer and fewer stable, high-paying jobs. Thus, more of the training for specific occupations is occurring in two-year colleges and postsecondary technical institutes.

In high schools, new forms of career-related education are creating options for many students, ranging from students with disabilities to students who are gifted. Among the new models are career academies, youth apprenticeships, and tech prep and career major programs. These models rely on work-related themes to focus the curriculum and prepare students for postsecondary education, including four-year colleges and universities.

College College students can participate in cooperative education programs, or part-time or summer work relevant to their field of study. This experience can be critical in helping students obtain the job they want when they graduate (Martinez, 2006). Many employers expect job candidates to have this type of experience. One survey found that almost 60 percent of employers said their entry-level college hires had co-op or internship experience (Collins, 1996).

More than 1,000 colleges offer co-op (cooperative education) programs. A co-op is a paid apprenticeship in a career that a college student is interested in pursuing. Many college students are not allowed to participate in co-op programs until their junior year.

developmental **connection**

Identity. Emerging adulthood is characterized by identity exploration, especially in work and love, and by instability, in work, love, and education. Chapter 1, p. 19

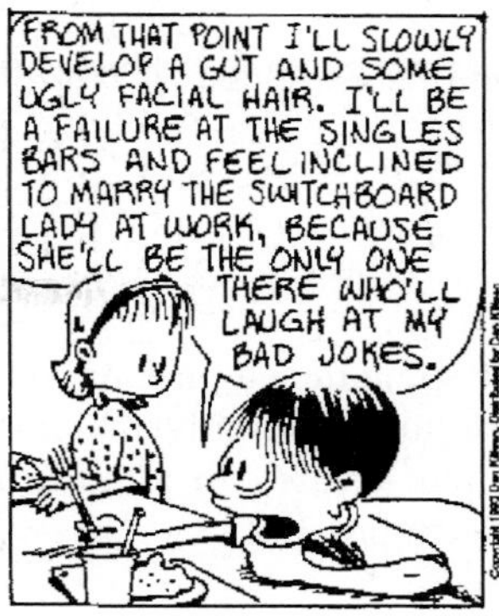

Source: Copyright by Dan Killeen. Used by permission

WORK IN EMERGING ADULTHOOD

The work patterns of emerging adults have changed over the course of the last 100 years (Hamilton & Hamilton, 2006). As an increasing number of emerging adults have participated in higher education, many leave home and begin their career work at later ages. Changing economic conditions have made the job market more competitive for emerging adults and increased the demand for more skilled workers (Gauthier & Furstenberg, 2005).

A diversity of school and work patterns characterize emerging adults (Fouad & Bynner, 2008). Some emerging adults are going to college full-time, others are working full-time. Some emerging adults work full-time immediately after high school, others after they graduate from college. Many emerging adults who attend college drop out and enter the workforce before they complete their degree; some of these individuals return to college later. Some emerging adults are attending two-year colleges, others four-year colleges; some are working part-time while going to college, others are not.

These emerging adults are college graduates who started their own business. Emerging adults follow a diversity of work and educational pathways. *What are some of these variations in education and work that characterize emerging adults?*

Review *Connect* Reflect

 Describe the role of work in adolescence and in college.

Review

- What is the sociohistorical context of adolescent work? What are the advantages and disadvantages of part-time work in secondary school and college? What is the profile of adolescent work around the world?
- How does work during college influence students' academic success?
- What are some aspects of work/career-based learning?
- What characterizes work in emerging adulthood?

Connect

- How does this section's discussion of the recent sociohistorical context of adolescent work compare with the historical nature of adolescent work described in Chapter 1?

Reflect *Your Own Personal Journey of Life*

- Did you work during high school? What were some of the pluses and minuses of the experience if you did work? Are you working part-time or full time now while you are going to college? If so, what effect does the work experience have on your academic success?

3 Career Development

LG3 Characterize career development in adolescence.

Developmental Changes | Cognitive Factors | Identity Development | Social Contexts

What are some developmental changes that characterize adolescents' career choices? What are some cognitive factors that affect career development? How is career development related to identity development? How do sociocultural factors affect career development?

DEVELOPMENTAL CHANGES

"Your son has made a career choice, Mildred. He's going to win the lottery and travel a lot."
© 2009. Reprinted courtesy of Bunny Hoest and *Parade* Magazine.

Many children have idealistic fantasies about what they want to be when they grow up. For example, many young children want to be superheroes, sports stars, or movie stars. In the high school years, they often have begun to think about careers on a somewhat less idealistic basis. In their late teens and early twenties, their career decision making has usually turned more serious as they explore different career possibilities and zero in on the career they want to enter. In college, this path often means choosing a major or specialization that is designed to lead to work in a specific field. By their early and mid-twenties, many individuals have completed their education or training and started to enter a full-time occupation. From the mid-twenties through the remainder of early adulthood, individuals often seek to establish their emerging career in a certain field. They may work hard to move up the career ladder and improve their financial standing.

William Damon (2008) maintains that it is not only children who have idealistic fantasies about careers but that too many of today's adolescents also dream about fantasy careers that may have no connection to reality. Too often the adolescents have no idea about what it takes to become such a career star, and usually there is no one in their lives who can help them to reach this career pinnacle. Consider adolescents playing basketball who dream of becoming the next Kobe Bryant and adolescents participating in theater who want to become the next Angelina Jolie, for example.

COGNITIVE FACTORS

Exploration, decision making, and planning play important roles in adolescents' career choices (Hirschi, Niles, & Akos, 2011). In countries where equal employment opportunities have emerged—such as the United States, Canada, Great Britain, and France—exploration of various career paths is critical in adolescents' career development. Adolescents often approach career exploration and decision making with considerable ambiguity, uncertainty, and stress. Many of the career decisions made by youth involve floundering and unplanned changes. Many adolescents do not adequately explore careers on their own and also receive little direction from guidance counselors at their schools. On the average, high school students spend less than three hours per year with guidance counselors, and in some schools the average is even less. In many schools, students not only do not know what information to seek about careers, they do not know how to seek it.

developmental **connection**

Cognitive Development. Adolescence is a time of increased decision making, and decision making appears to improve through the early adulthood years. Chapter 3, p. 106

William Damon (2008) described in *The Path to Purpose* how most high school students aren't lacking in ambition when it comes to careers but rather don't have anywhere near an adequate plan for how to reach their career goals. Too many youth drift and aimlessly go through their high school years, Damon says, behavior placing them at risk for not fulfilling their potential and not finding a life pursuit that energizes them.

In a large-scale longitudinal investigation, Mihaly Csikszentmihalyi and Barbara Schneider (2000) studied how U.S. adolescents develop attitudes and acquire skills to achieve their career goals and expectations. They assessed the progress of more than 1,000 students from 13 school districts across the United States. Students recorded at random moments their thoughts and feelings about what they did, and they filled out questionnaires regarding school, family, peers, and career aspirations. The researchers also interviewed the adolescents, as well as their friends, parents, and teachers. Among the findings of the study:

- Girls anticipated the same lifestyles as boys in terms of education and income.
- Lower-income minority students were more positive about school than more affluent students were.
- Students who got the most out of school—and had the highest future expectations—were those who perceived school to be more playlike than worklike.
- Clear vocational goals and good work experiences did not guarantee a smooth transition to adult work. Engaging activities—with intensive involvement regardless of content—were essential to building the optimism and resilience that are important for achieving a satisfying work life. This finding fits with Csikszentmihalyi's concept of flow, which we explored earlier in the chapter.

In another study, adolescents were more ambitious in the 1990s than adolescents in other studies conducted in the 1970s and 1980s (Schneider & Stevenson, 1999). The rising ambitions of adolescents were not confined to those from non-Latino White middle-income families but also characterized adolescents from low-income and ethnic minority families.

Today, more than 90 percent of high school seniors expect to attend college, and more than 70 percent anticipate working in professional jobs. Four decades ago, the picture was substantially different, with only 55 percent expecting to go to college and 42 percent anticipating working in professional jobs. In the study on adolescent ambitions in the 1990s, parents shared their adolescents' ambitious visions (Schneider & Stevenson, 1999). However, both adolescents and their parents often failed to make meaningful connections between educational credentials and future work opportunities. Parents can improve this relationship by becoming more knowledgeable about which courses their adolescents are taking in school, developing a better understanding of the college admissions process, providing adolescents with better information about various careers, and realistically evaluating their adolescents' abilities and interests in relation to these careers.

During college, students can benefit from the advice of college counselors, not only about careers but about many other aspects of life (Murphy & others, 2010). To read about the work of one college counselor, see the *Connecting with Careers* profile.

IDENTITY DEVELOPMENT

Career development is related to the adolescent's and emerging adult's identity development (Murrell, 2009). Career decidedness and planning are positively related to identity achievement, whereas career planning and decidedness are negatively related to identity moratorium and identity diffusion statuses (Wallace-Broscious, Serafica, & Osipow, 1994). Recall from Chapter 4 that identity moratorium describes individuals who have not yet made an identity commitment but are in the midst of exploring options, whereas identity diffusion identifies individuals who have neither made a commitment nor experienced a crisis (exploration of alternatives). Adolescents further along in the process of identity formation are better able to articulate their occupational choices and their next steps in obtaining short-term and long-term goals. By contrast, adolescents in the moratorium and diffusion statuses of identity are more likely to struggle with making occupational plans and decisions.

developmental **connection**

Identity. There is an increasing consensus that many of the key changes in identity development occur in emerging adulthood. Chapter 4, p. 145

One study focused on vocational identity development in relation to other identity domains (Skorikov & Vondracek, 1998). A cross-sectional study of 1,099 high school students in grades 7 through 12 revealed a developmental progression in adolescent vocational identity that was characterized by an increase in the proportion of students classified as diffused and foreclosed. (Recall from Chapter 4 that an

connecting with adolescents

Armando Ronquillo, High School Counselor/ College Adviser

Armando Ronquillo, counseling a Latina high school student about college.

Armando Ronquillo is a high school counselor and college adviser at Pueblo High School, which is in a low-socioeconomic-status area in Tucson, Arizona. More than 85 percent of the students have a Latino background. Armando was named top high school counselor in the state of Arizona for the year 2000. He has especially helped to increase the number of Pueblo High School students who go to college.

Ronquillo has an undergraduate degree in elementary and special education, and a master's degree in counseling. He counsels the students on the merits of staying in school and on the lifelong opportunities provided by a college education. Ronquillo guides students in obtaining the academic preparation that will enable them to go to college, including how to apply for financial aid and scholarships. He also works with parents to help them understand that their child going to college is not only doable but also affordable.

Ronquillo works with students on setting goals and planning. He has students plan for the future in terms of one-year (short-term), five-year (midrange), and ten-plus-year (long-term) time periods. Ronquillo says he does this "to help students visualize how the educational plans and decisions they make today will affect them in the future." He also organizes a number of college campus visitations for students from Pueblo High School each year.

To read further about the work of school counselors, see page 47 in the Careers in Adolescent Development appendix.

their career choices to careers that are gender stereotyped (Matlin, 2012). The motivation for work is the same for both sexes. However, females and males make different choices because of their socialization experiences and the ways that social forces structure the opportunities available to them (Tracey, Robbins, & Hofsess, 2005). For example, many girls and women stop taking math courses in high school or college, which restricts their career options (Watt & Eccles, 2008; Watt, Eccles, & Durik, 2006).

As growing numbers of young women pursue careers, they are faced with questions involving career and family (Matlin, 2012). Should they delay marriage and childbearing and establish their career first? Or should they combine their career, marriage, and childbearing in their twenties? Some females in the last decade have embraced the domestic patterns of an earlier historical period. They have married, borne children, and committed themselves to full-time mothering. These stay-at-home mothers have worked outside the home only intermittently, if at all, and have subordinated the work role to the family role.

Increasingly though, many other females have veered from this path and developed committed, permanent ties to the workplace that resemble the pattern once reserved only for males (Sax & Bryant, 2006). When they have children, it has been after their careers are well established, and rather than leaving the workforce to raise children, they have made efforts to combine a career and motherhood. Although there have always been professional women who pursued work instead of marrying, today's women are more likely to try to "have it all."

Socioeconomic Status and Ethnicity Many adolescents who have grown up in low-income or poverty conditions often face challenging circumstances in seeking upward mobility. These adolescents may have a difficult time deferring adult roles and may not be able to fully explore career opportunities.

Ethnic minority youth, especially those who grow up in low-income families, also may face problems in adequately being able to pursue successful careers (Banerjee, Harrell, & Johnson, 2011). A recent study with 18- to 20-year-old urban Latinos revealed that family obligation was a central theme in the decisions they made about their life and career after high school (Sanchez & others, 2011). In this study, financial circumstances were linked to whether they worked and/or took college classes.

To intervene effectively in the career development of ethnic minority youth, counselors need to increase their knowledge of communication styles, values regarding the importance of the family, the impact of language fluency, and achievement expectations in various ethnic minority groups (Waller, 2006). Counselors need to be aware of and respect the cultural values of ethnic minority youth, but such values need to be discussed within the context of the realities of the educational and occupational world (Ulloa & Herrera, 2006).

In this chapter, we have explored many aspects of achievement, careers, and work. One topic we examined was the influence of culture and ethnicity on achievement. In Chapter 12 we focus entirely on culture and adolescent development.

Review *Connect* Reflect

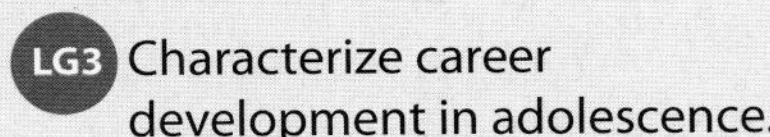

LG3 Characterize career development in adolescence.

Review

- What are some developmental changes that characterize adolescents' career choices?
- How are cognitive factors involved in adolescents' career development?
- How is identity development linked with career development in adolescence?
- What roles do social contexts play in adolescents' career development?

Connect

- Are there aspects of executive functioning (discussed in Chapter 3) that might be applied to understanding the cognitive factors involved in adolescents' career development?

Reflect *Your Own Personal Journey of Life*

- What are your career goals? Write down some of the specific work, job, and career goals that you have for the next 20, 10, and 5 years. Be as concrete and specific as possible. In creating your career goals, start from the farthest point—20 years from now—and work backward. If you start from a near point, you run the risk of adopting goals that are not precisely and clearly connected to your long-term career goals.

reach your **learning goals**

1 Achievement

LG1 Discuss achievement in the lives of adolescents.

The Importance of Achievement in Adolescence

- Social and academic pressures force adolescents to cope with achievement in new ways. Adolescents may perceive that their achievements are predictors of future, real-world outcomes in the adult world. Achievement expectations increase in secondary schools. Whether adolescents effectively adapt to these new pressures is determined in part by psychological, motivational, and contextual factors.

Achievement Processes

- Intrinsic motivation is based on internal factors such as self-determination, curiosity, challenge, and effort. Extrinsic motivation involves external incentives such as rewards and punishment. One view is that giving students some choice and providing opportunities for personal responsibility increase intrinsic motivation. It is important for teachers to create learning environments that encourage students to become cognitively engaged and develop a responsibility for their learning. Overall, the overwhelming conclusion is that it is a wise strategy to create learning environments that encourage students to become intrinsically motivated. However, in many real-world situations, both intrinsic and extrinsic motivation are involved, and too often intrinsic and extrinsic motivation have been pitted against each other as polar opposites. Attribution theory states that individuals are motivated to discover the underlying causes of behavior in an effort to make sense of the behavior. In attribution, calling on internal factors, such as effort, to explain performance is emphasized over calling on external factors, such as luck and blaming others. A mastery orientation is preferred over a helpless or a performance orientation in achievement situations. Mindset is the cognitive view, either fixed or growth, that individuals develop for themselves. Dweck argues that a key aspect of adolescents' development is to guide them in developing a growth mindset. Self-efficacy is the belief that one can master a situation and attain positive outcomes. Self-efficacy has been shown to be an important process in achievement. Goal setting, planning, and self-monitoring are important aspects of achievement. Students' expectations for success and the value they place on what they want to achieve influence their motivation. The combination of expectancy and value has been the focus of a number of efforts to understand students' achievement motivation. Adolescents benefit when their parents, teachers, and other adults have high expectations for their achievement. Recently, Damon has proposed that purpose is an especially important aspect of achievement that has been missing from many adolescents' lives.

Social Relationships and Contexts

- Social relationships and contexts play important roles in adolescents' achievement. In terms of social relationships, parents, peers, teachers, and mentors can be key aspects of adolescents' achievement. In terms of social contexts, ethnicity, socioeconomic status, and culture influence adolescents' achievement

Some Motivational Obstacles to Achievement

- Some motivational obstacles to achievement include procrastinating, being overwhelmed by anxiety, and protecting self-worth by avoiding failure. A special concern is adolescents having too much anxiety in achievement situations, which sometimes is linked to unrealistic parental expectations. The effort to avoid failure may involve self-handicapping strategies, such as deliberately not trying in school or putting off studying until the last minute. Ways to deal with motivational obstacles include identifying values and goals, using better time management, and dividing an overwhelming task into smaller parts.

2 Work

LG2 Describe the role of work in adolescence and in college.

Work in Adolescence

- Adolescents are not as likely to hold full-time jobs today as their counterparts from the nineteenth century were. The number of adolescents who work part-time, though, has increased dramatically. Advantages of part-time work in adolescence include learning how the business world works, how to get and keep a job, how to manage money, how to budget time, how to take pride in accomplishments, and how to evaluate goals. Disadvantages include giving up extracurricular activities at school, social affairs with peers, and sometimes sleep; as well as balancing the demands of school, family, peers, and work. Profiles of adolescent work vary around the world. In many developing countries, boys engage in considerably more paid labor than girls, who participate in more unpaid labor at home. U.S. adolescents engage in more work than their counterparts in many other developed countries. There appears to be little developmental advantage for most adolescents when they work 15 to 25 hours per week.

Working During College

- Working while going to college can help with schooling costs but can have a negative impact on students' grades and reduce the likelihood of graduation.

Work/Career-Based Learning

- Interest in work/career-based learning in high school is increasing. Many successful college students engage in cooperative learning or internship programs.

Work in Emerging Adulthood

- The work patterns of emerging adults have changed over the last 100 years, and a diversity of school and work patterns now characterize emerging adults. The nature of the transition from school to work is strongly influenced by the individual's education level. Many emerging adults change jobs, which can either involve searching or floundering.

3 Career Development

LG3 Characterize career development in adolescence.

Developmental Changes

- Many children have fantasies about what careers they want to enter when they grow up. In high school, these fantasies have lessened for many individuals, although still too many adolescents have a fantasy career they want to reach but don't have an adequate plan for how to reach their aspirations. In the late teens and early twenties, career decision making usually has turned more serious.

Cognitive Factors

- Exploration, decision making, and planning are important cognitive dimensions of career development in adolescence. Many adolescents have high aspirations but don't know how to reach these aspirations. Damon argues that adolescents and emerging adults need to incorporate thinking about purpose in their career decision making.

Identity Development

- Career development is linked to identity development in adolescence. Adolescents who are further along in the identity process are better able to articulate their career plans. In line with Erikson's theory, vocational identity plays a key role in overall identity development.

Social Contexts

- Among the most important social contexts that influence career development in adolescence are socioeconomic status, parents and peers, schools, gender, and ethnicity.

key terms

intrinsic motivation 364
extrinsic motivation 364
flow 365
attribution theory 366
mastery orientation 366
helpless orientation 366
performance orientation 366
mindset 367
self-efficacy 368
mentors 373
anxiety 376
self-handicapping 376

key people

Richard Ryan and Edward Deci 365
Mihaly Csikszentmihalyi 365
Carol Dweck 367
Albert Bandura 368
Dale Schunk 368
Jacquelynne Eccles 368
William Damon 370
Nel Noddings 372
Sandra Graham 374
Harold Stevenson 374

resources for improving the lives of adolescents

Handbook of Self-Regulation of Learning and Performance
Edited by Barry Zimmerman and Dale Schunk (2011)
New York: Routledge

A number of leading experts discuss many aspects of self-regulation, learning, and achievement processes.

Mindset
by Carol Dweck (2006)
New York: Random House

Extensive information and examples are provided about how adolescents can develop a growth mindset that will improve their achievement.

Mentoring in Adolescence
by Jean Rhodes and Sarah Lowe in R. M. Lerner and L. Steinberg (Eds.)
Handbook of Adolescent Psychology (2009, 3rd ed.)
New York: Wiley.

Leading experts describe research on mentoring and highlight the aspects of mentoring that are most successful in improving adolescents' achievement.

What Color Is Your Parachute?
by Richard Bolles (2012)
Berkeley, CA: Ten Speed Press

This is an extremely popular book on job hunting.

What Kids Need to Succeed
by Peter Benson, Judy Galbraith, and Pamela Espeland (2003)
Minneapolis: Search Institute

This easy-to-read book presents commonsense ideas for parents, educators, and youth workers that can help youth succeed.

self-assessment

The Student Online Learning Center includes the following self-assessments for further exploration:

- *Am I a Perfectionist?*
- *What Are My Academic and Personal Skills, Strengths, and Weaknesses?*
- *My Weekly Plan*
- *Evaluating My Career Interests*
- *Matching My Personality Type to Careers*
- *How Assertive Will I Be in Hunting for a Job?*

chapter 12 CULTURE

chapter **outline**

Culture, Adolescence, and Emerging Adulthoood

Learning Goal 1 Discuss the role of culture in the development of adolescents and emerging adults.

The Relevance of Culture for the Study of Adolescence and Emerging Adulthood

Cross-Cultural Comparisons

Rites of Passage

Socioeconomic Status and Poverty

Learning Goal 2 Describe how socioeconomic status and poverty are related to adolescent development.

What Is Socioeconomic Status?

Socioeconomic Variations in Families, Neighborhoods, and Schools

Poverty

Ethnicity

Learning Goal 3 Summarize how ethnicity is involved in the development of adolescents and emerging adults.

Immigration

Adolescence and Emerging Adulthood: A Special Juncture for Ethnic Minority Individuals

Ethnicity Issues

The Media and Technology

Learning Goal 4 Characterize the roles of the media and technology in adolescence and emerging adulthood.

Media Use

Television

The Media and Music

Technology, Computers, the Internet, and Cell Phones

Social Policy and the Media

A 16-year-old Japanese American girl (we will call her "Sonya") was upset over her family's reaction to her White American boyfriend. "Her parents refused to meet him and on several occasions threatened to disown her" (Sue & Morishima, 1982, p. 142). Her older brothers also reacted angrily to Sonya's dating a White American, warning that they were going to beat him up. Her parents also were disturbed that Sonya's grades, above average in middle school, were beginning to drop.

Generational issues contributed to the conflict between Sonya and her family (Nagata, 1989). Her parents had experienced strong sanctions against dating Whites when they were growing up and were legally prevented from marrying anyone but a Japanese. As Sonya's older brothers were growing up, they valued ethnic pride and solidarity. The brothers saw her dating a White as "selling out" her own ethnic group. Sonya's and her family members' cultural values obviously differ.

Michael, a 17-year-old Chinese American high school student, was referred to a therapist by the school counselor because he was depressed and had suicidal tendencies (Huang & Ying, 1989). Michael was failing several classes and frequently was absent from school. Michael's parents were successful professionals who expected Michael to excel in school and go on to become a doctor. They were disappointed and angered by Michael's school failures, especially because he was the firstborn son, who in Chinese families is expected to achieve the highest standards of all siblings.

The therapist encouraged the parents to put less academic pressure on Michael and to have more realistic expectations for Michael (who had no interest in becoming a doctor). Michael's school attendance improved and his parents noticed his improved attitude toward school. Michael's case illustrates how expectations that Asian American youth will be "whiz kids" can become destructive.

preview

Sonya's and Michael's circumstances underscore the importance of culture in understanding adolescent development. Although we have much in common with all humans who inhabit the earth, we also vary according to our cultural and ethnic backgrounds. The sociocultural worlds of adolescents and emerging adults are a recurrent theme throughout this book. And, because culture is such a pervasive dimension of adolescence and emerging adulthood, in this chapter we explore it in greater depth. We will consider cross-cultural comparisons, study ethnicity and socioeconomic status as major aspects of culture, and examine ways in which the dramatic growth of mass media and technology affect the lives of adolescents.

1 Culture, Adolescence, and Emerging Adulthood

LG1 Discuss the role of culture in development of adolescents and emerging adults.

The Relevance of Culture for the Study of Adolescence and Emerging Adulthood

Cross-Cultural Comparisons

Rites of Passage

In Chapter 1, we defined **culture** as the behavior, patterns, beliefs, and all other products of a specific group of people that are passed on from generation to generation. The products result from the interaction between groups of people and their environment over many years. Here we examine the role of culture in adolescents' and emerging adults' development.

developmental **connection**

Theories. In Bronfenbrenner's ecological theory, the macrosystem is the environmental system that involves the influence of culture on adolescent development. Chapter 1, p. 33

THE RELEVANCE OF CULTURE FOR THE STUDY OF ADOLESCENCE AND EMERGING ADULTHOOD

If the study of adolescence and emerging adulthood is to be a relevant discipline in the twenty-first century, increased attention will have to focus on culture and ethnicity (Bennett, 2011; Parke, Coltrane, & Schofield, 2011; Schlegel & Hewlett, 2011). Extensive contact between people from varied cultural and ethnic backgrounds is rapidly becoming the norm. Schools and neighborhoods are no longer the fortresses of a privileged group whose agenda is the exclusion of those with a different skin color or different customs. Immigrants, refugees, and ethnic minority individuals increasingly decline to become part of a homogeneous melting pot, instead requesting that schools, employers, and governments honor many of their cultural customs. Adult refugees and immigrants might find more opportunities and better-paying jobs here, but they are concerned that their children and adolescents might learn attitudes in school that challenge traditional authority patterns at home (Brislin, 2000).

In the twentieth century, the study of adolescents and emerging adults was primarily ethnocentric, emphasizing American values, especially middle-SES, non-Latino White, male values (Spencer, 2000). Cross-cultural psychologists point out that many of the assumptions about contemporary ideas in fields like adolescence were developed in Western cultures (Triandis, 2007). One example of **ethnocentrism**—the tendency to favor one's own group over other groups—is the American emphasis on the individual or self. Many Eastern countries, such as Japan, China, and India, are group-oriented. So is the Mexican culture. The pendulum may have swung too far in the individualistic direction in many Western cultures.

People in all cultures have a tendency to behave in ways that favor their cultural group, feel proud of their cultural group, and feel negatively toward other cultural groups. Over the past few centuries, and at an increasing rate in recent decades, technological advances in transportation, communication, and commerce have made these ways of thinking obsolete. Global interdependence is no longer a matter of belief or choice. It is an inescapable reality (UNICEF, 2011). Adolescents and emerging adults are not just citizens of the United States or Canada. They are citizens of the world, a world that has become increasingly interactive. By understanding the behavior and values of cultures around the world, the hope is that we can interact more effectively with each other and make this planet a more hospitable, peaceful place to live (Kottak & Kozaitis, 2012; Koppelman & Goodhart, 2011).

culture The behavior, patterns, beliefs, and all other products of a particular group of people that are passed on from generation to generation.

ethnocentrism A tendency to favor one's own group over other groups.

cross-cultural studies Studies that compare a culture with one or more other cultures. Such studies provide information about the degree to which development in adolescents and emerging adults is similar, or universal, across cultures, or about the degree to which it is culture-specific.

CROSS-CULTURAL COMPARISONS

As we saw in Chapter 1, **cross-cultural studies,** which involve the comparison of a culture with one or more other cultures, provide information about other cultures

Culture has a powerful impact on people's lives. In Xinjian, China, a woman prepares for horseback courtship. Her suitor must chase her, kiss her, and evade her riding crop—all on the gallop. A new marriage law took effect in China in 1981. The law sets a minimum age for marriage—22 years for males, 20 years for females. Late marriage and late childbirth are critical aspects of China's effort to control population growth.

developmental **connection**

Education. Recent international comparisons indicate that the highest achievement in math, science, and reading are held by students in Asian countries. Chapter 11, p. 374

Cross-cultural studies involve the comparison of a culture with one or more other cultures. Shown here is a 14-year-old !Kung girl who has added flowers to her beadwork during the brief rainy season in the Kalahari desert in Botswana, Africa. Delinquency and violence occur much less frequently in the peaceful !Kung culture than in most other cultures around the world.

individualism Emphasizes values that serve the self and gives priority to personal goals, not group goals.

collectivism Emphasizes values that serve the group by subordinating personal goals to preserve group integrity.

and the role of culture in development. This comparison reveals information about the degree to which adolescents' and emerging adults' development is similar, or universal, across cultures, or the degree to which it is culture-specific (Shiraev & Levy, 2010). In terms of gender, for example, the experiences of male and female adolescents continue to be worlds apart in some cultures (Larson, Wilson, & Rickman, 2009). In many countries, males have far greater access to educational opportunities, more freedom to pursue a variety of careers, and fewer restrictions on sexual activity than do females (UNICEF, 2011).

In Chapter 11, we discussed the higher math and science achievement of Asian adolescents when they are compared with U.S. adolescents. A recent study revealed that from the beginning of the seventh grade through the end of the eighth grade, U.S. adolescents valued academics less, and their motivational behavior also decreased (Wang & Pomerantz, 2009). By contrast, the value placed on academics by Chinese adolescents did not change across this time frame, and their motivational behavior was sustained.

Individualism and Collectivism In cross-cultural research, the search for basic traits has focused on the dichotomy between individualism and collectivism (Triandis, 2007):

- **Individualism** involves giving priority to personal goals rather than to group goals; it emphasizes values that serve the self, such as feeling good, personal distinction and achievement, and independence.
- **Collectivism** emphasizes values that serve the group by subordinating personal goals to preserve group integrity, interdependence of the members, and harmonious relationships.

Figure 12.1 summarizes some of the main characteristics of individualistic and collectivistic cultures. Many Western cultures, such as the United States, Canada, Great Britain, and the Netherlands, are described as individualistic; many Eastern cultures, such as China, Japan, India, and Thailand, are described as collectivistic. Mexican culture, too, is considered collectivistic.

Researchers have found that self-conceptions are related to culture. In one study, American and Chinese college students completed 20 sentences beginning with "I am ________" (Trafimow, Triandis, & Goto, 1991). As indicated in Figure 12.2, the American college students were much more likely to describe themselves with

Individualistic	Collectivistic
Focuses on individual	Focuses on groups
Self is determined by personal traits independent of groups; self is stable across contexts	Self is defined by in-group terms; self can change with context
Private self is more important	Public self is most important
Personal achievement, competition, power are important	Achievement is for the benefit of the in-group; cooperation is stressed
Cognitive dissonance is frequent	Cognitive dissonance is infrequent
Emotions (such as anger) are self-focused	Emotions (such as anger) are often relationship based
People who are the most liked are self-assured	People who are the most liked are modest, self-effacing
Values: pleasure, achievement, competition, freedom	Values: security, obedience, in-group harmony, personalized relationships
Many casual relationships	Few, close relationships
Save own face	Save own and other's face
Independent behaviors: swimming, sleeping alone in room, privacy	Interdependent behaviors: co-bathing, co-sleeping
Relatively rare mother-child physical contact	Frequent mother-child physical contact (such as hugging, holding)

FIGURE **12.1**

CHARACTERISTICS OF INDIVIDUALISTIC AND COLLECTIVISTIC CULTURES

personal traits ("I am assertive"), whereas the Chinese students were more likely to identify themselves by their group affiliations ("I am a member of the math club").

Human beings have always lived in groups, whether large or small, and have always needed one another for survival. Critics of the Western notion of psychology argue that the Western emphasis on individualism may undermine our basic species need for relatedness (Kagitcibasi, 2007). Some social scientists argue that many problems in Western cultures are intensified by their emphasis on individualism. Compared with collectivist cultures, individualistic cultures have higher rates of suicide, drug abuse, crime, teenage pregnancy, divorce, child abuse, and mental disorders.

A recent analysis proposed four values that reflect parents' beliefs in individualistic cultures about what is required for children's and adolescents' effective development of autonomy: (1) *personal choice;* (2) *intrinsic motivation;* (3) *self-esteem;* and (4) *self-maximization,* which consists of achieving one's full potential (Tamis-LeMonda & others, 2008). The analysis also proposed that three values reflect parents' beliefs in collectivistic cultures: (1) *connectedness to the family and other close relationships,* (2) *orientation to the larger group,* and (3) *respect and obedience.*

Critics of the individualistic and collectivistic cultures concept argue that these terms are too broad and simplistic, especially with the increase in globalization (Kagitcibasi, 2007). Regardless of their cultural background, people need both a positive sense of self and connectedness to others to develop fully as human beings. The analysis by Carolyn Tamis-LeMonda and her colleagues (2008) emphasizes that

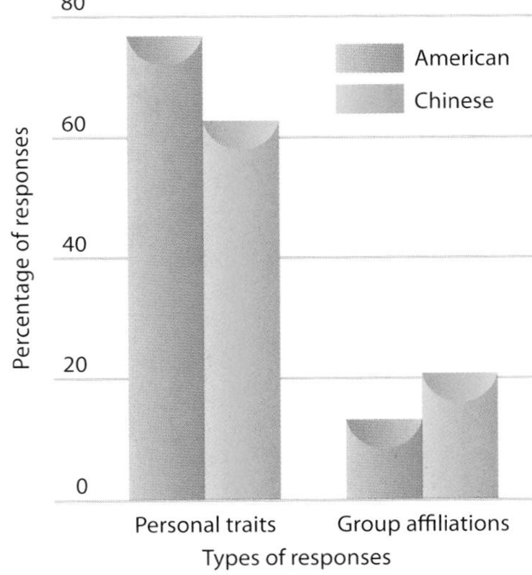

FIGURE **12.2**

AMERICAN AND CHINESE SELF-CONCEPTIONS. College students from the United States and China completed 20 "I am ________" sentences. Both groups filled in personal traits more than group affiliations. However, the U.S. college students more often filled in the blank with personal traits, the Chinese with group affiliations.

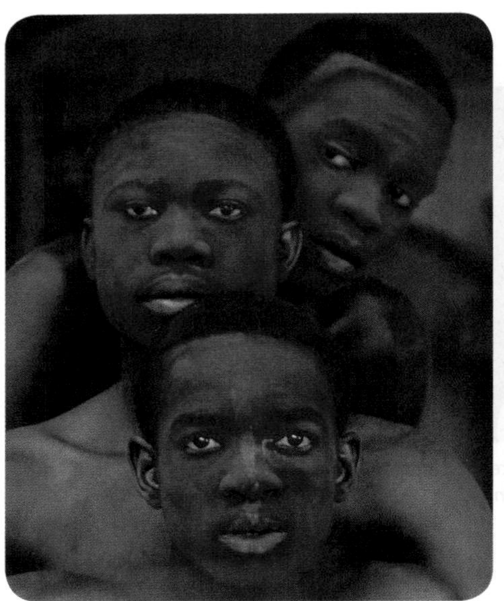

These Congolese Kota boys painted their faces as part of a rite of passage to adulthood. *What rites of passage do American adolescents have?*

The Apache Native Americans of the American Southwest celebrate a girl's entrance into puberty with a four-day ritual that includes special dress, day-long activities, and solemn spiritual ceremonies.

Maddie Miller, 13, sharing a prayer with her father, studied for a year to prepare for her bat mitzvah.

on them, and to be undecided about questions of career and lifestyle. Another rite of passage for increasing numbers of American adolescents is sexual intercourse (Halonen & Santrock, 1999). By the end of adolescence, more than 70 percent of American adolescents have had sexual intercourse.

The absence of clear-cut rites of passage makes the attainment of adult status so ambiguous that many individuals are unsure whether they have reached it or not. In Texas, for example, the legal age for beginning employment is 15, but many younger adolescents and even children are employed, especially Mexican immigrants. The legal age for driving is 16, but when emergency need is demonstrated, a driver's license can be obtained at age 15, and some parents might not allow their son or daughter to obtain a driver's license even at age 16, believing that they are too young for this responsibility. The legal age for voting is 18, and that for drinking recently has been raised to 21. In sum, exactly when adolescents become adults in the United States has not been clearly delineated as it has in primitive cultures where rites of passage are universal.

Review *Connect* Reflect

LG1 Discuss the role of culture in the development of adolescents and emerging adults.

Review

- What is culture? What is the relevance of culture in the study of development in adolescence and emerging adulthood?
- What are cross-cultural comparisons? What characterizes individualistic and collectivistic cultures? How do cultures vary in the time adolescents spend in various activities?
- What are rites of passage? How do cultures vary in terms of rites of passage?

Connect

- In this section you learned that U.S. adolescents have far more discretionary time at their disposal than do their European or Asian counterparts. Relate this fact to the discussion of expectations in Chapter 11.

Reflect *Your Own Personal Journey of Life*

- Have you experienced a rite of passage in your life? If so, what was it? Was it a positive or negative influence on your development? Is there a rite of passage you did not experience that you wished you had?

2 Socioeconomic Status and Poverty

 Describe how socioeconomic status and poverty are related to adolescent development.

What Is Socioeconomic Status? | Socioeconomic Variations in Families, Neighborhoods, and Schools | Poverty

Many subcultures exist within countries. For example, the values and attitudes of adolescents growing up in an urban ghetto or rural Appalachia may differ considerably from those of adolescents growing up in a wealthy suburb. A key difference between such subcultures is socioeconomic status.

WHAT IS SOCIOECONOMIC STATUS?

Socioeconomic status (SES) refers to a grouping of people with similar occupational, educational, and economic characteristics. Individuals with different SES have varying levels of power, influence, and prestige. In this chapter, for example, we evaluate what it is like for an adolescent to grow up in poverty. Socioeconomic status carries with it certain inequalities. Generally, members of a society have (1) occupations that vary in prestige, with some individuals having more access than others to higher-status occupations; (2) different levels of educational attainment, with some individuals having more access than others to better education; (3) different economic resources; and (4) different levels of power to influence a community's institutions. These differences in the ability to control resources and to participate in society's rewards produce unequal opportunities for adolescents (Conger & Conger, 2008). Socioeconomic differences are a "proxy for material, human, and social capital within and beyond the family" (Huston & Ripke, 2006, p. 425).

The number of visibly different socioeconomic statuses depends on the community's size and complexity. In most investigators' descriptions of SES, two categories, low and middle, are used, although as many as five categories have been delineated. Sometimes low SES is described as low-income, working class, or blue collar; sometimes the middle category is described as middle-income, managerial, or white collar. Examples of low-SES occupations are factory worker, manual laborer, welfare recipient, and maintenance worker. Examples of middle-SES occupations include salesperson, manager, and professional (doctor, lawyer, teacher, accountant, and so on). Professionals at the pinnacle of their field, high-level corporate executives, political leaders, and wealthy individuals are among those in the upper-SES category.

SOCIOECONOMIC VARIATIONS IN FAMILIES, NEIGHBORHOODS, AND SCHOOLS

The families, schools, and neighborhoods of adolescents have socioeconomic characteristics (Entwistle, Alexander, & Olson, 2010; Wright & others, 2012). Some adolescents have parents who have a great deal of money, and who work in prestigious occupations. These adolescents live in attractive houses and neighborhoods, enjoy vacations abroad and at high-quality camps, and attend schools where the mix of students is primarily from middle- and upper-SES backgrounds. Other adolescents have parents who do not have very much money and who work in less prestigious occupations. These adolescents do not live in very attractive houses and neighborhoods, rarely go on vacations, and attend schools where the mix of students is mainly from lower-SES backgrounds. Such variations in neighborhood settings can influence adolescents' adjustment and achievement (Hutson, 2008).

In America and most Western cultures, differences have been found in child rearing among different SES groups (Hoff, Laursen, & Tardif, 2002, p. 246):

- "Lower-SES parents (1) are more concerned that their children conform to society's expectations, (2) create a home atmosphere in which it is clear that

socioeconomic status (SES) Refers to a grouping of people with similar occupational, educational, and economic characteristics.

parents have authority over children," (3) use physical punishment more in disciplining their children, and (4) are more directive and less conversational with their children.

- "Higher-SES parents (1) are more concerned with developing children's initiative" and delay of gratification, (2) "create a home atmosphere in which children are more nearly equal participants and in which rules are discussed as opposed to being laid down" in an authoritarian manner, (3) are less likely to use physical punishment, and (4) "are less directive and more conversational" with their children.

Children and adolescents from low-SES backgrounds are at risk for experiencing low achievement and emotional problems, as well as lower occupational attainment in adulthood (McLoyd & others, 2009). Social maladaptation and psychological problems, such as depression, low self-confidence, peer conflict, and juvenile delinquency, are more prevalent among poor adolescents than among economically advantaged adolescents (Gibbs & Huang, 1989). Although psychological problems are more prevalent among adolescents from low-SES backgrounds, these adolescents vary considerably in intellectual and psychological functioning. For example, a sizable portion of adolescents from low-SES backgrounds perform well in school; some perform better than many middle-SES students. When adolescents from low-SES backgrounds are achieving well in school, it is not unusual to find a parent or parents making special sacrifices to provide the necessary living conditions and support to contribute to school success.

developmental **connection**

Education. Many adolescents in poverty face problems that present barriers to their learning. Chapter 10, p. 345

In Chapter 10, we read that schools in low-SES neighborhoods are more likely to have fewer resources than are schools in higher-SES neighborhoods. The schools in the low-SES areas also are more likely to have more students with lower achievement test scores, lower rates of graduation, and smaller percentages of students going to college (Engle & Black, 2008). In some instances, however, federal aid to schools has provided a context for enhanced learning in low-income areas.

So far we have focused on the challenges that many adolescents from low-income families face. However, research by Suniya Luthar and her colleagues (Ansary & Luthar, 2009; Ansary, McMahon, & Luthar, 2011; Luthar, 2006; Luthar & Goldstein, 2008) has found that adolescents from affluent families also face challenges. Adolescents in the affluent families Luthar has studied are vulnerable to high rates of substance abuse. In addition, her research has found that adolescent males from such families have more adjustment difficulties than do females, with affluent female adolescents especially more likely to attain superior levels of academic success.

POVERTY

What happens to a dream
deferred?
Does it dry up
Like a raisin in the sun?

—Langston Hughes
American Poet and Author, 20th Century

The world is a dangerous and unwelcoming place for too many of America's youth, especially those whose families, neighborhoods, and schools are low-income (Comer, 2010; Murry & others, 2011). Some adolescents are resilient and cope with the challenges of poverty without major setbacks, but many struggle unsuccessfully. Each adolescent who has grown up in poverty and reaches adulthood unhealthy, unskilled, or alienated keeps our nation from being as competent and productive as it can be.

What Is Poverty Like? Poverty is defined by economic hardship, and its most common marker is the federal poverty threshold. The poverty threshold was originally based on the estimated cost of food (a basic diet) multiplied by 3. This federal poverty marker is adjusted annually for family size and inflation.

In 2008, 19 percent of children under 18 years of age were living in families below the poverty line, the highest rate since 1998 but down from a peak of 23 percent in 1993 (Federal Interagency Forum on Child and Family Statistics, 2010). The

U.S. figure of 19 percent of children living in poverty is much higher than figures from other industrialized nations. For example, Canada has a child poverty rate of 9 percent and Sweden has a rate of 2 percent.

Poverty in the United States is demarcated along family structure and ethnic lines (Federal Interagency Forum on Child and Family Statistics, 2010). In 2008, 36.5 percent of female-headed families lived in poverty compared to only 6.4 percent of married-couple families. In 2008, 35 percent of African American families and 31 percent of Latino families lived in poverty, compared to only 10 percent of non-Latino White families. Compared with non-Latino White children, ethnic minority children are more likely to experience persistent poverty over many years and live in isolated poor neighborhoods where social supports are minimal and threats to positive development abundant (Jarrett, 1995) (see Figure 12.4).

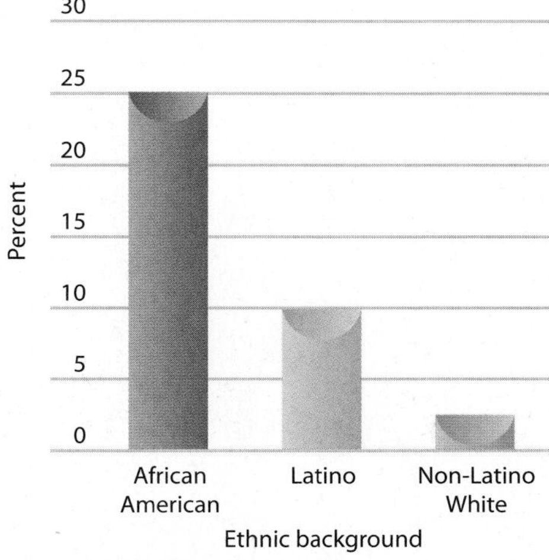

FIGURE **12.4**

LIVING IN DISTRESSED NEIGHBORHOODS.
Note: A distressed neighborhood is defined by high levels (at least one standard deviation above the mean) of (1) poverty, (2) female-headed families, (3) high school dropouts, (4) unemployment, and (5) reliance on welfare.

Living in poverty has many psychological effects on adolescents and emerging adults (Leventhal, Dupéré, & Brooks-Gunn, 2009; Miller & Taylor, 2011; Murry & others, 2011; Santiago & others, 2011). First, the poor are often powerless. In occupations, they rarely are the decision makers. Rules are handed down to them in an authoritarian manner. Second, the poor are often vulnerable to disaster. They are not likely to be given notice before they are laid off from work and usually do not have financial resources to fall back on when problems arise. Third, their range of alternatives is often restricted. Only a limited number of jobs are open to them. Even when alternatives are available, the poor might not know about them or be prepared to make a wise decision. Fourth, because of inadequate education and inability to read well, being poor means having less prestige.

One review concluded that compared with their economically more advantaged counterparts, poor children and adolescents experience widespread environmental inequities that include the following (Evans, 2004):

- They experience more conflict, violence, instability, and chaos in their homes (Emery & Laumann-Billings, 1998).
- They get less social support, and their parents are less responsive and more authoritarian (Bo, 1994).
- They watch more TV and have less access to books and computers (Bradley & others, 2001).
- Their schools and child-care facilities are inferior, and parents monitor their school activities less (Benveniste, Carnoy, & Rothstein, 2003).
- The air they breathe and the water they drink are more polluted, and their homes are more crowded and noisy (Myers, Baer, & Choi, 1996).
- They live in more dangerous and physically deteriorating neighborhoods with less adequate municipal services (Brody & others, 2001).

At a number of places in this text, the negative aspects and outcomes of poverty for adolescents are highlighted: as a risk factor for sexual problems (Chapter 6); running away from home (Chapter 8); reduction of income for divorced mothers, which can lead to poverty and its negative consequences for adolescents (Chapter 8); numerous school-related risks and problems, including inferior schools, increased risk of dropping out of school, and lower probability of going to college (Chapter 10); lower achievement expectations, lower achievement, lack of access to jobs, and entry into less desirable careers (Chapter 11); and higher rates of delinquency (Chapter 13).

developmental **connection**

Achievement. Many adolescents who have grown up in low-income or poverty conditions often face challenging circumstances in seeking upward mobility in a career. Chapter 11, p. 401

When poverty is persistent and long-standing, it can have especially damaging effects on children and adolescents (Chen, Howard, & Brooks-Gunn, 2011; Philipsen, Johnson, & Brooks-Gunn, 2009; Williams & Hazell, 2012). One study revealed that the more years 7- to 13-year-olds spent living in poverty, the more their physiological indices of stress were elevated (Evans & Kim, 2007).

Because of advances in their cognitive growth, adolescents living in poverty conditions likely are more aware of their social disadvantage and the associated stigma than are children (McLoyd & others, 2009). Combined with the increased

What characterizes socioeconomic variations in neighborhoods?

sensitivity to peers in adolescence, such awareness may cause them to try to hide their poverty status as much as possible from others.

A special concern is the high percentage of children and adolescents growing up in mother-headed households in poverty (Federal Interagency Forum on Child and Family Statistics, 2010). Vonnie McLoyd (1998) concluded that because poor, single mothers are more distressed than their middle-SES counterparts are, they tend to show low support, nurturance, and involvement with their children. Among the reasons for the high poverty rate of single mothers are women's low pay, infrequent awarding of alimony payments, and poorly enforced child support by fathers (Graham & Beller, 2002).

The term **feminization of poverty** refers to the fact that far more women than men live in poverty. Women's low income, divorce, and the resolution of divorce cases by the judicial system, which leaves women with less money than they and their children need to adequately function, are the likely causes of the feminization of poverty.

developmental **connection**

Social Policy. Reducing the poverty level and improving the lives of children and adolescents living in poverty are important goals of U.S. social policy. Chapter 1, p. 11

Countering Poverty's Effects One trend in antipoverty programs is to conduct two-generation interventions (McLoyd, Aikens, & Burton, 2006). This involves providing both services for children (such as educational child care or preschool education) and services for parents (such as adult education, literacy training, and job skill training). Evaluations of the two-generation programs suggest that they have more positive effects on parents than they do on children (St. Pierre, Layzer, & Barnes, 1996). Also discouraging, regarding children, is the finding that when the two-generation programs show benefits, they are more likely to be in health benefits than in cognitive gains.

Might intervention with families of children living in poverty improve children's school performance? In a recent experimental study, Aletha Huston and her colleagues (2006) evaluated the effects of New Hope, a program designed to increase parental employment and reduce family poverty, on adolescent development. They randomly assigned families with 6- to 10-year old children living in poverty to the New Hope program and a control group. New Hope offered adults living in poverty who were employed 30 or more hours a week benefits that were designed to increase family income (a wage supplement that ensured that net income increased as parents earned more) and to provide work supports through subsidized child care (for any child under age 13) and health insurance. Management services were provided to New Hope participants to assist them in job searches and other needs. The New Hope program was available to the experimental group families for three years (until the children were 9 to 13 years old). Five years after the program began and two years after it had ended, the program's effects on the children were examined when they were 11 to 16 years old. Compared to adolescents in the control group, New Hope adolescents were more competent at reading, had better school performance, were less likely to be in special-education classes, had more positive social skills, and were more likely to be in formal after-school arrangements. New Hope parents reported better psychological well-being and a greater sense of self-efficacy in managing their adolescents than control parents did. In a further assessment, the influence of the New Hope program on children 9 to 19 years after they left the program was evaluated (McLoyd & others, 2011). Positive outcomes especially occurred for African American boys, who were more optimistic about their future employment and career prospects.

What other programs are benefiting adolescents living in poverty? See the *Connecting with Health and Well-Being* interlude.

feminization of poverty Term reflecting the fact that far more women than men live in poverty. Women's low income, divorce, and the resolution of divorce cases by the judicial system, which leaves women with less money than they and their children need to function adequately, are the likely causes.

connecting with health and well-being

How Do the Quantum Opportunities Program and El Puente Help Youth in Poverty?

One potential positive path for youth living in poverty is to become involved with a caring mentor. The Quantum Opportunities program, funded by the Ford Foundation, was a four-year, year-round mentoring effort (Carnegie Council on Adolescent Development, 1995). The students were entering the ninth grade at a high school with high rates of poverty, were minorities, and came from families that received public assistance. Each day for four years, mentors provided sustained support, guidance, and concrete assistance to their students.

The Quantum program required students to participate in (1) academic-related activities outside school hours, including reading, writing, math, science, and social studies, peer tutoring, and computer skills training; (2) community service projects, including tutoring elementary school students, cleaning up the neighborhood, and volunteering in hospitals, nursing homes, and libraries; and (3) cultural enrichment and personal development activities, including life skills training, and college and job planning. In exchange for their commitment to the program, students were offered financial incentives that encouraged participation, completion, and long-range planning. A stipend of $1.33 was given to students for each hour they participated in these activities. For every 100 hours of education, service, or development activities, students received a bonus of $100. The average cost per participant was $10,600 for the four years, which is one-half the cost of one year in prison.

An evaluation of the Quantum project compared the mentored students with a nonmentored control group. Sixty-three percent of the mentored students graduated from high school, but only 42 percent of the control group did; 42 percent of the mentored students are currently enrolled in college, but only 16 percent of the control group are. Furthermore, control-group students were twice as likely as the mentored students to receive food stamps or welfare, and they had more arrests. Such programs clearly have the potential to overcome the intergenerational transmission of poverty and its negative outcomes.

The original Quantum Opportunities program no longer exists, but the Eisenhower Corporation (2010) recently began replicating the Quantum program in Alabama, South Carolina, New Hampshire, Virginia, Mississippi, Oregon, Maryland, and Washington, D.C.

Another effort to improve the lives of adolescents living in poverty is the El Puente program, which is primarily aimed at Latino adolescents living in low-SES areas. El Puente ("the bridge") was opened in New York City in 1983 because of community dissatisfaction with the health, education, and social services youth were receiving (Simons, Finlay, & Yang, 1991). El Puente emphasizes five areas of youth development: health, education, achievement, personal growth, and social growth.

El Puente is located in a former Roman Catholic church on the south side of Williamsburg in Brooklyn, a neighborhood made up primarily of low-income Latino families, many of which are far below the

Children participating in the Quantum Opportunities program at the Carver Center in Washington, D.C.

These adolescents participate in the programs of El Puente, located in a predominantly low-SES Latino neighborhood in Brooklyn, New York. The El Puente program stresses five areas of youth development: health, education, achievement, personal growth, and social growth.

(*continued*)

connecting with health and well-being

(*continued*)

poverty line. Sixty-five percent of the residents receive some form of public assistance. The neighborhood has the highest school dropout rate for Latinos in New York City and the highest felony rate for adolescents in Brooklyn.

When the youth, ages 12 through 21, first enroll in El Puente, they meet with counselors and develop a four-month plan that includes the programs they are interested in joining. At the end of four months, youth and staff develop a plan for continued participation. Twenty-six bilingual classes are offered in such subjects as music, theater, photography, and dance. In addition, a medical and fitness center, GED night school, and mental health and social services centers are also a part of El Puente.

How might the lessons learned from these successful programs be applied and studied in other cultural situations in which adolescents live in poverty?

Review *Connect* Reflect

LG2 Describe how socioeconomic status and poverty are related to adolescent development.

Review

- What is socioeconomic status?
- What are some socioeconomic variations in families, neighborhoods, and schools?
- How is poverty related to adolescent development?

Connect

- How does the idea of the family as a system (Chapter 8) connect with the experience of adolescents living in poverty?

Reflect *Your Own Personal Journey of Life*

- What was the socioeconomic status of your family as you were growing up? How did it impact your development?

3 Ethnicity

LG3 Summarize how ethnicity is involved in the development of adolescents and emerging adults.

Immigration

Adolescence and Emerging Adulthood: A Special Juncture for Ethnic Minority Individuals

Ethnicity Issues

Adolescents and emerging adults live in a world that has been made smaller and more interactive by dramatic improvements in travel and communication. U.S. adolescents and emerging adults also live in a world that is far more diverse in its ethnic makeup than it was in past decades: Ninety-three languages are spoken in Los Angeles alone!

Ethnicity is based on cultural heritage, nationality characteristics, race, religion, and language. A striking feature of the United States today is the increasing ethnic diversity of America's adolescents and emerging adults. In this section, we study African American adolescents, Latino adolescents, Asian American adolescents, and Native American adolescents, and the sociocultural issues involved in their development.

ethnicity A dimension of culture based on cultural heritage, national characteristics, race, religion, and language.

IMMIGRATION

Relatively high rates of immigration are contributing to the growth in the proportion of ethnic minority adolescents and emerging adults in the United States (Grigorenko & Takanishi, 2010; Wright & others, 2012). Immigrants often experience stressors uncommon to or less prominent among longtime residents such as language barriers, dislocations and separations from support networks, the dual struggle to preserve identity and to acculturate, and changes in SES status (Chao & Otsuki-Clutter, 2011; Ko & Perreira, 2010; Landale, Thomas, & Van Hook, 2011). Consequently, when working with adolescents and their immigrant families, counselors need to adapt intervention programs to optimize cultural sensitivity (Suárez-Orozco & Suárez-Orozco, 2010).

developmental **connection**

Diversity. Projections indicate that in 2100 there will be more Latino than non-Latino White adolescents in the United States and more Asian American than African American adolescents. Chapter 1, p. 10

Latino immigrants in the Rio Grande Valley, Texas. *What are some of the adaptations immigrants make?*

Though the United States has always included significant immigrant populations, psychologists have been slow to study these families. One study examined the cultural values and intergenerational value discrepancies in immigrant (Vietnamese, Armenian, and Mexican) and nonimmigrant (African American and European American) families (Phinney, Madden, & Ong, 2000). Although in all groups family obligations were endorsed more by parents than by adolescents, the intergenerational value discrepancy generally increased with time in the United States.

Recent research increasingly shows links between acculturation and adolescent problems (Choi, He, & Harachi, 2008). For example, more acculturated Latino youth in the United States experience higher rates of conduct problems, substance abuse, depression, and risky sexual behavior than their less acculturated counterparts (Gonzales & others, 2006). Conflict between parents and adolescents that results from the cultural shifts that have taken place in immigrant families is likely responsible for the link between acculturation and adolescent problems (Gonzales & others, 2007). The conflict is often greatest when adolescents have acculturated more quickly than their parents.

Many of the families that have immigrated in recent decades to the United States, such as Mexican Americans and Asian Americans, come from collective cultures in which family obligation and duty to one's family are strong (Parke, Coltrane, & Schofield, 2011). Family obligation and duty may take the form of assisting parents in their occupations and contributing to the family's welfare (Parke & Buriel, 2006; van Geel & Vedder, 2011). This often occurs in service and manual labor jobs, such as those in construction, gardening, cleaning, and restaurants.

To read about the work of one individual who studies immigrant adolescents, see the *Connecting with Careers* profile.

ADOLESCENCE AND EMERGING ADULTHOOD: A SPECIAL JUNCTURE FOR ETHNIC MINORITY INDIVIDUALS

As we discussed in Chapter 4, for ethnic minority individuals, adolescence and emerging adulthood often represent a special juncture in their development (Fuligni, Hughes, & Way, 2009; Rivas-Drake, 2011). Although children are aware of some ethnic and cultural differences, most ethnic minority individuals first consciously confront their ethnicity in adolescence. In contrast to children, adolescents and emerging adults have the ability to interpret ethnic and cultural information, to reflect on the past, and to speculate about the future. As they mature cognitively, ethnic minority adolescents and emerging adults become acutely aware of how the majority non-Latino White culture evaluates their ethnic group. One researcher commented that the young African American child may learn that Black is beautiful but conclude as an adolescent that White is powerful (Semaj, 1985).

developmental **connection**

Identity. Researchers are increasingly finding that a positive ethnic identity is linked to positive outcomes for ethnic minority adolescents. Chapter 4, p. 148

connecting with careers

Carola Suárez-Orozco, Immigration Studies Researcher and Professor

Carola Suárez-Orozco currently is chair and professor of applied psychology and co-director of Immigration Studies at New York University. She formerly was co-director of the Harvard University Immigration Projects. Suárez-Orozco obtained her undergraduate degree (in development studies) and doctoral degree (in clinical psychology) at the University of California at Berkeley.

She has worked in both clinical and public school settings in California and Massachusetts. While at Harvard, Suárez-Orozco conducted a five-year longitudinal study of immigrant adolescents' (coming from Central America, China, and the Dominican Republic) adaptation to schools and society. She especially advocates more research at the intersection of cultural and psychological factors in the adaptation of immigrant and ethnic minority youth (Suárez-Orozco, 2007).

Carola Suárez-Orozco, with her husband, Marcelo, who also studies the adaptation of immigrants.

Ethnic minority youths' awareness of negative appraisals, conflicting values, and restricted occupational opportunities can influence their life choices and plans for the future (Diemer & others, 2006). As one ethnic minority youth stated, "The future seems shut off, closed. Why dream? You can't reach your dreams. Why set goals? At least if you don't set any goals, you don't fail."

For many ethnic minority youth, a special concern is the lack of successful ethnic minority role models. The problem is especially acute for inner-city youth. Because of the lack of adult ethnic minority role models, some ethnic minority youth may conform to middle-SES, non-Latino White values and identify with successful non-Latino White role models. However, for many ethnic minority adolescents, their ethnicity and skin color limit their acceptance within the non-Latino White culture. Thus, they face the difficult task of negotiating two value systems—that of their own ethnic group and that of the non-Latino White society. Some adolescents reject the mainstream, forgoing the rewards controlled by non-Latino White Americans; others adopt the values and standards of the majority non-Latino White culture; and still others take the path of biculturality (Suyemoto, 2009). One study of Mexican American and Asian American college students revealed that both ethnic groups expressed a bicultural identity (Devos, 2006).

Recent research indicates that many members of families that have recently immigrated to the United States adopt a bicultural orientation, selecting characteristics of the U.S. culture that help them to survive and advance, while still retaining aspects of their culture of origin (Cheah & Yeung, 2011; Marks, Patton, & Garcia Coll, 2011). Immigration also involves cultural brokering, which has increasingly occurred in the United States as children and adolescents serve as mediators (cultural and linguistic) for their immigrant parents (Villanueva & Buriel, 2010). In adopting characteristics of the U.S. culture, Latino families are increasingly embracing the importance of education. Although their school dropout rates have remained higher than for other ethnic groups, toward the end of the first decade of the twenty-first century they declined considerably (National Center for Education Statistics, 2010).

In retaining positive aspects of their culture of origin, as research by Ross Parke and his colleagues (2011) indicates, Latino families are retaining a strong commitment to family when they immigrate to the United States even in the face of often having low-paying jobs and challenges in advancing economically. For example, divorce rates for Latino families are lower than for non-Latino White families of similar socioeconomic status.

Margaret Beale Spencer, shown here (on the right) talking with adolescents, believes that adolescence is a critical juncture in the identity development of ethnic minority individuals. Most ethnic minority individuals consciously confront their ethnicity for the first time in adolescence.

ETHNICITY ISSUES

A number of ethnicity issues are involved in the development of adolescents and emerging adults. First, we explore the importance of considering SES when drawing conclusions about the role of ethnicity in the development of adolescents and emerging adults.

Ethnicity and Socioeconomic Status A higher percentage of ethnic minority children and youth live in families characterized by poverty than do non-Latino children and youth (McLoyd & others, 2009). As indicated earlier in this chapter, in 2008, 35 percent of African American children and adolescents and 31 percent of Latino children and adolescents lived in poverty compared to 10 percent of non-Latino White children and adolescents (Federal Interagency Forum on Child and Family Statistics, 2010).

Much of the research on ethnic minority adolescents and emerging adults has failed to identify distinctions between the dual influences of ethnicity and SES. Ethnicity and SES can interact in ways that exaggerate the influence of ethnicity because ethnic minority individuals are overrepresented in the lower socioeconomic levels of American society (Rowley, Kurtz-Costes, & Cooper, 2010; Miller & Taylor, 2011; Wright & others, 2012). Consequently, too often researchers have given ethnic explanations of adolescent and emerging adult development that were in reality based on SES rather than ethnicity.

A recent longitudinal study illustrated the importance of separating SES and ethnicity in determining the educational and occupational aspirations of individuals from 14 to 26 years of age (Mello, 2009). In this research, SES successfully predicted educational and occupational aspirations across ethnic groups. In this study, after controlling for SES, African American youth reported the highest educational expectations, followed by Latino and Asian American/Pacific Islander, non-Latino White, and American Indian/Alaska Native youth.

Some ethnic minority youth are from middle-SES backgrounds, but economic advantage does not entirely enable them to escape their ethnic minority status (Banks, 2010; Nieto & Bode, 2012). Middle-SES ethnic minority youth are still subject to much of the prejudice, discrimination, and bias associated with being a member of an ethnic minority group. Often characterized as a "model minority" because of their strong achievement orientation and family cohesiveness, Japanese Americans still experience stress associated with ethnic minority status (Sue, 1990). Although middle-SES ethnic minority adolescents have more resources available to counter the destructive influences of prejudice and discrimination, they still cannot completely avoid the pervasive influences of negative stereotypes about ethnic minority groups.

That being said, the fact remains that many ethnic minority families are poor, and poverty contributes to the stressful life experiences of many ethnic minority adolescents (Cooper, 2011; Wright & others, 2012). Vonnie McLoyd and her colleagues (McLoyd, Aikens, & Burton, 2006; McLoyd & others, 2009, 2011) have concluded

Consider the flowers of a garden: Though differing in kind, color, form, and shape, yet, inasmuch as they are refreshed by the waters of one spring, revived by the breath of one wind, invigorated by the rays of one sun, this diversity increases their charm and adds to their beauty. . . . How unpleasing to the eye if all the flowers and plants, the leaves and blossoms, the fruits, the branches, and the trees of that garden were all of the same shape and color! Diversity of hues, form, and shape enriches and adorns the garden and heightens its effect.

—ABDU'L BAHA

Persian Baha'i Religious Leader, 19th/20th Century

that ethnic minority youth experience a disproportionate share of the adverse effects of poverty and unemployment in America today. Thus, many ethnic minority adolescents experience a double disadvantage: (1) prejudice, discrimination, and bias because of their ethnic minority status; and (2) the stressful effects of poverty.

Differences and Diversity Historical, economic, and social experiences produce legitimate differences among various ethnic minority groups, and between ethnic minority groups and the majority non-Latino White group (Kottak & Kozaitis, 2012; Wright & others, 2012). Individuals belonging to a specific ethnic or cultural group conform to the values, attitudes, and stresses of that culture. Their behavior, while possibly different from that of the majority, is, nonetheless, often functional for them. Recognizing and respecting these differences are important aspects of getting along with others in a diverse, multicultural world. Every adolescent and adult needs to take the perspective of individuals from ethnic and cultural groups that are different from theirs and think, "If I were in their shoes, what kind of experiences might I have had?" "How would I feel if I were a member of their ethnic or cultural group?" "How would I think and behave if I had grown up in their world?" Such perspective taking is a valuable way to increase one's empathy and understanding of individuals from other ethnic and cultural groups.

For most of the twentieth century, the ways ethnic minority groups differed from non-Latino Whites were conceptualized as *deficits*, or inferior characteristics on the part of the ethnic minority group. In recent years, there has been an effort to increasingly emphasize positive aspects of many ethnic groups, such as the family connectedness that characterizes many Latino families (Parke, Coltrane, & Schofield, 2011).

Another important dimension of ethnic minority adolescents and emerging adults is their diversity (Cushner, McClelland, & Safford, 2012; Koppelman & Goodhart, 2011). Ethnic minority groups are not homogeneous; the individuals within them have different social, historical, and economic backgrounds. For example, Mexican, Cuban, and Puerto Rican immigrants are Latinos, but they had different reasons for migrating, came from varying socioeconomic backgrounds in their native countries, and experience different rates and types of employment in the United States. The U.S. federal government now recognizes the existence of 511 different Native

connecting with adolescents

Seeking a Positive Image for African American Youth

I want America to know that most of us black teens are not troubled people from broken homes and headed to jail. . . . In my relationships with my parents, we show respect for each other and we have values in our house. We have traditions we celebrate together, including Christmas and Kwanza.

—*Jason Leonard, age 15*

How can a positive self-image based on ethnicity, such as the one expressed here, influence an adolescent's development?

Jason Leonard.

American tribes, each having a unique ancestral background with differing values and characteristics. Asian Americans include the Chinese, Japanese, Filipinos, Koreans, and Southeast Asians, each group having distinct ancestries and languages. The diversity of Asian Americans is reflected in their educational attainment: Some achieve a high level of education, whereas many others do not. For example, more than 9 of 10 of Korean American males graduate from high school, but only 3 to 4 percent of Vietnamese American males do. Failure to recognize diversity and individual variations results in the stereotyping of an ethnic minority group.

Type of Racial Hassle	Percent of Adolescents Who Reported the Racial Hassle in the Past Year
Being accused of something or treated suspiciously	71.0
Being treated as if you were "stupid," being "talked down to"	70.7
Others reacting to you as if they were afraid or intimidated	70.1
Being observed or followed while in public places	68.1
Being treated rudely or disrespectfully	56.4
Being ignored, overlooked, not given service	56.4
Others expecting your work to be inferior	54.1
Being insulted, called a name, or harassed	52.2

FIGURE **12.5**

AFRICAN AMERICAN ADOLESCENTS' REPORTS OF RACIAL HASSLES IN THE PAST YEAR

Prejudice, Discrimination, and Bias **Prejudice** is an unjustified negative attitude toward an individual because of the individual's membership in a group. The group toward which the prejudice is directed can be made up of people of a specific ethnic group, sex, age, religion, or other detectable difference (Johnson, 2011; Scupin, 2012). Our concern here is prejudice against ethnic minority groups.

Many ethnic minority individuals continue to experience persistent forms of prejudice, discrimination, and bias (Chao & Otsuki-Clutter, 2011; Martin & others, 2011; Nieto & Bode, 2012). Ethnic minority adolescents are taught in schools that often have a middle-SES, White bias (Holladay, 2011). Discrimination and prejudice continue to be present in the media, interpersonal interactions, and daily conversations (Alvarez, 2009). Crimes, strangeness, poverty, mistakes, and deterioration can be mistakenly attributed to ethnic minority individuals or foreigners. A recent study revealed that adolescents' perceived racial discrimination was linked to negative views that the broader society has about African Americans (Seaton, Yip, & Sellers, 2009).

Research studies provide insight into the discrimination experienced by ethnic minority adolescents (Berkel & others, 2010; Govia, Jackson, & Sellers, 2012; Martin & others, 2011; Seaton & others, 2010). Consider the following three studies:

- Discrimination of seventh- to tenth-grade African American students was related to their lower level of psychological functioning, including perceived stress, symptoms of depression, and lower perceived well-being; more positive attitudes toward African Americans were associated with more positive psychological functioning in adolescents (Sellers & others, 2006). Figure 12.5 shows the percentage of African American adolescents who reported experiencing different types of racial hassles in the past year.
- Chinese American sixth-graders experienced discrimination from their peers that was comparable to discrimination faced by African American sixth-graders (Rivas-Drake, Hughes, & Way, 2009).
- Latino adolescents encountered more discrimination than did Asian American adolescents, and the discrimination was linked to lower grade point averages and self-esteem and to more depressive symptoms and physical complaints (Huynh & Fuligni, 2010).
- African American adolescents' perceived personal racial discrimination was linked to their higher level of delinquency (Martin & others, 2011).

Progress has been made in ethnic minority relations, but discrimination and prejudice still exist, and equality has not been achieved. Much remains to be accomplished (Bennett, 2011; Govia, Jackson, & Sellers, 2011).

So far in this chapter, we have examined the role of culture, socioeconomic status, and ethnicity. In the next section, you will see that there are substantial variations across countries, socioeconomic groups, and ethnic groups in the use of media and technology.

prejudice An unjustified negative attitude toward an individual because of the individual's membership in a group.

Review *Connect* Reflect

Summarize how ethnicity is involved in the development of adolescents and emerging adults.

Review

- How has immigration affected ethnic minority adolescents and emerging adults?
- Why are adolescence and emerging adulthood a special juncture in the development of ethnic minority individuals?
- What are some important ethnicity issues that occur in adolescence and emerging adulthood?

Connect

- How can the concepts of individualism and collectivism, described earlier in this chapter, help us understand the immigrant experiences of adolescents and emerging adults?

Reflect *Your Own Personal Journey of Life*

- Think for a few moments about your ethnic background. How did your ethnicity influence the way you experienced adolescence?

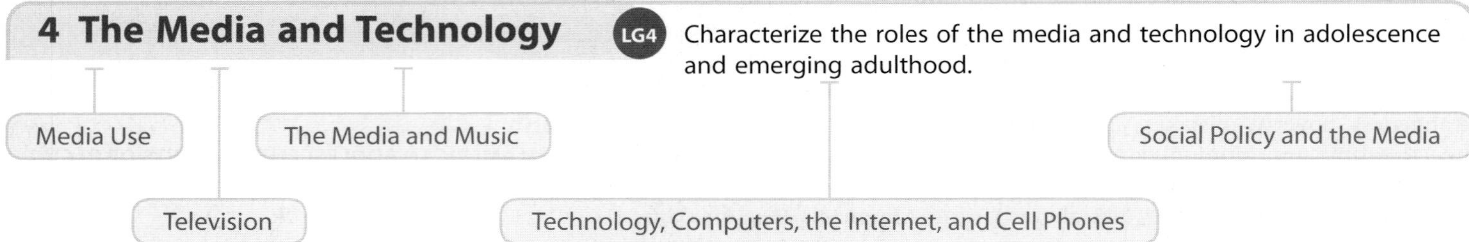

Few developments in society over the last 40 years have had a greater impact on adolescents than television and the Internet (Brown & Bobkowski, 2011; Jackson, 2012; Maloy & others, 2011). The persuasion capabilities of television and the Internet are staggering. Many of today's adolescents have spent more time since infancy in front of a television set, and more recently in front of a computer, than with their parents or in the classroom.

MEDIA USE

If the amount of time spent in an activity is any indication of its importance, there is no doubt that media play important roles in adolescents' lives (Brown & Bobkowski, 2011). To better understand various aspects of U.S. adolescents' media use, the Kaiser Family Foundation funded three national surveys, in 1999, 2004, and 2009. The 2009 survey included more than 2,000 8- to 18-year-olds and documented that adolescent media use has increased dramatically in the last decade (Rideout, Foehr, & Roberts, 2010). Today's youth live in a world in which they are encapsulated by media, and media use increases dramatically in adolescence. According to the survey conducted in 2009, 8- to 11-year-olds used total media 5 hours and 29 minutes a day, 11- to 14-year-olds an average of 8 hours and 40 minutes a day, and 15- to 18-year-olds an average of 7 hours and 58 minutes a day (see Figure 12.6). Thus, media use jumps more than 3 hours in early adolescence! The largest increases in media use in early adolescence are for TV and video game use. TV use by youth increasingly has involved watching TV on the Internet, on an iPod/MP3 player, and on a cell phone. As indicated in Figure 12.6, listening to music and using computers increase considerably in 11- to 14-year-old adolescents. And in the 2009 survey, adding up the daily media use figures to obtain weekly media use leads to the staggering levels of more than 60 hours a week of media use by 11-to 14-year-olds and almost 56 hours a week by 15- to 18-year-olds!

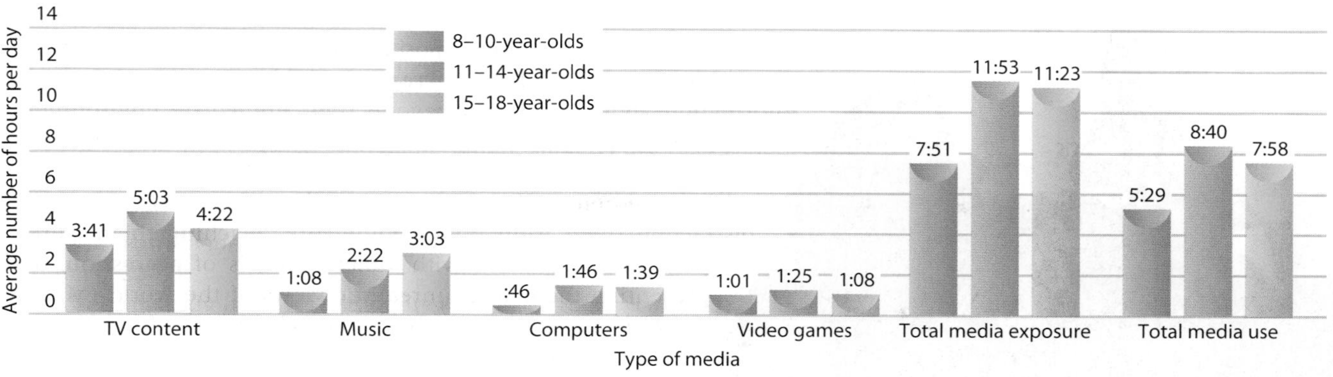

FIGURE **12.6**

TIME SPENT BY U.S. 8- TO 18- YEAR-OLDS IN A TYPICAL DAY

A major trend in the use of technology is the dramatic increase in media multitasking (Brown & Bobkowski, 2011). In the 2009 survey, when the amount of time spent multitasking was included in computing media use (in other words, when each task was counted separately), 11- to 14-year-olds spent a total of nearly 12 hours a day exposed to media (the total is almost 9 hours a day when the effect of multitasking is not included) (Rideout, Foehr, & Roberts, 2010)! In this survey, 39 percent of seventh- to twelfth-graders said "most of the time" they use two or more media concurrently, such as surfing the Web while listening to music. In some cases, media multitasking—such as text messaging, listening to an iPod, and updating a YouTube site—is engaged in at the same time as doing homework. It is hard to imagine that this allows a student to do homework efficiently, although there is little research on media multitasking. A recent study comparing heavy and light media multitaskers revealed that heavy media multitaskers were more susceptible to interference from irrelevant information (Ophir, Nass, & Wagner, 2010).

Mobile media, such as cell phones and iPods, are mainly driving the increased media use by adolescents. For example, in the 2004 survey, only 18 percent of youth owned an iPod or MP3 player; in 2009, 76 percent owned them. In 2004, 39 percent owned a cell phone; that figure jumped to 66 percent in 2009 (Rideout, Foehr, & Roberts, 2010).

Large individual differences characterize all forms of adolescent media use. In addition to the age differences described earlier, gender and ethnicity influence media use. Girls spend more time than boys on social networking sites and listening to music; boys spend more time than girls playing video games and computer games and going to video websites like YouTube (Rideout, Foehr, & Roberts, 2010).

In the recent national survey, African American and Latino youth used media daily more than did non-Latino white youth (Rideout, Foehr, & Roberts, 2010). The ethnic difference was especially pronounced in TV watching, with African American youth watching almost 6 hours a day, Latino youth more than 5 hours a day, and non-Latino White youth 3½ hours a day.

TELEVISION

Few developments during the second half of the twentieth century had a greater impact on children than television (Strasberger, 2009). Many children and adolescents spend more time in front of the television set than they do with their parents. The persuasive capabilities of television are staggering. The 20,000 hours of television watched by the time the average American adolescent graduates from high school are greater than the number of hours spent in the classroom.

THE MEDIA AND MUSIC

Anyone who has been around adolescents very long knows that many of them spend huge amounts of time listening to music on the radio, playing CDs of their favorite music, and watching music videos on television. Approximately two-thirds of all CDs are purchased by the 10- to 24-year-old age group. And one-third of the nation's 8,200 radio stations aim their broadcast rock music at adolescent listeners.

To date, no cause-and-effect studies exist to link either music or videos to an increased risk of early drug use in adolescence. For a small percentage of adolescents, though, certain music may provide a behavioral marker for psychological problems. For example, one study found that adolescents who spent more time listening to music with degrading sexual content were more likely to engage in sexual intercourse earlier than their peers who spent less time listening to this type of music (Martino & others, 2006). And a recent study revealed that higher use of music media was related to viewing the self as less physically attractive and having overall lower self-worth (Kistler & others, 2010). In this study, there were indications that adolescents may use music media as a source of social comparison against which they evaluate their own physical attractiveness and self-worth. Music media may also provide a context for modeling expectations about romantic relationships.

TECHNOLOGY, COMPUTERS, THE INTERNET, AND CELL PHONES

Culture involves change, and nowhere is that change greater than in the technological revolution. Today's adolescents are experiencing this revolution with increased use of computers, the Internet, and cell phones (Brown & Bobkowski, 2011; Jackson & others, 2012; Maloy & others, 2011). They are using these and a variety of other digital devices to communicate in the way their parents used pens, postage stamps, and telephones. The new information society still relies on some basic nontechnological competencies that adolescents need to develop: good communication skills, the ability to solve problems, to think deeply, to think creatively, and to have positive attitudes. However, how young people pursue these competencies is being challenged and extended in ways and at a speed unknown to previous generations (Maloy & others, 2011).

The Internet The **Internet** is the core of computer-mediated communication. The Internet is worldwide and connects thousands of computer networks, providing an incredible array of information—both positive and negative—that adolescents can access.

Internet Use by Adolescents Youth throughout the world are increasingly using the Internet, despite substantial variation in use in different countries around the world and in socioeconomic groups (Jackson & others, 2012; Uhls & Greenfield, 2009; Valkenburg & Peter, 2011). Special concerns have emerged about children's and adolescents' access to information on the Internet, which has been largely unregulated. Youth can access adult sexual material, instructions for making bombs, and other information that is inappropriate for them (Mesch, 2008). A further concern is peer bullying and harassment on the Internet (called *cyberbullying*) (Brown & Bobkowski, 2011; Sontag & others, 2011). A recent survey found that peer bullying offline and online were the most frequent threats that children and adolescents encountered (Palfrey & others, 2009). Another recent study revealed that victimization in both online and school settings were linked to lower self-esteem and higher stress and depression (Fredstrom, Adams, & Gilman, 2011). And yet another recent study found that offline relational aggression and having beliefs that support aggression predicted whether adolescents were likely to engage in Internet aggression (Werner, Bumpus, & Rock, 2010).

Internet The core of computer-mediated communication. The Internet system is worldwide and connects thousands of computer networks, providing an incredible array of information—both positive and negative—that adolescents can access.

A recent study of college students—mean age 20 years—found that when the Internet was used for shopping, entertainment, and pornography, negative outcomes resulted: higher level of drinking and drug use, greater number of sexual partners, worse relationships with friends and parents, and lower self-worth; however, when college students used the Internet for schoolwork, positive outcomes resulted: A lower level of drug use and higher self-worth (Padilla-Walker & others, 2010).

In one study, approximately half of parents reported that being online is more positive than watching TV for adolescents (Tarpley, 2001). However, a national survey indicated that 42 percent of U.S. 10- to 17-year-olds had been exposed to Internet pornography in the past year, with 66 percent of the exposure being unwanted (Wolak, Mitchell, & Finkelhor, 2007).

The Digitally Mediated Social Environment of Adolescents and Emerging Adults

The digitally mediated social environment of adolescents and emerging adults includes e-mail, instant messaging, social networking sites such as Facebook, chat rooms, videosharing and photosharing, multiplayer online computer games, and virtual worlds (O'Keefe, & others, 2011; Rideout, Foehr, & Roberts, 2010; Subrahmanyam & Greenfield, 2008). The remarkable increase in the popularity of Facebook was reflected in its recent replacement of Google in 2010 as the most frequently visited Internet site. Most of these digitally mediated social interactions began on computers but more recently have also shifted to cell phones, especially smartphones (Blair & Fletcher, 2011; Ridehout, Foehr, & Roberts, 2010; Valkenburg & Peter, 2011).

Recent national surveys revealed dramatic increases in adolescents' use of social media and text messaging (Lenhart & others, 2010a,b; Rideout, Foehr, & Roberts, 2010). In 2009, nearly three-fourths of U.S. 12- to 17-year-olds reported that they use social networking sites (Lenhart & others, 2010b). Eighty-one percent of 18- to 24-year-olds had created a profile on a social networking site and 31 percent of them visit a social networking site at least several times a day (Lenhart & others, 2010a). More emerging adult women visit a social networking site several times a day (33 percent) than do their male counterparts (24 percent).

In another report from the recent national survey, 75 percent of U.S. 12- to 17-year-olds had a cell phone (Lenhart & others, 2010a). In this survey, daily text messaging increased from 38 percent who texted friends daily in 2008 to 54 percent in 2009. Also in this survey, half of the adolescents sent 50 or more text messages a day with one-third sending 100 or more a day. Adolescent girls 14 to 17 years of age sent the most text messages, averaging more than 100 a day! The 12- to 13-year-old boys sent the fewest, approximately 20 a day. However, the 12- to 17-year-olds did not use Twitter to a great extent—just 8 percent of those who go online said they have tweeted. And fewer adolescents are blogging now: in 2006, 28 percent of adolescents said they blogged; by 2009 that percentage had dropped to 14 percent.

Text messaging has now become the main way that adolescents connect with their friends, surpassing face-to-face contact, e-mail, instant messaging, and voice calling (Lenhart & others, 2010b). However, voice-mailing is the primary way that most adolescents prefer to connect with parents.

A recent study examined the sequence of using electronic communication technologies that college students in a midwestern university used in managing their social networks (Yang & Brown, 2009). In this study, female college students followed a consistent sequence as their relationships developed, typically beginning by contacting new acquaintances on Facebook, then moving on to instant messaging, after which they may "exchange cell phone numbers, text each other, talk over their cell phone, and finally schedule a time to meet, if everything went well" (Yang & Brown, 2009, p. 2). Male college students were less likely to follow this sequence as consistently, although they did follow it more when communicating with females than males, suggesting that females may maintain more control over communication patterns.

Recent research has found that approximately one of three adolescents self-disclose better online than in person; in this research, boys report that they feel more comfortable self-disclosing online than do girls (Schouten, Valkenburg, & Peter, 2007; Valkenburg & Peter, 2009, 2011). In contrast (as we saw in Chapter 9), girls are more likely to feel comfortable self-disclosing in person than are boys. Thus, boys' self-disclosure may benefit from online communication with friends (Valkenburg & Peter, 2009, 2011). A recent study revealed that adolescents who were better adjusted at 13 to 14 years of age were more likely to use social networking sites at 20 to 22 years of age (Mikami & others, 2010). In this study, young adolescents' friendship quality and behavioral adjustment predicted similar qualities of interaction and problem behavior on social networking sites in emerging adulthood.

developmental **connection**

Peers. Girls' friendships are more likely to focus on intimacy while boys' friendships tend to emphasize power and excitement. Chapter 9, p. 311

Facebook provides opportunities for adolescents and emerging adults to communicate with others who share their interests. Facebook is the most popular way that adolescents and emerging adults communicate on the Internet.

Many adolescents and emerging adults who use Facebook apparently thought that the information they placed on the Web sites was private. However, social networking sites such as Facebook are not as secure in protecting private information as is often believed. Thus, if you are a Facebook user, you should never put your social security number, address, phone number, or date of birth information on the website. Another good strategy is not to put information on Facebook that current or future employers might use against you in any way. And a final good strategy is to be aware that college administrators and personnel may be able to use the information you place on Facebook to evaluate whether you have violated college policies (such as college drug and language harassment policies).

Clearly, parents need to monitor and regulate adolescents' use of the Internet (Jackson & others, 2012; Pujazon-Zazik & Park, 2010). Consider Bonita Williams, who began to worry about how obsessed her 15-year-old daughter, Jade, had become with MySpace (Kornblum, 2006). She became even more concerned when she discovered that Jade was posting suggestive photos of herself and had given her cell phone number out to people in different parts of the United States. She grounded her daughter, blocked MySpace at home, and moved Jade's computer from her bedroom into the family room.

What characterizes the online social environment of adolescents and emerging adults?

The following recent studies explored the role of parents in guiding adolescents' use of the Internet and media:

- Parents' high estimates of online dangers were not matched by their low rates of setting limits and monitoring their adolescents' online activities (Rosen, Cheever, & Carrier, 2008). Also in this study, adolescents who perceived that their parents had an indulgent parenting style (high warmth and involvement but low in strictness and supervision) reported engaging in the most risky online behavior, such as meeting someone in person whom they had initially contacted on the Internet.

- Both maternal and paternal authoritative parenting predicted proactive monitoring of adolescent media use (Padilla-Walker & Coyne, 2011). As part of the authoritative parenting style, parental regulation included the use of active and restrictive mediation. Active mediation encourages parent/adolescent discussion of exposure to questionable media content; restrictive mediation involves parents' efforts to restrict certain media from adolescents' use.
- Problematic mother-adolescent (age 13) relationships that involved undermining attachment and autonomy predicted emerging adults' preference for online communication and greater probability of forming a relationship with someone met online, yet poorer quality in online relationships (Szwedo, Mikami, & Allen, 2011).

SOCIAL POLICY AND THE MEDIA

Adolescents are exposed to an expanding array of media that carry messages that shape adolescents' judgments and behavior (Roberts, Henriksen, & Foehr, 2009). The following social policy initiatives were recommended by the Carnegie Council on Adolescent Development (1995):

- *Encourage socially responsible programming.* There is good evidence of a link between media violence and adolescent aggression. The media also shape many other dimensions of adolescents' development—gender, ethnic, and occupational roles, as well as standards of beauty, family life, and sexuality. Writers, producers, and media executives need to recognize how powerful their messages are to adolescents and work with experts on adolescent development to provide more positive images to youth.
- *Support public efforts to make the media more adolescent-friendly.* Essentially, the U.S. media regulate themselves in regard to their influence on adolescents. All other Western nations have stronger regulations than the United States to foster appropriate educational programming.
- *Encourage media literacy programs as part of school curricula, youth and community organizations, and family life.* Many adolescents do not have the knowledge and skills to critically analyze media messages. Media literacy programs should focus not only on television, but also on the Internet, newspapers, magazines, radio, videos, music, and electronic games.
- *Increase media presentations of health promotions.* Community-wide campaigns using public service announcements in the media have been successful in reducing smoking and increasing physical fitness in adolescents. Use of the media to promote adolescent health and well-being should be increased.
- *Expand opportunities for adolescents' views to appear in the media.* The media should increase the number of adolescent voices in their presentations by featuring editorial opinions, news stories, and videos authored by adolescents. Some schools have shown that this strategy of media inclusion of adolescents can be an effective dimension of education.

A review of social policy and the media by leading expert Amy Jordan (2008) concluded that a difficult challenge involves being able to protect the First Amendment right of free speech while still providing parents with adequate ways to protect their children and youth from unwanted content in their homes. Other experts argue that the government clearly can and should promote positive programming and provide more funding for media research (Brooks-Gunn & Donahue, 2008). For example, government can produce more public service media campaigns that focus on reducing risky behavior by adolescents.

developmental **connection**

Social Policy. The United States needs a developmentally attentive youth policy that applies to many areas of adolescents' lives. Chapter 1, p. 11

Review *Connect* Reflect

LG4 Characterize the roles of the media and technology in adolescence and emerging adulthood.

Review

- How extensively do adolescents use the media? How does their use vary across different types of media?
- How is watching television related to adolescent development?
- What roles do music and the media play in adolescents' lives?
- How are technology, computers, the Internet, and cell phones linked to adolescent development?
- What are some social policy recommendations regarding media use by adolescents?

Connect

- What influence might heavy media use have on adolescents' goal setting as described in Chapter 11?

Reflect *Your Own Personal Journey of Life*

- What was your use of various media in middle/junior and high school like? Did your use of the media in adolescence influence your development in positive or negative ways? Explain.

reach your **learning goals**

1 Culture, Adolescence, and Emerging Adulthood

Discuss the role of culture in the development of adolescents and emerging adults.

The Relevance of Culture for the Study of Adolescence and Emerging Adulthood

- Culture is the behavior, patterns, beliefs, and all other products of a specific group of people that are passed on from generation to generation. If the study of adolescence and emerging adulthood is to be a relevant discipline in the twenty-first century, increased attention will need to be focused on culture and ethnicity because there will be increased contact among people from varied cultural and ethnic backgrounds. For too long, the study of adolescence and emerging adulthood has been ethnocentric in the sense that the main participants in research studies have been middle-socioeconomic-status adolescents and emerging adults from the United States.

Cross-Cultural Comparisons

- Cross-cultural studies involve the comparison of a culture with one or more other cultures—they provide information about the degree to which information about adolescent and emerging adult development is culture-specific. Cross-cultural comparisons reveal information such as variations in the time adolescents spend in different activities, in achievement, and in sexuality. Individualistic cultures focus on the individual—personal goals are more important than group goals, and values (feeling good, achievement, independence) are self-focused. Collectivistic cultures center on the group—the self is defined by in-group contexts, and personal goals are subordinated to preserve group integrity. U.S. adolescents have more discretionary time than do adolescents in other countries. In the United States, adolescents are more achievement-oriented than adolescents in many other countries, but East Asian adolescents spend more time on schoolwork.

Rites of Passage

- Rites of passage are ceremonies that mark an individual's transition from one status to another, especially into adult status. In many primitive cultures, rites of passage are well defined and provide an entry into the adult world. Western industrialized countries lack clearly delineated formal rites of passage that mark the transition to adulthood.

2 Socioeconomic Status and Poverty

Describe how socioeconomic status and poverty are related to adolescent development.

What Is Socioeconomic Status?

- Socioeconomic status (SES) is the grouping of people with similar occupational, educational, and economic characteristics. Socioeconomic status often involves certain inequalities.

Socioeconomic Variations in Families, Neighborhoods, and Schools

- The families, neighborhoods, and schools of adolescents have socioeconomic characteristics that are related to the adolescent's development. Parents in low-SES families are more concerned that their children and adolescents conform to society's expectations; have an authoritarian parenting style; use physical punishment more in disciplining; and are more directive and less conversational with their children and adolescents than higher-SES parents are. Neighborhood variations such as housing quality and mix of high-, middle-, or low-SES residents can influence adolescents' adjustment and achievement. Schools in low-SES areas have fewer resources and are more likely to have students with lower achievement test scores and fewer students going on to college than schools in high-SES areas. Adolescents from affluent families also face adjustment challenges, especially showing high rates of substance use.

Poverty

- Poverty is defined by economic hardship, and its most common marker is the federal poverty threshold (based on the estimated cost of food multiplied by 3). Based on this threshold, the percentage of children under 18 years of age living in poverty increased from 17 percent in 2006 to 19 percent in 2008. The subculture of the poor often is characterized not only by economic hardship, but also by social and psychological difficulties. When poverty is persistent and long-standing, it can have especially devastating effects on adolescent development.

3 Ethnicity

Summarize how ethnicity is involved in the development of adolescents and emerging adults.

Immigration

- Relatively high rates of immigration among minorities are contributing to the growth in the proportion of ethnic minority adolescents and emerging adults in the United States. Immigrants often experience stressors uncommon to or less prominent among longtime residents (such as language barriers, dislocations, and separations from support networks).

Adolescence and Emerging Adulthood: A Special Juncture for Ethnic Minority Individuals

- Adolescence and emerging adulthood are often a critical juncture in the development of ethnic minority individuals. Most ethnic minority individuals first consciously confront their ethnicity in adolescence. As they cognitively mature, ethnic minority adolescents and emerging adults become acutely aware of how the non-Latino White culture evaluates their ethnic group.

Ethnicity Issues

- Too often researchers do not adequately tease apart SES and ethnicity when they study ethnic minority groups, with the result that conclusions about ethnicity are sometimes made that are not warranted. Historical, economic, and social experiences produce many legitimate differences among ethnic minority groups, and between ethnic minority groups and the White majority. Too often differences have been interpreted as deficits in ethnic minority groups. Failure to recognize the diversity within an ethnic minority group can lead to stereotyping. Many ethnic minority adolescents continue to experience prejudice, discrimination, and bias.

4 The Media and Technology

Characterize the roles of the media and technology in adolescence and emerging adulthood.

Media Use

- In terms of exposure, a significant increase in media use has occurred recently, especially in 11- to 14-year-olds. Adolescents are increasing the amount of time they spend in media multitasking. The social environment of adolescents has increasingly become digitally mediated. Older adolescents reduce their TV viewing and video game playing and increase their music listening and computer use. There are large individual variations in adolescent media use.

Television

- Television can have a positive influence on adolescents by presenting motivating educational programs, increasing adolescents' information about the world beyond their immediate environment, and providing models of prosocial behavior. Negative aspects of television include promoting passive learning, being a distraction from homework, teaching stereotypes, providing violent models of aggression, presenting unrealistic views of the world, and increasing obesity. TV violence is not the only cause of adolescents' aggression, but most experts agree that it can induce aggression and antisocial behavior. There also is concern about adolescents' playing violent video games. A special concern is the way sex is portrayed on television and the influence this can have on adolescents' sexual attitudes and behaviors. In general, TV viewing is negatively related to children's mental ability and achievement.

The Media and Music

- Adolescents are heavy consumers of CDs, spend huge amounts of time listening to music on the radio, and watch music videos on television.

Technology, Computers, the Internet, and Cell Phones

- Today's adolescents are experiencing a technology revolution through computers, the Internet, and sophisticated cell phones. The social environment of adolescents and emerging adults has increasingly become digitally mediated. The Internet continues to serve as the main focus of digitally mediated social interaction for adolescents and emerging adults but increasingly involves a variety of digital devices, including cell phones (especially smartphones). Adolescents' online time can have positive or negative outcomes. Large numbers of adolescents and college students engage in social networking on MySpace and Facebook.

Social Policy and the Media

- Social policy recommendations regarding the media include encouraging socially responsible programming, supporting public efforts to make the media more adolescent-friendly, and encouraging media literacy campaigns.

key terms

culture 393
ethnocentrism 393
cross-cultural studies 393
individualism 394
collectivism 394
rites of passage 397
socioeconomic status (SES) 399
feminization of poverty 402
ethnicity 404
prejudice 409
Internet 414

key people

Carolyn Tamis-LeMonda 395
Reed Larson and Suman Verma 396
Suniya Luthar 400
Vonnie McLoyd 402
Carola Suárez-Orozco 406
Ross Parke 407
Amy Jordan 417

resources for improving the lives of adolescents

The Eisenhower Foundation
www.eisenhowerfoundation.org

This foundation provides funds for a number of programs designed to improve the lives of children and adolescents living in low-income circumstances. The foundation is replicating in a number of states the successful Quantum Opportunities program of the Ford Foundation.

Poverty and Socioeconomic Disadvantage in Adolescence
by Vonnie McLoyd, Rachel Kaplan, Kelly Purcell, Erika Bagley, Cecily Hardaway, and Clara Smalls
in R. M. Lerner and L. Steinberg (Eds.), *Handbook of Adolescent Psychology* (2009, 3rd ed.)
New York: Wiley

An excellent, up-to-date chapter on poverty, ethnicity, and policies that are needed to improve the lives of children and adolescents who live in poverty conditions.

The World's Youth
edited by Bradford Brown, Reed Larson, and T. S. Saraswathi (2002)
Fort Worth, TX: Harcourt Brace

This is an excellent book on adolescent development in eight regions of the world.

Generation M²: Media in the Lives of 8- to 18-Year-Olds.
by Victoria Rideout, Ulla Foehr, and Donald Roberts (2010)
Menlo Park, CA: Kaiser Family Foundation

The detailed report of the latest national survey of adolescents' media use provides valuable information for understanding adolescent media use and ways for improving their health.

self-assessment

The Online Learning Center includes the following self-assessment for further exploration:

- *Stereotyping*

and coping involved with these problems? What characterizes resilient adolescents?

connecting with health and well-being

What Coping Strategies Work for Adolescents and Emerging Adults?

Here are some effective coping strategies that can benefit adolescents and emerging adults:

- ***Think positively and optimistically.*** Thinking positively and avoiding negative thoughts are good strategies when adolescents and emerging adults are trying to handle stress in just about any circumstance. Why? A positive mood improves the ability to process information efficiently and enhances self-esteem. In most cases, an optimistic attitude is superior to a pessimistic one. It provides a sense of controlling the environment, much like what Albert Bandura (2001, 2009, 2010a) talks about when he describes the importance of self-efficacy in coping.
- ***Increase self-control.*** Developing better self-control is an effective coping strategy. Coping successfully with a problem usually takes time—weeks, months, even years in some cases. Many adolescents and emerging adults who engage in problematic behavior have difficulty maintaining a plan for coping because their problematic behavior provides immediate gratification (such as eating, smoking, drinking, going to a party instead of studying for an exam). To maintain a self-control program over time, it is important to be able to forgo immediate satisfaction.
- ***Seek social support.*** Researchers consistently have found that social support helps adolescents and emerging adults cope with stress (Taylor, 2011a,b,c). For example, depressed adolescents and emerging adults usually have fewer and less supportive relationships with family members, friends, and co-workers than do their counterparts who are not depressed (Nolen-Hoeksema, 2011).
- ***See a counselor or therapist.*** If adolescents and emerging adults are not able to cope with the problem(s) they are encountering, it is very important for them to seek professional help from a counselor or therapist. Most colleges have a counseling service that provides unbiased, professional advice to students.
- ***Use multiple coping strategies.*** Adolescents and emerging adults who face stressful circumstances have many strategies from which to choose (Greenberg, 2011). Often it is wise to choose more than one because a single strategy may not work in a particular context. For example, an adolescent or emerging adult who has experienced a stressful life event or a cluster of such life events (such as the death of a parent or the breakup of a romantic relationship) might see a mental health professional, seek social support, exercise regularly, reduce drinking, and practice relaxation.

When used alone, no one of these strategies might be adequate, but their combined effect may allow the adolescent or emerging adult to cope successfully with stress. Recall what you have learned from reading about research on peers, family, and ethnicity as you consider any other strategies that might be helpful.

Masten and her colleagues (2006) concluded that being resilient in adolescence is linked to continuing to be resilient in emerging adulthood, but that resilience can develop in emerging adulthood. They also indicated that during emerging adulthood some individuals become motivated to better their lives and develop an improved ability to plan and make more effective decisions that place their lives on a more positive developmental course. In some instances, a specific person may influence an emerging adult in very positive ways, as was the case in Michael Maddaus' life, which we considered at the beginning of Chapter 1. You might recall that after a childhood and adolescence filled with stress, conflict, disappointment, and problems, his connection with a very competent mentor in emerging adulthood helped him to turn his life around, and he went on to become a successful surgeon. According to Masten and her colleagues (2006), a romantic relationship or the birth of a child may stimulate change and lead an emerging adult to develop a stronger commitment to a positive future.

Review *Connect* Reflect

LG1 Discuss the nature of problems in adolescence and emerging adulthood.

Review

- How can the biopsychosocial approach be characterized?
- What is the developmental psychopathology approach like?
- What are some general characteristics of adolescent and emerging adult problems?
- What is the nature of stress and coping in adolescence and emerging adulthood?
- How can the resilience of some adolescents and emerging adults be explained?

Connect

- How might friendships (described in Chapter 9) contribute to both stress and coping?

Reflect ***Your Own Personal Journey of Life***

- What were the most significant stressors that you experienced as an adolescent? How effectively did you cope with them? Explain.

2 Problems and Disorders

LG2 Describe some problems and disorders that characterize adolescents and emerging adults.

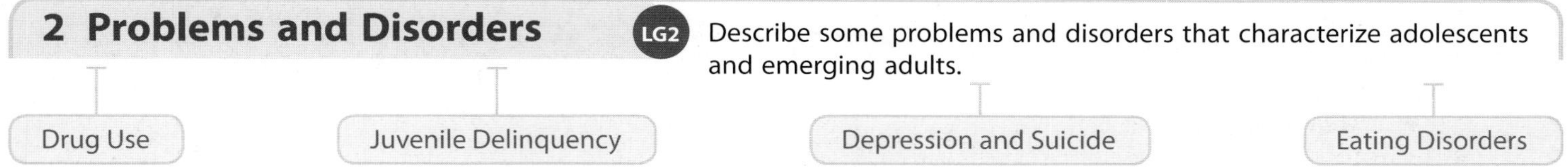

What are some of the major problems and disorders in adolescence and emerging adulthood? They include drugs and alcohol abuse, juvenile delinquency, school-related problems, high-risk sexual behavior, depression and suicide, and eating disorders. We discussed school-related and sexual problems in earlier chapters. Here we examine the other problems, beginning with drugs.

DRUG USE

How pervasive is adolescent and emerging adult drug use in the United States? What are the nature and effects of various drugs taken by adolescents and emerging adults? What factors contribute to adolescent and emerging adult drug use? Let's now explore these questions.

Trends in Overall Drug Use The 1960s and 1970s were a time of marked increases in the use of illicit drugs. During the social and political unrest of those years, many youth turned to marijuana, stimulants, and hallucinogens. Increases in adolescent and emerging adult alcohol consumption during this period also were noted (Robinson & Greene, 1988). More precise data about drug use by adolescents and emerging adults have been collected in recent years. Each year since 1975, Lloyd Johnston and his colleagues, working at the Institute of Social Research at the University of Michigan, have carefully monitored the drug use of America's high school seniors in a wide range of public and private high schools. Since 1991, they also have surveyed drug use by eighth- and tenth-graders and from time to time have assessed drug use in emerging adults and followed it into the middle adulthood years. The University of Michigan study is called the Monitoring the Future Study. In 2010, the study surveyed more than 46,000 secondary school students in more than 400 public and private schools (Johnston & others, 2011).

According to this study, the proportions of eighth-, tenth-, and twelfth-grade U.S. students who used any illicit drug declined in the late 1990s and first years of the twenty-first century (Johnston & others, 2011) (see Figure 13.4). The use of drugs among U.S. secondary school students declined in the 1980s but began to increase in the early 1990s (Johnston & others, 2011). In the late 1990s and early

FIGURE **13.4**

TRENDS IN DRUG USE BY U.S. EIGHTH-, TENTH-, AND TWELFTH-GRADE STUDENTS. This graph shows the percentage of U.S. eighth-, tenth-, and twelfth-grade students who reported having taken an illicit drug in the last 12 months, from 1991 to 2010 for eighth- and tenth-graders, and from 1975 to 2010 for twelfth-graders (Johnston & others, 2011).

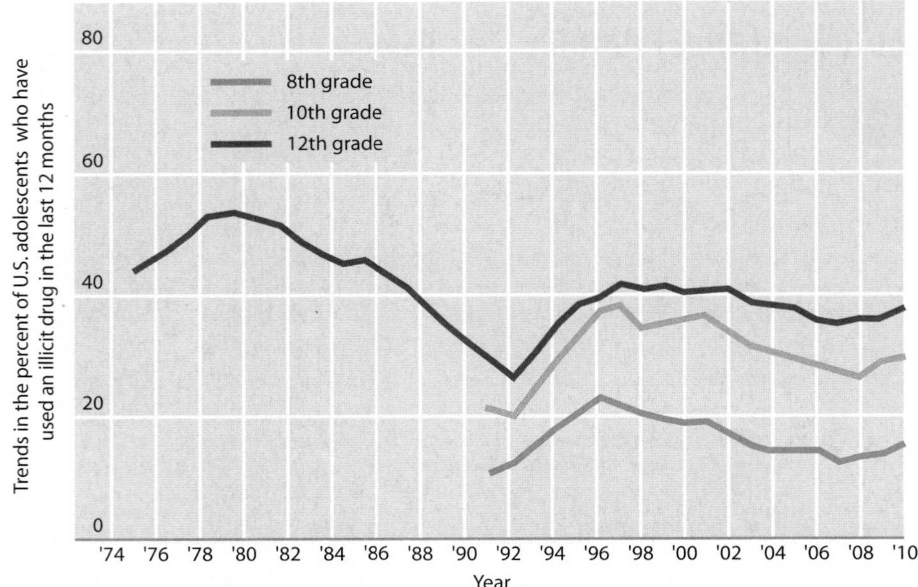

part of the twenty-first century, the proportion of secondary school students reporting the use of any illicit drug has been declining. The overall decline in the use of illicit drugs by adolescents during this time frame is approximately one-third for eighth-graders, one-fourth for tenth-graders, and one-eighth for twelfth-graders. Figure 13.4 shows the overall trends in drug use by U.S. high school seniors since 1975 and by U.S. eighth- and tenth-graders since 1991. The most notable declines in drug use by U.S. adolescents in the twenty-first century have occurred for LSD, cocaine, cigarettes, sedatives, tranquilizers, and Ecstasy. Marijuana is the illicit drug most widely used in the United States and Europe (Hibell & others, 2004; Johnston & others, 2011).

As shown in Figure 13.4, in which marijuana is included, an increase in illicit drug use by U.S. adolescents occurred in 2009 and 2010. However, when marijuana use is subtracted from the illicit drug index, no increase in U.S. adolescent drug use occurred in 2009 and 2010 (Johnston & others, 2011).

Johnston and his colleagues (2005) noted that "generational forgetting" contributed to the rise of adolescent drug use in the 1990s, as adolescents' beliefs about the dangers of drugs eroded considerably. The recent downturn in drug use by U.S. adolescents has been attributed to an increase in the perceived dangers of drug use on youth (Johnston & others, 2011).

Let's now consider separately a number of drugs that are abused by some adolescents and emerging adults.

Alcohol To learn more about the role of alcohol in adolescents' and emerging adults' lives, we examine the use and abuse of alcohol by adolescents and emerging adults, and risk factors in alcohol abuse.

Alcohol Use in Adolescence and Emerging Adulthood How extensive is alcohol use by U.S. adolescents? Sizable declines in adolescent alcohol use have occurred in recent years (Johnston & others, 2011). The percentage of U.S. eighth-graders saying that they had any alcohol to drink in the past 30 days fell from a 1996 high of 26 percent to 14 percent in 2010. The 30-day prevalence fell among tenth-graders from 39 percent in 2001 to 29 percent in 2010 and among high school seniors from 72 percent in 1980 to 41 percent in 2010. Binge drinking (defined in the University of Michigan surveys as having five or more drinks in a row in the last two weeks) by high school seniors declined from 41 percent in 1980 to 27 percent in 2010. Binge drinking by eighth- and tenth-graders also has dropped in recent years. A

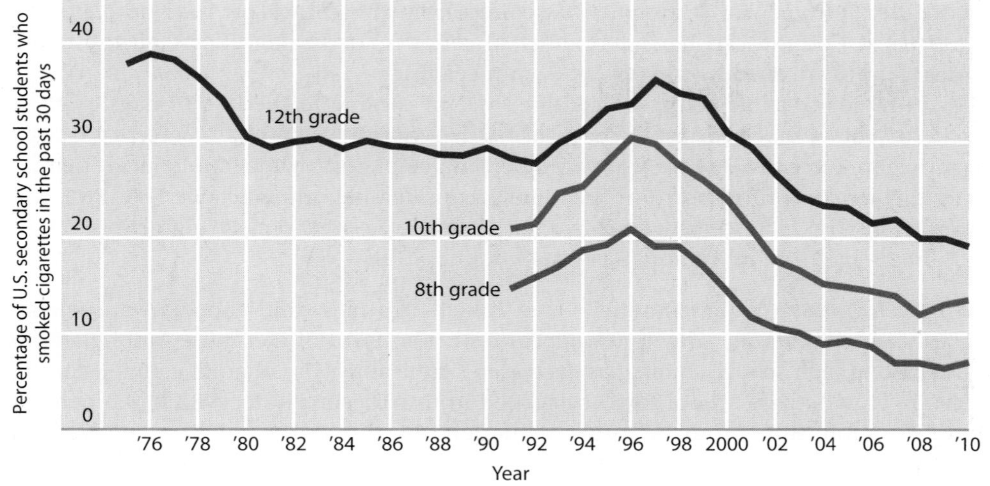

FIGURE **13.6**
TRENDS IN CIGARETTE SMOKING BY U.S. SECONDARY SCHOOL STUDENTS

establishing regular smoking habits during high school and college. Since the national surveys by Johnston and others began in 1975, cigarettes have been the substance most frequently used on a daily basis by high school seniors (Johnston & others, 2011).

The peer group especially plays an important role in smoking (Metzger & others, 2011). In one study, the risk of current smoking was linked with peer networks in which at least half of the members smoked, one or two best friends smoked, and smoking was common in the school (Alexander & others, 2001). And in a recent study, early smoking was predicted better by sibling and peer smoking than by parental smoking (Kelly & others, 2011).

Cigarette smoking is decreasing among adolescents (see Figure 13.6). Cigarette smoking among U.S. adolescents peaked in 1996 and 1997 and has gradually declined since then (Johnston & others, 2011). Following peak use in 1996, smoking rates for U.S. eighth-graders have fallen by 50 percent. In 2010, the percentages of adolescents who said they smoked cigarettes in the last 30 days were 19 percent (twelfth grade), 14 percent (tenth grade), and 7 percent (eighth grade). Since the mid-1990s an increasing percentage of adolescents have reported that they perceive cigarette smoking as dangerous, that they disapprove of it, that they are less accepting of being around smokers, and that they prefer to date nonsmokers (Johnston & others, 2011).

"I'll tell you one thing. As soon as I'm thirteen I'm gonna stop!"
Wayne Stayskal © 1979 Tribune Media Services, Inc. All Rights Reserved. Reprinted with permission.

The devastating effects of early smoking were brought home in a research study that found that smoking in the adolescent years causes permanent genetic changes in the lungs and forever increases the risk of lung cancer, even if the smoker quits (Wiencke & others, 1999). The damage was much less likely among smokers in the study who started in their twenties. One of the remarkable findings in the study was that the early age of onset of smoking was more important in predicting genetic damage than how heavily the individuals smoked.

A number of researchers have developed strategies for interrupting behavioral patterns that lead to smoking. In one investigation, high school students were recruited to help seventh-grade students resist peer pressure to smoke (McAlister & others, 1980). The high school students encouraged the younger adolescents to resist the influence of high-powered ads suggesting that liberated women smoke by saying, "She is not really liberated if she is hooked on tobacco." The students also engaged in role-playing exercises called "chicken." In these situations, the high school students called the younger adolescents "chicken" for not trying a cigarette. The seventh-graders practiced resistance to the peer pressure by saying, "I'd be a real chicken if I smoked just to impress you." Following several sessions, the students in the smoking prevention group were 50 percent less likely to begin smoking compared with a group of seventh-grade students in a neighboring junior high school, even though the parents of both groups of students had the same smoking rate.

Cocaine *Cocaine* is a stimulant that comes from the coca plant, native to Bolivia and Peru. Cocaine can have a number of seriously damaging effects on the body, including heart attacks, strokes, and brain seizures.

How many adolescents use cocaine? Use of cocaine in the last 30 days by high school seniors dropped from a peak of 6.7 percent in 1985 to 1.3 percent in 2010 (Johnston & others, 2011). A growing percentage of high school students are reaching the conclusion that cocaine use entails considerable unpredictable risk. Still, the percentage of adolescents who have used cocaine is precariously high. About 1 of every 13 high school seniors has tried cocaine at least once.

Amphetamines Amphetamines, often called "pep pills" and "uppers," are widely prescribed stimulants, sometimes appearing in the form of diet pills. Amphetamine use among high school seniors has decreased significantly. Use of amphetamines in the last 30 days by high school seniors declined from 10.7 percent in 1982 to 3.3 percent in 2010 (Johnston & others, 2011). Although use of over-the-counter diet pills has decreased in recent years, 40 percent of today's females have tried using diet pills by the time they graduate from high school.

Ecstasy *Ecstasy*, the street name for the synthetic drug MDMA, has both stimulant and hallucinogenic effects. Ecstasy produces euphoric feelings and heightened sensations (especially touch and sight). Ecstasy use can lead to dangerous increases in blood pressure, as well as a stroke or a heart attack.

Ecstasy use by U.S. adolescents began in the 1980s and then peaked in 2000 to 2001. Thirty-day prevalence of use in 2008 by eighth-, tenth-, and twelfth-graders was 1.1, 1.9, and 1.4 percent, respectively (down from 1.8, 2.6, and 2.8 percent in 2001) (Johnston & others, 2011). The downturn in reported use of Ecstasy in 2002 coincides with adolescents' increasing knowledge that Ecstasy use can be dangerous. However, in 2010, an upturn in Ecstasy use occurred, possibly because today's youth have heard less about the dangers of Ecstasy than did their predecessors.

Depressants **Depressants** are drugs that slow down the central nervous system, bodily functions, and behavior. Medically, depressants have been used to reduce anxiety and to induce sleep. Among the most widely used depressants is alcohol, which we discussed earlier; barbiturates; and tranquilizers. Though used less frequently than other depressants, the opiates are especially dangerous.

Eighteen-year-old Paul Michaud (*above*) began taking OxyContin in high school. Michaud says, "I was hooked." Now he is in drug treatment.

depressants Drugs that slow down the central nervous system, bodily functions, and behavior.

Barbiturates, such as Nembutal (pentobarbital) and Seconal (secobarbital), are depressant drugs that induce sleep or reduce anxiety. *Tranquilizers*, such as Valium (diazepam) and Xanax (alprazolam), are depressant drugs that reduce anxiety and induce relaxation. They can produce symptoms of withdrawal when an individual stops taking them. Since the initial surveys, begun in 1975, of drug use by high school seniors, use of depressants has decreased. For example, use of barbiturates by high school seniors at least every 30 days in 1975 was 4.7 percent; in 2010, it was 2.2 percent (Johnston & others, 2011). Over the same time period, tranquilizer use also decreased, from 4.1 percent to 2.5 percent, for 30-day prevalence.

Opiates, which consist of opium and its derivatives, depress the activity of the central nervous system. They are commonly known as narcotics. Many drugs have been produced from the opium poppy, among them morphine and heroin (which is converted to morphine when it enters the brain). For several hours after taking an opiate, an individual feels euphoria and pain relief; however, the opiates are among the most physically addictive drugs. The person soon craves more heroin and experiences very painful withdrawal unless he or she takes more.

The rates of heroin use among adolescents are quite low, but they rose significantly for grades 8, 10, and 12 in the 1990s (Johnston & others, 2009). In 2010, 0.4 percent of high school seniors said they had used heroin in the last 30 days (Johnston & others, 2011).

An alarming trend has recently emerged in adolescents' use of prescription painkillers. Many adolescents cite the medicine cabinets of their parents or of friends'

Drug Classification	Medical Uses	Short-term Effects	Overdose	Health Risks	Risk of Physical/ Psychological Dependence
DEPRESSANTS					
Alcohol	Pain relief	Relaxation, depressed brain activity, slowed behavior, reduced inhibitions	Disorientation, loss of consciousness, even death at high blood-alcohol levels	Accidents, brain damage, liver disease, heart disease, ulcers, birth defects	Physical: moderate; psychological: moderate
Barbiturates	Sleeping pill	Relaxation, sleep	Breathing difficulty, coma, possible death	Accidents, coma, possible death	Physical and psychological: moderate to high
Tranquilizers	Anxiety reduction	Relaxation, slowed behavior	Breathing difficulty, coma, possible death	Accidents, coma, possible death	Physical: low to moderate; psychological: moderate to high
Opiates (narcotics)	Pain relief	Euphoric feelings, drowsiness, nausea	Convulsions, coma, possible death	Accidents, infectious diseases such as AIDS (when the drug is injected)	Physical: high; psychological: moderate to high
STIMULANTS					
Amphetamines	Weight control	Increased alertness, excitability; decreased fatigue, irritability	Extreme irritability, feelings of persecution, convulsions	Insomnia, hypertension, malnutrition, possible death	Physical: possible; psychological: moderate to high
Cocaine	Local anesthetic	Increased alertness, excitability, euphoric feelings; decreased fatigue, irritability	Extreme irritability, feelings of persecution, convulsions, cardiac arrest, possible death	Insomnia, hypertension, malnutrition, possible death	Physical: possible; psychological: moderate (oral) to very high (injected or smoked)
HALLUCINOGENS					
LSD	None	Strong hallucinations, distorted time perception	Severe mental disturbance, loss of contact with reality	Accidents	Physical: none; psychological: low

FIGURE **13.7**

PSYCHOACTIVE DRUGS: DEPRESSANTS, STIMULANTS, AND HALLUCINOGENS

parents as the main source for their prescription painkillers. A 2004 survey revealed that 18 percent of U.S. adolescents had used Vicodin (acetaminophen and hydrocodone) at some point in their lifetime, whereas 10 percent had used OxyContin (oxycodone) (Partnership for a Drug-Free America, 2005). In the University of Michigan survey, a significant drop in Vicodin use occurred in 2010, down to 8 percent in grade 12 from 9.7 percent in 2009 (Johnston & others, 2011). These drugs fall into the general class of drugs called narcotics, and they are highly addictive. In this national survey, 9 percent of adolescents also said they had abused cough medications to intentionally get high. The University of Michigan began including OxyContin in its survey in 2002. For twelfth-graders, 4 percent reported using OxyContin on an annual basis in 2002, a figure that peaked in 2005 at 5.5 percent, but has turned slightly downward recently to 5.1 percent in 2010 (Johnston & others, 2011).

At this point, we have discussed a number of depressants, stimulants, and hallucinogens. Their medical uses, short-term effects, overdose symptoms, health risks, physical addiction risk, and psychological dependence risk are summarized in Figure 13.7.

What characterizes the use of inhalants by adolescents?

Anabolic Steroids **Anabolic steroids** are drugs derived from the male sex hormone, testosterone. They promote muscle growth and increase lean body mass. Nonmedical uses of these drugs carry a number of physical and psychological health risks (National Clearinghouse for Alcohol and Drug Information, 1999). Both males and females who take large doses of anabolic steroids usually experience changes in sexual characteristics. Psychological effects in both males and females can involve irritability, uncontrollable bursts of anger, severe mood swings (which can lead to depression when individuals stop using the steroids), impaired judgment stemming from feelings of invincibility, and paranoid jealousy.

In the University of Michigan study, in 2010, 0.3 percent of eighth-graders, 0.5 percent of tenth-graders, and 1.1 percent of twelfth-graders said they had used anabolic steroids in the past 30 days (Johnston & others, 2011). The rate of steroid use by twelfth-graders is a decline from 2004 (1.6 percent).

Inhalants Inhalants are ordinary household products that are inhaled or sniffed by children and adolescents to get high. Examples of inhalants include model airplane glue, nail polish remover, and cleaning fluids. Short-term use of inhalants can cause intoxicating effects that last for several minutes or even several hours if the inhalants are used repeatedly. Eventually the user can lose consciousness. Long-term use of inhalants can lead to heart failure and even death.

Use of inhalants is higher among younger than older adolescents. In the University of Michigan national survey, inhalant use by U.S. adolescents has decreased in the twenty-first century (Johnston & others, 2011). Use in the last 30 days by twelfth-graders was 1.4 percent in 2010, having peaked at 3.2 percent in 1995. The prevalence of inhalant use in the last 30 days by eighth-graders was 3.6 percent in 2010, down from a peak of 6.1 percent in 1995.

Factors in Adolescent and Emerging Adult Drug Abuse Earlier, we discussed the factors that place adolescents and emerging adults at risk for alcohol abuse. Researchers also have examined the factors that are related to drug use in general in adolescence and emerging adulthood, especially the roles of early substance use; parents, peers, and schools; and changes in substance use from adolescence through emerging and early adulthood.

Early Substance Use Most adolescents become drug users at some point in their development, whether their use is limited to alcohol, caffeine, and cigarettes, or extended to marijuana, cocaine, and hard drugs. A special concern involves adolescents who begin to use drugs early in adolescence or even in childhood (Buchmann & others, 2009; Trucco, Colder, & Wieczorek, 2011). One study revealed that individuals who began drinking alcohol before 14 years of age were more likely to become alcohol dependent than their counterparts who began drinking alcohol at 21 years of age or older (Hingson, Heeren, & Winter, 2006). A longitudinal study found that onset of alcohol use before 11 years of age was linked to increased adult alcohol dependence (Guttmannova & others, 2011).

What are ways that parents have been found to influence whether their adolescents take drugs?

Parents, Peers, and Schools Parents play an important role in preventing adolescent drug abuse (Kinney, 2012). Positive relationships with parents, siblings, peers and others can reduce adolescents' drug use (Harakeh & others, 2010: Kelly & others, 2011; Marti, Stice, & Springer, 2010). Researchers have found that parental monitoring is linked with a lower incidence of drug use (Tobler & Komro, 2010). A recent research review concluded that the more frequently adolescents ate dinner with their family, the less likely they were to have substance abuse problems (Sen, 2010). And a recent study revealed that negative interactions with parents were linked to increased adolescent drinking and smoking, while positive identification with parents was related to declines in use of these substances (Gutman & others, 2011).

anabolic steroids Drugs derived from the male sex hormone, testosterone. They promote muscle growth and increase lean body mass.

A longitudinal study conducted by Kenneth Dodge and his colleagues (2006) examined the joint contributions of parents and peers to early substance use. The sequence of factors that were related to whether an adolescent would take drugs by 12 years of age was:

- Being born into a high-risk family (especially with a poor, single, or teenage mother)
- Experiencing an increase in harsh parenting in childhood
- Having conduct problems in school and getting rejected by peers in childhood
- Experiencing increased conflict with parents in early adolescence
- Having low parental monitoring
- Hanging out with deviant peers in early adolescence and engaging in increased substance use

developmental **connection**

Families. Parental monitoring is a key aspect of parental management of adolescent lives. Chapter 8, p. 261

Educational success is also a strong buffer for the emergence of drug problems in adolescence (Henry & others, 2009). An analysis by Jerald Bachman and his colleagues (2008) revealed that early educational achievement considerably reduced the likelihood that adolescents would develop drug problems, including those involving alcohol abuse, smoking, and abuse of various illicit drugs.

Emerging Adulthood and Early Adulthood Fortunately, by the time individuals reach their mid-twenties, many have reduced their use of alcohol and drugs (Johnston & others, 2010). That is the conclusion reached by Jerald Bachman and his colleagues (2002) in a longitudinal analysis of more than 38,000 individuals (see Figure 13.8). The subjects were evaluated from the time they were high school seniors through their twenties. Some of the main findings in the study were as follows:

- College students drink more than youth who end their education after high school.
- Those who don't go to college smoke more.
- Singles use marijuana more than married individuals do.
- Drinking is heaviest among singles and divorced individuals. Becoming engaged, married, or even remarried quickly brings down alcohol use. Thus, living arrangements and marital status are key factors in alcohol and drug use rates during the twenties.
- Individuals who considered religion to be very important in their lives and who frequently attended religious services were less likely to take drugs than were their less-religious counterparts.

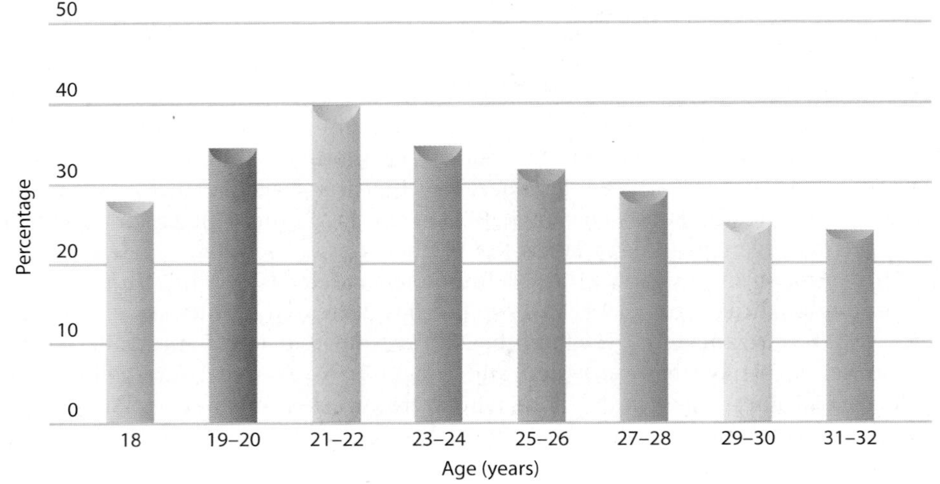

FIGURE **13.8**

BINGE DRINKING IN THE TRANSITION FROM ADOLESCENCE TO ADULTHOOD. This figure shows the percentage of individuals from age 18 through 32 who said they had engaged in binge drinking (having five or more drinks on any one occasion) during the past two weeks. Notice the decline in binge drinking in the mid-twenties.

JUVENILE DELINQUENCY

Thirteen-year-old Arnie, in the section that opened this chapter, is a juvenile delinquent with a history of thefts and physical assaults. What is a juvenile delinquent? What are the antecedents of delinquency? What types of interventions have been used to prevent or reduce delinquency?

What Is Juvenile Delinquency? The term **juvenile delinquency** refers to a broad range of behaviors, from socially unacceptable behavior (such as acting out in school) to status offenses (such as running away) to criminal acts (such as burglary). For legal purposes, a distinction is made between index offenses and status offenses:

- **Index offenses** are criminal acts, whether they are committed by juveniles or adults. They include such acts as robbery, aggravated assault, rape, and homicide.
- **Status offenses,** such as running away, truancy, underage drinking, sexual promiscuity, and uncontrollability, are less serious acts. They are performed by youth under a specified age, which classifies them as juvenile offenses. One study found that status offenses increased through adolescence.

States often differ in the age used to classify an individual as a juvenile or an adult. Approximately three-fourths of the states have established age 18 as a maximum for defining juveniles. Two states use age 19 as the cutoff, seven states use age 17, and four states use age 16. Thus, running away from home at age 17 may be an offense in some states but not in others.

One issue in juvenile justice is whether an adolescent who commits a crime should be tried as an adult. Some psychologists have proposed that individuals 12 and under should not be evaluated under adult criminal laws and that those 17 and older should be (Steinberg & Cauffman, 2001; Steinberg, 2009). They also recommend that individuals 13 to 16 years of age be given some type of individualized assessment in terms of whether to be tried in a juvenile court or an adult criminal court. This framework argues strongly against court placement based solely on the nature of an offense and takes into account the offender's developmental maturity. The Society for Adolescent Medicine has argued that the death penalty should not be used with adolescents (Morreale, 2004).

In addition to the legal classifications of index offenses and status offenses, many of the behaviors considered delinquent are included in widely used classifications of abnormal behavior. **Conduct disorder** is the psychiatric diagnostic category used when multiple behaviors occur over a six-month period. These behaviors include truancy, running away, fire setting, cruelty to animals, breaking and entering, excessive fighting, and others (Burke, 2011; Capaldi, 2012). When three or more of these behaviors co-occur before the age of 15, and the child or adolescent is considered unmanageable or out of control, the clinical diagnosis is conduct disorder. A recent study revealed that young adolescents' school connectedness served as a protective factor for early adolescent conduct problems (Loukas, Roalson, & Herrera, 2010).

In sum, most children or adolescents at one time or another act out or do things that are destructive or troublesome for themselves or others. If these behaviors occur often in childhood or early adolescence, psychiatrists diagnose them as conduct disorders (Farrington, 2009; Loeber & Burke, 2011). If these behaviors result in illegal acts by juveniles, society labels the offenders as *delinquents.*

The number of juvenile court delinquency caseloads in the United States increased dramatically from 1960 to 1996 but has decreased slightly since 1996 (see Figure 13.9) (Puzzanchera & Sickmund, 2008). Note that this figure reflects only adolescents who have been arrested and assigned to juvenile court delinquency caseloads and does not include those who were arrested and not assigned to the delinquency caseloads, nor does the figure include youth who committed offenses but were not apprehended.

juvenile delinquency A broad range of behaviors, including socially unacceptable behavior, status offenses, and criminal acts.

index offenses Criminal acts, such as robbery, rape, and homicide, whether they are committed by juveniles or adults.

status offenses Juvenile offenses, performed by youth under a specified age, that are not as serious as index offenses. These offenses may include such acts as underage drinking, truancy, and sexual promiscuity.

conduct disorder The psychiatric diagnostic category for the occurrence of multiple delinquent activities over a six-month period. These behaviors include truancy, running away, fire setting, cruelty to animals, breaking and entering, and excessive fighting.

Males are more likely to engage in delinquency than are females (Colman & others, 2009). However, U.S. government statistics revealed that the percentage of delinquency caseloads involving females increased from 19 percent in 1985 to 27 percent in 2005 (Puzzanchera & Sickmund, 2008).

As adolescents become emerging adults, do their rates of delinquency and crime change? Analyses indicate that theft, property damage, and physical aggression decrease from 18 to 26 years of age (Schulenberg & Zarrett, 2006). The peak for property damage is 16 to 18 years of age for males, 15 to 17 years of age for females. However, the peak for violence is 18 to 19 years of age for males and 19 to 21 years of age for females (Farrington, 2004).

A distinction is made between early-onset (before age 11) and late-onset (after age 11) antisocial behavior. Early-onset antisocial behavior is associated with more negative developmental outcomes than late-onset antisocial behavior (Schulenberg & Zarrett, 2006). Early-onset antisocial behavior is more likely to persist into emerging adulthood and is associated with more mental health and relationship problems (Loeber & Burke, 2011; Loeber, Burke, & Pardini, 2009).

FIGURE **13.9**

NUMBER OF U.S. JUVENILE COURT DELINQUENCY CASELOADS FROM 1960 TO 2005

Antecedents of Juvenile Delinquency Predictors of delinquency include conflict with authority, minor covert acts that are followed by property damage and other more serious acts, minor aggression followed by fighting and violence, identity (negative identity), self-control (low degree), cognitive distortions (egocentric bias), age (early initiation), sex (male), expectations for education (low expectations, little commitment), school achievement (low achievement in early grades), peer influence (heavy influence, low resistance), socioeconomic status (low), parental role (lack of monitoring, low support, and ineffective discipline), siblings (having an older sibling who is a delinquent), and neighborhood quality (urban, high crime, high mobility). A summary of these antecedents of delinquency is presented in Figure 13.10.

Let's look in more detail at several other factors that are related to delinquency. Erik Erikson (1968) notes that adolescents whose development has restricted their access to acceptable social roles or made them feel that they cannot measure up to the demands placed on them may choose a negative identity. Adolescents with a negative identity may find support for their delinquent image among peers, reinforcing the negative identity. For Erikson, delinquency is an attempt to establish an identity, although it is a negative identity.

Parenting factors play a key role in delinquency (Roche & others, 2011). Recall from earlier in this chapter the description of the developmental cascade approach of Gerald Patterson and his colleagues (2010) and research indicating that high levels of coercive parenting and low levels of positive parenting lead to the development of antisocial behavior in children, which in turn connect children to negative experiences in peer and school contexts.

Let's further explore the role that family processes play in the development of delinquency. Parents of delinquents are less skilled in discouraging antisocial behavior and in encouraging skilled behavior than are parents of nondelinquents. Parental monitoring of adolescents is especially important in determining whether an adolescent becomes a delinquent (Laird & others, 2008). A longitudinal study found that the less parents knew about their adolescents' whereabouts, activities, and peers, the more likely the adolescents were to engage in delinquent behavior (Laird & others, 2003). Family discord and inconsistent and inappropriate discipline are also associated with delinquency (Capaldi & Shortt, 2003). A recent study found that early parental monitoring in adolescence and ongoing parental support were linked to a lower incidence of criminal behavior in emerging adulthood (Johnson & others, 2011).

What are some characteristics of conduct disorder?

Antecedent	Association with Delinquency	Description
Authority conflict	High degree	Youth show stubbornness prior to age 12, then become defiant of authority.
Covert acts	Frequent	Minor covert acts, such as lying, are followed by property damage and moderately serious delinquency, then serious delinquency.
Overt acts of aggression	Frequent	Minor aggression is followed by fighting and violence.
Identity	Negative identity	Erikson argues that delinquency occurs because the adolescent fails to resolve a role identity.
Cognitive distortions	High degree	The thinking of delinquents is frequently characterized by a variety of cognitive distortions (such as egocentric bias, externalizing of blame, and mislabeling) that contribute to inappropriate behavior and lack of self-control.
Self-control	Low degree	Some children and adolescents fail to acquire the essential controls that others have acquired during the process of growing up.
Age	Early initiation	Early appearance of antisocial behavior is associated with serious offenses later in adolescence. However, not every child who acts out becomes a delinquent.
Sex	Male	Boys engage in more antisocial behavior than girls do, although girls are more likely to run away. Boys engage in more violent acts.
Expectations for education and school grades	Low expectations and low grades	Adolescents who become delinquents often have low educational expectations and low grades. Their verbal abilities are often weak.
Parental influences	Monitoring (low), support (low), discipline (ineffective)	Delinquents often come from families in which parents rarely monitor their adolescents, provide them with little support, and ineffectively discipline them.
Sibling relations	Older delinquent sibling	Individuals with an older delinquent sibling are more likely to become delinquent.
Peer influences	Heavy influence, low resistance	Having delinquent peers greatly increases the risk of becoming delinquent.
Socioeconomic status	Low	Serious offenses are committed more frequently by low-socioeconomic-status males.
Neighborhood quality	Urban, high crime, high mobility	Communities often breed crime. Living in a high-crime area, which also is characterized by poverty and dense living conditions, increases the probability that a child will become a delinquent. These communities often have grossly inadequate schools.

FIGURE **13.10**
THE ANTECEDENTS OF JUVENILE DELINQUENCY

Rare are the studies that actually demonstrate in an experimental design that changing parenting practices in childhood is related to a lower incidence of juvenile delinquency in adolescence. However, one recent study by Marion Forgatch and her colleagues (2009) randomly assigned divorced mothers with sons to an experimental group (mothers received extensive parenting training) and a control group (mothers received no parenting training) when their sons were in the first to third grades. The parenting training consisted of 14 parent group meetings that especially focused on improving parenting practices with their sons (skill encouragement, limit setting, monitoring, problem solving, and positive involvement). Best practices for emotion regulation, managing interparental conflict, and talking with children about divorce also were included in the sessions. Improved parenting practices and reduced contact with deviant peers were linked with lower rates of delinquency in the experimental group than in the control group at a nine-year follow-up assessment.

An increasing number of studies have found that siblings can have a strong influence on delinquency (Buist, 2010). In one study, high levels of hostile sibling relationships and older sibling delinquency were linked with younger sibling delinquency in both brother pairs and sister pairs (Slomkowski & others, 2001).

Having delinquent peers increases the risk of becoming delinquent (Brook & others, 2011; Loeber & Burke, 2011). For example, one study revealed that peer rejection and having deviant friends at 7 to 13 years of age were linked with increased delinquency at 14 to 15 years of age (Vitaro, Pedersen, & Brendgen, 2007).

Although delinquency is less exclusively a phenomenon of lower socioeconomic status than it was in the past, some characteristics of the low-SES culture might promote delinquency. Getting into and staying out of trouble are prominent features of life for some adolescents in low-income neighborhoods. Adolescents from low-income backgrounds may sense that they can gain attention and status by performing antisocial actions. Further, adolescents in communities with high crime rates observe many models who engage in criminal activities. Quality schooling, educational funding, and organized neighborhood activities may be lacking in these communities. A recent study revealed that engaged parenting and the mothers' social network support were linked to a lower level of delinquency in low-income families (Ghazarian & Roche, 2010). And another recent study found that youth whose families had experienced repeated poverty were more than twice as likely to be delinquent at 14 and 21 years of age (Najman & others, 2010).

Cognitive factors, such as low self-control, low intelligence, poor decision making, and lack of sustained attention, also are implicated in delinquency (Wolf & Crockett, 2011). For example, a recent study revealed that low-IQ habitual delinquents were characterized by low self-control (Koolhof & others, 2007). Another recent study found that at age 16 nondelinquents were more likely to have a higher verbal IQ and engage in sustained attention than were delinquents (Loeber & others, 2007). And in a longitudinal study, one of the strongest predictive factors of reduced likelihood of engaging in serious theft and violence was high academic achievement (Loeber & others, 2008).

Effective Prevention and Intervention Programs In a recent research review, effective juvenile delinquency prevention and intervention programs were described (Greenwood, 2008). The most successful programs are those that prevent juvenile delinquency from occurring in the first place. Home visiting programs that provide services to pregnant adolescents and their at-risk infants have been found to reduce the risk of delinquency for both the adolescent mothers and their offspring. For example, in the Nurse Family Partnership program, nurses provide child-care recommendations and social-skills training for the mother in a sequence of 20 home visits beginning during prenatal development and continuing through the child's first two years of life (Olds & others, 2004, 2007). Quality preschool education that involves home visits and working with parents also reduces the likelihood children will become delinquents. Later in the chapter, we will discuss one such program—the Perry Preschool program.

The most successful programs once adolescents have engaged in delinquency focus on improving family interactions and providing skills to adults who supervise and train the adolescent. One of these effective programs is Functional Family Therapy, in which the focus is on changing interaction among family members by improving family problem-solving skills, developing more positive emotional connections,

developmental **connection**

Research Methods. Experimental research designs, but not correlational research designs, allow researchers to determine cause-and-effect links. Chapter 1, p. 37

developmental **connection**

Peers. An important aspect of studying adolescents is to assess the company they keep—that is, who their friends are. Chapter 9, p. 305

What are some factors that are linked to whether adolescents engage in delinquent acts?

developmental **connection**

Research Methods. An important issue in the study of adolescent development is the role of early and later experiences. Chapter 1, p. 26

connecting with careers

Rodney Hammond, Health Psychologist

Rodney Hammond described his college experiences: "When I started as an undergraduate at the University of Illinois, Champaign–Urbana, I hadn't decided on my major. But to help finance my education, I took a part-time job in a child development research program sponsored by the psychology department. There, I observed inner-city children in settings designed to enhance their learning. I saw first-hand the contribution psychology can make, and I knew I wanted to be a psychologist" (American Psychological Association, 2003, p. 26).

Rodney Hammond went on to obtain a doctorate in school and community psychology with a focus on children's development. For a number of years, he trained clinical psychologists at Wright State University in Ohio and directed a program to reduce violence in ethnic minority youth. There, he and his associates taught at-risk youth how to use social skills to effectively manage conflict and to recognize situations that could lead to violence. Today, Hammond is director of Violence Prevention at the Centers for Disease Control and Prevention in Atlanta. Hammond says that if you are interested in people and problem solving, psychology is a wonderful way to put these together.

Rodney Hammond talking with an adolescent about strategies for coping with stress and avoiding risk-taking behaviors.

and strengthening parents' monitoring, guidance, and limits for their youth (Alexander & others, 1998). The least effective programs for reducing juvenile delinquency are those that emphasize punishment or attempt to scare youth.

To read about the work of one individual who has a commitment to reducing adolescent problems, including delinquency, see the *Connecting with Careers* profile.

DEPRESSION AND SUICIDE

As we saw earlier in the chapter, one of the most frequent characteristics of adolescents referred for psychological treatment is sadness or depression, especially among girls. In this section, we discuss the nature of adolescent depression and adolescent suicide.

Depression An adolescent who says "I'm depressed" or "I'm so down" may be describing a mood that lasts only a few hours or a much longer-lasting mental disorder. In **major depressive disorder,** an individual experiences a major depressive episode and depressed characteristics, such as lethargy and hopelessness, for at least two weeks or longer and daily functioning becomes impaired. According to the *Diagnostic and Statistical Manual of Mental Disorders—Fourth Edition (DSM-IV)* classification of mental disorders (American Psychiatric Association, 1994), nine symptoms define a major depressive episode, and to be classified as having major depressive disorder, at least five of these must be present during a two-week period:

major depressive disorder The diagnosis when an individual experiences a major depressive episode and depressed characteristics, such as lethargy and depression, for two weeks or longer and daily functioning becomes impaired.

1. Depressed mood most of the day
2. Reduced interest or pleasure in all or most activities
3. Significant weight loss or gain, or significant decrease or increase in appetite
4. Trouble sleeping or sleeping too much

5. Psychomotor agitation or retardation
6. Fatigue or loss of energy
7. Feeling worthless or guilty in an excessive or inappropriate manner
8. Problems in thinking, concentrating, or making decisions
9. Recurrent thoughts of death and suicide

In adolescence, pervasive depressive symptoms might be manifested in such ways as tending to dress in black clothes, writing poetry with morbid themes, or being preoccupied with music that has depressive themes. Sleep problems can appear as all-night television watching, difficulty in getting up for school, or sleeping during the day. Lack of interest in usually pleasurable activities may show up as withdrawal from friends or staying alone in the bedroom most of the time. A lack of motivation and energy level can show up in missed classes. Boredom might be a result of feeling depressed. Adolescent depression also can occur in conjunction with conduct disorder, substance abuse, or an eating disorder.

How serious a problem is depression in adolescence? Rates of ever experiencing major depressive disorder range from 1.5 to 2.5 percent in school-age children and 15 to 20 percent for adolescents (Graber & Sontag, 2009). By about age 15, adolescent females have a rate of depression that is twice that of adolescent males. Some of the reasons for this sex difference that have been proposed are these:

- Females tend to ruminate in their depressed mood and amplify it.
- Females' self-images, especially their body images, are more negative than males'.
- Females experience more stress about weight-related concerns than do males.
- Females face more discrimination than males do.
- Hormonal changes alter vulnerability to depression in adolescence, especially among girls.

Do gender differences in adolescent depression hold for other cultures? In many cultures the gender difference of females experiencing more depression does hold, but a recent study of more than 17,000 Chinese 11- to 22-year-olds revealed that the male adolescents and emerging adults experienced more depression than did their female counterparts (Sun & others, 2010). Explanation of the greater depression by males in China focused on stressful life events and a less positive coping style.

Mental health professionals note that depression often goes undiagnosed in adolescence (Nolen-Hoeksema, 2011). Why is this so? According to conventional wisdom, normal adolescents often show mood swings, ruminate in introspective ways, express boredom with life, and indicate a sense of hopelessness. Thus, parents, teachers, and other observers may see these behaviors as simply transitory and reflecting not a mental disorder but rather normal adolescent behaviors and thoughts.

Family factors are involved in adolescent depression (Gladstone, Beardslee, & O'Connor, 2011; Hamza & Willoughby, 2011; Roche & others, 2011). Reflecting the developmental cascade approach, Deborah Capaldi, Gerald Patterson, and their colleagues (Capaldi, 1992; Capaldi & Stoolmiller, 1999; Patterson, DeBaryshe, & Ramsey, 1989; Patterson, Reid, & Dishion, 1992) have proposed that behavior problems arising in the family in the early childhood years that are connected to inept parenting are carried forward into school contexts, producing problems in academics (poor grades, for example) and social competence (difficulty in peer relations, for example). This cascade of connecting relationships and contexts is expected to contribute to depressive symptoms.

Consider also the following research studies, which identify the roles that parents can have in the development of adolescent depression:

- Parent-adolescent conflict and low parental support were linked to adolescent depression (Sheeber & others, 2007).

What are some characteristics of adolescents who become depressed? What are some factors that are linked with suicide attempts by adolescents?

- Mother-daughter co-rumination (extensively discussing, rehashing, and speculating about problems) was linked to an increase in anxiety and depression in adolescent daughters (Waller & Rose, 2010).
- Exposure to maternal depression by age 12 predicted risk processes during development (higher stress and difficulties in family relationships), which set the course for the development of the adolescent's depression (Garber & Cole, 2010).

Poor peer relationships also are associated with adolescent depression (Conley & Rudolf, 2009). Not having a close relationship with a best friend, having less contact with friends, and being rejected by peers increase depressive tendencies in adolescents (Vernberg, 1990). A recent study revealed that four types of bullying—between bullies themselves, victims of bullying, those who were both bullies and victims, and the victims of cyberbullying—were all linked to adolescents' depression (Wang, Nansel, & Iannotti, 2011). Problems in adolescent romantic relationships can also trigger depression (Sternberg & Davila, 2008).

Friendship often provides social support. A recent study found that friendship provided a protective effect to prevent an increase in depressive symptoms in adolescents who avoided peer relations or were excluded from them as children (Bukowski, Laursen, & Hoza, 2010). However, researchers have found that one aspect of social support—the tendency to co-ruminate by frequently discussing and rehashing problems—is a risk factor for the development of depression in adolescent girls (Rose, Carlson, & Waller, 2007). For example, a recent study revealed that adolescent girls who had a high level of co-rumination were more likely two years later to develop depressive symptoms earlier, have more severe symptoms, and be depressed for a longer period of time (Stone & others, 2011). One implication of this research is that some girls who are vulnerable to developing internalized problems may go undetected because they have supportive friendships.

Being stressed about weight-related concerns in increasingly thought to contribute to the greater incidence of depression in adolescent girls than in adolescent boys (Touchette & others, 2011). A recent study revealed that one explanation for adolescent girls' higher level of depressive symptoms is a heightened tendency to perceive oneself as overweight and to diet (Vaughan & Halpern, 2010).

What type of treatment is most likely to reduce depression in adolescence? One study revealed that depressed adolescents recovered faster when they took an antidepressant and received cognitive behavior therapy that involved improving their coping skills than when they only took an antidepressant or only received cognitive behavior therapy (TADS, 2007). However, a safety concern has emerged with regard to taking antidepressants such as Prozac (fluoxetine). In 2004, the U.S. Food and Drug Administration assigned warnings to such drugs, stating that they slightly increase the risk of suicidal behavior in adolescents. In the study just described, 15 percent of depressed adolescents who only took Prozac had suicidal thoughts or attempted suicide compared with 6 percent who only received cognitive behavior therapy and 8 percent who received both Prozac and cognitive behavior therapy.

Suicide Depression is linked to an increase in suicidal ideation and suicide attempts in adolescence (Thompson & Light, 2011; Verona & Javdani, 2011). Suicidal behavior is rare in childhood but escalates in adolescence and then increases further in emerging adulthood (Park & others, 2006). Suicide is the third leading cause of death in 10- to 19-year-olds today in the United States (National Center for Health Statistics, 2009). After increasing to high levels in the 1990s, suicide rates in adolescents have declined in recent years. Approximately 4,400 adolescents commit suicide each year (Eaton & others, 2010). Emerging adults have triple the rate of suicide than that of adolescents (Park & others, 2006).

Although a suicide threat should always be taken seriously, far more adolescents contemplate or attempt it unsuccessfully than actually commit it. In a national study, in 2009, 15 percent of adolescents reported seriously considering suicide, 11 percent said that they had completed a plan for suicide, and 7 percent indicated that they had tried to take their life in the 12 months preceding the survey (Eaton & others, 2010). As shown in Figure 13.11, the percentage of ninth- to twelfth-grade students who seriously considered attempting suicide has declined since 1991. Females were more likely to attempt suicide than males, but males were more likely to succeed in committing suicide.

In emerging adulthood, males are six times as likely to commit suicide as females (National Center for Injury Prevention and Control, 2006). Males use more lethal means, such as guns, in their suicide attempts, whereas adolescent females are more likely to cut their wrists or take an overdose of sleeping pills—methods less likely to result in death.

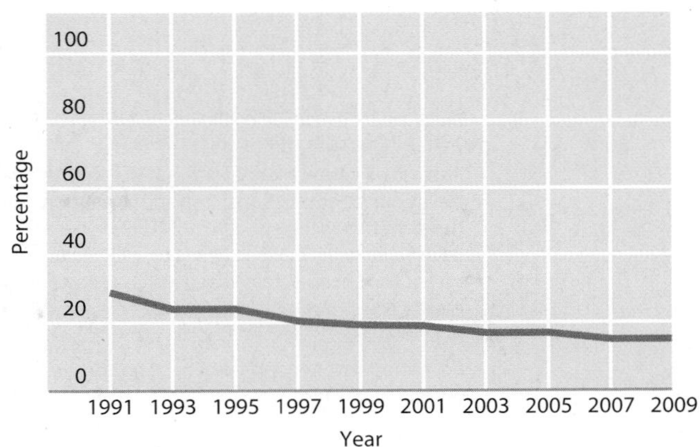

FIGURE **13.11**

PERCENTAGE OF U.S. NINTH- TO TWELFTH-GRADE STUDENTS WHO SERIOUSLY CONSIDERED ATTEMPTING SUICIDE IN THE PREVIOUS 12 MONTHS FROM 1991 TO 2009

Cultural contexts also are related to suicide attempts, and adolescent suicide attempts vary across ethnic groups in the United States. As indicated in Figure 13.12, more than 20 percent of Native American/Alaska Native (NA/AN) female adolescents reported that they had attempted suicide in the previous year, and suicide accounts for almost 20 percent of NA/AN deaths in 15- to 19-year olds (Goldston & others, 2008). African American and non-Latino White males reported the lowest incidence of suicide attempts. A major risk factor in the high rate of suicide attempts by NA/AN adolescents is their elevated rate of alcohol abuse.

Both early and later experiences may be involved in suicide attempts. The adolescent might have a long-standing history of family instability and unhappiness. Lack of affection and emotional support, high control, and pressure for achievement by parents during childhood are likely to show up as factors in suicide attempts. One research review found a link indicating that adolescents who had been physically or sexually abused were more likely to have suicidal thoughts than were adolescents who had not experienced such abuse (Evans, Hawton, & Rodham, 2005).

Adolescents' peer relations also are linked to suicide attempts (Matlin, Molock, & Tebes, 2011). A research review concluded that prior suicide attempts by a member of an adolescent's social groups were linked to the probability the adolescent also would attempt suicide (de Leo & Heller, 2008). The adolescent might also lack supportive friendships. For example, a recent study revealed that family support, peer support, and community connectedness was linked to a lower risk of suicidal tendencies in African American adolescents (Matlin, Molock, & Tebes, 2011). Recent and current stressful circumstances, such as getting poor grades in school and experiencing the breakup of a romantic relationship, may trigger suicide attempts (Antai-Otong, 2003).

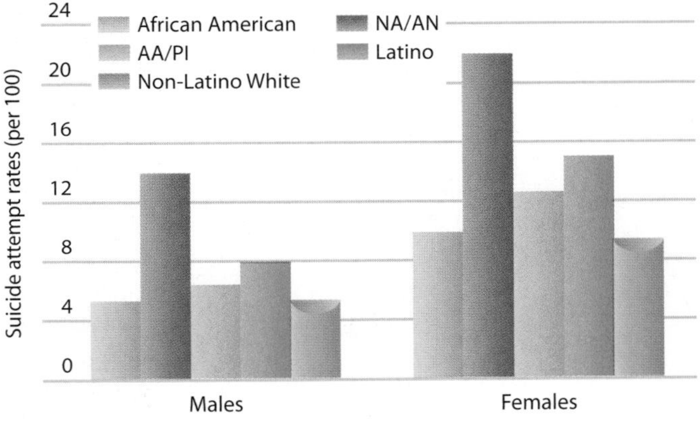

FIGURE **13.12**

SUICIDE ATTEMPTS BY U.S. ADOLESCENTS FROM DIFFERENT ETHNIC GROUPS. *Note:* Data shown are for one-year rates of self-reported suicide attempts. NA/AN = Native American/Alaska Native; AA/PI = Asian American/Pacific Islander.

What is the psychological profile of the suicidal adolescent? Suicidal adolescents often have depressive symptoms (Verona & Javdani, 2011). Although not all depressed adolescents are suicidal, depression is the most frequently cited factor associated with adolescent suicide (Bethell & Rhoades, 2008; Thompson & Light, 2011). A sense of hopelessness, low self-esteem, and high self-blame also are associated with adolescent suicide (O'Donnell & others, 2004). The following studies document a number of factors linked with adolescent suicide attempts:

- Overweight middle school students were more likely to think about, plan, and attempt suicide than their counterparts who were not overweight (Whetstone, Morrissey, & Cummings, 2007). Preteen alcohol use was linked to suicide attempts in adolescence (Swahn, Bossarte, & Sullivent, 2008).
- Adolescents who used alcohol while they were sad or depressed were at risk for making a suicide attempt (Schilling & others, 2009).

What to do	What not to do
1. Ask direct, straightforward questions in a calm manner: "Are you thinking about hurting yourself?" 2. Assess the seriousness of the suicidal intent by asking questions about feelings, important relationships, who else the person has talked with, and the amount of thought given to the means to be used. If a gun, pills, a rope, or other means have been obtained and a precise plan has been developed, clearly the situation is dangerous. Stay with the person until help arrives. 3. Be a good listener and be very supportive without being falsely reassuring. 4. Try to persuade the person to obtain professional help and assist him or her in getting this help.	1. Do not ignore the warning signs. 2. Do not refuse to talk about suicide if a person approaches you about it. 3. Do not react with humor, disapproval, or repulsion. 4. Do not give false reassurances by saying such things as "Everything is going to be OK." Also do not give out simple answers or platitudes, such as "You have everything to be thankful for." 5. Do not abandon the individual after the crisis has passed or after professional help has commenced.

FIGURE **13.13**

WHAT TO DO AND WHAT NOT TO DO WHEN YOU SUSPECT SOMEONE IS LIKELY TO ATTEMPT SUICIDE

- Data from the National Longitudinal Study of Adolescent Health indicated that the following were indicators of suicide risk: depressive symptoms, a sense of hopelessness, engaging in suicidal ideation, having a family background of suicidal behavior, and having friends with a history of suicidal behavior (Thompson, Kuruwita, & Foster, 2009).
- Another analysis based on the National Longitudinal Study of Adolescent Health also found that parental loss predicted an increase in suicide attempts one year later but not seven years later (Thompson & Light, 2011).
- Frequent, escalating stress, especially at home, was linked with suicide attempts in young Latinas (Zayas & others, 2010).
- Sexual victimization was linked to a risk for suicide attempts in adolescence (Plener, Singer, & Goldbeck, 2011).

In some instances, suicides in adolescence occur in clusters. That is, when one adolescent commits suicide, other adolescents who find out about this also commit suicide. Such "copycat" suicides raise the issue of whether or not suicides should be reported in the media; a news report might plant the idea of committing suicide in other adolescents' minds.

Figure 13.13 provides valuable information about what to do and what not to do when you suspect someone is likely to commit suicide.

EATING DISORDERS

Eating disorders have become increasingly common among adolescents (Schiff, 2011; Wardlaw & Smith, 2011). Here are some research findings involving adolescent eating disorders:

- *Body image*. Body dissatisfaction and distorted body image play important roles in adolescent eating disorders (Eichen & others, 2011). One study revealed that in general, adolescents were dissatisfied with their bodies, with males desiring to increase their upper body and females wanting to decrease the overall size of their body (Ata, Ludden, & Lally, 2007). In this study, low self-esteem and social support, weight-related teasing, and pressure to lose weight were linked to adolescents' negative body image. In another study, girls who felt negatively about their bodies in early adolescence were more likely to develop eating disorders, two years later, than their counterparts who did not feel negatively about their bodies (Attie & Brooks-Gunn, 1989). And a recent study found that the key aspect of explaining depression in overweight adolescents involved body dissatisfaction (Mond & others, 2011).

- *Parenting*. Adolescents who reported observing more healthy eating patterns and exercise by their parents had more healthy eating patterns and exercised more themselves (Pakpreo & others, 2004). Negative parent-adolescent relationships were linked with increased dieting by girls over a one-year period (Archibald, Graber, & Brooks-Gunn, 1999).
- *Sexual activity*. Girls who were both sexually active with their boyfriends and in pubertal transition were the most likely to be dieting or engaging in disordered eating patterns (Cauffman, 1994).
- *Role models and the media*. Girls who were highly motivated to look like same-sex figures in the media were more likely than their peers to become very concerned about their weight (Field & others, 2001). Watching commercials with idealized thin female images increased adolescent girls' dissatisfaction with their bodies (Hargreaves & Tiggemann, 2004). And a study of adolescent girls revealed that frequently reading magazine articles about dieting and weight loss was linked with unhealthy weight-control behaviors such as fasting, skipping meals, and smoking more cigarettes five years later (van den Berg & others, 2007).

Let's now examine different types of eating problems in adolescence, beginning with overweight and obesity.

developmental **connection**

Health. In general, throughout puberty girls are less happy with their bodies and have more negative body images than do boys. Chapter 2, p. 59

Overweight and Obese Adolescents The Centers for Disease Control and Prevention (2011) has a category of obesity for adults but does not have an obesity category for children and adolescents because of the stigma the label *obesity* may bring. Rather, they have categories for being overweight or at risk for being overweight in childhood and adolescence. These categories are determined by *body mass index (BMI)*, which is computed by a formula that takes into account height and weight. Only children and adolescents at or above the 95th percentile of BMI are included in the category of overweight, and those at or above the 85th percentile are included in the category of at risk for being overweight.

developmental **connection**

Health. A special concern is the high amount of fat and low amount of vegetables in adolescents' diets. Chapter 2, pp. 67–68

The percentage of overweight adolescents and emerging adults increased dramatically in the 1980s, 1990s, and into the early part of the first decade of the twenty-first century (Spruijt-Metz, 2011). For example, the incidence of being overweight increased from 11 to 17 percent for U.S. 12- to 19-year-olds from the early 1990s through 2004 (Eaton & others, 2006). However, recent research indicates that a leveling off began occurring about midway through the first decade of the twenty-first century (Ogden, Carroll, & Flegal, 2008). A recent analysis concluded that the leveling off in adolescents being overweight not only is occurring in the United States, but also in Europe, Japan, and Australia (Rokholm, Baker, & Sorensen, 2010). However, in this analysis, the leveling off was less likely to occur in adolescents living in low-income conditions. Despite the recent leveling off in being overweight for some adolescents, overweight and obesity in adolescents remains at epidemic levels.

Being overweight as a child is a strong predictor for being overweight as an adolescent. One study computed the BMI of more than 1,000 children at seven different times from 2 to 12 years of age (Nader & others, 2006). Eighty percent of the children who were at risk for being overweight at 3 years of age were also at risk for being overweight or were overweight at 12 years of age.

An increase in being overweight also has occurred in emerging adulthood (Park & others, 2006). The average BMI of U.S. 20- to 29-year-old males increased from 24.3 in the early 1960s to 26.6 in 2002, and in the same time frame the average BMI of 20- to 29-year-old females increased from 22.2 to 26.6. Approximately 17 percent of emerging adults are estimated to be obese (Brown, Moore, & Bzostek, 2005). A recent longitudinal study tracked more than 1,500 adolescents who were classified as not overweight, overweight, or obese when they were 14 years of age (Patton & others, 2011b). Across the 10-year period of the study, the percentage of overweight individuals increased from 20 percent at 14 years of age to 33 percent at 24 years of age. Obesity increased from 4 percent to 7 percent across the 10 years.

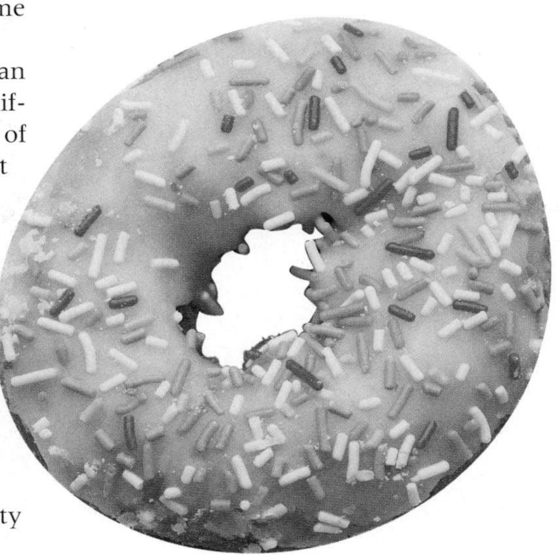

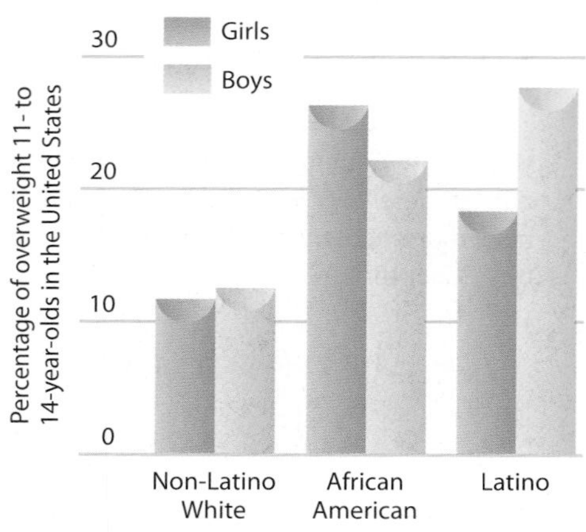

FIGURE **13.14**

PERCENTAGE OF OVERWEIGHT U.S. ADOLESCENT BOYS AND GIRLS IN DIFFERENT ETHNIC GROUPS

Are there ethnic variations in being overweight during adolescence in the United States? A survey by the National Center for Health Statistics (2002) found that African American girls and Latino boys have especially high risks of being overweight during adolescence (see Figure 13.14). Another study of 2,379 girls from 9 to 19 years of age found that the prevalence of being overweight was considerably higher for African American girls than for non-Latino White girls (Kimm & others, 2002). One study revealed that the higher obesity rate for African American females is linked with a diet higher in calories and fat, as well as sedentary behavior (Sanchez-Johnsen & others, 2004).

U.S. children and adolescents are more likely to be overweight or obese than their counterparts in most other countries (Spruijt-Metz, 2011). One comparison of 34 countries found that the United States had the second highest rate of child obesity (Janssen & others, 2005). In another study, U.S. children and adolescents (6 to 18 years of age) were four times more likely to be classified as obese than their counterparts in China and almost three times as likely to be classified as obese than their counterparts in Russia (Wang, 2000).

Eating patterns established in childhood and adolescence are strongly linked to obesity in adulthood. One study revealed that 62 percent of the male and 73 percent of the female adolescents in the 85th to 94th percentile of BMI became obese adults (Wang & others, 2008). In this study, of those at the 95th percentile and higher for BMI, 80 percent of the males and 92 percent of the females became obese adults. A recent study of more than 8,000 12- to 21-year-olds found that obese adolescents were more likely to develop severe obesity in emerging adulthood than were overweight or normal weight adolescents (The & others, 2010).

Both heredity and environmental factors are involved in obesity (Hahn, Payne, & Lucas, 2011). Some individuals inherit a tendency to be overweight. Only 10 percent of children who do not have obese parents become obese themselves, whereas 40 percent of children who become obese have one obese parent, and 70 percent of children who become obese have two obese parents. Identical twins, even when they are reared apart, have similar weights.

Strong evidence of the environment's role in obesity is the doubling of the rate of obesity in the United States since 1900, as well as the significant increase in adolescent obesity since the 1960s, which was described earlier. This dramatic increase in obesity likely is due to greater availability of food (especially food high in fat), energy-saving devices, and declining physical activity.

These overweight adolescent girls are attending a weight-management camp. *What are some factors that contribute to whether adolescents become overweight?*

Being overweight or obese has negative effects on adolescent health, in terms of both biological development and socioemotional development (Schiff, 2011; Spruijt-Metz, 2011). In terms of biological development, being overweight in adolescence is linked with high blood pressure, hip problems, pulmonary problems, and type 2 (adult-onset) diabetes (Kavey, Daniels, & Flynn, 2010). Researchers have found that U.S. adolescents' blood pressure has increased in the twenty-first century, and this increase is linked with the increase in being overweight in adolescence (Sun & others, 2008). In terms of socioemotional development, adolescents who are overweight are more likely than their normal-weight counterparts to have lower self-esteem, be depressed, and they have more problems in relationships with peers (Vaughan & Halpern, 2010). A recent study revealed that adolescents indicated that in most cases girls who were overweight were teased about it more than boys who were overweight (Taylor, 2011).

What types of interventions have been successful in reducing overweight in adolescents? Research indicates that regular exercise is a key component of weight reduction in adolescence (Ingul & others, 2010; Spruijt-Metz, 2011). One research review indicated that clinical approaches that focus on the individual adolescent and include a combination of caloric restriction, exercise (walking or biking to school, participating in a regular exercise program), reduction of sedentary activity (watching TV, playing video games), and behavioral therapy (such as keeping weight-loss diaries and receiving rewards for meeting goals) have been moderately effective in helping overweight adolescents lose weight (Fowler-Brown & Kahwati, 2004). A recent research review concluded that interventions targeted at changing family lifestyle were the most effective in helping children and adolescents lose weight (Oude Luttikhuis & others, 2009). In general, school-based approaches (such as instituting a school-wide program to improve eating habits) have been less effective than clinically based individual approaches (Dobbins & others, 2009; Lytle, 2009). A research review concluded that school-based approaches for reducing adolescents' weight have modest results, with TV watching the easiest behavior to change, followed by physical activity and then nutrition (Sharma, 2006).

developmental **connection**

Health. Researchers have found that as boys and girls reach and progress through adolescence, they become less active. Chapter 2, p. 68

A concern is that as schools are under increasing pressure to spend more time on academic topics, health-oriented programs are likely to be shortchanged (Paxson & others, 2006). When this is an impediment, one possibility is to include obesity prevention in after-school programs, which conflict less with schools' academic mandates (Story, Kaphingst, & French, 2006). Another promising strategy is to provide students with healthier foods to eat at school (Briefel & others, 2009; Reinehr & Wabitsch, 2010). In 2005, several states began enacting laws that require more healthy foods and less nonhealthy foods be sold in vending machines at schools. Schools also can play an important role by implementing programs that increase the amount of time children exercise (Dumith & others, 2010).

Anorexia Nervosa, Bulimia Nervosa, and Binge Eating Disorder Three eating disorders that may appear in adolescence and emerging adulthood are anorexia nervosa, bulimia nervosa, and binge eating disorder.

Anorexia Nervosa **Anorexia nervosa** is an eating disorder that involves the relentless pursuit of thinness through starvation. Anorexia nervosa is a serious disorder that can lead to death (Hebebrand & Bulik, 2011; Knoll, Bulik, & Hebebrand, 2011). Three main characteristics of anorexia nervosa are:

- Weighing less than 85 percent of what is considered normal for age and height.
- Having an intense fear of gaining weight. The fear does not decrease with weight loss.
- Having a distorted image of body shape. Even when they are extremely thin, anorexics see themselves as too fat. They never think they are thin enough, especially in the abdomen, buttocks, and thighs. They usually weigh themselves frequently, often take their body measurements, and gaze critically at themselves in mirrors.

anorexia nervosa An eating disorder that involves the relentless pursuit of thinness through starvation.

Anorexia nervosa has become an increasing problem for adolescent girls and emerging adult women. *What are some possible causes of anorexia nervosa?*

Anorexia nervosa typically begins in the early to middle teenage years, often following an episode of dieting and some type of life stress. It is about ten times more likely to characterize females than males. Although most U.S. adolescent girls have been on a diet at some point, slightly less than 1 percent ever develop anorexia nervosa (Walters & Kendler, 1994). When anorexia nervosa does occur in males, the symptoms and other characteristics (such as a distorted body image and family conflict) are usually similar to those reported by females who have the disorder.

Most anorexics are non-Latino White adolescents or young adult females from well-educated, middle- and upper-income families that are competitive and high-achieving. They set high standards, become stressed about not being able to reach the standards, and are intensely concerned about how others perceive them. Unable to meet these high expectations, they turn to something they can control: their weight. Problems in family functioning are increasingly being found to be linked to the appearance of anorexia nervosa in adolescent girls (Benninghoven & others, 2007), and recent research reviews indicate that family therapy is often the most effective treatment of adolescent girls with anorexia nervosa (Agras & Robinson, 2008; Fisher, Hetrick, & Rushford, 2010; Halmi, 2009).

The fashion image in U.S. culture contributes to the incidence of anorexia nervosa. The media portray thin as beautiful in their choice of fashion models, whom many adolescent girls strive to emulate. And many adolescent girls who strive to be thin hang out together. A recent study of adolescent girls revealed that friends often share similar body image and eating problems (Hutchinson & Rapee, 2007). In this study, an individual girl's dieting and extreme weight-loss behavior could be predicted from her friends' dieting and extreme weight-loss behavior. In addition, social-networking websites, such as Facebook, connect thousands of anorexics who are able to share pro-ana (pro-anorexic) information on how to deprive their bodies and become unhealthily thin.

Bulimia Nervosa Although anorexics control their eating by restricting it, most bulimics cannot. **Bulimia nervosa** is an eating disorder in which the individual consistently follows a binge-and-purge eating pattern. The bulimic goes on an eating binge and then purges by self-inducing vomiting or using a laxative. Although some people binge and purge occasionally and some experiment with it, a person is considered to have a serious bulimic disorder only if the episodes occur at least twice a week for three months.

As with anorexics, most bulimics are preoccupied with food, have a strong fear of becoming overweight, and are depressed or anxious (Speranza & others, 2005). A recent study revealed that bulimics overvalued their body weight and shape, and this overvaluation was linked to higher depression and lower self-esteem (Hrabosky & others, 2007). Unlike anorexics, people who binge and purge typically fall within a normal weight range, a characteristic that makes bulimia more difficult to detect.

Bulimia nervosa typically begins in late adolescence or early adulthood. About 90 percent of the cases are women. Approximately 1 to 2 percent of women are estimated to develop bulimia nervosa. Many women who develop bulimia nervosa were somewhat overweight before the onset of the disorder, and the binge eating often began during an episode of dieting. One study of adolescent girls found that increased dieting, pressure to be thin, exaggerated importance of appearance, body dissatisfaction, depression symptoms, low self-esteem, and low social support predicted binge eating two years later (Stice, Presnell, & Spangler, 2002). A recent study of individuals with anorexia nervosa or bulimia nervosa revealed that attachment insecurity was linked with body dissatisfaction, which was a key aspect of predicting and perpetuating these eating disorders (Abbate-Daga & others, 2010). In this study, need for approval was an important predictor of bulimia nervosa. As with anorexia nervosa, about 70 percent of individuals who develop bulimia nervosa eventually recover from the disorder (Agras & others, 2004).

bulimia nervosa An eating disorder in which the individual consistently follows a binge-and-purge eating pattern.

binge eating disorder (BED) Involves frequent binge eating but without compensatory behavior like the purging that characterizes bulimics.

Binge Eating Disorder (BED) **Binge eating disorder (BED)** involves frequent binge eating but without compensatory behavior like the purging that characterizes bulimics. Because they don't purge, individuals with BED are frequently overweight (New, 2008). Adolescents and emerging adults who have BED feel like they have lost control over how much they eat and cannot stop eating. BED is more common in individuals who are overweight or obese, but it also can occur in individuals who are normal weight. While most adolescents and emerging adults who are anorexic or bulimic are female, approximately one-third of those with BED are male (New, 2008). A recent research review indicated that the two best predictors that differentiated BED from other eating disorders were eating in secret and feeling disgust after the episode (White & Grilo, 2011). A recent study also found that individuals with BED showed a more negative pattern of everyday emotions, with anger being the emotion most often reported before a bingeing episode (Zeeck & others, 2011).

Adults in treatment for BED number approximately 1 to 2 million people; they often say that their bingeing problems began in childhood or adolescence (New, 2008). Common health risks of BED are those related to being overweight or obese, such as high blood pressure, diabetes, and depression (Araujo, Santos, & Nardi, 2010). Recent research indicates that individuals with BED show a higher degree of concern about weight and shape than do their obese counterparts without BED (Ahrberg & others, 2011).

Review *Connect* Reflect

LG2 Describe some problems and disorders that characterize adolescents and emerging adults.

Review

- What are some trends in adolescent drug use? What are some characteristics of the use of alcohol, hallucinogens, stimulants, depressants, anabolic steroids, and inhalants by adolescents? What are the main factors that are related to adolescent and emerging adult drug use?
- What is juvenile delinquency? What are the antecedents of juvenile delinquency? What characterizes violence in youth?
- What characterizes adolescent depression? How common is suicide in adolescence and emerging adulthood? What are some possible causes of suicide in adolescence and emerging adulthood?
- What are some trends in eating disorders? What are the main eating disorders in adolescence and emerging adulthood? What are some of their characteristics?

Connect

- How might the development of values, described in Chapter 7, be related to an adolescent's or emerging adult's decision to engage in drug use or abstain?

Reflect *Your Own Personal Journey of Life*

- Imagine that you have just been appointed to head the U.S. President's Commission on Adolescent Drug Abuse. What would be the first program you would try to put in place? What would its components be?

3 Interrelation of Problems and Prevention/Intervention

Summarize the interrelation of problems and ways to prevent or intervene in problems.

Adolescents with Multiple Problems | Prevention and Intervention

What problems affect the largest number of adolescents? What are the best strategies for preventing or intervening in adolescent problems?

ADOLESCENTS WITH MULTIPLE PROBLEMS

The four problems that affect the largest number of adolescents are (1) drug abuse, (2) juvenile delinquency, (3) sexual problems, and (4) school-related problems

What characterizes the most at-risk adolescents?

(Dryfoos, 1990; Dryfoos & Barkin, 2006). The adolescents most at risk have more than one of these problems. Researchers are increasingly finding that problem behaviors in adolescence are interrelated (Elkington, Bauermeister, & Zimmerman, 2011). For example, heavy substance abuse is related to early sexual activity, lower grades, dropping out of school, and delinquency (Brady & others, 2008; Marti, Stice, & Springer, 2010). Early initiation of sexual activity is associated with the use of cigarettes and alcohol, use of marijuana and other illicit drugs, lower grades, dropping out of school, and delinquency (Harden & Mendle, 2011). Delinquency is related to early sexual activity, early pregnancy, substance abuse, and dropping out of school (Pedersen & Mastekaasa, 2011). As much as 10 percent of the adolescent population in the United States have serious multiple-problem behaviors (adolescents who have dropped out of school, or are behind in their grade level, are users of heavy drugs, regularly use cigarettes and marijuana, and are sexually active but do not use contraception). Many, but not all, of these very high-risk youth "do it all." In 1990, it was estimated that another 15 percent of adolescents participate in many of these same behaviors but with slightly lower frequency and less deleterious consequences (Dryfoos, 1990). These high-risk youth often engage in two or three problem behaviors (Dryfoos, 1990). It was estimated that in 2005 the figure for high-risk youth had increased to 20 percent of all U.S. adolescents (Dryfoos & Barkin, 2006).

developmental **connection**

Sexuality. Early sexual initiation is a risk factor in adolescent development. Chapter 6, p. 194

PREVENTION AND INTERVENTION

In addition to understanding that many adolescents engage in multiple-problem behaviors, it also is important to develop programs that reduce adolescent problems (Weissberg, Kumpfer, & Seligman, 2003). We considered a number of prevention and intervention strategies for specific adolescent problems, such as drug abuse and juvenile delinquency, earlier in the chapter. Here we focus on some general strategies for preventing and intervening in adolescent problems. In a review of the programs that have been successful in preventing or reducing adolescent problems, adolescent researcher Joy Dryfoos (1990, 1997; Dryfoos & Barkin, 2006) described the common components of these successful programs. The common components include these:

1. *Intensive individualized attention.* In successful programs, high-risk youth are attached to a responsible adult who gives the youth attention and deals with the child's specific needs (Glidden-Tracey, 2005; Nation & others, 2003). This theme occurred in a number of different programs. In a substance-abuse program, a student assistance counselor was available full-time for individual counseling and referral for treatment. Programs often require highly trained personnel, and they extend over a long period to remain successful. (Dryfoos & Barkin, 2006).
2. *Community-wide, multiagency collaborative approaches.* The basic philosophy of community-wide programs is that a number of different programs and services have to be in place. In one successful substance-abuse program, a community-wide health promotion campaign was implemented that used local media and community education in concert with a substance-abuse curriculum in the schools. Community programs that include policy changes and media campaigns are more effective when they are coordinated with family, peer, and school components (Wandersman & Florin, 2003).
3. *Early identification and intervention.* Reaching children and their families before children develop problems, or at the beginning of their problems, is a successful strategy (Aber & others, 2006).

Here are three prevention programs/research studies that merit attention:

- *High Scope*. One preschool program serves as an excellent model for the prevention of delinquency, pregnancy, substance abuse, and dropping out of school. Operated by the High Scope Foundation in Ypsilanti, Michigan, the Perry Preschool has had a long-term positive impact on its students (Schweinhart & others, 2005; Weikert, 1993). This enrichment program, directed by David Weikert, services disadvantaged African American children. They attend a high-quality two-year preschool program and receive weekly home visits from program personnel. Based on official police records, by age 19 individuals who had attended the Perry Preschool program were less likely to have been arrested and reported fewer adult offenses than a control group. The Perry Preschool students also were less likely to drop out of school, and teachers rated their social behavior as more competent than that of a control group who did not receive the enriched preschool experience. In a more recent assessment, at age 40 those who had been in the Perry Preschool program were more likely to be in the workforce, own their own homes, and had fewer arrests (Schweinhart & others, 2005).
- *Fast Track*. A program that attempts to lower the risk of juvenile delinquency and other problems is Fast Track (Conduct Problems Prevention Research Group, 2007, 2010a,b; 2011; Dodge & McCourt, 2010; Jones & others, 2010; Miller & others, 2011). Schools in four areas (Durham, North Carolina; Nashville, Tennessee; Seattle, Washington; and rural central Pennsylvania) were identified as high risk based on neighborhood crime and poverty data. Researchers screened more than 9,000 kindergarten children in the four schools and randomly assigned 891 of the highest-risk and moderate-risk children to intervention or control conditions. The average age of the children when the intervention began was 6.5 years of age. The 10-year intervention consisted of behavior management training of parents, social cognitive skills training of children, reading tutoring, home visitations, mentoring, and a revised classroom curriculum that was designed to increase socioemotional competence and decrease aggression.

  The extensive intervention was most successful for children and adolescents who were identified as the highest risk in kindergarten, lowering their incidence of conduct disorder, attention deficit hyperactivity disorder, any externalized disorder, and antisocial behavior. Positive outcomes for the intervention occurred as early as the third grade and continued through the ninth grade. For example, in the ninth grade the intervention reduced the likelihood that the highest-risk kindergarten children would develop conduct disorder by 75 percent, attention deficit hyperactivity disorder by 53 percent, and any externalized disorder by 43 percent. Recently, data have been reported through age 19 (Miller & others, 2011). Findings indicate that the comprehensive Fast Track intervention was successful in reducing youth arrest rates (Conduct Problems Prevention Research Group, 2010a).
- *National Longitudinal Study on Adolescent Health*. This study is based on interviews with 12,118 adolescents and has implications for the prevention of adolescent problems (Aronowitz & Morrison-Beedy, 2008; Allen & MacMillan, 2006; Beaver & others, 2009; Cubbin & others, 2005). Perceived adolescent connectedness to a parent and to a teacher were the main factors that were linked with preventing these adolescent problems: emotional distress, suicidal thoughts and behavior, violence, use of cigarettes, use of alcohol, use of marijuana, and early sexual intercourse. This study also provides support for the

What are some strategies for preventing and intervening in adolescent problems?

first component of successful prevention/intervention programs as described under number 1 in the list at the beginning of this section. That is, intensive individualized attention is especially important when coming from important people in the adolescent's life, such as parents and teachers (Greenberg & others, 2003; Kumpfer & Alvarado, 2003).

Review *Connect* Reflect

LG3 Summarize the interrelation of problems and ways to prevent or intervene in problems.

Review

- Which four problems affect the largest number of adolescents? How are adolescent problems interrelated?
- What are the three main ways to prevent or intervene in adolescent problems?

Connect

- What role can parents play in preventing and intervening in adolescent problems (Chapter 8)?

Reflect *Your Own Personal Journey of Life*

- Did you have any of the problems in adolescence that were described in this chapter? If so, what factors do you think contributed to the development of the problem(s)? If you didn't experience any of the problems, what do you think protected you from developing the problems?

We have arrived at the end of this book. I hope this book and course have been a window to improving your understanding of adolescence and emerging adulthood, including your own development in these key time frames in your life. I wish you all the best in the remaining years of your journey through the human life span.

John W. Santrock

reach your **learning goals**

1 Exploring Adolescent and Emerging Adult Problems

LG1 Discuss the nature of problems in adolescence and emerging adulthood.

The Biopsychosocial Approach

- Biological, psychological, and social factors have been proposed as causes of problems that adolescents, emerging adults, and others can develop. The biopsychosocial approach emphasizes that problems develop through an interaction of biological, psychological, and social factors.

The Developmental Psychopathology Approach

- In the developmental psychopathology approach, the emphasis is on describing and exploring developmental pathways of problems. One way of classifying adolescent and emerging adult problems is as internalizing (for example, depression and anxiety) or externalizing (for example, juvenile delinquency).

Characteristics of Adolescent and Emerging Adult Problems

- The spectrum of adolescent and emerging adult problems is wide, varying in severity, developmental level, sex, and socioeconomic status. Middle-SES adolescents and females have more internalizing problems; low-SES adolescents and males have more externalizing problems. Adolescents who have a number of external and internal assets have fewer problems and engage in fewer risk-taking behaviors than their counterparts with few external and internal assets.

Stress and Coping

- Stress is the response of individuals to stressors, which are circumstances and events that threaten them and tax their coping abilities. Sources of stress include life events, daily hassles, and sociocultural factors (such as gender, acculturative stress, and poverty). Coping involves managing taxing circumstances, expending effort to solve life's problems, and seeking to master or reduce stress. Successful coping has been linked to a sense of personal control, positive emotions, personal resources, and the strategies used. One way of classifying coping strategies focuses on problem-focused coping and emotion-focused coping. In most situations, problem-focused coping is recommended over emotion-focused coping. Among the strategies for coping effectively are thinking positively and having support from others. Coping is influenced by the demands and resources of the environment, and individuals who face stressful circumstances often benefit from using more than one strategy.

Resilience

- Three sets of characteristics are reflected in the lives of adolescents and emerging adults who show resilience in the face of adversity and disadvantage: (1) individual factors—such as good intellectual functioning; (2) family factors—such as a close relationship with a caring parent figure; and (3) extrafamilial factors—bonds to prosocial adults outside the family. Resilience in adolescence is linked to continuing to be resilient in emerging adulthood, but resilience can develop in emerging adulthood.

2 Problems and Disorders

Describe some problems and disorders that characterize adolescents and emerging adults.

Drug Use

- The 1960s and 1970s were a time of marked increases in the use of illicit drugs. Drug use began to decline in the 1980s but increased again in the 1990s. Since the late 1990s, there has been a decline in the overall use of illicit drugs by U.S. adolescents. Understanding drug use requires an understanding of physical dependence and psychological dependence. Alcohol abuse is a major problem, although its use in adolescence has begun to decline. There is an increase in alcohol use and binge drinking during emerging adulthood. Binge drinking by college students is a continuing concern. Use of alcohol and drugs typically declines by the mid-twenties. Risk factors for alcohol use include heredity and negative family and peer influences. Other drugs that can be harmful to adolescents include hallucinogens (LSD and marijuana—their use increased in the 1990s), stimulants (such as nicotine, cocaine, and amphetamines), and depressants (such as barbiturates, tranquilizers, and alcohol). A special concern is cigarette use by adolescents, although the good news is that it has been declining in recent years. An alarming trend has recently occurred in the increased use of prescription painkillers by adolescents. Use of anabolic steroids has been linked with strength training, smoking, and heavy use of alcohol. Adolescents' use of inhalants has decreased in recent years. Drug use in childhood and early adolescence has more negative long-term effects than when it first occurs in late adolescence. Parents and peers can provide important supportive roles in preventing adolescent drug use. Being born into a high-risk family, having conduct problems at school, and being rejected by peers are factors related to drug use by 12-year-olds. Early educational achievement by adolescents has a positive influence in reducing the likelihood of developing problems with drug and alcohol abuse. Substance use peaks in emerging adulthood but begins declining by the mid-twenties.

Juvenile Delinquency

- Juvenile delinquency consists of a broad range of behaviors, from socially undesirable behavior to status offenses. For legal purposes, a distinction is made between index and status offenses. Conduct disorder is a psychiatric diagnostic category used to describe multiple delinquent-type behaviors occurring over a six-month period. Predictors of juvenile delinquency include authority conflict, minor covert acts such as lying, overt acts of aggression, a negative identity, cognitive distortions, low self-control, early initiation of delinquency, being a male, low expectations for education and school grades, low parental monitoring, low parental support and ineffective discipline, having an older delinquent sibling, heavy peer influence and low resistance to peers, low socioeconomic status, and living in a high-crime, urban area. Effective juvenile delinquency prevention and intervention programs have been identified.

Depression and Suicide

- Adolescents have a higher rate of depression than children do. Female adolescents are far more likely to develop depression than adolescent males are. Parent-adolescent conflict, low parental support, poor peer relationships, and problems in romantic relationships are factors associated with adolescent depression. Treatment of depression has involved both drug therapy and psychotherapy. Emerging adults have triple the rate of suicide than that of adolescents. The U.S. adolescent suicide rates increased in the 1990s but have fallen in recent years. Both early and later experiences may be involved in suicide. Family instability, lack of affection, poor grades in school, lack of supportive friendships, and romantic breakups may trigger suicide attempts.

Eating Disorders

- Eating disorders have become increasing problems in adolescence and emerging adulthood. The percentage of adolescents who are overweight increased dramatically in the 1980s and 1990s, but began leveling off in the middle of the first decade of the twenty-first century. Being obese in adolescence is linked with being obese as an adult. An increase in obesity has also occurred in emerging adulthood. Both heredity and environmental factors are involved in obesity. Being overweight in adolescence has negative effects on physical health and socioemotional development. Clinical approaches that focus on the individual adolescent and involve a combination of caloric restriction, exercise, reduction of sedentary behavior, and behavioral therapy have been moderately effective in helping overweight adolescents lose weight. Anorexia nervosa is an eating disorder that involves the relentless pursuit of thinness through starvation. Anorexics weigh less than 85 percent of weight considered normal, intensely fear weight gain, and even when very thin see themselves as too fat. Bulimia nervosa is an eating disorder in which the individual consistently follows a binge-and-purge eating pattern. Most bulimics are depressed or anxious, overvalue their body weight and shape, and typically fall within a normal weight range. Binge eating disorder (BED) involves frequent binge eating but without compensatory behavior like the purging that characterizes bulimics.

3 Interrelation of Problems and Prevention/Intervention

Summarize the interrelation of problems and ways to prevent or intervene in problems.

Adolescents with Multiple Problems

- The four problems that affect the most adolescents are (1) drug abuse, (2) juvenile delinquency, (3) sexual problems, and (4) school-related problems. Researchers are finding that adolescents who are the most at risk often have more than one problem and that the highest-risk adolescents often have all four of these problems.

Prevention and Intervention

- In Dryfoos' analysis, these were the common components of successful prevention/intervention programs: (1) extensive individual attention, (2) community-wide intervention, and (3) early identification and intervention.

key terms

biopsychosocial approach 424
developmental psychopathology approach 425
developmental cascades 426
internalizing problems 426
externalizing problems 426
stress 429
acculturative stress 431
coping 431
problem-focused coping 431
emotion-focused coping 432
hallucinogens 438
stimulants 438
depressants 440
anabolic steroids 442
juvenile delinquency 444
index offenses 444
status offenses 444
conduct disorder 444
major depressive disorder 448
anorexia nervosa 455
bulimia nervosa 456
binge eating disorder (BED) 456

key people

resources for **improving the lives of adolescents**

Adolescence
by Joy Dryfoos and Carol Barkin (2006)
New York: Oxford University Press

An outstanding book on adolescent problems and the programs and strategies that can successfully prevent and intervene in these problems.

Developmental Psychopathology
edited by Dante Cicchetti and Donald Cohen (2006)
New York: Wiley

This three-volume set provides extensive information about many aspects of developmental psychopathology.

Development and Psychopathology, 2010, Volume 22, Issues 3 and 4

An up-to-date presentation of theory and research on the increasing interest in the role of developmental cascades in predicting adolescent problems.

The Future of Children
(Vol. 18, No. 2, 2008)

Coverage of many aspects of juvenile delinquency, including effective prevention and intervention programs.

National Adolescent Suicide Hotline
800-621-4000

This hotline can be used 24 hours a day by teenagers contemplating suicide, as well as by their parents.

National Clearinghouse for Alcohol Information
www.health.org

This clearinghouse provides information about a wide variety of issues related to drinking problems, including adolescent drinking.

glossary

A

accommodation An adjustment of a schema to new information.

acculturative stress The negative consequences that result from contact between two distinctive cultural groups.

active (niche-picking) genotype-environment correlations Correlations that occur when children seek out environments that they find compatible and stimulating.

adaptive behavior A modification of behavior that promotes an organism's survival in the natural habitat.

adolescence The developmental period of transition from childhood to adulthood; it involves biological, cognitive, and socioemotional changes. Adolescence begins at approximately 10 to 13 years of age and ends in the late teens.

adolescent egocentrism The heightened self-consciousness of adolescents, which is reflected in their belief that others are as interested in them as they themselves are, and in their sense of personal uniqueness and invulnerability.

adolescent generalization gap Adelson's concept of generalizations about adolescents based on information regarding a limited, often highly visible group of adolescents.

adolescents who are gifted Adolescents who have above-average intelligence (usually defined as an IQ of 130 or higher) and/or superior talent in some domain, such as art, music, or mathematics.

adoption study A study in which investigators seek to discover whether the behavior and psychological characteristics of adopted children are more like their adoptive parents, who have provided a home environment, or more like those of their biological parents, who have contributed their heredity. Another form of adoption study involves comparing adopted and biological siblings.

adrenarche Puberty phase involving hormonal changes in the adrenal glands, which are located just above the kidneys. These changes occur from about 6 to 9 years of age in girls and about one year later in boys, before what is generally considered the beginning of puberty.

affectionate love Love occurring when an individual desires to have another person near and has a deep, caring affection for that person; also called companionate love.

AIDS Stands for acquired immunodeficiency syndrome, a sexually transmitted infection caused by the human immunodeficiency virus (HIV), which destroys the body's immune system.

altruism Unselfish interest in helping another person.

amygdala A portion of the brain's limbic system that is the seat of emotions such as anger.

anabolic steroids Drugs derived from the male sex hormone, testosterone. They promote muscle growth and increase lean body mass.

androgens The main class of male sex hormones.

androgyny The presence of a high degree of desirable feminine and masculine characteristics in the same individual.

anorexia nervosa An eating disorder that involves the relentless pursuit of thinness through starvation.

anxiety A vague, highly unpleasant feeling of fear and apprehension.

assimilation The incorporation of new information into existing knowledge.

attention Concentration and focusing of mental resources.

attention deficit hyperactivity disorder (ADHD) A disability in which children or adolescents consistently show one or more of the following characteristics over a period of time: (1) inattention, (2) hyperactivity, and (3) impulsivity.

attribution theory The theory that in their effort to make sense of their own behavior or performance, individuals are motivated to discover its underlying causes.

authoritarian parenting A restrictive, punitive style in which the parent exhorts the adolescent to follow the parent's directions and to respect work and effort. Firm limits and controls are placed on the adolescent, and little verbal exchange is allowed. This style is associated with adolescents' socially incompetent behavior.

authoritarian strategy of classroom management A teaching strategy that is restrictive and punitive. The focus is mainly on keeping order in the classroom rather than on instruction and learning.

authoritative parenting A style encouraging adolescents to be independent but still placing limits and controls on their actions. Extensive verbal give-and-take is allowed, and parents are warm and nurturant toward the adolescent. This style is associated with adolescents' socially competent behavior.

authoritative strategy of classroom management A teaching strategy that encourages students to be independent thinkers and doers but still involves effective monitoring. Authoritative teachers engage students in considerable verbal give-and-take and show a caring attitude toward them. However, they still declare limits when necessary.

average children Children who receive an average number of both positive and negative nominations from their peers.

B

behavior genetics The field that seeks to discover the influence of heredity and environment on individual differences in human traits and development.

bicultural identity Identity formation that occurs when adolescents identify in some ways with their ethnic group and in other ways with the majority culture.

Big Five factors of personality Five core traits of personality: openness to experience, conscientiousness, extraversion, agreeableness, and neuroticism (emotional stability).

binge eating disorder Involves frequent binge eating but without compensatory behavior like the purging that characterizes bulimics.

biological processes Physical changes in an individual's body.

biopsychosocial approach Approach that emphasizes that problems develop through an interaction of biological, psychological, and social factors.

bisexual A person who is attracted to people of both sexes.

boundary ambiguity The uncertainty in stepfamilies about who is in or out of the family and who is performing or responsible for certain tasks in the family system.

Bronfenbrenner's ecological theory A theory focusing on the influence of five environmental systems: microsystem, mesosystem, exosystem, macrosystem, and chronosystem.

bulimia nervosa An eating disorder in which the individual consistently follows a binge-and-purge eating pattern.

C

care perspective The moral perspective of Carol Gilligan, which views people in terms of their connectedness with others and emphasizes interpersonal communication, relationships with others, and concern for others.

case study An in-depth look at a single individual.

character education A direct moral education approach that involves teaching students a basic moral literacy to prevent them from engaging in immoral behavior or doing harm to themselves or others.

chlamydia One of most common sexually transmitted infections, named for *Chlamydia trachomatis,* an organism that spreads by sexual contact and infects the genital organs of both sexes.

chromosomes Threadlike structures that contain deoxyribonucleic acid, or DNA.

cliques Small groups that range from 2 to about 12 individuals and average about 5 to 6 individuals. Members are usually of the same sex and are similar in age; cliques can form because of similar interests, such as sports, and also can form purely from friendship.

cognitive control Involves effective control and flexible thinking in a number of areas, including controlling attention, reducing interfering thoughts, and being cognitively flexible.

cognitive moral education An approach based on the belief that students should learn to value things like democracy and justice as their moral reasoning develops; Kohlberg's theory has been the basis for many of the cognitive moral education approaches.

cognitive processes Changes in an individual's thinking and intelligence.

cohabitation Living together in a sexual relationship without being married.

cohort effects Refers to effects due to a person's date of birth, era, or generation, but not to actual chronological age.

collectivism Emphasizes values that serve the group by subordinating personal goals to preserve group integrity.

commitment The part of identity development in which adolescents show a personal investment in what they are going to do.

concrete operational stage Piaget's third stage, which lasts approximately from 7 to 11 years of age. In this stage, children can perform operations. Logical reasoning replaces intuitive thought as long as the reasoning can be applied to specific or concrete examples.

conduct disorder The psychiatric diagnostic category for the occurrence of multiple delinquent activities over a six-month period. These behaviors include truancy, running away, fire setting, cruelty to animals, breaking and entering, and excessive fighting.

conglomerate strategies The use of a combination of techniques, rather than a single approach, to improve adolescents' social skills; also called coaching.

connectedness An important element in adolescent identity development. It consists of two dimensions: mutuality, sensitivity to and respect for others' views; and permeability, openness to others' views.

conscience The component of the superego that involves behaviors disapproved of by parents.

constructivist approach A learner-centered approach that emphasizes the adolescent's active, cognitive construction of knowledge and understanding with guidance from the teacher.

contexts The settings in which development occurs. These settings are influenced by historical, economic, social, and cultural factors.

continuity-discontinuity issue Issue regarding whether development involves gradual, cumulative change (continuity) or distinct stages (discontinuity).

controversial children Children who are frequently nominated both as a best friend and as being disliked.

conventional reasoning The second, or intermediate, level in Kohlberg's theory. Individuals abide by certain standards (internal), but they are the standards of others (external), such as parents or the laws of society. The conventional level consists of two stages: mutual interpersonal expectations, relationships, and interpersonal conformity (stage 3) and social systems morality (stage 4).

convergent thinking A pattern of thinking in which individuals produce one correct answer; characteristic of the items on conventional intelligence tests; coined by Guilford.

coping Managing taxing circumstances, expending effort to solve life's problems, and seeking to master or reduce stress.

corpus callosum A large bundle of axon fibers that connect the brain's left and right hemispheres.

correlational research Research whose goal is to describe the strength of the relationship between two or more events or characteristics.

correlation coefficient A number based on a statistical analysis that is used to describe the degree of association between two variables.

creativity The ability to think in novel and unusual ways and discover unique solutions to problems.

crisis A period of identity development during which the adolescent is choosing among meaningful alternatives.

critical thinking Thinking reflectively and productively and evaluating the evidence.

cross-cultural studies Studies that compare a culture with one or more other cultures. Such studies provide information about the degree to which development in adolescents and emerging adults is similar, or universal, across cultures, or about the degree to which it is culture-specific.

cross-sectional research A research strategy that involves studying people all at one time.

crowds A larger group structure than cliques. Adolescents are usually members of a crowd based on reputation and may or may not spend much time together.

culture The behavior, patterns, beliefs, and all other products of a particular group of people that are passed on from generation to generation.

D

date, or **acquaintance, rape** Coercive sexual activity directed at someone whom the perpetrator knows.

dating scripts The cognitive models that adolescents and adults use to guide and evaluate dating interactions.

dependent variable The factor that is measured in experimental research.

depressants Drugs that slow down the central nervous system, bodily functions, and behavior.

descriptive research Research that aims to observe and record behavior.

development The pattern of change that begins at conception and continues through the life span. Most development involves growth, although it also includes decay (as in death and dying).

developmental cascades A developmental psychopathology approach that emphasizes connections across domains over time to influence developmental pathways and outcomes

developmental psychopathology approach Approach that focuses on describing and exploring the developmental pathways of problems.

difficult child A child who reacts negatively to many situations and is slow to accept new experiences.

direct instruction approach A teacher-centered approach characterized by teacher direction and control, mastery of academic skills, high expectations for students, and maximum time spent on learning tasks.

dismissing/avoidant attachment An insecure attachment category in which individuals deemphasize the importance of attachment. This category is associated with consistent experiences of rejection of attachment needs by caregivers.

divergent thinking A pattern of thinking in which individuals produce many answers to the same question; more characteristic of creativity than convergent thinking; coined by Guilford.

divided attention Concentration on more than one activity at the same time.

DNA A complex molecule that contains genetic information.

domain theory of moral development States that there are different domains of social knowledge and reasoning, including moral, social conventional, and personal domains. These domains arise from children's and adolescents' attempts to understand and deal with different forms of social experience.

dual-process model States that decision making is influenced by two systems—one analytical and one experiential, which compete with each other; in this model, it is the experiential system—monitoring and managing actual experiences—that benefits adolescent decision making.

E

early adolescence The developmental period that corresponds roughly to the middle school or junior high school years and includes most pubertal change.

early adulthood The developmental period beginning in the late teens or early twenties and lasting through the thirties.

early childhood The developmental period extending from the end of infancy to about 5 or 6 years of age; sometimes called the preschool years.

early-later experience issue Issue focusing on the degree to which early experiences (especially early in childhood) or later experiences are the key determinants of development.

easy child A child who generally is in a positive mood, quickly establishes regular routines, and adapts easily to new experiences.

eclectic theoretical orientation An orientation that does not follow any one theoretical approach but rather selects from each theory whatever is considered the best in it.

ego ideal The component of the superego that involves ideal standards approved by parents.

emerging adulthood The developmental period occurring from approximately 18 to 25 years of age; this transitional period between adolescence and adulthood is characterized by experimentation and exploration.

emotion Feeling, or affect, that occurs when a person is in a state or an interaction that is important to the individual, especially to his or her well-being.

emotional autonomy The capacity to relinquish childlike dependence on parents.

emotional intelligence The ability to perceive and express emotion accurately and adaptively, to understand emotion and emotional knowledge, to use feelings to facilitate thought, and to manage emotions in oneself and others.

emotion-focused coping Lazarus' term for responding to stress in an emotional manner, especially by using defense mechanisms.

empathy Reaction to another's feelings with an emotional response that is similar to the other's feelings.

epigenetic view Belief that development is the result of an ongoing bidirectional interchange between heredity and environment.

equilibration A mechanism in Piaget's theory that explains how individuals shift from one state of thought to the next. The shift occurs as individuals experience cognitive conflict or a disequilibrium in trying to understand the world. Eventually, the individual resolves the conflict and reaches a balance, or equilibrium, of thought.

Erikson's theory Theory that includes eight stages of human development. Each stage consists of a unique developmental task that confronts individuals with a crisis that must be faced.

estrogens The main class of female sex hormones.

ethnic gloss Use of an ethnic label such as African American or Latino in a superficial way that portrays an ethnic group as being more homogeneous than it really is.

ethnic identity An enduring, basic aspect of the self that includes a sense of membership in an ethnic group and the attitudes and feelings related to that membership.

ethnicity A dimension of culture based on cultural heritage, national characteristics, race, religion, and language.

ethnocentrism A tendency to favor one's own group over other groups.

evocative genotype-environment correlations Correlations that occur because an adolescent's genetically shaped characteristics elicit certain types of physical and social environments.

evolutionary psychology An approach that emphasizes the importance of adaptation, reproduction, and "survival of the fittest" in explaining behavior.

executive attention Type of attention that involves action planning, allocating attention to goals, error detection and compensation, monitoring progress on tasks, and dealing with novel or difficult circumstances.

executive functioning An umbrella-like concept that involves higher-order, complex cognitive processes that include exercising cognitive control, making decisions, reasoning, thinking critically, thinking creatively, and metacognition.

experience sampling method (ESM) Research method that involves providing participants with electronic pagers and then beeping them at random times, at which point they are asked to report on various aspects of their lives.

experimental research Research that involves an experiment, a carefully regulated procedure in which one or more of the factors believed to influence the behavior being studied are manipulated while all other factors are held constant.

externalizing problems Develop when individuals turn problems outward. An example is juvenile delinquency.

extrinsic motivation External motivational factors such as rewards and punishments.

F

female athlete triad A combination of disordered eating, amenorrhea, and osteoporosis that may develop in female adolescents and college students.

feminization of poverty Term reflecting the fact that far more women than men live in poverty. Women's low income, divorce, and the resolution of divorce cases by the judicial system, which leaves women with less money than they and their children need to function adequately, are the likely causes.

flow Csikszentmihalyi's concept of optimal life experiences, which he believes occur most often when people develop a sense of mastery and are absorbed in a state of concentration when they're engaged in an activity.

forgiveness An aspect of prosocial behavior that occurs when an injured person releases the injurer from possible behavioral retaliation.

formal operational stage Piaget's fourth and final stage of cognitive development, which he argued emerges at 11 to 15 year of age. It is characterized by abstract, idealistic, and logical thought.

friends A subset of peers who engage in mutual companionship, support, and intimacy.

G

gender The characteristics of people as males or females.

gender bias A preconceived notion about the abilities of females and males that prevents individuals from pursuing their own interests and achieving their potential.

gender intensification hypothesis Hypothesis stating that psychological and behavioral differences between boys and girls become greater during early adolescence because of increased socialization pressure to conform to masculine and feminine gender roles.

gender role A set of expectations that prescribes how females and males should think, act, and feel.

gender-role transcendence The belief that, when an individual's competence is at issue, it should be conceptualized not on the basis of masculinity, femininity, or androgyny but, rather, on a person basis.

gender schema theory Theory stating that an individual's attention and behavior are guided by an internal motivation to conform to gender-based sociocultural standards and stereotypes. Females are often portrayed in sexually provocative ways on MTV and in rock videos.

gender stereotypes Broad categories that reflect our impressions and beliefs about females and males.

gene × environment (G × E) interaction The interaction of a specific measured variation in the DNA and a specific measured aspect of the environment.

genes The units of hereditary information, which are short segments composed of DNA.

genital herpes A sexually transmitted infection caused by a large family of viruses of different strains. These strains produce other, nonsexually transmitted diseases such as chicken pox and mononucleosis.

genital warts An STI caused by the human papillomavirus; genital warts are very contagious and are the most common acquired STI in the United States in the 15- to 24-year-old age group.

genotype A person's genetic heritage; the actual genetic material.

gonadarche Puberty phase involving the maturation of primary sexual characteristics (ovaries in females, testes in males) and secondary sexual characteristics (pubic hair, breast, and genital development). This period follows adrenarche by about two years and is what most people think of as puberty.

gonorrhea A sexually transmitted infection caused by the bacterium *Neisseria gonorrhoeae,* which thrives in the moist mucous membranes lining the mouth, throat, vagina, cervix, urethra, and anal tract. This STI is commonly called the "drip" or the "clap."

goodness of fit The match between an individual's temperament style and the environmental demands the individual must cope with.

gratitude A feeling of thankfulness and appreciation, especially in response to someone doing something kind or helpful.

H

hallucinogens Drugs that alter an individual's perceptual experiences and produce hallucinations; also called psychedelic (mind-altering) drugs.

helpless orientation An outlook in which individuals seem trapped when experiencing difficulty and attribute their difficulty to a lack of ability. This orientation undermines performance.

hidden curriculum The pervasive moral atmosphere that characterizes every school.

homophobia Having irrational negative feelings against individuals who have same-sex attractions.

hormones Powerful chemicals secreted by the endocrine glands and carried through the body by the bloodstream.

hostile environment sexual harassment Sexual harassment in which students are subjected to unwelcome sexual conduct that is so severe, persistent, or pervasive that it limits the students' ability to benefit from their education.

hypotheses Specific assertions and predictions that can be tested.

hypothetical-deductive reasoning Piaget's term for adolescents' ability, in the formal operational stage, to develop hypotheses, or best guesses, about ways to solve problems; they then systematically deduce, or conclude, the best path to follow in solving the problem.

I

identity Who a person is, representing a synthesis and integration of self-understanding.

identity achievement Marcia's term for an adolescent who has undergone an identity crisis and made a commitment.

identity diffusion Marcia's term for the state adolescents are in when they have not yet experienced an identity crisis or made any commitments.

identity foreclosure Marcia's term for the state adolescents are in when they have made a commitment but have not experienced an identity crisis.

identity moratorium Marcia's term for the state of adolescents who are in the midst of an identity crisis but who have not made a clear commitment to an identity.

identity versus identity confusion Erikson's fifth developmental stage, which occurs during adolescence. At this time, individuals are faced with deciding who they are, what they are all about, and where they are going in life.

inclusion Educating a child or adolescent with special education needs full-time in the regular classroom.

independent variable The factor that is manipulated in experimental research.

index offenses Criminal acts, such as robbery, rape, and homicide, whether they are committed by juveniles or adults.

individualism Emphasizes values that serve the self and gives priority to personal goals, not group goals.

individuality An important element in adolescent identity development. It consists of two dimensions: self-assertion, the ability to have and communicate a point of view; and separateness, the use of communication patterns to express how one is different from others.

Individuals with Disabilities Education Act (IDEA) Act spelling out broad mandates for services to all children and adolescents with disabilities. These include evaluation and eligibility determination, appropriate education and an individualized education plan (IEP), and education in the least restrictive environment.

induction A discipline technique in which a parent uses reason and explanation of the consequences for others of the adolescent's actions.

indulgent parenting A style in which parents are highly involved with their adolescents but place few demands or controls on them. This is associated with adolescents' social incompetence, especially a lack of self-control.

infancy The developmental period that extends from birth to 18 or 24 months of age.

information-processing theory A theory emphasizing that individuals manipulate information, monitor it, and strategize about it. Central to this approach are the processes of memory and thinking.

insecure attachment Attachment pattern in which infants either avoid the caregiver or show considerable resistance or ambivalence toward the caregiver. This pattern is theorized to be related to difficulties in relationships and problems in later development.

intelligence The ability to solve problems and to adapt to and learn from everyday experiences; not everyone agrees on what constitutes intelligence.

intelligent quotient (IQ) A person's tested mental age divided by chronological age, multiplied by 100.

internalizing problems Develop when individuals turn problems inward. Examples include anxiety and depression.

Internet The core of computer-mediated communication. The Internet system is worldwide and connects thousands of computer networks, providing an incredible array of information—both positive and negative—that adolescents can access.

intimacy in friendship In most research studies, this concept is defined narrowly as self-disclosure, or sharing of private thoughts.

intimacy versus isolation Erikson's sixth developmental stage, which individuals experience during the early adulthood years. At this time, individuals face the developmental task of forming intimate relationships with others.

intrinsic motivation Internal motivational factors such as self-determination, curiosity, challenge, and effort.

inventionist view The view that adolescence is a sociohistorical creation. Especially important in this view are the sociohistorical circumstances at the beginning of the twentieth century, a time when legislation was enacted that ensured the dependency of youth and made their move into the economic sphere more manageable.

J

jigsaw classroom A classroom strategy in which students from different cultural backgrounds are placed in a cooperative group in which, together, they have to construct different parts of a project to reach a common goal.

justice perspective A moral perspective that focuses on the rights of the individual. Individuals independently make moral decisions.

juvenile delinquency A broad range of behaviors, including socially unacceptable behavior, status offenses, and criminal acts.

L

laboratory A controlled setting in which many of the complex factors of the "real world" are removed.

late adolescence The developmental period that corresponds approximately to the latter half of the second decade of life. Career interests, dating, and identity exploration are often more pronounced in late adolescence than in early adolescence.

late adulthood The developmental period that lasts from about 60 to 70 years of age until death.

learning disabilities Disabilities in which children experience difficulty in learning that involves understanding or using spoken or written language; the difficulty can appear in listening, thinking, reading, writing, and spelling. A learning disability also may involve difficulty in doing mathematics. To be classified as a learning disability, the learning problem is not primarily the result of visual, hearing, or motor disabilities; mental retardation; emotional disorders; or environmental, cultural, or economic disadvantage.

least restrictive environment (LRE) A setting that is as similar as possible to the one in which the children or adolescents without a disability are educated; under the IDEA, efforts to educate the child or adolescent with a disability in this setting has been given a legal basis.

longitudinal research A research strategy in which the same individuals are studied over a period of time, usually several years or more.

love withdrawal A discipline technique in which a parent removes attention or love from the adolescent.

M

major depressive disorder The diagnosis when an individual experiences a major depressive episode and depressed characteristics, such as lethargy and depression, for two weeks or longer and daily functioning becomes impaired.

mastery orientation An outlook in which individuals focus on the task rather than on their ability; they concentrate on learning strategies and the process of achievement instead of the outcome.

menarche A girl's first menstrual period.

mental age (MA) An individual's level of mental development relative to others; a concept developed by Binet.

mentors Individuals who are usually older and more experienced and are motivated to improve the competence and character of a younger person.

metacognition Cognition about cognition, or "knowing about knowing."

middle adulthood The developmental period that is entered at about 35 to 45 years of age and exited at about 55 to 65 years of age.

middle and late childhood The developmental period extending from about 6 to about 10 or 11 years of age; sometimes called the elementary school years.

Millennials The generation born after 1980, the first to come of age and enter emerging adulthood in the new millennium. Two characteristics of Millennials stand out: (1) their ethnic diversity, and (2) their connection to technology.

mindset The cognitive view, either fixed or growth, that individuals develop for themselves.

moral development Thoughts, feelings, and behaviors regarding standards of right and wrong.

moral exemplars People who have lived exemplary lives.

moral identity An aspect of personality that is present when individuals have moral notions and commitments that are central to their lives.

multicultural education Education that values diversity and includes the perspectives of a variety of cultural groups.

multiple developmental trajectories Concept that adults follow one trajectory and children and adolescents another one; how these trajectories mesh is important.

myelination The process by which the axon portion of the neuron becomes covered and insulated with a layer of fat cells, which increases the speed and efficiency of information processing in the nervous system.

N

narcissism A self-centered and self-concerned approach toward others.

naturalistic observation Observation of behavior in real-world settings.

nature-nurture issue Issue involving the debate about whether development is primarily influenced by an organism's biological inheritance (nature) or by its environmental experiences (nurture).

neglected children Children who are infrequently nominated as a best friend but are not disliked by their peers.

neglectful parenting A style in which the parent is very uninvolved in the adolescent's life. It is associated with adolescents' social incompetence, especially a lack of self-control.

neo-Piagetians Theorists who argue that Piaget got some things right but that his theory needs considerable revision. In their revision, they give more emphasis to information processing that involves attention, memory, and strategies; they also seek to provide more precise explanations of cognitive changes.

neurons Nerve cells, which are the nervous system's basic units.

nonshared environmental experiences The adolescent's own unique experiences, both within a family and outside the family, that are not shared by a sibling.

normal distribution A symmetrical distribution of values or scores, with a majority of scores falling in the middle of the possible range of scores and few scores appearing toward the extremes of the range.

O

optimism Involves having a positive outlook on the future and minimizing problems.

P

passive genotype-environment correlations Correlations that occur because biological parents, who are genetically related to the child, provide a rearing environment for the child.

peers Individuals who are about the same age or maturity level.

performance orientation An outlook in which individuals are focused on winning rather than achievement outcome. For performance-oriented students, winning results in happiness.

permissive strategy of classroom management A teaching strategy that offers students considerable autonomy but provides them with little support for developing learning skills or managing their behavior.

personality The enduring personal characteristics of individuals.

phenotype The way an individual's genotype is expressed in observed and measurable characteristics.

Piaget's theory A theory stating that children actively construct their understanding of the world and go through four stages of cognitive development.

popular children Children who are frequently nominated as a best friend and are rarely disliked by their peers.

possible self What individuals might become, what they would like to become, and what they are afraid of becoming.

postconventional reasoning The third and highest level in Kohlberg's theory. At this level, morality is more internal. The postconventional level consists of two stages: social contract or utility and individual rights (stage 5) and universal ethical principles (stage 6).

postformal thought Thought that is reflective, relativistic, and contextual; provisional; realistic; and open to emotions and subjective.

power assertion A discipline technique in which a parent attempts to gain control over the adolescent or the adolescent's resources.

precocious puberty The very early onset and rapid progression of puberty.

preconventional reasoning The lowest level in Kohlberg's theory of moral development. At this level, morality is often focused on reward and punishment. The two stages in preconventional reasoning are punishment and obedience orientation (stage 1) and individualism, instrumental purpose, and exchange (stage 2).

prefrontal cortex The highest level of the brain's frontal lobes that is involved in reasoning, decision making, and self-control.

prejudice An unjustified negative attitude toward an individual because of the individual's membership in a group.

prenatal period The time from conception to birth.

preoccupied/ambivalent attachment An insecure attachment category in which adolescents are hyperattuned to attachment experiences. This is thought mainly to occur because parents are inconsistently available to the adolescents.

preoperational stage Piaget's second stage, which lasts approximately from 2 to 7 years of age. In this stage, children begin to represent their world with words, images, and drawings.

problem-focused coping Lazarus' term for the strategy of squarely facing one's troubles and trying to solve them.

psychoanalytic theories Theories that describe development as primarily unconscious and heavily colored by emotion. Behavior is merely a surface characteristic, and the symbolic workings of the mind have to be analyzed to understand behavior. Early experiences with parents are emphasized.

psychometric/intelligence view A view that emphasizes the importance of individual differences in intelligence; many advocates of this view also argue that intelligence should be assessed with intelligence tests.

psychosocial moratorium Erikson's term for the gap between childhood security and adult autonomy that adolescents experience as part of their identity exploration.

puberty A period of rapid physical maturation involving hormonal and bodily changes that take place primarily in early adolescence.

Public Law 94-142 The Education for All Handicapped Children Act, which requires all students with disabilities to be given a free, appropriate public education.

Q

quid pro quo sexual harassment Sexual harassment in which a school employee threatens to base an educational decision (such as a grade) on a student's submission to unwelcome sexual conduct.

R

rape Forcible sexual intercourse with a person who does not give consent.

rapport talk The language of conversation, establishing connections and negotiating relationships.

reciprocal socialization The process by which children and adolescents socialize parents, just as parents socialize them.

rejected children Children who are infrequently nominated as a best friend and are actively disliked by their peers.

religion An organized set of beliefs, practices, rituals, and symbols that increases an individual's connection to a sacred or transcendent other (God, higher power, or higher truth).

religiousness The degree of affiliation with an organized religion, participation in prescribed rituals and practices, connection with its beliefs, and involvement in a community of believers.

report talk Talk that gives information; public speaking is an example.

resilience Adapting positively and achieving successful outcomes in the face of significant risks and adverse circumstances.

rites of passage Ceremonies or rituals that mark an individual's transition from one status to another, such as the entry into adulthood.

romantic love Love that has strong sexual and infatuation components; also called passionate love or eros. It often predominates in the early part of a love relationship.

S

schema A mental concept or framework that is useful in organizing and interpreting information.

secular trends Patterns of the onset of puberty over historical time, especially across generations.

secure attachment Attachment pattern in which infants use their primary caregiver, usually the mother, as a secure base from which to explore the environment. Secure attachment is theorized to be an important foundation for psychological development later in childhood, adolescence, and adulthood.

selective attention Focusing on a specific aspect of experience that is relevant while ignoring others that are irrelevant.

self All of the characteristics of a person.

self-concept Domain-specific evaluations of the self.

self-efficacy The belief that one can master a situation and produce positive outcomes.

self-esteem The global evaluative dimension of the self; also referred to as self-worth, or self-image.

self-handicapping Use of failure avoidance strategies such as not trying in school or putting off studying until the last minute so that circumstances, rather than a lack of ability, will be seen as the cause of low-level performance.

self-understanding The individual's cognitive representation of the self; the substance and content of self-conceptions.

sensorimotor stage Piaget's first stage of development, lasting from birth to about 2 years of age. In this stage, infants construct an understanding of the world by coordinating sensory experiences with physical, motoric actions.

service learning A form of education that promotes social responsibility and service to the community.

sexually transmitted infections (STIs) Infections that are contracted primarily through sexual contact. This contact is not limited to vaginal intercourse but includes oral-genital contact and anal-genital contact as well.

sexual minority Someone who identifies with being lesbian, gay, or bisexual.

sexual script A stereotyped pattern of role prescriptions for how individuals should sexually behave. Females and males have been socialized to follow different sexual scripts.

shared environmental experiences Siblings' common experiences such as their parents' personalities and intellectual orientation, the family's socioeconomic status, and the neighborhood in which they live.

slow-to-warm-up child A child who has a low activity level, is somewhat negative, and displays a low intensity of mood.

social cognition The way individuals conceptualize and reason about their social worlds—the people they watch and interact with, their relationships with those people, the groups they participate in, and the way they reason about themselves and others.

social cognitive theory The view that behavior, environment, and cognition are the key factors in development.

social cognitive theory of gender Theory emphasizing that children's and adolescents' gender development occurs through observation and imitation of gender behavior, and through rewards and punishments they experience for gender-appropriate and gender-inappropriate behavior.

social cognitive theory of moral development The theory that distinguishes between moral competence (the ability to produce moral behaviors) and moral performance (enacting those behaviors in specific situations).

social constructivist approach Approach that emphasizes the social contexts of learning and the construction of knowledge through social interaction.

social conventional reasoning Thoughts about social consensus and convention, as opposed to moral reasoning that stresses ethical issues.

social policy A national government's course of action designed to influence the welfare of its citizens.

social role theory Theory stating that gender differences mainly result from the contrasting roles of females and males, with females having less power and status and controlling fewer resources than males.

socioeconomic status (SES) Refers to a grouping of people with similar occupational, educational, and economic characteristics.

socioemotional processes Changes in an individual's personality, emotions, relationships with other people, and social contexts.

sociometric status The extent to which children and adolescents are liked or disliked by their peer group.

spermarche A boy's first ejaculation of semen.

spirituality Experiencing something beyond oneself in a transcendent manner and living in a way that benefits others and society.

standardized test A test with uniform procedures for administration and scoring. Many standardized tests allow a person's performance to be compared with the performance of other individuals.

status offenses Juvenile offenses, performed by youth under a specified age, that are not as serious as index offenses. These offenses may include such acts as underage drinking, truancy, and sexual promiscuity.

stereotype A generalization that reflects our impressions and beliefs about a broad group of people. All stereotypes refer to an image of what the typical member of a specific group is like.

stimulants Drugs that increase the activity of the central nervous system.

storm-and-stress view G. Stanley Hall's concept that adolescence is a turbulent time charged with conflict and mood swings.

stress The response of individuals to stressors, which are circumstances and events that threaten and tax their coping abilities.

sustained attention The ability to maintain attention to a selected stimulus for a prolonged period of time.

synapses Gaps between neurons, where connections between the axon and dendrites occur.

syphilis A sexually transmitted infection caused by the bacterium *Treponema pallidum,* a spirochete.

T

temperament An individual's behavioral style and characteristic way of responding.

theory An interrelated, coherent set of ideas that helps explain phenomena and make predictions.

top-dog phenomenon The circumstance of moving from the top position (in elementary school, the oldest, biggest, and most powerful students) to the lowest position (in middle or junior high school, the youngest, smallest, and least powerful).

triarchic theory of intelligence Sternberg's view that intelligence comes in three main forms: analytical, creative, and practical.

twin study A study in which the behavioral similarity of identical twins is compared with the behavioral similarity of fraternal twins.

U

unresolved/disorganized attachment An insecure category in which the adolescent has an unusually high level of fear and is disoriented. This can result from such traumatic experiences as a parent's death or abuse by parents.

V

values Beliefs and attitudes about the way things should be.

values clarification An educational approach that focuses on helping people clarify what is important to them, what is worth working for, and what purpose their lives are to serve. Students are encouraged to define their own values and understand others' values.

Vygotsky's theory A sociocultural cognitive theory that emphasizes how culture and social interaction guide cognitive development.

W

wisdom Expert knowledge about the practical aspects of life that permits excellent judgment about important matters.

Z

zone of proximal development (ZPD) Vygotsky's concept that refers to the range of tasks that are too difficult for an individual to master alone, but that can be mastered with the guidance or assistance of adults or more-skilled peers.

references

A

Aalsma, M. C., Lapsley, D. K., & Flannery, D. J. (2006). Personal fables, narcissism, and adolescent adjustment. *Psychology in the Schools, 43,* 481–491.

Abbate-Daga, G., Gramaglia, C., Amianto, F., Marzola, E., & Fassino, S. (2010). Attachment insecurity, personality, and body dissatisfaction in eating disorders. *Journal of Nervous and Mental Disease, 198,* 520–524.

Abbott, B. D., & Barber, B. L. (2010). Embodied image: Gender differences in functional and aesthetic body image among Australian adolescents. *Body Image, 7,* 22–31.

Aber, J. L., Bishop-Josef, S. J., Jones, S. M., McLern, T., & Phillips, D. A. (2006). *Child development and social policy*. Washington, DC: American Psychological Association.

Abruscato, J. A., & DeRosa, D. A. (2010). *Teaching children science: A discovery approach* (7th ed.). Boston: Allyn & Bacon.

Achenbach, T. M., & Edelbrock, C. S. (1981). Behavioral problems and competencies reported by parents of normal and disturbed children aged four through sixteen. *Monographs of the Society for Research in Child Development, 46* (1, Serial No. 188).

Achenbach, T. M., Howell, C. T., Quay, H. C., & Conners, C. K. (1991). National survey of problems and competencies among four- to sixteen-year-olds. *Monographs for the Society for Research in Child Development, 56* (3, Serial No. 225).

Ackerman, A., Thornton, J. C., Wang, J., Pierson, R. N., & Horlick, M. (2006). Sex differences in the effect of puberty on the relationship between fat mass and bone mass in 926 healthy subjects, 6 to 18 years old. *Obesity, 14,* 819–825.

Ackerman, P. L. (2011). Intelligence and expertise. In R. J. Sternberg & S. B. Kaufman (Eds.), *Cambridge handbook of intelligence*. New York: Cambridge University Press.

Adelson, J. (1979, January). Adolescence and the generalization gap. *Psychology Today, 13,* 33–37.

Adie, J. W., Duda, J. L., & Ntoumanis, N. (2010). Achievement goals, competition appraisals, and the well-being of elite youth soccer players over two competitive seasons. *Journal of Sport and Exercise Psychology, 32,* 555–579.

Adler, N. E., Ozer, E. J., & Tschann, J. (2003). Abortion among adolescents. *American Psychologist, 58,* 211–217.

Afterschool Alliance. (2009). *America after 3pm.* Washington, DC: Author.

Agras, W. S., & others. (2004). Report of the National Institutes of Health workshop on overcoming barriers to treatment research in anorexia nervosa. *International Journal of Eating Disorders, 35,* 509–521.

Agras, W. S., & Robinson, A. H. (2008). Four years of progress in the treatment of the eating disorders. *Nordic Journal of Psychiatry, 62*(Suppl 47), S19–S24.

Ahn, N. (1994). Teenage childbearing and high school completion: Accounting for individual heterogenicity. *Family Planning Perspectives, 26,* 17–21.

Ahrberg, M., Trojca, D., Nasrawi, N., & Vocks, S. (2011, in press). Body image disturbance in binge eating disorder: A review. *European Eating Disorders Review.*

Ahrons, C. R. (2004). *We're still family.* New York: HarperCollins.

Ahrons, C. R. (2007). Family ties after divorce: Long-term implications for children. *Family Process, 46,* 53–65.

Ainsworth, M. D. S. (1979). Infant-mother attachment. *American Psychologist, 34,* 932–937.

Alan Guttmacher Institute. (1995). *National survey of the American male's sexual habits.* New York: Author.

Alan Guttmacher Institute. (2010, January 26). *U.S. teenage pregnancies, births, and abortions.* New York: Author.

Albert, D., & Steinberg, L. (2011a, in press). Judgment and decision making in adolescence. *Journal of Research on Adolescence.*

Albert, D., & Steinberg, L. (2011b, in press). Peer influences on adolescent risk behavior. In M. Bardo, D. Fishbein, & R. Milich (Eds.), *Inhibitory control and drug abuse prevention: From research to translation.* New York: Springer.

Alexander, C., Piazza, M., Mekos, D., & Valente, T. (2001). Peers, schools, and cigarette smoking. *Journal of Adolescent Health, 29,* 22–30.

Alexander, J., & others. (1998). *Blueprints for violence prevention: Functional family therapy.* Boulder: University of Colorado.

Alexander, P. A., & Mayer, R. E. (Eds.). (2011). *Handbook of research on learning and instruction.* New York: Routledge.

Ali, M. M., & Dwyer, D. S. (2011). Estimating peer effects in sexual behavior among adolescents. *Journal of Adolescence, 34,* 183–190.

Allen, G., & MacMillan, R. (2006). *Depression, suicidal behavior, and strain: Extending strain theory.* Paper presented at the meeting of the American Sociological Association, Montreal.

Allen, J., & Allen, C. (2009). *Escaping the endless adolescence.* New York: Ballantine.

Allen J. P., & Miga, E. M. (2010). Attachment in adolescence: A move to the level of emotion relation. *Journal of Social and Personal Relationships, 27,* 181–190.

Allen, J. P., & others. (2009, April). *Portrait of the secure teen as an adult.* Paper presented at the meeting of the Society for Research in Child Development, Denver.

Allen, M., Svetaz, M. V., Hardeman, R., & Resnick, M. D. (2008, February). *What research tells us about parenting practices and their relationship to youth sexual behavior.* Campaign to Prevent Teen and Unplanned Pregnancy. Retrieved December 2, 2008, from www.TheNationalCampaign.org

Alleyne, B., Coleman-Cowger, V. H., Crown, L., Gibbons, M. A., & Vines, L. N. (2011). The effects of dating violence, substance use, and risky sexual behavior among a diverse sample of Illinois youth. *Journal of Adolescence, 34,* 11–18.

Almeida, D. (2011). Stress and aging. In K. W. Schaie & S. L. Willis (Eds.), *Handbook of the psychology of aging* (7th ed.). New York: Elsevier.

Alsaker, F. D., & Flammer, A. (1999). *The Adolescent experience: European and American adolescents in the 1990s.* Mahwah, NJ: Erlbaum.

Altarac, M., & Saroha, E. (2007). Lifetime prevalence of learning disability among U.S. children. *Pediatrics, 119*(Suppl 1), S77–S83.

Alvarez, A. (2009). Racism: "It isn't fair." In N. Tewari & A. Alvarez (Eds.), *Asian American psychology.* Clifton, NJ: Psychology Press.

Amabile, T. M. (1993). (Commentary). In D. Goleman, P. Kafman, & M. Ray (Eds.), *The creative spirit.* New York: Plume.

Amabile, T. M., & Hennessey, B. A. (1992). The motivation for creativity in children. In A. K. Boggiano & T. S. Pittman (Eds.), *Achievement and motivation.* New York: Cambridge University Press.

Amato, P. R. (2006). Marital discord, divorce, and children's well-being: Results from a 20-year longitudinal study of two generations. In A. Clarke-Stewart & J. Dunn (Eds.), *Families count*. New York: Cambridge University Press.

Amato, P. R. (2010). Research on divorce: Continuing trends and new developments. *Journal of Marriage and the Family, 72,* 650–666.

Amato, P. R., & Dorius, C. (2010). Fathers, children, and divorce. In M. E. Lamb (Ed.), *The role of the father in child development* (5th ed.). New York: Wiley.

Ambrose, D., Sternberg, R. J., & Sriraman, B. (Eds.). (2012). *Confronting dogmatism in gifted education*. New York: Routledge.

American Academy of Pediatrics. (2010). Policy statement—sexuality, contraception, and the media. *Pediatrics, 126,* 576–582.

American Academy of Pediatrics & Reiff, M. I. (2011). *ADHD: What every parent needs to know* (2nd ed.). Washington, DC: Author.

American Association of University Women. (1992). *How schools shortchange girls: A study of major findings on girls and education.* Washington, DC: Author.

American Association of University Women. (2006). *Drawing the line: Sexual harassment on campus.* Washington, DC: Author.

American College Health Association. (2008). American College Health Association—National College Health Assessment spring 2007 reference group data report (abridged). *Journal of American College Health, 56,* 469–479.

American Psychiatric Association. (1994). *Diagnostic and statistical manual of mental disorders* (4th ed.). Washington, DC: Author.

American Psychological Association (2003). *Psychology: Scientific problem solvers.* Washington, DC: Author.

Amsel, E., & Smetana, J. G. (Eds.). (2011, in press). *Adolescent vulnerabilities and opportunities: Constructivist and developmental perspectives.* New York: Cambridge University Press.

Amstadter, A. B., & others (2011). Self-rated health in relation to rape and mental health disorders in a national sample of women. *American Journal of Orthopsychiatry, 81,* 202–210.

Anderman, E. M. (2012, in press). Adolescence. In K. Harris, S. Graham, & T. Urdan (Eds.), *APA handbook of educational psychology*. Washington, DC: American Psychological Association.

Anderman, E. M., & Anderman, L. H. (2010). *Classroom motivation*. Upper Saddle River, NJ: Pearson.

Anderman, E. M., & Dawson, H. (2011). Learning and motivation. In P. Alexander & R. Mayer (Eds.), *Handbook of learning and instruction*. New York: Routledge.

Anderman, E. M., & Murdock, T. B. (Eds.). (2007). *Psychology of academic cheating*. San Diego: Academic Press.

Anderman, E. M., & Wolters, C. A. (2006). Goals, values, and affect: Influences on student motivation. In P. A. Alexander & P. H. Winne (Eds.), *Handbook of educational psychology* (2nd ed.). Mahwah, NJ: Erlbaum.

Anderson, D. R., Huston, A. C., Schmitt, K., Linebarger, D. L., & Wright, J. C. (2001). Early childhood viewing and adolescent behavior: The recontact study. *Monographs of the Society for Research in Child Development, 66* (1, Serial No. 264).

Anderson, E., Greene, S. M., Hetherington, E. M., & Clingempeel, W. G. (1999). The dynamics of parental remarriage. In E. M. Hetherington (Ed.), *Coping with divorce, single parenting, and remarriage*. Mahwah, NJ: Erlbaum.

Anderson, K. G., Tapert, S. F., Moadab, I., Crowley, T. J., & Brown, S. A. (2007). Personality risk profile for conduct disorder and substance use disorders in youth. *Addictive Behaviors, 32,* 2377–2382.

Anderson, P. L., & Meier-Hedde, R. (2011). *International case studies of dyslexia*. New York: Routledge.

Andersson, U. (2010). The contribution of working memory capacity to foreign language comprehension in children. *Memory, 18,* 458–472.

Ansary, N. S., & Luthar, S. S. (2009). Distress and academic achievement among adolescents of affluence: A study of externalizing and internalizing problem behaviors and school performance. *Development and Psychopathology, 21,* 319–341.

Ansary, N. S., McMahon, T. J., & Luthar, S. S. (2011, in press). Socioeconomic context and emotional-behavioral achievement links: Concurrent and prospective associations among low- and high-income youth. *Journal of Research on Adolescence.*

Antai-Otong, D. (2003). Suicide: Life span considerations. *Nursing Clinics of North America, 38,* 137–150.

Antonucci, T. C., Birditt, K. S., & Ajrouch, K. (2011). Convoys of social relations: Past, present, and future. In K. L. Fingerman, C. A. Berg, J. Smith, & T. C. Antonucci (Eds.), *Handbook of life-span development.* New York: Springer.

Appleton, J. J. (2012). Student engagement in school. In J. R. Levesque (Ed.), *Encyclopedia of adolescence.* New York: Springer.

Aquino, K., McFerran, B., & Laven, M. (2011). Moral identity and the experience of moral elevation in response to acts of uncommon goodness. *Journal of Personality and Social Behavior, 100,* 703–718.

Araujo, D. M., Santos, G. F., & Nardi, A. E. (2010). Binge eating disorder and depression: A systematic review. *World Journal of Biological Psychiatry, 11 (2, Pt 2),* 199–207.

Archibald, A. B., Graber, J. A., & Brooks-Gunn, J. (1999). Associations among parent-adolescent relationships, pubertal growth, dieting, and body image in young adolescent girls: A short-term longitudinal study. *Journal of Research on Adolescence, 9,* 395–415.

Ardelt, M. (2010). Are older adults wiser than college students: A comparison of two age cohorts. *Journal of Adult Development, 17,* 193–207.

Arends, R. I. (2012). *Learning to Teach* (9th ed.). New York: McGraw-Hill.

Arenkiel, B. R. (2011, in press). Genetic approaches to reveal the connectivity of adult-born neurons. *Frontiers in Neuroscience.*

Arim, R. G., & others. (2011, in press). The family antecedents and the subsequent outcomes of early puberty. *Journal of Youth and Adolescence.*

Arms, E., Bickett, J., & Graf, V. (2008). Gender bias and imbalance: Girls in U.S. special education programs. *Gender and Education, 20,* 349–359.

Armstrong, M. L., Roberts, A. E., Owen, D. C., & Koch, J. R. (2004). Contemporary college students and body piercing. *Journal of Adolescent Health, 35,* 58–61.

Armstrong, M. L. (1995). Adolescent tattoos: Educating and pontificating. *Pediatric Nursing, 21*(6), 561–564.

Arnett, J. (1990). Contraceptive use, sensation seeking, and adolescent egocentrism. *Journal of Youth and Adolescence, 19,* 171–180.

Arnett, J. J. (1995, March). *Are college students adults?* Paper presented at the meeting of the Society for Research in Child Development, Indianapolis.

Arnett, J. J. (2004). *Emerging adulthood*. New York: Oxford University Press.

Arnett, J. J. (2006). Emerging adulthood: Understanding the new way of coming of age. In J. J. Arnett & J. L. Tanner (Eds.), *Emerging adults in America*. Washington, DC: American Psychological Association.

Arnett, J. J. (2007). Socialization in emerging adulthood. In J. E. Grusec & P. D. Hastings (Eds.), *Handbook of socialization*. New York: Guilford.

Arnett, J. J. (2010). Oh, grow up! Generational grumbling and the new life stage of emerging adulthoods—Commentary on Trzesniewski & Donnellan (2010). *Perspectives on Psychological Science, 5,* 89–92.

Arnett, J. J., & Brody, G. H. (2008). A fraught passage: The identity challenges of African American emerging adults. *Human Development, 51,* 291–293.

Aronowitz, T., & Morrison-Beedy, D. (2008). Comparison of the maternal role in resilience among impoverished and non-impoverished early adolescent African American girls. *Adolescent & Family Health, 3,* 155–163.

Aronson, E. (1986, August). *Teaching students things they think they know all about: The case of prejudice and desegregation.* Paper presented at the meeting of the American Psychological Association, Washington, DC.

Arseth, A., Kroger, J., Martinussen, M., & Marcia, J. E. (2009). Meta-analytic studies of identity status and the relational issues of attachment and intimacy. *Identity, 9,* 1–32.

Asarnow, J. R., & Callan, J. W. (1985). Boys with peer adjustment problems: Social cognitive processes. *Journal of Consulting and Clinical Psychology, 53,* 80–87.

Ash, P. (2006). Adolescents in adult court: Does the punishment fit the criminal? *The Journal of the American Academy of Psychiatry and the Law, 34,* 145–149.

Ata, R. N., Ludden, A. B., & Lally, M. M. (2007). The effect of gender and family, friend, and media influences on eating behavior and body image during adolescence. *Journal of Youth and Adolescence, 36,* 1024–1037.

Attie, I., & Brooks-Gunn, J. (1989). Development of eating problems in adolescent girls: A longitudinal study. *Developmental Psychology, 25,* 70–79.

Avisar, A., & Shalev, L. (2011). Sustained attention and behavioral characteristics associated with ADHD in adults. *Applied Neuropsychology, 18,* 107–116.

B

Babbie, E. R. (2011). *The basics of social research* (5th ed.). Boston: Cengage.

Bachman, J. G., O'Malley, P. M., Schulenberg, J. E., Johnston, L. D., Bryant, A. L., & Merline, A. C. (2002). *The decline of substance abuse in young adulthood.* Mahwah, NJ: Erlbaum.

Bachman, J. G., O'Malley, P. M., Schulenberg, J. E., Johnston, L. D., Freedman-Doan, P., & Messersmith, E. E. (2008). *The education–drug use connection.* Clifton, NJ: Psychology Press.

Baddeley, A. D. (2008). What's new in working memory?*Psychology Review, 13,* 2–5.

Baddeley, A. D. (2010a). Long-term and working memory: How do they interact? In Lars Bäckman & Lars Nyberg (Eds.), *Memory, aging and the brain: A festschrift in honour of Lars-Göran Nilsson* (pp. 18–30). Hove, UK: Psychology Press.

Baddeley, A. D. (2010b). Working memory. *Current Biology, 20,* 136–140.

Baddeley, A. D. (2012). Working memory. *Annual Review of Psychology* (Vol. 63). Palo Alto, CA: Annual Reviews.

Bagwell, C. L., & Schmidt, C. L. (2011, in press). *Friendships in childhood and adolescence.* New York: Guilford.

Bakersmans-Kranenburg, M. J., & IJzendoorn, M. H. (2009). The first 10,000 adult attachment interviews: Distributions of adult attachment representations in clinical and non-clinical groups. *Attachment and Human Development, 11,* 223–263.

Baldwin, S., & Hoffman, J. P. (2002). The dynamics of self-esteem: A growth curve analysis. *Journal of Youth and Adolescence, 31,* 101–113.

Ball, B., Kerig, P. K., & Rosenbluth, B. (2009). "Like a family but better because you can actually trust each other": The Expect Respect dating violence program for at-risk youth. *Health Promotion Practices, 10,* S44–S58.

Ballentine, J. H., & Roberts, K. A. (2009). *Our social world* (2nd ed.). Thousand Oaks, CA: Sage.

Baltes, P. B., & Kunzmann, U. (2007). Wisdom and aging. In D. C. Park & N. Scharz (Eds.), *Cognitive aging* (2nd ed.). Philadelphia: Psychology Press.

Baltes, P. B., Lindenberger, U., & Staudinger, U. (2006). Life-span theory in developmental psychology. In W. Damon & R. Lerner (Eds.), *Handbook of child psychology* (6th ed.). New York: Wiley.

Baltes, P. B., & Smith, J. (2008). The fascination of wisdom: Its nature, ontogeny, and function. *Perspectives on Psychological Science, 3,* 56–64.

Bandura, A. (1986). *Social foundations of thought and action: A social cognitive theory.* Englewood Cliffs, NJ: Prentice Hall.

Bandura, A. (1991). Social cognitive theory of moral thought and action. In W. M. Kurtines & J. Gewirtz (Eds.), *Handbook of moral behavior and development* (Vol. 1). Hillsdale, NJ: Erlbaum.

Bandura, A. (1997). *Self-efficacy.* New York: W. H. Freeman.

Bandura, A. (1998, August). *Swimming against the mainstream: Accentuating the positive aspects of humanity.* Paper presented at the meeting of the American Psychological Association, San Francisco.

Bandura, A. (1999). Moral disengagement in the perpetuation of inhumanities. *Personality and Social Psychology Review, 3,* 193–209.

Bandura, A. (2001). Social cognitive theory. *Annual Review of Psychology* (Vol. 52). Palo Alto, CA: Annual Reviews.

Bandura, A. (2002). Selective moral disengagement in the exercise of moral agency. *Journal of Moral Education, 31,* 101–119.

Bandura, A. (2004, May). *Toward a psychology of human agency.* Paper presented at the meeting of the American Psychological Society, Chicago.

Bandura, A. (2009). Self-efficacy. In D. Carr (Ed.), *Encyclopedia of the life course and human development.* Boston: Gale Cengage.

Bandura, A. (2009). Social and policy impact of social cognitive theory. In M. Mark, S. Donaldson, & B. Campbell (Eds.), *Social psychology and program/policy evaluation.* New York: Guilford.

Bandura, A. (2010a). Self-efficacy. In D. Matsumoto (Ed.), *Cambridge dictionary of psychology.* New York: Cambridge University Press.

Bandura, A. (2010b). Vicarious learning. In D. Matsumoto (Ed.), *Cambridge dictionary of psychology.* New York: Cambridge University Press.

Banerjee, M., Harrell, Z. A. T., & Johnson, D. J. (2011). Racial/ethnic socialization and parental involvement in education as predictors of cognitive ability and achievement in African American children. *Journal of Youth and Adolescence, 40,* 595–605.

Bank, L., Burraston, B., & Snyder, J. (2004). Sibling conflict and ineffective parenting as predictors of boys' antisocial behavior and peer difficulties: Additive and international effects. *Journal of Research on Adolescence, 14,* 99–125.

Bankole, A., Singh, S., Woog, V., & Wulf, D. (2004). *Risk and protection: Youth and HIV/AIDS in sub-Saharan Africa.* New York: Alan Guttmacher Institute.

Banks, J. A. (2008). *Introduction to multicultural education* (4th ed.). Boston: Allyn & Bacon.

Banks, J. A. (2010). Multicultural education: Dimensions and paradigms. In J. A. Banks (Ed.), *The Routledge international companion to multicultural education.* New York: Psychology Press.

Bapat, S. A., Krishnan, A., Ghanate, A. D., Kusumbe, A. P., & Kaira, R. S. (2010). Gene expression: Protein interaction systems network modeling identifies transformation-associated molecules and pathways in ovarian cancer. *Cancer Research, 5,* 716–729.

Barber, B. L., & Demo, D. (2006). The kids are alright (at least most of them): Links to divorce and dissolution. In M. A. Fine & J. H. Harvey (Eds.), *Handbook of divorce and relationship dissolution.* Mahwah, NJ: Erlbaum.

Barker, R., & Wright, H. F. (1951). *One boy's day.* New York: Harper.

Barnes, G. M., Farrell, M. P., & Banerjee, S. (1995). Family influences on alcohol abuse and other problem behaviors among Black and White Americans. In G. M. Boyd, J. Howard, & R. A. Zucker (Eds.), *Alcohol problems among adolescents.* Hillsdale, NJ: Erlbaum.

Barnouw, V. (1975). *An introduction to anthropology: Vol. 2. Ethnology.* Homewood, IL: Dorsey Press.

Basow, S. A. (2006). Gender role and gender identity development. In J. Worell & C. D. Goodheart (Eds.), *Handbook of girls' and women's psychological health.* New York: Oxford University Press.

Bassi, M., Steca, P., Della Fave, A., & Caprara, G. V. (2007). Academic self-efficacy beliefs and quality of experience on learning. *Journal of Youth and Adolescence, 36,* 301–312.

Bathgate, K., & Silva, E. (2010, Fall). Joining forces: The benefits of integrating schools and community providers. *New Directions in Youth Development, 127,* 63–73.

Battistich, V. A. (2008). The Child Development Project: Creating caring school communities. In L. Nucci & D. Narváez (Eds.), *Handbook of moral and character education.* Clifton, NJ: Psychology Press.

Bauerlein, M. (2008). *The dumbest generation: How the digital age stupefies young Americans and jeopardizes our future (Or, don't trust anyone under 30).* New York: Tarcher.

Baumeister, R. F., Campbell, J. D., Krueger, J. I., & Vohs, K. D. (2003). Does high self-esteem cause better performance, interpersonal success, happiness, or healthier lifestyles? *Psychological Science in the Public Interest, 4*(1), 1–44.

Baumrind, D. (1971). Current patterns of parental authority. *Developmental Psychology Monographs, 4*(1, Pt. 2).

Baumrind, D. (1991). Effective parenting during the early adolescent transition. In P. A. Cowan & E. M. Hetherington (Eds.), *Advances in family research* (Vol. 2). Hillsdale, NJ: Erlbaum.

Bauserman, R. (2003). Child adjustment in joint-custody versus sole-custody arrangements: A meta-analytic review. *Journal of Family Psychology, 16,* 19–102.

Beaulieu, J. M., & Gainetdinov, R. R. (2011). The physiology, signaling, and pharmacology of dopamine receptors. *Pharmacology Review, 63,* 182–217.

Beaver, K. M., Wright, J. P., DeLisi, M., & Vaughn, M. G. (2009). Gene-environment interplay and delinquent involvement: Evidence of direct, indirect, and interactive effects. *Journal of Adolescent Research, 24* (March): 147–168.

Bednar, R. L., Wells, M. G., & Peterson, S. R. (1995). *Self-esteem* (2nd ed.). Washington, DC: American Psychological Association.

Beebe, D. W. (2011). Cognitive, behavioral, and functional consequences of inadequate sleep in children and adolescents. *Pediatric Clinics of North America, 58,* 649–665.

Beebe, D. W., Rose, D., & Amin, R. (2010). Attention, learning, and arousal of experimentally sleep-restricted adolescents in a simulated classroom. *Journal of Adolescent Health, 47,* 523–525.

Beghetto, R. A., & Kaufman, J. C. (Eds.). (2011). *Nurturing creativity in the classroom.* New York: Cambridge University Press.

Begley, S., & Interlandi, J. (2008, July 2). The dumbest generation? Don't be dumb. *Newsweek.* Retrieved July 15, 2008, from www.newsweek.com/id/138536

Bell, M. A., Greene, D. R., & Wolfe, C. D. (2010). Psychobiological mechanisms of cognition-emotion integration in early development. In S. D. Calkins & M. A. Bell (Eds.), *Child development at the intersection of cognition and emotion.* New York: Psychology Press.

Bellmore, A., Jiang, X. U., & Juvonen, J. (2010). Utilizing peer nominations in middle school: A longitudinal comparison between complete classroom-based and random list methods. *Journal of Research in Adolescence, 20,* 538–550.

Bellmore, A., Villarreal, V. M., & Ho, A. Y. (2011, in press). Staying cool across the first year of middle school. *Journal of Youth and Adolescence.*

Belsky, J. (1981). Early human experience: A family perspective. *Developmental Psychology, 17,* 3–23.

Belsky, J., & Beaver, K. M. (2011). Cumulative-genetic plasticity, parenting, and adolescent self-regulation. *Journal of Child Psychology and Psychiatry, 52,* 619–626.

Belsky, J., Jaffe, S., Hsieh, K., & Silva, P. (2001). Child-rearing antecedents of intergenerational relations in young adulthood: A prospective study. *Developmental Psychology, 37,* 801–813.

Belsky, J., Steinberg, L., Houts, R. M., Halpern-Felsher, B. L., & the NICHD Child Care Research Network. (2010). The development of reproductive strategy in females: Early maternal harshness → earlier menarche → increased sexual risk. *Developmental Psychology, 46,* 120–128.

Bem, S. L. (1977). On the utility of alternative procedures for assessing psychological androgyny. *Journal of Consulting and Clinical Psychology, 45,* 196–205.

Benner, A. D. (2011). Latino adolescents' loneliness, academic performance, and the buffering nature of friendships. *Journal of Youth and Adolescence, 5,* 556–567.

Bennett, C. I. (2011). *Comprehensive multicultural education* (7th ed.). Boston: Allyn & Bacon.

Benninghoven, D., Tetsch, N., Kunzendorf, S., & Jantschek, G. (2007). Body image in patients with eating disorders and their mothers, and the role of family functioning. *Comprehensive Psychiatry, 48,* 118–123.

Benokratis, N. (2011). *Marriages and families* (7th ed.). Upper Saddle River, NJ: Prentice Hall.

Benson, P. L. (2006). *All kids are our kids.* San Francisco: Jossey-Bass.

Benson, P. L. (2010). *Parent, teacher, mentor, friend: How every adult can change kids' lives.* Minneapolis: Search Institute Press.

Benson, P. L., Mannes, M., Pittman, K., & Ferber, T. (2004). Youth development, developmental assets, and public policy. In R. Lerner & L. Steinberg (Eds.), *Handbook of adolescent psychology* (2nd ed.). New York: Wiley.

Benson, P. L., & Scales, P. C. (2009). The definition and preliminary measurement of thriving in adolescence. *Journal of Positive Psychology, 4,* 85–104.

Benson, P. L., & Scales, P. C. (2011, in press). Thriving and sparks: Development and emergence of new core concepts in positive youth development. In R. J. R. Levesque (Ed.), *Encyclopedia of adolescence.* Berlin: Springer.

Benson, P. L., Scales, P. C., Hamilton, S. F., & Sesma, A. (2006). Positive youth development. In W. Damon & R. Lerner (Eds.), *Handbook of child psychology* (6th ed.). New York: Wiley.

Benveniste, L., Carnoy, M., & Rothstein, R. (2003). *All else equal.* New York: Routledge-Farmer.

Berecz, J. M. (2009). *Theories of personality.* Boston: Allyn & Bacon.

Berkel, C., & others. (2010). Discrimination and adjustment for Mexican American adolescents: A prospective examination of the benefits of culturally related values. *Journal of Research on Adolescence, 20,* 893–915.

Berkowitz, M. W., Battistich, V. A., & Bier, M. (2008). What works in character education: What is known and what needs to be known. In L. Nucci & D. Narváez (Eds.), *Handbook of moral and character education.* Clifton, NJ: Psychology Press.

Berkowitz, M. W., & Gibbs, J. C. (1983). Measuring the developmental features of moral discussion. *Merrill-Palmer Quarterly, 29,* 399–410.

Bernard, K., & Dozier, M. (2008). Adoption and foster placement. In M. M. Haith & J. B. Benson (Eds.), *Encyclopedia of infant and early childhood development.* Oxford, UK: Elsevier.

Berndt, T. J. (1979). Developmental changes in conformity to peers and parents. *Developmental Psychology, 15,* 608–616.

Berndt, T. J., & Perry, T. B. (1990). Distinctive features and effects of early adolescent friendships. In R. Montemayor (Ed.), *Advances in adolescent research.* Greenwich, CT: JAI Press.

Berninger, V. W. (2006). Learning disabilities. In W. Damon & R. Lerner (Eds.), *Handbook of child psychology* (6th ed.). New York: Wiley.

Berninger, V. W., & O'Malley, M. M. (2011). Evidence-based diagnosis and treatment for specific learning disabilities involving impairments in written and/or oral language. *Journal of Learning Disabilities, 44,* 167–183.

Bernstein, N. (2004, March 7). Young love, new caution. *New York Times,* p. A22.

Bersamin, M. M., Bourdeau, B., Fisher, D. A., & Grube, J. W. (2010). Television use, sexual behavior, and relationship status at last oral sex and vaginal intercourse. *Sexuality and Culture, 14,* 157–168.

Berscheid, E. (2010). Love in the fourth dimension. *Annual Review of Psychology* (Vol. 61). Palo Alto, CA: Annual Reviews.

Berscheid, E., Snyder, M., & Omoto, A. M. (1989). Issues in studying close relationships. In C. Hendrick (Ed.), *Close relationships.* Newbury Park, CA: Sage.

Best, D. L. (2010). *Gender.* In M. H. Bornstein (Ed.), *Handbook of cultural developmental science.* New York: Oxford University Press.

Best, J. R. (2011, in press). Effects of physical activity on children's executive function: Contributions of experimental research on aerobic exercise. *Developmental Review.*

Bethell, J., & Rhoades, A. E. (2008). Adolescent depression and emergency department use: The roles of suicidality and deliberate self-harm. *Current Psychiatry Reports, 10,* 53–59.

Beyers, E., & Seiffge-Krenke, I. (2011, in press). Does identity precede intimacy? Testing Erikson's theory on romantic development in emerging adults of the 21st century. *Journal of Adolescent Research.*

Beznos, G. W., & Coates, V. (2007, March). *Piercing and tattooing in adolescence: Psychological aspects.* Workshop at the meeting of the Society for Adolescent Medicine, Denver.

Bill and Melinda Gates Foundation. (2006). *The silent epidemic: Perspectives on high school dropouts.* Seattle: Author.

Bill and Melinda Gates Foundation. (2008). *Report gives voice to dropouts.* Retrieved August 31, 2008, from www.gatesfoundation.org/UnitedStates/Education/TransformingHighSchool/Related....

Birman, B. F., & others. (2007). *State and local implementation of the "No Child Left Behind Act." Volume II—Teacher quality under "NCLB": Interim report.* Jessup, MD: U.S. Department of Education.

Biro, F. M., & others. (2006). Pubertal correlates in black and white girls. *Journal of Pediatrics, 148,* 234–240.

Bjorklund, D. F. (2006). Mother knows best: Epigenetic inheritance, maternal effects, and the evolution of human intelligence. *Developmental Review, 26,* 213–242.

Bjorklund, D. F. (2012). *Children's thinking* (6th ed.). Boston: Cengage.

Bjorklund, D. F., & Pellegrini, A. D. (2002). *The origins of human nature.* New York: Oxford University Press.

Blackwell, L. S., & Dweck, C. S. (2008). *The motivational impact of a computer-based program that teaches how the brain changes with learning.* Unpublished manuscript. Department of Psychology, Stanford University, Palo Alto, CA.

Blackwell, L. S., Trzesniewski, K. H., & Dweck, C. S. (2007). Implicit theories of intelligence predict achievement across an adolescent tradition: A longitudinal study and an intervention. *Child Development, 78,* 246–263.

Blair, B. L., & Fletcher, A. C. (2011, in press). "The only 13-year-old on planet Earth without a cell phone": Meanings of cell phones in early adolescents' lives. *Journal of Adolescent Research.*

Blake, J. S. (2011). *Nutrition and you.* Upper Saddle River, NJ: Pearson.

Blakemore, J. E. O., Berenbaum, S. A., & Liben, I. S. (2009). *Gender development.* New York: Psychology Press.

Blakemore, S. J. (2010). The developing social brain: Implications for education. *Neuron, 65,* 744–747.

Blakemore, S. J., Dahl, R. E., Frith, U., & Pine, D. S. (2011, in press). Developmental cognitive neuroscience. *Developmental Cognitive Neuroscience.*

Blasi, A. (2005). Moral character: A psychological approach. In D. K. Lapsley & F. C. Power (Eds.), *Character psychology and character education.* Notre Dame, IN: University of Notre Dame Press.

Bleakley, A., Hennessy, M., Fishbein, M., & Jordan, A. (2009). How sources of sexual information relate to adolescents' beliefs about sex. *American Journal of Health Behavior, 33,* 37–48.

Bleakley, A., Hennessy, M., Fishbein, M., & Jordan, A. (2011, in press). Using the integrative model to explain how exposure to sexual media content influences adolescent sexual behavior.*Health Education and Behavior.*

Block, J. (1993). Studying personality the long way. In D. Funder, R. D. Parke, C. Tomlinson-Keasey, & K. Widaman (Eds.), *Studying lives through time.* Washington, DC: American Psychological Association.

Block, J. H., & Block, J. (1980). The role of ego-control and ego-resiliency in the organization of behavior. In W. A. Collins (Ed.), *Minnesota symposium on child psychology* (Vol. 13). Minneapolis: University of Minnesota Press.

Blomeyer, D., Treutlein, J., Esser, G., Schmidt, M. H., Schumann, G., & Laucht, M. (2008). Interaction between CRHRI gene and stressful life events predicts adolescent heavy alcohol use. *Biological Psychiatry, 63,* 146–151.

Blomfield, C. J., & Barber, B. L. (2011). Developmental experiences during extracurricular activities and Australian adolescents' self-concept: Particularly important for youth from disadvantaged schools. *Journal of Youth and Adolescence, 40,* 582–594.

Bloom, B. (1985). *Developing talent in young people.* New York: Ballantine.

Blos, P. (1989). The inner world of the adolescent. In A. H. Esman (Ed.), *International annals of adolescent psychiatry* (Vol. 1). Chicago: University of Chicago Press.

Blumenfeld, P. C., Kempler, T. M., & Krajcik, J. S. (2006). Motivation and cognitive engagement in learning environments. In R. K. Sawyer (Ed.), *The Cambridge handbook of the learning sciences.* New York: Cambridge University Press.

Blumenfeld, P. C., Marx, R. W., & Harris, C. J. (2006). Learning environments. In W. Damon & R. Lerner (Eds.), *Handbook of child psychology* (6th ed.). New York: Wiley.

Blumenthal, H., & others. (2011, in press). Elevated social anxiety among early maturing girls. *Developmental Psychology.*

Bo, I. (1994). The sociocultural environment as a source of support. In F. Nestmann & K. Hurrelmann (Eds.), *Social networks and social support in childhood and adolescence.* New York: Walter de Gruyter.

Bonci, C. M., & others. (2008). National Athletic Trainers' Association position statement: Preventing, detecting, and managing disordered eating in athletes. *Journal of Athletic Training, 43,* 80–108.

Bonney, C., & Sternberg, R. J. (2011). Learning to think critically. In P. A. Alexander & R. E. Mayer (Eds.), *Handbook of research on learning and instruction.* New York: Routledge.

Boonstra, H. (2002, February). Teen pregnancy: Trends and lessons learned. *The Guttmacher Report on Public Policy,* pp. 7–10.

Booth, A., Johnson, D. R., Granger, D. A., Crouter, A. C., & McHale, S. (2003). Testosterone and child and adolescent adjustment: The moderating role of parent-child relationships. *Developmental Psychology, 39,* 85–98.

Booth, A., Rustenbach, E., & McHale, S. (2011, in press). Early family transitions and depressive symptom changes from adolescence to early adulthood. *Journal of Marriage and Family.*

Booth-LaForce, C., & Kerns, K. A. (2009). Child-parent attachment relationships, peer relationships, and peer-group functioning. In K. H. Rubin, W. M. Bukowksi, & B. Laursen (Eds.), *Handbook of peer interactions, relationships, and groups.* New York: Guilford.

Booth, M. (2002). Arab adolescents facing the future: Enduring ideals and pressures to change. In B. B. Brown, R. W. Larson, & T. S. Saraswathi (Eds.), *The world's youth.* New York: Cambridge University Press.

Borich, G. D. (2011). *Effective teaching methods* (7th ed.). Boston: Allyn & Bacon.

Borjas, G. J. (2011). Poverty and program participation by immigrant children. *Future of Children, 21,* 247–266.

Bos, H., & Gartrell, N. (2010). Adolescents of the USA National Longitudinal Lesbian Family Study: Can family characteristics counteract the negative effects of stigmatization? *Family Process, 49,* 559–572.

Bowker, J. C., Rubin, K., & Coplan, R. (2012). Social withdrawal during adolescence. In J. R. Levesque (Ed.), *Encyclopedia of adolescence.* New York: Springer.

Bowker, J. C., & Spencer, S. V. (2010). Friendship and adjustment: A focus on mixed-grade friendships. *Journal of Youth and Adolescence, 39,* 1318–1329.

Bowlby, J. (1989). *Secure and insecure attachment.* New York: Basic Books.

Boyce, W. F., Davies, D., Gallupe, O., & Shelley, D. (2008). Adolescent risk taking, neighborhood social capital, and health. *Journal of Adolescent Health, 43,* 246–252.

Boyle, J. R., & Provost, M. C. (2012). *Strategies for teaching students with disabilities in inclusive classrooms.* Upper Saddle River, NJ: Pearson.

Brabeck, M. M., & Brabeck, K. M. (2006). Women and relationships. In J. Worell & C. D. Goodheart (Eds.), *Handbook of girls' and women's psychological health.* New York: Oxford University Press.

Bradley, R. H., Corwyn, R. F., McAdoo, H., & Coll, C. (2001). The home environments of children in the United States: Part I. Variations by age, ethnicity, and poverty status. *Child Development, 72,* 1844–1867.

Brady, S. S., & Halpern-Felsher, B. (2007). Adolescents' reported consequences of having oral sex versus vaginal sex. *Pediatrics, 119,* 229–236.

Brady, S. S., Tschann, J. M., Pasch, L. A., Flores, E., & Ozer, E. J. (2008). Violence involvement, substance use, and sexual activity among Mexican-American and European-American adolescents. *Journal of Adolescent Health, 43,* 285–295.

Brandon, P. D. (2009). Poverty, childhood and adolescence. In D. Carr (Ed.), *Encyclopedia of the life course and human development.* Boston: Gale Cengage.

Brand, S., & others. (2010). High exercise levels are related to favorable sleep patterns and psychological functioning in adolescents: A comparison of athletes and controls. *Journal of Adolescent Health, 46,* 133–141.

Brannon, L. (2012). *Gender* (6th ed.). Boston: Allyn & Bacon.

Bransford, J., & others. (2006). Learning theories in education. In P. A. Alexander & P. H. Winne (Eds.), *Handbook of educational psychology* (2nd ed.). Mahwah, NJ: Erlbaum.

Braun-Courville, D. K., & Rojas, M. (2009). Exposure to sexually explicit web sites and adolescent sexual attitudes and behaviors. *Journal of Adolescent Health, 45,* 156–162.

Braver, S. L., Ellman, I. M., & Fabricus, W. V. (2003). Relocation of children after divorce and children's best interests: New evidence and legal considerations. *Journal of Family Psychology, 17,* 206–219.

Bray, J. H., Berger, S. H., & Boethel, C. L. (1999). Marriage to remarriage and beyond. In E. M. Hetherington (Ed.), *Coping with divorce, single parenting, and remarriage.* Mahwah, NJ: Erlbaum.

Bray, J. H., & Kelly, J. (1998). *Stepfamilies.* New York: Broadway.

Brechwald, W. A., & Prinstein, M. J. (2011). Beyond homophily: A decade of advances in understanding peer influence processes. *Journal of Research on Adolescence, 21,* 166–179.

Brecklin, L. R., & Ullman, S. E. (2010). The roles of victim and offender substance use in sexual assault outcomes. *Journal of Interpersonal Violence, 25,* 1503–1522.

Brendgen, M., Lamarche, V., Wanner, B., & Vitaro, F. (2010). Links between friendship relations and early adolescents' trajectories of depressed mood. *Developmental Psychology, 46,* 491–501.

Brewster, K. L., & Harker Tillman, K. (2008). Who's doing it? Patterns and predictors of youths' oral sexual experiences. *Journal of Adolescent Health, 42,* 73–80.

Bridgeland, J. M., Dilulio, J. J., & Wulsin, S. C. (2008). *Engaged for success.* Washington, DC: Civic Enterprises.

Briefel, R. R., Crespinsek, M. K., Cabili, C., Wilson, A., & Gleason, P. M. (2009). School food environments and practices affect dietary behaviors of U.S. public school children. *Journal of the American Dietetic Association, 100*(Suppl 2), S91–S107.

Brislin, R. W. (2000). Cross-cultural training. In A. Kazdin (Ed.), *Encyclopedia of psychology.* New York: Oxford University Press.

Broderick, R. (2003, July/August). A surgeon's saga. *Minnesota: The magazine of the University of Minnesota Alumni Association,* 26–31.

Brody, G. H., & others (2001). The influence of neighborhood disadvantage, collective socialization, and parenting on African American children's affiliation with deviant peers. *Child Development, 72,* 1231–1246.

Brody, G. H., & Schaffer, D. R. (1982). Contributions of parents and peers to children's moral socialization. *Developmental Review, 2,* 31–75.

Brody, G. H., Stoneman, Z., & Burke, M. (1987). Child temperaments, maternal differential behavior and sibling relationships. *Developmental Psychology, 23,* 354–362.

Brody, N. (2007). Does education influence intelligence? In P. C. Kyllonen, R. D. Roberts, & L. Stankov (Eds.), *Extending intelligence.* Mahwah, NJ: Erlbaum.

Brodzinsky, D. M., & Pinderhughes, E. (2002). Parenting and child development in adoptive families. In M. H. Bronstein (Ed.), *Handbook of parenting* (Vol. 1). Mahwah, NJ: Erlbaum.

Bronfenbrenner, U. (1986). Ecology of the family as a context for human development: Research perspectives. *Developmental Psychology, 22,* 723–742.

Bronfenbrenner, U. (2004). *Making human beings human.* Thousand Oaks, CA: Sage.

Bronfenbrenner, U., & Morris, P. (1998). The ecology of developmental processes. In W. Damon (Ed.), *Handbook of child psychology* (5th ed., Vol. 1). New York: Wiley.

Bronfenbrenner, U., & Morris, P. A. (2006). The ecology of developmental processes. In W. Damon & R. Lerner (Eds.), *Handbook of child psychology* (6th ed.). New York: Wiley.

Bronstein, P. (2006). The family environment: Where gender role socialization begins. In J. Worell & C. D. Goodheart (Eds.), *Handbook of girls' and women's psychological health.* New York: Oxford University Press.

Brooker, R. (2011). *Biology* (2nd ed.). New York: McGraw-Hill.

Brook, J. S., Brook, D. W., Gordon, A. S., Whiteman, M., & Cohen, P. (1990). The psychological etiology of adolescent drug use: A family interactional approach. *Genetic Psychology Monographs, 116*(2).

Brooks-Gunn, J., & Donahue, E. H. (2008). Introducing the issue. *The Future of Children, 18*(1), 3–10.

Brooks-Gunn, J., Han, W-J., & Waldfogel, J. (2010). First-year maternal employment and child development in the first seven years. *Monographs of the Society for Research in Child Development, 75*(2), 1–147.

Brooks-Gunn, J., & Warren, M. P. (1989). The psychological significance of secondary sexual characteristics in 9- to 11-year-old girls. *Child Development, 59,* 161–169.

Brophy, J. (2004). *Motivating students to learn* (2nd ed.). New York: Routledge.

Broughton, J. (1983). The cognitive developmental theory of adolescent self and identity. In B. Lee & G. Noam (Eds.), *Developmental approaches to self.* New York: Plenum.

Broverman, L., Vogel, S., Broverman, D., Clarkson, F., & Rosenkranz, P. (1972). Sex-role stereotypes: A current appraisal. *Journal of Social Issues, 28,* 59–78.

Brown, B. B. (2011). Popularity in peer group perspective: The role of status in adolescent peer systems. In A. H. N. Cillessen, D. Schwartz, & L. Mayeux (Eds.), *Popularity in the peer system.* New York: Guilford.

Brown, B. B., & Bakken, J. P. (2011). Parenting and adolescent peer relationships: Reinvigorating research on family-peer linkages in adolescence. *Journal of Research on Adolescence, 1,* 153–165.

Brown, B. B., Bakken, J. P., Amerigner, S. W., & Mahon, S. D. (2008). A comprehensive conceptualization of the peer influence process in adolescence. In M. J. Prinstein & K. A. Dodge (Eds.), *Understanding peer influences in children and adolescents.* New York: Guilford.

Brown, B. B., & Dietz, E. L. (2009). Informal peer groups in middle childhood and adolescence. In K. H. Rubin, W. M. Bukowski, & B. Laursen (Eds.), *Handbook of peer interaction, relationships, and groups.* New York: Guilford.

Brown, B. B., & Larson, J. (2009). Peer relationships in adolescence. In R. L. Lerner & L. Steinberg (Eds.), *Handbook of adolescent psychology* (3rd ed.). New York: Wiley.

Brown, B. B., & Larson, R. W. (2002). The kaleidoscope of adolescence: Experiences of the world's youth at the beginning of the 21st century. In B. B. Brown, R. W. Larson, & T. S. Saraswathi (Eds.), *The world's youth.* New York: Cambridge University Press.

Brown, B. B., & Lohr, M. J. (1987). Peer-group affiliation and adolescent self-esteem: An integration of ego-identity and symbolic-interaction theories. *Journal of Personality and Social Psychology, 52,* 47–55.

Brown, B. B., & Prinstein, M. (Ed.). (2011, in press). *Encyclopedia of adolescence.* New York: Elsevier.

Brown, B., Moore, K., & Bzostek, S. (2005). A portrait of well-being in early adulthood: A report to the William and Flora Hewlett Foundation. Retrieved November 15, 2005, from http://www.hewlett.org/Archives/Publications/portraitOfWellBeing.htm

Brown, E. R., & Diekman, A. B. (2010). What will I be? Exploring gender differences in near and distant possible selves. *Sex Roles, 63,* 568–579.

Brown, J. D. (2011). Older and new media: Patterns of use and effects on adolescents' health and well-being. *Journal of Research on Adolescence, 21,* 95–113.

Brown, J. D., & Bobkowski, P. S. (2011). Older and newer media: Patterns of use and effects on adolescents' health and well-being. *Journal of Research on Adolescence, 21,* 95–113.

Brown, J. D., & Strasberger, V. C. (2007). From Calvin Klein to Paris Hilton and MySpace: Adolescents, sex, and the media. *Adolescent Medicine: State of the Art Reviews, 18,* 484–507.

Brownridge, D. A. (2008). The elevated risk for violence against cohabiting women: A comparison of three nationally representative surveys of Canada. *Violence Against Women, 14,* 809–832.

Brunstein Klomek, A., Marrocco, F., Kleinman, M., Schofeld, I. S., & Gould, M. S. (2007). Bullying, depression, and suicidality in adolescents. *Journal of the American Academy of Child and Adolescent Psychiatry, 46,* 40–49.

Buchanan, C. M., Maccoby, E. E., & Dornbusch, S. (1992). Adolescents and their families after divorce: Three residential arrangements compared. *Journal of Research on Adolescence, 2,* 261–291.

Buchmann, A. F., & others. (2009). Impact of age of first drink on vulnerability to alcohol-related problems: Testing the marker hypothesis in a prospective study of young adults. *Journal of Psychiatric Research, 43,* 1205–1212.

Bucx, F., Raaijmakers, Q., & van Wel, F. (2010). Life course stage in young adulthood and intergenerational congruence in family attitudes. *Journal of Marriage and the Family, 72,* 117–134.

Bucx, F., & van Wel, F. (2008). Parental bond and life course transitions from adolescence to young adulthood. *Adolescence, 43,* 71–88.

Budde, H., Voelcker-Rehage, C., Pietrabyk-Kendziorra, P., Ribeiro, P., & Tidow, G. (2008). Acute aerobic exercise improves attentional performance in adolescence. *Neuroscience Letters, 441,* 219–223.

Bugental, D. B., & Goodnow, J. J. (2006). Socialization processes. In W. Damon & R. Lerner (Eds.), *Handbook of child psychology* (6th ed.). New York: Wiley.

Buhi, E. R., & others. (2010). Quality and accuracy of sexual health information web sites visited by young people. *Journal of Adolescent Health, 47,* 206–208.

Buhl, H. M., & Lanz, M. (2007). Emerging adulthood in Europe: Common traits and variability across five European countries. *Journal of Adolescent Research, 22,* 439–443.

Buhrmester, D. (1990). Friendship, interpersonal competence, and adjustment in preadolescence and adolescence. *Child Development, 61,* 1101–1111.

Buhrmester, D. (1998). Need fulfillment, interpersonal competence, and the developmental contexts of early adolescent friendship. In W. M. Bukowski & A. F. Newcomb (Eds.), *The company they keep: Friendship in childhood and adolescence.* New York: Cambridge University Press.

Buhrmester, D. (2001, April). *Does age at which romantic involvement starts matter?* Paper presented at the meeting of the Society for Research in Child Development, Minneapolis.

Buhrmester, D., & Chong, C. M. (2009). Friendship in adolescence. In H. Reis & S. Sprecher (Eds.), *Encyclopedia of human relationships.* Thousand Oaks, CA: Sage.

Buist, K. L. (2010). Sibling relationship quality and adolescent delinquency: A latent growth curve analysis. *Journal of Family Psychology, 24,* 400–410.

Bukowski, W. M., Buhrmester, D., & Underwood, M. K. (2011). Peer relations as a developmental context. In M. K. Underwood & L. H. Rosen (Eds.), *Social development.* New York: Guilford.

Bukowski, W. M., Laursen, B., & Hoza, B. (2010). The snowball effect: Friendship moderates escalations in depressed affect among avoidant and excluded children. *Development and Psychopathology, 22,* 749–757.

Bukowski, W. M., Motzoi, C., & Meyer, F. (2009). Friendship process, function, and outcome. In K. H. Rubin, W. M. Bukowski, & B. Laursen (Eds.), *Handbook of peer interaction, relationships, and groups.* New York: Guilford.

Bumpas, M. F., Crouter, A. C., & McHale, S. M. (2001). Parental autonomy granting during adolescence: Gender differences in context. *Developmental Psychology, 37,* 163–173.

Burchinal, M. R., Peisner-Feinberg, E., Pianta, R., & Howes, C. (2002). Development of academic skills from preschool through second grade: Family and classroom predictors of developmental trajectories. *Journal of School Psychology, 40*(5), 415–436.

Bureau, J-F., Easterbrooks, M. A., & Lyons-Ruth, K. (2009). Maternal depressive symptoms in infancy: Unique contribution to children's depressive symptoms in childhood and adolescence? *Development and Psychopathology, 21,* 519–537.

Burgess-Champoux, T. L., Larson, N., Neumark-Sztainer, D., Hannan, P. J., & Story, M. (2009). Are family meal patterns associated with overall diet quality during the transition from early to middle adolescence? *Journal of Nutrition Education and Behavior, 41,* 79–86.

Burk, L. R., & others. (2011). Sex, temperament, and family contexts: How the interaction of early factors differentially predicted adolescent alcohol use and are mediated by proximal adolescent factors. *Psychology of Addictive Behaviors, 25,* 1–15.

Burke, J. D. (2011, in press). The relationship between conduct disorder and oppositional defiant disorder and their continuity with antisocial behaviors. In D. Shaffer, E. Leibenluft, & L. A. Rohde (Eds.), *Externalizing disorders of childhood: Refining the research agenda for DSM-V.* Arlington, VA: American Psychiatric Association.

Burnett, S. M., Weaver, M. R., Mody-Pan, P. N., Reynolds Thomas, L. A., & Mar, C. M. (2011). Evaluation of an intervention to increase human immunodeficiency virus testing among youth in Manzini, Swaziland: A randomized control trial. *Journal of Adolescent Health, 48,* 507–513.

Burnett, S., Sebastian, C., Cohen-Kadosh, K., & Blakemore, S. J. (2011, in press). The social brain in adolescence: Evidence from functional magnetic resonance imaging and behavioral studies. *Neuroscience and Biobehavioral Reviews.*

Bursuck, W. D., & Damer, M. (2011). *Teaching reading to students who are at-risk or have disabilities* (2nd ed.). Upper Saddle River, NJ: Merrill.

Burt, K. B., & Roisman, G. I. (2010). Competence and psychopathology: Cascade effects in the NICHD Study of Early Child Care and Youth Development. *Developmental Psychopathology, 22,* 557–567.

Burton, R. V. (1984). A paradox in theories and research in moral development. In W. M. Kurtines & J. L. Gewirtz (Eds.), *Morality, moral behavior, and moral development.* New York: Wiley.

Buss, D. (2000). Evolutionary psychology. In A. Kazdin (Ed.), *Encyclopedia of psychology.* New York: Oxford University Press.

Buss, D. M. (2008). *Evolutionary psychology* (3rd ed.). Boston: Allyn & Bacon.

Buss, D. M. (2012). *Evolutionary psychology* (4th ed.). Boston: Allyn & Bacon.

Buss, D. M., & Schmitt, D. P. (1993). Sexual strategies theory: An evolutionary perspective on human mating. *Psychological Review, 100,* 204–232.

Busseri, M. A., Costain, K. A., Campbell, K. M., Rose-Krasnor, L., & Evans, J. (2011, in press). Brief report: Engagement in sport and identity status. *Journal of Adolescence.*

Busséri, M. A., Willoughby, T., Chalmers, H., & Bogaert, A. R. (2006). Same-sex attraction and successful adolescent development. *Journal of Youth and Adolescence, 35,* 563–575.

Bussey, K., & Bandura A. (1999). Social cognitive theory of gender development and differentiation. *Psychological Review, 106,* 676–713.

Butcher, K., Sallis, J. F., Mayer, J. A., & Woodruff, S. (2008). Correlates of physical activity guideline compliance for adolescents in 100 U.S. cities. *Journal of Adolescent Health, 42,* 360–368.

Buzwell, S., & Rosenthal, D. (1996). Constructing a sexual self: Adolescents' sexual self-perceptions and sexual risk-taking. *Journal of Research on Adolescence, 6,* 489–513.

Byrnes, H. F., Miller, B. A., Chen, M-J., & Grube, J. W. (2011). The roles of mothers' neighborhood perceptions and specific monitoring strategies in youths' problem behaviors. *Journal of Youth and Adolescence, 36,* 649–659.

C

Cacioppo, J. T., Ernst, J. M., Burleson, M. H., McClintock, M. K., Malarkey, W. B., Hawkley, L. C., & others. (2000). Lonely traits and concomitant physiological processes: The MacArthur Social Neuroscience Studies. *International Journal of Psychophysiology, 35,* 143–154.

Calvert, S. L. (2008). Children as consumers: Advertising and marketing. *The Future of Children, 18,* 205–234.

Cameron, J. L. (2004). Interrelationships between hormones, behavior, and affect during adolescence: Understanding hormonal, physical, and brain changes occurring in association with pubertal activation of the reproductive axis. Introduction to Part III. *Annals of the New York Academy of Sciences, 1021,* 110–123.

Cameron, J. M., Heidelberg, N., Simmons, L., Lyle, S. B., Kathakali, M-V., & Correia, C. (2010). Drinking game participation among undergraduate students attending National Alcohol Screening Day. *Journal of American College Health, 58,* 499–506.

Cameron, J., & Pierce, D. (2008). Intrinsic versus extrinsic motivation. In N. J. Salkind (Ed.), *Encyclopedia of educational psychology.* Thousand Oaks, CA: Sage.

Campbell, B. (2008). *Handbook of differentiated instruction using the multiple intelligences.* Boston: Allyn & Bacon.

Campbell, C. Y. (1988, August 24). Group raps depiction of teenagers. *Boston Globe,* p. 44.

Campbell, L., Campbell, B., & Dickinson, D. (2004). *Teaching and learning through multiple intelligences* (3rd ed.). Boston: Allyn & Bacon.

Capaldi, D. M. (1992). Co-occurrence of conduct problems and depressive symptoms in early adolescent boys: II. A 2-year follow-up at grade 8. *Development and Psychopathology, 4,* 125–144.

Capaldi, D. M., & Shortt, J. W. (2003). Understanding conduct problems in adolescence from a lifespan perspective. In G. R. Adams & M. D. Berzonsky (Eds.), *Blackwell handbook of adolescence.* Malden, MA: Blackwell.

Capaldi, D. M., & Stoolmiller, M. (1999). Co-occurrence of conduct problems and depressive symptoms in early adolescent boys: III. Prediction to young-adult adjustment. *Development and Psychopathology, 11,* 59–84.

Capaldi, D. M., Stoolmiller, M., Clark, S., & Owen, L. D. (2002). Heterosexual risk behaviors in at-risk young men from early adolescence to young adulthood: Prevalence, prediction, and association with STD contraction. *Developmental Psychology, 38,* 394–406.

Caplan, P. J., & Caplan, J. B. (1999). *Thinking critically about research on sex and gender* (2nd ed.). New York: Longman.

Caprara, G. V., Vechhione, M., Alessandri, G., Gerbino, M., & Barbaranelli, C. (2011). The contribution of personality traits and self-efficacy beliefs to academic achievement: A longitudinal study. *British Journal of Educational Psychology, 81,* 78–96.

Cardelle-Elawar, M. (1992). Effects of teaching metacognitive skills to students with low mathematics ability. *Teaching & Teacher Education, 8,* 109–121.

Carlo, G., Knight, G. P., McGinley, M., Zamboanga, B. L., & Jarvis, L. H. (2010). The multidimensionality of prosocial behaviors and evidence of measurement equivalence in Mexican American and

European American early adolescents. *Journal of Research on Adolescence, 20,* 334–358.

Carlson, K. S., & Gjerde, P. F. (2010). Preschool personality antecedents of narcissism in adolescence and emerging adulthood: A 20-year longitudinal study. *Journal of Research in Personality, 43,* 570–578.

Carlson, M. J., Pilkauskas, N. V., McLanahan, S. S., & Brooks-Gunn, J. (2011). Couples as partners and parents over children's early years. *Journal of Marriage and the Family, 73,* 317–334.

Carnegie Council on Adolescent Development. (1989). *Turning points: Preparing American youth for the twenty-first century.* New York: Carnegie Foundation.

Carnegie Council on Adolescent Development. (1995). *Great transitions.* New York: Carnegie Foundation.

Carroll, J. (1993). *Human cognitive abilities.* Cambridge, UK: Cambridge University Press.

Carroll, J. L. (2010). *Sexuality now* (3rd ed.). Boston: Cengage.

Carroll, J. S., & Doherty, W. J. (2003). Evaluating the effectiveness of premarital prevention programs: A meta-analytic review of outcome research. *Family Relations, 52,* 105–118.

Carskadon, M. A. (Ed.). (2002). *Adolescent sleep patterns.* New York: Cambridge University Press.

Carskadon, M. A. (2004). Sleep difficulties in young people. *Archives of Pediatric and Adolescent Medicine, 158,* 597–598.

Carskadon, M. A. (2006, March). *Too little, too late: Sleep bioregulatory processes across adolescence.* Paper presented at the meeting of the Society for Research on Adolescence, San Francisco.

Carskadon, M. A. (2011). Sleep in adolescents: The perfect storm. *Pediatric Clinics of North America, 58,* 637–647.

Cartwright, K. B., Galupo, M. P., Tyree, S. D., & Jennings, J. G. (2009). Reliability and validity of the Complex Postformal Thought questionnaire: Assessing adults' cognitive development. *Journal of Adult Development, 16,* 183–189.

Carver, K., Joyner, K., & Udry, J. R. (2003). National estimates of romantic relationships. In P. Florsheim (Ed.), *Adolescent romantic relations and sexual behavior.* Mahwah, NJ: Erlbaum.

Casas, M. (2011). *Enhancing student learning in middle school.* New York: Routledge.

Case, R. (2000). Conceptual development. In M. Bennett (Ed.), *Developmental psychology.* Philadelphia: Psychology Press.

Case, R. (Ed.). (1992). *The mind's staircase: Exploring the conceptual underpinnings of children's thought and knowledge.* Hillsdale, NJ: Erlbaum.

Casey, B. J., Duhoux, S., & Malter Cohen, M. (2010). Adolescence: What do transmission, transition, and translation have to do with it? *Neuron, 67,* 749–760.

Casey, B. J., Getz, S., & Galvan, A. (2008). The adolescent brain. *Developmental Review, 28,* 62–77.

Casey, B. J., Jones, R. M., & Somerville, L. H. (2011). Braking and accelerating of the adolescent brain. *Journal of Research on Adolescence, 21,* 21–33.

Caspers, K. M., Paraiso, S., Yucuis, R., Troutman, B., Arndt, S., & Philibert, R. (2009). Association between the serotonin transporter polymorphism (5-HTTLPR) and adult unresolved attachment. *Developmental Psychology, 45,* 64–76.

Caspi, A. (1998). Personality development across the life course. In W. Damon (Series Ed.) & N. Eisenberg (Ed.), *Handbook of child psychology: Vol. 3. Social, emotional, and personality development* (5th ed.). New York: Wiley.

Caspi, A., Hariri, A. R., Holmes, A., Uher, R., & Moffitt, T. E. (2011). Genetic sensitivity to the environment: The case of the serotonin transporter gene and its implications for studying complex diseases and traits. In K. A. Dodge & M. Rutter (Eds.), *Gene-environment interaction and developmental psychopathology.* New York: Guilford.

Caspi, A., & others. (2003). Influence of life stress on depression: Moderation by a polymorphism in the 5-HTT gene. *Science, 301,* 386–389.

Caspi, A., & Shiner, R. (2006). Personality development. In W. Damon & R. Lerner (Eds.), *Handbook of child psychology* (6th ed.). New York: Wiley.

Cassidy, J., Woodhouse, S. S., Sherman, L. J., Stupica, B., & Lejuez, C. W. (2011). Enhancing infant attachment security: An examination of treatment efficacy and differential susceptibility. *Development and Psychopathology, 23,* 131–148.

Castle, J., & others. (2010). Parents' evaluation of adoption success: A follow-up study of intercountry and domestic adoptions. *American Journal of Orthopsychiatry, 79,* 522–531.

Catalano, R. F., Gavin, L. E., & Markham, C. M. (2010). Future directions for positive youth development as a strategy to promote adolescent sexual and reproductive health. *Journal of Adolescent Health, 46*(Suppl 1), S92–S96.

Cauffman, B. E. (1994, February). *The effects of puberty, dating, and sexual involvement on dieting and disordered eating in young adolescent girls.* Paper presented at the meeting of the Society for Research on Adolescence, San Diego.

Cauffman, E., & others. (2010). Age differences in affective decision making as indexed by performance on the Iowa Gambling Task. *Developmental Psychology, 46,* 193–207.

Cavanagh, S. (2007, October 3). U.S.-Chinese exchanges nurture ties between principals. *Education Week.* Retrieved July 15, 2008, from www.edweek.org

Cavanagh, S. E. (2009). Puberty. In D. Carr (Ed.), *Encyclopedia of the life course and human development.* Boston: Gale Cengage.

Ceballo, R., Huerta, M., & Ngo, Q. E. (2010). Schooling experiences of Latino students. In J. L. Meece & J. S. Eccles (Eds.), *Handbook of schools, schooling, and human development.* New York: Routledge.

Ceci, S. J., & Gilstrap, L. L. (2000). Determinants of intelligence: Schooling and intelligence. In A. Kazdin (Ed.), *Encyclopedia of Psychology.* New York: Oxford University Press.

Centers for Disease Control and Prevention. (2009a, November). *Sexually transmitted disease surveillance, 2008.* Atlanta, GA: U.S. Department of Health and Human Services.

Centers for Disease Control and Prevention. (2009b). *AIDS.* Atlanta: U.S. Department of Health and Human Services.

Centers for Disease Control and Prevention. (2011). *Body mass index for children and teens.* Atlanta, GA: Author.

Chandra, A., & others. (2009). Does watching sex on television predict teen pregnancy? Findings from a national longitudinal study of youth. *Pediatrics, 122,* 1047–1054.

Chao, R. (2001). Extending research on the consequences of parenting style for Chinese Americans and European Americans. *Child Development, 72,* 1832–1843.

Chao, R. K. (2005, April). *The importance of Guan in describing control of immigrant Chinese.* Paper presented at the meeting of the Society for Research in Child Development, Atlanta.

Chao, R. K. (2007, March). *Research with Asian Americans: Looking back and moving forward.* Paper presented at the meeting of the Society for Research in Child Development, Boston.

Chao, R. K., & Otsuki-Clutter, M. (2011). Racial and ethnic differences: Sociocultural and contextual explanations. *Journal of Research on Adolescence, 21,* 47–60.

Charles, C. M. (2011). *Building classroom discipline* (10th ed.). Boston: Allyn & Bacon.

Cheah, C. S. L., & Yeung, C. (2011). The social development of immigrant children: A focus on Asian and Hispanic children in the U.S. In P. K. Smith & C. H. Hart (Eds.), *Wiley-Blackwell handbook of childhood social development* (2nd ed.). New York: Wiley.

Chedraui, P. (2008). Pregnancy among young adolescents: Trends, risk factors, and maternal-perinatal outcome. *Journal of Perinatal Medicine, 36,* 256–259.

Chen, C., & Stevenson, H. W. (1989). Homework: A cross-cultural examination. *Child Development, 60,* 551–561.

Chen, J. J., Howard, K. S., & Brooks-Gunn, J. (2011). Neighborhoods matter: How neighborhood context influences individual development. In K. Fingerman, C. Berg, T. Antonucci, & J. Smith (Eds.), *Handbook of life-span psychology.* New York: Springer.

Chen, M. J., Grube, J. W., Nygaard, P., & Miller, B. A. (2008). Identifying social mechanisms for the prevention of adolescent drinking and driving. *Accident Analysis and Prevention, 40,* 576–585.

Chen, X., Chung, J., Lechcier-Kimel, R., & French, D. (2011). Culture and social development. In P. K. Smith & C. H. Hart (Eds.), *Wiley-Blackwell handbook of social development* (2nd ed.). New York: Wiley.

Chen, X., Tyler, K. A., Whitbeck, L. B., & Hoyt, D. R. (2004). Early sexual abuse, street adversity, and drug use among female homeless and runaway adolescents in the Midwest. *Journal of Drug Issues, 34,* 1–20.

Cherlin, A. J. (2009). *The marriage-go-round.* New York: Random House.

Cherlin, A. J., & Furstenberg, F. F. (1994). Stepfamilies in the United States: A reconsideration. In J. Blake & J. Hagen (Eds.), *Annual Review of Sociology,* Vol. 20. Palo Alto, CA: Annual Reviews.

Cherutich, P., & others. (2008). Condom use among sexually active Kenyan female adolescents at risk for HIV-1 infection. *AIDS Behavior, 12,* 923–929.

Chess, S., & Thomas, A. (1977). Temperamental individuality from childhood to adolescence. *Journal of Child Psychiatry, 16,* 218–226.

Chia-Chen, C. A., & Thompson, E. A. (2007). Preventing adolescent risky behavior: Parents matter! *Journal for Specialists in Pediatric Nursing, 12,* 119–122.

Chiappe, D., & MacDonald, K. (2005). The evolution of domain-general mechanisms in intelligence and learning. *Journal of General Psychology, 132,* 5–40.

Childstats.gov. (2010). Retrieved October 21, 2010, from www.childstats.gov/americaschildren/eco.asp

Chi, M. T. H. (1978). Knowledge structures and memory development. In R. S. Siegler (Ed.), *Children's thinking: What develops?* Hillsdale, NJ: Erlbaum.

Chira, S. (1993, June 23). What do teachers want most? Help from parents. *New York Times,* p. 17.

Chmielewski, C. (1997, September). Sexual harassment meet Title IX. *NEA Today, 16*(2), 24–25.

Choi, H., & Marks, N. F. (2011). Socioeconomic status, marital status continuity and change, and mortality. *Journal of Aging and Health, 23,* 714–742.

Choi, N. (2004). Sex role group differences in specific, academic, and general self-efficacy. *Journal of Psychology, 138,* 149–159.

Choi, Y., He, M., & Harachi, T. W. (2008). Intergenerational cultural dissonance, parent-child conflict and bonding, and youth problem behaviors among Vietnamese and Cambodian immigrant families. *Journal of Youth and Adolescence, 37,* 85–96.

Chouinard, R., Karsenti, T., & Roy, N. (2007). Relations among competence beliefs, utility value, achievement goals, and effort in mathematics. *British Journal of Educational Psychology, 77,* 501–517.

Christensen, K. Y., & others. (2010). Progression through puberty in girls enrolled in a contemporary British cohort. *Journal of Adolescent Health, 47,* 282–289.

Church, A. T. (2010). Current perspectives in the study of personality across cultures. *Perspectives on Psychological Science, 5,* 441–449.

Cillessen, A. H. N., & Bellmore, A. D. (2011). Social skills and social competence in interactions with peers. In P. K. Smith & C. H. Hart (Eds.), *Wiley-Blackwell handbook of childhood social development* (2nd ed.). New York: Wiley.

Cillessen, A. H. N., Schwartz, D., & Mayeux, L. (Eds.). (2011). *Popularity in the peer system.* New York: Guilford.

Clark, B. (2008). *Growing up gifted* (7th ed.). Upper Saddle River, NJ: Prentice Hall.

Clarke-Stewart, A., & Brentano, C. (2006). *Divorce: Causes and consequences.* New Haven, CT: Yale University Press.

Clark, M. S., Powell, M. C., Ovellette, R., & Milberg, S. (1987). Recipient's mood relationship type, and helping. *Journal of Personality and Social Psychology, 43,* 94–103.

Clark, R. D., & Hatfield, E. (1989). Gender differences in receptivity to sexual offers. *Journal of Psychology and Human Sexuality, 2,* 39–55.

Cleland, V., & Venn, A. (2010). Encouraging physical activity and discouraging sedentary behavior in children and adolescents. *Journal of Adolescent Health, 47,* 221–222.

Cleverley, K., & Kidd, S. A. (2011, in press).Resilience and suicidality among homeless youth. *Journal of Adolescence.*

Clinkinbeard, S. S., Simi, P., Evans, M. K., & Anderson, A. L. (2011, in press). Sleep and delinquency: Does amount of sleep matter? *Journal of Youth and Adolescence.*

Coatsworth, J. D., & Conway, D. E. (2009). The effects of autonomy-supportive coaching need satisfaction, and self-perceptions on initiative and identity in youth swimmers. *Developmental Psychology, 45,* 320–328.

Cochran, S. D., & Mays, V. M. (1990). Sex, lies, and HIV. *New England Journal of Medicine, 322*(11), 774–775.

Cohen, G. L., & Prinstein, M. J. (2006). Peer contagion of aggression and health-risk behavior among adolescent males: An experimental investigation of effects on public conduct and private attitudes. *Child Development, 77,* 967–983.

Cohen, P., Kasen, S., Chen, H., Hartmark, C., & Gordon, K. (2003). Variations in patterns of developmental transitions in the emerging adulthood period. *Developmental Psychology, 39,* 657–669.

Cohn, A., & Canter, A. (2003). *Bullying: Facts for schools and parents.* Washington, DC: National Association of School Psychologists Center.

Coie, J. (2004). The impact of negative social experiences on the development of antisocial behavior. In J. B. Kupersmidt & K. A. Dodge (Eds.), *Children's peer relations: From development to intervention.* Washington, DC: American Psychological Association.

Coker, T. R., Austin, S. B., & Schuster, M. A. (2010). The health and health care of lesbian, gay, and bisexual adolescents. *Annual Review of Public Health, 31,* 457–477.

Colangelo, N. C., Assouline, S. G., & Gross, M. U. M. (2004). *A nation deceived: How schools hold back America's brightest students.* Retrieved March 6, 2005, from http://nationdeceived.org/

Colby, A., Kohlberg, L., Gibbs, J., & Lieberman, M. (1983). A longitudinal study of moral judgment. *Monographs of the Society for Research in Child Development, 48*(21, Serial No. 201).

Cole, A. K., & Kerns, K. A. (2001). Perceptions of sibling qualities and activities of early adolescents. *Journal of Early Adolescence, 21,* 204–226.

Cole, M. (2006). Culture and cognitive development in phylogenetic, historical, and ontogenetic perspective. In W. Damon & R. Lerner (Eds.), *Handbook of child psychology* (6th ed.). New York: Wiley.

Coley, R. (2001). *Differences in the gender gap: Comparisons across/racial/ ethnic groups in the United States.* Princeton, NJ: Educational Testing Service.

Coley, R. L., Morris, J. E., & Hernandez, D. (2004). Out-of-school care and problem behavior trajectories among low-income adolescents: Individual, family, and neighborhood characteristics as added risks. *Child Development, 75,* 948–965.

Collins, M. (1996, Winter). The job outlook for 96 grads. *Journal of Career Planning, 23,* 51–54.

Collins, R. L., & others. (2004). Watching sex on television predicts adolescent initiation of sexual behavior. *Pediatrics, 114,* e280–e289.

Collins, W. A., Hennighausen, K. H., & Sroufe, L. A. (1998, June). *Developmental precursors of intimacy in romantic relationships: A longitudinal analysis.* Paper presented at the International Conference on Personal Relationships, Saratoga Springs, NY.

Collins, W. A., & Steinberg, L. (2006). Adolescent development in interpersonal context. In W. Damon & R. Lerner (Eds.), *Handbook of child psychology* (6th ed.). New York: Wiley.

Collins, W. A., & van Dulmen, M. (2006). Friendship and romance in emerging adulthood. In J. J. Arnett & J. L. Tanner (Eds.), *Emerging adults in America.* Washington, DC: American Psychological Association.

Collins, W. A., Welsh, D. P., & Furman, W. (2009). Adolescent romantic relationships. *Annual Review of Psychology* (Vol. 60). Palo Alto, CA: Annual Reviews.

Colman, R. A., Kim, D. H., Mitchell-Herzfeld, S., & Shady, T. A. (2009). Delinquent girls grown up: Young adult offending patterns and their relation to early legal, individual, and family risk. *Journal of Youth and Adolescence, 38,* 355–366.

Colrain, I. M., & Baker, F. C. (2011). Changes in sleep as a function of adolescent development. *Neuropsychology Review, 21,* 5–21.

Comer, J. (2010). Comer School Development Program. In J. Meece & J. Eccles (Eds.), *Handbook of research on schools, schooling, and human development.* New York: Routledge.

Comer, J. P. (2004). *Leave no child behind.* New Haven, CT: Yale University Press.

Comer, J. P. (2006). Child development: The under-weighted aspect of intelligence. In P. C. Kyllonen, R. D. Roberts, & L. Stankov (Eds.), *Extending intelligence.* Mahwah, NJ: Erlbaum.

Comer, J. P. (2010). Comer School Development Program. In J. Meece & J. Eccles (Eds.), *Handbook of research on schools, schooling, and human development.* New York: Routledge.

Commoner, B. (2002). Unraveling the DNA myth: The spurious foundation of genetic engineering. *Harper's Magazine, 304,* 39–47.

Commons, M. L., & Richards, F. A. (2003). Four postformal stages. In J. Demick & C. Andreoletti (Eds.), *Handbook of adult development.* New York: Kluwer.

Compas, B. E. (2004). Processes of risk and resilience during adolescence: Linking contexts and individuals. In R. Lerner & L. Steinberg (Eds.), *Handbook of adolescent psychology* (2nd ed.). New York: Wiley.

Compas, B. E., & Reeslund, K. L. (2009). Processes of risk and resilience during adolescence. In R. M. Lerner & L. Steinberg (Eds.), *Handbook of adolescent psychology* (3rd ed.). New York: Wiley.

Comstock, G., & Scharrer, E. (2006). Media and popular culture. In W. Damon & R. Lerner (Eds.), *Handbook of child psychology* (6th ed.). New York: Wiley.

Condry, J. C., Simon, M. L., & Bronfenbrenner, U. (1968). *Characteristics of peer- and adult-oriented children.* Unpublished manuscript. Cornell University, Ithaca, NY.

Conduct Problems Prevention Research Group. (2007). The Fast Track randomized controlled trial to prevent externalizing psychiatric disorders: Findings from grades 3 to 9. *Journal of the American Academy of Child and Adolescent Psychiatry, 46,* 1250–1262.

Conduct Problems Prevention Research Group. (2010a, in press). The effects of the Fast Track preventive intervention on the development of conduct disorder across childhood. *Child Development.*

Conduct Problems Prevention Research Group. (2010b, in press). The difficulty of maintaining positive intervention effect: A look at disruptive behavior, deviant peer relations, and social skills during the middle school years. *Journal of Early Adolescence.*

Conduct Problems Prevention Research Group (2011). The effects of Fast Track preventive intervention on the development of conduct disorder across childhood. *Child Development, 82,* 331–345.

Conger, J. J. (1988). Hostages to the future: Youth, values, and the public interest. *American Psychologist, 43,* 291–300.

Conger, K. J., & Kramer, L. (2010). Introduction to the special section: Perspectives on sibling relationships: Advancing child development research. *Child Development Perspectives, 4,* 69–71.

Conger, R. D., & Chao, W. (1996). Adolescent depressed mood. In R. L. Simons (Ed.), *Understanding differences between divorced and intact families: Stress, interaction, and child outcome.* Thousand Oaks, CA: Sage.

Conger, R. D., & Conger, K. J. (2008). Understanding the processes through which economic hardship influences rural families and children. In D. R. Crane & T. B. Heaton (Eds.), *Handbook of families and poverty.* Thousand Oaks, CA: Sage.

Conger, R. D., & others. (2012). Resilience and vulnerability of Mexican origin youth and their families: A test of a culturally-informed model of family economic stress. In P. K. Kerig, M. S. Schulz, & S. T. Hauser (Eds.), *Adolescence and beyond.* New York: Oxford University Press.

Conley, C. S., & Rudolph, K. D. (2009). The emerging sex difference in adolescent depression: Interacting contributions of puberty and peer stress. *Developmental Psychopathology, 21,* 593–620.

Connolly, J. A., Goldberg, A., Pepler, D., & Craig, W. (2004) Mixed-gender groups, dating, and romantic relationships in early adolescence. *Journal of Research on Adolescence, 14,* 185–207.

Connolly, J. A., & McIsaac, C. (2009). Romantic relationships in adolescence. In R. M. Lerner & L. Steinberg (Eds.), *Handbook of adolescent psychology* (3rd ed.). New York: Wiley.

Connolly, J., Furman, W., & Konarski, R. (2000). The role of peers in the emergence of heterosexual romantic relationships in adolescence. *Child Development, 71,* 1395–1408.

Connolly, J., & Stevens, V. (1999, April). *Best friends, cliques, and young adolescents' romantic involvement.* Paper presented at the meeting of the Society for Research in Child Development, Albuquerque.

Constantine, J. M., Seftor, N. S., Martin, E. S., Silva, T., & Myers, D. (2006). *A study of the effect of the Talent Search program on secondary and postsecondary outcomes in Florida, Indiana, and Texas: Final report from phase II of the national evaluation.* Washington, DC: U.S. Department of Education.

Constantine, N. A. (2008). Editorial: Converging evidence leaves policy behind: Sex education in the United States. *Journal of Adolescent Health, 42,* 324–326.

Constantine, N. A., Jerman, P., & Juang, A. (2007). California parents' preferences and beliefs on school-based sexuality education policy. *Perspectives on Sexual and Reproductive Health, 39,* 167–175.

Cook, P. J., MacCoun, R., Muschkin, C., & Vigdor, J. (2008). The negative impacts of starting middle school in the sixth grade. *Journal of Policy Analysis and Management, 27,* 104–121.

Cook, T. D., Deng, Y., & Morgano, E. (2007). Friendship influences during early adolescence: The special role of friends' grade point average. *Journal of Research on Adolescence, 17,* 325–356.

Cooksey, E. C. (2009). Sexual activity, adolescent. In D. Carr (Ed.), *Encyclopedia of the life course and human development.* Boston: Gale Cengage.

Cooper, C. R. (2011). *Bridging multiple worlds.* New York: Oxford University Press.

Cooper, C. R., & Ayers-Lopez, S. (1985). Family and peer systems in early adolescence: New models of the role of relationships in development. *Journal of Early Adolescence, 5,* 9–22.

Cooper, C. R., Behrens, R., & Trinh, N. (2009). Identity development. In R. A. Shweder, T. R. Dailey, S. D. Dixon, P. J. Miller, & J. Model (Eds.), *The Chicago companion to the child.* Chicago: University of Chicago Press.

Cooper, C. R., Cooper, R. G., Azmitia, M., Chavira, G., & Gullatt, Y. (2002). Bridging multiple worlds: How African American and Latino youth in academic outreach programs navigate math pathways to college. *Applied Developmental Science, 6,* 73–87.

Cooper, C. R., & Grotevant, H. D. (1989, April). *Individuality and connectedness in the family and adolescent's self and relational competence.* Paper presented at the meeting of the Society for Research in Child Development, Kansas City.

Cooper, M. L. (2002). Alcohol use and risky sexual behavior among college students and youth: Evaluating the evidence. *Journal of Studies on Alcohol, 14,* 101–107.

Coopersmith, S. (1967). *The antecedents of self-esteem.* San Francisco: W. H. Freeman.

Copeland, W., Shanahan, L., Miller, S., Costello, E. J., Angold, A., & Maughan, B. (2010). Outcomes of early pubertal timing in young women: A prospective population-based study. *American Journal of Psychiatry, 167,* 1218–1225.

Cornelius, J. R., Clark, D. B., Reynolds, M., Kirisci, L., & Tarter, R. (2007). Early age of first sexual intercourse and affiliation with deviant peers predict development of SUD: A prospective longitudinal study. *Addictive Behavior, 32,* 850–854.

Cosmides, L. (2011). Evolutionary psychology. *Annual Review of Psychology* (Vol. 62). Palo Alto, CA: Annual Reviews.

Coté, J. E. (2006). Emerging adulthood as an institutionalized moratorium: Risks and benefits to identity formation. In J. J. Arnett & J. L. Tanner (Eds.), *Emerging adults in America.* Washington, DC: American Psychological Association.

Coté, J. E. (2009). Identity formation and self-development. In R. M. Lerner & L. Steinberg (Eds.), *Handbook of adolescent psychology* (3rd ed.). New York: Wiley.

Covington, M. V. (2002). Patterns of adaptive learning study: Where do we go from here? In C. Midgley (Ed.), *Goals, goal structures, and patternts of adaptive learning.* Mahwah, NJ: Erlbaum.

Covington, M. V., & Teel, K. T. (1996). *Overcoming student failure.* Washington, DC: American Psychological Association.

Cowan, C. P., Cowan, P. A., & Barry, J. (2011). Couples' groups for parents of preschoolers: Ten-year outcomes of a randomized trial. *Journal of Family Psychology, 25,* 240–250.

Coyne, S. M., Nelson, D. A., & Underwood, M. (2011). Aggression in children. In P. K. Smith & C. H. Hart (Eds.), *Wiley-Blackwell handbook of childhood social development* (2nd ed.). New York: Wiley.

Crean, H. F. (2008). Conflict in the Latino parent-youth dyad: The role of emotional support from the opposite parent. *Journal of Family Psychology, 22,* 484–493.

Crespo, C., Kielpikowski, M., Jose, P. E., & Pryor, J. (2010). Relationships between family connectedness and body satisfaction: A longitudinal study of adolescent girls and boys. *Journal of Youth and Adolescence, 39,* 1392–1401.

Crissey, S. R. (2009). Dating and romantic relationships, childhood and adolescence. In D. Carr (Ed.), *Encyclopedia of the life course and human development.* Boston: Gale Cengage.

Crockett, L. J., Raffaelli, M., & Shen, Y-L. (2006). Linking self-regulation and risk proneness to risky sexual behavior: Pathways through peer pressure and early substance use. *Journal of Research on Adolescence, 16,* 503–525.

Crooks, R. L., & Baur, K. (2011). *Our sexuality* (11th ed.). Boston: Cengage.

Crouter, A. C. (2006). Mothers and fathers at work. In A. Clarke-Stewart & J. Dunn (Eds.), *Families count.* New York: Cambridge University Press.

Crouter, A. C., Bumpus, M. F., Head, M. R., & McHale, S. M. (2001). Implications of overwork and overload for the quality of men's family relationships. *Journal of Marriage and Family, 63,* 404–416.

Crowell, J. A., Treboux, D., & Brockmeyer, S. (2009). Parental divorce and adult children's attachment representations and marital status. *Attachment and Human Development, 11,* 87–101.

Crowley, S. J., & Carskadon, M. A. (2010). Modifications to weekend recovery sleep delay circadian phase in older adolescents. *Chronobiology International, 27,* 1469–1492.

Cruikshank, D. R., Jenkins, D. B., & Metcalf, K. K. (2012). *The act of teaching* (6th ed.). New York: McGraw-Hill.

Csikszentmihalyi, M. (1990). *Flow.* New York: HarperCollins.

Csikszentmihalyi, M. (1993). *The evolving self.* New York: Harper & Row.

Csikszentmihalyi, M., & Csikszentmihalyi, I. S. (Eds.). (2006). *A life worth living.* New York: Oxford University Press.

Csikszentmihalyi, M., & Nakamura, J. (2006). Creativity through the life span from an evolutionary systems perspective. In C. Hoare (Ed.), *Handbook of adult development and learning.* New York: Oxford University Press.

Csikszentmihalyi, M., & Schneider, B. (2000). *Becoming adult.* New York: Basic Books.

Cubbin, C., Brindis, C. D., Jain, S., Santelli, J., & Braveman, P. (2010). Neighborhood poverty, aspirations and expectations, and initiation of sex. *Journal of Adolescent Health, 47,* 399–406.

Cubbin, C., Santelli, J., Brindis, C. D., & Braveman, P. (2005). Neighborhood context and sexual behaviors among adolescents: Findings from the National Longitudinal Study of Adolescent Health. *Perspectives on Sexual and Reproductive Health, 37,* 125–134.

Cui, M., Fincham, F. D., & Pasley, B. K. (2008). Young adult romantic relationships: The role of parents' marital problems and relationship efficiency. *Personality and Social Psychology Bulletin, 34,* 1226–1235.

Cummings, E. M., & Davies, P. T. (2010). *Marital conflict and children: An emotional security perspective.* New York: Guilford.

Cummings, E. M., El-Sheikh, M., & Kouros, C. D. (2009). Children and violence: The role of children's regulation in the marital aggression–child adjustment link. *Clinical Child and Family Psychology Review, 12*(1), 3–15.

Cummings, E. M., & Kouros, C. D. (2008). Stress and coping. In M. M. Haith & J. B. Benson (Eds.), *Encyclopedia of infant and early childhood development. Vol. 3* (pp. 267–281). San Diego: Academic Press.

Currie, C., & others. (2008). *Inequalities in young people's health: HBSC international report from the 2005/2006 survey.* Geneva: World Health Organization.

Cushner, K. H., McClelland, A., & Safford, P. (2012). *Human diversity in education* (7th ed.). New York: McGraw-Hill.

D

Daddis, C. (2010). Adolescent peer crowds and patterns of belief in the boundaries of personal authority. *Journal of Adolescence, 33,* 699–708.

Dahl, R. E. (2004). Adolescent brain development: A period of vulnerabilities and opportunities. *Annals of the New York Academy of Sciences, 1021,* 1–22.

Dai, D. Y. (2012). The nature-nurture debate regarding high potential: Beyond dichotomous thinking. In D. Ambrose, R. J. Sternberg, & B. Sriraman (Eds.), *Confronting dogmatism in gifted education.* New York: Routledge.

Damon, W. (1988). *The moral child.* New York: Free Press.

Damon, W. (1995). *Greater expectations.* New York: Free Press.

Damon, W. (2008). *The path to purpose: Helping our children find their calling in life.* New York: Free Press.

D'Angelo, L. J., Halpern-Felsher, B. L., & Anisha, A. (2010). Adolescents and driving: Position paper of the Society for Adolescent Health and Medicine. *Journal of Adolescent Health, 47,* 212–214.

Daniels, H. (2011). Vygotsky and psychology. In U. Goswami (Ed.), *Wiley-Blackwell handbook of childhood cognitive development* (2nd ed.). New York: Wiley.

Darling, N. (2008). Commentary: Putting conflict in context. *Monographs of the Society for Research in Child Development, 73*(2), 169–175.

Darling-Hammond, N. (2011). Testing, No Child Left Behind, and educational equity. In L. M. Stulberg & S. L. Weinberg (Eds.), *Diversity in higher education.* New York: Routledge.

Darwin, C. (1859). *On the origin of species.* London: John Murray.

Das, A. (2009). Sexual harassment at work in the United States. *Archives of Sexual Behavior, 38,* 909–921.

D'Augelli, A. R. (1991). Gay men in college: Identity processes and adaptations. *Journal of College Student Development, 32,* 140–146.

Davidson, J., & Davidson, B. (2004). *Genius denied: How to stop wasting our brightest young minds.* New York: Simon & Schuster.

Davidson, M., Lickona, T., & Khmelkov, V. (2008). A new paradigm for high school character education. In L. Nucci & D. Narváez (Eds.), *Handbook of moral and character education.* Clifton, NJ: Psychology Press.

Davidson, W. S., Jimenez, T. R., Onifade, E., & Hankins, S. S. (2010). Student experiences of the adolescent diversion project: A community-based exemplar in the pedagogy of service-learning. *American Journal of Community Psychology, 46,* 442–458.

Davies, J., & Brember, I. (1999). Reading and mathematics attainments and self-esteem in years 2 and 6—an eight-year cross sectional study. *Educational Studies, 25,* 145–157.

Davis, A. E., Hyatt, G., & Arrasmith, D. (1998, February). "I Have a Dream" program. *Class One Evaluation Report,* Portland. OR: Northwest Regional Education Laboratory.

Davis, C. L., & others. (2007). Effects of aerobic exercise on overweight children's cognitive functioning: A randomized controlled trial. *Research Quarterly for Exercise and Sport, 78,* 510–519.

Davis, C. L., & others. (2011, in press). Exercise improves executive function and alters neural activation in overweight children. *Health Psychology.*

Davis, K., Christodoulou, Seider, S., & Gardner, H. (2011). The theory of multiple intelligences. In R. J. Sternberg & S. B. Kaufman (Eds.), *Cambridge handbook of intelligence.* New York: Cambridge University Press.

Davis, K. E., Norris, J., Hessler, D. M., Zawacki, T., Morrison, D. M., & George, W. H. (2010). College women's decision making: Cognitive mediation of alcohol expectancy effects. *Journal of American College Health, 58,* 481–488.

Davis, O. S. P., Arden, R., & Plomin, R. (2008). *g* in middle childhood: Moderate and genetic and shared environmental influence using diverse measures of cognitive ability at 7, 9, and 10 years in a large population sample of twins. *Intelligence, 36,* 68–80.

Day, J. M. (2010). Religion, spirituality, and positive psychology in adulthood: A developmental view. *Journal of Adult Development, 17,* 215–229.

de Ànda, D. (2006). Baby Think It Over: Evaluation of an infant simulation intervention for adolescent pregnancy prevention. *Health and Social Work, 31,* 26–35.

Deardorff, J., & others. (2011). Father absence, body mass index, and pubertal timing in girls: Differential effects by family income and ethnicity. *Journal of Adolescent Health, 48,* 441–447.

Deater-Deckard, K., & Dodge, K. (1997). Externalizing behavior problems and discipline revisited: Non-linear effects and variation by culture, context and gender. *Psychological Inquiry, 8,* 161–175.

de Bruin, W. B., Parker, A. M., & Fischhoff, B. (2007). Can adolescents predict significant life events? *Journal of Adolescent Health, 41,* 208–210.

deCharms, R. (1984). Motivation enhancement in educational settings. In R. Ames & C. Ames (Eds.), *Research on motivation in education* (Vol. 1). Orlando, FL: Academic Press.

Deci, E. L., Koestner, R., & Ryan, R. M. (2001). Extrinsic rewards and intrinsic motivation in education: Reconsidered once again. *Review of Educational Research, 71,* 1–28.

DeJong, W., DeRicco, B., & Schneider, S. K. (2010). Pregaming: An exploratory study of strategic drinking by college students in Pennsylvania. *Journal of American College Health, 58,* 307–316.

De La Paz, S., & McCutchen, D. (2011). Learning to write. In P. A. Alexander & R. E. Mayer (Eds.), *Handbook of research on learning and instruction.* New York: Routledge.

de Leo, D., & Heller, T. (2008). Social modeling in the transmission of suicide. *Crisis, 29,* 11–19.

Delisle, T. T., Werch, C. E., Wong, A. H., Bian, H., & Weiler, R. (2010). Relationship between frequency and intensity of physical activity and health behaviors of adolescents. *Journal of School Health, 80,* 134–140.

Dempster, F. N. (1981). Memory span: Sources of individual and developmental differences. *Psychological Bulletin, 89,* 63–100.

Denham, S., Waren, H., von Salisch, M., Benga, O., Chin, J-C., & Geangu, E. (2011). Emotions and social development in childhood. In P. K. Smith & C. H. Hart (Eds.), *Wiley-Blackwell handbook of childhood social development* (2nd ed.). New York: Wiley.

DePaulo, B. (2007). *Singled out.* New York: St. Martin's Griffin.

DePaulo, B. (2011). Living single: Lightening up those dark, dopey myths. In W. R. Cupach & B. H. Spitzberg (Eds.), *The dark side of close relationships.* New York: Routledge.

De Raad, B., & others. (2010). Only three factors of personality description are fully replicable across languages: A comparison of 14 trait taxonomies. *Journal of Personality and Social Psychology, 98,* 160–173.

DeRose, L., & Brooks-Gunn, J. (2008), Pubertal development in early adolescence: Implications for affective processes. In N. B. Allen & L. Sheeber (Eds.), *Adolescent emotional development and the emergence of depressive disorders.* New York: Cambridge University Press.

DeRose, L. M., Shiyko, M. P., Foster, H., & Brooks-Gunn, J. (2011, in press). Associations between menarcheal timing and behavioral developmental trajectories for girls from age 6 to age 15. *Journal of Youth and Adolescence.*

Deschesnes, M., Fines, P., & Demers, S. (2006). Are tattooing and body piercing indicators of risk-taking behaviors among high school students? *Journal of Adolescence, 29,* 379–393.

Devos, T. (2006). Implicit bicultural identity among Mexican American and Asian American college students. *Cultural Diversity and Ethnic Minority Psychology, 12,* 381–402.

Dewey, J. (1933). *How we think.* Lexington, MA: D. C. Heath.

DeZolt, D. M., & Hull, S. H. (2001). Classroom and schools climate. In J. Worell (Ed.), *Encyclopedia of women and gender.* San Diego: Academic Press.

Diamond, A. (2009). The interplay of biology and the environment broadly defined. *Developmental Psychology, 45,* 1–8.

Diamond, A. (2010). Commentary in Galinsky, E. (2010). *Mind in the making.* New York: Harper Collins.

Diamond, A., Casey, B. J., & Munakata, Y. (2011). *Developmental cognitive neuroscience.* New York: Oxford University Press.

Diamond, L. M. (2004). Unpublished review of J. W. Santrock's *Adolescence,* 11th ed. (New York: McGraw-Hill).

Diamond, L. M., Fagundes, C., & Butterworth, M. R. (2010). Intimate relationships across the life span. In M. E. Lamb, A. Freund, & R. M. Lerner (Eds.), *Handbook of life-span development.* New York: Wiley.

Diamond, L. M., & Savin-Williams, R. C. (2009). Adolescent sexuality. In R. M. Lerner & L. Steinberg (Eds.), *Handbook of adolescent psychology* (3rd ed.). New York: Wiley.

Diamond, L. M., & Savin-Williams, R. C. (2011, in press). Same-sex activity in adolescence: Multiple meanings and implications. In R. F. Fassinger & S. L. Morrow (Eds.), *Sex in the margins: Erotic experiences and behaviors of sexual minorities.* Washington, DC: American Psychological Association.

Diekman, A., & Schmidheiny, K. (2004). Do parents of girls have a higher risk of divorce? An eighteen-country study. *Journal of Marriage and the Family, 66,* 651–660.

Diemer, M. A., Kauffman, A., Koenig, N., Trahan, E., & Hsieh, C. A. (2006). Challenging racism, sexism, and social injustice: Support for urban adolescents' critical consciousness development. *Cultural Diversity and Ethnic Minority Psychology, 12,* 444–460.

Diener, E., & Seligman, M. E. P. (2002). Very happy people. *Psychological Science, 13,* 81–84.

Dindia, K. (2006). Men are from North Dakota, women are from South Dakota. In K. Dindia & D. J. Canary (Eds.), *Sex differences and similarities in communication.* Mahwah, NJ: Erlbaum.

Dishion, T. J., & Piehler, T. F. (2009). Deviant by design: Peer contagion in development, interventions, and schools. In K. H. Rubin, W. M. Bukowski, & B. Laursen (Eds.), *Handbook of peer interactions, relationships, and groups.* New York: Guilford.

Dishion, T. J., Piehler, T. F., & Myers, M. W. (2008). Dynamics and ecology of adolescent peer influence. In M. J. Prinstein & K. A. Dodge (Eds.), *Understanding peer influence in children and adolescents.* New York: Guilford.

Dishion, T. J., & Tipsord, J. M. (2011). Peer contagion in child and adolescent social and emotional development. *Annual Review of Psychology* (Vol. 62). Palo Alto, CA: Annual Reviews.

Dittman, C., & others. (2011). An epidemiological examination of parenting and family correlates of emotional problems in young children. *American Journal of Orthopsychiatry, 81,* 360–371.

Dixon, S. V., Graber, J. A., & Brooks-Gunn, J. (2008). The roles of respect for parental authority and parenting practices in parent-child conflict among African American, Latino, and European American families. *Journal of Family Psychology, 22,* 1–10.

Dobbins, M., & others. (2009). School-based physical activity programs for promoting physical activity and fitness in children and adolescents 6–18. *Cochrane Database of Systematic Reviews (1),* CD007651.

Dodge, K. A. (1993). Social cognitive mechanisms in the development of conduct disorder and depression. *Annual Review of Psychology* (Vol. 44). Palo Alto, CA: Annual Reviews.

Dodge, K. A. (2011a). Context matters in child and family policy. *Child Development, 82,* 433–442.

Dodge, K. A. (2011b). Social information processing models of aggressive behavior. In M. Mikulncer & P. R. Shaver (Eds.), *Understanding and reducing aggression, violence, and their consequences.* Washington, DC: American Psychological Association.

Dodge, K. A., Coie, J. D., & Lynam, D. R. (2006). Aggression and antisocial behavior in youth. In W. Damon & R. Lerner (Eds.), *Handbook of child psychology* (6th ed.). New York: Wiley.

Dodge, K. A., Malone, P. S., Lansford, J. E., Miller-Johnson, S., Pettit, G. S., & Bates, J. E. (2006). Toward a dynamic developmental model of the role of parents and peers in early onset substance abuse. In A. Clarke-Stewart & J. Dunn (Eds.), *Families count.* New York: Cambridge University Press.

Dodge, K. A., & McCourt, S. N. (2010). Translating models of antisocial behavioral development into efficacious intervention policy to prevent adolescent violence. *Developmental Psychobiology, 52,* 277–285.

Dodge, K. A., & Rutter, M. (Eds.). (2011). *Gene-environment interaction and developmental psychopathology.* New York: Guilford.

Dohrenwend, B. S., & Shrout, P. E. (1985). "Hassles" in the conceptualization and measurement of life event stress variables. *American Psychologist, 40,* 780–785.

Dolcini, M. M., & others. (1989). Adolescent egocentrism and feelings of invulnerability: Are they related? *Journal of Early Adolescence, 9,* 409–418.

Donnellan, M. B., & Robins, R. W. (2009). The development of personality across the life span. In G. Matthews & P. Corr (Eds.), *Cambridge Handbook of Personality.* Cambridge, UK: Cambridge University Press.

Donnellan, M. B., & Trzesniewski, K. H. (2010). Groundhog Day versus Alice in Wonderland, red herrings versus Swedish fishes, and hopefully something constructive: A reply to comments. *Perspectives on Psychological Science, 5,* 103–108.

Doremus-Fitzwater, T. L., Varlinskaya, E. I., & Spear, L. P. (2010). Motivational systems in adolescence: Possible implications for age differences in substance abuse and other risk-taking behaviors. *Brain and Cognition, 72,* 114–123.

Dorn, L. D., Dahl, R. E., Woodward, H. R., & Biro, F. (2006). Defining the boundaries of early adolescence: A user's guide to assessing pubertal status and pubertal timing in research with adolescents. *Applied Developmental Science, 10,* 30–56.

Dorn, L. H., & Biro, F. M. (2011). Puberty and its measurement: A decade in review. *Journal of Research on Adolescence, 21,* 180–195.

Dorn, L. H., Dahl, R. E., Woodward, H. R., & Biro, F. (2006). Defining the boundaries of early adolescence: A user's guide to assessing pubertal status and pubertal timing in research with adolescents. *Applied Developmental Science, 10,* 30–56.

Dranovsky, A., & Leonardo, E. D. (2011, in press). Is there a role for young hippocampal neurons in adaptation to stress? *Behavioral Brain Research.*

Dregan, A., & Armstrong, D. (2010). Adolescent sleep disturbances as predictors of adult sleep disturbances—A cohort study. *Journal of Adolescent Health, 46,* 482–487.

Drummond, R. J., & Jones, K. D. (2010). *Assessment procedures* (7th ed.). Upper Saddle River, NJ: Pearson.

Dryfoos, J. G. (1990). *Adolescents at risk: Prevalence and prevention.* New York: Oxford University Press.

Dryfoos, J. G. (1997). The prevalence of problem behaviors: Implications for programs. In R. P. Weissberg, T. P. Gullotta, R. L. Hampton, B. A. Ryan, & G. R. Adams (Eds.), *Healthy children 2010:* Enhancing children's wellness. Thousand Oaks, CA: Sage.

Dryfoos, J. G., & Barkin, C. (2006). *Adolescence.* New York: Oxford University Press.

Dugan, S. A. (2008). Exercise for preventing childhood obesity. *Physical Medicine and Rehabilitation Clinics of North America, 19,* 205–216.

Duggan, P. M., Lapsley, D. K., & Norman, K. (2000, April). *Adolescent invulnerability and personal uniqueness: Scale development and* *initial construct validation*. Paper presented at the 8th Biennial Meeting of the Society for Research on Adolescence, Chicago.

Duke, N. N., Skay, C. L., Pettingell, S. L., & Borowsky, I. W. (2011). Early death perception in adolescence: Identifying factors associated with change from pessimism to optimism about life expectancy. *Clinical Pediatrics, 50,* 21–28.

Dumith, S. C., & others. (2010). Overweight/obesity and physical fitness among children and adolescents. *Journal of Physical Activity and Health, 7,* 641–648.

Duncan, S. C., Duncan, T. E., Strycker, L. A., & Chaumeton, N. R. (2007). A cohort-sequential latent growth model of physical activity from 12 to 17 years. *Annals of Behavioral Medicine, 33,* 80–89.

Dunlop, S. M., & Romer, D. (2010). Adolescent and young adult car crash risk: Sensation seeking, substance use propensity, and substance use behaviors. *Journal of Adolescent Health, 46,* 90–92.

Dunn, J. (2005). Commentary: Siblings in their families. *Journal of Family Psychology, 19,* 654–657.

Dunn, J. (2007). Siblings and socialization. In J. E. Grusec & P. D. Hastings (Eds.), *Handbook of socialization*. New York: Guilford.

Dunphy, D. C. (1963). The social structure of urban adolescent peer groups. *Society, 26,* 230–246.

Dupre, M. E., & Meadows, S. O. (2007). Disaggregating the effects of marital trajectories on health. *Journal of Family Issues, 28,* 623–652.

Durik, A. M., Hyde, J. S., Marks, A. C., Roy, A. L., Anaya, D., & Schultz, G. (2006). Ethnicity and gender stereotypes of emotion. *Sex Roles, 54,* 429–445.

Durston, S. (2010). Imaging genetics in ADHD. *Neuroimage, 68,* 1114–1119.

Durston, S., & others. (2006). A shift from diffuse to focal cortical activity with development. *Developmental Science, 9,* 1–8.

Duschl, R., & Hamilton, R. (2011). Learning science. In P. A. Alexander & R. E. Mayer (Eds.), *Handbook of research on learning and instruction*. New York: Routledge.

Dusek, J. B., & McIntyre, J. G. (2003). Self-concept and self-esteem development. In G. Adams & M. Berzonsky (Eds.), *Blackwell handbook of adolescence*. Malden, MA: Blackwell.

Dweck, C. S. (2006). *Mindset*. New York: Random House.

Dweck, C. S. (2007). Boosting achievement with messages that motivate. *Education Canada, 47,* 6–10.

Dweck, C. S. (2012, in press). Social development. In P. Zelazo (Ed.), *Oxford handbook of developmental psychology*. New York: Oxford University Press.

Dweck, C. S., Mangels, J. A., & Good, C. (2004). Motivational effects on attention, cognition, and performance. In D. Yun Dai & R. J. Sternberg (Eds.), *Motivation, emotion, and cognition*. Mahwah, NJ: Erlbaum.

Dweck, C. S., & Master, A. (2009). Self-theories and motivation: Students' beliefs about intelligence. In K. R. Wentzel & A. Wigfield (Eds.), *Handbook of motivation at school*. New York: Routledge.

Dworkin, S. L., & Santelli, J. (2007). Do abstinence-plus interventions reduce sexual risk behavior among youth? *PLoS Medicine, 4,* 1437–1439.

Dyson, R., & Renk, K. (2006). Freshman adaptation to university life: Depressive symptoms, stress, and coping. *Journal of Clinical Psychology, 62,* 1231–1244.

E

Eagly, A. H. (2001). Social role theory of sex differences and similarities. In J. Worell (Ed.), *Encyclopedia of women and gender.* San Diego: Academic Press.

Eagly, A. H. (2010). Gender roles. In J. Levine & M. Hogg (Eds.), *Encyclopedia of group processes and intergroup relations.* Thousand Oaks, CA: Sage.

Eagly, A. H., & Crowley, M. (1986). Gender and helping behavior: A meta-analytic review of the social psychological literature. *Psychological Bulletin, 100,* 283–308.

Eagly, A. H., & Steffen V. J. (1986). Gender and aggressive behavior: A meta-analytic review of the social psychological literature. *Psychological Bulletin, 100,* 309–330.

Eagly, A. H., & Wood, W. (2011, in press). Gender roles in a biosocial world. In P. van Lange, A. Kruglanski, & E. T. Higgins (Eds.), *Handbook of theories in social psychology.* Thousand Oaks, CA: Sage.

East, P. (2009). Adolescent relationships with siblings. In R. M. Lerner & L. Steinberg (Eds.), *Handbook of adolescent psychology* (3rd ed.). New York: Wiley.

East, P., & Adams, J. (2002). Sexual assertiveness and adolescents' sexual rights. *Perspectives on Sexual and Reproductive Health, 34,* 198–202.

Eaton, D. K., & others. (2008). Youth risk behavior surveillance—United States, 2007. *MMWR,* 57, 1–131.

Eaton, D. K., & others. (2010). Youth risk behavior surveillance—United States 2009. *MMWR Surveillance Summary, 59*(5), 1–142.

Ebata, A. T., & Moos, R. H. (1989, April). *Coping and adjustment in four groups of adolescents*. Paper presented at the biennial meeting of the Society for Research in Child Development, Kansas City.

Eby, J. W., Herrell, A. L., & Jordan, M. L. (2011). *Teaching in elementary school: A reflective approach* (6th ed.). Boston: Allyn & Bacon.

Eccles, J. S. (1987). Gender roles and women's achievement-related decisions. *Psychology of Women Quarterly, 11,* 135–172.

Eccles, J. S. (1993). School and family effects on the ontogeny of children's interests, self-perceptions, and activity choice. In J. Jacobs (Ed.), *Nebraska Symposium on Motivation, 1992: Developmental perspectives on motivation*. Lincoln: University of Nebraska Press.

Eccles, J. S. (2004). Schools, academic motivation and stage-environment fit. In R. Lerner & L. Steinberg (Eds.), *Handbook of adolescent psychology*. New York: Wiley.

Eccles, J. S. (2007). Families, schools and developing achievement-related motivations and engagement. In J. E. Grusec & P. D. Hastings (Eds.), *Handbook of socialization*. New York: Guilford.

Eccles, J. S., Brown, B. V., & Templeton, J. (2008). A developmental framework for selecting indicators of well-being during the adolescent and young adult years. In B. V. Brown (Ed.), *Key indicators of child and youth well-being.* Clifton, NJ: Psychology Press.

Eccles, J. S., & Gootman, J. (2002). *Community programs to promote youth development*. Washington, DC: National Research Council Institute of Medicine, National Academy Press.

Eccles, J. S., & Roeser, R. W. (2009). Schools, academic motivation, and stage-environment fit. In R. M. Lerner & L. Steinberg (Eds.), *Handbook of adolescent psychology* (3rd ed.). New York: Wiley.

Eccles, J. S., & Roeser, R. W. (2010). Schools, academic motivation, and stage-environment fit. In J. Meece & J. Eccles (Eds.), *Handbook of research on schools, schooling, and human development*. New York: Routledge.

Eccles, J. S., & Roeser, R. W. (2011). Schools as developmental contexts during adolescence. *Journal of Research on Adolescence, 21,* 225–241.

Eccles, J. S., Wigfield, A., & Schiefele, U. (1998). Motivation to succeed. In W. Damon (Ed.), *Handbook of child psychology* (5th ed., Vol. 3). New York: Wiley.

Eckersley, R. (2010). Commentary on Trzesniewski and Donnellan (2010): A transdisciplinary perspective on young people's well being. *Perspectives on Psychological Science, 5,* 76–80.

Edelbrock, C. S. (1989, April). *Self-reported internalizing and externalizing problems in a community sample of adolescents*. Paper presented at the meeting of the Society for Research in Child Development, Kansas City.

Edwards, A. R., Esmonde, I., & Wagner, J. F. (2011). Learning mathematics. In P. A. Alexander & R. E. Mayer (Eds.), *Handbook of research on learning and instruction*. New York: Routledge.

Edwards, R., & Hamilton, M. A. (2004). You need to understand my gender role: An empirical test of Tannen's model of gender and communication. *Sex Roles, 50,* 491–504.

Eichen, D. M., Conner, B. T., Daly, B. P., & Faubar, R. L. (2011, in press). Weight perception, substance use, and disordered eating behaviors: Comparing normal weight and overweight high-school students. *Journal of Youth and Adolescence.*

Ein-Dor, T., Mikulincer, M., Doron, G., & Shaver, P. R. (2010). The attachment paradox: How can so many of (the insecure ones) have no adaptive advantages? *Perspectives on Psychological Science, 5,* 123–141.

Eisenberg, M. E., Bernat, D. H., Bearinger, L. H., & Resnick, M. D. (2008). Support for comprehensive sexuality education: Perspectives from parents of school-aged youth. *Journal of Adolescent Research, 42,* 352–359.

Eisenberg, N., & Fabes, R. A. (1998). Prosocial development. In N. Eisenberg (Ed.), *Handbook of child psychology* (5th ed., Vol. 3). New York: Wiley.

Eisenberg, N., Fabes, R. A., Guthrie, I. K., & Reiser, M. (2002). The role of emotionality and regulation in children's social competence and adjustment. In L. Pulkkinen & A. Caspi (Eds.), *Paths to successful development.* New York: Cambridge University Press.

Eisenberg, N., Fabes, R. A., & Spinrad, T. L. (2006). Prosocial development. In W. Damon & R. Lerner (Eds.), *Handbook of child psychology* (6th ed.). New York: Wiley.

Eisenberg, N., & Morris, A. S. (2004). Moral cognitions and prosocial responding in adolescence. In R. Lerner & L. Steinberg (Eds.), *Handbook of adolescent psychology* (2nd ed.). New York: Wiley.

Eisenberg, N., Morris, A. S., McDaniel, B., & Spinrad, T. L. (2009). Moral cognitions and prosocial responding in adolescence. In R. M. Lerner & L. Steinberg (Eds.), *Handbook of adolescent psychology* (3rd ed.). New York: Wiley.

Eisenberg, N., Spinrad, T. R., & Eggum, N. D. (2010). Emotion-focused self-regulation and its relation to children's maladjustment. *Annual Review of Clinical Psychology* (Vol. 6). Palo Alto, CA: Annual Reviews.

Eisenberg, N., & Valiente, C. (2002). Parenting and children's prosocial and moral development. In M. H. Bornstein (Ed.), *Handbook of parenting* (2nd ed.). Mahwah, NJ: Erlbaum.

Eisenhower Corporation. (2010). *Quantum Opportunities program.* Retrieved January 10, 2010 from http://www.eisenhowerfoundation.org/qop.php

Elkind, D. (1961). Quantity conceptions in junior and senior high school students. *Child Development, 32,* 531–560.

Elkind, D. (1976). *Child development and education: A Piagetian perspective.* New York: Oxford University Press.

Elkind, D. (1985). Egocentrism redux. *Developmental Review, 5,* 218–226.

Elkind, D., & Bowen, R. (1979). Imaginary audience behavior in children and adolescents. *Developmental Psychology, 15,* 38–44.

Elkington, K. S., Bauermeister, J. A., & Zimmerman, M. A. (2011, in press). Do parents and peers matter? A prospective socio-ecological examination of substance use and sexual risk among African American youth. *Journal of Adolescence.*

Elks, C. E., & Ong, K. K. (2011). Whole genome associated studies for age of menarche. *Briefings in Functional Genomics, 2,* 91–97.

Elks, C. E., & others. (2010). Thirty new loci for age at menarche identified by a meta-analysis of genome-wide association studies. *Nature Genetics, 42,* 1077–1085.

Elliot, D. L., Cheong, J., Moe, E., & Goldberg, L. (2007). Cross-sectional study of female athletes reporting anabolic steroid use. *Archives of Pediatric and Adolescent Medicine, 161,* 572–577.

Ellis, B. J., Shirtcliff, E. A., Boyce, W. T., Deardorff, J., & Essex, M. J. (2011). Quality of early family relationships and the timing and tempo of puberty: Effects depend on biological sensitivity to context. *Development and Psychopathology, 23,* 85–99.

Ellis, L., & Ames, M. A. (1987). Neurohormonal functioning and sexual orientation: A theory of homosexuality-heterosexuality. *Psychological Bulletin, 101,* 233–258.

Elmore, R. F. (2009). Schooling adolescents. In R. M. Lerner & L. Steinberg (Eds.), *Handbook of adolescent psychology* (3rd ed.). New York: Wiley.

Else-Quest, N. M., Hyde, J. S., & Linn, M. C. (2010). Cross-national patterns of gender differences in mathematics: A meta-analysis. *Psychological Bulletin, 136,* 103–127.

Emery, R. E. (1999). *Renegotiating family relationships* (2nd ed.). New York: Guilford.

Emery, R. E., & Laumann-Billings, L. (1998). An overview of the nature, causes, and consequences of abusive family relationships. *American Psychologist, 53,* 121–135.

Enea, C., Boissea, N., Fargeas-Gluck, M. A., Diaz, V., & Duque, B. (2011, in press). Circulating androgens in women: Exercise-induced changes. *Sports Medicine.*

Enfield, A., & Collins, D. (2008). The relationship of service-learning, social justice, multicultural competence, and civic engagement. *Journal of College Student Development, 49,* 95–109.

Engle, P. L., & Black, M. M. (2008). The effect of poverty on child development and educational outcomes. *Annals of the New York Academy of Science, 1136.*

Englund, M. M., Egeland, B., & Collins, W. A. (2008). Exceptions to high school dropout predictions in a low-income sample: Do adults make a difference? *Journal of Social Issues, 64*(1), 77–93.

Englund, M. M., Luckner, A. E., & Whaley, G. (2003, April). *The importance of early parenting for children's long-term educational attainment.* Paper presented at the meeting of the Society for Research in Child Development, Tampa.

Enright, R. D., Santos, M. J. D., & Al-Mabuk, R. (1989). The adolescent as forgiver. *Journal of Adolescence, 12,* 95–110.

Ensembl Human. (2008). *Explore the Homo sapiens genome.* Retrieved April 14, 2008, from www.ensembl.org/Homo_sapiens/index.html

Entwistle, D., Alexander, K., & Olson, L. (2010). The long reach of socioeconomic status in education. In J. L. Meece & J. S. Eccles (Eds.), *Handbook of research on schools, schooling, and human development.* New York: Routledge.

Enyeart Smith, T. M., & Wessel, M. T. (2011). Alcohol, drugs, and links to sexual risk behaviors among a sample of Virginia college students. *Journal of Drug Education, 41,* 1–16.

Epstein, J. L. (2001). *School, family, and community partnerships.* Boulder, CO: Westview Press.

Epstein, J. L. (2005). Results of the Partnership Schools-CSR model for student achievement over three years. *Elementary School Journal, 106,* 151–170.

Epstein, J. L. (2007a). Family and community involvement. In K. Borman, S. Cahill, & B. Cotner (Eds.), *American high school: An encyclopedia.* Westport, CT: Greenwood.

Epstein, J. L. (2007b). Homework. In K. Borman, S. Chaill, & B. Cotner (Eds.), *American high school: An encyclopedia.* Westport, CT: Greenwood.

Epstein, J. L. (2009). *School, family, and community partnerships.* Thousand Oaks, CA: Sage.

Erickson, J. B. (1982). *A profile of community youth organization members, 1980.* Boys Town, NE: Boys Town Center for the Study of Youth Development.

Ericsson, K. A., Charness, N., Feltovich, P. J., & Hoffman, R. R. (2006). *The Cambridge handbook of expertise and expert performance.* New York: Cambridge University Press.

Ericsson, K. A., Krampe, R., & Tesch-Römer, C. (1993). The role of deliberate practice in the acquisition of expert performance. *Psychological Review, 100,* 363–406.

Erikson, E. H. (1950). *Childhood and society*. New York: W. W. Norton.

Erikson, E. H. (1968). *Identity: Youth and crisis*. New York: W. W. Norton.

Erikson, E. H. (1969). *Gandhi's truth*. New York: W. W. Norton.

Erikson, E. H. (1970). Reflections on the dissent of contemporary youth. *International Journal of Psychoanalysis, 51,* 11–22.

Ernst, M., & Spear, L. P. (2009). Reward systems. In M. de Haan & M. R. Gunnar (Eds.), *Handbook of developmental social neuroscience*. New York: Guilford.

Escobar-Chaves, S. L., & Anderson, C. A. (2008). Media and risky behavior. *Future of Children, 18*(1), 147–180.

Espelage, D., Holt, M., & Poteat, P. (2010). The school context, bullying, and victimization. In J. Meece & J. Eccles (Eds.), *Handbook of research on schools, schooling, and human development*. New York: Routledge.

Etaugh, C., & Bridges, J. S. (2010). *Women's lives* (2nd ed.). Boston: Allyn & Bacon.

Euling, S. Y., & others. (2008). Examination of U.S. puberty-timing data from 1940 to 1994 for secular trends: Panel findings. *Pediatrics, 121*(Suppl 3), S172–S191.

Evans, E., Hawton, K., & Rodham, K. (2005). Suicidal phenomena and abuse in adolescents: A review of epidemiological studies. *Child Abuse and Neglect, 29,* 45–58.

Evans, G. W. (2004). The environment of childhood poverty. *American Psychologist, 59,* 77–92.

Evans, G. W., & Kim, P. (2007). Childhood poverty and health: Cumulative risk exposure and stress dysregulation. *Psychological Science, 18,* 953–957.

F

Fabiano, G. A., Pelham, W. E., Coles, E. K., Gnagy, E. M., Chronis-Tuscano, A., & O'Connor, B. C. (2009). A meta-analysis of behavioral treatments for attention deficit/hyperactivity disorder. *Clinical Psychology Review, 29*(2), 129–140.

Fabricus, W. V., Braver, S. L., Diaz, P., & Schenck, C. (2010). Custody and parenting time: Links to family relationships and well-being after divorce. In M. E. Lamb (Ed.), *The role of the father in child development* (5th ed.). New York: Wiley.

Fair, C. D., & Vanyur, J. (2011). Sexual coercion, verbal aggression, and condom use consistency among college students. *Journal of American College Health, 59,* 273–280.

Fairweather, E., & Cramond, B. (2011). Infusing creative and critical thinking into the classroom. In R. A. Beghetto & J. C. Kaufman (Eds.), *Nurturing creativity in the classroom*. New York: Cambridge University Press.

Fakier, N., & Wild, L. G. (2011, in press). Associations among sleep problems, learning difficulties, and substance use in adolescence. *Journal of Youth and Adolescence*.

Fallon, D. (2011). Reducing teen pregnancy. *Practicing Midwife, 14,* 23–24.

Fang, L., Schinke, S. P., & Cole, K. C. (2010). Preventing substance use among early Asian-American girls: Initial evaluation of a web-based mother-daughter program. *Journal of Adolescent Health, 47,* 529–532.

Fantasia, H. C. (2008). Concept analysis: Sexual decision-making in adolescence. *Nursing Forum, 43,* 80–90.

Faraone, S. V., & Mick, E. (2010). Molecular genetics of attention deficit hyperactivity disorder. *Psychiatric Clinics of North America, 33,* 159–180.

Farrington, D. P. (2004). Conduct disorder, aggression, and delinquency. In R. M. Lerner & L. Steinberg (Eds.), *Handbook of adolescent psychology* (2nd ed.). New York: Wiley.

Fasick, F. A. (1994). On the "invention" of adolescence. *Journal of Early Adolescence, 14,* 6–23.

Fatusi, A. O., & Hindin, M. J. (2010). Adolescents and youth in developing countries: Health and development issues in context. *Journal of Adolescence, 33,* 499–508.

Fatusi, A. O., & Hindin, M. J. (2010). Adolescents and youths in developing countries: Health and development issues in context. *Journal of Adolescence, 33,* 499–508.

Federal Interagency Forum on Child and Family Statistics. (2010). *America's children brief: Key national indicators of well-being 2010*. Retrieved October 21, 2010, from www.childstats.gov/americaschildren/eco.asp

Feeney, B. C., & Monin, J. K. (2008). An attachment-theoretical perspective on divorce. In J. Cassidy & P. R. Shaver (Eds.), *Handbook of attachment* (2nd ed.). New York: Guilford.

Feinberg, M. E., Kan, M. L., & Hetherington, E. M. (2007). The longitudinal influence of coparenting conflict on parental negativity and adolescent maladjustment. *Journal of Marriage and the Family, 69,* 687–702.

Feinstein, L., & Peck, S. C. (2008). Unexpected pathways through education: Why do some students not succeed in school and what helps others beat the odds? *Journal of Social Issues, 64*(1), 1–20.

Feiring, C. (1996). Concepts of romance in 15-year-old adolescents. *Journal of Research on Adolescence, 6,* 181–200.

Feldman, S. S., & Elliott, G. R. (1990). Progress and promise of research on normal adolescent development. In S. S. Feldman & G. Elliott (Eds.), *At the threshold: The developing adolescent*. Cambridge, MA: Harvard University Press.

Feldman, S. S., & Rosenthal, D. A. (1999). *Factors influencing parents' and adolescents' evaluations of parents as sex communicators.* Unpublished manuscript, Stanford Center on Adolescence, Stanford University.

Feldman, S. S., & Rosenthal, D. A. (Eds.). (2002). *Talking sexually: Parent-adolescent communication.* San Francisco: Jossey-Bass.

Feldman, S. S., Turner, R., & Araujo, K. (1999). Interpersonal context as an influence on sexual timetables of youths: Gender and ethnic effects. *Journal of Research on Adolescence, 9,* 25–52.

Feniger, Y. (2011, in press). The gender gap in advanced math and science course taking: Does same-sex education make a difference? *Sex Roles.*

Field, A. E., Cambargo, C. A., Taylor, C. B., Berkey, C. S., Roberts, S. B., & Colditz, G. A. (2001). Peer, parent, and media influences on the development of weight concerns and frequent dieting among preadolescent and adolescent girls and boys. *Pediatrics, 107,* 54–60.

Field, T., Diego, M., & Sanders, C. E. (2001). Exercise is positively related to adolescents' relationships and academics. *Adolescence, 36,* 105–110.

Fingerhut, A. W., & Peplau, L. A. (2012, in press). Sexual orientation and romantic relationships. In C. J. Patterson & A. R. D'Augelli (Eds.), *Handbook of psychology and sexual orientation.* New York: Oxford University Press.

Fingerman, K. L., & Birditt, K. S. (2011). Adult children and aging parents. In K. W. Schaie (Ed.), *Handbook of the psychology of aging* (7th ed.). New York: Elsevier.

Fingerman, K. L., Chan, W., Pitzer, L. M., Birditt, K. S., Franks, M. M., & Zarit, S. (2011). Who gets what and why: Help middle-aged adults provide to parents and grown children. *Journal of Gerontology B: Psychological Sciences and Social Sciences, 66,* 87–98.

Finn, A. S., Sheridan, M. A., Kam, C. L., Hinshaw, S., & D'Esposito, M. (2010). Longitudinal evidence for functional specialization of the neural circuit supporting working memory in the human brain. *Journal of Neuroscience, 18,* 11062–11067.

Fischer, K. W., & Immordino-Yang, M. H. (2008). The fundamental importance of the brain and learning for education. In *The Jossey-Bass reader on the brain and learning*. San Francisco: Jossey-Bass.

Fischhoff, B., Bruine de Bruin, W., Parker, A. M., Millstein, S. G., & Halpern-Felsher, B. L. (2010). Adolescents' perceived risk of dying. *Journal of Adolescent Health, 46,* 265–269.

Fisher, B. S., Cullen, F. T., & Turner, M. G. (2000). *The sexual victimization of college women.* Washington, DC: National Institute of Justice.

Fisher, C. A., Hetrick, S. E., & Rushford, N. (2010, April 14). Family therapy for anorexia nervosa. *Cochrane Database of Systematic Reviews, 4,* CD004780.

Fisher, T. D. (1987). Family communication and the sexual behavior and attitudes of college students. *Journal of Youth and Adolescence, 16,* 481–495.

Fitzpatrick, K. M., Dulin, A., & Piko, B. (2010). Bullying and depressive symptomatology among low-income African youth. *Journal of Youth and Adolescence, 39,* 634–645.

Flanagan, A. S. (1996, March). *Romantic behavior of sexually victimized and nonvictimized women.* Paper presented at the meeting of the Society for Research on Adolescence, Boston.

Flanagan, C. A. (2004). Volunteerism leadership, political socialization, and civic engagement. In R. Lerner & L. Steinberg (Eds.), *Handbook of adolescent psychology* (2nd ed.). New York: Wiley.

Flanagan, C. A., & Faison, N. (2001). Youth civic development: Implications for social policy and programs. *SRCD Social Policy Report, XV*(1), 1–14.

Flannery, D. J., Rowe, D. C., & Gulley, B. L. (1993). Impact of pubertal status, timing, and age on adolescent sexual experience and delinquency. *Journal of Adolescent Research, 8,* 21–40.

Flavell, J. H. (2004). Theory-of-mind development: Retrospect and prospect. *Merrill-Palmer Quarterly, 50,* 274–290.

Fleming, C. B., White, H. R., Oesterie, S., Haggerty, K. P., & Catalano, R. F. (2010). Romantic relationship status changes and substance abuse among 18- to 20-year-olds. *Journal of Studies on Alcohol and Drugs, 71,* 847–856.

Flint, M. S., Baum, A., Chambers, W. H., & Jenkins, F. J. (2007). Induction of DNA damage, alteration of DNA repair, and transcriptional activation by stress hormones. *Psychoneuroendocrinology, 32,* 470–479.

Florence, N. (2010). *Multiculturalism 101.* New York: McGraw-Hill.

Florsheim, P., Moore, D., & Edgington, C. (2003). Romantic relationships among adolescent parents. In P. C. Florsheim (Ed.), *Adolescent romantic relations and sexual behavior*. Oxford, UK: Routledge.

Flouri, E. (2004). Correlates of parents' involvement with their adolescent children in restructured and biological two-parent families: Role of child characteristics. *International Journal of Behavioral Development, 28,* 148–156.

Flynn, J. R. (1999). Searching for justice: The discovery of 1Q gains over time. *American Psychologist, 54,* 5–20.

Flynn, J. R. (2007). The history of the American mind in the 20th century: A scenario to explain gains over time and a case for the irrelevance of *g*. In P. C. Kyllonen, R. D. Roberts, & L. Stankov (Eds.), *Extending intelligence*. Mahwah, NJ: Erlbaum.

Flynn, J. R. (2011). Secular changes in intelligence. In R. J. Sternberg & S. B. Kaufman (Eds.), *Cambridge handbook of intelligence.* New York: Cambridge University Press.

Folkman, S., & Moskowitz, J. T. (2004). Coping: Pitfalls and promises. *Annual Review of Psychology* (Vol. 55). Palo Alto, CA: Annual Reviews.

Forbes, E. E., & Dahl, R. E. (2010). Pubertal development and behavior: Hormonal activation of social and motivational tendencies. *Brain and Cognition, 72,* 66–72.

Ford, M. E., & Smith, P. E. (2007). Thriving with social purpose: An integrative approach to the development of optimal human functioning. *Educational Psychologist, 42,* 153–171.

Forgatch, M. S., & Patterson, G. R. (2010). Parent Management Training—Oregon Model: An intervention for antisocial behavior in children and adolescents. In J. R. Weisz & A. E. Kazdin (Eds.), Evidence-based psychotherapies for children and adolescents (2nd ed.). New York: Guilford.

Forgatch, M. S., Patterson, G. R., DeGarmo, D. S., & Beldavs, Z. G. (2009). Testing the Oregon delinquency model with 9-year follow-up of the Oregon Divorce Study. *Development and Psychopathology, 21,* 637–660.

Fortenberry, J. D., & others. (2010). Sexual behaviors and condom use at last vaginal intercourse: A national sample of adolescents ages 14 to 17 years. *Journal of Sexual Medicine, 7,* 305–314.

Fosco, G. M., & Grych, J. H. (2010). Adolescent triangulation into parental conflicts: Longitudinal implications for appraisals and adolescent-parent relations. *Journal of Marriage and the Family, 72,* 254–266.

Fouad, N. A., & Bynner, J. (2008). Work transitions. *American Psychologist, 63,* 241–251.

Fowler-Brown, A., & Kahwati, L. C. (2004). Prevention and treatment of overweight in children and adolescents. *American Family Physician, 69,* 2591–2598.

Francis, J., Fraser, G., & Marcia, J. E. (1989). *Cognitive and experimental factors in moratorium-achievement (MAMA) cycles.* Unpublished manuscript. Department of Psychology, Simon Fraser University, Burnaby, British Columbia.

Franz, C. E. (1996). The implications of preschool tempo and motoric activity level for personality decades later. Reported in Caspi, A. (1998). Personality development across the life course. In W. Damon (Ed.), *Handbook of child psychology* (Vol. 3, p. 337). New York: Wiley.

Fraser, S. (Ed.). (1995). *The bell curve wars: Race, intelligence, and the future of America.* New York: Basic Books.

Frederikse, M., Lu, A., Aylward, E., Barta, P., Sharma, T., & Pearlson, G. (2000). Sex differences in inferior lobule volume in schizophrenia. *American Journal of Psychiatry, 157,* 422–427.

Fredricks, J. A., & Eccles, J. S. (2006). Is extracurricular participation associated with beneficial outcomes? Concurrent and longitudinal relations. *Developmental Psychology, 42,* 698–713.

Fredstrom, B. K., Adams, R. E., & Gilman, R. (2011). Electronic and school-based victimization: Unique contexts for adjustment difficulties during adolescence. *Journal of Youth and Adolescence, 40,* 405–415.

Freeman, D. (1983). *Margaret Mead and Samoa.* Cambridge, MA: Harvard University Press.

Freud, A. (1966). Instinctual anxiety during puberty. In *The writings of Anna Freud: The ego and the mechanisms of defense.* New York: International Universities Press.

Freud, S. (1917). *A general introduction to psychoanalysis.* New York: Washington Square Press.

Friedman, H. S., & Schustack, M. W. (2011). *Personality* (5th ed.). Upper Saddle River, NJ: Pearson.

Friedman, L., & others. (2011). Human papillomavirus vaccine: An updated position of the Society for Adolescent Health and Medicine. *Journal of Adolescent Health, 48,* 215–216.

Friend, M. (2011). *Special education* (3rd ed.). Upper Saddle River, NJ: Merrill.

Friend, M., & Bursick, W. D. (2012). *Including students with special needs: A practical guide for classroom teachers* (6th ed.). Upper Saddle River, NJ: Pearson.

Friesch, R. E. (1984). Body fat, puberty and fertility. *Biological Review, 59,* 161–188.

Frimer, J. A., Walker, L. J., Dunlop, W. L., Lee, B., & Riches, A. (2011, in press). The integration of agency and communion in moral personality: Evidence of enlightened self-interest. *Journal of Personality and Social Psychology.*

Frisen, A., & Holmqvist, K. (2010). What characterizes early adolescents with a positive body image? A qualitative investigation of Swedish boys and girls. *Body Image, 7,* 205–212.

Froh, J. J., Yurkewicz, C., & Kashdan, T. B. (2009). Gratitude and subjective well-being in early adolescence: Examining gender differences. *Journal of Adolescence, 32,* 633–650.

Fromme, K., Corbin, W. R., & Kruse, M. I. (2008). Behavioral risks during the transition from high school to college. *Developmental Psychology, 44,* 1497–1504.

Frost, J., & McKelvie, S. (2004). Self-esteem and body satisfaction in male and female elementary school, high school, and university students. *Sex Roles, 51,* 45–54.

Frye, D. (2004). Unpublished review of J. W. Santrock's *Child development,* 11th ed. (New York: McGraw-Hill).

Fuligni, A., Hughes, D. L., & Way, N. (2009). Ethnicity and immigration. In R. M. Lerner & L. Steinberg (Eds.), *Handbook of adolescent psychology* (3rd ed.). New York: Wiley.

Fuligni, A. J., Hughes, D. L., & Way, N. (2009). Ethnicity and immigration. In R. M. Lerner & L. Steinberg (Eds.), *Handbook of adolescent psychology* (3rd ed.). New York: Wiley.

Fuligni, A. J., Tseng, V., & Lamb, M. (1999). Attitudes toward family obligations among American adolescents from Asian, Latin American, and European backgrounds. *Child Development, 70,* 1030–1044.

Fuligni, A., & Stevenson, H. W. (1995). Time use and mathematics achievement among American, Chinese, and Japanese high school students. *Child Development, 66,* 830–842.

Fung, H. (2011). Cultural psychological perspectives on social development in childhood. In P. K. Smith & C. H. Hart (Eds.), *Wiley-Blackwell handbook of childhood social development* (2nd ed.). New York: Wiley.

Furman, E. (2005). *Boomerang nation.* New York: Fireside.

Furman, W (2002). The emerging field of adolescent romantic relationships. *Current Directions in Psychological Science, 11,* 177–180.

Furman, W., & Collins, W. A. (2009). Adolescent romantic relationships and experiences. In K. H. Rubin, W. M. Bukowski, & B. Laursen (Eds.), *Handbook of peer interactions, relationships, and groups.* New York: Wiley.

Furman, W., Low, S., & Ho, M. J. (2009). Romantic experience and psychosocial adjustment in middle adolescence. *Journal of Clinical Child and Adolescent Psychology, 38,* 75–90.

Furman, W., & Shaeffer. L. (2003). The role of romantic relationships in adolescent development. In P. Florsheim (Ed.), *Adolescent romantic relations and sexual behavior.* Mahwah. NJ: Erlbaum.

Furman, W., & Simon, V. A. (2008). Homophily in adolescent romantic relationships. In M. J. Prinstein & K. A. Dodge (Eds.), *Understanding peer influence in children and adolescents.* New York: Guilford.

Furman, W., & Wehner, E. A. (1998). Adolescent romantic relationships: A developmental perspective. In S. Shulman & W. A. Collins (Eds.), *New directions for child development: Adolescent romantic relationships.* San Francisco: Jossey-Bass.

Furman, W., & Winkles, J. K. (2010). Predicting romantic involvement, relationship cognitions, and relational styles regarding friends and parents. *Journal of Adolescence, 33,* 827–836.

Furstenberg, F. F. (2006). Growing up healthy: Are adolescents the right target group? *Journal of Adolescent Health, 39,* 303–304.

Furstenberg, F. F. (2007). The future of marriage. In A. S. Skolnick & J. H. Skolnick (Eds.), *Family in transition* (14th ed.). Boston: Allyn & Bacon.

Fussell, E., & Greene, M. E. (2002). Demographic trends affecting youth around the world. In B. B. Brown, R. W. Larson, & T. S. Saraswathi (Eds.), *The world's youth.* New York: Cambridge University Press.

G

Galambos, N. L., Barker, E. T., & Krahn, H. J. (2006). Depression, self-esteem, and anger in emerging adulthood: Seven-year trajectories. *Developmental Psychology, 42,* 350–365.

Galambos, N. L., Berenbaum, S. A., & McHale, S. M. (2009). Gender development in adolescence. In R. M. Lerner & L. Steinberg (Eds.), *Handbook of adolescent psychology.* New York: Wiley.

Galambos, N. L., Howard, A. L., & Maggs, J. L. (2011). Rise and fall of sleep quality with student experiences across the first year of the university. *Journal of Research on Adolescence, 21,* 342–349.

Galambos, N. L., & Maggs, J. L. (1991). Out-of-school care of young adolescents and self-reported behavior. *Developmental Psychology, 27,* 644–655.

Galinsky, E. (2010). *Mind in the making.* New York: HarperCollins

Galupo, M. P., Cartwright, K. B., & Savage, L. S. (2010). Cross-category friendships and postformal thought among college students. *Journal of Adult Development, 17,* 208–214.

Galvan, A., Hare, T., Voss, H., Glover, G., & Casey, B. J. (2007). Risk-taking and the adolescent brain: Who is at risk? *Developmental Science, 10,* F8–F14.

Ganahl, D. J., Prinsen, T. J., & Netzly, S. B. (2003). A content analysis of prime time commercials: A contextual framework of gender representation. *Sex Roles, 49,* 545–551.

Ganong, L., Coleman, M., & Jamison, T. (2011). Patterns of stepchild-stepparent relationship development. *Journal of Marriage and the Family, 73,* 396–413.

Garai, E. P., McKee, L. G., & Forehand, R. (2012). Discipline. In J. R. Levesque (Ed.), *Encyclopedia of adolescence.* New York: Springer.

Garber, J., & Cole, D. A. (2010). Intergenerational transmission of depression: A launch and grow model of change across adolescence. *Development and Psychopathology, 22,* 819–830.

Gardner, H. (1983). *Frames of mind.* New York: Basic Books.

Gardner, H. (1993). *Multiple intelligences.* New York: Basic Books.

Gardner, H. (2002). The pursuit of excellence through education. In M. Ferrari (Ed.), *Learning from extraordinary minds.* Mahwah, NJ: Erlbaum.

Gardner, H. (2012). Foreword. In D. Ambrose, R. Sternberg, & B. Sriraman (Eds.), *Confronting dogmatism in gifted education.* New York; Routledge.

Gardner, M., Roth, J., & Brooks-Gunn, J. (2008). Adolescents' participation in organized activities and developmental success 2 and 8 years after high school: Do sponsorship, duration, and intensity matter? *Developmental Psychology, 44,* 814–830.

Gardner, M., & Steinberg, L. (2005). Peer influence on risk taking, risk preference, and risky decision making in adolescence and adulthood: An experimental study. *Developmental Psychology, 41,* 625–635.

Garofalo, R., Wolf, R. C., Wissow, L. S., Woods, E. R., & Goodman, E. (1999). Sexual orientation and risk of suicide attempts among a representative sample of youth. *Archives of Pediatrics and Adolescent Medicine, 153,* 487–493.

Garrod, A., Smulyan, L., Powers, S. I., & Kilenny, R. (1992). *Adolescent portraits.* Boston: Allyn & Bacon.

Gates, W. (1998, July 20). Charity begins when I'm ready (interview). *Fortune magazine.*

Gaudineau, A., Ehlinger, V., Vayssiere, C., Jouret, B., Arnaud, C., & Godeau, E. (2010). Factors associated with early menarche: Results from the French Health Behavior in School-Aged Children (HBSC) Study. *BMC Public Health, 10,* 175.

Gaudreau, P., Amiot, C. E., & Vallerand, R. J. (2009). Trajectories of affective states in adolescent hockey players: Turning point and motivational antecedents. *Developmental Psychology, 45,* 307–319.

Gault-Sherman, M. (2011, in press). It's a two-way street: The bidirectional relationship between parenting and delinquency. *Journal of Youth and Adolescence.*

Gauthier, A. H., & Furstenberg, F. F. (2005). Historical trends in the patterns of time use among young adults in developed countries. In R. A. Setterson, F. F. Furstenberg, & R. G. Rumbaut (Eds.), *On the frontier of adulthood: Theories, research, and social policy.* Chicago: University of Chicago Press.

Gauvain, M. (2008). Vygotsky's sociocultural theory. In M. M. Haith & J. B. Benson (Eds.), *Encyclopedia of infant and early childhood development.* Oxford, UK: Elsevier.

Gauvain, M. (2011). Applying the cultural approach to cognitive development. *Journal of Cognition and Development, 12,* 121–133.

Gauvain, M., & Parke, R. D. (2010). Socialization. In M. H. Bornstein (Ed.), *Handbook of cultural developmental science.* New York: Psychology Press.

Gauvain, M., & Perez, S. M. (2007). The socialization of cognition. In J. E. Grusec & P. D. Hastings (Eds.), *Handbook of socialization.* New York: Guilford.

Gavin, L. E., Catalano, R. F., David-Ferdon, C., Gloppen, K. M., & Markham, C. M. (2010). A review of positive youth development programs that promote adolescent sexual and reproductive health. *Journal of Adolescent Health, 46*(Suppl 1), S75–S91.

Geary, D. C. (2010). *Male, female: The evolution of sex differences.* Washington, DC: American Psychological Association.

Gecas, V., & Seff, M. (1990). Families and adolescents: A review of the 1980s. *Journal of Marriage and the Family, 52,* 941–958.

Gentile, D. A. (2011). The multiple dimensions of video game effects. *Child Development Perspectives, 5,* 75–81.

Gentile, D. A., Mathieson, L. C., & Crick, N. R. (2010, in press). Media violence associations with the form and function of aggression among elementary school children. *Social Development.*

Gentile, D. A., & others. (2009). The effects of prosocial video games on prosocial behaviors: International evidence from correlational, longitudinal, and experimental studies. *Personality and Social Psychology Bulletin, 35,* 752–763.

George, C., Main, M., & Kaplan, N. (1984). *Attachment interview with adults.* Unpublished manuscript, University of California, Berkeley.

Gerrard, M., Gibbons, F. X., Houlihan, A. E., Stock, M. L., & Pomery, E. A. (2008). A dual-process approach to health risk decision-making: The prototype willingness model. *Developmental Review, 28,* 29–61.

Gestsdottir, S., Lewin-Bizan, S., von Eye, A., Lerner, J. V., & Lerner, R. M. (2009). The structure and function of selection, optimization, and compensation in adolescence: Theoretical and applied implications. *Journal of Applied Developmental Psychology, 30*(5), 585–600.

Ghazarian, S. R., & Roche, K. M. (2010). Social support and low-income, urban mothers: Longitudinal associations with delinquency. *Journal of Youth and Adolescence, 39,* 1097–1108.

Gibbons, J. L. (2000). Gender development in cross-cultural perspective. In T. Eckes & H. M. Trautner (Eds.), *The developmental social psychology of gender.* Mahwah, NJ: Erlbaum.

Gibbons, R. D., Hedeker, D., & DuToit, S. (2010). Advances in analysis of longitudinal data. *Annual Review of Clinical Psychology* (Vol. 6). Palo Alto, CA: Annual Reviews.

Gibbs, J. C. (2010). *Moral development and reality: Beyond the theories of Kohlberg and Hoffman* (2nd ed.). Boston: Allyn & Bacon.

Gibbs, J. C., Basinger, K. S., Grime, R. L., & Snarey, J. R. (2007). Moral judgment across cultures: Revisiting Kohlberg's universality claims. *Developmental Review, 27,* 443–500.

Gibbs, J. T. (1989). Black American adolescents. In J. T. Gibbs & L. N. Huang (Eds.), *Children of color.* San Francisco: Jossey-Bass.

Gibbs, J. T., & Huang, L. N. (1989). A conceptual framework for assessing and treating minority youth. In J. T. Gibbs & L. N. Huang (Eds.), *Children of color.* San Francisco: Jossey-Bass.

Giedd, J. N. (2007, September 27). Commentary in S. Jayson "Teens driven to distraction." *USA Today,* pp. D1–D2.

Giedd, J. N. (2008). The teen brain: Insights from neuroimaging. *Journal of Adolescent Health, 42,* 335–343.

Gilligan, C. (1982). *In a different voice.* Cambridge, MA: Harvard University Press.

Gilligan, C. (1992, May). *Joining the resistance: Girls' development in adolescence.* Paper presented at the symposium on development and vulnerability in close relationships, Montreal.

Gilligan, C. (1996). The centrality of relationships in psychological development: A puzzle, some evidence, and a theory. In G. G. Noam & K. W. Fischer (Eds.), *Development and vulnerability in close relationships.* Hillside, NJ: Erlbaum.

Gilligan, C., Brown, L. M., & Rogers, A. G. (1990). Psyche embedded: A place for body, relationships, and culture in personality theory. In A. I. Rabin, R. A. Zuker, R. A. Emmons, & S. Frank (Eds.), *Studying persons and lives.* New York: Springer.

Gilligan, C., Spencer, R., Weinberg, M. K., & Bertsch, T. (2003). On the listening guide: A voice-centered relational model. In P. M. Carnie & J. E. Rhodes (Eds.), *Qualitative research in psychology.* Washington, DC: American Psychological Association.

Gillig, P. M., & Sanders, R. D. (2011). Higher cortical functions: Attention and vigilance. *Innovations in Clinical Neuroscience, 8,* 43–46.

Gilmartin, S. K. (2006). Changes in college women's attitudes toward sexual intimacy. *Journal of Research on Adolescence, 16,* 429–454.

Gil-Olarte Marquez, P., Palomera Martin, R., & Brackett, M. (2006). Relating emotional intelligence to social competence and academic achievement in high school students. *Psicothema, 18,* 118–123.

Ginorio, A. B., & Huston, M. (2001). *Si! Se Puede! Yes, we can: Latinas in school.* Washington, DC: AAUW.

Girls, Inc. (1991). *Truth, trusting, and technology: New research on preventing adolescent pregnancy.* Indianapolis, IN: Author.

Gladstone, T. R., Beardslee, W. R., & O'Connor, E. E. (2011). The prevention of adolescent depression. *Psychiatric Clinics of North America, 34,* 35–52.

Glasper, E. R., Schoenfeld, T. J., & Gould, E. (2011, in press). Adult neurogenesis: Optimizing hippocampal function to suit the environment. *Behavioral Brain Research.*

Glenn, N. D. (2005). *Fatherhood in America.* Report to the National Fatherhood Initiative, Washington, DC.

Glidden-Tracey, C. (2005). *Counseling and therapy with clients who abuse alcohol or other drugs.* Mahwah, NJ: Erlbaum.

Glover, M. B., Mullineaux, P. Y., Deater-Deckard, K., & Petrill, S. A. (2010). Parents' feelings toward their adoptive and non-adoptive children. *Infant and Child Development, 19*(3), 238–251.

Gogtay, N., & Thompson, P. M. (2010). Mapping grey matter development: Implications for typical development and vulnerability to psychopathology. *Brain and Cognition, 72,* 6–15.

Goji, K., & others. (2009). Gonadotropin-independent precocious puberty associated with somatic activation mutation of the LH receptor gene. *Endocrine, 35,* 397–401.

Goldberg, W. A., & Lucas-Thompson, R. (2008). Maternal and paternal employment, effects of. In M. M. Haith & J. B. Benson (Eds.), *Encyclopedia of infant and early childhood development.* Oxford, UK: Elsevier.

Gold, M. A., & others. (2010). Associations between religiosity and sexual and contraceptive behaviors. *Journal of Pediatric and Adolescent Gynecology, 23,* 290–297.

Goldston, D. B., & others. (2008). Cultural considerations in adolescent suicide prevention and psychosocial treatment. *American Psychologist, 63,* 14–31.

Goleman, D. (1995). *Emotional intelligence.* New York: Basic Books.

Golombok, S. (2011a, in press). Why I study lesbian families. In S. Ellis, V. Clarke, E. Peel, & D. Riggs (Eds.), *LGBTQ Psychologies.* New York: Cambridge University Press.

Golombok, S. (2011b, in press). Children in new family forms. In R. Gross (Ed.), *Psychology* (6th ed.). London: Hodder Education.

Golombok, S., & Tasker, F. (2010). Gay fathers. In M. E. Lamb (Ed.), *The role of the father in child development* (5th ed.). New York: Wiley.

Gonzales, N. A., Deardorff, J., Formoso, D., Barr, A., & Barrera, M. (2006). Family mediators of the relation between acculturation and adolescent mental health. *Family Relations, 55,* 318–330.

Gonzales, N. A., Dumka, L. E., Muaricio, A. M., & German, M. (2007). Building bridges: Strategies to promote academic and psychological resilience for adolescents of Mexican origin. In J. E. Lansford, K. Deater Deckhard, & M. H. Bornstein (Eds.), *Immigrant families in contemporary society.* New York: Guilford.

Goodenough, J., & McGuire, B. A. (2012). *Biology of humans* (4th ed.). Upper Saddle River, NJ: Pearson.

Goodman, W. B., & others. (2011). Parental work stress and latent profiles of father-infant parenting quality. *Journal of Marriage and the Family, 73,* 588–604.

Good, M., & Willoughby, T. (2008). Adolescence as a sensitive period for spiritual development. *Child Development Perspectives, 2,* 32–37.

Good, M., & Willoughby, T. (2010). Evaluating the direction of effects in the relationship between religious versus non-religious activities, academic success, and substance use. *Journal of Youth and Adolescence, 40,* 680–693.

Goodnow, C., Szalacha, L. A., Robin, L. E., & Westheimer, K. (2008). Dimensions of sexual orientation and HIV-related risk among adolescent females: Evidence from a statewide survey. *American Journal of Public Health, 98,* 1051–1058.

Goodwin, P. Y., Mosher, W. D., & Chandra, A. (2010). Marriage and cohabitation in the United States: A statistical portrait based on cycle 6 (2002) of the National Survey of Family Growth. *Vital Health Statistics, 23,* 1–45.

Goossens, L. (2006, March). *Parenting, identity, and adjustment in adolescence.* Paper presented at the meeting of the Society for Research on Adolescence, San Francisco.

Goossens, L., Beyers, W., Emmen, M., & van Aken, M. A. G. (2002). The imaginary audience and personal fable. Factor analyses and concurrent validity of the "new look" measures. *Journal of Research on Adolescence, 12,* 193–215.

Goossens, L., & Luyckx, K. (2007). Identity development in college students: Variable-centered and person-centered analysis. In M. Watzlawik & A. Born (Eds.), *Capturing identity.* Lanham, MD: University of America Press.

Gottfried, A. E., Marcoulides, G. A., Gottfried, A. W., & Oliver, P. H. (2009). A latent curve model of motivational practices and developmental decline in math and science academic intrinsic motivation. *Journal of Educational Psychology, 101,* 729–739.

Gottlieb, G. (2007). Probabilistic epigenesis. *Developmental Science, 10,* 1–11.

Gottlieb, G., Wahlsten, D., & Lickliter, R. (2006). The significance of biology for human development: A developmental psychobiological systems view. In W. Damon & R. Lerner (Eds.), *Handbook of child psychology* (6th ed.). New York: Wiley.

Gottman, J. M., & Parker, J. G. (Eds.). (1987). *Conversations of friends.* New York: Cambridge University Press.

Gould, S. J. (1981). *The mismeasure of man.* New York: W. W. Norton.

Gove, W. R., Style, C. B., & Hughes, M. (1990). The effect of marriage on the well-being of adults: A theoretical analysis. *Journal of Health and Social Behavior, 24,* 122–131.

Govia, I. O., Jackson, J. S., & Sellers, S. L. (2011). Social inequalities. In K. L. Fingerman, C. A. Berg, J. Smith, & T. C. Antonucci (Eds.), *Handbook of life-span development.* New York: Springer.

Grabe, S., & Hyde, J. S. (2009). Body objectification, MTV, and psychological outcomes among female adolescents. *Journal of Applied Social Psychology, 39,* 2840–2858.

Graber, J. A., Brooks-Gunn, J., & Warren, M. P. (2006). Pubertal effects on adjustment in girls: Moving from demonstrating effects to identifying pathways. *Journal of Youth and Adolescence, 35,* 391–401.

Graber, J. A., Nichols, T. R., & Brooks-Gunn, J. (2010). Putting pubertal timing in developmental context: Implications for prevention. *Developmental Psychobiology, 52,* 254–262.

Graber, J. A., & Sontag, L. M. (2009). Internalizing problems during adolescence. In R. M. Lerner & L. Steinberg (Eds.), *Handbook of adolescent psychology* (3rd ed.). New York: Wiley.

Gradisar, M., Gardner, G., & Dohnt, H. (2011). Recent worldwide sleep patterns and problems during adolescence: A review and meta-analysis of age, region, and sleep. *Sleep Medicine, 12,* 110–118.

Graham, E. A. (2005). Economic, racial, and cultural influences on the growth and maturation of children. *Pediatrics in Review, 26,* 290–294.

Graham, J. H., & Beller, A. H. (2002). Non-resident fathers and their children: Child support and visitation from an economic perspective. In C. S. Tamis-LeMonda & N. Cabrera (Eds.), *The handbook of father involvement.* Mahwah, NJ: Erlbaum.

Graham, S. (1986, August). *Can attribution theory tell us something about motivation in blacks?* Paper presented at the meeting of the American Psychological Association, Washington, DC.

Graham, S. (1990). Motivation in Afro-Americans. In G. L. Berry & J. K. Asamen (Eds.), *Black students: Psychosocial issues and academic achievement.* Newbury Park, CA: Sage.

Graham, S. (1995, February 16). Commentary in *USA TODAY,* p. D2.

Graham, S. (2005, February 16). Commentary in *USA Today,* p. 2D.

Graham, S. (2011). School racial/ethnic diversity and disparities in mental health and academic outcomes. *Nebraska Symposium on Motivation, 57,* 73–96.

Graham, S., & Perin, D. (2007). A meta-analysis of writing instruction for adolescent students. *Journal of Educational Psychology, 99,* 445–476.

Graham, S., & Taylor, A. Z. (2001). Ethnicity, gender, and the development of achievement values. In A. Wigfield & J. S. Eccles (Eds.), *Development of achievement motivation.* San Diego: Academic Press.

Granqvist, P., & Dickie, J. R. (2006). Attachment and spiritual development in childhood and adolescence. In E. C. Roehlkepartain, P. E. King, & L. M. Wegener (Eds.), *The handbook of spiritual development in childhood and adolescence.* Thousand Oaks, CA: Sage.

Grant, A. M., & Gino, F. (2010). A little thanks goes a long way: Explaining why gratitude expressions motivate prosocial behavior. *Journal of Personality and Social Psychology, 98,* 946–955.

Grant, C. A., & Sleeter, C. E. (2011). *Doing multicultural education for achievement and equity.* New York: Routledge.

Grant, K. E., & others. (2006). Stressors and adolescent psychopathology: Evidence of moderating and mediating effects. *Clinical Psychology Review, 26,* 257–283.

Graves, K. N., Sentner, A., Workman, J., & Mackey, W. (2011). Building positive life skills the Smart Girls Way: Evaluation of a school-based sexual responsibility program for adolescent girls. *Health Promotion Practice, 12,* 463–471.

Gravetter, R. J., & Forzano, L. B. (2012). *Research methods for the behavioral sciences* (4th ed.). Boston: Cengage.

Gray, J. (1992). *Men are from Mars, women are from Venus.* New York: HarperCollins.

Greenberger, E., & Chu, C. (1996). Perceived family relationships and depressed mood in early adolescence: A comparison of European and Asian Americans. *Developmental Psychology, 32,* 707–716.

Greenberger, E., & Steinberg, L. (1986). *When teenagers work: The psychological social costs of adolescent employment.* New York: Basic Books.

Greenberg, J. S. (2011). *Comprehensive stress management* (12th ed.). New York: McGraw-Hill.

Greenberg, M. T., & others. (2003). Enhancing school-based prevention and youth development through coordinated social, emotional, and academic learning. *American Psychologist, 58,* 466–474.

Greene, B. (1988, May). The children's hour. *Esquire,* 47–49.

Greenwood, P. (2008). Prevention and intervention programs for juvenile offenders. *The Future of Children, 18*(2), 185–210.

Gregory, A. M., Ball, H. A., & Button, T. M. M. (2011). Behavioral genetics. In P. K. Smith & C. H. Hart (Eds.), *Wiley-Blackwell handbook of childhood social development* (2nd ed.). New York: Wiley.

Grigorenko, E. (2000). Heritability and intelligence. In R. J. Sternberg (Ed.), *Handbook of intelligence.* New York: Cambridge University Press.

Grigorenko, E. L., & Takanishi, R. (Eds.). (2010). *Immigration, diversity, and education.* New York: Routledge.

Gross, J. J., Fredrickson, B. L., & Levenson, R. W. (1994). The psychophysiology of crying. *Psychophysiology, 31,* 460–468.

Grusec, J. E. (2006). Development of moral behavior and a conscience from a socialization perspective. In M. Killen & J. G. Smetana (Eds.), *Handbook of moral development.* Mahwah, NJ: Erlbaum.

Grusec, J. E. (2011). Socialization processes in the family: Social and emotional development. *Annual Review of Psychology* (Vol. 62). Palo Alto, CA: Annual Reviews.

Grusec, J. E., Hastings, P., & Almas, A. (2011). Prosocial behavior. In P. K. Smith & C. H. Hart (Eds.), *Wiley-Blackwell handbook of childhood social development* (2nd ed.). New York: Wiley.

Grusec, J. E., & Sherman, A. (2011). Prosocial behavior. In M. K. Underwood & L. Rosen (Eds.), *Social development.* New York: Guilford.

Grych, J. H. (2002). Marital relationships and parenting. In M. H. Bornstein (Ed.), *Handbook of parenting.* Mahwah, NJ: Erlbaum.

Guerin, D. W., Gottfried, A. W., Oliver, P. H., & Thomas, C. W. (2003). *Temperament: Infancy through adolescence.* New York: Kluwer.

Guerra, N. G., & Williams, K. R. (2010). Implementing bullying prevention in diverse settings: Geographic, economic, and cultural influences. In E. M. Vernberg & B. K. Biggs (Eds.), *Preventing and treating bullying and victimization.* New York: Oxford University Press.

Guerra, N. G., Williams, K. R., & Sadek, S. (2011). Understanding bullying and victimization during childhood and adolescence: A mixed methods study. *Child Development, 82,* 295–310.

Guilamo-Ramos, V., Jaccard, J., Dittus, P., & Collins, S. (2008). Parent-adolescent communication about sexual intercourse: An analysis of maternal reluctance to communicate. *Health Psychology, 27,* 760–769.

Guilford, J. P. (1967). *The structure of intellect.* New York: McGraw-Hill.

Gumora, G., & Arsenio, W. (2002). Emotionality, emotion regulation, and school performance in middle school children. *Journal of School Psychology, 40,* 395–413.

Gunderson, E. A., Ramirez, G., Levine, S. C., & Beilock, S. L. (2011, in press). The role of parents and teachers in the development of math attitudes. *Sex Roles.*

Gutman, L. M., Eccles, J. S., Peck, S., & Malanchuk, O. (2011, in press). The influence of early family relations on trajectories of cigarette and alcohol use from early to late adolescence. *Journal of Adolescence.*

Guttentag, M., & Bray, H. (1976). *Undoing sex stereotypes: Research and resources for educators.* New York: McGraw-Hill.

Guttmannova, K., & others. (2011). Sensitive periods for adolescent alcohol use initiation: Predicting the lifetime occurrence and chronicity of alcohol problems in adulthood. *Journal of Studies on Alcohol and Drugs, 72,* 221–231.

H

Hahn, D. B., Payne, W. A., & Lucas, E. B. (2011). *Focus on health* (10th ed.). New York: McGraw-Hill.

Hale, S. (1990). A global developmental trend in cognitive processing speed. *Child Development, 61,* 653–663.

Haley, C. C., Hedberg, K., & Leman, R. F. (2010). Disordered eating and unhealthy weight loss practices: Which adolescents are at highest risk? *Journal of Adolescent Health, 47,* 102–105.

Halford, G. S., & Andrews, G. (2011). Information-processing models of cognitive development. In U. Goswami (Ed.), *Wiley-Blackwell handbook of childhood cognitive development* (2nd ed.). New York: Wiley.

Hallahan, D. P., Kauffman, J. M., & Pullen, P. C. (2012). *Exceptional learners* (12th ed.). Boston: Allyn & Bacon.

Hall, G. N. (2010). *Multicultural psychology* (2nd ed.). Upper Saddle River, NJ: Prentice Hall.

Hall, G. S. (1904). *Adolescence* (Vols. 1 & 2). Englewood Cliffs, NJ: Prentice Hall.

Halmi, K. A. (2009). Anorexia nervosa: An increasing problem in children and adolescents. *Dialogues in Clinical Neuroscience, 11,* 100–103.

Halonen, J. A., & Santrock, J. W. (1999). *Psychology: Contexts and applications* (3rd ed.). New York: McGraw-Hill.

Halonen, J. A., & Santrock, J. W. (2012, in press). *Your guide to college success* (7th ed.). Boston: Cengage.

Halpern, C. T. (2011). Same-sex attraction and health disparities: Do sexual minority youth really need something different for healthy development? *Journal of Adolescent Health, 48,* 5–6.

Halpern, D. F. (2006). Girls and academic success: Changing patterns of academic achievement. In J. Worell & C. D. Goodheart (Eds.), *Handbook of girls' and women's psychological health.* New York: Oxford University Press.

Halpern, D. F., Benbow, C. P., Geary, D. C., Gur, R. C., & Hyde, J. S. (2007). The science of sex differences in science and mathematics. *Psychological Science in the Public Interest, 8,* 1–51.

Halpern, D. F., Straight, C. A., & Stephenson, C. L. (2011). Beliefs about cognitive gender differences: Accurate for direction, underestimated for size. *Sex Roles, 64,* 336–347.

Halpern-Felsher, B. (2008). Editorial. Oral sexual behavior: Harm reduction or gateway behavior? *Journal of Adolescent Health, 43,* 207–208.

Hamilton, B. E., Martin, J. A., & Ventura, S. J. (2010, April 6). Births: Preliminary data for 2008. *National Vital Statistics Reports, 58*(16), 1–17.

Hamilton, S. F., & Hamilton, M. A. (2006). School, work, and emerging adulthood. In J. J. Arnett & J. L. Tanner (Eds.), *Emerging adults in America*. Washington, DC: American Psychological Associaton.

Hamilton, S. F., & Hamilton, M. A. (2009). The transition to adulthood: Challenges of poverty and structural lag. In R. M. Lerner & L. Steinberg (Eds.), *Handbook of adolescent psychology* (3rd ed.). New York: Wiley.

Hampton, J. (2008). Abstinence-only programs under fire. *Journal of the American Medical Association, 17,* 2013–2015.

Hamza, C. A., & Willoughby, T. (2011). Perceived parental monitoring, adolescent disclosure, and adolescent depressive symptoms: A longitudinal examination. *Journal of Youth and Adolescence, 40,* 902–915.

Han, J. S., Rogers, M. E., Nurani, S., Rubin, S., & Blank, S. (2011, in press). Patterns of chlamydia/gonorrhea positivity among voluntarily screened New York City public high school students. *Journal of Adolescent Health.*

Hannish, L. D., & Guerra, N. G. (2004). Aggressive victims, passive victims, and bullies: Developmental continuity or developmental change? *Merrill-Palmer Quarterly, 50,* 17–38.

Han, W-J. (2009). Maternal employment. In D. Carr (Ed.), *Encyclopedia of the life course and human development.* Boston: Gale Cengage.

Harakeh, Z., Scholte, R. H. J., Vermulst, A. A., de Vries, H., & Engels, R. C. (2010). The relations between parents' smoking, general parenting, parental smoking communication, and adolescents' smoking. *Journal of Research on Adolescence, 20,* 140–165.

Harden, K. P., & Mendle, J. (2011, in press). Adolescent sexual activity and the development of delinquent behavior: The role of relationship context. *Journal of Youth and Adolescence.*

Hardy, S. A., Bhattacharjee, A., Reed, A., & Aquino, K. (2010). Moral identity and psychological distance: The case of adolescent socialization. *Journal of Adolescence, 33,* 111–123.

Hargreaves, D. A., & Tiggemann, M. (2004). Idealized body images and adolescent body image: "Comparing" boys and girls. *Body Image, 1,* 351–361.

Harmon, O. R., Lambrinos, J., & Kennedy, P. (2008). Are online exams an invitation to cheat? *Journal of Economic Education, 39,* 116–125.

Harold, R. D., Colarossi, L. G., & Mercier, L. R. (2007). *Smooth sailing or stormy waters: Family transitions through adolescence and their implications for practice and policy.* Mahwah, NJ: Erlbaum.

Harrison-Hale, A. O., McLoyd, V. C., & Smedley, B. (2004). Racial and ethnic status: Risk and protective processes among African-American families. In K. L. Maton, C. J. Schellenbach, B. J. Leadbetter, & A. L. Solarz (Eds.), *Investing in children, families, and communities.* Washington, DC: American Psychological Association.

Harris, Y. R., & Graham, J. A. (2007). *The African American child.* New York: Springer.

Hart, C. L., Ksir, C. J., & Ray, O. S. (2011). *Drugs, society, and behavior* (14th ed.). New York: McGraw-Hill.

Hart, C. N., Cairns, A., & Jelalian, E. (2011). Sleep and sleep quality in children and adolescents. *Pediatric Clinics of North America, 58,* 715–733.

Hart, D., Matsuba, M. K., & Atkins, R. (2008). The moral and civic effects of learning to serve. In L. Nucci & D. Narváez (Eds.), *Handbook of moral and character education.* Clifton, NJ: Psychology Press.

Harter, S. (1986). Processes underlying the construction, maintenance, and enhancement of the self-concept of children. In J. Suls & A. Greenwald (Eds.), *Psychological perspective on the self* (Vol. 3). Hillsdale, NJ: Erlbaum.

Harter, S. (1989). *Self-perception profile for adolescents.* Denver: University of Denver, Department of Psychology.

Harter, S. (1990a). Self and identity development. In S. S. Feldman & G. R. Elliott (Eds.), *At the threshold: The developing adolescent,* Cambridge, MA: Harvard University Press.

Harter, S. (1990b). Processes underlying adolescent self-concept formation. In R. Montemayor, G. R. Adams, & T. P. Gullotta (Eds.), *From childhood to adolescence: A transitional period?* Newbury Park, CA: Sage.

Harter, S. (1998). The development of self-representations. In W. Damon (Ed.), *Handbook of child psychology* (5th ed., Vol. 3). New York: Wiley.

Harter, S. (1999). *The construction of the self.* New York: Guilford.

Harter, S. (2006). The development of self-representations in childhood and adolescence. In W. Damon & R. Lerner (Eds.), *Handbook of child psychology* (6th ed.). New York: Wiley.

Harter, S., & Lee, L. (1989). *Manifestations of true and false selves in adolescence.* Paper presented at the meeting of the Society for Research in Child Development, Kansas City.

Harter, S., & Monsour, A. (1992). Developmental analysis of conflict caused by opposing attributes in the adolescent self-portrait. *Developmental Psychology, 28,* 251–260.

Harter, S., Stocker, C., & Robinson, N. S. (1996). The perceived directionality of the link between approval and self-worth: The liabilities of a looking glass self orientation among young adolescents. *Journal of Research on Adolescence, 6,* 285–308.

Harter, S., Waters, P., & Whitesell, N. (1996, March). *False self behavior and lack of voice among adolescent males and females.* Paper presented at the meeting of the Society for Research on Adolescence, Boston.

Hartshorne, H., & May, M. S. (1928–1930). *Moral studies in the nature of character: Studies in deceit* (Vol. 1); *Studies in self-control* (Vol. 2); *Studies in the organization of character* (Vol. 3). New York: Macmillan.

Hartup, W. W. (1983). The peer system. In P. H. Mussen (Ed.), *Handbook of child psychology* (4th ed., Vol. 4). New York: Wiley.

Hartup, W. W. (1996). The company they keep: Friendships and their developmental significance. *Child Development, 67,* 1–13.

Hartup, W. W. (2005). Peer interaction: What causes what? *Journal of Abnormal Child Psychology, 33,* 387–394.

Hartwell, L. (2011). *Genetics* (4th ed.). New York: McGraw-Hill.

Harwood, R., Leyendecker, B., Carlson, V., Asencio, M., & Miller, A. (2002). Parenting among Latino families in the U.S. In M. H. Bornstein (Ed.), *Handbook of parenting* (2nd ed.). Mahwah, NJ: Erlbaum.

Hastings, P. D., Utendale, W. T., & Sullivan, C. (2007). The socialization of prosocial development. In J. E. Grusec & P. D. Hastings (Eds.), *Handbook of socialization.* New York: Guilford.

Hatton, H., Donnellan, M. B., Maysn, K., Feldman, B. J., Larsen-Rife, D., & Conger, R. D. (2008). Family and individual difference predictors of trait aspects of negative interpersonal behaviors during emerging adulthood. *Journal of Family Psychology, 22,* 448–455.

Hawkins, J. A., & Berndt, T. J. (1985, April). *Adjustment following the transition to junior high school.* Paper presented at the biennial meeting of the Society for Research in Child Development, Toronto.

Hawley, P. H. (2011). The evolution of adolescence and the adolescence of evolution: The coming of age of humans and the theory about the forces that made them. *Journal of Research on Adolescence, 21,* 307–316.

Hayashino, D., & Chopra, S. B. (2009). Parenting and raising families. In N. Tewari & A. Alvarez (Eds.), *Asian American psychology.* Clifton, NJ: Psychology Press.

Haydon, A., & Halpern, G. T. (2010). Older romantic partners and depressive symptoms during adolescence. *Journal of Youth and Adolescence, 39,* 1240–1251.

Hazan, C., & Shaver, P. R. (1987). Romantic love conceptualized as an attachment process. *Journal of Personality and Social Psychology, 52,* 522–524.

Heath, S. B. (1999). Dimensions of language development: Lessons from older children. In A. S. Masten (Ed.), *Cultural processes in child development: The Minnesota symposium on child psychology* (Vol. 29). Mahwah, NJ: Erlbaum.

Heath, S. B., & McLaughlin, M. W. (Eds.). (1993). *Identity and inner-city youth: Beyond ethnicity and gender.* New York: Teachers College Press.

Hebebrand, J., & Bulik, C. M. (2011, in press). Critical appraisal of provisional DSM-5 criteria for anorexia nervosa and an alternative proposal. *International Journal of Eating Disorders.*

Heiman, G. W. (2012). *Basic statistics for the behavioral sciences* (6th ed.). Boston: Cengage.

Heitzler, C. D., Martin, S., Duke, J., & Huhman, M. (2006). Correlates of physical activity in a national sample of children aged 9–13 years. *Preventive Medicine, 42,* 254–260.

Helwig, C. C., & Turiel, E. (2011). Children's social and moral reasoning. In P. K. Smith & C. H. Hart (Eds.), *Wiley-Blackwell handbook of childhood social development* (2nd ed.). New York: Wiley.

Hemphill, S. A., & others. (2010). Pubertal stage and the prevalence of violence and social/relational aggression. *Pediatrics, 126,* e298–e305.

Henderson, V. L., & Dweck, C. S. (1990). Motivation and achievement. In S. S. Feldman & G. R. Elliott (Eds.), *At the threshold: The developing adolescent.* Cambridge, MA: Harvard University Press.

Hendriks, A. A., Kuyper, H., Offringa, G. J., & Van der Werf, M. P. (2008). Assessing young adolescents' personality with the Five-Factor Personality Inventory. *Assessment, 15,* 304–316.

Hendry, J. (1999). *Social anthropology.* New York: Macmillan.

Hennesey, B. A. (2011). Intrinsic motivation and creativity: Have we come full circle? In R. A Beghetto & J. C. Kaufman (Eds.), *Nurturing creativity in the classroom.* New York: Cambridge University Press.

Hennessy, M., Bleakley, A., Fishbein, M., & Jordan, A. (2009). Estimating the longitudinal association between adolescent sexual behavior and exposure to sexual media content. *Journal of Sexual Research, 46,* 586–596.

Henretta, J. C. (2010). Lifetime marital history and mortality after age 50. *Journal of Aging and Health, 22,* 1198–1212.

Henry, K. L., Stanley, L. R., Edwards, R. W., Harkabus, L. C., & Chapin, L. A. (2009). Individual and contextual effects of school adjustment on adolescent alcohol use. *Prevention Science, 10,* 236–247.

Heppner, M. J., & Heppner, P. P. (2003). Identifying process variables in career counseling: A research agenda. *Journal of Vocational Behavior, 62,* 429–452.

Heppner, P., & Lee, D. (2001). Problem-solving appraisal and psychological adjustment. In C. R. Snyder & S. J. Lopez (Eds.), *Handbook of positive psychology.* New York: Oxford University Press.

Herman-Giddens, M. E. (2007). The decline in the age of menarche in the United States: Should we be concerned? *Journal of Adolescent Health, 40,* 201–203.

Herman-Giddens, M. E., Kaplowitz, P. B., & Wasserman, R. (2004). Navigating the recent articles on girls' puberty in *Pediatrics:* What do we know and where do we go from here? *Pediatrics, 113,* 911–917.

Hernandez, B. C., Vigna, J. F., & Kelley, M. L. (2010). The Youth Coping Responses Inventory: Developmental and initial validation. *Journal of Clinical Psychology, 66,* 1008–1025.

Herrera, C., Grossman, J. B., Kauh, T. J., Feldman, A. F., & McMaken, J. (2007). *Making a difference in schools: The Big Brothers Big Sisters school-based mentoring impact study.* Philadelphia, PA: Public/Private Ventures.

Herrera, C., Grossman, J. B., Kauh, T. J., & McMaken, J. (2011). Mentoring in schools: An impact study of Big Brothers Big Sisters school-based mentoring. *Child Development, 82,* 346–361.

Hershenberg, R., & others. (2011, in press). What I like about you: The association between attachment security and emotional behavior in a relationship promoting context. *Journal of Adolescence.*

Hertenstein, M. J., & Keltner, D. (2011). Gender and the communication of emotion via touch. *Sex Roles, 64,* 70–80.

Hess, L., Lonky, E., & Roodin, P. A. (1985, April). *The relationship of moral reasoning and ego strength to cheating behavior.* Paper presented at the meeting of the Society for Research in Child Development, Toronto.

Hetherington, E. M. (1972). Effects of father-absence on personality development in adolescent daughters. *Developmental Psychology, 7,* 313–326.

Hetherington, E. M. (1977). *My heart belongs to daddy: A study of the remarriages of daughters of divorcees and widows.* Unpublished manuscript, University of Virginia.

Hetherington, E. M. (1989). Coping with family transitions: Winners, losers, and survivors. *Child Development, 60,* 1–14.

Hetherington, E. M. (2005). Divorce and the adjustment of children. *Pediatrics in Review, 26,* 163–169.

Hetherington, E. M. (2006). The influence of conflict, marital problem solving, and parenting on children's adjustment in nondivorced, divorced, and remarried families. In A. Clarke-Stewart & J. Dunn (Eds.), *Families count.* New York: Cambridge University Press.

Hetherington, E. M., & Clingempeel, W. G. (1992). Coping with marital transitions: A family systems perspective. *Monographs of the Society for Research in Child Development, 57*(2–3, Serial No. 227).

Hetherington, E. M., Cox, M., & Cox, R. (1982). Effects of divorce on parents and children. In M. E. Lamb (Ed.), *Nontraditional families: Parenting and child development.* Hillsdale, NJ: Erlbaum.

Hetherington, E. M., & Kelly, J. (2002). *For better or for worse: Divorce reconsidered.* New York: Norton.

Hetherington, E. M., & others. (1999). Adolescent siblings in stepfamilies: Family functioning and adolescent adjustment. *Monographs of the Society for Research in Child Development, 64,* No. 4.

Hetherington, E. M., & Stanley-Hagan, M. (2002). Parenting in divorced and remarried families. In M. Bornstein (Ed.), *Handbook of parenting* (2nd ed.). Mahwah, NJ: Erlbaum.

Hewlett, B. S., & Macfarlan, S. J. (2010). Fathers' roles in hunter-gatherer and other small-scale cultures. In M. E. Lamb (Ed.), *The role of the father in child development* (5th ed.). New York: Wiley.

Hibell, B., & others. (2004). *The ESPAD report 2003.* The Swedish Council for Information on Alcohol and Other Drugs (CAN) and Council of Europe Pompidou Group. Stockholm, Sweden: CAN.

Hill, J. P., & Lynch, M. E. (1983). The intensification of gender-related role expectations during early adolescence. In J. Brooks-Gunn & A. C. Petersen (Eds.), *Girls at puberty: Biological and psychosocial perspectives.* New York: Plenum.

Hill, N. E., & Witherspoon, D. P. (2011). Race, ethnicity, and social class. In M. K. Underwood & L. H. Rosen (Eds.), *Social development.* New York: Guilford.

Hill, P. L., Duggan, P. M., & Lapsley, D. K. (2011, in press). Subjective invulnerability, risk behavior, and adjustment in early adolescence. *Journal of Early Adolescence.*

Hill, P. L., & Lapsley, D. K. (2011). Adaptive and maladaptive narcissism in adolescent development. In C. T. Barry, P. Kerig, K. Stellwagen, & T. D. Berry (Eds.), *Implications of narcissism and Machiavellianism for the development of prosocial and antisocial behavior in youth.* Washington, DC: American Psychological Association.

Hillis, S. D., & others. (2010). The protective effect of family strengths in childhood against adolescent pregnancy and its long-term psychological consequences. *The Permanente Journal, 4,* 18–27.

Hillman, C. H., & others. (2009). The effect of acute treadmill walking on cognitive control and academic achievement in preadolescent children. *Neuroscience, 3,* 1044–1054.

Hillman, J. B., & Biro, F. M. (2010). Dynamic changes of adiposity during puberty: Life may not be linear. *Journal of Adolescent Health, 47,* 322–323.

Hingson, R. W., Heeren, T., & Winter, M. R. (2006). Age at drinking onset and alcohol dependence: Age at onset, duration, and severity. *Archives of Pediatric and Adolescent Medicine, 160,* 739–746.

Hinkle, J. S., Tuckman, B. W., & Sampson, J. P. (1993). The psychology, physiology, and the creativity of middle school aerobic exercisers. *Elementary School Guidance & Counseling, 28,* 133–145.

Hipwell, A. E., Keenan, K., Loeber, R., & Battista, D. (2010). Early predictors of intimate sexual behaviors in an urban sample of young girls. *Developmental Psychology, 46,* 366–378.

Hipwell, A. E., Stepp, S. D., Keenan, K., Chung, T., & Loeber, R. (2011). Brief report: Parsing the heterogeneity of adolescent girls' sexual behavior: Relationships to individual and interpersonal factors. *Journal of Adolescence, 34,* 589–592.

Hirsch, B. J., & Rapkin, B. D. (1987). The transition to junior high school: A longitudinal study of self-esteem, psychological symptomatology, school life, and social support. *Child Development, 58,* 1235–1243.

Hirsch, J. K., Wolford, K., Lalonde, S. M., Brunk, L., & Parker-Morris, A. (2009). Optimistic explanatory style as a moderator of the association between negative life events and suicide ideation. *Crisis, 30,* 48–53.

Hirschi, A., Niles, S. G., & Akos, P. (2011). Engagement in adolescent career preparation: Social support, personality, and the development of choice decidedness and congruence. *Journal of Adolescence, 34,* 173–182.

Hoeksema, E., & others. (2010). Enhanced neural activity in frontal and cerebellar circuits after cognitive training in children with attention deficit hyperactivity disorder. *Human Brain Mapping, 31,* 1942–1950.

Hoelter, L. (2009). Divorce and separation. In D. Carr (Ed.), *Encyclopedia of the life course and human development.* Boston: Gale Cengage.

Hoeve, M., Dubas, J. S., Gerris, J. R. M., van der Laan, P. H., & Smeenk, W. (2011, in press). Maternal and paternal parenting styles: Unique and combined links to adolescent and early adulthood delinquency. *Journal of Adolescence.*

Hoff, E., Laursen, B., & Tardiff, T. (2002). Socioeconomic status and parenting. In M. H. Bornstein (Ed.), *Handbook of parenting* (2nd ed.). Mahwah, NJ: Erlbaum.

Hofferth, S. L., & Reid, L. (2002). Early childbearing and children's achievement behavior over time. *Perspectives on Sexual and Reproductive Health, 34,* 41–49.

Hoffman, M. L. (1970). Moral development. In P. H. Mussen (Ed.), *Manual of child psychology* (3rd ed., Vol. 2). New York: Wiley.

Hoffman, M. L. (1988). Moral development. In M. H. Bornstein & E. Lamb (Eds.), *Developmental psychology: An advanced textbook* (2nd ed.). Hillsdale, NJ: Erlbaum.

Holladay, J. (2011, in press). Promoting tolerance and equity in schools. In J. Marsh, R. Mendoza-Denton, & J. A. Smith (Eds.), *Are we born racist?* Boston: Beacon Press.

Holland, A. S., & Roisman, G. I. (2010). Adult attachment security and young adults' dating relationships over time: Self-reported, observational, and physiological evidence. *Developmental Psychology, 46,* 552–557.

Holmes, L. D. (1987). *Quest for the real Samoa: The Mead-Freeman controversy and beyond.* South Hadley, MA: Bergin & Garvey.

Holtz, P., & Appel, M. (2011, in press). Internet use and video gaming predict problem behavior in early adolescence. *Journal of Adolescence.*

Holzman, L. (2009). *Vygotsky at work and play.* Clifton, NJ: Psychology Press.

Hommel, B., Li, K. Z. H., & Li, S-C. (2004). Visual search across the life span. *Developmental Psychology, 40,* 545–558.

Hoover, K. W., Tao, G., Berman, S., & Kent, C. K. (2010). Utilization of health services in physician offices and outpatient clinics by adolescents and young women in the United States: Implications for improving access to reproductive services. *Journal of Adolescent Health, 46,* 324–330.

Hope, D. A. (2009). Contemporary perspectives on lesbian, gay, and bisexual identities: Introduction. *Nebraska Symposium on Motivation, 54,* 1–4.

Horowitz, F. D. (2009). Introduction: A developmental understanding of giftedness and talent. In F. D. Horowitz, R. F. Subotnik, & D. J. Matthews (Eds.), *The development of giftedness and talent across the life span.* Washington, DC: American Psychological Association.

Horwitz, A. G., Hill, R. M., & King, C. A. (2011, in press). Specific coping behaviors in relation to adolescent depression. *Journal of Adolescence.*

House, L. D., Mueller, T., Reininger, B., Brown, K., & Markham, C. M. (2010). Character as a predictor of reproductive health outcomes for youth: A systematic review. *Journal of Adolescent Health, 46*(Suppl 1), S59–S74.

Howe, A., & Richards, V. (2011). *Bridging the transition from primary to secondary school.* New York: Routledge.

Howe, M. J. A., Davidson, J. W., Moore, D. G., & Sloboda, J. A. (1995). Are there early childhood signs of musical ability? *Psychology of Music, 23,* 162–176.

Howe, N., Ross, H. S., & Recchia, H. (2011). Sibling relationships in early and middle childhood. In P. K. Smith & C. H. Hart (Eds.), *Wiley-Blackwell handbook of childhood social development* (2nd ed.). New York: Wiley.

Howe, W. A. (2010). Unpublished review of J. W. Santrock's *Educational psychology,* 5th ed. (New York: McGraw-Hill).

Hrabosky, J. I., Masheb, R. M., White, M. A., & Grilo, C. M. (2007). Overvaluation of shape and weight in binge eating disorder. *Journal of Consulting and Clinical Psychology, 75,* 175–180.

Huang, L. N. (1989). Southeast Asian refugee children and adolescents. In J. T. Gibbs & L. N. Huang (Eds.), *Children of color.* San Francisco: Jossey-Bass.

Huang, L. N., & Ying, Y. (1989). Chinese American children and adolescents. In J. T. Gibbs & L. N. Huang (Eds.), *Children of color.* San Francisco: Jossey-Bass.

Huang, P. M., Smock, P. J., Manning, W. D., & Bergstrom-Lynch, C. A. (2011). He says, she says: Gender and cohabitation. *Journal of Family Issues, 32,* 876–905.

Huebner, A. M., & Garrod, A. C. (1993). Moral reasoning among Tibetan monks: A study of Buddhist adolescents and young adults in Nepal. *Journal of Cross-Cultural Psychology, 24,* 167–185.

Huerta, M., Cortina, L. M., Pang, J. S., Torges, C. M., & Magley, V. J. (2006). Sex and power in the academy: Modeling sexual harassment in the lives of college women. *Personality and Social Psychology Bulletin, 32,* 616–628.

Huesmann, L. R. (1986). Psychological processes promoting the relation between exposure to media violence and aggressive behavior by the viewer. *Journal of Social Issues, 42,* 125–139.

Huesmann, L. R., Moise-Titus, J., Podolski, C., & Eron, L. D. (2003). Longitudinal relations between children's exposure to TV violence and their aggressive and violent behavior in young adulthood: 1977–1992. *Developmental Psychology, 39,* 201–221.

Hunt, E. (2011). Where are we? Where are we going? Reflections on the current and future state of research on intelligence. In R. J. Sternberg & S. B. Kaufman (Eds.),*Cambridge handbook of intelligence.* New York: Cambridge University Press.

Hunter, S. B., Barber, B. K., Olsen, J. A., McNeely, C. A., & Bose, K. (2011). Adolescents' self-disclosure across cultures: Who discloses and why. *Journal of Adolescent Research, 26,* 447–478.

Huston, A. C., & Bentley, A. C. (2010). Human development in societal context. *Annual Review of Psychology* (Vol. 61). Palo Alto, CA: Annual Reviews.

Huston, A. C., & Ripke, N. N. (2006). Experiences in middle and late childhood and children's development. In A. C. Huston & M. N. Ripke (Eds.), *Developmental contexts in middle childhood.* New York: Cambridge University Press.

Hutchinson, D. M., & Rapee, R. M. (2007). Do friends share similar body image and eating problems? The role of social networks and peer influences in early adolescence. *Behavior Research and Therapy 45,* 1557–1577.

Hutson, R. A. (2008). Poverty. In N. J. Salkind (Ed.), *Encyclopedia of educational psychology.* Thousand Oaks, CA: Sage.

Huttenlocher, P. R., & Dabholkar, A. S. (1997). Regional differences in synaptogenesis in human cerebral cortex. *Journal of Comparative Neurology, 37,* 167–178.

Huynh, V. W., & Fuligni, A. J. (2010). Discrimination hurts: The academic, psychological, and physical well-being of adolescents. *Journal of Research on Adolescence, 20,* 916–941.

Hyde, J. S. (2005). The gender similarities hypothesis. *American Psychologist, 60,* 581–592.

Hyde, J. S. (2007). New directions in the study of gender similarities and differences. *Current Directions in Psychological Science, 16,* 259–263.

Hyde, J. S., & DeLamater, J. D. (2011). *Human sexuality* (11th ed.). New York: McGraw-Hill.

Hyde, J. S., Lindberg, S. M., Linn, M. C., Ellis, A. B., & Williams, C. C. (2008). Gender similarities characterize math performance. *Science, 321,* 494–495.

Hyman, I., Kay, B., Tabori, A., Weber, M., Mahon, M., & Cohen, I. (2006). Bullying: Theory, research, and interventions. In C. M. Evertson & C. S. Weinstein (Eds.), *Handbook of classroom management: Research, practice, and contemporary issues.* Mahwah, NJ: Erlbaum.

Hymel, S., Closson, L. M., Caravita, C. S., & Vaillancourt, T. (2011). Social status among peers: From sociometric attraction to peer acceptance to perceived popularity. In P. K. Smith & C. H. Hart (Eds.), *Wiley-Blackwell handbook of childhood social development* (2nd ed.). New York: Wiley.

I

Ibanez, L., & de Zegher, F. (2006). Puberty after prenatal growth restraint. *Hormone Research, 65*(Suppl 3), 112–115.

Ibanez, L., Lopez-Bermejo, A., Diaz, M., & de Zegher, F. (2011, in press). Catch-up growth in girls born small for gestational age precedes childhood progression to high adiposity.*Fertility and Sterility.*

Idkowiak, J., & others. (2011, in press). Premature adrenarche—novel lessons from early onset androgen excess. *European Journal of Endocrinology.*

"I Have a Dream" Foundation. (2011). *About us.* Retrieved June 22, 2011, from www.ihad.org

Ingul, C. B., Tjonna, A. E., Stolen, T. O., Stoylen, A., & Wisloff, U. (2010). Impaired cardiac function among obese adolescents: Effect of aerobic interval training. *Archives of Pediatric and Adolescent Medicine, 164,* 852–859.

Irwin, C. E. (2010). Young adults are worse off than adolescents. *Journal of Adolescent Health, 46,* 405–406.

Irwin, C. E., Adams, S. H., Park, M. J., & Newacheck, P. W. (2009). Preventive care for adolescents: Few get visits and fewer get services. *Pediatrics, 123,* e565–e572.

Ito, K. E., & others. (2006). Parent opinion of sexuality education in a state with mandated abstinence education: Does policy match parental preference? *Journal of Adolescent Health, 39,* 634–641.

Ivanova, K., Mills, M., & Veenstra, R. (2011, in press). The initiation of dating in adolescence: The effect of parental divorce. The TRAILS study. *Journal of Research on Adolescence.*

J

Jackson, A., & Davis, G. (2000). *Turning points 2000.* New York: Teachers College Press.

Jackson, L. A., & others. (2012). The digital divide. In J. R. Levesque (Ed.), *Encyclopedia of adolescence.* New York: Springer.

Jackson, S. L. (2011). *Research methods* (2nd ed.). Boston: Cengage.

Jacobson, L. A., & others. (2011, in press). Working memory influences processing speed and reading fluency in ADHD. *Child Neuropsychology.*

Jaffee, S., & Hyde, J. S. (2000). Gender differences in moral orientation: A meta-analysis. *Psychological Bulletin, 126,* 703–726.

Jamieson, P. E., & Romer, D. (2008). Unrealistic fatalism in U.S. youth ages 14 to 22: Prevalence and characteristics. *Journal of Adolescent Health, 42,* 154–160.

Jamison, J., & Myers, L. B. (2008). Peer-group and price influence students drinking along with planned behavior. *Alcohol and Alcoholism, 43,* 492–497.

Jamner, M. S., Spruit-Meitz, D., Bassin, S., & Cooper, D. M. (2004). A controlled evaluation of a school-based intervention to promote physical activity among sedentary adolescent females: Project FAB. *Journal of Adolescent Health, 34,* 279–289.

Janssen, I., & others. (2005). Comparison of overweight and obesity prevalence in school-aged youth from 34 countries and their relationships with physical activity and dietary patterns. *Obesity Research, 6,* 123–132.

Jarrett, R. L. (1995). Growing up poor: The family experience of socially mobile youth in low-income African-American neighborhoods. *Journal of Adolescent Research, 10,* 111–135.

Jayakody, A., & others. (2011, in press). Early sexual risk among Black and minority ethnicity teenagers: A mixed methods study. *Journal of Adolescent Health.*

Jayson, S. (2006, June 29). The "millennials" come of age. *USA Today,* pp. 1D–2D.

Jekielek, S., & Brown, B. (2005). *The transition to adulthood: characteristics of young adults ages 18 to 24 in America.* Washington, DC: Child Trends and the Annie E. Casey Foundation.

Jenni, O. G., & Carskadon, M. A. (2007). Sleep behavior and sleep regulation from infancy through adolescence: Normative aspects. In O. G. Jenni & M. A. Carskadon (Eds.), *Sleep Medicine Clinics: Sleep in Children and Adolescents.* Philadelphia: W. B. Saunders.

Jensen, A. R. (2008). Book review. *Intelligence, 36,* 96–97.

Jenson-Campbell, L. A., & Malcolm, K. T. (2007). The importance of conscientiousness in adolescent interpersonal relationships. *Personality and Social Psychology Bulletin, 33,* 368–383.

Jessor, R. (Ed.). (1998). *New perspectives on adolescent risk behavior.* Cambridge, UK: Cambridge University Press.

Jeynes, W. H. (2003). A meta-analysis: The effects of parental involvement on minority children's academic achievement. *Education and Urban Society, 35,* 202–218.

Jhally, S. (1990). *Dreamworlds: Desire/sex/power in rock video* (Video). Amherst: University of Massachusetts at Amherst, Department of Communications.

Johns Hopkins University. (2006a, February 17). Undergraduate honored for launching health programs in India. Baltimore: Johns Hopkins University News Releases.

Johns Hopkins University. (2006b). Research: Tribal connections. Retrieved January 31, 2008, from www.krieger.jhu.edu/research/spotlight/prabhakar.html

Johnson, B. T., Scott-Sheldon, L. A., Huedo-Medina, T. B., & Carey, M. P. (2011). Interventions to reduce sexual risk for human immunodefiency virus in adolescents: A meta-analysis of trials, 1985–2008. *Archives of Pediatric and Adolescent Medicine, 165,* 177–184.

Johnson, D. R., & Johnson, F. P. (2009). *Joining together* (10th ed.). Upper Saddle River, NJ: Prentice Hall.

Johnson, K. (2011, in press). Prejudice vs. positive thinking. In J. Marsh, R. Mendoza-Denton, & J. A. Smith (Eds.), *Are we born racist?* Boston: Beacon Press.

Johnson, L., Giordano, P. C., Manning, W. D., & Longmore, M. A. (2011, in press). Parent-child relations and offending during young adulthood. *Journal of Youth and Adolescence.*

Johnson, M. D. (2012). *Human biology* (6th ed.). Upper Saddle River, NJ: Pearson.

Johnson, W. L., Giordano, P. C., Manning, W. D., & Longmore, M. A. (2010). Parent-child relations and offending during young adulthood. *Journal of Youth and Adolescence.*

Johnston, L. D., O'Malley, P. M., & Bachman, J. G. (2004). *Monitoring the Future national survey results on drug use, 1975–2003: Volume II, College students and adults ages 19–45* (NIH Publication No. 04-5508). Bethesda, MD: National Institute on Drug Abuse.

Johnston, L. D., O'Malley, P. M., Bachman, J. G., & Schulenberg, J. E. (2005). *Monitoring the Future national results on adolescent drug use: Overview of key findings, 2004* (NIH Publication No. 05-5726). Bethesda, MD: National Institute on Drug Abuse.

Johnston, L. D., O'Malley, P. M., Bachman, J. G., & Schulenberg, J. E. (2009). *Monitoring the Future national results on adolescent drug use: Overview of key findings, 2008.* Bethesda, MD: National Institute on Drug Abuse.

Johnston, L. D., O'Malley, P. M., Bachman, J. G., & Schulenberg, J. E. (2010). *Monitoring the Future national survey results on drug use, 1975–2009: Volume II, College students and adults ages 19–50* (NIH Publication No. 10-7585). Bethesda, MD: National Institute on Drug Abuse.

Johnston, L. D., O'Malley, P. M., Bachman, J. G., & Schulenberg, J. E. (2011). *Monitoring the Future national results on adolescent drug use: Overview of key findings, 2010.* Institute for Social Research, University of Michigan, Ann Arbor.

Jones, J. M. (2005, October 7). *Gallup Poll: Most Americans approve of interracial dating.* Princeton, NJ: Gallup.

Jones, M. C. (1965). Psychological correlates of somatic development. *Child Development, 36,* 899–911.

Jones, M. D., & Galliher, R. V. (2007). Navajo ethnic identity: Predictors of psychosocial outcomes in Navajo adolescents. *Journal of Research on Adolescence, 17,* 683–696.

Jones, V. (2011). *Practical classroom management.* Boston: Allyn & Bacon.

Jordan, A. B. (2008). Children's media policy. *The Future of Children, 18*(1), 235–253.

Jose, A., O'Leary, K. D., & Moyer, A. (2010). Does premarital cohabitation predict subsequent marital stability and marital quality? A meta-analysis. *Journal of Marriage and the Family, 72,* 105–116.

Josephson Institute of Ethics. (2006). *2006 Josephson Institute report card on the ethics of American youth. Part one—integrity.* Los Angeles: Josephson Institute.

Joy, E. A. (2009). Health-related concerns of the female athlete: A lifespan approach. *American Family Physician, 79,* 489–495.

Joyner, K. (2009). Transition to parenthood. In D. Carr (Ed.), *Encyclopedia of the life course and human development.* Boston: Gale Cengage.

Juang, L., & Syed, M. (2010). Family cultural socialization practices and ethnic identity in college-going emerging adults. *Journal of Adolescence, 33,* 347–354.

Juffer, F., & van IJzendoorn, M. H. (2005). Behavior problems and mental health referrals of international adoptees: A meta-analysis. *Journal of the American Medical Association, 293,* 2501–2513.

Juffer, F., & van IJzendoorn, M. H. (2007). Adoptees do not lack self-esteem: A meta-analysis of studies on self-esteem of transracial, international, and domestic adoptees. *Psychological Bulletin, 133,* 1067–1083.

Jussim, L., Cain, T. R., Crawford, J. T., Harber, K., & Cohen, F. (2009). The unbearable accuracy of stereotypes. In T. D. Nelson (Ed.), *Handbook of prejudice, stereotyping, and discrimination.* New York: Psychology Press.

Jussim, L., & Eccles, J. S. (1993). Teacher expectations II: Construction and reflection of student achievement. *Journal of Personality and Social Psychology, 63,* 947–961.

Jylhava, J., & others. (2009). Genetics of C-reactive protein and complement factor H have an epistatic effect on carotid artery compliance: The Cardiovascular Risk in Young Finns Study. *Clinical and Experimental Immunology, 155,* 53–58.

K

Kagan, J. (1992). Yesterday's premises, tomorrow's promises. *Developmental Psychology, 28,* 990–997.

Kagan, J. (2000). Temperament. In A. Kazdin (Ed.), *Encyclopedia of psychology.* New York: Oxford University Press.

Kagan, J. (2010). Emotions and temperament. In M. H. Bornstein (Ed.), *Handbook of cultural developmental science.* New York: Psychology Press.

Kagitcibasi, C. (2007). *Family, self, and human development across cultures.* Mahwah, NJ: Erlbaum.

Kahn, A., & Fraga, M. F. (2009). Epigenetics and aging: Status, challenges, and needs for the future. *Journals of Gerontology A: Biological Sciences and Medical Sciences, 64,* 195–198.

Kahn, J. A., & others. (2008). Patterns and determinants of physical activity in U.S. adolescents. *Journal of Adolescent Health, 42,* 369–377.

Kail, R. V. (2007). Longitudinal evidence that increases in processing speed and working memory enhance children's reasoning. *Psychological Science, 18,* 312–313.

Kang, P. P., & Romo, L. F. (2011, in press). The role of religious involvement on depression, risky behavior, and academic performance among Korean American adolescents. *Journal of Adolescence.*

Kann, L., & others. (2011). Sexual identity, sex of sexual contacts, and health-risk behaviors among students in grades 9–12—youth risk behavior surveillance, selected sites, 2001–2009. *MMWR Surveillance Summary, 60,* 1–133.

Kanner, A. D., Coyne, J. C., Schaeter, C., & Lazarus, R. S. (1981). Comparisons of two modes of stress measurement: Daily hassles and uplifts versus major life events. *Journal of Behavioral Medicine, 4,* 1–39.

Kaplowitz, P. B. (2009). Treatment of central precocious puberty. *Current Opinion in Endocrinology, Diabetes, and Obesity, 16,* 13–16.

Karnes, F. A., & Stephens, K. R. (2008). *Achieving excellence: Educating the gifted and talented.* Upper Saddle River, NJ: Prentice Hall.

Karnick, P. M. (2005). Feeling lonely: Theoretical perspectives. *Nursing Science Quarterly, 18,* 7–12.

Karniol, R., Gabay, R., Ochioin, Y., & Harari, Y. (1998). *Sex Roles, 39,* 45–58.

Karpov, Y. V. (2006). *The neo-Vygotskian approach to child development.* New York: Cambridge University Press.

Kato, T. (2005). The relationship between coping with stress due to romantic break-ups and mental health. *Japanese Journal of Social Psychology, 20,* 171–180.

Kauffman, J. M., McGee, K., & Brigham, M. (2004). Enabling or disabling? Observations on changes in special education. *Phi Delta Kappan, 85,* 613–620.

Kaufman, J. C., & Sternberg, R. J. (2007). Resource review: Creativity. *Change, 39,* 55–58.

Kavale, K. A., & Spaulding, L. S. (2011). Efficacy of special education. In M. A. Bray & T. J. Kehle (Eds.), *Oxford handbook of school psychology.* New York: Oxford University Press.

Kavey, R. E., Daniels, S. R., & Flynn, J. T. (2010). Management of high blood pressure in children and adolescents. *Cardiology Clinics, 28,* 597–607.

Keating, D. P. (1990). Adolescent thinking. In S. S. Feldman & G. R. Elliott (Eds.), *At the threshold: The developing adolescent.* Cambridge, MA: Harvard University Press.

Keating, D. P. (2007). Understanding adolescent development: Implications for driving safety. *Journal of Safety Research, 38,* 147–157.

Keating, D. P. (2009). Developmental science and giftedness: An integrated life-span framework. In F. D. Horowitz, R. F. Subotnik, & D. J. Matthews (Eds.), *The development of giftedness and talent across the life span.* Washington, DC: American Psychological Association.

Keating, D. P., & Halpern-Felsher, B. L. (2008). Adolescent drivers: A developmental perspective on risk, proficiency, and safety. *American Journal of Preventive Medicine, 35,* S272–S277.

Keijsers, L., & Laird, R. D. (2010). Introduction to special issue. Careful conversations: Adolescents managing their parents' access to information. *Journal of Adolescence, 33,* 255–259.

Kellogg, R. T. (1994). *The psychology of writing.* New York: Oxford University Press.

Kelly, A. B., & others. (2011). The influence of parents, siblings, and peers on pre- and early-teen smoking: A multilevel model. *Drug and Alcohol Review, 30,* 381–387.

Kelly, G. F. (2011). *Sexuality today* (10th ed.). New York: McGraw-Hill.

Kelly, J. B., & Lamb, M. E. (2003). Developmental issues in relocation cases involving young children: When, whether, and how? *Journal of Family Psychology, 17,* 193–205.

Kerig, P. K., Swanson, J. A., & Ward, R. M. (2012). Autonomy with connection: Influences of parental psychological control on mutuality in emerging adults' close relationships. In P. K. Kerig, M. S. Schulz, & S. T. Hauser (Eds.), *Adolescence and beyond.* New York: Oxford University Press.

Kessels, U., & Hannover, B. (2008). When being a girl matters less: Accessibility of gender-related self-knowledge in single-sex and coeducational classes and its impact on students' physics-related self-concept of ability. *British Journal of Educational Psychology, 78,* 273–289.

Keyes, K. M., Hatzenbuehler, M. L., & Hasin, D. S. (2011, in press). Stressful life experiences, alcohol consumption, and alcohol use disorders: The epidemiological evidence for four main types of stressors. *Psychopharmacology.*

Khashan, A. S., Baker, P. N., & Kenny, L. C. (2010, in press). Preterm birth and reduced birthweight in first and second teenage pregnancies: A register-based cohort study. *BMC Pregnancy and Childbirth.*

Kia-Keating, M., Dowdy, E., Morgan, M. L., & Noam, G. G. (2011). Protecting and promoting: An integrative conceptual model for healthy development of adolescents. *Journal of Adolescent Health, 48,* 220–228.

Kiang, L., & Fuligni, A. J. (2010). Meaning in life as a mediator of ethnic identity and adjustment among adolescents from Latin, Asian, and European American backgrounds. *Journal of Youth and Adolescence, 39,* 1253–1264.

Kiefer, S. M., & Ryan, A. M. (2008). Striving for social dominance over peers: The implications for academic adjustment during early adolescence. *Journal of Educational Psychology, 100,* 417–428.

Kimble, M., Neacsiu, A. D., Flack, W. F., & Horner, J. (2008). Risk of unwanted sex for college women: Evidence for a red zone. *Journal of American College Health, 57,* 331–338.

Kim, J.-Y., McHale, S. M., Crouter, A. C., & Osgood, D. W. (2007). Longitudinal linkages between sibling relationships and adjustment from middle childhood through adolescence. *Developmental Psychology, 43,* 960–973.

Kim, K. H. (2010, July 10). Interview. In P. Bronson & A. Merryman. The creativity crisis. *Newsweek,* 42–48.

Kimm, S. Y., & others. (2002). Obesity development during adolescence in a biracial cohort: The NHLBI Growth and Health Study. *Pediatrics, 110,* e54.

King, B. M. (2012). *Human sexuality today* (7th ed.). Upper Saddle River, NJ: Pearson.

King, L. A. (2011). *Psychology: An appreciative view* (2nd ed.). New York: McGraw-Hill.

King, P. E., Carr, A., & Boiter, C. (2011, in press). Spirituality, religiosity, and youth thriving. In R. M. Lerner, J. V. Lerner, & J. B. Benson (Eds.), *Advances in child development and behavior: Positive youth development.* New York: Elsevier.

King, P. E., Ramos, J. S., & Clardy, C. E. (2012, in press). Searching for the sacred: Religious and spiritual development among adolescents. In K. I. Pargament, J. Exline, & J. Jones (Eds.), *APA handbook of psychology, religion, and spirituality.* Washington, DC: American Psychological Association.

King, P. E., & Roeser, R. W. (2009). Religion and spirituality in adolescent development. In R. M. Lerner & L. Steinberg (Eds.), *Handbook of adolescent psychology* (3rd ed.). New York: Wiley.

Kinney, J. (2012). *Loosening the grip: A handbook of alcohol information* (10th ed.). New York: McGraw-Hill.

Kins, E., & Beyers, W. (2010). Failure to launch, failure to achieve criteria for adulthood? *Journal of Adolescent Research, 25,* 743–777.

Kirby, D. B., Laris, B. A., & Rolleri, L. A. (2007). Sex and HIV education programs: Their impact on sexual behavior of young people throughout the world. *Journal of Adolescent Health, 40,* 206–217.

Kirk, S. A., Gallagher, J. J., Coleman, M. R., & Anastaslow, N. J. (2012). *Educating exceptional children* (13th ed.). Boston: Cengage.

Kirkman, M., Rosenthal, D. A., & Feldman, S. S. (2002). Talking to a tiger: Fathers reveal their difficulties in communicating sexually with adolescents. In S. S. Feldman & D. A. Rosenthal (Eds.), *Talking sexually: Parent-adolescent communication.* San Francisco: Jossey-Bass.

Kistler, M., Rodgers, B., Power, T., Austin E. W., & Hill, L. G. (2010). Adolescents and music media: Toward an involvementmediational model of consumption and self-concept. *Journal of Research on Adolescence, 20,* 616–630.

Kistner, J., Counts-Allan, C., Dunkel, S., Drew, C. H., David-Ferton, C., & Lopez, C. (2010). Sex differences in relational and overt aggression in the late elementary school years. *Aggressive Behavior, 36,* 282–291.

Kiuru, N., Kovisto, P., Mutanen, P., Vuori, J., & Nurmi, J-E. (2011, in press). How do efforts to enhance career preparation influence peer groups? *Journal of Research on Adolescence.*

Klaczynski, P. (2001). The influence of analytic and heuristic processing on adolescent reasoning and decision making. *Child Development, 72,* 844–861.

Klaczynski, P. A., Byrnes, J. P., & Jacobs, J. E. (2001). Introduction to the special issue: The development of decision making. *Applied Developmental Psychology, 22,* 225–236.

Klaczynski, P. A., & Narasimham, G. (1998). Development of scientific reasoning biases: Cognitive versus ego-protective explanations. *Developmental Psychology, 34,* 175–187.

Klassen, R. M., Krawchuk, L. L., & Hannok, W. (2012). Academic procrastination in adolescence. In J. R. Levesque (Ed.), *Encyclopedia of adolescence.* New York: Springer.

Klatt, J., & Enright, R. (2009). Investigating the place of forgiveness within the positive youth development paradigm. *Journal of Moral Education, 38,* 35–52.

Klimstra, T. A., Hale, W. W., Raaijmakers, Q. A. W., Branje, S. J. T., & Meeus, W. H. H. (2010). Identity formation in adolescence: Change or stability? *Journal of Youth and Adolescence, 39,* 150–162.

Kling, K. C., Hyde, J. S., Showers, C., & Buswell, B. (1999). Gender differences in self-esteem: A meta-analysis. *Psychological Bulletin,* 125, 470–500.

Kloep, M., & Hendry, L. B. (2010). Letting go or holding on? Parents' perceptions of their relationships with their children during emerging adulthood. *British Journal of Developmental Psychology, 28,* 817–834.

Kloss, J. D., Nash, C. O., Horsey, S. E., & Taylor, D. J. (2011, in press). The delivery of sleep medicine to college students. *Journal of Adolescent Health.*

Knoll, S., Bulik, C. M., & Hebebrand, J. (2011, in press). Do the currently proposed DSM-5 criteria for anorexia nervosa adequately consider developmental aspects of children and adolescents? *European Child and Adolescent Psychiatry.*

Knopik, V. S. (2009). Maternal smoking during pregnancy and child outcomes: Real or spurious effect? *Developmental Neuropsychology, 34,* 1–36.

Knox, D., & Wilson, K. (1981). Dating behaviors of university students. *Family Relations, 30,* 255–258.

Kochanska, G., Barry, R. A., Stellern, S. A., & O'Bleness, J. J. (2010a). Early attachment organization moderates the parent-child mutually coercive pathway to children's antisocial conduct. *Child Development, 80,* 1288–1300.

Kochanska, G., Woodard, J., Iim, S., Koenig, J. L., Yoon, J. E., & Barry, R. A. (2010b). Positive socialization mechanisms in secure and insecure parent-child dyads: Two longitudinal studies. *Journal of Child Psychology and Psychiatry, 51,* 998–1009.

Koenig, L. B., McGue, M., & Iacono, W. G. (2008). Stability and change in religiousness during emerging adulthood. *Developmental Psychology, 44,* 523–543.

Kohlberg, L. (1958). *The development of modes of moral thinking and choice in the years 10 to 16.* Unpublished doctoral dissertation, University of Chicago.

Kohlberg, L. (1969). Stage and sequence: The cognitive-developmental approach to socialization. In D. A. Goslin (Ed.), *Handbook of socialization theory and research.* Chicago: Rand McNally.

Kohlberg, L. (1976). Moral stages and moralization: The cognitive developmental approach. In T. Lickona (Ed.), *Moral development and behavior.* New York: Holt, Rinehart, & Winston.

Kohlberg, L. (1986). A current statement on some theoretical issues. In S. Modgil & C. Modgil (Eds.), *Lawrence Kohlberg.* Philadelphia: Falmer.

Kohler, P. K., Manhart, L. E., &. Lafferty, W. E. (2008). Abstinence-only and comprehensive sex education and the initiation of sexual activity and teen pregnancy. *Journal of Adolescent Health, 42,* 344–351.

Kohn, M. L. (1977). *Class and conformity: A study in values* (2nd ed.). Chicago: University of Chicago Press.

Ko, L. K., & Perreira, K. M. (2010). "It turned my world upside down": Latino youths' perspectives on immigration. *Journal of Adolescent Research, 25,* 465–493.

Koolhof, R., Loeber, R., Wei, E. H., Pardini, D., & D'escury, A. C. (2007). Inhibition deficits of serious delinquent boys with low intelligence. *Criminal Behavior and Mental Health, 17,* 274–292.

Koppelman, K., & Goodhart, L. (2011). *Understanding human differences* (3rd ed.). Boston: Allyn & Bacon.

Kornblum, J. (2006, March 9). How to monitor the kids? *USA Today,* p. 1D.

Koropeckyj-Cox, T. (2009). Singlehood. In D. Carr (Ed.), *Encyclopedia of the life course and human development.* Boston: Gale Cengage.

Kort-Butler, L. A., & Hagewen, K. J. (2011). School-based extracurricular activity involvement and adolescent self-esteem: A growth-curve analysis. *Journal of Youth and Adolescence, 40,* 568–581.

Koskinen, S. M., & others. (2011, in press). A longitudinal twin study of effects of adolescent alcohol abuse on the neurophysiology of attention and orienting. *Alcoholism, Clinical and Experimental Research.*

Kottak, C. P., & Kozaitis, K. A. (2012). *On being different* (4th ed.). New York: McGraw-Hill.

Kozol, J. (2005). *The shame of a nation.* New York: Crown.

Kramer, L. (2010). The essential ingredients of successful sibling relationships: An emerging framework for advancing theory and practice. *Child Development Perspectives, 4,* 80–86.

Kring, A. M. (2000). Gender and anger. In A. H. Fischer (Ed.), *Gender and emotion: Social psychological perspectives.* New York: Cambridge University Press.

Kroger, J. (2007). *Identity development: Adolescence through adulthood* (2nd ed.). Thousand Oaks, CA: Sage.

Kroger, J., Martinussen, M., & Marcia, J. E. (2010). Identity change during adolescence and young adulthood: A meta-analysis. *Journal of Adolescence, 33,* 683–698.

Krueger, J. I., Vohs, K. D., & Baumeister, R. F. (2008). Is the allure of self-esteem a mirage after all? *American Psychologist, 63,* 64–65.

Kucian, K., & others. (2011, in press). Mental number line training in children with developmental dyscalculia. *NeuroImage.*

Kuhlberg, J. A., Pena, J. B., & Zayas, L. H. (2010). Familism, parent-adolescent conflict, self-esteem, internalizing behaviors, and suicide attempts among adolescent Latinas. *Child Psychiatry and Human Development, 41,* 425–440.

Kuhn, C., & others. (2010). The emergence of gonadal hormone influences on dopaminergic function during puberty. *Hormones and Behavior, 58,* 122–137.

Kuhn, D. (2009). Adolescent thinking. In R. M. Lerner & L. Steinberg (Eds.), *Handbook of adolescent psychology* (3rd ed.). New York: Wiley.

Kuhn, D., & Franklin, S. (2006). The second decade: What develops (and how)? In W. Damon & R. Lerner (Eds.), *Handbook of child psychology* (6th ed.). New York: Wiley.

Kumar, R., & Maehr, M. (2010). Schooling, cultural diversity, and student motivation. In J. L. Meece & J. S. Eccles (Eds.), *Handbook* *of research on schools, schooling, and human development*. New York: Routledge.

Kumpfer, K. L., & Alvarado, R. (2003). Family-strengthening approaches for the prevention of youth problem behaviors. *American Psychologist, 58,* 457–465.

Kunz, J. (2011). *THINK marriages and families*. Upper Saddle River, NJ: Pearson.

Kupersmidt, J. B., & Coie J. D. (1990). Preadolescent peer status, aggression, and school adjustment as predictors of externalizing problems in adolescence. *Child Development, 61,* 1350–1363.

Kuppens, S., Grietens, H., Onghena, P., & Michiels, D. (2009). Relations between parental psychological control and childhood relational aggression: Reciprocal in nature? *Journal of Clinical Child and Adolescent Psychology, 38,* 117–131.

Kurdek, L. A. (2008). Change in relationship quality for partners from lesbian, gay male, and heterosexual couples. *Journal of Family Psychology, 22,* 701–711.

Kurth, S., Jenni, O. G., Riedner, B. A., Tononi, G., Carskadon, M. A., & Huber, R. (2010). Characteristics of sleep slow waves in children and adolescents. *Sleep, 33,* 475–480.

L

Labouvie-Vief, G. (1986, August). *Modes of knowing and life-span cognition*. Paper presented at the meeting of the American Psychological Association, Washington, DC.

Labouvie-Vief, G. (2006). Emerging structures of adult thought. In J. J. Arnett & J. L. Tanner (Eds.), *Emerging adults in America*. Washington, DC: American Psychological Association.

Labouvie-Vief, G. (2009). Cognition and equilibrium regulation in development and aging. In V. Bengtson & others (Eds.), *Handbook of theories of aging*. New York: Springer.

Labouvie-Vief, G., Gruhn, D., & Studer J. (2010). Dynamic integration of emotion and cognition: Equilibrium regulation in development and aging. In M. E. Lamb, A. Freund, & R. M. Lerner (Eds.), *Handbook of life-span development* (Vol. 2). New York: Wiley.

Labrie, J. W., Hummer, J., Kenney, S., Lac, A., & Pedersen, E. (2011). Identifying factors that increase the likelihood for alcohol-induced blackouts in the prepartying context. *Substance Use and Misuse, 46,* 992–1002.

Ladd, G. W., Kochenderfer-Ladd, B., & Rydell, A-M. (2011). Children's interpersonal skills and school-based relationships. In P. K. Smith & C. H. Hart (Eds.), *Wiley-Blackwell handbook of social development* (2nd ed.). New York: Wiley.

Laflin, M. T., Wang, J., & Barry, M. (2008). A longitudinal study of adolescent transition from virgin to nonvirgin status. *Journal of Adolescent Health, 42,* 228–236.

LaFontana, K. M., & Cillessen, A. H. N. (2010). Developmental changes in the priority of perceived status in childhood and adolescence. *Social Development, 19,* 130–147.

LaFrance, M., Hecht, M. A., & Paluck, E. L. (2003). The contingent smile: A meta-analysis of sex differences in smiling. *Psychological Bulletin, 129,* 305–334.

Lagus, K. A., Bernat, D. H., Bearinger, L. H., Resnick, M. D., & Eisenberg, M. E. (2011). Parental perspectives on sources of sex information for young people. *Journal of Adolescent Health.*

Laird, R. D., Criss, M. M., Pettit, G. S., Dodge, K. A., & Bates, J. A. (2008). Parents' monitoring knowledge attenuates the link between antisocial friends and adolescent delinquent behavior. *Journal of Abnormal Psychology, 36,* 299–310.

Laird, R. D., & Marrero, M. D. (2010). Information management and behavior problems: Is concealing misbehavior necessarily a sign of trouble? *Journal of Adolescence, 33,* 297–308.

Laird, R. D., & Marrero, M. D. (2011). Mothers' knowledge of early adolescents' activities following the middle school transition and pubertal maturation. *Journal of Early Adolescence, 31,* 209–233.

Laird, R. D., Marrero, M. D., & Sentse, M. (2010). Revisiting parental monitoring: Evidence that parental solicitation can be effective when needed most. *Journal of Youth and Adolescence, 39,* 1431–1441.

Laird, R. D., Marrero, M. D., & Sherwood, J. K. (2010). Developmental and interactional antecedents of monitoring in early adolescence. In V. Guilamo-Ramos, J. Jaccard, & P. Dittus (Eds.), *Parental monitoring of adolescents: Current perspectives for researchers and practitioners*. New York: Columbia University Press.

Laird, R. D., Pettit, G. S., Bates, J. E., & Dodge, K. A. (2003). Parents' monitoring-relevant knowledge and adolescents' delinquent behavior: Evidence of correlated developmental changes and reciprocal influences. *Child Development, 74,* 752–768.

Lalonde, C., & Chandler, M. (2004). Culture, selves, and time. In C. Lightfoot, C. Lalonde, & M. Chandler (Eds.), *Changing conceptions of psychological life*. Mahwah, NJ: Erlbaum.

Landale, N. S., Thomas, K. J., & Van Hook, J. (2011). The living arrangements of children of immigrants. *Futu re of Children, 21,* 43–70.

Landor, A., Simons, L. G., Simons, R. L., Brody, G. H., & Gibbons, F. X. (2011). The role of religiosity in the relationship between parents, peers, and adolescent risky sexual behavior. *Journal of Youth and Adolescence, 40,* 296–309.

Langston, W. (2011). *Research methods laboratory manual for psychology* (3rd ed.). Boston: Cengage.

Langstrom, N., Rahman, Q., Carlstrom, E., & Lichtenstein, P. (2010). Genetic and environmental effects on same-sex behavior: A population study of twins in Sweden. *Archives of Sexual Behavior, 39,* 75–80.

Lansford, J. E. (2009). Parental divorce and children's adjustment. *Perspectives on Psychological Science, 4,* 140–152.

Lansford, J. E., Malone, P. S., Castellino, D. R., Dodge, K. A., Pettit, G. S., & Bates, J. E. (2006). Trajectories of internalizing, externalizing, and grades for children who have and have not experienced their parents' divorce or separation. *Journal of Family Psychology, 20,* 292–301.

Lansford, J. E., Yu, T., Erath, S. A., Pettit, G. S., Bates, J. E., & Dodge, K. A. (2010). Developmental precursors of number of sexual partners from ages 16 to 22. *Journal of Research on Adolescence, 20,* 651–677.

Lapsley, D. K. (1990). Continuity and discontinuity in adolescent social cognitive development. In R. Montemayor, G. Adams, & T. Gulotta (Eds.), *From childhood to adolescence: A transitional period?* Newbury Park, CA: Sage.

Lapsley, D. K. (2010). Moral agency, identity, and narrative in moral development. *Human Development, 53,* 87–97.

Lapsley, D. K., & Aalsma, M. C. (2006). An empirical typology of narcissism and mental health in late adolescence. *Journal of Adolescence, 29,* 53–71.

Lapsley, D. K., Enright, R. D., & Serlin, R. C. (1985). Toward a theoretical perspective on the legislation of adolescence. *Journal of Early Adolescence, 5,* 441–466.

Lapsley, D. K., & Hill, P. L. (2010). Subjective invulnerability, optimism bias, and adjustment in emerging adulthood. *Journal of Youth and Adolescence, 39,* 847–857.

Lapsley, D. K., Rice, K. G., & Shadid, G. E. (1989). Psychological separation and adjustment to college. *Journal of Counseling Psychology, 36,* 286–294.

Lapsley, D. K., & Stey, P. (2012, in press). Adolescent narcissism. In R. Levesque (Ed.), *Encyclopedia of adolescence.* New York: Springer.

Larrivee, B. (2009). *Authentic classroom management* (3rd ed.). Upper Saddle River, NJ: Prentice Hall.

Larson, N. I., & others. (2008). Fast food intake: Longitudinal trends during the transition to young adulthood and correlates of intake. *Journal of Adolescent Health, 43,* 79–86.

Larson, R., & Lampman-Petraitis, C. (1989). Daily emotional states as reported by children and adolescents. *Child Development, 60,* 1250–1260.

Larson, R., & Richards, M. H. (1994). *Divergent realities.* New York: Basic Books.

Larson, R. W. (1999, September). Unpublished review of J. W. Santrock's *Adolescence,* 8th ed. (New York: McGraw-Hill).

Larson, R. W. (2000). Toward a psychology of positive youth development. *American Psychologist, 55,* 170–183.

Larson, R. W. (2001). How U.S. children and adolescents spend time: What it does (and doesn't) tell us about their development. *Current Directions in Psychological Science, 10,* 160–164.

Larson, R. W. (2008). Development of the capacity for teamwork in youth development. In R. K. Silbereisen & R. M. Lerner (Eds.), *Approaches to positive youth development.* Thousand Oaks, CA: Sage.

Larson, R. W. (2011). Positive development in a disorderly world. *Journal of Research on Adolescence, 21,* 317–334.

Larson, R. W., & Angus, R. M. (2011, in press). Pursuing paradox: The role of adults in creating empowering settings for youth. In M. Aber, K. Maton, & E. Seidman (Eds.), *Empowerment settings and voices for social change.* New York: Oxford University Press.

Larson, R., Wilson, S., & Rickman, A. (2009). Globalization, societal change, and adolescence across the world. In R. M. Lerner & L. Steinberg (Eds.), *Handbook of adolescent psychology* (3rd ed.). New York: Wiley.

Larson, R. W., & Richards, M. H. (1994). *Divergent realities.* New York: Basic Books.

Larson, R. W., Rickman, A. N., Gibbons, C. M., & Walker, K. C. (2011, in press). Practitioner expertise: Creating quality within the tumble of events in youth settings. *New Directions in Youth Development.*

Larson, R. W., & Verma, S. (1999). How children and adolescents spend time across the world: Work, play, and developmental opportunities. *Psychological Bulletin, 125,* 701–736.

Larson, R. W., & Walker, K. C. (2010). Dilemmas of practice: Challenges to program quality encountered by youth program leaders. *American Journal of Community Psychology, 45,* 338–349.

Larson, R. W., Wilson, S., & Rickman, A. (2009). Globalization, societal change, and adolescence across the world. In R. M. Lerner & L. Steinberg (Eds.), *Handbook of adolescent psychology* (3rd ed.). New York: Wiley.

Laursen, B. (1995). Conflict and social interaction in adolescent relationships. *Journal of Research on Adolescence, 5,* 55–70.

Laursen, B., & Collins, W. A. (2009). Parent-child relationships during adolescence. In R. M. Lerner & L. Steinberg (Eds.), *Handbook of adolescent psychology* (3rd ed.). New York: Wiley.

Laursen, B., Coy, K. C., & Collins, W. A. (1998). Reconsidering changes in parent-child conflict across adolescence: A meta-analysis. *Child Development, 69,* 817–832.

LaVoie, J. (1976). Ego identity formation in middle adolescence. *Journal of Youth and Adolescence, 5,* 371–385.

Lawler, M., & Nixon, E. (2011). Body dissatisfaction among adolescent boys and girls: The effects of body mass, peer appearance culture, and internalization of appearance ideals. *Journal of Youth and Adolescence, 40,* 59–71.

Lawyer, S., Resnick, H., Bakanic, V., Burkett, T., & Kilpatrick, D. (2010). Forcible, drug-facilitated, and incapacitated rape and sexual assault among undergraduate women. *Journal of American College Health, 58,* 453–460.

Lazarus, R. S. (2000). Toward better research on stress and coping. *American Psychologist, 55*(6), 665–673.

Leadbeater, B. J., & Way, N. (2000). *Growing up fast.* Mahwah, NJ: Erlbaum.

Leadbeater, B. J., Way, N., & Raden, A. (1994, February). *Barriers to involvement of father of the children of adolescent mothers.* Paper presented at the meeting of the Society for Research on Adolescence, San Diego.

Leaper, C., & Bigler, R. H. (2011). Gender. In M. K. Underwood & L. H. Rosen (Eds.), *Social development.* New York: Guilford.

Leaper, C., & Brown, C. S. (2008). Perceived experience of sexism among adolescent girls. *Child Development, 79,* 685–704.

Leaper, C., & Friedman, C. K. (2007). The socialization of gender. In J. E. Grusec & P. D. Hastings (Eds.), *Handbook of socialization.* New York: Guilford.

Leatherdale, S. T. (2010). Factors associated with communication-based sedentary behaviors among youth: Are talking on the phone, texting, and instant messaging new sedentary behaviors to be concerned about? *Journal of Adolescent Health, 47,* 315–318.

Lecke, S. B., Morsch, D. M., & Spritzer, P. M. (2011). Leptin and adiponectiin in the female life course. *Brazilian Journal of Medical and Biological Research, 44,* 381–387.

Lee, K., & Ashton, M. C. (2008). The HEXACO personality factors in the indigenous personality lexicons and 11 other languages. *Journal of Personality, 76,* 1001–1054.

Lee, L. A., Sarra, D. A., Mason, A. E., & Law, R. W. (2011). Attachment anxiety, verbal immediency, and blood pressure: Results from a laboratory-analogue study following marital separation. *Personal Relationships, 18,* 285–301.

Lee, S. S. (2011). Deviant peer affiliation and antisocial behavior: Interaction with Monoamine Oxidase A (MAOA) genotype. *Journal of Abnormal Child Psychology, 39,* 321–332.

Leedy, P. D., & Ormrod, J. E. (2010). *Practical research* (9th ed.). Upper Saddle River, NJ: Prentice Hall.

Lefkowitz, E. S., Boone, T. L., & Shearer, T. L. (2004). Communication with best friends about sex-related topics during emerging adulthood. *Journal of Youth and Adolescence, 33,* 339–351.

Lefkowitz, E. S., & Espinosa-Hernandez, G. (2006). *Sexual related communication with mothers and close friends during the transition to university.* Unpublished manuscript, Department of Human Development and Family Studies, Pennsylvania State University, University Park, PA.

Lefkowitz, E. S., & Gillen, M. M. (2006). "Sex is just a normal part of life": Sexuality in emerging adulthood. In J. J. Arnett & J. L. Tanner (Eds.), *Emerging adults in America.* Washington, DC: American Psychological Association.

Lehr, C. A., Hanson, A., Sinclair, M. F., & Christensen, S. I. (2003). Moving beyond dropout prevention towards school completion. *School Psychology Review, 32,* 342–364.

Leitenberg, H., Detzer, M. J., & Srebnik, D. (1993). Gender differences in masturbation and the relation of masturbation experience in preadolescence and/or early adolescence to sexual behavior and adjustment in young adulthood. *Archives of Sexual Behavior, 22,* 87–98.

Lenhart, A., Ling, R., Campbell, S., & Purcell, K. (2010a, April 20). *Teens and mobile phones.* Washington, DC: Pew Research Center.

Lenhart, A., Purcell, K., Smith, A., & Zickuhr, K. (2010b, February 3). *Social media and young adults.* Washington, DC: Pew Research Center.

Lenroot, R. K., & Giedd, J. N. (2010). Sex differences in the human brain. *Brain and Cognition, 72,* 46–55.

Leondari, A., & Gonida, E. (2007). Predicting academic self-handicapping in different age groups: The role of personal achievement goals and social goals. *British Journal of Educational Psychology, 77,* 595–611.

Lepper, M. R., Corpus, J. H., & Iyengar, S. S. (2005). Intrinsic and extrinsic orientations in the classroom: Age differences and academic correlates. *Journal of Educational Psychology, 97,* 184–196.

Lerner, J. V., Phelps, E., Forman, Y., & Bowers, E. P. (2009). Positive youth development. In R. M. Lerner & L. Steinberg (Eds.), *Handbook of adolescent psychology* (3rd ed.). New York: Wiley.

Lerner, J. W., & Johns, B. (2012). *Learning disabilities and related mild disabilities* (12th ed.). Boston: Cengage.

Lerner, R. M., Boyd, M., & Du, D. (2008). Adolescent development. In I. B. Weiner & C. B. Craighead (Eds.), *Encyclopedia of psychology* (4th ed.). Hoboken, NJ: Wiley.

Lerner, R. M., & others. (2011, in press). Positive youth development: Contemporary theoretical perspectives. In A. C. Fonseca (Ed.), *Criancas e adolescentes,* Coimbra, Portugal: Nova Almedina.

Lerner, R. M., & Steinberg, L. (2009). The scientific study of adolescent development. In R. M. Lerner & L. Steinberg (Eds.), *Handbook of adolescent psychology* (3rd ed.). New York: Wiley.

Lerner, R. M., von Eye, A., Lerner, J. V., Lewin-Bizan, S., & Bowers, E. P. (2010). Special issue introduction: The meaning and measurement of thriving: A view of the issues. *Journal of Youth and Adolescence, 39,* 707–719.

Levant, R. F. (2001). Men and masculinity. In J. Worell (Ed.), *Encyclopedia of women and gender.* San Diego: Academic Press.

Leventhal, J., Dupéré, V., & Brooks-Gunn, J. (2009). Neighborhood influences on adolescent development. In R. M. Lerner & L. Steinberg (Eds.), *Handbook of adolescent psychology* (3rd ed.). New York: Wiley.

Levstik, L. (2011). Learning history. In P. A. Alexander & R. E. Mayer (Eds.), *Handbook of research on learning and instruction.* New York: Routledge.

Levykh, M. G. (2008). The affective establishment and maintenance of Vygotsky's zone of proximal development. *Educational Theory, 58,* 83–101.

Lewin-Bizan, S., Bowers, E., & Lerner, R. M. (2010). One good thing leads to another: Cascades of positive youth development among American adolescents. *Development and Psychopathology, 22,* 759–770.

Lewis, A. C. (2007). Looking beyond NCLB. *Phi Delta Kappan, 88,* 483–484.

Lewis, C., & Carpendale, J. (2011). Social cognition. In P. K. Smith & C. C. Hart (Eds.), *Wiley-Blackwell handbook of childhood social development.* New York: Wiley.

Lewis, C. G. (1981). How adolescents approach decisions: Changes over grades seven to twelve and policy implications. *Child Development, 52,* 538–554.

Lewis, M., Feiring, C., & Rosenthal, S. (2000). Attachment over time. *Child Development, 71,* 707–720.

Lewis, V. G., Money, J., & Bobrow, N. A. (1977). Idiopathic pubertal delay beyond the age of 15: Psychological study of 12 boys. *Adolescence, 12,* 1–11.

Liben, L. S. (1995). Psychology meets geography: Exploring the gender gap on the national geography bee. *Psychological Science Agenda, 8,* 8–9.

Lieberman, A. F., Chu, A., Van horn, P., & Harris, W. W. (2011). Trauma in early childhood: Empirical evidence and clinical implications. *Development and Psychopathology, 23,* 397–410.

Limber, S. P. (2004). Implementation of the Olweus Bullying Prevention program in American schools: Lessons learned from the field. In D. L. Espelage & S. M. Swearer (Eds.), *Bullying in American schools.* Mahwah, NJ: Erlbaum.

Li, M. D., Lou, X. Y., Chen, G., Ma, J. Z., & Elston, R. C. (2008). Gene-gene interactions among CHRNA4, CHRNB2, BDNF, and NTRK2 in nicotine dependence. *Biological Psychiatry, 64,* 951–957.

Lindberg, S. M., Hyde, S. S., Petersen, J. L., & Lin, M. C. (2010). New trends in gender and mathematics performance: A meta-analysis. *Psychological Bulletin, 136,* 1123–1135.

Lindblad, F., & Hjern, A. (2010). ADHD after fetal exposure to maternal smoking. *Nicotine and Tobacco Research, 12,* 408–415.

Lindley, F. A. (2009). *The portable mentor.* Thousand Oaks, CA: Corwin Press

Linley, P. A., & Joseph, S. (2004). Positive change following trauma and adversity: A review. *Journal of Traumatic Stress, 17,* 11–21.

Linver, M. R., Roth, J. L., & Brooks-Gunn, J. (2009). Patterns of adolescents' participation in organized activities: Are sports best when combined with other activities? *Developmental Psychology, 45,* 354–367.

Lippman, L. A., & Keith, J. D. (2006). The demographics of spirituality among youth: International perspectives. In E. Roehlkepartain, P. E. King, L. Wagener, & P. L. Benson (Eds.), *The handbook of spirituality in childhood and adolescence.* Thousand Oaks, CA: Sage.

Lipsitz, J. (1980, March). *Sexual development in young adolescents.* Invited speech given at the American Association of Sex Educators, Counselors, and Therapists, New York City.

Lipsitz, J. (1983, October). *Making it the hard way: Adolescents in the 1980s.* Testimony presented at the Crisis Intervention Task Force. House Select Committee on Children, Youth, and Families, Washington, DC.

Little, T. D., Card, N. A., Preacher, K. J., & McConnell, E. (2009). Modeling longitudinal data from research on adolescence. In R. M. Lerner & L. Steinberg (Eds.), *Handbook of adolescence* (3rd ed.). New York: Wiley.

Littleton, K., Scanlon, E., & Sharples, M. (Eds.). (2011). *Orchestrating personal inquiry learning.* New York: Routledge.

Liu, F. F., & others. (2011). Family stress and coping for Mexican origin adolescents. *Journal of Clinical Child and Adolescent Psychology, 40,* 385–397.

Lobelo, F., Pate, R. R., Dowda, M., Liese, A. D., & Daniels, S. R. (2010). Cardiorespiratory fitness and clustered cardiovascular disease risk in U.S. adolescents. *Journal of Adolescent Health, 47,* 352–359.

Loeber, R., & Burke, J. D. (2011). Developmental pathways in juvenile externalizing and internalizing problems. *Journal of Research on Adolescence, 21,* 34–46.

Loeber, R., Burke, J., & Pardini, D. (2009). The etiology and development of antisocial and delinquent behavior. *Annual Review of Psychology* (Vol. 60). Palo Alto, CA: Annual Reviews.

Loeber, R., Farrington, D. P., Stouthamer-Loeber, M., & White, H. R. (2008). *Violence and serious theft: Development and prediction from childhood to adulthood.* New York: Routledge.

Loeber, R., Pardini, D. A., Stouthamer-Loeber, M., & Raine, A. (2007). Do cognitive, physiological, and psychosocial risk and promotive factors predict desistance from delinquency in males? *Development and Psychopathology, 19,* 867–887.

Loehlin, J. C., Horn, J. M., & Ernst, J. L. (2007). Genetic and environmental influences on adult life outcomes: Evidence from the Texas adoption project. *Behavior Genetics, 37,* 463–476.

Lohman, D. F., & Lakin, J. M. (2011). Intelligence and reasoning. In R. J. Sternberg & S. B. Kaufman (Eds.), *Cambridge handbook of intelligence.* New York: Cambridge University Press.

Lomas, J., Stough, C., Hansen, K., & Downey, L. A. (2011, in press). Brief report: Emotional intelligence, victimization, and bullying in adolescents. *Journal of Adolescence.*

Lonardo, R. A., Giordano, P. C., Longmore, M. A., & Manning, W. D. (2009). Parents, friends, and romantic partners: Enmeshment in deviant networks and adolescent delinquency involvement. *Journal of Youth and Adolescence, 38,* 367–383.

Lord, S. E., & Eccles, J. S. (1994, February). *James revisited: The relationship of domain self-concepts and values to Black and White adolescents' self-esteem.* Paper presented at the meeting of the Society for Research on Adolescence, San Diego.

Loukas, A., Roalson, L. A., & Herrera, D. E. (2010). School connectedness buffers the effects of negative family relations and poor effortful control on early adolescent conduct problems. *Journal of Research on Adolescence, 20,* 13–22.

Lounsbury, J. W., Levy, J. J., Leong, F. T., & Gibson, L. W. (2007). Identity and personality: The big five and narrow personality traits in relation to sense of identity. *Identity, 7,* 51–70.

Lubart, T. I. (2003). In search of creative intelligence. In R. J. Sternberg, J. Lautrey, & T. I. Lubert (Eds.), *Models of intelligence: International perspectives.* Washington, DC: American Psychological Association.

Lucas, R. E., & Donnellan, M. B. (2009). Age differences in personality: Evidence from a nationally representative sample of Australians. *Developmental Psychology, 45,* 1353–1363.

Luders, E., & others. (2004). Gender differences in cortical complexity. *Nature Neuroscience, 7,* 799–800.

Luna, B., Padmanabhan, A., & O'Hearn, K. (2010). What has fMRI told us about the development of cognitive control in adolescence. *Brain and Cognition, 72,* 101–113.

Lunday, A. (2006, December 4). Two Homewood seniors collect Marshall, Mitchell scholarships. *The JHU Gazette, 36.*

Lund, H. G., Reider, B. D., Whiting, A. B., & Prichard, J. R. (2010). Sleep patterns and predictors of disturbed sleep in a large population of college students. *Journal of Adolescent Health, 46,* 124–132.

Lunkenheimer, E. S., Olson, S. L., Hollenstein, T., Sameroff, A. J., & Winter, C. (2011). Dyadic flexibility and positive affect in parent-child coregulation and the development of child behavior problems. *Development and Psychopathology, 23,* 577–591.

Luria, A., & Herzog, E. (1985, April). *Gender segregation across and within settings.* Paper presented at the biennial meeting of the Society for Research in Child Development, Toronto.

Luthar, S. S. (2006). Resilience in development: A synthesis of research across five decades. In D. Cicchetti & D. J. Cohen (Eds.), *Developmental psychopathology: Vol 3. Risk, disorders, and adaptation* (2nd ed.). Hoboken, NJ: Wiley.

Luthar, S. S., & Goldstein. A. S. (2008). Substance use and related behaviors among suburban late adolescents: The importance of perceived parent containment. *Development and Psychopathology, 20,* 591–614.

Luyckx, K. (2006). *Identity formation in emerging adulthood: Developmental trajectories, antecedents, and consequences.* Doctoral Disseration, Katholieke Universiteit Leuven, Leuven, Belgium.

Luyckx, K., Schwartz, S. J., Berzonsky, M. D., Soenens, B., Vansteenkiste, M., Smits, I., & Goossens, L. (2008). Capturing ruminative exploration: Extending the four-dimensional model of identity formation in late adolescence. *Journal of Research in Personality, 42,* 58–62.

Luyckx, K., Schwartz, S. J., Goossens, L., Soenens, B., & Beyers, W. (2008). Developmental typologies of identity formation and adjustment in female emerging adults: A latent class growth analysis approach. *Journal of Research on Adolescence, 18,* 595–619.

Luyckx, K., Schwartz, S. J., Soenens, B., Vansteenkiste, M., & Goossens, L. (2010). The path from identity commitments to adjustment: Motivational underpinnings and mediating mechanisms. *Journal of Counseling and Development, 88,* 52–60.

Lynch, M. E. (1991). Gender intensification. In R. M. Lerner, A. C. Petersen, & J. Brooks-Gunn (Eds.), *Encyclopedia of adolescence* (Vol. 1). New York: Garland.

Lynne-Landsman, S. D., Bradshaw, C. P., & Ialongo, N. (2010). Testing a developmental cascade model of adolescent substance use trajectories and young adult adjustment. *Development and Psychopathology, 22,* 933–948.

Lynne-Landsman, S. D., Graber, J. A., Nichols, T. R., & Botvin, G. J. (2010, in press). Is sensation seeking a stable trait or does it change over time? *Journal of Youth and Adolescence.*

Lyons, H., Giordano, P. C., Manning, W. D., & Longmore, M. A. (2010). Identity, peer relationships, and adolescent girls' sexual behavior: An exploration of the contemporary double standard. *Journal of Sex Research, 47,* 1–13.

Lytle, L. A. (2009). School-based interventions: Where do we go from here? *Archives of Pediatric and Adolescent Medicine, 163,* 388–389.

M

Maccoby, E. E. (1987, November). Interview with Elizabeth Hall: All in the family. *Psychology Today,* 54–60.

Maccoby, E. E. (1998). *The two sexes.* Cambridge, MA: Harvard University Press.

Maccoby, E. E. (2002). Gender and group process: A developmental perspective. *Current Directions in Psychological Science, 11,* 54–57.

Maccoby, E. E. (2007). Historical overview of socialization theory and research. In J. E. Grusec & P. D. Hastings (Eds.), *Handbook of socialization.* New York: Guilford.

Maccoby, E. E., & Jacklin, C. N. (1974). *The psychology of sex differences.* Palo Alto, CA: Stanford University Press.

Maccoby, E. E., & Martin, J. A. (1983). Socialization in the context of the family. In E. M. Hetherington (Ed.), *Handbook of Child Psychology: Vol. 4, Socialization, personality, and social development.* New York: Wiley.

MacDonald, K. (1987). Parent-child physical play with rejected, neglected, and popular boys. *Developmental Psychology, 23,* 705–711.

MacGeorge, E. L. (2004). The myth of gender cultures: Similarities outweigh differences in men's and women's provisions of and responses to supportive communication. *Sex Roles, 50,* 143–175.

Mac Iver, D., Balfanz, R. W., Ruby, A., & Byrnes, V. (2010). Talent development in the middle school. In J. L. Meece & J. S. Eccles (Eds.), *Handbook of research on schools, schooling, and human development.* New York: Routledge.

Maclean, A. M., Walker, L. J., & Matsuba, M. K. (2004). Transcendence and the moral self: Identity, integration, religion, and moral life. *Journal for the Scientific Study of Religion, 43,* 429–437.

Macy, R. J., Nurius, P. S., & Norris, J. (2006). Responding in their best interests: Contextualizing women's coping with acquaintance sexual aggression. *Violence Against Women, 12,* 478–500.

Mader, S. S. (2011). *Biology* (10th ed.). New York: McGraw-Hill.

Madison, B. E., & Foster-Clark, F. S. (1996, March). *Pathways to identity and intimacy: Effects of gender and personality.* Paper presented at the meeting of the Society for Research on Adolescence, Boston.

Madkour, A. S., Farhat, T., Halpern, C. T., Godeu, E., & Gabhainn, S. N. (2010). Early adolescent sexual initiation as a problem behavior: A comparative study of five nations. *Journal of Adolescent Health, 47,* 389–398.

Madsen, S. D., & Collins, W. A. (2011, in press). The salience of romantic experiences for romantic relationship qualities in young adulthood. *Journal of Research on Adolescence.*

Maehr, M. L., & Zusho, A. (2009). Goal-directed behavior in the classroom. In K. Wentzel & A. Wigfield (Eds.), *Handbook of motivation at school.* New York: Routledge.

Mael, F. A. (1998). Single-sex and coeducational schooling: Relationships to socioemotional and academic development. *Review of Educational Research, 68*(2), 101–129.

Magno, C. (2010). The role of metacognitive skills in developing critical thinking. *Metacognition and Learning, 5,* 137–156.

Mahmoudi-Gharaei, J., Dodangi, N., Tehrani-Doost, M., & Faghihi, T. (2011, in press). Duloxetine in the treatment of adolescents with attention deficit/hyperactivity disorder: An open-label study. *Human Psychopharmacology.*

Mahoney, J., Vandell, D., Simpkins, S., & Zarrett, N. (2009). Adolescent out-of-school activities. In R. M. Lerner & L. Steinberg (Eds.), *Handbook of adolescent psychology* (3rd ed.). New York: Wiley.

Malamitsi-Puchner, A., & Boutsikou, T. (2006). Adolescent pregnancy and perinatal outcome. *Pediatric Endocrinology Reviews, 3*(Suppl 1), 170–171.

Malik, N. M., & Furman, W. (1993). Practitioner review: Problems in children's peer relations: What can the clinician do? *Journal of Child Psychology and Psychiatry, 34,* 1303–1326.

Maloy, R. W., Verock-O'Loughlin, R-E., Edwards, S. A., & Woolf, B. P. (2011). *Transforming learning with new technologies.* Boston: Allyn & Bacon.

Malti, T., & Buchmann, M. (2010). Socialization and individual antecedents of adolescents' and young adults' moral motivation. *Journal of Youth and Adolescence, 39,* 138–149.

Malti, T., & Latzko, B. (2010). Children's moral emotions and moral cognition: Towards an integrative perspective. *New Directions for Child and Adolescent Development, 129,* 1–10.

Mandara, J. (2006). The impact of family functioning on African American males' academic achievement: A review and clarification of the empirical literature. *Teachers College Record, 108,* 206–233.

Mandelman, S. D., & Grigorenko, E. L. (2011). Intelligence: Genes, environments, and their interactions. In R. J. Sternberg & S. B. Kaufman (Eds.), *Cambridge handbook of intelligence.* New York: Cambridge University Press.

Manis, F. R., Keating, D. P., & Morrison, F. J. (1980). Developmental differences in the allocation of processing capacity. *Journal of Experimental Child Psychology, 29,* 156–169.

Manongdo, J. A., & Garcia, J. I. R. (2011). Maternal parenting and mental health of Mexican American youth: A bidirectional and prospective approach. *Developmental Psychology, 25,* 261–270.

Marceau, K., Ram, N., Houts, R. M., Grimm, K. J., & Susman, E. J. (2011, in press). Individual differences in boys' and girls' timing and tempo of puberty: Modeling development with nonlinear growth models. *Developmental Psychology.*

Marcell, A. V., & Halpern-Felsher, B. L. (2007). Adolescents' beliefs about preferred resources for help vary depending on the health issue. *Journal of Adolescent Health, 41,* 61–68.

Marcell, A. V., Klein, J. D., Fischer, I., Allan, M. J., & Kokotailo, P. K. (2002). Male adolescent use of health care services: Where are the boys? *Journal of Adolescent Health Care, 30,* 35–43.

Marcell, A. V., & Millstein, S. G. (2001, March). *Quality of adolescent preventive services: The role of physician attitudes and self-efficacy.* Paper presented at the meeting of the Society for Adolescent Medicine, San Diego.

Marcia, J. E. (1980). Ego identity development. In J. Adelson (Ed.), *Handbook of adolescent psychology.* New York: Wiley.

Marcia, J. E. (1987). The identity status approach to the study of ego identity development. In T. Honess & K. Yardley (Eds.), *Self and identity: Perspectives across the lifespan.* London: Routledge & Kegan Paul.

Marcia, J. E. (1994). The empirical study of ego identity. In H. A. Bosma, T. L. G. Graafsma, H. D. Grotevant, & D. J. De Levita (Eds.), *Identity and development.* Newbury Park, CA: Sage.

Marcia, J. E. (1996). Unpublished review of J. W. Santrock's *Adolescence,* 7th ed. (Dubuque, IA: Brown & Benchmark).

Marcia, J. E. (2002). Identity and psychosocial development in adulthood. *Identity: An International Journal of Theory and Research, 2,* 7–28.

Marcia, J. E., & Carpendale, J. (2004). Identity: Does thinking make it so? In C. Lightfoot, C. Lalonde, & M. Chandler (Eds.), *Changing conceptions of psychological life.* Mahwah, NJ: Erlbaum.

Marcovitch, H. (2004). Use of stimulants for attention deficit hyperactivity disorder: AGAINST. *British Medical Journal, 329,* 908–909.

Marecek, J., Finn, S. E., & Cardell, M. (1988). Gender roles in the relationships of lesbians and gay men. In J. P. De Cecco (Ed.), *Gay relationships.* New York: Harrington Park Press.

Markey, C. N. (2010, in press). Invited commentary: Why body image is important to adolescent development. *Journal of Youth and Adolescence.*

Markey, C. N. (2010). Invited commentary: Why body image is important to adolescent development. *Journal of Youth and Adolescence, 39,* 1387–1391.

Markham, C. M., & others. (2010). Connectedness as a predictor of sexual and reproductive health outcomes for youth. *Journal of Adolescent Health, 46*(Suppl 3), S23–S41.

Marks, A. K., Patton, F., & Garcia Coll, C. (2011). Being bicultural: A mixed-methods study of adolescents' implicitly and explicitly measured ethnic identities. *Developmental Psychology, 47,* 270–288.

Markstrom, C. A. (2010). *Empowerment of North American Indian girls.* Lincoln: University of Nebraska Press.

Markstrom, C. A. (2011, in press). Identity formation of American Indian adolescents: Local, national, and global considerations. *Journal of Research on Adolescence.*

Markus, H. R., & Kitayama, S. (2010). Cultures and selves: A cycle of mutual constitution. *Perspectives on Psychological Science, 5,* 420–430.

Markus, H. R., Mullally, P. R., & Kitayama, S. (1999). *Selfways: Diversity in modes of cultural participation.* Unpublished manuscript, Department of Psychology, University of Michigan.

Markus, H. R., & Nurius, P. (1986). Possible selves. *American Psychologist, 41,* 954–969.

Markus, H. R., Uchida, Y., Omoregi, H., Townsend, S. S., & Kitayama, S. (2006). Going for the gold: Models of agency in Japanese and American contexts. *Psychological Science, 17,* 103–112.

Marlatt, M. W., Lucassen, P. J., & van Pragg, H. (2010, in press). Comparison of neurogenic effects of fluoxetine, duloxetine, and running in mice. *Brain Research.*

Marshall Scholarships. (2007). Scholar profiles: 2007. Retrieved January 31, 2008, from www.marshallscholarship.org/profiles2007.html

Marsiglio, W., & Hinojsoa, R. (2010). Stepfathers' lives: Exploring social context and interpersonal complexity. In M. E. Lamb (Ed.), *The role of the father in child development* (5th ed.). New York: Wiley.

Marti, C. N., Stice, E., & Springer, D. W. (2010). Substance use and abuse trajectories across adolescence: A latent trajectory analysis of a community-recruited sample of girls. *Journal of Adolescence, 33,* 449–461.

Martin, C. L., & Ruble, D. N. (2010). Patterns of gender development. *Annual Review of Psychology* (Vol. 61). Palo Alto, CA: Annual Reviews.

Martin, C. L., Ruble, D. N., & Szkrybalo, J. (2002). Cognitive theories of early gender development. *Psychological Bulletin, 128,* 903–933.

Martinez, A. (2006). In the fast lane: Boosting your career through cooperative education and internships. *Careers and Colleges, 26,* 8–10.

Martini, T. S., & Bussèri, M. A. (2010). Emotion regulation strategies and goals as predictors of older mothers' and daughters' helping-related subjective well-being. *Psychology and Aging, 25*(1), 48–59.

Martin, L. R., Friedman, H. S., & Schwartz, J. E. (2007). Personality and mortality risk across the lifespan: The importance of conscientiousness as biopsychosocial attribute. *Health Psychology, 26,* 428–436.

Martin, M. J., & others. (2011, in press). The enduring significance of racism: Discrimination, and delinquency among Black American youth. *Journal of Research on Adolescence.*

Martino, S. C., & others. (2006). Exposure to degrading versus nondegrading music lyrics and sexual behavior among youth. *Pediatrics, 118,* e430–e431.

Mascalo, M. F., & Fischer, K. W. (2010). The dynamic development of thinking, feeling, and acting over the life span. In W. F. Overton & R. M. Lerner (Eds.), *Handbook of life-span development* (Vol. 1). New York: Wiley

Mash, E. J., & Wolfe, D. A. (2009). *Abnormal child psychology* (4th ed.). Belmont, CA: Cengage.

Masten, A. S. (2001). Ordinary magic: Resilience processes in development. *American Psychologist, 56*(3), 227–238.

Masten, A. S. (2004). Regulatory processes, risk and resilience in adolescent development. *Annals of the New York Academy of Sciences, 1021,* 310–319.

Masten, A. S. (2006). Developmental psychopathology: Pathways to the future. *International Journal of Behavioral Development, 31,* 46–53.

Masten, A. S. (2007). Resilience in developing systems: Progress and promise as the fourth wave rises. *Development and Psychopathology, 19,* 921–930.

Masten, A. S. (2009). Ordinary Magic: Lessons from research on resilience in human development. Retrieved October 15, 2009, from www.cea-ace.ca/media/en/Ordinary_Magic_Summer09.pdf

Masten, A. S. (2011). Resilience in children threatened by extreme adversity: Frameworks for research, practice, and translational synergy. *Development and Psychopathology, 23,* 493–506.

Masten, A. S., & Cicchetti, D. (2010). Developmental cascades. *Development and Psychopathology, 22,* 491–495.

Masten, A. S., Cutull, J. J., Herbers, J. E., & Gabrielle-Reed, M. J. (2009). Resilience in development. In C. R. Snyder & S. J. Lopez (Eds.), *The handbook of positive psychology* (2nd ed.). New York: Oxford University Press.

Masten, A. S., Desjardins, C. D., McCormick, C. M., Kuo, S. I., & Long, J. D. (2010). The significance of childhood competence and problems for adult success in work: A developmental casade analysis. *Developmental Psychopathology, 22,* 679–694.

Masten, A. S., Obradovic, J., & Burt, K. B. (2006). Resilience in emerging adulthood: Developmental perspectives on continuity and transformation. In J. J. Arnett & J. L. Tanner (Eds.), *Emerging adults in America.* Washington, DC: American Psychological Association.

Masten, A. S., & Reed, M. G. (2002). Resilience in development. In C. R. Snyder & S. J. Lopez (Eds.), *The handbook of positive psychology.* New York: Oxford University Press.

Masten, A. S., & Wright, M. O. (2009). Resilience over the lifespan: Developmental perspective on resistance, recovery, and transformation. In J. W. Reich, A. J. Zautra, & J. S. Hall (Eds.), *Handbook of adult resilience.* New York: Wiley.

Match.com. (2011). The Match.com Single in America Study. Retrieved February 7, 2011, from http://blog.match.com/singles-study

Matlin, M. W. (2012). *Psychology of women* (7th ed.). Boston: Cengage.

Matlin, S. L., Molock, S. D., & Tebes, J. K. (2011). Suicidality and depression among African American adolescents: The role of family and peer support and community connectedness. *American Journal of Orthopsychiatry, 81,* 108–117.

Matsuba, M. K., & Walker, L. J. (2004). Extraordinary moral commitment: Young adults involved in social organizations. *Journal of Personality, 72,* 413–436.

Matthews, G., Zeidner, M., & Roberts, R. D. (2006). Models of personality and affect for education: A review and synthesis. In P. A. Alexander & P. H. Wynne (Eds.), *Handbook of educational psychology* (2nd ed.). Mahwah, NJ: Erlbaum.

Matthews, G., Zeidner, M., & Roberts, R. D. (2011). *Emotional intelligence 101.* New York: Springer.

Mayer, J. D., Salovey, P., Caruso, D. R., & Cherkasskiy, L. (2011). Emotional intelligence. In R. J. Sternberg & S. B. Kaufman (Eds.), *Cambridge handbook of intelligence.* New York: Cambridge University Press.

Mayer, R. E. (2008). *Learning and instruction* (2nd ed.). Upper Saddle River, NJ: Prentice Hall.

Mayer, R. E., & Wittrock, M. C. (2006). Problem solving. In P. A. Alexander & P. H. Winne (Eds.), *Handbook of educational psychology* (2nd ed.). Mahwah, NJ: Erlbaum.

Mayers, L. B., & Chiffriller, S. H. (2008). Body art (body piercing and tattooing) among undergraduate university students: "Then and now." *Journal of Adolescent Health, 42,* 201–203.

McAdams, D. P. (2011). Life narratives. In K. L. Fingerman, C. A. Berg, J. Smith, & T. C. Antonucci (Eds.), *Handbook of life-span development.* New York: Springer.

McAdams, D. P., & Cox, K. S. (2010). Self and identity across the life span. In R. M. Lerner, A. Freund, & M. Lamb (Eds.), *Handbook of life-span development* (Vol. 2). New York: Wiley.

McAdams, D. P., Josselson, R., & Lieblich, A. (Eds.). (2006). *Identity and story: Creating self in narrative.* Washington, DC: American Psychological Association Press.

McAdoo, H. P. (2006). *Blackwell families* (4th ed.). Thousand Oaks, CA: Sage.

McAlister, A., Perry, C., Killen, J., Slinkard, L. A., & Maccoby, N. (1980). Pilot study of smoking, alcohol, and drug abuse prevention. *American Journal of Public Health, 70,* 719–721.

McCarty, C. A., Violette, H. D., & McCauley, E. (2011, in press). Feasibility of the positive thoughts and actions prevention program for middle schoolers at risk for depression. *Depression Research and Treatment.*

McClain, L. R. (2011). Cohabitation: Parents following in their children's footsteps. *Sociological Inquiry, 81,* 260–271.

McClure, J. B., & others. (2006). Chlamydia screening in at-risk adolescent females: An evaluation of screening practices and modifiable screening correlates. *Journal of Adolescent Health, 38,* 726–733.

McCombs, B. (2010). Learner-centered practices. In J. L. Meece & J. S. Eccles (Eds.), *Handbook of research on schools, schooling, and human development.* New York: Routledge.

McCormick, C. M., Kuo, S. I-C., & Masten, A. S. (2011). Developmental tasks across the life span. In K. L. Fingerman, C. A. Berg, J. Smith, & T. C. Antonucci (Eds.), *Handbook of life-span development.* New York: Springer.

McCrae, R. R., & Costa, P. T. (2006). Cross-cultural perspectives on adult personality trait development. In D. K. Mroczek & T. D. Little (Eds.), *Handbook of personality development.* Mahwah, NJ: Erlbaum.

McElhaney, K. B., & Allen, J. P. (2012). Sociocultural perspectives on adolescent autonomy. In P. K. Kerig, M. S. Schulz, & S. T. Hauser (Eds.), *Adolescence and beyond.* New York: Oxford University Press.

McElhaney, K. B., Allen, J. P., Stephenson, J. C., & Hare, A. L. (2009). Attachment and autonomy during adolescence. In R. M. Lerner & L. Steinberg (Eds.), *Handbook of adolescent psychology* (3rd ed.). New York: Wiley.

McElhaney, K. B., Antonishak, J., & Allen, J. P. (2008). "They like me, they like me not": Popularity and adolescents' perceptions of acceptance predicting social functioning over time. *Child Development, 79,* 720–731.

McHale, S. M., Kim, J. Y., Dotterer, A., Crouter, A. C., & Booth, A. (2009). The development of gendered interests and personality qualities from middle childhood through adolescence: A bio-social analysis. *Child Development, 80,* 482–495.

McHale, S. M., Kim, J. Y., Kan, M., & Updegraff, K. A. (2010). Sleep in Mexican-American adolescents: Social ecological and well-being correlates. *Journal of Youth and Adolescence, 40,* 666–679.

McHale, S. M., Updegraff, K. A., Helms-Erikson, H., & Crouter, A. C. (2001). Sibling influences on gender development in middle childhood and early adolescence: A longitudinal study. *Developmental Psychology, 37,* 115–125.

McHale, S. M., Updegraff, K. A., & Whiteman, S. D. (2011, in press). Sibling relationships. In G. W. Peterson & K. R. Bush (Eds.), *Handbook of marriage and family* (3rd ed.). New York: Springer.

McKinney, C., & Renk, K. (2011, in press). A multivariate model of parent-adolescent relationship variables in early adolescence. *Child Psychiatry and Human Development.*

McLaughlin, K. A., & Hatzenbuehler, M. L. (2009). Mechanisms linking stressful life events and mental health problems in a prospective, community-based sample of adolescents. *Journal of Adolescent Health, 44,* 153–160.

McLean, K. C., Breen, A. V., & Fournier, M. A. (2010). Constructing the self in early, middle, and late adolescent boys: Narrative identity, individuation, and well-being. *Journal of Research on Adolescence, 20,* 166–187.

McLean, K. C., & Pasupathi, M. (Eds.). (2010). *Narrative development in adolescence: Creating the storied self.* New York: Springer.

McLean, K. C., & Pratt, M. W. (2006). Life's little (and big) lessons: Identity statuses and meaning-making in the turning point narratives of emerging adults. *Developmental Psychology, 42,* 714–722.

McLean, K. C., & Thorne, A. (2006). Identity light: Entertainment stories as vehicle for self-development. In D. P. McAdams, R. Josselson, & A. Lieblich (Eds.), *Identity and story.* Washington, DC: American Psychological Association.

Mclellan, R., & Remedios, R. (2011). *Psychology for the classroom: Motivation.* New York: Routledge.

McLoyd, V. C. (1998). Children in poverty. In I. E. Siegel & K. A. Renninger (Eds.), *Handbook of child psychology* (5th ed., Vol. 4). New York: Wiley.

McLoyd, V. C., Aikens, N. L., & Burton, L. M. (2006). Childhood poverty, policy, and practice. In W. Damon & R. Lerner (Eds.), *Handbook of child psychology* (6th ed.). New York: Wiley.

McLoyd, V. C., Kaplan, R., Purtell, K. M., Bagley, E., Hardaway, C. R., & Smalls, C. (2009). Poverty and social disadvantage in adolescence. In R. M. Lerner & L. Steinberg (Eds.), *Handbook of adolescent psychology* (3rd ed.). New York: Wiley.

McLoyd, V. C., Kaplan, R., Purtell, K. M., & Huston, A. C. (2011). Assessing the effects of a work-based antipoverty program for parents on youth's future orientation and employment experiences. *Child Development, 82,* 113–132.

McMurray, R. G., Harrell, J. S., Creighton, D., Wang, Z., & Bangdiwala, S. I. (2008). Influence of physical activity on change in weight status as children become adolescents. *International Journal of Pediatric Obesity, 3,* 69–77.

McNeely, C. A., & Barber, B. K. (2010). How do parents make adolescents feel loved? Perspectives on supportive parenting from adolescents in 12 cultures. *Journal of Adolescent Research, 25,* 601–631.

McWilliams, L. A., & Bailey, S. J. (2010). Associations between adult attachment ratings and health conditions: Evidence from the National Comorbidity Survey replication. *Health Psychology, 29,* 446–453.

Meade, C. S., Kershaw, T. S., & Ickovics, J. R. (2008). The intergenerational cycle of teenage motherhood: An ecological approach. *Health Psychology, 27,* 419–429.

Mead, M. (1928). *Coming of age in Samoa.* New York: Morrow.

Meece, J. L., Anderman, E. M., & Anderman, L. H. (2006). Classroom goal structure, student motivation, and academic achievement. *Annual Review of Psychology* (Vol. 57). Palo Alto, CA: Annual Reviews.

Meeus, W. (2011). The study of adolescent identity formation 2000–2010: A review of longitudinal research. *Journal of Research in Adolescence, 21,* 75–84.

Meeus, W., van de Schoot, R., Keijser, L., Branje, S., & Schwartz, S. J. (2010). On the progression and stability of adolescent identity formation: A five-wave longitudinal study in early-to-middle and middle-to-late adolescence. *Child Development, 81,* 1565–1581.

Mehta, C. M., & Strough, J. (2009). Sex segregation in friendships and normative contexts across the life span. *Developmental Review, 29,* 201–220.

Mehta, C. M., & Strough, J. (2010). Gender segregation and gender-typing in adolescence. *Sex Roles, 63,* 251–263.

Meichenbaum, D., & Butler, L. (1980). Toward a conceptual model of the treatment of test anxiety: Implications for research and treatment. In I. G. Sarason (Ed.), *Test anxiety.* Mahwah, NJ: Erlbaum.

Meijs, N., Cillessen, A. H. N., Scholte, R. H. J., Segers, E., & Spikjkerman, R. (2010). Social intelligence and academic achievement as predictors of adolescent popularity. *Journal of Youth and Adolescence, 39,* 62–72.

Mellor, J. M., & Freeborn, B. A. (2011, in press). Religious participation and risky health behaviors among adolescents. *Health Economics.*

Mello, Z. R. (2009). Racial/ethnic group and socioeconomic status variation in educational and occupational expectations from adolescence to adulthood. *Journal of Applied Developmental Psychology, 30,* 494–504.

Merrill, D. M. (2009). Parent-child relationships: Later-life. In D. Carr (Ed.), *Encyclopedia of the life course human development.* Boston: Gale Cengage.

Mesch, G. S. (2008). Social bonds and Internet pornographic exposure among adolescents. *Journal of Adolescence, 32,* 601–618.

Metz, E. C., & Youniss, J. (2005). Longitudinal gains in civic development through school-based required service. *Political Psychology, 26,* 413–437.

Metzger, A., Dawes, N., Mermelstein, R., & Wakschlag, L. (2011). Longitudinal modeling of adolescents' activity involvement, problem peer associations, and youth smoking. *Journal of Applied Developmental Psychology, 32,* 1–9.

Meyer-Bahlburg, & others. (1995). Prenatal estrogens and the development of homosexual orientation. *Developmental Psychology, 31,* 12–21.

Meyer, I. H. (2003). Prejudice, social stress, and mental health in gay, lesbian, and bisexual populations: conceptual issues and research evidence. *Psychological Bulletin, 129,* 674–697.

Meyers, J. (2010, April 1). Suicides open eyes to bullying. *Dallas Morning News,* pp. 1A–2A.

Michael, R. T., Gagnon, J. H., Laumann, E. O., & Kolata, G. (1994). *Sex in America.* Boston: Little, Brown.

Michaud, P-A., & others. (2009). To say or not to say: A qualitative study on the disclosure of their condition by human immunodeficiency virus-positive adolescents. *Journal of Adolescent Health, 44,* 356–362.

Mikami & others. (2010). Adolescent peer relationships and behavior problems predict young adults' communication on social networking sites. *Developmental Psychology, 46,* 46–56.

Mikkelsson, L., Kaprio, J., Kautiainen, H., Kujala, U., Mikkelsson, M., & Nupponen, H. (2006). School fitness tests as predictors of adult health-related fitness. *American Journal of Human Biology, 18,* 342–349.

Mikulincer, M., Shaver, P. R., Bar-On, N., & Ein-Dor, T. (2010). The pushes and pulls of close relationships: Attachment insecurities and relational ambivalence. *Journal of Personality and Social Psychology, 98,* 450–468.

Milevsky, A. (2011). *Sibling relations in childhood and adolescence.* New York: Columbia University Press.

Milevsky, A. (2012). Parenting styles in adolescence. In J. R. Levesque (Ed.), *Encyclopedia of adolescence.* New York: Springer.

Miller, B., & Taylor, J. (2011, in press). Racial and socioeconomic status differences in depressive symptoms among Black and White youth: An examination of the mediating effects of family structure, stress, and support. *Journal of Youth and Adolescence.*

Miller, B. C., Benson, B., & Galbraith, K. A. (2001). Family relationships and adolescent pregnancy risk: A research synthesis. *Developmental Review, 21,* 1–38.

Miller, B. C., Fan, X., Christensen, M., Grotevant, H. D., & von Dulmen, M. (2000). Comparisons of adopted and nonadopted adolescents in a large, nationally representative sample. *Child Development, 71,* 1458–1473.

Miller, J. G. (2007). Insights into moral development from cultural psychology. In M. Killen & J. G. Smetana (Eds.), *Handbook of moral development.* Mahwah, NJ: Erlbaum.

Miller, P. H. (2011). Piaget's theory: Past, present, and future. In U. Goswami (Ed.), *Wiley-Blackwell handbook of childhood cognitive development* (2nd ed.). New York: Wiley-Blackwell.

Miller, W. L. (2008). Androgen synthesis in adrenarche. *Reviews in Endocrine and Metabolic Disorders, 10,* 3–17.

Mills, B., Reyna, V., & Estrada, S. (2008). Explaining contradictory relations between risk perception and risk taking. *Psychological Science, 19,* 429–433.

Miltenberger, R. G. (2012). *Behavior modification* (5th ed.). Boston: Cengage.

Minuchin, P. P., & Shapiro, E. K. (1983). The school as a context for social development. In P. H. Mussen (Ed.), *Handbook of child psychology* (4th ed., Vol. 4). New York: Wiley.

Mischel, W. (1968). *Personality and assessment.* New York: Wiley.

Mischel, W. (2004). Toward an integrative science of the person. *Annual Review of Psychology* (Vol. 55). Palo Alto, CA: Annual Reviews.

Mischel, W., & Mischel, H. (1975, April). *A cognitive social-learning analysis of moral development.* Paper presented at the meeting of the Society for Research in Child Development, Denver.

Misra, M. (2008). Bone density in the adolescent athlete. *Reviews in Endocrine and Metabolic Disorders, 9,* 139–144.

MMWR. (2006a, June 9). Youth risk behavior surveillance—United States 2005, Vol. 255. Atlanta, GA: Centers for Disease Control and Prevention.

MMWR. (2006b, August 11). The global HIV/AIDS pandemic, 2006. *MMWR, 55,* 841–844.

Molina, R. C., Roca, C. G., Zamorano, J. S., & Araya, E. G. (2010). Family planning and adolescent pregnancy. *Best Practices and Research: Clinical Obstetrics and Gynecology, 24,* 209–222.

Monahan, K. C., Lee, J. M., & Steinberg, L. (2011). Revisiting the impact of part-time work on adolescent adjustment: Distinguishing between selection and socialization using propensity score matching. *Child Development, 82,* 96–112.

Mond, J., van den Berg, P., Boutelle, K., Hannan, P., & Neumark-Sztainer, D. (2011, in press). Obesity, body dissatisfaction, and emotional well-being in early and late adolescence: Findings from the Project EAT study. *Journal of Adolescent Health.*

Montemayor, R. (1982). The relationship between parent-adolescent conflict and the amount of time adolescents spend with parents, peers, and alone. *Child Development, 53,* 1512–1519.

Montgomery, M. (2005). Psychosocial intimacy and identity: From early adolescence to emerging adulthood. *Journal of Adolescent Research, 20,* 346–374.

Moore, D. (2001). *The dependent gene.* New York: W. H. Freeman.

Morreale, M. C. (2004). Executing juvenile offenders: A fundamental failure of society. *Journal of Adolescent Health, 35,* 341.

Morris, M. C., Ciesla, J. A., & Garber, J. (2010). A prospective study of stress and autonomy versus stress sensitization in adolescents at varied risk for depression. *Journal of Abnormal Psychology, 119,* 341–354.

Morrison, G. S. (2009). *Teaching in America* (5th ed.). Upper Saddle River, NJ: Prentice Hall.

Morris, P., & Kalil, A. (2006). Out of school time use during middle childhood in a low-income sample: Do combinations of activities affect achievement and behavior? In A. Huston & M. Ripke (Eds.), *Middle childhood: Contexts of development.* New York: Cambridge University Press.

Mortimer, J. T., & Larson, R. W. (2002). Macrostructural trends and the reshaping of adolescence. In J. T. Mortimer & R. W. Larson (Eds.), *The changing adolescent experience.* New York: Cambridge University Press.

Mosher, W. D., Chandra, A., & Jones, J. (2005). *Sexual behavior and selected health measures: Men and women 15–44 years of age, United States, 2002.* Hyattsville, MD: National Center for Health Statistics.

Moshman, D. (2011). *Adolescent rationality and development: Cognition, morality, and identity* (3rd ed.). New York: Psychology Press.

Mounts, N. S. (2007). Adolescents' and their mothers' perceptions of parental management of peer relationships. *Journal of Research on Adolescence, 17,* 169–178.

Mounts, N. S. (2011). Parental management of peer relationships and early adolescents' social skills. *Journal of Youth and Adolescence, 40,* 416–427.

Mueller, S. C., & others. (2010). Psychiatric characterization of children with genetic causes of hyperandrogenism. *European Journal of Endocrinology, 163,* 801–810.

Mullis, I. V. S., Martin, M. O., Beaton, A. E., Gonzales, E. J., Kelly, D. L., & Smith, T. A. (1998). *Mathematics and science achievement in the final year of secondary school.* Chestnut Hill, MA: Boston College, TIMSS International Study Center.

Murnane, R. J., & Levy, F. (1996). *Teaching the new basic skills.* New York: Free Press.

Murphy, K. A., Blustein, D. L., Bohlig, A. J., & Platt, M. G. (2010). The college-to-career transition: An exploration of emerging adulthood. *Journal of Counseling and Development, 88,* 174–181.

Murray, J. P., & Murray, A. D. (2008). Television: Use and effects. In M. M. Haith & J. B. Benson (Eds.), *Encyclopedia of infant and early childhood development.* New York: Elsevier.

Murray, K. M., Byrne, D. C., & Rieger, E. (2011). Investigating adolescent stress and body image. *Journal of Adolescence, 34,* 269–278.

Murrell, P. C. (2009). Identity, agency, and culture: Black achievement and educational attainment. In L. C. Tillman (Ed.), *The SAGE handbook of African American Education.* Thousand Oaks, CA: Sage.

Murry, V. B., Berkel, C., Gaylord-Harden, N. K., Copeland-Linder, N., & Nation, M. (2011). Neighborhood poverty and adolescent development. *Journal of Research on Adolescence, 21,* 114–128.

Mussen, P. H., Honzik, M., & Eichorn, D. (1982). Early adult antecedents of life satisfaction at age 70. *Journal of Gerontology, 37,* 316–322.

Myers, D. (2008, June 2). Commentary in S. Begley & J. Interlandi, The dumbest generation? Don't be dumb. Retrieved July 22, 2008, from www.newsweek.com/id/138536/

Myers, D., Baer, W., & Choi, S. (1996). The changing problem of overcrowded housing. *Journal of the American Planning Association, 62,* 66–84.

Myers, D. G. (2010). *Psychology* (9th ed.). New York: Worth.

N

Nader, P., & others. (2006). Identifying risk for obesity in early childhood. *Pediatrics, 118,* e594–e601.

Nader, P. R., Bradley, R. H., Houts, R. M., McRitchie, S. L., & O'Brian, M. (2008). Moderate-to-vigorous physical activity from 9 to 15 years. *Journal of the American Medical Association, 300,* 295–305.

Nagata, P. K. (1989). Japanese American children and adolescents. In J. T. Gibbs & L. N. Huang (Eds.), *Children of color.* San Francisco: Jossey-Bass.

Nagel, B. J., & others. (2011). Altered white matter microstructure in children with attention-deficit/hyperactivity disorder. *Journal of the American Academy of Child and Adolescent Psychiatry, 50,* 283–292.

Najman, J. M., & others. (2010). Timing and chronicity of family poverty and development of unhealthy behaviors in children: A longitudinal study. *Journal of Adolescent Health, 46,* 538–544.

Nakamoto, J., & Schwartz, D. (2010). Is peer victimization associated with academic achievement? A meta-analytic review. *Social Development, 19,* 221–242.

Nansel, T. R., Overpeck, M., Pilla, R., Ruan, W., Simons-Morton, B., & Scheidt, P. (2001). Bullying behaviors among U.S. youth. *Journal of the American Medical Association, 285,* 2094–2100.

Narusyte, J., & others. (2011). Parental criticism and externalizing behavior problems in adolescents: The role of environment and genotype-environment correlation. *Journal of Abnormal Psychology, 120,* 365–376.

Narváez, D. (2006). Integrative moral education. In M. Killen & J. Smetana (Eds.), *Handbook of moral development.* Mahwah, NJ: Erlbaum.

Narváez, D. (2008). Four Component Model. In F. C. Power, R. J. Nuzzi, D. Narváez, D. K. Lapsley, & T. C. Hunt (Eds.), *Moral education: A handbook.* Westport, CT: Greenwood.

Narváez, D. (2010a). Moral complexity: The fatal attraction of truthiness and the importance of mature moral functioning. *Perspectives on Psychological Science, 5*(2), 163–181.

Narváez, D. (2010b). The embodied dynamism of moral becoming. *Perspectives on Psychological Science, 5*(2), 185–186.

Narváez, D., Bock, T., Endicott, L., & Lies, J. (2004). Minnesota's Community Voices and Character Education Project. *Journal of Research in Character Education, 2,* 89–112.

Narváez, D., & Hill, P. L. (2010). The relation of multicultural experiences to moral judgment and mindsets. *Journal of Diversity in Higher Education, 3,* 43–55.

Narváez, D., & Lapsley, D. K. (Eds.). (2009). *Personality, Identity, and Character: Explorations in Moral Psychology.* New York: Cambridge University Press.

National Assessment of Educational Progress. (2005). *The nation's report card: 2005.* Washington, DC: U.S. Department of Education.

National Assessment of Educational Progress. (2007). *The nation's report card: 2007.* Washington, DC: U.S. Department of Education.

National Center for Education Statistics. (1997). *School-family linkages.* Unpublished manuscript. Washington, DC: U.S. Department of Education.

National Center for Education Statistics. (1998). *Postsecondary financing strategies: How undergraduates combine work, borrowing, and attendance.* Washington, DC: U.S. Department of Education.

National Center for Education Statistics. (2002). *Contexts of postsecondary education: Earning opportunities.* Washington, DC: U.S. Department of Education.

National Center for Education Statistics. (2010). *The condition of education 2010.* Washington, DC: U.S. Department of Education.

National Center for Education Statistics. (2011). *The condition of education 2011.* Washington, DC: U.S. Department of Education.

National Center for Health Statistics. (2000). *Health United States, 1999.* Atlanta, GA: Centers for Disease Control and Prevention.

National Center for Health Statistics. (2002). Prevalence of overweight among children and adolescents: United States 1999–2000 (Table 71). *Health United States, 2002.* Atlanta, GA: Centers for Disease Control and Prevention.

National Center for Health Statistics. (2002). *Sexual behavior and selected health measures: Men and women 15–44 years of age, United States, 2002,* PHS 2003–1250. Atlanta, GA: Centers for Disease Control and Prevention.

National Center for Health Statistics. (2009). *Death rates.* Atlanta, GA: Centers for Disease Control and Prevention.

National Center for Health Statistics. (2010). *Health United States 2010.* Atlanta, GA: Centers for Disease Control and Prevention.

National Center for Health Statistics (2011). Vital signs: teen pregnancy—United States, 1991–2009. *MMWR, 60,* 414–420.

National Center for Injury Prevention and Control. (2006). Fatal injury reports [online database]. Retrieved March 16, 2006, from www.cdc.gov/ncipc/wisqars/

National Clearinghouse for Alcohol and Drug Information. (1999). *Physical and psychological effects of anabolic steroids.* Washington, DC: Substance Abuse and Mental Health Services Administration.

National Research Council. (1999). *How people learn.* Washington, DC: National Academic Press.

National Research Council. (2004). *Engaging schools: Fostering high school students motivation to learn.* Washington, DC: National Academies Press.

National Sleep Foundation. (2006). *2006 Sleep in America poll.* Washington, DC: National Sleep Foundation.

National Vital Statistics Reports (2010). Births, marriages, divorces, deaths: Provisional data for November 2009. *National Vital Statistics Reports, 58*(23), 1–5.

National Youth Risk Behavior Surveillance System (YRBSS). (2007). *National trends in risk behaviors.* Atlanta, GA: Centers for Disease Control and Prevention.

Nation, M., & others. (2003). What works in prevention: Principles of effective prevention programs. *American Psychologist, 58,* 449–456.

Natsuaki, M. N., & others. (2010). Early pubertal maturation and internalizing problems in adolescence: Sex differences in the role of cortical reactivity to interpersonal stress. *Journal of Clinical Child and Adolescent Psychology, 38,* 513–524.

Negriff, S., Susman, E. J., & Trickett, P. K. (2011, in press). The development pathway from pubertal timing to delinquency and sexual activity from early to late adolescence. *Journal of Youth and Adolescence.*

Neisser, U., & others. (1996). Intelligence: Knowns and unknowns. *American Psychologist, 51,* 77–101.

Nelson, C. A. (2003). Neural development and lifelong plasticity. In R. M. Lerner, F. Jacobs, & D. Wertlieb (Eds.), *Handbook of applied developmental science* (Vol. 1). Thousand Oaks, CA: Sage.

Nelson, C. A. (2011). Brain development and behavior. In A. M. Rudolph, C. Rudolf, L. First, G. Lister, & A. A. Gershon (Eds.), *Rudolph's pediatrics* (22nd ed.). New York: McGraw-Hill.

Nelson, L. J., & others. (2011). Parenting in emerging adulthood: An examination of parenting clusters and correlates. *Journal of Youth and Adolescence, 40,* 730–743.

Nelson, L. J., Padilla-Walker, L. M., Carroll, J. S., Madsen, S. D., Barry, C. M., & Badger, S. (2007). "If you want me to treat you like an adult, start acting like one!" Comparing the criteria that emerging adults and their parents have for adulthood. *Journal of Family Psychology, 21,* 665–674.

Nelson, M. C., & Gordon-Larsen, P. (2006). Physical activity and sedentary behavior patterns are associated with selected adolescent health risk behaviors. *Pediatrics, 117,* 1281–1290.

New, M. (2008, October). *Binge eating disorder.* Retrieved February 27, 2011, from http://kidshealth.org/parent/emotions/behavior/binge_eating.html

Newman, B. S., & Muzzonigro, P. G. (1993). The effects of traditional family values on the coming out process of gay male adolescents. *Adolescence, 28,* 213–226.

Nichols, J. F., Rauh, M. J., Lawson, M. J., Ji, M., & Barkai, H. S. (2006). Prevalence of female athlete triad syndrome among high school athletes. *Archives of Pediatric and Adolescent Medicine, 160,* 137–142.

Nieto, S. (2010). Multicultural education in the United States: Historical realities, ongoing challenges, and transformative possibilities. In J. A. Banks (Ed.), *The Routledge international companion to multicultural education.* New York: Routledge.

Nieto, S., & Bode, P. (2012). *Affirming diversity* (6th ed.). Boston: Allyn & Bacon.

Nie, Y., & Lau, S. (2009). Complementary roles of care and behavioral control in classroom management: The self-determination theory perspective. *Contemporary Educational Psychology, 34,* 185–194.

Nishina, A., Bellmore, A., Witkow, M. R., & Nylund-Gibson, K. (2010). Longitudinal consistency of adolescent ethnic identification across varying school ethnic contexts. *Developmental Psychology, 46,* 1389–1401.

Nitko, A. J., & Brookhart, S. M. (2011). *Educational assessment of students* (6th ed.). Boston: Allyn & Bacon.

Noddings, N. (1992). *The challenge to care in the schools.* New York: Teachers College Press.

Noddings, N. (2001). The care tradition: Beyond "add women and stir." *Theory into Practice, 40,* 29–34.

Noddings, N. (2006). *Critical lessons: What our schools should teach.* New York: Cambridge University Press.

Noddings, N. (2008). Caring and moral education. In L. Nucci & D. Narváez (Eds.), *Handbook of moral and character education.* Clifton, NJ: Psychology Press.

Noftle, E. E., & Robins, R. W. (2007). Personality predictors of academic outcomes: Big five correlates of GPA and SAT scores. *Journal of Personality and Social Psychology, 93,* 116–130.

Nolen-Hoeksema, S. (2011). *Abnormal psychology* (5th ed.). New York: McGraw-Hill.

Nosko, A., Tieu, T. T., Lawford, H., & Pratt, M. W. (2011). How do I love thee? Let me count the ways: Parenting during adolescence, attachment styles, and romantic narratives in emerging adulthood. *Developmental Psychology, 47,* 645–657.

Nottelmann, E. D., & others. (1987). Gonadal and adrenal hormone correlates of adjustment in early adolescence. In R. M. Lerner & T. T. Foch (Eds.), *Biological-psychological interactions in early adolescence.* Hillsdale, NJ: Erlbaum.

Nsamenang, A. B. (2002). Adolescence in sub-Saharan Africa: An image constructed from Africa's triple heritage. In B. B. Brown, R. W. Larson, & T. S. Saraswathi (Eds.), *The world's youth.* New York: Cambridge University Press.

Nucci, L. (2006). Education for moral development. In M. Killen & J. Smetana (Eds.), *Handbook of moral development.* Mahwah, NJ: Erlbaum.

Nucci, L., & Gingo, M. (2011). Moral reasoning. In U. Goswami (Ed.), *Wiley-Blackwell handbook of childhood cognitive development* (2nd ed.). New York: Wiley.

Nucci, L., & Narváez, D. (2008). *Handbook of moral and character education.* New York: Psychology Press.

O

Oberle, E., Schonert-Reichl, K. A., & Zumbo, B. D. (2011). Life satisfaction in early adolescence: Personal, neighborhood, school, family, and peer influences. *Journal of Youth and Adolescence, 40,* 889–901.

O'Brien, L., Albert, D., Chein, J., & Steinberg, L. (2010, in press). Adolescents prefer more immediate rewards when in the presence of their peers. *Journal of Research on Adolescence.*

O'Brien, M., & Moss, P. (2010). Fathers, work, and family policies in Europe. In M. E. Lamb (Ed.), *The father's role in child development* (5th ed.). New York: Wiley.

Occupational Outlook Handbook. (2010–2011). Washington, DC: U.S. Department of Labor, Bureau of Labor Statistics.

O'Connor, M., & others. (2010). Predictors of positive development in emerging adulthood. *Journal of Youth and Adolescence, 40,* 860–874.

O'Donnell, L., O'Donnell, C., Wardlaw, D. M., & Stueve, A. (2004). Risk and resiliency factors influencing suicidality among urban African American and Latino youth. *American Journal of Community Psychology, 33,* 37–49.

OECD. (2010). *Strong performers and successful reformers in education: Lessons from PISA for the United States.* Paris, France: OECD.

Offer, D., Ostrov, E., Howard, K. I., & Atkinson, R. (1988). *The teenage world: Adolescents' self-image in ten countries.* New York: Plenum.

Ogden, C. L., Carroll, M. D., & Flegal, K. M. (2008). High body mass index for age among U.S. children and adolescents, 2003–2006. *Journal of the American Medical Association, 299,* 2401–2405.

O'Keefe, G. S., & others. (2011). The impact of social media on children, adolescents, and families. *Pediatrics, 127,* 800–804.

Oldehinkel, A. J., Ormel, J., Veenstra, R., De Winter, A., & Verhulst, F. C. (2008). Parental divorce and offspring depressive symptoms: Dutch developmental trends during early adolescence. *Journal of Marriage and the Family, 70,* 284–293.

Olds, D. L., & others. (2004). Effects of home visits by paraprofessionals and nurses: Age four follow-up of a randomized trial. *Pediatrics, 114,* 1560–1568.

Olds, D. L., & others. (2007). Effects of nurse home visiting on maternal and child functioning: Age-9 follow-up of a randomized trial. *Pediatrics, 120,* e832–e845.

Oliva, A., Jimenez, J. M., & Parra, A. (2008). Protective effect of supportive family relationships and the influence of stressful life events on adolescent adjustment. *Anxiety, Stress, and Coping, 12,* 1–15.

Olson, M., & Hergenhahn, B. R. (2011). *Introduction to theories of personality* (8th ed.). Upper Saddle River, NJ: Pearson.

Olweus, D. (2003). Prevalence estimation of school bullying with the Olweus bully/victim questionnaire. *Aggressive Behavior, 29*(3), 239–269.

Ong, K. K. (2010). Early determinants of obesity. *Endocrine Development, 19,* 53–61.

Ong, K. K., Ahmed, M. L., & Dunger, D. B. (2006). Lesson from large population studies on timing and tempo of puberty (secular trends and relation to body size): The European trend. *Molecular and Cellular Endocrinology, 254–255,* 8–12.

Ophir, E., Nass, C., & Wagner, A. D. (2009). Cognitive control in media multitaskers. *Proceedings of the National Academy of Sciences USA, 106,* 15583–15587.

Orobio de Castro, B., Merk, W., Koops, W., Veerman, J. W., & Bosch, J. D. (2005). Emotions in social information processing and their relations with reactive and proactive aggression in referred aggressive boys. *Journal of Clinical Child and Adolescent Psychology, 34,* 105–116.

Orr, A. J. (2011, in press). Gendered capital: Childhood socialization and the "boy crisis" in education. *Sex Roles.*

Ortet, G., & others. (2011, in press). Assessing the Five Factors of personality in adolescence: The Junior Version of the Spanish NEO-PI-R. *Assessment.*

Oser, F., Scarlett, W. G., & Bucher, A. (2006). Religious and spiritual development through the lifespan. In W. Damon & R. Lerner (Eds.), *Handbook of child psychology* (6th ed.). New York: Wiley.

Osofsky, J. D. (1990, Winter). Risk and protective factors for teenage mothers and their infants. *SRCD Newsletter,* pp. 1–2.

Oswald, D. L., & Clark, E. M. (2003). Best friends forever? High school best friendships and the transition to college. *Personal Relationships, 10,* 187–196.

Oude Luttikhuis, H., & others. (2009). Interventions for treating obesity in children. *Cochrane Database of Systematic Reviews (1),* CD001872.

Overvelde, A., & Hulstijn, W. (2011). Handwriting development in grade 2 and grade 3 primary school children with normal, at risk, or dysgraphic characteristics. *Research in Developmental Disabilities, 32,* 540–548.

Owen, J. J., Rhoades, G. K., Stanley, S. M., & Markman, H. J. (2011). The role of leaders' working alliance in premarital education. *Journal of Family Psychology, 25,* 49–57.

Owens, J. A., Belon, K., & Moss, P. (2010). Impact of delaying school start time on adolescent sleep, mood, and behavior. *Archives of Pediatric and Adolescent Medicine, 164,* 608–614.

Oxford, M. L., Gilchrist, L. D., Gillmore, M. R., & Lohr, M. J. (2006). Predicting variation in the life course of adolescent mothers as they enter adulthood. *Journal of Adolescent Health, 39,* 20–36.

P

Padilla-Walker, L. M., & Coyne, S. M. (2011, in press). "Turn that thing off!" Parent and adolescent predictors of proactive media monitoring. *Journal of Youth and Adolescence.*

Padilla-Walker, L. M., Nelson, L. J., Carroll, J. S., & Jensen, A. C. (2010). More than just a game: Video game and Internet use during emerging adulthood. *Journal of Youth and Adolescence, 39,* 103–113.

Pakpreo, P., Ryan, S., Auinger, P., & Aten, M. (2004). The association between parental lifestyle behaviors and adolescent knowledge, attitudes, intentions, and nutritional and physical activity behaviors. *Journal of Adolescent Health, 34,* 129–130.

Palfrey, J., Sacco, D., Boyd, D., & DeBonis, L. (2009). *Enhancing child safety and online technologies.* Cambridge, MA: Berkman Center for Internet & Society.

Pals, J. L. (2006). Constructing the "springboard effect": Causal connections, self-making, and growth within the life story. In D. P. McAdams, R. Josselson, & A. Lieblich (Eds.), *Identity and story.* Washington, DC: American Psychological Association.

Paludi, M. A. (2002). *The psychology of women* (2nd ed.). Upper Saddle River, NJ: Prentice-Hall.

Papadimitriou, A., Nicolaidou, P., Fretzayas, A., & Chrousos, G. P. (2010). Clinical review: Constitutional advancement of growth, a.k.a., early growth acceleration, predicts early puberty and childhood obesity. *Journal of Clinical Endocrinology and Metabolism, 95,* 4535–4541.

Papini, D., & Sebby, R. (1988). Variations in conflictual family issues by adolescent pubertal status, gender, and family member. *Journal of Early Adolescence, 8,* 1–15.

Parade, S. H., Leerkes, E. M., & Blankson, A. N. (2010). Attachment to parents, social anxiety, and close relationships of female students over the transition to college. *Journal of Youth and Adolescence, 39,* 127–137.

Parens, E., & Johnston, J. (2009). Facts, values, and attention-deficit hyperactivity disorder (ADHD): An update on the controversies. *Child and Adolescent Psychiatry and Mental Health, 3,* 1.

Parent, J., Forehand, R. L., Merchant, M. J., Long, N., & Jones, D. J. (2011). Predictors of outcome of a parenting group curriculum: A pilot study. *Behavior Modification, 35,* 370–378.

Paris, F., & others. (2010). Premature pubarche in Mediterranean girls: High prevalence of heterozygous CYP21 mutation carriers. *Gynecological Endocrinology, 26,* 319–324.

Park, D. (2011). Neuroplasticity of cognitive function with age. In K. W. Schaie & S. L. Willis (Eds.), *Handbook of the psychology of aging* (7th ed.). New York: Elsevier.

Park, M. J., Brindis, C. D., Chang, F., & Irwin, C. E. (2008). A midcourse review of the healthy people 2010: 21 critical health objectives for adolescents and young adults. *Journal of Adolescent Health, 42,* 329–334.

Park, M. J., Paul Mulye, T., Adams, S. H., Brindis, C. D., & Irwin, C. E. (2006). The health status of young adults in the United States. *Journal of Adolescent Health, 39,* 305–317.

Parkay, F. W., & Stanford, B. H. (2010). *Becoming a teacher* (8th ed.). Upper Saddle River, NJ: Prentice Hall.

Parke, R. D., & Buriel, R. (2006). Socialization in the family: Ethnic and ecological perspectives. In W. Damon & R. Lerner (Eds.), *Handbook of child psychology* (6th ed.). New York: Wiley.

Parke, R. D., & Clarke-Stewart, K. A. (2011). *Social development.* New York: Wiley.

Parke, R. D., Coltrane, S., & Schofield, T. (2011, in press). The bicultural advantage. In J. Marsh, R. Mendoza-Denton, & J. A. Smith (Eds.), *Are we born racist?* Boston: Beacon Press.

Parker, J. D., Keefer, K. V., & Wood, L. M. (2011, in press). Toward a brief multidimensional assessment of emotional intelligence: Psychometric properties of the Emotional Quotient Inventory-Short form. *Psychological Assessment.*

Parkes, A., & others. (2011). Comparison of teenagers' early same-sex and heterosexual behavior: UK data from the SHARE and RIPPLE studies. *Journal of Adolescent Health, 48,* 27–35.

Parritz, R. H., & Troy, M. F. (2011). *Disorders of childhood.* Boston: Cengage.

Partnership for a Drug-Free America. (2005). *Partnership Attitude Tracking Study.* New York: Author.

Patel, D. R., & Baker, R. J. (2006). Musculoskeletal injuries in sports. *Primary Care, 33,* 545–579.

Pate, R. R., & others. (2009). Age-related change in physical activity in adolescent girls. *Journal of Adolescent Health, 44,* 275–282.

Patterson, C. J. (2009). Lesbian and gay parents and their children: A social science perspective. *Nebraska Symposium on Motivation, 54,* 142–182.

Patterson, C. J., & Wainright, J. L. (2010). Adolescents with same-sex parents: Findings from the National Longitudinal Study of Adolescent Health. In D. Brodzinsky, A. Pertman, & D. Kunz (Eds.), *Lesbian and gay adoption: A new American reality.* New York: Oxford University Press.

Patterson, G. R., DeBaryshe, B. D., & Ramsey, E. (1989). A developmental perspective on antisocial behavior. *American Psychologist, 44,* 239–335.

Patterson, G. R., Forgatch, M. S., & DeGarmo, D. S. (2010). Cascading effects following intervention. *Development and Psychopathology, 22,* 949–970.

Patterson, G. R., Reid, J. B., & Dishion, T. J. (1992). Antisocial boys (Vol. 4). Eugene, OR: Castalia.

Patton, G. C., & others. (2010). Mapping a global agenda for adolescent health. *Journal of Adolescent Health, 47,* 427–432.

Patton, G. C., & others. (2011a). A prospective study of the effects of optimism on adolescent health risks. *Pediatrics, 127,* 308–316.

Patton, G. C., & others. (2011b, in press). Overweight and obesity between adolescence and young adulthood: A 10-year prospective study. *Journal of Adolescent Health.*

Paul, E. L., McManus, B., & Hayes, A. (2000). "Hookups": Characteristics and correlates of college students' spontaneous and anonymous sexual experiences. *The Journal of Sexual Research, 37,* 76–88.

Paul, E. L., & White, K. M. (1990). The development of intimate relationships in late adolescence. *Adolescence, 25,* 375–400.

Paul, P. (2003, Sept/Oct). The PermaParent trap. *Psychology Today, 36*(5), 40–53.

Paulhus, D. L. (2008). Birth order. In M. M. Haith & J. B. Benson (Eds.), *Encyclopedia of infant and early childhood development.* Oxford, UK: Elsevier.

Paus, T. (2010). Growth of white matter in the adolescent brain: Myelin or axon? *Brain and Cognition, 72,* 26–35.

Paus, T., & others. (2007). Morphological properties of the action-observation cortical network in adolescents with low and high resistance to peer influence. *Social Neuroscience 3*(3), 303–316.

Paxson, C., Donahue, E., Orleans, C. T., & Grisso, J. A. (2006). Introducing the issue. *The Future of Children, 16,* 3–17.

Pearson, N., Biddle, S. J., & Gorely, T. (2009). Family correlates of breakfast consumption among children and adolescents: A systematic review. *Appetite, 52,* 1–7.

Peck, J. D., Peck, B. M., Skaggs, V. J., Fukushima, M., & Kaplan, H. B. (2011). Socio-environmental factors associated with pubertal development in female adolescents: The role of prepubertal tobacco and alcohol use. *Journal of Adolescent Health, 48,* 241–246.

Peck, S. C., Roeser, R. W., Zarrett, N., & Eccles, J. S. (2008). Exploring the roles of extracurricular activity quantity and quality in the educational resilience of vulnerable adolescents: Variable- and pattern-centered approaches. *Journal of Social Issues, 64,* 135–155.

Pedersen, W., & Mastekaasa, A. (2011, in press). Conduct disorder symptoms and subsequent pregnancy, child-birth, and abortion: A population-based longitudinal study of adolescents. *Journal of Adolescence.*

Peeters, M., Cillessen, A. H. N., & Scholte, R. H. J. (2010). Clueless or powerful? Identifying subtypes of bullies in adolescence. *Journal of Youth and Adolescence, 39,* 1041–1052.

Perez-Brena, N. J., Updegraff, K. A., & Umana-Taylor, A. J. (2011, in press). Father- and mother-adolescent decision-making in Mexican-origin families. *Journal of Youth and Adolescence.*

Perry, D. G., & Pauletti, R. E. (2011). Gender and adolescent development. *Journal of Research on Adolescence, 21,* 61–74.

Perry, N. E., & Rahim, A. (2011). Supporting self-regulated learning in classrooms. In B. J. Zimmerman & D. H. Schunk (Eds.), *Handbook of self-regulation of learning and performance.* New York: Routledge.

Perry, W. G. (1970). *Forms of intellectual and ethical development in the college years.* New York: Holt, Rinehart & Winston.

Perry, W. G. (1999). *Forms of ethical and intellectual development in the college years: A scheme.* San Francisco: Jossey-Bass.

Pesce, C., Crova, L., Cereatti, L., Casella, R., & Bellucci, M. (2009). Physical activity and mental performance in preadolescents: Effects of acute exercise on free-recall memory. *Mental Health and Physical Activity, 2,* 16–22.

Peskin, H. (1967). Pubertal onset and ego functioning. *Journal of Abnormal Psychology, 72,* 1–15.

Petersen, A. C. (1987, September). Those gangly years. *Psychology Today, 21,* 28–34.

Petersen, A. C., & Crockett, L. (1985). Pubertal timing and grade effects on adjustment. *Journal of Youth and Adolescence, 14,* 191–206.

Petersen, J. L., & Hyde, J. S. (2010). A meta-analytic review of research on gender differences in sexuality, 1973–2007. *Psychological Bulletin, 136,* 21–38.

Pettit, G. S., Bates, J. E., Dodge, K. A., & Meece, D. W. (1999). The impact of after-school peer contact on early adolescent externalizing problems is moderated by parental monitoring, perceived neighborhood safety, and prior adjustment. *Child Development, 70,* 768–778.

Pew Research Center. (2010). *Millennials: Confident, Connected, Open to Change.* Washington, DC: Pew Research Center.

Pew Research Center. (2010). *The decline of marriage and rise of new families.* Washington, DC: Pew Research Center.

Pfaffle, R., & Klammt, J. (2011). Pituitary transcription factors in the etiology of combined pituitary hormone deficiency. *Best Practices & Research: Clinical Endocrinology & Metabolism, 25,* 43–60.

Phares, V., & Rojas, A. (2012). Parental involvement. In R. Levesque (Ed.), *Encyclopedia of adolescence.* New York: Springer.

Philipsen, N. M., Johnson, A. D., & Brooks-Gunn, J. (2009). Poverty, effects on social and emotional development. *International Encyclopedia of Education* (3rd ed.). St. Louis, MO: Elsevier.

Phillips, D. A., & Lowenstein, A. (2011). Early care, education, and child development. *Annual Review of Psychology* (Vol. 62). Palo Alto, CA: Annual Reviews.

Phinney, J. S. (2006). Ethnic identity exploration in emerging adulthood. In J. J. Arnett & J. L. Tanner (Eds.), *Emerging adults in America.* Washington, DC: American Psychological Association.

Phinney, J. S., & Baldelomar, O. A. (2011). Identity development in multiple developmental contexts. In L. Jensen (Ed.), *Bridging cultural and developmental approaches to psychology.* New York: Oxford University Press.

Phinney, J. S., Madden, T., & Ong, A. (2000). Cultural values and intergenerational discrepancies in immigrant and non-immigrant families. *Child Development, 71,* 528–539.

Piaget, J. (1952). *The origins of intelligence in children.* (M. Cook, Trans.). New York: International Universities Press.

Piaget, J. (1954). *The construction of reality in the child.* New York: Basic Books.

Piaget, J. (1972). Intellectual evolution from adolescence to adulthood. *Human Development, 15,* 1–12.

Pleck, J. H. (1983). The theory of male sex role identity: Its rise and fall, 1936–present. In M. Levin (Ed.), *In the shadow of the past: Psychology portrays the sexes.* New York: Columbia University Press.

Pleck, J. H. (1995). The gender-role strain paradigm. In R. F. Levant & S. Pollack (Eds.), *A new psychology of men.* New York: Basic Books.

Plener, P. L., Singer, H., & Goldbeck, L. (2011). Traumatic events and suicidality in a German adolescent community sample. *Journal of Traumatic Stress, 24,* 121–124.

Plomin, R. (2004). Genetics and developmental psychology. *Merrill-Palmer Quarterly, 50,* 341–352.

Plomin, R., & Davis, O. S. P. (2009). The future of genetics in psychology and psychiatry: Microarrays, genome-wide association, and non-coding RNA. *Journal of Child Psychology and Psychiatry, 50,* 63–71.

Plomin, R., DeFries, J. C., McClearn, G. E., & McGuffin, P. (2009). *Behavioral genetics* (5th ed.). New York: W. H. Freeman.

Plucker, J. (2010). Interview. In P. Bronson & A. Merryman. The creativity crisis. *Newsweek,* 42–48.

Polce-Lynch, M., Myers, B. J., Kliewer, W., & Kilmartin, C. (2001). Adolescent self-esteem and gender: Exploring relations to sexual harassment, body image, media influence, and emotional expression. *Journal of Youth and Adolescence, 30,* 225–244.

Pollack, W. (1999). *Real boys.* New York: Henry Holt.

Pope, L. M., Adler, N. E., & Tschann, J. M. (2001). Post-abortion psychological adjustment: Are minors at increased risk? *Journal of Adolescent Health, 29,* 2–11.

Popenoe, D. (2008). *Cohabitation, marriage, and child wellbeing: A cross-national perspective.* Piscataway, NJ: The National Marriage Project, Rutgers University.

Popenoe, D. (2009). *The state of our unions: 2008. Updates of social indicators: Tables and charts.* New Brunswick, NJ: The National Marriage Project, Rutgers University.

Popenoe, D., & Whitehead, B. D. (2008). *The state of our unions: 2008.* New Brunswick, NJ: Rutgers University.

Popham, W. J. (2011). *Classroom assessment* (6th ed.). Boston: Allyn & Bacon.

Portes, A., & Rivas, A. (2011). The adaptation of migrant children. *The Future of Children, 21,* 219–246.

Potard, C., Courtois, R., & Rusch, E. (2008). The influence of peers on risky behavior during adolescence. *European Journal of Contraception and Reproductive Health Care, 13,* 264–270.

Poulin, F., Kiesner, J., Pedersen, S., & Dishion, T. J. (2011). A short-term longitudinal analysis of friendship selection on early adolescent substance use. *Journal of Adolescence,34,* 249–256.

Poulin, F., & Pedersen, S. (2007). Developmental changes in gender composition of friendship networks in adolescent girls and boys. *Developmental Psychology, 43,* 1484–1496.

Power, F. C., & Higgins-D'Alessandro, A. (2008). The Just Community Approach to moral education and moral atmosphere of the school. In L. Nucci & D. Narváez (Eds.), *Handbook of moral and character education.* New York: Psychology Press.

Powers, S. K., Dodd, S. L., & Jackson, E. M. (2011). *Total fitness and wellness.* Upper Saddle River, NJ: Pearson.

Prabhakar, H. (2007). Hopkins interactive guest blog: The public health experience at Johns Hopkins. Retrieved January 31, 2008, from http://hopkins.typepad.com/guest/2007/03/the_public_heal.html

Pressley, M. (2003). Psychology of literacy and literacy instruction. In I. B. Weiner (Ed.), *Handbook of psychology* (Vol. 7). New York: Wiley.

Pressley, M. (2007). An interview with Michael Pressley by Terri Flowerday and Michael Shaughnessy. *Educational Psychology Review, 19,* 1–12.

Pressley, M., Allington, R., Wharton-McDonald, R., Block, C. C., & Morrow, L. M. (2001). *Learning to read: Lessons from exemplary first grades.* New York: Guilford.

Pressley, M., Dolezal, S. E., Raphael, L. M., Welsh, L. M., Bogner, K., & Roehrig, A. D. (2003). *Motivating primary-grades teachers.* New York: Guilford.

Pressley, M., & Hilden, K. (2006). Cognitive strategies. In W. Damon & R. Lerner (Eds.), *Handbook of child psychology* (6th ed.). New York: Wiley.

Pressley, M., Mohan, L., Reffitt, K., Raphael-Bogaert, L. R. (2007). Writing instruction in engaging and effective elementary settings. In S. Graham, C. A. MacArthur, & J. Fitzgerald (Eds.), *Best practices in writing instruction.* New York: Guilford.

Pressley, M., Raphael, L., Gallagher, D., & DiBella, J. (2004). Providence–St. Mel School: How a school that works for African-American students works. *Journal of Educational Psychology, 96,* 216–235.

Priess, H. A., Lindberg, S. M., & Hyde, J. S. (2009). Adolescent gender-role identity and mental health: Gender intensification revisited. *Child Development, 80,* 1531–1544.

Prinstein, M. J. (2007). Moderators of peer contagion: A longitudinal examination of depression socialization between adolescents and their best friends. *Journal of Clinical Child and Adolescent Psychology, 36,* 159–170.

Prinstein, M. J., & Dodge, K. A. (2008). Current issues in peer influence. In M. J. Prinstein & K. A. Dodge (Eds.), *Understanding peer influence in children and adolescents.* New York: Guilford.

Prinstein, M. J., & Dodge, K. A. (2010). Current issues in peer influence research. In M. J. Prinstein & K. A. Dodge (Eds.), *Understanding peer influence in children and adolescents.* New York: Guilford.

Prinstein, M. J., Rancourt, D., Guerry, J. D., & Browne, C. B. (2009). Peer reputations and psychological adjustment. In K. H. Rubin, W. M. Bukowski, & B. Laursen (Eds.), *Handbook of peer interactions, relationships, and groups.* New York: Guilford.

Pryor, J. H., Hurtado, S., DeAngelo, L., Blake, L. P., & Tran, S. (2010). *The American freshman: National norms for fall 2010.* Los Angeles: Higher Education Institute, UCLA.

Pryor, J. H., Hurtado, S., Saenz, V. B., Lindholm, J. A., Korn, W. S., & Mahoney, K. M. (2005). *The American freshman: National norms for fall 2005.* Los Angeles: Higher Education Research Institute, UCLA.

Pudrovska, T. (2009). Midlife crises and transitions. In D. Carr (Ed.), *Encyclopedia of the life course and human development.* Boston: Gale Cengage.

Pujazon-Zazik, M., & Park, M. J. (2010). To tweet or not to tweet: Gender differences and potential positive and negative health outcomes of adolescents' social Internet use. *American Journal of Men's Health, 4,* 77–85.

Pulkkinen, L., & Kokko, K. (2000). Identity development in adulthood: A longitudinal study. *Journal of Research in Personality, 34,* 445–470.

Purper-Ouakil, D., & others. (2011). Neurobiology of attention deficit/hyperactivity disorder. *Pediatric Research, 69,* 69R–76R.

Putallaz, M., Grimes, C. L., Foster, K. J., Kupersmidt, J. B., Clie, J. D., & Dearing, K. (2007). Overt and relational aggression and victimization: Multiple perspectives within the school setting. *Journal of School Psychology, 45,* 523–547.

Putnam, S. P., Sanson, A. V., & Rothbart, M. K. (2002). Child temperament and parenting. In M. Bornstein (Ed.), *Handbook of parenting* (2nd ed.). Mahwah, NJ: Erlbaum.

Puzzanchera, C., & Sickmund, M. (2008, July). *Juvenile court statistics 2005.* Pittsburgh: National Center for Juvenile Justice.

Q

Qui, M. G., & others. (2011, in press). Changes of brain structure and function in ADHD children. *Brain Topography.*

Quinlan, S. L., Jaccard, J., & Blanton, H. (2006). A decision theoretic and prototype conceptualization of possible selves: Implications for the prediction of risk behavior. *Journal of Personality, 74,* 599–630.

Quinton, D., Rutter, M., & Gulliver, L. (1990). Continuities in psychiatric disorders from childhood to adulthood in the children of psychiatric patients. In L. Robins & M. Rutter (Eds.), *Straight and*

devious pathways from childhood to adulthood. New York: Cambridge University Press.

Quinton, W., Major, B., & Richards, C. (2001). Adolescents and adjustment to abortion: Are minors at greater risk? *Psychology, Public Policy, and Law, 7,* 491–514.

R

Raffaelli, M., & Ontai, L. (2001). "She's sixteen years old and there's boys calling over to the house": An exploratory study of sexual socialization in Latino families. *Culture, Health, and Sexuality, 3,* 295–310.

Raffaelli, M., & Ontai, L. L. (2004). Gender socialization in Latino/a families: Results from two retrospective studies. *Sex Roles, 50,* 287–299.

Randolph, M. E., Torres, H., Gore-Felton, C., Lloyd, B., & McGarvey, E. L. (2009). Alcohol use and sexual risk behavior among college students: Understanding gender and ethnic differences. *American Journal of Drug and Alcohol Abuse, 35,* 80–84.

Rao, U., Sidhartha, T., Harker, K. R., Bidesi, A., Chen, L-A., & Ernst, M. (2011). Relationship between adolescent risk preferences on a laboratory task and behavioral measures of risk-taking. *Journal of Adolescent Health, 48,* 151–158.

Rathunde, K., & Csikszentmihalyi, M. (2006). The developing person: An experiential perspective. In W. Damon & R. Lerner (Eds.), *Handbook of child psychology* (6th ed.). New York: Wiley.

Raven, P. H. (2011). *Biology* (9th ed.). New York: McGraw-Hill.

Read, J. P., Merrill, J. E., & Bytschkow, K. (2010). Before the party starts: Risk factors and reasons for "pregaming" in college students. *Journal of American College Health, 58,* 461–472.

Realini, J. P., Buzi, R. S., Smith, P. B., & Martinez, M. (2010). Evaluation of "big decisions": An abstinence-plus sexuality. *Journal of Sex and Marital Therapy, 36,* 313–326.

Ream, G. L., & Savin-Williams, R. (2003). Religious development in adolescence. In G. Adams & M. Berzonsky (Eds.), *Blackwell handbook of adolescence*. Malden, MA: Blackwell.

Regenerus, M., & Uecker, J. (2011). *Premarital sex in America: How Americans meet, mate, and think about marrying.* New York: Oxford University Press.

Reich, S. M., & Vandell, D. L. (2011). The interplay between parents and peers as socializing influences in children's development. In P. K. Smith & C. H. Hart (Eds.), *Wiley-Blackwell handbook of childhood social development* (2nd ed.). New York: Wiley.

Reid, P. T., & Zalk, S. R. (2001). Academic environments: Gender and ethnicity in U.S. higher education. In J. Worell (Ed.), *Encyclopedia of women and gender*. San Diego: Academic Press.

Reimuller, A., Hussong, A., & Ennett, S. T. (2011, in press). The influence of alcohol-specific communication on adolescent alcohol use and alcohol-related consequences. *Prevention Science.*

Reinehr, T., & Wabitsch, M. (2010, in press). Childhood obesity. *Current Opinion in Lipidology.*

Reinisch, J. M. (1990). *The Kinsey Institute new report on sex: What you must know to be sexually literate.* New York: St. Martin's Press.

Reis, O., & Youniss, J. (2004). Patterns of identity change and development in relationships with mothers and friends. *Journal of Adolescent Research, 19,* 31–44.

Remafedi, G., Resnick, M., Blum, R., & Harris, L. (1992). Demography of sexual orientation in adolescents. *Pediatrics, 89,* 714–721.

Renju, J. R., & others. (2011). Scaling up adolescent sexual and reproductive health interventions through existing government systems? A detailed process evaluation of a school-based intervention in the Mwanza region in the northwest of Tanzania. *Journal of Adolescent Health, 48,* 79–86.

Resnick, M. D., Wattenberg, E., & Brewer, R. (1992, March). *Paternity avowal/disavowal among partners of low income mothers.* Paper presented at the meeting of the Society for Research on Adolescence, Washington, DC.

Rest, J. R. (1986). *Moral development: Advances in theory and research.* New York: Praeger.

Rest, J. R. (1995). *Concerns for the social-psychological development of youth and educational strategies: Report for the Kaufmann Foundation.* Minneapolis: University of Minnesota, Department of Educational Psychology.

Rest, J. R., Narváez, D., Bebeau, M., & Thoma, S. (1999). *Postconventional moral thinking: A neo-Kohlbergian approach.* Hillsdale, NJ: Erlbaum.

Rey-Lopez, J. P., Vicente-Rodriguez, G., Biosca, M., & Moreno, L. A. (2008). Sedentary behavior and obesity development in children and adolescents. *Nutrition, Metabolism, and Cardiovascular Diseases, 18,* 242–251.

Reyna, V. F., Estrada, S. M., DeMarinis, J. A., Myers, R. M., Stanisz, J. M., & Mills, B. A. (2011, in press). Neurobiological and memory models of risky decision making in adolescents versus young adults. *Journal of Experimental Psychology: Learning, Memory, and Cognition.*

Reyna, V. F., & Farley, F. (2006). Risk and rationality in adolescent decision-making: Implications for theory, practice, and public policy. *Psychological Science in the Public Interest, 7,* 1–44.

Reyna, V. F., & Rivers, S. E. (2008). Current theories of risk and rational decision making. *Developmental Review, 28,* 1–11.

Rhoades, G. K., Stanley, S. M., & Markman, H. J. (2009). The pre-engagement cohabitation effect: A replication and extension of previous finding. *Journal of Family Psychology, 23,* 107–111.

Rhodes, J. E., & DuBois, D. L. (2008). Mentoring relationships and programs for youth. *Current Directions in Psychological Science, 17,* 254–258.

Rhodes, J. E., & Lowe, S. R. (2009). Mentoring in adolescence. In R. M. Lerner & L. Steinberg (Eds.), *Handbook of adolescent psychology* (3rd ed.). New York: Wiley.

Richards, M. H., & Larson, R. (1990, July). *Romantic relations in early adolescence*. Paper presented at the Fifth International Conference on Personal Relations, Oxford University, England.

Richmond, E. J., & Rogol, A. D. (2007). Male pubertal development and the role of androgen therapy. *Nature General Practice: Endocrinology and Metabolism, 3,* 338–344.

Rickards, T., & deCock, C. (2003). Understanding organizational creativity: Toward a paradigmatic approach. In M. A. Runco (Ed.), *Creativity research handbook.* Cresskill, NJ: Hampton Press.

Rickert, V. I., Sanghvi, R., & Wiemann, C. M. (2002). Is lack of sexual assertiveness among adolescent women a cause for concern? *Perspectives on Sexual and Reproductive Health, 34,* 162–173.

Rideout, V., Foehr, U. G., & Roberts, D. P. (2010). *Generation M2: Media in the lives of 8- to 18-year-olds.* Menlo Park, CA: Kaiser Family Foundation.

Rideout, V., Roberts, D. P., & Foehr, U. G. (2005). *Generation M.* Menlo Park, CA: Kaiser Family Foundation.

Rimsza, M. E., & Moses, K. S. (2005). Substance abuse on the college campus. *Pediatric Clinics of North America, 52,* 307–319.

Rinsky, J. R., & Hinshaw, S. P. (2011, in press). Linkages between childhood executive functioning and adolescent social functioning and psychopathology in girls with ADHD. *Child Neuropsychology.*

Risch, N., & others. (2009). Interaction between the serotonin transporter gene (5-HTTLPR), stressful life events, and risk of depression: A meta-analysis. *Journal of the American Medical Association, 301,* 2462–2471.

Rivas-Drake, D. (2011). Ethnic-racial socialization and adjustment among Latino college students: The mediating roles of ethnic centrality, public regards, and perceived barriers to opportunity. *Journal of Youth and Adolescence, 40,* 606–619.

Rivas-Drake, D., Hughes, D., & Way, N. (2009). Public ethnic regard and perceived socioeconomic stratification: Associations with well-being among Dominican and Black American youth. *Journal of Early Adolescence, 29,* 122–141.

Rivers, S. E., Reyna, V. F., & Mills, B. (2008). Risk taking under the influence: A fuzzy-trace theory of emotion in adolescence. *Developmental Review, 28,* 107–144.

Roberts, B. W., Edmonds, G., & Grijaiva, E. (2010). It is developmental me, not generation me: Developmental changes are more important than generational changes in narcissism—Commentary on Trzesniewski & Donnellan (2010). *Perspectives on Psychological Science,* 97–102.

Roberts, B. W., Jackson, J. J., Fayard, J. V., Edmonds, G., & Meints, J. (2009). Conscientiousness. In M. Leary & R. Hoyle (Eds.), *Handbook of individual differences in social behavior.* New York: Guilford.

Roberts, D. F., & Foehr, U. G. (2008). Trends in media use. *Future of Children, 18*(1), 11–37.

Roberts, D. F., Henriksen, L., & Foehr, U. G. (2004). Adolescents and the media. In R. Lerner & L. Steinberg (Ed.), *Handbook of adolescent psychology* (2nd ed.). New York: Wiley.

Roberts, D. F., Henriksen, L., & Foehr, U. G. (2009). Adolescence, adolescents, and the media. In R. M. Lerner & L. Steinberg (Eds.), *Handbook of adolescent psychology* (3rd ed.). New York: Wiley.

Roberts, G. C., Treasure, D. C., & Kavussanu, M. (1997). Motivation in physical activity contexts: An achievement goal perspective. *Advances in Motivation and Achievement, 10,* 413–447.

Roberts, M. A. (2010). Toward a theory of culturally relevant critical teacher care: African American teachers' definitions and perceptions of care for African American students. *Journal of Moral Education, 39,* 449–467.

Robins, R. W., Trzesniewski, K. H., Tracey, J. L., Potter, J., & Gosling, S. D. (2002). Age differences in self-esteem from age 9 to 90. *Psychology and Aging, 17,* 423–434.

Robinson, D. P., & Greene, J. W. (1988). The adolescent alcohol and drug problem: A practical approach. *Pediatric Nursing, 14,* 305–310.

Robinson, N. S. (1995). Evaluating the nature of perceived support and its relation to perceived self-worth in adolescents. *Journal of Research on Adolescence, 5,* 253–280.

Roche, K. M., Ghazarian, S. R., Little, T. D., & Leventhal, T. (2011). Understanding links between punitive parenting and adolescent adjustment: The relevance of context and reciprocal associations. *Journal of Research on Adolescence, 21,* 448–460.

Rogers, C. R. (1950). The significance of the self regarding attitudes and perceptions. In M. L. Reymart (Ed.), *Feelings and emotions.* New York: McGraw-Hill.

Rogoff, B., & others. (2011). Developing destinies: A Mayan midwife and town. New York: Oxford University Press.

Rogol, A. D., Roemmich, J. N., & Clark, P. A. (1998, September). *Growth at Puberty.* Paper presented at a workshop, Physical Development, Health Futures of Youth II: Pathways to Adolescent Health, Maternal and Child Health Bureau, Annapolis, MD.

Rohner, R. P., & Rohner, E. C. (1981). Parental acceptance-rejection and parental control: Cross-cultural codes. *Ethnology, 20,* 245–260.

Rokholm, B., Baker, J. L., & Sorensen, T. I. (2010). The leveling off of the obesity epidemic since the year 1999—a review of evidence and perspectives. *Obesity Reviews, 11,* 835–846.

Romas, J. A., & Sharma, M. (2010). *Practical stress management* (5th ed.). Upper Saddle River, NJ: Pearson.

Rönnlund, M., & Nilsson, L. G. (2008). The magnitude, generality, and determinants of Flynn effects on forms of declarative memory and visuospatial ability: Time-sequential analyses of data from a Swedish cohort study. *Intelligence, 36,* 192–209.

Rose, A. J., Carlson, W., & Waller, E. M. (2007). Prospective associations of co-rumination with friendship and emotional adjustment: Considering the socioemotional trade-offs of co-rumination. *Developmental Psychology, 43,* 1019–1031.

Rose, A. J., & Rudolph, K. D. (2006). A review of sex differences in peer relationship processes: Potential trade-offs for the emotional and behavioral development of girls and boys. *Psychological Bulletin, 132,* 98–132.

Rose, A. J., & Smith, R. L. (2009). Sex differences in peer relationships. In K. H. Rubin, W. M. Bukowski, & B. Laursen (Eds.), *Handbook of peer interactions, relationships, and groups.* New York: Guilford.

Rose, S., & Frieze, I. R. (1993). Young singles contemporary dating scripts. *Sex Roles, 28,* 499–509.

Rosenberg, M. (1979). *Conceiving the self.* New York: Basic Books.

Rosenberg, M. S., Westling, D. L., & McLeskey, J. (2011). *Special education for today's teachers* (2nd ed.). Upper Saddle River, NJ: Merrill.

Rosenblum, G. D., & Lewis, M. (2003). Emotional development in adolescence. In G. Adams & M. Berzonsky (Eds.), *Blackwell handbook of adolescence.* Malden, MA: Blackwell.

Rosenblum, S., Aloni, T., & Josman, N. (2010). Relationships between handwriting performance and organizational abilities among children with and without dysgraphia: A preliminary study. *Research in Developmental Disabilities, 31,* 502–509.

Rosengard, C. (2009). Confronting the intendedness of adolescent rapid repeat pregnancy. *Journal of Adolescent Health, 44,* 5–6.

Rosen, L., Cheever, N., & Carrier, L. M. (2008). The association of parenting style and child age with parental limit setting and adolescent MySpace behavior. *Journal of Applied Developmental Psychology, 29,* 459–471.

Rosenthal, N. L., & Kobak, R. (2010). Assessing adolescents' attachment hierarchies: Differences across developmental periods and associations with individual adaptation. *Journal of Research on Adolescence, 20,* 678–706.

Rosner, B. A., & Rierdan, J. (1994, February). *Adolescent girls' self-esteem: Variations in developmental trajectories.* Paper presented at the meeting of the Society for Research on Adolescence, San Diego.

Ross, H., & Howe, N. (2009). Family influences on children's peer relationships. In K. H. Rubin, W. M. Bukowski, & B. Laursen (Eds.), *Handbook of peer interactions, relationships, and groups.* New York: Guilford.

Rossiter, M. (Ed.). (2008). Possible selves and adult learning: Perspectives and potential. *New Directions for Adult and Continuing Education, 114,* 1–96.

Rostosky, S. S., Riggle, E. D., Horner, S. G., Denton, F. N., & Huellemeier, J. D. (2010). Lesbian, gay, and bisexual individuals' psychological reactions to amendments denying access to civil marriage. *American Journal of Orthopsychiatry, 80,* 302–310.

Rothbart, M. K. (2011). *Becoming who we are.* New York: Guilford.

Rothbart, M. K., & Bates, J. E. (1998). Temperament. In W. Damon (Ed.). *Handbook of child psychology* (5th ed., Vol. 3). New York: Wiley.

Rothbaum, F., Poll, M., Azuma, H., Miyake, K., & Weisz, J. (2000). The development of close relationships in Japan and the United States: Paths of symbiotic harmony and generative tension. *Child Development, 71,* 1121–1142.

Rothbaum, F., & Trommsdorff, G. (2007). Do roots and wings complement or oppose one another?: The socialization of relatedness and autonomy in cultural context. In J. E. Grusec & P. D. Hastings (Eds.), *Handbook of Socialization.* New York: Guilford.

Roth, J., Brooks-Gunn, J., Murray, L., & Foster, W. (1998). Promoting healthy adolescents: Synthesis of youth development program evaluations. *Journal of Research on Adolescence, 8,* 423–459.

Roustit, C., Campoy, E., Chaix, B., & Chauvin, P. (2010). Exploring mediating factors in the association between parental psychological distress and psychosocial maladjustment in adolescence. *European Child and Adolescent Psychiatry, 19,* 597–604.

Rowden, P., Matthews, G., Watson, B., & Biggs, H. (2011). The relative impact of work-related stress, life stress, and driving environment stress on driving outcomes. *Accident; Analysis and Prevention, 43,* 1332–1340.

Rowley, J. B. (2009). *Becoming a high-performance mentor*. Thousand Oaks, CA: Corwin Press.

Rowley, S., Kurtz-Costes, B., & Cooper, S. M. (2010). The role of schooling in ethnic minority achievement and attainment. In J. Meece & J. Eccles (Eds.), *Handbook of research on schools, schooling, and human development.* New York: Routledge.

Rubie-Davies, C. M. (2007). Classroom interactions: Exploring the practices of high- and low-expectation teachers. *British Journal of Educational Psychology, 77,* 289–306.

Rubie-Davies, C. M. (Ed.). (2011). *Educational psychology*. New York: Routledge.

Rubin, K. H., Bukowski, W., & Parker, J. G. (1998). Peer interactions, relationships, and groups. In N. Eisenberg (Ed.), *Handbook of child psychology* (5th ed., Vol. 3). New York: Wiley.

Rubin, K. H., Bukowski, W., & Parker, J. G. (2006). Peer interactions, relationships, and groups. In W. Damon & R. Lerner (Eds.), *Handbook of child psychology* (6th ed.). New York: Wiley.

Rubin, K. H., Coplan, R. J., Bowker, J. C., & Menzer, M. (2011). Social withdrawal and shyness. In P. K. Smith & C. H. Hart (Eds.), *Wiley-Blackwell handbook of childhood social development* (2nd ed.). New York: Wiley.

Rubin, Z., & Slomon, J. (1994). How parents influence their children's friendships. In M. Lewis (Ed.), *Beyond the dyad.* New York: Plenum.

Ruble, D. N., Boggiano, A. K., Feldman, N. S., & Loebl, J. H. (1980). Developmental analysis of the role of social comparison in self evaluation. *Developmental Psychology, 16,* 105–115.

Rumberger, R. W. (1995). Dropping out of middle school: A multilevel analysis of students and schools. *American Education Research Journal, 3,* 583–625.

Runco, M., & Spritzker, S. (Eds.). (2011). *Encyclopedia of creativity* (2nd ed.). New York: Elsevier.

Russell, A. (2011). Parent-child relationships and influences. In P. K. Smith & C. H. Hart (Eds.), *Wiley-Blackwell handbook of childhood social development* (2nd ed.). New York: Wiley.

Russell, S. T., Card, N. A., & Susman, E. J. (2011). Introduction: A decade review of research on adolescence. *Journal of Research on Adolescence, 21,* 1–2.

Russell, S. T., Crockett, L. J., & Chao, R. K. (2010). *Asian American parenting and parent-adolescent relationships*. New York: Springer.

Russell, S. T., & Joyner, K. (2001). Adolescent sexual orientation and suicide risk: Evidence from a national study. *American Journal of Public Health, 91,* 1276–1281.

Ruthsatz, J., Detterman, D., Griscom, W. S., & Cirullo, B. A. (2008). Becoming an expert in the musical domain: It takes more than just practice. *Intelligence, 36,* 330–338.

Rutter, M. (1979). Protective factors in children's response to stress and disadvantage. In M. W. Kent & J. E. Rolf (Eds.), *Primary prevention in psychopathology* (Vol. 3). Hanover: University of New Hampshire Press.

Rutter, M., & Dodge, K. A. (2011). Gene-environment interaction: State of the science. In K. A. Dodge & M. Rutter (Eds.), *Gene-environment interaction and developmental psychopathology.* New York: Guilford.

Rutter, M., & Garmezy, N. (1983). Developmental psychopathology. In P. H. Mussen (Ed.), *Handbook of child psychology* (4th ed., Vol. 4). New York: Wiley.

Ryan, A. M. (2011). Peer relationships and academic adjustment during early adolescence. *Journal of Early Adolescence, 31,* 5–12.

Ryan, C., Huebner, D., Diaz, R. M., & Sanchez, J. (2009). Family rejection as a predictor of negative health outcomes in white and Latino lesbian, gay, and bisexual young adults. *Pediatrics, 123,* 346–352.

Ryan, M. K. (2003). Gender differences in ways of knowing: The context dependence of the Attitudes Toward Thinking and Learning Survey. *Sex Roles, 49,* 11–12.

Ryan, R. M., & Deci, E. L. (2009). Promoting self-determined school engagement: Motivation, learning, and well-being. In K. Wentzel & A. Wigfield (Eds.), *Handbook of motivation at school.* New York: Routledge.

Ryan, S. M., & others. (2011, in press). Parenting strategies for reducing adolescent alcohol use: A Delphi consensus study. *BMC Public Health.*

S

Saarni, C. (1999). *The development of emotional competence*. New York: Guilford.

Saarni, C., Campos, J. J., Camras, L., & Witherington, D. (2006). Emotional development. In W. Damon & R. Lerner (Eds.), *Handbook of child psychology* (6th ed.). New York: Wiley.

Sadker, M. P., & Sadker, D. M. (2005). *Teachers, schools, and society* (7th ed.). New York: McGraw-Hill.

Saewyc, E. M. (2011). Research on adolescent sexual orientation: Development, health disparities, stigma, and resilience. *Journal of Research on Adolescence, 21,* 256–272.

Sagan, C. (1977). *The dragons of Eden*. New York: Random House.

Sakamaki, R., Toyama, K., Amamoto, R., Liu, C. J., & Shinfuku, N. (2005). Nutritional knowledge, food habits, and health attitude of Chinese university students—a cross-sectional study. *Nutrition Journal, 9,* 4.

Salazar, L. F., & others. (2011). Personal and social influences regarding oral sex among African American female adolescents. *Journal of Women's Health, 20,* 161–167.

Salmivalli, C., & Peets, K. (2009). Bullies, victims, and bully-victim relationships in middle childhood and adolescence. In K. H. Rubin, W. M. Bukowski, & B. Laursen (Eds.), *Handbook of peer interactions, relationships, and groups.* New York: Guilford.

Salmivalli, C., Peets, K., & Hodges, E. V. E. (2011). Bullying. In P. K. Smith & C. H. Hart (Eds.), *Wiley-Blackwell handbook of childhood social development* (2nd ed.). New York: Wiley.

Salovey, P., & Mayer, J. D. (1990). Emotional intelligence. *Imagination, Cognition, and Personality, 9,* 185–211.

Salzinger, S., Rosario, M., Feldman, R. S., & Ng-Mak, D. S. (2011). Role of parent and peer relationships and individual characteristics in middle school children's behavioral outcomes in the face of community violence. *Journal of Research on Adolescence, 21,* 395–407.

Sanchez, B., Esparza, P., Colon, Y., & Davis, K. E. (2011, in press). Tryin' to make it during the transition from high school: The role of family obligation attitudes and economic context for Latino-emerging adults. *Journal of Adolescent Research.*

Sanchez-Johnsen, L. A., Fitzgibbon, M. L., Martinovich, Z., Stolley, M. R., Dyer, A. R., & Van Horn, L. (2004). Ethnic differences in correlates of obesity between Latin-American and black women. *Obesity Research, 12,* 652–660.

Sandler, I., Wolchik, S., & Schoenfelder, E. (2011). Evidence-based family-focused prevention programs for children. *Annual Review of Psychology* (Vol. 62). Palo Alto, CA: Annual Reviews.

Sanson, A., Hempill, S. A., Yagmurlu, B., & McClowry, S. (2011). Temperament and social development. In P. K. Smith & C. H. Hart (Eds.), *Wiley-Blackwell handbook of childhood social development* (2nd ed.). New York: Wiley.

Santa Maria, M. (2002). Youth in Southeast Asia: Living within the continuity of tradition and the turbulence of change. In B. B. Brown, R. W. Larson, & T. S. Saraswathi (Eds.), *The world's youth*. New York: Cambridge University Press.

Santelli, J. S., Abraido-Lanza, A. F., & Melnikas, A. J. (2009). Migration, acculturation, and sexual and reproductive health of Latino adolescents. *Journal of Adolescent Health, 44,* 3–4.

Santelli, J., Sandfort, T. G., & Orr, M. (2009). U.S./European differences in condom use. *Journal of Adolescent Health, 44,* 306.

Santiago, C. D., Etter, E. M., Wadsworth, M. E., & Raviv, T. (2011, in press). Predictors of responses to stress among families coping with poverty-related stress. *Anxiety, Stress, and Coping.*

Santrock, J. W., & Halonen, J. S. (2009). *Your guide to college success* (6th ed.). Belmont, CA: Wadsworth.

Santrock, J. W., Sitterle, K. A., & Warshak, R. A. (1988). Parent-child relationships in stepfather families. In P. Bronstein & C. P. Cowan (Eds.), *Fatherhood today: Men's changing roles in the family*. New York: Wiley.

Savin-Williams, R. C. (2001). A critique of research on sexual minority youths. *Journal of Adolescence, 24,* 5–13.

Savin-Williams, R. C. (2011, in press).Identity development in sexual-minority youth. In S. Schwartz, K. Luyckx, & V. Vignoles (Eds.), *Handbook of identity theory and research*. New York: Springer.

Savin-Williams, R. C., & Demo, D. H. (1983). Conceiving or misconceiving the self: Issues in adolescent self-esteem. *Journal of Early Adolescence, 3,* 121–140.

Savin-Williams, R. C., Pardo, S. B., Vrangalova, Z., Mitchell, R. S., & Cohen, K. M. (2011, in press). Sexual and gender prejudice. In D. McCreary & J. Chrisler (Eds.), *Handbook of gender research in psychology*. New York: Springer.

Savin-Williams, R. C., & Ream, G. L. (2007). Prevalence of stability of sexual orientation components during adolescence and young adulthood. *Archives of Sexual Behavior, 36,* 385–394.

Sawyer, M. G., Pfeiffer, S., & Spence, S. H. (2009). Life events, coping, and depressive symptoms among young adolescents: A one-year prospective study. *Journal of Affective Disorders, 117,* 48–54.

Sax, L. J., & Bryant, A. N. (2006). The impact of college on sex-atypical career choices of men and women. *Journal of Vocational Behavior, 68.* 52–63.

Sayer, L. C. (2006). Economic aspects of divorce and relationship dissolution. In M. A. Fine & J. H. Harvey (Eds.), *Handbook of divorce and relationship dissolution*. Mahwah, NJ: Erlbaum.

Sbarra, D. A. (2006). Predicting the onset of emotional recovery following nonmarital relationship dissolution: Survival analysis of sadness and anger. *Personality and Social Psychology Bulletin, 32,* 298–312.

Sbarra, D. A., & Ferrer, E. (2006). The structure and process of emotional experience following nonmarital relationship dissolution: Dynamic factor anslysis of love, anger, and sadness. *Emotion, 6,* 224–238.

Scales, P. C., Benson, P. L., & Roehlkepartain, E. C. (2011, in press). Adolescent thriving: The role of sparks, relationships, and empowerment. *Journal of Youth and Adolescence.*

Scarr, S. (1993). Biological and cultural diversity: The legacy of Darwin for development. *Child Development, 64,* 1333–1353.

Schaie, K. W. (2011). Developmental influences on adult intellectual development: The Seattle Longitudinal Study. New York: Oxford University Press.

Schaie, K. W., & Willis, S. L. (2012). Adult development and aging (6th ed.). Upper Saddle River, NJ: Prentice Hall.

Schalet, A. T. (2011). Beyond abstinence and risk: A new paradigm for adolescent sexual health. *Women's Health Issues, 21*(Suppl 3), S5–S7.

Schermerhorn, A. C., Chow, S-M., & Cummings, E. M. (2010). Developmental family processes and interparental conflict: Patterns of micro-level influences. *Developmental Psychology, 46,* 869–885.

Schiff, W. J. (2011). *Nutrition for healthy living* (2nd ed.). New York: McGraw-Hill.

Schilling, E. A., Aseltine, R. H., Glanovsky, J. L., James, A., & Jacobs, D. (2009). Adolescent alcohol use, suicidal ideation, and suicide attempts. *Journal of Adolescent Health, 44,* 335–341.

Schlegel, A., & Hewlett, B. L. (2011). Contributions of anthropology to the study of adolescence. *Journal of Research on Adolescence, 21,* 281–289.

Schmalz, D. L., Deane, G. D., Leann, L., Birch, L. L., & Krahnstoever Davison, K. (2007). A longitudinal assessment between physical activity and self-esteem in early adolescent non-Hispanic females. *Journal of Adolescent Health, 41,* 559–565.

Schmidt, M. E., Marks, J. L., & Derrico, L. (2004). What a difference mentoring makes: Service learning and engagement for college students. *Mentoring and Tutoring Partnership in Learning, 12,* 205–217.

Schmidt, M. E., & Vandewater, E. A. (2008). Media and attention, cognition, and school achievement. *Future of Children, 18*(1), 64–85.

Schmottiach, N., & McManama, J. (2010). *Physical education activity handbook* (12th ed.). Upper Saddle River, NJ: Pearson.

Schneider, B., & Stevenson, D. (1999). *The ambitious generation.* New Haven, CT: Yale University Press.

Schneider, M., Dunton, G. F., & Cooper, D. M. (2008). Physical activity and physical self-concept among sedentary adolescent females: An intervention study. *Psychology of Sport and Exercise, 9,* 1–14.

Schofield, H. L., Bierman, K. L., Heinrichs, B., Nix, R. L., & the Conduct Problems Prevention Research Group. (2008). Predicting early sexual activity with behavior problems exhibited at school entry and in early adolescence. *Journal of Abnormal Child Psychology, 36,* 1175–1188.

Schouten, A. P., Valkenburg, P. M., & Peter, J. (2007). Precursors and underlying processes of adolescents' online self-disclosure: Developing and testing an "Internet-attribute-perception" model. *Media Psychology, 10,* 292–314.

Schulenberg, J. E., & Zarrett, N. R. (2006). Mental health during emerging adulthood: Continuities and discontinuities in course, content, and meaning. In J. J. Arnett & J. Tanner (Eds.), *Advances in emerging adulthood.* Washington, DC: American Psychological Association.

Schunk, D. H. (2008). *Learning theories* (5th ed.). Upper Saddle River, NJ: Prentice Hall.

Schunk, D. H. (2012). *Learning theories* (6th ed.). Upper Saddle River, NJ: Prentice Hall.

Schunk, D. H., Pintrich, P. R., & Meece, J. L. (2008). *Motivation in education* (3rd ed.). Upper Saddle River, NJ: Prentice Hall.

Schwartz, D., Kelly, B. M., Duong, M., & Badaly, D. (2010). Contextual perspective on intervention and prevention efforts for bully/victim problems. In E. M. Vernberg & B. K. Biggs (Eds.), *Preventing and treating bullying and victimization*. New York: Oxford University Press.

Schwartz, P. D., Maynard, A. M., & Uzelac, S. M. (2008). Adolescent egocentrism: A contemporary view. *Adolescence, 43,* 441–448.

Schwartz, S. J., & Finley, G. E. (2010). Troubled ruminations about parents: Conceptualization and validation with emerging adults. *Journal of Counseling & Development, 88,* 80–91.

Schwartz, S. J., & others. (2011). Examining the light and dark sides of emerging adults' identity: A study of identity status differences in positive and negative psychosocial functioning. *Journal of Youth and Adolescence, 40,* 839–859.

Schweinhart, L. J., Montie, J., Xiang, Z., Barnett, W. S., Belfield, C. R., & Nores, M. (2005). *Lifetime effects: The High/Scope Perry Preschool Study Through Age 40.* Ypsilanti, MI: High/Scope Press.

Sciberras, E., Ukoumunne, O. C., & Efron, D. (2011, in press). Predictors of parent-reported attention-deficit/hyperactivity disorder in children aged 6–7 years: A national longitudinal study. *Journal of Abnormal Child Psychology.*

Scott, M. E., Wildsmith, E., Welti, K., Ryan, S., Schelar, E., & Steward-Streng, N. R. (2011). Risky adolescent behaviors and reproductive health in young adulthood. *Perspectives on Sexual and Reproductive Health, 43,* 110–118.

Scourfield, J., Van den Bree, M., Martin, N., & McGuffin, P. (2004). Conduct problems in children and adolescents: A twin study. *Archives of General Psychiatry, 61,* 489–496.

Search Institute. (1995). *Barriers to participation in youth programs.* Unpublished manuscript, the Search Institute, Minneapolis.

Search Institute. (2010). *Teen's relationships.* Minneapolis, MN: Author.

Seaton, E. K. (2010). Developmental characteristics of African American and Caribbean Black Adolescents' regarding discrimination. *Journal of Research on Adolescence, 20,* 774–788.

Seaton, E. K., Caldwell, C. H., Sellers, R. M., & Jackson, J. S. (2010). Developmental characteristics of African American and Caribbean Black adolescents' attributions regarding discrimination. *Journal of Research on Adolescence, 20,* 774–788.

Seaton, E. K., Yip, T., & Sellers, R. M. (2009). A longitudinal examination of racial identity and racial discrimination among African American adolescents. *Child Development, 80,* 406–417.

Sebastian, C., Burnett, S., & Blakemore, S-J. (2010). Development of the self-concept in adolescence. *Trends in Cognitive Science, 12,* 441–446.

Sedikdes, C., & Brewer, M. B. (Eds.). (2001). *Individual self, relational self, and collective self.* Philadelphia: Psychology Press.

Seiffge-Krenke, I. (2011). Coping with relationship stressors: A decade review. *Journal of Research on Adolescence, 21,* 196–210.

Seiffge-Krenke, I., Aunola, K., & Nurmi, J-E. (2009). Changes in stress perception and coping during adolescence: The role of situational and personal factors. *Child Development, 80,* 259–279.

Seiter, L. N., & Nelson, L. J. (2011, in press). An examination of emerging adulthood in college students and nonstudents in India. *Journal of Adolescent Research.*

Selfhout, M., & others. (2010). Emerging late adolescence friendship networks and Big Five personality traits: A social network approach. *Journal of Personality, 78,* 509–538.

Seligman, M. E. P., & Csikszentmihalyi, M. (2000). Positive psychology. *American Psychologist, 55,* 5–14.

Seligson, T. (2005, February 20). They speak for success. *Parade Magazine.*

Sellers, R. M., Copeland-Linder, N., Martin, P. P., & Lewis, R. L. (2006). Racial identity matters: The relationship between racial discrimination and psychological functioning in African American adolescents. *Journal of Research on Adolescence, 16,* 187–216.

Semaj, L. T. (1985). Afrikanity, cognition, and extended self-identity. In M. B. Spencer, G. K. Brookins, & W. R. Allen (Eds.), *Beginnings: The social and affective development of Black children.* Hillsdale, NJ: Erlbaum.

Sen, B. (2010). The relationship between frequency of family dinner and adolescent problem behaviors after adjusting for other characteristics. *Journal of Adolescence, 33,* 187–196.

Seo, D-C., & Sa, J. (2010). A meta-analysis of obesity interventions among U.S. minority children. *Journal of Adolescent Health, 46,* 309–323.

Settersten, R. A., Furstenberg, F. F., & Rumbaut, R. G. (Eds.). (2005). *On the frontier of adulthood: Theory, research, and public policy.* Chicago: University of Chicago Press.

Sharma, A. R., McGue, M. K., & Benson, P. L. (1996). The emotional and behavioral adjustment of adopted adolescents: Part I: Age at adoption. *Children and Youth Services Reviews, 18,* 101–114.

Sharma, M. (2006). School-based interventions for childhood and adolescent obesity. *Obesity Review, 7,* 261–269.

Sharp, E. H., Coatsworth, J. D., Darling, N., Cumsille, P., & Ranieri, S. (2007). Gender differences in the self-defining activities and identity experiences of adolescents and emerging adults. *Journal of Adolescence, 30,* 251–269.

Shaver, P. R., & Mikulincer, M. (2007). Attachment theory and research. In A. W. Kruglanski & E. T. Higgins (Eds.), *Social psychology* (2nd ed.). New York: Guilford.

Shaw, P., & others. (2007). Attention-deficit/hyperactivity disorder is characterized by a delay in cortical maturation. *Proceedings of the National Academy of Sciences, 104*(49), 19649–19654.

Shaywitz, S. E., Gruen, J. R., & Shaywitz, B. A. (2007). Management of dyslexia, its rationale and underlying neurobiology. *Pediatric Clinics of North America, 54,* 609–623.

Shebloski, B., Conger, K. J., & Widaman, K. F. (2005). Reciprocal links among differential parenting, perceived partiality, and self worth: A three-wave longitudinal study. *Journal of Family Psychology, 19,* 633–642.

Sheeber, L. B., Davis, B., Leve, C., Hops, H., & Tildesley, E. (2007). Adolescents' relationships with their mothers and fathers: Associations with depressive disorder and subdiagnostic symptomatology. *Journal of Abnormal Psychology, 116,* 144–154.

Sher-Censor, E., Parke, R. D. & Coltrane, S. (2011). Parents' promotion of psychological autonomy, psychological control, and Mexican-American adolescents' adjustment. *Journal of Youth and Adolescence, 40,* 620–632.

Shernoff, D. J. (2009, April). *Flow in educational contexts: Creating optimal learning environments.* Paper presented at the meeting of the Society for Research in Child Development, Denver.

Shifren, K., Furnham, A., & Bauserman, R. L. (2003). Emerging adulthood in American and British samples: Individuals' personality and health risk behaviors. *Journal of Adult Development, 10,* 75–88.

Shiraev, E., & Levy, D. A. (2010). *Cross-cultural psychology* (4th ed.). Boston: Allyn & Bacon.

Shors, T. J., Anderson, M. L., Curlik, D. M., & Nokia, M. S. (2011, in press). Use it or lose it: How neurogenesis keeps the brain fit. *Behavioral Brain Research.*

Shulman, S., Davila, J., & Shachar-Shapira, L. (2011). Assessing romantic competence among older adolescents. *Journal of Adolescence, 34,* 397–406.

Shulman, S., Scharf, M., & Shachar-Shapira, S. (2012). The intergenerational transmission of romantic relationships. In P. K. Kerig, M. S. Schulz, & S. T. Hauser (Eds.), *Adolescence and beyond.* New York: Oxford University Press.

SIECUS (1999). *Public support for sex education.* Washington, DC: Author.

Siegel, D. M., Aten, M. J., & Roghmann, K. J. (1998). Self-reported honesty among middle and high school students responding to a sexual behavior questionnaire. *Journal of Adolescent Health, 23,* 20–28.

Siegler, R. S. (2006). Microgenetic analysis of learning. In W. Damon & R. Lerner (Eds.), *Handbook of child psychology* (6th ed.). New York: Wiley.

Sieving, R. E., & others. (2011, in press). A clinic-based youth development program to reduce sexual risk behaviors among adolescent girls: Prime Time Pilot Study. *Health Promotion Practice.*

Sigal, A., Sandler, I., Wolchik, S., & Braver, S. (2011). Do parent education programs promote healthy post-divorce parenting? Critical directions and distinctions and a review of the evidence. *Family Court Review, 49,* 120–129.

Silberg, J. L., Maes, H., & Eaves, L. J. (2010). Genetic and environmental influences on the transmission of parental depression to children's depression and conduct disturbance: An extended Children of Twins study. *Journal of Child Psychology and Psychiatry, 51,* 734–744.

Silva, C. (2005, October 31). When teen dynamo talks, city listens. *Boston Globe,* pp. B1, B4.

Silver, E. J., & Bauman, L. J. (2006). The association of sexual experience with attitudes, beliefs, and risk behaviors of inner-city adolescents. *Journal of Research on Adolescence, 16,* 29–45.

Silverman, J. G., Raj, A., Mucci, L. A., & Hathaway, J. E. (2001). Dating violence against adolescent girls and associated substance use, unhealthy weight control, sexual risk behavior, pregnancy, and suicidality. *Journal of the American Medical Association, 386,* 572–579.

Silver, S. (1988, August). *Behavior problems of children born into early-childbearing families.* Paper presented at the meeting of the American Psychological Association, Atlanta.

Silverstein, M., & Giarrusso, R. (2010). Aging and family life: A decade review. *Journal of Marriage and the Family, 72,* 1039–1058.

Simmons, R. G., & Blyth, D. A. (1987). *Moving into adolescence.* Hawthorne, NY: Aldine.

Simons, J. M., Finlay, B., & Yang, A. (1991). *The adolescent and young adult fact book.* Washington, DC: Children's Defense Fund.

Simon, V. A., Aikins, J. W., & Prinstein, M. J. (2008). *Homophily in adolescent romantic relationships.* Unpublished manuscript, College of Arts and Sciences, Wayne State University, Detroit.

Simpson, R. L. (1962). Parental influence, anticipatory socialization, and social mobility. *American Sociological Review, 27,* 517–522.

Singh, S., Wulf, D., Samara, R., & Cuca, Y. P. (2000). Gender differences in the timing of first intercourse: Data from 14 countries. *International Family Planning Perspectives, 26,* 21–28, 43.

Sinha, J. W., Cnaan, R. A., & Gelles, R. J. (2007). Adolescent risk behaviors and religion: Findings from a national study. *Journal of Adolescence, 30,* 231–249.

Sinnott, J. D. (2003). Postformal thought and adult development: Living in balance. In J. Demick & C. Andreoletti (Eds.), *Handbook of adult development.* New York: Kluwer.

Sinnott, J. D., & Johnson, L. (1997). Brief report: Complex postformal thought in skilled, research administrators. *Journal of Adult Development, 4*(1), 45–53.

Sirsch, U., Dreher, E., Mayr, E., & Willinger, U. (2009). What does it take to be an adult in Austria? Views of adulthood in Austrian adolescents, emerging adults and adults. *Journal of Adolescent Research, 24,* 275–292.

Sisson, S. B., Broyles, S. T., Baker, B. L., & Katzmarzyk, P. T. (2010). Screen time, physical activity, and overweight in U.S. youth: National Survey of Children's Health 2003. *Journal of Adolescent Health, 47,* 309–311.

Skinner, B. F. (1938). *The behavior of organisms: An experimental analysis.* New York: Appleton-Century-Crofts.

Skorikov, V., & Vondracek, F. W. (1998). Vocational identity development: Its relationship to other identity domains and to overall identity development. *Journal of Career Assessment, 6*(1), 13–35.

Slavin, R. E. (2011). Instruction based on cooperative learning. In P. A. Alexander & R. E. Mayer (Eds.), *Handbook of research on learning and instruction.* New York: Routledge.

Slavin, R. E. (2012). *Educational psychology* (10th ed.). Upper Saddle River, NJ: Prentice Hall.

Slomkowski, C., Rende, R., Conger, K. J., Simons, R. L., & Conger, R. D. (2001). Sisters, brothers, and delinquency: Social influence during early and middle adolescence. *Child Development, 72,* 271–283.

Smaldino, S. E., Lowther, D. L., & Russell, J. D. (2012). *Instructional technology and media for learning* (10th ed.). Boston: Allyn & Bacon.

Smetana, J. G. (2008). Commentary: Conflicting views of conflict. *Monographs of the Society for Research in Child Development, 73*(2), 161–168.

Smetana, J. G. (2008). "It's 10 o'clock: Do you know where your children are?" Recent advances in understanding parental monitoring and adolescents' information management. *Child Development Perspectives, 2,* 19–25.

Smetana, J. G. (2010). The role of trust in adolescent-parent relationships: To trust is to tell you. In K. Rotenberg (Ed.), *Trust and trustworthiness during childhood and adolescence.* New York: Cambridge University Press.

Smetana, J. G. (2011a, in press). *Adolescents, families, and social development: How adolescents construct their worlds.* New York: Wiley-Blackwell.

Smetana, J. G. (2011b, in press). Adolescents' social reasoning and relationships with parents: Conflicts and coordinations within and across domains. In E. Amsel & J. Smetana (Eds.), *Adolescent vulnerabilities and opportunities: Constructivist and developmental perspectives,* New York: Cambridge University Press.

Smetana, J. G., & Gaines, C. (1999). Adolescent-parent conflict in middle-class African-American families. *Child Development, 70,* 1447–1463.

Smetana, J. G., Gettman, D. C., Villalobos, M., & Tasopoulos, M. (2007, March). *Daily variations in African American, Latino, and European American teens' disclosure with parents and best friends.* Paper presented at the biennial meeting of the Society for Research in Child Development, Boston.

Smetana, J. G., Villalobos, M., Tasopoulos-Chan, M., Gettman, D. C., & Campione-Barr, N. (2009). Early and middle adolescents' disclosure to parents about activities in different domains. *Journal of Adolescence, 32,* 693–713.

Smith, A. B., Halari, R., Giampetro, V., Brammer, M., & Rubia, K. (2011, in press). Developmental effects of reward on sustained attention networks. *NeuroImage.*

Smith, C., & Denton, M. (2005). *Soul searching: The religious and spiritual lives of American teenagers.* New York: Oxford University Press.

Smith, J. B. (2009). High school organization. In D. Carr (Ed.), *Encyclopedia of the life course and human development.* Boston: Gale Cengage.

Smith, M. A., & Berger, J. B. (2010). Women's ways of drinking: College women, high-risk alcohol use, and negative consequences. *Journal of College Student Development, 51,* 35–49.

Smith, P. K., & Hart, C. A. (Eds.). (2011). *Wiley-Blackwell handbook of childhood social development* (2nd ed.). New York: Wiley.

Smith, R. E., & Smoll, F. L. (1997). Coaching the coaches: Youth sports as a scientific and applied behavioral setting. *Current Directions in Psychological Science, 6,* 16–21.

Smith, R. L., Rose, A. J., & Schwartz-Mette, R. A. (2010). Relational and overt aggression in childhood and adolescence:

Clarifying mean-level gender differences and associations with peer acceptance. *Social Development, 19,* 243–269.

Smith, T. E., Polloway, E. A., Patton, J. R., & Dowdy, C. A. (2012). *Teaching students with special needs in inclusive settings* (6th ed.). Upper Saddle River, NJ: Pearson.

Smits, I. A., & others. (2011). Cohort differences in the Big Five personality factors over a period of 25 years. *Journal of Personality and Social Psychology, 100,* 1124–1138.

Snarey, J. (1987, June). A question of morality. *Psychology Today, 21,* 6–8.

Snarey, J., & Samuelson, P. (2008). Moral education in the cognitive developmental tradition: Lawrence Kohlberg's revolutionary ideas. In L. P. Nucci & D. Narváez (Eds.), *Handbook of moral and character education.* New York: Routledge.

Solmeyer, A. R., McHale, S. M., Killoren, S. E., & Updegraff, K. A. (2011). Coparenting around siblings' differential treatment in Mexican-origin families. *Developmental Psychology, 25,* 251–260.

Solomon, D., Watson, P., Schapes, E., Battistich, V., & Solomon, J. (1990). Cooperative learning as part of a comprehensive program designed to promote prosocial development. In S. Sharan (Ed.), *Cooperative learning.* New York: Praeger.

Somerville, L. H., Jones, R. M., & Casey, B. J. (2010). A time of change: Behavioral and neural correlates of adolescent sensitivity to appetitive and aversive environmental cues. *Brain and Cognition, 72,* 124–133.

Sommer, B. B. (1978). *Puberty and adolescence.* New York: Oxford University Press.

Sommer, M. (2011). An overlooked priority: Puberty in sub-Saharan Africa. *American Journal of Public Health, 101,* 979–981.

Song, A. V., & Halpern-Felsher, B. L. (2010). Predictive relationship between adolescent oral and vaginal sex: Results from a prospective, longitudinal study. *Archives of Pediatric and Adolescent Medicine,165,* 243–249.

Song, L. J., & others. (2010). The differential effects of general mental ability and emotional intelligence on academic performance and social interactions. *Intelligence, 38,* 137–143.

Sontag, L. M., Clemans, K. H., Graber, J. A., & Lyndon, S. T. (2011). Traditional and cyber aggressors and victims: A comparison of social characteristics. *Journal of Youth and Adolescence, 40,* 392–404.

Sontag, L. M., Graber, J., Brooks-Gunn, J., & Warren, M. P. (2008). Coping with social stress: Implications for psychopathology in young adolescent girls. *Journal of Abnormal Child Psychology, 36,* 1159–1174.

Soto, C. J., John, O. P., Gosling, S. D., & Potter, J. (2011). Age differences in personality traits from 10 to 65: Big Five domains and facets in a large cross-cultural sample. *Journal of Personality and Social Psychology, 100,* 330–348.

Sousa, D. A. (1995). *How the brain learns: A classroom teacher's guide.* Reston, VA: National Association of Secondary School Principals.

Sowell, E. (2004, July). Commentary in M. Beckman, "Crime, culpability, and the adolescent brain." *Science Magazine, 305,* 599.

Sparling, P., & Redican, K. (2011). *MP iHealth.* New York: McGraw-Hill.

Spatz, C. (2012). *Basic statistics* (10th ed.). Boston: Cengage.

Spence, J. T., & Helmreich, R. (1978). *Masculinity and femininity: Their psychological dimensions.* Austin: University of Texas Press.

Spencer, M. B. (2000). Ethnocentrism. In A. Kazdin (Ed.), *Encyclopedia of psychology.* New York: Oxford University Press.

Speranza, M., & others. (2005). Depressive personality dimensions and alexithymia in eating disorders. *Psychiatry Research, 135,* 153–163.

Spiegler, M. D., & Guevremont, D. C. (2010). *Contemporary behavior therapy* (5th ed.). Boston: Cengage.

Spring, J. (2010). *Deculturalization and the struggle for equality* (6th ed.). New York: McGraw-Hill.

Spruijt-Metz, D. (2011). Etiology, treatment, and prevention of obesity in childhood and adolescence: A decade in review. *Journal of Research on Adolescence, 21,* 129–152.

Srabstein, J. C., McCarter, R. J., Shao, C., & Huang, Z. J. (2006). Morbidities associated with bullying behaviors in adolescents: School based study of American adolescents. *International Journal of Adolescent Medicine and Health, 18,* 587–596.

Sroufe, L. A. (2007). Commentary: The place of development in developmental psychology. In A. S. Masten (Ed.), *Multilevel dynamics in developmental psychology.* Mahwah, NJ: Erlbaum.

Sroufe, L. A., Coffino, B., & Carlson, E. A. (2010). Conceptualizing the role of early experience: Lessons from the Minnesota longitudinal study. *Developmental Review, 30,* 36–51.

Sroufe, L. A., Egeland, B., Carlson. E., & Collins, W. (2005). *The development of the person: The Minnesota Study of Risk and Adaptation from birth to maturity.* New York: Guilford.

Staff, J., Messersmith, E. E., & Schulenberg, J. E. (2009). Adolescents and the world of work. In R. M. Lerner & L. Steinberg (Eds.), *Handbook of adolescent psychology* (3rd ed.). New York: Wiley.

Stake, J. E. (2000). When situations call for instrumentality and expressiveness: Resource appraisal, coping strategy choice, and adjustment. *Sex Roles, 42,* 865–885.

Stangor, C. (2011). *Research methods for the behavioral sciences* (4th ed.). Boston: Cengage.

Stanley, S. M., Amato, P. R., Johnson, C. A., & Markman, H. J. (2006). Premarital education, marital quality, and marital stability: Findings from a large, household survey. *Journal of Family Psychology, 20,* 117–126.

Stanley, S. M., Rhoades, G. K., Amato, P. R., Markman, H. J., & Johnson, C. A. (2010). The timing of cohabitation and engagement: Impact on first and second marriages. *Journal of Marriage and the Family, 72,* 906–918.

Stanovich, K. E., West, R. F., & Toplak, M. E. (2011). Intelligence and rationality. In R. J.Sternberg & S. B. Kaufman (Eds.), *Cambridge handbook of intelligence.* New York: Cambridge University Press.

Stansfield, K. H., & Kirstein, C. L. (2006). Effects of novelty on behavior in the adolescent and adult rat. *Developmental Psychobiology, 48,* 273.

Starr, C. (2011). *Biology* (8th ed.). Boston: Cengage.

Starr, L. R., & Davila, J. (2009). Clarifying co-rumination: Associations with internalizing symptoms and romantic involvement among adolescent girls. *Journal of Adolescence, 32,* 19–37.

Staudinger, U. M., & Gluck, J. (2011). Psychological wisdom research. *Annual Review of Psychology* (Vol. 62). Palo Alto, CA: Annual Reviews.

Steca, P., Bassi, M., Caprara, G. V., & Fave, A. D. (2011, in press). Parents' self-efficacy beliefs and their children's psychosocial adaptation during adolescence. *Journal of Youth and Adolescence.*

Steel, P. (2007). The nature of procrastination: A meta-analytic and theoretical review of quintessential self-regulatory failure. *Psychological Bulletin, 133,* 65–94.

Steele, J., Waters, E., Crowell, J., & Treboux, D. (1998, June). *Self-report measures of attachment: Secure bonds to other attachment measures and attachment theory.* Paper presented at the meeting of the International Society for the Study of Personal Relationships, Saratoga Springs, NY.

Steinberg, L. (1986). Latchkey children and susceptibility to peer pressure: An ecological analysis. *Developmental Psychology, 22,* 433–439.

Steinberg, L. (2008). A neurobehavioral perspective on risk-taking. *Developmental Review, 28,* 78–106.

Steinberg, L. (2009). Adolescent development and juvenile justice. *Annual Review of Clinical Psychology* (Vol. 5). Palo Alto, CA: Annual Reviews.

Steinberg, L. (2010). A behavioral scientist looks at the science of adolescent brain development. *Brain and Cognition, 72,* 160–164.

Steinberg, L. (2011a). Adolescent risk-taking: A social neuroscience perspective. In E. Amsel & J. Smetana (Eds.), *Adolescent vulnerabilities and opportunities: Constructivist developmental perspectives*. New York: Cambridge University Press.

Steinberg, L. (2011b). *You and your adolescent: The essential guide for ages 10 to 25.* New York: Simon & Schuster.

Steinberg, L, Albert, D., Cauffman, E., Banich, M., Graham, S., & Woolard. J. (2008). Age differences in sensation-seeking and impulsivity as indexed by behavior and self-report: Evidence for a dual systems model. *Developmental Psychology, 44,* 1764–1778.

Steinberg, L., Graham, S., O'Brien, L., Woolard, J., Cauffman, E., & Banich, M. (2009). Age differences in future orientation and delay discounting. *Child Development, 80,* 28–44.

Steinberg, L. D. (1986). Latchkey children and susceptibility to peer pressure: An ecological analysis. *Developmental Psychology, 22,* 433–439.

Steinberg, L. D. (1988). Reciprocal relation between parent-child distance and pubertal maturation. *Developmental Psychology, 24,* 122–128.

Steinberg, L. D. (2004). Risk taking in adolescence: What changes, and why? *Annals of the New York Academy of Sciences, 1021,* 51–58.

Steinberg, L. D., & Cauffman, E. (2001). Adolescents as adults in court. *SRCD Social Policy Report, XV*(4), 1–13.

Steinberg, L. D., & Silk, J. S. (2002). Parenting adolescents. In M. Bornstein (Ed.), *Handbook of parenting* (2nd ed., Vol. 1). Mahwah, NJ: Erlbaum.

Steinberg, S. J., & Davila, J. (2008). Romantic functioning and depressive symptoms among early adolescent girls: The moderating role of parental emotional availability. *Journal of Clinical Child and Adolescent Psychology, 37,* 350–362.

Stein, C. J., & Micheli, L. J. (2010). Overuse injuries in youth sports. *Physician and Sportsmedicine, 38,* 102–108.

Stephens, J. M. (2008). Cheating. In N. J. Salkind (Ed.), *Encyclopedia of educational psychology*. Thousand Oaks, CA: Sage.

Sternberg, R. J. (1985, December). Teaching critical thinking, Part 2: Possible solutions. *Phi Delta Kappan,* 277–280.

Sternberg, R. J. (1986). *Intelligence applied*. Fort Worth: Harcourt Brace.

Sternberg, R. J. (1998). A balance theory of wisdom. *Review of General Psychology, 2,* 347–365.

Sternberg, R. J. (2004). Individual differences in cognitive development. In P. Smith & C. Hart (Eds.), *Blackwell handbook of cognitive development*. Malden, MA: Blackwell.

Sternberg, R. J. (2009). Intelligence. In M. E. Laur (Ed.), *Chicago companion to the child*. Chicago: University of Chicago Press.

Sternberg, R. J. (2010). The triarchic theory of successful intelligence. In B. Kerr (Ed.), *Encyclopedia of giftedness, creativity, and talent*. Thousand Oaks, CA: Sage.

Sternberg, R. J. (2011a). Personal wisdom in the balance. In M. Ferrari & N. Weststrate (Eds.), *Personal wisdom*. New York: Springer.

Sternberg, R. J. (2011b). Individual differences in cognitive development. In U. Goswami (Ed.), *Blackwell handbook of childhood cognitive development*. Malden, MA: Blackwell.

Sternberg, R. J. (2011c, in press). Intelligence. In B. McGaw, P. Peterson, & E. Baker (Eds.), *International encyclopedia of education* (3rd ed.). New York: Elsevier.

Sternberg, R. J. (2012). *Cognitive psychology* (6th ed.). Boston: Cengage.

Sternberg, R. J., & Ben-Zeev T. (2001). *Complex cognition*. New York: Oxford University Press.

Sternberg, R. J., Grigorenko, E. L., & Jarvin, L. (2011). *Explorations in giftedness*. New York: Cambridge University Press.

Sternberg, R. J., Jarvin, L., & Reznitskaya, A. (2011, in press). Teaching for wisdom through history: Infusing wise thinking skills in the school curriculum. In M. Ferrari (Ed.), *Teaching for Wisdom*. Amsterdam: Springer.

Sternberg, R. J., & Williams, W. M. (1996). *How to develop student creativity*. Alexandria, VA: ASCD.

Sternberg, S. J., & Davila, J. (2008). Romantic functioning and depressive symptoms among early adolescent girls: The moderating role of parental emotional availability. *Journal of Clinical Child and Adolescent Psychology, 37,* 350–362.

Steur, F. B., Applefield, J. M., & Smith, R. (1971). Televised aggression and the interpersonal aggression of preschool children. *Journal of Experimental Child Psychology, 11,* 442–447.

Stevenson, H. W. (1995). Mathematics achievement of American students: First in the world by the year 2000? In C. A. Nelson (Ed.), *Basic and applied perspectives on learning, cognition, and development*. Minneapolis: University of Minnesota Press.

Stevenson, H. W., Lee, S., Chen, C., Stigler, J. W., Hsu, C., & Kitamura, S. (1990). Contexts of achievement. *Monograph of the Society for Research in Child Development, 55* (Serial No. 221).

Stevenson, H. W., & Zusho, A. (2002). Adolescence in China and Japan: Adapting to a changing environment. In B. B. Brown, R. W. Larson, & T. S. Saraswathi (Eds.), *The world's youth*. New York: Cambridge University Press.

Stewart, A. J., Ostrove, J. M., & Helson, R. (2001). Middle aging in women: Patterns of personality change from the 30s to the 50s. *Journal of Adult Development, 8,* 23–37.

Stice, F., Presnell, K., & Spangler, D. (2002). Risk factors for binge eating onset in adolescent girls: A 2-year prospective investigation. *Health Psychology, 21,* 131–138.

Stiggins, R. (2008). *Introduction to student-involved assessment for learning* (5th ed.). Upper Saddle River, NJ: Prentice Hall.

Stipek, D. J. (2002). *Motivation to learn* (4th ed.). Boston: Allyn & Bacon.

Stipek, D. J. (2005, February 16). Commentary in *USA TODAY,* p. D1.

Stokes, C. E., & Raley, R. K. (2009). Cohabitation. In D. Carr (Ed.), *Encyclopedia of the life course and human development*. Boston: Gale Cengage.

Stone, L. B., Hankin, B. L., Gibb, B. E., & Abela, J. R. (2011, in press). Co-rumination predicts the onset of depressive disorders during adolescence. *Journal of Abnormal Psychology.*

Stoppa, T. M., & Lefkowitz, E. S. (2010). Longitudinal changes in religiosity among emerging adult college students. *Journal of Research on Adolescence, 20,* 23–38.

Story, M., Kaphingst, K. M., & French, S. (2006). The role of schools in obesity prevention. *Future of Children, 16*(1), 109–142.

St. Pierre, R., Layzer, J., & Barnes, H. (1996). *Regenerating two-generation programs*. Cambridge, MA: Abt Associates.

Strahan, D. B. (1983). The emergence of formal operations in adolescence. *Transcendence, 11,* 7–14.

Strasberger, V. C. (2009). Why do adolescent health researchers ignore the impact of the media? *Journal of Adolescent Health, 44,* 203–205.

Strasburger, V. C. (2010). Children, adolescents, and the media: Seven key issues. *Pediatric Annals, 39,* 556–564.

Strasburger, V. C., Wilson, B. J., & Jordan, A. (2008). *Children, adolescents, and the media*. Thousand Oaks, CA: Sage

Strati, A. D., Shernoff, D., & Kackar, H. Z. (2012). Flow. In J. R. Levesque (Ed.), *Encyclopedia of adolescence*. New York: Springer.

Straubhaar, J., LaRose, R., & Davenport, L. (2011). *Media now* (7th ed.). Boston: Cengage.

Stray, L. L., Ellertsen, B., & Stray, T. (2010). Motor function and methylphenidate effect in children with attention deficit hyperactivity disorder. *Acta Pediatrica, 99,* 1199–1204.

Streib, H. (1999). Off-road religion? A narrative approach to fundamentalist and occult orientations of adolescents. *Journal of Adolescence, 22,* 255–267.

Stroth, S., Kubesch, S., Dieterie, K., Ruchsow, M., Heim, R., & Kiefer, M. (2009). Physical fitness, but not acute exercise modulates event-related potential indices for executive control in healthy adolescents. *Brain Research, 1269,* 114–124.

Stroud, L. R., Papandonatos, G. D., Williamson, D. E., & Dahl, R. E. (2011, in press). Sex differences in cortisol response to corticotrophin releasing hormone challenge over puberty: Pittsburgh Pediatric Neurobehavioral Studies. *Psychoneuroimmunology.*

Stukenborg, J. B., Colon, E., & Soder, O. (2010). Ontogenesis of testis development population-based study. *Sexual Development, 4,* 199–212

Stulberg, L. M., & Weinberg, S. L. (Eds.). (2011). *Diversity in higher education*. New York: Routledge.

Su, R., Rounds, J., & Armstrong, P. I. (2009). Men and things, women and people: A meta-analysis of sex differences in interests. *Psychological Bulletin, 135,* 859–884.

Suárez-Orozco, C. (2007, March). *Immigrant family educational advantages and challenges*. Paper presented at the meeting of the Society for Research in Child Development, Boston.

Suarez-Orozco, M., & Suarez-Orozco, C. (2010). Globalization, immigration, and schooling. In J. A. Banks (Ed.), *The Routledge international companion to multicultural education*. New York: Routledge.

Subrahmanyam, K., & Greenfield, P. (2008). Online communication and adolescent relationships. *Future of Children, 18*(1), 119–146.

Sue, S. (1990, August). *Ethnicity and culture in psychological research and practice*. Paper presented at the meeting of the American Psychological Association, Boston.

Sue, S., & Morishima, J. K. (1982). *The mental health of Asian Americans: Contemporary issues in identifying and treating mental problems*. San Francisco: Jossey-Bass.

Sullivan, H. S. (1953). *The interpersonal theory of psychiatry*. New York: W. W. Norton.

Sullivan, P. J., & Larson, R. W. (2010). Connecting youth to high resource adults: Lessons from effective youth programs. *Journal of Adolescent Research, 25*(1), 99–123.

Sun, S. S., & others. (2008). Childhood obesity predicts adult metabolic syndrome: The Fels Longitudinal Study. *Journal of Pediatrics, 152,* 191–200.

Sun, Y., Tao, F., Hao, J., & Wan, Y. (2010). The mediating effects of stress and coping on depression among adolescents in China. *Journal of Child and Adolescent Psychiatric Nursing, 23,* 173–180.

Sund, A. M., Larsson, B., & Wichstrom, L. (2011). Role of physical and sedentary activities in the development of depressive symptoms in early adolescence. *Social Psychiatry and Psychiatric Epidemiology, 46,* 431–441.

Suris, J. C., Jeannin, A., Chossis, I., & Michaud, P. A. (2007). Piercing among adolescents: Body art as a risk marker: A population-based approach. *Journal of Family Practice, 56,* 126–120.

Susman, E. J. (2001). Unpublished review of J. W. Santrock's *Adolescence,* 9th ed. (New York: McGraw-Hill).

Susman, E. J., & Dorn, L. D. (2009). Puberty: Its role in development. In R. M. Lerner & L. Steinberg (Eds.), *Handbook of adolescent psychology* (3rd ed.). New York: Wiley.

Susman, E. J., Dorn, L. D., & Schiefelbein, V. L. (2003). Puberty, sexuality, and health. In R. M. Lerner, M. A. Easterbrooks, & J. Mistry (Eds.), *Comprehensive handbook of psychology: Developmental psychology* (Vol. 6). New York: Wiley.

Susman, E. J., & others. (2010). Longitudinal development of secondary sexual characteristics in girls and boys between ages 9½ and 15½ years. *Archives of Pediatric and Adolescent Medicine, 164,* 166–173.

Sutton-Smith, B. (1982). Birth order and sibling status effects. In M. E. Lamb & B. Sutton-Smith (Eds.), *Sibling relationships: Their nature and significance across the life span*. Hillsdale, NJ: Erlbaum.

Suyemoto, K. L. (2009). Multiracial Asian Americans. In N. Tewari & A. Alvarez (Eds.), *Asian American psychology*. Clifton, NJ: Psychology Press.

Swaab, D. F., Chung, W. C., Kruijver, F. P., Hofman, M. A., & Ishunina, T. A. (2001). Structural and functional sex differences in the human hypothalamus. *Hormones and Behavior, 40,* 93–98.

Swahn, M., Bossarte, R. M., & Sullivent, E. E. (2008). Age of alcohol use initiation, suicidal behavior, and peer and dating violence victimization and perpetration among high-risk, seventh-grade adolescents. *Pediatrics, 121,* 297–305.

Swanson, D. P. (2010). Adolescent psychosocial processes: Identity, stress, and competence. In D. P. Swanson, M. C. Edwards, & M. B. Spencer (Eds.), *Adolescence: Development in a global era*. San Diego: Academic Press.

Swanson, H. L. (1999). What develops in working memory? A life-span perspective. *Developmental Psychology, 35,* 986–1000.

Swartz, T. T., Kim, M., Uno, M. Mortimer, J., & O'Brien, K. B. (2011). Safety nets and scaffolds: Parental support in the transition to adulthood. *Journal of Marriage and the Family, 73,* 414–429.

Syed, M. (2010). Memorable everyday events in college: Narratives of the intersection of ethnicity and academia. *Journal of Diversity in Higher Education, 3,* 56–69.

Syed, M. (2011, in press). Developing an integrated self: Academic and ethnic identities among ethnically-diverse college students. *Developmental Psychology.*

Syed, M., & Azmitia, M. (2008). A narrative approach to ethnic identity in emerging adulthood: Bringing life to the identity status model. *Developmental Psychology, 44,* 1012–1027.

Syed, M., & Azmitia, M. (2009). Longitudinal trajectories of ethnic identity during the college years. *Journal of Research on Adolescence, 19*(4), 601–624.

Syed, M., & Azmitia, M. (2010). Narrative and ethnic identity exploration: A longitudinal account of emerging adults' ethnicity-related experiences. *Developmental Psychology, 46*(1), 208–219.

Syed, M., Azmitia, M., & Cooper, C. R. (2011, in press). Identity and academic success among under-represented ethnic minorities: An interdisciplinary review and integration. *Journal of Social Issues.*

Sykes, C. J. (1995). *Dumbing down our kids: Why America's children feel good about themselves but can't read, write, or add*. New York: St. Martin's Press.

Szulwach, K. E., & others. (2010). Cross talk between microRNA and epigenetic regulation in adult neurogenesis. *Journal of Cell Biology, 189,* 127–141.

Szwedo, D. E., Mikami, A. Y., & Allen, J. P. (2011, in press). Qualities of peer relations on social networking websites: Predictions from negative mother-teen interactions. *Journal of Research on Adolescence.*

T

TADS. (2007). The Treatment for Adolescents with Depression Study: Long-term effectiveness and safety outcomes. *Archives of General Psychiatry, 64,* 1132–1143.

Takeuchi, H., & others. (2011, in press). Regional gray matter density associated with emotional intelligence: Evidence from voxel-based morphometry. *Human Brain Mapping.*

Talpade, M. (2008). Hispanic versus African American girls: Body image, nutrition, and puberty. *Adolescence, 43,* 119–127.

Tamis-LeMonda, C. S., & Cabrera, N. (Eds.). (2002). *The handbook of father involvement.* Mahwah, NJ: Erlbaum.

Tamis-LeMonda, C. S., & McFadden, K. E. (2010). The United States of America. In M. H. Bornstein (Ed.), *Handbook of cultural developmental science.* New York: Psychology Press.

Tamis-LeMonda, C. S., Way, N., Hughes, D., Yoshikawa, H., Kallman, R. K., & Niwa, E. Y. (2008). Parents' goals for children: The dynamic coexistence of individualism and collectivism in cultures and individuals. *Social Development, 17,* 183–209.

Tannen, D. (1990). *You just don't understand: Women and men in conversation.* New York: Ballantine.

Tanner, J. M. (1962). *Growth at adolescence* (2nd ed.). Oxford, UK: Blackwell.

Tarokh, L., & Carskadon, M. A. (2008). Sleep in adolescents. In L. R. Squire (Ed.), *New Encyclopedia of Neuroscience.* Oxford, UK: Elsevier.

Tarokh, L., & Carskadon, M. A. (2010). Developmental changes in the human sleep EEG during early adolescence. *Sleep, 33,* 801–809.

Tarokh, L., Carskadon, M. A., & Achermann, P. (2011). Developmental changes in brain connectivity assessed using the sleep EEG. *Neuroscience, 31,* 6371–6378.

Tarpley, T. (2001). Children, the Internet, and other new technologies. In D. Singer & J. Singer (Eds.), *Handbook of children and the media.* Thousand Oaks, CA: Sage.

Tashiro, T., & Frazier, P. (2003). "I'll never be in a relationship like that again": Personal growth following romantic relationship breakups. *Personal Relationships, 10,* 113–128.

Tashiro, T., Frazier, P., & Berman, M. (2005). Stress-related growth following divorce and relationship dissolution. In M. A. Fine & J. H. Harvey (Eds.), *Handbook of divorce and relationship dissolution.* Mahwah, NJ: Erlbaum.

Tavris, C., & Wade, C. (1984). *The longest war: Sex differences in perspective* (2nd ed.). Fort Worth, TX: Harcourt Brace.

Taylor, B., Stein, N., & Burden, F. (2010). The effects of gender violence/harassment prevention programming in middle schools: A randomized experimental evaluation. *Violence and Victims, 25,* 202–203.

Taylor, J. H., & Walker, L. J. (1997). Moral climate and the development of moral reasoning: The effects of dyadic discussions between young offenders. *Journal of Moral Education, 26,* 21–43.

Taylor, L. M., & Fratto, J. M. (2012). *Transforming learning through 21st century skills.* Boston: Allyn & Bacon.

Taylor, N. L. (2011, in press). "Guys, she's humongous!": Gender and weight-based teasing in adolescence. *Journal of Adolescent Research.*

Taylor, R. D. (1996). Kinship support, family management, and adolescent adjustment and competence in African American families. *Developmental Psychology, 32,* 687–695.

Taylor, R. D. (2010). Risk and resilience in low-income African American families: Moderating effects of kinship social support. *Cultural Diversity and Ethnic Minority Psychology, 16,* 344–351.

Taylor, R. D., & Lopez, E. I. (2005). Family management practice, school achievement, and problem behavior in African American adolescents: Mediating processes. *Applied Developmental Psychology, 26,* 39–49.

Taylor, S. E. (2006). Tend and befriend: Biobehavioral bases of affiliation under stress. *Current Directions in Psychological Science, 15,* 273–277.

Taylor, S. E. (2011a). *Health Psychology* (8th ed.). New York: McGraw-Hill.

Taylor, S. E. (2011b). Tend and befriend theory. In A. M. van Lange, A. W. Kruglanski, & E. T. Higgins (Eds.), *Handbook of theories of social psychology.* Thousand Oaks, CA: Sage.

Taylor, S. E. (2011c). Affiliation and stress. In S. Folkman (Ed.), *Oxford handbook of stress, health, and coping.* New York: Oxford University Press.

Teenage Research Unlimited. (2004, November 10). *Diversity in word and deed: Most teens claim multicultural friends.* Northbrook, IL: Teenage Research Unlimited.

Teilmann, G., Juul, A., Skakkebaek, N. E., & Toppari, J. (2002). Putative effects of endocrine disruptors on pubertal development in the human. *Best Practices in Research and Clinical Endocrinology and Metabolism, 16,* 105–121.

Templeton, J. L., & Eccles, J. S. (2006). The relation between spiritual development and identity processes. In E. Roehlkepartain, P. E. King, L. Wagener, & P. L. Benson (Eds.), *The handbook of spirituality in childhood and adolescence.* Thousand Oaks, CA: Sage.

Terman, L. (1925). *Genetic studies of genius: Vol. 1. Mental and physical traits of a thousand gifted children.* Stanford, CA: Stanford University Press.

Terry-McElrath, Y. M., O'Malley, P. M., & Johnston, L. D. (2011). Exercise and substance among American youth, 1991–2009. *American Journal of Preventive Medicine, 40,* 530–540.

Testa, M., Hoffman, J. H., & Livingston, J. A. (2010). Alcohol and sexual risk behaviors as mediators of the sexual victimization-revictimization relationship. *Journal of Consulting and Clinical Psychology, 78,* 249–259.

The, N. S., & others. (2010). Association of adolescent obesity with risk of severe obesity in adulthood. *Journal of the American Medical Association, 304,* 2042–2047.

Thoma, S. J. (2006). Research on the Defining Issues Test. In M. Killen & J. Smetana (Eds.), *Handbook of moral development.* Mahwah, NJ: Erlbaum.

Thomaes, S., Bushman, B. J., Stegge, H., & Olthof, T. (2008). Trumping shame by blasts of noise: Narcissism, self-esteem, shame, and aggression in young adolescents. *Child Development, 18,* 758–765.

Thomas, A., & Chess, S. (1991). Temperament in adolescence and its functional significance. In R. M. Lerner, A. C. Petersen, & J. Brooks-Gunn (Eds.), *Encyclopedia of adolescence* (Vol. 2). New York: Garland.

Thomas, C. R., & Gadbois, S. A. (2007). Academic self-handicapping: The role of self-concept clarity and students' learning strategies. *British Journal of Educational Psychology, 77,* 109–119.

Thomas, C. W., Coffman, J. K., & Kipp, K. L. (1993, March). *Are only children different from children with siblings? A longitudinal study of behavioral and social functioning.* Paper presented at the biennial meeting of the Society for Research in Child Development, New Orleans.

Thompson, J., Manore, M., & Vaughn, L. (2011). *Science of nutrition* (2nd ed.). Upper Saddle River, NJ: Pearson.

Thompson, M., Kuruwita, C., & Foster, E. M. (2009). Transitions in suicide risk in a nationally representative sample of adolescents. *Journal of Adolescent Health, 44,* 458–463.

Thompson, M. P., & Light, L. S. (2011, in press). Examining gender differences in risk factors in suicide attempts made 1 and 7 years later in a nationally representative sample. *Journal of Adolescent Health.*

Thompson, R. A. (2008). Unpublished review of J. W. Santrock's *Life-span development,* 12th ed. (New York: McGraw-Hill).

Thompson, R. A. (2009). Early foundations: Conscience and the development of moral character. In D. Narváez & D. Lapsley (Eds.), *Personality, identity, and character: Explorations in moral psychology.* New York: Cambridge University Press.

Thompson, R. A. (2012, in press). Attachment and development: Precis and prospect. In P. Zelazo (Ed.), *Oxford handbook of developmental psychology*. New York: Oxford University Press.

Thompson, R. A., & Goodman, M. (2011). The architecture of social developmental science: Theoretical and historical perspectives. In M. K. Underwood & L. H. Rosen (Eds.), *Social development.* New York: Guilford.

Thompson, R. A., & Newton, E. K. (2010). Emotion in early conscience. In W. Arsenio & E. Lemerise (Eds.), *Emotions, aggression, and morality: Bridging development and psychopathology.* Washington, DC: American Psychological Association.

Thompson, R. A., Winer, A. C., & Goodvin, R. (2011). The individual child: Temperament, emotion, self, and personality. In M. Bornstein & M. E. Lamb (Eds.), *Developmental science: An advanced textbook* (6th ed.). New York: Psychology Press/Taylor & Francis.

Timperio, A., Salmon, J., & Ball, K. (2004). Evidence-based strategies to promote physical activity among children, adolescents, and young adults: Review and update. *Journal for Science and Medicine in Sport, 7*(Suppl), 20–29.

Tobler, A. L., & Komro, K. A. (2010). Trajectories of parental monitoring and communication and effects on drug use among urban young adolescents. *Journal of Adolescent Health, 46,* 560–568.

Tolan, P. H., Gorman-Smith, D., Henry, D., Chung, K., & Hunt, M. (2004). The relation of patterns of coping of inner-city youth to psychopathology symptoms. *Journal of Research on Adolescence, 12,* 423–449.

Tolman, D. (2002). *Dilemmas of desire: Teenage girls talk about sexuality.* Cambridge, MA: Harvard University Press.

Tolman, D. L., & McClelland, S. I. (2011). Normative sexuality development in adolescence: A decade in review, 2000–2009. *Journal of Research on Adolescence, 21,* 242–255.

Tomfohr, L., & others. (2011). Uplifts and sleep. *Behavioral Sleep Medicine, 9,* 31–37.

Tomlinson-Keasey, C. (1972). Formal operations in females from 11 to 54 years of age. *Developmental Psychology, 6,* 364.

Tompkins, T. L., Hockett, A. R., Abraibes, N., & Witt, J. L. (2011, in press). A closer look at co-rumination: Gender, coping, peer functioning, and internalizing/externalizing problems. *Journal of Adolescence.*

Tortolero, S. R., & others. (2010). It's your game. Keep it real: Delaying sexual behavior with an effective middle school program. *Journal of Adolescent Health, 46,* 169–179.

Touchette, E., & others. (2011). Subclinical eating disorders and their comorbidity with mood and anxiety disorders in adolescent girls. *Psychiatry Research, 185,* 185–192.

Townsend, M. (2011). Motivation, learning, and instruction. In C. M. Rubie-Davies (Ed.), *Educational psychology*. New York: Routledge.

Tracey, T. J. G., Robbins, S. B., & Hofsess, C. D. (2005). Stability and change in interests: A longitudinal study of adolescents from grades 8 through 12. *Journal of Vocational Behavior, 66,* 1–25.

Trafimow, D., Triandis, H. C., & Goto, S. G. (1991). Some tests of the distinction between the private and collective self. *Journal of Personality and Social Psychology, 60,* 649–655.

Triandis, H. C. (2007). Culture and psychology: A history of their relationship. In S. Kitayama & D. Cohen (Eds.), *Handbook of cultural psychology*. New York: Guilford.

Trucco, E. M., Colder, C. R., & Wieczorek, W. F. (2011). Vulnerability to peer influence: A moderated mediation study of early adolescent alcohol initiation. *Addictive Behaviors, 36,* 729–736.

Trzesniewski, K. H., & Donnellan, M. B. (2010). Rethinking "generation me": A study of cohort effects from 1976–2006. *Perspectives on Psychological Science, 5,* 58–75.

Trzesniewski, K. H., Donnellan, M. B., Moffitt, T. E., Robins, R. W., Poulton, R., & Caspi, A. (2006). Low self-esteem during adolescence predicts poor health, criminal behavior, and limited economic prospects during adulthood. *Developmental Psychology, 42,* 381–390.

Trzesniewski, K. H., Donnellan, M. B., & Robins, R. W. (2008a). Do today's young people really think they are so extraordinary? An examination of secular trends in narcissism and self-enhancement. *Psychological Science, 19,* 181–188.

Trzesniewski, M., Donnellan, M. B., & Robins, R. W. (2008b). Is "Generation Me" really more narcissistic than previous generations? *Journal of Personality, 76,* 903–918.

Tschann, J. M., Flores, E., de Groat, C. L., Deardorff, J., & Wibbelsman, C. J. (2010). Condom negotiation strategies and actual condom use among Latino youth. *Journal of Adolescent Health, 47,* 254–262.

Tseng, V. (2004). Family interdependence and academic adjustment in college: Youth from immigrant and U.S. born families. *Child Development, 75,* 966–983.

Tucker, C. J., McHale, S. M., & Crouter, A. C. (2001). Conditions of sibling support in adolescence. *Journal of Family Psychology, 15,* 254–271.

Tucker, C. J., & Winzeler, A. (2007). Adolescent siblings' daily discussions: Connections to perceived academic, athletic, and peer competency. *Journal of Research on Adolescence, 17,* 145–152.

Tucker, J. S., Edelen, M. O., Ellickson, P. L., & Klein, D. J. (2011). Running away from home: A longitudinal study of adolescent risk factors and adult outcomes. *Journal of Youth and Adolescence, 40,* 507–518.

Tung, R., & Ouimette, M. (2007). *Strong results, high demand: A four-year study of Boston's pilot high schools.* Boston: Center for Collaborative Education.

Turbin, M. S., Jessor, R., Costa, F. M., Dong, Q., Zhang, H., & Wang, C. (2006). Protective and risk factors in health-enhancing behavior among adolescents in China and the United States: Does social context matter? *Health Psychology, 25,* 445–454.

Twenge, J. M., & Campbell, W. K. (2001). Age and birth cohort differences in self-esteem: A cross-temporal meta-analysis. *Personality and Social Psychology Bulletin, 5,* 321–344.

Twenge, J. M., & Campbell, W. K. (2010). Birth cohort differences in the Monitoring the Future dataset and elsewhere: Further evidence for generation me—Commentary on Trzesniewski & Donnellan (2010). *Perspectives on Psychological Science, 5,* 81–88.

Twenge, J. M., Konrath, S., Foster, J. D., Campbell, W. K., & Bushman. B. J. (2008a). Egos inflating over time: A cross-temporal meta-analysis of the Narcissistic Personality Inventory. *Journal of Personality, 76,* 875–902.

Twenge, J. M., Konrath, S., Foster, J. D., Campbell, W. K., & Bushman, B. J. (2008b). Further evidence of an increase in narcissism among college students. *Journal of Personality, 76,* 919–928.

U

Udry, J. R. (1990). Hormonal and social determinants of adolescent sexual initiation. In J. Bancroft & J. M. Reinisch (Eds.), *Adolescence and puberty.* New York: Oxford University Press.

Ueno, K., & McWilliams, S. (2010). Gender-typed behaviors and school adjustment. *Sex Roles, 63,* 580–591.

Uhart, M., Chong, R. Y., Oswald, L., Lin, P. I., & Wand, G. S. (2006). Gender differences in hypothalamic-pituitary-adrenal (HPA) axis reactivity. *Psychoneuroendocrinology, 31,* 642–652.

Uhls, Y. T., & Greenfield, P. M. (2009). Adolescents and electronic communication. Retrieved June 25, 2010, from http://www.education.com/reference/article/adolescents-online-social-networking/

Ulloa, E. C., & Herrera, M. (2006). Strategies for multicultural student success: What about grad school? *Career Development Quarterly, 54,* 361–366.

Umana-Taylor, A. J., & Guimond, A. B. (2010). A longitudinal examination of parenting behaviors and perceived discrimination predicting Latino adolescents' ethnic identity. *Developmental Psychology, 46,* 636–650.

Umana-Taylor, A. J., Updegraff, K. A., & Gonzales-Bracken, M. A. (2011). Mexican-origin adolescent mothers' stressors and psychological functioning: Examining ethnic identity affirmation and familism as moderators. *Journal of Youth and Adolescence, 40,* 140–157.

Underhill, K., Montgomery, P., & Operario, D. (2007). Sexual abstinence programs to prevent HIV infection in high-income countries. *British Medical Journal, 335,* 248.

Underwood, M. K. (2011). Aggression. In M. K. Underwood & L. Rosen (Eds.), *Social development.* New York: Guilford.

UNICEF. (2003). *Annual report: 2002.* Geneva: Author.

UNICEF. (2007). *The state of the world's children 2007.* Geneva: Author.

UNICEF. (2011). *The state of the world's children 2011.* Geneva: Author.

University of Buffalo Counseling Services. (2011). *Procrastination.* Retrieved January 3, 2011, from http://ub-counseling.buffalo.edu/stressprocrast.shtml

University of Illinois Counseling Center. (1984). *Overcoming procrastination.* Urbana-Champaign, IL: Department of Student Affairs.

Updegraff, K. A., Kim, J-Y., Killoren, S. E., & Thayer, S. M. (2010). Mexican American parents' involvement in adolescent's peer relationships: Exploring the role of culture and adolescents' peer experiences. *Journal of Research on Adolescence, 20,* 65–87.

Updegraff, K. A., McHale, S., Whiteman, S. D., Thayer, S. M., & Delgado, M. Y. (2005). Adolescent sibling relationships in Mexican American families: Exploring the role of familism. *Journal of Family Psychology, 19,* 512–522.

Urban, J. B., Lewin-Bizan, S., & Lerner, R. M. (2010). The role of intentional self-regulation, lower neighborhood ecological assets, and activity involvement in youth developmental outcomes. *Journal of Youth and Adolescence.*

Urdan, T., & Midgley, C. (2001). Academic self-handicapping: What we know, what more is there to learn. *Educational Psychology Review, 13,* 115–138.

USA Today. (2001, October 10). All-USA first teacher team. Retrieved November 20, 2004, from www.usatoday/com/news/education2001

U.S. Census Bureau. (2008). *Population statistics.* Washington, DC: U.S. Department of Labor.

U.S. Census Bureau. (2010). *People.* Washington, DC: Author.

U.S. Department of Education. (1996). *International comparisons of education.* Washington, DC: Author.

U.S. Department of Energy. (2001). *The human genome project.* Washington, DC: Author.

V

Valkenburg, P. M., & Peter, J. (2009). Social consequences of the Internet for adolescents. *Current Directions in Psychological Science, 18,* 1–5.

Valkenburg, P. M., & Peter, J. (2011, in press). Online communication among adolescents: An integrated model of its attraction, opportunities, and risks. *Journal of Adolescent Health.*

Valle, J., & Connor, J. (2011). *Rethinking disability.* New York: McGraw-Hill.

Vandehey, M., Diekhoff, G., & LaBeff, E. (2007). College cheating: A 20-year follow-up and the addition of an honor code. *Journal of College Development, 48,* 468–480.

Vandell, D. L., Minnett, A., & Santrock, J. W. (1987). Age differences in sibling relationships during middle childhood. *Applied Developmental Psychology, 8,* 247–257.

van den Berg, P., Neumark-Sztainer, D., Hannan, P. J., & Haines, J. (2007). Is dieting advice from magazines helpful or harmful? Five-year associations with weight control behaviors and psychological outcomes in adolescents. *Pediatrics, 119,* e30–e37.

van den Dries, L., Juffer, F., van IJzendoorn, M. H., & Bakersman-Kranenburg, M. J. (2010). Infants' physical and cognitive development after international adoption from foster care or institutions in China. *Journal of Developmental and Behavioral Pediatrics, 31,* 144–150.

van der Stel, M., & Veenman, M. V. J. (2010). Development of metacognitive skillfulness: A longitudinal study. *Learning and Individual Differences, 20,* 220–224.

Van De Voorde, S., Roeyers, H., Verte, S., & Wiersema, J. R. (2011, in press). The influence of working memory load on response inhibition in children with attention-deficit/hyperactivity disorder or reading disorder. *Journal of Clinical Neuropsychology.*

van Geel, M., & Vedder, P. (2011, in press). The role of family obligations and school adjustment in explaining the immigrant paradox. *Journal of Youth and Adolescence.*

Van Goozen, S. H. M., Matthys, W., Cohen-Kettenis, P. T., Thisjssen, J. H. H., & van Engeland, H. (1998). Adrenal androgens and aggression in conduct disorder prepubertal boys and normal control. *Biological Psychiatry, 43,* 156–158.

van IJzendoorn, M. H., Kranenburg, M. J., Pannebakker, F., & Out, D. (2010). In defense of situational morality: Genetic, dispositional, and situational determinants of children's donating to charity. *Journal of Moral Education, 39,* 1–20.

Van Ryzin, M. J., Johnson, A. B., Leve, L. D., & Kim, H. K. (2011, in press). The number of sexual partners and health-risking sexual behavior: Prediction from high school entry to high school exit. *Archives of Sexual Behavior.*

van Soelen, I. L., & others. (2011). Heritability of verbal and performance intelligence in a pediatric longitudinal sample. *Twin Research and Human Genetics, 14,* 119–128.

Vansteenkiste, M., Timmermans, T., Lens, W., Soenens, B., & Van den Broeck, A. (2008). Does extrinsic goal framing enhance extrinsic goal-oriented individuals' learning and performance? An experimental test of the match perspective versus self-determination theory. *Journal of Educational Psychology, 100,* 387–397.

VanTassel-Baska, J. (2012). Curriculum as a system of thinking about learning: The dangers of dogmatic interpretation. In D. Ambrose, R. J. Sternberg, & B. Sriraman (Eds.), *Confronting dogmatism in education.* New York: Routledge.

Vasan, N. (2002). Commentary in "18-year-old inductees." Retrieved 4/24/09 from http://thekidshalloffame.com/CustomPage19.html

Vaughan, C. A., & Halpern, C. T. (2010). Gender differences in depressive symptoms during adolescence: The contributions of weight-related concerns and behaviors. *Journal of Research on Adolescence, 20,* 389–419.

Vaughn, M. G., Beaver, K. M., Wexler, J., DeLisi, M., & Roberts, G. J. (2011). The effect of school dropout on verbal ability in adulthood: A propensity score matching forward. *Journal of Youth and Adolescence, 40,* 197–206.

Veenman, M. V. J. (2011). Learning to self-monitor and self-regulate. In P. A. Alexander & R. E. Mayer (Eds.), *Handbook of research on learning and instruction*. New York: Routledge.

Veenstra, A., Lindenberg, S., Munniksma, A., & Dijkstra, J. K. (2010). The complex relationship between bullying, victimization, acceptance, and rejection: Giving special attention to status, affection, and sex differences. *Social Development, 19,* 480–486.

Velez, C. E., Wolchik, S. A., Tein, J. Y., & Sandler, I. (2011). Protecting children from the consequences of divorce: A longitudinal study of the effects of parenting on children's coping responses. *Child Development, 82,* 244–257.

Vermeersch, H., T'Sjoen, G., Kaufman, J. M., & Vincke, J. (2008). The role of testosterone in aggressive and non-aggressive risk-taking in boys. *Hormones and Behavior, 53,* 463–471.

Vernberg, E. M. (1990). Psychological adjustment and experience with peers during early adolescence: Reciprocal, incidental, or unidirectional relationships? *Journal of Abnormal Child Psychology, 18,* 187–198.

Verona, E., & Javdani, S. (2011, in press). Dimensions of adolescent psychopathology and relationships to suicide risk indicators. *Journal of Youth and Adolescence.*

Veronneau, M.-H., & Dishion, T. J. (2010). Predicting change in early adolescent problem behavior in the middle school years: A mesosystematic perspective on parenting and peer experiences. *Journal of Abnormal Child Psychology, 38,* 1125–1137.

Veronneau, M.-H., Vitaro, F., Pedersen, S., & Tremblay, R. E. (2008). Do peers contribute to the likelihood of secondary graduation among disadvantaged boys? *Journal of Educational Psychology, 100,* 429–442.

Verstraeten, K., Vasey, M. W., Raes, F., & Bitjtttebier, P. (2009). Temperament and risk for depressive symptoms in adolescence: Mediation by rumination and moderation by effortful control. *Journal of Abnormal Child Psychology, 37,* 349–361.

Veselka, L., Schermer, J. A., & Vernon, P. A. (2011). Beyond the big five: The Dark Triad and the supernumerary personality inventory. *Twin Research and Human Genetics, 14,* 158–168.

Veugelers, P. J., & Fitzgerald, A. L. (2005). Effectiveness of school programs in preventing obesity: A multilevel comparison. *American Journal of Public Health, 95,* 432–435.

Villanti, A., Boulay, M., & Juon, H. S. (2011). Peer, parent, and media influences on adolescent smoking by developmental stage. *Addictive Behaviors, 36,* 133–136.

Villanueva, C. M., & Buriel, R. (2010). Speaking on behalf of others: A qualitative study of the perceptions and feelings of adolescent Latina language brokers. *Journal of Social Issues, 66,* 197–210.

Vitaro, F., Pedersen, S., & Brendgen, M. (2007). Children's disruptiveness, peer rejection, friends' deviancy, and delinquent behaviors: A process-oriented approach. *Development and Psychopathology, 19,* 433–453.

Vondracek, F. W., & Porfeli, E. J. (2003). The world of work and careers. In G. Adams & M. Berzonsky (Eds.), *Blackwell handbook of adolescence*. Malden, MA: Blackwell.

Vreeman, R. C., & Carroll, A. E. (2007). A systematic review of school-based interventions to prevent bullying. *Archives of Pediatric and Adolescent Medicine, 161,* 78–88.

Vujeva, H. M., & Furman, W. (2011). Depressive symptoms and romantic relationship qualities from adolescence through emerging adulthood: A longitudinal examination of influences. *Journal of Clinical Child and Adolescent Psychology, 40,* 123–135.

Vygotsky, L. S. (1962). *Thought and language*. Cambridge, MA: MIT Press.

W

Waber, D. P. (2010). *Rethinking learning disabilities*. New York: Guilford.

Wachs, T. D. (1994). Fit, context and the transition between temperament and personality. In C. Halverson, G. Kohnstamm, & R. Martin (Eds.), *The developing structure of personality from infancy to adulthood*. Hillsdale, NJ: Erlbaum.

Wachs, T. D. (2000). *Necessary but not sufficient*. Washington, DC: American Psychological Association.

Wadsworth, M. E., Raviv, T., Santiago, C. D., & Etter, E. M. (2011). Testing the adaptation to poverty-related stress model: Predicting psychopathology symptoms in families facing economic hardship. *Journal of Clinical Child and Adolescent Psychology, 40,* 646–657.

Wahlstrom, D., Collins, P., White, T., & Luciana, M. (2010). Developmental changes in dopamine neurotransmission in adolescence: Behavioral implications and issues in assessment. *Brain and Cognition, 72,* 146–159.

Waite, L. J. (2009). Marriage. In D. Carr (Ed.), *Encyclopedia of the life course and human development*. Boston: Gale Cengage.

Walker, L. J. (2002). Moral exemplarity. In W. Damon (Ed.), *Bringing in a new era of character education*. Stanford, CA: Hoover Press.

Walker, L. J., deVries, B., & Bichard, S. L. (1984). The hierarchical nature of stages of moral development. *Developmental Psychology, 20,* 960–966.

Walker, L. J., deVries, B., & Trevethan, S. D. (1987). Moral stages and moral orientation in real-life and hypothetical dilemmas. *Child Development, 58,* 842–858.

Walker, L. J., & Frimer, J. A. (2011). The science of moral development. In M. K. Underwood & L. Rosen (Eds.), *Social development*. New York: Guilford.

Walker, L. J., & Hennig, K. H. (2004). Differing conceptions of moral exemplars: Just, brave, and caring. *Journal of Personality and Social Psychology, 86,* 629–647.

Walker, L. J., Hennig, K. H., & Krettenauer, R. (2000). Parent and peer contexts for children's moral reasoning development. *Child Development, 71,* 1033–1048.

Walker, L. J., Pitts, R. C., Hennig, K. H., & Matsuba, M. K. (1995). Reasoning about morality and real-life moral problems. In M. Killen & D. Hart (Eds.), *Morality in everyday life*. New York: Cambridge University Press.

Walker, L. J., & Taylor, J. H. (1991). Family interaction and the development of moral reasoning. *Child Development, 62,* 264–283.

Wallace-Broscious, A., Serafica, F. C., & Osipow, S. H. (1994). Adolescent career development: Relationships to self-concept and identity status. *Journal of Research on Adolescence, 4,* 127–150.

Waller, B. (2006). Math interest and choice intentions of non-traditional African-American college students. *Journal of Vocational Behavior, 68,* 538–547.

Waller, E. M., & Rose, A. J. (2010). Adjustment trade-offs of co-rumination in mother-adolescent relationships. *Journal of Adolescence, 33,* 487–497.

Wallerstein, J. S. (2008). Divorce. In M. M. Haith & J. B. Benson (Eds.), *Encyclopedia of infant and early childhood development*. Oxford, UK: Elsevier.

Wallis, C. (2011). Performing gender: A content analysis of gender display in music videos. *Sex Roles, 64,* 160–172.

Walsh, J. (2008). Self-efficacy. In N. J. Salkind (Ed.), *Encyclopedia of educational psychology*. Thousand Oaks, CA: Sage.

Walsh, R. (2011, in press). Lifestyle and mental health. *American Psychologist.*

Walsh, S. M., & Donaldson, R. E. (2010). Invited commentary: National Safe Place: Meeting the immediate needs of runaways and homeless youth. *Journal of Youth and Adolescence, 39,* 437–445.

Walter, C. A. (1986). *The timing of motherhood.* Lexington, MA: D. C. Heath.

Walters, E., & Kendler, K. S. (1994). Anorexia nervosa and anorexia-like symptoms in a population based twin sample. *American Journal of Psychiatry, 152,* 62–71.

Walvoord, E. C. (2010). The timing of puberty: Is it changing? Does it matter? *Journal of Adolescent Health, 47,* 433–439.

Wanakowska, M., & Polkowska, J. (2010). The pituitary endocrine mechanisms involved in mammalian maturation: Maternal and photoperiodic influences. *Reproductive Biology, 10,* 3–18.

Wandersman, A., & Florin, P. (2003). Community interventions and effective prevention. *American Psychologist, 58,* 441–448.

Wang, J., Nansel, T. R., & Iannotti, R. J. (2011, in press). Cyber and traditional bullying: Differential association with depression. *Journal of Adolescent Health.*

Wang, J. Q. (2000, November). *A comparison of two international standards to assess child and adolescent obesity in three populations.* Paper presented at the meeting of American Public Health Association, Boston.

Wang, L. Y., Chyen, D., Lee, L., & Lowry, R. (2008). The association between body mass index in adolescence and obesity in adulthood. *Journal of Adolescent Health, 42,* 512–518.

Wang, M. C., & others. (2010). Exposure to comprehensive school intervention increases vegetable consumption. *Journal of Adolescent Health, 47,* 74–82.

Wang, Q., & Pomerantz, E. M. (2009). The motivational landscape of early adolescence in the United States and China: A longitudinal study. *Child Development, 80,* 1272–1287.

Ward, L. M. (2002). Does television exposure affect emerging adults' attitudes and assumptions about sexual relationships? Correlational and experimental confirmation. *Journal of Youth and Adolescence, 31,* 1–15.

Ward, L. M., Day, K. M., & Epstein, M. (2006). Uncommonly good: Exploring how mass media may be a positive influence on young women's sexual health and development. *New Directions for Child and Adolescent Development, 112,* 57–70.

Ward, L. M., & Friedman, K. (2006). Using TV as a guide: Associations between television viewing and adolescents' sexual attitudes and behavior. *Journal of Research on Adolescence, 16,* 133–156.

Wardlaw, G. M., & Smith, A. M. (2011). *Contemporary nutrition* (8th ed.). New York: McGraw-Hill.

Warren, A., Lerner, R. M., & Phelps, E. (2011). *Thriving and spirituality among youth.* New York: Wiley.

Warren, J. T., & others. (2010). Do depression and low self-esteem follow abortion among adolescents? Evidence from a national study. *Perspectives on Sexual and Reproductive Health, 42,* 230–235.

Warrington, M., & Younger, M. (2003). "We decided to give it a twirl": Single-sex teaching in English comprehensive schools. *Gender and Education, 15,* 339–350.

Waterman, A. S. (1985). Identity in the context of adolescent psychology. In A. S. Waterman (Ed.), *Identity in adolescence: Processes and contents.* San Francisco: Jossey-Bass.

Waterman, A. S. (1992). Identity as an aspect of optimal psychological functioning. In G. R. Adams, T. P. Gullotta, & R. Montemayor (Eds.), *Adolescent identity formation.* Newbury Park, CA: Sage.

Watson, D. L., & Tharp, R. G. (2007). *Self-directed behavior* (9th ed.). Belmont, CA: Wadsworth.

Watson, J. B. (1930). *Behaviorism* (rev. ed.). Chicago: University of Chicago Press.

Watt, H. M. G. (2008). Gender and occupational outcomes: An introduction. In H. M. G. Watt & J. S. Eccles (Eds.), *Gender and occupational outcomes.* Washington, DC: American Psychological Association.

Watt, H. M. G., & Eccles, J. S. (Eds.). (2008). *Gender and occupational outcomes.* Washington, DC: American Psychological Association.

Watt, H. M. G., Eccles, J. S., & Durik, A. M. (2006). The leaking mathematics pipeline for girls: A motivational analysis of high school enrollments in Australia and the United States. *Equal Opportunities International, 25,* 642–659.

Way, N., & Silverman, L. R. (2012). The quality of friendships during adolescence: Patterns across context, culture, and age. In P. K. Kerig, M. S. Shulz, & S. T. Hauser (Eds.), *Adolescence and beyond.* New York: Oxford University Press.

Webb, J. T., Gore, J. L., Mend, E. R., & DeVries, A. R. (2007). *A parent's guide to gifted children.* Scottsdale, AZ: Great Potential Press.

Webster, N. S., & Worrell, F. C. (2008). Academically-talented adolescents' attitudes toward service in the community. *Gifted Child Quarterly, 52,* 170–179.

Wechsler, H., Davenport, A., Sowdall, G., Moetykens, B., & Castillo, S. (1994). Health and behavioral consequences of binge drinking in college. *Journal of the American Medical Association, 272,* 1672–1677.

Weikert, D. P. (1993). [Long-term positive effects in the Perry Preschool Head Start program.] Unpublished data. High Scope Foundation, Ypsilanti, MI.

Weiner, B. (2005). *Social motivation, justice, and the moral emotions.* Mahwah, NJ: Erlbaum.

Weinstein, C. S. (2007). *Middle and secondary management: Lessons from research and practice* (3rd ed.). New York: McGraw-Hill.

Weinstein, N., Deci, E. L., & Ryan, R. M. (2012). Motivational determinants of integrating positive and negative past identities. *Journal of Personality and Social Psychology, 100,* 527–544.

Weinstock, H., Berman, S., & Cates, W. (2004). Sexually transmitted diseases among American youth: Incidence and prevalence estimates, 2000. *Perspectives on Sexual and Reproductive Health, 36,* 6–10.

Weissberg, R., & Caplan, M. (1989, April). *A follow-up study of a school-based social competence program for young adolescents.* Paper presented at the meeting of the Society for Research in Child Development, Kansas City.

Weissberg, R. P., Kumpfer, K. L., & Seligman, M. E. P. (2003). Prevention that works for children and youth. *American Psychologist, 58,* 425–432.

Welch, K. J. (2011). *THINK human sexuality.* Upper Saddle River, NJ: Pearson.

Welti, C. (2002). Adolescents in Latin America: Facing the future with skepticism. In B. B. Brown, R. W. Larson, & T. S. Saraswathi (Eds.), *The world's youth.* New York: Cambridge University Press.

Wentzel, K. R. (1997). Student motivation in middle school: The role of perceived pedagogical caring. *Journal of Educational Psychology, 89,* 411–419.

Wentzel, K. R. (2004). Unpublished review of J. W. Santrock's *Adolescence,* 11th ed. (New York: McGraw-Hill).

Wentzel, K. R. (2009). Peers and academic functioning at school. In K. H. Rubin, W. M. Bukowski, & B. Laursen (Eds.), *Handbook of peer interactions, relationships, and groups*. New York: Guilford.

Wentzel, K. R. (2010). Teacher-student relationships and adjustment. In J. L. Meece & J. S. Eccles (Eds.), *Handbook of research on schools, schooling, and human development*. New York: Routledge.

Wentzel, K. R., & Asher, S. R. (1995). The academic lives of neglected, rejected, popular, and controversial children. *Child Development, 66,* 754–763.

Wentzel, K. R., Barry, C. M., & Caldwell, K. A. (2004). Friendships in middle school: Influences on motivation and school adjustment. *Journal of Educational Psychology, 96,* 195–203.

Wentzel, K. R., & Caldwell, K. (1997). Close friend and group influence on adolescent cigarette smoking and alcohol use. *Child Development, 31,* 540–547.

Wentzel, K. R., & Watkins, D. E. (2011). Instruction based on peer interaction. In P. A. Alexander & R. E. Mayer (Eds.), *Handbook of research on learning and instruction*. New York: Routledge.

Werner, N. E., Bumpus, M. F., & Rock, D. (2010). Involvement in Internet aggression during early adolescence. *Journal of Youth and Adolescence, 39,* 607–619.

Werner, N. E., & Hill, L. G. (2010). Individual and peer group normative beliefs about relational aggression. *Child Development, 81,* 826–836.

Wetherill, R. R., Neal, D. J., & Fromme, K. (2010). Parents, peers, and sexual values influence sexual behavior during the transition to college. *Archives of Sexual Behavior, 39,* 682–694.

Whetstone, L. M., Morrissey, S. L., & Cummings, D. M. (2007). Children at risk: The association between weight status and suicidal thoughts and attempts in middle school youth. *Journal of School Health, 77,* 59–66.

White, M. (1993). *The material child: Coming of age in Japan and America*. New York: Free Press.

White, M. A., & Grilo, C. M. (2011). Diagnostic efficiency of DSM-IV indicators for binge eating episodes. *Journal of Consulting and Clinical Psychology, 79,* 75–83.

White, S. W. (2010). The school counselor's role in dropout prevention. *Journal of Counseling and Development, 88,* 227–235.

Whitehead, B. D., & Popenoe, D. (2003). *The state of our unions*. Piscataway, NJ: The National Marriage Project, Rutgers University.

Whitehead, K. A., Ainsworth, A. T., Wittig, M. A., & Gadino, B. (2009). Implications of ethnic identity exploration and ethnic identity affirmation and belonging for intergroup attitudes among adolescents. *Journal of Research on Adolescence, 19,* 123–135.

Whiteman, S. D., Jensen, A., & Bernard, J. M. (2012). Sibling influences. In J. R. Levesque (Ed.), *Encyclopedia of adolescence.* New York: Springer.

Whiteman, S. D., McHale, S. M., & Soli, A. (2011, in press). Theoretical perspectives on sibling relationships. *Journal of Family Theory and Review.*

Whitfield, K. W. (2011). Health disparities, social class, and aging. In K. W. Schaie & S. L. Willis (Eds.), *Handbook of the psychology of aging* (7th ed.). New York: Elsevier.

Whiting, B. B. (1989, April). *Culture and interpersonal behavior.* Paper presented at the meeting of the Society for Research in Child Development, Kansas City.

Whitton, S. W., Waldinger, R. J., Schulz, M. S., Allen, J. P., Crowell, J. A., & Hauser, S. T. (2008). Prospective associations from family-of-origin interactions to adult marital interactions and relationship adjustment. *Journal of Family Psychology, 22,* 274–286.

Wiencke, J. K., & others. (1999). Early age at smoking initiation and tobacco carcinogen DNA damage in the lung. *Journal of the National Cancer Institute, 91,* 614–619.

Wigfield, A., & Cambria, J. (2010). Students' achievement values, goal orientations, and interest: Definitions, development, and relations to achievement outcomes. *Developmental Review, 30,* 1–35.

Wigfield, A., & Eccles, J. S. (1989). Test anxiety in elementary and secondary school students. *Journal of Educational Psychology, 24,* 159–183.

Wigfield, A., Eccles, J. S., Schiefele, U., Roeser, R., & Davis-Kean, P. (2006). Development of achievement motivation. In W. Damon & R. Lerner (Eds.), *Handbook of child psychology* (6th ed.). New York: Wiley.

Wigfield, A., Klauda, S. L., & Cambria, J. (2011). Motivational sources and outcomes of self-regulated learning and performance. In B. J. Zimmerman & D. H. Schunk (Eds.), *Handbook of self-regulation of learning and performance*. New York: Routledge.

Williams, A. L., & Merten, M. J. (2009). Adolescents' online social networking following the death of a peer. *Journal of Adolescent Research, 24,* 67–90.

Williams, K. M., Nathanson, C., & Paulhus, D. L. (2010). Identifying and profiling academic cheaters: Their personality, cognitive ability, and motivation. *Journal of Experimental Psychology: Applied, 16,* 293–307.

Williams, R., & Hazell, P. (2011). Austerity, poverty, resilience, and the future of mental health services for children and adolescents. *Current Opinion in Psychiatry, 24,* 263–266.

William T. Grant Foundation Commission on Work, Family, and Citizenship. (1988, February). *The forgotten half: Noncollege-bound youth in America.* New York: William T. Grant Foundation.

Wilson, B. J. (2008). Media and children's aggression, fear, and altruism. *Future of Children, 18*(1), 87–118.

Wilson-Shockley, S. (1995). *Gender differences in adolescent depression: The contribution of negative affect.* Unpublished master's thesis, University of Illinois at Urbana-Champaign.

Winerman, L. (2005). Leading the way. *Monitor on Psychology, 36,* 64–67.

Winn, I. J. (2004). The high cost of uncritical teaching. *Phi Delta Kappan, 85,* 496–497.

Winne, P. H. (2011). Cognitive and metacognitive factors in self-regulated learning. In B. J. Zimmerman & D. H. Schunk (Eds.), *Handbook of self-regulation of learning and performance*. New York: Routledge.

Winner, E. (1996). *Gifted children: Myths and realities*. New York: Basic Books.

Winner, E. (2006). Development in the arts. In W. Damon & R. Lerner (Eds.), *Handbook of child psychology* (6th ed.). New York: Wiley.

Winner, E. (2009). Toward broadening our understanding of giftedness: The spatial domain. In F. D. Horowitz, R. F. Subotnik, & D. J. Matthews (Eds.), *The development of giftedness and talent across the life span*. Washington, DC: American Psychological Association.

Witkow, M. R., & Fuligni, A. J. (2010). In-school versus out-of-school friendships and academic achievement among an ethnically diverse sample of adolescents. *Journal of Research on Adolescence, 20,* 631–650.

Witvliet, M., & others. (2010). Peer group affiliation in children: The role of perceived popularity, likeability, and behavioral similarity in bullying. *Social Development, 19,* 285–303.

Wolak, J., Mitchell, K., & Finkelhor, D. (2007). Unwanted and wanted exposure to online pornography in a national sample of youth Internet users. *Pediatrics, 119,* 247–257.

Wolf, S. A., Melnik, A., & Kempermann, G. (2011). Physical exercise increases adult neurogenesis and telomerase activity, and improves deficits in the mouse model of schizophrenia. *Brain, Behavior, and Immunology, 25,* 971–980.

Wolff, J. M., & Crockett, L. J. (2011, in press). The role of deliberative decision making, parenting, and friends in adolescent risk behaviors. *Journal of Youth and Adolescence.*

Wolfinger, N. H. (2011). More evidence for trends in the intergenerational transmission of divorce: A completed cohort approach using data from the general social survey. *Demography, 48,* 581–592.

Wolfgram, S. M. (2008). Openness in adoption: What we know so far—a critical review of the literature. *Social Work, 53,* 133–142.

Wolfson, A. R. (2010). Adolescents and emerging adults sleep patterns: New developments. *Journal of Adolescent Health, 46,* 97–99.

Wolitzky-Taylor, K. B., & others. (2011). Is reporting of rape on the rise? A comparison of women with reported versus unreported rape experiences in the National Women's Study-Replication. *Journal of Interpersonal Violence, 26,* 807–832.

Women in Academia (2011). *A historical summary of gender differences in college enrollment rates.* Retrieved on June 12, 2011, from www.wiareport.com

Wong Briggs, T. (1999, October 14). Honorees find keys to unlocking kids' minds. Retrieved July 22, 2004, from www.usatoday.com/education/1999

Wong Briggs, T. (2005, October 13). USA Today's 2005 all-USA teacher team. *USA Today,* p. 6D.

Wood, D., Larson, R. W., & Brown, J. R. (2009). How adolescents come to see themselves as more responsible through participation in youth programs. *Child Development, 80,* 295–309.

Wood, J. T. (2011). *Communication mosaics* (6th ed.). Boston: Cengage.

World Health Organization. (2000). *The world health report.* Geneva: Author.

Wright, R. H., Mindel, C. H., Tran, T. V., & Habenstein, R. W. (2012). *Ethnic families in America* (5th ed.). Upper Saddle River, NJ: Pearson.

X

Xi, H., Zhang, L., Guo, Z., & Zhao, L. (2011). Serum leptin concentration and its effect on puberty in Naqu Tibetian adolescents. *Journal of Physiological Anthropology, 30,* 111–117.

Xia, N. (2010). *Family factors and student outcomes.* Unpublished doctoral dissertation, RAND Corporation, Pardee RAND Graduate School, Pittsburgh.

Y

Yancey, A. K., Grant, D., Kurosky, S., Kravitz-Wirtz, N., & Mistry, R. (2011). Role modeling, risk, and resilience in California adolescents. *Journal of Adolescent Health, 48,* 36–43.

Yang, C., & Brown, B. (2009, April). *From Facebook to cell calls: Layers of electronic intimacy in college students' peer relations.* Paper presented at the meeting of the Society for Research in Child Development, Denver.

Yell, M. L., & Drasgow, E. (2009). *What every teacher should know about No Child Left Behind* (2nd ed.). Upper Saddle River, NJ: Prentice Hall.

Yen, H. L., & Wong, J. T. (2007). Rehabilitation for traumatic brain injury to children and adolescents. *Annals of the Academy of Medicine Singapore, 36,* 62–66.

Yi, S., & others. (2010,). Role of risk and protective factors in risky sexual behavior among high school students in Cambodia. *BMC Public Health, 10,* 477.

Young, M. A., & Vazsonyi, A. T. (2011). Parents, peers, and risky sexual behaviors in rural African American adolescents. *Journal of Genetic Psychology, 172,* 84–93.

Youngblade, L. M., & Curry, L. A. (2006). The people they know: Links between interpersonal contexts and adolescent risky and health-promoting behavior. *Developmental Science, 10,* 96–106.

Youngblade, L. M., Curry, L. A., Novak, M., Vogel, B., & Shenkman, E. A. (2006). The impact of community risks and resources on adolescent risky behavior and health care expenditures. *Journal of Adolescent Health, 38,* 486–494.

Youniss, J., McLellan, J. A., & Yates, M. (1999). Religion, community service, and identity in American youth. *Journal of Adolescence, 22,* 243–253.

Youniss, J., & Ruth, A. J. (2002). Approaching policy for adolescent development in the 21st century. In J. T. Mortimer & R. W. Larson (Eds.), *The changing adolescent experience.* New York: Cambridge University Press.

Yu, T., Pettit, G. S., Lansford, J. E., Dodge, K. A., & Bates, J. E. (2010). The interactive effects of marital conflict and divorce on parent-adult children's relationships. *Journal of Marriage and the Family, 72,* 282–292.

Yuan, A. S. V. (2010). Body perceptions, weight control behavior, and changes in adolescents' psychological well-being over time: A longitudinal examination of gender. *Journal of Youth and Adolescence, 39,* 927–939.

Yudof, M. G., Levin, B., Moran, R., & Ryan, J. M. (2012). *Educational policy and the law* (5th ed.). Boston: Cengage.

Yussen, S. R. (1977). Characteristics of moral dilemmas written by adolescents. *Developmental Psychology, 13,* 162–163.

Z

Zaff, J. F., Hart, D., Flanagan, C., Youniss, J., & Levine, P. (2010). Developing civic engagement within a civic context. In M. E. Lamb, A. M. Freund, & R. M. Lerner (Eds.), *Handbook of life-span development* (Vol. 2). New York: Wiley.

Zager, K., & Rubenstein, A. (2002). *The inside story on teen girls.* Washington, DC: American Psychological Association.

Zalewski, M., Lengau, L. J., Wilson, A. C., Trancik, A., & Bazinet, A. (2011). Associations of coping and appraisal styles with emotion regulation during preadolescence. *Journal of Experimental Child Psychology, 110,* 141–158.

Zamboanga, B. L., & others. (2011). Pregaming in high school students: Relevance to risky drinking practices, alcohol cognitions, and the social drinking context. *Psychology of Addictive Behaviors,* 25, 340–345.

Zarrett, N., Fay, K., Li, Y., Carrano, J., Phelps, E., & Lerner, R. M. (2009). More than child's play: Variable- and pattern-centered approaches for examining effects of sports participation on youth development. *Developmental Psychology, 45,* 368–382.

Zayas, L., Guibas, L. E., Fedoravicius, N., & Cabassa, L. J. (2010). Patterns of distress, precipitating events, and reflections on suicide attempts by young Latinas. *Social Science & Medicine, 70,* 1773–1779.

Zeeck, A., Stelzer, N., Linster, H. W., Joos, A., & Hartmann, A. (2011, in press). Emotion and eating in binge eating disorder and obesity. *European Eating Disorders Review.*

Zeiders, K. H., Roosa, M. W., & Tein, J. Y. (2011). Family structure and family processes in Mexican-American families. *Family Process, 50,* 77–91.

Zeifman, D., & Hazan, C. (2008). Pair bonds as attachments: Reevaluating the evidence. In J. Cassidy & P. R. Shaver (Eds.), *Handbook of attachment* (2nd ed.). New York: Guilford.

Zill, N., Morrison, D. R., & Coiro, M. J. (1993). Long-term effects of parental divorce on parent-child relationships, adjustment, and achievement in young adulthood. *Journal of Family Psychology, 7,* 91–103.

Zimmerman, B. J., & Schunk, D. H. (Eds.). (2011). *Handbook of self-regulation of learning and performance*. New York: Routledge.

Zinn, M. B., & Wells, B. (2000). Diversity within Latino families: New lessons for family social science. In D. M. Demo, K. R. Allen, & M. A. Fine (Eds.), *Handbook of family diversity*. New York: Oxford University Press.

Zinzow, H. M., & others. (2010). Drug- or alcohol-facilitated, incapacitated, and forcible rape in relationship to mental health among a national sample of women. *Journal of Interpersonal Violence, 25,* 2217–2236.

Zinzow, H. M., & others. (2011, in press). Prevalence and risk of psychiatric disorders as a function of variant rape histories: Results from a national sample of women. *Social Psychiatry and Psychiatric Epidemiology.*

Ziol-Guest, K. M. (2009). Child custody and support. In D. Carr (Ed.), *Encyclopedia of the life course and human development.* Boston: Cengage.

Zittleman, K. (2006, April). *Being a girl and being a boy: The voices of middle schoolers.* Paper presented at the meeting of the American Educational Research Association, San Francisco.

credits

PHOTO CREDITS

p. xvi: © Rubberball/Punchstock

Chapter 1

p. 1: © Comstock/Getty RF; p. 2 (top): © AP Photo; (middle): © AP Photo/Noah Berger, File; (bottom): © Michael Maddaus, University of Minnesota, Division of Thoracic & Foregut Surgery; p. 3: © Archives of the History of American Psychology, University of Akron, Akron, OH; p. 4: Courtesy of the American Anthropological Association, Arlington, VA 22201; p. 6 (top): © Ramin Talaie/Corbis; (bottom): © McGraw-Hill Companies/Suzie Ross, Photographer; p. 7: © Rolf Bruderer/Getty Images/Blend Images; p. 12: Courtesy of Peter Benson; p. 13 (top): © Naser Siddique/UNICEF Bangladesh 2007; (bottom): © AFP/Getty; p. 14 (top): © Dain Gair Photographer/Index Stock/PhotoLibrary; (bottom): © AP Photo/Ricardo Mazalan; p. 18 (top, left-right): Courtesy of Landrum Shettles; John Santrock; © Dynamics Graphics Group/PunchStock RF; © Corbis RF; © Comstock/PictureQuest RF; © Vol. 155/Corbis RF; © Corbis RF; © Corbis RF; (bottom left): © Ariel Skelley/Blend Images LLC; (bottom right): © Ariel Skelley/Blend Images/Getty Images; p. 19: © Andrew Councill; p. 22: © Juice Images/Cultura/Getty Images RF; p. 25 (left): © Stockbyte/Getty RF; (right): © Photodisc/Getty RF; p. 27: © Bettmann/Corbis; p. 28: © Barton Silverman/New York Times/Redux Pictures; p. 29: © Sarah Putnam/Index Stock Imagery/PhotoLibrary; p. 30: © Yves Debraine/Black Star/Stock Photo; p. 31 (top): © A. R. Lauria/Dr. Michael Cole, Laboratory of Human Cognition; (bottom): © Creatas/Jupiter Iamges RF; p. 32: Courtesy of Albert Bandura; p. 33: Courtesy of Cornell University, Dept. of Human Development and Family Services; p. 35: © Michael Newman/Photo Edit; p. 36: © Dr. Susan Tapert, p. 36: © Dr. Susan Tapert; p. 37 (top): © David Grubin Productions, Inc., Reprinted by Permission; (bottom): Image Courtesy of Dana Boatman, Ph.D., Department of Neurology, John Hopkins University. Reprinted with permission from *The Secret Life of the Brain* © 2001 by the National Academy of Sciences. Courtesy of the National Academies Press, Washington, D.C.; p. 40 (left): © Syndicated Features Limited/The Image Works; (right): © Thomas Craig/Index Stock/PhotoLibrary; p. 41: Courtesy Pamela Trotman Reid

Chapter 2

p. 49: © Nicolas Russell/Getty Images/The Image Bank; p. 54 (top): © Value RF/Corbis RF; (bottom): © Buddy Mays/Corbis; p. 59: © Jon Feingersh/The Stock Market/Corbis; p. 60 (top): © VSS 22/Getty RF; (bottom): © Corbis RF; p. 61: © Britt Erlanson/Getty Images/Cultura RF; p. 63: © Courtesy of Anne Petersen, W. K. Kellogg Foundation; p. 65 (top): © Chris Garrett/Photonica/Getty Images; (bottom): © Thomas Barwik/Getty; p. 66 (top): © Spencer Grant/Photo Edit; (bottom): © AP Photo/Kyle Ericson; p. 68: © Image Source/PunchStock RF; p. 69: Dallas Morning News, photographer Vernon Bryant; p. 71(top): © Richard T. Nowitz/Corbis; (bottom): © PhotoDisc/Getty RF; p. 72: © Lisa Peardon/Getty; p. 74: © Jim Lo Scalzo; p. 75: © Tom Brakefield/Getty RF; p. 79: © Tony Freeman/Photo Edit; p. 81: © Duomo/Corbis

Chapter 3

p. 88: © Vol. RFDC697/Corbis RF; p. 89 (left): © Steve Gschmeissner/Photo Researchers; p. 90: © Davis Turner-Pool/Getty Images; p. 92: © Archives Jean Piaget, Universite De. Geneve, Switzerland; p. 93 (left to right): © Stockbyte/Getty Images RF; © BananaStock/PunchStock RF; © image100/Corbis RF; © Corbis RF; p. 94: © David Young-Wolf/Photo Edit; p. 96: © Wendy Stone/CORBIS; p. 97: © Johnny Le Fortune/Corbis; p. 99: © ImageSource/Corbis RF; p. 100: © Jose Luis Pelaez, Inc/Blend Images/Getty Images; p. 101 (left): © A.R. Lauria/Dr. Michael Cole, Laboratory of Human Cognition; (right): © Bettmann/Corbis; p. 103: © John Henley/Corbis; p. 104: © Yellow Dog Productions/Getty; p. 107: © Big Cheese Photo/SuperStock RF; p. 108: © Scott Houston/Corbis; p. 110: Courtesy of Laura Bickford; p. 111: © Gideon Mendel/Corbis; p. 112: © Rayman/Digital Vision/Getty RF; p. 115: © National Library of Medicine; p. 117 (top): © Courtesy of Robert Sternberg; (bottom): © Tom Stewart/Corbis; p. 121: © Stewart Cohen/Stone/Getty; p. 122: © Car Culture/Getty

Chapter 4

p. 128: © Masterfile RF; p. 131 (top): © A. Huber/U. Starke/Corbis; (bottom): © Hugh Arnold/The Image Bank/Getty; p. 132 (left): © M. Regine/The Image Bank/Getty; (right): © RandyFaris/Corbis; p. 133: © M. L. Harris/Ionica/Getty; p. 134 (left): © Tim Pannell/Corbis RF; (right): © Charles Gupton/Getty; p. 136: © Klawitter Productions/Corbis; p. 139: © Anthony Redpath/Corbis; p. 141 (top): © Bettmann/Corbis; (bottom): © Bettmann/Corbis; p. 142: © Somos/Veer/Getty RF; p. 145: © Masterfile RF; p. 147: © Mike Watson Images/Corbis RF; p. 148: © 1997 USA Today Library, photo by Robert Deutsch; p. 149 (top): © Patrick Sheandell/Photo Alto; (bottom): © Mark edward Atkinson/Getty RF; p. 151: © C. Devan/zefa/Corbis; p. 152: © iStock RF; p. 153: © Jonathan Cavendish/Corbis; p. 155: © Steve Smith/Getty

Chapter 5

p. 161: © Blend Images/Masterfile; p. 166 (left): © Charles Gullung/Corbis; (right): © Dylan Ellis/Corbis RF; p. 167 (top): © David Young-Wolf/Getty; (bottom): © Dann Tardif/LWA/Corbis; p. 168: © Joeri DE ROCKER/Alamy; p. 174: © Ariel Skelley/Blend Images/Corbis RF; p. 175: © Reuters/Corbis; p. 178: Courtesy Cynthia de las Fuentes, Our Lady of the Lakes University, San Antonio, Texas; p. 179: © Image100/Corbis RF; p. 180: © Tony Freeman/Photo Edit; p. 181: © Keith Carter Photography

Chapter 6

p. 186: Masterfile RF; p. 189: © The McGraw-Hill Companies/John Fournoy, photographer; p. 190: Courtesy Everett Collection; p. 193: © Photomorgana/Corbis; p. 194: © Stockbyte/Punchstock; p. 196: © Getty RF; p. 198: © AP Photo/Nati Harnik; p. 201 (top): © Michael Ray; (bottom): © Patrick Steele/Alamy; p. 205 (top): © Geoff Manasse/Getty Images RF; (bottom): © Suzanne DeChillo/New York Times/Redux Pictures; p. 206: © Karen Kasmauski/Corbis; p. 207 (top): Courtesy Lynn Blankinship; p. 207 (bottom): © Rosemarie Gearhart/iStockphoto RF; p. 208: © 1998 Frank Fournier; p. 209 (left): © Wendy Stone/Corbis; (right): © Louise

Gubb/Corbis SABA; p. 213: © Creasource/Corbis; p. 217: © James D. Wilson/Woodfin Camp & Associates; p. 218 (top): © Li Ge/ China Feature/Corbis Sygma; (bottom): © Steve Raymer/Corbis

Chapter 7

p. 223: Corbis; p. 224: © Matthew J. Lee/The Boston Globe/Getty; p. 225: © Unknown; p. 228: © Randy Faris/Corbis; p. 230: © Sean Adair/Reuters/Corbis; p. 231: © Raghu-Rai/Magnum Photos; p. 234: © Angela Hampton Picture Library/Alamy; p. 236: © ThinkStock/Corbis RF; p. 237 (left): © Bettmann/Corbis; (right): © Alain Nogues/Sygma/Corbis; p. 240 © Nancy Ney/Getty Images/ Digital Vision; p. 242 (top): © Ronald Cortes; (bottom): © Tony Freeman/Photo Edit; p. 243: © Rubberball/Nicole Hil/Getty RF; p. 245: Courtesy Connie Flanagan; p. 246: Courtesy Nina Vasan; p. 247 (top): © Digital Vision/Getty Images; (bottom): © Big Stock Photo RF; p. 248: © Paul Chesley/Stone/Getty

Chapter 8

p. 252: © Paul Barton/Corbis; p. 254: © Michael Newman/Photo Edit; p. 256 (top left): © David Young-Wolf/Photo Edit; (top right): © David Young-Wolf/Photo Edit; (bottom): © Jack Hollingsworth/ Corbis RF; p. 258: © Pat Vasquez-Cunningham 1999; p. 260: © Ryan McVay/Getty RF; p. 261: © 2011 Photo Library RF; p. 262: © JGI/Tom Grill/Blend Images/Corbis RF; p. 264: © BananaStock/ PunchStock; p. 265: © BananaStock/PunchStock; p. 266: © Tom Stewart/Corbis; p. 267: © Bill Aron/Photo Edit; p. 269: © UpperCut Images/Getty RF; p. 270: © Corbis RF; p. 272: © David Young Wolff/Photo Edit; p. 273: © Digital Vision/Getty Images; p. 275: © James G. White Photography; p. 276: © Jason Hosking/ Stone/Getty; p. 279: © Bananastock/PunchStock; p. 282: © Todd Wright/Blend Images/Getty Images RF; p. 283: © The Photo Works/Alamy; p. 284: © Kathy Heister/Index Stock/PhotoLibrary; p. 287 (left): © Bob Daemmrich/The Image Works; (right): © Erika Stone/Peter Arnold/PhotoLibrary; p. 289: © Tim Fareell/ Star Ledger/Corbis

Chapter 9

p. 294: © Huntstock, Inc/Alamy; p. 296: Getty Images RF; p. 297 (top): © Creatas/PunchStock; (bottom left): © Tom Grill/Corbis RF; (bottom right): © Creasource/Corbis; p. 299 (left): © Mary Kate Denny/Photo Edit; (right): © Michael Newman/Photo Edit; p. 300 (top): © Bob Jacobson/Corbis RF; (bottom): © Images100/ Corbis RF; p. 302 (top): © Tony Freeman/Photo Edit; (bottom): © PhotoDisc/Getty RF; p. 304: Corbis; p. 305: © Toney Freeman/ Photo Edit; p. 306: © Corbis RF; p. 307: © Tim Pannell/Corbis; p. 309 (top): © Punchstock/Brand X Pictures; (bottom): Courtesy of Boys and Girls Club of America; p. 311(top): © Kevin Dodge/ Corbis; (bottom): © Michael A. Keller/zefa/Corbis; p. 312: © Eri Morita/Getty; p. 313 (top): © Photo by Bob Barrett/FPG/Hulton Archive/Getty Images; © PhotoDisc/Getty RF; p. 314: © Image Source/PictureQuest; p. 315: © Pinto/Corbis; p. 316: © Pascal Broze/Getty RF; p. 318: © Ronnie Kaufmann/Corbis; p. 319: © Mike Watson/Corbis RF; p. 320: © Jenny Acheson/Getty Images; p. 322 (top): © Reed Kaestner/Corbis RF; (bottom): © Stockdisc/ PunchStock RF; p. 323 (left): © Mats Widen/Johner Images/Getty RF; (right): © David Hanover/Stone/Getty; p. 325: © Digital Vision/Getty Images

Chapter 10

p. 330: © Image Source/Alamy; p. 331 (top left): © Andrew Itkoff; p. 331 (top right): © Dale Sparks; (middle): © Michael A. Schwarz Photography, Inc.; (bottom): © Patty Wood; p. 332: © Tony Cordoza/Alamy; p. 333 (top): © Teacher's Curriculum Institute; (bottom): © Jose Luis Pelaez, Inc./Corbis; p. 335 (top): © Creatas/PunchStock; (bottom): © PictureQuest RF; p. 337 (top): © Ed Kashi/Corbis; (bottom): Courtesy of I Have a Dream-Houston, Houston, TX; p. 338 (top): © Stockbyte/ Punchstock; (bottom): © Wally McNamee/Corbis; p. 340: © Gill Ross/Corbis; p. 342: © Vol. 71/Photodisc/Getty RF; p. 344: © Photodisc/Getty RF; p. 345 (left): © Hill Street Studios/Blend Images/Getty Images; (right): © The Image Bank/Getty; p. 346: © Tommie Lindsey; p. 347: © Vera Berger/zefa/Corbis RF; p. 348: © James Ransome; p. 349: © John S. Abbott; p. 350: © Fujifots/ The Image Works; p. 352: © AP Photo/Manuel Balce Ceneta; p. 353: © JupiterImages; p. 354: © Milton Hinnart/The Dallas Morning News; p. 355: © Koichi Kamoshida/Newsmakers/Getty; p. 356: © Doug Wilson/Corbis

Chapter 11

p. 361: © PhotoAlto Agency/Getty RF; p. 363: © 2007 USA Today Library, photo by Kevin Moloney; p. 367: brainology.com; p. 369 (top): © AP Photo/Michael Tweed; (bottom): © Ralf-Finn Hestoft/ Corbis; p. 370 (top): © Martin Meyer/Corbis; (bottom): Courtesy William Damon, Standford University; p. 371: © Adivasi munnetra sangam gudalur; p. 372: © Comstock/Punch/Stock RF; p. 373: © Irwin Thompson/The Dallas Morning News; p. 374: Courtesy Sandra Graham; p. 375: © Robert A. Isaacs/Photo Researchers; p. 379: © Dennis MacDonald/Photo Edit; p. 381: © Jose Luis Perez/Corbis; p. 384: Courtesy Grace Leaf; p. 385: © Photodisc/ Getty RF; p. 386: Courtesy of Armando Ronquillo

Chapter 12

p. 391: © Rolf Bruderer/Blend Images/Corbis RF; p. 393: © Tom Grill/Corbis RF; p. 394 (top): © Jay Dickman; (bottom): © Marjorie Shostak/Anthro Photos; p. 397: © Shine Pictures/Corbis; p. 398 (left): © Daniel Lainé; (middle): © Bill Gillette/Stock Boston; (right): © Sylvia Plachy/Redux Pictures; p. 402: © BananaStock/ PunchStock; p. 403 (left): Courtesy Quantum Opportunities Program at the Carver Center in Washington, D.C.; (right): Courtesy El Puente; p. 405: © Alison Wright/Corbis; p. 406 (bottom): Courtesy of Carola Suarez-Orozco and photographer Kris Snibble/Harvard News Office, © President and Fellows of Harvard College; p. 406 (top): Courtesy Margaret Beal Spencer; p. 408: © 1997 USA Today Library, photo by H. Darr Beiser; p. 412 (top): © Tom Stewart/Crobis; p. 412 (middle): © BananaStock/ PunchStock; p. 412 (bottom): © imagebroker.net/PhotoLibrary; p. 415: © Idealink Photography/Alamy; p. 416: © L. Clarke/Corbis

Chapter 13

p. 422: © BananaStock/PunchStock; p. 425 (top): © Adam Gault/ Digital Vision/Getty RF; p. 425 (bottom): © Taxi/Getty RF; p. 427 (top): © Brand X Pictures/Jupiter Images RF; p. 427 (bottom): © Photodisc/Getty RF; p. 431: © Stephanie Maze/Corbis; p. 432: © Gary Houlder/Corbis; p. 433: Courtesy Luis Vargas; p. 437 (top): © Joe Raedle/Newsmakers/Getty; p. 437 (bottom): © Daniel Allan/ Taxi/Getty; p. 440: © Josh Reynolds; p. 442 (top): © BananaStock/ JupiterImages/i2i/Alamy; p. 442 (bottom): © Charles Gullung/zefa/ Corbis; p. 444 (top): © Corbis RF; p. 444 (bottom): © Stockdisc/ PunchStock; p. 447: © Chuck Savage/Corbis; p. 448: Courtesy of Dr. Rodney Hammond, Director, Division of Violence Prevention, Centers for Disease Control and Prevention; p. 450: © BananaStock/ PunchStock; p. 453: © Jules Frazier/Getty RF; p. 454: © Karen Kasmausk/Corbis; p. 456: © Ian Thraves/Alamy; p. 458: © Peter Beavis/Getty; p. 459: © Image Source/Getty RF

TEXT/LINE ART CREDITS

Chapter 1

Fig. 1.1: After data presented by the U.S. Census Bureau (2002). *National population projections I. Summary Files*. Washington, DC: U.S. Bureau of the Census. **Fig. 1.2:** After data presented by the U.S. Census Bureau (2002). *National population projections I. Summary Files*. Washington, DC: U.S. Bureau of the Census. **Fig. 1.3:** John W. Santrock, *Life-Span Development*, 9e, p. 19, fig. 1.5. Copyright © 2004 The McGraw-Hill Companies, Inc. Used with permission of The McGraw-Hill Companies, Inc. **Fig. 1.4:** (line art) John W. Santrock, *Life-Span Development*, 9e, p. 21, fig. 1.6. Copyright © 2004 The McGraw-Hill Companies, Inc. Used with permission of The McGraw-Hill Companies, Inc. **Fig. 1.5:** Schulenberg, J. E. & Zarrett, N. R. (2006). Mental health during emerging adulthood: Continuity and discontinuity in courses, causes, and consequences. In J. J. Arnett & J. L. Tanner (Eds.), *Emerging adults in America: Coming of age in the 21st Century*. Washington, DC: American Psychological Association, Figure 6.1, p. 136. Copyright © 2006 by the American Psychological Association. Adapted with permission. Source of data: Monitoring the Future study, Institute of Social Research, University of Michigan. **Fig. 1.6:** Schulenberg, J. E. & Zarrett, N. R. (2006). Mental health during emerging adulthood: Continuity and discontinuity in courses, causes, and consequences. In J. J. Arnett & J. L. Tanner (Eds.), *Emerging adults in America: Coming of age in the 21st Century*. Washington, DC: American Psychological Association, Figure 6.4, p. 139. Copyright © 2006 by the American Psychological Association. Adapted with permission. Source of data: Monitoring the Future study, Institute of Social Research, University of Michigan. **Fig. 1.7:** Eccles, J. S., & Gootman, J. (2002). Community programs to promote youth development, Box 3-1. Washington, DC: National Academies Press. Reprinted with permission from the National Academies Press, Copyright © 2002 National Academy of Sciences. **Fig. 1.9:** John W. Santrock, *Life-Span Development*, 9e, p. 45, Fig. 2.1. Copyright © 2004 The McGraw-Hill Companies, Inc. Used with permission of The McGraw-Hill Companies, Inc. **Fig. 1.11:** John W. Santrock, *Psychology*, 7e, p. 129, fig. 4.7. Copyright © 2003 The McGraw-Hill Companies, Inc. Used with permission of The McGraw-Hill Companies, Inc. **Fig. 1.12:** John W. Santrock, *Psychology*, 7e, p. 487, fig. 12.6. Copyright © 2003 The McGraw-Hill Companies, Inc. Used with permission of The McGraw-Hill Companies, Inc. **Fig. 1.17:** John W. Santrock, *Psychology*, 7e, fig. 2.4. Copyright © 2003 The McGraw-Hill Companies, Inc. Used with permission of The McGraw-Hill Companies, Inc. **Fig. 1.18:** John W. Santrock, *Psychology*, 7e, Fig. 2.5. Copyright © 2003 The McGraw-Hill Companies, Inc. Used with permission of The McGraw-Hill Companies, Inc.

Chapter 2

Fig. 2.4: Reproduced from J. M. Tanner, R. H. Whitehouse, and M. Takaishi, "Standards from Birth to Maturity for Height, Weight, Height Velocity, and Weight Velocity: British Children 1965," *Archives of Disease in Childhood*, v. 41, pp. 613–633, copyright © 1966 with permission from the BMJ Publishing Group Ltd. **Fig. 2.6:** John W. Santrock, *Children*, p. 447, fig. 15.5. Copyright © The McGraw-Hill Companies, Inc. Used with permission of The McGraw-Hill Companies, Inc. **Fig. 2.7:** From A. F. Roache, "Secular Trends in Stature, Weight and Maturation," *Monographs of the Society for Research in Child Development*, n. 179. © 1977 The Society for Research in Child Development, Inc. Reprinted with permission of the Society for Research in Child Development. **Fig. 2.8:** Reprinted from *Journal of Adolescent Health*, 39(3), M. Jane Park, Tina Paul Mulye, Sally H. Adams, Claire D. Brindis and Charles E. Irwin, Jr., "The Health Status of Young Adults in the United States," p. 310, Copyright 2006, with permission from Elsevier. **Fig. 2.9:** After data presented by *MMWR: Morbidity and Mortality Weekly Report*, Vol. 55, No. SS-5 (June 9, 2006). U.S. Department of Health and Human Services. **Fig. 2.10:** After Table 52 from *MMWR: Morbidity and Mortality Weekly Report*, Vol. 55, No. SS-5 (June 9, 2006). U.S. Department of Health and Human Services. **Fig. 2.11:** After Table 95 from Eaton, D. K., et al. "Youth risk behavior surveillance—United States, 2007." *MMWR Surveillance Summaries*. 57(SS04):1–131. June 6, 2008. **Fig. 2.12:** From John T. Bonner, *The Evolution of Culture in Animals*. © 1980 Princeton University Press. Reprinted by permission of Princeton University Press. **Fig. 2.13:** John W. Santrock, *A Topical Approach to Life-Span Development*, 3rd ed., fig. 2.3. Copyright © 2007 The McGraw-Hill Companies, Inc. Used with permission of The McGraw-Hill Companies, Inc. **Fig. 2.14:** John W. Santrock, *Children*, 7e, fig. 3.14. Copyright © 2003 The McGraw-Hill Companies, Inc. Used with permission of The McGraw-Hill Companies, Inc.

Chapter 3

Fig. 3.1: John W. Santrock, *Child Development*, 10e, p. 131, fig. 5.1. Copyright © 2004 The McGraw-Hill Companies, Inc. Used with permission of The McGraw-Hill Companies, Inc. **Fig. 3.3:** John W. Santrock, *Life-Span Development*, 13th ed., p. 357, fig. 11.4. Copyright © 2011 The McGraw-Hill Companies, Inc. Used with permission of The McGraw-Hill Companies, Inc. **Fig. 3.4:** John W. Santrock, *Child Development*, 13e, p. 174, fig. 6.1. Copyright © 2010 The McGraw-Hill Companies, Inc. Used with permission of The McGraw-Hill Companies, Inc. **Fig. 3.5:** Reprinted by permission from Dr. Jan Sinnott. **Fig. 3.7:** John W. Santrock, *Life-Span Development*, 9e, p. 248, Fig. 8.11. Copyright © 2004 The McGraw-Hill Companies, Inc. Used with permission of The McGraw-Hill Companies, Inc. **Fig. 3.8:** John W. Santrock, *Educational Psychology*, 2e, fig. 8.5. Copyright © 2004 The McGraw-Hill Companies, Inc. Used with permission of The McGraw-Hill Companies, Inc. Data is from Dempster, F. N. (1981). "Memory Span: Sources of Individual Variation and Developmental Differences," *Psychological Bulletin, 89*, p. 63–100. **Fig. 3.9:** John W. Santrock, *Psychology*, 7e, p. 314, fig. 8.8. Copyright © 2003 The McGraw-Hill Companies, Inc. Used with permission of The McGraw-Hill Companies, Inc. **Fig. 3.10:** John W. Santrock, *Educational Psychology*, 3rd ed., p. 275, fig. 8.6. Copyright © 2008 The McGraw-Hill Companies, Inc. Used with permission. Data is from H. Lee Swanson, "What Develops in Working Memory? A Life Span Perspective" in *Developmental Psychology*, July 1999, 35, 4, 986–1000. **Fig. 3.11:** From Ellen Galinsky, *Mind in the Making*, p. 19. Copyright © 2010. Reprinted by permission of HarperCollins Publishers. **Fig. 3.13:** John W. Santrock, *Educational Psychology*, 3rd ed., p. 275, Fig. 8.6. Copyright © 2008 The McGraw-Hill Companies, Inc. Used with permission of The McGraw-Hill Companies, Inc. Data is from Ronald T. Kellogg, "Observations on the Psychology of Thinking and Writing," *Composition Studies*, vol. 21 (1993), pp. 3–41. **Fig. 3.14:** John W. Santrock, *Children*, 5th ed., Fig. 10.1. Copyright © 1997 The McGraw-Hill Companies, Inc. Used with permission of The McGraw-Hill Companies, Inc. **Fig. 3.16:** John W. Santrock, *Psychology*, 7e, p. 405, Fig. 10.5. Copyright © 2003 The McGraw-Hill Companies, Inc. Used with permission of The McGraw-Hill Companies, Inc. **Fig. 3.17:** Robert Sternberg, *Handbook of Intelligence*. Copyright © Cambridge University Press 2000. Reprinted with permission of Cambridge University Press. **Fig. 3.18:** Ulric Neisser, "The Increase in IQ Scores from 1932–1997." Used with permission.

Chapter 4

p. 129: From "Self and Identity Development" by Susan Harter. In S. S. Feldman and G. R. Elliott (eds.), *At the Threshold: The Developing Adolescent*. Cambridge, MA: Harvard University Press, 1990, pp. 352–353. Used with permission of Dr. Susan Harter. **Fig. 4.2:** R. W. Robins, K. H. Trzesniewski, J. L. Tracy, S. D. Gosling, and J. Potter (2002). "Global Self-Esteem Across the Life Span," *Psychology and Aging,* 17(3), 423–434 (Figure 1). Copyright © 2002 by the American Psychological Association. Adapted with permission. **Fig. 4.3:** S. Harter (1999). *The Construction of The Self,* Table 6.1. New York: The Guilford Press. Reprinted with permission. **Fig. 4.4:** John W. Santrock, *Educational Psychology,* 2e, Fig. 3.7. Copyright © 2004 The McGraw-Hill Companies, Inc. Used with permission of The McGraw-Hill Companies, Inc. **Fig. 4.5:** John W. Santrock, *Children,* 7e, p. 542. McGraw-Hill, 2003. Copyright © 2003 The McGraw-Hill Companies, Inc. Used with permission of The McGraw-Hill Companies, Inc. **Fig. 4.6:** John W. Santrock, *Psychology,* 7e, p. 499, fig. 12.11. Copyright © 2003 The McGraw-Hill Companies, Inc. Used with permission of The McGraw-Hill Companies, Inc.

Chapter 5

p. 163: From Zager, K., & Rubenstein, A. (2002). *The Inside Story on Teen Girls*. Washington, DC: American Psychological Association, pp. 21–22. Copyright © 2002 by the American Psychological Association. Reproduced with permission. **Fig. 5.1:** John W. Santrock, *A Topical Approach to Life-Span Development,* 3rd ed., Fig. 12.4. Copyright © 2007 The McGraw-Hill Companies, Inc. Used with permission of The McGraw-Hill Companies, Inc. **Fig. 5.2:** National Assessment of Educational Progress (2007). *The Nation's Report Card*. Washington, DC: U.S. Department of Education, Figure 6, p. 12. **Fig. 5.4:** John W. Santrock, *A Topical Approach to Life-Span Development,* 3rd ed., fig. 12.5. Copyright © 2007 The McGraw-Hill Companies, Inc. Used with permission of The McGraw-Hill Companies, Inc. **Fig. 5.5:** From Pryor, J. H., Hurtado, S., Saenz, V. B., Lindholm, J. A., Korn, W. S., & Mahoney, K. M. (2005). *The American freshman: National norms for fall 2005*. Los Angeles: Higher Education Research Institute, UCLA. Reprinted with permission.

Chapter 6

Fig. 6.2: John W. Santrock, *Life-Span Development,* 12e, Fig. 11.5. Copyright © 2009 The McGraw-Hill Companies, Inc. Used with permission of The McGraw-Hill Companies, Inc. **Fig. 6.4:** After data presented by the National Center for Health Statistics (2002). *Sexual behavior and selected health measures: Men and women 15–44 years of age, United States 2002*. PH2003-1250. Atlanta: Centers for Disease Control and Prevention. **Fig. 6.5:** From Hamilton, Martin, and Ventura (2000), National Vital Statistics Reports, Centers for Disease Control and Prevention. **p. 196:** Gilmartin, S. K. (2006). Changes in college women's attitudes toward sexual intimacy. *Journal of Research on Adolescence,* 16(3): 444, 447. **pp. 202–203:** Boonstra, H., Teen pregnancy: trends and lessons learned, *The Guttmacher Report on Public Policy,* 2002, 5(1): 9–10. **Fig. 6.6:** Figure from Child Trends, *Facts at a Glance, 2008,* http://www.childtrends.org. Washington, DC: Child Trends. Used with permission. **Fig. 6.7:** National Center for Health Statistics, Births to Teenagers in the United Sates, 1940–2000, *National Vital Statistics Report,* Vol. 49, No. 10. **Fig. 6.9:** B. S. Fisher, F. T. Cullen, & M. G. Turner (2000). *The Sexual Victimization of College Women*. Washington, DC: National Institute of Justice, Exhibit 8, p. 19.

Chapter 7

Fig. 7.1: From Selman, R. S. (1976). "Social-Cognitive Understanding." In Thomas Lickona (Ed.) *Moral Development and Behavior*. Reprinted with permission of Thomas Lickona. **Fig. 7.2:** From Kohlberg, L. (1969). "Stage and Sequence: The Cognitive-Developmental Approach to Socialization." In D. A. Goslin (Ed.), *Handbook of Socialization Theory and Research*. Chicago: Rand McNally. Reprinted with permission of David Goslin. **Fig.7.3:** From Colby, A. et al. (1983). "A Longitudinal Study of Moral Judgment," *Monographs for the Society for Research in Child Development,* Serial #201. Reprinted with the permission of the Society for Research in Child Development. **Fig. 7.4:** Yussen, S. R. (1977). "Characteristics of Moral Dilemmas Written by Adolescents," *Developmental Psychology,* 13(2), 162–163 (Table 1). Copyright © 1977 by the American Psychological Association. Adapted with permission. **Fig. 7.6:** From Pryor, J. H., Hurtado, S., Saenz, V. B., Lindholm, J. A., Korn, W. S., & Mahoney, K. M. (2005). *The American freshman: National norms for fall 2005.* Los Angeles: Higher Education Research Institute, UCLA. Reprinted with permission. **Fig. 7.7:** John W. Santrock, *Child Development,* 12e, fig. 13.5. Copyright © The McGraw-Hill Companies, Inc. Used with permission of The McGraw-Hill Companies, Inc.

Chapter 8

Fig. 8.1: Belsky, J. (1981). Early human experience: A family perspective. *Developmental Psychology,* 17(1), 3-23 (Figure 1). Copyright © 1981 by the American Psychological Association. Reproduced with permission. **Fig. 8.4:** John W. Santrock, *Children,* p. 306, fig. 11.5. Copyright © The McGraw-Hill Companies, Inc. Used with permission. **Fig. 8.5:** John W. Santrock, *Child Development,* 10e, p. 495, fig. 15.6. Copyright © 2004 The McGraw-Hill Companies, Inc. Used with permission of The McGraw-Hill Companies, Inc. **p. 280** Excerpts from Clarke-Stewart, A., & Brentano, C. (2006). *Divorce: Causes and Consequences, pp. 127, 129, 137, 169.* Copyright © 2006 by Alison Clarke-Stewart and Cornelia Brentano. All rights reserved. New Haven, CT: Yale University Press. Used with permission.

Chapter 9

Fig. 9.3: John W. Santrock, *Life-Span Development,* 11e, p. 513, fig. 16.4. Copyright © 2008 The McGraw-Hill Companies, Inc. Used with permission of The McGraw-Hill Companies, Inc. **Fig. 9.4:** From Dexter C. Dunphy, "The Social Structure of Urban Adolescent Peer Groups," *Sociometry,* Vol. 26. Washington, DC: American Sociological Association, 1963. **Fig. 9.5:** From "Romantic Development: Does Age at Which Romantic Involvement Starts Matter?" by Duane Burhmester, April 2001. Paper presented at the meeting of the Society for Research in Child Development, Minneapolis, MN. Reprinted with permission of the author. **Fig. 9.6:** From Popenoe, D., *The State of Our Unions 2008.* Figure 7, Copyright © 2008 by the National Marriage Project at the University of Virginia. Reprinted by permission of the National Marriage Project.

Chapter 10

Fig. 10.1: National Center for Education Statistics (2010). The condition of education 2010. Washington, D.C.: U.S. Department of Education. **Fig. 10.2:** From Nansel, T. R. et al., (2001, April 25). "Bullying Behaviors Among U.S. Youth," *Journal of the American*

Medical Association, 285 (16): 2094–2100. **Fig. 10.3:** John W. Santrock, *Life-Span Development,* 11e, p. 320, fig. 10.3. Copyright © 2008 The McGraw-Hill Companies, Inc. Used with permission of The McGraw-Hill Companies, Inc. **Fig. 10.5:** John W. Santrock, *Educational Psychology,* 4e, Fig. 6.3. Copyright © 2009 The McGraw-Hill Companies, Inc. Used with permission of The McGraw-Hill Companies, Inc.

Chapter 11

Fig. 11.2: From Deborah Stipek, *Motivation to Learn: Integrating Theory and Practice,* 4e. Published by Allyn and Bacon, Boston, MA. Copyright © 2002 by Pearson Education. Reprinted by permission of the publisher. **Fig. 11.3:** Data from 2009 assessment of 65 countries by the Organization for Economic Cooperation and Development. **Fig. 11.4:** From H. W. Stevenson, S. Lee, & J. W. Stigler, "Mathematics Achievement of Chinese, Japanese and American Children," *Science,* Vol. 231, No. 4739 (February 14, 1986), pp. 693–699, figure 6. Reprinted with permission from AAAS. http://www.aaas.org. Readers may view, browse, and/or download material for temporary copying purposes only, provided these uses are for noncommercial personal purposes. Except as provided by law, this material may not be further reproduced, distributed, transmitted, modified, adapted, performed, displayed, published, or sold in whole or in part, without prior written permission from the publisher. **Fig. 11.5:** Staff, J., Messersmith, E. E., & Schulenberg, J. E. (2009). Adolescents and the world of work. In R. M. Lerner & L. Steinberg (Eds.), *Handbook of adolescent psychology* (3rd Ed.), p. 277, Fig. 8.1. New York: Wiley. Copyright © 2009 by John Wiley & Sons, Inc. All rights reserved. Reprinted with permission of John Wiley & Sons, Inc.

Chapter 12

Fig. 12.3: Reed W. Larson and Suman Verma (1999). "How Children and Adolescents Spend Time Across the World: Work, Play, and Developmental Opportunities," *Psychological Bulletin,* 125(6), 701–736 (Table 6). Copyright © 1999 by the American Psychological Association. Reproduced with permission. **Fig. 12.5:** After Table 1 from Sellers, R. M. et al. (2006). Racial Identity Matters: The Relationship Between Racial Discrimination and Psychological Functioning in African American Adolescents. *Journal of Research on Adolescence,* 16(2): 187–216. Malden, MA: Blackwell Publishers. Used with permission. **Fig. 12.6:** "Generation M: Media in the Lives of 8-18 Year-olds—Executive Summary" (#7250), The Henry J. Kaiser Family Foundation, March 2005. This information was reprinted with permission from the Henry J. Kaiser Family Foundation. The Kaiser Family Foundation is a non-profit private operating foundation, based in Menlo Park, California, dedicated to producing and communicating the best possible information, research and analysis on health issues. **p. 400:** Harlem (2) ["What happens to a dream deferred..."]", from *The Collected Poems of Langston Hughes* by Langston Hughes, edited by Arnold Rampersad with David Roessel, Associate Editor. Copyright © 1994 by the Estate of Langston Hughes. Used by permission of Alfred A. Knopf, a division of Random House, Inc., and by permission of Harold Ober Associates Incorporated. **Fig. 12.7:** John W. Santrock, *Child Development,* 10e, p. 598, Fig. 18.7. Copyright © 2004 The McGraw-Hill Companies, Inc. Used with permission of The McGraw-Hill Companies, Inc.

Chapter 13

p. 427: From "Desert Places" in *The Poetry of Robert Frost,* edited by Edward Connery Lathem. Copyright © 1969 by Henry Holt and Company. Copyright © 1936 by Robert Frost, © Copyright 1964 by Lesley Frost Ballantine. Reprinted by arrangement with Henry Holt and Company, LLC. **Fig. 13.2:** From Achenback, T. M., & Edelbrock, C. S. (1981). "Behavioral Problems and Competencies Reported by Parents of Normal and Disturbed Children Aged Four through Sixteen," *Monographs for the Society for Research in Child Development,* 46 (1, Serial No. 188). © Society for Research in Child Development. Reprinted with permission of the Society for Research in Child Development. **p. 429:** From Zager, K., & Rubenstein, A. (2002). *The Inside Story on Teen Girls.* Washington, DC: American Psychological Association, pp. 141. Copyright © 2002 by the American Psychological Association. Reproduced with permission. **Fig. 13.3:** Masten, A. S., & Coatsworth, J. D. (1998). "The Development of Competence in Favorable and Unfavorable Environments: Lessons from Research on Successful Children," *American Psychologist,* 53(2), 205–220 (Table 2). Copyright © 1998 by the American Psychological Association. Reproduced with permission. **Fig. 13.4:** Johnston, L. D., O'Malley, P. M., Bachman, J. G., & Schulenberg, J. E. (2011). *Monitoring the Future: National results on adolescent drug use: Overview of key findings, 2010,* Ann Arbor, Mich., Institute for Social Research, The University of Michigan. **Fig. 13.5:** Johnston, L. D., O'Malley, P. M., Bachman, J. G., & Schulenberg, J. E. (2011). *Monitoring the Future: National results on adolescent drug use: Overview of key findings, 2010,* Ann Arbor, Mich., Institute for Social Research, The University of Michigan. **Fig. 13.9:** Puzzanchera,C., & Sickmund, M. (2008, July). Figure from *Juvenile Court Statistics 2005, p. 6.* Pittsburgh: National Center for Juvenile Justice. **Fig. 13.11:** From Centers for Disease Control and Prevention. (2006, June 8). *National Youth Risk Behavior Survey 1991–2005: Trends in the Prevalence of Suicide Ideation and Attempts.* Atlanta, GA: Centers for Disease Control and Prevention. **Fig. 13.14:** From Selye, H. *The Stress of Life.* Copyright © 1976 The McGraw-Hill Companies, Inc. Used with permission.

name index

A

B

C

D

E

F

G

H

L

M

N

O

P

Q

R

S

T

W

Z

subject index

B

C

D

E

F

G

H

I

M

N

O

P

Q

R

S

T

U

V